Communications
in Computer and Information Science 243

Chunfeng Liu   Jincai Chang   Aimin Yang (Eds.)

Information Computing and Applications

Second International Conference, ICICA 2011
Qinhuangdao, China, October 28-31, 2011
Proceedings, Part I

Springer

Volume Editors

Chunfeng Liu
College of Sciences
Hebei United University
Tangshan 063000, Hebei, China
E-mail: liucf403@163.com

Jincai Chang
College of Sciences
Hebei United University
Tangshan 063000, Hebei, China
E-mail: jincai@heuu.edu.cn

Aimin Yang
College of Sciences
Hebei United University
Tangshan 063000, Hebei, China
E-mail: aimin_heut@163.com

ISSN 1865-0929 e-ISSN 1865-0937
ISBN 978-3-642-27502-9 e-ISBN 978-3-642-27503-6
DOI 10.1007/978-3-642-27503-6
Springer Heidelberg Dordrecht London New York

Library of Congress Control Number: Applied for

CR Subject Classification (1998): C.2, D.2, C.2.4, I.2.11, C.1.4, D.4.7, H.3-4

Typesetting: Camera-ready by author, data conversion by Scientific Publishing Services, Chennai, India

Printed on acid-free paper

Springer is part of Springer Science+Business Media (www.springer.com)

Preface

Welcome to the proceedings of the International Conference on Information Computing and Applications (ICICA 2011), which was held in Qinhuangdao, China, October 28-30, 2011.

As future-generation information technology, information computing and applications become specialized, information computing and applications including hardware, software, communications and networks are growing with ever increasing scale and heterogeneity, and becoming overly complex. The complexity is getting more critical along with the growing applications. To cope with the growing and computing complexity, information computing and applications focus on intelligent, self-manageable, scalable computing systems and applications to the maximum extent possible without human intervention or guidance.

With the rapid development of information science and technology, information computing has become the third approach for scientific research. Information computing and applications is the field of study concerned with constructing intelligent computing, mathematical models, numerical solution techniques and using computers to analyze and solve natural scientific, social scientific and engineering problems. In practical use, it is typically the application of computer simulation, intelligent computing, Internet computing, pervasive computing, scalable computing, trusted computing, autonomy-oriented computing, evolutionary computing, mobile computing, applications and other forms of computation to problems in various scientific disciplines and engineering. Information computing and applications is an important underpinning for techniques used in information and computational science and there are many unresolved problems worth studying.

The ICICA 2011 conference provided a forum for engineers and scientists in academia, industry, and government to address the most innovative research and development issues including technical challenges and social, legal, political, and economic issues, and to present and discuss their ideas, results, work in progress and experience on all aspects of information computing and applications.

There was a very large number of paper submissions (865), representing six countries and regions. All submissions were reviewed by at least three Program or Technical Committee members or external reviewers. It was extremely difficult to select the presentations for the conference because there were so many excellent and interesting submissions. In order to allocate as many papers as possible and keep the high quality of the conference, we finally decided to accept 289 papers for presentation, reflecting a 33.2% acceptance rate. And 96 papers are included in this volume. We believe that all of these papers and topics not only provided novel ideas, new results, work in progress and state-of-the-art techniques in this field, but also stimulated future research activities in the area of information computing and applications.

The exciting program of this conference was the result of the hard and excellent work of many individuals, such as the Program and Technical Committee members, external reviewers and Publication Chairs, all working under a very tight schedule. We are also grateful to the members of the local Organizing Committee for supporting us in handling so many organizational tasks, and to the keynote speakers for accepting to come to the conference with enthusiasm. Last but not least, we hope you enjoy the conference proceedings.

October 2011

Chunfeng Liu
Jincai Chang
Aimin Yang

Organization

ICICA2011 was organized by the Hebei Applied Statistical Society (HASS), College of Science of Hebei United University, and sponsored by the National Natural Science Foundation of China, Northeastern University at Qinhuangdao, Yanshan University and Nanyang Technological University. It was held in cooperation with *Communications in Computer and Information Science* (CCIS) of Springer.

Executive Committee

Honorary Chair

Qun Lin	Chinese Academy of Sciences, China

General Chairs

Yanchun Zhang	Victoria University, Australia
Baoxiang Liu	Hebei United University, China
Yiming Chen	Yanshan University, China

Program Chairs

Chunfeng Liu	Hebei United University, China
Leizhen Wang	Northeastern University at Qinhuangdao, China
Chunlai Chai	Zhejiang Gongshang University, China

Local Arrangements Chairs

Jincai Chang	Hebei United University, China
Aimin Yang	Hebei United University, China

Steering Committee

Qun Lin	Chinese Academy of Sciences, China
Yuhang Yang	Shanghai Jiao Tong University, China
MaodeMa	Nanyang Technological University, Singapore
Nadia Nedjah	State University of Rio de Janeiro, Brazil
Lorna Uden	Staffordshire University, UK
Xingjie Hui	Northeastern University at Qinhuangdao, China
Xiaoqi Li	Northeastern University at Qinhuangdao, China

Xiaomin Wang	Northeastern University at Qinhuangdao, China
Yiming Chen	Yanshan University, China
Maohui Xia	Yanshan University, China
Chunxiao Yu	Yanshan University, China
Yajuan Hao	Yanshan University, China
Dianxuan Gong	Hebei United University, China
Yajun Zhang	Northeastern University, China

Publicity Chairs

Aimin Yang	Hebei United University, China
Chunlai Chai	Zhejiang Gongshang University, China

Publication Chairs

Yuhang Yang	Shanghai Jiao Tong University, China

Financial Chair

Chunfeng Liu	Hebei United University, China
Jincai Chang	Hebei United University, China

Local Arrangements Committee

Li Feng	Hebei United University, China
Songzhu Zhang	Northeastern University at Qinhuangdao, China
Jiao Gao	Northeastern University at Qinhuangdao, China
Yamian Peng	Hebei United University, China
Lichao Feng	Hebei United University, China
Dianxuan Gong	Hebei United University, China
Yuhuan Cui	Hebei United University, China

Secretaries

Jingguo Qu	Hebei United University, China
Huancheng Zhang	Hebei United University, China
Yafeng Yang	Hebei United University, China

Program/Technical Committee

Yuan Lin	Norwegian University of Science and Technology, Norway
Yajun Li	Shanghai Jiao Tong University, China
Yanliang Jin	Shanghai University, China
Mingyi Gao	National Institute of AIST, Japan

Yajun Guo	Huazhong Normal University, China
Haibing Yin	Peking University, China
Jianxin Chen	University of Vigo, Spain
Miche Rossi	University of Padova, Italy
Ven Prasad	Delft University of Technology, The Netherlands
Mina Gui	Texas State University, USA
Nils Asc	University of Bonn, Germany
Ragip Kur	Nokia Research, USA
On Altintas	Toyota InfoTechnology Center, Japan
Suresh Subra	George Washington University, USA
Xiyin Wang	Hebei United University, China
Dianxuan Gong	Hebei United University, China
Chunxiao Yu	Yanshan University, China
Yanbin Sun	Beijing University of Posts and Telecommunications, China
Guofu Gui	CMC Corporation, China
Haiyong Bao	NTT Co., Ltd., Japan
Xiwen Hu	Wuhan University of Technology, China
Mengze Liao	Cisco China R&D Center, China
Yangwen Zou	Apple China Co., Ltd., China
Liang Zhou	ENSTA-ParisTech, France
Zhanguo Wei	Beijing Forestry University, China
Hao Chen	Hu'nan University, China
Lilei Wang	Beijing University of Posts and Telecommunications, China
Xilong Qu	Hunan Institute of Engineering, China
Duolin Liu	ShenYang Ligong University, China
Xiaozhu Liu	Wuhan University, China
Yanbing Sun	Beijing University of Posts and Telecommunications, China
Yiming Chen	Yanshan University, China
Hui Wang	University of Evry, France
Shuang Cong	University of Science and Technology of China, China
Haining Wang	College of William and Mary, USA
Zengqiang Chen	Nankai University, China
Dumisa Wellington Ngwenya	Illinois State University, USA
Hu Changhua	Xi'an Research Insti. of Hi-Tech, China
Juntao Fei	Hohai University, China
Zhao-Hui Jiang	Hiroshima Institute of Technology, Japan
Michael Watts	Lincoln University, New Zealand
Tai-hon Kim	Defense Security Command, Korea

Muhammad Khan	Southwest Jiaotong University, China
Seong Kong	The University of Tennessee, USA
Worap Kreesuradej	King Mongkuts Institute of Technology Ladkrabang, Thailand
Uwe Kuger	Queen's University Belfast, UK
Xiao Li	CINVESTAV-IPN, Mexico
Stefa Lindstaedt	Division Manager, Knowledge Management, Austria
Paolo Li	Polytechnic of Bari, Italy
Tashi Kuremoto	Yamaguchi University, Japan
Chun Lee	Howon University, Korea
Zheng Liu	Nagasaki Institute of Applied Science, Japan
Michiharu Kurume	National College of Technology, Japan
Sean McLoo	National University of Ireland, Ireland
R. McMenemy	Queens, University Belfast, UK
Xiang Mei	The University of Leeds, UK
Cheol Moon	Gwangju University, Korea
Veli Mumcu	Technical University of Yildiz, Turkey
Nin Pang	Auckland University of Technology, New Zealand
Jian-Xin Peng	Queens University of Belfast, UK
Lui Piroddi	Technical University of Milan, Italy
Girij Prasad	University of Ulster, UK
Cent Leung	Victoria University of Technology, Australia
Jams Li	University of Birmingham, UK
Liang Li	University of Sheffield, UK
Hai Qi	University of Tennessee, USA
Wi Richert	University of Paderborn, Germany
Meh shafiei	Dalhousie University, Canada
Sa Sharma	University of Plymouth, UK
Dong Yue	Huazhong University of Science and Technology, China
YongSheng Ding	Donghua University, China
Yuezhi Zhou	Tsinghua University, China
Yongning Tang	Illinois State University, USA
Jun Cai	University of Manitoba, Canada
Sunil Maharaj Sentech	University of Pretoria, South Africa
Mei Yu	Simula Research Laboratory, Norway
Gui-Rong Xue	Shanghai Jiao Tong University, China
Zhichun Li	Northwestern University, China
Lisong Xu	University of Nebraska-Lincoln, USA
Wang Bin	Chinese Academy of Sciences, China
Yan Zhang	Simula Research Laboratory and University of Oslo, Norway

Table of Contents – Part I

Computational Statistics

Social Networking and Computing

Evolutionary Computing and Applications

Information Education and Application

Internet and Web Computing

Scientific and Engineering Computing

System Simulation Computing

Table of Contents – Part II

Computational Statistics

Bio-inspired and DNA Computing

Evolutionary Computing and Applications

Information Education and Application

Internet and Web Computing

Multimedia Networking and Computing

Parallel and Distributed Computing

Scientific and Engineering Computing

Monotone Positive Solutions for Singular Third-Order m-Point Boundary Value Problems

Hai-E Zhang[1], Cheng Wang[1], Wen-Feng Huo[2], and Guo-Ying Pang[3]

[1] Department of Basic Teaching, Tangshan College, Hebei 063000, P.R. China
[2] Kaiyuan Autowelding System Co.,Ltd, Hebei 063000, P.R. China
[3] Department of General Courses, Academy of Military Transportation, Tianjin, 300161, P.R. China
{haiezhang,huowenfeng2009}@126.com, 149960953@qq.com,
d:gy_pang2006@163.com

Abstract. To investigate the existence results of single and multiple monotone positive solutions for a class of nonlinear singular m-point boundary value problems of third-order differential equations with a positive parameter. Firstly, Green's function for the associated linear boundary value problem is constructed, and then, some useful properties of the Green's function are obtained. Finally, To establish intervals of the parameter which yield the existence of at least one, two and infinitely many monotone positive solutions under suitable conditions for the above problem. The main tool is the well-known Guo-Krasnoselskii's fixed point theorem.

Keywords: Singular, Boundary value problem, Monotone positive solutions, Guo-Krasnoselskii's fixed point theorem.

1 Introduction

This paper is concerned with the singular third-order m-point BVP

$$\begin{cases} u'''(t) + \lambda a(t) f(t, u(t)) = 0, & 0 < t < 1, \\ u(0) = \sum\limits_{i=1}^{m-2} k_i u(\xi_i), u'(0) = u'(1) = 0, \end{cases} \tag{1}$$

where λ is a positive parameter, $0 < \xi_1 < \xi_2 < \ldots < \xi_{m-2} < 1$, $k_i \in R^+$ $(i = 1, 2, \ldots, m-2)$ and $\sum\limits_{i=1}^{m-2} k_i < 1$.

Third-order differential equations arise in a variety of different areas of applied mathematics and physics, e.g., in the deflection of a curved beam having a constant or varying cross section, a three layer beam, electromagnetic waves or gravity driven flows and so on [1].

Recently, third-order two-point or three-point boundary value problems (BVPs for short) have received much attention [2,3,4,5,6,7]. To the best of my knowledge, only few papers deal with more general m-point BVPs of third-order differential

C. Liu, J. Chang, and A. Yang (Eds.): ICICA 2011, Part I, CCIS 243, pp. 1–8, 2011.

equations. One may see [8,9,10,11,12]. Motivated greatly by the above-mentioned excellent works, the aim of this paper is to establish some criteria for the existence of one, two and infinitely positive solutions for BVP (1) in an explicit interval of λ by using the following well-known Guo-Krasnoselskii' s fixed point theorem.

Theorem 1. *[13,14] Let E be a Banach space and $K \subset E$ be a cone in E. Assume Ω_1 and Ω_2 are open subsets of E with $0 \in \Omega_1$ and $\overline{\Omega}_1 \subset \Omega_2$, $T : K \cap (\overline{\Omega}_2 \setminus \Omega_1) \to K$ be a completely continuous operator such that*
(i) $\|Tu\| \le \|u\|, \forall\, u \in K \cap \partial\Omega_1$ and $\|Tu\| \ge \|u\|, \forall\, u \in K \cap \partial\Omega_2$; or
(i) $\|Tu\| \ge \|u\|, \forall\, u \in K \cap \partial\Omega_1$ and $\|Tu\| \le \|u\|, \forall\, u \in K \cap \partial\Omega_2$.
Then T has a fixed point in $K \cap (\overline{\Omega}_2 \setminus \Omega_1)$.

2 Preliminary Lemmas

In arriving our main results, the following preliminary lemmas are necessary.

Lemma 1. *[11] Let $h \in C[0,1]$. Then the BVP*

$$\begin{cases} u'''(t) + h(t) = 0, \quad t \in (0,1), \\ u(0) = \sum\limits_{i=1}^{m-2} k_i u(\xi_i), \; u'(0) = u'(1) = 0 \end{cases} \tag{2}$$

has a unique solution $u(t) = \int_0^1 G(t,s) h(s) ds$, which satisfies $u'(t) = \int_0^1 G_1(t,s) h(s) ds$, in which

$$G(t,s) = G_0(t,s) + \frac{1}{1 - \sum\limits_{i=1}^{m-2} k_i} \sum_{i=1}^{m-2} k_i G_0(\xi_i, s), \; 0 \le t, s \le 1,$$

$$G_1(t,s) = \begin{cases} s(1-t), 0 \le s \le t \le 1, \\ t(1-s), 0 \le t \le s \le 1 \end{cases}$$

are called Green's function, where

$$G_0(t,s) = \begin{cases} \frac{2st - s^2 - st^2}{2}, & 0 \le s \le t \le 1, \\ \frac{(1-s)t^2}{2}, & 0 \le t \le s \le 1. \end{cases}$$

Lemma 2. *[11] For all $(t,s) \in [0,1] \times [0,1]$,*
(i) $\delta g(s) \le G(t,s) \le g(s)$;
(ii) $G(t,s) \le G(x,s)$ for $x \in [0,1]$ and $t \le x$;
(iii) $G_1(t,s) \le s(1-s)$,
where $g(s) = \frac{1}{2\left(1 - \sum\limits_{i=1}^{m-2} k_i\right)} s(1-s)$, $s \in [0,1]$ and $0 < \delta = \sum\limits_{i=1}^{m-2} k_i \xi_i^2 < 1$.

This paper will use the classical Banach space $E = C[0,1]$ equipped with sup norm $\|u\| = \max_{t\in[0,1]} |u(t)|$. Denote

$$K = \left\{ u \in E |\, u(t) \geq 0, \min_{0\leq t\leq 1} u(t) \geq \delta \|u\|,\ t \in [0,1] \right\}.$$

Then it is obvious that K is a cone in E.

Define

$$T_\lambda u(t) = \int_0^1 G(t,s)\, a(s)\, f(s, u(s))\, ds,\ t \in [0,1].$$

Obviously, if u is a fixed point of T_λ in K, then u is a solution of the BVP (1).

Lemma 3. *[11] Each fixed point of T_λ is nondecreasing.*

In remainder of this paper, the following assumptions are hold:

$(H1)$ $a : (0,1) \to R^+$ is continuous and $0 < \int_0^1 s(1-s)\, a(s)\, ds < \infty$.
$(H2)$ $f : [0,1] \times R^+ \to R^+$ is continuous.
$(H3)$ The function $f(t,u)$ is nondecreasing in u and satisfies $(H2)$.
Following $(H1)$, $0 < \int_0^1 g(s)\, a(s)\, ds < \infty$ obviously.

Lemma 4. *Assume that $(H1)$, $(H2)$ hold. Then $T_\lambda : K \to K$ is completely continuous.*

Proof. Suppose that $u \in K$. Let $M_0 = \sup_{s\in[0,1], u\in[0,\|u\|]} f(s,u)$. Then it follows from Lemma 2, $(H1)$ and $(H2)$ that

$$0 \leq T_\lambda u(t) = \lambda \int_0^1 G(t,s)\, a(s)\, f(s,u(s))\, ds \leq M_0 \lambda \int_0^1 g(s)\, a(s)\, ds,\ t \in [0,1],$$

which implies that T_λ is well defined. Furthermore, by Lemma 2, it is to see that $T_\lambda(K) \subset K$.

Now prove that T_λ is a compact operator. Let $D \subset K$ be a bounded set. We will show that $T_\lambda(D)$ is relatively compact in K. Suppose that $\{w_k\}_{k=1}^{\infty} \subset T_\lambda(D)$ is an arbitrary sequence. Then there is $\{u_k\}_{k=1}^{\infty} \subset D$ such that $Tu_k = w_k$. Set

$$M = \sup\{\|u\| : u \in D\}.$$

Let $M_1 = \sup_{s\in[0,1], u\in[0,M]} f(s,u)$. With the similar arguments as above,

$$|w_k(t)| = |T_\lambda u_k(t)| = \left| \lambda \int_0^1 G(t,s)\, a(s)\, f(s,u(s)) \right| \leq M_1 \lambda \int_0^1 g(s)\, a(s)\, ds,\ t \in [0,1],$$

which shows that $\{w_k\}_{k=1}^{\infty}$ is uniformly bounded. Similarly, for $t \in [0,1]$,

$$|w_k'(t)| = |(T_\lambda u_k)'(t)| = \left| \lambda \int_0^1 G_1(t,s)\, a(s)\, f(s,u(s)) \right| \leq M_1 \lambda \int_0^1 s(1-s)\, a(s)\, ds,$$

which implies that $\{w_k'\}_{k=1}^{\infty}$ is also uniformly bounded. Therefore, $\{w_k\}_{k=1}^{\infty}$ is equicontinuous. By Arzela-Ascoli theorem, $\{w_k\}_{k=1}^{\infty}$ has a convergent subsequence, so T_λ is compact.

Finally, we claim that T_λ is continuous. Suppose $u_m,\ u \in K$ and $u_m \to u\,(m \to \infty)$. Then there exists $M_2 > 0$ such that $\|u\| < M_2$.

Let $M_3 = \sup\limits_{s,u \in [0,1]\times[0,M_2]} f(s,u)$. Then we have

$$\lambda G(t,s)\,a(s)\,f(s,u(s)) \le M_3 \lambda g(s)\,a(s)\,, \quad (t,s) \in [0,1] \times (0,1)$$

By applying the Lebesgue Dominated Convergence theorem,

$$\begin{aligned}\lim_{m\to\infty} T_\lambda u_m(t) &= \lim_{m\to\infty} \lambda \int_0^1 G(t,s)\,a(s)\,f(s,u_m(s))\,ds \\ &= \lambda \int_0^1 G(t,s)\,a(s)\,f(s,u(s))\,ds = T_\lambda u(t)\,,\ t \in [0,1]\,,\end{aligned}$$

which implies that T_λ is continuous. Therefore, $T_\lambda : K \to K$ is completely continuous.

3 Existence Results

Denote: $f^0 = \lim\limits_{u\to 0^+} \sup\limits_{t\in[0,1]} \frac{f(t,u)}{u}$, $f_0 = \lim\limits_{u\to 0^+} \inf\limits_{t\in[0,1]} \frac{f(t,u)}{u}$, $f^\infty = \lim\limits_{u\to +\infty} \sup\limits_{t\in[0,1]} \frac{f(t,u)}{u}$, $f_\infty = \lim\limits_{u\to\infty} \inf\limits_{t\in[0,1]} \frac{f(t,u)}{u}$, and $A = \int_0^1 g(s)\,a(s)\,ds$.

Assume that $\frac{1}{\delta^2 A f_\infty} = 0$ if $f_\infty = \infty$, $\frac{1}{Af^0} = \infty$ if $f^0 = 0$, $\frac{1}{\delta^2 A f_0} = 0$ if $f_0 = \infty$ and $\frac{1}{Af^\infty} = \infty$ if $f^\infty = 0$.

Now, the existence of at least one positive solution for the BVP (1) is obtained by applying the well-known Guo-Krasnoselskii's fixed point theorem.

Theorem 2. *Suppose $(H1)$, $(H2)$ hold. If there exist two positive constants $R_1 \ne R_2$ such that*

$(A1)$ $f(t,u) \le \frac{R_1}{\lambda A}$, $\forall\ (t,u) \in [0,1]\times[0,R_1]$; $(A2)$ $f(t,u) \ge \frac{R_2}{\lambda\delta A}$, $\forall\ (t,u) \in [0,1]\times[\delta R_2, R_2]$. Then BVP (1) has at least one positive solution $u^* \in K$ with $\min\{R_1,R_2\} \le \|u^*\| \le \max\{R_1,R_2\}$.

Proof. Without loss of generality, we may assume that $R_1 < R_2$. Let $\Omega_1 = \{u \in E\,|\,\|u\| < R_1\}$, $\Omega_2 = \{u \in E\,|\,\|u\| < R_2\}$. It follows from $(A1)$ and Lemma 2.2 that for any $u \in K \cap \partial\Omega_1$,

$$T_\lambda u = \lambda \int_0^1 G(t,s)\,a(s)\,f(s,u(s))\,ds \le \lambda \int_0^1 g(s)\,a(s)\,\frac{R_1}{\lambda A}ds = R_1 = \|u\|\,,$$

so $\|T_\lambda u\| \le \|u\|\,, foru \in K \cap \partial\Omega_1$. On the other hand, for any $u \in K \cap \partial\Omega_2$, $\delta R_2 \le \min\limits_{t\in[0,1]} u(t) \le R_2$, it follows from $(A1)$ and Lemma 2.2 that

$$T_\lambda u = \lambda \int_0^1 G(t,s)\,a(s)\,f(s,u(s))\,ds \ge \lambda\delta \int_0^1 g(s)\,a(s)\,\frac{R_2}{\lambda\delta A}ds = R_2 = \|u\|\,,$$

therefore, $\|T_\lambda u\| \geq \|u\|$, *for* $u \in K \cap \partial\Omega_2$. Applying the first part of Theorem 1 yields that T_λ has a fixed point $u^* \in K \cap \left(\overline{\Omega}_2 \backslash \Omega_1\right)$, which is a desired positive solution of BVP (1).

In the remainder of the paper, we define $\Omega_r = \{u \in E \,|\, \|u\| < r\}$, for any $r > 0$.

Theorem 3. *Suppose (H1), (H2) hold. Then for each* $\lambda \in \left(\frac{1}{\delta^2 A f_\infty}, \frac{1}{A f^0}\right)$ *or* $\lambda \in \left(\frac{1}{\delta^2 A f_0}, \frac{1}{A f^\infty}\right)$, *BVP (1) has at least one positive solution.*

Proof. If $\lambda \in \left(\frac{1}{\delta^2 A f_\infty}, \frac{1}{A f^0}\right)$, then we can choose sufficiently small $\varepsilon_1 > 0$ such that $\frac{1}{\delta^2 A(f_\infty - \varepsilon_1)} \leq \lambda \leq \frac{1}{A(f^0+\varepsilon_1)}$. By the definition of f^0, there exists $r_1 > 0$ such that $f(t,u) \leq (f^0 + \varepsilon_1) u$, for $t \in [0,1]$, $u \in [0, r_1]$. So, for any $u \in K \cap \partial\Omega_{r_1}$,

$$\begin{aligned} T_\lambda u(t) &= \lambda \int_0^1 G(t,s)\, a(s)\, f(s, u(s))\, ds \leq \lambda \int_0^1 g(s)\, a(s) \left(f^0 + \varepsilon_1\right) u(s)\, ds \\ &\leq \lambda \|u\| \int_0^1 g(s)\, a(s) \left(f^0 + \varepsilon_1\right) ds = \lambda \|u\| A \left(f^0 + \varepsilon_1\right) \leq \|u\|. \end{aligned}$$

Consequently, $\|T_\lambda u\| \leq \|u\|$, *for* $u \in K \cap \partial\Omega_{r_1}$. Next, in view of the definition of f_∞, there exists R_1' such that $f(t,u) \geq (f_\infty - \varepsilon_1) u$, for $t \in [0,1]$, $u \in [R_1', \infty]$. Let $R_1 = \max\{2r_1, \delta^{-1} R_1'\}$. If $u \in K \cap \partial\Omega_2$, then $\min\limits_{t\in[0,1]} u(t) \geq \delta R_1 \geq R_1'$. Thus,

$$\begin{aligned} T_\lambda u(t) &= \lambda \int_0^1 G(t,s)\, a(s)\, f(s, u(s))\, ds \geq \lambda\delta \int_0^1 g(s)\, a(s) (f_\infty - \varepsilon_1)\, u(s)\, ds \\ &\geq \lambda\delta^2 A (f_\infty - \varepsilon_1) \|u\| \geq \|u\|. \end{aligned}$$

Hence, $\|T_\lambda u\| \geq \|u\|$, *for* $u \in K \cap \partial\Omega_{R_1}$. Applying the first part of Theorem 1 yields that T_λ has a fixed point $u^* \in K \cap \left(\overline{\Omega}_{R_1} \backslash \Omega_{r_1}\right)$, which is a desired positive solution of BVP (1).

If $\lambda \in \left(\frac{1}{\delta^2 A f_0}, \frac{1}{A f^\infty}\right)$, then choosing sufficiently small $\varepsilon_2 > 0$ such that $\frac{1}{\delta^2 A(f_0 - \varepsilon_2)} \leq \lambda \leq \frac{1}{A(f^\infty + \varepsilon_2)}$. Similar to the above argument, from the definition of f_0, there exists $r_2 > 0$ such that $f(t,u) \geq (f_0 - \varepsilon_2) u$, for $t \in [0,1]$, $u \in [0, r_2]$. So, for any $u \in K \cap \partial\Omega_{r_2}$ and $t \in [0,1]$,

$$\begin{aligned} T_\lambda u(t) &= \lambda \int_0^1 G(t,s)\, a(s)\, f(s, u(s))\, ds \geq \lambda\delta \int_0^1 g(s)\, a(s) (f_0 - \varepsilon_2)\, u(s)\, ds \\ &\geq \lambda\delta^2 A (f_0 - \varepsilon_2) \|u\| \geq \|u\|. \end{aligned}$$

Thus, $\|T_\lambda u\| \geq \|u\|$, *for* $u \in K \cap \partial\Omega_{r_2}$. Now, considering the definition of f^∞, there exist $R_2' > 0$ such that $f(t,u) \geq (f^\infty + \varepsilon_2) u$, for $t \in [0,1]$, $u \in [R', \infty]$. Consider two cases: f is bounded or f is unbounded.

Case 1. Suppose that f is bounded, say $f(t,u) \leq N$, for $t \in [0,1]$, $u \in [0, \infty]$. In this case we may choose $R_2 = \max\{2R_2', \lambda N A\}$ such that for any $u \in K \cap \partial\Omega_{R_2}$ and $t \in [0,1]$,

$$T_\lambda u(t) = \lambda \int_0^1 G(t,s)\, a(s)\, f(s,u(s))\, ds \le \lambda N \int_0^1 g(s)\, a(s)\, ds = \lambda N A \le R_2 = \|u\|.$$

So, $\|T_\lambda u\| \le \|u\|$. Case 2. If f is unbounded, then we may choose $R_2 \ge R_2'$ such that $f(t,u) \le f(t,R_2)$, $for\ t \in [0,1], u \in [0,R_2]$. Then for any $u \in K \cap \partial\Omega_{R_2}$,

$$\begin{aligned} T_\lambda u(t) &= \lambda \int_0^1 G(t,s)\, a(s)\, f(s,u(s))\, ds \le \lambda \int_0^1 g(s)\, a(s)\, f(t,R_2)\, ds \\ &\le \lambda R_2 \int_0^1 g(s)\, a(s) \left(f^\infty + \varepsilon_2\right) ds = \lambda \|u\| \int_0^1 g(s)\, a(s) \left(f^\infty + \varepsilon_2\right) ds \\ &= \lambda A \left(f^\infty + \varepsilon_2\right) \|u\| \le \|u\|. \end{aligned}$$

So $\|T_\lambda u\| \le \|u\|$. Hence, we have $\|T_\lambda u\| \le \|u\|$, $for\ u \in K \cap \partial\Omega_{R_2}$. Applying the second part of Theorem 1 yields that T_λ has a fixed point $u^* \in K \cap \left(\overline{\Omega}_{R_2} \setminus \Omega_{r_2}\right)$, which is a desired positive solution of BVP (1).

4 Multiplicity Results

This section discusses the existence of multiplicity positive solutions for BVP (1).

Theorem 4. *Suppose that (H1), (H3) hold. In addition, assume that $f_0 = f_\infty = \infty$. Then for each $\lambda \in (0, \lambda_1)$, BVP (1) has at least two positive solutions, where $\lambda_1 = \sup\limits_{m>0} \frac{m}{A \max\limits_{t\in[0,1],u\in[0,m]} f(t,u)}$.*

Proof. Define a function h by $h(m) = \frac{m}{A \max\limits_{t\in[0,1],u\in[0,m]} f(t,u)}$.

It is easy to see that $h : (0,\infty) \to (0,\infty)$ is continuous and $\lim\limits_{m\to+0} h(m) = \lim\limits_{m\to\infty} h(m) = 0$. Thus there exists $m_0 \in (0,\infty)$ such that $h(m_0) = \sup\limits_{m>0} h(m) = \lambda^*$.

For $\lambda \in (0, \lambda^*)$, there exist constants c_1, c_2 $(0 < c_1 < m_0 < c_2 < \infty)$ with $h(c_1) = h(c_2) = \lambda$. Thus

$$f(t,u) \le \frac{c_1}{\lambda A}, \forall (t,u) \in [0,1] \times [0,c_1]\ and\ f(t,u) \le \frac{c_2}{\lambda A}, \forall (t,u) \in [0,1] \times [0,c_2].$$

On the other hand, from $0 < f_0 = f_\infty = \infty$, there exist constants d_1, d_2 $(0 < d_1 < c_1 < c_2 < d_2 < \infty)$ with $\frac{f(t,u)}{u} \ge 1/\left(\lambda \frac{1}{2}\delta^2 A\right)$ for $(t,u) \in [0,1] \times (0,d_1) \cup \left(\frac{1}{2}\delta^2 d_2, \infty\right)$. Thus

$$f(t,u) \ge \frac{d_1}{\lambda A}, \forall (t,u) \in [0,1] \times \left[\frac{1}{2}\delta^2 d_1, d_1\right]\ and\ f(t,u) \ge \frac{d_2}{\lambda A}, \forall (t,u) \in [0,1] \times \left[\frac{1}{2}\delta^2 d_2, d_2\right].$$

By Theorem 2, there exist two positive solutions u_1, $u_2 \in P$ with $d_1 \le \|u_1\| \le c_1$ and $c_2 \le \|u_2\| \le d_2$.

Theorem 5. *Suppose that* $(H1)$, $(H3)$ *hold. In addition, assume that* $f_0 = f_\infty = 0$. *Then for each* $\lambda \in (\lambda_2, \infty)$, *BVP* (1) *has at least two positive solutions, where* $\lambda_2 = \sup\limits_{m>0} \frac{m}{A \min\limits_{t\in[0,1], u\in\left[\frac{1}{2}\delta^2 m, m\right]} f(t,u)}$.

Proof. Define a function p by $p(m) = \frac{m}{A \min\limits_{t\in[0,1], u\in\left[\frac{1}{2}\delta^2 m, m\right]} f(t,u)}$.

It is easy to see that $h : (0,\infty) \to (0,\infty)$ is continuous and $\lim\limits_{m\to+0} h(m) = \lim\limits_{m\to\infty} h(m) = \infty$. Thus there exists $m_0 \in (0,\infty)$ such that $h(m_0) = \inf\limits_{m>0} h(m) = \lambda_2$.

For $\lambda \in (\lambda_2, \infty)$, there exist constants d_1, d_2 $(0 < d_1 < m_0 < d_2 < \infty)$ with $p(d_1) = p(d_2) = \lambda$. Thus

$$f(t,u) \geq \frac{d_1}{\lambda A}, \forall (t,u) \in [0,1] \times \left[\frac{1}{2}\delta^2 d_1, d_1\right] \; and \; f(t,u) \geq \frac{d_2}{\lambda A}, \forall (t,u) \in [0,1] \times \left[\frac{1}{2}\delta^2 d_2, d_2\right]$$

On the other hand, because $f_0 = 0$, there exist constant c_1 $(0 < c_1 < d_1)$ with $\frac{f(t,u)}{u} \leq \frac{1}{\lambda A}$ for any $(t,u) \in [0,1] \times (0, c_1)$. Thus

$$f(t,u) \leq \frac{c_1}{\lambda A}, \forall (t,u) \in [0,1] \times [0, c_1].$$

By $f_\infty = 0$, there exists constant c $(d_2 < c < \infty)$ with $\frac{f(t,u)}{u} \leq \frac{1}{\lambda A}$ for any $(t,u) \in [0,1] \times (0,\infty)$. Let $M = \sup\limits_{x\in[0,c]} f(x)$ and $c_2 \geq \max\{\lambda M A, c\}$. It is easy to see that

$$f(t,u) \leq \frac{c_2}{\lambda A}, \forall (t,u) \in [0,1] \times [0, c_2].$$

By Theorem 2, there exist two positive solutions u_1, $u_2 \in P$ with $c_1 \leq \|u_1\| \leq d_1$ and $d_2 \leq \|u_2\| \leq c_2$.

Now we discuss the existence of infinitely many positive solutions for BVP (1).

Theorem 6. *Suppose that* $(H1)$, $(H3)$ *hold. In addition, assume that* $0 < f^0$, $f_0 < \infty$. *Then for each* $\lambda \in \left(\frac{1}{\delta^2 A f^0}, \frac{1}{A f_0}\right)$, *BVP* (1) *has infinitely many small enough positive solutions.*

Proof. For $\lambda \in \left(\frac{1}{\delta^2 A f^0}, \frac{1}{A f_0}\right)$ we have $f_0 < \frac{1}{\lambda A}$ and $f^0 > \frac{1}{\lambda \delta^2 A}$. Therefore, there are positive constant sequences $\{a_k\}$, $\{b_k\}$ with $a_k \to 0$, $b_k \to 0$ $(k \to \infty)$ such that

$$\sup_{t\in[0,1]} f(t, a_k) \leq \frac{a_k}{\lambda A}, \quad \inf_{t\in[0,1]} f(t, \delta b_k) \geq \frac{b_k}{\lambda \delta A}, \quad k = 1, 2, \cdots.$$

Without loss of generality, we assume that $a_1 > b_1 > a_2 > b_2 > \cdots > a_k > b_k > \cdots$. In a completely analogous argument, Theorem 2 implies the conclusion of the theorem holds.

In the same way, the following theorem is obvious.

Theorem 7. *Suppose that* $(H1)$, $(H3)$ *hold. In addition, assume that* $0 < f^\infty, f_\infty < \infty$. *Then for each* $\lambda \in \left(\frac{1}{\delta^2 A f^\infty}, \frac{1}{A f_\infty}\right)$, *BVP* (1) *has infinitely many large enough positive solutions.*

References

1. Gregus, M.: Third Order Linear Differential Equations. Math. Appl. Reidel, Dordrecht (1987)
2. Infante, G., Zima, M.: Positive solutions of multi-point boundary value problems at resonance. Nonlinear Anal. 69, 2458–2465 (2008)
3. Anderson, D.R., Davis, J.M.: Multiple solutions and eigenvalues for three-order right focal boundary value problems. J. Math. Anal. Appl. 267, 135–157 (2002)
4. El-Shahed, M.: Positive solutions for nonlinear singular third order boundary value problems. Commun. Nonlinear Sci. Numer. Simul. 14, 424–429 (2009)
5. Li, S.: Positive solutions of nonlinear singular third-order two-point boundary value problem. J. Math. Anal. Appl. 323, 413–425 (2006)
6. Avery, R.I., Henderson, J., O'Regan, D.: Four functionals fixed point theorem. Math. Comput. Modelling 48, 1081–1089 (2008)
7. Yao, Q.: The existence and multiplicity of positive solutions for a third-order three-point boundary value problem. Acta Math. Appl. Sinica 19, 117–122 (2003)
8. Du, Z.J., Ge, W.G., Zhou, M.R.: Singular perturbations for third-order nonlinear multi-point boundary value problem. J. Differential Equations 218, 69–90 (2005)
9. Du, Z.J., Lin, X.J., Ge, W.G.: On a third order multi-point boundary value problem at resonance. J. Math. Anal. Appl. 302, 217–229 (2005)
10. Sun, J.P., Zhang, H.E.: Exsitence of solutions to third-order m-point boundary value problems. Electronic J. Differential Equations 125, 1–9 (2008)
11. Zhang, H.E., Sun, J.P.: A generalization of Leggett-Williams fixed point theorem and its application (submitted)
12. Shi, A.L., Zhang, H.E., Sun, J.P.: Singular third-order m-point boundary value problems. Communications in Applied Analysis 12, 353–364 (2008)
13. Guo, D., Lakshmikantham, V.: Nonlinear Problems in Abstract Cones. Academic Press, San Diego (1988)
14. Krasnoselskii, M.A.: Positive Solutions of Operator Equations, Noordhoff, Groningen (1964)

Time Asymptotically Almost Periodic Viscosity Solutions of Hamilton-Jacobi Equations

Shilin Zhang*

School of Mathematics, Shandong University, Jinan , 250100, China
shilinzhang@yahoo.cn

Abstract. To investigate the uniqueness and existence of viscosity solutions of Hamilton-Jacobi equations in the time asymptotically almost periodic case, this paper use the comparison theorem of Hamilton-Jacobi equations and the property of the asymptotically almost periodic functions to get such results.

Keywords: Hamilton-Jacobi equations, time asymptotically almost periodic viscosity solutions, asymptotically almost periodic functions.

1 Introduction

In this paper we consider the viscosity solutions of first order Hamilton-Jacobi equations of the form

$$\partial_t u + H(x, u, Du) = f(t), \ (x,t) \in \mathbb{R}^N \times \mathbb{R} \tag{1.1}$$

This problem was studied in paper [1] in the time periodic and almost periodic cases. And papers by Crandall and Lions (see [2-4]) proved the uniqueness and stability of viscosity solutions for a large class of equations, in particular for the initial value problem

$$\begin{cases} \partial_t u + H(x,t,u,Du) = 0, \ (x,t) \in \mathbb{R}^N \times]0,T[, \\ u(x,0) = u_0(x), \ x \in \mathbb{R}^N \end{cases} \tag{1.2}$$

and also for the stationary problem

$$H(x,u,Du) = 0, x \in \mathbb{R}^N. \tag{1.3}$$

Recently many papers concerning on the viscosity solutions of Hamilton-Jacobi equations have been published (see [5-8]), also the author of this article have studied the time almost-periodic viscosity solutions of parabolic equations (see [9]) and time remotely almost periodic viscosity solutions of Hamilton-Jacobi equations (see [10]).

Now in this paper we study this problem in a more regular condition, i.e. in the time asymptotically almost periodic case. That is we will look for such

* Supported by National Science Foundation of China (Grant No.11001152).

C. Liu, J. Chang, and A. Yang (Eds.): ICICA 2011, Part I, CCIS 243, pp. 9–15, 2011.

viscosity solutions when the hamiltonian H and f are continuous functions, f is asymptotically almost periodic in t. The asymptotically almost periodic functions were first introduced in [11,12] by Fréchet. There are other papers concern on such functions (see [13,14]).

Let X be a Banach space. Let Ω be a closed subset of X, let $J \in \{\mathbb{R}^+, \mathbb{R}\}$ and let $\phi(J \times \Omega, X)$ (respectively, $\phi(J, X)$) be the space of bounded continuous functions from $J \times \Omega$ (respectively, J) to X with supremum norm.

Definition 1.1. $f(t) \in C(\mathbb{R}^+)$ is said to be a asymptotically almost periodic function on $\mathbb{R}^+$, if it is a sum of a continuous almost periodic function $g(t)$ defined on $\mathbb{R}$ and a continuous function $\varphi(t)$ defined on $\mathbb{R}^+$ which satisfied $\lim_{t\to+\infty} \varphi(t) = 0$, that is

$$f(t) = g(t) + \varphi(t),$$

in which $g(t)$ is called the almost periodic part of $f(t)$. Denote by $AAP(\mathbb{R}^+)$ all such functions.

Definition 1.2. Let $f(t) \in C(\mathbb{R}^+)$, for any $\varepsilon > 0$, there exists $l(\varepsilon) > 0$ and $N(\varepsilon) \geq 0$, such that any interval of length $l(\varepsilon)$ in $\mathbb{R}^+$ contains τ satisfies

$$|f(t+\tau) - f(t)| < \varepsilon,$$

for any $t \geq N(\varepsilon)$, denote by $T(f, \varepsilon)$ all such τ. Then we call $f(t)$ is a asymptotically almost periodic function on $\mathbb{R}^+$.

Theorem 1.3. If $f(t) \in AAP(\mathbb{R}^+)$, then $f(t)$ is bounded and uniformly continuous on $\mathbb{R}^+$.

Definition 1.4. A function $f \in \phi(J \times \Omega, X)$ is said to be asymptotically almost periodic in $t \in J$ and uniform on compact subsets of Ω if for every $\varepsilon > 0$ and every compact subset K of Ω, there exist a relatively dense subset P and a bounded subset C of J such that

$$\|f(t+\tau, x) - f(t, x)\| < \varepsilon(\tau \in P, t, t+\tau \in J \setminus C, x \in K).$$

Denote by $AAP(J \times \Omega, X)$ all such functions.

Proposition 1.5. Assume that $f(t)$ is asymptotically almost periodic. Then $\frac{1}{T}\int_a^{a+T} f(t)dt$ converges as $T \to +\infty$ uniformly with respect to $a \in R$. Moreover the limit does not depend on a and it is called the average of f

$$\exists\langle f\rangle := \lim_{T\to+\infty} \frac{1}{T}\int_a^{a+T} f(t)dt, \quad uniformly\ with\ respect\ to\ a \in R.$$

Proof. As $f(t) \in AAP(R)$, then $f(t)$ is bounded, and $\forall\varepsilon > 0, \forall\tau \in T(f, \varepsilon), \exists s_0 > 0$, when $|t| > s_0, |f(t+\tau) - f(t)| < \varepsilon$. Let $G = \sup_{t\in R} |f(t)|$, take $\varepsilon > 0$, assume $l = l(\frac{\varepsilon}{4})$ is an interval length of $T(f, \frac{\varepsilon}{4})$. Take $\tau \in T(f, \frac{\varepsilon}{4}) \cap [a, a+l]$, then for any $a, s \in R$

$$\begin{aligned}|\int_a^{a+s} f(t)dt - \int_0^s f(t)dt| &= |(\int_\tau^{\tau+s} - \int_0^s + \int_{\tau+s}^{a+s} + \int_a^\tau)f(t)dt| \\ &\le \int_0^s |f(t+\tau)-f(t)|dt + \int_{\tau+s}^{a+s}|f(t)|dt + \int_0^\tau |f(t)|dt \\ &= \int_0^{s_0} |f(t+\tau)-f(t)|dt + \int_{s_0}^{s}|f(t+\tau)-f(t)|dt \\ &\quad + \int_{\tau+s}^{a+s}|f(t)|dt + \int_0^\tau |f(t)|dt \\ &\le \sup_{[s_0,s]} |f(t+\tau)-f(t)|\cdot(s-s_0) + 2G(l+s_0) \\ &< \tfrac{\varepsilon}{4}(s-s_0) + 2G(l+s_0)\end{aligned}$$

so

$$|\frac{1}{T}\int_a^{a+T} f(t)dt - \frac{1}{T}\int_0^T f(t)dt| \le \frac{\varepsilon}{4T}(T-T_0) + \frac{2G(l+T_0)}{T}, \tag{1.4}$$

and

$$\begin{aligned}|\tfrac{1}{nT}\int_0^{nT} f(t)dt - \tfrac{1}{T}\int_0^T f(t)dt| &= \tfrac{1}{n}|\Sigma_{k=1}^n \tfrac{1}{T}[\int_{(k-1)T}^{kT} f(t)dt - \int_0^T f(t)dt]| \\ &\le \tfrac{\varepsilon}{4T}(T-T_0) + \tfrac{2G(l+T_0)}{T},\end{aligned} \tag{1.5}$$

By passing $n \to +\infty$ in (1.5), we get

$$|\langle f\rangle - \frac{1}{T}\int_0^T f(t)dt| \le \frac{\varepsilon}{4T}(T-T_0) + \frac{2G(l+T_0)}{T}, \tag{1.6}$$

Using Triangle Inequality from (1.4) and (1.6) we deduce

$$|\frac{1}{T}\int_a^{a+T} f(t)dt - \langle f\rangle| \le \frac{\varepsilon}{2T}(T-T_0) + \frac{4G(l+T_0)}{T} < \varepsilon,$$

if only $T > \frac{8G(l+T_0)}{\varepsilon} - T_0$. That is : when $T \to \infty$, $\frac{1}{T}\int_a^{a+T} f(t)dt$ converges at $\langle f\rangle$ uniformly with respect to $a \in R$. Moreover notice the identical equation

$$\frac{1}{T}\int_a^{a+T} f(t)dt = \frac{1}{T}\int_0^T f(t+a)dt,$$

This means the limit does not depend on a.

Let $h(t) = \int_{-\infty}^t e^{\gamma(\sigma-t)} f(\sigma)d\sigma$, where $\gamma > 0$ is a constant, $t \in \mathbb{R}$, then we have

Proposition 1.6. If $f(t) \in AAP(\mathbb{R})$, then $h(t) \in AAP(\mathbb{R})$.

Proof. As $f(t) \in AAP(\mathbb{R})$, then

$$f = g + \varphi,$$

where $g \in AP(\mathbb{R})$ and $\lim_{|t|\to\infty} \varphi(t) = 0$. Next we will prove $h(t) \in AAP(\mathbb{R})$.

$$\begin{aligned}h(t) &= \int_{-\infty}^t e^{\gamma(\sigma-t)} f(\sigma)d\sigma \\ &= \int_{-\infty}^t e^{\gamma(\sigma-t)} g(\sigma)d\sigma + \int_{-\infty}^t e^{\gamma(\sigma-t)}\varphi(\sigma)d\sigma\end{aligned}$$

Let $I(t) = \int_{-\infty}^t e^{\gamma(\sigma-t)} g(\sigma)d\sigma$, $II(t) = \int_{-\infty}^t e^{\gamma(\sigma-t)}\varphi(\sigma)d\sigma$. By the proposition of almost periodic functions and $g \in AP(\mathbb{R})$, we know that $I(t) \in AP(\mathbb{R})$. Using the boundedness of φ, we can easily prove that $\lim_{|t|\to\infty} II(t) = 0$. So we have the conclusion $h(t) \in AAP(\mathbb{R})$.

2 Main Results and Proofs

This paper states on the following main hypotheses.

Let us list some hypotheses in the stationary case.

$$\begin{aligned}&\forall 0 < R < +\infty, \exists \gamma_R > 0 : H(x,u,p) - H(x,v,p) \geq \gamma_R(u-v),\\ &for\ all\ x \in \mathbb{R}^N, -R \leq v \leq u \leq R, p \in \mathbb{R}^N;\end{aligned} \tag{2.1}$$

$$\begin{aligned}&\forall R > 0, \exists m_R, \lim_{z\to 0} m_R(z) = 0 : |H(x,u,p) - H(y,u,p)| \leq m_R(|x-y| \cdot (1+|p|)),\\ &for\ all\ x,y \in \mathbb{R}^N, -R \leq u \leq R, p \in \mathbb{R}^N;\end{aligned} \tag{2.2}$$

$$\forall 0 < R < +\infty, \lim_{|p|\to+\infty} H(x,u,p) = +\infty, uniformly\ for\ (x,u) \in \mathbb{R}^N \times [-R,R]; \tag{2.3}$$

$$\forall 0 < R < +\infty, H\ is\ uniformly\ continous\ on\ \mathbb{R}^N \times [-R,R] \times \overline{B}_R; \tag{2.4}$$

$$\exists M > 0 : H(x,-M,0) \leq 0 \leq H(x,M,0), \forall x \in \mathbb{R}^N. \tag{2.5}$$

From paper [1] we know that hypotheses (2.1), (2.2 or 2.3), (2.4), (2.5) ensure the existence of a unique solution for the stationary equation (1.3). And more regularly (2.1) can be replaced by

$$H(x,u,p) - H(x,v,p) \geq 0, \forall x \in \mathbb{R}^N, v \leq u, p \in \mathbb{R}^N, \tag{2.6}$$

(which comes to taking $\gamma_R = 0$ in (2.1).

When the hamiltonian is time dependent the corresponding assumptions are

$$\begin{aligned}&\forall 0 < R < +\infty, \exists \gamma_R > 0 : H(x,t,u,p) - H(x,t,v,p) \geq \gamma_R(u-v),\\ &for\ all\ x \in \mathbb{R}^N, 0 \leq t \leq T, -R \leq v \leq u \leq R, p \in \mathbb{R}^N;\end{aligned} \tag{2.7}$$

$$\begin{aligned}&\forall R > 0, \exists m_R : |H(x,t,u,p) - H(y,t,u,p)| \leq m_R(|x-y| \cdot (1+|p|)),\\ &for\ all\ x,y \in \mathbb{R}^N, t \in [0,T], -R \leq u \leq R, p \in \mathbb{R}^N, where \lim_{z\to 0} m_R(z) = 0;\end{aligned} \tag{2.8}$$

$$\forall 0 < R < +\infty, H\ is\ uniformly\ continous\ on\ \mathbb{R}^N \times [0,T] \times [-R,R] \times \overline{B}_R; \tag{2.9}$$

$$\exists M > 0 : H(x,t,-M,0) \leq 0 \leq H(x,t,M,0), \forall x \in \mathbb{R}^N, t \in [0,T]. \tag{2.10}$$

Now we present two results of viscosity solutions (see [1]).

Theorem 2.1. Assume that (2.7), (2.8), (2.9), (2.10) hold (with $\gamma_R \in \mathbb{R}, \forall R > 0$). Then for every $u_0 \in BUC(\mathbb{R}^N)$ there is a unique viscosity solution $u \in BUC(\mathbb{R}^N \times [0,T])$ of (1.2), $\forall T > 0$.

Theorem 2.2. Let u be a bounded time periodic viscosity u.s.c. subsolution of $\partial_t u + H(x,t,u,Du) = f(x,t)$ in $\mathbb{R}^N \times \mathbb{R}$ and v a bounded time periodic viscosity l.s.c. supersolution of $\partial_t v + H(x,t,v,Dv) = g(x,t)$ in $\mathbb{R}^N \times \mathbb{R}$, where $f, g \in BUC(\mathbb{R}^N \times \mathbb{R})$ and H are T periodic such that (2.7), (2.8), (2.9) hold. Then we have

$$\sup_{x\in\mathbb{R}^N} (u(x,t) - v(x,t)) \leq \sup_{s\leq t} \int_s^t \sup_{x\in\mathbb{R}^N} (f(x,\sigma) - g(x,\sigma)) d\sigma,$$

Moreover, the hypothesis (2.8) can be replaced by $u \in W^{1,\infty}(\mathbb{R}^N \times \mathbb{R})$ or $v \in W^{1,\infty}(\mathbb{R}^N \times \mathbb{R})$.

Now we will prove the uniqueness and existence of asymptotically almost periodic viscosity solutions. For the uniqueness we have the following result.

Theorem 2.3. *Let u a bounded u.s.c. viscosity subsolution of $\partial_t u + H(x,t,u,Du) = f(x,t)$, in $\mathbb{R}^N \times \mathbb{R}$ and v a bounded l.s.c. viscosity supersolution of $\partial_t v + H(x,t,v,Dv) = g(x,t)$, in $\mathbb{R}^N \times \mathbb{R}$ where $f, g \in BUC(\mathbb{R}^N \times \mathbb{R})$ and (2.7), (2.8), (2.9) hold uniformly for $t \in \mathbb{R}$. Then we have for all $t \in \mathbb{R}$*

$$\sup_{x\in\mathbb{R}^N} (u(x,t) - v(x,t))_+ \le e^{-\gamma t} \int_{-\infty}^{t} \sup_{x\in\mathbb{R}^N} (f(x,\sigma) - g(x,\sigma))_+ d\sigma$$

Moreover the hypotheses (2.8) can be replaced by $u \in W^{1,\infty}(\mathbb{R}^N \times \mathbb{R})$ or $v \in W^{1,\infty}(\mathbb{R}^N \times \mathbb{R})$.

Proof. This proposition is similar to the Proposition 6.5 in paper [1].

Now we concentrate on the existence part.

Theorem 2.4. *Assume that $f : \mathbb{R} \to \mathbb{R}$ is asymptotically almost periodic and that the hamiltonian $H = H(x,z,p)$ satisfying the hypotheses (2.1), (2.2), (2.4) and $\exists M > 0$ such that $H(x,-M,0) \le f(t) \le H(x,M,0), \forall (x,t) \in \mathbb{R}^N \times \mathbb{R}$. Then there is a time asymptotically almost periodic viscosity solution in $BC(\mathbb{R}^N \times \mathbb{R})$ of $\partial_t u + H(x,u,Du) = f(t)$, in $\mathbb{R}^N \times \mathbb{R}$.*

Proof. We consider the unique viscosity solution of the problem

$$\begin{cases} \partial_t u_n + H(x,u_n,Du_n) = f(t), \ (x,t) \in \mathbb{R}^N \times]-n,+\infty[, \\ u_n(x,-n) = 0, \ x \in \mathbb{R}^N \end{cases}$$

for all $n \ge 1$. Such a solution exists by Theorem 2.1. Next we will prove that for all $t \in \mathbb{R}$, $(u_n(t))_{n\ge -t}$ converges to a asymptotically almost periodic viscosity solution of $\partial_t u + H(x,u,Du) = f(t)$, in $\mathbb{R}^N \times \mathbb{R}$. As f is asymptotically almost periodic, then for any $\varepsilon > 0$, take $\tau \in P_{\varepsilon_1}$, where $\varepsilon_1 = \frac{\gamma\varepsilon}{2}$. Set $C_{\varepsilon_2} = \{t \in \mathbb{R} : \|\varphi\| \ge \varepsilon_2\}$, where $\varepsilon_2 = \frac{\gamma\varepsilon}{4}$. Similar to the proof of Proposition 6.6 in paper [1], we obtain in $\mathbb{R}^N \times \mathbb{R} \setminus C_{\varepsilon_2}$ by fixing $t, t+\tau \in \mathbb{R} \setminus C_{\varepsilon_2}$ and n large enough

$$|u_n(x,t) - u_n(x,t+\tau)| \le 2M \cdot e^{-\gamma(t-t_n)} + e^{-\gamma t} \int_{t_n}^{t} e^{\gamma\sigma} |f(\sigma+\tau) - f(\sigma)| d\sigma,$$

By passing $n \to +\infty$ we have $t_n \to -\infty$ and using Proposition 1.6 we deduce

$$|u(x,t) - u(x,t+\tau)| \le \varepsilon, (x,t) \in \mathbb{R}^N \times \mathbb{R} \setminus C_{\varepsilon_2}.$$

By Definition 1.4 we conclude that $u(x,t) \in BC(\mathbb{R}^N \times \mathbb{R})$ is asymptotically almost periodic.

Now we study the asymptotic behaviour of time asymptotically almost periodic viscosity solutions of

$$\partial_t u_n + H(x,u_n,Du_n) = f_n(t), \ (x,t) \in \mathbb{R}^N \times \mathbb{R}. \tag{2.11}$$

where $f : \mathbb{R} \to \mathbb{R}$ is a asymptotically almost periodic function. For all $n \geq 1$ notice that $f_n(t) = f(nt), \forall t \in \mathbb{R}$ is asymptotically almost periodic and has the same average as f. Now suppose that such a hypothesis exists

$$\exists M > 0 \text{ such that } H(x, -M, 0) \leq f(t), \forall (x,t) \in \mathbb{R}^N \times \mathbb{R}. \tag{2.12}$$

We introduce also the stationary equation

$$H(x, u, Du) = \langle f \rangle := \frac{1}{T} \int_0^T f(t)dt, \ x \in \mathbb{R}^N. \tag{2.13}$$

Theorem 2.7 *Let $H = H(x,z,p)$ be a hamiltonian satisfying (2.6), (2.2), (2.4), (2.12) where f is asymptotically almost periodic function. Suppose also that there is a bounded l.s.c viscosity supersolution $\tilde{V} \geq -M$ of (2.13), that $t \to F(t) = \int_0^t \{f(s) - \langle f \rangle\}ds$ is bounded and denote by V, v_n the minimal stationary, resp. time asymptotically almost periodic l.s.c. viscosity supersolution of (2.13), resp. (2.11). Then the sequence $(v_n)_n$ converges uniformly on $\mathbb{R}^N \times \mathbb{R}$ towards V and $\|v_n - V\|_{L^\infty(\mathbb{R}^N \times \mathbb{R})} \leq \frac{2}{n}\|F\|_{L^\infty(\mathbb{R})}, \forall n \geq 1$.*

Proof. As $v_n = \sup_{\alpha>0} v_{n,\alpha}$ is asymptotically almost periodic, we introduce $w_{n,\alpha}(x,t) = v_{n,\alpha}(x, \frac{t}{n}), (x,t) \in \mathbb{R}^N \times \mathbb{R}$, which is also asymptotically almost periodic. Similar to Theorem 5.1 in paper [1] and by using Theorem 2.2 we deduce that

$$w_{n,\alpha}(x,t) - V_\alpha(x) \leq \sup_{s \leq t} \frac{1}{n} \int_s^t (f(\sigma) - \langle f \rangle)d\sigma \leq \frac{2}{n}\|F\|_{L^\infty(\mathbb{R})},$$

and similarly $V_\alpha(x) - w_{n,\alpha}(x,t) \leq \frac{2}{n}\|F\|_{L^\infty(\mathbb{R})}, \forall n \geq 1$. We have for all $n \leq 1$

$$|w_{n,\alpha}(x,t) - V_\alpha(x)| \leq \frac{2}{n}\|F\|_{L^\infty(\mathbb{R})},$$

and after passing to the limit for $\alpha \searrow 0$ one gets for all $(x,t) \in \mathbb{R}^N \times \mathbb{R}$

$$|w_n(x,t) - V(x)| \leq \frac{2}{n}\|F\|_{L^\infty(\mathbb{R})}.$$

Finally we deduce that $\|v_n - V\|_{L^\infty(\mathbb{R}^N \times \mathbb{R})} \leq \frac{2}{n}\|F\|_{L^\infty(\mathbb{R}^N \times \mathbb{R})}$ for all $n \geq 1$.

References

1. Bostan, M., Namah, G.: Time periodic viscosity solutions of Hamilton-Jacobi equaitons. Commun. Pure Appl. Anal. 6(2), 389–410 (2007)
2. Crandall, M.G., Lions, P.-L.: Condition d'unicité pour les solutions génćralisées des équations de Hamilton-Jacobi du premier order. C. R. Acad. Sci. Paris, Sér. I Math. 292, 183–186 (1981)
3. Crandall, M.G., Lions, P.-L.: Viscosity solutions of Hamilton-Jacobi equations. Trans. Amer. Math. Soc. 277, 1–42 (1983)

4. Crandall, M.G., Evans, L.C., Lions, P.-L.: Some properties of viscosity solutions of Hamilton-Jacobi equations. Trans. Amer. Math. Soc. 282, 487–502 (1984)
5. Feng, J., Katsoulakis, M.: A Comparison Principle for Hamilton-Jacobi Equations Related to Controlled Gradient Flows in Infinite Dimensions. Arch. Rational Mech. Anal. 192, 275–310 (2009), doi:10.1007/s00205-008-0133-5
6. Strömberg, T.: A counterexample to uniqueness of generalized characteristics in Hamilton-Jacobi theory. Nonlinear Analysis 74, 2758–2762 (2011)
7. Azagra, D., Ferrera, J., López-Mesas, F.: A maximum principle for evolution Hamilton-Jacobi equations on Riemannian manifolds. J. Math. Anal. Appl. 323, 473–480 (2006)
8. Ibrahim, H.: Existence and uniqueness for a nonlinear parabolic/Hamilton-Jacobi coupled system describing the dynamics of dislocation densities. Ann. I. H. Poincaré-AN 26, 415–435 (2009)
9. Zhang, S., Piao, D.: Almost periodic viscosity solutions of nonlinear parabolic equations. Boundary Value Problems 2009, Article ID 873526, 15 pages (2009), doi:10.1155/2009/873526
10. Zhang, S., Piao, D.: Time remotely almost-periodic viscosity solutions of Hamilton-Jacobi equations. ISRN Mathematical Analysis 2011, Article ID 415358, 13 pages (2011), doi:10.5402/2011/415358
11. Fréchet, M.: Les fonctions asymptotiquement presque-périodiques. Revue Sci (Rev. Rose Illus.) 79, 341–354 (1941)
12. Fréchet, M.: Les fonctions asymptotiquement presque-périodiques continues. C. R. Acad. Sci. Paris 213, 520–522 (1941)
13. Zhang, C.: Ergodicity and asymptotically almost periodic solutions of some differential equations. International Journal of Mathematics and Mathematical Sciences 25(12), 787–800 (2001)
14. Buse, C.: A spectral mapping theorem for evolution semigroups on asymptotically almost periodic functions defined on the half line. Electronic Journal of Differential Equations 2002(70), 111 (2002)

Fuzzy Mathematics Method in the Evaluation of Teaching Ability

Youchu Huang

College of Mathematics and Information Science, Wenzhou University,Wenzhou China
hyc@wzu.edu.cn

Abstract. Educational evaluation will get fuzzy information in most time, which limits us to judge who is good and bad. In this article the author give a new method, which is built by fuzzy mathematics. The method can reduce personal disturbances, contribute to comparison, bring educational evaluation into scientific. The author used the method in the evaluation of teaching ability, obtained satisfactory results.

Keywords: Fuzzy mathematics, Education, Evaluation.

1 Introduction

Teacher's teaching ability is very important for education. In order to improve teacher's teaching ability, many schools have held teaching ability competition. But the information that the judges received is vague, such as good language, write a good word, good instructional design, etc. It's difficult for them to distinguish whose teaching ability is the best, whose teaching ability is the worst.

To solve these problems, we give a new method. The method is built by fuzzy mathematics, which can transform fuzzy information into numerical information [1]. Fuzzy mathematics is founded by the professor Zadeh in 1965, who is come from the University of California U.S. Initially, fuzzy mathematics is used in the field of the control and other related engineering research. In recent years, fuzzy mathematics are widely used in the humanities and social sciences fields [2].

In this article the author built a fuzzy mathematics method, which can reduce the influence of human factors, improve the fairness and accuracy of the evaluation. The method made the result of teaching ability evaluation easy to sort. We use the method in teaching ability evaluate can obtain a satisfactory results.

2 The Fuzzy Mathematics Method

Education evaluation must be clear evaluation objectives, evaluation of content and weight. The model is built around these areas as the evaluation factor, evaluation weight, evaluation grade and evaluation result.

C. Liu, J. Chang, and A. Yang (Eds.): ICICA 2011, Part I, CCIS 243, pp. 16–22, 2011.

2.1 Establishment of the Set of Evaluation Factors $U=(u_1,u_2,\cdots,u_n)$

In the first, we should select some factors to evaluate teaching ability. The factors constitute a set

$$U=(u_1,u_2,\cdots,u_n),$$

n equal to the number of factors [3]. For example, if we select five factors, such as language performance, blackboard-writing, instructional design, teaching attitudes and classroom atmosphere to evaluate teaching ability, we will get the set of evaluation factor

$$U=(u_1,u_2,u_3,u_4,u_5).$$

In the set, u_1 means language performance, u_2 means blackboard-writing, u_3 means instructional design, u_4 means teaching attitudes and u_5 means classroom atmosphere.

2.2 Give Each Factor a Weight, Get a Set of Weight $A=(a_1,a_2,\cdots,a_n)$

The importance of each factor is different to teaching ability. To distinguish the importance of each factor, we should give each factor a weight. We will get a set of weight

$$A=(a_1,a_2,\cdots,a_n)$$

Each weight a_i corresponds to each factor u_i ($1\le i\le n$) [4]. The greater of the weight indicate that the more important of the factor. In order to standardize operations, we should let $\sum_{i=1}^{n} a_i = 1$.

2.3 Establishment the Set of Evaluation Grade $V=(v_1,v_2,\cdots,v_m)$

We should give each factor a grade, when we evaluate someone's teaching ability. All grades what we can be selected constitute a set of evaluation grade

$$V=(v_1,v_2,\cdots,v_m),$$

m equal to the number of grades [5]. For example, if we can select excellent, good, medium, pass and bad to measure each factors, we will get a set of evaluation grade

$$V=(v_1,v_2,v_3,v_4,v_5).$$

In the set, v_1 means excellent, v_2 means good, v_3 means medium, v_4 means pass and v_5 means bad.

2.4 Establishment of Fuzzy Evaluation Matrix $R_{n\times m}$

When the judges evaluate someone's teaching ability, they will give each factor a grade. After statistics, we will get that person's evaluation result. The person's each factor is an evaluation fuzzy sets

$$R_i=(r_{i1},r_{i2},\cdots,r_{im}),$$

i corresponds to the factor u_i, r_{ij} corresponds to the grade of v_j, In order to standardize operations, we should let $\sum_{j=1}^{m} r_{ij}=1$ $(i=1,2,\cdots,n)$[6].

For example, the fuzzy sets

$$R_1=(0.1,0.2,0.3,0.2,0.2)$$

show that 10% judges give the person's first factor (u_1) is v_1, 20% judges give v_2, 30% judges give v_2, 20% judges give v_3 and 20% judges give v_5. Similarly, we can get the person's every factor's evaluation fuzzy set. Then we get the person's fuzzy evaluation matrix [7]:

$$R=\begin{pmatrix} r_{11} & r_{12} & \cdots & r_{1m} \\ r_{21} & r_{22} & \cdots & r_{2m} \\ \cdots & \cdots & \cdots & \cdots \\ r_{n1} & r_{n2} & \cdots & r_{nm} \end{pmatrix}$$

n equal to the number of the factor. m equal to the number of the evaluation grade.

2.5 Get the Set of Evaluation Result $B=(b_1,b_2,\cdots,b_m)$

Let the set of weight A and the fuzzy comparison matrix R be fuzzy operation, we will get a preliminary results of the person's evaluation.

$$B=A\circ R_{n\times m}=(a_1,a_2,\cdots,a_n)\circ\begin{pmatrix} r_{11} & r_{12} & \cdots & r_{1m} \\ r_{21} & r_{22} & \cdots & r_{2m} \\ \cdots & \cdots & \cdots & \cdots \\ r_{n1} & r_{n2} & \cdots & r_{nm} \end{pmatrix}=(b_1,b_2,\cdots,b_m)$$

In which,

$$b_j=(a_1\wedge r_{1j})\vee(a_2\wedge r_{2j})\vee\cdots(a_n\wedge r_{nj}),$$

$$a_i\wedge r_{ij}=\max\{a_i,r_{ij}\},\ a_i\vee r_{ij}=\min\{a_i,r_{ij}\}\ [8].$$

If we normalized the results, we will obtain standardized vector of fuzzy evaluation .

$$b_j' = \frac{b_j}{\sum_{j=1}^{m} b_j},$$

then we will get the result set $B' = (b_1', b_2', \cdots, b_m')$. Obvious, $\sum_{j=1}^{m} b_j' = 1$.

In the set B', b_i' corresponds to the person's teaching ability is grade v_i [9]. If we get every grade a point, we can get a number of the result of the person's teaching ability [10].

3 Application Examples

3.1 Establishment of the Set of Evaluation Factors $U = (u_1, u_2, u_3, u_4, u_5)$

We think the teaching ability should include language performance, blackboard-writing, instructional design, teaching attitudes and classroom atmosphere. Then we will build a set of evaluation factors

$$U = (u_1, u_2, u_3, u_4, u_5)$$

3.2 Give Each Factor a Weight, Get a Set of Weight $A = (a_1, a_2, a_3, a_4, a_5)$

After discussion, we give every factor a weight and get a set of weight

$$A = (0.25, 0.15, 0.35, 0.1, 0.15).$$

Then

$$0.25+0.15+0.35+0.1+0.15=1.$$

Which means language performance's weight is 0.25, blackboard-writing's weight is 0.15, instructional design's weight is 0.35, teaching attitudes' weight is 0.1, classroom atmosphere's weight is 0.15.

3.3 Establishment the Set of Evaluation Grade $V = (v_1, v_2, v_3, v_4, v_5)$

We give five levels to each evaluation factors. Then we get a set of evaluation grade V = (excellent, good, medium, pass, bad).

3.4 Establishment of Fuzzy Evaluation Matrix $R_{5\times5}$

If the result of a teacher's language performance evaluation is 15 percent of the judges think the person's language performance is excellent, 30 percent of the judges think the person's language performance is good, 35 percent of the judges think the person's language performance is medium, 20 percent of the judges think the person's language performance is pass, 0 percent of the judges think the person's language performance is bad.

We will get

$$R_1 = (0.15, 0.3, 0.35, 0.2, 0).$$

Similarly, we will get the result of blackboard-writing instructional design, teaching attitudes and classroom atmosphere evaluation grade is

$$R_2 = (0.1, 0.3, 0.3, 0.25, 0.05),$$

$$R_3 = (0, 0.15, 0.35, 0.35, 0.15),$$

$$R_4 = (0.3, 0.35, 0.3, 0.05, 0),$$

$$R_5 = (0.1, 0.25, 0.35, 0.3, 0)。$$

Then, we will get the matrix

$$R = \begin{pmatrix} 0.15 & 0.3 & 0.35 & 0.2 & 0 \\ 0.1 & 0.3 & 0.3 & 0.25 & 0.05 \\ 0 & 0.15 & 0.35 & 0.35 & 0.15 \\ 0.3 & 0.35 & 0.3 & 0.05 & 0 \\ 0.1 & 0.25 & 0.35 & 0.3 & 0 \end{pmatrix},$$

3.5 Get the Set of Evaluation Result B and B'

$$B = A \circ R = (0.15, 0.3, 0.35, 0.2, 0) \circ \begin{pmatrix} 0.15 & 0.3 & 0.35 & 0.2 & 0 \\ 0.1 & 0.3 & 0.3 & 0.25 & 0.05 \\ 0 & 0.15 & 0.35 & 0.35 & 0.15 \\ 0.3 & 0.35 & 0.3 & 0.05 & 0 \\ 0.1 & 0.25 & 0.35 & 0.3 & 0 \end{pmatrix}$$

$$= (0.2, 0.3, 0.35, 0.35, 0.15)$$

We get the set Standardization,

$$b_1' = \frac{b_1}{b_1 + b_2 + b_3 + b_4 + b_5} = \frac{0.2}{0.2 + 0.3 + 0.35 + 0.35 + 0.15} = 0.15$$

Similarly, we will get

$$b_2' = 0.22, b_3' = 0.26, b_4' = 0.26, b_5' = 0.11.$$

Which made

$$b_1' + b_2' + b_3' + b_4' + b_5' = 1 \circ$$

Then, we get the result of the person's teaching ability, the result set is

$$B' = (0.15, 0.22, 0.26, 0.26, 0.11).$$

That's mean 15% judges evaluate the teacher's teaching ability is excellent, 22% judges evaluate he teacher's teaching ability is good, 26% judges evaluate the teacher's teaching ability is medium, 26% judges evaluate he teacher's teaching ability is pass, and 11% judges evaluate he teacher's teaching ability is bad.

If we let excellent equal to 95, good equal to 80, medium equal to 70, pass equal to 60 and bad equal to 50, we will get the set of score

$$C = (95, 80, 70, 60, 50).$$

Then, we will get a score to the result of the teacher's teaching ability:

$$d = B' \cdot C^T = 95 \times 0.15 + 80 \times 0.22 + 70 \times 0.26 + 60 \times 0.26 + 50 \times 0.11 = 71.15.$$

That's mean the teacher's teaching ability evaluate get a number of 71.15.

4 Conclusion

This model can be used for a variety of evaluation with fuzzy information, such as some kinds of ability test, professional title assessment etc. The model can do with fuzzy information and let evaluation results quantization, which will reduce the human factors impact on the evaluation results and improve the evaluation of scientific [11]. It's an effective model of educational assessment.

References

1. Li, A., Wu, D.: Fuzzy Mathematics and Its Application. Xinjiang People's Publishing House, Wulumuqi (1986) (in Chinese)
2. Li, Y.: Method of Fuzzy Synthetic Judgment Using in the Assessment of the Title of Technical Post. Mathematics in Practice and Theory 34(12), 13–15 (2004) (in Chinese)

3. Huang, Y.: Fuzzy Mathematics Using in Educational Evaluation. College Mathematics 1, 134–137 (2009) (in Chinese)
4. Feng, M.: A Model for Fuzzy Comprehensive Assessment of Teacher Work. Mathematics in Practice and Theory 34(11), 35–37 (2004) (in Chinese)
5. Hong, C., Teng, Y.: Application of Fuzzy Comprehensive Evaluation in the Tenders Decision. Journal of Jilin Architectural and Civil Engineering Institute 24(2), 74–77 (2007) (in Chinese)
6. Lai, S., Yin, G.: The application of fuzzy comprehensive evaluation theory on engineering bidding evaluation. Journal of Heilongjiang Institute of Technology 21(2), 15–17 (2007) (in Chinese)
7. Fu, L.: Research on the Construction of Fuzzy Evaluation System of College Students Based on the Dominant Position of Students. Journal of Chongqing Technology Business University (Nat. Sci. Ed) 27(2), 202–207 (2010) (in Chinese)
8. Xue, W., Wang, L.: A fuzzy evaluation of supply chain information risk under Ecommerce. Journal of Dalian Maritime University 37(1), 99–102 (2011) (in Chinese)
9. Mo, S.: Evaluation model of competitiveness of agricultural wholesale market based on Fuzzy Comprehensive Evaluation. Guangdong Agricultural Sciences 1, 174–177 (2011) (in Chinese)
10. Wang, Q., Jiao, B.: Optimal Route Selection Based on Grey Fuzzy Comprehensive Evaluating. Technology & Economy in Areas of Communications 1, 57–59+68 (2010) (in Chinese)
11. Peng, Z.: Fuzzy Mathematics and Application. Wuhan University Publishing House, Wuhan (2002) (in Chinese)

Hamilton Non-holonomic Momentum Equation of the System and Conclusions

Hongfang Liu[1], Ruijuan Li[2], and Nana Li[1]

[1] Tangshan College, Tangshan, P.R. China
[2] Langfang Normal College, Langfang, P.R. China
lhf_gir@tom.com, {liruijuan03,lalazinana}@126.com

Abstract. Mechanical system nonholonomic constraint by more and more international wide attention and sparked the modern technology china-africa complete constraint technology is widely used. The article take poisson opinions on nonholonomic constraint mechanics poisson theory to study, with the conservation of momentum equations are given nonholonomic constraint Hamilton mechanical system equation, gets some conclusion.

Keywords: Nonholonomic systems, dynamic analysis, Lagrange-d'Alembert variational principle, Lyapunov stability of equilibrium, stability of motion.

1 Introduction

Non-holonomic system originated in the Lagrange-d'Alembert principles. Ferrers by adding constraints in the form of Euler-Lagrange equations derived non-holonomic system of equations of motion. In recent years, with the theoretical development of the perfect, modern mathematics, engineering and other specialized, non-holonomic system, more and more widespread international concern and led to modern technology, technology is widely applied nonholonomic constraints .

Lagrange mechanics according to some basic principles, we now consider the non-holonomic system of Hamilton. This requires the use of law of conservation of momentum equation, the value of the momentum is changing, it is natural to take the Poisson point of view is reasonable [1], on this basis, the following non-holonomic theory of Poisson [2].

First, the symmetry does not necessarily lead to conservation laws, it is a momentum equation. Secondly, the usual Poisson operator does not meet the Jacobi identity. In fact, the so-called Jacobian (when to meet the Jacobi equation, the cycle sum to zero) or the equivalent of saying, Schouten said nonholonomic constraints computing the curvature of the distribution function. Therefore, in the non-holonomic system, there is always recent Poisson structure.

2 Poisson Representation

Van der schaft and Maschke's approach is based on the configuration space Q Lagrange function L , where the mean kinetic energy minus potential energy, that is,

C. Liu, J. Chang, and A. Yang (Eds.): ICICA 2011, Part I, CCIS 243, pp. 23–29, 2011.

$$L(q,\dot{q})=\frac{1}{2}<<q,\dot{q}>>-V(q)$$

Which $<<\cdot,\cdot>>$ As defined in the configuration space Q metric, V is the potential energy function.As noted above, the distribution of non-holonomic constraint is given by $D\subset TQ$.Make $D^{\circ}\subset T^{*}Q$ its annihilator, annihilator with ω^{α} that the base is zero, You can write a constraint can be writed

$$\omega^{\alpha}(\dot{q})=0\ ,\ \alpha=1,\cdots,k$$

Cotangent bundle by $T^{*}Q$ the canonical Poisson bracket installed, its coordinates is (q,p), then

$$\{F,G\}(q,p)=\frac{\partial F}{\partial q^{i}}\frac{\partial G}{\partial p^{i}}-\frac{\partial F}{\partial p^{i}}\frac{\partial G}{\partial q^{i}}=\left(\frac{\partial F}{\partial q},\frac{\partial G}{\partial p}\right)^{T}J\begin{pmatrix}\frac{\partial G}{\partial q}\\ \frac{\partial G}{\partial p}\end{pmatrix}$$

In which J is canonical Poisson tensor

$$J=\begin{pmatrix}0_{n} & I_{n}\\ -I_{n} & 0_{n}\end{pmatrix}$$

In the Lagrange system with different Lagrange multipliers do not describe the Hamilton equation, But with $T^{*}Q$ vector field Submanifolds said. Van der schaft and Maschkle is achieved by coordinate transformation [1], Bloch and others I have used the following approach [3].

First, phase space constraints $M=FL(D)\subset T^{*}Q$,Hamilton method with the constraint that $p\in M$,Under the local coordinate

$$M=\left\{(q,p)\in T^{*}Q\mid\omega^{\alpha}\frac{\partial H}{\partial p_{i}}=0\right\}$$

Make $\{X_{\alpha}\}$ the base for the constraint distribution D, $\{\omega^{a}\}$ is Ground zero annihilator D°, $\{\omega_{a}\}$ is the complement of the subspace D, Makes $\langle\omega^{a},\omega_{b}\rangle=\delta_{b}^{a}$, δ_{b}^{a} is Kronecker function, $a=1,\cdots,k$, $\alpha=1,\cdots,n-k$, Coordinate transformation defined as $(q,p)\rightarrow(q,\tilde{p}_{\alpha},\tilde{p}_{a})$,which

$$\tilde{p}_{\alpha}=X_{\alpha}^{i}p_{i}\ ,\ \tilde{p}_{a}=\omega_{\alpha}^{i}p_{i} \tag{2.1}$$

This is caused by Van der schaft and Maschkle new coordinates given $(q,\tilde{p}_{\alpha},\tilde{p}_{a})$ [1], The Poisson tensor is

$$\tilde{J}(q,\tilde{p})=\begin{pmatrix}\{q^i,q^j\} & \{q^i,\tilde{p}_j\}\\ \{\tilde{p}_i,q^j\} & \{\tilde{p}_i,\tilde{p}_j\}\end{pmatrix} \tag{2.2}$$

So that $(\tilde{p}_\alpha,\tilde{p}_a)$ satisfies the constraint equations $\frac{\partial\tilde{H}}{\partial\tilde{p}_a}(q,\tilde{p})=0$, There

$$M=\left\{(q,\tilde{p}_\alpha,\tilde{p}_a)\mid\frac{\partial\tilde{H}}{\partial\tilde{p}_a}(q,\tilde{p}_\alpha,\tilde{p}_a)=0\right\}$$

Use $(q,\tilde{p}_\alpha)$ to express the coordinates of M , There

$$\frac{\partial\tilde{H}}{\partial q^j}(q,\tilde{p}_\alpha,\tilde{p}_a)=\frac{\partial H_M}{\partial q^j}(q,\tilde{p}_\alpha)$$

$$\frac{\partial\tilde{H}}{\partial\tilde{p}_\beta}(q,\tilde{p}_\alpha,\tilde{p}_a)=\frac{\partial H_M}{\partial\tilde{p}_\beta}(q,\tilde{p}_\alpha)$$

H_M is the induction of coordinates for the restricted Hamilton function of M . Remove the formula (2.2) k rows and k columns in the back, Constraint in M tensor induced on the coordinates of $(q^i,\tilde{p}_\alpha)$ can be expressed as

$$\begin{pmatrix}\dot{q}^i\\ \dot{\tilde{p}}_\alpha\end{pmatrix}=J_M(q,\tilde{p}_\alpha)\begin{pmatrix}\frac{\partial H_M}{\partial q^j}(q,\tilde{p}_\alpha)\\ \frac{\partial H_M}{\partial\tilde{p}_\beta}(q,\tilde{p}_\alpha)\end{pmatrix},\begin{pmatrix}q^i\\ \tilde{p}_\alpha\end{pmatrix}\in M \tag{2.3}$$

J_M is the matrix $\tilde{J}$ in k rows and k columns removed after the $(2n-k)$ - $(2n-k)$ matrix.

In the constraint matrix J_M defined $\{\cdot,\cdot\}_M$ on the submanifold, there

$$\{F_M,G_M\}_M(q,\tilde{p}_\alpha):=\begin{pmatrix}\frac{\partial F_M}{\partial q^i} & \frac{\partial F_M}{\partial\tilde{p}_\alpha}\end{pmatrix}^T J_M(q^i,\tilde{p}_\alpha)\begin{pmatrix}\frac{\partial G_M}{\partial q_j}\\ \frac{\partial G_M}{\partial\tilde{p}_\beta}\end{pmatrix}$$

In the constrained sub-manifold M , F_M,G_M is a smooth function, Obviously $\{\cdot,\cdot\}_M$ is to meet the first and second conditions of Poisson operator, the anti-symmetry and Leibniz rule. If and only if constraint operation is bound to complete the Jacobian of., In addition, H_M notice by the anti-symmetry is integrable.

3 Constrained Hamilton Equations

As in the full mechanics, Poisson representation and representation in the Lagrange Lagrange transformation are equivalent. Nature can be thought of in the non-holonomic whether such a relationship. The following can be used Van der schaft and Maschkle general method gives the dynamic equations of non-holonomic constraint theorem.

Theorem 1. Make $q^i = (r^\alpha, s^a)$ for the local coordinate, then ω^α can be expressed as:

$$\omega^a(q) = ds^a + A^a_\alpha(\dot{r}, s)dr^\alpha \tag{3.1}$$

This $A^a_\alpha(r,s)$ is the Ehresmann contact coordinates. In M nonholonomic constraint on the Hamilton equations of motion can be written as

$$\dot{s}_\alpha = -A^a_\beta \frac{\partial H_M}{\partial \tilde{p}_\beta}$$

$$\dot{r}_\alpha = \frac{\partial H_M}{\partial \tilde{p}_\alpha}$$

$$\dot{\tilde{p}}_\alpha = \frac{\partial H_M}{\partial r^\alpha} + A^b_\beta \frac{\partial H_M}{\partial s^b} - p_b B^b_{\alpha\beta} \frac{\partial H_M}{\partial \tilde{p}_\beta}$$

Where $B^b_{\alpha\beta}$ is the contact in the curvature coefficient Ehresmann, p_b is to M the limit, denoted by $(p_b)_M$.

Can prove Theorem 1 in the equation and the Lagrange-d'Alembert equation is equivalent [3]. It should be noted that, after some of the non-holonomic systems theory approach in the intrinsic speed of the phase space under the constraints induced by the kinetic energy of the D/G said the introduction of the induction phase space constraints on the Lagrange function:

$$l_c : D/G \to R$$

Here we do not discuss their reasons, in Bloch, Marsden and Ratiu, who have given the equations of motion about the Lagrange and Hamilton equations of motion and some of the analysis [3,4,5]. Tangent bundle on the basis of which parallel the right move, given the freedom to coordinate intrinsic mode formula also gives a simple explanation on the momentum equations, in particular, while the intrinsic method clearly shows the reduction equation, but The coordinates of the form is still very complicated.

4 Lie Security Measure on the Power System and the Asymptotic

Nonholonomic dynamic does not necessarily guarantee measure, by contrast, Hamilton is guaranteed and the volume of the system. Nonholonomic system is Poisson, there is energy security, indicating that Hamilton system in both the energy and volume to maintain. Kozolov that integrable nonholonomic systems is a necessary condition for the existence of invariant measures.

About a class of special importance of the non-holonomic constraint equation is the generalized rigid body dynamic equations. Generalized configuration space is a rigid body Lie G ,Lagrange function $L:TG \to R$ is left invariant of lie metric G , Namely: $L(g,\dot{g}) = l(g^{-1}\dot{g})$,there $l: g \to R$ is defined by the formula of a reduction of the Lagrange function in the Lie algebra g , I_{ab} is positive definite inertia tensor $I: g \to g^*$, By the Euler-Poincar equations can be given some of the generalized rigid body dynamic

$$\dot{p}_b = C^c_{ab} I^{ad} p_c p_d = C^c_{ab} p_c \Omega^a \tag{4.1}$$

Where $p_b = I_{ab}\Omega^a$ is the momentum component, C^c_{ab} is the Lie algebra structure constant in the system (4.1) is Hamiltonian. The following theorem shows that in the phase space volume does not have security of.

Theorem 2. Euler-Poincar equations have an invariant measure if and only if G is unimodular group, the constraint is a generalized rigid body dynamic system (4.1) must satisfy the left invariant nonholonomic constraints

$$\langle a, \Omega \rangle = a_i \Omega^i = 0 \tag{4.2}$$

Where a is the dual Lie algebra g^* of the fixed element, $\langle \cdot,\cdot \rangle$ refers to the dual Lie algebra and Lie algebra elements in the natural pairing. Qiapu Lei Jin sled and Suslov problem is a typical example.

Constrained power generalized rigid body can be reduced by the Euler-Poincar-Suslov equations

$$\dot{p}_b = C^c_{ab} I^{ad} p_c p_d + \lambda a_b = C^c_{ab} p_c \Omega^a + \lambda a_b \tag{4.3}$$

and constraints (4.2) to decide. If you eliminate the Lagrange multiplier, then (4.3) into the momentum equation.

Now, given so Euler-Poincar-Suslov equations are invariant measure of the condition.

Theorem 3. Equation (4.3) has a invariant measure if and only if

$$KC_{ij}^{k}I^{ig}a_{g}a_{k}+C_{jk}^{k}=\mu a_{j}\text{, } K=1/\langle a,I^{-1}a\rangle,\mu\in R \tag{4.4}$$

Theorem 4. If the constraint vector a is the inertia tensor of the feature vector, or restraint system on all spindle is symmetrical Z_2, the compact Euler-Poincaré-Suslov system is a security measure, if the maximum exchange is one-dimensional sub-algebra, then this condition is also necessary.

5 The Euler-Poincaré-Suslov Problem on $SO(3)$

Consider the classical Suslov problem, can be seen as the standard Euler put the power to meet the following constraints

$$\langle a,\Omega\rangle=a_1\Omega^1+a_2\Omega^2+a_3\Omega^3=0 \tag{5.1}$$

Where $\Omega=(\Omega^1,\Omega^2,\Omega^3)\in SO(3)$ is the pendulum angular velocity.

Constraints (4.1) along the direction of the angular velocity relative to the $a=(a_1,a_2,a_3)$ projection of the object frame is zero. The reduction of non-holonomic constraint equations of motion by (4.3) and given the following conditions

$$C_{12}^{3}=C_{23}^{1}=C_{31}^{2}=-C_{21}^{3}=-C_{32}^{1}=-C_{13}^{2}=1$$

the remaining $C_{ij}^{k}=0$.

Therefore, the momentum force is measure-preserving if and only if the constraint vector a is the inertia tensor I eigenvalues. Get this conclusion another way is to calculate the linear momentum balance of flow of the intrinsic value. When $a_2=a_3=0$, the zero eigenvalue, under normal circumstances, can be a non-zero real eigenvalues and two zero eigenvalues, and the measure-preserving phase-contradiction.

In order to prove theorems, multiplier elimination λ, the system of differential equations for the second right. Homogeneous polynomial differential equations is the right measure-preserving if and only if it is any divergence [6]. When (4.3) right zero divergence can get (4.4).

On non-holonomic system control is an important issue, Bloch discussed it in detail, and gives some applications [3]. Nonlinear control systems and the distribution of non-holonomic constraints has a natural link between, when the resulting distribution function is not integrable, the control system is given control vector field controllability, which provides a new direction in A typical example is the nonholonomic integrator. Brockett gives the definition of the Heisenberg group on the two control systems on the introduction and research .

References

1. Van der Schaft, A.J., Maschke, B.M.: On the Hamiltonian formulation of nonholonomic mechanical systems. Rep. on Math. Phys. 34, 225–233 (1994)
2. Koon, W.S., Marsden, J.E.: The Hamiltonian and Lagrangian approaches to the dynamics of nonholonomic systems. Reports on Math. Phys. 40, 21–62 (1997)
3. Bloch, A.M., Baillieul, J., Crouch, P.E., Marsden, J.E.: Nonholonomic Mechanics and Control. Springer, Berlin (2003)
4. Cendra, H., Marsden, J.E., Ratiu, T.S.: Geometric mechanics,Lagrangian reduction and nonholonomic systems. In: Enguist, B., Schmid, W. (eds.) Mathematics Unlimited: 2001 and Beyond, pp. 221–273. Springer, New York (2001)
5. Bloch, A.M., Krishnaprasad, P.S., Marsden, J.E., Murray, R.: Nonholonomic mechanical systems with symmetry. Arch. Rat. Mech. An. 136, 21–99 (1996)
6. Arnold, V.I., Kozlov, V.V., Neishtadt, A.I.: Dynamical Systems III. Encyclopedia of Mathematics, vol. 3. Springer, Berlin (1988)
7. Dong, Y.-F., Duan, W.-F.: Theoretical Mechanics. Tsinghua University Press, Beijing (2006)
8. Liang, L.-F., Hu, H.C.: HUNAN FINANCIAL AND. Lagrange dynamics of nonholonomic systems theoretical framework. Chinese Science (G Series: Physics, Mechanics & Astronomy) (01) (2007)
9. Zhang, X.W.: A complete high-order mechanical system Hamilton canonical equations. Journal of Anhui University (Natural Science) (02) (2006)
10. Yao, W.: Containing non-ideal non-holonomic constraints of the complete system to combat the problem. Journal of Peking University (Natural Science) (05) (2010)
11. Shi, S.: Discrete dynamical systems symmetry constraints and conserved quantities, vol. (01). Shanghai University (2008)
12. Ding, G.: Lagrange function is equivalent to changing the system of symmetries and conserved quantities of mechanical effect. Anhui Normal University (Natural Science) (01) (2009)

The Analytical Solution of Residual Stress in the Axial Symmetry Object

Qiumei Liu[1], Guanghui Wang[1], and Junling Zheng[2]

[1] He Bei United University, Tangshan, Hebei Province, China
[2] E&A College of Hebei Normal University of Science&Technology
Qinhuangdao, Hebei Province, China
liuqiumei1981@163.com

Abstract. The analytical solution can promote the extensive generation of the numerical solution as a standard solution. The paper analyzes the retaining ring residual stress of the axial symmetry object and constructs stress function satisfied with boundary conditions and biharmonic equation, then works out the corresponding analytical solution and the limit of the axial symmetry object when it infinite long, it is the famous Sachs formula. Exporting Sachs formula shows that Sachs way is an especial form of stress function way, also shows stress function way has more comprehensive applicability.

Keywords: residual stress stress function analytical solution.

1 Introduction

The analytical solution can illuminate the mechanics views that it wants to convey, and also can promote the extensive generation of the numerical solution as a standard solution. Therefore it has very great value in the theory and the engineering. This paper is devoted to studying the analytical solution, which is often used in theory and engineering, in terms of mechanics, combining the mathematics with elasticity. We analyzes the retaining ring residual stress of the axis asymmetry object and constructs stress function satisfied with boundary conditions and biharmonic equation, then works out the corresponding analytical solution and the limit of the axis asymmetry object when it infinite long, it is the famous Sachs formula. Exporting Sachs formula shows that Sachs way is an especial form of stress function way, also shows stress function way has more comprehensive applicability.

2 Boundary Conditions

Axial symmetry is gradually shelled, when strips off the internal wall from the radius a to the radius ρ, the radial direction residual stress T_{rr} and the cutting residual stress T_{rz} in the radius place ρ is released at the same time. This process is equal after stripping off in the radius for the axial symmetry internal surface has exerted $-T_{rr}$ and $-T_{rz}$ stress which shows in Fig. 1-3 and thinks T_{rr} with T_{rz} along the coordinate z change.

C. Liu, J. Chang, and A. Yang (Eds.): ICICA 2011, Part I, CCIS 243, pp. 30–36, 2011.

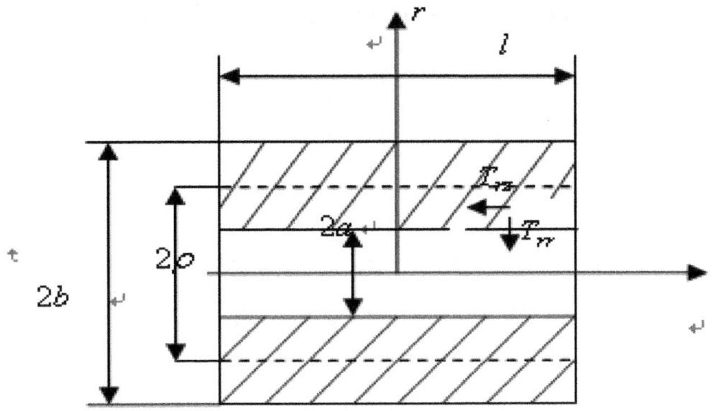

Fig. 1. Residual stress in ρ when the layer is not shelled

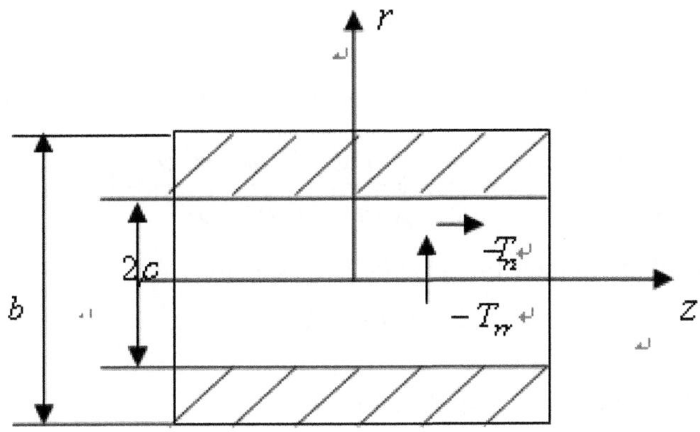

Fig. 2. Residual stress in ρ is released and distorted when the layer is shelled

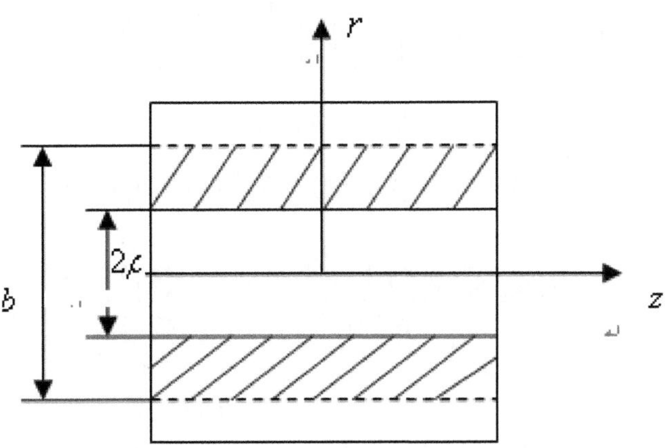

Fig. 3. Keep the instance of fixedness

According to the above models, we have the flowing boundary conditions

$$\text{When } r = \rho \begin{cases} \sigma_r = -T_{rr} \\ \tau_{rz} = -T_{rz} \end{cases} \tag{1}$$

$$\text{When } r = b \begin{cases} \sigma_r = 0 \quad \tau_{rz} = 0 \\ \sigma_\theta = \sigma_{\theta b} \quad \sigma_z = \sigma_{zb} \end{cases} \tag{2}$$

$$\text{When } z = \pm\frac{l}{2} \begin{cases} \iint_S \sigma_z ds = 0 \\ \iint_S \tau_{rz} ds = 0 \end{cases} \tag{3}$$

3 Construct Stress Function

The stress function ϕ of the space axis asymmetric satisfied with biharmonic equation

$$\left(\frac{\partial^2}{\partial r^2}+\frac{1}{r}\frac{\partial}{\partial r}+\frac{\partial^2}{\partial Z^2}\right)\left(\frac{\partial^2\phi}{\partial r^2}+\frac{1}{r}\frac{\partial\phi}{\partial r}+\frac{\partial^2\phi}{\partial Z^2}\right)=0 \tag{4}$$

The solution of the formula (4) is the flowing formula

$$\phi = f(r)\sin kz \tag{5}$$

$k=\frac{\pi}{l}$, $f(r)$ is the function of the radius r.

We can obtain the following result when the formula (5) substitution(4)

$$f^{(4)}(r)+\frac{2}{r}f'''(r)-\left(\frac{1}{r^2}+2k^2\right)f''(r)+\left(\frac{1}{r^3}-\frac{2k^2}{r}\right)f'(r)+k^4 f(r)=0 \tag{6}$$

The general solution of (6) is the flowing formula

$$\phi = \sin kz[A_1 f_1(r) + A_2 f_2(r) + A_3 f_3(r) + A_4 f(r)] \tag{7}$$

$$f_1(r)=\sum_{i=0}^{\infty}\frac{(i+1)k^{2i}r^{2i}}{4^i(i!)^2},\; f_2(r)=\sum_{i=1}^{\infty}\frac{ik^{2i-2}r^{2i}}{4^{i-1}(i!)^2}$$

$$f_3(r)=f_1(r)\ln r-\sum_{i=1}^{\infty}\frac{(i+1)k^{2i}\sum_{m=1}^{i}\frac{1}{m}}{(2i)^2[2(i-1)]^2\cdots 4^2\cdot 2^2}r^{2i},$$

$$f_4(r)=f_2(r)\ln r-\sum_{i=1}^{\infty}\frac{(i+1)k^{2i}\sum_{m=1}^{i}\frac{1}{m+1}}{[2(i+1)]^2(2i)^2\cdots 6^2\cdot 4^2}r^{2i+2}.$$

4 Analytical Solution Satisfied with Boundary Conditions

Put(7)into the flowing formulas

$$\begin{cases}\sigma_r=\frac{\partial}{\partial z}\left(\mu\nabla^2\varphi-\frac{\partial^2\varphi}{\partial r^2}\right) & \sigma_\vartheta=\frac{\partial}{\partial z}\left(\mu\nabla^2\varphi-\frac{1}{r}\frac{\partial\varphi}{\partial r}\right)\\ \sigma_z=\frac{\partial}{\partial z}\left((2-\mu)\nabla^2\varphi-\frac{\partial^2\varphi}{\partial z^2}\right) & \tau_{rz}=\frac{\partial}{\partial r}\left((1-\mu)\nabla^2\varphi-\frac{\partial^2\varphi}{\partial z^2}\right)\end{cases} \tag{8}$$

We can obtain the flowing results

$$\begin{cases}\sigma_r=k\cos kz[A_1w_{11}(r)+A_2w_{12}(r)+A_3w_{13}(r)+A_4w_{14}(r)]\\ \sigma_\theta=k\cos kz[A_1w_{21}(r)+A_2w_{22}(r)+A_3w_{23}(r)+A_4w_{24}(r)]\\ \sigma_z=-k\cos kz[A_1w_{31}(r)+A_2w_{32}(r)+A_3w_{33}(r)+A_4w_{34}(r)]\\ \tau_{rz}=\sin kz[A_1w_{41}(r)+A_2w_{42}(r)+A_3w_{43}(r)+A_4w_{44}(r)]\end{cases} \tag{9}$$

$$\begin{cases}w_{1i}(r)=(\mu-1)f_i''+\frac{\mu}{r}f_i'-k^2\mu f_i\\ w_{2i}(r)=\mu f_i''+\frac{\mu-1}{r}f_i'-k^2\mu f_i\\ w_{3i}(r)=(2-\mu)f_i''+\frac{2-\mu}{r}f_i'-k^2(1-\mu)f_i\\ w_{4i}(r)=(1-\mu)f_i'''+\frac{1-\mu}{r}f_i''-\frac{1-\mu}{r^2}f_i'+k^2\mu f_i'\end{cases} \quad i=1,2,3,4 \tag{10}$$

Put (7) into the boundary conditions (1)~ (3),we can obtain the flowing results

$$\begin{cases}k\cos kz[A_1w_{11}(\rho)+A_2w_{12}(\rho)+A_3w_{13}(\rho)+A_4w_{14}(\rho)]=-T_{rr}\\ \sin kz[A_1w_{41}(\rho)+A_2w_{42}(\rho)+A_3w_{43}(\rho)+A_4w_{44}(\rho)]=-T_{rz}\\ k\cos kz[A_1w_{11}(b)+A_2w_{12}(b)+A_3w_{13}(b)+A_4w_{14}(b)]=0\\ \sin kz[A_1w_{41}(b)+A_2w_{42}(b)+A_3w_{43}(b)+A_4w_{44}(b)]=0\\ k\cos kz[A_1w_{21}(b)+A_2w_{22}(b)+A_3w_{23}(b)+A_4w_{24}(b)]=\sigma_{\theta b}\\ -k\cos kz[A_1w_{31}(b)+A_2w_{32}(b)+A_3w_{33}(b)+A_4w_{34}(b)]=\sigma_{zb}\end{cases} \tag{11}$$

The solution of (11) is the flowing formulas

$$\begin{cases} A_1 w_{11}(b) + A_2 w_{12}(b) + A_3 w_{13}(b) + A_4 w_{14}(b) = 0 \\ A_1 w_{41}(b) + A_2 w_{42}(b) + A_3 w_{43}(b) + A_4 w_{44}(b) = 0 \\ A_1 w_{21}(b) + A_2 w_{22}(b) + A_3 w_{23}(b) + A_4 w_{24}(b) = \dfrac{\sigma_{\theta b}}{k\cos kz} \\ A_1 w_{31}(b) + A_2 w_{32}(b) + A_3 w_{33}(b) + A_4 w_{34}(b) = \dfrac{\sigma_{zb}}{-k\cos kz} \end{cases} \tag{12}$$

$$\Delta = \begin{vmatrix} w_{11}(b) & w_{12}(b) & w_{13}(b) & w_{14}(b) \\ w_{41}(b) & w_{42}(b) & w_{43}(b) & w_{44}(b) \\ w_{21}(b) & w_{22}(b) & w_{23}(b) & w_{24}(b) \\ w_{31}(b) & w_{32}(b) & w_{33}(b) & w_{34}(b) \end{vmatrix}$$

$$\Delta_1 = \begin{vmatrix} 0 & w_{12}(b) & w_{13}(b) & w_{14}(b) \\ 0 & w_{42}(b) & w_{43}(b) & w_{44}(b) \\ \dfrac{\sigma_{\theta b}}{k\cos kz} & w_{22}(b) & w_{23}(b) & w_{24}(b) \\ \dfrac{\sigma_{zb}}{-k\cos kz} & w_{32}(b) & w_{33}(b) & w_{34}(b) \end{vmatrix} \quad \Delta_2 = \begin{vmatrix} w_{11}(b) & 0 & w_{13}(b) & w_{14}(b) \\ w_{41}(b) & 0 & w_{43}(b) & w_{44}(b) \\ w_{21}(b) & \dfrac{\sigma_{\theta b}}{k\cos kz} & w_{23}(b) & w_{24}(b) \\ w_{31}(b) & \dfrac{\sigma_{zb}}{-k\cos kz} & w_{33}(b) & w_{34}(b) \end{vmatrix}$$

$$\Delta_3 = \begin{vmatrix} w_{11}(b) & w_{12}(b) & 0 & w_{14}(b) \\ w_{41}(b) & w_{42}(b) & 0 & w_{44}(b) \\ w_{21}(b) & w_{22}(b) & \dfrac{\sigma_{\theta b}}{k\cos kz} & w_{24}(b) \\ w_{31}(b) & w_{32}(b) & \dfrac{\sigma_{zb}}{-k\cos kz} & w_{34}(b) \end{vmatrix} \quad \Delta_4 = \begin{vmatrix} w_{11}(b) & w_{12}(b) & w_{13}(b) & 0 \\ w_{41}(b) & w_{42}(b) & w_{43}(b) & 0 \\ w_{21}(b) & w_{22}(b) & w_{23}(b) & \dfrac{\sigma_{\theta b}}{k\cos kz} \\ w_{31}(b) & w_{32}(b) & w_{33}(b) & \dfrac{\sigma_{zb}}{-k\cos kz} \end{vmatrix}$$

$$A_i = \frac{\Delta_i}{\Delta}, \quad i = 1, 2, 3, 4 \tag{13}$$

Put (13) into (11), we get the following results

$$\begin{cases} T_{rr} = -\dfrac{k\cos kz}{\Delta}\left[\Delta_1 w_{11}(\rho) + \Delta_2 w_{12}(\rho) + \Delta_3 w_{13}(\rho) + \Delta_4 w_{14}(\rho)\right] \\ T_{rz} = -\dfrac{\sin kz}{\Delta}\left[\Delta_1 w_{41}(\rho) + \Delta_2 w_{42}(\rho) + \Delta_3 w_{43}(\rho) + \Delta_4 w_{44}(\rho)\right] \end{cases} \tag{14}$$

The equilibrium equation of the residual stress

$$\begin{cases} \dfrac{\partial T_{rr}}{\partial \rho} + \dfrac{\partial T_{rz}}{\partial z} + \dfrac{1}{\rho}\left(T_{rr} - T_{\theta\theta}\right) = 0 \\ \dfrac{\partial T_{rz}}{\partial \rho} + \dfrac{\partial T_{zz}}{\partial z} + \dfrac{1}{\rho} T_{rz} = 0 \end{cases} \tag{15}$$

Then with the same methods we can infer the flowing formulas

$$T_{\theta\theta} = \rho\frac{\partial T_{rr}}{\partial \rho} + \rho\frac{\partial T_{rz}}{\partial z} + T_{rr}, T_{zz} = -\int\left(\frac{\partial T_{rz}}{\partial \rho} + \frac{1}{\rho}T_{rz}\right)dz .$$

5 The Limit of $k \to 0$

When $k \to 0\left(k = \frac{\pi}{l}\right)$

$$\begin{cases} f_1(r)=1,\ f_1'(r)=0,\ f_1''(r)=0,\ f_1'''(r)=0 \\ f_2(r)=r^2,\ f_2'(r)=2r,\ f_2''(r)=2,\ f_2'''(r)=0 \\ f_3(r)=\ln r,\ f_3'(r)=\frac{1}{r},\ f_3''(r)=-\frac{1}{r^2},\ f_3'''(r)=\frac{2}{r^3} \\ f_4(r)=r^2\ln r,\ f_4'(r)=2r\ln r+r,\ f_4''(r)=3+2\ln r,\ f_4'''(r)=\frac{2}{r} \end{cases} \tag{16}$$

Put (16) into (10),we get the following results

$$\begin{cases} w_{11}(r)=0,\ w_{12}(r)=4\mu-2,\ w_{13}(r)=\frac{1}{r^2},\ w_{14}(r)=4\mu\ln r-2\ln r+4\mu-3 \\ w_{21}(r)=0,\ w_{22}(r)=4\mu-2,\ w_{23}(r)=-\frac{1}{r^2},\ w_{24}(r)=4\mu\ln r-2\ln r+4\mu-1 \\ w_{31}(r)=0,\ w_{32}(r)=4(2-\mu),\ w_{33}(r)=0,\ w_{34}(r)=4(\ln r+1)(2-\mu) \\ w_{41}(r)=0,\ w_{42}(r)=0,\ w_{43}(r)=0,\ w_{44}(r)=\frac{4(1-\mu)}{r} \end{cases} \tag{17}$$

Put (17) into (12), we get the following results

$$A_2 = \frac{\sigma_{\theta b}}{k\cos kz}\frac{1}{2(4\mu-2)}, A_3 = -\frac{\sigma_{\theta b}}{k\cos kz}\frac{b^2}{2}, A_4 = 0 \tag{18}$$

Put (18) into (14), we get the following results

$$T_{rr} = -k\cos kz\left[\frac{\sigma_{\theta b}}{k\cos kz}\frac{1}{2(4\mu-2)}(4\mu+2) - \frac{\sigma_{\theta b}}{k\cos kz}\frac{b^2}{2}\frac{1}{\rho^2}\right]$$

$$= \sigma_{\theta b}\frac{b^2-\rho^2}{2\rho^2} = \frac{E}{1-\mu^2}\frac{f_b-f}{2f}H$$

Then we have the following formula in the same way

$$T_{\theta\vartheta} = \frac{E}{1-\mu^2}\left[(f_b-f)\frac{dH}{dh} - \frac{f_b+f}{2f}H\right]$$

$$H = \varepsilon_{\theta b} + \mu\varepsilon_{zb}, f = \pi\rho^2, f_b = \pi b^2$$

It is the famous Sachs formula. Exporting Sachs formula shows that Sachs way is an especial form of stress function way, also shows stress function way has more comprehensive applicability.

References

1. Timoshenko, S., Goodier, J.N.: Theory of Elasticity, vol. 39, pp. 422–430. MoGrawhill Book Co., New York (1970)
2. Liu, Z., Shan, R., Liu, W., Ni, L.: Solution of a Hollow Thick-wall Cylinder Subject to Quadric Function Pressures and Its Limit when ℓ→ ∞. Science in China (Series E) 47(2), 229–236 (2004)
3. Duó, P., Liu, J., Dini, D., Golshan, M., Korsunsky, A.M.: Evaluation and analysis of residual stresses due to foreign object damage. Mechanics of Materials 39(3), 199–211 (2007)
4. Ding, H., Huang, D., Wang, H.: Analytical Solution for Fixed-end Beam Subjected to Uniform Load. Journal of Zhejiang University Science 6A(8), 779–783 (2005)
5. James, M.N., Hughes, D.J., Chen, Z., Lombard, H., Hattingh, D.G., Asquith, D., Yates, J.R., Webster, P.J.: Residual stresses and fatigue performance. Engineering Failure Analysis 14(2), 384–395 (2007)
6. Alegre, J.M., Bravo, P., Preciado, M.: Fatigue behaviour of an autofrettaged high-pressure vessel for the food industry. Engineering Failure Analysis 14(2), 396–407 (2007)
7. Sosa, A.D., Echeverría, M.D., Moncada, O.J., Sikora, J.A.: Residual stresses, distortion and surface roughness produced by grinding thin wall ductile iron plates. International Journal of Machine Tools and Manufacture 47(2), 229–235 (2007)
8. Spiteri, P., Ho, S., Lee, Y.-L.: Assessment of bending fatigue limit for crankshaft sections with inclusion of residual stresses. International Journal of Fatigue 29(2), 318–329 (2007)
9. Kim, J.W., Lee, D.G.: Measurement of residual stresses in thick composite cylinders by the radial-cut-cylinder-bending method. Composite Structures 77(4), 444–456 (2007)
10. Kim, H.S., Lee, D.G.: Reduction of thermal residual stress of the hybrid co-cured structure using a dielectrometry. Composites Science and Technology 67(1), 29–44 (2007)

An Estimation for the Average Error of the Chebyshev Interpolation in Wiener Space

Liu Xiong[1] and Gong Dianxuan[2]

[1] School of Mathematics and Computational Science,
Zhanjiang Normal College Zhanjiang, Guangdong, 524048 China
[2] College of Science, Hebei United Universtiy, Tangshan , 063009 China
liuxiong980211@yahoo.com.cn

Abstract. In this paper, the first kind of Chebyshev interpolation in the Wiener space are discussed. under the L_p norm, the convergence properties of Chebyshev interpolation polynomials base on the zeros of the Chebyshev polynomials are proved. Furthermore, the estimation for the average error of the first kind of Chebyshev interpolation polynomials are weakly equivalent to the average errors of the corresponding best polynomial approximation. while $p=4$,the weakly asypmtotic order $e^4(H_n,G_4)\approx 1/\sqrt{n}$ of the average error in the Wiener space is obtained.

Keywords: Chebyshev interpolation polynomials, average error, L_2-norm, Wiener-space.

1 Introduction

Let F be a real separable Banach space equipped with a probability measures μ on the Borelsets of F. Let G be another normed space such that F is continuously embedded in G By $\|\bullet\|$ we denote the norm in G . Any $A:F\to G$ such that $f\mapsto\|f-A(f)\|$ is a measurable mapping called an approximation operator (or just approximation). The average error of A is defined as

$$e_p(A,H)=(\int_F\|f-A(f)\|^p\mu(df))^{\frac{1}{p}} \tag{1.1}$$

Since the target function in practical problems is usually given by its(exact or noisy) values at finitely many points, the approximation operator $A(f)$ is often considered depending on some function values about f only. Many papers such as [1], [2] studied the complexity of computing an ε-approximation in average case setting.

C. Liu, J. Chang, and A. Yang (Eds.): ICICA 2011, Part I, CCIS 243, pp. 37–43, 2011.

Papers [3], [4] obtained the weak asymptotic order of the average error of Lagrange interpolation and Hermite-Fej´er interpolation in the Wiener space.

In this paper, we will show an estimation of the average error (in the $L_2 - norm$) of Chebyshev polynomial of the first kind in the Wiener space when $p = 4$. Now we turn to show the result.

Let X be the space of continuous function f defined on $[0,1]$ such that $f(0) = 0$. The space X is equipped with the sup norm. The Wiener measure ω is uniquely defined by the following property

$$\omega(f \in C[-1,1] : (f(t_1), \cdots f(t_n)) \in B) = \prod_{j=1}^{n} \frac{1}{\sqrt{2\pi(t_j - t_{j-1})}} \bullet$$

$$\int_B \exp\left[\sum_{j=1}^{n} \frac{-(u_j - u_{j-1})^2}{2(t_j - t_{j-1})}\right] du_1 du_2 \cdots du_n \tag{1.2}$$

For every $0 = t_0 < t_1 < t_2 < \cdots < t_n \le 1$ with $u_0 = 0$ and $n \ge 1, B \in \mathrm{B}(\Re^n)$, in which $\mathrm{B}(\Re^n)$ is the class of all Borel subsets of $\Re^n$. It follows from [1] that:

$$\int_X f(x_1) f(x_2) ud(f) = \min\{x_1, x_2\}, \forall x_1, x_2 \in [0,1] \tag{1.3}$$

Let $F = \{f \in C[-1,1] : g(t) = f(2t-1) \in X\}$ and for every measurable subset $A \subset F$, we define

$$\mu(A) = \omega(\{g(t) = f(2t-1) : f \in A\}) \tag{1.4}$$

Where $1 \le p \le \infty$, let $G_p[-1,1]$ be the linear normed space of all $L_p - \text{int}\,egrable$ functions f on $[-1,1]$ with the following finite norm

$$\|f\|_p = \left(\int_{-1}^{1} |f(x)|^p \frac{d(x)}{\sqrt{1 - x^2}} \right)^{\frac{1}{p}} \tag{1.5}$$

Let $t_k = t_{nk} = \cos\dfrac{k\pi}{n+1}, k = 1, 2, \cdots n$ be the zeros of $T_n(x) = \cos n\theta$, $x = \cos\theta$ which is the n-th degree Chebyshev polynomial of the first kind. The Chebyshev interpolation polynomial based on the zeros above is as follows

$$H_n(f,x)=\sum_{k=1}^{n} f(t_k)h_k(x) \tag{1.6}$$

Where $H_k(x)=(1-xt_k)(\frac{T_n(x)}{n(x-t_k)})^2 \ge 0, \sum_{k=1}^{n} h_k(x)=1$.

2 Theorem

Theorem 1. For any $0 \le x_1 \le x_2 \le x_3 \le x_4 \le 1$, we can we can derive

$$\int_X f(x_1)f(x_2)f(x_3)f(x_4)\omega d(f)=2x_1x_2+x_1x_3$$

Theorem 2. Let $H_n(f,x)$ be defined above, then we can obtain $e_4(H_n,G_4)\approx\frac{1}{\sqrt{n}}$ where $A_n \approx B_n$ means that there exist n- independent constants c_1,c_2, satisfied with $C_1A_n \le B_n \le C_2A_n$.

3 The Proof of the Theorem

From [1] ,we can obtain the proof of the theorem 1, now we turn to give the proof of the theorem 2. we can obtain the lower-bounds estimation according to [2], we consider sup-bounds estimation as follows: denote $p=4$,obtained by $\sum_{k=1}^{n} l_k(x)=1$; It can be checked that:

$$e^4(L_n,G_4)=\int_F\int_{-1}(\sum_{k=1}^{m}(f(x)-f(t_k))l_k(x))^4\frac{dx}{\sqrt{1-x^2}}u(df) \tag{3.1}$$

$$=\sum_{k_1=1}^{n}\sum_{k_2=1}^{n}\sum_{k_3=1}^{n}\sum_{k_4=1}^{n}\int_{-1}^{1} l_{k1}(x)l_{k2}(x)l_{k3}(x)l_{k4}(x)\frac{dx}{\sqrt{1-x^2}}\bullet$$

$$\int_F(f(x)-f(t_{k1}))(f(x)--f(t_{k2}))(f(x)-f(t_{k3}))(f(x)-f(t_{k4}))\mu(df)$$

Where $0 \le k_1 \le k_2 \le k_3 \le k_4 \le 1$, from the result of Theorem 1, we can obtain the following:

$$\int_{-1}^{t} l_{k1}(x)l_{k2}(x)l_{k3}(x)l_{k4}(x)\frac{dx}{\sqrt{1-x^2}} \bullet$$

$$\int_F (f(x)-f(t_{k1}))(f(x)-f(t_{k2}))(f(x)-f(t_{k3}))(f(x)-f(t_{k4}))u(df)$$

$$=\frac{1}{4}\int_{-1}^{t_{k4}}[2(x-t_{k4})(x-t_{k3})+(x-t_{k4})(x-t_{k2})]l_{k1}(x)l_{k2}(x)l_{k3}(x)l_{k4}(x)\frac{dx}{\sqrt{1-x^2}} \quad (3.2)$$

$$-\frac{1}{4}\int_{t_{k3}}^{t_{k2}}(x-t_{k3})(x-t_{k2})l_{k1}(x)l_{k2}(x)l_{k3}(x)l_{k4}(x)\frac{dx}{\sqrt{1-x^2}}$$

$$+\frac{1}{4}\int_{t_{k1}}^{1}[2(x-t_{k2})(x-t_{k1})+(x-t_{k3})(x-t_{k1})]l_{k1}(x)l_{k2}(x)l_{k3}(x)l_{k4}(x)\frac{dx}{\sqrt{1-x^2}}$$

Rearrange k_1, k_2, k_3, k_4 to $\overline{k}_1 \le \overline{k}_2 \le \overline{k}_3 \le \overline{k}_4$, we can obtain the below from (3.2)

$$4e^4(L_n, G_4)=\sum_{k_1=1}^{n}\sum_{k_2=1}^{n}\sum_{k_3=1}^{n}\sum_{k_4=1}^{n}\int_{-1}^{t_{\overline{k}4}}[2(x-t_{\overline{k}4})(x-t_{\overline{k}3})+$$

$$(x-t_{\overline{k}4})(x-t_{\overline{k}2})]l_{\overline{k}1}(x)l_{\overline{k}2}(x)l_{\overline{k}3}(x)l_{\overline{k}4}(x)\frac{dx}{\sqrt{1-x^2}}$$

$$-\sum_{k_1=1}^{n}\sum_{k_2=1}^{n}\sum_{k_3=1}^{n}\sum_{k_4=1}^{n}\int_{t_{\overline{k}3}}^{t_{\overline{k}2}}(x-t_{\overline{k}3})(x-t_{\overline{k}2})l_{\overline{k}1}(x)l_{\overline{k}2}(x)l_{\overline{k}3}(x)l_{\overline{k}4}(x)\frac{dx}{\sqrt{1-x^2}} \quad (3.3)$$

$$+\sum_{k_1=1}^{n}\sum_{k_2=1}^{n}\sum_{k_3=1}^{n}\sum_{k_4=1}^{n}\int_{t_{\overline{k}1}}^{1}[2(x-t_{\overline{k}2})(x-t_{\overline{k}1})+(x-t_{\overline{k}3})(x-t_{\overline{k}1})]\bullet$$

$$l_{\overline{k}1}(x)l_{\overline{k}2}(x)l_{\overline{k}3}(x)l_{\overline{k}4}(x)\frac{dx}{\sqrt{1-x^2}}$$

$$=I_1+I_2+I_3$$

where

$$
\begin{aligned}
I_3 &= 3\sum_{k=1}^{n}\int_{t_k}^{1}(x-t_k)^2 h_k^4(x)\frac{dx}{\sqrt{1-x^2}} + 12\sum_{k=1}^{n}\int_{t_k}^{1}(x-t_k)^2 h_k^3(x)\sum_{j=k+1}^{n}h_j(x)\frac{dx}{\sqrt{1-x^2}} \\
&+12\sum_{k=1}^{n}\int_{t_k}^{1}(x-t_k)h_k(x)[(x-t_k)h_k(x)\sum_{m=k+1}^{n}h_m(x)]^2 \\
&+2\sum_{j=k+1}^{n}(x-t_j)h_j(x)[\sum_{m=j}^{n}h_m(x)]^2\frac{dx}{\sqrt{1-x^2}} \\
&+6\sum_{k=1}^{n}\int_{t_k}^{1}(x-t_k)h_k^2(x)\sum_{j=k+1}^{n}(x-t_j)h_j(x)(h_j(x)+2\sum_{s=k+1}^{n}h_s(x))\frac{dx}{\sqrt{1-x^2}} \\
&+12\sum_{k=1}^{n}\int_{t_k}^{1}(x-t_k)h_k(x)\sum_{j=k+1}^{n}h_j(x)\sum_{i=j}^{n}(x-t_i)h_i(x)(h_i(x)+2\sum_{s=j+1}^{n}h_s(x))\frac{dx}{\sqrt{1-x^2}} \\
&= D_1 + D_2 + 12D_3 + 6D_4 + 12D_5
\end{aligned}
\tag{3.4}
$$

For $\left|x-t_k\right|h_k(x) \le \frac{\sqrt{1-t_k^2}\left|l_k(x)\right|}{n} + \frac{\left|x_k\right|T_n^2(x)}{n2} \le \frac{2}{n}$ and $0 \le h_k(x) \le 1$, we can obtain:

$$
0 < D_1 \le \frac{12}{n^2}\sum_{k=1}^{n}\int_{t_k}^{1} h_k^2(x)\frac{dx}{\sqrt{1-x^2}} \le \frac{12}{n^2}\int_{-1}^{1}\sum_{k=1}^{n}h_k(x)\frac{dx}{\sqrt{1-x^2}} = \frac{12\pi}{n^2} \tag{3.5}
$$

Because of $0 \le \sum_{j=k+1}^{n} h_j(x) \le 1$ and (3.5), we can obtain the below;

$$
\left|D_2\right| \le \frac{48}{n^2}\sum_{k=1}^{n}\int_{t_k}^{1} h_k(x)\frac{dx}{\sqrt{1-x^2}} \le \frac{48}{n^2}\int_{-1}^{1}\sum_{k=1}^{n}h_k(x)\frac{dx}{\sqrt{1-x^2}} = \frac{48\pi}{n^2} \tag{3.6}
$$

Denote $t_0 = 1$, we can drive:

$$
\begin{aligned}
D_3 &= \sum_{k=1}^{n}\sum_{i=1}^{k}\int_{t_i}^{t_{i-1}}(x-t_k)h_k(x)(x-t_k)h_k(x)[\sum_{m=k+1}^{n}h_m(x)]^2 \\
&+2\sum_{j=k+1}^{n}(x-t_j)h_j(x)[\sum_{m=j}^{n}h_m(x)]^2\frac{dx}{\sqrt{1-x^2}} \\
&= \sum_{i=1}^{n}\int_{t_i}^{t_{i-1}}\sum_{k=i}^{n}(x-t_k)h_k(x)(x-t_k)h_k(x)[\sum_{m=k+1}^{n}h_m(x)]^2 \\
&+2\sum_{j=k+1}^{n}(x-t_j)h_j(x)[\sum_{m=j}^{n}h_m(x)]^2\frac{dx}{\sqrt{1-x^2}}
\end{aligned}
\tag{3.7}
$$

For any $j > i$, let $x = \cos\theta$, combining

$$\frac{\sin\frac{2s-1}{2n}\pi}{\sin\frac{s+i-1}{2n}\pi} \le 2, \sin\frac{s-i}{2n}\pi \le \sin\frac{s+i-1}{2n}\pi$$

and $\sin x \ge \frac{2x}{\pi}$, $0 \le x \le \frac{\pi}{2}$, we can obtain:

$$|D_3| \le \frac{48\pi}{n^2} \tag{3.8}$$

Similar to(3.8), we can obtain $0 \le D_4 \le \frac{36}{n^2}$ and

$$0 \le D_5 \le \frac{28}{n^2} \tag{3.9}$$

combined the obover D_1, D_2, D_3, D_4, D_5 ,we can driver

$$I_3 \le \frac{1788\pi}{n^2} \tag{3.10}$$

in a similar way, $I_1 \le \frac{1788\pi}{n^2}$ and

$$0 \le I_2 \le \frac{864\pi}{n^2} \tag{3.11}$$

As a conclusion, while $P = 4$, the sup bound estimation errors are given as follows:

$$e^4(H_n, G_4) \approx \frac{1}{\sqrt{n}} \tag{3.12}$$

Acknowledgments. Foundation item: Supported by the Youth Project Foundation of Zhanjiang Nomal College Natural Science (No.QL0901). The second author is supported by the Educational Commission of Hebei Province of China (Grant No. Z2010260)

References

1. Traub, J.F., Wasilkowski, G.W., Wozniakowski, H.: Information-Based Complexity. Academic Press, New York (1988)
2. Klaus, R.: Approximation and optimization on the wiener space. J. Complexity 6, 337–364 (1990)

3. Xu, G.-Q.: An average error of lagrange interpolation and Hermite-Fejér interpolation in the wienerspace. Acta Mathematica Sinica in Chinese 50(5), 1–3 (2007)
4. Zhao, H.-J.: An average error of lagrange interpolation in the wiener space. Journal of Tianjin NormalUniversity (Natural Science Edition) 27(1), 1–2 (2007)
5. Xu, G.-Q.: The rate of weighted Lp convergence of interpolators operators. Chinese Journal of Engineering Mathematics 5, 1–3 (2006) (in Chinese)
6. Liu, Y., Xu, G.-Q.: An Estimation for the Average Error of the Quasi-Grünwald Interpolation in the Wiener Space. Chin. Quart. J. of Math. 24(1), 94–101 (2009)

A Numerical Method for Two-Dimensional Schrödinger Equation Using MPS*

Tao Li[1,4], Guo-Dong Wang[2], and Zi-Wu Jiang[3]

[1] Department of Mathematics, Linyi University, Linyi, 276005, P.R. China
[2] Department of Mathematics, Qufu Normal University, Rizhao, 276826, P.R. China
[3] School of Informatics, Linyi University, Linyi, 276005, P.R. China
[4] Department of Mathematics, Shangdong Normal University, Jinan, 250014, P.R. China
taoliemail@126.com

Abstract. In this paper, we propose a numerical scheme to solve the two-dimensional (2D) time-dependent Schrödinger equation by using the method of particular solution(MPS) and radial basis function(RBF). The scheme works in a similar fashion as finite-difference methods. The results of numerical experiments are presented, and compared with analytical solutions to confirm the good accuracy of the presented scheme.

Keywords: Schrödinger equation, Radial Basis Function (RBF), Method of particular solution(MPS).

1 Introduction

This paper is devoted to the numerical computation of the two-dimensional (2D) time-dependent Schrödinger equation:

$$-i\frac{\partial u}{\partial t} = \frac{\partial^2 u}{\partial x^2} + \frac{\partial^2 u}{\partial y^2} + \omega(x, y)u, \tag{1}$$

in some continuous domain with suitable initial and Dirichlet boundary conditions and an arbitrary potential function $\omega(x, y)$. The solution for such a kind of equation is of fundamental importance in quantum mechanics (modeling of quantum devices [1]), electromagnetic wave propagation [2], underwater acoustics (paraxial approximations to the wave equation [3]) and design of certain optoelectronic devices [4] as it models an electromagnetic wave equation in a two-dimensional weakly guiding structure. It has also found its application in various quantum dynamics calculations [5,6].

* This work was supported by the National Natural Science Foundation of China (Nos. 10671086, 11071031, U0935004), and the Natural Science Foundation of Shandong Province, China (NO. ZR2010AM014).

C. Liu, J. Chang, and A. Yang (Eds.): ICICA 2011, Part I, CCIS 243, pp. 44–51, 2011.

There have been attempts to develop numerical schemes for equations similar to system (1). Several secondorder spatial accurate schemes including fully explicit scheme, fully explicit method, fully implicit technique, fully implicit formula, Crank-Nicolson finite-difference procedure, alternating direction implicit (ADI) method, the Barakat and Clark explicit finite-difference scheme were discussed by Dehghan [9]. The authors of [8,10] studied models similar to the present problem but they used finite-difference techniques.

In the current work we investigate a different approach to find the solution of the system (1). Dehghan [7] paper presents a numerical scheme to solve the system (1) using the collocation method and approximating the solution directly using multiquadrics and the thin plate splines radial basis function. Wang [11] uses the method of particular solution (MPS) with the inverse multiquadrics (IMQ) and the thin plate splines(m=1,2) radial basis function to solve the system (1). This paper develop the multiquadrics (MQ) and the thin plate splines (TPS) (m=3) radial basis function in the MPS. The scheme is similar to finite-difference methods. To test the accuracy of the scheme, it is applied to one example having analytical solutions. Our results exhibit good comparison with analytical solutions.

2 The Method of Particular Solutions

Consider following boundary value problem

$$\Delta u(x,y) = f(x,y), \qquad x,y \in \Omega, \tag{2}$$

$$Bu(x,y) = b(x,y), \qquad x,y \in \Gamma, \tag{3}$$

where Δ and B are the Laplace operator and boundary differential operators respectively, $\Omega \subseteq \mathbb{R}^d$, is the solution domain, Γ is its boundary, and $f(x,y)$ and $b(x,y)$ are given functions.

In the method[13], the RBFs interpolation constructed as linear combinations of a finite series of basis $\{\phi_j\}_1^n$ is used to approximate $f(x,y)$, and the interpolants $\hat{f}_n(x,y)$ of $f(x,y)$ can be represented as

$$f(x,y) \simeq \hat{f}_n(x,y) = \sum_{j=1}^{n} \lambda_j \phi(r_j), \tag{4}$$

where $r_j = \|(x,y) - (x,y_j)\|$ is Euclidean distance, $\{x_j, y_j\}_1^n$ are interpolation points, and the real coefficients $\{\lambda_j\}_1^n$ can be determined by solving

$$\sum_{j=1}^{n} \lambda_j \phi(r_j) = f(x_k, y_k), \qquad 1 \leq k \leq n, \tag{5}$$

as long as the real coefficient matrix $A_\phi = (\phi(r_{kj}))_{n\times n}$ is invertible.

Therefore, according to (5), it is easy to know that an approximate particular solution $u(x, y)$ to (2) is given by

$$u(x, y) \simeq \sum_{j=1}^{n} \lambda_j \Phi(r_j), \tag{6}$$

where $\Phi(r_j)$ is obtain by analytically solving

$$\Delta\Phi(r_j) = \phi(r_j). \tag{7}$$

If we impose $u(x, y)$ in (6) to satisfy the governed equation (2) and boundary conditions (3), then $u(x, y)$ becomes the approximate solution of the original partial differential equation (2)–(3). To be more specific, we have

$$\sum_{j=1}^{n} \lambda_j \phi(r_j) = f(x_k, y_k), \qquad x_k, y_k \in \Omega, \tag{8}$$

$$\sum_{j=1}^{n} \lambda_j B\Phi(r_j) = b(x_k, y_k), \qquad x_k, y_k \in \Gamma. \tag{9}$$

Let $\{x_k, y_k\}_1^{n_I}$ and $\{x_k, y_k\}_{n_I+1}^{n}$ are interior points and boundary points respectively, here $n = n_I + n_B$, according to (8) and (9), we have

$$\sum_{j=1}^{n} \lambda_j \phi(r_j) = f(x_k, y_k), \qquad 1 \le k \le n_I,$$

$$\sum_{j=1}^{n} \lambda_j B\Phi(r_j) = b(x_k, y_k)), \qquad n_I + 1 \le k \le n.$$

The above linear system can be easily solved by standard matrix solver. If $\{\lambda_j\}_1^n$ is determined, the approximate particular solution becomes the approximate solution $u(x, y)$ of equation (2)-(3), i.e.,

$$u(x, y) = \sum_{j=1}^{n} \lambda_j \Phi(r_j). \tag{10}$$

Note that an accurate approximation of the particular solution $u(x)$ depends on the appropriate choice of radial basis function ϕ. In the RBF literatures [12,14,15], some of the globally defined RBFs are only conditionally positive definite. The unique solvability of the interpolation problem can be obtained by adding a polynomial term to the interpolation (4), giving

$$f(x, y) \simeq \hat{f}_n(x, y) = \sum_{j=1}^{n} \lambda_j \phi(r_j) + \sum_{k=1}^{K} \mu_k p_k(x, y), \tag{11}$$

along with the constraints

$$\sum_{j=1}^{n} \mu_k p_k(x_j, y_j) = 0, \quad 1 \leq k \leq K, \tag{12}$$

where $\{p_k\}_1^K$ is a basis of $\mathcal{P}_{m-1}$, the space of d-variate polynomials of order not exceeding than $m-1$, and

$$K = \binom{m-1+d}{d}$$

is the dimension of $\mathcal{P}_{m-1}$.

3 Application

We consider the following two-dimensional time-dependent Schrödinger equation[9]:

$$-i\frac{\partial u}{\partial t} = \Delta u + \omega(x,y)u, \quad (x,y) \in \Omega \subset \mathbb{R}^2, \ \ 0 < t \leq T, \tag{13}$$

with the initial condition

$$u(x,y,0) = u_0(x,y), \quad (x,y) \in \Omega, \tag{14}$$

and Dirichlet boundary condition

$$u(x,y,t) = g(x,y), \quad (x,y) \in \partial\Omega, \ \ 0 < t \leq T, \tag{15}$$

where u_0, g and ω are known functions, Δ is equal to $(\frac{\partial^2}{\partial x^2} + \frac{\partial^2}{\partial y^2})$, and the function u is unknown.

First, let us discretize (13) according to the following θ-weighted scheme:

$$\begin{aligned} -i\frac{u(x,y,t+dt) - u(x,y,t)}{dt} &= \theta[\Delta u(x,y,t+dt) + \omega(x,y)u(x,y,t+dt)] + \\ &\quad (1-\theta)[\Delta u(x,y,t) + \omega(x,y)u(x,y,t)], \end{aligned} \tag{16}$$

where $0 \leq \theta \leq 1$, and dt is the time step size. Rearranging (16), using the notation $u^n = u(x,y,t)$ where $t^n = t^{n-1} + dt$, we obtain

$$-iu^{n+1} - \theta dt[\Delta u^{n+1} + \omega(x,y)u^{n+1}] = -iu^n + (1-\theta)dt[\Delta u^n + \omega(x,y)u^n]. \tag{17}$$

Then

$$\Delta u^{n+1} = -(\frac{i}{\theta dt} + \omega(x,y))u^{n+1} + \frac{i}{\theta dt} - \frac{1-\theta}{\theta}[\Delta u^n + \omega(x,y)u^n]. \tag{18}$$

Assume $u^{n+1}(x,y)$ is a sought solution to the elliptic PDE. We can represent the right hand side of (18) as a function $F(x)$. This means that (18) is a standard Poisson-type differential equation

$$\Delta u^{n+1} = F(x,y). \tag{19}$$

Therefore, if the fictitious function $F(x,y)$ is known, (18) is equivalent to the Poisson-type equation (19) under the same boundary conditions.

Then approximating the function $F(x,y)$ by RBFs $\{\phi_j\}_1^n$, we get

$$F(x,y) \simeq \sum_{j=1}^{n} \lambda_j^{n+1} \phi_j(r_{kj}), \quad k,j = 1,2,\cdots,n \tag{20}$$

where r_{kj} is Euclidean distance. Then we can approximate $u(x,y)$ at time step $n+1$ as follows

$$u^{n+1}(x,y) \simeq \sum_{j=1}^{n} \lambda_j^{n+1} \Phi_j(r_j), \tag{21}$$

where Φ_j is obtain by analytically solving

$$\Delta\Phi = \phi. \tag{22}$$

In this paper, two kinds of RBFs are adopted, ie. MQ and TPS [16]

$$\phi_j(r) = \sqrt{(r^2+c^2)}, \qquad \phi_k(r) = r^{2m}\ln(r), \quad m = 3. \tag{23}$$

Note that (18) is a recursion formula and we can solve each elliptic PDE step by step starting with initial condition (14). As is well known, it is difficult to obtain accurate numerical derivative from scatter data. Therefore, we choose $\theta = 1$ in our method we call Euclidean scheme. In this case, we can reformulate (17).

Write (17) together with boundary condition (15) in a matrix form

$$[u]^n = A[\lambda]^n, \tag{24}$$

where $[u]^n = [u_1^n,\ u_2^n,\ \cdots,u_n^n]$, $[\lambda]^n = [\lambda_1^n, \lambda_2^n, \cdots, \lambda_n^n]$ and $A = [a_{kj}], 1 \le k,j \le n$. The matrix A can be split into $A = A_d + A_b$, where

$$A_d = \begin{cases} (a_{kj}), & 1 \le k \le p, 1 \le j \le n, \\ a_{kj} = 0, & \text{otherwise.} \end{cases}$$

$$A_b = \begin{cases} (a_{kj}), & p+1 \le k \le n, 1 \le j \le n, \\ a_{kj} = 0, & \text{otherwise.} \end{cases}.$$

By applying to the domain points and boundary points, there are $p < (N-3)$ internal points and $(N-3-p)$ boundary points, (15) and (17) can be reformulated in the following matrix form:

$$(-iA_d + B)[\lambda]^{n+1} = (-iA_d + C)[\lambda]^n + [G]^{n+1}, \tag{25}$$

where

$$B = -\theta dt(\Delta A_d + W * A_d) + A_b, \qquad C = (1-\theta)dt(\Delta A_d + W * A_d),$$
$$[G]^n = [0 \cdots 0, G^n_{p+1} \cdots G^n_{N-3}], \qquad W = [\omega_1, \omega_2 \cdots \omega_p].$$

The symbol '*' means that the ith component of vector W is multiplied to all components of ith row of matrix A_d. Assume that $[\lambda]^n = [\lambda_r]^n + i[\lambda_i]^n$ and $[G]^n = [G_r]^n + i[G_i]^n$. Indices r and i represent the real part and imaginary part of complex vectors, respectively. Using this notation, (25) can be written as

$$\begin{aligned} &B[\lambda_r]^{n+1} + A_d[\lambda_i]^{n+1} + i(-A_d[\lambda_r]^{n+1} + B[\lambda_i]^{n+1}) \\ &= C[\lambda_r]^n + A_d[\lambda_i]^n + [G_r]^{n+1} + i(-A_d[\lambda_r]^n + C[\lambda_i]^n + [G_i]^{n+1}). \end{aligned} \tag{26}$$

The complex equations (26) can be rewritten in the following real variable form:

$$\begin{pmatrix} B & A_d \\ -A_d & B \end{pmatrix} \begin{bmatrix} \lambda_r \\ \lambda_i \end{bmatrix}^{n+1} = \begin{pmatrix} C & A_d \\ -A_d & C \end{pmatrix} \begin{bmatrix} \lambda_r \\ \lambda_i \end{bmatrix}^{n} + \begin{bmatrix} G_r \\ G_i \end{bmatrix}^{n+1}. \tag{27}$$

Note that (27) is obtained by equalizing the real and imaginary parts of the right and left sides. Thus, the solution of the complex system has been reduced to solving the real variable system. Since the coefficient matrix is unchanged in time steps, we use the LU factorization to the coefficient matrix only once and use this factorization in our algorithm.

4 Numerical Example

In order to study the validity and effectiveness of the proposed scheme, we choose a example with the presence of the potential function.

We consider (13) in the region $0 \le x, y \le 1$ with potential function

$$\omega(x,y) = 3 - 2\tanh^2 x - 2\tanh^2 y$$

The analytical solution of the equation is

$$u(x,y,t) = \frac{i\exp(it)}{\cosh(x)\cosh(y)}.$$

The initial and boundary conditions can be found from the analytical solution as

$$u(x,y,0) = \frac{i}{\cosh(x)\cosh(y)}, \quad 0 \le x, y \le 1,$$

and

$$u(0,y,t) = \frac{i\exp(it)}{\cosh(y)}, \qquad u(1,y,t) = \frac{i\exp(it)}{\cosh(1)\cosh(y)},$$
$$u(x,0,t) = \frac{i\exp(it)}{\cosh(x)}, \qquad u(x,1,t) = \frac{i\exp(it)}{\cosh(1)\cosh(x)}.$$

Table 1 presents the maximum absolute error for the real part and imaginary part of solution at different t up to 1.0 by using multiquadrics and the thin plate splines. In this paper, we use the maximum error defined as

$$\epsilon = \max \left| \frac{u_{exact}(x, y, t) - u_{approximate}(x, y, t)}{u_{exact}(x, y, t)} \right|.$$

The results obtained show the very good accuracy and efficiency of the new approximate scheme. Note that we can't distinguish the exact solution from the estimated solution in Fig. 1.

It is worth pointing that we employed this test problem which is taken from the literature [11]. This enables us to compare our results with the earlier works.

Table 1. Numerical errors using MQs and TPS represented by the first and the second rows respectively at different times, where $dx = dy = 0.1, dt = 0.001, \theta = 1$

t	Real part	Imaginary part	ϵ
0.1	4.0806×10^{-9}	7.2506×10^{-7}	6.5355×10^{-5}
	4.5028×10^{-5}	3.2322×10^{-5}	5.3562×10^{-5}
0.3	2.0135×10^{-8}	1.7422×10^{-5}	2.6624×10^{-5}
	9.7267×10^{-6}	1.9260×10^{-5}	2.1558×10^{-5}
0.5	3.4365×10^{-8}	3.8886×10^{-7}	7.8949×10^{-5}
	5.9068×10^{-5}	2.1889×10^{-5}	6.2993×10^{-5}
0.7	5.6348×10^{-6}	4.5641×10^{-7}	1.8781×10^{-5}
	8.7405×10^{-6}	1.7289×10^{-5}	1.7964×10^{-5}
1.0	6.4248×10^{-8}	1.8763×10^{-6}	8.5240×10^{-6}
	1.1032×10^{-5}	6.0615×10^{-6}	1.2588×10^{-5}

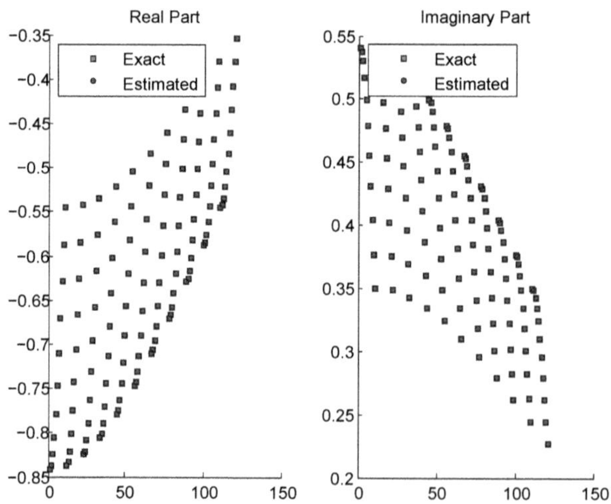

Fig. 1. Real and imaginary parts of numerical and analytical solutions at time t = 1 with dx = dy = 0.1, dt = 0.001 and using MQ (with c = 0.7) as the radial basis function for example

5 Conclusion

In this paper, we proposed a numerical scheme to solve the two-dimensional (2D) time-dependent Schrödinger equation using the method of particular solution(MPS) using multiquadrics (MQ) and the thin plate splines (TPS)(m=3) radial basis function.The numerical results given in the previous section demonstrate the good accuracy of this scheme.

References

1. Arnold, A.: Numerically absorbing boundary conditions for quantum evolution equations. VLSI Design 6, 313–319 (1998)
2. Levy, M.: Parabolic Equation Methods for Electromagnetic Wave Propagation. IEEE (2000)
3. Tappert, F.D.: The parabolic approximation method. In: Keller, J.B., Papadakis, J.S. (eds.) Wave Propagation and Underwater Acoustics. Lecture Notes in Physics, vol. 70, pp. 224–287. Springer, Berlin (1977)
4. Huang, W., Xu, C., Chu, S.T., Chaudhuri, S.K.: The finite-difference vector beam propagation method. J. Lightwave Technol. 10(3), 295–304 (1992)
5. Hajj, F.Y.: Solution of the Schrodinger equation in two and three dimensions. J. Phys. B At. Mol. Phys. 18, 1–11 (1985)
6. Ixaru, L.G.: Operations on oscillatory functions. Comput. Phys. Comm. 105, 1–9 (1997)
7. Dehghan, M.: A numerical method for two-dimensional Schrödinger equation using collocation and radial basis functions. Com. and Math. 54, 136–146 (2007)
8. Kalita, J.C., Chhabra, P., Kumar, S.: A semi-discrete higher order compact scheme for the unsteady two-dimensional Schrödinger equation. J. Comput. Appl. Math. 197, 141–149 (2006)
9. Dehghan, M.: Finite difference procedures for solving a problem arising in modeling and design of certain optoelectronic devices. Math. Comput. Simulation 71, 16–30 (2006)
10. Subasi, M.: On the finite-difference schemes for the numerical solution of two dimensional Schrödinger equation. Numer. Methods Partial Differential Equations 18, 752–758 (2002)
11. Wang, G., Jiang, T.: A numerical method for two-dimensional time-dependent Schrödinger equation. The Acdemic Journal of LinYi University 6, 1–4 (2011)
12. Micchelli, C.A.: Interpolation of scattered data: distance matrices and conditionally positive definite functions. Constructive Approximation 2, 11–12 (1986)
13. Chen, C.S., Fan, C.M., Wen, P.H.: The method of particular solutions for solving elliptic problems with variable coefficients. Communication in Numerical Methods in Engineering (2010)
14. Quan, S.: A meshless method of lines for the numerical solution of KdV equation using radial basis functions. Engineering Analysis with Boundary Elements 33, 1171–1180 (2009)
15. Dehghan, M., Shokri, A.: A meshless method for numerical solution of the one-dimensional wave equation with an integral condition using radial basis functions. Numer. Algor. 52, 461–477 (2009)
16. Dereli, Y., Irk, D., Dağ, İ.: Soliton solutions for NLS equation using radial basis functions. Chaos, Solitons and Fractals 42, 1227–1233 (2009)

Dynamical Systems Method for Solving First Kind of Operator Equations with Disturbance Item

Jiang Cheng-Shun[1] and Wang Xian-Chao[2]

[1] Wuhan College, Zhongnan University of Economics and Law, Wuhan, 430079
[2] Institute of Information and Engineering, Information Engineering University, Zhengzhou, 450002

Abstract. In this paper, the dynamical systems method (DSM) for solving the first kind of operator equations with noise in the right-hand data is studied. The convergence of the discrete form of DSM is proved, and then the convergence rate of the approximate solution is obtained under certain prior assumption. The experimental results of first kind of Fredholm integral equations show that DSM is more accurate and faster than Tikhonov regularization method.

Keywords: DSM, ill-posed problems, Fredholm integral equations, Tikhonov regularization method.

1 Introduction

Affected by the drivers of the urgent needs in many subjects and engineering fields, the study of inverse problems achieved great development in the past two decades. The solutions of many inverse problems finally belong to the solutions of the first kind of operator equations[1].

Set H is Hilbert space and K is the boundary operator on H. The first kind of operator equations can be denoted as

$$Kx = y. \tag{1}$$

Specially, (1) is the first kind of Fredholm integral operator equations, if K is

$$Kx(l) := \int_a^b k(l,s)x(s)ds = y(l), \quad l \in [a,b], \tag{2}$$

Usually such operator equations are ill-posed problems. To solve them, regularization strategy is a feasible method [2,3].

DSM is a newly developed method for solving operator equations, which is determined by solving well-posed initial value problems of ordinary differential equations to obtain the original operator equations [4-9]. In this article, a proof of the convergence is given based on the discrete form, and the error of approximate solutions is also estimated. Finally the first kind of Fredholm integral equation is numerically solved to the advantages of DSM.

C. Liu, J. Chang, and A. Yang (Eds.): ICICA 2011, Part I, CCIS 243, pp. 52–59, 2011.

2 Theory and Iterative Form of DSM

2.1 Theory of DSM

We suppose that (H): *K* is boundary operator on Hilbert space, $\|K\| \le \sqrt{m}$, $m > 0$ is constant, R(A) is open. There is *u* which satisfies *Ku=y*, $u \perp N(K)$, *N(K)* is zero space of operator *K*.

To solve problem (1), we construct the following initial value problem.

$$\dot{x}(t) = \Phi(t,x), \ \ x(0) = x_0, \ \ t > 0, \tag{3}$$

where $\Phi(t,x)$ is continuous, $x(t) \in H$ satisfies Lipschitz condition, there is a constant $c > 0$, for all $t \ge 0$, we have

$$\sup_{x_1,x_2 \in H} \|\Phi(t,x_1) - \Phi(t,x_2)\| \le c\|x_1 - x_2\|, \tag{4}$$

then the initial problem (3) has unique solution. DSM of solving the operator equation (1) is to select suitable function $\Phi(t,x)$. By solving the Cauchy problem (3), the solution satisfied the following conditions can be obtained.

$$\exists x(t), \ \forall t > 0; \ \exists u := x(\infty); \ Ku = y, \tag{5}$$

Set y_δ is the data with disturbance, which satisfies the error estimate $\|y - y_\delta\| \le \delta$. Then (3) turns into

$$\dot{x}_\delta(t) = \Phi_\delta(t, x_\delta), \ \ x_\delta(0) = x_0, \ \ t > 0. \tag{6}$$

The stop time t_δ satisfies $\lim_{\delta \to 0} \|x_\delta(t_\delta) - u\| = 0.$

2.2 A Kind of Iterative Form of DSM

Consider the following dynamical system[6]

$$\dot{x}_\delta(t) = \Phi_\delta(t, x_\delta) = -x_\delta(t) + \left(T + \varepsilon(t)I\right)^{-1} K^* y_\delta, \ \ x_\delta(0) = x_\delta^0, \tag{7}$$

where $T = K^*K$, $\varepsilon(t) > 0$ is continuous on $[0,\infty)$ which tends to 0 monotonously and satisfies $\int_0^\infty \varepsilon(s)ds = \infty$. Commonly we can set $\varepsilon(t) = \dfrac{\varepsilon_0}{1+t}$, then

$$x_\delta(t) = x_\delta^0 e^{-t} + e^{-t} \int_0^t e^s \left(T + \varepsilon(s)I\right)^{-1} K^* y_\delta ds, \tag{8}$$

and the stop time t_δ can be confirmed by the solution of the next equation

$$\varepsilon(t) = \delta^b, \ \ b \in (0,1). \tag{9}$$

Obviously, from (9) we have

$$\lim_{\delta\to 0}\frac{\delta}{\varepsilon(t)}=0. \tag{10}$$

Therefore it is proved that the solution of operation equation (1) can be obtained from the solution of the Cauchy problem (7)[4]. In order to increase the calculation speed, the continuous function $\varepsilon(t)$ is replaced by step function $\tilde{\varepsilon}(t)$.

$$\tilde{\varepsilon}(t)=\varepsilon_n=\varepsilon(t_n),\ \ t_n\le t\le t_{n+1}, \tag{11}$$

Applying the (8), the next iterative form can be obtained

$$w_\delta^{n+1}=e^{-h_n}w_\delta^n+(1-e^{-h_n})(T+\varepsilon_n I)^{-1}K^*y_\delta, \tag{12}$$

where $w_\delta^0=x_\delta^0$, $h_n=t_{n+1}-t_n=q^n$, $1\le q\le 2$.

From the analysis of the iterative form (12), the convergence is proved based on the discrete form, and then the error of approximate solutions is estimated.

Theorem 1. Suppose (H) is established, u is the minimum norm solution of (1) and satisfies (5), then for any $x_\delta^0\in H$, the iterative solution w_δ^{n+1} satisfies

$$\lim_{n\to\infty}\lim_{\delta\to 0}\left\|w_\delta^{n+1}-u\right\|=0. \tag{13}$$

Before the proof of the theorem 1, the following lemmas are given.

Lemma 1[5]. Set $T=K^*K$, K is an arbitrary boundary linear operator on Hilbert space. If $\varepsilon>0$, then

$$\left\|(T+\varepsilon I)^{-1}K^*\right\|\le\frac{1}{2\sqrt{\varepsilon}}. \tag{14}$$

Lemma 2. $\varepsilon_n>0$, w_δ^n is the iterative solution determined by (12), then for all $n>0$, there is a constant M which satisfies $\left\|w_\delta^n\right\|\le M$.

Proof. Set $f_n=(1-e^{-h_n})(T+\varepsilon_n I)^{-1}K^*y_\delta$, then

$$\left\|f_n\right\|\le\left\|(T+\varepsilon_n I)^{-1}K^*y_\delta\right\|\le\left\|(T+\varepsilon_n I)^{-1}K^*(y-y_\delta)\right\|+\left\|(T+\varepsilon_n I)^{-1}Tu\right\|$$

$$\le\frac{\delta}{2\sqrt{\varepsilon_n}}+\left\|\int_0^m\frac{\lambda}{\lambda+\varepsilon_n}dE_\lambda u\right\|\le\frac{\delta}{2\sqrt{\varepsilon_n}}+\left\|\int_0^m dE_\lambda u\right\|=\frac{\delta}{2\sqrt{\varepsilon_n}}+\left\|u\right\|$$

where $\{E_\lambda\}$ is the spectral set of self-adjoint operator T, $\left\|T\right\|=m$, u is the minimum norm solution of (1). From (10), $\dfrac{\delta}{2\sqrt{\varepsilon_n}}\to 0$. So there is a positive number M_1, we have $\left\|f_n\right\|\le M_1$. From (12), then

$$w_\delta^n = e^{-h_{n-1}} w_\delta^{n-1} + f_{n-1} = e^{-h_{n-1}} \left(e^{-h_{n-2}} w_\delta^{n-2} + f_{n-2}\right) + f_{n-1}$$

$$= e^{-(h_{n-1}+h_{n-2})} w_\delta^{n-2} + e^{-h_{n-1}} f_{n-2} + f_{n-1}$$

$$= e^{-\sum_{i=0}^{n-1} h_i} w_\delta^0 + \left(e^{-\sum_{i=1}^{n-1} h_i} f_0 + e^{-\sum_{i=2}^{n-1} h_i} f_1 + \ldots + e^{-h_{n-1}} f_{n-2} + f_{n-1} \right)$$

$$\le e^{-\sum_{i=0}^{n-1} h_i} w_\delta^0 + \left[1 + (n-1) e^{-h_{n-1}}\right] M_1 = I_1 + I_2,$$

For $h_n = q^n$, $1 \le q \le 2$, it is obvious that when $n \to \infty$, $I_1 \to 0$, $(n-1)e^{-q^{n-1}} \to 0$. Thus, for any $\varepsilon_n > 0$, there is a positive number M, we have $w_\delta^n \le M$.

Next we prove the theorem 1.

Proof. From (12) and Lemma 1, then

$$\left\|w_\delta^{n+1} - u\right\| = \left\|e^{-h_n} w_\delta^n + (1 - e^{-h_n})(T + \varepsilon_n I)^{-1} K^* y_\delta - u\right\|$$

$$\le \left\|e^{-h_n} w_\delta^n\right\| + (1 - e^{-h_n}) \left\{ \left\|(T + \varepsilon_n I)^{-1} K^* (y_\delta - y)\right\| + \left\|(T + \varepsilon_n I)^{-1} K^* y - u\right\| \right\} + \left\|e^{-h_n} u\right\|$$

$$\le \left\|e^{-h_n} w_\delta^n\right\| + (1 - e^{-h_n}) \left\{ \frac{\delta}{2\sqrt{\varepsilon_n}} + \left\|(T + \varepsilon_n I)^{-1} K^* y - u\right\| \right\} + \left\|e^{-h_n} u\right\|$$

$$\le \left\|e^{-h_n} w_\delta^n\right\| + \frac{\delta}{2\sqrt{\varepsilon_n}} + \left\|(T + \varepsilon_n I)^{-1} K^* y - u\right\| + \left\|e^{-h_n} u\right\|$$

$$= I_1 + I_2 + I_3 + I_4.$$

From Lemma 2, when $n \to \infty$, $I_1 \le e^{-h_n} M \to 0$. Considering I_3,

$$I_3^2 = \left\|(T + \varepsilon_n I)^{-1} K^* y - u\right\|^2 = \left\|(T + \varepsilon_n I)^{-1} T u - u\right\|^2 = \left\|\varepsilon_n (T + \varepsilon_n I)^{-1} u\right\|^2$$

$$= \int_0^m \frac{\varepsilon_n^2}{(\lambda + \varepsilon_n)^2} d(E_\lambda u, u),$$

When $n \to \infty$, $\varepsilon_n \to 0$. So $\dfrac{\varepsilon_n}{\lambda + \varepsilon_n} \to 0$. From $u \in N(K)^\perp = N(T)^\perp$, we have

$$I_3^2 = \int_0^m \frac{\varepsilon_n^2}{(\lambda + \varepsilon_n)^2} d(E_\lambda u, u) \to \left\|P_N u\right\|^2 = 0,$$

where P_N is orthogonal projection operator on $N(T)$. Thus $\left\|w_\delta^{n+1}-u\right\| \le \frac{\delta}{2\sqrt{\varepsilon_n}}$. If we select $2\sqrt{\varepsilon_n}=2\sqrt{\varepsilon(t_n)}=\delta^b$, $b\in(0,1)$, then when $\delta\to 0$, $\frac{\delta}{2\sqrt{\varepsilon_n}}\to 0$. It is clear when $n\to\infty$, $I_4\to 0$.

From above discussions, we have $\lim_{n\to\infty}\lim_{\delta\to 0}\left\|w_\delta^{n+1}-u\right\|=0$. The proof is completed.

3 The Error Estimate of Approximate Solution

In order to estimate the error of approximate solution, we assume that the solution of the original operator equation satisfies some smoothness conditions, and then we have the following theorem.

Theorem 2. Set $u\in S_v$, $S_v=\{u:u=T^v h,\|h\|\le R, v>0\}$, R is a positive number. Set $\phi(\delta)$ is the convergence order of the error of the approximate solution, then

$$\phi(\delta)=\begin{cases} O(\delta^{\frac{2v}{2v+1}}), & 0<v<1, \\ O(\delta^{\frac{2}{3}}), & v\ge 1, \end{cases} \qquad \delta\to 0.$$

Proof. From the proof of theorem 1, we know

$$\begin{aligned}\left\|w_\delta^{n+1}-u\right\| &= \left\|e^{-h_n}w_\delta^n+(1-e^{-h_n})(T+\varepsilon_n I)^{-1}K^* y_\delta-u\right\| \\ &\le \frac{\delta}{2\sqrt{\varepsilon_n}}+\left\|(T+\varepsilon_n I)^{-1}K^* y_\delta-u\right\|,\end{aligned} \tag{15}$$

where

$$\begin{aligned}\left\|(T+\varepsilon_n I)^{-1}K^* y_\delta-u\right\| &= \left\|(T+\varepsilon_n I)^{-1}K^* y_\delta-\int_0^m dE_\lambda u\right\| \\ &= \left\|(T+\varepsilon_n I)^{-1}K^* y_\delta-\int_0^m \frac{\lambda}{\lambda+\varepsilon_n}dE_\lambda u-\int_0^m \frac{\varepsilon_n}{\lambda+\varepsilon_n}dE_\lambda u\right\| \\ &\le \left\|(T+\varepsilon_n I)^{-1}K^* y_\delta-(T+\varepsilon_n I)^{-1}Tu\right\|+\left\|\int_0^m \frac{\varepsilon_n}{\lambda+\varepsilon_n}dE_\lambda u\right\|=I_1+I_2,\end{aligned} \tag{16}$$

From Lemma 1, we have

$$I_1=\left\|(T+\varepsilon_n I)^{-1}K^*(y_\delta-y)\right\|\le\frac{\delta}{2\sqrt{\varepsilon_n}}. \tag{17}$$

Applying the theorem condition,

$$I_2 \le \varepsilon_n \left\| \sup_{\|h\|\le R} \int_0^m \frac{dE_\lambda T^v h}{\lambda+\varepsilon_n} \right\| = \varepsilon_n \sup_{\|h\|\le R} \left\| (T+\varepsilon_n I)^{-1} T^v h \right\| = \varepsilon_n \sup_{\|h\|\le R} \left\| \int_0^m \frac{\lambda^v}{\lambda+\varepsilon_n} dE_\lambda h \right\|. \tag{18}$$

If $v \ge 1$, $I_2 \le \varepsilon_n m^{v-1} R$. From (15), (17), (17) and (18), we have

$$\left\| w_\delta^{n+1} - u \right\| \le \frac{\delta}{\sqrt{\varepsilon_n}} + \varepsilon_n m^{v-1} R, \tag{19}$$

When $\varepsilon_n = (2m^{v-1}R)^{-\frac{2}{3}} \delta^{\frac{2}{3}}$, (21) has the minimum $3\left(\frac{m^{v-1}R}{4}\right)^{\frac{1}{3}} \delta^{\frac{2}{3}}$, so $\phi(\delta) = O(\delta^{\frac{2}{3}})$.

If $0 < v < 1$,

$$I_2 \le \varepsilon_n \sup_{\|h\|\le R} \left\| \int_0^m \frac{\lambda^v}{\lambda+\varepsilon_n} dE_\lambda h \right\| = \varepsilon_n \sup_{\|h\|\le R} \left\| \int_0^m \frac{1}{\lambda^{1-v}+\varepsilon_n \lambda^{-v}} dE_\lambda h \right\| \le R v^v (1-v)^{1-v} \varepsilon_n^v.$$

Set $C = R v^v (1-v)^{1-v}$,

$$\frac{\delta}{\sqrt{\varepsilon_n}} + C\varepsilon_n^v \ge (v+\frac{1}{2}) \left(\frac{\delta}{v}\right)^{\frac{2v}{2v+1}} (2C)^{\frac{1}{2v+1}} = O\left(\delta^{\frac{2v}{2v+1}}\right).$$

The proof is completed.

4 Numerical Experiments

In this section, we solve the first kind of Fredholm integral operator equations with DSM and compare the numerical results with Tikhonov regularization method. The form of the integral equation is

$$Kx(l) := \int_0^1 (1+ls)e^{ls} x(s) ds = e^l, \quad l \in [0,1]. \tag{20}$$

It is clear (20) has the unique solution $x(l) = 1$. Set $f(l,s) = (1+ls)e^{ls}$. The interval $0 \le s \le 1$ is averagely divided into n segments. $s_0, s_1, \ldots, s_{n+1}$ are the nodes. Set $x_i = x(s_i)$, Using composite trapezoidal formula to solve the equation (20), then

$$Kx(l) \approx \frac{h}{2}\left[f(l,s_0)x_0 + 2\sum_{i=1}^{n} f(l,s_i)x_i + f(l,s_{n+1})x_{n+1} \right].$$

Suppose the right-hand data is y_δ with perturbation and satisfies $\|y_\delta - y\| \le \delta$. We solve the equation (20) with DSM and Tikhonov regularization method respectively. From the iterative course of DSM we find the calculations focus on the inverse matrix $(T+\varepsilon_n I)^{-1}$ in equation (12). The Tikhonov regularization method is similar. So we use the iterative time N_{iter} to denote the computation of the algorithms. The error result x_δ is described as $Err = \|x_\delta - x\|_2 / \|x\|_2$. We use the relative error $\delta_{rel} = \|y_\delta - y\|_2 / \|y\|_2$ to describe the perturbation amplitude of the right-hand data y_δ. To reduce the impact of random factors on the results, we examine the two methods using the average of multiple calculations. The number of nodes are n=32. The calculation process is repeated 10 times and generates a random disturbance each time. The results are shown in Table 1.

Table 1. The numerical results using DSM and Tikhonov regularization (TR), $\delta_{rel} = 0.1$

Times	DSM		TR	
	N_{iter}	Err	N_{iter}	Err
1	4	0.1082	8	0.1288
2	5	0.1357	7	0.1446
3	3	0.2092	7	0.2261
4	5	0.1196	7	0.1004
5	4	0.2434	6	0.2561
6	3	0.3142	7	0.3083
7	2	0.2980	5	0.2983
8	2	0.2475	5	0.2538
9	5	0.1360	7	0.1661
10	3	0.1963	5	0.2094
Average	3.6	0.2009	6.4	0.2089

From Table 1, we can find that the iterative times of DSM are less than TR and the accuracy of DSM is higher than TR. For the effect of random factors, although the accuracy of DSM in fourth and sixth times is lower than TR, it doesn't affect the overall performance of DSM.

Table 2. The numerical results using DSM and Tikhonov regularization (TR), $\delta_{rel} = 0.05$

Times	DSM		TR	
	N_{iter}	Err	N_{iter}	Err
1	3	0.08076	6	0.09870
2	5	0.06609	7	0.06635
3	3	0.05983	6	0.05224
4	5	0.06602	7	0.05741
5	4	0.07345	6	0.07157
6	3	0.05003	5	0.05758
7	3	0.04628	6	0.04937
8	3	0.08462	6	0.08462
9	3	0.05858	5	0.09979
10	3	0.05990	5	0.06209
Average	3.5	0.0646	5.9	0.0700

We change the accuracy of the right-hand data and set the relative error $\delta_{rel} = 0.05$, and then repeat similar calculations. Table 2 shows DSM still has a higher accuracy and less computation than TR.

5 Conclusion

In this article, we prove the convergence of the solution of the first kind of operator equations with DSM and calculate the convergence speed of approximate solution under certain prior conditions. The results of theory and numerical experiments demonstrate that DSM is an efficient way to solve ill-posed linear boundary operator equations.

Acknowledgments. This work was supported by the National High Technology Research and Development Program of China (2009AA012200).

References

1. Kirsch, A.: An Introduction to the Mathematical Theory of Inverse Problems. Springer, New York (1996)
2. Groetsch, C.W.: The Theory of Tikhonov Regularization for Fredholm Equations of the First Kind. Pitman, Boston (1984)
3. Engl, H.W., Kunisch, K., Neubauer, A.: Convergence Rates for Tikhonov Regularization of Nonlinear Ill-posed Problems. Inverse Problems 5, 523–540 (1989)
4. Airapetyan, R.G., Ramm, A.G.: Dynamical Systems and Discrete Methods for Solving Nonlinear Ill-posed Problem. Applied Mathematics Reviews, 491–536 (2000)
5. Ramm, A.G.: Linear Ill-posed Problems and Dynamical Systems. J. Math. Anal. Appl. 258, 448–456 (2001)
6. Ramm, A.G.: Dynamical Systems Method for Solving Operator Equations. Commun. Nonlinear Sci. Numer. Simul. 9, 383–402 (2004)
7. Hoang, N.S., Ramm, A.G.: Dynamical Systems Gradient Method for Solving Ill-conditioned Linear Algebraic Systems. Acta Applicandae Mathematicae 111, 189–204 (2010)
8. Hoang, N.S., Ramm, A.G.: Dynamical Systems Gradient Method for Solving Nonlinear Equations with Monotone Operators. Acta Applicandae Mathematicae 106, 473–499 (2009)
9. Hoang, N.S.: Dynamical Systems Method of Gradient Type for Solving Nonlinear Equations with Monotone Operators. BIT Numerical Mathematics 50, 751–780 (2010)

Numerical Simulation of One Dimensional Heat Conduction Equation for Inverse Problem

Dongmei Li[1], Qiuna Zhang[1], Yan Gao[2], and Rongcui Zheng[1]

[1] Qinggong College, Hebei United University, Tangshan, China, 063000
[2] College of Science, Hebei United University, Tangshan, China, 063000
lidm_qyheut@163.com

Abstract. Boundary integral method was adopted to deal with ill-conditions occurred while solving inverse problem of heat conduction equation. Given initial value and boundary value, and fundamental solution of differential equations, the integral equation was obtained, which was needed to solve on the boundary of the region Ω . In the end, we give numerical results.

Keywords: Heat conduction equation, Boundary integral method, Inverse problem, Numerical simulation.

1 Introduction

Heat conduction equation appears in a wide range of science and industrial fields. Its research in industry is of great significance, particularly with regard to inverse problem of heat conduction equation. Such as air fields, measuring the surface temperature of space capsule during the atmosphere is a typical inverse problem of heat conduction equation, through part of the boundary or the internal data to determine the heat of anther part of the boundary. Usually, inverse problem of heat conduction equation solving is ill-conditioned. A small perturbation will bring the solution to the problem a great deal of error[1].

Boundary integral method was adopted to deal with ill-conditions. Given initial value and boundary value, and fundamental solution of differential equations, the integral equation was obtained, which was needed to solve on the boundary of the region Ω. Then solution of the problem is obtained. By solving the boundary integral equation, the value of the unknown integral kernel can be earned. Then solution of the problem to be solved is constructed by convolution of the fundamental solution and the integral kernel. Compared with other methods, the advantages of this approach lie in that calculation is realized on the border. Thus the problem is fall from two-dimensional to one-dimensional. So that we can expect that the calculation can largely save the computing time and storage space, and bring great convenience to calculation.

C. Liu, J. Chang, and A. Yang (Eds.): ICICA 2011, Part I, CCIS 243, pp. 60–66, 2011.

2 Mathematical Model of One-Dimensional Heat Conduction Equation

2.1 Direct Problem

Consider the following problem

$$\begin{cases} u_t(x,t) - a^2 u_{xx}(x,t) = 0, & 0 \le x \le 1, 0 \le t \le T \\ u(x,0) = u_0(x), & 0 \le x \le 1 \\ -u_x\big|_{x=0} = f(t), & 0 \le t \le T \\ u_x\big|_{x=1} = g(t), & 0 \le t \le T \end{cases} \tag{1}$$

Where $u(x,t)$ is the temperature distribution function, T is the length of time interval, $f(t)$ and $g(t)$ are piecewise continuous functions. Given $f(t)$, $g(t)$, $u_0(x)$ or their discrete values to get the solution to this problem is the direct problem.

2.2 Inverse Problem

Here the inverse problem is

$$\begin{cases} u_t(x,t) - a^2 u_{xx}(x,t) = 0, & 0 \le x \le 1, 0 \le t \le T \\ u(x,0) = u_0(x), & 0 \le x \le 1 \\ u(1,t) = h(t), & 0 \le t \le T \\ u_x\big|_{x=1} = g(t), & 0 \le t \le T \end{cases} \tag{2}$$

Where $u(x,t)$ is the temperature distribution function, T is the length of time interval, $h(t)$ and $g(t)$ are piecewise continuous functions. Given $h(t)$, $g(t)$ or their discrete values to get the solution $u(x,t)$ or the value of u_x at the point $x = 0$. This is an ill-posed problem.

3 Boundary Integral Method for This Problem

Boundary integral method is the fundamental of the method. Only consider the case of one-dimensional homogeneous heat conduction equation of the initial conditions.

Given a specific form of one-dimensional

$$\begin{cases} u_t(x,t) - a^2 u_{xx}(x,t) = 0, & 0 \le x \le 1, 0 \le t \le T \\ u(x,0) = u_0(x), & 0 \le x \le 1 \\ -u_x\big|_{x=0} = f(t), & 0 \le t \le T \\ u_x\big|_{x=1} = g(t), & 0 \le t \le T \end{cases}$$

Suppose $G(x,t)$ is the fundamental solution of the heat conduction equation, then

$$G(x,t)=\frac{H(t)}{2a\sqrt{\pi t}}\exp\{-x^2/(4at)\}$$

where $H(t)=\begin{cases}1, & t>0\\ 0, & else\end{cases}$

Simple layer potential V is as follow

$$(V\sigma)(x,t)=\int_0^t\int_\Gamma \sigma(y,\tau)G(x-y,t-\tau)d\Gamma_y d\tau$$

$$=\int_0^t \sigma(0,\tau)G(x-0,t-\tau)d\tau+\int_0^t \sigma(1,\tau)G(x-1,t-\tau)d\tau$$

where $(x,t)\in\Omega\times[0,T]$, $\Gamma=\partial\Omega$.

Defined operator

$$(U\sigma)(x,t)=\int_0^t\int_\Gamma \sigma(y,\tau)\partial_{n_x}G(x-y,t-\tau)d\Gamma_y d\tau$$

By solving the integral equation

$$\begin{cases}(\frac{1}{2}I+U)\mu=g\\ u=V\mu\end{cases}$$

where $\mu=\partial_n u^- -\partial_n u^+$, then the solution of the problem can be earned.

Using simple layer potential method, there is

$$u=\int_0^t \sigma(0,\tau)G(x,t-\tau)d\tau+\int_0^t \sigma(1,\tau)G(x-1,t-\tau)d\tau \tag{3}$$

Denote $\sigma(0,\tau)$, $\sigma(1,\tau)$ as $\varphi_1(\tau)$, $\varphi_2(\tau)$ then $\mu=(\sigma(0,\tau),\sigma(1,\tau))^T$.

Corresponding equations are

$$\begin{aligned}\frac{1}{2}\varphi_1(t)-\int_0^t G_x(-1,t-\tau)\varphi_2(\tau)d\tau=f(t)\\ \frac{1}{2}\varphi_2(t)+\int_0^t G_x(1,t-\tau)\varphi_1(\tau)d\tau=g(t)\end{aligned} \tag{4}$$

to get $\varphi_1(\tau)$, $\varphi_2(\tau)$, substituting into(3), then $u(x,t)$ can be obtained.

4 Algorithms of the Problem

4.1 Direct Problem

The subdivision of x and t is

$$x_0=0,\ x_j=x_0+jd,\ j=1,2,\cdots,M,\ d=1/M;$$
$$t_0=0,\ t_i=t_0+ih,\ i=1,2,\cdots,N,\ h=1/N;$$

where M, N are positive integers. Equations(4) can be discretized into

$$\frac{1}{2}\varphi_1(t_i) - hG_x(-1, t_i - t_j)\varphi_2(t_j) = f(t_i)$$
$$\frac{1}{2}\varphi_2(t_i) + hG_x(1, t_i - t_j)\varphi_1(t_j) = g(t_i) \qquad i = 1,2,\cdots,N$$

Discrete values of φ_1, φ_2 can be obtained by solving linear equations.

Values of φ_1, φ_2 are substituted into discretized form of (3), then discrete values of $u(x,t)$ can be obtained.

$$u(x_j, t_i) = \sum_{k=1}^{i} h\varphi_1(t_k)G(x_j, t_i - t_k) + \sum_{k=1}^{i} h\varphi_2(t_k)G(x_j - 1, t_i - t_k) \quad (5)$$
$$i = 1,2,\cdots,N\ ;\ j = 1,2,\cdots,M$$

4.2 Inverse Problem

Take the data obtained from direct problem as raw data of inverse problem. Similarly to direct problem, we have

$$\int_0^t \varphi_1(\tau)G(1, t-\tau)d\tau + \int_0^t \varphi_2(\tau)G(0, t-\tau)d\tau = h(t)$$
$$\frac{1}{2}\varphi_2(\tau) + \int_0^t \varphi_1(\tau)G_x(1, t-\tau)d\tau = g(t)$$

Using subdivision of x and t, this formula can be discretized into

$$\sum_{j=1}^{i} h\varphi_1(t_j)G(1, t_i - t_j) + \sum_{j=1}^{i} h\varphi_2(t_j)G(0, t_i - t_j) = h(t_i)$$
$$\frac{1}{2}\varphi_2(t_i) + \sum_{j=1}^{i} h\varphi_1(t_j)G_x(1, t_i - t_j) = g(t_i) \qquad i = 1,2,\cdots,N$$

Discrete values of φ_1, φ_2 can be obtained by solving linear equations.

Values of φ_1, φ_2 are substituted into(5), then discrete values of $u(x,t)$ can be obtained.

5 Numerical Simulation

Consider the problem

$$\begin{cases} u_t(x,t) - 100u_{xx}(x,t) = 0, & 0 \le x \le 1, 0 \le t \le 1 \\ u(x,0) = 0, & 0 \le x \le 1 \\ -u_x\Big|_{x=0} = 5\sin(30t), & 0 \le t \le 1 \\ u_x\Big|_{x=1} = 1, & 0 \le t \le 1 \end{cases}$$

The solution $u(1,t)$ of direct problem can be got by difference method. Using the same algorithm as above, we can get the value of $u(x,t)$ and $u_x(x,t)$ at $x=0$.

Here is the difference scheme.

$$\begin{cases} u_{i,j+1} = a^2 h \dfrac{u_{i+1,j} - 2u_{i,j} + u_{i-1,j}}{d^2} + u_{i,j} \\ u_{i,0} = 0 \\ u_{0,j} = u_{1,j} + df_j \\ u_{M,j} = u_{M-1,j} + dg_j \end{cases}$$

This is an explicit scheme, which is convergence when $\dfrac{a^2 h}{d^2} < \dfrac{1}{2}$ [2].

In the computation of inverse problem, Tikhonov regularization method is used to deal with singular matrix of the linear equations, in order to obtain the approximate solution near the exact solution.

The pictures of numerical simulation are as follows

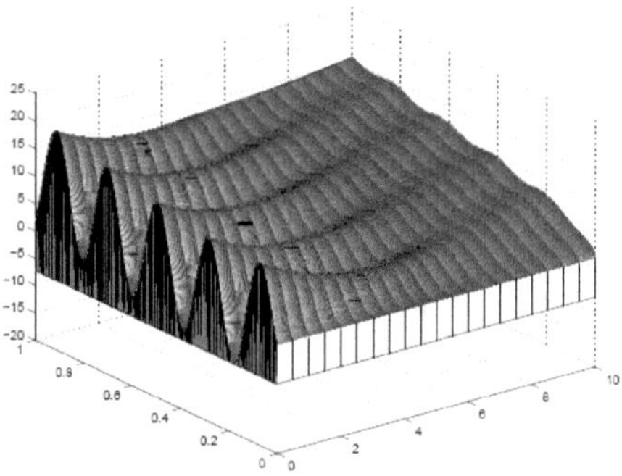

Fig.1

Fig. 1. The distribution image of the temperature function u obtained from the difference scheme

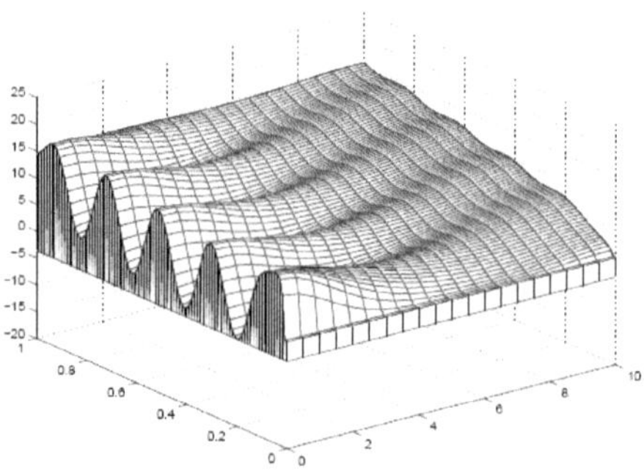

Fig.2

Fig. 2. Solving the direct problem to get u(1, t), and then the temperature function u is obtained by boundary integral method, the distribution image of u is above

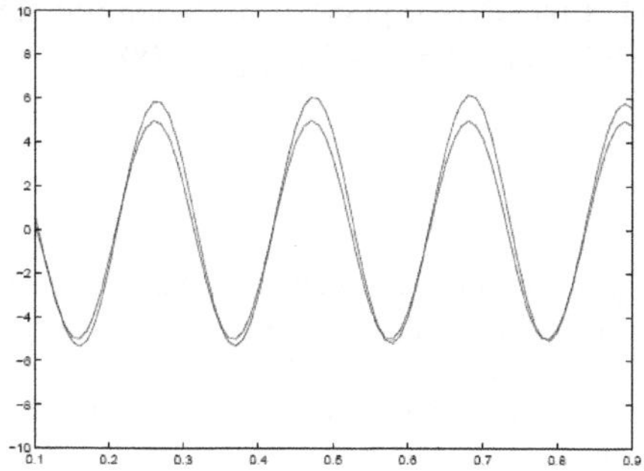

Fig.3

Fig. 3. The error image of boundary function f 1 obtained from the inverse problem and the original boundary function f

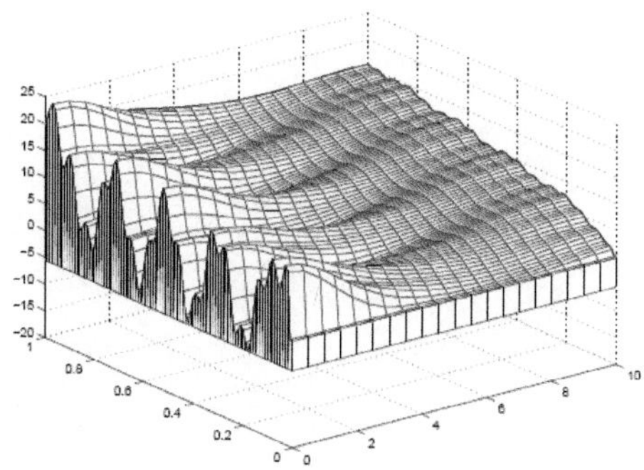

Fig.4

Fig. 4. The distribution image of temperature function u obtained with the disturbance δ=1 to the boundary function u(1, t)

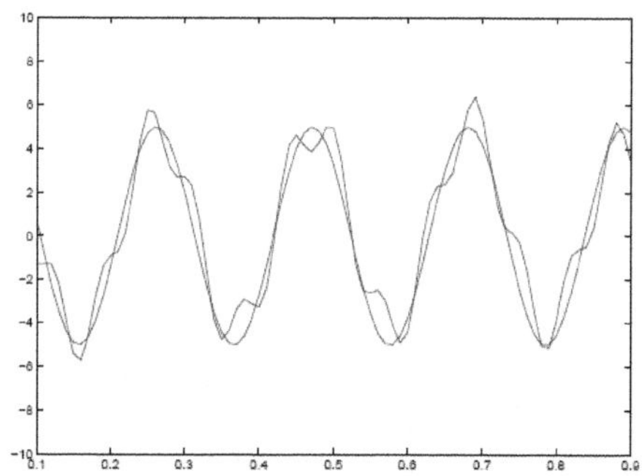

Fig.5

Fig. 5. The error image of boundary function f 1 obtained from the inverse problem and the original boundary function f, with the disturbance δ=1 to u(1, t)

Acknowledgments. This paper is supported by Scientific Research Fund Project of Qinggong College, Hebei United University, (qy201002).

References

1. Jia, X.: Some inverse problems of heat conduction equations, p. 9. Fudan University (2005)
2. Li, R., Feng, G.: Numerical Solution of Differential Equations, p. 4. Higher Education Press (2001)
3. Kirsch, A.: An Introduction to the Mathematical Theory of Inverse Problems. Applied Mathematical Sciences 120, 10 (1999)
4. Ma, F.: Finite difference domain decomposition method for two dimensional heat equation. Numerical Computation and Application of Computers 27(2), 96–105 (2006)
5. Jia, X., Wang, Y.: Solving inverse heat conduction problem by boundary integral method. Journal of Ningxia University 24(3), 9 (2003)

Improved Reaching Law Sliding Mode Control Applied to Active Power Filter

Xiao Zhang, Jing Li, and Xiaolei Liu

Department of Information and Electrical Engineering,
China University of Mining and Technology, Xuzhou, China
Alice5681987@163.com

Abstract. For the shunt active power filter (SAPF), the stability of DC-side voltage plays a very important role in its performance. Considering the large overshoot, static error and poor robustness of traditional P-I control method, an improved reaching law sliding mode control strategy is proposed and applied to three-phase three-wire shunt active power filter for its DC-side voltage control. The simulation experiment shows that the proposed method effectively improves the robustness of DC-side voltage control and evidently suppresses overshoot and has high practical value in three-phase three-wire SAPF.

Keywords: DC-side voltage control, Shunt active power filter, Reaching law sliding mode control, Status point.

1 Introduction

Currently, in the design of shunt active power filter, the DC side usually adopts DC-link capacitors rather than DC power supply as the energy storage device. But during the procedure for active power filter to track the instruction compensation current, the inherent line resistance and switching loss will cause active power consumption. Besides, the APF needs to absorb a certain amount of active power with the working state changing, which can also lead to the fluctuation of DC-side voltage, thus resulting in under-voltage or over-voltage., which may endanger the operation of the APF [1]. So, the maintenance of voltage stability on DC side plays a very important role in the performance of APF.

Traditional P-I control applied to APF DC-side voltage regulation can suppress harmonics to some degree, but it takes a relatively longer time to achieve voltage stability as well as has overshoot. So, in this way, the effect of P-I control is not that satisfactory, which is mainly due to the fact that P-I controller largely depends on the precise mathematical model of the system, thus presenting poor robustness and tending to cause voltage overshoot and current shock [2]. The reaching law sliding mode controller proposed in this paper has good robustness and can suppress voltage overshoot effectively.

C. Liu, J. Chang, and A. Yang (Eds.): ICICA 2011, Part I, CCIS 243, pp. 67–74, 2011.

2 Brief Introduction of System Structure and Working Principle of SAPF

The main circuit diagram of three-phase active power filter is shown in Fig. 1. The system includes two controllers: the outer loop is reaching law sliding mode controller, which regulates the output voltage to track the desired value; the inner loop is the P-I current controller, which controls the compensation current to track the instruction value and helps produce the driving signals for the IGBTs.

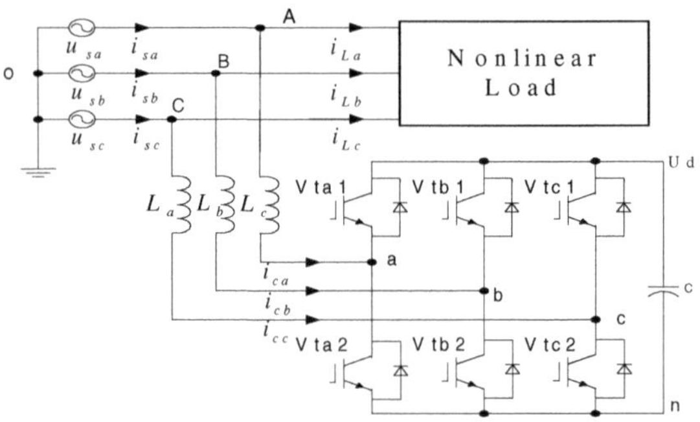

Fig. 1. Main circuit diagram of SAPF

3 DC-Side Voltage Analysis

In the following section, p_s and q_s denote the instantaneous active power and instantaneous reactive power respectively on the AC side of shunt APF. And p_L and q_L denote the instantaneous active power and instantaneous reactive power of the load respectively. Due to the harmonics in the load current, p_L and q_L both contain certain mount of AC component, which means p_L and q_L are composed of DC component $\overline{p_L}$, $\overline{q_L}$ and AC component $\tilde{p}_L$ $\tilde{q}_L$ [3].That is,

$$p_L = \overline{p_L} + \tilde{p}_L \tag{1}$$

$$q_L = \overline{q_L} + \tilde{q}_L \tag{2}$$

If the shunt APF is meant to compensate the harmonics, then the following equations should be satisfied

$$p_A = -\tilde{p}_L \tag{3}$$

$$q_A = -\tilde{q}_L \tag{4}$$

Then, equations (5) and (6) can be obtained.

$$p_S = p_A + p_L = \overline{p_L} \tag{5}$$

$$q_S = q_A + q_L = \overline{q_L} \tag{6}$$

Under this circumstance, the power source only needs to provide the DC component of instantaneous active power and instantaneous reactive power, whose required source current, if the source voltage is symmetrical and distortionless, equals to the fundamental positive-sequence component of the load current. The average value of p_A, the instantaneous active power of APF, is zero, which keeps the DC-side voltage stable. But as a result of the AC component in p_A, the DC-side voltage U_d will fluctuate.

If the APF is merely used for reactive power compensation, then the following equations should be satisfied.

$$p_A = 0 \tag{7}$$

$$q_A = -q_L \tag{8}$$

Under this circumstance, p_A constantly equals to zero. And there is no energy exchange between the DC and AC side of APF. Therefore, U_d can always keep constant and stable. Based on the analysis above, it can be concluded that the APF DC side doesn't need any energy storage device when merely compensating reactive power. As far as capacitors, only very small capacity is required.

If a decreased U_d is expected, the result can be achieved by the condition $p_A = \Delta p > 0$, where $\Delta p = e\Delta i_p$ and e is the source voltage connected to the grid and Δi_p is the additional active component of the APF output current. Under this condition, the APF can continuously gain energy from the power source on the AC side and transfer it to the DC-side energy storage device to increase U_d. So, theoretically speaking, if $p_A > 0$ is satisfied, U_d can keep increasing to any larger value [4]. On the contrary, if $p_A < 0$ then the electrical energy on the DC-link capacitors will decrease, thus making U_d decreased.

4 The Design of Sliding Mode Controller

Based on the analysis above, the voltage deviation on the capacitor is set as the negative feedback. That is to take the deviation between the actual capacitor voltage and its reference value as input of reaching law sliding mode controller and the output of reaching law sliding mode controller as the reference current transferred into the current control module. As a general, the design of sliding-mode variable structure controller basically includes two parts: one is to design the switching function $s(x)$, based on which the designed sliding mode tends to be asymptotically stable and presents satisfactory dynamic quality; the other is to design sliding mode control law $u(x)$ to satisfy the reaching condition, thus forming sliding mode area on the switching surface [5].

In case the switching function $s(x)$ and the sliding mode control law $u(x)$ are obtained, the sliding mode control system can be soundly established.

As it has been mentioned above, U_d is given as the voltage on the DC-link capacitor. And here U^*_d is given as the desired voltage on DC-link capacitors. x_1 and x_2 are defined as follows,

$$x_1 = \Delta v(k) = V^*_{DC} - V_{DC} \tag{9}$$

$$x_2 = \dot{x}_1 = \frac{x_1}{T} = \frac{\Delta v(k)}{T} = \frac{V^*_{DC} - V_{DC}}{T} \tag{10}$$

The state equation is given by (11)

$$\dot{x} = \begin{bmatrix} \dot{x}_1 \\ \dot{x}_2 \end{bmatrix} = \begin{bmatrix} 0 & 1 \\ 0 & 0 \end{bmatrix} \begin{bmatrix} x_1 \\ x_2 \end{bmatrix} + \begin{bmatrix} 0 \\ -k \end{bmatrix} u \tag{11}$$

Where k is a constant, $k > 0$ and u is the control law function to be defined.

According to the state equation, the equation of the sliding mode plane is given by (12)

$$s = \begin{bmatrix} c & 1 \end{bmatrix} \begin{bmatrix} x_1 \\ x_2 \end{bmatrix} = cx_1 + x_2 \tag{12}$$

Where c is a constant and equation (13) can be derived

$$\dot{s} = \begin{bmatrix} c & 1 \end{bmatrix} \begin{bmatrix} \dot{x}_1 \\ \dot{x}_2 \end{bmatrix} = c\,\dot{x}_1 + \dot{x}_2 \tag{13}$$

According to the principle of sliding mode control, only under ideal condition, will the controlled target slide exactly along the sliding plane. And even very tiny undesirable factors can cause high-frequency jitter, which will in turn generate disturbance to the system and may probably provoke the high-frequency components that constantly exists but has not been modeled in the system, thus causing greater interference and even instability to the system.

From a physical perspective, the generation of jitter in the system is due to the fact that when the system status point moves toward the switching surface with its inherent inertia, it still has a certain nonzero speed. In order to control this speed, various reaching law can be designed. According to the general reaching law designing rules that when far from the switching surface, the system status point should move toward the switching surface with a relatively greater speed and when the status point is near to the switching surface, the speed should gradually to be zero. In this way, not only the dynamic characteristic can be guaranteed, but the jitter of the control signal can also be reduced [6].

So, in this article, the improved exponential reaching law sliding mode control with a boundary layer is adopted, namely,

$$\begin{aligned} \dot{s} &= c\dot{x}_1 + \dot{x}_2 \\ &= -\varepsilon sat(s(x_1, x_2)) - qs(x_1, x_2) \end{aligned} \tag{14}$$

Where ε and q are constant, $\varepsilon > 0$ and $q > 0$.

If equation (11) is substituted into equation (14) then equation (15) can be acquired

$$u = \frac{1}{k}[cx_2 + \varepsilon sat(s(x_1, x_2)) + qs(x_1, x_2)] \tag{15}$$

Where

$$sat(s(x_1, x_2)) = \begin{cases} 1 & , \quad s > \Delta \\ \dfrac{s}{\Delta}, & -\Delta \le s \le \Delta \\ -1 & , \quad s < -\Delta \end{cases} \tag{16}$$

The saturation function $sat(s)$ in formula (16) can attract the system status point within a certain range to the Δ region, in which the status point can change linearly and reduces the switching frequency. Compared with the common exponential reaching law, the improved design can reduce jitter effectively. The newly designed reaching law control method can correct the largest deviation with a relatively shorter time, thus guaranteeing fast tracking control. The proposed method can guarantee fast track in just one control cycle as well as avoid jittering of large amplitude.

5 Simulation and Experiment Research

With the purpose of verifying the correctness of the proposed control scheme, the Matlab simulation and experiment are conducted. The parameters are as follows: the power line voltage is 380V, 50Hz; the load is an uncontrollable three-phase rectifier bridge with series resistor and inductance of 10Ω and 0.6mH on the DC side; the desired voltage on DC side is set as 1000V; the output inductor of SAPF is 2.5mH and the sampling frequency is 10K Hz; when the simulation runs to 0.17s, a series resistance-inductance load of 16Ω,0.5mH is put in parallel. P-I current controller is set as the inner loop, $i_p - i_q$ [7] [8] method is adopted for harmonic detection and SVPWM [9] [10] is the control strategy. The simulation results are shown is Fig. 2 to Fig. 6, and the experiment result is shown in Fig. 7 and Fig. 8, which have verified the feasibility of the proposed scheme.

From the waveforms above, it can be concluded that with reaching law sliding mode controller applied in the control of DC side voltage, the SAPF can have satisfactory compensation effects. The total harmonic distortion has been reduced to 2.57%, which improves the power quality a lot. Besides, the improved reaching law sliding mode controller has better dynamic performance and robustness [11], which improves the dynamic compensation performance of the shunt APF.

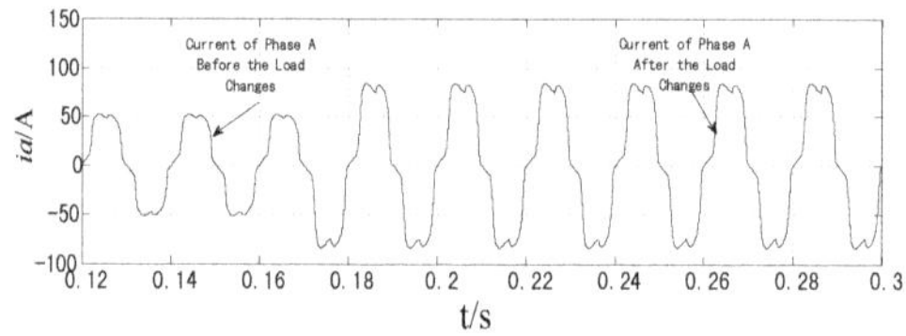

Fig. 2. Source current waveform of phase A before compensation

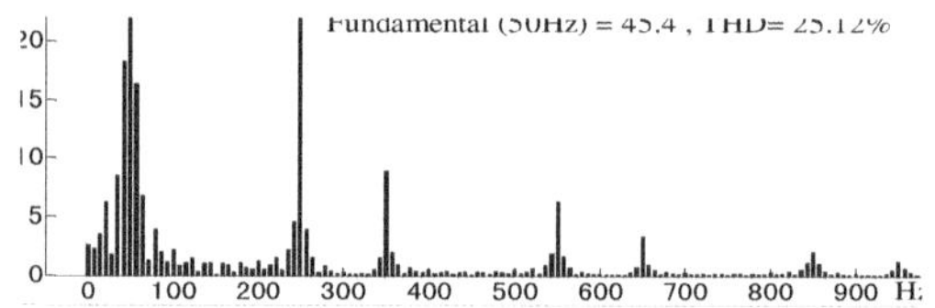

Fig. 3. FFT analysis of source current of phase A before compensation

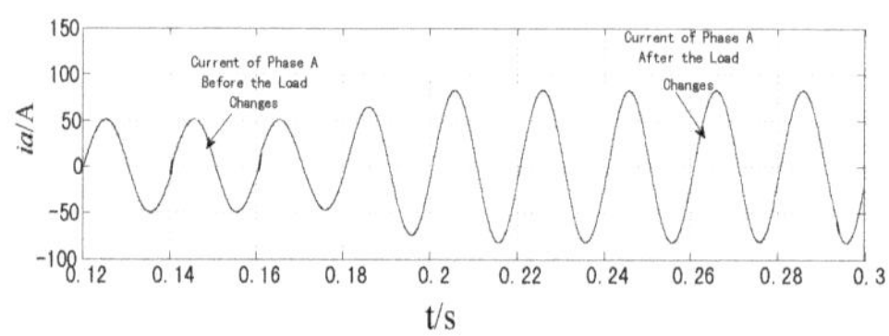

Fig. 4. Source current waveform of phase A after compensation

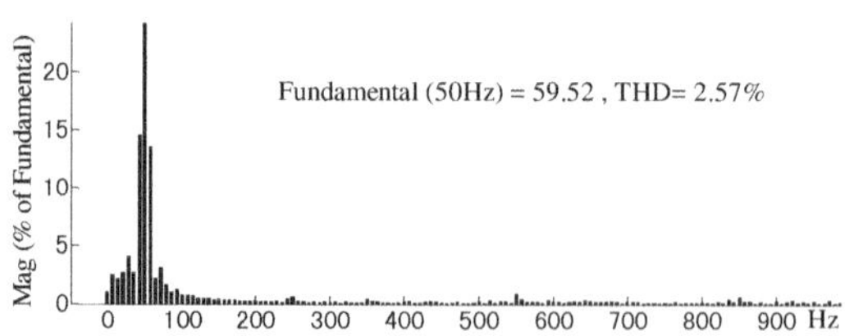

Fig. 5. FFT analysis of source current of phase A after compensation

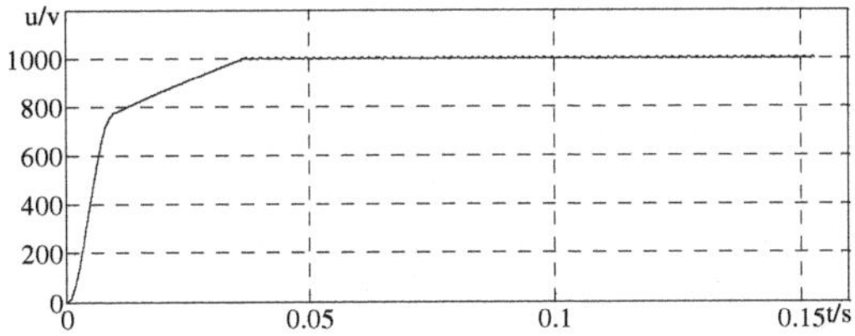

Fig. 6. Capacitor voltage waveform on DC side after compensation

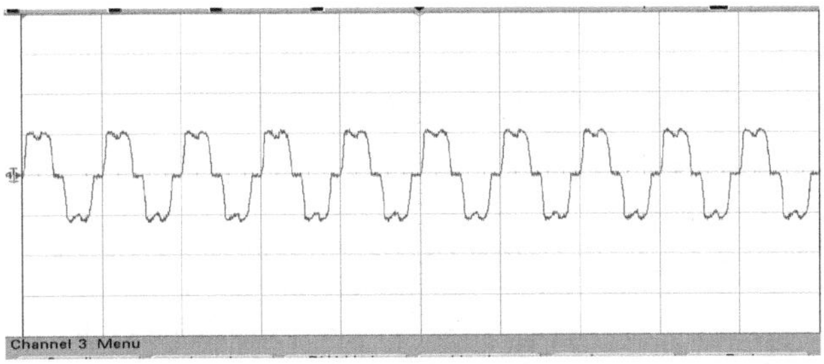

Fig. 7. System current of Phase A before compensation and adding load

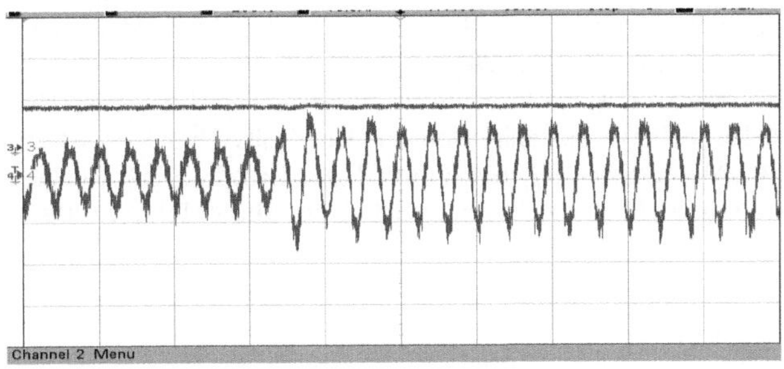

Fig. 8. DC-side voltage and system current of Phase A after compensation and with load adding

From the simulation and experimental results above, it can be concluded that with reaching law sliding mode controller applied in the control of DC side voltage, the SAPF can present satisfactory compensation effects. The total harmonic distortion has been reduced to 2.57%, which improves the power quality a lot. Besides, the improved reaching law sliding mode controller has better dynamic performance and robustness, which improves the dynamic compensation performance of SAPF.

6 Conclusion

In this paper, the DC-side voltage of SAPF is analyzed thoroughly and the improved reaching law sliding mode control is applied to the control of DC-side voltage. Simulation results verify the correctness of the proposed control method and indicate that the proposed method requires less computation, has satisfactory dynamic performance with good robustness and can suppress jitter, thus suitable for the application in APF.

References

1. Zhang, D., Lv, Z.-Y., Chen, G.-Z.: Capacitor Voltage Control of Shunt Active Power Filter. Power Electronics 41(10), 77–79 (2007)
2. Zhou, X.-S., Zhou, Y.-B., Ma, Y.-B., et al.: Analysis on DC side voltage of shunt active power filter. Electric Power 42(2), 24–29 (2009)
3. Wang, Z.-A., Yang, J., Liu, J.-J.: Harmonic Suppresion and Reactive Power Compensation. Machinery Industry Press, Beijing (1998)
4. Liu, H.: Analysis of SVPWM in the Context of Nonorthogonal Coordinates and Study on the Hybird Active Power Filter. North China Electric Power University Thesis for P.H.D Degree (2004)
5. Wang, F.-R.: Sliding Mode Variable Structure Control. Machinery Industry Press, Beijing (1995)
6. Wang, C.: Variable Structure Control of Shunt Active Power Filter. Southwest Jiaotong University, Chengdu (2006)
7. Li, Z.-Y., Pan, L.: Harmonic Detection of the Grid Current Based on Instantaneous Reactive Power Techniques of Automation & Applications, vol. 27(7) (2008)
8. Xiao, Y.-Q., Xiong, Z.-Y., Jiang, K.-S.: Simulink Simulation on harmonic detection of power system based on the theory of instantaneous reactive power. Experiment Technology and Management 25(11) (2008)
9. Qiu, J.-Y., Song, W.-X., Han, Y., Yao, G., Zhou, L.-D., Chen, C.: Study on Three-level PWM Rectifier Based on Voltage Space Vector Pulse Width Modulation. Power System Protection and Control 37(13) (2009)
10. Yang, Y.: Research on Three-level Inverter System Based on Space Vector Pulse Width Modulation Technology. Shanghai: Donghua University Thesis for Master Degree (2008)
11. Zhang, J.-B.: Application of Active Power Filter Based on H∞ Robust Control Theory. Chengdu: Southwest Jiaotong University Thesis for Master Degree (2007)

Multiple Integrals and the Calculating Method of Its Limit

Ma Xing-Hua[1], Li Dong-Mei[2], and Zhang Huan-Cheng[3]

[1] College of Science, Hebei United University, Tangshan, Hebei, 063009, China
[2] Department of Automation Engineering, Tangshan Industrial Vocational Technical College, Tangshan, Hebei, 063000, China
[3] Qinggong College, Hebei United University, Tangshan, Hebei, 063000, China
{mxh332,nhnhldm}@163.com, zhanghuancheng0@yahoo.com.cn

Abstract. It can be generalized to multiple integrals by calculating double integrals and triple integrals. Doing some calculation about multiple integrals suitably can broaden knowledge and one's outlook. Furthermore, the result of multiple integrals have something to do with n, so the limit of n-lay Integrations can be calculated. These will be help to understand the limit ideas by calculating limit and analyzing the significance of limit. Based on several sample problem of multiple integrals, this paper analyzed the calculating method, the solving method and the significance of limit.

Keywords: Multiple integrals, Integral Domain, Integrand, Limit.

1 Calculation of Multiple Integrals

1.1 Direct Calculation

If the function $f(x_1,x_2,\cdots,x_n)$ is determined by the following inequality within the region Ω is a bounded continuous:

$$\begin{cases} a \le x_1 \le b \\ \psi_1(x_1) \le x_2 \le \varphi_1(x_1) \\ \psi_2(x_1,x_2) \le x_3 \le \varphi_2(x_1,x_2) \\ \qquad\qquad \cdots\cdots \\ \psi_{n-1}(x_1,x_2,\cdots,x_{n-1}) \le x_n \le \varphi_{n-1}(x_1,x_2,\cdots,x_{n-1}) \end{cases}$$

Where a and b are constants,

$\psi_1(x_1)$, $\varphi_1(x_1)$, $\psi_2(x_1,x_2)$, $\varphi_2(x_1,x_2)$, ..., $\psi_{n-1}(x_1,x_2,\cdots,x_{n-1})$,

$\varphi_{n-1}(x_1,x_2,\cdots,x_{n-1})$ is a continuous function, and the corresponding multiple integral is calculated by the following formula:

$$\iint\limits_{\Omega}\cdots\int f(x_1,x_2,\cdots,x_n)dx_1dx_2\cdots dx_n$$

C. Liu, J. Chang, and A. Yang (Eds.): ICICA 2011, Part I, CCIS 243, pp. 75–81, 2011.

$$= \int_a^b dx_1 \int_{\psi_1(x_1)}^{\varphi_1(x_1)} dx_2 \int_{\psi_2(x_1,x_2)}^{\varphi_2(x_1,x_2)} dx_{n-1} \cdots \int_{\psi_{n-1}(x_1,x_2,\cdots,x_{n-1})}^{\varphi_{n-1}(x_1,x_2,\cdots,x_{n-1})} f(x_1,x_2,\cdots,x_n)dx_n.$$

1.2 Variable Substitution

If (1) the function $f(x_1,x_2,\cdots,x_n)$ is continuous within the Bounded region Ω;(2)Continuously differentiable function.

$x_i = u_i(\xi_1,\xi_2,\cdots,\xi_n)$ $(i=1,2,\cdots,n)$, bijectively mapped bounded region Ω of space $Ox_1x_2\cdots x_n$ into bounded region Ω' of space $O'\xi_1\xi_2\cdots\xi_n$;(3)Jacobian formula on region Ω':

$$J = \frac{\partial(x_1,x_2,\cdots,x_n)}{\partial(\xi_1,\xi_2,\cdots,\xi_n)} \neq 0$$

Then have the following formula:

$$\iint_{\Omega}\cdots\int f(x_1,x_2,\cdots,x_n)dx_1dx_2\cdots dx_n$$
$$= \iint_{\Omega'}\cdots\int f(\xi_1,\xi_2,\cdots,\xi_n)|J|d\xi_1 d\xi_2\cdots d\xi_n.$$

2 Typical Example Analysis

Example one: calculation $\iint\limits_{\substack{x_1\ge 0,x_2\ge 0,\cdots,x_n\ge 0\\ x_1+x_2+\cdots+x_n\le a}}\cdots\int dx_1dx_2\cdots dx_n$. $(a>0)$

Analysis:by promoting principles of triple integral the integral region is expressed as:

$$\begin{cases} 0\le x_1 \le a \\ 0\le x_2 \le a-x_1 \\ \quad\cdots\cdots \\ 0\le x_{n-1} \le a-x_1-\cdots-x_{n-2} \\ 0\le x_n \le a-x_1-\cdots-x_{n-1} \end{cases}$$

Which can be directly calculated by changing n-lay integration into repeated integral.

Solution: let $I_n = \iint\limits_{\substack{x_1\ge 0,x_2\ge 0,\cdots,x_n\ge 0\\ x_1+x_2+\cdots+x_n\le a}}\cdots\int dx_1dx_2\cdots dx_n$, there

$$I_n = \int_0^a dx_1 \int_0^{a-x_1} dx_2 \ldots \int_0^{a-x_1-\cdots-x_{n-2}} dx_{n-1} \int_0^{a-x_1-\cdots-x_{n-1}} dx_n$$

Integrating from the inside out, formula is obtained with recurrence:

$$\int_0^{a-x_1} dx_2 \cdots \int_0^{a-x_1-\cdots-x_{n-2}} dx_{n-1} \int_0^{a-x_1-\cdots-x_{n-1}} dx_n = \frac{1}{(n-1)!}(a-x_1)^{n-1}$$, then

$$I_n = \int_0^a \frac{1}{(n-1)!}(a-x_1)^{n-1} dx_1 = \frac{a^n}{n!}$$

That is

$$\underset{\substack{x_1 \geq 0, x_2 \geq 0, \cdots, x_n \geq 0 \\ x_1+x_2+\cdots+x_n \leq a}}{\iint\cdots\int} dx_1 dx_2 \cdots dx_n = \frac{a^n}{n!}.$$

Specially, when $a = 1$, $\underset{\substack{x_1 \geq 0, x_2 \geq 0, \cdots, x_n \geq 0 \\ x_1+x_2+\cdots+x_n \leq 1}}{\iint\cdots\int} dx_1 dx_2 \cdots dx_n = \frac{1}{n!}.$

Example Two: seek volume of n-dimensional pyramid

$$\frac{x_1}{a_1} + \frac{x_2}{a_2} + \cdots + \frac{x_n}{a_n} \leq 1, x_i \geq 0, (i = 1, 2, \cdots, n)$$
$$(a_i > 0, i = 1, 2, \cdots, n)$$

Solution: knowing from geometric meaning of multiple integral, volume $V_n = \underset{\substack{\frac{x_1}{a_1}+\frac{x_2}{a_2}+\cdots+\frac{x_n}{a_n} \leq 1, \\ x_i \geq 0, (i=1,2,\cdots,n)}}{\iint\cdots\int} dx_1 dx_2 \cdots dx_n$

Set $x_i = a_i \xi_i$, $(i = 1, 2, \cdots, n)$, then Jacobian formula

$$J = a_1 a_2 \cdots a_n$$

Therefore

$$V_n = a_1 a_2 \cdots a_n \underset{\substack{\xi_1+\xi_2+\cdots+\xi_n \leq 1, \\ \xi_i \geq 0, (i=1,2,\cdots,n)}}{\iint\cdots\int} d\xi_1 d\xi_2 \cdots d\xi_n.$$

Due to

$$\underset{\substack{\xi_1+\xi_2+\cdots+\xi_n \leq 1, \\ \xi_i \geq 0, (i=1,2,\cdots,n)}}{\iint\cdots\int} d\xi_1 d\xi_2 \cdots d\xi_n = \frac{1}{n!}.$$

So

$$V_n = \frac{a_1 a_2 \cdots a_n}{n!}.$$

Example Three: calculation $\underset{x_1^2+x_2^2+\cdots+x_n^2 \leq a^2}{\iint\cdots\int} dx_1 dx_2 \cdots dx_n$.

Solution: let $V_n = \underset{x_1^2+x_2^2+\cdots+x_n^2\le a^2}{\iint\cdots\int} dx_1 dx_2 \cdots dx_n$

For transformation,

$$\begin{cases} x_1 = ar\cos\varphi_1 \\ x_2 = ar\sin\varphi_1\cos\varphi_2 \\ \qquad\cdots\cdots \\ x_{n-1} = ar\sin\varphi_1\sin\varphi_2\cdots\sin\varphi_{n-2}\cos\varphi_{n-1} \\ x_n = ar\sin\varphi_1\sin\varphi_2\cdots\sin\varphi_{n-2}\sin\varphi_{n-1} \end{cases}$$

Therefore, region $\Omega: x_1^2 + x_2^2 + \cdots + x_n^2 \le a^2$ is expressed by

$$0 \le r \le 1, 0 \le \varphi_1 \le \pi, 0 \le \varphi_2 \le \pi, \cdots, 0 \le \varphi_{n-2} \le \pi, 0 \le \varphi_{n-1} \le 2\pi,$$

Also, Jacobian formula

$$J = a^n r^{n-1} \sin^{n-2}\varphi_1 \sin^{n-3}\varphi_2 \cdots \sin\varphi_{n-2}$$

Thereupon

$$V_n = a^n \int_0^{2\pi} d\varphi_{n-1} \int_0^{\pi} \sin^{n-2}\varphi_1 d\varphi_1 \int_0^{\pi} \sin^{n-3}\varphi_2 d\varphi_2 \cdots \int_0^{\pi} \sin\varphi_{n-2} d\varphi_{n-2} \int_0^1 r^{n-1} dr$$

$$= \frac{2\pi a^n}{n} \frac{\Gamma(\frac{n-1}{2})\Gamma(\frac{1}{2})}{\Gamma(\frac{n}{2})} \cdot \frac{\Gamma(\frac{n-2}{2})\Gamma(\frac{1}{2})}{\Gamma(\frac{n-1}{2})} \cdots \frac{\Gamma(\frac{2}{2})\Gamma(\frac{1}{2})}{\Gamma(\frac{3}{2})}$$

$$= \frac{2}{n} a^n \frac{\pi^{\frac{n}{2}}}{\Gamma(\frac{n}{2})} = \frac{a^n \pi^{\frac{n}{2}}}{\frac{n}{2}\Gamma(\frac{n}{2})} = \frac{a^n \pi^{\frac{n}{2}}}{\Gamma(\frac{n}{2}+1)}$$

For n is odd and even, respectively have the formula

$$V_{2m} = \frac{\pi^m}{m!} a^{2m}, V_{2m+1} = \frac{2\cdot(2\pi)^m}{(2m+1)!} a^{2m+1}.$$

3 Limits of Multiple Integrals

In general, the results of multiple integrals with n, and therefore we can research on the limit. when $n \to \infty$. Significance will be analyzed by calculating the limit of the following several cases of multiple integrals.

Example Four: calculation $\lim\limits_{n\to\infty} \underset{\substack{x_1\ge0,x_2\ge0,\cdots,x_n\ge0\\ x_1+x_2+\cdots+x_n\le a}}{\iint\cdots\int} dx_1dx_2\cdots dx_n$. ($a>0$)

Solution: knowing from the example one,

$$I_n = \underset{\substack{x_1\ge0,x_2\ge0,\cdots,x_n\ge0\\ x_1+x_2+\cdots+x_n\le a}}{\iint\cdots\int} dx_1dx_2\cdots dx_n = \frac{a^n}{n!}.$$

Because $\frac{a^n}{n!} = \frac{a}{1}\cdot\frac{a}{2}\cdots\frac{a}{n}$, Let k be a natural number greater than 2a, then

$$0 < \frac{a^n}{n!} = \frac{a}{1}\cdot\frac{a}{2}\cdots\frac{a}{n} = (\frac{a}{1}\cdot\frac{a}{2}\cdots\frac{a}{k})(\frac{a}{k+1}\cdot\frac{a}{k+2}\cdots\frac{a}{n}) < a^k(\frac{1}{2})^{n-k} = \frac{(2a)^k}{2^n},$$

$\lim\limits_{n\to\infty}\frac{(2a)^k}{2^n} = 0$, therefore, $\lim\limits_{n\to\infty}\frac{a^n}{n!} = 0$. That is

$$\lim_{n\to\infty} \underset{\substack{x_1\ge0,x_2\ge0,\cdots,x_n\ge0\\ x_1+x_2+\cdots+x_n\le a}}{\iint\cdots\int} dx_1dx_2\cdots dx_n = 0.$$

Since the n re-integration of the integrand $f(x_1,x_2,\cdots,x_n)\equiv 1$, according to the promotion of triple integral, we can see that the significance of n-lay integration in the sense that the measure of integral region

$\Omega: x_1\ge0, x_2\ge0,\cdots,x_n\ge0, x_1+x_2+\cdots+x_n\le a$, And the limit of zero can be seen: the time when certain values with increasing n, the measure will get smaller.

Specially, when $a=1$, we obtain

$$\lim_{n\to\infty} \underset{\substack{x_1\ge0,x_2\ge0,\cdots,x_n\ge0\\ x_1+x_2+\cdots+x_n\le 1}}{\iint\cdots\int} dx_1dx_2\ldots dx_n = \lim_{n\to\infty}\frac{1}{n!} = 0$$

Example Five: calculation $\lim\limits_{n\to\infty} \underset{\substack{\frac{x_1}{1}+\frac{x_2}{2}+\cdots+\frac{x_n}{n}\le1,\\ x_i\ge0,(i=1,2,\cdots,n)}}{\iint\cdots\int} dx_1dx_2\cdots dx_n$

Solution: knowing from the example two,

$$\underset{\substack{\frac{x_1}{1}+\frac{x_2}{2}+\cdots+\frac{x_n}{n}\le1,\\ x_i\ge0,(i=1,2,\cdots,n)}}{\iint\cdots\int} dx_1dx_2\cdots dx_n = 1\cdot2\cdots n \underset{\substack{\xi_1+\xi_2+\cdots+\xi_n\le1,\\ \xi_i\ge0,(i=1,2,\cdots,n)}}{\iint\cdots\int} d\xi_1d\xi_2\cdots d\xi_n = n!\frac{1}{n!} = 1$$

Therefore,

$$\lim_{n\to\infty} \underset{\substack{\frac{x_1}{1}+\frac{x_2}{2}+\cdots+\frac{x_n}{n}\le1,\\ x_i\ge0,(i=1,2,\cdots,n)}}{\iint\cdots\int} dx_1dx_2\cdots dx_n = 1.$$

Example Six: calculation $\lim_{n\to\infty} \underset{x_1^2+x_2^2+\cdots+x_n^2\le a^2}{\iint\cdots\int} dx_1dx_2\cdots dx_n$.

Solution: knowing from the example three,

$$V_n = \begin{cases} V_{2m} = \dfrac{\pi^m}{m!}a^{2m}, n \text{ is even} \\ V_{2m+1} = \dfrac{2\cdot(2\pi)^m}{(2m+1)!}a^{2m+1}, n \text{ is odd} \end{cases}$$

When $a^2 \le \pi$, $V_{2m} = \dfrac{\pi^m}{m!}a^{2m} \le \dfrac{\pi^{2m}}{m!} \to 0$; when $a^2 > \pi$, $V_{2m} = \dfrac{\pi^m}{m!}a^{2m} < \dfrac{a^{4m}}{m!} \to 0$,

Therefore, $\lim_{m\to\infty} V_{2m} = 0$. Same reason, $\lim_{m\to\infty} V_{2m+1} = 0$, $\lim_{n\to\infty} V_n = 0$. That is,

$$\lim_{n\to\infty} \underset{x_1^2+x_2^2+\cdots+x_n^2\le a^2}{\iint\cdots\int} dx_1dx_2\cdots dx_n = 0.$$

Since the n re-integration of the integrand $f(x_1, x_2, \cdots, x_n) \equiv 1$, n-lay integration expresses the measure points on the region of $\Omega: x_1^2 + x_2^2 + \cdots + x_n^2 \le a^2$. If $x_1^2 + x_2^2 + \cdots + x_n^2 = a^2$ is called n-dimensional spherical equation, a is the radius of the sphere,n-lay integration $\underset{x_1^2+x_2^2+\cdots+x_n^2\le a^2}{\iint\cdots\int} dx_1dx_2\cdots dx_n$ is presented the volume of the n-dimensional sphere, and the limit of zero shows that: n-dimensional sphere radius is fixed, the value of its volume with the increase of n will be getting smaller.

References

1. Fei, D., Zhou, X.: B.P.Demidovich. Exercise Book of Mathematical Analysis, 2nd edn. Shandong Science and Technology Press (January 2004)
2. Xu, X.: Probability Method of Acquiring the Sum of Infinite Series and the Limit of Multi-integral. Engineering Mathematics (2) (2002)
3. Ma, X.-H., Wei, L.-G., Peng, Z.-Q.: The Method of How to Solve the Probability Density of Two Function Which is N-dimension Random Variable. Engineering Mathematics (4) (2006)
4. Zhao, L.: On "Double Integral Method" in the selection of a new variable of integration. Journal of Liaoning Teachers College(Natural Science Edition) (June 2004)
5. Zhang, L., Sun, H.: The Introduction of Double integral element integral method. Studies in College Mathematics (March 2003)
6. Zhao, H., Zhang, Y.: The Symmetry of Multiple Integrals. The Research Journal of China Educational Development (June 2010)

7. Shi, Y.: A Proof of Multiple Integral Substitution Theorem by Arc Diferential Vector. Journal of Shanxi Datong University (Natural Science Edition) (August 2010)
8. Shen, Y.: Practical Mathematics Handbook. Science Press (August 1992)
9. Zhang, H.: The application of probabilistic model method in Summation of series. Journal of Dalian Education University 16(1), 54–56 (2000)
10. Zhang, S.: The limit Method of a class of the probability of sequence. Mathematics in Engineering 15(2), 155–156 (1999)

Cubic B-Spline Interpolation and Realization

Zhijiang Wang, Kaili Wang, and Shujiang An

College of Science, Hebei United University, Tangshan Hebei 063009, China
kaili@heuu.edu.cn

Abstract. The word "spline" originates from the tool which the project cartography personnel to use in order to connects destination to a light fair curve, namely elastic scantling or thin steel bar. The curve by such spline has the continual slope and curvature in the function. The interpolation which partial and low order polynomial has certainly smooth in the partition place the function is simulates above principle to develop, it has overcome the oscillatory occurrences which the higher mode polynomial interpolation possibly appears, and has the good value stability and the astringency, the function by this kind of interpolation process is the polynomial spline function.

Keywords: cubic spline, interpolation, partial supporting.

1 Introduction

The word "spline" originates from the tool which the project cartography personnel to use in order to connects destination to a light fair curve, namely elastic scantling or thin steel bar. The curve by such spline has the continual slope and curvature in the function. The interpolation which partial and low order polynomial has certainly smooth in the partition place the function is simulates above principle to develop, it has overcome the oscillatory occurrences which the higher mode polynomial interpolation possibly appears, and has the good value stability and the astringency, the function by this kind of interpolation process is the polynomial spline function.

The spline is the piecewise polynomial and a active branch on approximation theory of function, and one important foundations of computational method. It was side by American mathematician I.J. Schoenberg in on century 40's for the light fair curve. But until 1967 the first books that system introduction spline function was published. Afterwards, the spline theory develop rapidly internationally, it obtained the promoted application in computation physics, optimum control, computer-aided design as well as computation mechanics.

2 The Basic Concept of Spline

The spline refers to one kind of tool which was used by the plotter originally, usually thin sliver which is makes of the lignin or other elastic material, its function coordinates group of data points on the clamp plate connection diagram to form a

C. Liu, J. Chang, and A. Yang (Eds.): ICICA 2011, Part I, CCIS 243, pp. 82–89, 2011.

corona curve. The concept of spline curve or the spline function is extends from that at first. From the view in mechanical point, that curve Real is that Can withstand the load on more flexible beam deflection deformation curve. According to the pure curved theory:

$$EI\frac{1}{R(x)} = M(x) \tag{2.1}$$

Under the assumption that in a small deflection,

$$R(x) = \frac{(1+y'^2)^{3/2}}{y''} \approx \frac{1}{y''(x)}$$

and resist curved stiffness EI of beam is constant, so(2.1)become:

$$y''(x) = \frac{1}{EI}M(x) \tag{2.2}$$

Because $M(x)$ along beam is linear variation, that essence of curve $y(x)$ is piecewise cubic polynomial. The load application of centralized point is junctions of partitions respectively cubic polynomial in between. This second derivative of curve is continual in the junction. This is cubic spline curve. The spline function has the explicit significance of mechanics: first spline function may represent elastic string under the centralism action of force; quadric spline function may represent the deflection curve under centralism couple function; cubic spline function represent deflection curve under the central load function.

2.1 Definition and Nature of Spline

Definition: For a partition in part $[a,b]$:

$$\Delta :< x_0 < x_1 < x_2 < \cdots < x_n < b$$

If function $S(x)$ satisfy following condition:

(1) $S(x)$ is n order polynomial in every set interval (x_i, x_{i+1});

(2) $S(x)$ and it's $1,2,\cdots,n-1$ derivative continue in $[a,b]$

$S(x)$ is n order polynomial spline. x_i is spline node.

To partition Δ in $[a,b]$, the different equation of $n+1$ order:

$$S^{(n+1)}(x) = \sum_{i=1}^{n-1} b_i \delta(x - x_i) \tag{2.3}$$

May create n order spline:

$$S(x) = \sum_{k=0}^{n} \frac{a_k x^k}{k!} + \sum b_i \frac{(x - x_i)_+^n}{n!} \tag{2.4}$$

Nature:

1. It is n order polynomial in (x_i, x_{i+1});
2. $S(x) \in C^{n-1}(-\infty, \infty)$, $C^{n-1}(-\infty, \infty)$ express set on all function of the $n-1$ order derivative in real axis;
3. $S^{(n)}(x)$ have left and right limit on point x, but unequal, its leap quantity $[S^{(n)}(x_i)] = S^{(n)}(x_i + 0) - S^{(n)}(x_i - 0) = b_i$, $S^{(n)}(x)$ is derivative with x of $S(x)$;
4. When $b_i = 0$, (2.4) degenerate to ordinary n order polynomial.

Apply the above n spline function to approach the arbitrary function, it has good compatibility and flexibility, and may make many questions to obtain satisfactory solution.

3 Interpolation of Cubic B-Spline

3.1 B-Spline and Its Main Nature

B-spline has kinds of equal definition. In reason it more use the definition of difference coefficient on section end power function. B- spline is K order piecewise polynomial by sequence $U: u_0 \le u_1 \le \cdots \le u_{i+k+1}$ decide which non-decreasing parameter on a joint point rector, namely K order polynomial spline. De Boor and Cox as standard algorithm who calculate the recursive definition of B-spline. Its formulation as following:

$$\begin{cases} N_{i,0}(u) = \begin{cases} 1, u \in [u_i, u_{i+1}) \\ 0, otherwise \end{cases} \\ N_{i,p}(u) = \dfrac{u - u_i}{u_{i+p} - u_i} N_{i,p-1}(u) + \dfrac{u_{i+p+1} - u}{u_{i+p+1} - u_{i+1}} N_{i+1,p-1}(u), \ p \ge 2 \\ \dfrac{0}{0} = 0 \end{cases} \tag{3.1}$$

The B-spline have support in part, the basis of B-spline is a group that have the most smallest supporting polynomial spine space, it is called Basic spline.

We may promote higher degree B-spline. Commonly used the graph of quadric and cubic B-spline, as Fig1 and 2:

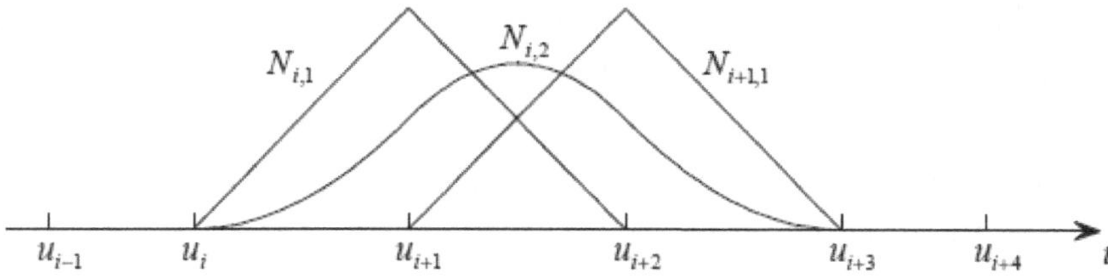

Fig. 1. The 2 degree B-spline

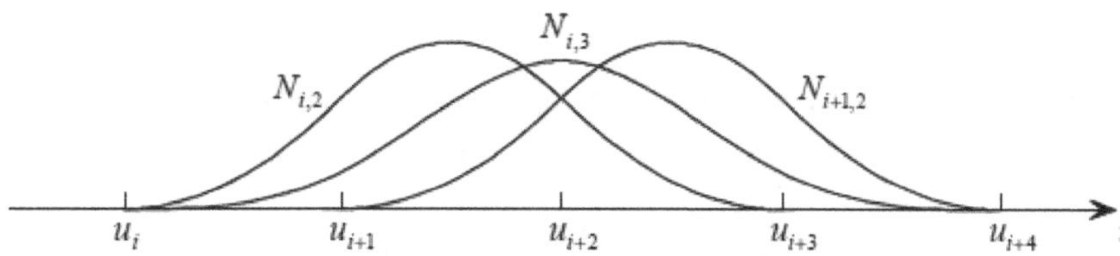

Fig. 2. The 3 degree B-spline

By the chart in obviously, the high of spline follow raise and drop power degree, but the squire of spline surrounds is invariable.

The B-spline has main nature: The partial supporting, the power, the B-spline function continuity in the point place, the derivative and recursion. The partial supporting has the very vital role in the B-spline curve fitting.

(1) Partial supporting

$$B_{i,k}(u)\begin{cases} \geq 0, u \in [u_i, u_{i+k+1}] \\ = 0, otherwise \end{cases}$$

It has also contained the no negativity. According to the partial supporting, although B-spline $B_{i,k}(u)$ defines in the entire parameter axis, but only in the supporting interval $[u_i, u_{i+k+1}]$ has bigger than 0 outside the supporting interval is 0.

(2) Positive

$$B_{i,k}(u) \geq 0$$

3.2 B-Spline Curve Interpolation

The method of B-spline still used the control apex to define the curve. In order to can describe the complex shape and partial supporting, uses the B-spline to take the primary function. Therefore, equation of the B-spline curve may write that:

$$c(u) = \sum_{i=0}^{n} d_i B_{i,k}(u) \tag{3.2}$$

$d_i \left(i = 0,1,\cdots,n\right)$ is control top. Broken line with link in turn is called B-spline control polygon, and may called control polygon.

$B_{i,k}(u), i = 0,1,...,n$ is called k order standard B-spline base function.

The important nature of B-spline curve is part nature. Because of B-spline basic having the partial supporting, the support interval of $B_{i,k}(u)$ is (u_i, u_{i+k+1}) and the joint point number by support interval contained is relevant to order k, and the support interval of k order B-spline contain $k+1$ joint point interval. A willful point on parameter u axis, $u \in [u_i, u_{i+1}]$,it have $k+1$ non-zer k order B-spline $B_{i,k}(u)$, $\left(j = i-k, i-k+1,\cdots,i\right)$,other k order B-spline is 0 at that.

So that section in $[u_i, u_{i+1}]$ on the definition of B-spline curve, omit term which its basic function get 0,it show:

$$c(u) = \sum_{j=i-k}^{i} d_i B_{j,k}(u), u \in [u_i, u_{i+1}] \tag{3.3}$$

Above form show a part about part nature of B-spline curve, and parameter in domain on k order B-spline curve is a point of $u \in [u_i, u_{i+1}]$. $c(u)$ has $k+1$ control top d_i, $j = i-k, i-k+1,...,i$ at most, it relevant to other top.

The part nature also show in domain of curve,k order B-spline curve section on non-zero joint point $u \in [u_i, u_{i+1}]$,it is decided by $k+1$ top $d_{i-k}, d_{i-k+1},..., d_i$ and relevant base function of B-spline. It moves a top to reduced lower sign, namely $d_{i-k+1}, d_{i-k+2},..., d_{i+1}$ of the $k+1$ control top decide above section B-spline curve, in contrast, it decide below section B-spline curve. When revising some section curve, you adjust in $k+1$ control top.

Adjacent four control tops decide each section cubic B-spline curve segment. The joint point of adjacent curve segment is called knot point, as S_i in Fig2 and 4,it correspond joint point u_i on joint point interval. To curve segment on joint point interval $u \in [u_i, u_{i+1}]$,as $S_{i+1}S_{i+2}$,it decide by four control top $P_{i+1}P_{i+2}P_{i+3}P_{i+4}$.

Another aspect of part nature is part which revising some control top P_i affect to the chap of curve.

Partial supporting is one of important nature which B-spline curve is governable position. The important nature is differentiability or parameter continuity, B-spline curve is infinite differential in each curve segment, it denote C^{∞} .it is $k-r$ order differentiable in end point of curve segment on corresponding joint point, it denote C^{k-r} , r is repeat degree of knot point.

B-spline curve interpolation is called B-spline interpolation curve, in order to make k order B-spline curve through a group data $q(i = 0,1,...,m)$, generally the end point of curve and its data is identical, and the segment joint point of curve and joint point in domain of B-spline curve is corresponding, as q_i have knot point u_{k+1} $(i = 0,1,\cdots,m)$ N control top d_i $(i = 0,1,\cdots,n)$ and joint point vector definite B-spline interpolation curve. In that $n = m + k - 1$,the number of control point is more than $k+1$ data, it has $m + k$ unknown top. According to request of interpolation in end point, it take $k+1$ secure support of important joint point. As a result, it has $u_0 = u_1 \cdots u_k = 0$, $u_{n+1} = u_{n+2} \cdots u_{n+k+1} = 1$. Then the accumulation of data points for regulating parameters of a long string $\overline{u_i}$ $(i = 0,1,\cdots,m)$corresponding definition of the region to determine the value of nodes $u_{k+1} = \overline{u_i}(i = 0,1,...,m)$. $n+1$ control point which interpolation condition show is linear equation group which make $m+1$ linear equation group of unknown rector.

$$p(u_i) + \sum_{j=0}^{n} d_j B_{j,k}(u_i) = \sum_{j=i-k}^{i} d_j B_{j,k}(u_i) = q_{i-k}$$

$$u \in [u_i, u_{i+1}] \subset [u_k, u_{n+1}]; i = k, k+1,...,n \tag{3.4}$$

When create B-spline interpolation curve, to degree k , using B-spline curve of C^2 Continuous as interpolation curve.

4 Run Spline Function by MATLAB

Cases 1: Know the relation of $y = F(x)$:when y=[1 3 0 20 20 4 18],

for $x = 0$: length $y - 1$.

Using cubic interpolation and cubic B-spline interpolation, compute the value of function when $x_1 = -5:0.2:5.5$, then draw curve.

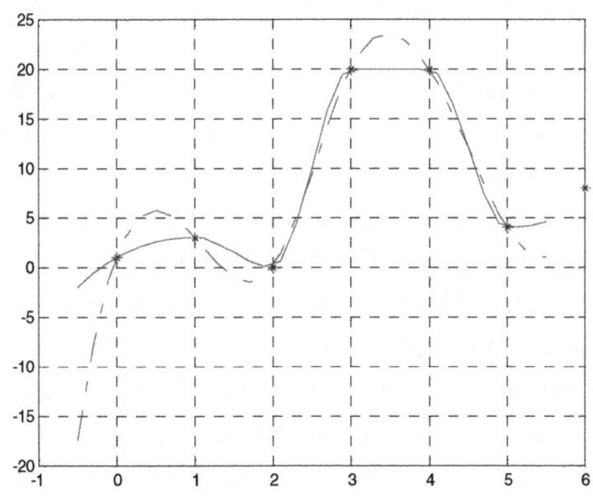

Fig. 3. Line is cubic interpolation, dotted line is cubic B-spline interpolation

Difference: The figure shows using two methods to draw curve between the samples the value is difference, the curve smooth degree is better with curve interpolations. Another, when independent variable when definition sector on bound curve, curve B-spline interpolation and curve interpolation extension tendency is different that is more obvious.

Cases 2: Data have been used to study interpolation

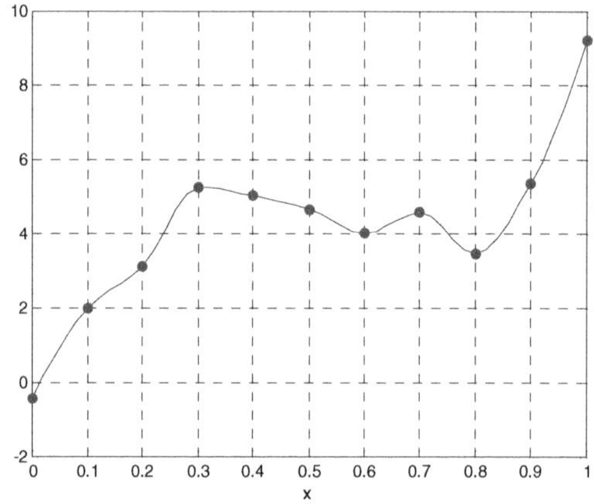

Fig. 4. The curve interpolations

5 Conclusion

Through the study and the teacher's help, I know the spline、B-spline and spline interpolation more. It computer-aided geometric design and in the integration of the contour design (motor vehicles, aircraft, etc.) get a successful application. Research of spline theory through continuous development and then be a powerful tool as a function approximation. Their applications are gradually extended to all types of data interpolation, fitted and smooth, numerical differential and integral, differential equations and integral equations of the numerical solution, and so on.

In the text, I introduce spline theory, research the B-spline study of the nature, describing the interpolation methods of the function, and through mathematical software MATLAB, and make B-spline interpolation of some function, obtain some conclusions, see the advantages of B-spline interpolation.

At present, with research deeply, many new theories gradually came to the surface, for example, spline function in the way of structural mechanics was developed; it has been applied and developed in leaps and bounds in solid mechanics, fluid mechanics, the foundation and basic, structural movement mechanics, shell thickness, high-rise building structure, dynamics and other aspects of the structure.

References

1. Kadalbajoo, M.K., Kumar, V.: B-spline solution of singular boundary value problems. Applied Mathematics and Computation 182, 1509–1513 (2006)
2. Kadalbajoo, M.K., Arorar, P.: B-splines with artificial viscosity for solving singularly perturbed boundary value problems. Mathematical and Computer Modelling 52, 654–666 (2010)
3. Kadalbajoo, M.K., Arorar, P., Gupta, V.: Collocation method using artificial viscosity for solving stiff singularly perturbed turning point problem having twin boundary layers. Computers and Mathematics with Applications 61, 1595–1607 (2011)
4. Wang, R.-H., Li, C.-J., Zhu, C.-G.: Computational Geometry. Science Press, BeiJing (2008)
5. Ren, Y.-J.: Numerical Analysis and MATLAB Implementation. Higher Education Press (2008)
6. Kadalbajoo, M.K., Yadaw, A.S., Kumar, D., Gupta, V.: Comparative study of singularly perturbed two-point BVPs via:Fitted-mesh finite difference method, B-spline collocation method and finite element method. Applied Mathematics and Computation 204, 713–725 (2008)
7. Bawa, R.K., Natesan, S.: A Computational Method for Self-Adjoint Singular Perturbation Problems Using Quintic Spline, vol. 50, pp. 1371–1382 (2005)
8. Chang, J., Wang, Z., Yang, A.: Construction of Transition Curve Between Nonadjacent Cubic T-B Spline Curves. In: Zhu, R., Zhang, Y., Liu, B., Liu, C. (eds.) ICICA 2010. LNCS, vol. 6377, pp. 454–461. Springer, Heidelberg (2010)
9. Chang, J., Wang, Z., Wu, Z.: The Smooth Connection Between Adjacent Bicubic T-B Spline Surfaces. Journal of Information and Computational Science 7(N9), 2155–2164 (2010)
10. Chang, J., Wang, R., Yuan, J.: Random Splines and Random Empirical Mode Decomposition. Journal of Information and Computational Science 7(N10), 1987–1997 (2010)

Statistical Analysis and Some Reform Proposals of Statistics Education

Lichao Feng[1], Shaohong Yan[1], Yanmei Yang[1], Yafeng Yang[2], and Huancheng Zhang[2]

[1] College of Science, Hebei United University, NO.46 Xinhua West Street, Tangshan 063009, Hebei Province, China
[2] College of Light Industry, Hebei Polytechnic University, Tangshan 063000, Hebei Province, China
flch19820520@yahoo.cn

Abstract. With rapid growth of national economy, Statistics has played a more and more significant role in real life, which has been widely applied to natural science, experimental science, economic science, management science and other application fields. But the paper analyses many practical problems in Chinese Statistics education, including problems of Statistical textbooks, problems of teachers and problems of students. And the paper proposes some reform proposals about Statistics education as follows: strengthen combination of Statistics education and computer, perfect teaching material system, update practical teaching contents, use case-based teaching method and strengthen construction of statistical teaching staff and so on.

Keywords: Statistical Education, Statistical Textbooks, Reform Proposals, Case-based Teaching Method.

1 Introduction

Originated from Politics and Economics, "Statistics" is a course about how to collect data, organize data and analyze data properly and effectively, is a science to study random data. Statistics has played a more and more significant role in real life, which has been widely applied to natural science, experimental science, economic science, management science and other application fields. As a result, to embody significant role of discipline of Statistics, Chinese twelfth five-year plans separate Statistics from mathematics as a dependent subject.

2 Role and Status of Statistics

According to statistical data published State Statistics Bureau in April 25 2010, we know that: consumer price of entire population goes down by 0.7%, where price of food goes up by 0.7%; price of agricultural products goes down by 2.4%; means of agricultural production drops bby 2.5%; price of houses go up by 1.5%, where one of

C. Liu, J. Chang, and A. Yang (Eds.): ICICA 2011, Part I, CCIS 243, pp. 90–95, 2011.

new houses goes up by 1.3% and one of second-hand houses goes up by 2.4%. And the consumer price index (CPI) in 2005-2009 is shown in fig.1. In a word, Statistics has played a more and more significant role in real life

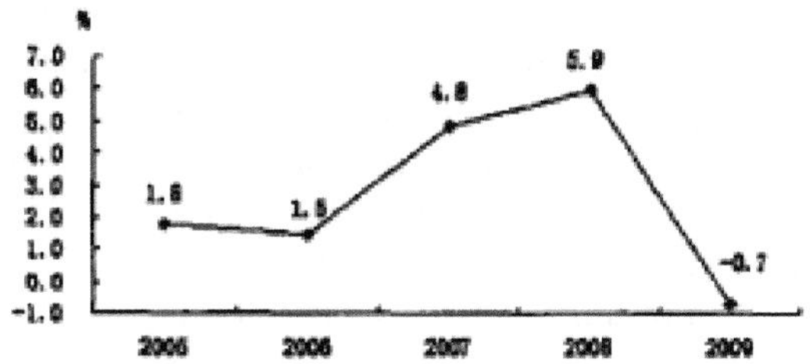

Fig. 1. Ups and downs of consumer price index (CPI) in 2005-2009

It is manifested that Statistics is a thinking method of exploring nature, understanding society and inferring the unknown. Statistics is not a purely profession, but has been fused in natural science, experiment science, economical science and management science and other application fields.

Statistical Process, the process of solving practical problems by using statistical methods, mainly includes the following three sections: collecting data, organizing data and analyzing data. And the section of collecting data is the base, while the other sections construct main body of descriptive Statistics and inferential Statistics. From the point of calculation, Statistical Process includes section of constructing mathematics model, section of collecting data and organizing data, and section of Statistical inferring, predicting and decision making.

The significant role and important status of Statistics are mainly attributed to section of inferential Statistics. That is to say, Statistical inferring mainly analyze sample data from different fields using unique statistical methods, and then explain statistical results using professional language to research the essence and the inherent law of corresponding fields from plentiful phenomena. And significant role and important status of Statistics are attributed to fusion with application fields to solve difficult problems of corresponding fields using statistical methods.

3 Existing Problems of Statistical Education

As to significant role and important status of Statistics, Statistics education in colleges has drawn more attention from many application fields, but there are many problems in Chinese Statistics education at present. We would list the problems as follows:

3.1 Existing Problems of Statistical Textbooks

At present, most of statistical textbooks in Chinese universities are written by traditional teaching mode, which pay more attention to deduction process of statistical theorems and whose content are relatively old. The main drawbacks include:

(1) most of statistical textbooks have foxed module structure, and are lack of the contents of statistical softwares and applications of programming. Foxed module structures of textbooks mainly include statistical Indexes, parameters estimation, hypothesis test, related analysis, regression analysis, variance analysis and so on, but statistical textbooks rarely involve statistical forecasting and statistical analysis, and most of statistical textbooks are lack of theoretical innovation and extension; most of appendixes of textbooks rarely introduce SPSS software、 SAS software、 R software and other statistical softwares in detail, and rarely introduce MATLAB software and other non-statistical mathematical softwares. The drawbacks make students lose the opportunity of calculation and analysis of plentiful practical data by statistical softwares. As a result, students couldn't develop practical ability of solving real problems.

(2) Most of statistical textbooks are short of practically statistical cases. In general, the materials of statistical textbooks are simple data designed by authors, which convenience teachers and students to understand and practice. The simple examples of statistical textbooks simply the conditions of real data, which result in practical simulation effect of dealing with plentiful data and reduce abilities of judging, thinking and innovation.

3.2 Existing Problems of Teachers

From the point of years' teaching practice, Statistics is one of most difficult courses. Most of teachers still take traditional teaching mode which stress explanation of various statistical knowledge and statistical methods, while students also always study theorems and do exercises using formula directly. The teaching method above and monotony exercises and monotony examinations could not harmonize with statistical softwares, computer applications and practical cases, leading to that students can't understand and apply content very well. At the same time, the qualities of teachers need to be improved. Some teachers are not familiar with SPSS, SAS and R statistical softwares, let alone make analyzing and applying by those softwares. Meeting real problems, some teachers couldn't solve real problems using statistical thoughts and statistical methods; some teachers are lack of ability to adapt and change and couldn't select and use statistical theorems and statistical technologies neatly.

3.3 Existing Problems of Students

From the point of years' teaching practice, students only know dealing with second-hand materials by using statistical softwares, but don't know how to deal with first-hand materials. Students usually collect second-hand materials from newspapers, magazines and networks. While second-hand materials are very important, first–hand materials show more changing realities. Students could not collect first-hand materials very well: first, students don't know how to design investigation plans and questionnaires according to investigation purposes; second, students don't know how to collect statistical data and most students are not familiar with methods of collecting first-hand materials. Many corporations always need professional statisticians to do regular and irregular investigations and get first-hand materials, which provide many opportunities for students to practice. At the same time, students also wish to participate the investigations in their spare times to understand the process of investigations. Students need opportunities to understand the content of sample investigation, key-point investigation and general investigation, to understand the surveying methods of questioning, observation, experimentation and Telphi, to learn to communicate with investigating subjects, and understand source, collecting methods, examinations, summary, analysis of materials.

4 Some Reform Proposals of Statistics Education

Practice teaching is an import sector of realization of colleges' personnel training goal, which play an significant part in improving students' overall qualify, culturing students' creative spirit and practical ability. The aim of Statistics education is to cultivate "application-type" talents. Form the point of practice, first introduce problems, and then solve problems by guiding students to use corresponding statistical theories and different disposal methods. In the process of solving problems, divide students into several groups to discuss in detail; and every group sums up conclusions and methods and communicate with other groups; in the end teachers provide appropriate method to solve problems with students. In the Harmony, happy and free circumstance, students could consider and research questions independently, could express their opinions without hesitations by referring plentiful literatures, and propose their conclusions. When students meet with difficulties, they could discuss with teachers together to search the method of solving problems, which plays an important role in cultivating students' creative spirit and practical ability. We propose some suggestions about Statistics education as follows:

4.1 Strengthen Combination of Statistics Education and Computer

Statistics is a science about studying data, which can't deal with data without computer in the information society. In the process of teaching Statistics, we must strengthen combination of Statistics and computer. We should deal with random data using EXCEL software, SPSS software and other modern statistical softwares. As improvement of colleges' teaching conditions and population of Multimedia classrooms, colleges introduce electrical audio-visual aids teaching system, which provide some conditions for reforming teaching methods. Teachers should show the operations of EXCEL software, SPSS software and other statistical softwares, should show the operations of collecting network data using modern methods, which compensate drawbacks of traditional teaching media and could enrich teaching content, expand student's field of vision, convenience students hold current statistical researches and statistical developments correctly in time, help students understand statistical knowledge well.

4.2 Perfect Teaching Material System and Update Practical Teaching Contents

According to different requirements for different professions about statistical knowledge and different professional students' cultivating aims, we should update practical teaching contents continuously, and then perfect teaching material system further. Statistical materials of Statistical profession not only stress explanation and reasoning of statistical theories and statistical knowledge, but also cultivate practical ability of solving practical problems using statistical softwares; Statistical materials of non-statistical profession mainly stress the cultivation of ability of solving practical problems, stress introduction of statistical softwares' knowledge in textbooks, and pay attention to show how to solve practical problems using statistical knowledge and statistical softwares. In choosing statistical cases, if the authors of textbooks could connect with practice, the authors should consider cases close to our daily life, daily study and daily work to the greatest extent. At the same time, on the base of inheriting the original materials' highlights, it is needed to delete nuanced teaching contents, to develop students' knowledge fields, to expand the knowledge of statistical inference, regression analysis and statistical prediction. In a summary, Statistical materials of Statistical profession put reasoning front and centre and pay attention to reasoning of statistical theories; Statistical materials of non-Statistical profession pay attention to practical applications and need to delete difficult theories' proofs.

4.3 Use Case-Based Teaching Method and Strengthen Construction of Statistical Teaching Staff

Because Statistics is a science with strong utility and maneuverability, statistical teachers should teach Statistics by using case-based teaching method. Case-based teaching method could guide students to study how to collect, arrange and analyze data. Case-based teaching method doesn't only lay foundation for students' principle-- "apply their knowledge, learning to use with a long", but also strengthen students' comprehensive ability of statistical materials, students' practical application ability of analyzing and solving problems using statistical materials, students' potential sense of connecting with facts. As a direct result, there are more requirements for teachers.

But there exists a perilous reality: on one hand, most colleges don't attach importance to practical teaching resulting shortage of statistical teaching staff; on the other hand, young teachers couldn't afford the task of practical teaching without enough practical experience. As to the status above, colleges must strengthen construction of statistical teaching staff through different ways. Statistical teachers doesn't only master basic computer knowledge and statistical softwares, but also need to connect with corporations to collect related statistical cases and organize students to analyze feasibility of practical cases. Statistical teachers should tell students experiment cases and experiment aim, supervise students' operation, give students' appropriate guide and discuss with students about problems. Statistical teachers should pay attention to circumstance of "teacher acts as guide and students act interactively" and stimulate self learning ability of students. For example, list social hot problems, require students to do investigations and do some basic statistical analysis to consolidate students' statistical knowledge.

5 Conclusion

This paper introduces origination of Statistics and significant role and important status of Statistics which has been widely applied to natural science, experimental science, economic science, management science and other application fields. But there exist many problems in Chinese Statistics education, including problems of Statistical textbooks, teachers and students. At last, we propose some reform proposals about Statistics education.

Acknowledgement. This paper is supported a project sponsored by Tangshan Science and Technology Bureau Program of Hebei Province (NO. 11110228a).

References

1. Yang, X.: Study on Educational Reform of Statistics under the Informational Age. Journal of Jiangsu Institute of Education (Natural Sciences) 27(2) (2007)
2. Wu, L.Y.: Problems of countermeasures of statistics teaching in our country. China Science and Technology Information 2, 16–19 (2005)
3. Huang, B.: Teaching Reform of Statistics for the Non-statistic Majors. Science and Technology of West China 5, 75–76 (2005)
4. Zhang, X.Q.: A Tentative Study on Teaching Reform of Statistics for the Non-statistic Majors. Statistics & Information Tribune 09, 25–27 (2001)
5. Zhang, X.Q.: Perfection and Development of Statistics Textbooks for Non-statistics Majors in Universities. Journal of Dalian Nationalities University 11(2) (2009)
6. Ling Zhang, J.L.: Statistics of Non-statistics-major on Higher Educationals. Journal of Guangxi Commercial College 19(4) (2002)

Research on SPSS' Application in Probability and Statistics Course with Principal Components Analysis

Yafeng Yang, Shujuan Yuan, and Li Feng

Qinggong College, Hebei United University, Tangshan, China, 063000
{www1673,yuanshujuan1980,fengli3}@163.com

Abstract. With the growing popularity of information technology, statistical software application of statistical knowledge has become the main tool to solve practical problems. Therefore, statistical software, teaching oriented model has become the modern "Probability and Statistics" teaching trends. This paper describes an example principal component analysis in SPSS software application of probability and statistics courses.

Keywords: SPSS, Principal Components Analysis, Probability and Statistics.

1 Introduction

Today, the information is highly developed and economic activity is increasing, wealth of information and data processing is needed. How to extract useful information from these data to guide people's social practice becomes increasingly necessary and urgent. So probability theory and mathematical statistics provides increasingly broad prospects, which requires us to strengthen the teaching of probability theory and mathematical statistics, enriches its content, and then provides better service for social practice.

Probability and statistics course is a strong discipline to study the statistical regularity of random phenomena and apply, the course of thinking in dealing with the problem is different from the other students in math courses, so students find it difficult to grasp. According to the author's many years' teaching practice, in the teaching process, we should give top priority, such as training students to master the basic idea of probability and statistics, methods, and solving practical problems. To solve the above problems, we can use SPSS software to aid teaching, it provides virtually every aspect of the module, such as parameter estimation, hypothesis testing, analysis of variance, regression analysis, mathematical statistics, and most areas of the calculation of probability theory, and then calling format of each functional module is very simple and convenient to complete the appropriate calculations and mapping.

2 Principal Components Analysis

2.1 Basic Principles

Setting the original variables are $x_1, x_2, \ldots, x_n$. New variables after principal component analysis are $z_i(i=1\cdots m, m<n)$, then $z_i = l_{i1}x_1 + l_{i2}x_2 + \cdots + l_{in}x_n$, z_i as

C. Liu, J. Chang, and A. Yang (Eds.): ICICA 2011, Part I, CCIS 243, pp. 96–101, 2011.

the first i principal component analysis to the original variable indicator $x_1, x_2, \ldots, x_n$. It frequently selects several of the largest principal component factors when dealing with the actual problems, but in some question must been paid attention to, such as:

(1) z_i and z_j $(i \neq j, i, j = 1 \cdots m)$ are independent;

(2) z_1 is the largest variance of linear combination of $x_1, x_2, \ldots, x_n$; z_2 is the largest variance of linear combination of $x_1, x_2, \ldots, x_n$, and not related to $z_1, z_2, \ldots, z_m$ is the largest variance of linear combination of $x_1, x_2, \ldots, x_n$, and not related to $z_1, z_2, \ldots, z_{m-1}$.

2.2 Calculated Steps

The calculating of Principal Components Analysis can be divided into the following five steps:

(1) Data standardization.

In order to rule out the impact of different dimensions, raw based data needed to be standardization. Standardized formulation is: $x_{ij}^{'} = \frac{x_{ij} - \overline{x}_j}{s_j}$.

In the formulation, $x_{ij}^{'}$ as the standardized data, $\overline{x}_j$, $s_j (j = 1, 2, \cdots n)$ express the mean and standard deviation of the j factor respectively.

(2) Calculate related coefficient matrix.

After the raw data has been processed, it obtained standardized data matrix $(x_{ij}^{'})_{p \times n}$, then calculate the corresponding correlation coefficient matrix $R = (x_{ij}^{'})_{n \times n}$. In the formulation, R is n symmetric matrix of order.

(3) Calculating the eigenvalues and eigenvectors of related coefficient matrix R.

Counting out the eigenvalues $\lambda_i (i = 1, 2, \cdots n)$ and the corresponding eigenvectors $u_i (i = 1, 2, \cdots n)$ of R , and $\lambda_1 \geq \lambda_2 \geq \cdots \geq \lambda_n$. λ_i is the variance of principal component z_i, if variance is larger and the contribution is greater to total variance.

(4) Calculating the contribution ratio, determining the principal component.

Design $e_i = \lambda_i / \sum_{i=1}^{n} \lambda_i \times 100\%$ as the contribution ratio of the principal component z_i and $\sum_{i=1}^{n} e_i$ as the cumulative variance contribution rate. We usually select m principal component when the total $\sum_{i=1}^{n} e_i$ is greater than or equal to 85%.

Then n principal component reduce to m major principal component.

(5) Comprehensive analysis.

The standardized data were substituted into the expression of the principal component, and then calculated $F_k(k = 1,2,\cdots p)$ principal component values of the various sections. Last the Comprehensive value of various sections got with weights of variance contribution rate of each principal component.

3 Application of SPSS in Principal Components Analysis

3.1 The Data Standardization

Choose the button “Descriptive Statistics”, and select the standardization variables into “Variable”. Then check the button “OK”.

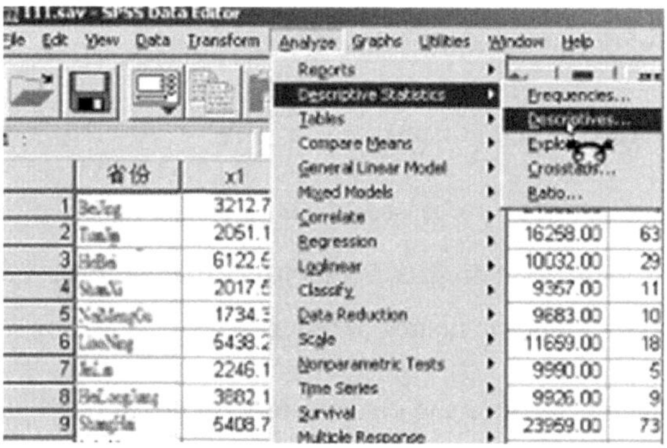

Fig. 1. Descriptive Statistics

3.2 Basic Operations

According to the calculating steps of Principal Components Analysis shown in below, we should reduce the data firstly.

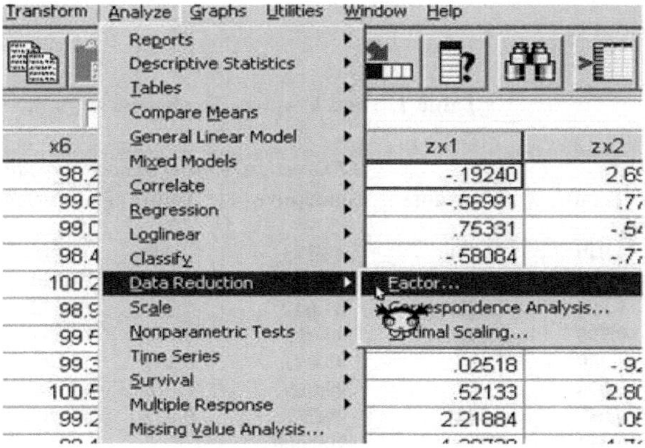

Fig. 2. Data Reduction

Then, selecting data standardizated into Variables and checking the button Extraction...

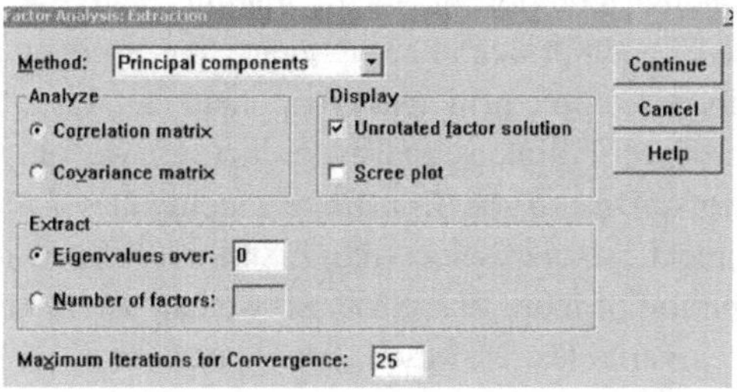

Fig. 3. Factor Analysis Extraction

Fill in the "Extract" box with the number 0. Then, checking the button "continues", and return to the last box. If the related coefficient matrix is needed, you should check the button Descriptives... .

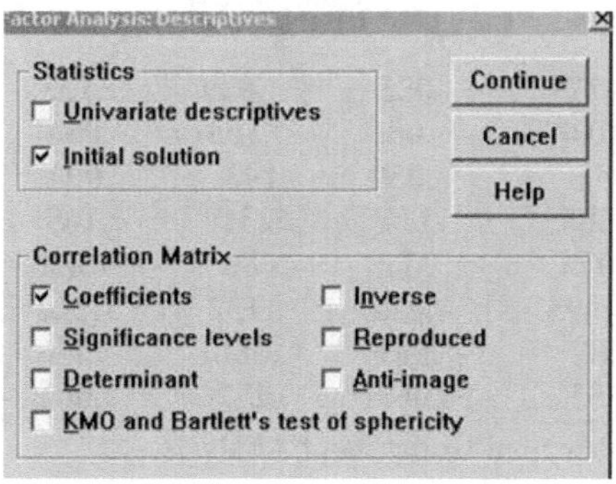

Fig. 4. Factor Analysis Descriptives

So we can get

Table 1. Total Variance Explained

Initial Eigenvalue				*s Extraction Sums of Squared Loadings*		
Component	**Total**	**% of Variance**	**Cumulative %**	**Total**	**% of Variance**	**Cumulative %**
1	3.849	48.118	48.118	3.849	48.118	48.118
2	1.808	22.594	70.712	1.808	22.594	70.712
3	1.306	16.329	87.042	1.306	16.329	87.042
4	0.595	7.443	94.485	0.595	7.443	94.485
5	0.289	3.608	98.092	0.289	3.608	98.092
6	0.078	0.977	99.069	0.078	0.977	99.069
7	0.057	0.718	99.787	0.057	0.718	99.787
8	0.017	0.213	100.000			

Extraction Method: Principal Component Analysis.

3.3 Calculating the Eigenvalues

In the steps of principal component, factor loading matrix will appear, and we can obtain the variance of each principal component, that is eigenvalues. Their size show that how much information the principal component can describe. In general, in order to achieve the purpose of dimensionality reduction, we only extract the first few principal components. Due to the first three eigenvalues' cumulative contribution rate is 87.042 percent, so we select the first three eigenvalues according to the cumulative contribution of more than 85%. So we can use three new variables instead of the original seven variables. However, the expression of three new variable cannot obtained directly from the output window, because "Component Matrix" refers to the factor loading matrix, and each load refers to the correlation coefficient between the principal component and the corresponding variable.

Table 2. Component Matrix a

	Component						
	1	2	3	4	5	6	7
x1	**.855**	**.477**	**-.025**	**.049**	**.133**	**.098**	**.069**
x2	**.747**	**.614**	**.083**	**.103**	**.086**	**.179**	**.088**
x3	**.916**	**.352**	**-.030**	**.103**	**.094**	**.007**	**.089**
x4	**.554**	**-.688**	**.330**	**.231**	**.169**	**-.169**	**-.031**
x5	**.627**	**-.078**	**.371**	**-.680**	**.028**	**-.009**	**-.021**
x6	**-.379**	**-.095**	**.851**	**.132**	**-.325**	**.027**	**.000**
x7	**.285**	**.682**	**.569**	**.086**	**.346**	**.024**	**.046**
x8	**.893**	**.355**	**.063**	**.179**	**.001**	**.081**	**.183**

Extraction Method: Principal Component Analysis.
7components extracted

Input the first three factor loading matrix to the data editor window (variables B1, B2, B3), then check the button "Transform compute". In the dialog box, input "A1 = B1/SQR (3.849) ","A2 = B2/SQR (1.808) "and "A3 = B3/SQR (130.6) ", can be obtained eigenvectors A1. Then, we can obtain the available A1, A2 and A3 and the expression of principal components.

3.4 Principal Component Ranking

First, the eigenvectors is multiplied with the normalized data. We can get the principal components' scores Z1, Z2, Z3. Second, if comprehensive evaluation function is needed, we still need input a comprehensive evaluation function in the "Transform compute" box.

4 Conclusion

Putting the SPSS into probability and statistics teaching, makes probability and statistics becomes easy in numerical data processing, so we can focus on clarifying the deal with the problem of thinking and greatly, which improves teaching efficiency, while enhancing the students' ability to apply to meet the needs of social development.

References

1. Zhang, S.: Research and probe on experiment teaching mode of Probability and Statistics based on SPSS under network environment. Journal of Xi'an University of Posts and Telecommunications 16(1), 145–148
2. Li, X., Xu, Z.: Dominant Position and Application of SPSS Software in Probability and Statistics Curriculum Set. Journal of Shenyang Normal University (Natural Science) 128(1), 24–26
3. Li, X., Chen, Z.: Correctly Using SPSS Software for Principal Components Analysis. Statistical Research 27(8), 28–32
4. Su, Y.: The Application of SPSS in the Statistic Teaching. Computer Knowledge and Technology 6(31), 8892-8893 (2010)
5. Zhou, M.: Exploring on Problem and Solution of University Students' Career Planning-Survey and Analysis. Journal of Nanjing University of Finance and Economics (2), 102–105 (2009)
6. Xu, Q.: Explorations and Practice on the Probability Theory and Mathematical Statistics. College Mathematics 26(1), 10–13

Empirical Analysis on Relation between Domestic Tourism Industry and Economic Growth in China*

Wang Liangju[1,2], Li Wanlian[1], and Wang Yongpei[2]

[1] School of Business Administration, Anhui University of Finance and Economics, Bengbu, Anhui, P.R. China, 233030
[2] School of Business, Renmin University of China, Beijing, P.R. China, 100872
acwlj@163.com

Abstract. Based on the data from 1984 to 2009, this paper takes an empirical analysis on the relation between China's economic growth and the development of China's domestic tourism industry in accordance with cointegration theory and Granger causality Test. The results show that there is a stable and long-term relation between China's economic growth and the development of China's domestic tourism industry. Moreover, there is a two-way Granger causality between the development of China's domestic tourism industry and China's economic growth. Economic growth is the Granger cause of the development of domestic tourism and domestic tourism is the Granger cause of economic growth. That's to say China's economic growth has promoted the development of China's domestic tourism industry and the development of China's domestic tourism industry has boosted China's economic growth.

Keywords: Domestic tourism Industry, Economic growth, Cointegration theory, Granger causality test.

1 Introduction

Tourism industry consists of six factors of travel, sightseeing, accommodation, food, shopping and entertainment. It is an industry with strong comprehensiveness, high industrial relevance and large pull function. Tourism consumption directly stimulates traditional industries such as civil aviation, railway, highway, commerce, food and accommodation. Besides, tourism consumption plays an important role in promoting the development of modern service industries such as international finance, logistics, information consultation, cultural originality, movie production, entertainment, conferences and exhibitions. Domestic tourism has become a main body of China's three tourism markets. Total income of China's tourism industry is about 1.26 trillions Yuan in 2009. Among which, the income of domestic tourism industry is 1.02 trillions Yuan and accounts for 80.95 % of the total income of China's tourism industry. The

* This paper is sponsored by sustentation fund for youth college teachers in Anhui, China (2008jqw059zd). A special graduate is expressed to Zhou Mo for his helpful remark on the original edition of the paper, who is a PhD candidate at Renmin University of China.

C. Liu, J. Chang, and A. Yang (Eds.): ICICA 2011, Part I, CCIS 243, pp. 102–109, 2011.

development of domestic tourism industry can expand domestic demand, drive the development of related industries, promote the adjustment of industrial structure and industrial upgrade, and promote the transformation of economic growth mode. In December 2009, State Council of People's Republic of China issued an opinion of speeding up the development of China's tourism industry, which put forward taking domestic tourism industry as priority, actively developing inbound tourism and orderly developing outbound tourism. Since China's reforming and opening, the rapid development of China's national economy has supported the development of China's domestic tourism industry. With the constant improvement of living standard of Chinese people, resident consumption changes from material object mainly to both material object and services. China's domestic tourism industry will benefit much from China's resident consumption upgrade.

China's domestic tourism industry started from reforming and opening, and grew rapidly since the 1990s. China's domestic tourist arrivals added from 200 millions person times in 1984 to 1.902 billions person times in 2009 with an average annual increasing rate at 9.36 per cent. Since reforming and opening, China keeps a long-term and high-speed economic growth. China's gross domestic product (GDP) added from 720.8 billions Yuan in 1984 to 3.35 trillions Yuan in 2009 with an average annual increasing rate at 9.86 per cent (has eliminated the effect of inflation). China's domestic tourism industry seems to keep increasing with the development of China's national economy. It is necessarily to introduce empirical data to tell the true story between them.

2 Literature Review

With the rapid development of China's domestic tourism industry, there is a little literature trying to study the relation between the development of China's domestic tourism industry and China's economic growth. However, these studies have not drawn a coincident conclusion. Wu's research (2003) found that the development of tourism industry has largely promoted China's economic growth. Yang's research (2006) indicated domestic tourism industry has little pulling effects on economic growth, but economic growth had significant driving effects on domestic tourism industry. These researches directly took regression analysis on non-stationary variables such as domestic tourism income, inbound tourism income and GDP, thus spurious regression may occur. Chen et al. (2006) took a Granger causality test on the relation between the development of China's tourism industry and China's economic growth based on the time series data of domestic tourism income, inbound tourism income and GDP from 1985 to 2003.This research showed that the development of China's tourism industry had a significantly promoting effects on China's economic growth, but China's economic growth had little promoting effects on the development of China's tourism industry. Since 1993, China started to implement sampling survey on domestic tourism industry and the data in 1993 is incomparable with previous year. In addition, the statistical method on international tourism income has changed with the reform of foreign exchange management system in China and the data is also incomparable with previous year. So the sample data quality in this research exist serious defects. Zhang et al. (2009) took a cointegration analysis on the relation between urban and rural residents' tourism consume and economic growth with times series data from 1994 to 2006.The results from this study were unreliable because the sample size was too small.

Classical regression analysis is based on the hypothesis that the time series is stationary. However, time series data in practice is often non-stationary. To take a directly regression analysis on these non-stationary data may induce to spurious regression and draw a false conclusion. Furthermore, the regression analysis may loose some information through difference transformation. Cointegration theory in dynamic econometrics analysis can overcame the deficiency of these methods mentioned above and can effectively deal with nonstationary time series. Since the series of variables in this paper may be non-stationary, we firstly take a unit root test on these variables to examine whether they are stationary. If they are non-stationary, we can introduce cointegration theory to analysis the relation between them. On the basis of cointegration test, we take Granger causality test to examine whether there is causality between these variables. Granger (1988) pointed out that there would be a one-way Granger cause at least if these variables were cointegration.

Based on the data of China's GDP and domestic tourist arrivals from 1984 to 2009, this paper analyses the long-term equilibrium relation (namely cointegration relation) between the development of China's domestic tourism industry and China's economic growth in accordance with cointegration theory. Moreover, this paper builds an error correction model to analysis the short-term equilibrium relation between the development of China's domestic tourism industry and China's economic growth, and examines whether there is causality between them via Granger cause tests.

3 Empirical Results

3.1 Variables Selection and Data Specification

Considering the data on China's domestic tourism industry before 1984 being unavailable, the sampling period in this paper is during 1984 to 2009. All data derives from The Yearbook of China Statistics and The Yearbook of China Tourism Statistics in relevant years. This paper selects the following two indexes to measure the development of China's domestic tourism industry and China's economic growth. ①The sign Y denotes China's GDP (100 millions Yuan is the unit), which reflects the aggregate macro-economy and its change reflects economic growth. The GDP is calculated at constant price of 1978 to eliminate the effect of inflation. ② the sign R denotes China's domestic tourist arrivals (100 millions person times is the unit), which reflects the development of China's domestic tourism industry. Because the logarithmic transformation does not influence the cointegration relation between raw data and can eliminate heteroscedasticity, China's GDP and domestic tourism arrivals are both in the form of natural logarithm. The signs lnY and lnR respectively denote China's GDP and domestic tourist arrivals after the transformation of natural logarithm. Figure 1 intuitively describes changing trend of lnY and lnR. However, it's necessary to construct an econometric model to examine the real relation between lnY and lnR.

Classical regression analysis is based on the hypothesis that the data is stationary. However, time series data in practice is often non-stationary. To take a directly regression analysis on these non-stationary data may induce to spurious regression and draw a false conclusion. From the scatter diagram of lnY and lnR, we can find that the two series keep an appropriately same trend of change on the whole. But further study is necessary to examine whether there is a long-term equilibrium relation or cointegration relation between lnY and lnR.

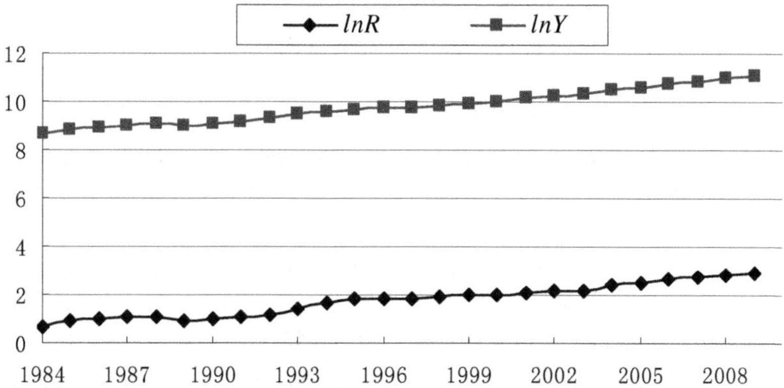

Fig. 1. Changing trend of lnY and lnR

3.2 Unit Root Test

The cointegration relation between two variables is based on that they have same orders of integration. So, we firstly test the stationary of the series of *lnY* and *lnR* with unit root test. This paper tests the stationary of *lnY* and *lnR* as well as their orders of integration by *ADF* (Augment Dickey-Fuller) test. The lagged order is determined on the rule of *AIC* (Akaike Information Criterion). The software of *Eviews*6.0 is employed to take *ADF* test on ln*Y* and ln*R* (the results of *ADF* test reported in table 1). The results show that *lnY* and *lnR* are both non-stationary because each *ADF* value of them exceeds the critical value on the significant level of 10 percent. Each *ADF* value of their first-order difference is less than the critical value on the significant level of 5 percent, which shows that their first-order difference are stationary, that is to say *lnY* and *lnR* are both first-order integration, namely *lnY* and *lnR*~*I*(1) . Therefore, we can take a cointegration analysis on the relation between them.

Table 1. Results of unit uoot test on variables (*ADF* test)

Variable	Test type (*c, t, p*)	*ADF* value	critical value 1%	5%	10%	conclusion
lnY	(c,t,1)	3.074	4.394	3.612	3.243	non-stationary
lnR	(c,t,1)	2.501	4.394	3.612	3.243	non-stationary
△*lnY*	(c,0,1)	3.009	3.753	2.998	2.639	stationary
△*lnR*	(c,0,0)	4.289	3.738	2.992	2.636	stationary

Note: (1) test type (*c, t, p*), *c* denotes drift term, *t* denotes time trend, *p* denotes lag length;
(2) △denotes first-order difference.

3.3 Cointegration Test

The results of unit root test indicate that lnY and lnR are both first-order integration series. So, we can examine whether there is a cointegration relation between them. This paper tests whether there is a cointegration relation between lnY and lnR based on the method of Engel-Granger two-step test.

The first step, running OLS regression on lnY and lnR, we have

$$\ln Yt = 7.945 + 1.041 \ln Rt \quad (1)$$
$$(153.626) \quad (38.021)$$
$$R^2 = 0.984 \qquad DW = 0.726$$

DW=0.726 indicates that there is first-order autocorrelation. Adding lagged terms to the above mentioned model, we can obtain the following dynamic distributed lag model

$$lnY_t = -0.455 + 0.244 lnR_t - 0.295\, lnR_{t-1} + 1.063 lnY_{t-1} \quad (2)$$
$$(-0.768) \quad (3.390) \quad (-3.965) \quad (14.194)$$
$$R^2=0.998 \quad DW=1.567 \quad SSE = 0.029 \quad LM_1=0.752 \quad LM_2=5.972 \quad ARCH_1=1.723$$

The results of *LM* test on serial correlation show that there is no autocorrelation. The results of *ARCH* test indicate there is no heteroscedasticity. Hence, formula (2) can be considered to be the long-term equilibrium relation between *lnY* and *lnR*.

The second step, we take unit root test on residual series ($\hat{e}_t$) in model (2). The results reported in table 2. The *ADF* value is less than the critical value on the significant level of 1 percent. Therefore, we can consider residual series being a stationary series, that is to say $\hat{e}_t \sim I(0)$. Furthermore, the hypothesis that *lnY* and *lnR* is cointegration can not be rejected, that is to say *lnY* and *lnR* are (1, 1) cointegration. Formula (2) is the long-term equilibrium relation between *lnY* and *lnR*. The long-term elasticity of *lnY* changing to *lnR* equals to 0.810(the value is calculated by the expression [(0.244-0.295)/ (1-1.063)]), which indicates China's GDP will add 0.810 percent if China's domestic tourist arrivals increase 1 percent in the long term.

Table 2. Results of unit root test on residual series (*ADF* Test)

Variable	Test type(c, t, p)	*ADF* value	Critical value at 1 percent level	Conclusion
$\hat{e}_t$	(0,0,0)	-4.029	-2.665	stationary

3.4 Error Correction Model

Error correction model (ECM) is an econometric model with specific form. The main form of ECM model is put forward by Davidson, Hendry, Srba and Yeo in 1978, and which can be called DHSY model. If two variables are cointegration, the short-term disequilibrium relation between them can be represented with an ECM model (Engle & Granger, 1987). With OLS method, we can obtain the following ECM model to represent the short-term disequilibrium relation between lnY and lnR:

$$\triangle lnY_t = 0.229\triangle lnR_t - 0.280\triangle lnR_{t-1} + 1.500\triangle lnY_{t-1} - 0.436\triangle lnY_{t-2} - 1.025ecm_{t-1} \quad (3)$$

(4.289) (-3.767) (7.754) (-3.138) (-4.313)

R^2=0.7372 DW=1.969 SSE = 0.023 LM_1=0.540 $ARCH_1$=0.163

Where ecm_t can be representd by the expression(lnY_t-0.244lnR_t +0.295lnR_{t-1}-1.063lnY_{t-1}+0.455). The relevent statistic indicates error correction model can pass the test. The *ECM* model describes how the equilibrium error impacts GDP in the short term. The coefficient of the *ECM* term equals -1.025 (less than zero), which is in accordence with the reverse correction mechanism. The short-term elasticity of *lnY* changing to *lnR* equals to 0.229, which indicates China's GDP will add 0.229 percent if China's domestic tourist arrivals increase 1 percent in the short term.

3.5 Granger Causality Test

Cointegration test can examine whether there is a long-term equilibrium relation, however, it can not test whether there is causality between them. Granger causality test provided a good method to resolve such problem. We can consider variable X is variable Y's Granger cause if the lagged term of X included can significantly improve the accuracy of the predicted variable Y.

The results of cointegration test show that there is a long-term equilibrium relation between lnY and lnR. However, further study is needed to examine whether there is causality between them. Based on the method of Granger causality test, this paper tests whether there is a causality relation between lnY and lnR (the results of this test reported in table 3). The results indicate that there is a two-way Granger causality between the development of China's domestic tourism industry and China's economic growth. The development of China's domestic tourism industry is the Granger cause of China's economic growth. Meanwhile, China's economic growth is also the Granger cause of the development of China's domestic tourism industry.

Table 3. Results of Granger causality test

Lags	Null Hypothesis	F-Statistic	Probability	Conclusion
1	*lnR* does not Granger Cause *lnY*	5.206	0.033	rejected
	lnY does not Granger Cause *lnR*	7.942	0.010	rejected

4 Conclusions and Discussion

Based on the empirical analysis mentioned above, we can draw the following conclusion. First of all, there is a significant correlativity between the development of China's domestic tourism industry and China's economic growth. Although the growth of each of them is non-stationary, there is a long-term stable equilibrium relation between them. The long-term elasticity of lnY changing to lnR equals to 0.810, which indicates China's GDP will add 0.810 percent if China's domestic tourist arrivals increase 1 percent in the long term. Secondly, there is a short-term equilibrium relation between the development of China's domestic tourism industry and China's economic growth in the short term. The short-term elasticity of lnY changing to lnR equals to 0.229, which indicates China's GDP will add 0.229 percent if China's domestic tourist arrivals increase 1 percent in the short term. From error correction term, we can find that there is an adjustment mechanism from short term to long term in the relation between the development of China's domestic tourism industry and China's economic growth. Thirdly, there is a two-way Granger causality between the development of China's domestic tourism industry and China's economic growth. The development of China's domestic tourism has pulled China's economic growth. Meanwhile, China's economic growth has promoted the development of China's domestic tourism industry.

At the present, China's domestic tourism market has become largest in the world and China's domestic tourism has been entering a popular stage. China's domestic tourists were 1.90 billions person times and domestic tourism income was 1.02 trillions Yuan in 2009. China's tourism industry has played an important role in maintaining China's economic growth, expanding China's domestic demand and adjusting China's industrial structure under the circumstance of international financial crisis. The prosperity of China's domestic tourism industry laid a stable groundwork for China's tourism industry being a growth point in China's economy. As well as, the sustaining and stable growth of China's economy provided a good deal capital for the development of China's domestic tourism industry and promoted the improvement of China's tourism infrastructure. With China's economy growing continually, the income of the population rising steadily and their leisure time increasing step by step, increasing popular and diversifying demand of tourism consume provides an opportunity to the development of China's domestic tourism industry. The sustaining and stable growth of China's economy will keep on driving the development of China's domestic tourism industry.

References

1. Wu, G.: Analysis of Coherency between Tourism Development and Economic Growth in China. Journal of Shanghai Institute of Technology 3(4), 238–241 (2003) (in Chinese)
2. Yang, Z.: An Empirical Analysis on the Interaction Effect between Tourism Consume and Economic Growth. Journal of Inner Mongolia Finance and Economics College 4(2), 27–30 (2006) (in Chinese)
3. Chen, Y., Liu, P., Xu, C.: Research on Causality between Development of Tourism and Economic Growth in China. Journal of Hengyang Normal University 27(1), 93–97 (2006) (in Chinese)
4. Zhang, L., Liu, B.: Analysis on Influence of Tourism Consumption on Economic Growth in China. Technology Economics 28(5), 81–85 (2009) (in Chinese)
5. Shao, Q.: Developing Tourism Industry is an Important Path to Confront International Financial Crisis. QIUSHI 16, 35–37 (2009) (in Chinese)
6. Zhao, L., Quan, H.: An Empirical Study on Relation between Domestic Tourism Consumption and Economic Growth in China. On Economic Problems 33(4), 32–38 (2011) (in Chinese)

7. Wu, Z.: Cointegration and Granger Causality Analysis between Tourism and GDP. The Theory and Practice of Finance and Economics 30(3), 116–118 (2009) (in Chinese)
8. Jeffrey, W.: Introductory Econometrics: a Modern Approach, 4th edn. Renming University of China Press, Beijing (2010) (in Chinese)
9. Sun, J.: The Tutorial to Econometrics, 2nd edn. Tsinghua University Press, Beijing (2009) (in Chinese)
10. Zhang, X.: Guide to Using Eviews of Econometrics software. Nankai University Press, Tianjin (2004) (in Chinese)

Study of Coordinated Development between Urban Human Settlement and Economy Based on Entropy Weight Method

Wenyi Zhang, Cuilan Mi, and Shuming Guan

College of Science, Hebei United University, Tangshan, China
shuxuellzt@yahoo.com.cn, micuilan@163.com, smguan@126.com

Abstract. This paper take Hebei province 11 cities as the object of study, combined with city actual condition selecting urban habitat environmental and economic characteristics of the evaluation index, establish coordination development model. Model to determine the weighing values for assessment index of weighting method of the information entropy, urban living environment of Hebei province with the level of economic development for evaluation and analysis. Finally makes the pointed analysis to the environment and the economy of the urban people, puts forward the proposal to the urban development, and achieves the urban sustainable development ultimate objective.

Keywords: entropy weight, coordinated development, coordination degree.

1 Introduction

With the rapid development of industrialization and urbanization, the large-scale concentration of industry and population, urban environment contamination, ecological damage and resident health problems increasingly get worse. It has become the prominent problems of human development which coordinating the relationship between with residential environment and speeding up the economic development simultaneously. Now, the urban human settlement which being concerned by architecture, geography, environtology and ekistics is becoming one of hot topics.

The improvement of urban human settlement and economic development is the system's two factors who interaction, mutual promotion and mutual restraint. Economic development is the basis and premise of urban human settlement improvement, the improvement of urban human settlement is the primary motivator of economic development. But the economic development likes a double-edged sword. People's one-sided pursuit of economic growth which results in resource destruction and pollution make urban human settlement to be faced with unprecedented challenge and that environment protection, infrastructure need too much money which restrict the improvement of urban human settlement. We must create a pleasant good living environment before we can import advanced technique and equipment, attract mastering emerging technology and management's talents,

C. Liu, J. Chang, and A. Yang (Eds.): ICICA 2011, Part I, CCIS 243, pp. 110–117, 2011.

increase jobs and promote economic structure adjustment. In contrast, if the urban human settlement is polluted and damaged, there will make the society by economic losses, environmental resource exhaustion and limiting the further development of economics [1].

This paper takes the 11 cities of Hebei Province as the object of study. On the basis of practical situation we structure the evaluation index of human settlement and economic characteristics and establish the coordinate coefficient models.

2 The Construction of the Evaluation Index System

The urban human settlement and economic development system is enormous. It includes society, environment, economics, culture and other aspects [3]. The estimate of harmonious state is not exhaustive. For reflecting the two subsystems comprehensively, we must set up the composite index which contains the major influencing factors. When selecting and designing the evaluation index, we need to not only follow the universality principle of objectivity, scientific, integrity and representativeness, but also follow the principle of humanist, hierarchy, locality, comparability and dynamics. According to above principle and hebei province's practical situation, two subsystems select the following index which see table 1.

Table 1. Living environment and economic characteristics of evaluation indexes

Code Urban living environment index	code Economic characteristics index
X1 The per-capita practical area(sq.m.)	Y1 GDP(Billion yuan)
X2 Population density (person / square kilometers)	Y2 Industrial added value (Billion yuan)
X3 Per capita have road area(sq.m.)	
X4 Every million people have doctors number	Y3 fixed investments (Billion yuan) Y4 All revenue(Billion yuan)
X5 Per capita public green area(sq.m.)	Y5 Financial institutions of foreign currency of account balance(Billion yuan)
X6 The finished green coverage(%)	
X7 Urban sewage concentration adolescent(%)	Y6 Trade(Billion dollars)
X8 Motor vehicle environmental regular detection rate(%)	Y7 CONSUM(Billion yuan)
X9 The industrial solid wastes utilization rate(%)	Y8 CPI
X10 College students with every million counted	Y9 Urban per capita disposable income(Yuan)
X11 Every million people have several books(volume)	Y10 Herdsmen per capita cash income(Yuan)

3 Theory Basis

3.1 Coordinative Degree Assessment

Coordination is a concept to describe the harmonious relations among different systems or system components, which indicates that different systems or system components function together efficiently (Yang, 1994). Due to the dynamic change of system, the relations among system components are in a state of constant adjustment, so coordinative degree is a quantitative measure of the coordinative relations among different systems or system components. There are mutual interactions and feedbacks between economy and environment, but whether the relations between them are in the state of coordination need to be judged by quantitative assessment. Coordinative degree between economy and environment is a quantitative measure of the coupled relations between urban development and urban environment in different stages of urban growth [5], the objectives of which are to discuss whether the relations between them are in the state of coordination and to coordinate the relations between them so as to realize the sustainable development of urban.

Referring to related researches in this domain D is used to denote the coordinative degree [2] between economy and environment of the urban.

$$f(x)=\sum_{i=1}^{m}a_i x_i' . \tag{1}$$

$$g(y)=\sum_{i=1}^{m}b_i y_i' .. \tag{2}$$

Where, a_i and b_i are respectively the value of their index weights, x_i' and y_i' are respectively standardized value of Urban living environment and economic indicators;

$$x_i' = \begin{cases} x_i/\lambda_{\max};\textit{when } x_i \textit{ the bigger the better} \\ \lambda_{\min}/x_i;\textit{when } x_i \textit{ the lower the better} \end{cases} . \tag{3}$$

Where, $\lambda_{\max}$ and $\lambda_{\min}$ are respectively the maximum and minimum value in a same standard. y_i' is using the same processing method.

$$C' = \frac{f(x)\bullet g(y)}{\left[\frac{f(x)+g(y)}{2}\right]^2} . \tag{4}$$

$$C = \left\{ \frac{f(x)\bullet g(y)}{\left(\frac{f(x)+g(y)}{2}\right)^2} \right\}^k . \tag{5}$$

Where, C is coordinative degree, k is coordinate coefficient, $k \geq 2$.

$$T=\alpha f(x)+\beta g(y) . \tag{6}$$

$$D=\sqrt{C\bullet T} . \tag{7}$$

Where D is the coordinate development, T is comprehensive evaluation index, $\alpha=\beta=0.5$.

The standard [6] of coordinative degree assessment is as Table 2:

Table 2. Standard of coordinative degree assessment

D	type
0.00-0.09	Extreme discoordination recession
0.10-0.19	Serious discoordination recession
0.20-0.29	Moderate discoordination recession
0.30-0.39	Mild discoordination recession
0.40-0.49	Endangered discoordination recession
0.50-0.59	Barely coordinated development
0.60-0.69	Primary coordinated development
0.70-0.79	Intermediate coordinated development
0.80-0.89	good Coordination
0.90-1.00	high quality Coordination

3.2 Human Settlement and Economic Development Model

Judging by development model of human settlement and economic, we can compare $f(x_j)$ and $g(y_j)$, as Table 3:

Table 3. Living environment and economic development model

$f(x_j)$ relationship with $g(y_j)$	Development mode
$f(x_j) > g(y_j)$	Economic lag environment model
$f(x_j) = g(y_j)$	Economic environment harmonious mode
$f(x_j) < g(y_j)$	Environmental lag economic models

4 Weight Calculation Using Entropy Value Methods

In the information field , Entropy is usually used to measure the degree of disorder or dispersion for a closed system , and it is an excellent indication of concentration or uncertainty[4], The bigger is the entropy value , the more disorderly is the data in the system , the smaller is the entropy value , the more orderly and 'purely' is the data . The decision matrix built by n schemes and m evaluating indexes is clearly an information carrier, so entropy is used to evaluate the degree of ordering and utility in the system. According to its essence to assess the effective degree of information, we can apply information entropy to calculate weight coefficient, the higher the utility value is, and the greater its importance of assessment is. The main calculation steps are shown as follows:

Comparison matrix R composed by n schemes and m evaluating indexes is built:

$$R = (v_{ij})_{mn} \ (i = 1,2,\ldots,m;\ j = 1,2,\ldots,n)$$

Comparison matrix R is normalized to construct normalized matrix B : $B=(b_{ij})_{mn}$, $b_{ij}=\dfrac{v_{ij}-v_{\min}}{v_{\max}-v_{\min}}$, Where, $v_{\max}$ and $v_{\min}$ is respectively the most satisfied and the most dissatisfied under the same indicator.

According to the information entropy principle, the entropy coefficient of indicator can be defined:

$$P_{ij}=\frac{b_{ij}}{\sum_{j=1}^{m} b_{ij}},\quad H_i=-\frac{1}{\ln m}\left(\sum_{j=1}^{m} p_{ij}\ln p_{ij}\right)\ i=1,2,\ n;\ j=1,2,\ldots m;$$

Where, $P_{ij}=0$, $\ln p_{ij}$ is meaningless to be amended, is defined as:

$$p_{ij}\ \ln p_{ij}=0.$$

The entropy [7] coefficient of the indicators is calculated:

$$\omega_i=\frac{1-H_i}{\sum_{i=1}^{n}(1-H_i)},\ \sum_{i=1}^{n}\omega_i=1\ .$$

5 Empirical Analysis –Take Hebei Province 11 Cities for Example

5.1 The Original Data for the System of Evaluation

The original data for the evaluation index of urban human settlement and the index of economic characteristics comes from the 2008th statistic annals of Hebei province.

5.2 The Confirming for the Weight of Index

1. The calculation for the entropy weight of urban human settlement index
   Set up the judgment matrix $R(v_{11\times 11})$; the normalization of the matrix, we have $B(x)$.
   Calculating every index's evaluation proportion is p_{X_j} and calculating every index's entropy is H_{X_j} .
2. The calculation for the entropy weight of economic characteristics index
   Set up the judgment matrix $R(v_{10\times 11})$; the normalization of the matrix, we have $B(y)$.
   Every index's evaluation proportion is p_{Y_j} and calculating every index's entropy is H_{Y_j} .

5.3 Data Normalization

For eliminating ill effects which is occasioned by the different of variable's dimension, the index is standardized before the analysis. The original data is standardized by formula (4).

5.4 Calculating Results

Using formula (1) to calculate the estimating function value of every city's comprehensive urban human settlement $f(x_j)$; using formula (2) to calculate the estimating function value of every city's comprehensive economic $g(y_j)$.

Using formula (6) to calculate the comprehensive estimating index of every city's economic and urban human settlement.

Using formula (5) to calculate the harmony degree [11,12] of every city, take $k = 2$.

Using formula (7) to calculate the harmony development degree of every city.

5.5 Results Analysis

We make the calculating results for the table 4 and 5:

Table 4. The harmony development degree of urban human settlement and economics

index	TS	SJZ	BD	CZ	XT	LF	HS	QHD	ZJK	CD	HD
$f(x_j)$	0.593	0.699	0.479	0.517	0.498	0.517	0.490	0.657	0.526	0.738	0.539
$g(y_j)$	0.976	0.738	0.369	0.416	0.334	0.418	0.220	0.336	0.256	0.245	0.435
D_j	0.832	0.847	0.640	0.675	0.620	0.676	0.510	0.631	0.551	0.525	0.690

Table 5. The coordinated development status of environment and economics

city	the type of coordinated degree	development pattern
TS	good coordinated development	economic model of environmental hysterics
SJZ	good coordinated development	economic model of environmental hysterics
BD	primary coordinated development	environmental model of economical hysterics
CZ	primary coordinated development	environmental model of economical hysterics
XT	primary coordinated development	environmental model of economical hysterics
LF	primary coordinated development	environmental model of economical hysterics
HS	reluctant coordinated development	environmental model of economical hysterics
QHD	primary coordinated development	environmental model of economical hysterics
ZJK	reluctant coordinated development	environmental model of economical hysterics
CD	reluctant coordinated development	environmental model of economical hysterics
HD	primary coordinated development	environmental model of economical hysterics

The above table is only the generally analysis and assessment of the coordinated development status, below is the targeted analysis of urban human settlement and economics.

For the data of table 4, we give a ranking table 6 of every city's urban human settlement and economics.

Table 6. The ranking of urban human settlement and economics

position	the rank of urban human settlement	the rank of economics
1st	Cheng De	Tangshan
2nd	Shi Jiazhuang	Shi Jiazhuang
3rd	Qinhuangdao	Han Dan
4th	Tangshan	Lang Fang
5th	Han Dan	Cang Zhou
6th	Zhang Jiakou	Bao Ding
7th	Cang Zhou	Qinhuangdao
8th	Lang Fang	Xing Tai
9th	Xing Tai	Zhang Jiakou
10th	Heng Shui	Chengde
11th	Bao Ding	Heng Shui

6 Conclusion and Suggestions

Urban human settlement and economic system exist in the whole urban ecological system. Because of the complexity of systems, uncertainty factors remain widespread. Although the study of urban human settlement have obtained great progresses, the quantitative study between urban human settlement and balanced economic development[8,9] yet not pay enough attention to it. This paper use entropy method and coordinate development model which make coordinate development as the level of urban human settlement and economic coordinated development to quantitative evaluation [10]. Evaluate results is broadly in line with the practical situation which explain this method reflecting objective truly.

Hebei province's cities should use advantages of itself, establish itself development strategy on the evaluate result and reality [13], made urbanism, reconstruction and management for the basic industry and leading industry. We must make the industrial cluster which covered by urban environmental economic for chain development, walk industry way and form industrial system. Developed urban construction industry foster new growth areas in the economy, bring up important urban human settlement. Consequently, it will maintain steady, rapid, coordinated development of the urban economic. Simultaneously, we will expand publicity, enhance education, boost the awareness of ecological protection, inspires resident's lifestyles changing to ecotypic sustainable model.

In addition, urban human settlement and economic system have close interconnection. Reinforcing the analysis of the two systems' development evolution mechanism, forecast and warning will help discover the law between them, reveal the internal relations and make better coordinated development of the urban human settlement and economic development.

References

1. Liu, Q., Lin, Z., Feng, N.: The differential quantitative evaluation research of urban human settlement for Jiang Su province. Areal Research and Development 24(5), 30–33 (2005)
2. Yang, S.: A study on the forecast and regulation of coordinated development of urban environment and economy in Guang Zhou. Scientia Geographica Sinica 14(2), 136–143 (1994)
3. Li, B.: The evaluation research of urban human settlement construction. Ecological Economy 5, 34–37 (2005)
4. Guo, X.: Application of Improved Entropy Method in Evaluation of Economic Result. Systems Engineering Theory & Practice 12 (1998)
5. Liu, S., Liu, B.: The study on the sustainable development evaluation system of urban human settlement. Urban Planning Forum 5, 35–39 (1999)
6. Liao, C.: The quantitative evaluation and category systems of coordinated development between environment and economics. Tropical Geography 19(2), 171–177 (1999)
7. Qiu, W.: Administrative decision and applied entropy. China Machine Press, Beijing (2001)
8. Yan, W., Gu, L.: The application of entropy decision method in engineering evaluation. Journal of Xi'an University of Architecture and technology 36(1), 98–100 (2004)
9. Liang, Z.: Coordinated Development Evaluation of Economy-environment System in Shandong Province. Resource Development & Market 2 (2009)
10. Luan, X.: Economic and Environmental Development in Xi'an Strategy. Xi'an University of Science and Technology 5 (2010)
11. Yin, F., He, X., Wang, L., Yan, D.: A New Method of Achievement Evaluation based on Coordination Degree and Entropy. Journal of Environmental Management College of China 1 (2011)
12. Xue, N., Gong, L., Aniwar, A.: Coordination degree evaluation of energy-economy-environment composite system in Xinjiang. Journal of Arid Land Resources and Environment 5 (2009)
13. Zhou, R., Liu, L., Wang, G.: Research on the Countermeasures of Promoting Energy-Economic-Environment System to Coordinating development in Hebei Province. Hebei Academic Journal 1 (2011)

An Empirical Study on Influence Factors of Earnings Forecast Disclosure Willingness

Xu Nan, Zhang Wei-li, and Wang Li-yan

School of Economics & Management, Yanshan University,
Qinhuangdao, China
xn96051092@126.com

Abstract. The paper does an empirical study on influence factors of earnings forecast disclosure willingness of listed companies using Logist regression model. The results show that the board size relates with the earnings forecast disclosure willingness significant negative, managers changes, asset-liability ratio and managers stockholdings relate with the earnings forecast disclosure willingness significant positive, other variables of management characteristic have no significant influence to earnings forecast disclosure willingness.

Keywords: earnings forecast, disclosure willingness, management characteristic, influence factors.

1 Introduction

Earnings forecast means that listed companies disclose their earnings roughly before disclosing final financial reports to the public, it belongs to the future profitability forecast of enterprise management. Earnings forecast is not required to compulsory disclosure as final financial reports and management holds the choice right whether or not to disclose.

After 2006, with the improving of earnings forecast system of listed companies, more and more listed companies begin to disclose the earnings forecast information. The proportion of disclosure companies to the total listed companies were 48.10%, 52.20% and 57.87% on December 31, 2007, December 31, 2008, and December 31, 2009 respectively. This phenomenon shows that listed companies emphasize and strengthen the executive power to earnings forecast system. It is worth of discussion about what factors influence earnings forecast disclosure willingness.

2 Literature Review

The study on earnings forecast of foreign scholars mainly includes five aspects: earnings forecast motivation, earnings forecast disclosure strategy, the market reaction of earnings forecast, the accuracy of earnings forecast and the relationship between the securities analysts predict and earnings forecast. Waymire (2003) drew two conclusions through studying the earnings forecast of 1997-2001:(1)the disclosure of good news and bad news yield significant positive supra-normal return

C. Liu, J. Chang, and A. Yang (Eds.): ICICA 2011, Part I, CCIS 243, pp. 118–125, 2011.

and significant negative supra-normal return respectively, (2)the more difference between forecast earnings and the market expected earnings, the greater the supra-normal return[1]. Pownall, Wasley and Waymire (2005) analyzed the market reaction of different forecast type information employing 1252 times earnings forecast of 91 listed companies from July of 1996 to December of 2004 as research samples[2]. Holthausen and Verrecchia (2003)[3], Kim and Verrecchia (2005)[4] found that: the higher accuracy of earnings forecast information is, the more the investors depend on earnings forecast. Robert Libby Hum-tong Tan (1999) carried on the questionnaire survey and case testing for 28 financial analysis institution in order to study the securities analysts' preference, feeling and evaluation to earnings forecast[5].

Currently there is few study about influence factors of earnings forecast disclosure willingness. Yang Ping (2010) analyzed the accuracy, timeliness and correction results of listed company earnings forecast information. Yang employed earnings forecast from 2006 to 2008 as research samples and made three conclusions: (1)the accuracy of earnings forecast is increasing, meanwhile the timeliness is decreasing, (2)managers tend to optimistic estimation when facing bad news, (3)there was still a large gap between revised earnings forecast and actual results[6]. Guo Na, Qi Huai-jin (2010) analysed the relationship between earnings forecast disclosure and earnings management using 2579 samples of Chinese A-stock market from 2007 and 2008 and drew three conclusions: (1)the earnings management level of the companies of disclosing earnings forecast was higher than the companies of not disclosing earnings forecast significantly, (2)the earnings management level of the companies of mandatory disclosing earnings forecast was higher than the companies of voluntary disclosing earnings forecast significantly, (3)companies such as assets in small scale, profitability in low level and liabilities more likely engaged in earnings management[7].

3 Empirical Analysis

3.1 Sample Selection and Data Sources

We take earnings forecast of Chinese A-stock market from 2007-2009 as study subject excluding the new companies in the List in 2009, ST companies, PT companies, financial listed companies, listed companies issuing B-shares and H-shares, and listed companies of data missing and changing in severe abnormalities. 3992 samples are obtained after such treatment, 1210 of which is from the year of 2007, 1339 from 2008, and 1443 from 2009.

The basic information of listed companies and information about corporate governance structure derives from CSMAR database. Earnings forecast information of listed companies, laws and regulations, and some supporting information are from the Securities Star Website (http://www. Stockstar.com), Shanghai Stock Exchange Website (http://www.sse.com.cn) and the Shenzhen Stock Exchange website (http://www.szse.cn). The relevant information about the accounting firm is from Chinese Institute of CPAs Website (http://www.cicpa.org.cn). EXCEL and SPSS18.0 are employed in data processing.

3.2 Variable Definition, Hypothesis and Model

3.2.1 Variable Definition

The name, meaning and definitions of each variable are shown in Table 1.

Table 1. Variable List

Variable type	Variable name	Variable meaning	Variable definitions
Endogenous variable	P	Earnings forecast disclose or not	Disclosure, then P is 1, not disclosure, then P is 0
Exogenous variable	BDSize	Board size	total number of directors of the board
	BDIndep	Independent directors proportion	The number of independent directors/ total number of the board
	BDlead	Leadership structure	Dumb variables, when the same person who is chairman and general manager, the variable is 1, otherwise 0
	ManagSL	Managers' salaries	Ln(The average of managers' salaries)
	ManagSH	Managers stockholdings	Ln(The average of managers stockholdings number)
	ManagAge	Managers' age	The average age of managers
	IND	Industry type	Dumb variables, when industry type is one of the following: computer and related equipment manufacturing, computer application services, medical and biological products, the variable is 1, otherwise 0
	ManagChg	Managers changes	Dumb variables, if managers change the variable is 1, otherwise 0
	TDebt	Asset-liability ratio	Total liabilities / total assets
	Audit10	Accounting firm type	Dumb variables, if the listed companies hired accounting firms of the top 10, the variable is 1, otherwise 0
Control variables	Size	Firm size	Ln(Total assets)
	Growth	Operating profit growth ratio	(Operating profit of this year - operating profit last year)/ operating profit last year
	ROE	Return on equity	Net profit / net assets

3.2.2 Hypothesis

Through analyzing the influence factors of earnings forecast disclosure willingness from the existing literature and considering our unique system background, the present study deems that the influence factors of earnings forecast disclosure willingness can be divided into two kinds of factors: internal drivers and external governance mechanisms[8-10]. Internal drivers includes the management structural features, management incentive features and management background features. External factors include the industry in which the enterprise lays, the managers competitiveness, creditors governance and audit institutions of and the intermediary market. This paper proposes the following 13 hypothesis.

Hypothesis 1: Earnings forecast disclosure willingness negatively related with the board size.

Hypothesis 2: Earnings forecast disclosure willingness positively related with the proportion of independent directors.

Hypothesis 3: When the same person who is chairman and general manager, earnings forecast disclosure willingness of the listed companies intend to be low.

Hypothesis 4a: Earnings forecast disclosure willingness positively related with the managers' salaries.

Hypothesis 4b: Earnings forecast disclosure willingness positively related with the managers stockholdings level.

Hypothesis 5: Earnings forecast disclosure willingness negatively related with the average age of Managers.

Hypothesis 6: Earnings forecast disclosure willingness positively related with the industry risk.

Hypothesis 7: Earnings forecast disclosure willingness positively related with the managers market competitiveness.

Hypothesis 8: Earnings forecast disclosure willingness positively related with Asset-liability ratio.

Hypothesis 9: The degree of earnings forecast disclosure is higher made by the top 10 accounting firms than other accounting firms.

Hypothesis 10: Earnings forecast disclosure willingness positively related with the firm size.

Hypothesis 11: Earnings forecast disclosure willingness positively related with the growth of the listed companies.

Hypothesis 12: Earnings forecast disclosure willingness positively related with the profitability of the listed companies.

3.2.3 Model

The paper adopts Logist regression model and Maximum Likelihood Method is used to estimate parameters. Model expressions are as follows:

$$\lambda = \mathrm{Ln}\left(\frac{p}{1-p}\right) = \beta_0 + \beta_1 \mathrm{X}_1 + \cdots + \beta_i \mathrm{X}_i \tag{1}$$

Based on the above analysis of the influence factors of earnings forecast disclosure willingness, Logistic regression model is as follows:

$$\begin{aligned} \ln\left(\frac{p}{1-p}\right) &= \beta_0 + \beta_1 BDSize + \beta_2 BDIndep + \beta_3 BDLead + \beta_4 ManagSL \\ &+ \beta_5 ManagSH + \beta_6 ManagAge + \beta_7 IND + \beta_8 ManagChg + \beta_9 TDebt \\ &+ \beta_{10} Audit10 + \beta_{11} Size + \beta_{12} Growth + \beta_{13} ROA + \varepsilon \end{aligned} \tag{2}$$

β_0 is the constant term, β_i (i = 0,1, ...,13) is the Coefficient to be estimated of exogenous variables, ε is random component in Equation 2.

3.3 Result

3.3.1 Descriptive Results

(1) Descriptive statistics of the management characteristics

Descriptive results of the management characteristics are shown in Table 2.

Table 2. Descriptive results of the management characteristics

	sample size	minimum	maximum	mean	standard deviation
BDSize	3 992	2	18	9.30	1.937
BDIndep	3 992	0.0909	0.5714	0.3560	0.0482
ManagSH	3 992	0	336 012 251	3 558 765.1	1.678E7
ManagSL	3 992	2.6971	20.7884	11.7639	0.9782
ManagAge	3 992	36.64	73.54	47.4412	3.1315
TDebt	3 992	0.0178	1.7712	0.4909	0.1828
Size	3 992	18.2659	27.4877	21.7392	1.1627
Growth	3 992	-148.2933	493.5518	0.8371	16.9742
ROE	3 992	-2.7736	12.228	0.1174	0.3279

The results show that: ①The mean number of directors of the board is 9.30, and typically the size of 7-9 people is ideal, indicating that the board size of the sample companies is reasonable. ②The mean of independent directors proportion is 0.356, slightly larger than one-third which is the required proportion of China Securities Regulatory Commission(CSRC), indicating that sample companies comply with the basic requirements of the CSRC. ③Managers holdings number vary from the minimum of 0 to the maximum of 336,012,251, with the mean being 3,558,765.10. It is found in the data collection that companies in which managers hold share are not many in the samples. ④Ln(the mean number of managers' salaries) vary from the minimum of 2.6971 to the maximum of 20.7884, indicating that the differences exist in the management salaries of the sample companies. ⑤Managers' age range from 36.64 to 73.54, and the mean of managers' age is 48. ⑥Asset-liability ratio is 0.4909, less than 0.5, indicating that the sample companies may be restrained by creditors, and therefore carried out disclosing earnings forecast. ⑦The average asset size is 21.7392, and there is a bit distance between the maximum and minimum. ⑧Operating profit growth ratio ranged from the minimum of -148.2933 to the maximum of 493.5518, with the mean number of 0.8371, indicating that significant differences in the growth of the sample companies. ⑨The mean number of ROE is 0.1174, with the maximum of 12.228 and the minimum of -2.7736, indicating that a larger difference of profitability in the sample companies.

(2) Dummy variable frequency statistical analysis
Descriptive statistical analysis can not be used to analyze dummy variable, frequency statistical analysis is employed. The results of dummy variable frequency are shown in Table 3.

Table 3. Dummy variable frequency

dummy variable	assignment	frequency	percentage
	1	578	14.48%
BDlead	0	3 414	85.52%
	total	3 992	100%
	1	457	11.45%
IND	0	3 535	88.55%
	total	3 992	100%
	1	1 059	26.53%
ManagChg	0	2 933	73.47%
	total	3 992	100%
	1	1 163	29.13%
Audit10	0	2 829	70.84%
	total	3 992	100%

The statistical analysis of frequency indicates that: ①Chairman and general manager is the same person in14.48% of sample companies, indicating that some board of listed companies may lack independence. ②26.53% of sample companies have replaced managers, showing that the managers are faced with certain pressure of market competition. ③The proportion is moderate in computer and related equipment manufacturing, computer application services, medical and biological products. ④ 29.13% of sample companies are audited by the top 10 accounting firms, indicating that most listed companies in China tend to hire non-top 10 accounting firms to audit.

3.3.2 Regression Analysis

After correlation test, tolerance test and variance inflation factor analysis, 3 variables namely firm size (Size), managers' age (ManagAge) and leadership structure (BDlead) are excluded, and the remaining 10 variables are integrated into the regression model. Therefore, the last 10 variables entering the model includes: Board Size (BDSize), Independent directors proportion (BDIndep), Managers' salaries (ManagSL), Managers stockholdings (ManagSH), Industry Type (IND), Managers changes (ManagChg), Asset-liability ratio (TDebt), Accounting firm Type (Audit10), Operating profit growth ratio (Growth) and Return on equity (ROE). The results of Logistic regression are shown in Table 4.

From the above results of regression analysis, regression coefficients of independent directors proportion, industry type and accounting firm type are contrary to the original hypothesis and the rest variables regression coefficients are consistent with the original hypothesis. The Sig value of managers changes and the asset-liability ratio are less than 0.01, and the Sig value of the board size is less than 0.05, indicating that the impact of managers market competitiveness intensity, creditors governance and board size on earnings forecast disclosure willingness of listed companies is quite significant. The Sig value of managers stockholdings is more than 0.05 but less than 0.1, indicating that the impact of managers stockholdings on earnings forecast disclosure willingness exists. The Sig value of independent directors proportion, operating profit growth ratio, industry type, accounting firm type, return on equity and managers' salaries are not significant.

Table 4. Regression results of Logistic model

	B	S.E,	Wals	df	Sig.	Exp (B)
Board Size	-.036**	.025	4.002	1	.045	.965
Independent directors proportion	-.188	.964	.038	1	.846	1.207
Managers stockholdings	.005*	.000	3.084	1	.079	1.000
Operating profit growth ratio	.002	.003	.715	1	.398	1.002
Industry type	-.004	.136	.001	1	.974	.996
Managers changes	.060***	.015	15.112	1	.001	.942
Accounting firm type	-.034	.099	.120	1	.729	1.035
Managers' salaries	.042	.048	.784	1	.376	1.043
Asset-liability ratio	.783***	.265	8.762	1	.003	2.188
Return on equity	.358	.247	2.095	1	.148	1.430
Constant	1.544	.967	2.549	1	.110	4.682

***(P=0.01) **(2-tailed).**,** (P=0.05) **(2-tailed).**,*(P=0.1) **(2-tailed)**

The evaluation of the logistic regression models includes the adequacy and accuracy. The Sig value of HL test is 0.64, more than 0.05, indicating that the model is more appropriate. The value of R^2 is 0.31, close to 0.4, indicating that the model is accurate.

4 Discussion and Conclusions

The results of this study indicate that the four indicators of managers changes, asset-liability ratio, the board size and managers stockholdings are the important influence factors of earnings forecast disclosure willingness of listed companies.

It is significant for managers changes to earnings forecast disclosure willingness of listed companies, so the hypothesis 7 was supported. The stronger intensity of the managers market competitiveness, the more dismissal risk of service managers are faced. Therefore, managers would be more conscientious and communicate with outside investors actively, thus disclose the earnings forecast timely.

Asset-liability ratio made a significant contribution to the earnings forecast disclosure willingness of listed companies, so the hypothesis 8 was supported.

Creditors pay close attention to the companies of high asset-liability ratio and require listed companies to disclosure their earnings information timely in order to make decisions timely and safeguard their claims' value.

Board size made a significant contribution to the earnings forecast disclosure willingness of listed companies and support the hypothesis 1.The board of larger size are likely to be controlled by general manager owing to the poor communication and coordination between board members. But the board of smaller size work efficiency and reduce information asymmetry between listed companies and investors.

Managers stockholdings made a significant contribution to the earnings forecast disclosure willingness of listed companies and support the hypothesis 4b. Managers stockholdings can make the benefit accordance between managers and shareholders. Managers are concerned with the performance and values of listed companies.

Other explanatory variables of independent directors proportion, leadership structure, managers' salaries, managers' age, industry type and accounting firm type didn't affect the earnings forecast disclosure willingness of listed companies significantly and do not support the original hypothesis.

Three control variables of firm size, operating profit growth ratio and return on equity didn't affect the earnings forecast disclosure willingness of listed companies significantly and do not support the original hypothesis.

References

1. Waymire, G.: Additional Evidence on the Information Content of Management Earnings Forecasts. Journal of Accounting Research 22, 19–34 (2003)
2. Pownall, G., Wasley, C., Waymire, G.: The Stock Price Effect of Alternative Types of Management Earnings Forecasts. The Accounting Review 10, 231–250 (2005)
3. Holthausen, V.: The Effects of Sequential Information Releases on the Variance of Price Changes in an Intertemporal Multi Asset Market. Journal of Accounting Research 3, 210–243 (2003)
4. Kim, O., Verrecchia, R.E.: Trading Volume and Price Reactions to Public Announcements. Journal of Accounting Research 9, 65–83 (2005)
5. Robert Libby, H.-T.: TanAnalysts' Reaction to Warnings of Negative Earnings Surprises. Journal of Accounting Research 15, 415–435 (2009)
6. Yang, P.: Earnings Forecasts Characteristics Analysis Based on the Earnings Forecasts of Listed Companies. Journal of Northwestern Polytechnical University (social science edition) 6, 19 (2010)
7. Guo, N., Qi, H.-J.: An Empirical Research on the Relationship Between Earnings Forecasts Disclosure and Earnings Management 2, 34 (2010)
8. Liu, C.: Earnings Preannouncement, Earnings Change and Auditors Governance Effect. Journal of Shanghai Lixin University of Commerce 4, 62–69 (2010)
9. Guo, N.: Errors in Management Achievement Forecast and Surplus Management—— Evidence from Chinese Listed Companies. Economic Survey 6, 76–80 (2010)
10. Bai, X.: The Multiple Influence of Corporate Disclosure Policy on Analyst Forecast. Journal of Financial Research 4, 92–112 (2009)

Study on Critical Technologies of Earth-Fill Shore-Protection Structure in the Three Gorges Reservoir*

Xiaoying He[1], Hongkai Chen[1], and Hudui Liu[2]

[1] Institute of Geotechnical Engineering, Chongqing Jiaotong University, Chongqing, 400074
xiaoying_he@yahoo.com, chk39520@163.com
[2] NanJiang Hydrogelolgical&Engineering Geology Brigade, Chongqing
wodeyingzi0410@163.com

Abstract. Earth-fill shore-protection technology is organic bonded by making artificial island and bank slope protection. While, during the building progress of the bank-protection works, three problems are inevitable: the water level fluctuation deteriorate the stability of the bank slope; the effective combination between original bank slope and the fill; intensive fluctuation of the bank slope caused by the reservoir water level's cyclic soak. Adopted critical technologies such as spray drain, synchro drainage technology, excavating inverse steps at the surface between the fill and original bank slope, etc solve the key problems. These critical technologies are applied on the Ningjiang island project. The results show that the stability of the bank slope in Ningjiang island enhanced, the urban land augmented.

Keywords: Earth-fill shore-protection structure, cyclic soak, synchro drainage technology, the Three Gorges Reservoir.

1 Introduction

With the completion of the Three Gorges Reservoir, more than 20 towns' residents migrate from existing inhabitancies, which makes the pinch of land use becomes more and more nakedness. Meanwhile, the area and the extent of Water-Level-Fluctuating Zone (WLFZ) whose area reaches 348.93km2 in the Three Gorges Reservoir is the biggest in the world. Meanwhile, the stability of the slope in Water-Level-Fluctuating Zone threatens the safety of the bank slope and the constructions in it.

The research and utilization of the WLFZ can take full advantage of the land resource in the reservoir for development, be the supply of production goods for immigration in the same time.

The current earth-fill island is build at the beach. Charlier and DeMeyer(1988)studied the influence of man-made island to the ocean environment in the aim of garbage

* This work was financially supported by the Chongqing Natural Science Foundation (2008BA0015).

C. Liu, J. Chang, and A. Yang (Eds.): ICICA 2011, Part I, CCIS 243, pp. 126–135, 2011.

disposal[1];JETRO(2004)did research on the feasibility to build man-made island on the big ditch entrance to the Pacific Ocean[2];Bayyinahsalahuddin(2006)did researches on the influence between Bubai Fortunes Windmill Palm island and Persian Gulf ocean circumstance, the influence between man-made island and halobios, sediment movement. For the circumstance of the man-made island is much worse than wharf, it is necessary to consider the soak and undercutting effect[3].

Shore protection can reduce the water's erosion effect on the bank slopes[4],while, as the 20 towns such as WuShan,Fengjie,Yunyang,WanZhou, etc implement "backward immigrate from current place's policy, the earth-fill shore protection technology which can sugar up and consummate the city foundation as well as increase the land use of city is in need. Then the earth-fill shore-protection technology is in need.

2 Earth-Fill Shore Protection Structure in NingJiang Island

NingJiang island is a earth-fill bank protection structure in WuShan country[5], planned to be build in the entrance of DaNing river for flood prevention combine with protect the roadbed of NingJiang road and make use oft the large amount of soil abandoned during the operation of the immigration. As the construction is completed, a byland formed. Therefore, NingJiang project is a comprehensive treatment project which is main for bank protection, utilize th land resource as well as decorating the WLFZ area. Current landform of the Ningjiang island project is shown in Fig.1.NingJiang project in WuShan county adopts earth-fill shore protection structure who combines artificial island with bank slope protection, the design mode is peninsula, designing plane figure of the project is shown in figure2.

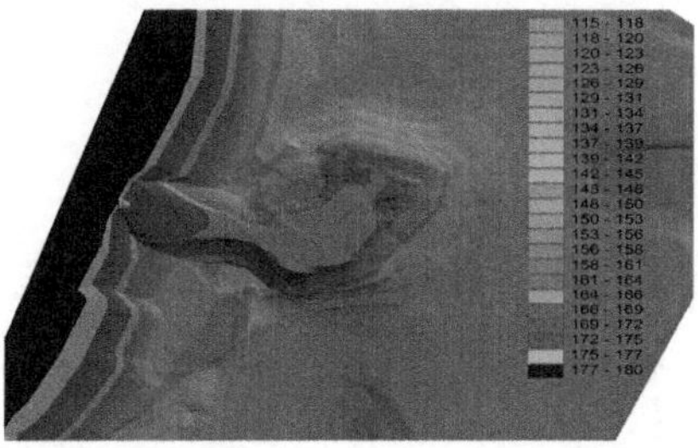

Fig. 1. Existing landform of the Ningjiang project

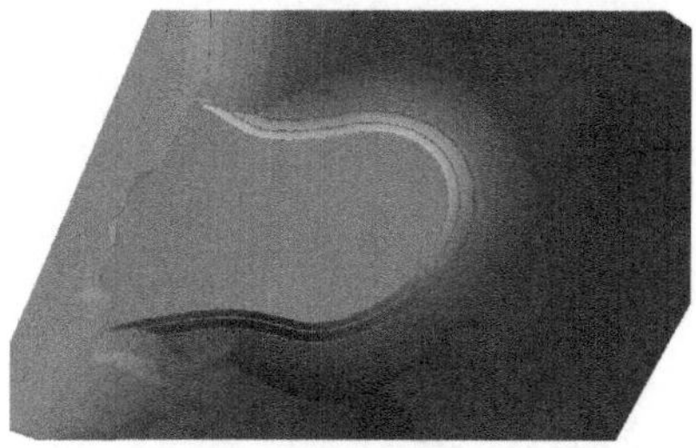

Fig. 2. Designing plane figure of the Ningjiang island project

2.1 Engineering Geological Conditions

Multi-year average precipitation in WuShan country is 1222mm,rainfall is concentrate in May to September, daily maximum precipitation reaches to 199mm.

Stratum layers in NingJiang project is Quaternary artificial loose soil, allucial-proluvial clay stratification and residual gravel soil,bedrock is aubergine silty mudstone of the secondary BaDong series in middle Triassic.Karst is quite developing in the field.

2.2 Geotechnical Physical and Mechanical Properties

Adopted fifteen undisturbed soil samples to take soil mechanics experiments, where standard penetration test(SPT) and 9 groups field shearing tests consist of the in-situ test.Soil samples is consist of fill, silty clay and gravel soil.Shearing intensive parameter's variation of the solum inNingjiang island is shown in Table.1.

Table 1. Shearing intensive parameter's variation of the solum inNingjiang island

Soil samples	Natural parameters		Saturate parameters	
	c (KPa)	φ(°)	c(KPa)	φ(°)
Fill	20	20	15.0	20
Siltyclay	25	18	21	14
Gravelsoil	25	25	20	22

2.3 Original Treatment Schemes for NingJiang Project

According to geotechnical physical and mechanical properties,original treatment schemes for NingJiang project are foundation treatment with rip rapping apron, rock-fill dam, backfill compaction, slope prevention and cantilever retaining wall. According to flood prevention standard, it is dyke building in grade four. The engineering plane figure of the Ningjiang island project and design chart of 0+50 pile of the Ningjiang island project are shown in Fig.3 and Fig.4.

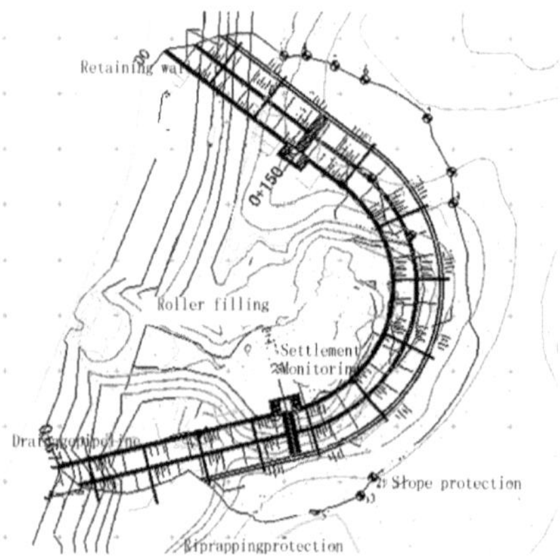

Fig. 3. Engineering plane of the Ningjiang island project

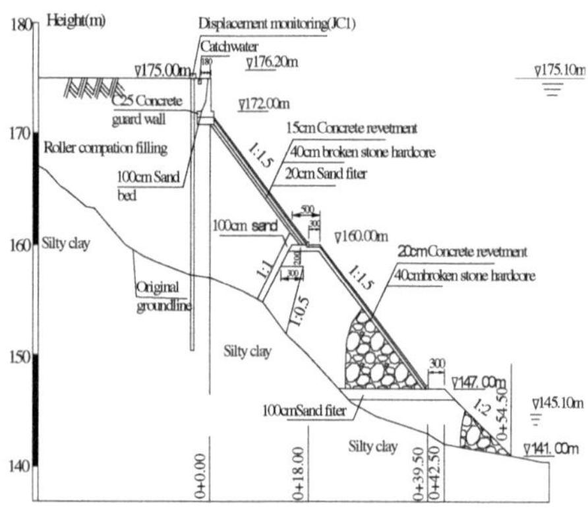

Fig. 4. The 0+50 pile design chart of the Ningjiang project

2.4 Stability Calculation

Taking typical cross section 1-1' and 2-2' as examples to calculate the stability of filling construct section. For NingJiang project is build in the Three Gorges Reservoir, the stability calculation must be taken in four operating modes: natural state(considering sole weight of bank slope and building load);high water level state(considering sole weight, building load and 175m water level);low water level state(considering sole weight, building load and 145m water level);water level decrease state(sole weight, building load and the osmotic pressure dropping from 175m to 145m),The stability calculation results is shown in Tab.2.

Table 2. The stability calculation results

Cross section		Sliding plane	Natural state	High water level state(175m)	Low water level state(145m)	water level decrease state (175m→145m)
1-1'	Before fill	1	1.3875	1.1461	1.2162	0.9587
		2	1.6848	1.4066	1.4925	1.2329
	After fill	1	1.4358	1.3752	1.3827	1.1025
		2	1.4042	1.1495	1.2442	1.0249
2-2'	Before fill	1	1.4648	1.2289	1.2921	1.1128
	After fill	1	1.3875	1.1461	1.2162	0.9587

It is vividly shown in the table that the stability of the bank slope increased after the filling project, while, during the water level decrease period, the stability of the NingJiang project decreased in the same way. Accordingly, as the completion of the Three Gorges Reservoir, most part of man made island will soak in water, cyclical soak will affect the stability of NingJiang project.

3 The Water Level Fluctuation Affects the Stability of Shore Protections

The cyclical fluctuation of water level in the Three Gorges Reservoir affect stability of the shore protections inevitably, it deteriorates shore protections' physical parameters, reduces shore protections' ability to resist external loads [6].Moreover, as the water level in reservoir subsidents, tensile force on the pore surface, cohesive strength and friction force of the bank slope affect groundwater in the shore protection structure. This phenomenon increases a imbalance hydrostatic pressure and hydrodynamic pressure, which increase the sliding effect of the shore protection structures, reduces the stability of shore protection structures even more.

Based on this, three critical technologies will be faced during the build process of the earth-fill bank protection structure in high water level fluctuation reservoir:

Earth-Fill Bank Slope's Stability Deteriorated under Water Level Fluctuation. As the Three Gorges Reservoir impounded, soil bank slopes' shear strength reduces for immersed in water when the reservoir level and groundwater rose. Meanwhile, cyclically scouring by reservoir water, bank slopes deforming and damaged as well as falls back until form new stable ones[7.8].Constructing reservoir leads to surface water and groundwater environment and their dynamic action system variation which aggravate water-rock effect, changes rock mass structure and component, deteriorates rock and soil mechanics properties.Finally,rock and soil mass of bank slope can not keep balance with surrounding environment anymore, bank slope damaged.

Effective Combination between Original Bank Slope and the Fill. Material of the fill and the bank slope are different. The osmosis and scouring of the reservoir water and the uneven settlement between fill and bank slope induce damage breaks out along the interface of fill and original bank slope during the fluctuation process of the reservoir water level on the condition that effective combination between original bank slope and the fill is not proper handed.

Intensive Deterioration of the Bank Slope Caused by the Reservoir Water Level's Cyclic Soak. To the aim of flood prevention, the Three Gorges Reservoir's water level changes annually between 175m and 145m.Then,the affection between water and bank slope is the hotspot during the operation the it[9].Component of the fill is complicated for its distribution proportion between macadam and soil, cementation, particle diameter, arrange style and compactness are different. Meanwhile, seepage field of groundwater changes cyclically in the same ways, which dramatically deteriorate the stability of the earth-fill bank protection structures.

4 Critical Technologies of Earth-Fill Shore-Protection Structure

4.1 Resolving for Earth-Fill Bank Slope's Stability Deterioration under Water Level Fluctuation

Underground Channel for Drainage. To cut underground channel for drainage at the interface between fill and original bank slope in certain width (commonly be 2.5m to 3.0m),lay permeable earthwork cloth in the drainage and fill with macadam to equal to the drainage. Meanwhile, laying permeable earthwork at the top to form a underfround channel for drainage shown in figure 5,which can reduce the softening effect to the fill under the decrease of the water level.

Synchro Drainage Technology. To filling bank slope, synchro drainage technology can reduce strong penetrability created during the landing process of the reservoir water level.Synchro drainage technology must be combine with the retaining wall, typical bank protecting retaining wall is shown in Figure 6.

Optimizing filling in the back of retaining wall.
Internal factors affects the soil pressure of retaining wall is the filling property. The only path to improve the stability and security of the retaining wall is the amelioration of filling property. Selectting prime fill whose internal friction angle is even bigger can effectively decrease load transmission and the acting force affect on the retaining wall.

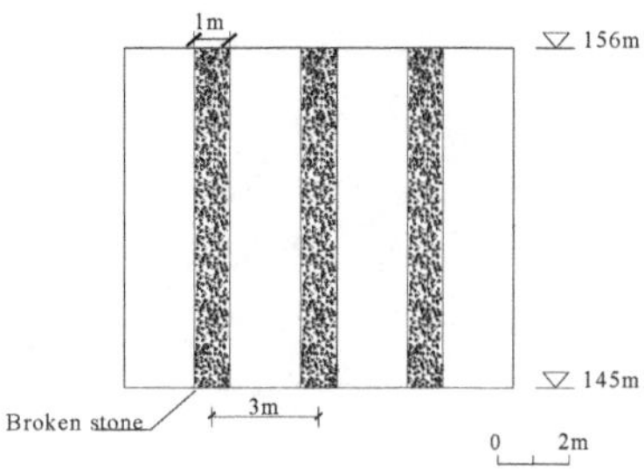

Fig. 5. The spray drain under the fill

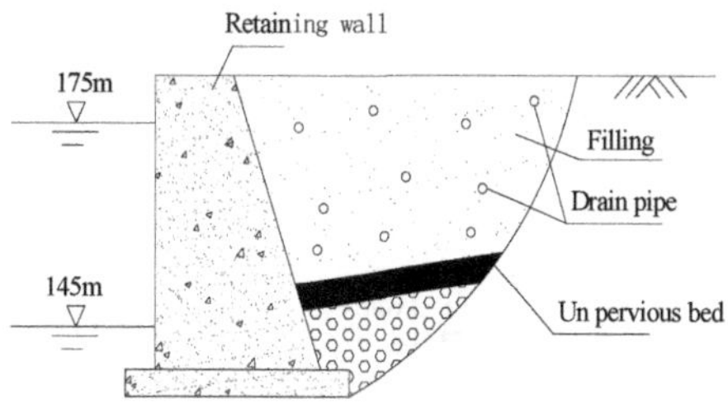

Fig .6. The reverting retaining wall

Drainage technology on retaining wall.
Hydraulic gradient of underground percolation is proportional to water head and inversely proportional to the flowing distance.Cutting down the flowing distance can increase the hydraulic gradient in the condition that the water head is a constant. The effective method to cut down the flowing distance is imbed drainage pipeline in the fill. According to principle of minimum potential energy and principle of minimum potential energy.underground water in infiltration flow field will choose the shortest path to flow into drainage pipeline and flow into reservoir through built-in pipeline.

To drastically discharge underground water, it is necessary to select appropriate diameter and arrangement mode of drainage pipeline based on the maximal lowering speed ensured by synchro drainage technology's request. Drainage pipeline must dip into natural soil, whose dimension has to no less than 2.0m for further intercept underground water in bank slope. Arrangement plan of drainage pipeline in the rewetting retaining wall is shown in Figure 7.

Catchwater and spray drain.
Retaining wall is usually built with concrete, who makes its low hydraulic permeability. Meanwhile, as the hydraulic permeability of bank slope is poor in the same way, underground water in the fill is hard to be discharged through the wall when the reservoir water level decreased. Therefore, it is necessary to adopt engineering measures to drainage underground water and prevent underground water or pore water storing below the lowest exhaust outlet of retaining wall to form a inverse trapezoid area. Accordingly, a water-resisting layer can be build below the lowest exhaust outlet with impermeable materials or weak impermeable clay soil, the cut and draining facility of groundwater after the retaining wall is shown in Figure 8.For the facility of cutting underground water, the water-resisting layer can be made as funnel type hood face with exhaust outlet as its center.

4.2 Effective Combination between Original Bank Slope and the Fill

Resolving methods are divided to three steps. Firstly, clean out organic mass on the interface between fill and original bank slope. Secondly, excavate stages along the slope, the width of stage is about 2m.Thirdly, lays macadam on the stage, whose thickness is about 30cm.

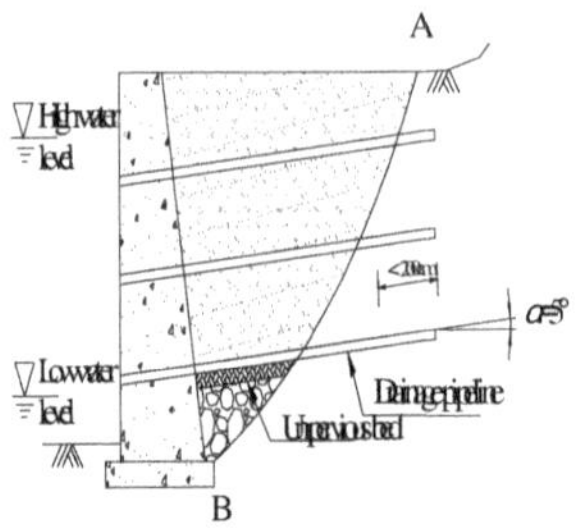

Fig. 7. Arrangement plan of drainage pipeline

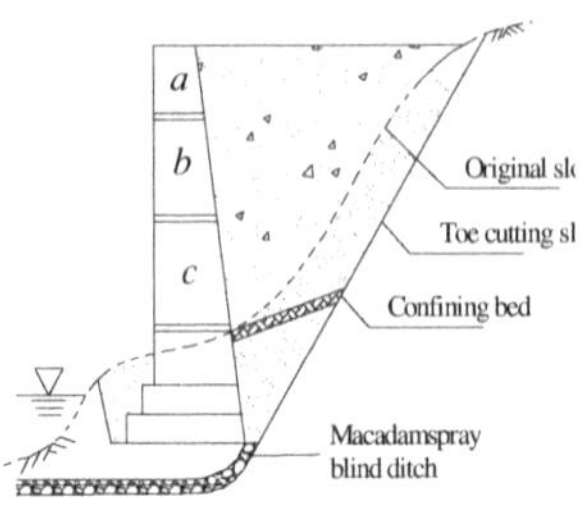

Fig. 8. The cut and draining facility

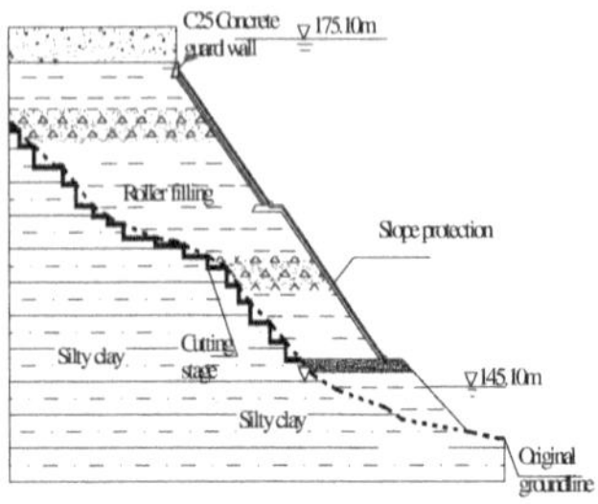

Fig. 9. The dentate processing in revetting retaining wall of groundwater after the retaining wall surface between fill and original slope

Though this resilient, the fill can be effectively wedging into original bank slope, enhancing the frictional strength between the fill and original bank slope. The dentate processing at the surface between the fill and original bank slope is shown in Figure 9.

4.3 Resolve for Intensive Fluctuation of Bank Slope Caused by Reservoir Water Level's Cyclic Soak

Selecting Filling with Good Water Physical Properties. Filling must be chosen to satisfy the request of strength and transformation must be ones whose coefficient of permeability is low. Enhancing filling's compacted density and deformation modulus using compaction and rolling technology to reduce the cyclical soak influence affect on bank slope.

Implement Underground Water Synchrony Drainage Technology Effectively. Installing drainage pipeline in the filling to reduce flowing pressure created in rapid drawdown through cutting down reservoir water's retention time in the filling.

Reclaiming the Filling Laminated Following Different Osmosis. Consulting the designing cross section plane, filling is reclaimed as their osmosis to achieve enough stability. Meanwhile, the thickness of each layer of the filling is ensured according as the soil property, effective compacting depth of compactor and compaction requirements.

5 Optimization Scheme for NingJiang Earth-Fill Shore-Protection Project

5.1 Optimization Scheme Design

To realize the optimization scheme of NingJiang earth-fill shore-protection project,it is necessary to combine the three critical technologies together. Cross-sectional drawing of the cantilever retaining wall is shown in figure 10.Blind drainage can be suitable to either drainage reservoir water during the decrease of the water level or drainage pore water flowing from the bank slope to the lowest exhaust outlet in the retaining wall. Cross-sectional drawing of the blind drainage is shown in figure 11.

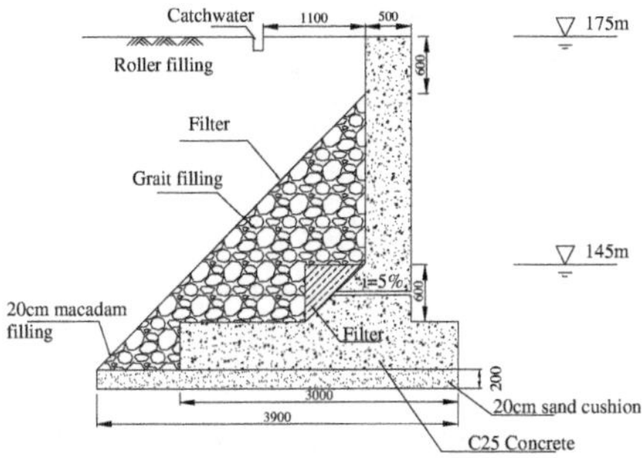

Fig. 10. Cross-sectional drawing of cantilever retaining wall

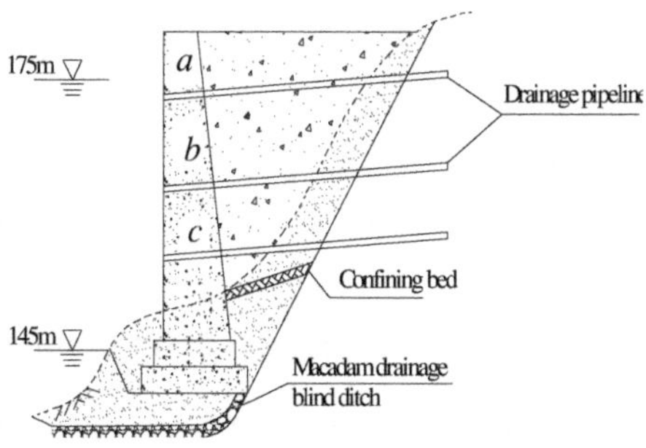

Fig. 11. Cross-sectional draw of cantilever retaining wall

Excavating stages at the surface of bank slope is the way to make fill wedding into the original bank slope in the purpose of enhance the coefficient of friction between the filling and bank slope,the detail drawing of dentate processing is shown in figure 12.Designing cross-sectional drawing of the cantilever retaining wall adopting critical technologies is shown in figure 13.

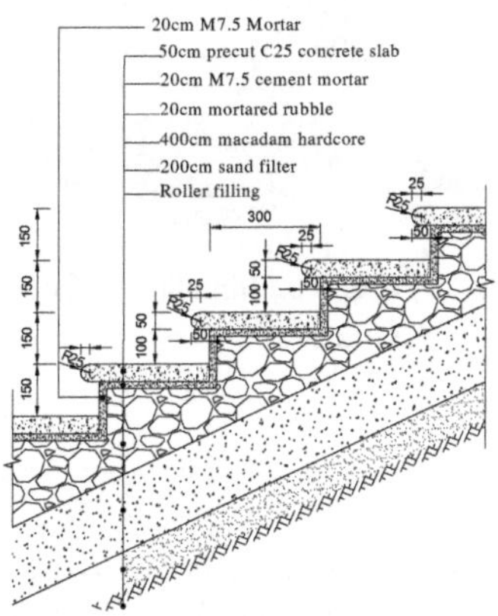

Fig. 12. The detail drawing of dentate processing

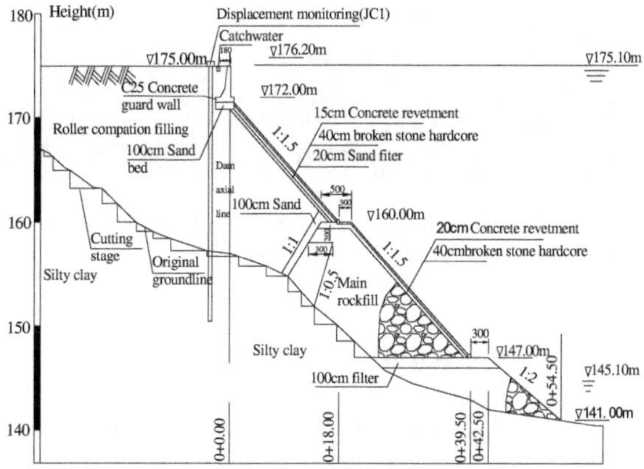

Fig. 13. Designing section plane (Taking the 0+50 pile as exanple)

5.2 Stability Analysis of NingJiang Project's Optimization Scheme

Taking typical 1-1' and 2-2' cross sections in the filling as example to analyze the stability of the project's optimization scheme.The result is shown in table 3.

Table 3. The stability calculation of the optimizing scheme (dropping state of the water level in reservoir)

Cross section	Sliding surface	Stability parameter
1-1'	1	1.2343
	2	1.2694
	3	1.2537
2-2'	1	1.1256
3-3'	1	1.2685

It is vividly shown in the table that, after taking the optimization scheme, in dropping state of water level in reservoir, the stability parameter increases about 0.15.

5.3 Regulating Effect of NingJiang Project

As the optimization scheme is well down, the NingJiang project can display great functions. Firstly, renovate Water-Level-Fluctuating Zone, sugar up tourist environment; secondly, bring up regional quality, form tourist landscape; thirdly, increase the protection of bank slopes, decrease water lose and soil erosion; fourthly, increase city area. The photograph before building is shown in figure 14,while,the regulating effect of NingJiang project is shown in figure 15 and figure16.

Fig. 14. Photograph before building

Fig. 15. Regulating effect of NingJiang project

Fig. 16. Simulate effect of project

6 Conclusion

Earth-fill shore-protection technology can protect the Water-Level-Fluctuating Zone in the Three Gorges Reservoir, while, water level fluctuation deteriorate the stability of the bank slope, effective combination between original bank slope, the fill and intensive fluctuation of bank slope caused by the reservoir water level's cyclic soak are the critical problems met in earth-fill shore-protection structure constructing process.

Critical technologies such as spray drain, synchro drainage technology, excavating inverse stages at the intersurface between the filling and original bank slope were applicated in Ningjiang island, the results show that the stability of bank slope in Ningjiang island increased, the urban land augmented.

References

1. Charlier, R.H., DeMeyer, C.P.: Artificial islands:environmental aspects off Beigium. International Journal of Environmental Studies 32(2&3) (December 1988)
2. JETRO. Feasibility Study of the Construetion of an Artifieial Island at the Pacific Entrance to the Panama Canal (2004)
3. Salahuddin, B.: The Marine Environmental ImPacts of Artificial Island Construction, Dubai, UAE (2006)
4. Younis, E.B.A.: Prediction of Bank Erosion in a Reach of the Sacramento River and its Mitigation with Groynes. Water Resour. Manage. 23, 3121–3147 (2009)
5. Architectural Engineering Design Institute, Beijing Iron Works, Integrated ecological regulation project reconnaissance report in NingJiang island project, WuShan county 9 (2007)
6. Chinese National Standards Code for design of levee project(GB50286-98) China planning press (1998)
7. Zhang, Z., Wang, S.: Principles of engineering geological analysis. Geological Press, Beijing (2005)
8. Mittal, S., Garg, K.G., Saran, S.: Analysis and design of retaining wall having reinforced cohesive frictional backfill. Geotechnical and Geological Engineering 24, 499–522 (2006)
9. Li, W.-S., Ding, X.-L., Wu, A.-Q., et al.: Shear strength degeneration of soil and rock mixture in Three Gorges Reservoir bank slopes under influence of impounding. Rock and soil mechanics 28(7), 1338–1342 (2007)

The Research on Lubricating Property of Piston Pin by AVL Excite Designer

Huo Ping[1], He Chuan[1], Li Yuhong[2], and Tian Lvzhu[1]

[1] College of Mechanical Engineering, Hebei United University, Tangshan, China
[2] Tangshan Iron and Steel Group Co, Ltd, Tangshan, China
huoping009@163.com, hechuan2010@yahoo.com.cn

Abstract. This paper uses dynamics analysis software AVL Excite Designer to build a simulation model of the connecting rod small end and proceed the calculations, with the connecting rod small end of a four-cylinder diesel engine as its researching object. Through the calculation and analysis of the oil film pressure between the piston pin and the connecting rod, we can find out the position's weak spots of the lubrication under different rotate speeds. And then it can provide guidance to the design of the engine's small head of the connecting rod and the correct using methods of the engine.

Keywords: engine, connecting rod small end, oil film, lubricating property, piston pin.

1 Introduction

The connecting rod bearing is one of the main friction pair in engine, mainly including the bearing, the connecting rod bearing and the piston pin bearing. The piston pin bearing plays an important role in the engine. The internal-combustion engine change heat energy into kinetic energy. The kinetic energy is transferred to connecting rod through the piston pin. The connecting rod small end running conditions is very bad. The temperature and pressure are very high, and it doesn't have an independent system of lubrication supply. As the engine long time running, the piston pin would be abraded and the gap between bearings would be enlarged. Lubrication conditions would be greatly changed as the engine's long time running. It will reduce the working performance of the engine seriously. So, it is necessary to research on engine and figure out various kinds of factors that affect the lubrication. So the property of engine can be improved.

The simulation model is built up by software AVL Excite Designer, Figure out the regular pattern of the creation of oil film on different rotate speed. Find out the weak link of lubrication.

2 The Lubrication Model of Connecting Rod Small End

The lubrication system of piston pin is splash lubrication, it doesn't has a oil supply system and it also doesn't has a oil filtration system, all the oil is taken by crank to piston pin. The structure chart of cylinder and crank is shown as figure 1.

C. Liu, J. Chang, and A. Yang (Eds.): ICICA 2011, Part I, CCIS 243, pp. 136–141, 2011.

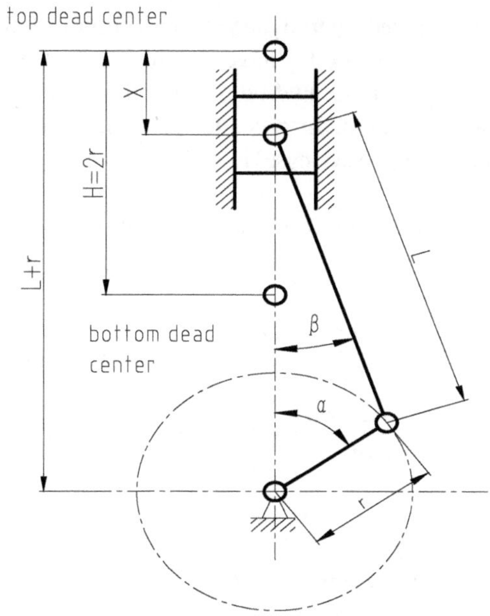

Fig. 1. The structure chart of cylinder and crank

In figure 1: Radius of crank is "r", length of connecting rod is "L", angle of crank is "α", angle of connecting rod is "β".

In the cylinder, there is a piston pin connecting the piston and crank. The temperature and pressure in the cylinder are very high, so the working environment of piston pin is very bad. The structure chart of connecting rod small end and the piston pin are as shown in figure 2.

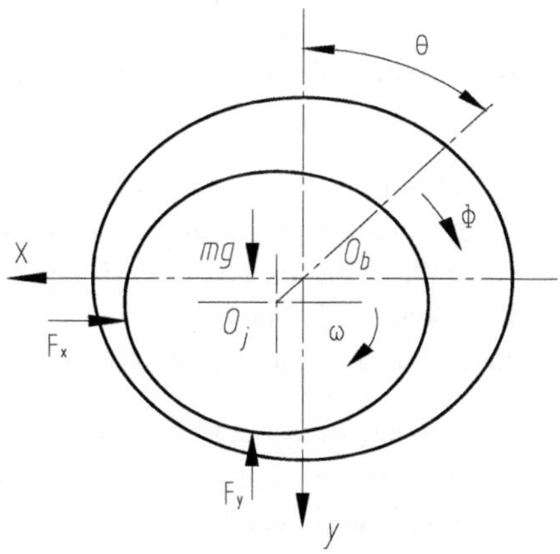

Fig. 2. The structure chart of connecting rod small end and piston pin

The oil lubrication included hydrodynamic lubrication and elastic hydrodynamic lubrication. With the thickness of oil film getting smaller and smaller, hydrodynamic lubrication will change into elastic hydrodynamic lubrication, then turn into part of elastic hydrodynamic lubrication. In order to make the model close to the actual engine, we can make a supposed case that the gap in the bearing is full filled lubricating oil.

The non-dimensional pressure distribution of oil film content with Reynolds equation as (1) and (2).

$$\frac{\partial}{\partial\phi}\left|(1+\varepsilon\cos\phi)^3\frac{\partial\pi}{\partial\phi}\right|+\left(\frac{D}{BR}\right)^2\frac{\partial}{\partial z}\left[(1+\varepsilon\cos\phi)^3\frac{\partial\pi}{\partial z}\right]$$
$$=-6\left|\varepsilon\sin(\phi-\delta)-\frac{2\varepsilon}{\omega^*}\frac{d\delta}{dt}\sin(\phi-\delta)-\frac{2}{\omega^*}-\frac{d\varepsilon}{dt}\cos(\phi-\delta)\right| \quad (1)$$

$$\begin{cases}\varepsilon=\sqrt{z_1^2+z_2^2}\\ \theta=\tan^{-1}(z_1/z_2)\\ \varepsilon'=z_3\sin\theta+z_4\cos\theta\\ \varepsilon\theta'=z_3\sin\theta-z_4\cos\theta\end{cases} \quad (2)$$

The equations shows the correlations of the diameter D, the width BR, the eccentricity ratio ε, the angle of displacement Θ, the engine oil power viscosity μ, the intermittent motion δ, , the rotate speed of shaft neck w* and the pressure of oil film π. The force on piston pin in direct X and Y are Fx and Fy.

3 Built Up the Model of System Dynamics and Oil Film

Make some assumptions for Theoretical Analysis and Calculation of connecting rod small end:

1) The gap in the bearing is full filled lubricating oil.
2) The lubricating oil is Newtonian fluid, it is incompressible.
3) The axis of bearing is parallel with the axis of shaft neck.
4) The bearing and shaft neck are rigid body.
5) The process of lubricating has no temperature variation.

Based on these hypotheses, the model of system dynamics and oil film can be built up. The research of the coupling effect between piston pin and connecting rod small end is just solved the simultaneous equations (1) and (2).

Built up the model with the use of the software AVL Excite Designer like figure 3.

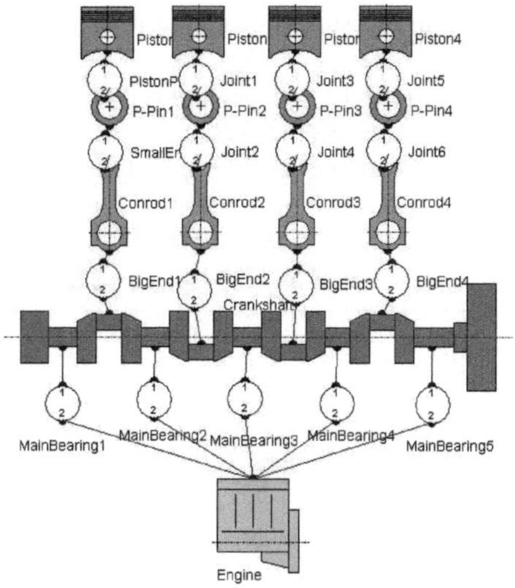

Fig. 3. The model of engine in AVL

At different rotate speeds, the pressures in cylinder are different. Take the different rotate speed in common use:2000r/min, 3000r/min and 4000r/min in the simulation model. The distribution of cylinder pressure at 3000r/min is shown in figure 4. The starting point in figure 4 is the beginning of inlet stroke and the ending point is the end of exhaust stroke.

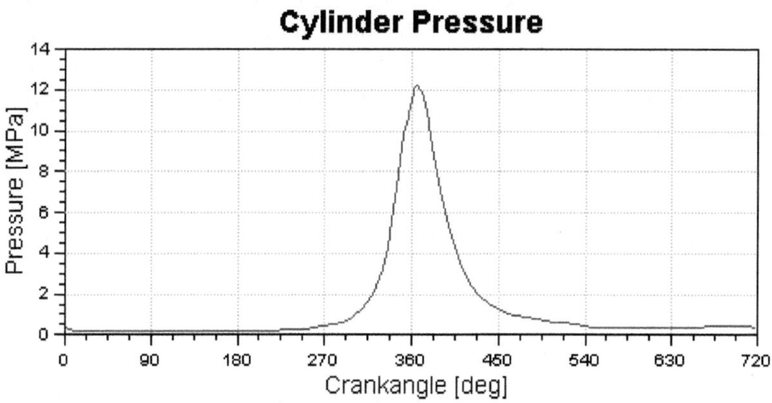

Fig. 4. The cylinder pressure distribution

In the diesel engine, a cylinder has 4 strokes in a working cycle: Inlet stroke, Compression stroke, Expansion stroke, Exhaust stroke. The crank angle in 0°-180° is Inlet stroke, 180°-360°is Compression stroke, 360°-540°is Expansion stroke, 540°-720°is Exhaust stroke. As the figure3 shows, the pressure in inlet stroke and exhaust stroke is very low, the compression stroke and expansion stroke have a very high pressure. The maximum pressure appeared at the end of compression stroke and the beginning of expansion stroke.

The pressure in cylinder transfer to connecting rod through piston pin and the press on piston pin is changed with time. So the pressure distribution of oil film on piston pin is changed with time. At the rotate speed 3000r/min, the pressure distribution on piston pin is showed in figure 5.

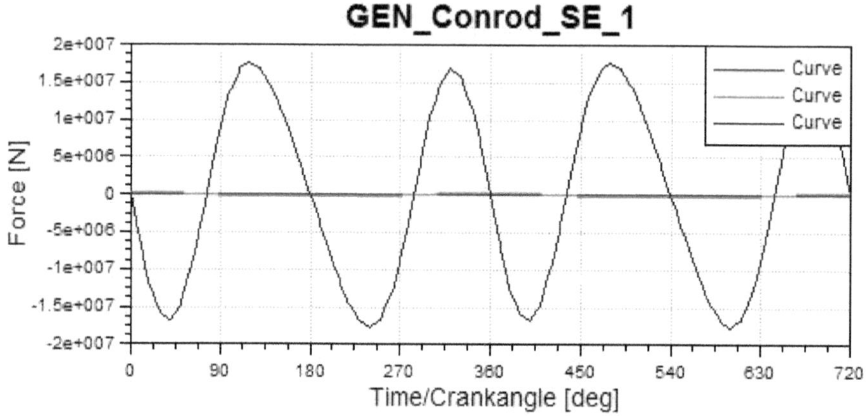

Fig. 5. The pressure distribution on piston pin (or connecting small rod)

Because the model is a four-cylinder diesel engine, the direct of force would change twice in a working cycle in one cylinder. Four piston pins connect to a crank, so the direct of force in one piston pin has changed eight times in a working cycle. By the change of pressure on a piston pin, the thickness of oil film on piston is changed with time. On the basis of calculation principle and computation model, figuring out the thickness of oil film on the bearing of connecting rod small end, the reckoning is showed in figure 6.

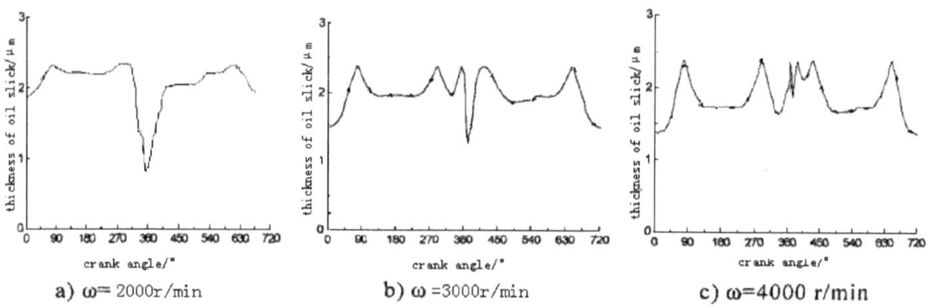

Fig. 6. The minimum thickness of oil film distribution

The starting point in figure 6 is the beginning of inlet stroke and the ending point is the end of exhaust stroke. Compare with figure 4, the position of minimum thickness of oil film is just the maximum cylinder pressure position. Observe these figures as a whole, no matter whether considering the effect of surface roughness, the minimum thickness of oil film is concerned bearing capacity, the thinner oil film the more bearing capacity. At different rotate speeds, the minimum thickness of oil film distribution is different. Compare in the three figures, at 2000r/min, the thickness of oil film mainly more than 1μm, but sometimes less than 1μm. It is under the allowable 1.0μm. At 3000r/min and 4000r/min, the thickness of oil film is more than 1μm. It is shown even in the same engine, at different rotate speeds, the thickness of oil film is different. The minimum thickness of oil film on piston pin increases with the increasing of the rotate speed, so diesel engine must be avoided working in a low speed.

4 Conclusion

1) At different rotate speed, the minimum thickness of oil film on piston pin has a same place. This position is the end of compression stroke, and it is also the acting stroke start. At this moment, the cylinder has the maximum pressure, the piston pin also has the maximum pressure. It makes the pressure of oil film increase and the thickness of oil film decrease. The lubricant performance of oil film becomes worse.
2) When the rotate speed at 2000r/min、 3000r/min or 4000r/min, the pressure distribution and the thickness of oil film distribution are different. The thickness of oil film related to rotate speed. When the crank is at a high rotate speed, the inertia force get higher and the thickness of oil film changes more. When the crank is at a low rotate speed, the inertia force get lower and the change of thickness of oil film is smooth.
3) At different rotate speeds, the thickness of oil film on piston is different. The rotate speed increase, the thickness of oil film increase too. So a diesel engine must be avoided working in a low speed.

References

1. Wang, H.: Study of strength of Diesel Engine Crankshaft and Lubrication on Main Bearing. Dalian Maritime University (2008)
2. Wen, S.: Tribological principle. BeiJing Tsinghua University Press (1990)
3. Xu, W.: Design of automotive engine. BeiJing China Communications Press (2007)
4. Naduvinamani, N.B., Hiremath, P.S.: Surface Roughness Effects in the Short Porous. Journal Bearing with a couple stress Fluid. Fluid Dynamics Research (2002)
5. Ram, T., Sekhar, A.S.: The Effect of Roughness Parameter on the Performance of Hydrodynamic. Journal Bearings with Rough surfaces. Tribology International (1999)
6. Duan, X.: The Research of WD615 Diesel Engine Crankshaft Bearing Lubrication Properties Based on AVL Excite Designer. Internal Combustion Engines (2010)
7. Liang, Z.: The Researching Status and Application Prospect of Remanufacturing Technology for Armored Equipment and Engines. Journal of Academy of Armored Force Engineering (2007)
8. Zhang, J., Zuo, Z., Wang, X., Dong, H.: Analysis of the Performance of Piston Pin Bearing in Mixed Lubrication. Transactions of CS ICE (2010)
9. Xu, B.: Surface engineering and reproduce engineering material protection (2000)
10. Duan, F.: Effect of Elastic Deformation on the Lubrication Performance of Journal Bearing. Lubrication Engineering (2000)

Application of Atmosphere-Environment Quality Assessment Based on Fuzzy Comprehensive Evaluation

Shufei Lin[1], Yongli Zhang[2], and Yanwei Zhu[3]

[1] College of Computer the North University for Ethnics,Yinchuan, China
[2] College of Light industry, Hebei United University,Tangshan, China
[3] Department of Mathematics and Information science
TangshanNormal University Tangshan, China
{linshufei197937,zhyl01,zhyw79}@163.com

Abstract. In this paper, the fuzzy composite appraisal method is used in the atmosphere-environment quality assessment. Take Da Tong as an example, synthesize the received fuzzy information and take the method of maximum subordination principle, make the objective and practical appraisal on the area of atmosphere-environment quality assessment. we can get the effects of all guided pollution factor upon the assessed area, which can provide reliable basis for the environmental planning and management.

Keyword: atmosphere-environment quality, fuzzy composite appraisal method, subordinate function.

1 Introduction

Atmospheric environmental pollution is one of the urban environment problems, which has called increasingly attention of the public people. Making an objective and composite appraisal on the Atmosphere-environment Quality based on the practical monitoring results have a great significance to have a correct understanding of atmospheric environmental pollution situation, thus conduct the effectively controlling and management on the pollution. In the working of environmental quality assessment, fuzzy mathematics has been used more and more widely. The fuzzy mathematics method is one of the calculations of the atmospheric quality synthetic appraisal index [1][2]. It cites the fuzzy matrix composite operation method which has three processes. Firstly, this method evaluates each single parameter. Then, it considers the status of various parameters in general and matches the parameters with appropriate weight. Lastly, we can obtain the comprehensive assessment results by reutilization of the fuzzy concept and the fuzzy matrix composite calculation. We can take an example of Da Tong for the urban atmospheric-environment quality appraisal. So it can present us the level of atmospheric environment quality based on the fuzzy mathematics maximum subjection principle[3] [4].

2 Fuzzy Composite Appraisal Method

In 1956, automatic control expert L.A.Z at the University of California published the famous paper named fuzzy sets, marking the birth of fuzzy mathematics. Fuzzy

C. Liu, J. Chang, and A. Yang (Eds.): ICICA 2011, Part I, CCIS 243, pp. 142–149, 2011.

mathematics is to research and deal with the fuzzy phenomena with quantitative method.

As a branch of fuzzy mathematics, Fuzzy composite appraisal method has been widely used in many fields. Although still exists the phenomenon of improper selection model, but you should believe, with the gradually understanding of its efficacy, it can bring convenience to solve the related problems. Meanwhile no other branches of mathematics and model can replace it.

Composite appraisal, also known as the so-called multi-objective decision making, is overall to evaluate things or phenomena affected by many factors refers. If these fuzzy factors involved in the appraisal process, this appraisal process will be called fuzzy composite appraisal[5][6].

2.1 Establish Factor Set

Various factors to affect the appraisal object are called the set of factors .That set is a common set, expressed by S: $S=\{S_1,S_2, \ldots,S_n\}$.

2.2 Establish the Appraisal Set

Appraisal set is the kind of set which is total collection of various appraisal results. It uses the T to express the set: $T=\{T_1,T_2, \ldots,T_n\}$.

2.3 Single-Factor Fuzzy Composite Appraisal

Starting from a single appraisal factor to determine that the subordination degree to appraisal set T of appraisal objects is called the single factor fuzzy appraisal. $\underset{\sim}{R}_i$ is called a single factor appraisal set, can be simplified to

$$\underset{\sim}{R}_i = (r_{i1}, r_{i2}, \cdots, r_{in}) \quad (1)$$

In the of matrix

$$\underset{\sim}{R} = \begin{bmatrix} \underset{\sim}{R}_1 \\ \underset{\sim}{R}_2 \\ \vdots \\ \underset{\sim}{R}_m \end{bmatrix} = \begin{bmatrix} r_{11} & r_{12} & \cdots & r_{1n} \\ r_{21} & r_{22} & \cdots & r_{2n} \\ \vdots & \vdots & & \vdots \\ r_{m1} & r_{m2} & \cdots & r_{mn} \end{bmatrix} \quad (2)$$

This matrix is called a single factor appraisal matrix.

2.4 Fuzzy Composite Appraisal

Single-factor fuzzy composite appraisal, just reflects the impact of a factor on the appraisal object, it is not complete. The purpose of appraisal is to take the influence of all factors into account, to obtain more reasonable appraisal result, the result is fuzzy composite appraisal will be carried out [7][8].

$\underset{\sim}{S_i}$ consisted in the set of factors $\underset{\sim}{S}$ can also be divided into $\underset{\sim}{S_i}=\{S_{i1},S_{i2},\ldots,S_{ik}\}$ (i=1,2, …,n), that is to say, there are ki factors in $\underset{\sim}{S_i}$ .Let $\underset{\sim}{A_i}$ is the importance of factors of the fuzzy set $\underset{\sim}{S_i}$, $\underset{\sim}{R_i}$ is to overall appraisal of ki factors in $\underset{\sim}{S_i}$, according to the initial model $M(\wedge,\vee)$for a preliminary composite appraisal, we can get

$$\underset{\sim}{A_i}\circ\underset{\sim}{R_i}=\underset{\sim}{B_i}=(\text{bi1bi2}\ldots\text{bin})(\text{i}=12\ldots\text{n}) \tag{3}$$

Where $\underset{\sim}{B_i}$ is the single-factor appraisal of $\underset{\sim}{S_i}$. Again let $\underset{\sim}{S_i}=\{S_1,S_2,\ldots,S_n\}$, $\underset{\sim}{A}$ is the importance of factors of the fuzzy set $\underset{\sim}{S}$,then, matrix $\underset{\sim}{B}$ is the overall appraisal of $\underset{\sim}{S}$:

$$\underset{\sim}{B}=\begin{bmatrix}\underset{\sim}{B_1}\\ \underset{\sim}{B_2}\\ \vdots\\ \underset{\sim}{B_n}\end{bmatrix}=\begin{bmatrix}\underset{\sim}{A_1}\circ\underset{\sim}{R_1}\\ \underset{\sim}{A_2}\circ\underset{\sim}{R_2}\\ \vdots\\ \underset{\sim}{A_n}\circ\underset{\sim}{R_n}\end{bmatrix} \tag{4}$$

So we get the results of composite appraisal II: $\underset{\sim}{Z}=\underset{\sim}{A}\circ\underset{\sim}{B}$

Take fuzzy relations $\underset{\sim}{R_i}$ (i=1,2,3,4) and $\underset{\sim}{B}$ as "fuzzy converter", while $\underset{\sim}{A_i}$ (i=1,2,3,4) and $\underset{\sim}{A}$ are the primary input and secondary input respectively, then $\underset{\sim}{B_i}$ (i=1,2,3,4) and $\underset{\sim}{Z}$ are the primary output and secondary output respectively [9][10].

3 Application

After the collection and collation of data for Da Tong city on the atmospheric environment, taking four air pollutants as appraisal factors, taking the factor set as $U=\{SO_2,TSP,NO_x,CO\}$ .Taking appraisal set as $V=\{\text{I},\text{II},\text{III},\text{IV}\}$,respectively refers to {clean, clear polluted, moderately polluted, seriously polluted}.Criteria used in the appraisal are listed in table 1:

Table 1. Appraisal criteria mg/m^3

object	I	II	III	IV
SO_2	0.05	0.15	0.25	0.50
TSP	0.12	0.30	0.50	1.00
NO_x	0.05	0.10	0.15	0.30
CO	4.00	5.00	6.00	10.00

3.1 Determinate Subordination Function and Distribution Graph

According to the every level standard at grading system to establish subordination function corresponding to different levels for each appraisal factor, make a combination of the actual situation of atmosphere-environment quality assessment in Da Tong city, then choose the more simple distribution of lower semi-trapezoid. The function distribution is shown in Figure 1.

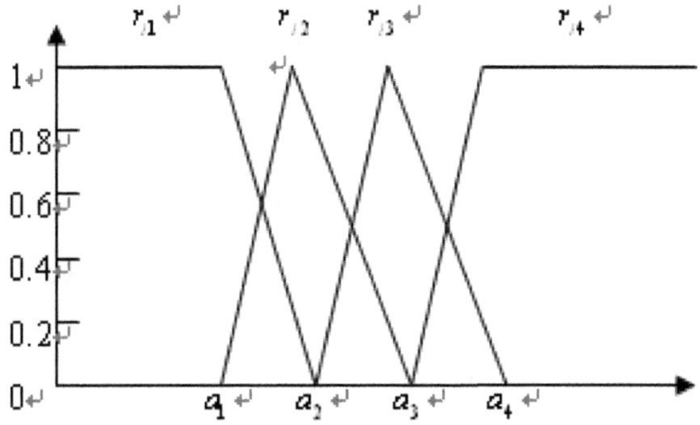

Fig. 1. Lower semi-trapezoid function distribution

The subordination function of the air quality for SO_2

$$U(x)_1=\begin{cases}1 & x\le 0.05\\ 10(0.15-x) & 0.05\le x\le 0.15\\ 0 & x\ge 0.15\end{cases},\quad U(x)_2=\begin{cases}10(x-0.05) & 0.05\le x\le 0.15\\ 10(0.25-x) & 0.15\le x\le 0.25\\ 0 & x\le 0.05, x\ge 0.25\end{cases}$$

$$U(x)_3=\begin{cases}10(x-0.15) & 0.15\le x\le 0.25\\ 4(0.5-x) & 0.25\le x\le 0.5\\ 0 & x\le 0.15, x\ge 0.5\end{cases},\quad U(x)_4=\begin{cases}4(x-0.25) & 0.25\le x\le 0.5\\ 1 & x\ge 0.5\\ 0 & x\le 0.25\end{cases}$$

The subordination function of the air quality for *TSP*

$$U(x)_1=\begin{cases}1 & x\le 0.15\\ \dfrac{20(0.3-x)}{3} & 0.15\le x\le 0.3\\ 0 & x\ge 0.3\end{cases},\quad U(x)_2=\begin{cases}\dfrac{20(x-0.15)}{3} & 0.15\le x\le 0.3\\ 5(0.5-x) & 0.3\le x\le 0.5\\ 0 & x\le 0.15, x\ge 1\end{cases}$$

$$U(x)_3=\begin{cases}5(x-0.3) & 0.3\le x\le 0.5\\ 2(1-x) & 0.5\le x\le 1\\ 0 & x\le 0.3, x\ge 1\end{cases},\quad U(x)_4=\begin{cases}2(x-0.5) & 0.5\le x\le 1\\ 1 & x\ge 1\\ 0 & x\le 0.5\end{cases}$$

The subordination function of the air quality for NO_x

$$U(x)_1 = \begin{cases} 1 & x \le 0.05 \\ 20(0.1-x) & 0.05 \le x \le 0.1 \\ 0 & x \ge 0.1 \end{cases}, \quad U(x)_2 = \begin{cases} 20(x-0.05) & 0.05 \le x \le 0.1 \\ 20(0.15-x) & 0.1 \le x \le 0.15 \\ 0 & x \le 0.05, x \ge 0.15 \end{cases}$$

$$U(x)_3 = \begin{cases} 20(x-0.1) & 0.1 \le x \le 0.15 \\ \dfrac{20(0.3-x)}{3} & 0.15 \le x \le 0.3 \\ 0 & x \le 0.1, x \ge 0.3 \end{cases}, \quad U(x)_4 = \begin{cases} \dfrac{20(x-0.15)}{3} & 0.15 \le x \le 0.3 \\ 1 & x \ge 0.3 \\ 0 & x \le 0.15 \end{cases}$$

The subordination function of the air quality for CO

$$U(x)_1 = \begin{cases} 1 & x \le 4 \\ 5-x & 4 \le x \le 5 \\ 0 & x \ge 5 \end{cases}, \quad U(x)_2 = \begin{cases} x-4 & 4 \le x \le 5 \\ 6-x & 5 \le x \le 6 \\ 0 & x \le 4, x \ge 6 \end{cases}$$

$$U(x)_3 = \begin{cases} x-5 & 5 \le x \le 6 \\ \dfrac{10-x}{4} & 6 \le x \le 10 \\ 0 & x \le 5, x \ge 10 \end{cases}, \quad U(x)_4 = \begin{cases} \dfrac{x-6}{4} & 6 \le x \le 10 \\ 1 & x \ge 10 \\ 0 & x \le 6 \end{cases}$$

3.2 Calculate the Subordination Degree of All the Parameters

According to subordination function and the real measured value *X*, respectively to calculate the subordination degree u_i to atmosphere-environment quality of I, II, III, IV for the individual components, to measure each individual index so that to evaluate results on subordination degree. We can make a fuzzy matrix by the subordination degree r_{ij}. Its expression is:

$$\underset{\sim}{R} = \begin{bmatrix} r_{11} & r_{12} & \cdots & r_{1n} \\ r_{21} & r_{22} & \cdots & r_{2n} \\ \cdots & \cdots & & \cdots \\ r_{m1} & r_{m2} & \cdots & r_{mn} \end{bmatrix} = (r_{ij})_{m \times n} = \begin{bmatrix} 0.5 & 0.5 & 0 & 0 \\ 0 & 0.25 & 0.75 & 0 \\ 0 & 0 & 0.83 & 0.17 \\ 0 & 0 & 0.30 & 0.70 \end{bmatrix} \tag{5}$$

3.3 Determinate the Weight Row Matrix $\underset{\sim}{A}$

Many methods to empower in fuzzy composite appraisal can be divided into two types, which are the standard weighting method and the main factors highlighted weighting method. For standard weighting method, because of only considering the difference in appraisal criteria, often produces absurd conclusion. Excessive multiples method is a main factor highlighted weighting method, but different weights are defined so that the appraisal is also vary greatly. Due to the extent that the appraisal factors impact on atmosphere-environment varies in size, this is also a vague phenomenon. The appraisal factors may be given a certain weights, to establish the fuzzy relationship $\underset{\sim}{A}$ between them. The model uses excessive multiple weighting method and normalizes the weights, this can highlight the role of the major pollutants in atmosphere-environmental quality assessment; also take the differences in standard values of different pollutants into account. The calculation is simple, the formula is:

$$W_i = \frac{x_i}{s_i} \quad \overline{W}_i = \frac{W_i}{\sum_{i=1}^{n} W_i} \quad s_i = \frac{1}{m}\sum_{i=j}^{m} s_{ij} \tag{6}$$

Where: W_i means the weight of the ith appraisal factor;

x_i means the measured daily average concentration of the ith appraisal factor;

s_i means the mathematical average of concentration standards at all levels of the ith appraisal factor;

$\overline{W}_i$ means the weight value of the ith normalized appraisal factor;

s_{ij} means the standard concentration of ith appraisal factor and j- level air quality;

n means the number of the appraisal factors;

m means the level of air quality classification;

In accordance with the formula above, the weight of all the appraisal factors of the atmospheric-environmental quality in Da Tong city is calculating. See table 2.

Table 2. The weight value of all the appraisal factors of the atmospheric-environmental quality in Da Tong city

object	SO_2	TSP	NO_x	CO
x_i	0.1	0.45	0.175	8.8
s_i	0.2375	0.4875	0.15	6.25
W_i	0.421	0.923	1.167	1.408
$\overline{W}_i$	0.107	0.236	0.298	0.359

The appraisal factors above form a weight row matrix $\underset{\sim}{A}$:

$$\underset{\sim}{A} = (\overline{W}_1,\overline{W}_2,\overline{W}_3,\overline{W}_4) = (0.1070.2360.2980.359) \tag{7}$$

3.4 Composite Calculation of Fuzzy Matrix

On the basis of obtaining two fuzzy matrix $\underset{\sim}{A}$ and $\underset{\sim}{R}$, make fuzzy matrix composite calculation between $\underset{\sim}{A}$ and $\underset{\sim}{R}$, we can get fuzzy composite appraisal results, which indicates atmospheric-environmental quality corresponding to different subordination degree at different levels of V set.

$$\underset{\sim}{B} = \underset{\sim}{A} \circ \underset{\sim}{R}, b_j = \bigvee_{i=1}^{n} (a_i \wedge r_{ij}) \quad j = 1, 2, \cdots, n$$

$$\underset{\sim}{B} = (\overline{W}_1, \overline{W}_2, \cdots, \overline{W}_4) \begin{bmatrix} r_{11}\ r_{12} \cdots r_{14} \\ r_{21}\ r_{22} \cdots r_{24} \\ \cdots\cdots \quad \cdots \\ r_{41}\ r_{42} \cdots r_{44} \end{bmatrix} = (b_1, b_2, b_3, b_4) \tag{8}$$

3.5 Fuzzy Composite Appraisal

When composite calculation uses the maximum and minimum method, elements of matrix $\underset{\sim}{A}$ and, respectively, correspond to elements of matrix $\underset{\sim}{R}$ in each column, in the way of taking small and then large, finally get the results.

$$\underset{\sim}{B} = \underset{\sim}{A} \circ \underset{\sim}{R} = [0.1070.2360.2980.359] \begin{bmatrix} 0.5 & 0.5 & 0 & 0 \\ 0 & 0.25 & 0.75 & 0 \\ 0 & 0 & 0.83 & 0.17 \\ 0 & 0 & 0.30 & 0.70 \end{bmatrix} \tag{9}$$

$$\begin{aligned} &= [(0.107 \wedge 0.5) \vee (0.236 \wedge 0) \vee (0.298 \wedge 0) \vee (0.359 \wedge 0) \\ &\quad [(0.107 \wedge 0.5) \vee (0.236 \wedge 0.25) \vee (0.298 \wedge 0) \vee (0.359 \wedge 0)] \\ &\quad [(0.107 \wedge 0) \vee (0.236 \wedge 0.75) \vee (0.298 \wedge 0.83) \vee (0.359 \wedge 0.30)] \\ &\quad [(0.107 \wedge 0) \vee (0.236 \wedge 0) \vee (0.298 \wedge 0.17) \vee (0.359 \wedge 0.70)]\} \\ &= [0.107\ 0.236\ 0.30\ 0.359] \\ \Sigma &= 1.002 \end{aligned}$$

Normalize the results, we have: $\underset{\sim}{B} = [0.107\ 0.236\ 0.299\ 0.358]$, $\Sigma = 1$

According to the maximum subordination principle, we take the biggest value from b_1, b_2, b_3, b_4. The level of corresponding appraisal set V is the fuzzy composite appraisal results of atmospheric-environmental quality assessment .We can know that b_4 is the biggest, so the appraisal of the level of this grade Ⅳ atmospheric-environmental quality is a serious pollution, the appraisal results are consistent with the actual situation.

4 Conclusions

This paper uses the fuzzy composite appraisal to assess the atmospheric-environment quality. Because the use of lower semi-trapezoidal subordination function and excessive multiple weighting method, it not only highlights the role of major pollutants, but also takes differences in standard values of different pollutants into account. Fuzzy subordination functions are used to describe atmospheric-environment quality in the fuzzy mathematics, this method reflects the ambiguity of the actual boundaries, makes the appraisal closer to the objective reality. Factor choice highlights the main factors, while no considering or less considering other secondary factors which could reflect the objective reality, also simplify the calculation. Fuzzy mathematics takes a large value, it is a "highlight the main factors" without regarding to other secondary factors, and the correct method of weight selection is simple and easy to master. The obtained appraisal results are basically consistent with the actual.

References

1. Li, C., Chen, Y., Zhang, H.: The application of the fuzzy comprehensive evaluation on the mine geologic enviroment evaluation. ShanXi Architecture (2), 44–46 (2011) (in Chinese)
2. Wang, M., Wang, D., Yang, X.: Aeroengine Performance Monitoring Based on Improved Fuzzy Synthetic Evaluation. Lubrication Engineering (1), 80–84 (2011) (in Chinese)
3. Xie, J.: Application of Fuzzy Synthesis Evaluation on Electronic Countermeasure Decision-making System. Radio Engineering (3), 49–52 (2011) (in Chinese)
4. Chen, N., Chen, H., Jin, H.: Model for Survivability in Mobile Communication Network. Designing Techniques of Posts and Telecommunications (3), 35–39 (2011) (in Chinese)
5. Cheng, S., Cheng, Y.: Design and Implementation of Universal Simulation Software for Fuzzy Comprehensive Judgement. Computer Engineering (3), 51–54 (2010) (in Chinese)
6. Li, D., Li, Y., Li, F.: Short-term Prediction and Warning of Regional Atmospheric Environment Quality by Artificial. Construction and Design for Project (7), 74–77 (2010) (in Chinese)
7. Zhang, H., Sun, S.: Quality Evaluation Model of Atmospheric Environment Based on BP Neural Network. Journal of Anhui Agricultural Sciences (31), 17657–17664 (2010) (in Chinese)
8. Zhu, X., Li, X.: Application of Correspondence Analysis Method in City Atmosphere Enviroment Quality Assessment. Journal of DaLian JiaoTong University (2), 89–94 (2010) (in Chinese)
9. Han, X., Zhang, G., Liu, Y.: Study and Application of General Tool of Fuzzy Comperhensive Evaluation. Computer Appliaction and Software (2), 188–190 (2010) (in Chinese)
10. Yang, W.: Environment Quality Assessment by Fuzzy Mathematics Method. Journal of WuHan University of Technology (12), 47–50 (2001) (in Chinese)

Numerical Simulation of Low-Speed Combustion Using OpenFOAM on Multi-core Cluster Systems

Liu Zhi-qin, Sun Zhao-guo, Chen Hao-nan, and Liu Tao

School of Computer Science and Technology, Southwest University of Science and Technology. Mianyang, Sichuan, 621010, China
lzq@swust.edu.cn

Abstract. This paper researched and developed a numerical simulation system of combustion flow on multi-core cluster systems and then a low-speed combustion solver was designed based on turbulent combustion model. In order to test the system and the solver, H2/O2 premixed combustion case was simulated using the solver. The simulation result indicated that this numerical simulation system was feasible and the low-speed combustion solver was highly accurate. At the same time, the computing time can be accelerated compared to sequential computing after using parallel computing technology.

Keywords: Numerical Simulation, Combustion Flow, Low-speed, Parallel Computing.

1 Introduction

Computational fluid dynamic (CFD) is a subject using numerical simulation methods to solve fluid flow problems[1]. Numerical simulation of combustion flow is one of the applications of CFD, and the low-speed combustion plays an important role in the applications of combustion field. At present, researchers focus the main work on the combustion experiment research, carrying out the investigation of numerical simulation is not only an important significance for investigating for the reaction mechanism but also a valuable tool and method for the comparative analysis with the experiment results.

The purpose of present work researched the numerical simulation of low-speed combustion and explored the applications of open software for the computational fluid dynamic.

2 System Architecture and Components

Figure 1 presents the architecture diagram of the numerical simulation system for low-speed combustion. It shows that the system is made use of OpenFOAM platform, and the design of the solve for low-speed combustion is based on the low-speed combustion models, while the combustion chamber mesh is using mesh software such as Gridgen and BlockMesh, then partition the mesh into several sub-domains based

C. Liu, J. Chang, and A. Yang (Eds.): ICICA 2011, Part I, CCIS 243, pp. 150–157, 2011.

on domain decomposition algorithm and assign the sub-domains to the corresponding computation nodes. In the end, we simulate the low-speed combustion on the parallel computing platform which was built based on MPI[2].

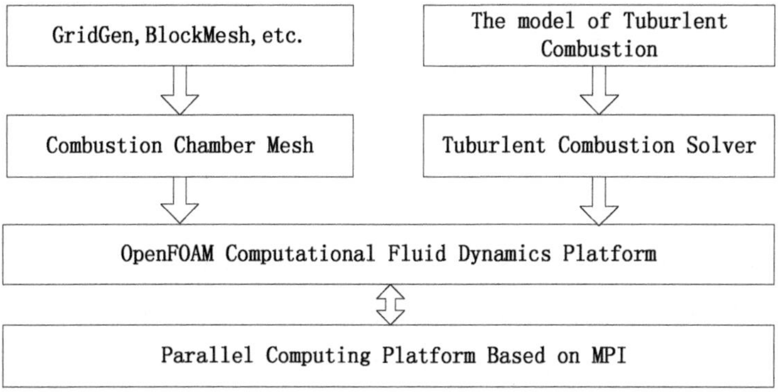

Fig. 1. This shows the framework of the numerical simulation system for combustion flow

3 Design and Implementation

3.1 The OpenFOAM CFD Tool

This chapter will give a main introduction of OpenFOAM CFD Tool. The simulation platform is based on the OpenFOAM CFD tool. "OpenFOAM is an established object-oriented library for Computational Continuum Mechanics, with emphasis on CFD. It implements physical models of fluid flow, structural analysis, heat and mass transfer using equation mimicking"[3].

OpenFOAM whose core is a flexible set of C++ written modules is an open source software, we can get its codes from internet. They are used to build solvers, to simulate specific problem in engineering mechanics. Domain decomposition parallelism is fundamental to the design of OpenFOAM and integrated at a low level so that solvers can generally be developed without the need for any "parallel-specific" coding[4].The structure of OpenFOAM can be seen in Figure 2 as follows, it has pre-processing, solving and post-processing three parts.

3.2 Combustion Model

In premixed combustion, the low-speed flow of the reactants and chemical reaction process interrelated and influence each other, low-speed flow component concentration and temperature fluctuations can enhance mixing and heat transfer components, thus affecting the average chemical reaction rate, chemical rapid exothermic reaction exothermic process caused by density variations, while the fluid transport coefficients, thereby affecting the process of low-speed flow. This interrelated and influence each other makes the combustion reaction is extremely complex. Please do not set running heads or page numbers. In this paper we use $k-\varepsilon$ turbulent model as the combustion the numerical simulation model.

$k-\varepsilon$ turbulent model, for general situations, such as flat-wall boundary layer, weak jet plane, both pipe flow and other flow process model can give very satisfactory results[5]. $k-\varepsilon$ turbulent model is as follows:

$$\rho\frac{Dk}{Dt}=\frac{\partial}{\partial x_i}\left[\left(\mu+\frac{\mu_t}{\sigma_k}\right)\frac{\partial k}{\partial x_i}\right]+G_k+G_b-\rho\varepsilon-Y_M \tag{1}$$

$$\rho\frac{D\varepsilon}{Dt}=\frac{\partial}{\partial x_i}\left[\left(\mu+\frac{\mu_t}{\sigma_k}\right)\frac{\partial \varepsilon}{\partial x_i}\right]+C_{1\varepsilon}\frac{\varepsilon}{k}(G_k+C_{3\varepsilon}G_b)-C_{2\varepsilon}\rho\frac{\varepsilon^2}{k} \tag{2}$$

In the equation, G_k expressed as the average velocity gradient caused by the low-speed kinetic energy, G_b is used for buoyancy effects caused by the low-speed kinetic energy; Y_M is compressible velocity low-speed fluctuation expansion of the total dissipation rate. Low-speed viscosity is $\mu_t=\rho C_\mu\frac{k^2}{\varepsilon}$.

In addition, during the chemical reaction model we used the kinetic reaction model of chemical libraries Cantera[6]. The H_2/O_2 combustion chemical reaction mechanism involves 9 components and 27 reactions.

The computational domain was discredited using finite volume method. In the combustion case, the transient term(ddt) was computed using LU-SGS implicit iteration method. The convection term(div) was computed using second-order upwind, difference of Gaussian scheme. The diffusion term(laplacian) was computed using second-order linear modified, difference of Gaussian scheme. In this paper, H_2/O_2 premixed combustion reactor was steady and compressible flow, so SIMPLE (Semi-Implicit Method for Pressure-Linked Equations)[7] algorithm was used to solve the equations.

3.3 Low-Speed Combustion Solver

At first, we installed OpenFOAM on the Linux operating system; the solver consists of make directories, header files and the main program. The make directory includes option and file. Option defines the compilation files to specify the location of header files which are used for compilation and dynamic link libraries. Header is used to pre-compiling the main program called lowFoam.C, mainly including hEqn.H, pEqn.H, UEqn.H, YEqn.H and other documents. Figure 2 is the composition diagram of the solver.

3.4 Parallel Computing Platform

It requires a large number of grids to get the details of the combustion chamber flow configuration, for example, the grid of our numerical computation is 10 000, serial running is not competent to the computation scale obviously, we need only through parallel running in order to meet research requirements.

Make	4.0 KB
chemistry.H	903 B
convergenceCheck.H	396 B
createFields.H	2.6 KB
hEqn.H	852 B
initConvergenceCheck.H	362 B
pEqn.H	1.3 KB
readChemistryProperties.H	2.7 KB
UEqn.H	509 B
YEqn.H	4.6 KB
lowFoam.C	3.2 KB
lowFoam.dep	50.2 KB

Fig. 2. This shows the composition diagram of the low-speed combustion solver. The main file is lowFoam.C, which consists the important steps of the program. hEqn.H, pEqn.H, UEqn.H, YEqn.H four files are the equations which will be used in the lowFoam.C file.

Our parallel programs used message passing model. Message passing parallel programs have two kinds which are called function decomposition and domain decomposition respectively. The principle of function decomposition is dividing a big problem into several sub-problems and then solves them particularly; domain decomposition is decomposing the computation domain into several smaller domains. In this paper we used domain decomposition methods, that decomposing domain into several small domains using partitioning algorithm[8], and then computed the small domains using the message passing library for information exchange.

The parallel programming language based on message passing parallel programming model has two kinds, one is called MPI and the other is PVM. At present, MPI is more popular than PVM because of its prominent advantage which can be found in [9]. We used OpenMPI[10] as the parallel programming which is one of the open source implementation of MPI.

The parallel computing platform, including eight PCs, configuration environments are INTEL P4 3.0G CPU, 512MB RAM, 80G hard drive and 100 Mb/s network adapter. Multi-core cluster system is formed by eight PCs and a local area network twisted-pair and switch. One machine is the master node, which is responsible for assigning allocation and process management, the other seven units is responsible for the calculation.

4 The Studied Case

4.1 Initial Conditions and Boundary Conditions

When the platform for numerical simulation of low-speed combustion was built successfully, the H_2/O_2 premixed combustion case was simulated with the platform on a specific combustion chamber mesh. Figure 5 is the configuration sketch of the combustion chamber mesh, whose length is 1 m and width is 0.1 m. The size of the mesh which was used 100 000 cells for the periodic runner computations. The boundary condition of the left is inlet, which will be injected H_2, O_2 and Ar. The boundary condition of the right is outlet. When the reaction started, the combustion chamber was filled with H_2O. The specific boundary conditions and initial conditions referred to Table 1.

Table 1. The bundary conditions and initial conditions of the combustion flow fiel

BC	Inlet	InternalField
T(K)	1600	1600
V(m/s)	1	-
P(bar)	101325	101325
H_2	0.009	0
O_2	0.026	0
Ar	0.965	0
H_2O	0	1

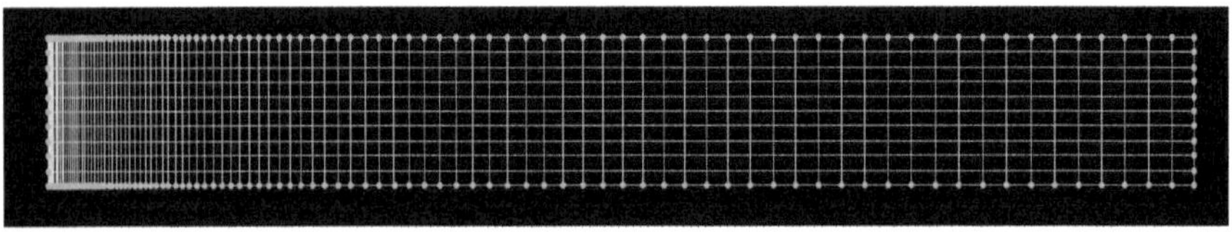

Fig. 3. This shows the configuration sketch of combustion chamber whose number of mesh is 10 000

4.2 Computations and Results

In the computation phase, the fuels were injected into the combustion chamber with 1 m/s velocity. After a period of computation the reacting was stability. Figure 4 presents the mass distribution of H_2O when the combustion began and Figure 5 presents the state of combustion chamber when it was steady. The figures demonstrated that when the combustion began, the head of the flame was filled with the H_2O. The export was full of the product H_2O. The simulation figures can show better response about the characteristics of low-speed combustion flows.

Temperature is the most important contrast in numerical research stage. Our simulation results would be compared with the obtained results of Chemkin software at the same conditions. Chemkin[11] is a large chemical kinetics software package which is developed by the U.S. Sandia laboratory. At present, Chemkin software is widely used in numerical simulation of combustion because of its reasonable structure, good reliability and it is easily to be transplanted. Figure 6 is the contrast of the result computed by our solver and results obtained by Chemkin and Chemapp respectively. It can be seen from the figure that changing trend of the temperature and the maximum of temperature obtained by our result is the same and the results obtained by Chemkin and Chemapp approximately. The initial temperature of the reaction is 1600.0K, when it is stable the maximum is 2181.2K. But at the beginning of the reaction the temperature is a little high than the curve of Chemkin, indicating that the solver should be further improved, in order to obtain better simulation results.

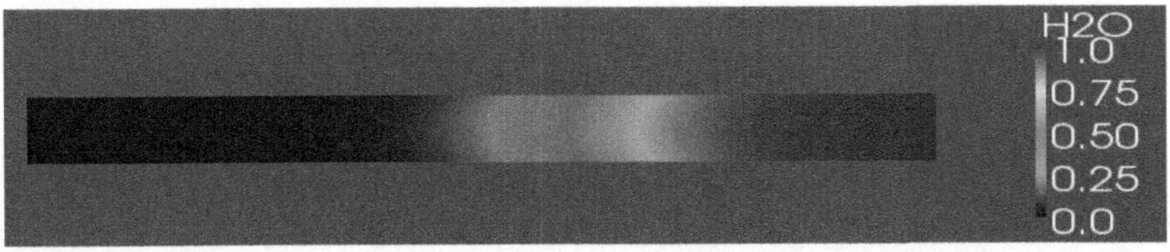

Fig. 4. This presents the configuration sketch of reacting state, the mass of H_2O changes radically and rapidly

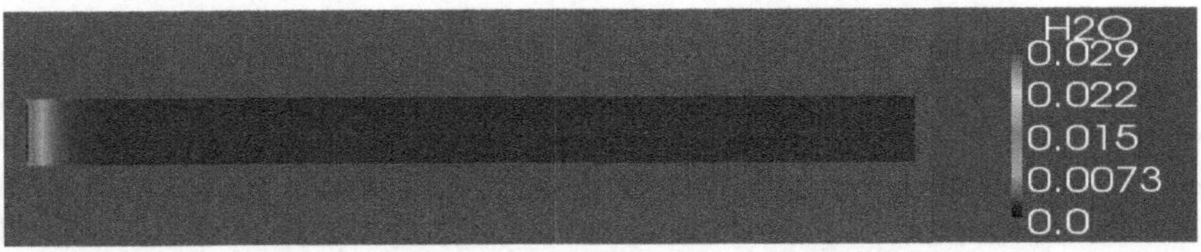

Fig. 5. This shows the configuration sketch of reacting state when the reactor was completed and steady, the chamber is full of H_2O

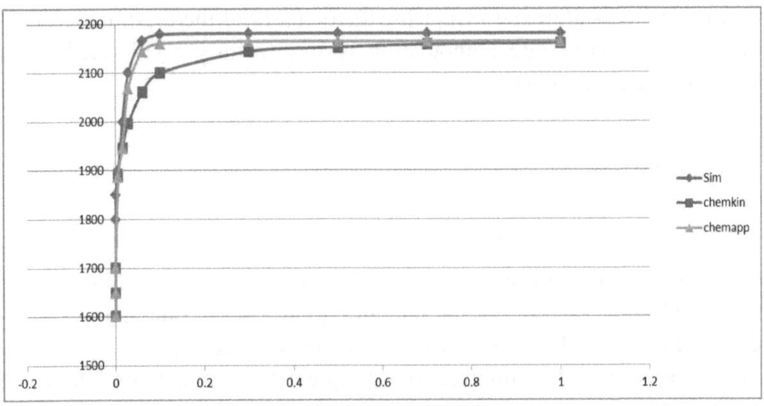

Fig. 6. The three lines shows the temperature contrast of combustion effects. The blue line is the result computed by the low-speed solver, the red and green line is the computed results by Chemkin and Chemapp at the same conditions.

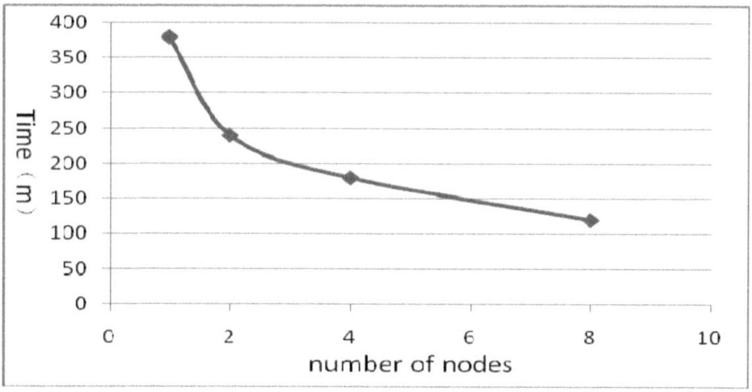

Fig. 7. This shows the accelerating effect of parallel computing. The vertical axis is the computing time consumed and the lateral axis is the number of the computing nodes.

5 Parallel Performance

Before computation, we should partition the mesh of the combustion chamber into sub-domains and assign sub-domains to each node respectively with their initial information, then start the computing process in the master node, this process will build several parallel computing sub-process in each nodes. Figure 7 shows the parallel computing time consumed using the parallel computing platform. When the number of the computing nodes increased, the computing time consumed decreased, the serial computation has consumed 380 minutes, in contrast the time consumed one twice than serial computation when partitioned two domains. When the number of nodes were increased the consumed rate become slowness. We should improve the mesh partitioning algorithm and increasing the quantity of the mesh in order to get the better results. In a word, the computation is significantly accelerated when using parallel computing technology.

6 Conclusions

According to the experiment, there are three conclusions as follows:

(1) We have designed solver for low-speed combustion using turbulent combustion model and built the numerical simulation platform of combustion system based on OpenFOAM toolbox and parallel computing successfully.
(2) Using the system to simulate H2/O2 premixed combustion under the grid environment in a particular combustion chamber, the results can show better response about the characteristics of low speed combustion flows.
(3) The computation can be accelerated after using parallel computing technology, which is good for large-scale numerical simulation works.

References

1. Abbott, M.B., Basco, D.R.: Computational Fluid Dynamics – An Introduction for Engineers. Longman Scientific & Technical, Harlow, England (1989)
2. The message passing interface (MPI) standard (2011), `http://www.mcs.anl.gov/research/projects/mpi/`
3. Jasak, H., Beaudoin, M.: OpenFOAM Tubro Tools: From General Purpose CFD to Turbomachinery Simulations. In: Proceedings of ASME-JSME-KSME Joint Fluids Engineering Conference (AJK2011-FED) (2011)
4. Nielsen, N.E.L.: Numerical investigation of a BFR using OpenFOAM. Fluids and Combustion Engineering (2008)
5. Tao, W.-Q.: Numerical Heat Transfer, 2nd edn. XI'AN Jiaotong University Press, Xi'an (2008)
6. Goodwin, D.G.: Cantera: Object-oriented software for reacting flows. Technical report, California Institute of Technology (2002)
7. Moulalled, F., Darwish, M.: A unified formulation of the staggered class of algorithms for fluid flow at all speeds. Numerical Heat transfer B 37, 103–139 (2000)
8. Kaiypis, G., Kumar, V.: METISA: Software Package for Partitioning Unstructured Graphs, Partitioning Meshes, and Computing Fill-Reducing Orderings of Sparse Matrices,Version 4.0, University of Minnesota, Department of Computer Science/Army HPC Research Center (1998)
9. Rabenseifner, G.J.R., Hager, G.: Hybrid MPI/OpenMP parallel programming on clusters of multi-core SMP nodes. In: 2009 Parallel, Distributed and Network-based Processing (2009)
10. OpenMPI: Open Source High Performance Computing, `http://www.open-mpi.org/,2011`
11. Kee, R.J., Rupley, F.M., Miller, J.A.: CHEMKIN Release 4.1.1. Reaction Design, San Diego, CA (2007)

AntiMalDroid: An Efficient SVM-Based Malware Detection Framework for Android

Min Zhao, Fangbin Ge, Tao Zhang, and Zhijian Yuan

Institute of Command and Automation,PLA University of Science and technology, Nanjing, China
{ezhouzhaomin,gefangbin,zhangtao421,nudt_yzj}@gmail.com

Abstract. Mobile handsets, especially smartphones, are becoming more open and general-purpose, thus they also become attack targets of malware. Threat of malicious software has become an important factor in the safety of smartphones. Android is the most popular open-source smartphone operating system and its permission declaration access control mechanisms can't detect the behavior of malware. In this work, AntiMalDroid, a software behavior signature based malware detection framework using SVM algorithm is proposed, AntiMalDroid can detect malicious software and there variants effectively in runtime and extend malware characteristics database dynamically. Experimental results show that the approach has high detection rate and low rate of false positive and false negative, the power and performance impact on the original system can also be ignored.

Keywords: smartphone, Android, malware detection, SVM.

1 Introduction

With the development of embedded system and high-speed mobile communication network of technology advances, smartphones become more and more common, these smartphones offer a new computing environment, due to the openness of its operating system, the network is easy of use that make it more vulnerable to malicious attacks and destruction, also brought new challenges for their security researchers.

As more and more smartphones stored a variety of private personal information, including personal address book, digital images, personal documents, it is easier to connect to the other terminal and access may types of network, terminal software can access the network without permission of its owner, the user privacy of information leak out by running this kinds of software. Meanwhile, Malware may also be without the authorization of owner to "hide" some of the high payment services and power-exhausted services. Traditional Malware detection theory proposed based on PC architecture is not applicable to smartphones, a new type of malware detection mechanism for smartphones is desirable.

This paper design of a SVM-based active learning framework named AntiMalDroid for smartphone malware detection, and in the Android system validated the effectiveness of the method, tests show that the proposed method has good applicability and scalability can be realized on a variety of popular malware

C. Liu, J. Chang, and A. Yang (Eds.): ICICA 2011, Part I, CCIS 243, pp. 158–166, 2011.

detection, and can detect unknown malware. It has less impact on system performance; cost impact on the original system capacity can also be ignored.

The Article is organized as follows: Section 2 introduces the related research work and evaluation; Section 3 describe the malware detection system on the Android model architecture overview; Section 4 describe the design and implement of the framework in detail; section 5 experimentally validate using this method to establish the effectiveness of the detection system; final summary of the full text, and describes future research ideas.

2 Related Work

The initial studies on smartphone malware [1,2,3,4] mainly focused on understanding the threats and behaviors of emerging malware. Guo et al. [1] examined various types of attacks that can be launched to a compromised smartphone, and suggested potential defenses. Radmilo et al. [2] revealed the vulnerability of MMS/SMS, which can be exploited to launch attacks on battery exhaustion. Mulliner et al. [3] demonstrated a proof-of-concept malware which crosses service boundaries in Windows CE phones. They also revealed buffer overflow vulnerabilities in MMS [4].

Forrest et al.[5] presented document host-based anomaly detection, in this way and by monitoring system call sequence stored in the database, if the behavior of the program is not system call sequence data that it is the invasion. Later, the introduction of the behavior of learning algorithms, finite state machines and hidden Markov chain to achieve from the system call sequence of knowledge mining. All these practices are based on the representation of the program's normal behavior and abnormal from the normal mode model. However, these methods ignore the semantics of system calls; their limitation is a simple procedure scrambled can escape detection.

Christorescu et al.[6] proposed a new semantic-aware static malware detection technique, and try to identify the same semantics to detect the scrambling code, they decompile the code and give anti-malicious software behavior predefined template to match malware, it can detect simple scrambled through malware, shortcomings of the software behavior detect approach is that it needs to precisely match a predefined template, limited the number of malware that can be detected.

Zhichao Zhu and Guohong Cao et al.[7] made use of social network to detect the spread of mobile cellular network worm. Smartphones through the network traffic between the social relations between the terminal drawn maps, the user usually open and download content from their friends and acquaintances; social network worms diagram describes the most likely mode of transmission. The Authors propose two segmentation algorithms graph of social relations: balance segmentation and clustering segmentation. Social network approach can solve the mobile network worm propagation detection, but the method can't be used to detect other types of smartphone malware.

Abhijit Bose, Xin Hu et al.[8,13] proposed a framework mobile for worms, viruses and Trojan horse detection. They first present a time domain sequence based on the logical order of program behavior, and then they give an effective representation of malware behaviors. Each one of these behaviors may not be threatened if a single look. The authors validated the framework in Symbian OS. They stored 25 kinds of typical behavior of malicious software coding sequence into the database, and then proposed a two-stage mapping technology with the knowledge of the run-time system monitoring events and procedures based API .They use support vector machine classifier to distinguish between malware and normal software.

3 Overview of AntiMalDroid

Fig.1 illustrates the architecture of AntiMalDroid. The upper side is the learning component, including characteristic monitoring module , characteristic learning module, behavior characteristics signature module and signature database. Characteristics monitor module monitored all running software to get their running characteristics, forming the original characteristics of the normal software behavior and malware behavior. Characteristics of these two types are put into learning modules to generate the behavioral characteristics. The behavior signature module signed the behavior into behavior signatures and stored them in the signature database. The bottom half of Fig 1 is part of malware detection, including run-time behavior monitoring module, behavior signature module, decision module and the response module. Running behavior Characteristics monitor module monitored the key points of service managers and intent users of Android, and then sign the behavior sequences with the same algorithm above. Comparing the behavior signatures with the signatures in the signature database, response module will give a response if the signature matched the malware signature in the database.

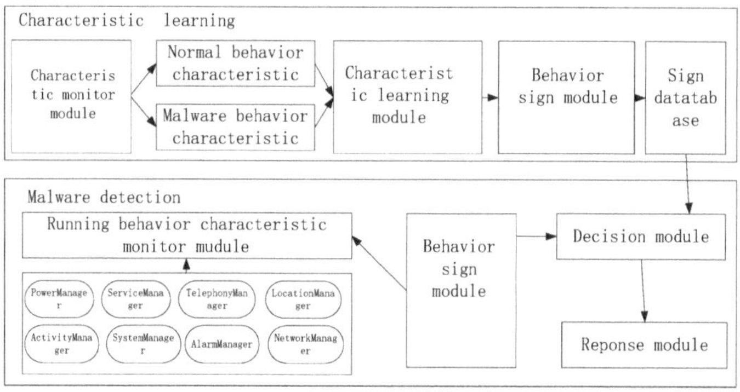

Fig. 1. AntiMalDroid Malware detection framework overview

4 Design and Implement

4.1 Software Behavior Signature and Algorithm

In smartphone operating systems, the behavior of malware may occur in multiple locations, the occurrence of these acts combined according to certain timing in order to constitute malicious software behavior, one or a few of these separate behavior can't determine whether they are malicious behaviors. This collection is then processed by temporal relations, after all the behaviors are abstracted and signed to software behavior patterns. Code packing, simple scrambling does not change the behavior of software, malware and its variants are generally in the same run-time behavior patterns, the signature of them can be detected through the same behavior. Compared with feather-based malware detection method, the signature database of behavior signature based is much smaller, so the behavior-based detection of malicious code signature is ideal for resource-constrained mobile devices. New malware usually include new behavior signature that is inconsistent with the known normal behavior, so behavior-based malware detection signatures can detect new, unknown malware.

This paper defines software behavior as Intent issued and system resources access by applications in Android-based smartphone operating systems. Software behavior signature can be get as follows: First, insert monitoring points in every service managers in Android framework. Every monitor collects manager call by process identifier based on timestamp and write manager call logs. Finally, classify logs by process identifier and sort them by timestamp. Fig 2 shows typical behavioral characteristics of the process of collection of the original process:

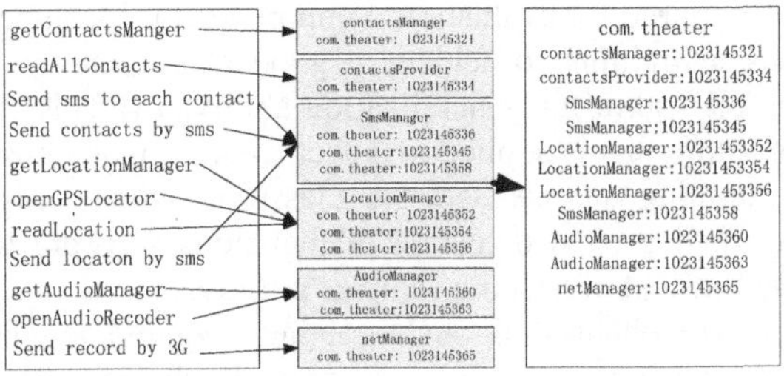

Fig. 2. A typical behavioral characteristics of the process diagram

The Behavioral characteristics of the process collecting algorithm is described as follows:

```
For (each manager)
  If (PID get this manager)
    timestamp ← now;
    Log(PID,manager,timestamp);
  end if;
classify logs by PID;
sort logs based on timestamp;
```

Log (PID, MID, timestamp) said it would write to the log file when process PID access service manager MID in time timestamp. After a while, the process behavior sequence will be collected in chronological order.

4.2 Learning Algorithm for Malware Signatures

Currently, most malicious software detection approaches are rule-based detection technology[15]; such detection approaches can only detect predefined rule database of malicious software and can't detect a good number of known malwares and new malwares' variants. Therefore, intelligent anomaly detection technology is put forward and becomes a research hotspot. Anomaly detection techniques commonly used the following theories: probability and statistics, artificial neural networks, genetic algorithms, fuzzy recognition and artificial immune method.

The traditional rule-based anomaly detection approaches using statistical methods mostly divide collected data into normal and abnormal categories. To solve such problems, you first need to mark the type of samples to build the training sample set, the establishment of the training sample set depends on security experts, and the cost is much expensive. To improve the classification accuracy in the learning process needs enough training samples, on one hand increases the cost of building the training sample set, on the other hand, collecting a large number of learning samples is also difficult. To address this problem, you need a learning method in the case of a small number of training samples, access to better classification results.

Active learning as a way to solve this problem have been proposed, it is proposed by Lewis and Gale et al.[9], and it changed the traditional focus from a known sample of passive learning methods, which according to the learning process, take the initiative to choose the most Good sample to study, thus effectively reducing the number of samples required for evaluation. Support Vector Machine (SVM) is a small number of samples in training to achieve a good classification of the case of the intelligent learning algorithm for generalization ability.[14] This article give a SVM active learning algorithm that is applied to detect Android malicious software, making less need of the training sample set, the classifier achieve higher classification accuracy, resulting in improved detection of malicious software training speed and reduce the construction cost of training samples purposes.

SVM parameters are obtained through training, required to obtain two types of training samples that the signature patterns of normal behavior and abnormal behavior signature patterns. This paper defines the behavior of the signature track the behavior of the software, used with a window of length k behavior of the software to obtain the signature track on the sliding short sequences of system resource access. How to choose the size of the sliding window is the key issue. If the selected sequence length is too short will lose resource access order relation, if the length is too large and can't reflect the context of normal and abnormal conditions of local order. Hofmeyr SA et al.[5] draw conclusions from the experiment: when the window is greater than 30, the call sequence from the program behavior can't be determined for useful information. Lee W et al.[10] suggests that the most appropriate resource access short sequence length is 6 or 7. The short sequence length is 6 in this paper, the experimental result shows this selection is proper. The following algorithm is used to generate normal short sequences:

```
NCS← slidewindow(nobs);
NCL← NCS;
MCS← slidewindow(mobs);
for (mcs in MCS)
  for (ncs in NCS)
    if (mcs = ncs) del mcs from MCS;
    for (mcs in MCS) {
```

```
d← MAX;
for (ncs in NCS) {
  d(mcs,ncs)← Harmin(mcs,ncs);
  if (d(mcs,ncs)<d) d←d(mcs,ncs); }
if d>D del mcs from MCS; }
```

In the algorithm, NCS represent normal characteristic sequence database, ncs represent a normal characteristic sequence instance, MCS represent malware characteristic sequence database, mcs represent a malware characteristic sequence instance. When using a sliding window of length 6 on the behavior signatures of normal software, the normal characteristic sequences will be get. When using to malicious ones, the result will include both the normal sequence and malicious sequences. Because the number of malware is far smaller than the normal, the size of MCS is far smaller than NCS. When a sequence appears in both NCS and MCS, delete it from NCS. When a sequence is not included in MCS and not completely match any ncs in NCS, using Hamming distance measure its similarity with the normal samples. For the two short sequences i and j, the Hamming distance between them is denoted by d(i,j). For each new sequence i, the definition of the minimum Hamming distance $d_{min(i)}$ is min{d (i, j)}. $d_{min(i)}$ is the value of the expression of the sequence and extent of deviation from normal mode.

Finally, for a not match sequence i, compare $d_{min(i)}$ with D that is a predetermined comparison threshold to determine if it is abnormal, that is, if $d_{min(i)}$ equals or larger than D, the sequence i is a ncs, whereby abnormal short sequences available sample set.

4.3 Malware Detection

The SVM active learning algorithm is used for detection, SVM's most prominent feature is based on the principle of structural risk minimization. Vapnik et al.[11] maximize the generalization ability of learning, that is a limited training sample set can still guarantee an independent test set that maintain a small error.

The characteristics of the learning process as a normal sample of short sequence is not complete, resulting in short sequences based on the normal access to the abnormally short sequence in the sample may contain normal intermittent, the SVM classifier generate classification error, so the introduction of detection module, which presented below the level of risk using malware to make decisions.

Taking into account the different smartphone behavior of malicious software on the system and the user is different from the losses caused by the introduction of a risk factor (Risk Factor, referred to as RF), RF is used for each short sequence of a malicious act to give a weight, the right base Value is set to 1, if the behavior of the system and user security threat is greater, giving a greater than 1 RF. The introduction of risk (Risk Rank, referred to as RR) is a software as a measure of the quantitative identification as malware, RR is defined as follows:

$$RR = \sum_{i=1}^{n} ncs_i \times RF_{ncs_i} \tag{1}$$

Set a malware detection threshold D, the value determined by the experimental results, our results show that the D value of 17 is the best detection threshold. When the RR is greater than the calculated D, the software is ultimately determined as malware.

5 Evaluation

The computational complexity and battery consumption are two essential factors of security system of mobile devices. They are needed to be considered when making any changes to the software stack on these devices. We have evaluated both these aspects for the malware detection framework presented in this paper. As a test system, we have taken the Android Froyo that kernel version is 2.6.25 operating on the htc hero handset. Evaluation of the framework presented below.

5.1 Malware Detection

As Android market is most famous Android software sharing place, we choose the most popular 100 software in Android market as our normal software test swatches, choose the following popular malware as our malicious software test swatches.

Table 1. Malicious software swatches

name	Infected software	Report time
Geinimi	Monkey Jump 2, President vs. Aliens, City Defense, Baseball 2010	2011.1
DroidDream	Sexy Girls: Hot Japanese, Sex Sound, Super StopWatch and Timer, Super Color Flashlight	2011.3
Plankton	Angry birds, DroidKungfu, YZHCSMS	2011.5

Google Inc. announces that much famous and popular software has been infected by these three types of malware. We put the 100 normal software and selected 2 of each type of malware to characteristic learning module to taint the detect engine, then another 200 software are sent to detect engine to test the effective of the detect framework. The test result is described as follows:

Table 2. Malware detection evaluation result

Malware type	Infected num	Correct detected	False positive	False negative	Detection rate
Geinimi	30	28	3.7%	3%	93.3%
DroidDream	30	27	5.4%	4.6%	90%
Plankton	30	27	4.3%	5.7%	90%

Table 2 shows the result when applying the detection framework to different famous malware. An SVM active learning engine is built for each type of malware. We can see that the framework can detect most of these three types of malware, and the false positive rate and false negative rate are small, because the behavior of these three type of malware are very distinct.

5.2 Performance Evaluation

The primary users of smartphones in general and Android in particular are usually unable or unwilling to sacrifice performance for security. Moreover, the computational power of most smartphones, while being superior to traditional cell phones, is still lower than desktop computers. It is therefore necessary that the security policy model not overly tax the computational capabilities of the phone.

Message service, location service and shell script are three import executable program while using Android smartphones. These three programs can also candidate our three types protected object. TABLE 3 shows the spending time that with and without the malware detection system. The result shows that the performance decrease is bearable.

Table 3. Time Consumption Evaluation

Action	Application	Time no detection(ms)	Time with detection(ms)
Send SMS	SMS(Java app)	56	87
Access GPS	GPS Viewer(Java app+native app)	78	113
Exec shell	Init.sh	23	34

5.3 Power Consumption Evaluation

Measurement of battery consumption on Android is difficult due to the fact that the battery charge level reported by the Android hardware is at a very coarse grained level. Using software for measurement of battery consumption during Access GPS simply yields ‘no change’ in battery level. However, note that since we use hash table to store normal and abnormal software behavior signature information, the decision-making time consumption is linear.

Therefore, using the same arguments as those for time consumption, we can conclude that the battery consumption overhead caused by our decision making mechanism is also bearable.

6 Conclusion and Future Work

In this paper, we design and implement a SVM active learning algorithm based Android malware detection framework named AntiMalDroid; it can detect and restrict the most popular and some unknown malwares running on Android platform. Our performance evaluation shows that that the time consumption is a little more. Future work will continue to find more optimal algorithm to decrease the time consumption.

This work is simply the first step in a longer journey towards realizing practical smartphone malware detection system. We plan to extend our mechanism to other Linux-based embedded systems.

References

1. Guo, C., Wang, H., Zhu, W.: Smartphone attacks and defenses. In: HotNets-III, UCSD (November 2004)
2. Racic, R., Ma, D., Chen, H.: Exploiting mms vulnerabilities to stealthily exhause mobile phone's battery. In: IEEE SecureComm (2006)
3. Mulliner, C., Vigna, G., Dagon, D., Lee, W.: Using Labeling to Prevent Cross-Service Attacks Against Smart Phones. In: Büschkes, R., Laskov, P. (eds.) DIMVA 2006. LNCS, vol. 4064, pp. 91–108. Springer, Heidelberg (2006)
4. Mulliner, C., Vigna, G.: Vulnerability analysis of mms user agents. In: Proc. of ACM ACSAC (2006)
5. Forrest, S., Pearlmutter, B.: Detecting instructions using system calls: Alternative data models. In: IEEE Symposium on Security and Privacy (1999)
6. Mihai, C., Somesh, J., et al.: Semantic-aware malware detection. In: IEEE Symposim of Security and Privacy (2005)
7. Zhu, Z., Cao, G., et al.: A Social Network Based Patching Scheme for Worm Containment in Cellular Networks. In: Infocomm (2009)
8. Bose, A., Hu, X., et al.: Behavioral Detection of Malware on Mobile Handsets. In: MobiSys 2008, June 17-20 (2008)
9. Lewis, D., Gale, W.: A sequential algorithm for training text classifiers. In: Proceedings of the ACM SIGIR Conference on Research and Development in Information Retrieval, pp. 3–12. ACM/Springer (1994)
10. Lee, W., Dong, X.: Informatiion-Theoretic Measures for Anomaly Detection. In: Proc of the 2001 IEEE Symp. on Security and Privacy, pp. 130–143 (2001)
11. Vapnik, V.N.: The Nature of Statistical Learning Theory. Spring, New York (1995)
12. Xie, L., Zhang, X., Chaugule, A., Jaeger, T., Zhu, S.: Designing System-level Defenses against Cellphone Malware. In: Proc. of 28th IEEE International Symposium on Reliable Distributed Systems, SRDS (2009)
13. Xie, L., Zhang, X.: pBMDS: A Behavior-based Malware Detection System for Cellphone Devices. In: WiSec 2010, Hoboken, New Jersey, USA, March 22-24 (2010)
14. Sommer, R., Paxson, V.: Outside the Closed World: On Using Machine Learning For Network Intrusion Detection. In: IEEE Symposium of Security and Privacy, Oakland, California, USA (2010)
15. Enck, W., Ongtang, M., McDaniel, P.: On Lightweight Mobile Phone Application Certification. In: ACM CCS 2009, Chicago, Illinois, USA (2009)

Mining the Concise Patterns for Service Reliability Prediction

Ying Yin, Xizhe Zhang, and Bin Zhang*

College of Information Science and Engineering, Northeastern University
Shengyang, 110004, China
yy_00000000@163.com

Abstract. As more and more Web service become available, large-scale and open distributed systems enable participants to share resources and services with each other via the Web. However, they always run in a highly dynamic change environment where various uncertain factors often emerge, such as server unavailable, internet interrupt or temporarily interrupt and so on. In order to make the composite service run normally and minimize the interrupt time by the exceptional handling, it is necessary for the system to own the ability to predict the reliability of composite service in advance. This paper proposes an efficient prediction model by mining concise patterns to predict service reliability. Experiments show that the efficiency of proposed method.

Keywords: Concise Pattern, Prediction, Service Reliability.

1 Introduction

Web services can be composed together as composite Web service. They often interact with each other to carry out complex transactions or workflows[9]. However, Web service always run in a highly dynamic change environment(The Web)[1], with more and more Web service available and various uncertain factors(such as environment, requirement etc) emerging, the reliability of deployed composite service will not guarantee during remote service invocation[8]. It is inevitable that one component service fails or becomes overloads[10]. On this basis, composite Web service reliable and correct execution has become one of the major challenges in the area of Service-oriented Computing(SOC). Therefore, reliability evaluation is an important step for building stable service system and reducing the service interruption or expensive roll-back operations in the long-running business process. In order to make the composite service run normally and minimal the interrupt time by the exceptional factor, the system need to own the ability of predicting the reliability of composite service in advance.

Traditional solutions for service stable evaluation are construct a reliability prediction model. Many researches have been done to prediction based on QoS-aware[2,3]. However, QoS-aware prediction method need real-time monitor

* Corresponding author.

C. Liu, J. Chang, and A. Yang (Eds.): ICICA 2011, Part I, CCIS 243, pp. 167–173, 2011.

service QoS values[2,3], the process will be high cost. Another is collaborative filter[4,6] based approach for making QoS prediction based on the similar users. However, the methods are not enough efficiency by leaking the relationship identification among different QoS attributes.

To attack this critical challenge, this paper proposes an efficient prediction model by mining concise patterns to predict service reliability. Experiments show that the performance outperforms previous method.

The remainder of this paper is organized as follows: Section 2 states the process of extracting execution instances from execution logs. In Section 3, we present the basic definitions related. Section 4 gives an efficient method for identifying CP based on interesting measure. Experimental results are described in Section 5. We summarize our research and discuss some future work directions in Section 6.

2 Extracting Execution Instances from Execution Logs

Once a service-oriented application or a composite service is deployed in a runtime execution environment, the application can be executed in many execution instances. Each execution instance is uniquely identified with an identifier (i.e., id). In each execution instance, a set of service sequence can be triggered. Due to various uncertain factors which make the same execution instance success or fail. Reason for this phenomenon is that there are much execution status information under different uncertain factors. We record the triggered events in the log using the logging facility provided by the execution environment. An execution log contains different types execution information. For example, resource adapter events record the interaction between the service-oriented application and a legacy system. Business rule events track the runtime status of business rules. Service invocation events indicate the timeline of a web service execution. We are interested in service invocation events. In particular, for a component service, its running quality will fluctuate with the change of its status. The same service will produce different effect by running in the different status(such as internet environment). sometimes successful, sometimes fails. For example table 1, It is helpful to predict the service reliability by extracting the execute status information from execution log for service management.

Table 1. Composite QoS status Information

A	*CompositeQoS*	*Descriptinon*
S^0	$< AV^0, EXE^0 >$	Server Unavailable, Runtime delay
S^1	$< AV^{0.5}, EXE^0 >$	Server available intermittently, Runtime delay
S^2	$< AV^1, EXE^0 >$	Server available, Runtime delay
$\times$	$< AV^0, EXE^1 >$	Server Unavailable, Normal Execution
S^3	$< AV^{0.5}, EXE^1 >$	Server available intermittently, Normal Execution
S^4	$< AV^1, EXE^1 >$	Server available, Normal Execution

There are many attributes for each component service. In order to depict the various execution status information clearly, for each component service, we only consider two QoS attributes as an example, such as available attribute and execution time attribute. Available attribute has three options: av^0 means server is unaccessible, $av^{0.5}$ means server is accessible intermittently and av^1 means server is accessible normally; execution time attribute has two options: exe^1 and exe^0. exe^1 means the component service was implemented within expected execution time, otherwise the option is exe^0. Under these situation, we obtain five groups of service composed execution status information which shows in table 1: $< AV^0, EXE^0 >$ represents server unavailable but runtime delay, $< AV^{0.5}, EXE^0 >$ represents server available intermittently but runtime delay, $< AV^1, EXE^0 >$ represents server available but runtime delay, $< AV^{0.5}, EXE^1 >$ represents server available intermittently but normal execution and $< AV^1, EXE^1 >$ represents server available but normal execution. However, for the status information $< AV^0, EXE^1 >$ represents server unavailable but normal execution, we do not consider this situation because it does not hold the practical significance.

Table 2. An example of service execution instances

ID	$ExecuteLog$	$Count$	$Class$
1	S_1^0	3	$failed$
2	S_1^1, S_2^1, S_3^1	2	$failed$
3	S_1^2, S_2^2, S_3^2	2	$failed$
4	S_1^1, S_2^1, S_3^1	3	$failed$
5	$S_1^4, S_2^2, S_3^2, S_4^2$	2	$failed$
6	S_1^4, S_2^2, S_3^2	1	$failed$
7	$S_1^4, S_2^3, S_3^4, S_4^2$	2	$successful$
8	S_1^4, S_2^3, S_3^4	2	$successful$

Based on the assumption above and execution instances, there are a large collection of composite service execute records D which are stored as sequential data shows in table 2. S={$S_1, S_2, ..., S_n$}, and T={successful, failed} be the complete set of class of D, then each record consists of one or more component services from S and a class label from T. Note that every component service have different QoS expression values, which can evaluate the execute status of the component service. For simplify, we let the capital letters with subscript, such as S_1, S_2, S_3, S_4, denotes different abstract service class and the superscript, such as 0, 1, 2, 3, 4, denotes different QoS status of the component service. Table 2 shows a service execute data with 17 users and four abstract service class. For brevity, we partitions execution instances into two types: "successful" and "failed" shows in table 2. Bellow are some definitions related.

3 Basic Definition

Definition 1. *Let D be an execute service log with service set S, S=*{$S_1, S_2, ..., S_n$}. *Let* $P = \{S_1^i S_2^j ... S_l^k\} \subseteq S(l{=}1,2,...,n)$ *be a component service or a subset of execute* *sequence with status information, where* $\{i,j,k\} \in [0,1,2,3,4]$. *We called a component service with status information or a set of component pairs a* **Pattern**. **P** *is an abbreviation of* **Pattern**.

Definition 2. *Let P be a pattern and C_k be one of the category of fault. The intra-class support of pattern P in class C_k is the ratio of the number of records containing P with the class C_k to the number of class C_k in the data set,* **IS** *is an abbreviation of* **Intra_Support**.

$$IS(P|C_k) = \frac{Support(P \bigcup C_k)}{Support(C_k)}$$

Based on the definition above, if given a pattern P, then Pa denotes the superset of pattern P, Pab denotes the superset of pattern P and Pa, Pabc is the superset of pattern P, Pa and Pab. Therefore, we can obtain a set I in which each item is the superset of P except itself, i.e.I={P,Pa,Pab,...}. we say the set I is the ***Prefix Rule Sets*** with common prefix P.

Definition 3. Discriminate Pattern *is abbreviated to* ***DP***. *The discriminate pattern evaluate the classify capability of pattern P occurring in different class That is say, it estimate the correlation about the pattern with the class.*

A pattern′s DP for specific C_k is defined as:

$$DP(P|C_k) = \frac{\sigma + Supp(P \cup C_k)}{\sigma + Supp(P \cup \neg C_k)}$$

Supp is abbreviation of Support. $Supp(P{\cup}C_k)$ denotes the support of pattern P and C_k emerging simultaneously, $Supp(P \cup \neg C_k)$ denotes the support of pattern P and $\neg C_k$ emerging simultaneously. i.e. $Supp(P{\cup}\neg C_k){=}Supp(P){-}Supp(P{\cup}C_k)$. σ is close to zero.

Definition 4. *For a given class C_k, an* **concise pattern (CP)** *should satisfy: (1)Pattern P should be frequent in given class; (2)Pattern P should have the higher confidence than the threshold specified by user; (3)Pattern P should have the ability to distinguish in different class. All the optimal patterns combination as* **Concise Pattern Sets**.

4 Concise Pattern Mining

We discuss the detail of CP mining algorithm below, taking Table 2 as the example, where the minimum intra-class support threshold γ=2.

The mining process is conducted on a prefix tree as shown in Figure 1, which is build on Table 2. Limited by space, we omit the description of constructing such a prefix tree structure. From figure 1, we can see there are four abstract service class s_1, s_2, s_3 and s_4 at level 1. Next, we generate the candidate patterns for the second level. We can see 11 candidate 1-patterns at level 2, where the number within brackets denotes the count of patterns. For example, $s_1^1(4)$ denotes the total count of s_1^1 is 4. The pattern p with solid box represents the corresponding rule. For example, class f with solid box under $s_1^1(4)$ means the rule $s_1^1 \rightarrow f$ can be deduce.

At first, we look at some pruning techniques that are used in CP. These pruning rules prevent unnecessary patterns generation efficiently and only preserve the concise patterns.

Pruning Rule 1. *Given IS, Pattern Px denotes pattern P and all its possible proper supersets, class* $C_k \in C$ *(k=1,2,3,...) denotes one types of the diseases. If* $0 \leqslant IS(P \rightarrow C_k) \leqslant \gamma$, *then pattern P and its supersets for their's corresponding class* C_k *will not be the concise pattern.*

Pruning Rule 2. *If pattern P satisfy Supp(P)=Supp(Px), Pa denotes its proper superset, then pattern Pa and all its possible proper supersets will not be useful for concise pattern.*

Pruning Rule 3. *Given Pattern P, when* $IS(P \rightarrow (C_k/\neg C_k)) \geq \gamma$, *if* $(1-\delta) \leq CP(P) \leq (1+\delta)$ *then P will not be the concise pattern.*

Limited by space, we omit the proof. The above pruning rules are very efficient since it only generates a subset of frequent patterns with maximal interestingness instead of all ones.

We can use the support-based pruning 1(see the details in section3.3) to prune some rules(line 2-5). We can pruning some redundancy rules by applying pruning rule 1(line 8~10), such as candidateS_1^0,S_2^1,$S_1^1S_2^1$, $S_2^1S_3^1$ are remove since IS($^0_1$)=1< γ, IS($^1_2$)=1< γ, IS($S_1^1S_2^1$,)=1< γ, IS($S_2^1S_3^1$,)=1< γ. It is marked by red ① where the prune rule 1 is applied. Further, if all c under some pattern are pruned, then rules containing this pattern will be pruned.

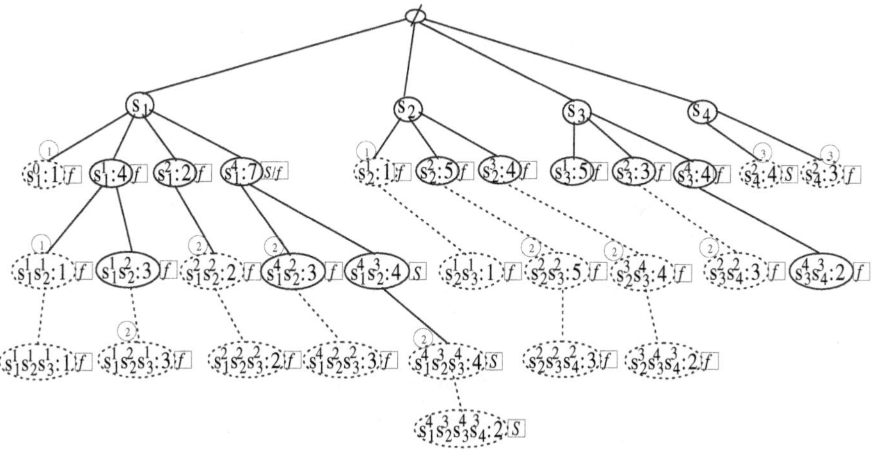

Fig. 1. The Concise Patterns Tree

Then, we perform the confidence-based pruning rule 2(line 13), which will also be explained in subsection 3.3. For instance, $(S_1^2 S_2^2)$ in candidate$(S_1^2 S_2^2; f)$ is terminated because of Supp$(^2_1)$=Supp$(S_1^2 S_2^2)$=2. It is marked by red ② where the prune rule 2 is applied. At last, CP-based pruning rule 3 is very important but not difficult understand (see subsection 3.2). For example, candidate pattern S_4^2 is removed by line 14 because Supp$(S_4^2 \rightarrow f)$ = Supp$(S_4^2 \rightarrow c)$ hold. It is marked by red ③ where the prune rule 3 is applied. Limited by space, we omit complete pseudo-code for mining optimal CP sets.

Finally, the optimal CP sets are significantly smaller than an association rule set, but is still too big for decision practitioners to review them all. We may only return top-k concise patterns, but they may all come from a section of the data set and lack the representation for all class. In order to account for all known class, we aim to retain one contrast pattern sets for each class C_k. Limited by space, we don′t list the top-k algorithm in details.

5 Experiments

The following experiments mainly analysis the efficiency and reliability of proposed prediction model. We are simulate network environment and generate network topology graph by BRITE tool. The number of web services are 400 belongs to 50 classes which distributing 400 network nodes. The periods of execution is 10 weeks. The system select composite services by matching I/O operation.

Fig.2 shows the scalability for CPA under different number of services, when the number of candidate services is increasing. That is, when the value of the parameter (represented by the X axis) increases, the prediction times of CPA (represented by the Y axis) goes up. The shorter of the candidate services, the less of the run times. We can see that CPA algorithm always consume the least time, because it need't to compute the composite service QoS and compare it with SLA.

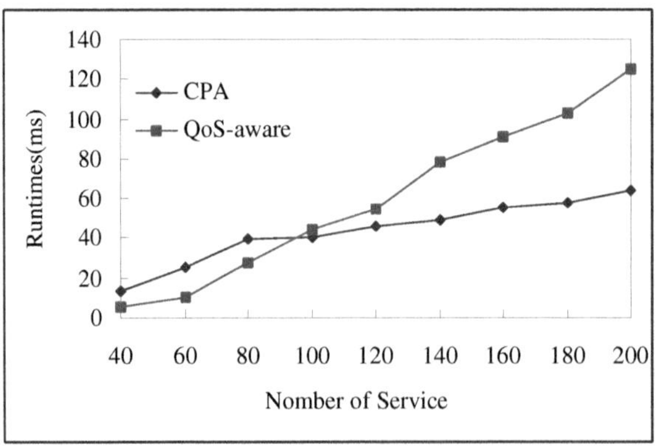

Fig. 2. Runtime of Prediction

6 Conclusion

In this paper, we discuss the concise patterns which are important for predict service reliability, and propose an interesting measure in order to decide whether the patterns are interesting for distinguish the multiple class. Based on the interesting measure, we propose a new algorithm with pruning rules to mine all optimal concise patterns efficiently. Our experimental results confirm that our approach is effective and efficient for CP generating.

Acknowledgments. National Natural Science Foundation of China under grants (No. 61100028,61073062,60903009,60803026); This work was supported by China Postdoctoral Science Foundation (No. 20100481204); The Fundamental Research Funds for the Central Universities under grants (No. N090304006); Industry tackle key problem plan of Liaoning Province(No.2010216005); Natural Science Foundation of Liaoning Province(No. 20102061).

References

1. Yu, Q., Liu, X.M., Bouguettaya, A., Medjahed, B.: Deploying and managing Web services: issues, solutions, and directions. The VLDB Journal 17, 537–572 (2008)
2. Yu, T., Zhang, Y., Lin, K.J.: Efficient Algorithms for Web Services Selection with End-to-End QoS Constraints. ACM Trans. Web 1(1), 1–25 (2007)
3. Leitner, P., Michlmayr, A., Rosenberg, F., Dustdar, S.: Monitoring, Prediction and Prevention of SLA Violations in Composite Services. In: Proc. of IEEE International Conference on Web Services, pp. 369–376. IEEE Press, Miami (2010)
4. Zheng, Z.B., Ma, H., Michael, R., King, I.: QoS-Aware Web Service Recommendation by Collaborative Filtering. IEEE Transactions on Service Computing (TSC) 4(2), 140–152 (2011)
5. Chen, L., Feng, Y.P., Wu, J., Zheng, Z.B.: An Enhanced QoS Prediction Approach for Service Selction. In: Proc. of the 5th IEEE International Conference on Web Services. IEEE Press, Washington (accepted 2011)
6. Xie, Q., Wu, K., Xu, J., He, P., Chen, M.: Personalized Context-Aware QoS Prediction for Web Services Based on Collaborative Filtering. In: Cao, L., Zhong, J., Feng, Y. (eds.) ADMA 2010, Part II. LNCS, vol. 6441, pp. 368–375. Springer, Heidelberg (2010)
7. Shao, L., Zhang, J., Wei, Y., Zhao, J., Xie, B., Mei, H.: Personalized QoS Prediction for Web Services via Collaborative Filtering. In: Proc. of the 5th IEEE International Conference on Web Services, pp. 439–446. IEEE Press, Beijing (2007)
8. Zhang, G., Liu, L., Seshadri, S., Bamba, B., Wang, B.: Scalable and Reliable Location Services through Decentralized Replication. In: Proc. of the 7th IEEE International Conference on Web Services, pp. 632–638. IEEE Press, Los Angeles (2009)
9. Zhang, L., Zhang, J., Hong, C.: Services Computing. TSingHua University Press, Beijing (2007)
10. Ge, J., Hu, H., Lu, J.: Service Discovery and Substitution According to Inheritance of Behavior with Invariant Analysis. In: Proc. of the 8th IEEE/ACIS International Conference on Computer and Information Science, pp. 971–976. IEEE Press, Shanghai (2009)

Study on the Current Situation and Coordination Policies Concerning the Regional Differences in Tourism Investment Environment of Hebei Province

Wei Guo, Fang Lv, and Na Song

Tourism Department, School of Economics & Management, Yanshan University,
Qinhuangdao, China
guowei@ysu.edu.cn

Abstract. To examine the current situation concerning the regional differences in tourism investment environment in Hebei province, the research findings show that there are overall differences and spatial differences in creating tourism investment environment among 11 cities in Hebei provinces. The differences go to two opposing extremes with the absolute differences increasing greatly and relative differences increasing slowing down. Following an analysis of the reasons for the differences, by examining both the internal and external environment, some policies for coordinating those differences are put forward so as to attract more tourism investments and promote the improvement of the investment environment and the development of tourism in Hebei province.

Keywords: tourism investment environment, regional differences, coordination policies, Hebei province.

1 Introduction

The travel investment environment quality directly affect the introduction of tourism investment and investment effect, so all the regional differences of tourism investment environment of Hebei province in understanding will help each other to improve their tourism investment promotion of environmental quality, to attract tourist investing. In this paper, the research of tourism investment environment in Hebei province, the present situation of the regional differences as the starting point, analysis the gap in Hebei cities, for better building of tourism investment environment, and to attract more investment to provide the reference.

2 Analysis of Regional Differences in Hebei Tourism Investment Environment

To observe the changes of overall differences of tourism investment environment in Hebei Province, in 2005 -2009 is now selected as a measure of the amount of

C. Liu, J. Chang, and A. Yang (Eds.): ICICA 2011, Part I, CCIS 243, pp. 174–180, 2011.

Table 1. 2005 -2009 tourist Investment in each city of Hebei Province(10000yuan)

	2005	2006	2007	2008	2009
Shijiazhuang	107577	2210	12756	257971	480245
Chengde	15499	4568	17030	45609	108639
Zhangjiakou	21598	4763	12933	37402	103408
Qinhuangdao	64264	2050	4271	57071	72817
Tangshan	26375	21892	12222	211348	298041
Langfang	40616	10191	12130	126948	274735
Baoding	124937	9216	8332	124857	192035
Cangzhou	13802	10670	7476	56814	82950
Hengshui	7490	116	9100	5600	7492
Xingtai	14839	3085	5581	35444	77876
Handan	76200	21712	12520	142728	200516

Data source : 2006-2010, "Hebei Economic Yearbook"

investment in tourism indicators of eleven cities in Hebei Province (see Table I). The use of standard deviation to estimate the amount of regional tourism investment and the standard deviation of the absolute differences in regional tourism investment estimated coefficient of relative differences, to show regional differences in changes in the overall profile. Use deviation, and relative growth rate ratio of each city to show trends and magnitude in the last five years,. The formula is as follows:

a. Standard deviation

$$S = \sqrt{\sum_{i=1}^{n}(y_i - \bar{y})^2 / N} \quad (1)$$

Where: y_i is regional tourism investment, $\bar{y}$ is the province's average of cities to tourism investment, N is the number of cities.

b. Coefficient of standard deviation

$$V = \sqrt{\frac{\sum_{i=1}^{n}(y_i - \bar{y})^2}{N}} \Big/ \bar{y} \quad (2)$$

Where: y_i is regional tourism investment, $\bar{y}$ is the province's average of cities to tourism investment, N is the number of cities.

c. Deviation

$$\eta = y_i - \bar{y} \quad (3)$$

Where: y_i is regional tourism investment, $\bar{y}$ is the province's average of cities to tourism investment.

d. Ratio

$$\mu = \frac{y_i}{\bar{y}} \tag{4}$$

Where: y_i is regional tourism investment, $\bar{y}$ is the province's average of cities to tourism investment.

e. Relative growth rate

$$\text{Nich}=\frac{x_{2i}-x_{1i}}{x_2-x_1} \tag{5}$$

Where: x_{2i},x_{1i} respectively on behalf of the tourism investment of city i at time 1and at time 2, x_2,$x_1$representing the Hebei Province tourist investment in time 2 and time 1.

2.1 Hebei Tourism Investment Environment Analysis of the Overall Features of Regional Differences

The Absolute Gap Increased. The results can be seen (Table 2), in addition to the standard deviation calculated in 2007 the relatively slow growth, the other four-year data showed faster growth rate. This shows that the absolute amount of investment in the tourist areas, Hebei eleven cities the gap is increasing, and that regional differences in tourism investment environment increases, showing a polarization trend.

The Relative Gap between Seems Slow. It can be seen(Table 2), except for 2007 data significantly smaller, the other four years of data show a weak decreasing trend, which shows the various cities to create a better investment environment for active travel to their starting point are increased tourism investment. So, relatively speaking, the regional tourism investment environment, the relative differences are narrowing the gap.

Table 2. In recent years, changes in Hebei regional tourism investment gap

	2005	2006	2007	2008	2009
Standard deviation	40858	7558	3768	80116	136042
Coefficient of standard deviation	0.876	0.919	0.363	0.800	0.788

2.2 Hebei Tourism Investment Environment Analysis of Regional Differences in the Spatial Characteristics

Through the deviation indicator data, ratio and relative growth rate is calculated (Table 3), we can see:

Shijiazhuang, Tangshan, Langfang on the Amount of Investment in the Tourism Growth Rate Increased. These three cities in 2009 are positive deviation, and ratios greater than 159%.

Chengde, Zhangjiakou, Qinhuangdao, Cangzhou, Hengshui and Xingtai on the Amount of Investment in Tourism has Shown a Relatively Negative Growth Trend. These cities in 2005 and 2009, two observation points are below the average amount of investment, and in these cities in the amount of investment in tourism in 2009 compared with the mean difference of Hebei Province farther.

Baoding Shows Growth Deceleration in Amount of Investment in Tourism. Baoding in 2005 and 2009, tourism investment are above average in Hebei Province, but the amount of investment in tourism in 2009, the mean difference is smaller.

Handan Remained Unchanged. 2005 and 2009, tourism investment and the level of the province's growth rate was essentially flat. It shows that the basic speed of Handan investment in the tourism development is keeping up with developments in Hebei Province.

Specific Ranking. Through the calculation of the relative speed of development, we can see that investment in tourism, the different pace of development of cities, specific ranking: Shijiazhuang, Tangshan, Langfang, Handan, Chengde, Zhangjiakou, Cangzhou, Baoding, Xingtai, Qinhuangdao, Hengshui.

Table 3. Cities and Hebei province average deviation, ratio and relative growth rate

	2005		2009		relative growth rate
	average deviation	ratio	average deviation	ratio	
Shijiazhuang	60922.73	2.3058	307631	2.78219	0.268966
Chengde	-31155.3	0.3322	-63975	0.629375	0.067222
Zhangjiakou	-25056.3	0.4629	-69206	0.599071	0.059045
Qinhuangdao	17609.73	1.3774	-99797	0.421849	0.006173
Tangshan	-20279.3	0.5653	125427	1.726633	0.19607
Langfang	-6038.27	0.8705	102121	1.591615	0.168971
Baoding	78282.73	2.6779	19421	1.112511	0.048427
Cangzhou	-32852.3	0.2958	-89664	0.480552	0.049906
Hengshui	-39164.3	0.1605	-165122	0.043403	0.0000014
Xingtai	-31815.3	0.3180	-94738	0.451157	0.045496
Handan	29545.73	1.6332	27902	1.161644	0.089723

3 Hebei Tourism Investment Environment Analysis of the Reasons for Regional Differences

Regional differences in the amount of investment in tourism can find reasons from two aspects: the travel industry environment itself and the external environment:

3.1 Travel Industry Environment

Tourism Resources Endowments. Hebei province owns huge tourism resource, but very uneven distribution between 11cities, 3A and above scenic spots, the number of Shijiazhuang, a total of 11, and Hengshui is zero. Similarly, Hebei Province, with key cultural heritage units 163, with 46 on Baoding, Langfang has only one.

Differences in Quality of Tourism Enterprises. There are more than 562 tourism enterprises in Shijiazhuang, while only 84 in Hengshui, while the performance of employees are different, in comparison of tourism human resources development index and the strength index, the quality of tourism workers in Qinhuangdao is the highest among the province.

Differences in the Level of Tourism Performance tourism performance mainly refer to two indicators, Travel and tourism income results and tourist receptions. The most annual income from tourism and hospitality of the city are Shijiazhuang and Qinhuangdao, a minimum of Hengshui and Xingtai cities. the highest city nearly 5 times more than the minimum City.

3.2 The External Environment

Different Economic Environment. Economic environment composed of the potential for economic development, regional spending power, potential of the urban development. Basic elements are: per capita GDP, retail sales, total fixed asset investment, green coverage, life garbage treatment rate. There is a certain gap between the economic environment in Hebei province, the attractiveness of investment in tourism are not the same.

Different Infrastructure Environment. Traffic is the most basic facilities. To passenger volume, for example, Baoding owns 110 million passengers per year, is Hengshui 2.35 million people, nearly five times. This has resulted in the traffic environment as well as tourism investment environment differences.

4 Coordinated Response to Regional Differences in Tourism Investment Environment in Hebei Province

Absolute difference in Hebei Province is increased, the relative speed difference in different cities slow down, and unbalanced status differences, can be considered from three aspects of coordination.

4.1 The Guidance and Coordination of Tourism Investors

In the case of increasing differences, from a macro point of view, the government should give financial and policy support to the city with less investment. For example Chengde, Zhangjiakou, Qinhuangdao, Cangzhou, Hengshui and Xingtai, in the amount of investment on growth is negative, Baoding is slow growth. This requires all levels of government and tourism businesses to be more emphasis on investment, increase tourism environment to optimize investment.

4.2 Tourism Investment Objects between Each Other

Objects have to do is to improve their ability to attract investment, learn from each other's experience to improve the tourism investment environment and methods of each other. Include: the optimization and development of tourism resources, improvement of business and tourism professionals and to improve the quality of improvement. At the same time the city needs to further optimize other investment environment, including: the improvement of infrastructure, enhance the overall image of the city and so on.

4.3 Joint Action of Tourism Investment Media

As a whole, Hebei Province, should also be joint tourism marketing, unified image of the publicity in various cities, it not only contribute to more help, more investment in tourism businesses for weak city', but also help for improve the overall understanding of Hebei province, it brings more possible for weaker city to attract large-scale tourism investment. To a certain extent, it plays a coordinating effect to low down the differences in various cities.

5 Conclusion

In this paper, starting with regional differences of tourism investment environment, use of tourism investment in Hebei Province, this index measured the differences and gaps of tourist investment environment in the cities, find reasons from two aspects, the travel industry environment itself and the external environment. And then, give recommendations to coordinate. Thus, finally, it promote tourism investment environment optimization.

References

1. Zhang, H., Yong, G., Liu, C.-Y.: Optimize the environment for foreign investment thinking Hebei. China Trade and Economic Tribune 3, 60–61 (2011)
2. Wu, Y., Zhang, Y.: Survey of Hebei province's investment environment and thinking. Hebei Normal University 9, 14–17 (2009)

3. Liu, X.: Xinjiang tourism investment climate study (master's degree thesis). Xinjiang University, Tourism Management (2008)
4. Zhang, H., Yong, G., Liu, C.-Y.: Optimize Hebei Provincial Foreign Investment. Environment of the Chinese Economic and Trade Herald 3, 60–61 (2011)
5. Zheng, Y.: Liaoning Provincial Tourism Investment Environment Evaluation. Resources and Industries 8, 73–77 (2008)
6. Zhang, R.: Hebei regional differences in analysis and coordination of economic development research. (Master thesis) Beijing Jiaotong University, Regional Economics (2007)
7. Wang, A.: Hunan Spa Hotel Investment Environment Evaluation study - in Chenzhou City, for example. (Master thesis): Hunan Normal University (2009)
8. Zhou, Y., Hunan, H.: Chongqing and Guizhou side of tourism investment climate study. Tourism Resources 26, 749–751 (2010)
9. Liu, X.: Xinjiang tourism investment climate study (master's degree thesis); Xinjiang University, Tourism Management (2009)
10. Jenny, C.: Supply-side investment: An international analysis of the return and risk relationship in the Travel and Leisure sector. Tourism Management, 665–673 (2009)

The Mathematical Model of the College Students' Employment and Analytical from the Perspective of Economy

Cheng Lijun, Kou Yilei, and Zhao Haiyan

Qinggong College, Hebei United University, Tangshan, Hebei, 063000
clj@qy.heuu.edu.cn, 18931539099@189.cn

Abstract. At present, the college students' employment situation is still very serious, but with this form strong contrast, labor shortage is increasingly fierce. The root cause of this phenomenon our country's regional and local development of internal imbalance, the mode of economic growth is hard to form an effective demand caused by college students. Fundamental policy of solution to the problem is: Implement development strategy and policy to promote development in less developed areas, narrowing the regional economic disparity, relieve employment density of college students' employment concentration areas; Change growth mode of regional economic, improve the ability of absorbing for university graduates.

Keywords: regional economic differences, college students, the difficult employment, countermeasures.

1 Introduction

For the cause of college students' employment difficult, academic circles have different point of view. A kind of ideas that caused the direct reason for university graduates is to college expansion of successive years (figure 1). A view of the personnel system and the household registration system weaken the market economy in talent allocation shall be brought into play, led to the basic role of human resources of the irrational distribution, the normal flow of bondage to the talents, restricted the university graduates of employment. Another kind of ideas that college students are planned economy and elite education long-term effects, part of the graduates' employment concept is misaligned, expectations and social needs, led to big gap college students' employment rate low, one of the important reasons. Some scholars from the standpoint of the labor both sides argued that some college.

Students, their own quality is insufficient, the competitiveness of the workplace and the accepting units from inadequate actual need, devotion to human capital, is also high consumption of university students' employment difficult important reasons. This paper from the balanced development of regional economy of the relative macro perspective, get a new discussion of university students' employment difficult.

C. Liu, J. Chang, and A. Yang (Eds.): ICICA 2011, Part I, CCIS 243, pp. 181–188, 2011.

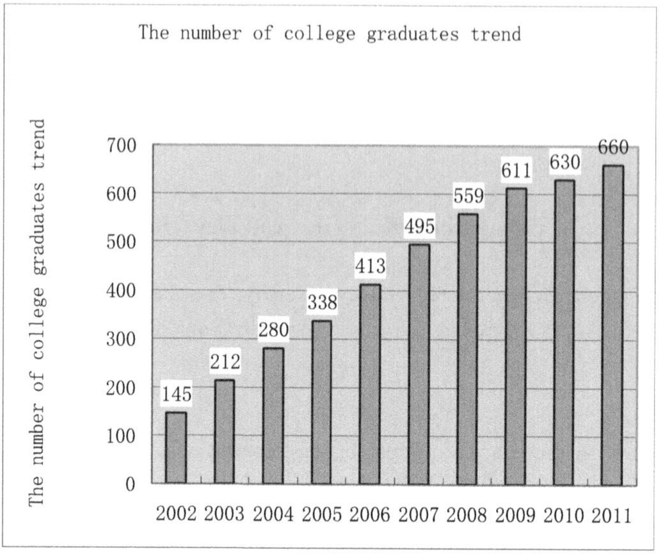

Fig. 1.

2 The Influence of Flow of University Students' Employment because of Chinese Regional Economic Development Level Is Not Balanced

Since the early 21s, China has formed "university student boom" from less developed areas to the developed areas. Every year, the year's graduates are to become large scale up to the relatively strong absorption capacity of Beijing and southeast coastal cities. According to the state personnel had published data show that in 2005, 70.7% of college graduates distribution in large and medium-sized cities in the county, 21.9% in towns, 5.5% in villages, and only 1.9% in rural accounted (figure 2). Only Beijing, Guangzhou, Shenzhen, Shanghai will receive the personnel department of the 15 provinces and cities random 10.9% of college graduates. Shenzhen absorb more than 30000 college students in 2005 for the first time. Even in recent years, Beijing area and the southeast coastal area absorbing the university graduates at least an half of the national university. 2008 by Michael think China's 2007 college graduates to the provincial flow of investigation shows, Guangdong, Shanghai, Zhejiang, Beijing four of the net inflow to graduate 185.2%, 130%, 117% and 70.8%, than any other greatly province, of which the rate is the net inflow of Guangdong talent is far ahead. [1]This long period of one-sided employment flow, which makes the city on the students demand tends gradually saturated, more weight in the college students' employment competition. On the other hand, for the urgent need of the college students in less developed areas, the talent flow quantity but far greater than inflow, especially young skeleton brain drain. This forms talents to keep talents, where digestion so many talents place where all talents who have crowded, causing the college students' employment difficulties and work positions and the paradox of the situation.

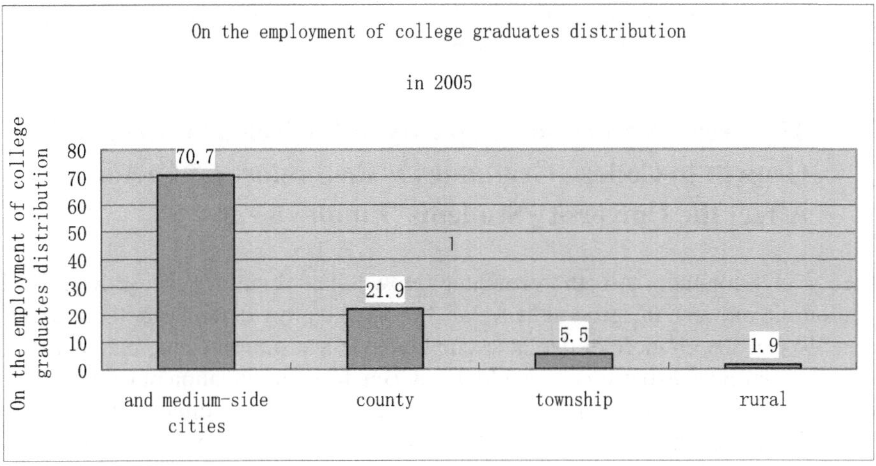

Fig. 2.

Investigate its reason, on the one hand, because the labor remuneration backward areas and development space and the eastern part of the actual cannot equate coastal areas. Many labor force and senior talents flow to the developed area. For example, since 1992, the migrant workers from other provinces to Guangdong in every year, more than 10 million people. In the 90s, is more than 15 million. At the same time, backward area of college students and mature senior personnel also into the coastal regions and high return industry, further weakening backward areas ability of development. In less developed areas "wage lowland" trouble, hard for "talents platform" provide rich nutrition, is caused by the root cause of the brain drain. On the other hand, the less developed areas and the general lack of talent, need intelligence investment and support, but because the distribution system, the household registration system, policy, security system, the preparation of quantity, the influence of such funds difficult, even if the thought of these graduates place employment also often hard to come by. This is causing the college students to the west in the objective, as the basic unit of the employment of the space is narrow, channel, also exacerbate the graduate employment difficulties. The reason of the phenomenon lies in the regional economic development levels. After the reform and open policy, our country executes the importance of the development of the coastal areas non-balanced development strategy, trying to make the unbalanced development of regional transformation to promote the power of the development of the whole national economy. In 70 s, China's focus on the advantage resources to the development of the pearl river delta area, and in 80 s lean strength to make the Yangtze river delta, in 90 s and focus on building the Jingjintang and the Bohai sea triangle region. The regional imbalance development strategy in the national economy as a whole to achieve the sustained and rapid development and, at the same time, leading to a series of social, economic and ecological environment. More outstanding between area is show obvious imbalance, the regional economic development gap between more and more remarkable. The regional economic differences, that university graduates will own ideal employment in developed areas to positioning, cause "the phenomenon of an army squeeze wooden bridge".

3 The Weak Absorption Capacity of the Regional Economic Growth to College Graduates Is the Important Factor to Affect the University Students' Employment

Theory of economic growth, economic growth and employment growth is the relationship between the general has related economic growth, the faster the speed, the more we can absorb more of the labor employment, a sustained economic growth can drive the continued expansion of employment. But, from the situation of China's reform and opening to the more than 30 years, the sustained, rapid economic growth have not well drive employment growth, employment is still more prominent contradiction, economic growth and employment growth trend of the agreement is obvious. Investigate its reason, regional economic structure change of the total amount of lag in regional economic growth, regional employment structure transformation lags behind regional industrial structure transformation, is impeding labor absorption capacity, especially influence economic growth to college students' labor absorption capacity basic reason. The specific performance in: On one hand, economic growth exist industry differences to labor absorption capacity. Absorption ability of economic growth about labor usually use employment elasticity to analysis. Obtain employment points to the elastic labor employment growth and economic growth ratio, it reflects the ratio between the economic growth to the strength of the labor absorption capacity. Generally speaking, the greater flexible employment, show that the economic system of labor ability to absorb better. The smaller the employment elastic, show that the economic system of labor ability to absorb weak. From three times industrial employment situation we can see, it growth to labor absorption capacity there exist obvious differences. In the first, second and third industry, the third industry is the main source of absorbing college students employment, is the main channel of labor obtain employment. In the western developed countries, the third industry labor has to 60 to 70% of total labor. The third industry of developed countries is more than two-thirds in the proportion of the general all. While in China, the third industry of GDP, 1990 ~ 2000, 11 years is around 30% or so, from 2002 up to 40.46% .After 10 years, it is the basic stagnation, (see table 1 figure 3). Thus cause of Chinese labor force in the three industries configuration, main performance for the first industry absorb redundant Labor force, but the secondary and tertiary industries absorbing labor shortages. So the high-speed growth of Chinese economy and not to produce more pulling power, but it produced extrusion effect in a certain extent to job growth produced extrusion effect, and is weak to the ability of absorbing of college graduates, then caused the college students' employment problems in a certain extent.

Table 1.

year	2001	2002	2003	2004	2005	2006	2007
The third industry in GDP (%)	39.02	40.46	41.47	41.23	40.38	40.5	40.94
year	2008	2009	2010				
The third industry in GDP (%)	41.9	43.43	42.97				

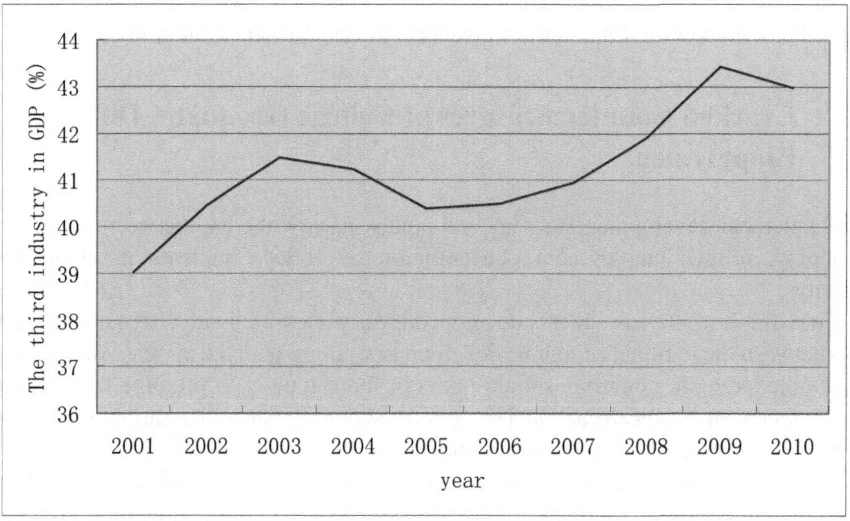

Fig. 3.

On the other hand, economic growth on labor absorption capacity exists industry differences. Economic growth to the influence of each industry employment is different too. According to the research shows that, from the pace of economic growth and employment growth in the relationship between the velocity of agricultural economic growth, see and employment growth is on the opposite direction changes, the agricultural economic growth for agricultural employment has obvious effect of rejection. The financial and insurance of the highest employment elasticity, the second is the real estate industry, and the third is the transportation, post and telecommunications warehousing later in order: health sports, scientific research and comprehensive technology services, wholesale and retail trade catering industry, construction, social services, education, culture, radio and television industry. For college students and the ability of absorbing some of the strongest is the quality of the labor demand higher industry, such as real estate and financial insurance, the scientific research and technical services, the comprehensive industry requirements have certain people employed the comprehensive quality and professional knowledge, if no professional knowledge, even if have jobs is also unable to obtain employment. But in China the current situation does the overall size of the small service, service level is not high, the structure unreasonable, the institutional reform and innovation in the lag, the social and economic coordination for the requirements of the development of health also does not adapt. According to the development and reform commission (NDRC) to provide the data, 2010 years of China's service industries to realize sector was from 1.71 billion up by 11.9% over the previous year. But the sluggish development of service industry situation has not changed fundamentally. The national service GDP does not increase the proportion of the fallen, from 43.43% in 2009 to 42.97%. Compared with the developed countries, China's services in the economy, the small proportion of economic growth to cause the needs of the college students is limited, intensifies the college students' employment pressure.

4 Cracked Countermeasures of College Graduates Difficult Employment

(1) Implement development strategy and policy, narrow the gap between the regional economy, relieve employment concentration of college students in employment density.

First of all, to increase in less developed areas policy inclination dynamics, narrow gap between the regional economic development. Along with the increase of the overall economic strength, countries should take out more money to promote the economic development of backward areas; The country should enhance the gap on the regional economic development, we should control power industry policy, investment policy and financial policy, tax policy and so on, strengthen policy support efforts to Low level of economic development of the region step by step. At the same time, we should create and use more means and ways to guide the space configuration of resources rationally, and gradually reduce regional economic development gap, provide more jobs for college students, attract more students to underdeveloped region development.

Secondly, actively promote underdeveloped region urbanization construction, promote the less developed areas urbanization process, improve the attraction of the less developed areas to the university graduates. Urbanization rate is the measure of a national and regional economic development level of important standard. Through the system reform and the policy adjustment, promoting urban and rural in construction planning, industrial development, market information, policy measures, ecological environment protection, development of social undertakings and gradually achieve the integration between urban and rural areas in economy, society, culture, the ecological coordinated development. Promoting urban and rural residents and the production method, way of life and living way mutual confluence, reduce the gap between urban and rural areas, ease college students' employment blindly to flow to the trend of the developed areas.

Third, promoting less developed areas of non-state-owned economy development, increase the vitality of the less developed areas for college graduates, provide more to the chance to choose. In the development of commodity economy, the construction process of market economy, the existence of the non-state-owned economy and the appropriate development is necessary. It is helpful for promoting the production, the active market and expand employment, renew the idea. The developed areas of the high speed economic development are largely because non-state-owned economy developed rapidly, and support the local economy has become an important part of growth. And less developed areas of non-state-owned economy development is relatively slowly. To make less developed areas and the developed areas as soon as possible the gap narrowing, countries should further emancipate the mind, renew the idea, vigorously promote undeveloped areas of non-state-owned economy, in order to enhance the development of regional economy, for the vitality of the university graduates to provide a lot of job opportunities.

(2)Regional economic growth mode transformation, speed up the economic structure adjustment, improve the ability of absorbing for university graduates.

Promote industry structure and employment structure coordination development is to keep sustained, rapid economic growth and labor force full employment basic way. We have to have a strategic adjustment of industrial structure, adhere to the people-oriented scientific development concept, form already can effectively absorb human resources, and in conformity with the requirements of the development of economy and society, competitive industrial structure. We not only to increase the human resources development strength, improve the quality of workers and professional strain ability, promoting the employment structure and industrial structure to adapt, gradually realize the fundamentals of the industrial structure. We must fully consider the present situation of the labor force and development process, considering each social level of labor obtain employment problem, realize the industry diversification, the discrepancy, promote industrial structure and employment.

At the same time, we could develop modern service industry, effectively increase the college students' employment. Modern service industry in high human capital content, high technology content and high added value, and other features, is absorbing the employment of college graduates channels. Some experts point out, in the next five years China will focus on developing six service industry: tourism, property management, homeowners, community service, education training industry and cultural industries. The industry demands the quality of the employees is higher, employees need to fully knowledge structure, good interpersonal skills, solid foreign language skills and computer operating capability, stable psychological quality and energetic, good ability in organization and coordination, and have strong sharpness and more rapid acceptance of information the new things, strong analysis, integration and processing power, also have strong innovation enthusiasm and spirit. However, the qualities are owned by the college students. Therefore, the modern service industry is the main channel of contemporary college students employment. Only in these industries, college students can manifest the due value, show the mien. Thus can ease college students' employment pressure, and can avoid the waste of talent.

References

1. Liu, Q., et al.: Factors and countermeasures of affect college students' employment. China's College Students' Employment (13) (2006)
2. Liu, S.: Chinese regional economic development. China statistical publishing house, Beijing (1994)
3. Cui, G.: Chinese regional economic differences and the empirical analysis of government behavior. Macro Economic Research (2006)
4. Yang, W.: College students' employment choice and policy stimulation. Chinese Higher Education Research (2004)
5. Yu, C.: The cause analysis and countermeasures study of college students' employment difficult. Chinese Employment (5) (2007)
6. Wang, H.: China's higher education quality crisis and management strategies in transformation. Tsinghua University Education Research (6) (2005)
7. Yu, C.: In college students' employment status and coping measures. Higher Education Building 16 (2007)
8. Development and reform commission web site of china, `http://www.sdpc.gov.cn/zjgx/t20110331_403287.htm`
9. Baidu library, `http://wenku.baidu.com/view/b4922525ccbff121dd368333.html`

The Foundation of the Mathematical Model of Economic Impact and the Analysis of the Effect on the Economy of Shanghai World Expo

Lijun Cheng[1] and Lina Wang[2]

[1] Qinggong College, Hebei United University, Tangshan, Hebei, 063000
[2] Tangshan Teachers College Tangshan, Hebei, 063000
clj@qy.heuu.edu.cn, 18931539099@189.cn

Abstract. This paper mainly use the macroeconomic theory, cost benefit analysis, Time Series forecasting method and the method of quantitative to get the World Expo on Shanghai's economic impact modeling and analysis. Using the Gallup's prediction of passenger volume get expected income and expenditure. Give a quantitative evaluation prediction about the Shanghai economy , separately from *GDP* and income spending the two macro angles and tourist arrivals and employment the two microscopic view. First, the application of macroeconomic theory in the multiplier effect model, using linear regression method, according to 1980--2002 in Shanghai's per capita income and consumption, forecast 2002 - 2010 increase of value of 4204.0601 billion, using time series methods, predicted Shanghai in 2010 from August to October the number of tourists were 585.56, 621.1, 659.16 million. Finally, the application of cost - benefit analysis, the establishment of forecast net income of Shanghai's economic model, based on the forecast of revenue and expenditure, obtained total revenue of 85.037 billion yuan and total expenditure of 91.95 billion yuan, during the operation of the Expo. And use the data to prove that the Shanghai World Expo will help boost the confidence of people around the world and the courage to accelerate and promote world economic recovery process.

Keywords: Macroeconomic Theory, Linear Regression, Cost Benefit Analysis.

1 Preface

2010 Shanghai world expo is the first world exposition that held in China .Since the1851 London's " All nations industrial exposition " start, the Expo is becoming the exchange of peoples history, culture, show scientific and technological achievements embodied the spirit of cooperation, future development of an important stage. Expo will not only marks of the strong economic development, and to some extent, also contributed to the host countries, particularly in the host city's economic development, promoting the growth of the city's economic, increased employment opportunities; Much earlier urban infrastructure construction and environmental improvement process; Led third industrial upgrading and structural optimization, especially to

C. Liu, J. Chang, and A. Yang (Eds.): ICICA 2011, Part I, CCIS 243, pp. 189–196, 2011.

promote the prosperity of high-tech industries; strengthen the surrounding economic cooperation, enhance the host city for the region's economic concentration and radiation; Improve the host city's reputation, image and visibility.

That the influence of World Expo to Shanghai's economy, will lead the promotion of urban culture, improvement of transport infrastructure, development of exhibition industry, the advertising industry to promote, improve the quality of urban culture and other aspects of the corresponding development.

2 Expo to Shanghai Economy Directly Effect Analysis

According to John Maynard Keynes macro economic theory, the multiplier effect, public spending and investment will stimulate effective demand, the increase of investment will drive the economic increase exponentially. In the Multiplier theory, the investment multiplier formula can be expressed as

$$K = \Delta Y / \Delta I \tag{1}$$

Investment decisions is boundary consumption tendency, with ΔC crepresents consumption increment, because $\Delta Y = \Delta C + \Delta I$, substituted $\Delta I = \Delta Y - \Delta C$ into the equation (1) was

$$K = \Delta Y / (\Delta Y - \Delta C) = 1/(1 - MPC)$$

where $MPC = \Delta C / \Delta Y$.

Shanghai consumers' MPC from the preparation period to the exhibition period, become the key to the world expo calculation multiplier effect. Through to the Shanghai world expo's bid for the former per capita income and the per capita consumption of regression analysis, calculates the consumption function, and by using the consumption function and the definition of MPC marginal consumption that specific value.

Per capita income for the income variables, per capita consumption as the dependent variable, city of Shanghai in 1980 - 2002, per capita income and per capita consumption statistics, see table 1.

According to the data table 1 linear regression analysis, use of MATLAB programming get Fig. 1.

Fig. 1 derived from the linear regression equation.

$$C = 231.31 + 0.7537Y$$

Where C is the per capita consumption, Y is per capita income.

The whole world expo investment include the park, the expo village of construction cost, operating costs and the expo will be an extension projects that support the construction cost, total 103.546 billion yuan, the added value caused by GDP is

$$\Delta Y = 1035.46/(1 - 0.7537)$$

The world expo in the investment multiplier calculated, the Shanghai world expo for an extension to the eight years time will be expected to make Shanghai an increase of

420.40601 billion yuan per year on average, and an increase of 52.55075 billion yuan. Consider the long-term investment and is time-lag, eight years of real value will be slightly lower than the calculated value.

Table 1. Shanghai 1980 - 2002 per capita income and per capita consumption

Year	Per Capita Disposable Income (Yuan)	Per capita Consumption Expenditure (Yuan)	Year	Per Capita Disposable Income (Yuan)	Per Capita Consumption Expenditure (Yuan)
In 1980	637	553	In 1991	2486	2167
In 1981	637	585	In 1992	3009	2509
In 1982	659	576	In 1993	4227	3530
In 1983	686	615	In 1994	5868	4669
In 1984	832	726	In 1995	7172	5868
In 1985	1075	992	In 1996	8159	6763
In 1986	1293	1170	In 1997	8439	6820
In 1987	1437	1282	In 1998	8773	6866
In 1988	1923	1648	In 1999	10932	8248
In 1989	1976	1812	In 2000	11718	8868
In 1990	2183	1937	In 2001	12883	9336
			In 2002	13250	10464

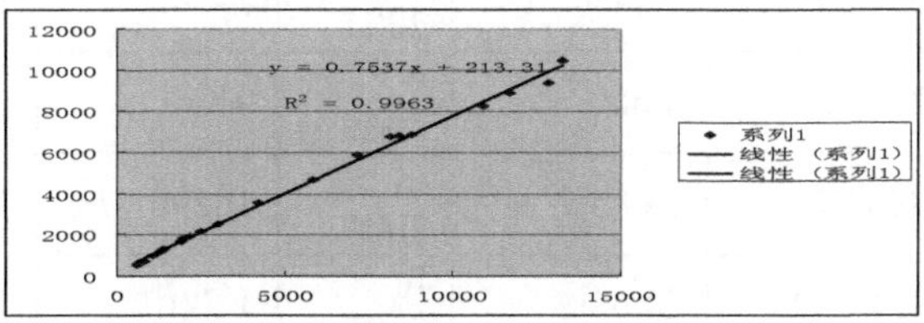

Fig. 1. Shanghai's per capita consumption and income of the linear regression graph

Statistics of Shanghai 1980 - 2009, the actual values of *GDP* and *GDP*'s growth rate, see table 2.[5]

Through the data in Table 2, using EXCEL to draw Fig. 2.

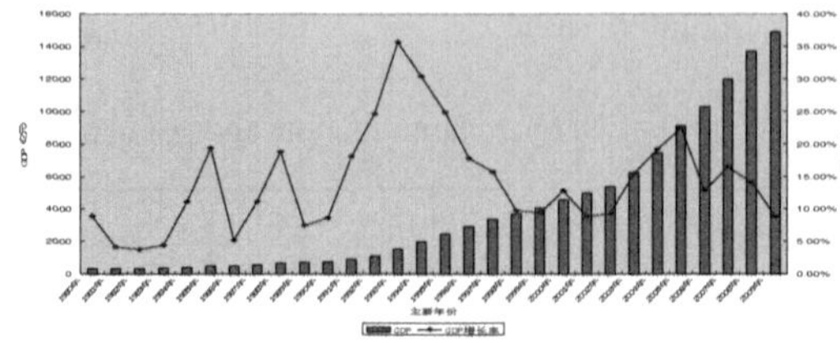

Fig. 2. Shanghai 1980-2009, the actual value of *GDP* and *GDP*'s growth rate

Table 2. Shanghai 1980-2009, the actual value of *GDP* and *GDP*'s growth rate

Year	GDP (Billion Yuan)	The GDP Growth Rate	Year	GDP (Billion Yuan)	The GDP Growth Rate
In 1980	311.89	8.89%	In 1995	2462.57	24.88%
In 1981	324.76	4.13%	In 1996	2902.2	17.85%
In 1982	337.07	3.79%	In 1997	3360.21	15.78%
In 1983	351.81	4.37%	In 1998	3688.2	9.76%
In 1984	390.85	11.10%	In 1999	4034.96	9.40%
In 1985	466.75	19.42%	In 2000	4551.15	12.79%
In 1986	490.83	5.16%	In 2001	4950.84	8.78%
In 1987	545.46	11.13%	In 2002	5408.76	9.25%
In 1988	648.3	18.85%	In 2003	6250.84	15.57%
In 1989	696.54	7.44%	In 2004	7450.27	19.19%
In 1990	756.45	8.60%	In 2005	9125	22.48%
In 1991	893.77	18.15%	In 2006	10296.97	12.84%
In 1992	1114.32	24.68%	In 2007	12001	16.55%
In 1993	1511.61	35.65%	In 2008	13698	14.14%
In 1994	1971.92	30.45%	In 2009	14901	8.78%

View Fig. 2, verify the investment is long-term and lag of the time, eight years of actual value will be slightly lower than the calculated value.

3 The Shanghai World Expo to Tourism Impact Analysis

In 2010 the Shanghai World Expo is Shanghai tourism development great opportunity. A country to host the World Expo, the most direct benefit is the tourism industry, which is a significant positive correlation. From two perspectives of tourism economic impact on Shanghai were considered, one for the Shanghai 2008 January to 2010 July, the number of visitors to the statistical data, see Table 3; using time series method for the prediction of Shanghai in 2010 8, October 9, the number of tourists, on the other hand is through to the Shanghai 2005 to 2009 May by October the number of tourists, see Table 4; using averaging method, respectively, predict Shanghai 2010 World Expo case in

Table 3. 2008 January to 2010 July in Shanghai, the number of visitors

Date	Immigration	Proportion	Total	Date	Immigration	Proportion	Total
In 2008 January	401581	11.70%	3432316	In 2009 April	499735	13.80%	3621268
In 2008 February	327035	12.70%	2575079	In 2009 May	442637	14.10%	3139270
In 2008 March	478190	14%	3415643	In 2009 June	411027	14.30%	2874315
In 2008 April	516922	16.34%	3163537	In 2009 July	462608	16.00%	2891300
In 2008 May	516922	15.80%	3271658	In 2009 August	439005	14.50%	3027621
In 2008 June	444217	15.70%	2829408	In 2009 September	506585	14.50%	3493690
In 2008 July	408386	15.50%	2634748	In 2009 October	459619	14.60%	3148075
In 2008 August	392210	15.20%	2580329	In 2009 November	546342	14.60%	3742068
In 2008 September	461311	14.90%	3096047	In 2009 December	472236	15.10%	3127391
In 2008 October	502791	15.30%	3286216	In 2010 January	439339	11.50%	3820339
In 2008 November	513309	16.50%	3110964	In 2010 February	354355	12.20%	2904549
In 2008 December	370212	15.90%	2328377	In 2010 March	694372	11.80%	5884508
In 2009 January	349518	12.08%	2893361	In 2010 Apri	677586	11.40%	5943737
In 2009 February	341893	14.11%	2423055	In 2010 May	620360	12.50%	4962880
In 2009 March	402730	13.80%	2918333	In 2008 June	730076	13.70%	5329022
				In 2008 July	674863	14.20%	4752556

May to October the number of visitors each month, according to the 5 Shanghai in 2010, 6, in July the actual number of tourists and the prediction of the 8 October, 9, the number of tourists, calculate because of the World Expo Shanghai May to October 2010 influence tourists increment. If a visitor to stay stay for a day, daily consumption of 2000 yuan, which calculated by the impact of increased tourism income.

According to data in Table 3, use of Matlab to get, using time series methods to predict the number of tourists in Shanghai In 2010 August ,September, October.

Table 4. Shanghai from 2005 to 2009, May to October the number of tourists

	May		June		July	
Year	Number of people	The percentage of traffic	Number of people	The percentage of traffic	Number of people	The percentage of traffic
2005	324114		363128		358887	
2006	401901		376738		368709	
2007	439811	18.30%	441796	17.80%	411777	18.20%
2008	448563	15.80%	444217	15.70%	408386	15.50%
2009	442637	14.10%	411027	14.30%	462608	16.00%
Average	411405	16.07%	407381	15.93%	402073	16.57%
Total	2560613		2556786		2427002	
	August		September		October	
Year	Number of people	The percentage of traffic	Number of people	The percentage of traffic	Number of people	The percentage of traffic
2005	373153		394518		426034	
2006	384193		412395		449292	
2007	423663	18.40%	456139	18.90%	493626	19.40%
2008	392210	15.20%	461311	15.20%	502791	15.30%
2009	439005	14.50%	506585	14.50%	459619	14.60%
Average	402445	16.03%	446190	16.20%	466272	16.43%
Total	2510051		2754257		2837357	

Table 5. No world expo case number of visitors **Table 6.** The increase number of tourists caused by the World Expo

Month	The number of visitors	Month	The incremental number of visitors
May	2560613	May	2402267
June	2556786	June	2772236
July	2427002	July	2325554
August	2510051	August	3345549
September	2754257	September	3456743
October	2837357	October	3754243

According to Fig. 3 get the fitting formula

$$y = 139.7x^3 - 1253x^2 - 5875x + 2749000 \tag{2}$$

According to the type (1) that the 2010 Shanghai August tourism population is 5855600 people, the September tourism population is 6211000 people, the October tourism population is 6591600 people.

Through to the Shanghai 2005 to 2009 May to October the number of visitors, see Table 4, using the averaging method, respectively, to predict the number of visitors in Shanghai 2010 from May to October each month without the Shanghai Expo, see table 5.

According to the actual Shanghai in 2010, May, June, July the number of visitors and the prediction of the August, September, October, the number of tourists, to calculate because of the World Expo Shanghai May to October 2010 influence tourists increment, see table 6.

And calculated because of the influence of the world expo 2010 Shanghai from may to October the increment is 18056592 visitors . According to assume that the number of days tourists stay for two days, daily consumption of 2,000 yuan, in order to estimate the impact of the increase due to the Expo is 722.26368 billion tourism revenue.

4 Conclusion

First of all, to Shanghai economy directly stimulate the establishment of mathematical model, more accurate forecast in 2002 to 2010 the growth of GDP value, practical to consider the Shanghai World Expo is the long-term investment limitation and lagging, eight years the actual GDP value added will be slightly lower than the calculated value. Then, using a mathematical time-series forecasting methods to predict the 2010 Shanghai 8,9,10 months of tourists, in practice, reflects the accuracy of the forecasts. Also whether to carry out the Expo by contrast, to carry out quantitative Shanghai World Expo will stimulate tourism. If a visitor will stay for two days, it increased.

Finally, the use of cost - benefit analysis method, to compare the accuracy of identified the Expo net earnings, the results show that the Expo will be a loss, this model does not consider the inadequacies of the hosting of the World Expo relocation costs, construction costs, construction costs, reserve, construction period interest, then the World Expo's economic benefits will be reduced, and Appear more losses.

In short, the 2010 Shanghai World Expo is the first world exposition that held in China. Expo will be of great significance to run for the boost market confidence, promote world economic, technological and cultural exchanges and cooperation to jointly cope with the financial crisis, sustainable development is of great significance.

References

1. Yang, J., Yang, X.: Western economics tutorial. East China University of Science and Technology press (2008)
2. Zhang, J.: A concise course of western economics. China Agricultural University Press (2000)

3. Jia, J., He, X., Jin, J.Y.: Statistics. Renmin University of China Press (2000)
4. Xue, D., Chen, Y.: Advanced application of MATLAB to solve mathematical problems. National Tsing Hua University Press (2008)
5. Shanghai statistical yearbook (2010), `http://www.stats-sh.gov.cn/2003shtj/tjnj/nj10.htm?d1=2010tjnj/C0811.htm`
6. Shanghai statistical yearbook (2003), `http://www.stats-sh.gov.cn/2003shtj/tjnj/2003tjnj/tables/2_1.htm`
7. Shanghai travel, `http://lyw.sh.gov.cn/message/information/content/gov_bulletin_new3.htm`
8. `http://www.expo2010.cn/` `http://www.expo2010.cn/`
9. Shanghai statistical yearbook (2004), `http://www.stats-sh.gov.cn/2004shtj/tjnj/tjnj2004.htm#`
10. Xiao, D.: Based on the theory of cost-benefit of Shanghai world expo economic impact study. East China Normal University Press (2008)
11. Mao, X., Wang, G.: The employment effects of Shanghai World Expo, S1 (2005)
12. Li, Y.: Correct understanding and input-output multiplier. Journal of Renmin University of China (6)
13. Zhao, Y.: Macroeconomic statistical analysis, Renmin University of China Press (2000)
14. Wang, H., Chen, X.: Shanghai World Expo, Analysis and Forecast of the main income. Shanghai Management Science (1) (2010)
15. Guo, Z.: 2010 Shanghai World Expo effects on the tourism development potential analysis, Tourism Tribune (2) (2003)

Research of Economic Growth Model of Shanghai World Expo Impact

Yunhua Qu

Finance Division Hebei United University Tangshan 063009Hebei P.R. China
hblgdxqyh@126.com

Abstract. 2010 World Expo in Shanghai is not only boost the economy but also driven around the city's economic growth. So that the whole Yangtze River Delta economic zone than in the past has been significantly improved. Accelerate the World Expo Shanghai as the center of the Yangtze River Delta region's infrastructure and industrial restructuring, improve the city's overall quality, promote tourism, catering, communications, transportation and other industries developed rapidly, increasing the secondary industry and tertiary industry demand for employees, creating a large number of employment opportunities. This paper analyzes the model for the Shanghai World Expo to promote cultural exchange and stimulate economic growth and drive around the Shanghai Yangtze River Delta economic analysis and quantitative evaluation of the Shanghai World Expo impact. The results show that the Expo will be organized during the 2003-2009 average annual GDP growth of 1.91 pull Shanghai percent, two years after the Expo will boost average annual GDP growth of 1.35 percentage points from Shanghai. In addition Expo radiation effects will drive the Yangtze River Delta region's rapid economic growth, driven in 2003-2009 the average annual value of the Yangtze River Delta region to increase the secondary industry 646.676 billion yuan, driving increased value of tertiary industry 274.577 billion yuan.

Keywords: Shanghai World Expo, Regression model, Economic growth, Industry value.

1 Introduction

The Expo is becoming the exchange of peoples history, culture, show scientific and technological achievements embodied the spirit of cooperation, future development of an important stage from 1851 London "World Industrial Exposition" Start. Host the 2010 Shanghai World Expo will further enhance China's international reputation, increase awareness and understanding of the world to Shanghai, which will improve the city in the world, Shanghai's international image and status. Expo in Shanghai, China will make the world more fully understand China, and witnessed great changes in China, and accelerate China's market-oriented economy, China will further deepen with the world economy, and can promote the Shanghai and its surrounding region and China's economic the rapid development. Therefore, in promoting China's economic development is of great significance. China has the world's fastest growing economy and one of the largest growth potential, combined with the World Expo is to promote the consumption of stimulating investment in the haste to speed up China's economic development.

C. Liu, J. Chang, and A. Yang (Eds.): ICICA 2011, Part I, CCIS 243, pp. 197–204, 2011.

In cultural terms, the Expo is a global event. Whether it is from space or from the content point of view, the scope of the Expo is very extensive. Participating countries are from around the world, participating countries and visitors from around the world for cultural exchange on learning. Each pavilion has its own national culture, participating countries and visitors, especially foreign tourists visited the exhibition hall through to get to know the history and culture of participating countries with advanced science and technology. At the same time by the participating countries also show their goods and scientific and technological achievements to the visitors from around the world to promote their own. The participating countries through these two aspects achieved cultural exchanges.

Shanghai World Expo Shanghai will boost the economy will play a significant role, so to Shanghai to create considerable employment opportunities, Hannover Expo 1996 will create 10 million jobs. Leading role in the Expo, as China's most economically developed regions of the Yangtze River Delta, Shanghai in the Yangtze River Delta region to take the lead position on the role of boosting the economy of the surrounding region is obvious, therefore, not only for the Shanghai World Expo is a rare development opportunities, impact on the Yangtze River Delta is also very large.

For the Shanghai World Expo impact of quantitative analysis, taking into account the influence can be reflected by the many, through the analysis mainly from the following considerations:

1)Cultural exchanges

Foreign visitors to Shanghai World Expo will see not only promote China's economic development, more importantly, get to know Chinese culture, Chinese culture, making more flourish. In the study of the Expo has attracted many foreign arrivals, we only collected from the opening of the Expo in May to July data. Taking into account the quarter of factors influence the number of foreign immigrants, in order to more accurately predict when the Expo is not the number of foreign immigrants, we collect network according to the Shanghai Tourism Bureau from 2004 to 2009 foreign immigrants each year the number of months 5,6,7, thus fitting the regression forecast in January 2010, the number 5,6,7. Then predicted and the actual number of arrivals compared to the increase in the number to be the impact of the Expo is the number of foreigners to increase awareness and understanding of Chinese culture, promote the exchange of Chinese culture.

2)Economic impact on the Shanghai

Shanghai World Expo led to more rapid development of Shanghai's economy and some infrastructure. Urban planning and transport infrastructure improvement and construction of each pavilion, which requires government investment. At the same time the construction of these facilities must be improved to a great extent, enhance the overall image of Shanghai to attract more tourists and create more economic benefits. It increased during the exhibition work to improve the employment rate. There is stimulating the rapid development of service industry. These will promote the rapid development of Shanghai's economy.

3)Expo radiation effects of the Yangtze River Delta

1970 Osaka World Expo in Osaka as the center for the Kansai economy with the rise. 1992 World Expo in Seville, southern Spain, the development of backward areas. World Expo 2000 in Hanover, Lower Saxony led economic recovery. Yangtze River Delta would be the first to benefit from the Shanghai World Expo.

2 Regression Model

Foreign visitors to Shanghai World Expo will see not only promote China's economic development, more importantly, get to know Chinese culture, Chinese culture, making more flourish. In the study of the Expo has attracted many foreign arrivals, when the use of the opening of the Expo from May to July data. Taking into account the quarter of factors influence the number of foreign immigrants, in order to more accurately predict when the Expo is not the number of foreign immigrants, our network according to the Shanghai Tourism Bureau. Collected from 2004 to 2009, foreign immigrants each year the number of months 5,6,7. Thus fitting the regression forecast in January 2010, the number 5,6,7, and then compared with the actual number of arrivals. Be to increase the number of the Expo is the number of people affected, thereby increasing the foreign knowledge and understanding of Chinese culture.

Suppose $f(x)$ is the return of tourist arrivals in May outside a function, $g(x)$ is the return of tourist arrivals in June outside a function, $h(x)$ is the number of tourists in July outside the regression function. Collected from Shanghai to the Shanghai Tourism Bureau network of 5,6,7 months each year 2004-2009 the number of foreign entry in Table 1:

Table 1. Number of foreign arrivals in Shanghai

Month	2004	2005	2006	2007	2008	2009
May	253427	291987	349356	375836	384154	365658
June	252619	307080	324301	375818	374257	336921
July	263493	301447	313854	342255	335396	383786

Fitted by regression forecast in January 2010,we can get the May and June and July entry number. Specific functions are as follows:

$f(x) = -8597.9x^2 + 84875x + 170075$,the goodness of fit is $R^2 = 0.979$.

$g(x) = -9537.7x^2 + 86037x + 172025$,the goodness of fit is $R^2 = 0.9303$.

$h(x) = -444.36x^2 + 24017x + 246053$,the goodness of fit is $R^2 = 0.9215$.

Where x is 1,2,3 ... (1 representatives on behalf of 2004,2 representatives on behalf of 2005, and so on). Predicted and real value of the contrast shown in Figure 1:

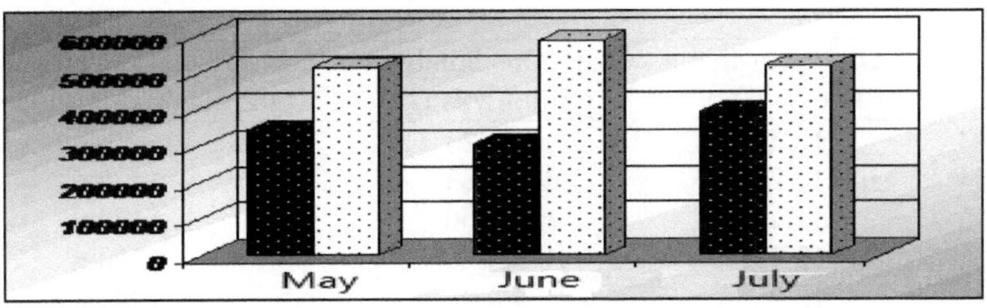

Fig. 1. Forecasts compared with the actual number of arrivals

It can be seen from Figure 1, the World Expo in just three months an increase of 575,181 people of knowledge and understanding of Chinese culture, contributed greatly to foreigners knowledge and understanding of Chinese culture.

It can be seen from the previous May June and July to three months for foreign visitors than the actual historical data fitting according to the data from more than a monthly average of the actual value of combined value of more than 191,727 people compared . Obviously the Expo has attracted many foreign people travel, World Expo is a global event. Whether it is from space, or from the content point of view, the scope of the Expo is very extensive. As the state system is not restricted, and less subject to regional influence, and no ethnic, religious, cultural and economic level and other factors, participating countries from around the world. Tourists to visit the Expo Hall to understand by advanced scientific and technological achievements. The culture of different countries to achieve the exchange of 67.15% increase in the number of immigrants more illustrates this point.

3 Expo-Effect Model

Shanghai World Expo in Shanghai led the rapid economic development and some infrastructure. At the same time the construction of these facilities must be improved to a great extent, enhance the overall image of Shanghai to attract more tourists and create more economic benefits. It increased during the exhibition to work to improve the employment rate. There is stimulating the rapid development of service industries, especially the hotel. These will promote the rapid development of Shanghai's economy. We are from the World Expo in Shanghai or two considerations GDP growth after the Expo to get the data to show GDP growth for Shanghai World Expo impact.

When not hosting the World Expo, Shanghai, the total investment in fixed assets will not result because of the Expo's investment, GDP growth would not be driven by investment in the Expo. So Shanghai's GDP growth rate minus the growth in investment due to the Expo is not when the Shanghai World Expo normal economic growth in GDP.

We compared the Expo held in Shanghai GDP or the growth rate of both cases and thus was born the quantitative analysis of the economic impact of the Shanghai Expo.

1) We calculate fixed asset investment contribution to GDP growth rate: S=E*F*100%. According to the Shanghai Bureau of Statistics, we get the following data.

Table 2. Shanghai GDP(2003-2009)

Year	GDP growth rate R(%)	GDP (One hundred million yuan)	GDPincrease amount F (One hundred million yuan)
2003	12.3	6 694.23	953.2
2004	14.2	8 072.83	1378.6
2005	11.4	9 247.66	1174.8
2006	12.7	10 572.24	1324.6
2007	15.2	12 494.01	1921.8
2008	9.7	14 069.87	1575.9
2009	8.2	15 046.45	976.6

Table 3. Total investment in fixed assets in Shanghai

Year	Total investment in fixed assets (One hundred million yuan)	Amount of fixed asset investment growth E (One hundred million yuan)	Fixed assets investment GDP growth rate S
2003	2452.11	265.05	27.81%
2004	3084.66	632.55	45.88%
2005	3542.55	457.89	38.98%
2006	3925.09	382.54	28.88%
2007	4458.61	533.52	27.76%
2008	4829.45	370.84	23.53%
2009	5273.33	443.88	45.45%

2) We calculate fixed asset investment to GDP ratio of driving: H=R*S

Table 4. Fixed-asset investment to GDP ratio of driving

Year	GDP Growth R(%)	Fixed asset investment growth to GDP S	Fixed assets investment to GDP ratio in driving H
2003	12.3	27.81%	3.420179396
2004	14.2	45.88%	6.515457711
2005	11.4	38.98%	4.443150073
2006	12.7	28.88%	3.667772426
2007	15.2	27.76%	4.219809863
2008	9.7	23.53%	2.282657089
2009	8.2	45.45%	3.727104794

3) We calculate the total fixed capital investment Expo ratio: P=B/E
According to official data Expo 2010 Shanghai World Expo will have a direct investment of about 28.6 billion yuan, and thus driving traffic, commerce, urban transformation of the extended field of 5-10 times the investment, assuming an extension of areas that require 5 times the investment, calculated total investment of 143 billion yuan.

Expo investment proportion of total investment =(Investment in fixed assets per year contribution to GDP growth * The total investment Expo)/ Contribution to total GDP growth rate of investment.

Table 5. The ratio of Expo investment in fixed capital

Year	Expo investment proportion of total investment	Expo Investment B (One hundred million yuan)	Expo investment in fixed capital ratio P
2003	11.67%	166.8670342	62.96%
2004	19.26%	275.3489079	43.53%
2005	16.36%	233.8906729	51.08%
2006	12.12%	173.3107224	45.31%
2007	11.65%	166.6004105	31.23%
2008	9.88%	141.2198392	38.08%
2009	19.07%	272.762413	61.45%

4) We calculate the investment-led Expo a few percentage points of GDP growth: Q=H*P

Table 6. GDP growth rate of investment-led Expo

Year	Expo investment-led GDP growth Q	Year	Expo investment-led GDP growth Q
2004	2.84%	2007	1.32%
2005	2.27%	2008	0.87%
2006	1.66%	2009	2.29%

Expo average GDP growth rate of investment-led is 1.91%.

5) We calculate the GDP growth rate:X=R-Q

Table 7. GDP growth

Year	GDP growth X(%)	Year	GDP growth X(%)
2003	10.1	2007	13.9
2004	11.4	2008	8.8
2005	9.1	2009	5.9

According to the 2000 to 2009 GDP data on time to return to the regression function:

$$y = 841.4 \times t^{0.9513} + 3447$$

(t = 1,2,3, ... 13,1 representatives on behalf of 2000,2 of 2001, and so on).And predicted 2010 and 2012 World Expo in no case the GDP growth rate, detailed in Table 10.

Table 8. 2011 to 2012 GDP growth forecast without Expo

Year	Real GDP (One hundred million yuan)	ForecastGDP(One hundred million yuan)	Forecast growth rate without Expo%
2003	6320.87403	6593	-
2004	7041.453669	7337	-
2005	7682.225953	8074	-
2006	8527.270808	8805	-
2007	9712.561451	9531	-
2008	10567.26686	10252	-
2009	11190.7356	10969	-
2010	-	11683	6.5%
2011	-	12394	6.1%
2012	-	13102	5.7%

Table 8 is based on the data in front of Shanghai's GDP growth rate calculated from 2000 to 2009 the real GDP. Then predicted by the regression function as follows:

$$y = 841.4 \times t^{0.9513} + 3447$$

(t = 1,2,3, ... 13,1 representatives on behalf of 2000,2 of 2001, and so on). We can calculate from 2000 to 2009 the GDP. Then calculate the free Expo 2011 GDP growth of 6.1% and 2012 GDP growth of 5.7%.

The data from the Shanghai Statistical Yearbook, at the same way, when the Shanghai Expo GDP regression function of time is as follows:

$$y = 2148 \times t^{0.8303} + 4229$$

(t = 1,2,3, ... 10,1 representatives on behalf of 2003,2 of 2004, and so on).Predict the results as follows:

Table 9. World Expo held from 2011 to 2012 GDP growth forecast table

t	Year	Real GDP (One hundred million yuan)	Forecast (One hundred million yuan)	Expo growth forecast
1	2003	6 694.23	6377	-
2	2004	8 072.83	8048	-
3	2005	9 247.66	9577	-
4	2006	10 572.24	11020	-
5	2007	12 494.01	12402	-
6	2008	14 069.87	13738	-
7	2009	15 046.45	15036	
8	2010	-	16303	8.4%
9	2011	-	17544	7.6%
10	2012	-	18761	6.9%

Table 9 is from 2003 to 2009 Shanghai World Expo preparation during the actual GDP data. According to data obtained regression function:

$$y = 2148 \times t^{0.8303} + 4229$$

(t = 1,2,3, ... 10,1 representatives on behalf of 2003,2 of 2004, and so on).We can calculate the predicted annual GDP data, and then calculate the corresponding post-Expo 2011 and 2012 growth rate was 7.6% and 6.9%.

According to Tables 8 and 9, we can get the following table.

Table 10. GDP growth rate of Expo and without Expo (%)

Year	Predict with Expo	Predict without Expo	Higher than the GDP growth rate
2011	7.6%	6.1%	1.5%
2012	6.9%	5.7%	1.2%
An average GDP growth rate		1.35%	

Above table of results can be seen, when the World Expo is always better than the GDP growth rate is not higher Expo 1.4 to 1.8 percentage points. The average GDP growth rate is 1.6%. Expo late (2011 - 2012) average growth rate of GDP of Shanghai World Expo will be no more than the GDP average of 1.35 percentage points. After the description of the Shanghai World Expo promoted economic development.

4 Regression Model

Based on the above model to be quantitatively, we get the influence of the Shanghai World Expo. In the promotion of cultural exchange, the World Expo in just three months increased of 575,200 between the people cultural exchange. Shanghai World Expo will greatly facilitate the foreigners to understand Chinese culture and knowledge.

Shanghai World Expo will also have an important economic impact. Shanghai World Expo will boost average annual GDP growth of 1.91 percent during the preparations for Expo (2003 ~ 2009). Shanghai World Expo will boost average annual GDP growth of 1.35 percentage points after the Expo two years (2011 ~ 2012). Shanghai World Expo to promote rapid economic development, a significant economic impact on Shanghai.

Radiation effects Expo will also bring rapid economic development in surrounding areas. Yangtze River Delta region is the Expo the first beneficiaries of radiation effects. Yangtze River Delta region of the second industry and tertiary industry during the Expo organizing the rapid development of the Yangtze River Delta region the average value of secondary industry, 646.676 billion yuan each year in preparation for the World Expo period (2003 ~ 2008). Value of the tertiary industry increased 274.577 billion yuan. Yangtze River Delta to speed up the pace of rapid economic development.

References

1. Jiang, Q., Xie, J., Ye, J.: Mathematical models, version 3. Higher Education Press, Beijing (2003)
2. Shanghai Municipal Tourism Bureau (September 10, 2010), http://lyw.sh.gov.cn/index.htm
3. China Tourism (September 12, 2010), http://www.cnta.com/html/rjy/index.html
4. Shanghai Statistics Bureau (September 10, 2010), http://www.stats-sh.gov.cn
5. China Bureau of Statistics (September 10, 2010), http://www.stats.gov.cn
6. Xu, B.: Research and forecast after World Expo. Shanghai Economic Research (1), 103–111 (2010)
7. Xu, G.: Statistics, 1st edn. Shanghai People's Publishing House, Shanghai (2007)

Based on AHP Quantitative Assessment of Tourism Impact

Jia Peipei[1], Zhang Tai[2], Cui Wei[1], Zhang Jie[1], and Shi Xiaoshuang[1]

[1] Fundamental Department, Hebei College of Finance, Baoding, Hebei, 071051
[2] Experimental training center, Hebei Software Institute, Baoding, Hebei, 071002,
Supported by the Youth Foundation of Hebei Finance University (JY201012)
peipeijia@yahoo.com.cn, zhangtai.ok@163.com

Abstract. The paper comprehensive analysis of the impact of the Expo will factor in the local tourism industry, construction industry of Shanghai World Expo in Shanghai will influence more comprehensive evaluation index system and fuzzy comprehensive evaluation and the combination of AHP, the establishment of the Shanghai World Expo impact of tourism quantitative assessment model.

Keywords: AHP, tourism, Multi-index comprehensive evaluation system, Fuzzy Comprehensive Evaluation.

1 Introduction

2010 Shanghai Expo in domestic, and international Shang are produced has huge of "Expo effect", including political, and economic, and culture technology, aspects, 2010 Shanghai Expo regardless of from characteristics, scale, movie stars force, angle see, are belonging to large flag sexual event, under event tourism theory, success of event tourism activities often to on held to has far-reaching of economic significance and social significance, especially greatly enhanced has tourism attractive and set distinct of city image.

2 Establishment of Multiple Index Comprehensive Evaluation System

In a scientific, comprehensive, testability and flexible principles of ease of operation, for statistical analysis of data published by authoritative departments, factors affecting the reference to the Shanghai tourism, based on analytic theories, the establishment of the Shanghai World Expo 2010 Shanghai multiple index comprehensive evaluation system of tourism impact.

2.1 Analysis of Influencing Factors

2.1.1 Improving Images

Tourism image is means for must of tourist destinations or tourism Enterprise expanded tourist and increased tourism consumption by for of series of information publicity and Expo on tourism of effect inevitable reflected in on Shanghai City of tourism image of effect, and tourism image of improve inevitable will promote tourism of development.[1]

C. Liu, J. Chang, and A. Yang (Eds.): ICICA 2011, Part I, CCIS 243, pp. 205–212, 2011.

2.1.2 Attracting Tourists

From the perspective of a market economy, tourism demand is constituted by tourists, and tourists are formed by the tourists. Expo new attraction to the tourists is very large, is under the Olympic information publicity, gain recognition for tourism resources of host through Expo. Tourist is the basis for development of tourism industry, of course, influence of tourists on tourism be imagined.

2.1.3 Creating a Tourist Environment

Tourism is a combination of relevant departments of the national economy or industry, is a comprehensive business industry, its core industry primarily by the hotel and guesthouse accommodation, transportation, travel agencies and tour entertainment industry and so on. Scenic spots in China including Shanghai, all of their corresponding facilities are still too many areas requiring improvement, including transport, guided tours.[2]

2.1.4 Increased Tourism Revenue

As one of the most fundamental objectives of the evaluation of tourism, increase tourism revenue has to be on the most direct impact of tourism in Shanghai World Expo in Shanghai and, to determine the influence of the Shanghai World Expo in Shanghai tourism; tourism income will be as an indispensable factor.

2.2 Establishment of Multiple Index Comprehensive Evaluation System

According to the analysis of influencing factors on the tourism industry, in the establishment of multiple index comprehensive evaluation system of the following:

Table 1. Font sizes of headings. Table captions should always be positioned above the tables.

Shanghai tourism industry influence of the World Expo 2010	Increased tourism revenue	Retail revenue(x_1)
		Residential income(x_2)
		Restaurant revenues(x_3)
		Entertainment industry income(x_4)
		Ticket revenue(x_5)
	Enhance the tourism image	Media awareness(x_6)
		To upgrade the industry personalize(x_7)
		Public awareness(x_8)
	To attract tourists	Number of domestic tourists(x_9)
		Number of inbound tourism(x_{10})
	Creating tourism environment	Number of hotels(x_{11})
		Number of transport(x_{12})
		Number of restaurant(x_{13})
		Number of travel agency(x_{14})
		Number of tours and entertainment industry(x_{15})

3 On Evaluation Index of Quantitative Treatment

Fuzzy comprehensive evaluation method is a method of broader application of fuzzy mathematics. During the evaluation of an item often encountered such a problem.

3.1 Membership Function of Tectonic Quantitative Methods to Influence the Strength Criteria of Quantitative Treatment [3]

Hypothesis evaluation is divided into A,B,C,D,E a total of five levels: {v1,v2,v3,v4,v5} respectively interpreted as {this influence is very strong, stronge, usual, weak, and very weak} corresponding to its five levels in turn as 5,4,3,2,1. Membership functions:

$$f(x) = \begin{cases} \left[1 + \alpha (x - \beta)^{-2}\right]^{-1} & ,1 \le x \le 3 \\ a \ln x + b & ,3 \le x \le 5 \end{cases};$$

Experience evaluation by experts in accordance with the assumption that:

(1) when the "influence is very strong", the membership to 1, that is, $f(5)=1$;

(2)when the "influence is strong", the membership to 0.8, that is, $f(3)=0.8$;

(3)when the "Influence is very weak", the membership to 0.01, that is $f(1)=0.01$.

Then, we have $\alpha=1.1086$, $\beta=0.8942$, $a=0.3915$, $b=0.3699$. The membership function is:

$$f(x) = \begin{cases} \left[1+1.1086(x-0.8942)^{-2}\right]^{-1} & ,1 \le x \le 3 \\ 0.3915\ln x + 0.3699 & ,3 \le x \le 5 \end{cases}$$

Therefore, for each evaluation are quantitative values, namely:

Table 2. Influence quantization tables

A	Influence is very strong	1
B	Influence the strong	0.9
C	Influence the General	0.8
D	Influence of weak	0.5
E	Very weak influence	0.01

3.2 On Quantitative Evaluation Factors of Treatment

3.2.1 Quantify the Impact Factor to Increase Tourism Revenue Processing

Table 3 data, compared with a year earlier to increase tourism revenue growth factor affecting the normalized, get the following increase tourism revenue impact factor of quantitative value table.

Table 3. Shanghai tourism statistics

month	March	April	May	June	July
Entertainment tourism,educational and cultural products	98.8	99.20	100.60	101.80	102.00
the same period than last year (%)	-1.20	———	0.60	———	2.00
Social total retail sales of consumer goods (billion)	474.66	474.78	512.46	501.58	505.98
last year the corresponding period grows (%)	15.5	16.5	18.9	19.5	18.1
catering	50.39	49.77	55.42	57.88	59.6
the same period than last year (%)	8.5	12.1	14.7	25	27.7
inbound tourism (million)	69.43	67.76	71.37	75.66	———
the same period than last year (%)	36	23.4	45.7	61.2	———

Table 4. Increase tourism revenue impact factor of quantitative value table

items	data	Evaluation grade	Quantitative evaluation grades	weight
Retail revenues (x1)	17.7%	C	0.8	22.163%
Accommodation income	41.575%	A	1	22.70%
Catering income (x3)	17.7%	C	0.8	22.163%
Entertainment income (x4)	0.4667%	E	0.01	0.274%
Tickets income (x5)	———	A	1	22.70%

3.2.2 Tourism Image to Ascend the Impact Factor Quantization Process

The domestic well-known third-party data companies-WanRui data using independent research and development of network communication effect of monitoring system, according to the 2010 world expo information we get the table 5:

Table 5. Tourism image to ascend the impact factor quantization process sheets

items	Evaluation grade	Quantitative evaluation grades	Each affecting factors and weighting
Media attention	A	1	37.04%
Public attention	B	0.9	33.33%
Personalized industry	C	0.8	29.63%

Table 6. Factors to attract tourist quantitative processing

items	growth than 2009	Evaluation grade	Quantitative evaluation grades	weight
Reception of domestic tourists	50%	A	1	55.6%
Reception tourist arrivals	17%	C	0.8	44.4%

3.2.3 Attract Tourist Influence Factor of the Quantization Process

City tourism bureau chief word book Ming reported this year Shanghai tourism work major goals: reception of domestic tourists than 1.8 million in 2009, up about 45 percent; According to the above information we can get table 6.

3.2.4 Tourism Environment to Create the Impact Factor Quantization Process

First, to the index survey passenger attention.

Table 7. Data survey results tables

Survey index	Accommo-dation	catering	entertainment	Shopping	traffic	guide	other
Attention	47.4%	14.9%	15.0%	7.0%	10.2%	2.4%	2.8%

According to the statistical data of above a few indexes can be obtained quantized treatment.

Table 8. Creating tourism environment impact factor quantization processing

items	Qualitative evaluation	Quantitative qualitative evaluation	weight
Hotel number	A	1	31.15%
Transportation quantity	D	0.5	15.58%
Catering number	C	0.8	24.92%
Travel club number	E	0.01	0.31%
Visit entertainment quantity	B	0.9	28.04%

3.3 The Evaluation Indexes of Four Quantization Process

According to the above data and information, we adopt the weighted fuzzy comprehensive analysis, the method of comprehensive evaluation for four index weight, but with data gives a comprehensive, accuracy, we still needs to be enhanced by structure fuzzy membership functions under the quantitative method for quantitative indexes, process.

Table 9. Tourism index evaluation table

	revenue	image	tourist	environment
Current economic benefits	A	D	A	C
Quantitative index	1	0.5	1	0.8
Long-term economic benefits	C	A	C	D
Quantitative index	0.8	1	0.8	0.5
Average economic benefits	0.9	0.75	0.9	0.65

To normalized data

Evaluation index	Increase tourism revenue	Ascending tourism image	Attract tourist	Create tourism environment
weight	0.28125	0.234375	0.28125	0.203125

3.4 For Multi-index Synthetic Evaluation System of the Impact Factor Four Index 15 Quantization Process to become Comprehensive

According to the above data results of data and information, normalized.

Table 10. The influence of the shadow make a unified normalized tables

items	Superior index weight	Itself weight	Combination weight coefficient
Retail revenues	0.28125	0.22163	0.062333
Accommodation income	0.28125	0.2270	0.063844
Catering income	0.28125	0.22163	0.062333
Entertainment income	0.28125	0.00274	0.000771
Tickets income	0.28125	0.2270	0.063844
Media attention	0.234375	0.3704	0.086813
Promoting industrial individuation	0.234315	0.3333	0.078097
Promoting industrial individuation	0.234375	0.2963	0.069445
Domestic tourism number	0.28125	0.556	0.156263
Tourist arrivals	0.28125	0.444	0.124988
Hotel number	0.203125	0.3115	0.063273
Transportation quantity	0.203125	0.1558	0.031647
Catering number	0.203125	0.2492	0.050619
Travel club number	0.203125	0.0031	0.00063
Visit entertainment quantity	0.203125	0.2804	0.056956

4 Evaluation Model of the Establishment and Application

4.1 Establishment of Model

This model is based on multivariate linear model, the weight of every evaluation factors obtained, unified level standard, get tourism impact quantitative evaluation model. Will Shanghai world expo related data analysis, according to the uniform level standard and get their income into model according to the uniform score, criterion to evaluate its effect. Will influence degree set to 1-5 gradient, respectively {influence very weak; Less influential; Influential general; Influence is stronger; Influence is very strong}[4].

According to the above analysis, we obtained based on the influence of the multivariate linear models of tourism expo quantitative evaluation model:

$$f(x_1,\ldots,x_n)=\beta_1\times x_1+\beta_2\times x_2+\cdots\cdots+\beta_n\times x_n\,.$$

Denote: β_n the index proportion, x_n the evaluation index, $n=1,2,\cdots,15$.

$\beta_1,\cdots,\beta_n=$ 0.062333,0.063844,0.062333,0.000771,0.063844,0.086813,0.078097, 0.069445,0.156263,0.124988,0.063273,0.031647,0.050619,0.00063,0.056956

Thus, the tourism influential evaluation model is:

$$\begin{aligned}f(x_n)=&0.062333\times x_1+0.063844\times x_2+0.062333\times x_3+0.000771\times x_4\\&+0.063844\times x_5+0.086813\times x_6+0.078097\times x_7+0.069445\times x_8\\&+0.156263\times x_9+0.124988\times x_{10}+0.063273\times x_{11}+0.031647\times x_{12}\\&+0.050619\times x_{13}+0.00063\times x_{14}+0.056956\times x_{15}\end{aligned}$$

Using the equation can be quantitatively calculated on the influence of the world expo in Shanghai tourism intensity.

4.2 The Influence of the Inspection

According to the data, we get to watch, referring to influence gradient 15 impact factors make a unified quantization to deal with:

x_1	x_2	x_3	x_4	x_5	x_6	x_7	x_8	x_9	x_{10}	x_{11}	x_{12}	x_{13}	x_{14}	x_{15}
C	A	C	E	A	A	B	C	A	C	A	D	C	E	B
3	5	3	1	5	5	4	3	5	3	5	2	3	1	4

Will more quantitative values and obtained the model of Shanghai expo in Shanghai, the influence of the tourism industry $f(x)=3.884246$. $f_{\min}(1)=0.971856$, $f_{\max}(5)=4.85928$, reference the satisfaction survey measurement method and evaluation standards formulated influence are shown below:

Influence is very strong	Influence strong	Influence general	Less influential
3.887—4.859	2.916—3.887	1.944—2.916	0.971—1.944

So, we finally get to Shanghai world expo Shanghai tourism influence. CePingBiao reference influence, and it can get to Shanghai world expo Shanghai tourism's influence is very strong.

5 Epilogue

Through the above analysis, we can conclude that of Shanghai world expo effect the influence of tourism industry is huge, especially for greatly increased the tourist attraction and establish a striking image of the city. The expo as a brand had formed a kind of intangible assets, in the future for a very long time will still as tourism resources produce long-term effects. 2010 world expo ends, for the expo and established urban infrastructure can continue for tourism, play used on the other.

References

1. Lin, X.-P.: Olympic host city influence of digital reading. Beijing Planning and Construction 2, 149–151 (2004)
2. Yang, L.-P., Zhang, J.-X.: Significant events project influence on urban development. Urban Problems 1, 11–15 (2008)
3. Wang, Z.-G., Yang, S.-S.: Based on fuzzy comprehensive evaluation information network system can survive evaluation. Network Security Technology and Application, 57–60 (2010)
4. Jiang, Q.-Y., Xie, J.-X., Ye, J.: Mathematical model. Higher Education Press, Beijing (2008)
5. Zhao, Y.-F., Chen, J.-F., Guo, W.-L.: The analytic hierarchy process and its application in power decision-making system. Power System Protection and Control 3, 134–136 (2005)
6. Wang, Y., Wu, Y.-J., Xiong, A.-Y., Liu, Y.: Hubei province summer travel climate comfort fuzzy comprehensive evaluation. Journal of Guizhou Meteorology 2, 28–29 (2009)
7. Yang, R.-R.: Heilongjiang province of tourism cycle economy evaluation index system structure. Northern Economy 5, 20–22 (2007)
8. Di, Q.-B., Han, Z.-L.: Discussion of the Assessment Indicators System of Sustainable Development of Marine Economy. Areal Research and Development 3, 117–121 (2009)
9. Zhang, Q.-D.: Planning environmental impact assessment difficulties analysis. Environment and Sustainable Development 1, 39–42 (2011)
10. Cui, F.: Coordinated Development Degree of Tourism Economy and Ecological Environment in Shanghai. China Population Resources and Environment 5, 64–69 (2008)

Influence of FDI on the Total Export of Shanxi Province

Li Miao

Schlool of Humanities, Economics and Law, Northwestern Polytechnical University
Xi'an, China 710072
limiao@nwpu.edu.cn

Abstract. Since the policy of reform and opening up, Foreign Direct Investment (FDI) in China has reached significant achievements. Foreign trade has also made worldwide known achievements. This paper, taking Shanxi Province, the major trade province of FDI and foreign trade, as the research subject, with the data from 1987 to 2010, adopts dummy variables, unit root test, cointegration test, Granger causality test and the method of regression models, to conduct an empirical research on the influence of FDI on the total export of Shanxi province. Regression results show that FDI has a long-term and significant role in promoting export growth of Shanxi province and there had been structural changes in the relationship between FDI stocks and exports of Shanxi Province in 1993 which is the significant turning point for Shanxi adopting FDI.

Keywords: FDI, total export, dummy variables, cointegration, Granger causality.

1 Introduction

Shanxi Province, as one of the leading provinces in development of the west regions, has made notable achievements. Compared with the coastal provinces and cities, Shanxi province is with a poor basis in its FDI utilization, but its developing speed is very fast. In recent ten years, its growing speed of adopting FDI ranks the top cities around the country. Since 2002, Shanxi has become the second leading province attracting FDI in the west regions, followed by Sichuan province. Therefore, this paper takes Shanxi as the research subject, applying Econometric analysis method to empirically study the influence of FDI on Shanxi's total export.

2 Brief Introduction to Econometric Analysis Method

Quantitative analysis of the influence of FDI on the foreign trade scope. Scholars generally measure FDI's influence on foreign trade through establishing econometric models which rarely reflect the influence of qualitative factors. After Deng Xiaoping's Southward tour speech in 1992, the amount of foreign investment in China surged to a maintained height afterward. The year 1993 and 1994 became the turning point of development. Since characteristics of FDI before and after 1993 are distinctly different, a single model cannot well reflect the different characteristics of these two phases and the different influential factors of policy and environmental. Therefore, the

C. Liu, J. Chang, and A. Yang (Eds.): ICICA 2011, Part I, CCIS 243, pp. 213–220, 2011.

author decides to introduce dummy variables in to the econometric model so as to measure the influence of qualitative factors such as the policy and environment factors at different stages. Such is to improve the model accuracy and eliminate the setting error of the model and ultimately to avoid reduction in sample size and accuracy caused by direct subsection regression. In addition, in existing studies, most models are directly established without unit root test, cointegration test and Granger test. Therefore, they are running the risk of "pseudo regression". The author will select related data from 1990 to 2010, on the basis of a series of tests to establish the econometric model to make the empirical analysis. The final goal is to reveal the promoting role and laws of FDI on Shanxi province's export growth. All of the model analysis in this paper is conducted by using measuring software Eviews5.0.

3 Empirical Research on the Influence of FDI on the Total Export of Shanxi Province

3.1 Variable Selection and Data Description

In establishing the relationship model between FDI and exports, variable selection is directly decides the success of the model. Generally speaking, to analyze the relationship between FDI and exports, according to experiences it is reasonable to directly selecting the actually utilized foreign capital as the explaining variable and exports as the explained variable. However, due to that the foreign-invested enterprises have to go through the process from investment to production, causing the time lag effect, so we can choose the one-year lagged FDI as the explaining variable; taking into account the capital cumulative effect, we will establish two models in FDI influence on Shanxi's total exports, respectively using FDI-1, FDIC-1 as the variables. FDI-1 is FDI of the previous year and FDIC-1 is the total utilization value of FDI in the previous year. The simple transforming of the variable values cannot affect their correlation, so we have conducted the logsrithmization on the data used to minimize the influence of heteroskedasticity problems occurred in time series on the results accuracy. Shanxi province does not have official FDI and exports statistics since 1985. The FDI amount and size before 1990 were very small (between 1990 and 2010, FDI projects did not have statistics, and the actual foreign capital utilization totaled only 1 billion U.S. dollars). Thus, this paper studies the data from 1990 to 2010, spanning 21 years. Among them, FDI adopts the actual amount of FDI utilization of each year as its statistic data and export is the total annual exports. All the unit is 0.1 billion dollars. After Deng Xiaoping's southern tour speech in 1992, foreign investment into our country surged rapidly, and then maintained a constant high position. The year 1993 and 1994 became the turning point of the developmen t. The influence of policy factor is qualitative, so the dummy variable introduced are as follows:

$$D_t = \begin{cases} 1, & 1993(\textit{before } 1993) \\ 0, & 1993(\textit{after } 1993) \end{cases}$$

The model of the entire sample duration can be written as follows:

$$\ln EX_t = b_0 + b_1 D_t + (b_2 + b_3 D_t)\ln FDI_{-1t} + U_t$$
$$\ln EX_t = b_0 + b_1 D_t + (b_2 + b_3 D_t)\ln FDIC_{-1t} + U_t$$

All data in this paper are from "Statistical Yearbook of Shanxi Province". Table 1 shows the raw data:

Table1. 1990-2010 Shanxi province FDI utilization na and exports

Year	(EX)	lnEX	FDI-1	lnFDI-1	FDIC-1	lnFDIC-1
1990	4.6059	1.527	0.3106	-1.169	4.5068	1.506
1991	6.0502	1.800	0.1133	-2.178	4.9259	1.595
1992	7.6531	2.035	0.2068	-1.576	5.2418	1.657
1993	9.9347	2.296	5.2290	1.654	5.7001	1.74
1994	12.1615	2.498	9.2204	2.221	8.0433	2.085
1995	12.8261	2.551	4.1142	1.414	10.4242	2.344
1996	12.6922	2.541	4.1521	1.424	13.6649	2.615
1997	12.3120	2.511	6.0056	1.793	16.9657	2.831
1998	11.1668	2.413	6.5990	1.887	23.2473	3.146
1999	11.5225	2.444	3.7582	1.324	26.2483	3.268
2000	13.1003	2.573	4.2693	1.451	28.9011	3.364
2001	11.1044	2.407	4.9931	1.608	31.9053	3.463
2002	13.7717	2.623	7.3009	1.988	35.4227	3.567
2003	17.3523	2.854	8.4064	2.129	44.1893	3.788
2004	23.9658	3.177	8.3428	2.121	48.8495	3.889
2005	30.7581	3.426	10.4877	2.35	54.1159	3.991
2006	36.2960	3.671	15.8273	2.761	60.39	984.111
2007	46.7244	3.844	20.3530	3.013	69.64	874.243
2008	53.8066	3.985	19.7311	2.982	91.60	034.517
2009	39.8815	3.686	18.1781	2.9	94.29	574.546
2010	62.07	4.128	14.0117	2.640	109	.4016.015

Note : Na stands for data loss.
Source: 1991 -2011 " the shanxi statistics year book "

3.2 Econometric Analysis Process

(1) Stationarity test

We need to apply the cointegration technique to analyze the impact of FDI on the total exports growth, aiming to reveal problems from two aspects: namely, if there is a long-term and stable relationship between Shanxi FDI and its exports; to what extent do they interact with each other. Since this variable is the time-series data, there may be non-stationarity. Thus we use ADF (Augmented Dickey-Fuller) unit root test method to test the stability of the variables.

From the output results of the above table, it can be seen that the original time series lnEX, ln lnFDI-1, ln lnFDIC-1 under the 1%, 5% and 10% significance levels are not stable, but the time series △lnEX and △lnFDIC-1 under the 5% significant level is stable, △FDI-1 under the 1% significant level is stable. Thus we can draw that, time series lnEX, ln FDI-1, ln FDIC-1 are all first-order single , whole I (1) sequence. There might be a cointegration relationship between them.

Table 2. ADF unit root test results

Variables	Test type (C,T, K)	ADF test value	Critical value at each significant level			Testing
			1%	5%	10%	
LNEX	(0,0,1)	-0.458952	-3.808546	-3.020686	-2.650413	unsteady
LNFDI- 1	(0,0,1)	-20184526	-3.831511	-3.029970	-2.655194	unsteady
LNFDIC-1	(0,0,1)	-0.922765	-3.808546	-3.020686	-2.650413	unsteady
△lnEX	(0,0,1)	-3.686014	-3.831511	-3.029970	-2.655194	Steady**
△lnFDI-1	(0,0,0)	-5.045402	-3.857386	-3.040391	-2.660551	Steady***
△lnFDIC-1	(0,0,0)	-3.397700	-3.831511	-3.029970	-2.655194	Steady**

Note: candt are the constant item and the tendency item. k is the lagged orders adopted. When an ADF value is larger than the critical value, it declares an unstable sequence. * * * is for under there 1 % significant leve l. * * is for under the 5 % significant level. * is for under the 10% signif icant leve l.

(2) Cointegration test

Unstable time series cannot directly go through simple regressions without the cointegration test to verify whether there is cointegration relationship among variables, namely, whether there is a long-term equilibrium relationship among variables. Because we separately inspect the co-integration relationship between lnEX and ln FDI-1, lnEX and ln FDIC-1, here we choose the E - G two-step inspection. Its principle is if multiple I (1) or I (0) variable have the cointegration relationship, after using the traditional econometric to conduct variable regressions, the residual should obey the I (0) process. Since the above variables are I (1) process, we can use E - G two-step regression analysis. First we use least-square method to have a regression analysis on ln FDI-1 and lnEX, lnEX and ln FDIC-1, and then we will have an ADF unit root test on the residual sequences of the regression equation. Finally, we determine whether the co-integration relationship exists or not according to the stableness of the residual sequences. Results of the ADF unit root test on LnEX and ln FDI-1 regression equations and the residual series are as follows:

$$\ln EX_t = 1.426 - 0.498D_t + (0.22 + 1.199D_t) \times \ln FDI_{-1t} \tag{1}$$

$$t \text{ value } [2.055] \quad [-0.661] \quad [-0.537] \quad [2.798]$$

$$R_2 = 0.8597 \qquad \overline{R_2} = 0.835 \qquad F = 34.722$$

Table 3. ADF unit root test results of equations(1) Residual series

ADF Test Statistics	-4.833885	1%critical value	-3.831511	stable
		5%critical value	-3.029970	
		10%critical value	-2.655194	

Results of ADF unit root test on LnEXt and ln FDIC-1 regression equations and the residual series are as follows:

$$\ln EX_t = -3.51 + 4.36D_t + (0.341 + 0.726D_t) \times \ln FDIC_{-1t} \tag{2}$$

$$t \text{ value } [-0.711] \quad [0.882] \quad [1.074] \quad [-0.876]$$

$$R_2 = 0.819 \qquad \overline{R_2} = 0.787 \qquad F = 25.675$$

$$\ln EX_t = 3.561 - 2.526D_t + (0.104 + 1.04D_t) \times \ln FDI_{-1t} \tag{3}$$

$$(0.089) \quad (0.360) \quad (0.037) \quad (0.108)$$

$$[40.035] \quad [-7.009] \quad [2.784] \quad [9.618]$$

$$\overline{R^2} = 0.953$$

Table 4. ADF unit root test results of equations (2) Residual series

ADF Test Statistics	-4.117357	1%critical value	-3.831511	steady
		5%critical value	-3.029970	
		10%critical value	-2.655194	

Judging from the testing results , both the results of the ADF unit root test on the residual series of equation (1) and equation (2) are less than the critical value under the 1% significant level, indicating that a co-integration relationship can be inferred respectively between lnEX and ln FDI-1, lnEX and ln FDIC-1 under the 99 % confidence level, that they have a long-term relationship, and that they can go for the next step of Granger causality test in order to find out their causal relationship.

(3) Granger causality test

The cointegration test results confirm that there is a long-term equilibrium relationship between the lnEX and FDI-1 , lnEX and ln FDIC-1, but to decide whether there is a causal relationship and what kind of causality there is, we still need further Granger causality tests on them. Granger causality tests are so sensitive to the changes in lag phases that it provides a powerful tool for us to study the short-term and long-term relationship between the economic variables. The inspection principle is: take the output P value as the probability value to be examined, and decide the probability of exist causality according to the P value. If P <0.1, it means under the 10% significant level, namely 90% confidence level, the Granger causality is accepted; If P> 0.1, it means the Granger causality is rejected under the 10% significant level or the 90% confidence level . This article chooses the 10% significant level, and P values of the second-order lag. The test results are shown in Table 5:

From the results of Granger causality tests we can see that at the 10% level of significance, for the two variables ln FDI-1 and lnEX, ln FDI-1 is the cause of lnEX, but lnEX is not the cause of ln FDI-11. For the two variables FDIC-1 and lnEX, ln FDIC-1 is the cause of lnEX's, while ln FDIC-1 is not the cause of lnEX's. That is to say, FDI growth caused exports growth, and they have the direct causality that FDI is the cause and export is the result. However, the contrary is not true.

Table 5. Granger causality test results

Test	P value of Second order lag	Result
lnFDI-1 is not the Granger cause for lnEX	0.58573	lnFDI-1→?lnEX
lnEX is not the Granger cause for lnFDI-1	0.04744	lnEX→lnFDI-1
lnFDIC-1 is not the Granger cause for lnEX	0.04389	lnFDIC-1→lnEX
lnEX is not the Granger cause for lnFDIC-1	0.34218	lnEX→? lnFDIC-1

Note: P value is the probability value. If P < 0.05, causality at the 5% significance level is accepted; if P< 0.1, causality at the 10% significant level is accepted; otherwise, the causal relationship can not be established. The conclusion decides whether or not to reject the null hypothesis under the 10% significant level. →says the former is the latter's Granger reason, →? says the former is not the latter's Granger reason.

Passed the Granger causality test, equations obtained from the cointegration test are established. Next is the analysis of the equations.

$$\ln EX_t = 1.426 - 0.498D_t + (0.22 + 1.199D_t) \times \ln FDI_{-1t} \tag{4}$$

t value [2.055] [–0.661] [–0.537] [2.798]

$R_2 = 0.8597 \qquad \overline{R_2} = 0.835 \qquad F = 34.722$

Regression equation (4.1.9) can be transformed into the following two sub-equations:

lnEXt=1.426 +0.22lnFDI-1t pre- 1993 (5)

lnEXt=0.928 +1.419lnFDI-1t post-1993 (6)

In Equation (1), the adjusted goodness-of-fit illustrates that the overall linear relationship of the equation is remarkably tenable. T value represents that ln FDI-1and dummy variable D as the explaining variables are appropriate. It can be seen from the regression results that FDI of Shanxi Province plays a relatively strong role in promoting the growth of export. Taking 1993 for the sector, there was a structural change on the relationship between Shanxi FDI and exports. Before 1993, every increase of 1 percentage point of Shanxi FDI will drive the exports growth of next year for 0.22 percentage points. After 1993, every increase of 1 percentage point of Shanxi FDI will lead an increase of 1.419 percent of exports in the next year. The contribution of FDI to export is obviously enhanced.

lnEX and lnFDIC-1 regression equation is as follows:

$$\ln EX_t = -3.51 + 4.36D_t + (0.341 + 0.726D_t) \times \ln FDIC_{-1t} \tag{7}$$

t value [–0.711] [0.882] [1.074] [–0.876]

$R_2 = 0.819 \qquad \overline{R_2} = 0.787 \qquad F = 25.675$

Regression equation (4.1.10) can be transformed into the following two sub-equations:

$$\ln EXt=-3.51+0.341\ln FDIC\text{-}1t \quad \text{pre- 1993} \tag{8}$$

$$\ln EXt=0.85+1.067\ln FDIC\text{-}1t \quad \text{post-1993} \tag{9}$$

In the equation (2), the adjusted goodness-of-fit illustrate equation overall linear relationship significantly established. t value indicates that the ln FDIC-1t and dummy variables Dt as the explanatory variable is appropriate. It can be seen from the regression results, that Shanxi FDI capital stock, to some degree, has promoted its exports growth. Similarly, taking 1993 for the sector, there also was a structural change in the relationship between FDI capital stock and exports. Before 1993, whenever capital stock of FDI in Shanxi Province increased by 1 percentage point, it would bring about exports growth in the next year by 0.34 percentage points. After 1993, every increase of 1 percentage point in capital stock of FDI in Shanxi Province will bring about exports growth in the next year by 1.67 percent.

6 Conclusion

First, the co-integration analysis shows that there is a long-term equilibrium relationship between FDI and Shanxi exports volume. FDI plays a remarkable role in promoting exports growth, and such role is the subject to the time lag effect. Meanwhile, FDI has a strong accumulative effect on promoting export growth, so Shanxi FDI's influence on exports is a long-term releasing process. Second, taking 2003 for the sector, both the amounts of Shanxi FDI and exports growth have notably increased. However, relatively exports grow faster than FDI, which indicates that the Western Development makes the huge contribution to the policy impetus of exports, and the year 2003 is a turning point for the development of export and FDI. In addition, seen from Granger causality test results, FDI growth have caused exports growth and they have direct causality relationship. FDI is the cause while export is the result. Yet FDI growth doesn't have an obvious effect on promoting exports increase, so the reverse causality cannot be established.

References

1. Xiao, D.: Foreign Trade Theory. Nankai University Press, Tianjin (2002)
2. Paul, K. (beauty): Krueman New Theory of International Trade, China Social Science Press (2002)
3. XiaoJuan, J., Shengming, Y., Lei, F.: Chinese Foreign Trade Theoretical Frontiers III. Social Sciences Academic Press (2003)
4. Wang, Z., Feng, L.: FDI in China and China's export competitiveness-to our country according to different technology category subdivision manufactured exports empirical analysis. The Nankai Economy Research (4), first 52–57 (2004)
5. Zhang, W., Wu, J.: FDI and empirical study of China's foreign trade. International trade issues of (3), first 80–90 (2005)

6. Chen, J., Qin, Z.: FDI for Chinese goods import and export influence empirical analysis. The International Trade 5th period, 62–68 (2006)
7. Shanxi, B.: The shanxi statistical yearbook. China Statistical Publishing House (1991-2011)
8. Kanta, M., Akbar, T.: The Effect of Foreign Capital and Imports on Economic Growth: Further Evidence from Four Asian Countries(1970-1998). Journal of Asian Economics (2004)
9. Fishwick, F.: Multinational Companies and Economic Concentration in Europe. Gower Publishing Company, England (1981)
10. Liu, X.H., Burridge, P.: Relationships between Economic Growth, Foreign Direct Investment and Trade: Evidence from China. Taylor and Francis Journals Applied Economics (2002)

Application of Fuzzy Cluster Analysis for Academic Title Evaluation

Baofeng Li and Donghua Wang

Department of Mathematics and Information Science,
Tangshan Normal University, Tangshan, China
lbf6713@sina.com

Abstract. In this paper, firstly fuzzy cluster analysis is introduced to make the performance evaluation of teaching level according to original data and standardized data respectively, which come from thirty-four teaching staffs who participate in the academic title evaluation of associate professor in 2010. And then for fully reflecting original information of the data and not losing the accuracy of the evaluation, a combination evaluation model based on the Borda method is established. At last a more scientific and rational result is get applying a new model to the data mention above.

Keywords: fuzzy cluster analysis, the method of Borda, combination evaluation, academic title evaluation.

1 Introduction

Evaluation work of the professional and technical positions involves the performance evaluation about the teaching staffs [1]. It not only helps improve the scientific and technological management level and efficiency, but also to mobilize the enthusiasm of teaching staffs [2]. So the establishment of a scientific, objective, fair and quantifiable evaluation method of performance is the exploration direction for many research scientists [3].

Essentially, the work of performance evaluation of teachers is a ranking job. In order to make the results more reasonable, credible and scientific, we can synthesize the fuzzy information of the teachers. Then a fuzzy mathematical model can be built using fuzzy cluster analysis method. At last, we can determine the ranking of performance about each teacher according fuzzy cluster analysis results.

In practical problems, different data generally have different dimensions. In order to make the quantities with different dimensions can be compared; the dates usually need to be standardized [4, 5]. However, the standardized data usually lose some information of the original data. Therefore, in order to fully reflect the original information of the data and the accuracy of the evaluation, this paper uses fuzzy cluster analysis to rank the performance of teachers applying original data s and standardized data and finally gets the results by the method of Borda [6].

C. Liu, J. Chang, and A. Yang (Eds.): ICICA 2011, Part I, CCIS 243, pp. 221–226, 2011.

2 Theory and Basic Steps of the Evaluation

Fuzzy cluster analysis [7, 8] is a basic method of mathematical statistics used in the study of multivariate statistical analysis. It can quantitatively determine the similarity relation between the samples based on the attributes or characteristics of the samples. From the fuzzy cluster analysis method we can know that after given the threshold level, the most similar objects gather in a class. If we construct a new object whose indexes take the optimal value(or worst value)of each index and cluster, then the object which first gather into a class with this constructed object is the best (or worst)evaluation object . Repeat this process, we can get the sorting from good to bad(or from poor into good).

Let $X = \{x_1, x_2, \cdots, x_n\}$ be the set of the objects which are need to be sorted. And the characters of each object is expressed by m indexes, ie

$$x_i = (x_{i1}, x_{i2}, \cdots, x_{im}), \quad i = 1,2,\cdots,n$$

Then, the steps of the evaluation based on fuzzy clustering are:

The first step Increase an new object x_{n+1}, whose indexes take the optimal value of each index;

The second step structure fuzzy similar matrix, that is, determine the level of similarity between those objects. There are many ways to do this job, for example, correlation coefficient method, distance method, the subjective evaluation method, etc.

The third step Do fuzzy clustering, that is, find out the object which is clustered into the same cluster with x_{n+1}, and write down the number;

The fourth step Remove the object in the same cluster with x_{n+1}, from the object set;

The fifth step Repeat the step (2) to step (4), until all objects sorting are finished.

In practical problems, to make use the quantities with different dimensions, we usually require to make suitable transformations to the date before the second step of data, namely standardization.

So in order to better use data and better evaluate, this article will respectively use original data and standardized data to calculate, where we will use the following formula to make standardization:

$$x_{ij}^{'} = \frac{x_{ij} - \min_j x_{ij}}{\max_j x_{ij} - \min_j x_{ij}}$$

where $x_{ij} (i = 1,2,\cdots,n; j = 1,2,\cdots,m)$ are original date and $x_{ij}^{'}$ $(i = 1,2,\cdots,n;$ $j = 1,2,\cdots,m)$ are standardized data.

After getting the two sort results, we can compose them by the mean value method or Borda method, then we will obtain the combination evaluation value. Borda method is applied widely and we take this method here. Its principle is as follow:

In the results obtained by different methods, if the number of that decision scheme A_i is better than A_j is greater than the number of that A_j is better than A_i, then .it note that A_iSA_j; If the number is equal, then note that A_iEA_j. So we can structure the Borda matrix as follow:

$$B=(b_{ij})_{m\times m}\text{, where } b_{ij}=\begin{cases}1, if\ A_iEA_j\\ 0\ other\,cases\end{cases}.$$

Define the score of A_i is

$$b_i=\sum_{j=1,j\neq i}^{m} b_{ij}$$

Then the b_i is the "excellent" (or "wins") number of A_i. Observe that, the greater b_i is, the better A_i is. If $b_i=b_j$, then we compare their variance. The variance is, the decision scheme is.

3 Case

Tangshan Normal University is a full-time regular undergraduate colleges of Hebei province of China. Every year there are many teachers to apply to participate in academic title evaluation. The number of applicants is always smaller than the given index, so how to choose from them is a painful problem.

Taking the information about thirty-four teaching staffs who participate in the academic title evaluation of associate professor in Tangshan Normal University in the 2010 as example, it uses fuzzy cluster analysis to evaluate and sort their capability. The original data can be seen in Table 1(The name of the teaching staffs are substitute by their second name).

Firstly supposes that there is a teacher, whose evaluation value of each index is not less than any one of the 34 teachers. Without loss of generality, his indexes can take 6, 70.81, 36.7, 9. Then we can determine the performance sorting in accordance with the order of the teachers clustering into one class with the virtual teacher. Using quantity product approach [9] we get the fuzzy similarity matrixes respectively. At last by transitive closure method [10] we can get the clustering results which are given in Table2.

By computing, the correlation coefficient between the two combination evaluation methods is 0.88. And the result of the combination evaluation value can be seen in the Table 3 which are computed by the method of Borda.

Table 1. The date of the 34 teaching staffs

Name	Educational background	Teaching quantity	Scientific research workload	Job performance
Cheng	5	47	30.31	9
Mou	4	51	21.585	7.75
Yingzi	5	32.4	10.805	7
Yufen	4	58	9.67	7
Dong	3	46.12	8.735	7
Junxia	5	48.5	22.19	7
Liqiang	5	44.1	11.09	7
Jining	5	60.3	15.92	7
Shugeng	5	44.62	6.5	8.75
Zhixin	6	57	21.48	7
Xiaohui	5	60	8.19	5
Wei	5	49	9.59	7.3
Baofeng	5	63	24.935	8
Gang	3	46	16.53	8.25
Haicheng	3	59	11	7.75
Jian	5	44.5	14.65	6.25
Yuanyuan	3	67	14.5	9
Fafen	5	59.57	9.1975	7
Junhong	4	58	19.645	9
Yanzhi	5	61	29.665	8
Xiangguo	3	47	8	9
Yongqing	4	51	22.5	5
Lina	5	44.11	21.19	7.5
Shengcai	5	55	16.7	7.5
Zhenling	5	60.12	36.7	7
Yanyu	3	54.5	12.85	9
Jing	6	55	30.68	5.25
Liying	4	58.8	5.73	7.35
Yuanjing	4	52.5	24.4	7.5
Yongping	6	41.8	20.145	5
Xin	5	65.73	26.17	8.65
Lili	6	58	15.145	7.75
Yan	5	70.81	15.525	7
Yuhua	5	54.5	15.735	9

Remark. The value of each index about the teaching staff is calculated by the same and fixed formula which is accepted by the teaching staffs in Tangshan Normal University.

Table 2. The results of the fuzzy cluster analysis

Name	The result of unstandardiz-ation	The result of standardization	Name	The result of unstandardiz-ation	The result of standardizati-on
Cheng	11	5	Fafen	19	19
Mou	16	17	Junhong	9	11
Yingzi	34	33	Yanzhi	3	3
Yufen	22	23	Xiangguo	30	32
Dong	32	34	Yongqing	17	31
Junxia	20	16	Lina	25	18
Liqiang	31	27	Shengcai	14	14
Jining	10	13	Zhenling	1	2
Shugeng	33	21	Yanyu	23	20
Zhixin	8	6	Jing	6	9
Xiaohui	21	29	Liying	24	26
Wei	28	22	Yuanjing	12	15
Baofeng	4	4	Yongping	27	24
Gang	26	30	Xin	2	1
Haicheng	18	25	Lili	13	7
Jian	29	28	Yan	5	8
Yuanyuan	7	12	Yuhua	15	10

Table 3. The results of the combination evaluation

Name	The result of Borda method	Name	The result of Borda method
Cheng	8	Fafen	18
Mou	16	Junhong	10
Yingzi	34	Yanzhi	3
Yufen	19	Xiangguo	32
Dong	33	Yongqing	23
Junxia	17	Lina	22
Liqiang	31	Shengcai	15
Jining	12	Zhenling	1
Shugeng	28	Yanyu	20
Zhixin	6	Jing	7
Xiaohui	26	Liying	24
Wei	25	Yuanjing	14
Baofeng	4	Yongping	27
Gang	29	Xin	2
Haicheng	21	Lili	11
Jian	30	Yan	5
Yuanyuan	9	Yuhua	13

4 Conclusion

In this paper, to the quantitative data of 34 teaching staff in Tangshan normal university, we firstly propose fuzzy cluster analysis to sort using original data and standardized data. Then it uses Borda method to combine their results and gets the comprehensive ranking results. At the same time, the correlation coefficient between the two evaluation methods are computed which show that the credibility of the results is high. In other word, the combined evaluation model not only considers the differences between the single method, but also consider the order factors. Therefore, the evaluation results are more comprehensive, scientific, rational, and more credible. In a word, this study provides new practical ideas and methods for the job of academic title evaluation.

Acknowledgment. The project supported by the Research and Development of Tangshan City (11140209a) and Natural Science Foundation of Tangshan Normal University (01D01).

References

1. Tian, Z.: The Historical Evolution of the Appraisement and Engagement System of the Professional Title of China's College and University Teachers. Journal of Hunan University of Science and Engineering 3, 265–268 (2006)
2. Zhao, Z.: Analysis of the Evaluation and Engagement of Professional Titles in Universities. Journal of Yangzhou University Higher Education Study Edition 5, 30–32 (2005)
3. Liu, T.: Title of University of fair competition assessment. Jiangsu Higher Education 6, 111–113 (2000)
4. Wu, S.: Linear Approximating Method in the Transacting Process of Nonlinear Standardization of Data. Journal of Information Engineering University 2, 1671–1673 (2007)
5. Reguo, F.: Entropy Weighting Ideal Point Method and its applications in investment decision making. J.Wuhan Univ. of Hydr.& Elec. Eng. 6, 105–107 (1998)
6. Zhu, B.: Application of combination evaluation for cities' comprehensive economic Power of delta of Pear River. Journal of Liaoning Technical University 25, 242–244 (2006)
7. Xie, J.: Fuzzy Mathematics and Its Applications. Huazhong University Press, Wuhan (2009)
8. Yu, C.: Adaptive Watermarking Algorithm Based on Fuzzy Clustering and Zernike Moments. Journal of Shantou University 4, 66–74 (2010)
9. Lu, Q.: The Research and Realization of Fuzzy Clustering Algorithm. Computer Knowledge and Technology 3, 1987–1990 (2008)
10. Luo, L.: Environment quality appraisal analysis based on transitive closure method with regard to 5 cities in southwestern area of China. J. University of Shanghai for Science and Technology 31, 303–306 (2009)

Research on Granularity Pair and It's Related Properties*

Li Feng[1], Chunfeng Liu[2], Jing Wang[3], and Dongzhong He[4]

[1] Qinggong College, Hebei Polytechnic University
[2] College of Science, Hebei Polytechnic University
[3] Tangshan College
[4] Shijiazhuang Tiedao University Sifang College,Tangshan Hebei 063009, China
fengli3@126.com

Abstract. According to the two major theory -Granularity Computing and Set Pair Analysis, a brief description is made and analysed, the potential link between them is mined, the concept of granularity pair is defined, which is the organic combination on Set Pair Analysis theory and Granularity Computing theory, and the basic properties and operation rules of granularity pair are advanced, and then its program is studied.

Keywords: Granularity Pair, Granular Computing, Set Pair Analysis.

1 Introduction

Granular Computing still has not a unified and precise definition so far. Granular Computing is a kind of new concept and computing paradigm of information processing, covering all the theory, tools, methods and technology research of the granularity, mainly applies in processing the mass, fuzzy, incomplete and uncertain information[1]. Granularity is a noun of physics, here refers to the measure method of granularity, and granularity is constructed by those modules which has the similar structure or similar functions. The nested relationship of granularity will form the level.

Set $K=(U,R)$ a knowledge base, $R\in \mathrm{R}$, where R is a equivalence relation, also called knowledge [2]. There is $R\subseteq U\times U$.

Set $R\in \mathrm{R}$,the knowledge granularity of R, remember it as $\mathrm{GD}(R)$, which has the following definition

$$\mathrm{GD}(R)=\frac{|R|}{|U^2|}=\frac{|R|}{|U|^2} \tag{1}$$

There, $|R|$ represents the base of $R\subseteq U\times U$.

* Project supported by National Natural Science Foundation of China (No.61170317) and Natural Science Foundation of Hebei Province of China (No. A2009000735).

C. Liu, J. Chang, and A. Yang (Eds.): ICICA 2011, Part I, CCIS 243, pp. 227–234, 2011.

Set Pair is a pair which has certain relation between the two sets[3]. The basic thought of the Set Pair Aanalysis is in the given background, analyzes the properties of the two sets, constrcts the identity, difference and opposite degree, it is connection degree $\mu = a + bi + cj$, there a is called the same degree, b is called the different degree, and c is called opposite degree, and satisfies $a + b + c = 1$. And extends it to $m > 2$, m is the number of sets. An, then the further research and study is based on the above.

2 The Correlated Analysis between Hierarchichy Knowledge Granularity and Set Pair Analysis

Suppose Human understanding of the world is in depth constantly, from a develop view, people's understanding will always be imprecise and ambiguous. But from a point of view it is accurate and clear in a certain level (or stage). The hierarchy (or more simple classification) model can reflect the delicate relationship better between the ambiguous and clear, the certainty and uncertainty, and describe people's understanding and analyze from different levels and requirements of things[4]. Many scholars put forward their ideas and algorithms for hierarchical model to realize things better from all levels. Baoxiang Liu has made layers from the angle of the set pair, using fuzzy clustering method[5]; Feng Ye's calculation based on fuzzy sets , which is a model of granular computing, can reduce computational complexity[6].

The uncertainty of knowledge is from two aspects: one is due to the uncertainty of the system, that is to say the border of the knowledge represent system is uncertain, the greater the border, the more rough and fuzzy the knowledge, the higher the level of knowledge; the other hand, the concept is uncertain, that is, the granularities divided are different by the different equivalent relations, the less attributes, the more rough of the granularity, the more inaccurate the knowledge, the higher the level. Many scholars have studied the uncertain system and achieve good results. Wenxiu Zhang, etc. have published Principles of Uncertainty Reasoning [7]; Duoqian Miao, Yu Wang have discussed the relationships between roughness and entropy, and provide a method dealing with the concept of uncertainty [8].

SPA theory is not studied that puts the uncertainty into certainty, but puts the certainty and uncertainty as a system to study. The system must have levels, and the definiton of connection degree in Set Pair Analysis theory is could also be used to get levels.

In view of the T structure in Set Pair Analysis theory handling certainty-uncertainty system, and hierarchy knowledge granularity in the Granularity Computing, this paper put them together, advances the concept of granularity pair. It is the granularity in Set Pair form, which views object sets and attribute sets as a pair, and inherits the properties of set pair and granularity.

3 The Define of Granularity Pair

Granularity pair connects the granular computing and the set pair analysis, is the definition of granularity to set pair. The specific definitions are as follows[9-11].

Definition 1 (granularity pair). Suppose object set X and attribute set Y constitute a set pair $H=(X,Y)$, R is the equivalent relation on $H=(X,Y)$, we call set pair $H=(X,Y)$ as a granularity pair on equivalent relation R .

Definition 2 (connection degree). In a specific information system, analyse the linkages of set pair $H=(X,Y)$ under the equivalent relation R . Suppose the base number of object sets is $|X|=m$, the base number of the attribute sets is $|Y|=n$, then the base number of the granularity pair is $H=(X,Y)$ composited by X and Y .

When the object has the properties definitely, make the pairing R , the identity degree is $\frac{|S|}{N}$.

When the object does not have the properties definitely, make the pairing $P(X,Y)$, the opposite degree is $\frac{|P|}{N}$.

When the objects and attributes have no clear relationship, make the pairing $F(X,Y)$, the difference degree is $\frac{|F|}{N}$, and $|F|=N-|S|-|P|$.

There $S(X,Y),P(X,Y),F(X,Y)\subseteq H(X,Y)$.

Then the connection degree of granularity pair is

$$\mu=\frac{|S|}{N}+\frac{|F|}{N}i+\frac{|P|}{N}j \tag{2}$$

Definition 3. Suppose granularity pair be $H=(X,Y)$,there X are object sets and Y are attribute sets, R are the equivalent relations on H , pair sets $L(X,Y)\subseteq H(X,Y)$. The specific definitions are as follows.

$$\underline{apr}(L)=\bigcup\{(x,y)\mid(x,y)\in H(X,Y),R(x,y)\subseteq L(X,Y)\}$$

$$\overline{apr}(L)=\bigcup\{(x,y)\mid(x,y)\in H(X,Y),R(x,y)\cap L(X,Y)\neq\Phi\}$$

Set $pos_R(L)=\{(x,y)\mid xRy,(x,y)\in H\}$ is known as the positive domain of granularity pair $L(X,Y)$;

set $neg_R(L)=\{(x,y)\mid x\not R y,(x,y)\in H\}$ is known as the negative domain of granularity pair $L(X,Y)$;

set $bn_R(L)=\{(x,y)\mid x\overline{R}y,(x,y)\in H\}$ is known as the border of granularity pair $L(X,Y)$.

Because of the existence of the border, the uncertainty is portrayed out. Use the confidence threshold β to describe the degree of positive region closed to the border, when β is different, the boundary will change to positive domain or negative domain, it is dynamic trend what we need.

Definition 4. Suppose granularity pair be $H = (X, Y)$,there X are object sets and Y are attribute sets, R are the equivalent relations on H , pair sets $L(X,Y) \subseteq H(X,Y)$. Given $0.5 < \beta \leq 1$, the specific definitions are as follows.

$$\underline{apr}^{\beta}(L) = \bigcup\{(x,y) \mid (x,y) \in pos_R(L), a > \beta\}$$

$$\overline{apr}^{\beta}(L) = \bigcup\{(x,y) \mid (x,y) \in pos_R(L) \bigcup bn_R(L), a + b \geq 1 - \beta\}$$

We call them $\beta-$down approximation set and $\beta-$up approximation set on $L(X,Y)$.

There

$$a = \frac{|pos_R(L)|}{N}, \quad b = \frac{|bn_R(L)|}{N}$$

are called the identity degree and the difference degree of granularity pair $L(X,Y)$.

$\beta-$down approximation of granularity pair $L(X,Y)$ reflects that the granularity pair can be classified correctly into L certainly, when β is given and the sets have the equivalent relation R clearly in granularity pair $H(X,Y)$; $\beta-$up approximation of granularity pair $L(X,Y)$ reflects that the granularity pair would be classified into L uncertainly, when β is given and the sets have the equivalent relation R not clearly in granularity pair $H(X,Y)$.

To describe the proportion of $\beta-$down, up approximation in the granularity pair $H(X,Y)$, the concept of clarity degree and ambiguity degree are introduced.

Definition 5. Call $\varphi^{\beta}(L)$ as $\beta-$clarity degree of granularity pair $H(X,Y)$, if

$$\varphi^{\beta}(L) = \frac{|\underline{apr}^{\beta}(L)|}{N};$$

call $\phi^{\beta}(L)$ as $\beta-$ambiguity degree of granularity pair $H(X,Y)$, if

$$\phi^{\beta}(L) = \frac{|\overline{apr}^{\beta}(L)|}{N}.$$

There $|\bullet|$ presents basic numbers.

Ambiguity is the necessary product that the root of knowledge granularity develops continuely. It is easy to see, with the increase of β, $|\underline{apr}^{\beta}(L)|$ is smaller, while $|\overline{apr}^{\beta}(L)|$ is increasing, which results in the decrease of $\beta-$particle clarity degree and the increase of $\beta-$ambiguity degree. This means, granularity pairs which could be correctly classified certainly reduce, while granularity pairs which may be classified to $L(X,Y)$ not clearly increase.

With the decrease of the positive and negative domain, there will be more and more granularity pairs included in boundaries. The idea of the dynamic hierarchical algorithm links the positive connection between the border and the confidence threshold β.

4 Algorithms Rulers

The By definition of $\underline{\text{apr}}L$ and $\overline{\text{apr}}L$, combining with the properties of the slower and upper approximation, it is not hard to get:

1) $\underline{\text{apr}}L \subseteq L \subseteq \overline{\text{apr}}L$
2) $\underline{\text{apr}}\Phi = \overline{\text{apr}}\Phi = \Phi$, $\underline{\text{apr}}U = \overline{\text{apr}}U = U$
3) $\overline{\text{apr}}(L \bigcup G) = \overline{\text{apr}}L \bigcup \overline{\text{apr}}G$
4) $\underline{\text{apr}}(L \bigcap G) = \underline{\text{apr}}L \bigcap \underline{\text{apr}}G$
5) $L \subseteq G \Rightarrow \underline{\text{apr}}L \subseteq \underline{\text{apr}}G$
6) $L \subseteq G \Rightarrow \overline{\text{apr}}L \subseteq \overline{\text{apr}}G$
7) $\underline{\text{apr}}(L \bigcup G) \supseteq \underline{\text{apr}}L \bigcup \underline{\text{apr}}G$
8) $\overline{\text{apr}}(L \bigcap G) \subseteq \overline{\text{apr}}L \bigcap \overline{\text{apr}}G$
9) $\underline{\text{apr}}(\sim L) = \sim \overline{\text{apr}}L$
10) $\overline{\text{apr}}(\sim L) = \sim \underline{\text{apr}}L$
11) $\underline{\text{apr}}(\underline{\text{apr}}L) = \overline{\text{apr}}(\underline{\text{apr}}L) = \underline{\text{apr}}L$
12) $\overline{\text{apr}}(\overline{\text{apr}}L) = \underline{\text{apr}}(\overline{\text{apr}}L) = \overline{\text{apr}}L$

5 Realization

1) Set Pair $H = (X,Y)$ is a granularity pair in an equivalence relation R , here equivalence relation R is differentiate relationship ind(R) , in not confusion circumstances, ind can be omitted. Establish ind.m files in MATLAB7.0, design corresponding program, which can avoid the mistake of the artificial calculation, and can accelerate the computing speed. The differentiate realization is as shown in figure 1.

2) By definition 3, if granularity pair $L(X,Y) \subseteq H(X,Y)$, then $\underline{\text{apr}}(L)$, $\overline{\text{apr}}(L)$ is called the lower approximation set and the upper approximation set of $L(X,Y)$, view each granularity pair $L(X,Y)$ as an element in matrix, the information system decision table can be thought a matrix composed of granularity pair. The program of the lower approximation set and the upper approximation set is below.

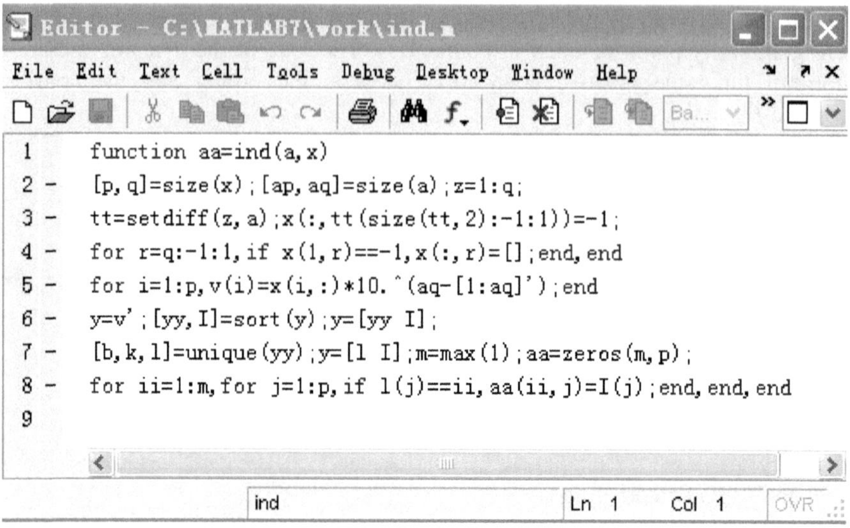

Fig. 1. The program of $\mathrm{ind}(R)$

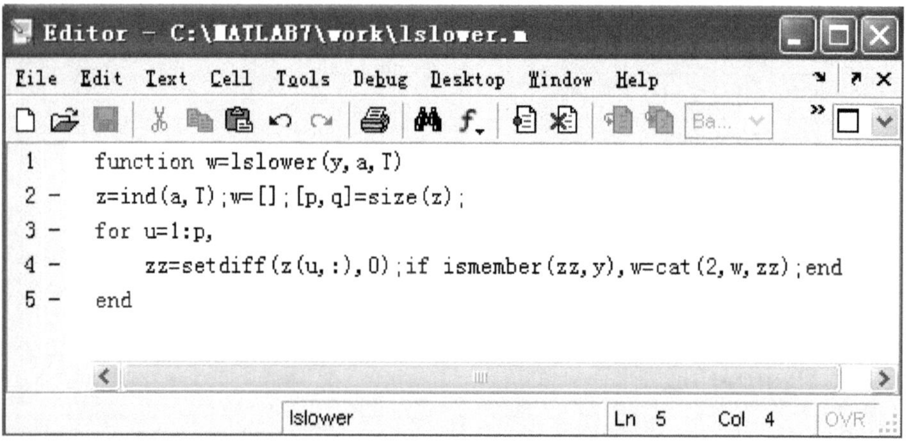

Fig. 2. The program of $\underline{\mathrm{apr}}(L)$

In program, y represents granularity pair set, a represents decision attribute, T stands for information system decision table matrix. The lower approximation set and the upper approximation set can call format.

S1= lslower = (X, a, S) % for lower approximation set
S2 = lsupper (X, a, S) % for upper approximation set
S = setdiff (S2, S1) % using differential set function for the boundary sets

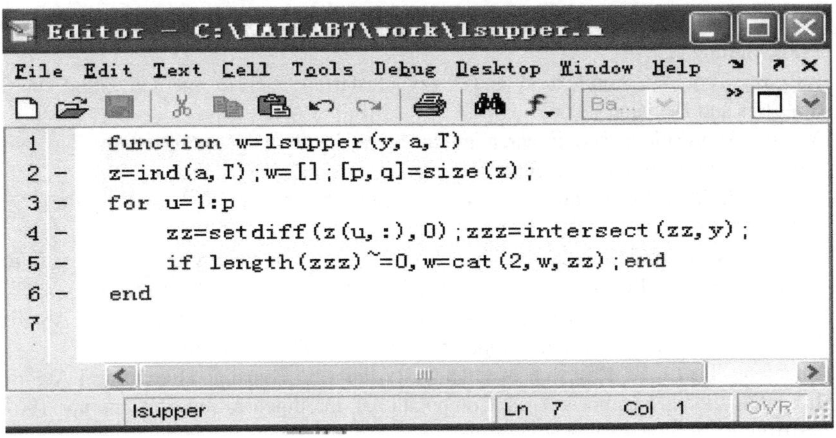

Fig. 3. The program of $\overline{\text{apr}}(L)$

3) Because of each contact vector of the granularity knowledge expression system made up by identity, opposite, and difference three parts, advice attribute reduction first when information system attributes are many, then set up the vector expression system knowledge. MATLAB can get attribute reduction made by funuction redu () , call format directly

Y = redu (c, d, S) % conditions about Jane

Y = core (c, d, S) % nuclear sets

6 Conclusion

Granular computing is a high and new research area, and Set Pair Analysis is 20 years old. As two young theory, the researchers are not many. For the research of the combination theory is more little. The granularity pair supplies a new research level for the GrC, which is valuable for the further improvement of Granularity Computing.

Set knowledge granularity is a new attempt for Granularity Computing, hope the granularity pair to put set knowledge granularity to promote. For the properties' perfection will be the next main point of research.

References

1. Li, D., Miao, D., Zhang, D., Zhang, H.: Research on Granularity Computing. Computer science 32(9), 1–12 (2005)
2. Miao, D., Fan, S.: Knowledge granularity and its application. System Engineering Theory and Practice 1, 48–56 (2002)
3. Zhao, K.: Set Pair Analysis and Its Application. Zhejiang Science Technology Press, Hangzhou (2000)

4. Zhang, B., Zhang, L.: Problem Solving Theory and Application. Tsinghua University Press, Beijing (1990)
5. Liu, B., Tan, Y.: Application and fuzzy clustering analysis method based on SPA. Statistics and Decision (2006)
6. Ye, F.: Applications and research in the hierarchical fuzzy control based on granular computing of fuzzy sets. Guangdong University Master's degree thesis (2008)
7. Zhang, W., Yi, L.: Uncertainty Theory Reasoning. Xi'an Jiaotong University Press, Xi'an (1996)
8. Miao, D., Wang, Y.: The relationship between information entropy and roughness in rough set theory. Pattern Recognition and Artificial Intelligence 11, 34–40 (1998)
9. Chunfeng, L., Li, F.: Research of Granularity Pair and Similar Hierarchical Algorithm. International Lecture Notes in Computer Science, pp. 371–378 (2010)
10. Chunfeng, L., Li, F.: Research of Granularity Pair and Dynamic Hierarchical Algorithm. In: International Symposium on Computational Intelligence and Design, pp. 190–193 (2010)
11. Chunfeng, L., Li, F.: Construction and Application of Hierarchical Knowledge Granularity. Advanced Materials Research Journal, 353–355 (2010)

Research and Application of Parallel Genetic Algorithm

Yamian Peng, Jianping Zheng, Chunfeng Liu, and Aimin Yang

Hebei United University Tangshan 063009Hebei P.R. China
pym806@163.com

Abstract. GA (genetic algorithm) is a simulation of natural evolution process and mechanism for solving the problem of a class of extreme self-organization, adaptive artificial intelligence techniques. It simulates Darwinian natural evolution and genetic variation of Bangladesh Lauderdale theory, has a solid biological basis; it provides views from the intelligence generation process simulation of biological intelligence, cognitive science has a distinct meaning; it for free expression or expression of any class function with parallel computing behavior can be realized; it can solve the practical problems of any kind, has extensive application value. This paper studies the genetic algorithm and parallel genetic algorithm problem, the historical origin of the algorithm, the biological basis of development and a rough description of the algorithm described in depth principle, theoretical analysis, and were illustrated using Matlab Genetic algorithm toolbox to solve, to make images, and finally summarized, and the genetic algorithm application in various fields are described.

Keywords: genetic algorithms, coding, selection, crossover, mutation.

1 Introduction

Genetic algorithm and parallel genetic algorithms have a rough idea, GA (genetic algorithm) is a kind of natural selection and genetics based on effective search methods, which start from a population using selection, crossover and mutation Genetic Operators and other evolving populations, and finally obtain the global optimal solution. The main carrier of genetic material of chromosomes, in the GA in solving the problem, said the same as "chromosome Chromosome", usually a binary string representation, which itself is not necessarily the solution. First of all, some randomly generated data, the initial chromosome, the chromosome composition of these randomly generated a population (Population), the number of chromosomes as the population size of population or population size. Second: the fitness function to evaluate the pros and cons of each chromosome, that chromosome level of adaptation to the environment, used as the basis for future genetic manipulation. Third: select (Selection), the selection process for the purpose of the fine selected from the current population of chromosomes, through the selection process to produce a new population. Fourth: the populations of the new crossover operation and mutation operation. Crossover and mutation operators aim is to tap the diversity of individual populations, avoid the possibility of falling into local solutions. Finally, the new population (ie, offspring) repeated selection, crossover and mutation operations, after

C. Liu, J. Chang, and A. Yang (Eds.): ICICA 2011, Part I, CCIS 243, pp. 235–242, 2011.

processing a given number of iterations since the best chromosome as the optimal solution of optimization problems. Parallel Genetic Algorithm (PGA) is used in the GA on the basis of one of the ways to improve search efficiency. Achieve PGA, not only to transform the serial GA into a parallel equivalent to the program, more importantly, is to modify the structure of GA into easy-to-Parallel Implementation of the form, the formation of parallel population model. Parallel population model changes the traditional GA involves two aspects: First, should the serial number of GA single population is divided into sub-populations, to divide and rule; second is to control and manage the exchange of information between sub-populations. Different methods produce different partition PGA structure. Such structural differences lead to different PGA models: global parallel model, coarse-grained model, fine-grained model and the hybrid model.

2 Global Parallel Genetic Algorithms

Serial global parallel GA is a direct parallel of the program, which is only one group, the fitness value of all individuals are based on the adaptation value of the whole group, can be any match between individuals, which made the group selection and matching is global. In this parallel model of global parallel, GA is an independent evaluation of the individual, without communication between individuals, therefore, generally parallel evaluation of the individual within the main process responsible for the selection, recombination and mutation operations, from the process responsible for the calculation of fitness function . In addition, crossover and mutation operators can be given from the process is complete. From the primary process and the communication between processes and individual performance evaluation in activities related to the main part of the group process will be sent to individuals from the process, individuals from the process evaluation completed after the value of sending them to adapt to the host. If the crossover and mutation are also assigned to from the process, you will need to send offspring to the main process. Most global models synchronous communication, all from the process until the fitness value to each individual to the main process, and then calculate the fitness value by the main process can be easily adapted to calculate the absolute value of the individual and for selection operation. Obviously, this is a better performance of the traditional genetic algorithm.

If using asynchronous communication, the main process does not wait for from the process, this approach is similar to natural evolution, but the calculation of individual fitness, and how to select the operation is more difficult, relatively easy to select the parallel competition of the match option. The results show that blindly increasing the number from the process will lead to a sharp increase in traffic overhead.

Global parallel is easy to implement, if the computing time is mainly used in the evaluation, this is a very efficient parallel method, it retains the simple genetic algorithm's search behavior, which can be applied directly to the theory of simple genetic algorithm results.

Coarse-grained model is the extension of the classical genetic algorithm structure, with different behaviors. In nature, species group system consists of a number of individuals. Less in the case of the processor, we can be divided into several sub-groups of groups, each sub-group contains a number of individuals, each sub-group is assigned a processor, namely, they are independent of each other in parallel implementation of evolution, each after a certain interval (ie number of evolutionary generation) put their best individuals to migrate to adjacent sub-groups to go. This coarse-grained parallel genetic algorithm is called transfer type or island model. In the coarse-grained model, we must address the important issue is parameter selection, including: migration topology, migration rate, migration cycles.

One. Regional structure
Divided into sub-groups in the community after a move to specify the topology for the group. Migration topology and structure of a particular parallel machine has a corresponding relationship between the internal, often taking the structure of parallel computers, if the computer in order to achieve coarse-grained model, you can use any structure.

(1) the number of regions

In most cases the number of regions is fixed, equal to the number of processors available, typically a power of 2 ranging from 4 to 64. In certain circumstances the number of groups, the number of regions also identified the number of individuals in all regions. Usually, the regional sub-groups in the number of individuals between 50 and 100.

(2) migration topology

Topology to determine the regional migration of individuals between the migration path and migration topology most similar to that of the given parallel processor interconnection topologies. Such as hypercube, two-dimensional network topology and so on.

Fewer in the region, the migration can be fully connected topology, so that individuals can move to migrate to other regions. But another view is: an isolated region in space optimization is beneficial.

Topology of the parallel genetic algorithm is an important aspect of performance is the main reason for migration costs. In the coarse-grained model, before running the specified topology remain unchanged after the static topology, is currently the major trend. More intensive in the topology and topology found loose, the former by less function evaluations to find the global optimum. Also in the dynamic topology, according to the diversity, the two groups in the genotype distance measure, which allows individuals to dynamically migrate to other sub-groups to go.

Two. Scale migration
The exchange of individuals between the regions controlled by two parameters: migration rate and migration cycles. Large-scale migration of coarse-grained model will enable global parallel model is similar to the way work, and the formation of small-scale migration of the GA with smaller groups operate independently.

(1) mobility

In each migration cycle, you can move one or several individuals, often in absolute mobility of population size or the percentage of children given in the form. Some implementations use more than 1 mobility on the grounds that individuals migrate to other regions in different individuals in the reorganization, the less chance of survival. Typical migration rate is the number of sub-groups, 10% to 20%.

(2) migration cycle

Migration cycle determines the time interval of individual migration, usually once every several generations of migration can also be a generation after the migration. Typically, the higher the migration rate, the longer the migration cycle.

Most of the coarse-grained parallel genetic algorithm for synchronous transfer mode, but there is also an asynchronous transfer mode, only when some event occurs only after communication between the regions. A certain kind of program is this: When GA to generate in the region (premature) convergence only when migration; Another solution is: Every time an improvement in a region that individual to perform migration operations asynchronously. The centralized solution is: all of its sub-groups from the process performed in the GA, and periodically some of the best results will be sent to the master process, the main process is to choose the most suitable individual to be broadcast to from the node on the network by the experiments show that the speed increase of close to linear speedup. The timing of migration further studies are needed.

Three. Migration Strategy

Migration can basically match the selection and survival selection with the same strategy. Although the area within the region tend to choose more the better individuals, but migrate selection and replacement, you can also use other standard difficult.

(1) migration options

Select the individual is responsible for choosing migration, usually best to select one or several individuals can be selected as the match, as ordered by fitness value ratio or the proportion of choices, there is also randomly selected and replaced.

(2) Replacement Migration

In most cases, is the worst, or a limited number of individuals replace the worst, and migration options similar to the proportion or the order can be adapt to the proportion of the value of options, determining the individual to be replaced in order to produce within the region a better individual selection pressure. There is an ongoing program to genotype Hamming distance as the similarity measure, who moved to replace those with the most similar individual. In a "migration model", with the move to replace the individual to move out in the individual regions. The starting point of the two programs is to maintain diversity within the region.

3 Numerical Simulations

The printing area is 122 mm × 193 mm. The text should be justified to occupy the full line width, so that the right margin is not ragged, with words hyphenated as appropriate. Please fill pages so that the length of the text is no less than 180 mm, if possible. Schubert function:

$$f(x_1,x_2)=\sum_{i=1}^{5} i\cdot\cos[(i+1)\cdot x_1+i]\cdot\sum_{i=1}^{5} i\cdot\cos[(i+1)\cdot x_2+i] \qquad -10\le x_1,x_2\le 10$$

To solve $\min f(x)$.

There Schubert function expression, and made this function with matlab image can be seen, Schubert function is a multi-multi-modal functions with multiple minima. In the traditional genetic algorithm, based on the initial population is divided into four sub-populations, migration probability is set to 0.2, every 20 generations and the current migration between sub-populations, that would put them at intervals of 20 generations the best individual migrate to adjacent sub-groups to go to improve the convergence speed.

Solving process is Matlab program and solution results is as follows:

$$x_1 = 11.1413, x_2 = -19.6497, \min f(x) = -186.7308$$

(1) The objective function of the image as shown below:

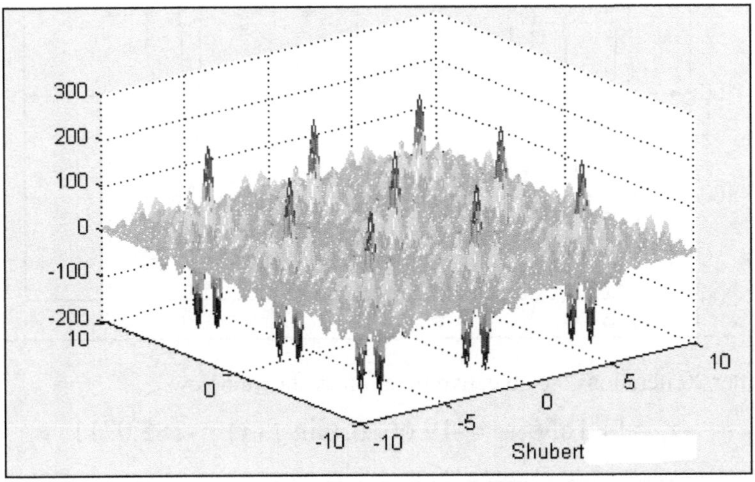

(2) objective function value of the distribution of the initial population as shown below:

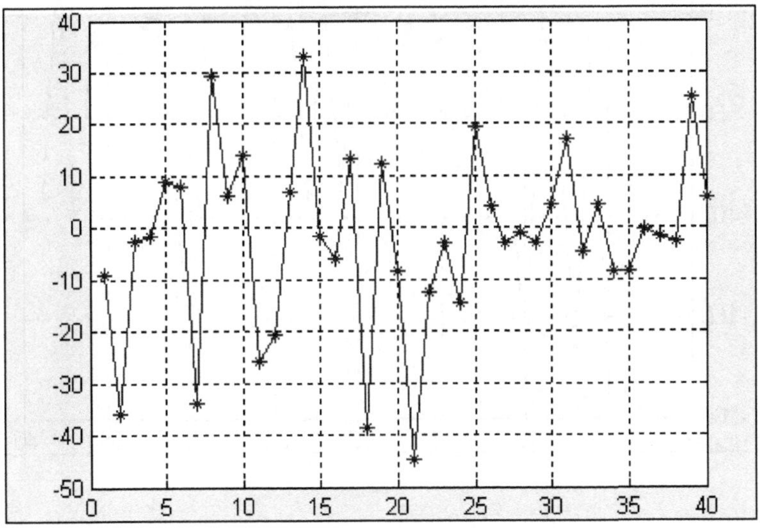

(3) After 10 iterations the objective function as shown below:

$$x_1 = 11.1907, x_2 = -19.6098, \min f(x) = -177.5717$$

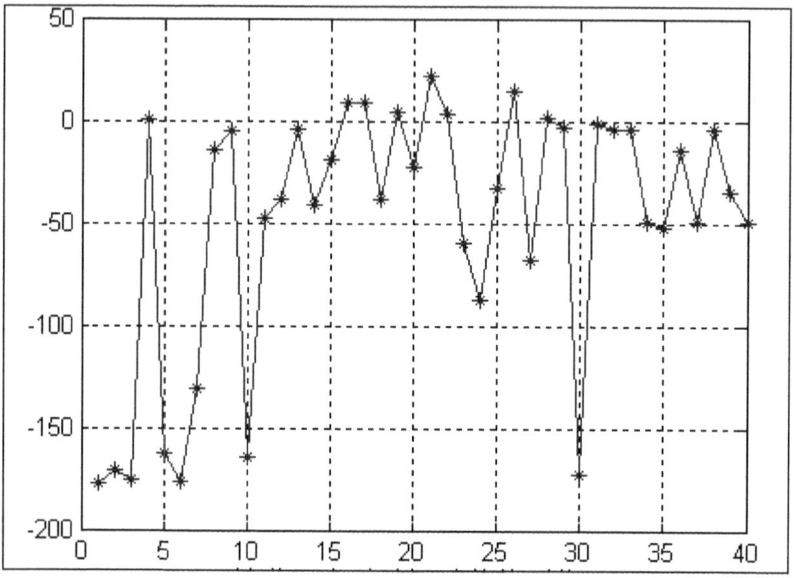

(4) after 20 iterations the objective function as shown below:

$$x_1 = 11.1656, x_2 = -19.6610, \min f(x) = -185.0711$$

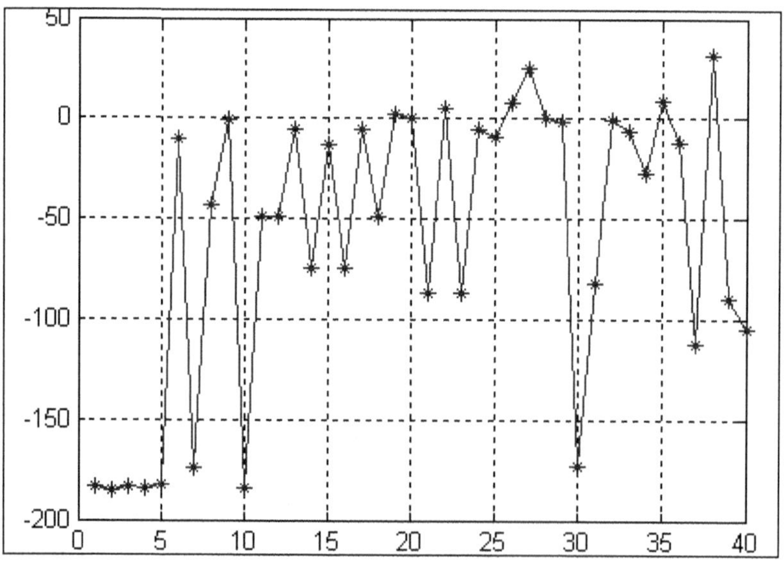

(5) After 30 iterations the objective function as shown below:

$$x_1 = 11.1356, x_2 = -19.6485, \min f(x) = -186.6528$$

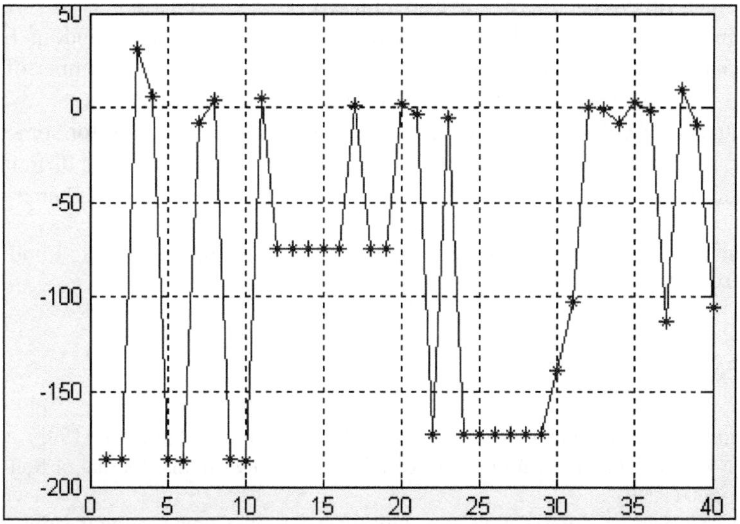

(6) after 50 iterations, the population mean of the objective function changes and changes in the optimal solution as shown below:

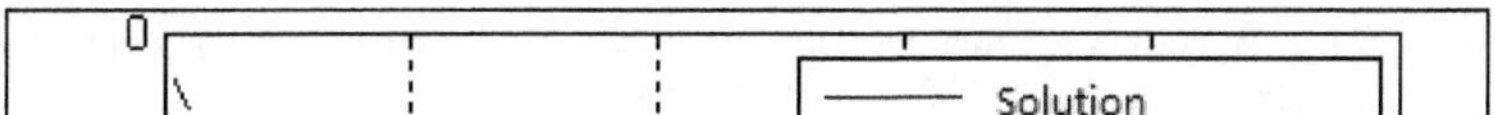

4 Summary

Genetic algorithms to solve complex provides a general framework for optimization problems, it does not depend on the specific problem areas, the types of problems has a strong robustness. Therefore, widely used in many disciplines. Function optimization is the classical application areas of genetic algorithm, genetic algorithm is also used for performance evaluation example. There are also continuous functions of discrete functions, there are also concave convex function, a low-dimensional function also has a high-dimensional functions, there are also random function to determine the function, a single peak of the peak function has a number of functions and so on. Distinctive geometric features with these functions to evaluate the performance of GA and better reflects the nature of the algorithm for some nonlinear effects, multi-model, multi-objective function optimization problem, difficult to solve by other optimization methods. The genetic algorithm is easy to get a better result.

Acknowledgement. This paper is supported by the Natural Scientific Fund Project in Hebei Province (A2011209019).

References

1. Cantu-Paz, E.: A Summary of Research on Parallel Genetic Algorithms (1995)
2. Hou, G., Luo, J.: An ideal model of parallel genetic algorithms. Journal of Software 10(5), 557–560 (1999)
3. Zeng, G., Ding, C.: Parallel genetic algorithm analysis. Computer Engineering (09), 23–26 (2001)
4. Wu, H.: The parallel genetic algorithm to solve constrained parallel machine scheduling problems. Computer Development (01) (2001)
5. Chang, P.-C.: A variety of mechanisms based on simulated annealing population parallel genetic algorithm. Journal of Software (03), 416–420 (2000)

Reform and Practice of Computational Intelligence

Haiyan Xie, Kelun Wang, and Xiaoju Huang

Department of Mathematics, Dalian Maritime University, Dalian 116026, China
winteriscoming@sina.com

Abstract. Computational Intelligence (CI) is one important research direction of artificial intelligence fields. According to the characteristics of CI, this paper discuss how to follow the teaching principles in reform and very good deal with the relationship between teaching and studying, how to improve the students' interest in curriculum in practice, and how to make students learn more knowledge in a limited class hour though using all kinds of teaching method, which effectively improve students ability to analyze and solve problems.

Keywords: Computational Intelligence (CI), Teaching method, multimedia courseware, examination mode.

1 Introduction

CI is one of the important courses for students majoring in information in universities of science and engineering. Nowadays it is an option course in Department of Mathematics, Dalian Maritime University. Teaching this course is of great importance because it plays a major role in students' subsequent study and in the process of solving practical problems. It is a noticeable issue during the whole teaching process to achieve the goals of developing students' interest in CI, making them not only master some theoretical knowledge but also gear their study to practical use and master the subject via a comprehensive study of surrounding areas, and fostering their ability of analyzing and solving problems. As a teacher of this course, I have some opinions on its teaching methods according to my experience and I hope to exchange views with my peers to raise education level.

2 Cultivating Students' Interest in CI

CI includes artificial neural network, fuzzy system and evolutionary computation. This course involves many other subjects, for example, Probability Theory and Mathematical Statistics, Operational Research, Higher Mathematics, Linear Algebra and so on, which makes it one of the difficult courses for undergraduates and more appropriate for senior undergraduates or postgraduates. On the one hand, for many students, their mathematical foundations are so week that they feel fearful, lacking confidence. On the other hand, students will consider CI as a mathematical course if the teacher talks too much about theoretical knowledge. "Interest is the best teacher." Therefore, the emphasis should be put on cultivating students' interest in CI,

C. Liu, J. Chang, and A. Yang (Eds.): ICICA 2011, Part I, CCIS 243, pp. 243–250, 2011.

enhancing their desire for knowledge and making teaching content vivid. The goal of stimulating students' interest in learning can be reached from the following aspects.

2.1 Setting Up Suspension

If a film is full of signs of danger and foreshadows everywhere, it will be the most likely to attract a large audience. Teacher is just like a director, that is, if we want the students to show great interest in the course, we should set up more suspensions, guiding them step by step into our teaching content. For example, when teaching about artificial neural network, we can ask the students what neural network is. Of course, most students don't know the exact answer but they do know there are a lot of neural networks in our brains. Then start from the neural networks in our brains. First we can introduce a modern fairy tale: Team A and Team B were two evenly matched football strong contingent. Before the decisive battle in the new season, both teams were eager to take the title. To ensure the matter was on the safe side, Team A painstakingly prepared a secret weapon---a robot A1 who acted as goalkeeper with a high-speed and large-capacity computer. However, the performance of A1 on court was disappointing. Faced with the quick-moving football, although it spared no efforts in calculating at a speed of ten billion per second to make a correct catching decision by dealing with orientation, velocity and other data transferred from the sensor, its competitors scored before it made the right response. While the experienced goalkeeper B1 from Team B, who reacted alertly and buttered his bread on both sides, frequently stopped the quick-moving football from all direction. Thus the outcome was plain to see for all.

After finishing the story, it is natural to bring up the main part, that is, telling the students that although that is a fairy tale, it shows an indubitable fact that despite the crazy computation speed of modern computers which can reach more than tens of billions per second, confronted with problems with continuous, fuzzy and random information processing, modern computers appear very slow and clumsy. In addition, some real examples can be given. A two or three year old child who even doesn't know that one plus one equals two can easily picks out his or her own parents in the crowd. If a computer tries to complete this easy task for the human being, however, it will cost the computer tremendous efforts. Next we tell them about the biological model of the human brain and the function of each part followed by bringing in an artificial neural network model. That is a magic model which can simulate many basic functions of the brain and simple ways of thinking, such as recognition, association, memory and so on. And about how to realize these functions will be presented in subsequent course.

Through such a method, we can lead the students into an unknown and mystical world. It is the thirst for knowledge that will make them grow to love this course. You have taken the first step toward success in this way. Of course, if at the first class, I will also point out that the application of computational intelligence exists everywhere and it is reflected in Graduation Design of both undergraduates and postgraduates as well. What's more, students will have a better understanding and mastery of MATLAB software (a programming tool) with the help of some experimental classes.

With those introductions above, we've settled the problem of "Why we should learn this course", which allows the students to notice the importance of CI and arouses their interest in it.

2.2 Case Teaching

Case Teaching means that the teacher puts forward some new questions from the very beginning, proceeding from practical examples and throwing out a minnow to catch a whale, and the students try to figure things out and deal with the issue via some theoretical knowledge. Many students during learning such basic courses as Higher Algebra, and Mathematical Analysis which generally have a higher theoretical level always have such a question---What are these courses for? In comparison, CI stresses application so that students won't think that theories they've learnt are castles in the air, but that they are very close to real life. Closing to real life means that they can learn to meet practical needs, which will award them a sense of accomplishment finally. For example, when giving instructions to the students in the applications of adaptive linear element (adaline) in signal processing [1], two questions should be asked first. One is that during the measurement of fetal heart rate (FHR), how we can gain the exact FHR by getting rid of mother's heart rate, for mother's heart rate is so strong that it has an impact on FHR. The other is that when we are making phone calls, how we can make the voice on the other end be heard explicitly by removing our own, for voices from the other end and ours will reach our ears together. Then students will consider them close to as well as far away from their lives because such cases can happen everywhere in life but they never try to use knowledge they've learnt to explain all these things. In this way, students' enthusiasm and curiosity are aroused, so the "minnow" is thrown out, then we come to the second part---catching a "whale", that is, we can use adaline to achieve noise cancellation to solve questions above. As a result, students will become clear suddenly and be excited about that such complex tasks can be completed by using simple knowledge. For another example, BP neural network (Fig.1.) has been widely applied in many fields ranging[2-5] from pattern recognition, curve fitting, data compression, and weather forecasting to many others. Then we can raise such questions before explaining BP Network [6], along with giving a brief introduction of the conception in advance. It enables students to learn theoretical knowledge with questions in mind and arouse their curiosity.

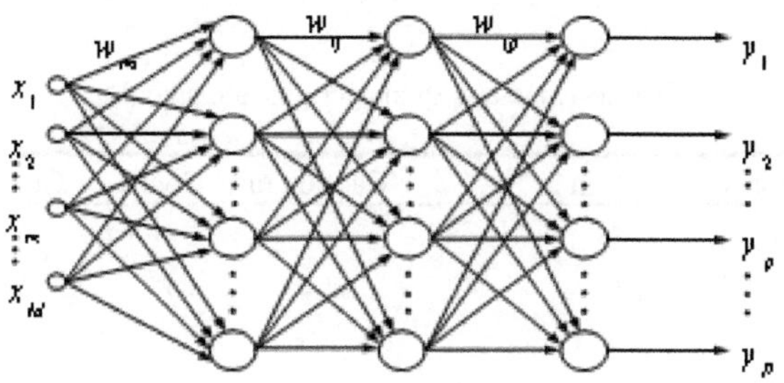

Fig. 1. BP Neural Network

2.3 Heuristic Models of Teaching

CI covers a lot of subjects, some of which students have learnt, but the problem is that they don't know what to do with them. So teachers should learn to skillfully fuse these fragments together by utilizing heuristic models of teaching, guiding the students to solve problems by themselves. In class, it will be helpful in encouraging and enlightening the students if the teacher designs several scene questions on the basis of every knowledge point and adopts some heuristic language. For instance, in a proof the teacher asks "what should we do next" or gives a conclusion ahead and then asks "why is this happening". That also puts the students into deep thinking and assists them to sweep away learning obstacles. Take the BP network as an example. We introduce a error function (equation (1)) whose main parameter is network's weights in BP Algorithm, and then ask "How can you modify the weights to make the error less and less?" Once after the question was put forward, many of my students just sat with a clueless look on their faces. At this moment, we can instruct them to answer the question "Which direction do a function changes the fastest along?" Of course, it's an easy case for a student from department of mathematics. Some have known the answer is the gradient direction. However, some have already forgotten the concept of gradient. While others have known how to calculate the gradient of a function but do not know how to use it. Then ask the students, "Is the gradient direction the direction to increase or decrease the fastest?" The answer is the direction decrease the fastest. So it's easy to come to the conclusion that if we want to make the error less and less, we should modify the weights along the gradient direction. That's the gradient descent method.

$$E(n)=\frac{1}{2}\sum_{p=1}^{P}e_{kp}^{2}(n)=\frac{1}{2}\sum_{p=1}^{P}\left(d_{kp}(n)-y_{kp}(n)\right)^{2} . \quad (1)$$

When finishing one example, it is essential that such results are extended to the general case by asking "What do you draw from here". For example, when the teacher leads the students to generalize data forecasting by RBF Neural Networks, giving n sets of data with m captions and s goals (table 1), the answer to the question---how to design the neurons in input layer and hidden layer, can be found by discussion, which benefits students' further mastery and grasp of knowledge.

Table 1. Data with m captions and s goals

	Caption 1	Caption 2	⋯	Caption m	Goal 1	Goal 2	⋯	Goal s
Data 1	x_{11}	x_{12}	⋯	x_{1m}	y_{11}	y_{12}	⋯	y_{1s}
Data 2	x_{21}	x_{22}	⋯	x_{2m}	y_{21}	y_{22}	⋯	y_{2s}
⋮	⋮	⋮	⋮	⋮	⋮	⋮	⋮	⋮
Data n	x_{n1}	x_{n2}	⋯	x_{nm}	y_{n1}	y_{n1}	⋯	y_{ns}

3 Improving Students' Ability to Solve Problems

To further enhance teachers' teaching effectiveness and improve students' practical ability, I choose MATLAB software to carry out experimental teaching of this course and heighten students' practical ability and design innovation. The application of CI is relatively wide, involving much more theoretical knowledge. In order to help the students further master CI knowledge, I give out some related assignments, most of which depend on students' experiment on the computer by themselves. To aid students in making better use of MATLAB software, I usually arrange two classes for MATLAB software and CI Toolbox before the students experiment on the computer, introducing to them some common MATLAB language statements related to CI, and presenting several complete code to help students to experience the power of MATLAB software and encourage them to further master the language by self-study.

As for every algorithm in CI, I will present corresponding MATLAB toolbox functions (of course that will increase task difficulty for teachers) to save students' time, and a specific application to enable students to learn to analyze issues and implement algorithms utilizing MATLAB. E.g., after learning the application of BP network in forecasting, we should give some factors and data about earthquakes to the students and ask them to design the BP network and simulate the network by MATLAB to gain the results. Additionally, after learning Radial Basis Function network (RBF)[7], we can assign the students to solve the same problem as that in the BP using RBF and compare these two methods. Moreover, I won't give them the specific usages of the parameters in the functions. Instead, I leave them to work things out for themselves. Practice has proved that under the guidance of the teacher, the majority of the students have a good command of the basic use of MATLAB software and CI toolbox. I can see that they master the skills and methods of using MATLAB software to analyze and solve problems via self-learning and experimenting on the computer. For the sake of different levels of students, sometimes I assign different levels of homework to be selected by the students. It's an obvious trend that good students choose more difficult problems, which will score some points for the final exam. While students who are bad at studies usually finish only some easier ones. This method is also one part of hierarchical teaching.

As to homework handed out by the students, I will correct their papers, reading their program item by item. Then I will highly praise those who did a good job and send a suggested correction of some complex ones. For some students who are not learning actively enough and even copy some other's homework, I will give a timely criticism and find out the reasons to help them finish their homework alone. In a word, homework can enhance students' understanding and grasp of knowledge and develop their ability of analyzing and solving problems.

Additionally, I pay close attention to developing students' ability to integrate theory with practice. For example, I divide the students into groups and assign each group to search on the Internet to access some related articles after school. Then each group picks out a representative to act as a teacher to explain to the whole class the paper they've read before and their experiment results. It turns out that such an act has been very successful in not only broadening their horizons, but also consolidating the knowledge they have learnt and enabling students to discover and solve problems. One of my students once applied neural networks to curve fitting in discrete electrical data and won the third prize in the Seventh Student Research and Innovation and "Haihui Cup" Student Research Topics last year in my school.

4 Taking the Advantage of Multimedia Courseware to Make the Course Vivid

So far, CI has developed rapidly in various fields. Limited by class hours (only 46 class hours), we can only teach students the basic methods of CI. But no matter which method we apply, if presented in the form of writing on the blackboard, it is merely a waste of time and an activator to make the students feel boring. Furthermore, teaching of CI aims to enable students to apply their knowledge and we should give them some application examples. But in most cases, those examples cannot be expressed well in a few words, which demand that the teacher spend a lot of time on writing on the blackboard. That means low class efficiency. Fortunately multimedia courseware shows its superiority here. With the improvement of teaching surroundings, all colleges and universities establish multimedia classrooms. What we should do is to make full use of these multimedia classrooms. In the process, making multimedia courseware is a very important part. CI courseware should include the main ideas and theories of CI, but not all. Otherwise, it will give students the feeling that the teacher is echoing every word in the book, and then they will lose interest in learning.

Besides, there's a problem of what should be taught and when to teach. Jialu Xu, Vice Chairman of the Standing Committee of the National People's Congress, famous educator, once said that the most important thing of being a teacher is not to know what should be taught, but what should not be taught. Therefore, we don't have to teach the students all that we know to puzzle them. We just need to teach them what they can understand then with suitable methods at the right time. Furthermore, although multimedia has a special sound, I never use it in order not to disturb the quality of teaching. What's more, every time I finish my class, I record in my notebook the number of slides, course ware problems and the degree of students' understanding of knowledge to making timely adjustments and modifications. There're many course wares on the Internet with many errors and irregularities, so I make the course ware by myself according to my teaching characteristics. I can say that each slide of my course ware has condensed my painstaking effort.

All in all, Applying multimedia courseware to classroom teaching can effectively increased the amount of teaching information, so that students learn more within the limited time. Meanwhile, the number of the examples increases by about one third and all the students receive adequate training. It is of great significance to train the students to solve practical problems and develop their creative thinking.

5 Paying Attention to the Guiding Effect of Exam Content and Form

Testing methods for students has a certain degree of guiding effect. The course is an option course in my school, and in the end students will be given an open-book exam. If the exam content is based on conceptions, gap-fillings and inference questions, it is bound to result in that the students hesitate rather than determine to get to the bottom of knowledge. What's worse, those who take good notes in class are probably to score high, but they even don't know what CI is for. Therefore, questions focused on the concepts and formulas appeared in the notes should be as little as possible and we should start from practical application, telling the students that if they don't spend any time in learning or do their homework in half-heartedly, they will fail in the exam though it is an open-book exam. I also record everyone's assignment quality and regard it as an important parameter for evaluating their final course grade. In fact, there are students failing in the exam every semester, but the number of students who attempt to pass the exam without any efforts is becoming less and less.

6 Summary

CI is a general study that draws upon many fields and has a great many of applications. Teachers need to make more efforts to teach this course well. In my teaching practice, I cultivated students' interest in learning and improved class efficiency. That has achieved a multiplier effect. I learned much knowledge and wrote some papers [8-11] related to my teaching course. I believe that with further exploration and practice, we can make greater progress.

References

1. Jun, G.: Artificial Computational Intelligence: Principles and Simulation Experiments. China Machine Press, Beijing (2007) (in Chinese)
2. Lili, R., Zhongtuo, W.: A Method to Determine the Structure and Parameters of BP Neural Network from Knowledge. Journal of Computer Research and Development 40(2), 169–176 (2003)
3. Yingrong, L., Yinsheng, Y., Hongxia, L.: Application of Nonlinear Combination Forecasting Model Based on BP Neural Networks in Grain Logistics Demand. Journal of Jilin University (Engineering and Technology Edition) 38, 61–64 (2008) (in Chinese)
4. GwoChing, L., TaPeng, T.: Application of a Fuzzy Neural Network Combined With a Chaos Genetic Algorithm and Simulated Annealing to Short-Term Load Forecasting. IEEE Transactions On Evolutionary Computation 10, 330–340 (2006)
5. Dongsheng, L., Chunhua, J.: Application of an Improved BP Neural Network in Business Forecasting. In: Proceedings of the 6th World Congress on Intelligent Control and Automation, pp. 2700–2704. IEEE Press, China (2006)
6. Flying Synopsys R & D Center: Computational Intelligence: Theory and MATLAB7 Application. Electronic Industry Press, Beijing (2005) (in Chinese)

7. Chunguang, Z., Yanchun, L.: Computational Intelligence. Jilin University Press, Jilin (2009) (in Chinese)
8. Haiyan, X., Depeng, Z., Xiaojie, Y., Kelun, W.: Port Supply ChainSupernetwork Optimization Based on Variational Inequalities. In: 2010 International Conference on Logistics Systems and Intelligent Management, pp. 1240–1245. IEEE Press, China (2010)
9. Haiyan, X., Depeng, Z., Fengying, M.: A Kind of Approximately Linear Support Vector Machine Based on Variational Inequality. In: Pacific-Asia Workshop on Comprtational Intelligence and Industrial Application, pp. 287–291. IEEE Press, China (2008)
10. Haiyan, X., Depeng, Z., Zhiping, W., Xin, T.: Linear Support Vector Machine Based on Variational Inequality. In: Fifth International Conference on Natural Computation, pp. 526–530. IEEE Press, China (2009)
11. Haiyan, X., Lining, Z., Fengying, M., Quanying, Z.: Research on Application of the Rough Neural Network in Freight Volume Forecast. The Advances in Information and Systems Sciences, 1129–1136 (2008)

Design and Research of Intelligent Electronic Scheduling Course Algorithm

Qing-yun Ru, Dan Liu, and Jing-yi Du

Computer Science and Technology Department Henan Mechanic and Electric Engineering College Xinxiang, Henan, China
{ruqingyun,liudan1005}@126.com, dujingyiww@yahoo.com.cn

Abstract. As the rapid development and popularization of computer technology, it has become an urgent need for major colleges and universities to develop university educational administration system. The foreground application of Education Management Information System uses the method combining modules into the application and each module is independent. The whole system includes several modules which are school management, classroom management, teaching project management, curriculum management. And all colleges and universities attach great importance to the construction of educational management information, and considers school construction as the core of its work. This paper takes the High School of Henan Mechanical and educational management system as example and elaborates on design and implementation of Intelligent Electronic Course Scheduling Algorithm.

Keywords: Teaching Management, Arranging Management, C/S, B/S.

With the rapid development of computer technology and Internet technology, it has become an important step to promote digital and intelligent technology to promote China's social development. Educational management is very important and a very complex management for college. With the depth reform education system and the rapid increase of the students' number, the curriculum setting has been developed to the depth and breadth. And the teaching system gradually transits from year to credit. The previous educational management system has been increasingly unable to meet the needs of modern Educational Administration. So all colleges and universities are looking for or developing a school educational management system meeting the educational institutions of college. The paper takes educational management system of Henan Mechanical and College as example to elaborate the arranging management module of current educational administration system in detail.

1 Choice of System Structure and Partition of Functions

Whether the design of the structure of the Academic Management System software is good or bad will directly affects the efficiency and security of the system. The current structure of computer networks in use are mainly two kinds: client / server architecture

C. Liu, J. Chang, and A. Yang (Eds.): ICICA 2011, Part I, CCIS 243, pp. 251–256, 2011.

(Client / Server, referred to as C / S) and browser / server architecture (Browser / Server. Because the college teaching management system covers a wide range, data capacity is bigger and functional characteristics are complex, the structure is chosen, using B / S structure or C / S structure singly is unscientific. So in the process of the system design, the paper uses hybrid solution.

2 The Need Analysis of Arrangement Management under the Credit System

Curricula School Administration Management System is an important part of the teaching management system. The arrangement process of credit system is very complex: And the system will take a lot of teaching resources in the allocation of resources. It is an important indicator to evaluate the teaching software whether resources can be allocated reasonably. The design of Curricula Management System involves several parts including the task of teaching, classes, arranging conditions, classroom type and teachers. These parts are interconnected and interrelated. Before the course scheduling algorithm is programmed, arrangement information must be set, and the operation can be completed by the client. The main keywords being set are process table, classroom type, the specific time and so on. In the macro programming design, the reasonableness of the allocation resources should be considered firstly. In order to program intelligent system, there will involve arranging courses, classes, and teachers, Week / Day views, classrooms and other factors to meet a variety of special requirements and integrate scheduling practices of curriculum. The details are as follows.

(1) The expectations of teaching task can be set artificially, and the constraints can be set arbitrarily in the teaching task. The expectation of the teaching task refers to the special requirements considered by system as a priority when the system arranges class automatically. For example, they wish or hope to have class on Monday and to have other classes in the morning. It the arranging expects is "fixed" which means that the request must be meted. If the system can not meet fixed expectations, the arranging is failed; if expectations are not "fixed", other options will be chosen when the hope can not be met.

(2) The system can arrange class automatically and manually. For large batches teaching tasks, automatically arranging can be used. And for special requirements or irregular curriculum, manually arranging courses can be used. The system can take advantage of comprehensive arranging to treat with emergencies, such as string processing, supply processing, temporary occupation and so on.

(3) The system can specify various ways to print the report, such as class schedule, classroom curriculum, teacher curriculum, the school curriculum and so on.

(4) The system has comprehensive search functions, such as querying the results of arranging, querying an empty classroom, querying the teaching tasks in certain period and so on.

(5) The system has automatic calibration function, such as verification by class, verification by teacher, validation by classroom and comprehensive validation and so on.
(6) The time of automatic arranging can not be too long, and the system should have the automatic optimization performance and achieve search through Web and print schedule function.

3 The Design and Implementation of Arranging Process

In the design of teaching management system, the design of arranging management is the core of the whole system. In order to specifically describe the process of arranging, the course units Coursei should be defined firstly before arranging. And each course corresponds to the following attributes set including class time Timei, school classes Classi, classroom teachers and classroom Roomi Teacheri. In which, Course is curriculum, the subscript i indicates that the i-class time of this course. The curriculum can be represents as a collection {Course1, Course2, ..., CourseN}. During arranging the curriculum, we set the class time, school classes set, a collection of classroom teachers and classrooms to accommodate courses as a collection of containers, and the course is divided into a number of hours in accordance with the specified vector (Week, Day, and Section) for decomposition. In which Week expresses the Week, Day expresses a certain day and Section is a lesson. Achieving course arrangement is to arrange class unit to the time property set Class∧Teacher∧Room according to certain rules constraints. So a complicated arranging course problem boils down to a permutation and combination problems.

3.1 Constraint Condition

The complexity of timetabling problems stem from a lot of constraints. Although the specific circumstances of each school is different, but most of the constraints is same. Generally, constraints consist of Course, Class, Teacher, classroom and Time. During the course arrangement, according to pre-set, the five elements can be found and then be made the appropriate combination. The constraints largely are conjunction item of Course + Class + Teacher + Room + Time conjunctive form. The whole constraints can be constructed with a relational database, and each class has to satisfy the constraints. The general constraints can be divided into two types of hard constraints and soft constraints. The constraints are often as follows.

(1) At the same time on the same day, a teacher can not be arranged two courses.
(2) At the same time on the same day, two courses can not be arranged in a classroom.
(3) At the same time on the same day, two courses can not be arranged for a class.
(4) A class can not be repeated a course on the same day.
(5) The classroom capacity must be greater than or equal to the number of school classes.
(6) A teacher in one day has not more than four courses.

The 1,2,3,4 constraint items can be known as hard constraints. If these constraints do not force, this will lead to the ultimate failure so as to influence the normal development of teaching. So 1, 2, 3, 4 constraint items should be meet, during the process of arranging. The 5, 6 items are known as soft constraints. If this constraint is not in force, this will not affect the normal teaching and it can only affect the quality of teaching and teaching effectiveness, so this constraint entry should be avoided occurring.

3.2 Key Solution

In the process of arrangement, the intension of solving is to rationally allocate of teaching resources based on meeting a variety of constraints to improve teaching quality and teaching effectiveness. In the course of the arrangement, in order to find the optimal solution, all solutions will be listed to choose the optimal solution. But the solution acquired in the process of solving procedures does not represent its optimal solution, but in certain cases the combined solution is the optimal solution. Therefore, getting the optimal solution is the ultimate goal. When the algorithm is designed, using of the idea of resource allocation the, the arranging problem can be seen as the process that a demander reasonably allocate resource and avoid resource conflicts. This process is done step by step. When the confliction occurs, adjustment will timely be made and be stepped back. If resources are lack, the system will stop and come back to re-adjust the parameters and constraints. In the actual algorithm, the following strategy can be used commonly.

(1) The number priority policy. The school programs which's number is more will precede over the courses of small number to avoid that big class lesson is not free time $Class1 \Lambda Class2 \Lambda Class3 \Lambda \ldots \Lambda Class\ N = 0$ because the single class is arranged firstly.
(2) Curriculum priority strategy is arranging the course with bigger span for the same number to avoid fragmentation caused by firstly arranging the course with small span.

Arranging algorithm can be described as follows.

(1) Test whether the system resources are adequacy, including detecting arranging information and checking the system information.
(2) According to the priority rules, the system will find the teaching task for sorting the priority of classes and arranging for priority classes.
(3) Find a total free area of classes and teachers. Namely, take the conjunction together of the time property for classes and teachers.
(4) Allocating classroom. Take the conjunction of free time for teaching classes, classroom teachers and classroom.
(5) Check and generate the arranging results, and write the arranging result to the database. For example, A,B,C,D teachers will be arranged two teachers to have class in the morning on Wednesday, how to arrange class according to the three conditions.

(1) B and C can not all be arranged
(2) Arrange C, do not arrange D
(3) If the system arranges A, then C and D will be arranged in one class

The answer method is to use of mathematical logic, which is as follows:

$$(A \rightarrow C \vee D) \wedge (\neg(B \wedge C)) \wedge (C \rightarrow \neg D) = \prod 3,6,7,8,B,C,E,F = \Sigma 0,1,2,4,5,9,A,D \quad (1)$$

Then according to the actual to discuss, 0 is not arranged, 1, 2,4 are arranged one-teacher classes, D is the arrangement of three teachers in school, which should be excluded. Finally, the paradigm will be drawn :

$$\Sigma 5,9,A = (\neg A \wedge B \wedge \neg C \wedge D) \vee (A \wedge \neg B \wedge \neg C \wedge D) \vee (A \wedge \neg B \wedge C \wedge \neg D) \quad (2)$$

The system can arrange B, D, or A, D, or A, C. Therefore, there are three election laws; the system can take any one.

Intelligent arranging is more flexible than automatic arranging which can always be processed on the specific task. Conjunction Intelligent Course Management System based on constraint adds new features in addition to achieving the function of the original manual system to ensure consistency and timeliness of data processing. The running of the program greatly reduces the strength of arranging work and improve work efficiency and quality so as to achieve the desired design results.

4 Conclusion

As the rapid development and popularization of computer technology, it has become an urgent need for major colleges and universities to develop university educational administration system. The foreground application of Education Management Information System uses the method combining modules into the application and each module is independent. The whole system includes several modules which are school management, classroom management, teaching project management, curriculum management. And all colleges and universities attach great importance to the construction of educational management information, and considers school construction as the core of its work. This paper takes the High School of Henan Mechanical and educational management system as example and elaborates on design and implementation of Intelligent Electronic Course Scheduling Algorithm.

References

1. Mou, S.-B.: The Study on the Algorithm of Curricula Arrangement in College Teaching Management System. Sichuan University of Science and Technology. J. Mol.Med. (4) (2004)
2. Zhang, J.: Implementation of University Course Timetabling on Graph Theory. Journal of Chongqing Teachers College (Natural Science Edition), J. Mol. Med. (1) (2005)
3. Yi, L.-R., Chen, Z.-G.: Development and Implementation of a Web Based Teaching Management System. Systems Engineering. J. Mol. Med. (2) (2002)

4. Huang, X., Wu, J., Zhang, S.: Architecture of Distance Learning Management System. Computer Engineering and Applications. J. Mol. Med. (12) (2003)
5. Sigart Bulletin, G.J.: Efficient Local Search for Very Large-scale Satisfiability Problems, vol. 3(1), pp. 8–12 (1992)
6. Li, Y.-J., Lu, C.-W.: The Use of Ant Colony Genetic Algorithm in Intelligent scheduling course of Colleges and Universities. Modern Electronic Technology. J. Mol. Med. (14) (2010)
7. Sun, X.-B., Xu, T.-Z., Li, W.: Study on Scheduling Course System Based on GIS on Campus. Computer and Digital Engineering. J. Mol. Med. (3) (2009)
8. Chen, X.-F.: Class Arrangement Algorithm Constraint Conditions and their Realization in Teaching Management System. Journal of Dongguan University of Technolegy. J. Mol. Med. 16(1) (2009)
9. Li, F.-L.: Design and Realization of Intelligent Scheduling Course System for Middle Vocation Schools. Beijing University of Technology. J. Mol. Med. (3) (2009)
10. Wang, L., Wen, W.-S.: Study and Realization of Scheduling Course System Based on Aglet platform. Computer Engineering and Science. J. Mol. Med. (9) (2009)
11. Xie, J.J., Liu, C.P.: Fuzzy mathematics methods and its application. Mol. Huazhong University of Science and Technology (2000)
12. Liu, X.L.: Composite fuzzy judge decision-making applied in the work of internship. J. Mathematics Communication (2003)
13. Liu, X.L., Yan, F.: Fuzzy Comprehensive Evaluation Model in work of Teacher Recruitment. In: 1st ACIS International Symposiums on CDEE, pp. 346–348 (2010)
14. Liu, X.L.: Fuzzy Decision in work of Confirming City Flower Candidates. Journal of Anhui Agricultural Sciences, 556–577 (2010)
15. Ye, Q.X.: College Mathematical Modeling Contest Guidance Materials (3). Mol. Hunan Education Publishing House (2002)
16. Ye, Q.X.: College Mathematical Modeling Contest Guidance Materials (4). Mol. Hunan Education Publishing House (2002)

How to Build a Harmonious-Classroom Based on Information Technology

Lin Jiang[1], Gelin Dai[2], Jiaxin Xu[3], and Guikao Yang[2]

[1] Department of Training, Xuzhou Air Force College, Xuzhou, China, 221000
[2] Department of Air Ammunition, Xuzhou Air Force College, Xuzhou, China, 221000
[3] Department of Logistics Command, Xuzhou Air Force College,Xuzhou, China, 221000
{quhuishui,xjx}@126.com, {dgl,ygk1127}@163.com

Abstract. Classroom is the major place in which the quality-oriented education is conducted by a teacher, and the reform of teaching method is tried out. Its environmental construction plays a significant role in both sides of "Teaching" and "Learning". This paper,through exploring about building good teacher-student relationship, reinforcing the cooperation between teachers and students, as well as the improvement of test system, sheds light on the significance of building a harmonious classroom and serves as a reference for conducting classroom teaching under the modern educational concept.

Keywords: Harmonious classroom, Teaching environment, Teacher-student relationship.

1 Introduction

Classroom is an important place in which a teacher implements quality education, and the vital breach for the reform of teaching method; at the same time, it is also the place where students demonstrate their abilities and develop their personalities. Setting up harmonious classroom is the platform and field for the realization of the two aspects talking above. People often say that, there are three states of mind for teachers: the first is to impart knowledge; the second is to enlighten wisdom and the third is to lighten the life. In my opinion, classroom also owns the three states of mind that we talk above. The classroom of imparting knowledge just like green grass, all green,which can be found everywhere. The classroom of enlightenment wisdom just like twinkling flowers, which let person yearn for. However, classroom of lightening the life is what can meet rather than beg. Teachers should comply with the individual development of students, implement effective teaching and build harmonious classroom, let the teachers and the students to roam and grow together in the areas of the thoughts accrete and wisdoms collide, and in the fields of the communication of the internal spirits and the scenery of melt feelings. Therefore, the exploration of building harmonious classroom is of great realistic significance.

C. Liu, J. Chang, and A. Yang (Eds.): ICICA 2011, Part I, CCIS 243, pp. 257–262, 2011.

2 Connotation and Feature of Harmonious Classroom

"Harmony" refers to a pleasing combination of elements in a whole. It is defined in the dictionary of contemporary Chinese language as "well cooperated; good symmetry". In terms of classroom teaching, "Harmony" means that various factors contributing to the teaching activities are well integrated under the educational concept of student-oriented. In this way, the students' self-inspiration, self-development and self-fulfillment can be largely insured. Harmonious classroom should bear the following feature:

2.1 Being Systematic

Harmonious classroom is a system consisting of teachers, students, teaching contents, teaching methods, teaching appraisement and the other essential factors. Not only do teachers, students and the classroom environment have mutual influence in the classroom, but also teachers and students may interact each other. Harmonious classroom required that each factor should give full play to form a joint effort.

2.2 Homeostasis

Harmonious classroom is an overall system, whose structure and function, material and the input and output of energy are in the relatively steady state.

This kind of balance denotes that the major part in the classroom, classroom environment, classroom teaching and the social environment comprises a comprehensive balance. Harmonious classroom needs optimizing internal teaching environment.

Through the spiritual communication between teachers and students, and mutual interaction among the teachers, students and teaching contents, the energy flowing and exchange will be realized during the process of transmitting the information. Besides, the teachers are required to optimize the external teaching environment, further insuring that the concept of the teaching keeps up with the development of times, then to enhance the students' ability of updating to the society.

2.3 Be Whole-Opening

Harmonious classroom should be open to all the students based on teachers' delicate design and arrangement. Teaching content should be changed from the book knowledge to the knowledge outside world. The teaching focus needed to be converted from certainty of attending to the teaching result into the uncertainty of teaching process. And, the teaching appraisement is opened to the various possibility of appraisal rather than the uniqueness of appraisement.

2.4 Be Sustainable

Harmonious classroom can help to realize the mutual development between teaching and learning. Teachers and students not only acquire knowledge and skills in the classroom, but also enrich their emotion and set up their new values. Furthermore, through upgrading the quality of their life and value, teachers and students realize the promotion of all-round and sustainable development.

3 Construction of the Harmonious Classroom

Student as the key power of classroom is the springboard and end-point of classroom teaching. In the realistic classroom, we can also often see such a scene: Some teacher likes asking top students to reply problems only; some lacks patience when students reply problems without giving them fully time to think out the question; and others forbid students to chip in etc.

Rogers, American educational psychologist said: "Success education lies on pure-hearted understanding, trustful teacher-student relationship and harmonious classroom atmosphere." Harmonious classroom is to pursue natural, harmonious, democratic, equal classroom atmosphere, to build a kind of free and healthy teaching environment for students' development, and to found a dynamic and animated teacher-student relationship and coordinate, mutual teacher-student relationship.

Modern educational thinking tells us that the democratic and equal teacher-student relationship is the strong catalyst which arouses students' learning interest, is also the key that teaching campaign carries out smoothly. Democratic, harmonious and healthy relationship between teachers and students can be just happy for students to accept education, just meeting "Qin Qi Shi, Xin Qi Dao".

3.1 Well-Developed Teacher-Etudent Relationship Is the Basis of Building the Harmonious Teaching Environment.

Do Not Bring in the Classroom the Teachers' Personal Likes and Dislikes As Well As the Self-emotion. The organization of classroom teaching is an art, the final pursuit of which is to be harmonious. As an organizer of the teaching process, it is of great importance for a teacher to manipulate the teaching "Venation". A teacher's personal likes, dislikes and the change of mood can affect his judgment, and then trigger unfavorable factors and the negative influence in the classroom.

To Well Know the Characteristics of the Students and Make Preparations for the Communication. In recent years, this classroom teaching mold -----"teachers function as a guider and students as major learner" has been universally approved. So, it is firmly proposed that understanding the characteristics of the students be the essential point for the classroom teaching. Without the familiarization with the students, the design of the teaching content is of no possibility, not to speak of the choice of teaching methods and the implementation of teaching reform. Therefore, what should be emphasized is that when preparing for the lessons, we should not only prepare the book knowledge, but also "prepare" our students. The whole teaching design should include the analysis of the students' characteristics (their starting point, learning attitude), teaching content(the function of the on-going course , the aim and effect of teaching, correlation of the on-going course to the others) ,teaching organization(the width and depth of the teaching content, key points and difficult points, orders、 mold and the method of teaching), etc.

To Trust Students and Appreciate Each One. To trust students is the core for the heuristic teaching. Students, both physically and mentally, are under the process of growing up, so they are easily influenced by the outside factors, especially at the times when science and technology is developing rapidly and much information jammed in their mind affects their reasonable judgment. So, teachers should permit and tolerate the mistakes committed by the students, and never abandon any student. Meanwhile, when appraising students, teachers need maximize their strong points and minimize their shortcomings. In this way can a teacher make no any deflection in terms of judging students.

To Build the Mechanism of Mutual Respect and Equal Participation Between Teachers and Students. As an individual, no matter being students or teachers, they are independent behaviors and thinkers. Each teacher is unique, and so is each student. The only difference between teachers and students are the experiences and the values toward the world they have. So, during the teaching process, we should get rid of the mechanical input of the theory and the validated imitation, and help students to develop scientific ways of thinking, sharp judgment, and to foster a good habit of learning coupled with active cooperative awareness. In this way, students may improve their ability to cater to the society with self-respect, dignity, harmony and philanthropism.

3.2 To Enhance the Cooperation between Teachers and Students Is an Effective Way of Building Harmonious Teaching Environment.

To Enhance the Interaction between Teachers and Students and Guide Students to Actively Participate in Teaching. Now, most students' attention in the class is shortened, making the teaching process more difficult to proceed. In order to attract students' attention, teachers need to guide students to fully participate in the teaching activities. For example, adopting the teaching mold "practise—explain---review" to help students digest what they have learned; at the same time, long-time explanation of the same problems should be avoided, for it may make students exhausted. On the other hand, the unified teaching mold of teaching and learning can make classroom teaching more intuitionistic and practical.

To Foster and Enhance Students' Self-confidence to RelieveTheir Pressure in the Classroom. During the teaching process, teachers should help students to set up two consciousnesses: one is allowing the individual to make mistakes during the cognitive process; the other is learning needs time, and deep understanding needs more. For example, teachers should point out the inevitability and chanciness of the mistakes before class, making students not feel embarrassed when they find they have done something wrong.

To Design a Novel Opening Remarks and Set Up a New Tunnel into the Teaching Content. Novel opening remarks can shorten the distance between the student and teacher and interest the students at the same time. Opening remarks can be or not be related to the course. What's the most important is that it can attract the students' attention. We can break through the traditional way of teaching: "preview---lead in----explain". Teachers can propose a question by giving a specific example or social phenomenon to let all classmates think deeply, then, discuss in groups. Finally, teachers choose one or two student to answer the questions. This mold not only engages the students' interest in participating in the classroom activities, but also encourages them to think actively.

To Set Up Group to Learn to Enhance Harmonious Relationship among Students. It is helpful to set up cooperative learning group. One is helping teachers o vacate time to solve students' problem; the other is serving to build a learning atmosphere. Students can get or strengthen their understanding more quickly in mutual explaining. The last point is to give students more opportunity to show them and to foster a good learning habit.

3.3 To Reform Testing System is Beneficial Supplement for Setting Up Harmonious Teaching Environment.

Traditional examination and scoring system can not reflect completely and objectively the students' ability, nor are them helpful in arousing students' interest along with fostering a good learning habit. Meanwhile, for those students who pay more efforts to prepare but get lower grade, it is undoubtedly a blow on their activity. Therefore, under the basis of the normal testing system, changing the ways of testing is worthwhile to engage students' learning motivation and form a good learning environment.

To Minimize the Examination. Teachers can replace the examination with after-class assignment and the periodic summarization to minimize the test and degrade the students' antipathy for the exam. The purpose of the test is not to threaten students but grant them the opportunity to sum up and show their learning result. So, we should judge students' performance through different ways and forms, ensuring that students may spend enough time in learning rather than in the exam passively. In this way can their pressure in the classroom be relieved.

To Attach Importance to the Individuation of Selecting the Course. Recently, it has been largely proposed that elective course should be reformed and the additive credits should be added to provide students more space to develop their personality. Our purpose is to pay more attention to the development of students' personality and the improvement of their comprehensive quality. As to the non-major courses, we should, according to students' characteristics and specialty, permit students to design their own additive credits to substitute those courses they are not interested in The major. Also, this system can be realized by holding lecture, the topic and the content of which will be come up with by full-time teachers at the end of term. After the approval of the school, the lecture can be held next term.

The reform of testing system thoroughly eases the students, and boosts the students' interest from the very beginning. At the same times, it provides a support for building harmonious teaching environment. At present, although students' enthusiasm will be affected by elimination system and allotment after graduation, building harmonious environment is vital for enhancing students' cognition and fostering the habit of life-long study. As the organizer of the classroom teaching, each of us should conduct a deep research and practice.

4 Conclusion

To sum up, classroom is the spirit place for students' self-development and value realization, and only harmonious classroom teaching can provide a good arena for free, all-around and harmonious development of students' ability. Harmony is the forever pursue of classroom teaching, and the wonderful state of mind.

References

1. Boyer, E.L.: Scholarship Reconsidered: Priorities of the Professoriate. The Carnegie Foundation for the Advancement of Teaching. Princeton University Press, New Jersey (1990)
2. Rice, R.E.: Beyond Scholarship Reconsidered: Toward an Enlarged Vision of the Scholarly Work of Faculty Members. New Directions for Teaching and Learning 90, 7–18 (2002)
3. Johnston, R.: The University of the Future: Boyer Revisited. Higher Education 36(3), 253–272 (1998)
4. Diamond, R.M.: Defining Scholarship for the Twenty-first Century. New Directions for Teaching and Learning 90, 73–80 (2002)
5. Heywood, J.: Assessment in Higher Education, 2nd edn. John Wiley & Sons Ltd, London (1989)
6. Kogan, M. (ed.): Evaluating Higher Education. Jessica Kingsley Publishers, London (1989)
7. Centra, J.A.: Reflective Faculty Evaluation. Jossey-Bass Publishers, San Franscisco (1993)
8. Tang, X.: On Building Harmonious and Effective Classroom Atmosphere. Science of Education Monthly (February 2010)
9. Wang, L.: Ethic Thoughts on Building Harmonious Classroom. Education Exploration (November 2010)
10. Can, S.: Exploration on Internal Traits of Harmonious Classroom. Global Outlook of Education (December 2007)
11. Trigwell, K., Martin, E., Benjamin, J., Prosser, M.: Scholarship of Teaching: A Mode. Hiher Education Research and Development 19(2), 155–168 (2000); Diamond R M. Defining
12. Neumann, R.: Research and Scholarship: Perceptions of senior Academic Administrators. High Education 25(2), 97–110 (1993)
13. Goldhaber, D.D., Brewer, D.J.: Dose teacher Certification Matter? High School Teacher Certification Status and Student Achievement. Educational Evaluation and Policy Analysis 22(2), 129–145 (2000)
14. Suell, J.Y., Piotrowski, C.: Alternative Teacher Education Programs: A Review of the Literature and Outcome Studies. Journal of Instructional Psychology (5) (2007); Bettencourt, L.U., Howard, L.: Alternatively Licensing Career Changers to be Teachers in the Field of Special Education: Their First-year Reflections. Exceptionality 12(4), 225–238 (2004)

Information Technology Research and Its Application on Physics

Zhang Haishan[1], Zhou Haiyun[2], and Li Wei[3]

[1] Modern Technology Education Centre, Hebei United University, Tangshan, Hebei, China
[2] Tangshan No.5 Middle School, Tangshan Hebei, China
[3] Information Engineering College, Hebei United University, Tangshan, Hebei, China
sea @heut.edu.cn, yunmail0372@sina.com.cn, heutliwei@163.com

Abstract. As the information technology develops rapidly and the reform in education continues to deepen, it permits middle school education to change greatly both in teaching content and teaching mode. Under the guidance of the new curriculum standards of physics in senior high school , by analyzing the current integrated situation and correctly grasping the meaning of the integration of information technology with physics, three physics teaching patterns about the of integration information technology with senior physics are proposed. I hope it will make a meaningful exploration in the integration of information technology with physics teaching in senior high school, providing some guidance to the future physics teaching of senior high school.

Keywords: information technology, integration, physics teaching.

1 Introduction

Information technology is one of the most active, the most rapidly growing, and the most influential factors in the field of science and technology all over the world, causing a comprehensive change in the content, form, methods and organization of education. The integration of information technology with curriculum has become a research focus and developing trends in national information technology education, the process of educational informatization, and even the whole reform in education and teaching. Currently, Now, our country is engaged in a vigorous basic education curriculum reform, whose entry point is the curriculum reform. It aims at exploring the organic integration of information technology and teaching of other subjects, changing the traditional ideas of education, teaching content and methods, and teaching evaluation and so on, so as to make teaching more efficient, realize the optimization of the teaching process, and foster the information literacy in students.

2 Current Situation of Research

Information technology and Curriculum integration developed from multimedia teaching based on audio-visual information and CAI. That how to realize the

C. Liu, J. Chang, and A. Yang (Eds.): ICICA 2011, Part I, CCIS 243, pp. 263–270, 2011.

integration of information technology in physics teaching has been experimented for nearly ten years at home and abroad, with different emphasis and effect. Along with the diverse needs of physics teaching, information technology and the integration of secondary school physics curriculum have been extensively carried out. [1] What's more, they are applied to physics teaching, the construction of curriculum resources, teaching evaluation and other aspects. But these are only simple applications, not the real "integration" of information technology with high school physics. So the effect is far from ideal, some even go to wrong way in teaching.

2.1 The Inadequate Breadth of View of the Integration of Information Technology with Physics Curriculum

Many physics teachers think that using computers in class is the curriculum integration, which is quite superficial, misunderstanding information technology as merely applying computers to teaching; or rest the use of curriculum integration only on the level of using courseware to "play" and "show content", giving first place to the single model type of classroom demonstration and classroom practice, overlooking two-way communication, and with poor interaction as well. [2] The introduction of information technology has only made some progress in helping reduce the teaching load. Compared to the traditional methods, no substantial progress in developing students' thinking abilities has been made, failing to realize the organic integration.

2.2 The Inaccurate Understanding for the Purpose of Curriculum Integration

There are two main views about the integration of information technology with curriculum. One tends to promote the study of the course; the other tends to train students in information literacy. Some physics teachers only understand the information literacy as Internet browsing, improving typing speed, being able to gather information, ignoring improving students' learning ability of the integrated use of information and cultivating the emotional awareness of physical information. Some physics teachers don't value students' information literacy. They do not care whether information literacy has organically combined with physics teaching or not.

2.3 The Abuse of Technology Standard Theory in Curriculum Integration

Some physics teachers hold a wrong view called Technology Standard Theory in curriculum integration. They don't start from the need of the course, regardless of whether the teaching effect is optimized or not. They use information technology frequently. It's common to use technology for the sake of technology itself in teaching. Instead of considering the characteristics of physics, they only emphasize the gorgeous form of the courseware. Generally speaking, they place too much emphasis on the sound, light, color and other kinds of stimuli that are produced by multimedia, neglecting the cognitive characteristics of learners. [3] As a result, they do not achieve the desired results, but distract the attention of students. Some teachers even use computers to simulate physical experiments, not realizing that the base of the physical research is experiments. They don't consider information technology as an important of physics teaching. Therefore, information technology does not play its desired role in teaching.

2.4 Unable to Handle the Relationship between Traditional Teaching and Curriculum Integration

Some teaches are not ready to accept changes and innovation. They do not or seldom use the new teaching methods by the integration of information technology with physics curriculum, thinking traditional teaching methods can entirely achieve the purpose of teaching. So it's not necessary to waste time in learning to use new technique. While some teachers exaggerate the role of information technology, thus replacing a lot of teaching of physics experiments with information technology, rejecting many excellent teaching methods and teaching media in traditional teaching. Both the two attitudes separate the relationship between information technology and traditional teaching, and fail to take advantage of their respective merits and complement each other. [4]

3 The Connotation of the Integration of Information Technology with Physics in New Curriculum

The new round of curriculum reform of high school physics put forward new requirements for students, asking students to shift from the pure ability to solve problems and experiment to learn scientific exploration methods, develop autonomous learning ability, form good thinking habits, and can use the physical knowledge and science inquiry methods to solve problem during which process exercise thinking and build application consciousness. [5]The integration of information technology with physics just provides a new developing direction for physics education in the new curriculum.

The integration of information technology with physics is to combine the advantages of information technology and physics organically according to its characteristics, applying information technology into all aspects of physics courses so as to optimize varieties of teaching resources, all kinds of teaching factors to promote fundamental changes in teaching methods. In this way, the contents, processes and evaluation of physics teaching can realize the purpose of information, enabling students to do better in physics, enabling students to apply information technology effectively to achieve the goal of learning physics better, thus training the students to have innovative spirit and practical abilities.

The information technology mainly composed of multimedia and network can be used as Cognitive and Affective Motivation instruments to promote students Independent Study and Creation Platform to enrich instructional environment. With students' comprehensive and harmonious development as ultimate goal, by the platform provided by information technology, students could gain a better understanding of physical knowledge coupled with information, form their own opinion, reorganize their own physical knowledge structure, expend their thinking, develop their ability in many aspects such as information literacy, collaboration awareness and so on while improving the physical literacy.

4 Ways and Means of Implementation

The integration of Information Technology physics should be considered mainly from the following aspects:

4.1 The Integration of Information Technology with Modern Education Concept

To implement the integration of information technology with curriculum, the educational thought and educational concept must change. The application of information technology in the traditional educational concept will be nothing but "put old wine in new wineskins", failing to achieve organic integration of information technology with curriculum. Integration should highlight people oriented, and students is the learning subjects so that teachers and external environment are all around to serve students, helping and promoting students' significant construction for knowledge. [6] Therefore, the selection and design of physics courseware should highlight students' initiative and experience in learning.

4.2 The Integration of Information Technology with Physics Teaching Content

Give play to the advantages of multimedia in helping physics teaching break some teaching points and difficulties, for example, to visualize and materialize some abstract concept, to display some microscopic processes, and to slow down the instantaneous and so on. Along the discussion of the integration of information technology and high school physics curriculum, information technology should be taken full use timely to supplement the latest content for physics teaching, and to install "interface" for physics learning.

4.3 The Integration of Information Technology with Various Teaching Methods

Physics is an experimental discipline, the knowledge and theories of which is explained and constructed on scientific research. Therefore, various teaching methods should be integrated based on the need of teaching, such as the explorative study, research-oriented learning, cooperative learning, etc. in information technology environment. [7] Through the combination of information technology and learning style, it promotes the adjustment of teaching methods, aiming at achieving the multi-level curriculum goal.

4.4 The Integration of Information Technology with Various Teaching Methods

Physics is an experimental discipline, the knowledge and theories of which is explained and constructed on scientific research. Therefore, various teaching methods should be integrated based on the need of teaching, such as the explorative study, research-oriented learning, cooperative learning, etc. in information technology environment[8]. Through the combination of information technology and learning style, it promotes the adjustment of teaching methods, aiming at achieving the multi-level curriculum goal.

4.5 The Integration of Information Technology with Traditional Education Media

Modern media should be organically combined with traditional teaching media, constructing the learning environment favorable to learning subjects, realizing reciprocal advantages, and bringing out the best in each other. By the data test and processing through computers, the law-discovering and problem-solving software should be regarded and developed. Discovery learning and problem solving learning should be carried out on that basis. In the process of the use of various teaching media, attention is paid to the irreplaceable role of modern teaching media. [9]

5 Construction of the Teaching Model for the Integration of Information Technology with Senior High School Physics

According to the role of information technology in physics teaching, the status of students in the learning process, and based on the analysis of the integration of information technology and teaching, we have proposed three modes for the information technology and senior high school physics teaching:

5.1 Information Technology-Based Multimedia Demo Integration Mode

The single integrated teaching mode "Multimedia demo model" is at present the most popular among physics teachers, and is also a widely applied pattern. Teachers make use of selfmade or purchased courseware, or appropriate information technology resources to assist the classroom instruction. The core of this pattern is to take advantage of technology to improve teachers' teaching. This integration teaching mode aims at the defects of the traditional classroom teaching. When technology means especially high information technology is adopted to support in classroom teaching, multi-media computers' presentation can turn the abstract into visualization at the situation where it is difficult for the teacher to clearly explain the content or for the students to understand [10]. This multi-media presentation provides students with the specific intuitive material, making students easy to perceive, understand and imagine and further able to understand and grasp the teaching content, and thus the teacher can effectively make breakthroughs towards the difficult and important points. This pattern is mainly conducted by the teachers' concentration explanation and the students' collective learning. Teachers and students can timely communicate with each other so that the teachers can have a prompt knowing of students' feedback. Meanwhile, there exist some limitations of this teaching mode which kills individual differences among students at the same time, the same schedule. This model is teacher centered while students are still in a passive position. It is a primary form of integrating information technology with curriculum, which is at the lowest level of integration as well.

5.2 Classroom-Based Integrative Model of Inquiry Collaboration

Inquiry-based instruction model in the teaching course, specially refers to the one provides students free enough chances to express, question, explore and discuss questions and permits them to utilize their learned knowledge to solve practical problems by all kinds of attempt activities such as individual, group, collective and so on, with the teachers' enlightening and guiding, the premise of the students' independent study and collaborative discussion, the existing instruction material as basic content to explore, the world and real life around students as reference object. The basic task of the classroom teaching reform is to change the traditional class group teaching form,reducing teaching time of the teacher in class, making the students actively participate in teaching process, and exerting students' initiative of independent exploration. [11]Modern information technology provides material base for explorative teaching. Multimedia and interactive and virtual reality technology information expression, greatly improve the learning efficiency and interest of students in exploring learning process. Exploratory integration teaching model can help students to develop the ability to analyze and solve the problems and creative thinking ability, so that students will gain knowledge systematized and structured, which makes it easier for students to understand knowledge, consolidate learning contents, and to put their knowledge into practice.

This kind of instruction model, on the one hand, pay attention to the students' extraction and application of the basic concepts and principles, on the other hand, to the students' development of thinking quality, inquiry ability and problem solving skills. It's a effective model to train innovation capacity and scientific spirit.

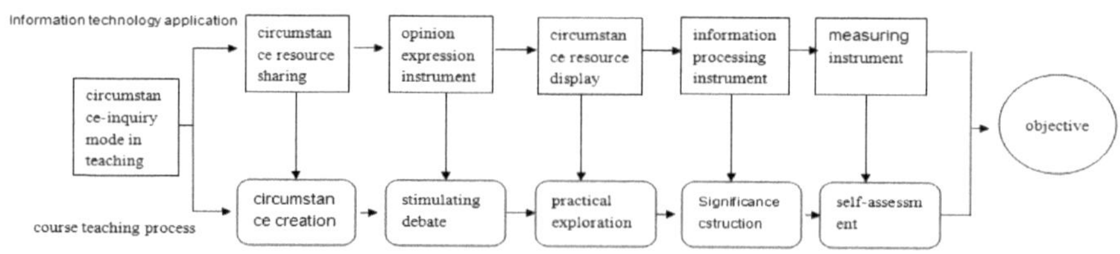

Fig. 1. Classroom-Based Integrative Model of Inquiry Collaboration

5.3 Integration Mode of Research-Oriented Physics Study Based on the Network

Resources online provide rich materials for physics subject-exploration that students can not only see, hear all kinds of information, but can go deep into the study content as well. In the process of course teaching, teachers can announce some exploring research topics occasionally on campus network, to motivate students to try to design experiments, and to solve specific problems, such as "mechanics on playground", "urban heat island effect", "the electromagnetic pollution in life" and so on, enabling research-oriented learning to get extended. Students search relevant materials around the topics through the network resources, sort their results, then write the essays and publish them online; or they discuss and communicate about the theme of researches by email or BBS [12]. They each form their own judgment; express their understanding of the problems and the different ways of thinking for problem solving.

They argue, evaluate, and cooperate mutually to solve various problems. On the internet, teachers put forward and design g research topics, while guiding students do exploring study in real life and through text information; lead students to exchange cross-space and time through the network, to integrate information of all aspects; these ways can greatly improve the students' study and research in the information age.

In this mode, teachers help to set up teaching situation by the use of information technology: with teachers' guidance, students and teachers interact mutually to do researching study. Students in the learning process are active and positive, while teachers coordinate and supervise in the teaching process. Information technology in this mode is a tool for students' studies, cooperation and communication, and is a kind of open integration way; and further integrated application.

6 Conclusion

The "integration" of information technology and physics is not a simple operation process, but a long-term complex study, investigation and practice process, a whole project from cellar to rafter multi-cooperationally. Standard of Physics Education reflecting the concept of "integration" , physics teaching materials embodying the spirit of "integration", physics teachers trained with "integration" thinking, library of teaching resources of multimedia convenient to teachers after scientific integration, and adaptable hardware facilities and so on are all needed. Only by the combination of physics curriculum, information technology, and the characteristics of teachers and students can we effectively integrate information technology and classroom physics teaching, and finally realizes the requirements for the goals of new curriculum of high school physics.

Acknowledgments. This paper is supported by the Scientific Research Foundation of Hebei Polytechnic University of China (Grant No. Z201016).

References

1. Sang, X., Zhang, Q.W.: Theory and practice of learning in the information age. Central Radio & TV University Press, Beijing (2000)
2. Zhu, Z.-T., Zhong, Z.-X.: Modern Educational Technology: Develop Multiple Intelligences. The Publishing House of East China Normal University, Shanghai (2003)
3. He, K.: Instructional System Design. Beijing Normal University Press, Beijing (2002)
4. Chen, Q., Liu, R.: Contemporary Educational Psychology. Beijing Normal University Press, Beijing (2003)
5. Li, S.-Y.: Teaching Strategies on Promoting Normal Tertiary Students Multi-intelligent Development in Information Technology Circumstances. In: 2010 International Conference on Optics, Photonics and Energy Engineering, OPEE 2010 (2010)
6. Matthews, M.R.: Construetivismandseieneeedueation: Afurthe
7. Guo, T.-T.: Level Information Technology Courses in the Teching of Task-driven. Shanxi Normal University, Shanxi (2010)
8. Lu, X.-S.: Inquiry Learning's Implementation and Evaluation in the Teaching of Information Technology. In: 2010 International Colloquium on Computing,Communication, Control, and Management, CCCM 2010 (2010)
9. Roblyer, M.D., Jack, E., Mary, A.H.: Integrating Educational technology into Teaching
10. The Power of Digital Learing. Integrating Content, The CEO Fourmon Education (March 2000)
11. Yin, S.-S.: Integrated Research of Information Technology and physics Teaching to Enhance Teaching Effectiveness. East China Normal University (2010)
12. Fang, D.: The Practice Study on Generative Teaching in Junior High School's Information Technology Course. GuangXi Normal University, GuangXi (2010)

Collaborative Filtering Algorithm Based on Improved Similarity Calculation

Yang Hongmei

Hebei United University, Tangshan, 063009
yanghongmei@heuu.edu.cn

Abstract. In collaborative filtering algorithm, the count of common rated items can indicate the effect of the similarity of both users. As similarity with larger count of common rated items can reflect the relationship of both users more precisely, larger similarity of small count of common rated items has higher weight in prediction is improper. The count of common rated items should be taken into account in neighbor selection. In this paper, an improved similarity calculation to collaborative filtering algorithm is proposed for neighbor selection. Experimental results demonstrate the approach can achieve better recommendation quality.

Keywords: Neighbor Selection, Similarity Calculation, Poisson Distribution.

1 Introduction

With the development of information technology, especially the development of internet, the information-overload problem becomes a challenge confronted by researchers. Personalized recommendation is one of the methods to ravel out the problem. In the field of recommendation research, collaborative filtering is the most popular approach, at the same time, content-based filtering and hybrid filtering are also two key approaches, and more and more researchers start to pay their attention to them. Content-based filtering compares profile of users with that of items using designated model, and offer similar products to users or provide a user with products that similar users have purchased[1-3]. Hybrid filtering is approaches which can enhance performances of recommendation quality by combining more than two recommendation techniques[4, 5].

In recommendation field, collaborative filtering is hot spot research. Due to the importance of neighbor selection to the recommendation quality, it attracts researchers more attention from the forepart of the research of collaborative filtering. The technique of k-nearest neighbors of collaborative filtering algorithm is a frequently-adopted method[6, 7]. The word, “nearest”, means that these neighbors have the largest similarity value with the designated user. K nearest neighbors are selected to predict unrated items in this technique if there are enough users who have common rated items. If the count of the users who have common rated items is less than the number k, these users are all selected as nearest neighbors. Although this technique is simple, it can also alleviate the effect of data sparsity.

C. Liu, J. Chang, and A. Yang (Eds.): ICICA 2011, Part I, CCIS 243, pp. 271–276, 2011.

The cluster-based technique is another neighbor selection approach and has attracted more attention from the researchers in recent years. Commonly, cluster-based technique selects neighbors according to some specific rules. These rules can alleviate the problem of data sparsity, or can improve the quality of recommendation, or else can affect both of them. In order to improve predict precision when data is sparse, R. Wang proposed a novel algorithm and resolve the data sparsity problem via the novel clustering approach-modified Bisecting K-means [8]. Quan et al proposed an approach based on stability of user similarity. As the diversity of items, users can have different preferences to them. In the approach these factors are all taken into account when clustering neighbors are selected [9]. S. Gong provides an method that utilizes the fuzzy similar-priority comparison to calculate the similarity of users and uses the fuzzy clustering technology to select neighbors, and the experimental results demonstrate that this algorithm can improve the quality of recommendation [10]. Incorporating content-based rules into cluster-based technique is another hot spot of research [11-13]. In these methods, content-based predictor is used to enhance existing user and item data and help to improve the quality of neighbor selection.

This paper will analyze the similarity calculation and neighbor selection. As item-based technique is similar to user-based technique, this research will focus on one technique, user-based collaborative filtering. Utilizing experiments demonstrate the effects which the count of common rated items imposes to the quality of recommendation. By the analysis of experimental results, an improved method to collaborative filtering is proposed and experiments indicate it can enhance the recommendation quality of collaborative filtering.

2 The Effect of the Count of Common Rated Items to Collaborative Filtering

Undeniably, similarity can reflect the relationship of two users and is an important factor in neighbor selection. However, similarity computed on small count of common rated items can not well indicate the relationship of two users. Accompanying with the count of common rated items which similarity computation is based on increasing larger, the similarity can reflect the relationship of two users better. To analyze the effect of the count of common rated items to collaborative filtering, the process of recommendation should be researched firstly.

2.1 Collaborative Filtering Algorithm

In order to describe data of collaborative filtering, two kinds of sets are defined, $U = \{u_1, u_2, ...u_m\}$ which represents users, and $I = \{i_1, i_2, ...i_n\}$ which denotes items. If a user u_x rates a item i_y with a score, the value of the score can be recorded r_{xy} which represents that the user u_x has rated item i_y and the rating score is r_{xy}. The rating scores of all items rated or unrated by all users can be denoted as a matrix $R = \{r_{xy}\}$. One common method to compute the similarity between two users is called correlation similarity and can denotes as[14]:

$$sim(u_a, u_b) = \frac{\sum_{c \in I_{ab}} (r_{a,c} - \overline{r_a})(r_{b,c} - \overline{r_b})}{\sqrt{\sum_{c \in I_{ab}} (r_{a,c} - \overline{r_a})^2} \sqrt{\sum_{c \in I_{ab}} (r_{b,c} - \overline{r_b})^2}} \tag{1}$$

I_{ab} is a set which includes all items which is the common rated items of u_a and u_b. c is a item in the set I_{ab}. The notations $\overline{r_a}$ a and $\overline{r_b}$ denote the average rating of the items rated by the users u_a and u_b, respectively. After similarities between users computed, the predicting score of $r_{a,y}$, if the item i_y has not rated by the user u_a, can be calculated by the following equation:

$$p(r_{a,y}) = \overline{r_a} + \frac{\sum_{b \in U_N} (r_{b,y} - \overline{r_b}) \times sim(u_a, u_b)}{\sum_{b \in U_N} sim(u_a, u_b)} \tag{2}$$

$p(r_{a,y})$ denotes the predicting score of $r_{a,y}$, and U_N is a set of the u_a's neighborhood users whose preferences are similar to u_a.

2.2 Probability of CCRI in Stochastic Conditions

From view of probability, to any of two users, the count of common rated item(CCRI) of them can be simulated as poison distribution. The Poisson distribution is a discrete probability distribution that expresses the probability of a number of events occurring in a fixed period of time if these events occur with a known average rate and independently of the time since the last event. Typical poison distribution depicts the following event: the number of customs who enter a bank in a fixed period of time. Disregarding of the preference of users, any of two users can be considered as a bank, and films (objects users rate) as customs. The count of films which "enter" the two users in a fixed period of time conforms to poison distribution.

In collaborative filtering, the probability of CCRI of two users can be expressed as follows disregarding of the preference:

$$p(CCRI) = \frac{e^{\lambda} \lambda^{CCRI}}{(CCRI)!} \tag{3}$$

To a given period of time, rating scores from users are stored in collaborative filtering system. The mean number of CCRI between two users can be achieved, and then the $p(CCRI)$ can also be achieved. The $p(CCRI)$ is the probability of CCRI disregarding of preference of users, and the CCRI of given two users indicates the CCRI does occur and it has preference information of users. If the CCRI of two users is k, and $p(k) = p$. If p is small and the CCRI of the two users k do occur, this means small probability event has occurred. On the contrary, if p is large, it means large probability event has occurred. In collaborative filtering, these two events represent important information. If a user a has two neighbor users, b and c, who have same similarity with a, the probability of CCRI of a and b is much smaller than that of a and c indicates a is more similar than a and b. The following two reasons can explain it. Firstly, the smaller probability of CCRI at stochastic condition has occurred infers special relationship between a and c. The more similar preference of a and c results in the occurrence of the events of smaller probability. Secondly, the same similarity is different in deed. The similarity between a and c is difficult to occur in stochastic condition, and it is more similar preferences that result in that.

2.3 Neighbors Selection

As two factors, similarity and CCRI, are taken into consideration in neighbor selection. How to determine the weight of them in neighbor selection is an important problem to solve. A neighbor selection index $I_{i,j}$ is chosen which combines the influence of similarity and CCRI and denotes the degree of preference similar of two user, i and j. $I_{i,j}$ is a comparative value, in other words, if the preferences of the users i and j is more similar than that of the users i and k, then $I_{i,j} > I_{i,k}$, the index is appropriate. $I_{i,j}$ is expressed as follows:

$$I_{i,j} = sim(u_i, u_j) f(p(CCRI_{i,j})) \tag{4}$$

Accordingly, a new prediction approach of unrated items by equation (2) can be modified as follows:

$$p(r_{a,y}) = \overline{r_a} + \frac{\sum_{u_b \in N_a} (r_{b,y} - \overline{r_b}) \times I_{a,b}}{\sum_{u_b \in N_a} I_{a,b}} \tag{5}$$

3 Experimental Results

Recommender systems provide recommendation by prediction of unrated items. If the prediction to unrated items is more accurate, the recommendation quality will be better. The commonly employed method to measure the quality of prediction in collaborative filtering is calculating the value of MAE (Mean Absolute error). MAE can be computed by the following equation:

$$MAE = \frac{1}{t} \sum_{y \in T} \left| r_{a,y} - p(r_{a,y}) \right| \tag{6}$$

T is a set of unrated items, t is the total number of unrated items in the set T. $r_{a,y}$ and $p(r_{a,y})$ are the actual and the predicted ratings, respectively.

Data sets used in these experiments are provided by MovieLens. In the experiments, The designated number of rating scores of the designated users to a certain items are abstracted as Table 1 and 80% of the rating scores are taken as training set which is used to predict the other 20% rating score. The experimental results are listed as Table 1 and indicate the proposed algorithm can always enhance the recommendation quality.

Table 1. Experimental Data and Experimental Results

Count of Users	Count of movies	MAE of the Traditional Algorithm	MAE of the Proposed Algorithm
235	420	0.76382	0.75663
310	580	0.76138	0.75224
470	820	0.75867	0.75109
785	1266	0.75239	0.74827

4 Conclusion

The count of common rated items is an important fact which has great influence to the recommendation quality in collaborative filtering. It means the similarity computed by it is more effective with its value larger. In the paper, an improved approach has been proposed which takes count of common rated items into account in neighbors selection and experimental results demonstrate it has better recommendation quality.

References

1. Phuong, N.D., Thang, L.Q., Phuong, T.M.: A graph-based method for combining collaborative and content-based filtering, Heidelberg, Germany, pp. 859–869 (2008)
2. Pasi, G., Bordogna, G., Villa, R.: A multi-criteria content-based filtering system, New York, NY, United States, pp. 775–776 (2007)
3. Wen, Z.-F., Yuan, H.: Novel algorithm for content-based image filtering. Tongxin Xuebao/Journal on Communication 27, 280–284 (2006)
4. Bezerra, B., De Carvalho, F.D.A.T.: A Symbolic hybrid approach to face the new user problem in recommender systems, Heidelberg, Germany, pp. 1011–1016 (2004)
5. Li, C., Liang, C., Ma, L.: Collaborative filtering recommendation algorithm based on domain nearest neighbor. Jisuanji Yanjiu yu Fazhan/Computer Research and Development 45, 1532–1538 (2008)
6. Chen, B., Zhou, M.: Rater maturity oriented k-nearest neighbor collaborative filtering algorithms. Chinese Journal of Electronics 16, 584–590 (2007)
7. Rashid, A.M., Lam, S.K., LaPitz, A., Karypis, G., Riedl, J.: Towards a scalable kNN CF algorithm: Exploring effective applications of clustering, Heidelberg, Germany, pp. 147–166 (2007)

8. Wang, R.: Improve recommendation quality via a novel clustering algorithm. Journal of Computational Information Systems 3, 1963–1970 (2007)
9. Quan, T.K., Fuyuki, I., Shinichi, H.: Improving accuracy of recommender system by clustering items based on stability of user similarity, Piscataway, NJ, United States, p. 4052704 (2007)
10. Gong, S.: The collaborative filtering recommendation based on similar-priority and fuzzy clustering, Piscataway, NJ, United States, pp. 248–251 (2008)
11. Puntheeranurak, S., Tsuji, H.: A multi-clustering hybrid recommender system, Piscataway, NJ, United States, pp. 223–228 (2007)
12. (k)Bezerra, B., Carvalho, F., Alves, G.: Collaborative Filtering based on Modal Symbolic user profiles: Knowing you in the first meeting, Heidelberg, Germany, pp. 235–245 (2004)
13. Tiraweerakhajohn, C., Pinngern, O.: Finding item neighbors in item-based collaborative filtering by adding item content, New York, NY, United States, pp. 1674–1678 (2004)
14. Karypis, G.: Evaluation of item-based top-N recommendation algorithms, Atlanta, GA, United States, pp. 247–254 (2001)

The Research and Application of Fuzzy EntropyWeight Comprehensive Evaluation Method in Paper Quality Evaluation

Cuilan Mi and Baoxiang Liu

College of Science, Hebei United University,Tangshan, Hebei, China
micuilan@163.com, liubx5888@126.com

Abstract. According to the fuzziness of Each index in Test quality evaluation, The entropy value theory of information will be used to test quality evaluation,use The difficulty, degree of differentiate, believe degree, validity and the standard deviation. As the impact of the test quality evaluation index. Establish a comprehensive evaluation index system, Using the information entropy as evaluation index weight coefficient, which can effectively solve the weight distribution difficulties. Weight is an objectivity, This method is a new test quality evaluation method, and connecting with the example of application, The results show that the method was simple, practical and reliable.

Keywords: fuzzy synthetic assessment method, entropy weight, paper quality, evaluation index.

1 Introduction

The exam as a teaching quality control of important link, its results reflect level of the students to master the knowledge and the teaching quality, the quality of teaching evaluation for the school teaching reform and provide to the forefront of information. And students' scores in addition to its own factors and the teacher by the influence on the quality of teaching, as well as by the test quality direct effect. The current most university examination papers rely mainly on the history of the proposition teachers experience, the analysis of the result of the exam scores of limited to simple calculation, it's hard to become an average measure of teaching quality and students' performance objective standard, the analytical results are also hard to say is accurate. Many scholars take a large number of trying to evaluation of examination paper quality of comprehensive, commonly used methods are: statistical description method of education statistics, fuzzy comprehensive evaluation method, the rough set theory, the principal component analysis and so on, but each method has some deficiencies.

And because the papers, the calculation method of quality evaluation index each are not identical, lead to test evaluation standard is different, so the comprehensive evaluation of examination paper quality, there is no uniform method. In this paper, the application of information entropy theory to test quality evaluation of the construction based on entropy weight test paper quality evaluation model, the objective of the

C. Liu, J. Chang, and A. Yang (Eds.): ICICA 2011, Part I, CCIS 243, pp. 277–283, 2011.

entropy weight method to determine the weight, overcome the weight of the subjective factors affect choice. And with our school 2009- 2010 annual the second term probability and mathematical statistics course final examination paper, for example, to test quality case study.

2 Evaluation Index of Paper Quality

The selection of evaluation indicators of examination paper quality evaluation plays an important role in the index selection, the rationality of the discretion of the test quality to influence. This paper in the scientific and reasonable and can be used to calculate the principle of construction, the influence of the five test quality index, difficulty, degree of differentiate, believe degree, validity and the standard deviation [3].

(1) The difficulty is to point to the test paper degree of difficulty. It reflects the subject to the student ability and knowledge of the level for degree, The whole of the difficulty of the test paper $P = \frac{1}{W}\sum_{i=1}^{n} P_i W_i$, W is the full score of the test, P_i and Wi are difficulty and Full score for the NO question, n is the total Title of the paper, $P_i = \overline{X} / X$, $\overline{X}$ is the average score of each title, X is full score of each title.

(2) Differentiate papers reflect the test of its different candidates questions the distinction between the degree. The whole of the examination paper of differentiate $D = \frac{1}{W}\sum_{i=1}^{n} D_i W_i$, w is the full score of the test, Di and Wi are difficulty and Full score for the NO question, n is the total Title of the paper,

(3) Papers standard deviations are a group of the values of the variable said discrete degree, reflect the volatility of the stability test scores, and calculation formula is $S = \sqrt{\frac{1}{N-1}\sum_{i=1}^{N}(x_i - \overline{x})^2}$, N is Sample size, xi is the Student's result. $\overline{x}$ is the result of each student.

(4) The reliability test used to describe the examination results, the reliability of the formulas $a = \left[\frac{K}{K-1}\right]\left[1 - \frac{\sum S_i^2}{S_t^2}\right]$, K is the question number of test, S_i^2 is The questions from squared residuals, S_t^2 is Overall score from the examination paper squared residuals.

(5) Validity refers to the validity of the test results and the correctness of the degree of examination paper, the whole efficiency degree for: $T = \frac{1}{100}\sum_{i=1}^{k} A_i T_i$. Ai is the full score of NO.i, T_i is efficiency degree for NO.i.

3 Based on Entropy Weight Test Quality of Fuzzy Comprehensive Evaluation

Fuzzy comprehensive evaluation is the more commonly used a evaluation method, which mainly is the application of fuzzy sets method, through the things the factors involved a single decision, and then, comprehensive all the circumstances, given the thing a general decision-making, and eliminate the influence of various things influence of uncertainty factors.

3.1 The Fuzzy Comprehensive Evaluation Method

Test quality the fuzzy comprehensive evaluation method of the procedure is as follows [1] :

(1) sure factors set $U = \{u_1, u_2, \cdots, u_m\}$

(2) Determine evaluation set $V = \{v_1, v_2, \cdots, v_n\}$

(3) Make a single factor evaluation between U and V, establish the fuzzy relation matrix $R = R_f = (r_{ij})_{m\times n}$,r_{ij} is level of v_j (i=1,2....m,,j=1,2....n)

(4) Establish fuzzy comprehensive evaluation model:

$$B = A \circ R = (b_1, b_2, \cdots, b_n \tag{1}$$

$b_j = \sum_{k=1}^{m} a_k r_{kj} (j = 1, 2, \cdots, n)$, Weight distribution vector $A = (a_1, a_2, \cdots, a_m)$. Normalization B, According to overall Evaluation vector B' and The maximum membership degree of the things, can make decisions.

3.2 The Method of Entropy Weight Coefficients Determined

To determine the weighing values of fuzzy comprehensive evaluation is the key link, directly affects the rationality of the evaluation results. In the application of the fuzzy comprehensive evaluation method, the method to determine the weight of a DuoZhong, each have its advantages and disadvantages. In this article, the entropy weight method to determine the weight. Entropy weight method is to use the information entropy reflects how much access to information to the weighting, the information entropy can comprehensively reflect the sample all the information, and the results from the high reliability, strong ability to adapt. The information entropy of empowerment main steps [9] :

(1) assumption that evaluated object has m evaluation index, n evaluation objects, construct judgment matrix $X = (x_{ij})_{m\times n}$

(2) will judgment matrix X normalization, get the normalized matrix $R = (r_{ij})_{m\times n}$,

Among them: $r_{ij} = \dfrac{x_{ij} - \min_i\{x_{ij}\}}{\max_i\{x_{ij}\} - \min_i\{x_{ij}\}}$

(3) from the traditional entropy concept available can define a definition of evaluation index of entropy $H_j = -k\sum_{i=1}^{m} p_{ij} Inp_{ij}$, $p_{ij} = r_{ij} \Big/ \sum_{j=1}^{n} r_{ij}$,when $p_{ij} = 0$, Inp_{ij} is meaningless,so fixed p_{ij} ,Modified computing formula for $p_{ij}^{'} = 1 + r_{ij} \Big/ \sum_{j=1}^{n} (1 + r_{ij})$, Probability matrix $P = (p_{ij}^{\prime})_{m \times n}$.

(4) the NO. j index calculation of entropy weight.

$$\omega_j = \frac{1 - H_j}{\sum_{j=1}^{n} (1 - H_j)} = \frac{1 - H_j}{n - \sum_{j=1}^{n} H_j}, j = 1, 2, \cdots, n \tag{2}$$

$\omega_j \in [0,1]$ and $\sum_{j=1}^{n} \omega_j = 1$.

4 The Empirical Analysis-The Fuzzy Entropy Comprehensive Evaluation in Test Quality Evaluation of Application

Probability and mathematical statistics course is our school undergraduate students, the final assessment of the important basic course of test quality relatively stable reliable source, material, the case will choose the course 2009 2010 annual the second term of the final examination papers material, including 17 students a professional of 1107 papers for test quality of examination paper analysis, with grade, and to illustrate the fuzzy entropy comprehensive evaluation in test quality evaluation, the application of standard university degree foundation course provides the theory basis for the establishment of the papers.

Calculation papers respect to: the difficulty for 0.738; Differentiate for 0.373268; Reliability is 0.847727; Validity of 0.573024; Standard deviation is 14.9. The general test quality into excellent, good, qualified and the unqualified four ranks, education statistics, ever by the scholars of examination paper evaluation criteria and to all experts opinion [7], establish evaluation standard sees Table 1:

Table 1. Evaluation standard table

	excellent	*Good*	*qualified*	*unqualified*
difficulty	0.50-0.55	0.45-0.50 0.55-0.60	0.35-0.45 0.60-0.70	Below 0.35 Over 0.70
Differentiate	Over 0.4	0.3-0.4	0.2-0.3	Below 0.2
Reliability	Over 0.85	0.80-0.85	0.75-0.80	Below 0.75
Validity	Over 0.80	0.70-0.80	0.60-0.70	Below 0.60
Standard deviation	Over 30	20-30	15-20	Below 15

4.1 Confirm Comprehensive Evaluation Matrix

Firstly, 10 experts to probability and mathematical statistics paper five index according to the standard of table 1 grade, and get the NO. i index of a level in the NO. j membership, which can get the normalized comprehensive evaluation matrix $R=(r_{ij})_{5\times4}$, see above 2:

Table 2. comprehensive evaluation matrix R

	excellent	*Good*	*general*	*Below Average*
difficulty	0.2	0.6	0.2	0.0
Differentiate	0.6	0.1	0.1	0.2
Reliability	0.3	0.2	0.2	0.3
Validity	0.5	0.4	0.1	0.0
Standard deviation	0.6	0.2	0.2	0.0

4.2 Each Index Calculation of Entropy Weight

In order to calculate the entropy weight of each index, according to professional students into a group of 17, and separately calculated each group index. The revised probability calculation formula get probability matrix $P=(p'_{ij})_{17\times5}$, see the table below 3:

Table 3. Probability matrix P

specialty	*difficulty*	*Differentiate*	*Reliability*	*Validity*	*Standard deviation*
calorifics	0.068994	0.057663	0.060778	0.055975	0.080329
network	0.043019	0.069411	0.066109	0.060454	0.060964
biological	0.057681	0.056502	0.046443	0.050409	0.048891
chemical	0.073301	0.051290	0.054656	0.051892	0.048882
Electrical science	0.047507	0.057340	0.058820	0.055053	0.053887
Material chemistry	0.070187	0.059916	0.067301	0.080259	0.057452
communication	0.060126	0.063122	0.062720	0.061140	0.055831
water	0.059695	0.058664	0.063279	0.065670	0.056148
steel	0.063866	0.051046	0.050388	0.043675	0.048976
Electronictechnology	0.052715	0.056577	0.058878	0.052781	0.086972
telecom	0.046749	0.066406	0.067400	0.075625	0.059380
construction	0.076406	0.040506	0.036576	0.042252	0.043486
computer	0.038203	0.081012	0.073152	0.084503	0.083859
packaging	0.058339	0.056514	0.055192	0.053406	0.051530
Civil engineering	0.060224	0.063960	0.065341	0.065584	0.058168
engineering	0.067450	0.053446	0.057749	0.049254	0.052087
machinery	0.055538	0.056623	0.055216	0.052068	0.053159

The calculating formula of the entropy get five index of the entropy value respectively:, , H1=0.9943, H2=0.9964, H3=0.9960,H4=0.9932,H5=0.9928.

By entropy weight calculation formula in test quality get the index weight in the evaluation of are: $\omega_1=0.2092$, $\omega_2=0.1319$ $\omega_3=0.1448$, $\omega_4=0.2489$, $\omega_5=0.2652$.

By (1) type can be for the comprehensive evaluation vector for: $B = A \circ R = (0.4480, 0.3203, 0.1692, 0.0698)$.

Due to the comprehensive evaluation of each component of vector for 1, so do not need to do is normalized, namely for final decision vector.

From the comprehensive evaluation vector can see: the total situation papers for: 44.80%, 32.03%, 16.92% good good qualified, 6.96% not qualified. Papers belonging to good quality and good degree is bigger, according to maximum subjection principle, this paper quality excellent, can comprehensively reflect the students to master the knowledge degree and the teachers' teaching level. The examination paper of more than 76% to more than the possibility of good, more than 93% of possibility, that is qualified the whole situation good paper.

Table 4. Comprehensive evaluation standard table

Evaluation results	*excellent*	*Good*	*qualified*	*unqualified*
score	1	0.85	0.75	0.6

Judge level and the corresponding points, with ZongPing scores that comprehensive evaluation score of:

$$N = B \cdot C^{\mathrm{T}} = (0.4480, 0.3203, 0.1692, 0.0698) \cdot (1, 0.85, 0.75, 0.6)^{\mathrm{T}} = 0.8836$$

Judging from the total score can draw the conclusion: the examination paper analysis on the whole is good, can reflect this semester students' knowledge of and teachers' teaching level, at the same time, from the index of the entropy weight can see: the difficulty and the validity and the standard deviation three index to the influence degree of the test quality most, it can reflect the index, so the test quality examination paper proposition to considered the difficulty of the questions and validity, and to ensure that the whole of the quality of the test paper, the results of the analysis, other type test quality analysis of great significance.

5 The Result Analysis

Test quality assessment is an important undergraduate teaching management work, also the quality of teaching evaluation is one of important index, it is to measure the volume level and teachers is an important basis of students' learning effect. This article through to the fuzzy comprehensive evaluation method and information entropy theory research, the establishment of a fuzzy entropy comprehensive evaluation model, this method overcomes the subjective factors of determining weight, can be more objective and reasonable evaluation of questions, and the practice proves that this method is more accurate evaluation result, high reliability of a kind of evaluation method. 2009 2010 annual the second term probability and mathematical statistics test paper quality is good, the overall index also reached the education measurement learn the general requirements, five evaluation index, the difficulty and the validity and standard deviations can reflect the examination paper quality, in short, to test quality for scientific evaluation and quantitative analysis, is to improve the quality of scientific and objective test questions, the important way of teaching this course and its practical significance proposition.

References

1. Li, A.G., Zhang, Z.H., et al.: Fuzzy Mathematics and Its Applications, 2nd edn., pp. 165–189. Metallurgical Industry Press, Beijing (2005)
2. Qu, S.H.: Management decision-making study and application of entropy, pp. 165–189. Machinery Industry Press, Beijing (2001)
3. Hang, J.M., Mei, C.C., He, X.W.: Fuzzy comprehensive evaluation model based on the quality of the paper evaluation system. Computer Science 31(2), 281–284 (2004)
4. Kong, L.Y.: Based on rough set theory, a comprehensive evaluation of the quality of papers. Sun Yat-sen University, Guangzhou (2007)
5. Chen, Q.B., Nie, R.: Based on entropy theory of open-ended investment fund performance evaluation. Business Times (24), 85–86 (2007)
6. Li, X.Q., Zhen, R.: Based on entropy weight coefficient of evaluation of urban information. Information Science (12), 15–19 (2007)
7. Li, Y.R.: Comprehensive evaluation for the evaluation of research papers in mathematics college entrance. Hebei University, Baoding (2005)
8. Wang, J., Zhang, J.S.: ComParing Several Methods of Assuring Weight Vector In Synthetical Evaluation. Journal of Hebei University of Technolojy 30(2), 52–57 (2001)
9. Yang, K.Y., Wang, L., et al.: Improved entropy fuzzy evaluation model in hydraulic engineering. Water-Saving Irrigation (8), 60–62 (2007)
10. Negoita, C.V.: Applications of Fuzzy Sets to Systems Analysis. Applied Economics Letters 4, 497–501 (1997)

Global Exponential Stability Analysis for Uncertain Stochastic Neural Networks with Discrete and Distributed Time-Varying Delays

Guan Wei and Zeng Hui

School of Sciences, Yanshan University, Qinhuangdao, China
guanwei@ysu.edu.cn

Abstract. In this paper, the global exponential stability is investigated for a class of stochastic neural networks with both discrete and distributed delays and norm-bounded uncertainties. Based on Lyapunov stability theory and stochastic analysis approaches, delay-dependent criteria are derived to ensure the global, robust, exponential stability of the addressed system in the mean square for all admissible parameter uncertainties. The criteria can be checked easily by the LMI Control Toolbox in Matlab. A numerical example is given to illustrate the effectiveness and improvement over some existing results.

Keywords: stochastic neural networks, discrete delays, distributed delay, norm-bounded uncertainties, global exponential stability.blocked matrix method.

1 Introduction

In recent years, neural networks have been investigated widely because of their extensive applications in pattern recognition, image processing, association and many other fields. Time delay will inevitably occur in electronic neural networks owing to the unavoidable finite switching speed of amplifiers. The delay is a source of instability and oscillatory response of networks, so the stability analysis of neural networks with delays attracts many researchers, see [1-5].

When performing the computation, there are many stochastic perturbations that affect the stability of neural networks. A neural network could be stabilized or destabilized by certain stochastic inputs. It implies that the stability analysis of stochastic neural networks also has primary significance in the research of neural networks. Recently, there are some research issues about stochastic neural networks, see [6-11] and references therein. But they don't give the convergence rate. In designing a neural networks, one concerns not only on the stability of the system but also on the convergence rate, that is to say, one usually desires a fast response in the network, so it is important to determine the exponential stability and to estimate the exponential convergence rate. This motivates our research.

Notations: The following notations will be used throughout this paper. For a real square matrix X , the notation $X > 0 \left(X \geq 0, X < 0, X \leq 0 \right)$ means that X is real symmetric and positive definite (positive semi-definite, negative definite, negative

C. Liu, J. Chang, and A. Yang (Eds.): ICICA 2011, Part I, CCIS 243, pp. 284–292, 2011.

semi-definite, respectively). $\lambda(X)$ denotes the set of eigenvalues of X, $\lambda_{\max}(X)$ and $\lambda_{\min}(X)$ denote the maximum and minimum eigenvalues of X, respectively. Let $(\Omega, \mathcal{F}, \{\mathcal{F}_t\}_{t\geq 0}, P)$ be a complete probability space with a filtration $\{\mathcal{F}_t\}_{t\geq 0}$ satisfying the usual conditions (i.e. it is right continuous and $\mathcal{F}_0$ contains all P-null sets). The mathematical expectation operator with respect to the given probability measure P is denoted by $\mathbf{E}\{\cdot\}$.

2 Problem Statement

In this paper, we consider the following uncertain stochastic neural networks with discrete and distributed time-varying delays:

$$\begin{aligned} \mathrm{d}x(t) = \Big[&-(C+\Delta C(t))x(t) + (A+\Delta A(t))f(x(t)) + (B+\Delta B(t))g(x(t-\sigma(t))) \\ &+ (D+\Delta D(t)) \int_{t-\tau(t)}^{t} h(x(s))\,\mathrm{d}s \Big]\mathrm{d}t + \big[\Delta H_1(t)x(t) + \Delta H_2(t)x(t-\sigma(t))\big]\mathrm{d}\omega(t) \end{aligned} \quad (1)$$

Where $x(t) = [x_1(t), \ldots, x_n(t)]^{\mathrm{T}} \in R^n$ is the neural state vector, $C = \mathrm{diag}\{c_1, \ldots, c_n\}$ is a positive diagonal matrix, A, B and D represent the connection weight matrix, the discretely delayed connection weight matrix and the distributive delayed connection weight matrix, respectively. $f(x(t))$, $g(x(t))$, $h(x(t))$ are the neuron activation function. $\omega(t) = [\omega_1(t), \ldots, \omega_m(t)]^{\mathrm{T}} \in R^m$ is a m-dimensional Brownian motion defined on a complete probability space $(\Omega, \mathcal{F}, \{\mathcal{F}_t\}_{t\geq 0}, P)$. $\sigma(t)$ and $\tau(t)$ denote the discrete time-varying delay and the distributed time-varying delay, respectively, and are assumed to satisfy $0 \leq \sigma(t) \leq \sigma$, $\dot{\sigma}(t) \leq \mu < 1$ and $0 \leq \tau(t) \leq \tau$.

Where $\Delta C(t)$, $\Delta A(t)$, $\Delta B(t)$, $\Delta D(t)$, $\Delta H_1(t)$ and $\Delta H_2(t)$ are the time-varying uncertainties of the form:

$$\begin{bmatrix}\Delta C(t) & \Delta A(t) & \Delta B(t) & \Delta D(t) & \Delta H_1(t) & \Delta H_2(t)\end{bmatrix} = MF(t)\begin{bmatrix}N_1 & N_2 & N_3 & N_4 & N_5 & N_6\end{bmatrix} \quad (2)$$

Where $M, N_i\ (i = 1,2,3,4,5,6)$ are known constant matrices with appropriate dimensions, $F(t)$ is the time-varying uncertain matrices, which satisfies

$$F^{\mathrm{T}}(t)F(t) \leq I \quad (3)$$

In addition, it is assumed that each neuron activation function in system (1) $f_i(\cdot), g_i(\cdot), h_i(\cdot)(i = 1,2,\ldots,n)$ is bounded and satisfies the following condition:

$$l_i^- \leq \frac{f_i(y_1) - f_i(y_2)}{y_1 - y_2} \leq l_i^+ \quad (4)$$

$$m_i^- \le \frac{g_i(y_1) - g_i(y_2)}{y_1 - y_2} \le m_i^+ \tag{5}$$

$$v_i^- \le \frac{h_i(y_1) - h_i(y_2)}{y_1 - y_2} \le v_i^+ \tag{6}$$

Where $l_i^-, l_i^+, m_i^-, m_i^+, v_i^-, v_i^+$ $(i = 1, 2, \ldots, n)$ are some constants, and they can be positive, negative, and zero. So it is less restrictive than the descriptions on both the sigmond activation functions and the Lipschitz-type activation functions.

Definition 1. The trivial solution of the neural networks (1) is said to be globally robustly stochastically exponentially stable with convergence rate k for all admissible uncertainties satisfying (2)-(3) in the mean square if there exist positive constants $\eta > 0$ and $k > 0$, then $\mathbf{E}\|x(t)\|^2 \le \eta e^{-2kt} \sup_{-\max\{\sigma,\tau\} \le s \le 0} \mathbf{E}\|x(s)\|^2$

Lemma 1. [1] Let U, V, W and M be real matrices of appropriate dimensions with M satisfying $M = M^{\mathrm{T}}$, then $M + UVW + W^{\mathrm{T}}V^{\mathrm{T}}U^{\mathrm{T}} < 0$, for all $V^{\mathrm{T}}V \le I$.

If and only if there exist a scalar $\varepsilon > 0$ such that $M + \varepsilon^{-1}UU^{\mathrm{T}} + \varepsilon W^{\mathrm{T}}W < 0$.

Lemma 2. [24] (Schur complement) For a given matrix $S = \begin{bmatrix} S_{11} & S_{12} \\ S_{12}^T & S_{22} \end{bmatrix}$ with $S_{11} = S_{11}^{\mathrm{T}}$, $S_{22} = S_{22}^{\mathrm{T}}$, then the following conditions are equivalent:

(1) $S < 0$
(2) $S_{22} < 0, S_{11} - S_{12}S_{22}^{-1}S_{12}^{\mathrm{T}} < 0$
(3) $S_{11} < 0, S_{22} - S_{12}^{\mathrm{T}}S_{11}^{-1}S_{12} < 0$

Lemma 3. [19] For any constant symmetric matrix M, $M = M^{\mathrm{T}} > 0$, scalar $\gamma > 0$, we have $\gamma \int_0^{\gamma} \omega^{\mathrm{T}}(s) M \omega(s) \mathrm{d}s \ge \left[\int_0^{\gamma} \omega(s) \mathrm{d}s\right]^{\mathrm{T}} M \left[\int_0^{\gamma} \omega(s) \mathrm{d}s\right]$.

Lemma 4. [20] Let A, D, E, F and P be real matrices of appropriate dimensions with $P > 0$ and satisfying $F^{\mathrm{T}}F \le I$ .Then for any scalar $\varepsilon > 0$ satisfying $P^{-1} - \varepsilon^{-1}DD^{\mathrm{T}} > 0$, we have

$$(A + DFE)^{\mathrm{T}} P (A + DFE) \le A^{\mathrm{T}} \left(P^{-1} - \varepsilon^{-1}DD^{\mathrm{T}}\right) A + \varepsilon E^{\mathrm{T}} E.$$

3 Main Results

In this section, we discuss global robust exponential stability of uncertain stochastic neural networks (1) in the mean square. Based on Lyapunov function and stochastic analysis approach, we get delay-dependent stability criteria in terms of LMI.

Our first result in this paper deals with the exponential stability of (1) with $\Delta C(t)=0, \Delta A(t)=0$, $\Delta B(t)=0$ and $\Delta D(t)=0$, i.e.

$$\mathrm{d}x(t)=\left[-Cx(t)+Af\left(x(t)\right)+Bg\left(x\left(t-\sigma(t)\right)\right)+D\int_{t-\tau(t)}^{t}h\left(x(s)\right)\mathrm{d}s\right]\mathrm{d}t \\ +\left[\Delta H_1(t)x(t)+\Delta H_2(t)x\left(t-\sigma(t)\right)\right]\mathrm{d}\omega(t) \tag{7}$$

Denote $L_1:=\mathrm{diag}\{l_1^-l_1^+,...,l_n^-l_n^+\}$, $L_2:=\mathrm{diag}\{l_1^-+l_1^+,...,l_n^-+l_n^+\}$, $M_1:=\mathrm{diag}\{m_1^-m_1^+,...,m_n^-m_n^+\}$, $M_2:=\mathrm{diag}\{m_1^-+m_1^+,...,m_n^-+m_n^+\}$, $V_1:=\mathrm{diag}\{v_1^-v_1^+,...,v_n^-v_n^+\}$, $V_2:=\mathrm{diag}\{v_1^-+v_1^+,...,v_n^-+v_n^+\}$

Theorem 1. The equilibrium point of system (7) is globally exponentially stable in the mean square, if there exist $P>0$, $Q_1>0$, $Q_2>0$, $R_1>0$, $R_2>0$, $U_1=\mathrm{diag}\{u_{11},...,u_{1m}\}\ge 0$, $U_2=\mathrm{diag}\{u_{21},...,u_{2n}\}\ge 0$, $U_3=\mathrm{diag}\{u_{31},...,u_{3n}\}\ge 0$, $\varepsilon_1>0$ such that

$$\begin{bmatrix} -P & PM \\ * & -\varepsilon_1 I \end{bmatrix}<0 \tag{8}$$

$$\Xi=\begin{bmatrix} \Psi_{11} & \varepsilon_1 N_5^{\mathrm{T}}N_6 & PA+L_2U_1 & M_2U_2 & PB & V_2U_3 & PD \\ * & \Psi_{22} & 0 & 0 & 0 & 0 & 0 \\ * & * & -2U_1 & 0 & 0 & 0 & 0 \\ * & * & * & R_1-2U_2 & 0 & 0 & 0 \\ * & * & * & * & -(1-\mu)\mathrm{e}^{-2k\sigma}R_1 & 0 & 0 \\ * & * & * & * & * & \tau^2R_2-2U_3 & 0 \\ * & * & * & * & * & * & -\mathrm{e}^{-2k\tau}R_2 \end{bmatrix}<0 \tag{9}$$

$$\Psi_{11}=2kP-PC-CP+Q_1+\sigma^2Q_2-2L_1U_1-2M_1U_2-2V_1U_3+\varepsilon_1N_5^{\mathrm{T}}N_5$$

$$\Psi_{22}=-(1-\mu)\mathrm{e}^{-2k\sigma}Q_1+\varepsilon_1N_6^{\mathrm{T}}N_6$$

Proof. For system (7), we choose the following Lyapunov-Krasovksii function

$$V(t)=\mathrm{e}^{2kt}x^{\mathrm{T}}(t)Px(t)+\int_{t-\sigma(t)}^{t}\mathrm{e}^{2ks}x^{\mathrm{T}}(s)Q_1x(s)\mathrm{d}s+\sigma\int_{-\sigma}^{0}\int_{t+\beta}^{t}\mathrm{e}^{2ks}x^{\mathrm{T}}(s)Q_2x(s)\mathrm{d}s\mathrm{d}\beta \\ +\int_{t-\sigma(t)}^{t}\mathrm{e}^{2ks}g^{\mathrm{T}}\left(x(s)\right)R_1g\left(x(s)\right)\mathrm{d}s+\tau\int_{-\tau}^{0}\int_{t+\beta}^{t}\mathrm{e}^{2ks}h^{\mathrm{T}}\left(x(s)\right)R_2h\left(x(s)\right)\mathrm{d}s\mathrm{d}\beta \tag{10}$$

Where P, Q_1, Q_2, R_1 and R_2 are positive matrices.

By Itô 's differential formula, the stochastic derivative of $V(t)$ along the trajectory of system (7) is

$$
\begin{aligned}
\mathrm{d}V(t) \le \mathrm{e}^{2kt}\Big\{&2kx^{\mathrm{T}}(t)Px(t) \\
&+2x^{\mathrm{T}}(t)P\Big[-Cx(t)+Af(x(t))+Bg(x(t-\sigma(t)))+D\int_{t-\tau(t)}^{t}h(x(s))\mathrm{d}s\Big] \\
&+\big[\Delta H_1(t)x(t)+\Delta H_2(t)x(t-\sigma(t))\big]^{\mathrm{T}}P\big[\Delta H_1(t)x(t)+\Delta H_2(t)x(t-\sigma(t))\big] \\
&+x^{\mathrm{T}}(t)Q_1x(t)-(1-\mu)\mathrm{e}^{-2k\sigma}x^{\mathrm{T}}(t-\sigma(t))Q_1x(t-\sigma(t))+\sigma^2x^{\mathrm{T}}(t)Q_2x(t) \\
&-\sigma\mathrm{e}^{-2k\sigma}\int_{t-\sigma}^{t}x^{\mathrm{T}}(s)Q_2x(s)\mathrm{d}s+g^{\mathrm{T}}(x(t))R_1g(x(t)) \\
&-(1-\mu)\mathrm{e}^{-2k\sigma}g^{\mathrm{T}}(x(t-\sigma(t)))R_1g(x(t-\sigma(t)))+\tau^2h^{\mathrm{T}}(x(t))R_2h(x(t)) \\
&-\tau\mathrm{e}^{-2k\tau}\int_{t-\tau}^{t}h^{\mathrm{T}}(x(s))R_2h(x(s))\mathrm{d}s\Big\}\mathrm{d}t \\
&+\big\{2x^{\mathrm{T}}(t)P\big[\Delta H_1(t)x(t)+\Delta H_2(t)x(t-\sigma(t))\big]\big\}\mathrm{d}\omega(t)
\end{aligned}
$$

From Lemma 3, we know

$$
\begin{aligned}
-\sigma\int_{t-\sigma}^{t}x^{\mathrm{T}}(s)Q_2x(s)\mathrm{d}s &\le -\sigma\int_{t-\sigma(t)}^{t}x^{\mathrm{T}}(s)Q_2x(s)\mathrm{d}s \\
&\le -\frac{\sigma}{\sigma(t)}\Big(\int_{t-\sigma(t)}^{t}x(s)\mathrm{d}s\Big)^{\mathrm{T}}Q_2\Big(\int_{t-\sigma(t)}^{t}x(s)\mathrm{d}s\Big) \\
&\le -\Big(\int_{t-\sigma(t)}^{t}x(s)\mathrm{d}s\Big)^{\mathrm{T}}Q_2\Big(\int_{t-\sigma(t)}^{t}x(s)\mathrm{d}s\Big)
\end{aligned}
$$

$$
\begin{aligned}
-\tau\int_{t-\tau}^{t}h^{\mathrm{T}}(x(s))R_2h(x(s))\mathrm{d}s &\le -\tau\int_{t-\tau(t)}^{t}h^{\mathrm{T}}(x(s))R_2h(x(s))\mathrm{d}s \\
&\le -\frac{\tau}{\tau(t)}\Big(\int_{t-\tau(t)}^{t}h(x(s))\mathrm{d}s\Big)^{\mathrm{T}}R_2\Big(\int_{t-\tau(t)}^{t}h(x(s))\mathrm{d}s\Big) \\
&\le -\Big(\int_{t-\tau(t)}^{t}h(x(s))\mathrm{d}s\Big)^{\mathrm{T}}R_2\Big(\int_{t-\tau(t)}^{t}h(x(s))\mathrm{d}s\Big)
\end{aligned}
$$

From Lemma 4, we know for any scalar $\varepsilon>0$ satisfying $P^{-1}-\varepsilon^{-1}DD^{\mathrm{T}}>0$, then

$$
\begin{aligned}
&\big[\Delta H_1(t)x(t)+\Delta H_2(t)x(t-\sigma(t))\big]^{\mathrm{T}}P\big[\Delta H_1(t)x(t)+\Delta H_2(t)x(t-\sigma(t))\big] \\
&=\big\{MF(t)\big[N_5x(t)+N_6x(t-\sigma(t))\big]\big\}^{\mathrm{T}}P\big\{MF(t)\big[N_5x(t)+N_6x(t-\sigma(t))\big]\big\} \\
&\le \varepsilon_1\big[N_5x(t)+N_6x(t-\sigma(t))\big]^{\mathrm{T}}P\big[N_5x(t)+N_6x(t-\sigma(t))\big]
\end{aligned}
$$

By Schur complement, we know $P^{-1}-\varepsilon^{-1}DD^{\mathrm{T}}>0$ is equivalent to (8).

From (4-6) we know that

$$\big[f_i(x_i(t))-l_i^-x_i(t)\big]\big[f_i(x_i(t))-l_i^+x_i(t)\big]\le 0,\ f_i(0)=0,\ i=1,2,\ldots,n$$

$$\big[g_i(x_i(t))-m_i^-x_i(t)\big]\big[g_i(x_i(t))-m_i^+x_i(t)\big]\le 0,\ g_i(0)=0,\ i=1,2,\ldots,n$$

$$\big[h_i(x_i(t))-v_i^-x_i(t)\big]\big[g_i(x_i(t))-v_i^+x_i(t)\big]\le 0,\ h_i(0)=0,\ i=1,2,\ldots,n$$

Then, for $U_1 = \mathrm{diag}\{u_{11},...,u_{1n}\} \geq 0$, $U_2 = \mathrm{diag}\{u_{21},...,u_{2n}\} \geq 0$ and $U_3 = \mathrm{diag}\{u_{31},...,u_{3n}\} \geq 0$, we have

$$\begin{aligned}
\mathrm{d}V(t) &\leq \mathrm{d}V(t) - 2\sum_{i=1}^{n} u_{1i}\left[f_i(x_i(t)) - l_i^- x_i(t)\right]\left[f_i(x_i(t)) - l_i^+ x_i(t)\right] \\
&\quad - 2\sum_{i=1}^{n} u_{2i}\left[g_i(x_i(t)) - m_i^- x_i(t)\right]\left[g_i(x_i(t)) - m_i^+ x_i(t)\right] \\
&\quad - 2\sum_{i=1}^{n} u_{3i}\left[h_i(x_i(t)) - v_i^- x_i(t)\right]\left[h_i(x_i(t)) - v_i^+ x_i(t)\right] \\
&\leq \left\{\xi^T(t)\Xi\xi(t)\right\}\mathrm{d}t + \left\{2x^{\mathrm{T}}(t)P\left[\Delta H_1(t)x(t) + \Delta H_2(t)x(t-\sigma(t))\right]\right\}\mathrm{d}\omega(t)
\end{aligned} \tag{11}$$

Where

$$\xi(t) = \Big[x^{\mathrm{T}}(t), x^{\mathrm{T}}(t-\sigma(t)), f^{\mathrm{T}}(x(t)),$$

$$g^{\mathrm{T}}(x(t)), g^{\mathrm{T}}(x(t-\sigma(t))), h^{\mathrm{T}}(x(t)), \left(\int_{t-\tau(t)}^{t} h(x(s))\mathrm{d}s\right)^{\mathrm{T}}\Big]^{\mathrm{T}}$$

From $\Xi < 0$, it is obvious that there must exist scalar $\gamma > 0$ such that

$$\Xi + \mathrm{diag}\{\gamma I, 0, 0, 0, 0, 0, 0\} < 0$$

Taking the mathematical expectation, we have $\dfrac{d\mathbf{E}V(t)}{dt} \leq \mathbf{E}\left[\xi^T(t)\Xi\xi(t)\right] \leq -\gamma\mathbf{E}\|x(t)\|^2$

Then $\mathbf{E}V(t) \leq \mathbf{E}V(0)$

$$\begin{aligned}
\mathbf{E}V(0) &= \mathbf{E}\Big\{x^{\mathrm{T}}(0)Px(0) + \int_{-\sigma(0)}^{0} \mathrm{e}^{2ks}x^{\mathrm{T}}(s)Q_1x(s)\mathrm{d}s + \sigma\int_{-\sigma}^{0}\int_{\beta}^{0}\mathrm{e}^{2ks}x^{\mathrm{T}}(s)Q_2x(s)\mathrm{d}s\mathrm{d}\beta \\
&\quad + \int_{-\sigma(0)}^{0}\mathrm{e}^{2ks}g^{\mathrm{T}}(x(s))R_1g(x(s))\mathrm{d}s + \tau\int_{-\tau}^{0}\int_{\beta}^{0}\mathrm{e}^{2ks}h^{\mathrm{T}}(x(s))R_2h(x(s))\mathrm{d}s\mathrm{d}\beta\Big\} \\
&\leq \Big(\lambda_{\max}(P) + (\lambda_{\max}(Q_1) + \lambda_{\max}(R_1)M^TM)\int_{-\sigma(0)}^{0}\mathrm{e}^{2ks}\mathrm{d}s + \lambda_{\max}(Q_2)\int_{-\sigma}^{0}\int_{\beta}^{0}\mathrm{e}^{2ks}\mathrm{d}s\mathrm{d}\beta \\
&\quad + \lambda_{\max}(R_2)V^TV\int_{-\tau}^{0}\int_{\beta}^{0}\mathrm{e}^{2ks}\mathrm{d}s\mathrm{d}\beta\Big)\sup_{-\max\{\sigma,\tau\}\leq s\leq 0}\mathbf{E}\|x(s)\|^2
\end{aligned} \tag{12}$$

Where $M = \mathrm{diag}\left\{\max\left(|m_i^-|, |m_i^+|\right)\right\}$, $V = \mathrm{diag}\left\{\max\left(|v_i^-|, |v_i^+|\right)\right\}$ $i = 1, 2, \ldots, n$

On the other hand, from the definition of $V(t)$, one obtains

$$\mathbf{E}V(t) \geq \lambda_{\min}(P)\mathrm{e}^{2kt}\mathbf{E}\|x(t)\|^2 \tag{13}$$

Combining (12) and (13), it can be easily obtained that

$$\mathbf{E}\|x(t)\|^2 \leq \eta\mathrm{e}^{-2kt}\sup_{-\max\{\sigma,\tau\}\leq s\leq 0}\mathbf{E}\|x(s)\|^2$$

This indicates that the stochastic neural networks system (7) is globally exponentially stable in the mean square.

Now we consider the global robust exponential stability for system (1).

Theorem 2. The equilibrium point of system (1) is globally exponentially stable in the mean square if there exist $P>0$, $Q_1>0$, $Q_2>0$, $R_1>0$, $R_2>0$, $U_1=\mathrm{diag}\{u_{11},\dots,u_{1m}\}\geq 0$, $U_2=\mathrm{diag}\{u_{21},\dots,u_{2n}\}\geq 0$, $U_3=\mathrm{diag}\{u_{31},\dots,u_{3n}\}\geq 0$, $\varepsilon_1>0$, $\varepsilon_2>0$ such that

$$\begin{bmatrix} -P & PM \\ * & -\varepsilon_1 I \end{bmatrix}<0 \tag{14}$$

$$\Omega=\begin{bmatrix}
\Psi_{11} & \varepsilon_1 N_5^{\mathrm{T}}N_6 & \Psi_{13} & M_2U_2 & PB-\varepsilon_2 N_1^{\mathrm{T}}N_3 & V_2U_3 & PD-\varepsilon_2 N_1^{\mathrm{T}}N_4 & PM \\
* & \Psi_{22} & 0 & 0 & 0 & 0 & 0 & 0 \\
* & * & -2U_1+\varepsilon_2 N_2^{\mathrm{T}}N_2 & 0 & \varepsilon_2 N_2^{\mathrm{T}}N_3 & 0 & \varepsilon_2 N_2^{\mathrm{T}}N_4 & 0 \\
* & * & * & R_1-2U_2 & 0 & 0 & 0 & 0 \\
* & * & * & * & \Psi_{55} & 0 & \varepsilon_2 N_3^{\mathrm{T}}N_4 & 0 \\
* & * & * & * & * & \tau^2 R_2-2U_3 & 0 & 0 \\
* & * & * & * & * & * & \Psi_{77} & 0 \\
* & * & * & * & * & * & * & -\varepsilon_2 I
\end{bmatrix}<0 \tag{15}$$

$$\Psi_{11}=2K-PC-CP+Q_1+\sigma^2Q_2-2L_1U_1-2M_1U_2-2V_1U_3+\varepsilon_1 N_5^{\mathrm{T}}N_5+\varepsilon_2 N_1^{\mathrm{T}}N_1$$
$$\Psi_{13}=PA+L_2U_1-\varepsilon_2 N_1^{\mathrm{T}}N_2$$
$$\Psi_{22}=-(1-\mu)\mathrm{e}^{-2k\sigma}Q_1+\varepsilon_1 N_6^{\mathrm{T}}N_6$$
$$\Psi_{55}=-(1-\mu)\mathrm{e}^{-2k\sigma}R_1+\varepsilon_2 N_3^{\mathrm{T}}N_3$$
$$\Psi_{77}=-\mathrm{e}^{-2k\tau}R_2+\varepsilon_2 N_4^{\mathrm{T}}N_4$$

Proof. Replacing C, A, B and D in (7) with $C+\Delta C(t)$, $A+\Delta A(t)$, $B+\Delta B(t)$ and $D+\Delta D(t)$, $\Delta C(t)$, $\Delta A(t)$, $\Delta B(t)$ and $\Delta D(t)$ are described in (2) and (3), we get

$$\begin{aligned}\Xi_1=\Xi&+\begin{bmatrix}M^{\mathrm{T}}P & 0 & 0 & 0 & 0 & 0 & 0\end{bmatrix}^{\mathrm{T}}F(t)\begin{bmatrix}-N_1 & 0 & N_2 & 0 & N_3 & 0 & N_4\end{bmatrix}\\ &+\begin{bmatrix}-N_1 & 0 & N_2 & 0 & N_3 & 0 & N_4\end{bmatrix}^{\mathrm{T}}F(t)\begin{bmatrix}M^{\mathrm{T}}P & 0 & 0 & 0 & 0 & 0 & 0\end{bmatrix}\end{aligned}$$

From Lemma 1, we know $\Xi_1<0$ is equivalent to

$$\begin{aligned}\Xi_2=\Xi&+\varepsilon_2^{-1}\begin{bmatrix}M^{\mathrm{T}}P & 0 & 0 & 0 & 0 & 0 & 0\end{bmatrix}^{\mathrm{T}}\begin{bmatrix}M^{\mathrm{T}}P & 0 & 0 & 0 & 0 & 0 & 0\end{bmatrix}\\ &+\varepsilon_2\begin{bmatrix}-N_1 & 0 & N_2 & 0 & N_3 & 0 & N_4\end{bmatrix}^{\mathrm{T}}\begin{bmatrix}-N_1 & 0 & N_2 & 0 & N_3 & 0 & N_4\end{bmatrix}<0\end{aligned}$$

Using Schur Complement, $\Xi_2<0$ is equivalent to $\Omega<0$. So, we have $\Xi_1<0$.

From Lyapunov theorem, the uncertain stochastic neural networks system (1) is exponentially stable.

4 Numerical Examples

In this section, a numerical example is presented to demonstrate the usefulness of the developed method on the exponential stability of the system (1) with time-varying delays.

Consider the stochastic neural networks with the following parameters:

$$C=\begin{bmatrix}3.5 & 0\\ 0 & 4.5\end{bmatrix},\ A=\begin{bmatrix}0.2 & 0.5\\ 0.9 & 1.2\end{bmatrix},\ B=\begin{bmatrix}-0.5 & 0.7\\ -0.8 & -1\end{bmatrix},\ D=\begin{bmatrix}0.4 & 0.8\\ 0.5 & 0.2\end{bmatrix},$$

$$M=\begin{bmatrix}0.5 & 0\\ 0 & 0.5\end{bmatrix},\ N_i=\begin{bmatrix}0.2 & 0\\ 0 & 0.2\end{bmatrix}(i=1,2,\ldots,6),\ l_i^-=m_i^-=v_i^-=0,\ l_i^+=0.5,$$

$$m_i^+=0.5,\ v_i^+=0.5,\ i=1,2,3,\sigma=0.2,\ \tau=0.5$$

For $\mu=0$, by Theorem 1 in [23], the stochastic neural network is exponential stable. Indeed it is a criterion to check the asymptotic stability of stochastic neural networks with constant time delays, so we can not get the convergence rate. And the condition given in [23] is discrete delay-independent. By solving an optimization problem, the upper bound of distribute delay is $\tau=5.0066$. By solving the LMIs (21) and (22), we not only obtain that the stochastic neural networks is exponentially stable but also get the convergence rate., we get the upper bound of convergence rate is $k=1.9552$. For $k=0$, we can obtain that stochastic neural network is asymptotic stable and the upper bound of delays is $\sigma=\tau=5.5965$ by Corollary 2. For $\sigma=0.2$, $\tau=0.5$, $k=1.9552$, the solution of LMIs is as follows:

$$P=\begin{bmatrix}8.4433 & 0.0195\\ 0.0195 & 6.2292\end{bmatrix},\ Q_1=\begin{bmatrix}0.3100 & -0.0002\\ -0.0002 & 0.3101\end{bmatrix},\ Q_2=\begin{bmatrix}0.0243 & -0.0209\\ -0.0209 & 0.0293\end{bmatrix},$$

$$R_1=\begin{bmatrix}26.9434 & -4.5397\\ -4.5397 & 18.7943\end{bmatrix},\ R_2=\begin{bmatrix}48.2275 & 11.9769\\ 11.9769 & 80.4345\end{bmatrix},\ U_1=\begin{bmatrix}12.3450 & 0\\ 0 & 22.3476\end{bmatrix},$$

$$U_2=\begin{bmatrix}25.4239 & 0\\ 0 & 16.9132\end{bmatrix},\ U_3=\begin{bmatrix}14.3646 & 0\\ 0 & 22.8039\end{bmatrix},\ \varepsilon_1=19.3317,\ \varepsilon_2=2.1114$$

5 Conclusions

Based on Lyapunov stability theory and LMI technique, a new criterion is derived as LMI to ensure the exponential stability of stochastic neural networks with both discrete and distributed time-varying delays in this letter. By the Theorems, we can not only determine the exponential stability but also get the maximum of exponential convergence rate. What is more, this approach is computational effective since it can be easily verified and solved by use of the LMI Control Toolbox in Matlab. The effectiveness of the proposed criterion is demonstrated in numerical example.

References

1. Singh, V.: Robust Stability of Cellular Neural Networks with Delay. IEEE Proc. Control Theory Appl. Linear Matrix Inequality Approach 151, 125–129 (2004)
2. He, Y., Wu, M., She, J.H.: An Improved Global Asymptotic Stability Criterion for Delayed Cellular Neural Networks. IEEE Trans. Neural Networks 17, 250–252 (2006)
3. Cho, H.J., Park, J.H.: Novel Delay-Dependent Robust Stability Criterion of Delayed Cellular Neural Networks. Chaos, Solitons and Fractals 32, 1194–1200 (2007)
4. Zhang, Q., Wei, X.P., Xu, J.: Delay-Dependent Global Stability Condition for Delayed Hopfield Neural Networks. Nonlinear Analysis: Real World Application 8, 997–1002 (2007)
5. Zhu, E.W.: Asymptotical Mean Square Stability of Cellular Neural Networks with Random Delay. Journal of Harbin Institute of Technology 3, 409–413 (2010)
6. Wei, L.: Global Exponential Stability of Fuzzy Cellular Neural Networks with Constant Delays. Journal of Communication and Computer 7, 30–34 (2010)
7. Shao, J.: A New Result on Global Exponential Robust Stability of Neural Networks with Time-Varying Delays. Journal of Control Theory and Applications 7, 315–320 (2009)
8. Qing, Z.: Global Exponential Stability of Cohen-Grossberg Neural Networks with Time-Varying Delays and Impulses. Journal of Shanghai University (English Edition) 3, 255–259 (2009)
9. Jing, Y.-W., Zhang, R., Wang, Z.-S.: Global Exponential Stability of Neural Network Models with Time-Varying Delay for Quadratic Programming Problem. Kongzhi yu Juece/Control and Decision 25(6), 921–924+928 (2010)
10. Qiu, F., Cui, B.-T.: A Delay-Decomposition Approach for Stability of Neural Network with Time-Varying Delay. Chinese Physics B 18(12), 5203–5211 (2009)
11. Huang, Z., Li, X., Mohamad, S., Lu, Z.: Robust Stability Analysis of Static Neural Network with S-type Distributed Delays. Applied Mathematical Modelling 33(2), 760–769 (2009)

Research on the Fuzzy Evaluation System in China's Sports Network Course Teaching

Yunzhi Peng

Physical Education Institute, Hunan University of Science and Technology 411201
Xiangtan, China
doctor2000@yeah.net

Abstract. Purpose: Discuss the application of fuzzy evaluation in China's sports network course teaching. Method: By means of Literature retrieval method and index system of assessment. First of all, it has studied the overall design philosophy of the system and determined to adopt the "three-layer model" of the Browser/Server structure. Then combined the database technology as well as web and database interconnecting technique. Result: An complete index system of fuzzy eveluation in China's sports network course teaching had been constructed. Conclusion: Index system of fuzzy evaluation will offer certain guidance to both the quality evaluation and the design of the network courses.

Keywords: fuzzy evaluation system, network course, research.

1 Introduction

In recent years, with the development of the multimedia network technology, distance education has entered the new stage based on network and network education has achieved greater potentials. Massachusetts Institute of Technology has carried out "OCW" since 2002, and by now, it has opened about 1,550 courses of the school to the world, so the learners can study on the Internet without stepping out of doors [1]. OCW conveys the high-quality courses of the world-renowned schools to every corner of the world and spreads the knowledge to more people, which will benefit all human beings. In China, network education has involved higher education, basic education and training institutions. Especially in colleges and universities, the 68 network education academies approved by the Ministry of Education have already had 2,400,000 registered students by 2004 [2].

However, in terms of the development process of the education, each step of the network course construction from course design to teaching implementation is not mature. [3, 4] Therefore, we should attach importance to the evaluation of network courses. Currently, people at home and abroad are very concerned about network course evaluation and the researches are focusing on the setting of the evaluation criterion. The current network course evaluation models rely mainly on linear model, and the evaluation experts give a quantitative estimate to each specific indicator and

C. Liu, J. Chang, and A. Yang (Eds.): ICICA 2011, Part I, CCIS 243, pp. 293–299, 2011.

use weighted averaging to calculate the final comprehensive evaluation results. The core of its evaluation philosophy is based on the hypotheses that the evaluation results can be superimposed and the evaluation factors are in linear relationship. However, in fact, in the criteria of network courses, many indexes usually have a certain degree of ambiguity, i.e. nonlinear characteristics, they neither have clear boundaries and extensions, nor have absolute and very accurate affirmation and negation. [5] To solve these problems, the paper has studied the applications and researches of the fuzzy evaluation system in China's sports multimedia teaching.

The fuzzy theory is to make fuzzy quantification of the membership function that the event belongs to the set degree, to get a membership degree to solve various problems [6]. The traditional physical education evaluation mainly adopts linear evaluation model, whose modeling and operation are easy and it is widely used in the field of education evaluation. However, in the network course evaluation, the evaluation objects have a certain degree of ambiguity, nonlinear characteristics, they neither have clear boundaries, nor have absolute affirmation and negation. The introduction of fuzzy theory has overcome the shortcomings of using classical mathematics to carry out accurate evaluation and neglecting the ambiguity and uncertainty of the education information, and provided objective and scientific evaluation tools for quantitative evaluation of network courses. [7]

2 Construction of Evaluation Index

The evaluation index system has researched the current evaluation criteria in and out of the network, referred to various information sources, including nearly 300 domestic and foreign papers and dozens of scale and evaluation index sets, made comprehensive analysis and processing of them and finally formed 4 first-class index systems and 27 second-class index systems; then adopted Delphi method, to get the weight of first-class index and second-class index of the sports network courses. [8] Through the consistency test, the weight is proved to be reasonable.

2.1 The Content and Framework of the Sports Network Course Index

The evaluation index system is the visible unity formed by evaluation indexes of different levels according to logic structure of the evaluation objects. [9] It is the volume calibration system measuring the development level and state of the education evaluation objects and it is the core of the education evaluation program. The construction of the network course is a systematic engineering, its design, development and implementation need to integrate and coordinate a variety of factors, so the core task of network course evaluation is to extract the evaluation dimensions of the network courses and analyze to get a complete set of evaluation index system. A complete evaluation index system is an organic collection composed of the evaluation indexes, index weights, evaluation standard elements and membership degrees that reflect the nature of the network courses. [10] Figure 1 shows the main framework of the network course evaluation index system.

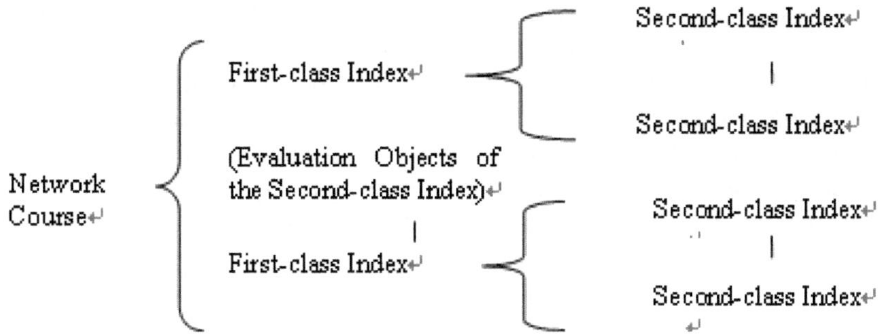

Fig. 1. The Main Framework of the Network Course Evaluation Index System

2.2 The Establishment of the Evaluation Index Dimensions

Collect evaluation indexes through documentation method, and these indexes have many repeated contents or contents of similar or related meanings. The work of this step is to filter and extract the mass and confused indexes and get a sensible order. The first step is to delete the repeated, that is, integrate the contents of the same meaning and little different expression into one index and choose the most clear and appropriate expression. Then identify the related items in the index, i.e. the indexes with little difference in the evaluation angle or evaluation criteria. Integrate the indicators of a kind to the same higher index. Adopt the method of systemization and analysis (induction and deduction), and finally form 4 first-class indexes, 27 second-class indexes and the preliminary framework of the index system.

2.3 The Establishment of the Evaluation Index Weight

The paper adopts Delphi method to determine the weight. Divide all the indexes in the criteria into three parts, i.e. required field, optional field and encouragement field. Then design the questionnaire and give out the questionnaire to the experts. Conduct statistical analysis to the returned questionnaires and then design the questionnaires of the next round. Give out the questionnaire again and feed back the results of the questionnaire of the last round to each member. Each member can refer to the others' opinions to answer the questionnaire of the next round. Repeat the process of the third step, until all the members reach agreement on the survey content, the weight distribution of the network course quality certification standard index system will complete the determination.

2.4 The Establishment of the Evaluation Criterion

For the fuzzy synthetic evaluation, the value of the comment field adopts graded scores and then uses the method of quantitative synthesis to confirm. The partition of the evaluation grade uses the membership function in the fuzzy theory, adopts the method of interval assignment of [0,1] to regulate the membership scope of each element grade. [11] The greatest advantage of the method is to be able to make the elements whose grades are difficult to be determined with exact number get relatively objective and reasonable evaluation, and thus improve the validity and reliability of the evaluation. The simplest quantization is firstly to assign a value of 7, 6, 5, 4, 3, 2 and 1 to each grade. The second step is to set the membership degree of each grade and the membership degree can be drawn by a membership function;The quantization of qualitative rating is set in accordance with Formula (4-1), as shown in Table 1.

Table 1. Membership Degree of the Evaluation Grade

Evaluation Grade	Special A	Very A	A	Relatively A	Relatively Not A	Very Not A	Special Not A
Value Assignment	7	6	5	4	3	2	1
μA	0.90	0.8	0.64	0.51	0.41	0.33	0.26

3 The Design of the Fuzzy Synthetic Evaluation System in Sports Network Courses

3.1 The Design of the Browser/Intermediate Layer/Server (B/DIS)-Based 3-Tier Model

The evaluation system adopts 3-tier-based design, and compared to the 2-tier structure model (B/S), its client is just for realizing the user interface, while the application logic is achieved by the transaction service layer, i.e. Data Broker. In this way, the purpose of sliming the client down can be achieved.

3.2 The Individualized Setting of the End Users

The evaluation system adopts the user registration and login mechanism, and each user uses the only user id and password to log in the system. When a new evaluation activity starts, the related evaluators will get the evaluation notice. Considering the difference in the evaluation purposes and evaluation objects, the system allows the users to delete, add and modify the evaluation indexes, as well as customize and save their evaluation criteria on the basis of the criterion besides adopting the "Network Course Evaluation Index System" to evaluate in the part of course certification. In the need of understanding the quality of a certain network course, the user can choose a certain evaluation criterion customized by him and invite certain registered users to carry out evaluation activities according to the features of the evaluation purposes and the network courses.

3.3 The Structural Analysis of the Network Course Evaluation System

User Management Module: The main function of the module is the management of the user information, including user registration, login and user authority setup The evaluation system adopts the user registration and login mechanism, and each user uses the only user id and password to log in the system. When a new evaluation activity starts, the related evaluators will get the evaluation notice. Considering the difference in the evaluation purposes and evaluation objects, the system allows the users to delete, add and modify the evaluation indexes, as well as customize and save their evaluation criteria on the basis of the criterion besides adopting the "Network Course Evaluation Index System" to evaluate in the part of course certification. In the need of understanding the quality of a certain network course, the user can choose a certain evaluation criterion customized by him and invite certain registered users to carry out evaluation activities according to the features of the evaluation purposes and the network courses., etc. For example, the administrator can add, delete and modify the system users.

Questionnaire Module: The module provides the evaluators the network course-related evaluation survey questionnaire, and the evaluation items of the questionnaire should be built on the basis of the network course evaluation index system (as shown in Table 3). After giving appropriate comments ("Very Suitable", "Relatively Suitable", "Uncertain" and "Not Suitable") to the evaluation items, the evaluator clicks the button of "Submit", and then the filled information can be saved to the system database as the basis for implementing evaluation in the future.

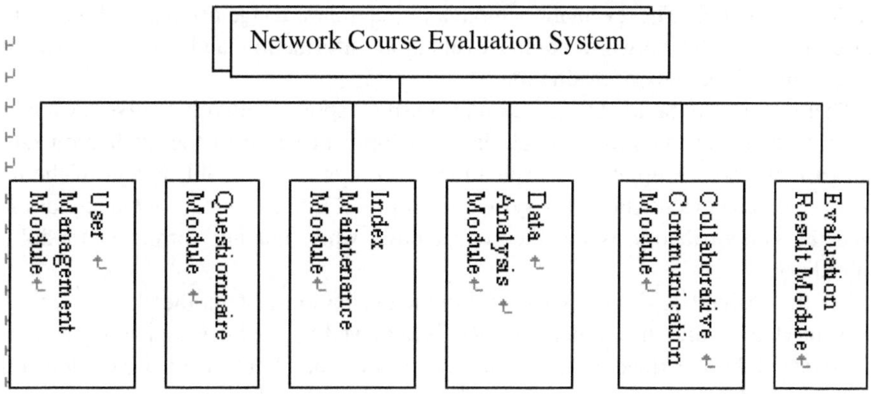

Fig. 2. The Functional Module of the Network Course Evaluation

Index System Maintenance Module: The module is used for the maintenance and management of the evaluation index system of the network courses. According to the setting of the user authority, the administrator and expert can add, delete, modify and browse the evaluation index system.

Data Processing Module: The user checks and modifies the index system after browsing the network courses; then the system can generate a questionnaire automatically and the user submits the questionnaire after filling; then the system makes unitary processing of the collected survey data as the fuzzy evaluation matrix, and evaluates the second-class indexes and first-class indexes through fuzzy evaluation; at last, make comprehensive evaluation to obtain the final evaluation results.

Collaborative Communication Module: The module has five topics of "Course Content", "Teaching Design", "Interface Design", "Technology" and "Others", and the evaluator can express their evaluation opinions on the relevant aspects of the courses by the way of message as well as browse the evaluations of others, or exchange the achievements and difficulties in participating the evaluation, and through the solution of the problems, to improve the network course evaluation system.

Evaluation Result Module: According to the collected survey information, the system carries out data analysis according to the information processing of fuzzy synthetic evaluation system, shows the evaluation scores of the first-class indexes and second-class indexes, modifies the corresponding aspects according to the score of the individual network course and makes a rating scale for the network courses, which has played a guiding role for students to select network courses and facilitated the identification and selection of the expert network courses.

4 Conclusion

Analyze the evaluation methods and procedures of network courses at home and abroad and put forward the fuzzy synthetic evaluation-based network course evaluation model. The evaluation model is put forward against the ambiguity and uncertainty of the network course evaluation information and has improved the science and objectivity of evaluation.

There is much faultiness in China's current sports network course evaluation criterion and there is still research and development space in the evaluation index dimensions, index weights and evaluation criteria, etc. The establishment of the new network course evaluation index system must proceed from China's actual conditions, take the system theory as the theoretical basis while making correct methodology subsidiary.

For the design based on 3-tier model in the evaluation system, the client is only for user interface, while the application logic is achieved by the intermediate layer, which has reduced the workload of the client. The constructed platform has basically met the features of adaptability, security and stability of the network courses.

References

1. Yin, Q.: Web Qos Service Discovery Model Based on Two-dimension Fuzzy Evaluation. Journal of Huaihai Institute of Technology (Natural Science Edition) 18, 34–36 (2009)
2. Xu, Y., Zhong, D.: Research on Network Security Evaluation Based on Fuzzy Method. Measurement and Control Technology 28, 79–82 (2009)
3. Bao, B., Wang, Y., Liu, C.: Research On Fuzzy Mathematics in Evaluating Teaching Quality of Higher Education. Journal of Anhui Science and Technology University 22, 73–80 (2008)
4. Zeng, Z., Zhang, Y., Yang, L.: Comprehesive Study on Performance Evaluation of Digital Resource Service. Library and Information Service 8, 55–57 (2008)

5. Wang, H., Peng, Y.: Multilevel indicator Evaluation Teclulique of network course based on fuzzy set. Computer Engineering and Design 30, 2061–2063 (2009)
6. Chang, Z.: Research on Multimedia Teaching Quality. Journal of ChangChun Institute of Technology (Social Sciences Edition) 3, 84 (2006)
7. Liu, G.: The Application of Multimedia Technology in PE Teaching. Journal of Leshan Normal College 19, 138–140 (2004)
8. Xie, J.: Thoughts on overall Teaching Reform of Normal Regular Colleges and Universities. Journal of Chengdu Sports University 35, 85–87 (2009)
9. Zhang, L., Wang, Y.: Design and Assessment of Teaching Courseware in P.E. Colleges. Journal of Inner Mongolia University for Nationalities 5, 111–115 (2005)
10. Xie, J.: Thoughts on overall Teaching Reform of Normal Regular Colleges and Universities. Journal of Chengdu Sports University 35, 85–87 (2009)
11. Chen, L.: The Quality of Social Interactions among Students in the Asynchronous Network Interactive Environment-Study of Example Cases Discussed Online in the Distance Teacher Training. Distance Education in China 4, 19–22 (2004)

The Application of Cloud Computing Technology in University Digital Libraries

Zhang Haishan[1], Zhou Haiyun[2], and Meng Kenan[3]

[1] Modern Technology Education Centre, Hebei United University, Tangshan, Hebei, China
sea @heut.edu.cn
[2] Tangshan No.5 Middle School, Tangshan Hebei, China
yunmail0372@sina.com.cn
[3] Modern Technology Education Centre, Hebei United University, Tangshan, Hebei, China
hblgdxdj@126.com

Abstract. Based on summarizing the concept of cloud computing and its characteristics, combining the problems they faced in the application of traditional libraries, through studying the cloud computing and the characteristics of book information system, this paper provides the design proposal of the new type of book information system with the cloud computing technology introduced, which can integrate university book information and improve information services level.

Keywords: cloud computing, digital libraries, information services.

1 Introduction

In recent years, cloud computing as a mixed product along the development of traditional computer technology and network technology, is gradually coming to our life. The library, as a highly dependant of IT technology, should also ride the wind and waves and seize the opportunity to actively respond to in the wave of cloud computing. How to organically integrate the concept of cloud computing with library services is one question we must consider. Chinese universities are numerous, but universities can neither share nor exchange between each other; because of diversified investment, most constructions of the hardware and software of the library lag behind; the traditional mode of the information services system is expensive with weak expansion ability, poor configurability, and difficult to upgrade. These all are the incurable chronic illness facing the current Chinese university libraries.

2 Cloud Computing Technology

2.1 The Concept of Cloud Computing

For the time being, cloud computing is not yet a unified authoritative definition. Cloud computing is service based on Internet. By transferring the mission executed

C. Liu, J. Chang, and A. Yang (Eds.): ICICA 2011, Part I, CCIS 243, pp. 300–307, 2011.

originally by personal computers and private data center to large computing centers shared by all users in the Internet to finish, realizing computing resources of the computer hardware and software, and the sufficient sharing of installation, configuration and maintenance to these computing resources. [1] Cloud Computing is a mixed product of traditional computers and Network technology development combining Grid Computing, distributed Computing, Parallel Computing, Utility Computing, Network Storage Technologies, Virtualization, Load Balance and so on.

2.2 The Characteristics of Cloud Computing

Safe and reliable. Cloud computing provides the most reliable and safe data storage center, and users don't have to worry about troubles like data loss, virus invasions and so on. Cloud computing employs measures like data multiple replica fault tolerance and computing node isomorphism interchangeable to guarantee the high reliability of services, and the centralized storage of data makes it much easier to implement safety monitoring.

Very low cost. Cloud computing sets low requirements to client equipment, thus the library need not pay high capital on hardware purchasing. [2] Only a small amount of money is necessary if the library chooses to rent the related services offered by cloud services, such as the hardware configuration and its upgrading. Lower maintenance cost can be got through the reduction of both the number and the cost of the software and hardware.

Excellent computing power. Cloud computing has provided us a software and hardware service to an unprecedented scale. Users connected to cloud computing system will no longer be limited to what a desktop alone can do; they will have control of thousands of computers and servers to carry out the task of the super computers. [3]

Data sharing. In the network application mode of the cloud computing, only one data is needed which is saved in the other side of the "cloud". Once your electronic equipments are connected to the Internet, you can visit and use the same data at the same time. Data and application sharing between different equipments can be easily achieved with cloud computing. With many users sharing the resources, circumstances like a single user assumes higher expenses or limited resources cannot be fully used can be avoided.

Infinite possibilities. Cloud computing provides us both an unlimited space for storage and data management, and an infinite computing power to accomplish all kinds of applications. Personal computers and other electronic equipment could not provide an unlimited amount of storage space and computing power, but in the other side of "cloud", that can be easily done with a huge cluster of thousands of, tens of thousands of or even more servers . [4] Personal and individual equipment ability is limited, but the potential of the clouds computing is almost limitless.

Dynamic expansion. With dynamic expansion of its scale, cloud computing can quickly responds to different applications. The resources under the cloud computing system can be dynamically expanded and reconfigured with the increase of applications and users.

3 The Transformation of the Application of Digital Libraries in Cloud Computing Environment

The present books information systems home and abroad are all adopting the traditional pattern design, and this structure of B/S system is only suitable to use in a small scale with less learners (such as a internal university). The books information system with cloud computing technology introduced can provide powerful ability of information services, very suitable for large-scale libraries and information services (such as several universities or a Mega Center), and they are mainly listed as follows:

3.1 Low Cost

In the cloud computing environment, there is no need for general medium or small libraries to buy expensive hardware device, but to rent computing power from cloud computing suppliers as the software system used by the end user. [5] The computer equipment in the library also need not install application system software, and they can use internet applications system as long as they connect the Internet. The upgrade and maintenance of software could also be operated directly on the Internet by the cloud service provider, thus the library imperceptibly enjoys the latest version of the software system. The universal property of "cloud" enables the utilization rate of resources to step up in a large degree much more than the traditional system, and then universities do not need to afford the high cost of data center management.

3.2 Resources Sharing

Cloud computing model can make information sharing space between libraries altogether; the related electronic resources in the library are stored in hundreds of millions of servers in the "cloud" instead of in a certain computer; relevant information can be accessed globally, or shared by some library groups, or simply used by the users of the library itself, realizing information resources sharing to the full. [6] Visitors don't need to know which server resources are stored in; the system manages all the resources as a whole, uses uniform resource list, and provides the most reasonable service, no longer subject to region and time.

3.3 Avoiding Repetitive Resources Construction

The traditional mode of the books information system is difficult to establish unified system due to structural problems; each library in the universities builds their own resources, easily leading to repetitive construction and causing a lot of unnecessary loss. The books information system introducing cloud computing technology can establish a unified national system, enable university libraries in university library from all parts of our country to put up unified plan and construction resources, and effectively avoid repetitive resources construction.

3.4 Exerting the Maximum Function of the Library

In the traditional library services model, users generally must use the computer to utilize the electronic resources of the library. And in the application of cloud computing model, users can also use the electronic resources services provided by the library through equipment like cell phones, PDA, etc. [7] As cloud computing model provides a powerful wireless access function, future users use the electronic resources of the library through all sorts of relevant terminals, and thus the role of library resource center get full play.

3.5 The Powerful Ability of Information Services

The books information system introducing cloud computing technology can give full play to the characteristics of cloud computing, can use software and hardware resources of various universities as a whole, consequently it provides powerful ability of information services and resources providing. [8] For instance, there exists the common phenomenon that hardware and software constructions in universities in the central and western underdeveloped region of China lag behind, and the problem can't be solved in the short term. By introducing the cloud computing technology to books information system can integrate the software and hardware of all around the east and west of our country, providing powerful service ability for universities from all parts in union.

4 The Design of Books Information System with Cloud Computing Technology Introduced

The resources of each university library form a "cloud", and the new mode of the book information system can automatically search all kinds of resources and choose the best route to transmit data, when a server is at fault, it can automatically turn to other servers; each module is designed to achieve efficient resources sharing, and visitors do not need to know which server the resources are by using the uniform resources list, and they can make any visit without the limit of region and time; it can realize the nearby visit to teaching resources, and to any one of the resources visitors, the system can automatically analyze its IP, determine the routing, look for the nearest resources from him, and establish a connection, and thus provides the fastest and best visit; it achieves the function of registering all resources and sharing the registration information all at once, without the need to repeated register. [9] This system can make full use of the software and hardware resources in the “cloud”, providing powerful service ability, and realizing the pattern of the general construction of book resources and sharing library materials among universities, which greatly improve the utilization rate of books and information, and reduce the repetitive construction.

For papery books, it’s also suitable for the book information system to introduce cloud computing technology. First, related information of papery books need to be collected and input into information system, and released to all the users both inside and outside school by the system; second, the users choose books of any universities, deal with relevant electronic formalities online, fill out information such as the name, address, contact information, and so on, pay lending deposit through Alipay or online bank, through the books information system; finally, the library will send books to its users by express company after confirming, and the user also send books back by express company after using up. The library will return the deposit through Alipay or online bank if the books are examined undamaged. [10] If there is, the deposit can be partly deducted only to return the rest. The whole process only requires users to pay a little express cost, while the borrow area and borrowing rate in university libraries are increased to a large degree.

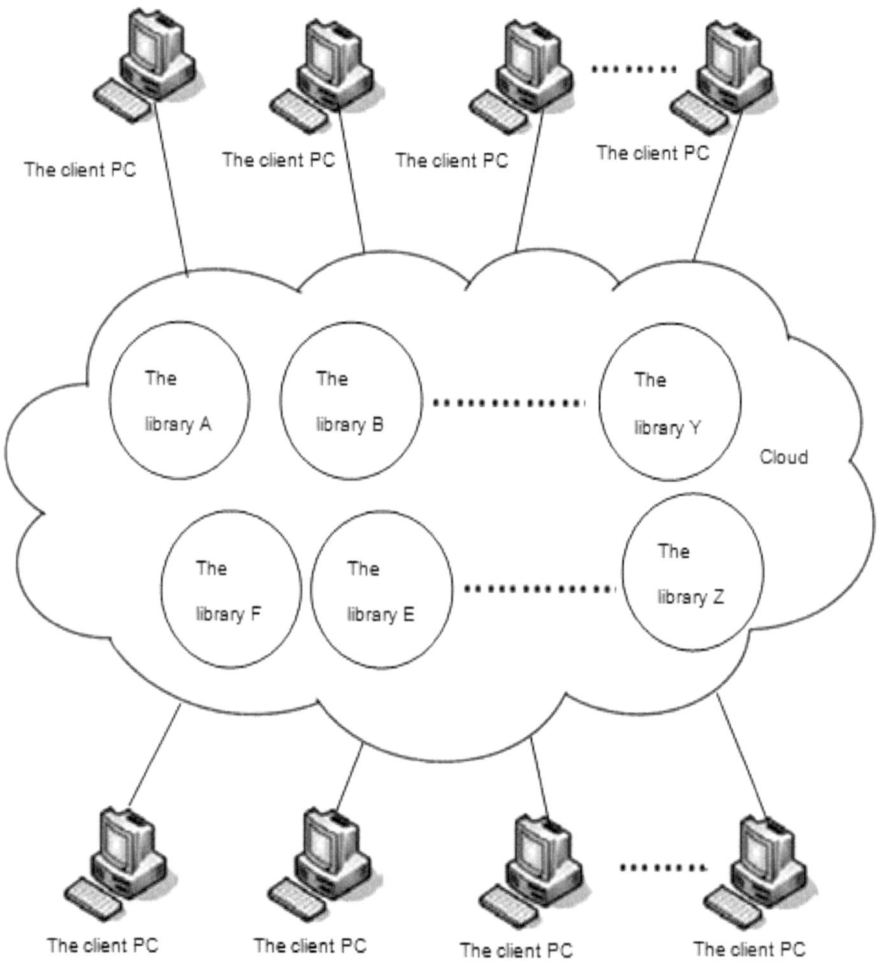

Fig. 1. Cloud-Based Logical Structure of Llibrary Information System

5 Notable Problems

Cloud computing could bring numerous benefits to the application of digital libraries, but as a new kind of technology, it still has some problems. As utilizing cloud computing in the construction of digital libraries, problems should be paid attention to are listed as follows.

5.1 Data Security

The biggest worry of the library to the cloud computing lies in the data security. The library data, programs are not stored in local machines, but in cloud computing data processing center. Many details haven't been provided to the users by the service provider of the center, such as the location of the center, staffing information, the technology adopted, and operation mode and so on. [11] Every cloud computing service provider emphasizes the encryption technology, the SSL for instance, used to protect user's data, but the data are encrypted by the SSL technology data, only when it's transferred on the network, the protection during processing and storage remains unresolved. The library should collect the existing data, and establish the data resources which can be stored in "cloud" and which must be stored in the existing mode of the library.

5.2 On Alternative

The library is supposed to not only be able to choose IT suppliers freely, transfer from a supplier to another at zero cost and at any time, but also be able to choose different services from different suppliers. Only this operating mode of cloud computing can be accepted by the library. If there is no substitutability and no free to move from a service provider to another, or the transfer cost is too high, then the dependence of library to the cloud will become very strong and bound to the cloud suppliers equivalently. [12] Without alternative, good quality may become worse, low prices are likely to rise. Even if the cloud computing enterprises are state-owned, the interest of the library is difficult to be ensured without corresponding regime. And once the clouds have the alternative, then the user's rights to choose IT suppliers freely can be approved and the safeguard mechanism to form marketization is built.

5.3 Interface

The cloud computing still has no open common criteria, and great difficulty is produced when the application program based on one company's cloud computing programming model are transferred to the other company's cloud computing platform. Due to the different conditions of the libraries, the server configurations and the sever operating systems are different. [13] In order to apply cloud computing technology better, the library should pay close attention to interface software aiming at different operating platforms supplied by cloud service provider, or cooperate with related units to develop the interface card which is suitable for itself.

5.4 Copyright

In the cloud computing mode, libraries joining in the cloud model could share each other's information resources through the related agreement, that is, users in "cloud" could use electronic resources of other libraries like using their own as well. [14] When the libraries provide customers conveniences and improve the degree of freedom in sharing information resources with the cloud model, the copyright disputes are brought about at the same time. Therefore, the author suggests library should study on the copyright disputes probably caused in the information resources sharing under the new cloud computing model, and develop practical and feasible scheme to help users use information resources in each library expediently.

5.5 The Industry Standard

At present, the country has not yet published corresponding policies and regulations for cloud computing, nor designated uniform industry standard, then it lacks effective legal means and industry norms to monitor and control its business operation. The quality of the cloud services fails to get effective guarantee. [15] The existing domestic cloud computing enterprises are mostly "private cloud" providers, and their mutual compatibility is poor, which makes digital libraries face the holding predicament in selecting their suppliers for once a conflict occurred between suppliers, it is difficult to replace because of the existence of incompatibility. Without common standards, it is impossible of the digital library to realize zero cost transfer between suppliers. To be able to realize the fungibility of different IT service providers, apart from the contract relationship formed by corresponding agreement with the supplier, technically speaking, it still needs IT service provider of cloud computing to follow common standards.

6 Conclusion

Although in the current we are facing many technology and service obstacles, we believe those difficulties will be solved neatly with the booming development of cloud computing technology in the IT field and the perfection of policies and regulations. The application of cloud computing technology and methods to the construction of the books information system can not only integrate the books information resources, increase the utilization rate of resources, and improve research and teaching level, but also bring new application area for cloud computing, enabling clouds services to get more close to our life and study and letting us personally feel the great change by technology. Since there are numerous Chinese colleges and universities, if university libraries can have coordination construction and be able to share resources, it will surely be saved a lot of the education funds, which have too many difficulties to cope with, and be able to concentrate funds to promote the software and hardware quality of each library, and then improve the overall strength of Chinese colleges and universities.

References

1. Wang, W., Chen, L.: The Model of CALIS's Cloud Service Platform for Distributed Digital Libraries. Journal of Academic Libraries (4), 13–18 (2009)
2. Liu, P.: Cloud Computing. Publishing House of Electronics Industry, Beijing (2010)
3. Shi, H.: On the Cloud Computing and the Mobile library. Library Development (9), 10–12 (2009)
4. Yang, M., Yuan, X.: Digital Libraries under the Cloud Computing Enviorment. Library Development (9), 7–9, 12 (2009) (Ch)
5. Wei, Z., Li, H., Zu, Y.: Library Information Services Research Influenced by Cloud Computing. Library (2), 87–88, 93 (2010) (Ch)
6. http://baike.baidu.com/view/327983.htm
7. Peter, F.: Dot Cloud: The 21st Century Business Platform Built on Cloud Computing. Publishing House of Electronics Industry, Beijing (2009)
8. Wang, C., Ai, F.: Thinking about the Information Security of the Digital Library in Cloud Computing Era. Library Development (1), 50–52 (2010) (Ch)
9. Wang, Q.: Virtualization and Cloud Computing. Publishing House of Electronics Industry, Beijing (2009)
10. Hu, X., Fan, B.: Cloud Computing:The Challenges to Library Management. Journal of Academic Libraries (4), 7–12 (2009) (Ch)
11. Qian, W., Deng, Z.: Cloud Computing and Management of Information Resource Sharing. Library and Information (4), 47–52 (2009) (Ch)
12. Youseff, L., Butrico, M., Da Silva, D.: Toward a Unified Ontology ofCloud Computing. IEEE Xplore, pp. 2–10 (2009)
13. Dong, B., Zheng, Q., Yang, J., Li, H., Qiao, M.: An E -learning Ecosystem Based on Cloud Computing Infrastructure. In: 2009 Ninth IEEE International Conference on Advanced Learning Technologies, pp. 125–127 (2009)
14. Kwok, T., Nguyen, T., Lam, L.: A Software as a Service with Multi tenancy Support for an Electronic Contract Management Application. In: 2008 IEEE International Conference on Services Computing, pp. 179–186 (2008)
15. Raman, T.V.: Cloud Computing And Equal Access For AI1. Communications of the ACM (7), 37–41 (2008)

A Quantum Genetic Algorithm to Solve the Problem of Multivariate

Bing Han[1], Junna Jiang[1], Yanhui Gao[2], and Junhong Ma[1]

[1] HeBei united University, School of Science, Tangshan, Hebei, China, 063009
[2]North China Institute of Science and Technology, Department of Basic Courses, East Yanjiao, Beijing, China, 101601
hanbcrane@126.com, jjn131313@tom.com

Abstract. In order to apply quantum genetic algorithm to solve multi-peak continuous function optimal problem, a novel quantum genetic algorithm referring to multi-variable problem is proposed. It operates variables upon a universal quantum chromosome collectively. Thus it can adjust evolutionary intensity dynamically and consider evolutionary orientation depending on generated function of rotation angle. Theoretical and experimental results show that, this quantum genetic algorithm can obtain better evolutionary speed and better performance of convergence on multi-variable problem.

Keywords: quantum genetic algorithm, rotation angle, generated function, quantum chromosome.

1 Introduction

Quantum information uses the quantum state as information unit (qubits), use the unitary transformation and quantum measurement complete information processing and extraction (Feynman[1]).With quantum computation theory ,The quantum genetic algorithm has been extensive attention. Quantum genetic algorithm (QGA) using qubits coding to represent chromosome, Using quantum revolving door strategy to complete the chromosomes of the update evolution, Both "exploration" and "developed" capability, its characteristic is the population scale is small, fast convergence rate and global optimization ability. But now, the update method for solving the quantum gate continuous functions, especially multivariable continuous function optimization problems also existed some shortage, For example the evolution of every generation algorithm of time slow, very long, so evolutionary algebra exploring new quantum evolutionary algorithm is very necessary.

This paper analyzed the mechanism of QGA for quantum update the revolving door, put forward a method of solving multivariable multi-peak continuous function quantum genetic algorithm. Algorithm with a multiple variable universal quantum, and with new chromosome said generating function rotation Angle to dynamically adjust the revolving door, thus achieved the refresh strategy, the calculating process

C. Liu, J. Chang, and A. Yang (Eds.): ICICA 2011, Part I, CCIS 243, pp. 308–314, 2011.

simplification multivariate the purpose, and received good optimum effect. The algorithm for solving multivariable problem can achieve rapid evolution speed and better convergent effect.

2 The Proposed Algorithm and Analysis

2.1 The Algorithm Is Introduced

Quantum genetic algorithm using qubits storage and express a genes that can is "0" state, "1" state or their any intermediate condition. Therefore, a quantum chromosome can also express more states of superposition, with better diversity features. Meanwhile, in the role of by QGA quantum gate ground probability amplitude of quantum ways that make use of population diversity to maintain and probability amplitude of comparison to complete quantum gate of updates. A state of qubits can be expressed as:

$$|\Phi\rangle = \alpha|0\rangle + \beta|1\rangle \tag{1}$$

α and β respectively is state of $|0\rangle$ and $|1>$ with probability amplitude, and satisfy the following normalization conditions:

$$|\alpha|^2 + |\beta|^2 = 1 \tag{2}$$

In type (2), the $|\alpha|^2$ said the probability of the quantum state observation value 0 , the $|\beta|^2$ said the probability of the quantum state observation value 1. Therefore, a contain m qubits quantum chromosome to include 2^m a characterization of state, they can say is:

$$|\Phi_i>=\sum_{k=1}^{2^m} C_k|S_k \tag{3}$$

Among them, C_k said the probability amplitude of S_k and meet the normalization conditions

$$|C_1|^2 + |C_2|^2 + \cdots |C_{2^m}|^2 = 1 \tag{4}$$

At the same time, with probability amplitude of α, β, tend to 1 or 0, the multiplicity of the chromosome disappear, the algorithm convergence.

This paper quantum revolving door

$$G = \begin{bmatrix} \cos\theta_i & -\sin\theta_i \\ \sin\theta_i & \cos\theta_i \end{bmatrix} \tag{5}$$

Among them, θ_i for quantum of the chromosome with the first I a qubits, it's rotation Angle value:

$$\theta_i = \Delta\theta_i \times s(\alpha_i, \beta_i) \tag{6}$$

In Type (6), $\Delta\theta_i$ is the effect of the convergent speed coefficient, is the selection of it must be reasonable. $\Delta\theta_i$ value too large, algorithm to search for the grid will be very big, easy to have "premature" phenomenon; And $\Delta\theta_i$ values of the small, i algorithm to search for the speed will slow, happen "stagnation" phenomenon. This $\Delta\theta_i$ is a change range from 0.005π to 0.05π adaptive variable, defined as:

$$\Delta\theta_i = 0.005\pi + (0.05\pi - 0.005\pi) \times \frac{|f(x_i) - f(b_i)|}{\max(f(x_i), f(b_i))} \tag{7}$$

Among them, $f(x_i)$ and $f(b_i)$ said the current respectively quantum chromosome observation and the current value of the optimal solution to. Function $s(\alpha_i, \beta_i)$ control algorithm, so that the algorithm can search direction to the optimal solution of evolutionary direction. This paper variable continuous function improved the strategy problem generating function $s(\alpha_i, \beta_i)$. Among them, the two variables continuous function of problem generating function $s(\alpha_i, \beta_i)$ the following table 1 shows:

Table 1. Two variables continuous function of problem generating function

$\prod_{a=1}^{2} x_i^a$	$\prod_{a=1}^{2} b_i^a$	$f(x_i) > f(b_i)$	$\Delta\theta_i$	$s(\alpha_i,\beta_i)$			
				$\alpha_i \bullet \beta_i > 0$	$\alpha_i \bullet \beta_i < 0$	$\alpha_i = 0$	$\beta_i = 0$
0	0	False	0.005	-1	+1	±1	0
0	0	True	0.005	+1	-1	0	±1
0	1	False	δ	+1	-1	0	±1
0	1	True	δ	-1	+1	±1	0
1	0	False	δ	-1	+1	±1	0
1	0	True	δ	+1	-1	0	±1
1	1	False	0	0	0	0	0
1	1	True	0	0	0	0	0

$\prod_{a=1}^{2} x_i^a$ 、 $\prod_{a=1}^{2} b_i^a$ Is the current respectively chromosome observation and the most optimal solution of the first I a of the two variables qubits the product of value.

This generation function basis $\prod_{a=1}^{2} x_i^a$ 、 $\prod_{a=1}^{2} b_i^a$ is the value of the current chromosome observation fitness f (xi) and the current value of the optimal solution to f (bi) carries on the comparison, if f (xi) > f (bi), then change the search direction, the method to the direction of the xi evolution; Otherwise, don't change the search direction, so that the algorithm the optimum solution approach direction. So, the update process for quantum chromosomes:

$$P_n^{k+1} = G(k) * P_n^k \tag{8}$$

Among them, P_n^{k+1} 、 P_n^k says the first k m quantum chromosome first generation after update and update the expression of the former , $G(k)$ is the first generation of quantum revolving door k matrix.

2.2 The Implementation Process of Algorithm

The quantum genetic algorithm for the implementation of the process:

(1) the initialization: given the population size of chromosome number n and qubits m and therefore involve n individual population for $P = \{p_1, p_2 \cdots, p_n\}$, among them, $p_j (j = 1, 2, \cdots n)$ is the individual j in a population of the individual, probability amplitude of $\alpha_i, \beta_i (i = 1, 2, \cdots, m)$ are $\frac{1}{\sqrt{2}}$, said in the initial search when all states to the same probability in stack.

(2) according to P probability amplitude of quantum superposition state constructed the observation state R, $R = a_1, a_2, \cdots a_n$, among them, $a_j (j = 1, 2, \cdots, n)$ is the state of each individual observation, that is, a binary string.

(3) choice: would observe state decoding the actual value, and by using fitness function evaluate each individual fitness, and retain the best individual value.

(4) according to the type (6) generation, and using quantum rotation Angle type (8) update quantum chromosomes.

(5)judge whether meet the conditions for the termination, if meet, the termination algorithm; Otherwise, evolution and converting it to the algebraic add 1 step (2).

3 Test

This paper use of the simulated annealing genetic algorithm with binary code of fixed length coding method; The selection process using roulette wheels method, and introducing selection pressure to enhance the choice of the algorithm effect; Cross the DuoWei crossover method (process of this paper take 0.8); crossover probability Variation process by binary take the operation (this mutation probability take 0.05). Through the assessment in the calculation of the test function optimization and comparative simulation .Annealing genetic algorithm (AGA) [9] and the quantum genetic algorithm (QGA) [7] to analyze the quantum genetic algorithm (MVQGA) performance. In the same termination conditions (the ε measurement accuracy) take average way repeatedly, different population scale were taken and the biggest evolution algebra, analyzed and compared, the algorithm convergence performance and efficiency (①said average evolution, ②said algebraic average running time, ③said convergence efficiency, ④ said the average evolution final value).

F1: (1) the Camel function (chromosomes length is 16, $\varepsilon = 0.005$)

$$f(x, y) = (4 - 2.1x^2 + \frac{1}{3}x^4) + xy + (-4 + 4y^2)y^2, -10 < x, y < 10$$

Camel function has six local minimum points, two of them for the global minima, minimum of 1.031628. As shown in table 2.

Table 2. Several performance comparison algorithm (Camel function)

	Psize=200,M_time=500				Psize=200,M_time=1000				Psize=300,M_time=1000			
	①	②	③	④	①	②	③	④	①	②	③	④
AGA	292	3.65	0.44	-0.7779	639	7.08	0.47	-0.6135	477	7.46	0.54	-0.8803
QGA	416	4.36	0.29	-1.0163	740	6.58	0.55	-1.0238	661	8.82	0.72	-1.0272
MVQGA	301	1.39	0.65	-1.0269	340	1.48	0.98	-1.0291	243	1.61	0.99	1.0293

(2) ShafferF6 function (chromosomes length is 32, = 0.0097)

$$f(x, y) = \frac{\sin^2 \sqrt{x^2 + y^2} - 0.5}{(1 + 0.001 \times (x^2 + y^2))^2} - 100.5, -10 < x, y < 10$$

ShafferF6 function with an infinite number of the local minimum points, of which only a (0, 0) for the global minimum, minimum of 101. This function is the minimum peak around a circle ridge, they are the value of 100.990283, it is easy to stagnation in the local minimum points. As shown in table 3.

Table 3. Several performance comparison algorithm (ShafferF6 function)

	Psize=200,M_time=500				Psize=200,M_time=1000				Psize=300,M_time=1000			
	①	②	③	④	①	②	③	④	①	②	③	④
AGA	491	8.44	0.06	-.55740	881	9.22	0.21	-.72860	873	17.3	0.25	-.70004
QGA	482	11.2	0.06	-.99064	919	12.9	0.16	-.99114	915	24.0	0.19	-.99138
MVQGA	477	4.84	0.10	-.99080	815	5.34	0.38	-.99230	831	7.6	0.45	-99254

Comparative analysis of the test results, above the AGA, QGA the two algorithm can greatly improve the convergent performance of genetic algorithm, but they each generation of evolutionary time is slower, evolutionary algebra is longer. Contrast the AGA and QGA, this MVQGA can in the same even smaller evolution algebra get better convergence efficiency under the terminal value and evolution. The important thing is, MVQGA relatively the AGA and QGA the algorithm can save much time, so as to express the superiority of the algorithm.

4 Conclusion

This paper proposes a multivariate problems to solve the quantum genetic algorithm. The quantum genetic algorithm is applicable to solve many variables peak continuous function optimization problem, its characteristic is running time is faster, convergence effect has been compared. Theoretical analysis and experimental results show that the quantum genetic algorithm for solving more variable problem has good performance.

References

1. Feynman, R.: Quantum mechanical computers. Foundations of Physics 16, 507–531 (1986)
2. Narayanan, A.: An introductory tutorial to quantum computing. The Institution of Electrical Engineers (1997)

3. Grover, L.K.: Quantum mechanics searching. In: Proceedings of the 1999 Congress on Evolutionary Computation, pp. 2255–2261 (1999)
4. Narayanan, A., Moore, M.: Quantum-inspired genetic algorithms. IEEE, 61–66 (1996)
5. Han, K.H., Kim, J.H.: Genetic Quantum Algorithm and its Application to Combinational Optimization Problem. IEEE, 1354–1360 (2000)
6. Talbi, H., Draa, A., Batouche, M.: A New Quantum-Inspired Genetic Algorithm for Solving the Travelling Salesman Problem. IEEE, 1192–1197 (2004)
7. Zhang, G.X.: A Novel Genetic Algorithm and Its Application to Digital Filter Design. IEEE, 1600–1605 (2002)
8. Yang, J.-A.: Multi-Universe Parallel Quantum Genetic Algorithm and Its Application to Blind Source Seperation. IEEE, 393–398 (2003)

The Perspective of Job Requirements on Teaching Reform of the CIM Major

Yuesheng Zhang

School of Management, Xinxiang University, Xinxiang 453003, China
xxtc2008@163.com

Abstract. To make information management personnel more in line with job requirements of the times, the paper takes the major of computer information management in higher vocational and technical institutions for example to re-examine the professional training objectives and curriculum system. By analyzing the training requirements of the new era and the ideas of professional settings, it points out the computer information management professionals should be educated as the comprehensive model of knowledge and ability, which is based on the actual job requirements, takes knowledge, ability and quality as the core of development. And this paper focuses on the requirements from the job of the professional quality to probe into the teaching reform, emphasizes the overall quality of the training of students, rather than the traditional purely on professional skills development.

Keywords: CIM, Teaching reform, scheme.

1 Introduction

Since the latter half of the 20th century, information industry has become the most potential economic growth point. At present the global information industry average growth of 15-20% in, far more than the speed of growth in the global economy. China's information industry in recent 10 years, on average, 30% of the speed of the rapid development of national economy, has become the first pillar industries.

2 Reform Major Teaching Goal

2.1 Reform Traditional Education Ideas

The higher vocational education objective for "training technology applied talents, theory for sufficient degree, emphasis on skills training and quality education as the core", emphasizing the education, the innovation education characteristic and lifelong education, professional technology required students practical ability love and respect, industrious, feels at ease in the first line of work.

C. Liu, J. Chang, and A. Yang (Eds.): ICICA 2011, Part I, CCIS 243, pp. 315–321, 2011.

2.2 Updating the Teaching Contents

A new teaching plan has of course system made two major adjustment, a theory course is the compressed with appropriate for sufficient degree, arranged for more practical training course); it is increased practical, novel, and can satisfy the industry and unit of choose and employ persons needs course. Features.

2.3 Reform Teaching Methods

Will be in professional teaching used in great quantities in the modern teaching means, improve class information capacity: based on laboratory practice and training base for students from experiment to deepen understanding and mastering knowledge, in practice training, improve skills. At the same time reform exam system, increase skills assessment to the skill levels of sex as a main assessment and evaluation of the main standard students.

2.4 Structure "Double Teachers" Team

Reform of teachers team strong theoretical knowledge, practice knowledge comparatively weak condition, strengthen the training of teachers' team and the introduction of higher vocational education, the establishment of a adapt to the characteristics of The Times, the hierarchy, the full-time and part-time combined with high quality high levels of double division teachers team, and a push for teachers' goal management, project management mechanism and incentive mechanism.

2.5 Reform Single Talent Training Mode

In adding course system plan relevant qualification authentication aspects of the curriculum, help students through the relevant qualification certification exams, the implementation of the "double card system", out of a degree education and the authentication education combined pathway.

2.6 Strengthen Theory with Practice

The reform of teaching theory and practical, enclosed not close contact of the tradition of enterprises, strengthen contact, will study and employment, enterprise, combined, and teaching, scientific research and industry combined, let the students during the period of school can join the real software industry in the whole process to exercise.

3 Design the Talent Training Scheme

3.1 Understand the Social Needs

To implement successful enterprise informatization for extensive social investigation, know a business in the first line of work in the information management and technical staff and managers to the content of the work, this type of work requires the necessary knowledge, ability and quality structure, and learn from the experience of the higher vocational education at home and abroad, the vocational education basic law, strengthen technology using ability, innovation ability and the basic quality of the training, get the training plan and make professional talent training mode first-hand material. Combined with the actual situation, information management professional main position (group), knowledge and ability structure required to design table 1:

Table 1. To post, knowledge and ability structure requirements

Professional post	knowledge structure	capacity requirements
Enterprise management information system maintenance and development	higher mathematics, professional English, data structure, the principle of the computer and assemblers, principle of operating system, principle and application of database, c++, computer network and the Internet, management, management information system, object-oriented technology	1) master management and the management information system of basic knowledge 2) master database principle and development technology 3) will maintain general management information system, and can do simple development 4) master a large database of host operating system of using and maintenance

3.2 Construct Professional Talents of Knowledge and Ability System

According to the information management professional main position (group) for professional talents, knowledge and ability request, to construct the ability training for the foundation of knowledge and ability structure, outstanding technical application ability and basic quality of the training. As shown in figure 1 below.

Post basic requirements:

Love the motherland, support the leadership of the Chinese communist party, political enthusiasm high love life, hard work, has the professional spirit set up the quality first thought, loving one's work, has the good professional ethics The above structure is based on computer information management specialized technical application ability training as the main line to design, the embodiment of the first national vocational teaching conference of the proposed four requirements: has the formation technology application ability necessary basic theoretical knowledge and professional knowledge; With strong comprehensive use of various knowledge and skills of the ability to solve practical problems; Have good professional ethics, love their work, work hard, industrious, and people in the spirit of cooperation, feels at ease in the production, construction, management and service first line work; Have strong

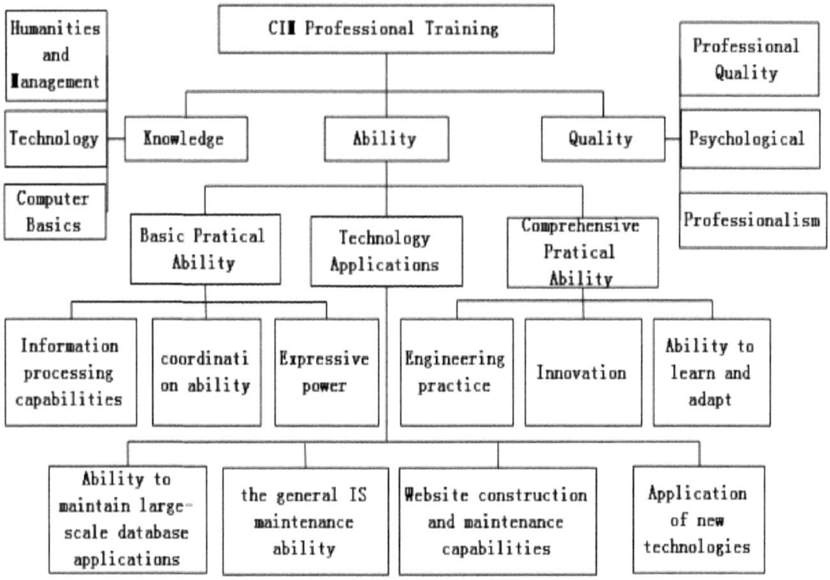

Fig. 1. CIM of knowledge, ability and quality structure model

psychological quality and good health. Highlight the general practice ability, technology application ability, the training of comprehensive developing ability, taking into consideration the computer information management work in the tools necessary to culture foundation knowledge, basic computer knowledge, large database and management information system of professional knowledge, also considered the students' individual character development, employment flexibility and ability of sustainable development quality requirements.

3.3 Design Theory Teaching System

According to the professional training target and "must be enough", "the principle of novel effect", in order to cluster course construction as the core, constructing theory teaching system. After the reform of the teaching system of cultural foundation theory, computer basic, management foundation, management information system, network and application five knowledge module. After the reform of teaching theory system weakened the course subject system, strengthen the knowledge of accumulating, applied and novelty, highlighted the basis of professional theory teaching application characteristics, pay attention to the humanities and social science and professional technical education combined and infiltration, takes into account both the personnel training pertinence, applicability, and consider the insurance industry and other employing units of amphibious sex and talents, the sustainable development.

3.4 Design Practice Teaching System

According to the professional training objectives and abroad experience, you design a new practice teaching system, including professional basis, computer technology training, training comprehensive practice three modules. In the new experiment practice teaching system, we pay attention to training of comprehensive practical skills, increase the experimental depth and the breadth, in order to make students further practice, from a wider and deeper levels of the train of thought of up to analyze and solve problems. According to production practice research situation optimization experiment content, according to the production practice and scientific research of the problems, and provide some research experiment practice, let students understand the experiment practice in production and research the role with Internet explorer, of the role of the experiment, the actual exercise, and has further improve its ability to solve practical problems. First let students to design scheme, and make the practice implementation steps, in the final analysis, goals and existing problems, and explores the solving methods.

4 Conclusion

The computer information management specialized teaching reform plan, is our present situation and the demand of talents in based on the research of the higher vocational education, according to the teaching theory and higher technology applied talents cultivation regularity, with regard to the teaching resources of the actual, the careful design formation. With a clear goal, the reform of the reform thought of clear, bright and modern information processing characteristics and higher vocational education features, believe to be able to become a computer information management specialty teaching reform of the success of the powerful guarantee.

References

1. Li, J.: International Vocational Education Trends. World vocational and technical education (2000)
2. Wen, Y.-M., Du, F.-M., Li, J.: Applying Projection Method in Practice Training of Computer Major Students. Computer Education (2010)
3. Wu, C., Cui, X.: Practical Teaching Exploration of the Computer Information Management System Course. Computer Education (2011)
4. Li, L., Wang, X., Huo, J.: Design and implementation of a physical experimental information teaching system based on Web. Journal of University of Science and Technology of China (2010)
5. Wei, L., Yuan, Q., Huo, J., Wang, X.: The design and implementation of unstructured data management system in e-learning teaching system. Journal of University of Science and Technology of China (2010)
6. Chen, S.-P., Hou, X.-L.: Teaching Method was Researched by Database System Theory Course. Computer Knowledge and Technology(Academic Exchange) (2007)

7. Zhan, W.: The Design and Implementation of Management System for Highway Vocational Skill Authentication. Computer Knowledge and Technology (2009)
8. Alexander, S., Golja, T.: Using students' experiences to derive quality in an e-learning system: An institution's perspective. Journal of Educational Technology & Society, 17–33 (2007)
9. Andrade, J., Ares, J., Garcia, R., Rodriguez, S., Seoane, M., Suarez, S.: Guidelines for the Development of E-learning Systems by means of Proactive Question. Computers & Education, 1510–1522 (2008)
10. Ani, G., Slavomir, S., Marko, R., Branko, I.: Controlled experiment replication in evaluation of e-learning system's educational influence. Computers & Education, 591–602 (2009)
11. Blin, F., Munro, M.: Why Hasn't Technology Disrupted academics' teaching Practices? Understanding Resistance to Change Through the Lens of Activity Theory. Computers & Education, 475–490 (2008)
12. Bostock, S.J., Wu, L.Z.: Gender in student online discussions. Innovations in Education and Teaching International, 73–85 (2005)
13. Chen, N.S., Ko, H.C., Kinshuk, Lin, T.: A model for synchronous learning using the Internet. Innovations in Education and Teaching International, 181–194 (2005)
14. Clark, W., Logan, K., Luckin, R., Mee, A., Oliver, M.: Beyond Web 2.0: mapping the technology landscapes of young learners. Journal of Computer Assisted Learning, 56–69 (2009)
15. Eynon, R.: The use of the world wide web in learning and teaching in higher education: reality and rhetoric. Innovations in Education and Teaching International, 15–23 (2008)
16. Ham, V., Davey, R.: Our first time: two higher education tutors reflect on becoming a 'virtual teacher'. Innovations in Education and Teaching International, 257–264 (2005)
17. Huang, C.J., Chu, S.S., Guan, C.T.: Implementation and performance evaluation of parameter improvement mechanisms for intelligent e-learning systems. Computers & Education, 597–614 (2007)
18. Huang, S.L., Yang, C.W.: Designing a semantic bliki system to support different types of knowledge and adaptive learning. Computers & Education, 701–712 (2009)
19. Hussin, V.: Supporting off-shore students: a preliminary study. Innovations in Education and Teaching International, 363–376 (2007)
20. Kim, C.J., Santiago, R.: Construction of E-learning Environments in Korea. Educational Technology Research & Development, 108–115 (2005)
21. Kim, S.W., Leet, M.G.: Validation of an evaluation model for Learning Management Systems. Journal of Computer Assisted Learning, 284–294 (2008)
22. Lee, I.: Korean Content Management in e-Higher Education: Here and Hereafter. Educational Technology Research & Development, 209–219 (2006)
23. Levy, P., Aiyegbayot, O., Little, S.: Designing for Inquiry-based Learning with the Learning Activity Management System. Journal of Computer Assisted Learning, 238–251 (2009)
24. Limniou, M., Papadopoulos, N., Whitehead, C.: Integration of Simulation into Pre-laboratory Chemical Course: Computer Cluster Versus WebCT. Computers & Education, 45–52 (2009)
25. Martín-Blas, T., Serrano-Fernández, A.: The role of new technologies in the learning process: Moodle as a teaching tool in Physics. Computers & Education, 35–44 (2009)
26. McGill, T.J., Klobas, J.E.: A Task-technology Fit View of Learning Management System Impact. Computers & Education, 496–508 (2009)
27. Pachler, N., Daly, C.: Narrative and Learning with Web 2.0 Technologies: Towards a Research Agenda. Journal of Computer Assisted Learning, 6–18 (2009)
28. Sabry, K., Barker, J.: Dynamic Interactive Learning Systems. Innovations in Education

29. Trentin, G.: Using a Wiki to Evaluate Individual Contribution to a Collaborative Learning Project. Journal of Computer Assisted Learning, 43–55 (2009)
30. Wang, W.T., Wang, C.C.: An empirical study of instructor adoption of web-based learning systems. Computers & Education, 761–774 (2009)
31. Zeng, Q., Zhao, Z., Liang, Y.: Course ontology-based user's knowledge requirement acquisition from behaviors within e-learning systems. Computers & Education, 809–818 (2009)
32. Shen, C.-C., Chuang, H.-M., Wang, L.-C.: Applications of knowledge-sharing blog concepts to the information teaching. International Journal of Continuing Engineering Education and Life Long Learning (2010)

Importing MB-OFDM Synchronization Approach into Core Curriculums for Postgraduates Education

Zhihong Qian*, Xiaohang Shang, Jin Huang, and Xue Wang

College of Communication Engineering, Jilin University, 5372 Nanhu Avenue, Changchun, Jilin 130012, P.R. China
dr.qzh@163.com, ilovemusic_sxh@yahoo.com.cn, huangjin09@mails.jlu.edu.cn, yeti_1019@yahoo.com.cn

Abstract. Postgraduate education is currently engaged in curriculum reform in China. With the on-going reform, many potential problems are exposed gradually. In this paper, the ideas and methods of reforming the postgraduate curriculum teaching and the way based on general education are presented, adopting ways such as strengthening the teaching materials, applying the heuristic teaching and bilingual teaching, as well as importing some novel approaches, like MB-OFDM synchronization approach the author of this paper made, into graduates core curriculums, Modern Digital Communication, as a trial. The postgraduates under such education would be trained into qualified talents and have a strong foundational knowledge, practical ability, spirit of innovation and integrated quality. As a consequence, the idea of this reformed postgraduate curriculum provides a specific direction for the further reform of postgraduate education in China.

Keywords: postgraduates education, core curriculum, digital communications, MB-OFDM, Synchronization.

1 Introduction

The curriculum refers to a system of various disciplines and diverse educational and instructional activities in schools in accordance with a certain educational purpose. And that the curriculum, heart of education, is unification in the teaching and learning activities between the content and the process of implementation. Therefore, it is only a means to achieve the educational aims. The postgraduate education is a systematic project, in any country in the world, which includes the curriculum teaching, social practice, degree thesis and many other links. The postgraduate curriculum teaching is the foundation of the graduate education, the quality of which directly decides the quality and the level of the postgraduate education, as well as obviously affects the cultivation of postgraduates' innovative ability [1]. With the further development of

* Corresponding author. Professor of Communication and Information System at the College of Communication Engineering, Jilin University, P.R. China. His research work focuses on wireless communication and networks.

C. Liu, J. Chang, and A. Yang (Eds.): ICICA 2011, Part I, CCIS 243, pp. 322–329, 2011.

China's higher education, postgraduate education is also confronting many new opportunities and challenges. There are plenty of problems modes to be solved in the current postgraduate curriculum system and teaching. Therefore, reviewing and estimating correctly the training level of postgraduate education is a key work whether graduate education can seize the opportunity and meet the challenge.

In the United States, general education has already became one of the most popular and practical issues about the study of higher education, which opens a window for American college students to wider world to obtain both broad vision and innovation, furthermore, to adapt to the social environment rapidly[2]. However, Chinese higher education especially the postgraduate education, fosters many excellent academic talented person, but inadvertently plays a negative role in the creative and management "generalists" that modern society needs.

This paper is about the enlightenment of American General Education on curriculum reformation of postgraduate education in China. This will be followed by a description of the general education and core curriculum, why the curriculum reformation is needed, and what method is adopted for the curriculum reformation take example by the general education. A synchronization issue and proposed approach of MB-OFDM systems is imported into core curriculums for postgraduates' education.

2 General Educations and Core Curriculum

General educations, in the United States, are originated from the promotion of President Elliott in Harvard University. General courses, with the spirit of pursuing the progress, through continuous reform and development, eventually establishes core curriculum of practical model in general education. The implementation of Core curriculum guarantees the development of the general education at Harvard University and enriches the theory of the general curriculum. The idea and practice of this course is imitated by many universities all over the world, and also should turn out to be the most helpful issues about the studies of higher education in China.

Burke, the President of Harvard University, has mentioned, "so far, the core curriculum is a curriculum enforcement mode which reflects the spirit of general education the most perfectly in concept." Core curriculums of a subject should be curriculums that aim at achieving the training goal of this subject, make a decisive role for students to grasp professional core knowledge and to obtain cultivate core ability, and improve the specialty core competitiveness. And the curriculums should not be overmuch [3]. In Webster New University Dictionary, the core curriculum is defined as a special curriculum which synthesizes the basic contents of the traditional course, and aims at providing the common knowledge background for all students. This definition delimits the connotation of the core curriculum according to the curriculum content and the course target. "The basic content of the traditional course" is the content of the core curriculum. "Aiming at providing the common knowledge background for all students" is the goal of the core curriculum. "Common knowledge background" does not only simply indicate that students obtain some certain specific common knowledge, but also include the same way of thinking and studying training that students acquire. Every course in the core curriculum has different contents and topics, in addition, two or three years' learning of the postgraduate education cannot cover the entire core curriculum in the school. Every course all emphasizes the learning of thinking training and methodology. Thus, students could get "common knowledge background" by means of the studying of the core curriculum.

3 Analysis on Postgraduate Curriculum of Universities in China

Deviation in Recognition of Postgraduate Teaching. Most Chinese colleges put forward to the development goal of building research-based university. Consequently, high level research work becomes a central task. In the very period, high quality papers and high level scientific projects turn into wind vane. Now the scale of postgraduates in each college is developing rapidly, at the same time, the problem of behindhand teaching infrastructures is more and more remarkable relatively due to the teaching disorder and the inefficiency of teaching management.

Deviation in the Relationship between the Grasp of the Curriculum Learning and Research. Some people deem that postgraduate curriculum and papers are two independent links, which is a misunderstanding of the recognition that laying stress on research papers by means of shortening the time of the curriculum to achieve the purpose of the research innovation. Unfortunately, some advisers also hold this view which exacerbates the pullulating of the postgraduate curriculum. On the contrary, the high quality of the curriculum learning can even yield twice the result with half the effort.

Imperfect Content, Methods and Means. Owing to the content obsolescence of the original curriculum, postgraduate curriculum teaching doesn't have much difference from graduate course, which seriously influences the function of postgraduate education and makes interests decrease. Furthermore, teaching methods should be flexibly chosen according to teaching content and student status. Nevertheless, teachers are accustomed to spoon-feeding education, and they always overlook the importance of heuristic teaching, and ignore the process, but directly deliver students the result. Traditional Chinese teachers regard the result much more important than the process of enlightenment which would cost much time, so they order students to memorize the result without the process of seeking [4].

4 Promoting Core Curriculum Quality

Generally, a core curriculum is multiple disciplines associated. Technology interacts with communication and culture in complex ways that go beyond the boundaries of individual disciplines. Students are expected to make growth in problem-solving by using concepts from multiple disciplines in the design of individual and group research projects. They make oral, written, multimedia and conference-style presentations. They choose material appropriate to interdisciplinary exploration, compare and contrast concepts, make arguments incorporating insights from across fields, learn to employ methods conducive to studying established and emerging communication technologies. They should have the opportunity to learn a variety of quantitative and qualitative approaches that are applicable across disciplines. They break new ground by exploring and developing new methodologies for analyzing communications phenomena that make use of digital technologies.

4.1 General Ideas

Reform the Curriculum Teaching Methods. Teaching content goes first in the way of teaching, which is the teaching and the learning bridge between teachers and students, the main substance means in carrying out the teaching method, and the key of the core curriculum. A good textbook or professional material should meet with the teaching requirements for rich-content, understandable, practical and facilitate [5]. Considering the core curriculum "the basic content of the traditional course" as well as the developing of the technology and the society, teachers should update and enrich the teaching content including professional new theories, new cases and new trends based on the forefront of the course development, in addition to multimedia courseware which can easily stimulate students' learning interest and enthusiasm through pictures, sounds, vivid and so on animation displays. Such forms of contents and expression may increase perceptual knowledge, deepen students' understanding, open up the thought and the professional knowledge of students and promote the professional level of the learning and research. However, key points must focus on imparting scientific thinking method, the ability of solving practical problems, and providing the foundation of exploring new problems and new research methods for students.

Scientific Thinking. The core curriculums are to train students to grasp the scientific thinking method and the ability to solve overall problems. Advanced teaching method is an important guarantee to improve the teaching quality, teachers should reform the obsolete and inefficient curriculum method that encourage the way of discussion, observation, research, and self-study used freely in the postgraduate curriculum. As a result, heuristic teaching is the key of the core curriculum. The core thought is mainly as following. To set up discussion and learning groups to take advantage of team cooperation method to complete a teaching practice. Usually, students form discussion and learning development groups voluntarily, while teachers assign each group to complete the mission about the curriculum on schedule and encourage them to do as much work as possible. And the group head is responsible for judging group work in meetings to check out the work of discussion and learning groups within the specified time. While each member of the group explains and replies to questions on his or her respective work. The advantage of public report is to eliminate the phenomenon of plagiarism in training projects. Through the above measures, students obtain the capability of self-study, independent-thinking, problem-solving, communication and cooperation with each other in the group, and understand the importance of teamwork in study or work.

Teaching in English. Nowadays, the curriculum of internationalization forms is crucial and significant due to the need of the senior talents adapting to the international circumstance. Chinese postgraduate students are faced with a unique language challenge that they are expected to master two languages: native language and English [6]. As a result, according to the connotation of the core curriculum, one of the most effective and practical teaching method is to adopt the bilingual teaching. Teachers can select original textbooks of English version of a wide comprehensiveness of both theory and practice. Afterwards, with the advancement of students ability to study in English, teachers can gradually increase the proportion of English language in teaching the course. By reading relevant textbooks in English, listening to the courses in English and discussing with each other in English, students can understand professional knowledge and improve English proficiency better. Consequently, bilingual teaching is worth widely using and being accepted.

Reform the Way of Exam. The modification of the exam evaluation form is a necessary requirement of core curriculums [7]. Whether in undergraduate education or postgraduate education in China, the terminal examination, which plays a determinative and crucial part in the students' total scores, used to be applied in the past testing system. While it was mostly in written and closed form which can hardly reflect the integrated connotation of students and also made students over-loaded pressure. However, nowadays, the more reasonable comprehensive evaluation in the testing method is highlighted starting from the teaching requirement of the core curriculum [8]. Besides written examination, the inspecting and evaluating methods also involve observing and recording the performance of students, the interview, homework, discussion, and paperwork.

4.2 MB-OFDM Synchronization Approach Imported into Core Curriculums

The core curriculum for communication major graduates in Jilin University, China, is Modern Digital Communication Principles, and MB-OFDM enclosed, but novel approaches are not. It is absolutely important for graduates to learn novel approaches every year in the fields of core curriculums around.

Multi-band orthogonal frequency division multiplexing (MB-OFDM) is a wonderful wideband technology, dividing the allocated 7.5 GHz ultra-wideband (UWB) spectrum into 14 bands, each with a bandwidth of 528 MHz whereby information is transmitted using OFDM modulation on each band. Although OFDM has several advantages such as low complexity equalization in dispersive channels and the spectral density scalability, it has some disadvantages such as larger susceptibility to nonlinear distortion at the transmit power amplifier and larger sensitivity to frequency offsets. Frequency offset causes a loss of orthogonality among the subcarriers thereby introducing sub-carrier interference and significantly degrading the error performance. The current work deals with the problems of carrier frequency offset estimation and compensation based on literature [9] for MB-OFDM systems [10].

A low-complexity frequency offset estimator is proposed, which utilizes a half-cycle Constant Amplitude Zero Auto Correlation (CAZAC) sequence $c(k)$ as the preamble sequence. The estimation is carried out under the mode of cross comparison for half period. The lth complex base band OFDM symbol in qth frequency band can be expressed as

$$s_{q,l}(k)=\begin{cases}\frac{1}{N}\sum_{m=0}^{\frac{N}{2}-1}c_{q,l}(m)e^{j2\pi km/N}, & 0\le n\le\frac{N}{2}-1\\ \frac{1}{N}\sum_{m=\frac{N}{2}}^{N-1}c_{q,l}\left(m-\frac{N}{2}\right)e^{j2\pi km/N}, & \frac{N}{2}\le n<N\\ 0,\ -N_{pre}\le n<0;\ N\le n<N+N_0 & \end{cases} \tag{1}$$

We assume perfect timing synchronization, and a normalized frequency offset $\varepsilon_q=\Delta f_q/f$, where Δf_q is the frequency offset in band q and f is the inter sub-carrier spacing.

Cross correlation between the first half cycle of the lth symbol and the second half of the $(l+d)th$ symbol in qth frequency band is

$$\begin{aligned}R_{q,l}(n)&=\sum_{(l,l+d\in L)}r_{q,l}^{*}(n)r_{q,l+d}\left(n+\frac{N}{2}\right)\\&=\sum e^{j(2\pi\varepsilon_q N_s d/N+\pi\varepsilon_q)}\left\{\left|x_{q,l}(n)\right|^2+G_{q,l}+W_{q,l}\right\}\end{aligned} \tag{2}$$

Define $N_{q,l}=\left|x_{q,l}(n)\right|^2+G_{q,l}+W_{q,l}$. The frequency offset estimation of lth OFDM symbol is derived as

$$\hat{\varepsilon}_{q,l}=\varepsilon_{q,l}+\frac{\frac{1}{M/2}\sum_{n=0}^{M/2-1}angle\left(N_{q,l}\right)}{2\pi\frac{N_s}{N}d+\pi} \tag{3}$$

The variance of the estimation within the lth OFDM symbol is derived as

$$Var(\hat{\varepsilon}_{q,l})=\frac{2N^2}{3M\,(2dN_s+N)^2} \tag{4}$$

The proposed algorithm implements the estimation by half cycle semi-cross contrast, which reduces the time of add and shift operation significantly. We derive the reducing rate of addition as

$$\eta_1 = \frac{\frac{M}{2}(L-1)}{M(L-1)+1} \overset{M(L-1)+1 \gg \frac{1}{2}}{\approx} 50\% \tag{5}$$

Similarly the reducing rate of arithmetic shift may be represented as

$$\eta_2 = \frac{\left(\frac{M}{2}-1\right)(L-1)}{(M-1)(L-1)} = \frac{1}{2} - \frac{1}{2(M-1)} \approx 50\% \tag{6}$$

The simulations are carried out to study the performance contrasting with [9]. We use the simulation parameters as: N =128, $N_{pre} = 32$, N_g =5, f =4.125MHz. We get L=2,4,6 to simulate and analyze the method. Fig 1 shows the CRLBs of the proposed method and [9] method as a function of SNR and L. With the increase of L, the algorithm performances better. The minimum could be lower than 10^{-7}, which is rather small. Meanwhile, the CRLB decreases with the increase of SNR. The algorithm performs well even in the environment of SNR=0.

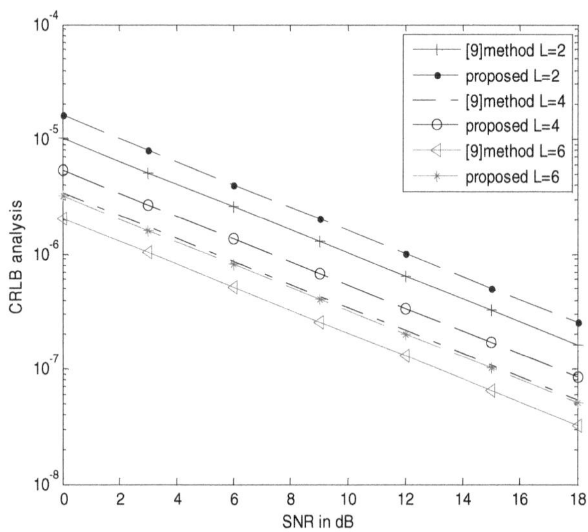

Fig. 1. CRLB analysis for different symbols length

Acknowledgments. This paper is supported by the National Natural Science Foundation of China (No.61071073), the Doctoral Fund of Ministry of Education of China (No. 20090061110043), the Graduate Innovation Fund of Jilin University (No. 20111059), and the Graduate Curriculum System and Core Curriculum Scheme Fund of Jilin University (No. 20101004 and No. 20102210).

References

1. Craig, H.C.: Theories of General Education: A Critical Approach, pp. 282–286. St. Martin Press, New York (1992)
2. Peng, S.Q.: Research on the Curricula Designing of College General Education. Doctoral Degree's Thesis, pp. 6–8. Xinan University, China (2006)
3. Yue, A.C., Gao, H.Q., Xiong, H.P.: Reseach and practice on the professional core courses in application engineering university. Research in Higher Education of Engineering, 47–49 (2007)
4. Cui, Q.E., Zhang, X.X., Shang, H.P.: Introspection on China's Curriculum Reform. In: 2010 International Conference on Education and Management Technology(ICEMT 2010), pp. 200–204 (2010)
5. Cai, W.: Reform and Practice of Core Curriculum Teaching in the Specialty of Building Environment and Facilities Engineering. In: 2010 International Conference on Optics, Photonics and Energy Engineering, pp. 68–71 (2010)
6. Neill-Carrillo, E.O., Collins, D.L., Garriga, J.L., Macchiavelli, R., Cruz, J.A.: Towards Student Success in General and STEM Education. In: 39th ASEE/IEEE Frontiers in Education Conference, Session M3F, pp. 18–21 (2009)
7. Victor, N.: Accessing the General Curriculum: Including Students with Disabilitities in Standards-Based Reform, pp. 89–91. Calif Corwin Press, Thousand Oaks (2000)
8. Edward, P., Epstein, A., Bursuck, M.H., William, D.: Testing Adaptions in the General Education Classroom. Challenges and Directions, Reading & Writing Quarterly 19, 189–194 (2003)
9. Sen, D., Chakrabarti, S., Kumar R.V.: A new frequency offset estimation scheme for ultra-wideband MB-OFDM Systems. In: IEEE ICACT, vol.3, pp.1929–1934 (2008)
10. Wang, X., Liu, D., Liu, Y., Wang, M.L., Qian, Z.H.: A Low Complexity Frequency Offset Estimation for MB-OFDM based UWB Systems. In: 2009 International Conference on Electrical and Communications Engineering (ICECE 2009), Venice, Italy, vol. 58, pp. 446–450 (2009)

Application of Modern Design Methods in the Graduation Designs of Mechanical Engineering Science

Fuxiang Zhang and Wenzhong Li

College of Mechanical and Electronic Engineering, Hebei University of Science and Technology, Shijiazhuang, Hebei 050018, P.R. China
zhang.fx.cn@foxmail.com, wenzhongli@163.com

Abstract. To guide more and better application of modern design methods in graduation designs in mechanical engineering science, the necessity of introducing modern design methods into graduation designs of mechanical engineering science was analyzed, and the commonly used modern design methods and their application area were also pointed out. Examples of application were then given to show their practical situation and effect. The teaching innovation showed that the application of modern design methods in graduation designs of mechanical engineering science can greatly improve the efficiency and the level of design.

Keywords: Modern Design Method, Mechanical Engineering Science, Graduation Design.

1 Introduction

The teaching process of graduation designs is an important stage to reach the undergraduate training objectives and it is the last teaching link of personnel training in institutes of higher education in P.R. China. Basic task of graduation designs is to train students to have the ability to analyze and solve practical problems by comprehensively using learned basic theories, knowledge and skills. The purpose of graduate designs is to improve students' comprehensive quality, cultivate their innovative spirit and practical ability. Completing one subject can enable students to master basic design methods and get primary engineering training. It can also help teachers comprehensively assess their teaching quality so as to improve the teaching management level.

College of Mechanical and Electronic Engineer of Hebei University of Science and Technology opened the course of "Modern Design Theory and Method" in 2008. For several years, the speaker teachers have inducted the students to use modern design theories and methods in their graduation designs and got good effects. Here, the application of modern design theory and method is introduced according to the actual situation of graduation designs of mechanical engineering science in Hebei University of Science and Technology.

C. Liu, J. Chang, and A. Yang (Eds.): ICICA 2011, Part I, CCIS 243, pp. 330–336, 2011.

2 Necessity Analysis

Many problems remains in traditional graduation design methods of mechanical engineering science [1],such as complex design process, low design quality, difficulty in design of complex curves and curved surface, design results cannot be tested in a short period, design methods is hard to cultivate students' enthusiasm etc. In addition, being short of innovative design ideas and methods by using traditional design methods, most students' graduation design schemes lack innovation [2].

Inheriting traditional design method, modern design method has developed by continuing absorbing modern theories, methods and up-to-date study fruits of relevant subjects. It mainly includes [3]: design methodology, CAD, industrial design, finite element method, optimum design, green design, reliability design, similarity design, fatigue design and man-machine engineering etc.

Characterized in innovative thinking, dynamic analysis, accurate calculating, optimized design and computer aided design (CAD) modern design method is a qualitative leap from traditional design methods [4]. At present, modern design method is actively pushed in under-graduate course in mechanical engineering science of institutes of higher education in our country [5]. For the present students majoring in mechanical engineering science, it is a key point to master modern design method and improve application ability before turning into innovative talents.

Inducting modern design method in graduation design of undergraduate course in mechanical engineering science can release students from mass calculation and plot work and enables them to put more effort into the innovative design, and improve the quality of their graduation designs as a result.

3 Common Used Modern Design Methods

3.1 Design Methodology

Design methodology study on the design process, design rules, and thinking and working methods of study by the view of system [6]. Its research contents include design object, design process and processes and procedures, design thinking, design evaluation, design information management and application of modern design theory and methods. Analysis from the system point of view, design system is looked as a three-dimensional system that consists of time dimension, logical dimension and method dimension. It also advocates to adopting parallel design instead of the process of serial design. Systematic design of the schemes is the important content of design methodology, in which function analysis method is the main method to search for function principle schemes. The design steps of function analysis method are consists of analysis, synthesis, evaluation and decision-making that its main content is doing functional analysis by using the tools of black box model, function tree etc based on the design demand, seeking function unit solution by using the tools of solutions directory etc and listing the morphological matrix and then finish the scheme design. Design methodology also aims at the research work of creative mechanism and creation techniques and advocates to realize advantageous design to improve the competitiveness of the products based on innovative design. In the design methodology, TRIZ theory an important innovation theory that uses the technical contradictions and their solution principles realize product innovation [7]. In TRIZ theory, 40 innovation principles and 39 technical conflicts are summarized and conflict solving matrix is list. Now, there are many computer aided innovation software products such as TechOptimizeer of Innovation Machine Co., Innovation Workbench (IWB) of Ideation International Co., computer aided innovation platform Pro/Innovator and innovation ability development platform CBT/NOVA of IWINT, Inc. [8]. By using design methodology, the students can bring forward innovate technical scheme and solve technical problems better in the process of scheme design.

3.2 Computer Aided Design

Computer aided design is a technology that use the ability of graphic processing and numerical calculation of the computers do design and analysis of engineering or products [9]. Intelligent CAD system can simulate specialists' design process of a field, band the technology of artificial intelligence, optimization, finite element method, computer drawing etc together, and let the computer participate in conventional design process of decision-making performance analysis of the scheme as much as possible. So it can greatly improve the design efficiency. CAD system integration is an important direction. For an example, we can integrate CAD, CAM, CAPP and CAT into a CAE system that make work of the design, manufacture, technics and test integrative. Now, there are many mature CAD products such as AutoCAD, SolidWorks, Pro/E, UG and CAXA etc. Now, AutoCAD usually is used in two-dimensional engineering drawings and secondary development; SolidWorks, Pro/E and UG usually are used in three-dimensional modeling; china-made software CAXA is widely used two-dimensional engineering drawings and secondary development because of its integration of national standard parts library etc. By using CAD software, students can visually design the parts and assemble them. Through virtual assembly, students can find the design faults and correct them in time.

3.3 Optimum Design

Optimum design is a design method that base on mathematical programming and take computers as the auxiliary tools [10]. In this method, first establish the optimization objective; second turn the design problem into the mathematical problem; and then select suitable optimization algorithm and program calculation program; last get optimal design by computer automatically. For the mechanical product design, usually need to select parameters such as weight, volume, velocity, bearing capacity and cost etc to reach the optimal design index. Practice shows that optimum design is an effective design method which can ensure the produces' quality, reduce the weight or volume, and reduce the cost etc. It can greatly improve the design efficiency and make the designers free from tedious and repetitive calculations. In addition, by using the optimum design, we can get the advantageous design under technical constraints which is actual optimization design. Common used optimum design methods are golden section method, Powell method, DFP method and penalty function method etc. There are corresponding BASIC, C and Matlab procedures have been developed and easy for use. The use of optimum design methods in a graduation design requires the design scheme is not only right but also optimal.

3.4 Finite Element Method

Finite element method is a modern numerical method that takes the computer as a tool. It can be used in solving complex nonlinear or non-steady-state problems, static and dynamic analysis of complex structure in engineering design. It also can be used to calculate stress distribution and deformation of parts of complex shape and becomes a useful tool of calculation of intensity and stiffness of complex parts [8]. Finite element method can not only be used to solve the displacement and stress of the structure but also be used to do analysis of stability and dynamics of the structure and then get the structure' dynamic response such as self-excited vibration frequency and mode shape etc; get dynamic deformation and stress etc. Now, widely used finite element software products are Ansysis and Abaqus etc. These software products have powerful pre-processing procedure (including generating cell and input file automatically) and post-processing procedure (including displaying results; plotting deformation figure, isoline figure, vibration mode and dynamic display structure's dynamic response etc.). In graduation designs, students usually faced is structure analysis.

4 Application and Analysis

4.1 Application in Graduation Designs

Here we introduce an excellent graduation design as an application example of modern design method [11]. The subject is "Innovate Design of a Surface Lapping Machine". Design background is: The main motion forms of surface lapping are circular motion, linear motion and swing etc. Equipments of precise surface lapping usually adopt cylindrical gear drive to complete planetary motion. Such problems as high weight, big noise and vibration etc exist in these equipments. Especially for the surface lapping machines of large radius of gyration, large diameter of cylindrical gear causes large weight of the whole equipment, which leads to high energy consumption. In addition, the lubricant which the gears used can cause pollution to the lapping liquid. The design task is: aiming at the shortcomings of current surface lapping machine, design a novel surface lapping machines of large radius of gyration by adopting modern design method to improve the efficiency of lapping. The design process is listed below.

The keystone of the design task is design of the main drive system. By using the systematic design method and taking the design object as a whole technology system, we began with function analysis, then found the input and output, finally established a black-box model (as shown in Fig. 1) by taking the surface lapping machine as a "black box", and finally establish the black-box model, as shown in Fig. 1.

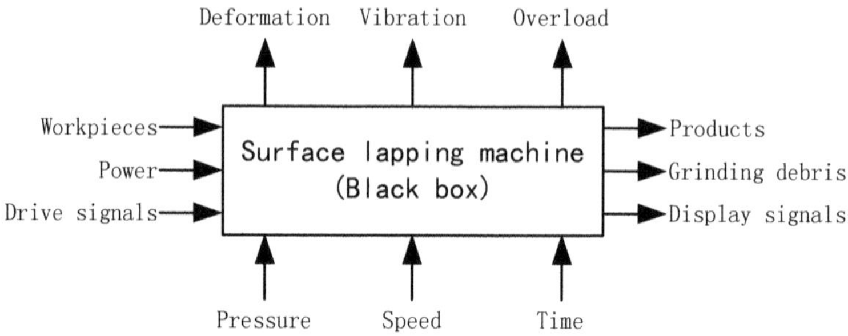

Fig. 1. Black-box model of the surface lapping machine

Type synthesis and number synthesis of the black-box model produced many function principle solutions and their corresponding technical schemes. The morphological matrix of their function principle is listed in Table 1. According to the morphological matrix, we can select a technology scheme.

Table 1. Morphological matrix of the surface lapping machine

Sub-function	Sol. 1	Sol. 2	Sol. 3	Sol. 4	Sol. 5	Sol. 6	Sol. 7
Power source	Motor	Air motor	Hydraulic motor	Oil machine	Steam engine		
Transmission	Gear	Bevel gear	Synchronous belt	Harmonic gear	Chain	Cycloid pin wheel	Worm gear
Control	Relay	SCM	PLC				
Grinding plate structure	Spiral	Gridding	Anti-triangle radiation	Triangle radiation			
Pressure adjustment	Bolt	Nuts	Differential spiral				

According to the morphological matrix list in Table 1, there are 1260 technology schemes ($5\times7\times3\times4\times3=1260$). We can select schemes by the following three selection principles: compatibility principle; preference for the solutions with best sub-functions; winkle the solutions that do not meet the design requirements or do not satisfy constraints or are not dissatisfied. The optimization technology scheme is: motor driving, synchronous belt transmission, SCM control, anti-triangle radiation grinding plate structure, differential spiral Pressure adjustment device.

Triz is always in the process of development and improvement. Triz experts have developed the 8 laws of product evolution brought forward by G. S. Altshuller into many evolutionary models of technology system [8]. These modes are fit for innovation of technology system and production process. The mode of system evolution to a higher level means the system evolutes from single system to multi-system. According to the theory, the scheme of synchronous belt drived four-work-station surface lapping machine was got, as shown in Fig. 2. In the whole design process, UG was used to do 3D design, by which design effect was shown intuitively and observe the spatial layout of mechanical parts and movement and space interference of moving parts. So, the design was revised efficiently. The 3D effect of machine is shown in Fig. 3.

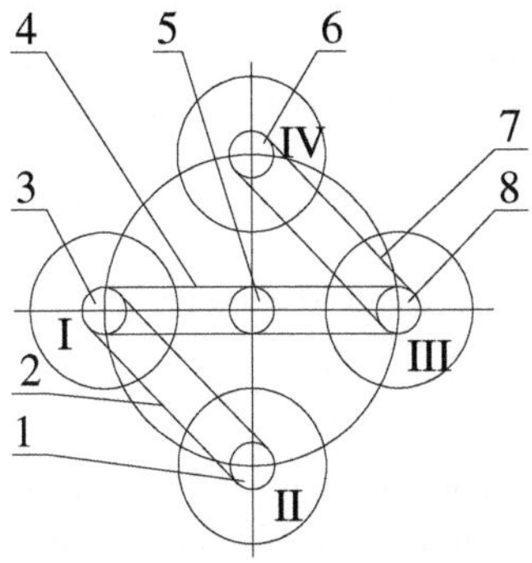

1. Driven pulley II 2. No.2 belt 3. Driven pulley I
4. No.1 belt 5. Driving pulley 6. Driven pulley
7. No.3 belt 8. Driven pulley III

Fig. 2. Transmission scheme

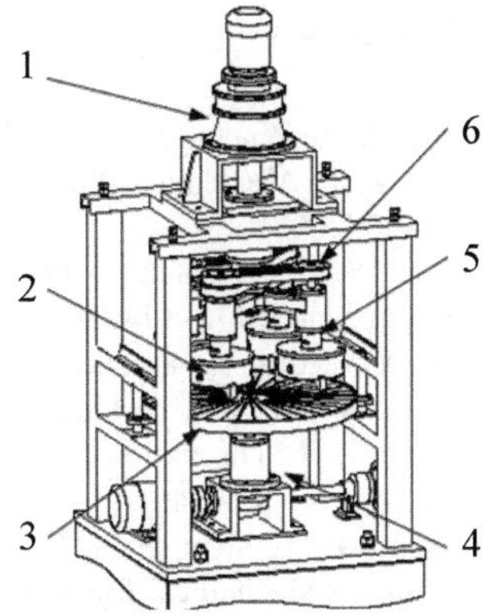

1. Geared Motor 2. Grinding fixture 3. Grinding plate
4. Lifting device 5. Pressure adjustment device
6. Synchronous belt drive device

Fig. 3. 3D effect graph

Upper beam of the surface lapping machine is sealed by channel beams and armor plates. Since the upper beam is the main part bear the force, its deformation can impact to surface lapping. So, the finite element analysis software Ansys was used to check the stress and deformation of the beam. In this graduation design, a variety of modern design methods were used, such as design methodology, CAD and finite element method. The design level was greatly improved.

4.2 Effect Analysis

Since 2008, College of Mechanical and Electronic Engineer of Hebei University of Technology opened the course of "Modern Design Theory and Method" for three years. The speak teachers have inducted the students to use modern design theories and methods in their graduation designs. As the experiments in reform at selected units of teaching practice, there are totally 21 students widely used modern design methods in their graduation designs. Their score is: 5 excellent, 10 good, middle 4 and pass 2, and totally 2 designs were excellent graduation designs of Hebei University of Science and Technology. In Table 2, it shows the comparison of score between test group and the other students. The result shows that the score of the test group was better than that of the other students.

Table 2. Contrast of gradate

Grade	Test group (%)	Required (%)
Excellent	23.8	15
Good	47.6	35
Medium	19	35
Pass	9.5	15

References

1. Bai, X.H., Zhang, Z.L., Xin, M.J.: Application of Modern Design Method in Graduation Design of Mechanical Engineering Profession. China Modern Educational Equipment 9, 25–26 (2008)
2. Wei, Y.X.: Research of Innovative Approaches of Modern Mechanical Design. China Equipment 5, 173–174 (2009)
3. Ni, X.N., Liu, Y.: Practice and Study of the Teaching Method of Modern design Method. China Science and Technology Information 10, 226–227 (2008)
4. Chen, Q.H.: Discussion on Teaching of Modern Design Theory and Method. Science and Technology Innovation Herald 4, 129 (2010)
5. Wang, L.Y., Shangguan, L.J., Ji, Z.L., et al.: The Exploration and Practice of Training Mode in Mechanical Engineering Innovation Talents. Journal of North China Institute of Water Conservancy and Hydroelectric Power (Social Science) 4, 161–162 (2010)
6. Lu, X.F.: The Definition and First Stage Classification of Modern Design Technique. Journal of Nanchang University (Engineering & Technology) 1, 75–79 (2009)
7. Wang, W.G., Zhang, Y., Lin, Y.J., et al.: Application Discussion of TRIZ in Graduation Designs in Mechanical Engineering Science. Journal of Yangtze University (Nat. Sci. Edit.) 1, 352–354 (2010)
8. Wang, F.Q.: Modern Design Methods and its Applications. Tianjin University Press, Tianjin (2008)
9. Wang, J.W., Xiong, W., Li, H.L., et al.: Developing Trend on Modern Optimal Design Methods. Machine Building & Automation 6, 5-6, 9 (2007)
10. Liu, G.Q.: Modern Mechanical Design using Computer Aided Design. China New Technologies and Products 11, 69 (2008)
11. Zhang, F.X., Liu, Z.Y.: Design of Surface Lapping Machine based on Modern Design Methodology. Hebei Journal of Industrial Science and Technology 1, 13–18 (2011)

On the Systematic Measures about the Innovative Education of the University Students

Yunsheng Cao

Department of the humanities, Shandong Traffic and Transport,University,
Jinan, 250023, China

Abstract. Nowadays the higher education is gradually changing from the elitists educating towards the masses education and the national higher education competition is also shifted from the number of educated people to the quality of the educated people, the core is to develop new talent. Our higher education should adopt practical and systematic measures to train the students' innovative consciousness and innovation ability so that we could make the university students to be the winners in the increasingly fierce international competition and to make a due contribution to build our innovative country.

Keywords: the university students, innovative education, systematic, measures.

1 Introduction

Innovative education is a new type of education, which is regarded as the process to guide students to digest, use information and knowledge and train their ability of independent thinking and creativity of the wisdom. In 1980, Shanghai Traffic University in the domestic firstly inaugurated the creative course to train consciously the students on innovation ability. Then, innovative education is soon brought out in other universities. In the past 20 years, the creation of learning in our country's science and technology, education and agricultural production and have been already playing an increasingly important role. However, the relative to the western developed countries, our innovative institutions of higher education, especially the education is a big gap, it is difficult to adapt to the economic globalization challenges and improve our overall national strength needs. Therefore, the university authorities should fully realize the significance of innovating education, and adopt practical measures to raise truly systematic university students' creativity and innovation ability.

1.1 The Analysis of the Current the University Students Innovation Ability

Our university students at school age are generally in the 19th ～ 23 years old, which is in a mental development of the important stage. Their thoughts are vigorous and active. However, the innovation ability of our university students are relatively weak, which is manifested in the following four aspects.

C. Liu, J. Chang, and A. Yang (Eds.): ICICA 2011, Part I, CCIS 243, pp. 337–344, 2011.

Innovation Cognitive Capacity Is Relatively Weak, Which Is the Basic Features of the University Students. The students affected by the traditional teaching method are easy to overlook their own innovation cognitive ability, and are not good at giving the scientific knowledge a partial or comprehensive arrangement, or making up a knowledge system, a thread is used to learn knowledge, understanding a smattering knowledge is often rote learning, and knowledge is usually applied or copied mechanically, thus the forgetting rate of knowledge is greatly increased.

Innovative Thinking Ability Is Evidently Deficient to the College Student Groups. Many college students of the lack of regular training and innovative thinking and they doesn't get into the habit of thinking and creativity, so they are only good at a one-way or a singleton toward ruddy vertical thought and analysis, they even have such innovative thinking on the sparks flashed, and it is not conducive to innovation, not to say in practice "more fruit and a good results".

The Lack of Practical Innovation Ability Is the Distinctive Features to College Student Groups. For a long time, as cognition of the arduous tasks and limitedness, and chance to practice in teaching for teachers of the practice and experimental method procedures and formulas to justice that the use of students copying, copy of the process of practice may phenomenon is often a lack of predictability, often to the dependence and not to do, too much emphasis on practical conclusions of the uniqueness and certainty. Because the above disadvantages generally exist, the students' quality and innovation ability to improve the practice are seriously hindered.

The Innovation Critical Ability Is Shortcoming, Which Is the Fundamental Characteristics to the College Students Group. In our adored "authorities" on the students in the creative and innovative thinking on the understanding and practice of the general lack of proper criticism and criticize the practice, not to authority or the teachers mentioned "aggressive", for fear of criticism and suggestions from the accused or failure ;And some students are under the illusion that that is a consequence, the intellectual rebellion, it is immoral, they dared not question, not to have their own ideas. Therefore, innovative and practical abilities to criticize are in no time trained and raised.

1.2 The Basic Responses to Implement the University Innovating Education

To Take Effective Measures to Eliminate the Prejudice and Somewhat Mystical in the Creative Aspects. Since human society, people began to create and innovative practice. But curiously, thousands of years the people in fact are strange to their very familiar creations, innovations, and they also strange to the essence of knowledge and innovation. Therefore, they gradually produced a variety of prejudice and misunderstanding to the creations and the innovations.

For a Long Time People Have Worshiped and Praised on the Creations Produced by the Great Man, but not on the Creation of the Ordinary People. As they mention the creation, consciously or unconsciously ,they always think of Newton and Einstein, Galileo and Edison, Darwin, Mendeleev, Lu Xun, Gordy, because all of them have a large number of contributions of distinction and they are the invention of the master of the giants of literature, science and the tycoon. However, few people think of the general people's creation, and fewer people would have thought of his own creation.

The Praise to the Great People are Usually on Part of the Results Gained by the Invention Process. For example, people used to praise Edison's a thousand invention, praise of Newton's third largest law, and worship of Darwin's theory of evolution and disposed of Einstein's theory of relativity, but neglected the details of their work, neglecting their mechanism. Even in the vast multitude of information recorded in literature, and they simply the creation of the results or at most are some of the experiment through. People have little interest concerned about the "big" in the process of thinking and approach that is to create the activities of their own laws and art of attention. Thus it caused some people think that "big" that they seldom meet with setbacks and failures in their creation process, because they were "big", so they made such significant achievements and ordinary people do not see things well, they study hard and the success of the hidden behind the creation of the skills and create laws, even mistakenly believed that as long as you study hard, you can obtain results.

People Mistakenly Think the More Knowledge, the More Creations and a Man Is not Good at Creations, Mainly because of Lack of Knowledge. It is the most common and most deep prejudice. In fact, it is an intellectual knowledge, knowledge is an important part of the people of all kinds of ability, but for creating, not all knowledge is essential to create ability, one size does not possess knowledge is totally dependent on him, that is knowledge and creation are nonlinearly related.

Based on the prejudice and misunderstanding, the people unconsciously make a mystery on creation, and they think the creations are high and seem to be created only a handful of genius, and exchanges with the ordinary people. These prejudices and misunderstanding, not only hinder the progress of science and technology, and seriously affected the overall development of the people. Therefore, the higher education priority is to eliminate the students are creations, innovations of the prejudice, misunderstanding and somewhat mystical.

2 To Update Education Concepts

The ideas are the leader of the action, and also the premises to train the creative personnel. The creativity education in the era of knowledge economy must present many different characteristics from the ones of the industrial age. The traditional educational ideas that the subjects and the inheritance and the doing things are regarded as the central must be replaced by the ideas that treat educating people and creations and the intelligence and coordinate development, human and work of the integration as the new ideas to educate. Therefore, in view of knowledge, we should fully realize that not only knowledge outside the book knowledge, which ought to include computer and network knowledge and experience of the invisible. However, we must foster interdisciplinary new ideas, knowledge and ability to create the overall quality of training and to harmonizing ; in the view, we will pay attention to training professionals of self-learning ability of innovation, research capacity, mental capacity or power of expression and the organization and management capability, and our ultimate goal is to improve the innovation ability. In the ideas of the development, we should think highly of the nonintellectual factors in the course of education and make the mental elements and nonintellectual factors mutual coordination and harmonious development. Further in view of quality talents we should pay attention that the students are engaged in a field of expertise, and we should teach our children to be true man. In short, our innovative education should face to the modernization, the world and geared to the future to provide guidance to strengthen the quality of education and training to develop morally, intellectually and physically innovation for objective, to develop innovative consciousness and innovation ability, a high level of success at the core, to increase educational quality come to the 21st century China's modernization drive and scientific and technological progress and the international competition of talents highly demand for the purpose. It is the knowledge economy time we should build up innovation education thoughts.

2.1 The Adjustment of the Talents' Training Model

For a long time, the division of disciplines in our universities are so excessive elaboration that innovation to train people with knowledge and ability moves very slowly. In recent years, we bringing up hybrids, but still ignore the problems to train the innovative capabilities. Now facing the challenges of the knowledge-based economy, our innovative education should be on the development of high technology and accomplish industrialization "the central task to adjust the mode of talent training, facing our country's economic development and social development, efforts to foster a number of and wide, knowledge, adaptable, high quality of the creative and feeling of times, senior personnel responsible. For this reason, the system shall be reformed according to categories. The management and entrance institutions are changed to the university students in order to let the students have the knowledge base and more students have to study freely. The students space should be a narrow subject, professional basis of expanded to a wide range of groups and subject to the realization of science, technology, science, social and the humanities between the pervasion and communication, and a solid foundation of education, and advocated the comprehensive, overall quality of education, a liberal education; From the people of the mechanism, we must encourage individuals to establish an incentive mechanism.

2.2 To Reform the Curriculum System of Teaching Contents

Presently the updating knowledge is increasing, and the edge subjects as well as interdisciplinary subjects are also coming up, the features of the digitized and informationized which are the main features of the information industry are the knowledge economy, to develop creative talents innovation ability focuses on teaching and the reform of the course and the reform aims are to implement teaching and course of modernization to meet the future social development for the people's needs. Therefore, we must follow the scientific, standardized, diversification "principle of the updating instruction content and improving the curriculum systems and establish a" loose "the education and curriculum systems. In arranging the integrative teaching contents, the following principles should be followed :(1) the subject of course, the strengthening of course well with the links between academic education and comprehensive, integrated with scientific education, and come to the development trend of the classical (2) to select excellent the teaching contents and develop new ones; (3) to put the frontiers of knowledge and expertise embodied in the modern scientific development of many subjects the knowledge of the cross between infiltration reflected in the teaching contents; (4) special attention should be paid to teaching plan for cultivating the students' ways of thinking, innovation, science and innovation ability in the teaching contents.

2.3 To Make Good Environments for the Innovation Education

Creative activities are conductive in certain circumstances. The creators or responsiveness to the environment usually referred to the environment. In philosophical terms, the creators of knowledge, abilities and qualities are to create nein and environmental factors, belongs to the external causes. in general, a good environmental factors conducive to the students create activity and creativity of development. Therefore, a favorable environment for the university students of innovating education is essential.

A Number of Creative Teachers, Whose Responsibility Is to Encourage and Train the Students to Continue to Stimulate the Creativity and Innovation Abilities. The teachers in the implementation of the process of innovating education are the dominant. Therefore, the first condition for the implementation of innovating education is to have a number of creative teachers. As a creative teacher should have the following conditions. the first is strong career-ambition and responsibility; The second is to have the fearless and pioneering spirit; The three is to have great creative thinking, and education and the way to the students' mental state and characterized emotional; the four is have a broad knowledge base, especially in the professional knowledge; the five is love and understanding, and appraisal of the students. The Teachers in the class teaching process, must create learn the principles and the teaching content, and will continue to encourage the students to ask many questions in classroom teaching process and make the students find the scene and live up lesson to enable the students to ask a question actively so as to increase their creativity. A number of creative supervisors are very necessary for the teachers to play their creation. As a creative management, enterprise shall have a high degree of enthusiasm and conscientiousness, support enterprise and development in the creative education and they should have tolerant attitudes to the teachers who have not been expected to be wrong.

To Use Innovative Teaching Materials to Cultivate the Ability of Independent Thinking and Innovation. In traditional education, the textbooks for students are too passive to accept this viewpoint and they often repressed the students' imagination and creativity. Japan chiropractors think that creative materials shall be made to understand the activities of the process and contents of the study, on the concept of the knowledge and skills, a full of things to be introduced to encourage the vigorous, and encourage the original. Japanese scholars' views are useful to our construction of the teaching materials.

To Offer Specialized Courses for the Students' Innovation. The schools should offer a series of special programs suitable to the training of the innovation. These courses are such kinds of subject as speculative science or psychological, methodology to explore the question of creative thinking. We should believe that the people's creative thinking is no mystery, but there are rules to follow. Human technology development in many vivid examples of invention is to reveal the secrets of creative thinking and creative thinking of the laws of good sum it up and consciously on young students , you can help them in the rough road gradually from the realm of necessity to the Realm of freedom.

To Develop Diverse Forms of the Second Class, to Develop the Students' Creativity and Innovation Abilities. Take advantage of innovation activities in education, we can put the classroom learning in the application in practice, to develop the students' interests and hobbies, so the students can train their exercise independent thinking abilities ; On the other hand, it can make up the classroom teaching's limitations brought up by the place, the time and the form of teaching so as to provide wider space for the students' innovation. A survey shows that college graduates work achievements are connected with the activities in which they participated in the stage of the secondary schools and universities. The reason is that the extra-curricular activities are different from the classroom teaching. The students usually select their favorite, certainly they will work hard at the field. This has changed the teaching model in the classroom. It is a big help for the students' development of creative thinking of science and technology. We are also made a survey, the results indicate that the students who often engage in extracurricular the interest group, their spirits of assiduous study and overcoming the difficulty with courage are more prominent. In future, all institutions should pay more attention to inviting the experts on an academic lectures, thus creating conditions to lead the students to make more science and technology innovations.

A Number of Creative Supervisors Are Very Necessary for the Teachers to Play Their Creation. As a creative management, enterprise shall have a high degree of enthusiasm and conscientiousness, support enterprise and development in the creative education and they should have tolerant attitudes to the teachers who have not been expected to be wrong.

3 The Qualities That the University Teachers Should Have to Improve the Innovative Education

3.1 The Charm of the Reputable Character

As a university teachers and charisma is the most important qualities, but also to the trust and respect. As the factor of charisma come from truth and easy to distinguish right from the stand firm, from deep thinking, from the teacher highly thought of it. The university teachers in their teaching process, the analysis of natural and social process, in view of the people to demonstrate that the process will be conveyed to the students some of his own ideas of the information that students will further consideration and decision and even will change the student's a decision, the decision is past and present and future. The teacher is a society in the leading groups and they represent a social conscience, pointing direction of young life, a nation in the future development of the track. They thought highly decided to a state of the future, they decided to a state of the future of their personalities determine the future generations, a nation's personality. Of noble nature and unsullied character should be no thought, this reason, not greedy for profit or benefit, and should be in conformity with the scientific truth, justice and fairness and maintaining social conscience and integrity, to keep in view of life and values.

3.2 The Deep Professional Quality

With the development of society, knowledge and technical areas, more and more, the university teachers in their specified field, have solid professional skill and abundant theoretical basis, and it is more important to get the capabilities to make the learning into natural, social and human. As the teacher's function is not only impart knowledge, the task is not only is learning to a heap of dead knowledge. The knowledge of the class into a form of thought, a natural tool for searching and social framework dialysis, a service to humankind happy, is teaching and learning is the ultimate goal. to achieve this, of course, the teacher to student, to give students a drop of water, and have a bucket of water. University teachers will not hear the ears, but read textbooks. the more rapid they fail to catch changes in social life, and therefore, the teacher must be concerned about it, society, nation and world affairs, the new knowledge, for his knowledge of the latest knowledge, will be charged to students, will the present and future tightly together.

3.3 Good Communicational Capacity

Teaching activities is not a one-way of social activity, but a two-way interpersonal activity. The power of expression, of course, is the most important power in exchange, with their knowledge and ideas of course, teachers use the language should be clear, accurate and fluent, humor, it is contagious, excited and inspire effort, to have thinking, logic and critically. Teachers and students in class, not only a language of communication and more important is the exchange and make eye contact, gesture of communication, which will only see the handouts, or sitting, balanced, the principals, there is no communication, of course, it's not teaching. Humorous language liven up lesson to attract the children's attention to interference from other matters. Therefore, a university teachers sense of humor is a classroom teaching and learning the key to success factor. A teacher liked by the students rarely is not a language teacher. A smile is more than a kind of fighting strength of every gram. Only in light of circumstances will quickly absorbed the information and the information, and memory the information will be involved in the desire, without the involvement of teaching activities will never achieve satisfactory results.

3.4 Broad Knowledge Reserves

The teacher is a part of the profession, not a monk chanted sutras turned the microphone. A single only understand their professional knowledge is not likely to become a qualified teacher. a university teaching astrophysical of the teachers don't understand philosophy is a hard to imagine that a lecture on art course of the teachers don't understand mathematical principles is also a weird experience. A civil engineering professional college teachers do not have the knowledge of physics, as a history of university teachers don't understand the study, can't find the civil engineering study the structure and physics, I don't find in history and learn the relationship between the longest. An environment of the design of the university, if he does not understand the psychology he will not find the design of the essence. Such circumstances, a university teachers simply know own professional knowledge, it would be impossible to use all kinds of knowledge to make the lessons impressed and charming. Therefore, as a teacher, such as a college teaches economics teacher, in addition to the professional knowledge, should be at least crude to understand many other subjects, including political science, mathematics, psychology and sociology, aesthetic, philosophy, history, etc.

References

1. Zhuang, S., Rong, Z.: The creation of The Ordinary. China's Mining University Press, Xuzhou (1997)
2. Pan, M., Shen, Z.: The WTO, The Editor of Higher Education Development of China. Beijing University Press (2001)
3. Zhang, K.: The Chinese University Education, vol. 36(1) (2000)
4. Wang, W.: The Humanism and Education. The Commercial Press, China (1983)
5. Mishing, Y.: Diffusion Processes in Advanced Technological Materials. In: Gupta, D. (ed.). Noyes Publications/William Andrew Publising, Norwich, NY (2004) (in press)
6. Information on, `http://www.tysy.net/manager/news/xcb/science`

Theory and Practice of Engineering Mathematics in Innovative Education of Computing Science Specialty

Youcai Xue

School of Science, Zhejiang University of Science and Technology, 318 Liuhe Road, Hangzhou 310023 China
xueyoucai@126.com

Abstract. This paper is to do research about some problems in the innovative education of engineering mathematics, discuss the significance of the innovative education from different aspects such as innovative consciousness, innovative quality and innovative capability, and investigate the function of the mathematics education in the innovative education, and report the practice exploration on the innovative education aspect such as mathematics education mode, mathematics teaching method etc.

Keywords: Engineering Mathematics, Innovative Education, Teaching Method.

Engineering mathematics has an important position in engineering and technical education, at the same time it's one of the innovative education key elements. How to play the role of engineering mathematics in engineering and technology innovation education, this is a problem should be seriously considered. The author believe, we should establish a new engineering mathematics education model that is composed by mathematical theory, mathematical modeling and applied, mathematics experiment and so on, and make full use of the function of mathematics education in the innovative consciousness, innovative quality and innovative capability to reinforce the students' basic knowledge, and improve their thinking ability and use of mathematical problem-solving ability to innovate. In this regard we have conducted a number of positive explorations for latest years, and have made some preliminary results in theory and practice.

1 The Significance of Innovation Capability

In general, the innovation capability is a dynamic system of multi-dimensional that is composed of innovative consciousness, quality and capability.

Two primal constituent of the innovative consciousness are personality and consciousness quality. Innovative personality is composed of the emotions, ideals, psychological and wills related to the innovation, of course includes personal gifts. Innovative consciousness quality means the strong innovation desire, which includes the hunger for knowledge, curiosity, explorations consciousness, critical consciousness, thoughts and ideas.

C. Liu, J. Chang, and A. Yang (Eds.): ICICA 2011, Part I, CCIS 243, pp. 345–352, 2011.

The innovative qualities include mainly the humanity qualities and the knowledge qualities. Humanity qualities include personal views on life and values, aesthetic ability, moral levels and so on. Knowledge qualities mainly refer to the educated man's all kinds of knowledge background and their constituent, certainly include their learning ability, especially the self-learning ability.

The primal constituent of innovative capability include mainly observation, attentiveness, imagination, memory, ability of thinking, creativity and so on., among them, the creativity is composed of methodological competence, theory application ability and problem-solving ability.

2 The Value of Mathematics Education and the Cultivation of Creative ability

Mathematics education plays an important part in engineering innovative education. That is embodied in that mathematics education has the important educational values of person quality, thoughtway, scientific language, esthetic education, application value and cultural value.

The personal quality educational value of mathematics education is primarily reflected in the critical spirit of mathematics and the training of will. Because we only believe those "proved" things, don't believe those "intuition" and "authority", that provide the most direct training for people's rational "critical spirit" in the process of study and research mathematics, and make people believe in science and rationality. In the process of mathematics training the proving and calculation of many propositions need patience and the conscientious spirit in addition to scientific method. Sometimes even a common question would be solved insistently, so mathematic education can train the person's will, such as person's patience, perseverance, conscientious these nonintellectual factors.

The thoughtway educational value of mathematics education is primarily reflected in some "mathematics rational" impact on human, such as "quantification thought and research method", "abstract thought and research method", "critical spirit and opening spirit ". The quantitative analysis method or the research method from quantification to qualitative is important science research method. The division of mathematics and physics of Chinese Academy of Sciences indicate that "the quantitative thinking is the process of people refine mathematical problem in practice, abstract it to be a mathematical model, and obtain the solution or approximate solution by solving the mathematical model, and then verify the solution back to the practice" in their report "Today's mathematics and its application" [2]. The mathematics research invented such as the abstraction, formalization and axiomatization research method, it is one of the most important science research method of humans. The "mathematics" is how to use the mathematics concept, symbol and so on, to performance targets of things and their relationship [1], that is we should be good at observing the world from the mathematics perspective and analyzing all kinds of things and phenomenon, in order to solve problem"[1]. So the famous educationist Frenduthal indicated that is mathematicization studying than mathematics studying.

The scientific language educational value of mathematics education is primarily reflected in the mathematics language approach, that is "actually mathematics provides the necessary language for the scientific cognitive activities which is the necessary concept frame" [1]. Mathematics not only revealed the quantitative rules, but also has great significance for humans' cognitive activities and practical activities. As Poincar pointed out that if no such language, we would not know the most closely similar of things for ever. And we would not know the concordance of world for ever [4].So from this point of view the mathematics learning can be seen as a language learning, the mathematics teaching is the mathematical language teaching. [5]

Mathematics Education has important scientific esthetic education function. The beauty of symmetry, simply, unity and singularity in mathematics reflects the abstract beauty of science. One of important standards in science research is "esthetic standard". For example, the theory of relativity was universally recognized, because of its mathematical beauty. In the process of mathematics education we should pay attention to the best combination between aesthetics and mathematics education.

The methodology value of mathematics education primarily is reflected in "problem solving". "Problem solving" is a basic form of mathematics learning and research. So that provides an effective way for people to learn solution strategy and thinking method of solving problem [1]. The characteristics of the modern mathematics development has been extended from the obviously intuitive background quantitative model to the possible quantitative model, so mathematics provides the best places to play humans' creativity [1]. In fact the modern mathematics includes many mathematical methods such as re-constructing, generalizing, specializing and axiomatizing the object of studying, which provide the most important method to create the new mathematical model. All these indicate, because of the particularity of the mathematics study method, Mathematics Education has the special meaning for the training of humans' creativity. The Japanese famous mathematician and mathematics educationist Yamakuni has pointed out that human has the inventiveness and creativity, but if you want to cultivate human's the most noble properties, you should make the best of mathematics education[7].

The application value of Mathematics Education is not only reflect in its important applicability but also the significance for the people's development referred to above is more important. "The cultural value of mathematics is embodied in the very important effect for the development of humans' rational spirituality", it convince people the world is regular (rationality), and it can be know (by the mathematical tools) [1]. And then, the rationality of mathematics is reflected in it's beyond perceptual experience, and we can achieve a more profound understanding of nature with the theoretical thinking.

3 The Exploring and Practice of "New Teaching Model of the Engineering Mathematics"

In view of the above points, we explore a new comprehensive course model that is mixed with mathematics theory, mathematical modeling, mathematical experiments and mathematics culture, and achieve a better teaching effect. The main approach is as follows:

3.1 Teaching Model of Mathematics Course

Because the traditional engineering mathematics attaches importance to theory, but looks down on practice, attaches importance to imitation, but looks down on innovation, attaches importance to knowledge, but looks down on diathesis, the engineering mathematics education can't satisfy. We mixed the mathematics theory, Mathematical Modeling, mathematical experiments and mathematics culture together to be a organic whole on the basis of the foreign successful experience of engineering mathematics education, and interpenetrate each other, support each other, and achieve a better effect.

Firstly, for the theoretical course of mathematics, we reorganized the content of teaching with problem as locomotive. Problem is the soul of mathematics. But it's a pity that almost mathematics materials become a union of concepts, theorems, examples and exercises after years of selecting, it's difficult to get the source of knowledge background. Even some easy application problems just imitate mathematics knowledge simply. In teaching we use the discovery teaching methods in problem situation, that is, bring up a problem in the process of teaching, after that we analysis some possible mathematical methods when we solve the problem, then repeat the process of the knowledge discovering with students. Secondly, for the proof of mathematics theorems, when we meet those more important method theory we must make an effort to clear it, let students understand the principle of that. When we meet the common theorems we just give the summary of proof, and then ask students complete it as homework to enhance students' ability.

For mathematical modeling, we think, firstly mathematics itself is a science of model. So, the point is how to abstract, simplify the practical problem to a mathematical problem. Secondly, we should try to students understand which mathematical methods are used in the process of solving the mathematical model. Thirdly we enhance the applicability education of mathematics theory. Because of these reasons, we collected and compiled lots of applicative problems, and let students solve it with the methods learned in the class selectively. And we carried out some extra-curricular teaching activities that are based of mathematics model, and has attracted students' attention.

With the heavy use of the modern calculate software, many calculating skill in the traditional mathematics education has lost their educational aim, and have been supplanted by the mathematical science computing methods and experiment. So we added the content on science computing methods and the corresponding experiment. Positive teaching effect has been achieved.

In the process of teaching we introduced the mathematics history, the experience of mathematician, the discovery and creation process of mathematics, the methods significance of mathematics, the contrast of the eastern and western mathematical cultures and so on, that are concerned with the mathematics knowledge. By this way a good culture educational effect was achieved, and enhanced the students' creation consciousness.

3.2 Mathematics Teaching Methods

Firstly, as mentioned above, we used the discovery teaching methods in problem situation. When students repeat the discovery processes of knowledge they can brush up the creative and discovery process of mathematics, and study the mathematical methods. We especially attached great importance to using different method to solve the same problem. So then students can experience the application of different mathematics methods, and enhance problem-solving abilities.

Secondly, we used the discussing uebung teaching method. For those strongly theoretical content that need to be profound understood, it's difficult to achieve the request of teaching if you only depend on the classroom teaching, homework and uebung. So we arranged some seminar, that is, let students research these problems be found in teaching, or some innovative problems and application problems by themselves, and then discussed and communicate them in the seminar with the purpose of enhancing students' analysis and problem-solving abilities. The teacher has to elaborately design the seminar, he has to select the appropriate content in advance, and work out the important, heuristic, typical and challenging discussing problem. And the students earnestly prepare, discuss in groups and discuss in class, finally the teacher make a summary. Through the discussion students not only has deepened the understanding of the abstract mathematical theory, but also greatly arouse their curiosity and innovational desire, and train students' innovation thought and creative consciousness, train students for the subjects who can independently, dynamically and creatively carry out the cognitive and practical activities, let students became the decision maker of studying, the subject of information process and the active constructivist of knowledge.

For example, in the study the following theorem later

Theorem1 [6] Let A be an $m \times n$ matrix with the r rank. Then there exist an $m \times r$ matrix B and an $r \times n$ matrix C whose ranks are m and n, respectively, such that $A = BC$.

We put forward a question: This theorem have what application?

As an example, we give its one of an application in communication:

For any given $m \times n$ matrix, we could perform elementary row operations on it to obtain a reduced row echelon form.

Therefore, we have

$$A=\begin{pmatrix}2&-1&-1&1&2\\1&1&-2&1&4\\4&-6&2&-2&4\\3&6&-9&7&9\end{pmatrix}\to\begin{pmatrix}1&0&-1&0&4\\0&1&-1&0&3\\0&0&0&1&-3\\0&0&0&0&0\end{pmatrix}\text{, and}$$

$$B=\begin{pmatrix}2&-1&1\\1&1&1\\4&-6&-2\\3&6&7\end{pmatrix},C=\begin{pmatrix}1&0&-1&0&4\\0&1&-1&0&3\\0&0&0&1&-3\end{pmatrix},$$

such that $A=BC$.

According to this procedure, we could thereby achieve a new encryption technique. Next, we will present several new methods in cryptography based on that idea.

Let B be an encrypted key matrix. Let C be an encrypted information matrix.

The First Method

We can do some tricks on the encrypted information matrix C . Let

$$C_1=\begin{pmatrix}-1&4\\-1&3\\0&-3\end{pmatrix}$$

, while the encrypted key matrix B remains the same. By manipulating of matrix multiplication, we could easily extract the third and fifth rows from the information matrix A, which is

$$D^T=BC=\begin{pmatrix}1&-2&2&-9\\2&4&4&9\end{pmatrix}.$$

The Second Method

Let A be an encrypted information matrix. The encrypted key matrix is just the product of several elementary matrices. Therefore, there exists a nonsingular matrix P such that $PA=C$, where C is an information matrix.

The Third Method

Let A be an encrypted information matrix, and let the encrypted key matrix undefined. We could perform elementary row operations on A, and then find out the information matrix C . Due to the non-uniqueness of orders of elementary operations, the sequence of manipulations must consent to two-sided correspondents at first. Otherwise, performers should need extra agreements to obtain information matrices. Hence this encryption technique can be easily accessible to us all!

Thirdly, the unit summaries review teaching method. We adhered to ask students to summarize the knowledge, methods and questions, and then write what one has learned from this chapter. By this way students can review the knowledge in time, and they can put the problems and the problem-solving methods in order systematically. Enhance students' mathematics capability and their capability for self-learning.

Fourthly, add the "large homework" of mathematical modeling. Assign some problems with broad information, and if you want to solve it you have to consult large reference material and dig into them. Or let students themselves raise some problem to study, discuss, make models, experiment by computer and complete a paper. Enhance students' capability of problem-solving and creativity ability.

Fifthly, the learning and using of modern mathematical software can interest students when they experiment. Students have learned the method to solve mathematical problem by modern science technology. In the process of experiment classes are solidarity, learn form each other, and overcome some students' afraid emotion for mathematics.

3.3 Effect of Practice

The practice of innovative teaching model of engineering mathematics has achieved expected results. The main performance is as follows:

(1) Increased the self-confidence of majority's studying mathematics, learning atmosphere become more and more deep. Many students are afraid to study mathematics course before, but now they can select the study method which they like, and study, discuss, research according to their interest and forte. Every student truly learns and earns, followed by the phenomenon of mass fail in college mathematics disappear gradually.

(2) Mathematical cultural education has played a positive role in guiding to increase students' attainments of creative consciousness and cultural spirits. For these years we had received 350 pieces of paper and studying notes. One female student had written that she once thought mathematics was only a pile of formula, definition, and the terrible proving and complicated calculation, she is very afraid of mathematics, but though the studying of mathematical culture she understood what is mathematics, reason why people study mathematics, and she knew the great role that mathematics played in the process of human civilization.

(3) Students at different levels meet the different needs of mathematics. For those students who will enhance the Graduate Record Examination or the college math competition In Zhejiang, the teaching model has taken a good effect. For these years our college accessed a large harvest in the college math competition In Zhejiang.

(4) Enhance the students' initiative to take part in all kinds of innovation activity. In the CUMCM our college has made breakthrough progress. For example, twelve teams of our college took part in the CUMCM in 2006, two teams won the state first prize and two teams won the state second prize. In 2007 two teams won the state second prize. In February 2008 two teams of our college took part in the Mathematical Contest in Modeling (MCM), one team won the second prize, one team won successful participant.

(5). Promote the all-round reforms of college mathematic, teaching research results continue emerge. The good news is that these teachers' teaching research results are not only theoretical, but also the practical project has been increasing year by year. So the teaching of mathematics is promoted.

4 Conclusion

Mathematics is the basic course in college, how to make the basic course play the role in the innovative education that is a project need to research seriously. We think, enhancing the teaching of basic course, reinforcing the students' knowledge base, improving the students' creative consciousness, creative quality, capability of thinking and application of knowledge, these are basic requirements and basic approach in the innovative education.

References

1. Zheng, Y.: Philosophy of Mathematics Education. Version 2, pp. 172–195, 228-229. Sichuan education Press, Chengdu (2001)
2. Department of Mathematics Physics in Chinese Academy of Sciences. Current Mathematics and its Application. Studies. Dialectics of Nature, 3-4, Version 1 (1994)
3. Poincaré, H., (write), Li, X. (translate): The Value of Science, p. 190. Guangming Daily Press, Beijing (1988)
4. Mathematics Pedagogy, p. 191. People Education Press, Beijing (1984)
5. Pólya, G.: How to Solve it, p. 2. Science Press, Beijing (1982)
6. Jin, Q.: An application of elementary transformation: a matrix of full rank decomposition. College Mathematics (5), 195–196 (2009)
7. Xiong, X.: The Application of Invertible Matrix in Secure Communication. College Mathematics (3), 108–112 (2007)
8. Stallings, W.: Cryptography and Network Security, 4th edn., pp. 28–30. Publishing House
9. Zhang, D., Zhang, Y.: New concept: Mathematics teaching with the question driving. Studies in College Mathematics (3), 8–12 (2004)
10. Chen, W.: Creation of problem situation in exploratory teaching of mathematics. Higher Education of Sciences (4), 43–45 (2009)
11. Zhang, W., Tang, C.: Computer Simulation Technology-aided Teaching and Creative Education. Higher Education of Sciences (4), 60–62 (2009)

Research on the Construction of Financial Information System after Universities' Merger

Jun Zheng[1], Guangbiao Sun[1], and Xiuli Hou[2]

[1] Finance Department, Hebei United University, Hebei Tangshan, 063000, P.R. China
[2] Qian'an College, Hebei United University, Hebei Qian'an, 064400, P.R. China

Abstract. The university created after merger needs to evolve rapidly. It should be matched by the Financial Information System (FIS), such as effective way of financing, scientific method of improve the capital efficiency, construction of financial information service system. These require the financial management of the university after merger keep pace with the time, and provide financial assurance for the university to rapid development, so as to further improve financial services and financial management capability. Based on the authors' practical work experience in the financial work after universities' merger, this paper discusses on the motivation of FIS, proposal ideas and measures of building a FIS of universities after merger, and gives an analysis to related issues of FIS.

Keywords: University and college, Financial information, Financial Information System.

1 Introduction

Merger of higher education institutions is the reform of Chinese higher education system. It aims at improving the comprehensive level of university through the restructuring of educational resources, and then optimizes elementary university size for effectiveness.

Chinese higher education experienced a larger scale, broader wave of universities' merger from the Middle and Late 1990s to the beginning of the 21st century. So far, the multi-campus universities in China have become a common phenomenon, the three main ways are mergers between universities, remote campus, and city universities. At the same time, compared with the traditional model, the financial management is accordingly involved in large in the universities after merger.

Situation calls for effective utilization of information technology in education. How to construct the financial information service system as soon as possible, to ensure financial information to better play the role of management in universities, is the new development trend of computerized accounting, and a necessary requirement to promote education Information Strategy.

C. Liu, J. Chang, and A. Yang (Eds.): ICICA 2011, Part I, CCIS 243, pp. 353–359, 2011.

2 The Major Problems Facing in Current Management of Combined Financial Information in Universities after Merger

In recent years, a common implementation method of Financial Management System is a unified leadership and decentralized management system. That is, colleges, campuses, and branch campus are at the secondary school level for hierarchical management. The following are major problems:

2.1 Accounts Differ

Campuses vary in size before merger. The management system is different, accounting models are not as the same. Larger scale universities may implement the "centralized management and decentralized accounting" or "classification management and accounting classification", and have achieved computerized accounting; Small scale universities may implement the "centralized management and centralized accounting", and even still at the stage of the account at hand.

2.2 The Overall Business in Multi-campus Distributed Separately, but Each Campus with Uneven Workload Distribution

There have relatively dispersed campus in the combined university, which increase the difficulty of accounting for reunification. Accounting bodies at all levels implement financial management mode of "self-contained and decentralized accounting ". Financial system of subordinate units is from different departments in accounting, financial expenses, income distribution and other aspects.

There is no clear division of work at all levels of accounting organizations in the financial responsibility and authority for use of funds. It does not form a reasonable accounting of the operating mechanism, which cause the upper and lower flow of capital and property management out of touch.

2.3 Uneven Quality of Staff

Impacted by the existing accounting system, they have formed a certain way of thinking and accounting treatment, they are not familiar with the situation outside except for their original campus.

In such a situation to rush into battle, it will lead the accounting information received, and difficult to reflect the financial situation to a certain extent. Also the coordination between the various positions is in poor internal controls. That weakened the financial sector, and is not conducive to an overall financial situation of the college to implement effective, comprehensive supervision. Further more, far away from the financial department, and business processing methods backward, will result in the precipitation and waste of funds.

3 Need for Implementing Financial Information Management in University and College

With the expansion of university education, multi-campus education and financial management at different levels have been more common. The financial position, cash flow, income and expenditure of secondary units must report to the primary financial units. Then the overall financial information can be processed, which resulted in low efficiency.

The primary financial units should establish a financial data processing center, Work out the same accounting standards and treat the same procedures through the establishment of real-time financial information service system for managers to provide supports.

Meanwhile, for secondary units input data to the system in accordance with the same accounting standards and procedures, data processing centers centralized financial information processing. Financial management costs are greatly reduced, which help to improve financial efficiency and service levels, thus enhance the scientific management of financial information.

4 The Idea of Constructing Financial Information Service System

To create a financial information service system, the following design should be fulfill.

4.1 Design of System Architecture

Information systems currently used consists of three subsystems: financial business processes subsystem, financial management information subsystem and financial decision support subsystem.

(1) Financial business processes subsystem.
The subsystem consists of the daily accounting and control subsystem of funds, liquidity planning and management subsystems, investment and budgetary decision-making subsystem, capital operation management subsystem, value stream management subsystems based on supply chain, and so on. All these subsystem are mainly used to deal with the counter business operations and daily affairs, their functions are to automate the manual processing of financial business, with the characteristics of fast and accurate, and be able to handle large quantities of information and original share information.

(2) Financial management information subsystem.
The subsystem is based on general accounting information subsystems and financial services subsystems. Through the collection, transmission, storage, processing of financial information, it provides decision support for leading services, and for the

financial management information services. It has two functions: collection and processing of financial data, as well as providing financial management, financial information for decision-making.

(3) Financial decision support subsystem.
Decision-making is the management process in which the people submit a variety of solutions to problems and perform, in order to achieve the desired objectives, they use scientific theories and method, give systematic analysis of subjective and objective conditions. Based on information provided by financial management information subsystem to establish effective financial data warehouse, the financial decision support subsystem uses various forecasting methods to give the status quo and future development trend analysis.

4.2 Design of Hardware Technical

Modern communications technology and advanced computer network technology provides a powerful technology base for the realization of a computerized financial management and University network. Especially in recent years, reorganization, merger, establishment of new campuses among all colleges and universities, have brought a lot of new content to the university financial management. Modern communications technology and advanced network technology are no doubt bring great convenience and efficiency to this new development model. It can be said, it is just with communications technology and network technology support, which makes true of achieving remote, real-time financial management in multi-campus, multi-sectors.

(1) Construction of Information Processing Center.
With construction of Integration finance into business in digital campus, school finance information database stored in a central data warehouse of information, it had become share information in campus to provide shared management and service authorization, just as other business information databases. Treasury set two Center server as the Finance Application Center server and backup server. WEB server of financial information is unified information center without regard to the financial sector. High reliability of the application server cluster and configure the disk array to form a hot standby of the results. At the End of every Business Day, the financial data take measure of tape backup to fully ensure data security and system stability.

(2) Construction of Networks and network system.
With the aids of Campus financial information data network (1000M), financial backbone network provide sufficient bandwidth for large amounts of data transfer, database replication and inquiries. Network system is based on the WAN B / S (Browser / Server) structure. That is, the application software installed on the server - network financial management system, users only install the browser client mode.

(3) To Purchase Remote office equipment.
It Include mobile office equipment to access server and firewall. Configure the remote access device, provide a safe and efficient operation of the remote query and functionality for remote branch leadership, and provide remote access control.

4.3 Design of Software Technical

With the quick development of IT technology, network technology and computer technology, the financial information increase every day followed along with the social economic development. It has become unstoppable trend to manage financial information with modern Network technology.

Especially in the Universities after merger, the campus network has been established to achieve the integration of financial management and operational work. That has enhanced the transparency of financial information. It is conducive to information users be able to understand information and make the appropriate decisions.

To achieve financial information services to the users face to face, would require financial data flow from a closed financial processing platform into the Internet. The accuracy, security and real-time performance are facing unprecedented challenges. Therefore, constructing financial information service system must be by means of advanced, reliable networking technology and more powerful financial software.

Finance Department needs to cooperation with the software company to archive functional expansion of financial software which was in mature application in the enterprise management, and develop financial software and information processing platform (Universities Version) for college financial accounting and service.

Through hierarchical authority, it makes all staff querying, using, and participating in financial management. Add functions (release, query, budget and control) to ensure that all financial activities are of budget, accounting and analysis in process.

In current computerized accounting systems, there has more mature, powerful software system in colleges and universities. The university financial department can choose the specific financial management software which appropriate one's own.

You need to do the following.

(1) Focus on the software functional requirements.
Universities can use the network financial software (WEB EDITION) as software of financial management information system, to build their own financial management system. The application modules include: accounts processing, system management, financial management, current account management, financial analysis, reporting system, payroll, tuition management, and bill management.

(2) Software based settings.
Since the accounting systems are different in various units within one University, you need to set up different sets of accounts. This design not only guarantees the integrity of the uniform financial information, while maintains the original characteristics of secondary units in the financial to meet the different needs; The centralized financial management makes secondary units only have right of using financial software but can't control it. The subjects, items, currency, and other system parameters encoded set by the university according to uniform standards. This avoids the financial information in a distributed system.

5 Measures in Constructing Financial Information Service System

5.1 Full Investigating with a Clear Target, and Making Scientific Planning

Make scientific planning is the key. Leaders in charge of financial information should enhance the sense of urgency and responsibility, say in important matters to make decision. A leading group of financial information should be set up to identify the needs of various parts of the financial information, to make a clear target, and to do scientific planning. In addition, strengthening staff training to enhance the ability of full use financial information is also planning should be considered.

5.2 Improving University Infrastructure Network, Expanding Financial Software Functionality to Further Enhance the Ability of Financial Information Released

Geographical isolation of the multi-campus mode led to the financial information data cannot be synchronized and cannot be unified managed. For now requires special technology to provide remote access, extranet and intranet security links, for reliability and security of data. How to improve the infrastructure network, is basis of building a financial information service system.

5.3 Update Financial Concepts, So As to Strengthen Technical Training and Financial Management Capacity of Staff

Technical training should do in financial officers to make them be aware of the importance of scientific management, to enhance information management capacity constantly, and to promote the construction work of good financial information in universities after merger.

6 Summary

Financial information is an important means to improve the university modern management level. Only to keep solving the problems in the information construction, to maintain and construct a new platform positively for financial information, financial information network can give full play to the strengths, and to better promote the healthy and orderly development of higher education.

References

1. Zheng, W., Yang, B., McLean, G.N.: Linking organizational culture, structure, strategy, and organizational effectiveness: Mediating role of knowledge management. Journal of Business Research 63(7), 763–771 (2010)

2. Kemeny, M.E.: Staff Development of Direct Care Workers in Pennsylvania: The Relationship between Organizational Structure and Culture and Best-Practices in Training (June 8, 2010), http://hdl.handle.net/2069/247
3. Hevner, A., March, S., Park, J., Ram, S.: Design Science Research in Information Systems. Management Information Systems Quarterly 28(1), 75–105 (2004)
4. Bailey, K.: Taking a Byte Out of M&A Failure. CMA Management Hamilton 75(3), 16–19 (2001)
5. McDonald, M., Mors, T.A., Phillips, A.: Management system integration: Can it be done? Quality Progress 36(10), 67 (2003)
6. Tsamenyi, M., Cullen, J., González, J.M.G.: Changes in accounting and financial information system in a Spanish electricity company: A new institutional theory analysis. Management Accounting Research 17(4), 409–432 (2006)
7. Jain, A.: Smart Legacy Modernization. Polaris Software Lab Limited (2005)
8. Bradley, R.V., Pridmore, J.L., Byrd, T.A.: Information Systems Success in the Context of Different Corporate Cultural Types: An Empirical Investigation. Journal of Management Information Systems 33(2), 267–294 (2006)
9. Lin, S.-R.: The Information Technology (IT) Integration of Bank Merger: An Exploratory Case Study, MBA Thesis. National Central University (2006)
10. Chou, S.-c.T.: Migrating to the web: a web financial information system server. Decision Support Systems 23(1), 29–40 (1998)
11. Brancheau, J., Janz, B., Wetherbe, J.: Key Issues in Information Systems Management: 1994-95 SIM Delphi Results. MIS Quarterly 20(2), 225–242 (1996)

Research on Academic and Performance of Teachers in Universities

Jing Tan, Yinlin Wu, and Yanan Li

Qinggong College, Hebei United University, Tangshan 063009, China
wanghui6819526@126.com

Abstract. The development of universities not only needs the good school condition, but also needs the first-class teacher troop. The higher education popularity took one kind of social tidal current, without doubt has the profound influence to our country each kind of universities's survival and the development. How does the universities through positively carry on the interior organizational reform, strengthens to the universities human resources management, raises the achievements level, then improves the teacher quality, strengths this school the competitive ability and the synthesis strength, is the current universities personnel system reform key point and the difficult.

Keywords: Scholarship of Teaching and Learning, teacher professional development, performance management system.

1 Introduction

Performance Management is a process to acquire and apply information that make out objective and equitable appraisal to department and department's employee with adopting scientific methods according to certain standard at certain time period and appraisal scope, then to revise arisen deviations of department and employee's work target according to appraisal results and do some indispensable rewards and punishment and other measures to department and employee.

In the universities, discussed academic, most of them to participate in research and published papers, monographs, scientific research has been recognized as the measure of the academic status of a university to evaluate the academic standards of a university teacher as well as only the most important indicators. However, as the main duties of university teachers - teaching is not academic activities, teaching activities, which include academic standards, how to evaluate. Looking at the status of university teaching, reflect content of vocational college teachers, the quality of the current problems of higher education, research activities of University Teachers, the level of research and teaching the profound meaning of learning, teaching and research given the same academic status far-reaching theoretical and practical significance.

C. Liu, J. Chang, and A. Yang (Eds.): ICICA 2011, Part I, CCIS 243, pp. 360–365, 2011.

2 Academic Status of College Teaching

At present all our universities for research evaluation activities are inseparable from the audit, whether it is job classification or performance assessment, in addition to teaching the provisions of a certain amount of work, difficult to measure the quality of teaching and learning activities. This is difficult to quantify the teaching methods used to evaluate, and bear fruit slowly, can not bring direct economic benefits of the activity, attention is very limited. Many teachers can not seriously into the teaching, do not want to spend time in teaching, teaching time, teaching quality are not guaranteed, leading to the quality of students fail to achieve the standard or even decline. Heavy task of teaching the teachers when not on the teacher, the teacher is not widespread on the undergraduate stage.

2.1 The Meaning of Academic Activities of Teaching Are Not Clear, University Teachers, Their Lack of Understanding of the Overall Scholarship of Teaching

For a long time, university teachers, limited understanding of the work of specialized academic disciplines to explore, think that teaching is not an academic activity, also used in specialized subject areas of scientific research about the academic work of university teachers, university teachers ignore what is in the The main professional activities - teaching in the academic level. Professional colleges of education, so most of the teachers on teaching limited understanding of "missionary, Tuition, FAQ," has generally believed that teaching the difference between the subjects, and teachers with high academic standards, to know more, study deep knowledge and master new technologies and new well is high academic standards, only concerned about what to teach, no one to teach and how to teach the reasons why. Also did not realize, is the study of university teachers to teach, the nature of learning activities that explore the nature of teaching, teaching is found in the teaching, integrated teaching and application of teaching, integrated teaching.

2.2 The Academic Level of Teaching Evaluation System Is Not Sound

Some colleges and universities rely on SECT; SECT mechanical results will be used as the sole criterion for the level of teaching. What is more, the test results to students and teachers linked to the quality of teaching and learning activities. The academic assessment system on teaching college teachers are facing the differences between disciplines, is faced with the academic freedom and administrative intervention in the conflict, university teachers, teaching is a kind of research activities, university teachers are deemed to be an "advanced knowledge "the incarnation of the evaluation of academic standards of teaching professional development of the subject is also a key issue.

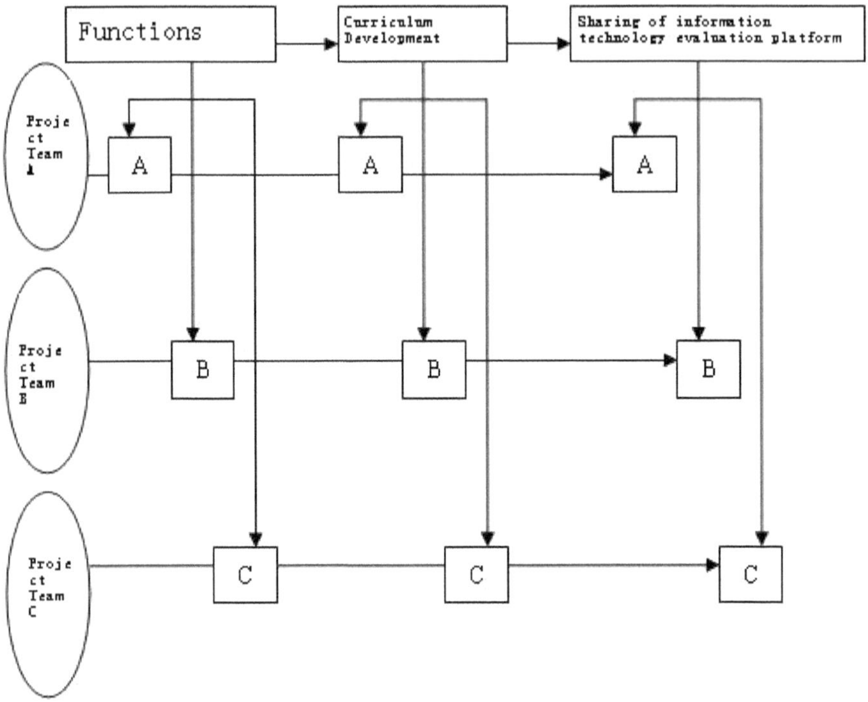

3 Improve the Academic Level of University Teaching Measures

3.1 Teacher Performance Management

First is the performance assessment data for TTF assessment system, can use two way to acquire data: one is the traditional way, namely the organization and the release of the paper to teachers fill in progress; 2 it is digital network means, that TFT system software, use assessment scarfing online campus, as in the open teaching assessment system provides assessment main body.

The first step is to identify the validity of the data, which of the three kinds of data collection (students, with their peers, experts) to identify, do not accord with the effectiveness of the overall assessment requirements invalid data screening; The second step is to data types are classified, that is, based on what the teacher is in the discipline nature and characteristics of the nature of the course or granted to effective data material classification, to ensure the objectivity and comparability evaluation; Third is the main body of the reliability evaluation test; Fourth step is to determine the opinions of main body weight assessment, namely from different sources of data for fuzzy data processing (C2-C11) and the common data processing (C1, C12 to C17).

Assessment of the main division of opinion of the weights

Index number	Issue number	Weight issues	Students weighted function	Weight counterparts	Leadership weighted function
C2	1	1.0	0	0.80	0.20
C3	2	1.0	0.45	0.35	0.20
C4	3	1.0	0.40	0.35	0.20
C5	4	0.6	0.35	0.45	0.20
	5	0.4	0.60	0.35	0.15
C6	6	0.5	0.45	0.40	0.25
	7	0.5	0.25	0.50	0.05
C7	8	1.0	0.65	0.30	0.05
C8	9	1.0	0.60	0.30	0.10
C9	10	1.0	0.60	0.30	0.10
C10	11	1.0	0.60	0.30	0.40

Modern science and technology and psychology studies have shown that the performance of teachers by the following four factors.

S-skill
O-opportunity
M-motive
E-environment
P-performance

You can use the following formula: $P = f(S, O, M, E)$

This formula shows that the performance of skills, opportunities, incentives, environment these four variables. In other factors under the condition of invariable, the teacher of the higher performance skills, the more obvious, therefore is proportional to the skills and performance. The skill level in turn depends on a variety of factors that include the individual's physical, mental, suffered the situation of education and training, teachers have the knowledge and experience.

3.2 Implementation of the Integrated Learning Programmer University

Integrated Learning means that learning is a whole, rather than the various parts of the comprehensive, integrated education, the knowledge to find the connection between the point contacts at the development of the students in the integration of knowledge and application of knowledge. Undergraduate experience is often a general school education; integrated learning programs help students establish good study habits, college career in a limited study to better benefit the future development of their knowledge and skills. Integrated Learning courses include: connecting different types of knowledge and experience of the curriculum; the use of theory to guide practice and then the ability to rise to theory courses; use of diverse and even conflicting views of issues of course; combination of situational awareness to understand issues and positions courses. In the implementation of integrated education of higher education in the curriculum, the curriculum is to contact the students experience, practical experience and effective way of all abilities.

3.3 Strengthening Teacher Education

The teacher is teaching "academic" executor, therefore, must strengthen the teacher education. On teachers education must first set up the teacher "teaching and learning" the idea, to realize the importance of university teaching, the university teaching as a academic to treat. Next, want to teach students to understand the method, move into the students know the existing knowledge and experience, in the study hope to get the knowledge and experience, so as to determine the need to adopt the teaching methods. Want to teach the use of knowledge production teaching method, using proper teaching method to guide the students to learn more. Good teaching method can help. Help students to knowledge into 'line of internal and external accumulation, collect reached the expected teaching goal. In addition, in the education of teachers to strengthen the communication between scholars, form community.

3.4 Knowledge-Sharing Platform for Building Higher Education

Knowledge sharing, refers to the organization or team of employees through various channels of knowledge exchange and discussion of the process of knowledge transfer in the transfer of knowledge, and expands knowledge of the use value. Topics include:

(1) Building the University network resources platform. Platform network resources in colleges and universities in various fields of academics and teachers can communicate, you can write your own experiences through the blog. Peers for evaluation, you can upload teaching resources for other teachers to download information in order to promote the sharing of resources of University Teachers.
(2) The construction platform for scholars. Growth in the logic of scientific knowledge is a special form of scientific thinking and innovative use of the results of community building platform for scholars to exchange space for teachers to promote the growth of scientific knowledge.

References

1. Boyer, E.: Scholarship Reconsidered (1990)
2. Boyer, E.-L.: Speech on education reform, The United States, Tu Yan State, Fang Tong translation. Education Science Press, Beijing (2002)
3. Wang, Y.J.: American higher education development and reform. People's Education Press (2008)
4. Richard, M.: The Scholarship of Teaching (2009)

5. Borko, H., Putnam, P.T.: Learning to teach. In: Berliner, D.C., et al. (eds.) Handbook of Educational Psychology, pp. 673–709. Simon& Schuster Macmillan (1996)
6. Tagg, J.: From teaching to learning: A new paradigm for Undergraduate education. Change 27(6), 13–25 (2008)
7. Weimmer: Teaching on solid ground: Using scholarship to improve practice, San Francisco, vol. 54 (1996)
8. Mezirow: Transformative dimensions of adult learning. San Francisco, vol. 23 (2010)
9. Ceta, K.: Exploring the scholarship of teaching. The Journal of Higher Education 71(4), 476–495 (2009)
10. Trigwel, K.: Scholarship of Teaching:higher education research and development, vol. (2) (2009)

Multi-dimension System of Imbarking Education in Colleges and Universities

YinLin Wu, Jing Tan, Yanan Li, and Mingxi Zhang

Qinggong College, Hebei United University, Tangshan 063009, China
18931571616@189.cn

Abstract. Imbarking education, as an important notion in current situation , has attracted more and more attention in the field of education. The relate d practical and theoretical studies increase rapidly in the higher education of China and yet , more effective imbarking education call s for the const ruction of a multi-dimension educational system taking into consideration the educational goal, the target educatees, the matching disciplines and the educational plat form.

Keywords: college imbarking education, system of imbarking education, platform of imbar king education.

1 Introduction

With higher education from elite education to mass education, college students at this stage difficult employment as a prominent social problem in China. The expert analysis, economic growth does not automatically bring about maximum employment, and only hope in the economic and social development in the growing status and role of higher education can make a difference. For the economic and social development, higher education must be to further deepen reform in all aspects, to "education to entrepreneurship education from employment," clearly entrepreneurship education and academic education and vocational education have the same status, strengthen education and awareness of entrepreneurship students start Ability to effectively solve the social problems Graduates Employment, which is cultivating innovative talents, building an innovative country's urgent need for the national strategy.

2 The Clear Purpose of Entrepreneurship Education

Actively guide students to change their concept of employment, and enhance innovation and entrepreneurship, to enable students to realize their own business is the social progress, the value of their own survival and self-actualization needs, a higher level of employment, students should also be strengthened against the risk of update their knowledge, resource integration, strategic planning and information resources development consciousness.

Entrepreneurial activity related to all aspects of knowledge. The production of a business from scratch and after the development process, involving many aspects,

C. Liu, J. Chang, and A. Yang (Eds.): ICICA 2011, Part I, CCIS 243, pp. 366–371, 2011.

including the idea of screening, market research, feasibility studies, business start, business preparation, marketing analysis, business growth and so on. Each link has a lot to learn, but also have a lot of exploration and summary of previous experience. These are the precious wealth of the entrepreneur. If the entrepreneur to prepare well in advance of knowledge is bound to accelerate the entrepreneurial process and avoid detours.

Entrepreneurship is the entrepreneur must have the basic quality. Generally include professional competence, management ability and comprehensive skills. The basis of professional competence is the business, including the professional ability and professional ability to innovate. Management capability is the key entrepreneurs, including an analysis of judgments, decision making, management, financial management capacity. Social integration capability is the guarantee business, including public relations, adaptability, team player, and entrepreneurs.

3 Build a Sound System of Entrepreneurship Education

Take the path of production and research integration of entrepreneurship education, both economic and social development of modern higher education requests, but also the entrepreneurial spirit of Higher Education and practical ability with people's needs. First, we must make full use of campus resources, building business practice base or guide students into the business entrepreneurs to open business practice base. The second is to start in the campus demonstration bases, such as the establishment of college students venture alliances, the establishment of the student body's educational consulting business, media companies and other entities to develop entrepreneurial management knowledge entrepreneurs. Third, through the University Student Association, the use of research laboratories to enable students to understand the frontier shows sophisticated equipment, showcase the latest scientific research, participate in teacher research, and enhance the practical ability of college students venture. Fourth, community college students based within the contact through community enterprises, and gradually establish characteristics consistent with community development needs and business practices for entrepreneurship education practice base.

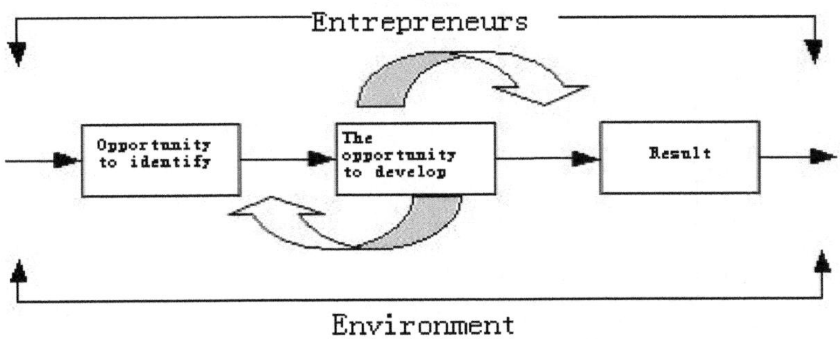

4 Improve the Education System of the Security System Entrepreneurship

Promote entrepreneurship education should be a corresponding system of guarantees. Such as the development policy of the development of entrepreneurship education teachers to encourage teachers to set up business education courses, research and education methods in order to expedite the pace of building entrepreneurship education teachers; revised school management approach, students can participate in various entrepreneurship education activities, elective courses and related business suspension , create the conditions for early graduation and other business; set practical lesson credits, relaxing credit restrictions to allow early graduation, delay graduation, are promoting entrepreneurship education and encourages students to start the effective policies, encouraging college students venture will help create a campus atmosphere; the establishment of various forms of entrepreneurship education funds can be thought of entrepreneurship education and teaching, scientific research, entrepreneurial support business growth.

4.1 Object Dimensions and Composition of Entrepreneurship Education System

According to different levels of entrepreneurship education goals, education, entrepreneurship education can include different objects: First, students learn and understand the business, the second is to develop entrepreneurial quality, and spirit and ability of students, the three enterprises with the ability to cultivate the entrepreneurial talent - of entrepreneurship education in different objects have different training requirements. Venture an indifference curve as follows:

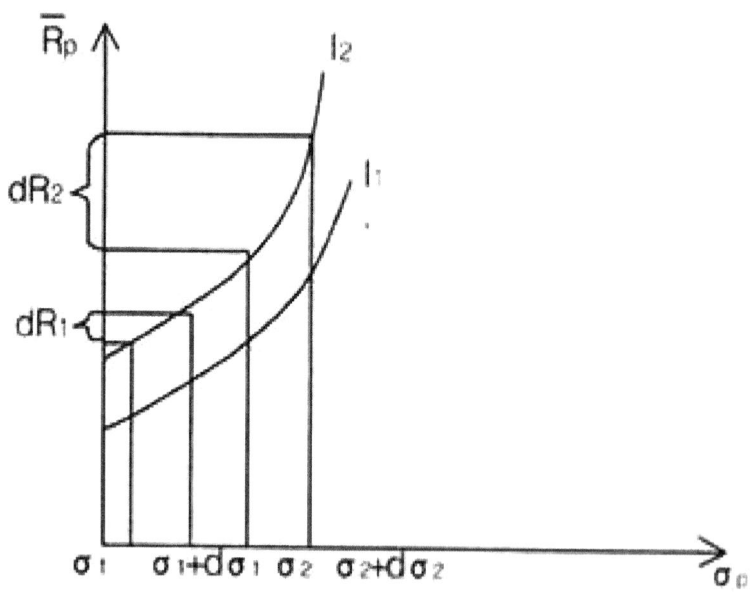

Fig. 1. Indifference curve

The first level of entrepreneurship education for the object, mainly spread basic knowledge of business, and creates a business atmosphere for the teaching objectives. Concrete can be set up within the school's entrepreneurship education compulsory and elective courses, conduct business seminars, student and other business practices, universal business knowledge, understand the business process. At the same time be aware of market economy development for the enterprise opportunities and challenges, to develop business-based skills, fostering entrepreneurial culture. The second level of entrepreneurship education for the object, mainly to develop students awareness of entrepreneurship and entrepreneurial spirit of the teaching objectives, counseling students to participate in business plan, organize entrepreneurs salon, participate in business simulation training, attend training classes and other entrepreneurs, entrepreneurs, students the habit of thinking, improve their innovative spirit, teamwork, professionalism, and with the increase of students in grades education efforts to increase this, so have the entrepreneurial personality traits. For a small number of third level students who have established business needs to start a business, train future entrepreneurs for the teaching objectives. A "project access, the whole truth management, business incubators, regular assessment," the form of entrepreneurship education through professional education site for students and entrepreneurial business start-up capital, start trying to actively promote the college students, fully support the entrepreneurial team, the business guide to success with business needs students to help them become the de facto entrepreneurs.

4.2 Entrepreneurship Education Platform Dimensions and Composition System

Any implementation of entrepreneurship education is inseparable from a certain platform support; the essential has three platforms, namely, education, entrepreneurship education and research platform for entrepreneurship education and practice of event management platform, business services, and education and guidance platform.

Entrepreneurship education in primary education and research platform for entrepreneurship education to complete the theoretical study and practical teaching management, specifically the development of entrepreneurship courses and professors, students, employability and entrepreneurial law entrepreneurship education research, teacher introduction, training and management. Entrepreneurship education and practice of event management platform is based on student management of the main body. Again, business services, education and protection platform. Entrepreneurship education and protection of the main platform for entrepreneurs to provide business information exchange, business advice and guidance, to provide venture capital fund, established to help achieve business goals, and business advice and guidance provided during the operation.

Tab Impact of the entrepreneurs' shareholding on the entrepreneurial performance						
Dependent	Model 5			Model 6		
variable	ROA	Mprofit	Growth	ROA	Mprofit	Growth
C	0.1359	0.4399	3.5417	0.1384	0.4546	3.9894
	(6.0052)	(16.3652)	(3.9732)	(5.8758)	16.4587)	(3.8310)
Gleve	-0.1050	-0.2071	-2.4484	-0.1115	-0.2166	-2.4241
	(-2.748)	(-4.2415)	(-1.1561	(-2.9021	(-4.3559	(-1.1159)
Assturn	0.0405	-0.0570	0.0171	0.0407	-0.0562	0.0334
	(5.1328)	(-7.8806)	0.0754	(5.0931)	(-7.7996	(0.1509)
Cfa	0.0849	0.0737	-6.5638	0.0919	0.0845	-6.5725
	(1.9236)	(1.6533)	(-1.3307)	(2.0664)	(1.8662)	(-1.3472)
Life	-0.0052	-0.0094	-0.0575	-0.0575	-0.0090	-0.0500
	-1.7127	-2.3690	-0.3427	-1.6484	-2.1671	-0.2902
EnFirst	0.0486	0.0689	-0.3256			
	(2.6885)	(3.2849)	(-0.5020)			
Enshare				0.0708	0.0712	-1.6752
				(1.9551)	(1.7654)	(-1.7036)
Adj-R2	0.1796	0.2450	0.0981	0.1718	0.2258	01.030

5 Summary

Entrepreneurship education has become an important part of reform of higher education, colleges and universities is a general trend of Enterprise Education. Entrepreneurship education is a comprehensive systems engineering, the purpose must be clear, the goals set under the premise of integrating internal and external resources, the establishment of multi-level, comprehensive entrepreneurship education system to ensure that entrepreneurship education in a good educational environment carried out in a planned way to develop entrepreneurial spirit and entrepreneurship students and business entrepreneurs business managers.

References

1. Burton, R.: Clark book, Building Entrepreneurial Universities: organizational restructuring of the way. People's Education Publishing House (2003)
2. St with Henry · Ezra: University of the global knowledge economy. Jiangxi Education Press (1999)
3. Wang, P.: British Universities and Entrepreneurship Education. Academia Press (2009)

4. Burton, R.: University of continuous change - new cases of Entrepreneurial Universities and the new concept. People's Education Press (2008)
5. Society For Scientific the``entrepreneurial university ecosystem of entrepreneurship". Higher Education Research (2009)
6. Yu, G.H.: Strengthens awareness of entrepreneurship research university Modern Education Science: Higher Education Research, vol. (004), pp. 15–153 (2009)
7. Song, Z.H., Liu, Q.G.: Study undertaking education. Chinese Adults Education (23), 78–79 (2009)
8. Muka, R.J.: Comparative research on macro—structures of online higher education between China and America. Open Education Research (4), 107–112 (2009) (in Chinese)
9. Yin, B.S.: Comparative research of online course between China and the United States:a comparative study between Beijing Normal University and University of New Mexico. Open Education Research (6), 104–110 (2009) (in Chinese)
10. Qiao, Q.: American distance higher education: characteristics and experience. China Distance Education (10), 73–78 (2009) (in Chinese)

Synthesized Reform Practice Links of Mechanical Basis Course Group for Applied-Typed College Students

Liyan Feng, Chunguang Lu, and Yingfei Gao

College of Mechanical Engineering, Hebei United University, Tangshan, Hebei, 063009, China
fengliyan65@126.com, jxlcg@heuu.edu.cn, breads@163.com

Abstract. With the renewal of course contents, as well as the rising demand of cultivating college students' knowledge, ability and quality, the original practice link already can not adapt to the need of current educational reform. To train student's the overall design ability and the innovative design ability, the synthesized reform to practice links of mechanical foundation curriculum group including "Theory of Machines and Mechanisms", "Machines Design" and "Mechanical Creative Design" was carried on. Its reform situation and implementing effects on several aspects, such as curriculum design, experimental teaching, extra-curricular technical creative design is introduced. The curriculum design after reform integrated the innovating design of whole scheme, design and analysis of the mechanism, structure design of the parts together, the 3D parametric model and 2D parametric drawing were constructed directly. Moreover, the actual design case is presented.

Keywords: Curriculum Group, Experimental Teaching, Curriculum Design, Extra-curricular Creative Design.

1 Introduction

Applied-typed college students is an education type which develops when higher education transits from elite education to popular education[1], it emphasizes the teaching of basic and systematic theories as well as the training of overall abilities[2].

"Theory of Machines and Mechanisms", "Mechanical Design", and "Mechanical Creative Design" are main courses for college students of mechanics major, they are basic but important courses and are closely associated with engineering as well. They can also strengthen the abilities for designing, engineering consciousness and creation. It's in no circumstance that we should build up the reform of the practical links for the basic mechanic courses. With a view to the main link of needs for engineering training, we consider the practical solutions for experimental teaching, curriculum design and innovation design, the details are in the followings.

2 Reform of Curriculum Design

Curriculum Design is a bridge from knowledge to power; it's a most important link of practical teaching.

C. Liu, J. Chang, and A. Yang (Eds.): ICICA 2011, Part I, CCIS 243, pp. 372–378, 2011.

"Theory of Machines and Mechanisms Curriculum Design" and "Mechanical Designing Curriculum Design" have been separated from each other for quite a long time, not only the content of the course but also attention and time, we just set one week for the former and three weeks for the latter. Besides, the tasks of each course are relatively independent. For example, we chose air piston compressor, power press and slotting machine as typical subjects for design and analysis. We design their planar linkage, flywheel, gear mechanism, and cam mechanism. But for the Mechanical Designing Curriculum Design, we focus on the speed reducers, designing the part drawing of axes, gears, and boxes, as well as the assembly drawing of the speed reducer [4].

We paid too much attention to training the abilities of calculating, basic skills of drawing, which greatly benefit the strength of the main knowledge point of the course. But this way that the students study and refer to data in schedule does no good to developing the student's creation sense. To meet the concept of the modern machinery design, Curriculum Design focuses on the sixth term, students are required to have an overall design of the machine selecting one from packing machine, shaping machine, power press and slotting machine, etc.

For view of the system, first of all, we design the kinetic scheme of the executed portions, select the prime mover, determine the scheme of the mechanism gearing, then we write computer programs for the design, the analysis, and the calculation of the switch mechanism, using the Adams software to do the work of the assembly organization. Finally, we would check strength and design the structure of the key parts, here, AutoCAD, Pro/E are recommended to do the two and three-dimensional design. And write the instruction of the overall design.

As a result, mechanism design, design of component parts, creation and plan determination being combined into an integrated design, this reform can have the students overall trained on the mechanical design, and this will surely benefit them a lot.

For example, We want to design a pair of gear transmission, firstly, input their transmission ratio, power, speed and operating conditions; secondly, make contact strength and bending strength calculation automatically, obtain basic parameters such as teeth, modulus, etc; thirdly, calculate the gear geometry dimensions; finally, VB and PRO/E will exchange data using the GATEWAY controls, obtain the 3d parametric modeling and 2d working drawing.

2.1 Strength Checking of Spiral Bevel Gear

ISO10300 C method has been used to check strength. We have derived contact stress and bending stress calculation formula.

2.1.1 Gear Surface Contact Fatigue Strength

The calculation standard of gear surface contact fatigue strength is: the contact stress σ_H is less than or equal to allowable contact stress $[\sigma_H]$, that is

$$\sigma_H = Z_{M\_B} Z_H Z_E Z_{LS} Z_\beta Z_K \sqrt{F_{mt}(1+\cos\delta_2/u\cos\delta_1)/d_{v1}l_b}\sqrt{K_A K_V K_{H\beta} K_{H\alpha}} \le [\sigma_H] = \frac{\sigma_{H\lim} Z_{NT} Z_X Z_L Z_R Z_V Z_W}{S_{H\lim}} \quad (1)$$

In the equation above, F_{mt} is defined as tangent force exerted midpoint of gear width; d_{v1} is defined as pitch diameter of Equivalent pinion; l_b is defined as the length of contact line on gear tooth; u is transmission ratio; δ_1、δ_2 are defined as angles at reference con of two meshing gears; $\sigma_{H\lim}$ is defined as contact fatigue limit ;the rest are coefficients used in contact strength.

2.1.2 Gear Bottom Bend Fatigue Strength

The calculation standard of gear bottom bend fatigue strength is : the bending stress σ_F is less than or equal to allowable bending stress $[\sigma_F]$,that is

$$\sigma_F = \frac{F_{mt} m_{mt} Y_{K\_C}}{b m_{et}^2 Y_j} K_A K_V K_{F\beta} K_{F\alpha} \le [\sigma_F] = \frac{\sigma_{F\lim} Y_{ST} Y_{NT} Y_{\delta relT} Y_{RrelT} Y_x}{S_{F\min}} \quad (2)$$

In the equation above, $\sigma_{F\lim}$ is defined as bending fatigue limit; F_{mt} is tangent force exerted midpoint of gear width; m_{mt} is defined as transverse modulus at the midpoint of gear width; b is effective width;the rest are coefficients used in bending strength.

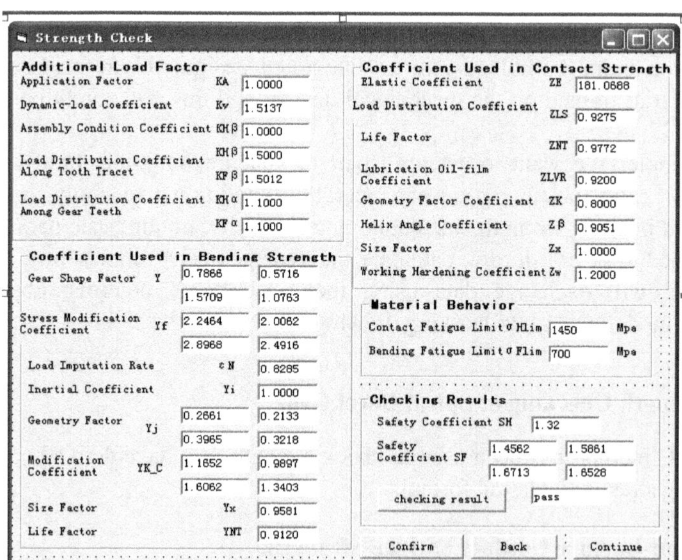

Fig. 1. Strength computation

For two meshing gears, the first step is to check the contact strength, then check the bending strength for pinion's concave and convex, finally, check the bending strengths for the larger one's concave and convex. Strength checking interface has been shown in fig. 1.

2.2 Geometrical Dimensions Calculation

To meet the needs of designing the working drawing, choosing the cutting dish, and calculating strength, we calculate four kinds of parameters: the basic dimensions, tooth width midpoint parameters, transverse parameters of the equivalent gears, and normal parameters of the equivalent gears.

A pair of spiral bevel gear used on MU train can be cited as a typical example. Confined to the length of the thesis, only the basic dimensions and main results of the gears are listed in Table 1.

Table 1. Gear's Main Parameters

Mean Spiral Angle $\beta_m = 35^\circ$	Normal Pressure Angle $\alpha_n = 20^\circ$	Transverse Module of Gear m_t =9.2mm	Addendum Coefficient h_a^* =0.85	Clearance Coefficient c^* =0.188

Gear	Helix Hand	Number of Teeth	Adde-ndum	Dede-ndum	Pitch Angle	Root Angle	Face Angle	Outside Diameter
pinion	Left	22	10.84	6.54	21°48"	20°25"	24°26"	222.52
gearwheel	Right	55	4.80	12.56	68°12"	65°33"	69°34"	509.57

2.3 Parameterization Drawing

The 3D geometry model is constructed according to its actual size based on PRO/E, the 2D Parameterization drawing based on AutoCAD platform is obtained directly. The mentioned above gearwheel's 3D and 2D working drawing have been shown in fig. 2 and fig. 3 respectively.

Fig. 2. The gearwheel's 3D model

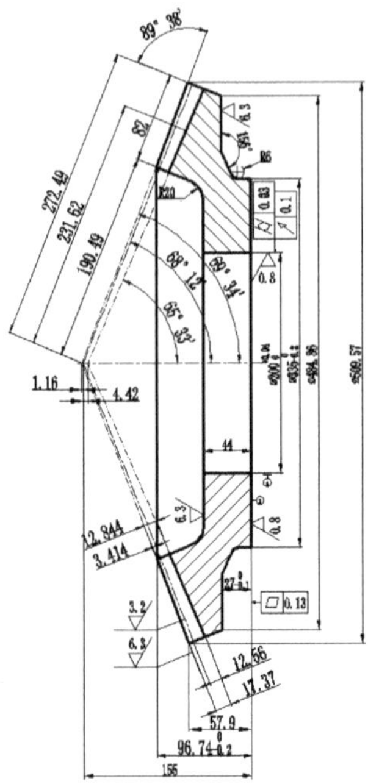

Fig. 3. The gearwheel's 2D drawing

From what is said above, it is convenient for designer to do many tasks for gear, including strength check, geometric parameter design and calculation, parameterized drawing, which greatly reduces the design processing cycle and improves design precision.

3 Experimental Teaching Reform

3.1 Construction of the Experimental Course

For the overall of the special training, in charge of training the integrated ability and innovation ability, we build the new experimental system of the basic mechanical courses and have a major reform of the content of the experiment; improving and adding something new into the experiment, there are required experiments and optional experiments for the students. This will reduce the evincive and demonstrating experiment, but increase comprehensive designing and research experiment.

3.2 Building up Special Experiments

3.2.1 Combinational Creation Design of Shafting

We start the experiment called combinational creation design of shafting in order to make the students master the key of the structure design of shafting. The experiment use modular design principle which divides step shafts into some modules according to different elements of structures, and change the categories and assembly position of the modules, in this way, we can get kinds of structural structure design plan of shafts.

3.2.2 Synthesized and Innovational Experiment

For some experiment of design on mechanism and machines, assignment will be assigned by teachers or decided by students themselves, students will design the mechanism kinetic scheme creatively by their own. This demands the students check their titles in groups according to their subjects, and work out a detailed plan of their designs, they are allowed to use the equipment in the lab to test their plan and get a result of the correctness and feasibility.

One of the most creative design titles is listed below.

Demands: Please design a two-way adding-press mechanism of a packing machine, when tightening the packet, the up-actuator and down-actuator should approach each other in a line in synchronism. In other words, when the up-actuator movers down, the down one should move up meanwhile, after packing, the two actuators should move backward.

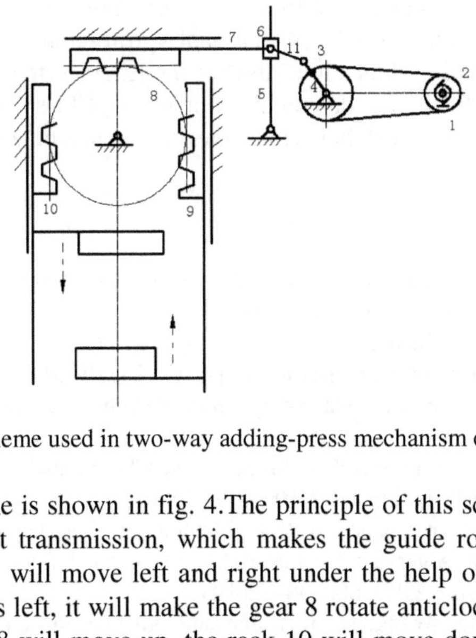

Fig. 4. Reference scheme used in two-way adding-press mechanism of a packing machine

A reference scheme is shown in fig. 4.The principle of this scheme is like this, the motor 1 drives a belt transmission, which makes the guide rod 5 moves back and forth, the rack gear 7 will move left and right under the help of the slipper 6. When the rack gear 7 moves left, it will make the gear 8 rotate anticlockwise. Rack 9 which is meshed with gear 8 will move up, the rack 10 will move down at the same time , which just finishes the action of packing, when the rack 7 move right, this will complete the action of loosing.

4 Some Extra-Curricular Technical Innovation Design

Based on the college experiment centre and the engineering training centre, we shall launch some technical innovation design. So we hold the annual innovation design competition regularly on the entire school. More and more are taking part in it, and the qualities of the works are becoming better, too.

In recent years, 39 innovation design works have won the provincial level prize, 3 have been listed on the national invention patent, and a lot of works won the national utility model patent. Meanwhile, 5 works won the first prize in Hebei innovation design; 12 works won the second prize.

In the process of the innovation design, students experienced the many procedures including selection of the topic, plan of the design, fabrication of the real objects, oral defense in scene, which teach students much knowledge that they can't get from the books, this guarantees the logicality and systematization of the subjects, the students improve themselves a lot in consulting and writing, the comprehensive abilities of design, cooperation, the abilities to solve practical problems, hands-on abilities and so on.

5 Implementing Effects

After years of reform practice, the didactic instruction have disappeared instead, the building of the autonomous study mode is promoted. Abilities of self-study, examination skills, and innovation abilities are improved overall. "Theory of Machines and Mechanisms" and "Mechanical Designing" of our school have been judged as the provincial fine course for two terms; in our school, "mechanical design manufacturing and automation" is national professional characteristics. "The Research of the Innovation Education Mode of the Engineering College Students" and "Reform of the Mechanic Fundamental Courses on Class Teaching and Practical Links" won the third prize in Hebei province excellent teaching achievements.

References

1. Wang, L.: Search Reform of the Applied-typed College Students Classroom Teaching. Search of Education, 64–65 (January 2004)
2. Ge, W.: Start s New Idea to Fabricate the National Great Course of the Principle of Mechanism. Education of University in China, 10–12 (July 2005)
3. Li, H.: On Construction of the University courses. Higher Education Press in Jiangsu, 73–74 (June 2006)
4. Feng, L., Gao, Q.: How to Search and Practice the Classroom Teaching of the Principle of Mechanics. University Forum., 108–109 (May 2008)
5. Xu, Y., Watanabe, K.: Classification Method of Coupler Curves of Nongrashof Mechanisms by an Algebraic Characteristic. Mechanical Science and Technology for Aerospace Engineering 23(5), 602–604 (2004)
6. Wang, J., Zhang, G., Wang, B.: Research and practice on "quality project" of quality construction of machinery basic courses. China Modern Educational Equipment 1, 103–105 (2011)
7. Wang, W., Wang, D., Shen, A.: Reform and Exploration of the Mechanical and Electronic Engineering Practice Teaching System Based on CDIO Training Model. Journal of ANHUI Normal of University 33(2), 136–138 (2010)
8. Zhang, C.: Mechanical Creative Design. Mechanical Industry Press (2010)
9. Shao, L.: Research and Development on Basic Courses Network Teaching System of Mechanics Engineering Speciality. Southeast University (2008)
10. Sun, Z., Shan, H., Zhuang, Y.: Reforming the Course Exercise of Machine Theory to Improve Students' Innovation Ability, vol. 11, pp. 98–99 (2007)

The Survey on the Teaching Methods of Mathematics Teachers from High Schools in Handan

Zhang Yanxia and Yang Cangyu

Handan College, Department of Mathematics, Handan, Hebei, China
{hdxyzyx,yangcangyu}@163.com

Abstract. The ways of teaching is the dynamic detail of the methods of teaching. In the essay, the author analyzed the reasons and necessities for changing the ways of teaching as well as the present situation with questionnaire and interview. The result shows that the ways of learning has gradually shifted to cooperative discussion and research which is badly needed. Meanwhile, the teachers' capability on teaching has been improved but they still need the ability requested by the new curriculum. According to the necessities for changing the ways of teaching, the objective of class should be the students' psychological acquisition, new recognition, self-improvement and self development. The essay is based on the experiences of teaching in Handan and provides reference to the ways of teaching.

Keywords: The city of Handan, Mathematics curriculum criteria, Mathematics classroom, Teaching methods, Conversion.

1 Introduction

With the continuous development of education reform as well as the advent of High School Mathematics Curriculum Criteria, and Mathematics Curriculum Criteria in Compulsory Education, the method of teaching is changing from time to time. In this essay, the author is to discuss the changing of mathematics class teaching method based on the teaching and learning in some high schools in Handan.

2 Definition of Teaching Method

So far, different recognitions on methods of teaching have resulted in different definitions. In common sense, teaching method is the dynamic detail of the teaching manner, such as explanation, elaboration and presentation. It is not an independent teaching task but the one with particular method. A teaching method contains different ways and so does the teaching way. In detail, teaching method is the application of various manners as well as the practice of teaching and learning. [1]

C. Liu, J. Chang, and A. Yang (Eds.): ICICA 2011, Part I, CCIS 243, pp. 379–386, 2011.

3 A Survey on Class Teaching Methods Carried Out among High Schools and the Result Analysis

3.1 Questionnaires on Students

Purpose and the Structure of the Questionnaire. The survey is carried out among the students from Grade 7 to 9 to know the students' satisfactory on teachers' teaching, to apprehend the actual teaching methods and provide suggestions to the teaching method research based on the student's advice.

There are 8 questions in the questionnaire, among which questions 1, 3, 4 are about the students' preferred teaching methods and their ways of learning, 3, 5, 6 are the survey on the teachers' teaching, 7 is on their opinions on their marks, and 8 is on the students' suggestions on teaching.

Result and Analysis. There are 272 students participated in the survey and 272 questionnaires are collected back.

Q1: What kind of Mathematics class do you prefer?

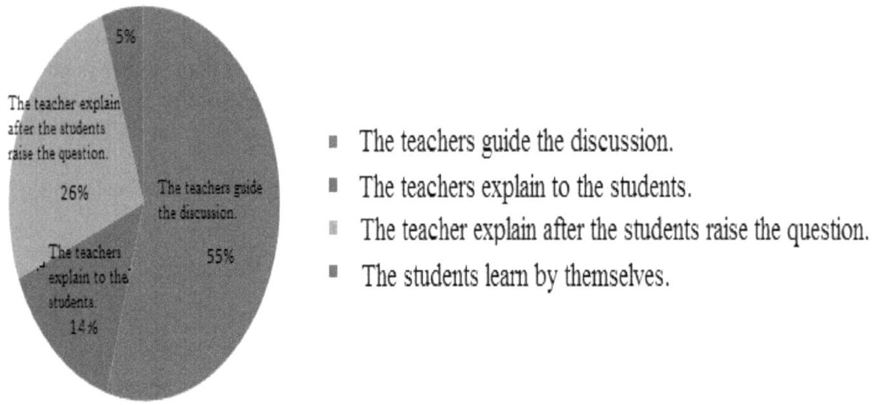

The result shows that a majority of students like their teachers to guide them during the discussion or explain the questions raised by the students after they learn by themselves. They will become increasingly interested in mathematics once they are to search for the ways of learning independently and enjoy the success. Meanwhile, the teaching is more importance-focused.

According to the feedbacks of Question 2(Which way is easy for you to learn?), 53% of the interviewees agree on the point that they should discuss the question then the teachers explain. 30% suggest the teachers' explanation come before their discussion, which shows the students' expectations on class discussion. As for Question 4(Do you often discuss with your classmates in class?), 62 % say that they sometimes discuss in mathematics class., which proves the importance of cooperative discussion.

Q3: As a teacher, how do you response when some students make mistakes in the same exercise?

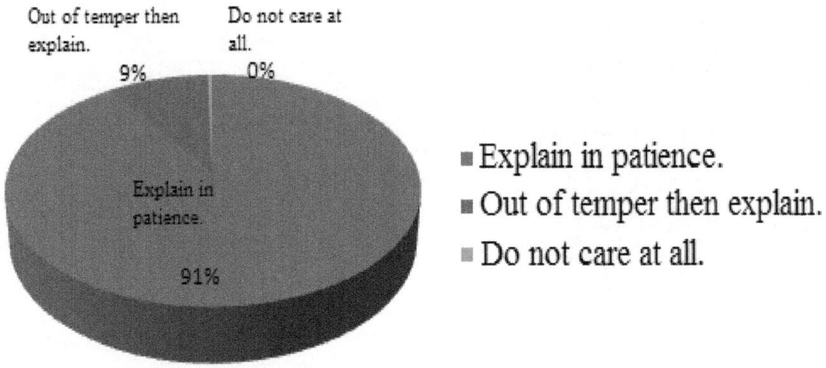

Judging from the diagram, what most of the teachers do complies with the initiative of new curriculum criteria, which is to study and discuss the questions together with the students.

For Question 6(How does your teacher teach the content in the textbook?), 63% of the students think that the teachers should fully take advantage of both the curriculum and extra-curriculum resources, adjust the teaching content and enrich the teaching resources, while 35% agree that the teachers should adjust, omit and add some contents. However, only 2% take the text books as professional. As a result, most of the teachers are able to adjust and enrich the teaching contents while the rest need improvement.

Q7: Among all the following issues, which one do you think impact the result most?

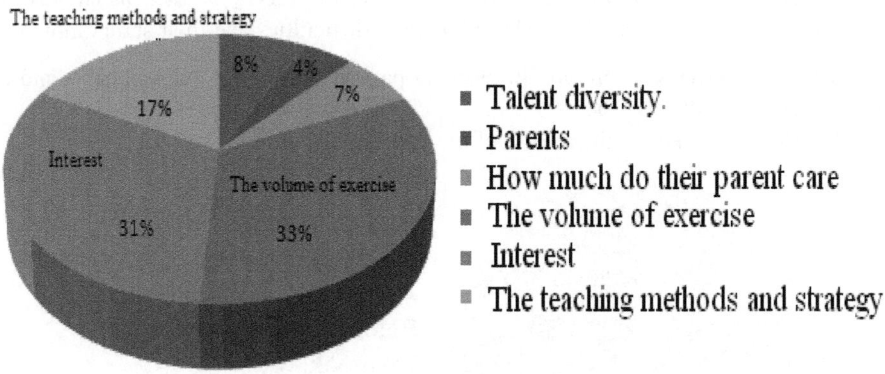

According to the diagram, a lot of students think that personal interest and the teachers' teaching method and strategy affect their study a lot. Therefore, they will make progress on their mathematics when their teachers adopt the teaching manners and strategy in the perspective of the students.

Q8: Do you have any suggestion on your mathematics teaching? This is an open question. The results are as follows:

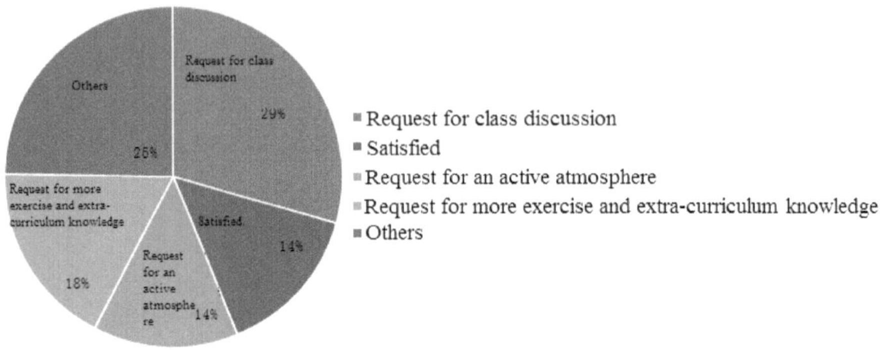

As reference to the chart, 43% of the students hope to improve the teaching methods, such as to provide an active atmosphere and discussion during class. In this way, the teachers should be dedicated on the change of teaching methods so as to meet the requirements of new curriculum and the students.

3.2 Questionnaires on Teachers

Purpose and the Structure of the Questionnaire. The survey is carried out among the teachers from Grade 7 to 9 to know their recognition on the necessity of the change of teaching methods and their ways of teaching, which helps to provide reference to the research on the mathematics teaching.

There are 10 questions in the questionnaire. Questions 1 and 4 are on their recognitions on the importance of the teaching method in the perspective of new curriculum concept. Questions 2, 5, 6, 7 and 8 are the survey on their usual ways of teaching. Question 3, 9 and 10 are based on their difficulties and their self comments.

Result and Analysis. There are 40 teachers participated in the questionnaire and all the surveys are collected back.

Q1: What is the key to the reform of the curriculum?

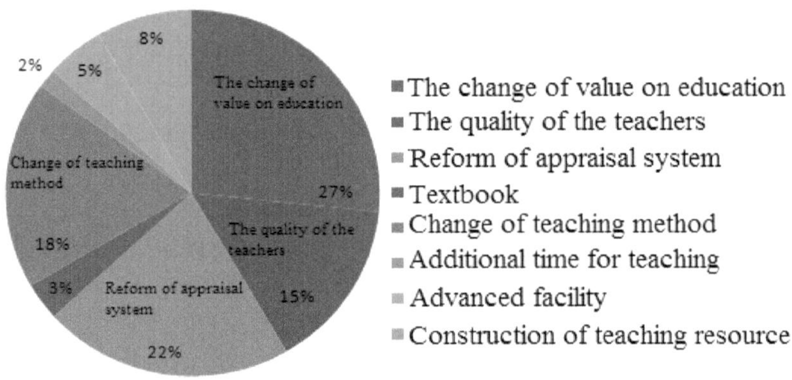

Judging from the charter, most of them think that the keys to the reform are the change of education ideas, reform of appraisal system, improvement of the teaching method and the character of the teachers themselves.

As far as the answers to Question 4(Does the way of teaching impact the learning?), 42% say that the ways of teaching impact their methods of learning while 58% think it impacts to some extent. Nobody do not think that the ways of teaching impact their learning at all, which shows the way of teaching is important and more attention should be paid on it.

Q3: What impacts the quality of teaching?

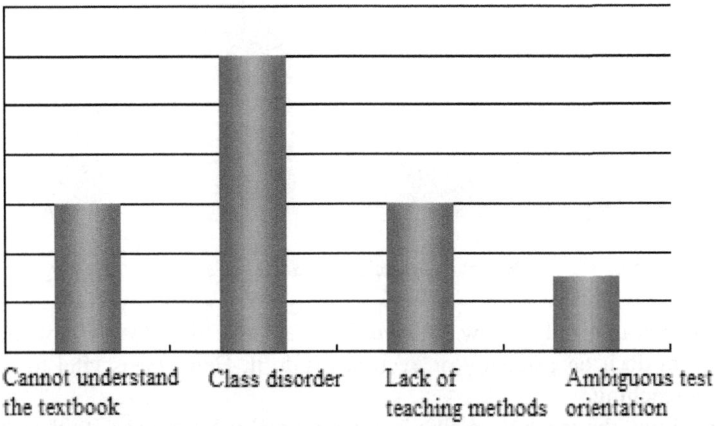

The issue that impacts the quality of teaching is the disorder of class.

According to the feedbacks of Question 9(Which ability do you need?), there are 3 skills that need improvement: efficient class organization, multimedia teaching and teaching adjustment according to the students., on which the teachers need to improve according the new curriculum.

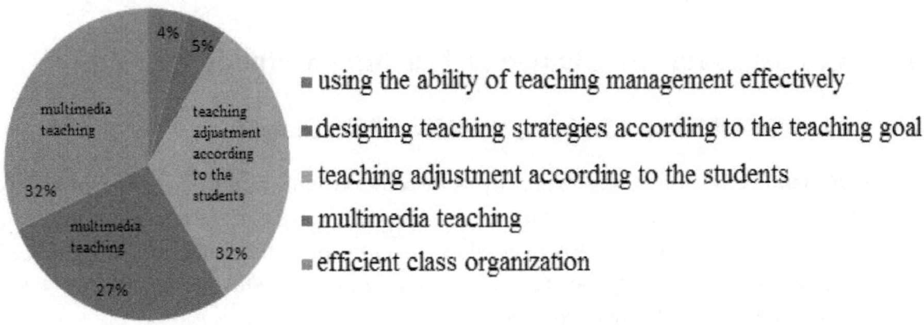

On Question 10(Are you satisfied with your teaching?), most of the teachers are satisfied with their ways of teaching which a few think their ways should be improved.

Q6: The new curriculum idea recommends the ways of learning such as spontaneous research and teamwork, have you put them into practice?

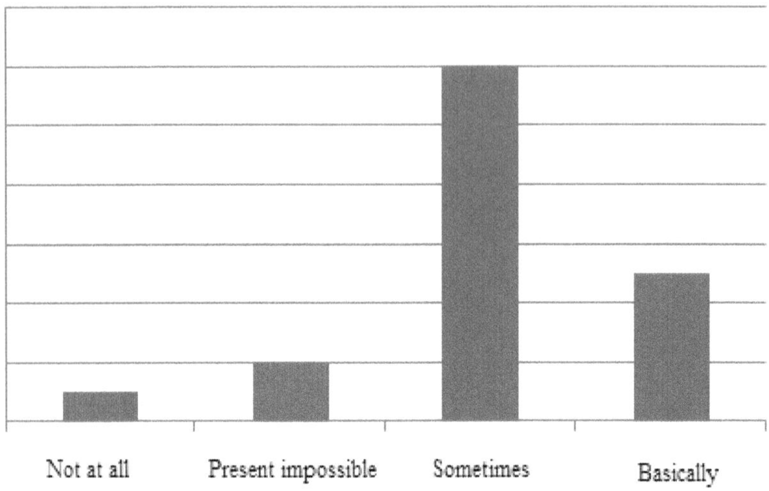

It is obvious that only a few teachers have achieve the idea of new curriculum. Most of them do it occasionally or even never do it. Hence, it is vital to change the methods of teaching.

For one thing, the teaching methods have gradually complied with the concepts of new curriculum since its establishment. The ways of learning has been changed and it is the same with the teaching methods; on the other, some teachers still do not possess all the abilities requested by new curriculum, which can not meet the students' desire for class discussion re. As a result, great efforts should be put into the change of teaching methods though the new curriculum has been accepted by the mass.

4 Proposals for the Change of Teaching Methods

4.1 The Necessities for Changing the Ways of Teaching[2]

Social Reason. Nowadays, the economy is developed with rapid pace. The model is shifted from extensive one into intensive one. During the transitional period, talents of innovation are badly needed. However, it is a shame that the education falls behind the development of economy because the people educated with the traditional ways cannot meet the request of modern times.

School Reason. There are so many issues in education. In compulsory education, the students are over loaded. As a result, the teachers focus on the training of examination skill, the acquisition of knowledge and the criteria of reference rather than the integrated skill, development of talent and multi ways of exploitation. However, some teachers only like the students, who do as they are told to, while taking the “trouble-makers” and the curiosity for new knowledge as disadvantages, which frustrates their enthusiasm and kills their innovations.

Student Reason. The reform and opening up brings great treasure and the one-child policy slows down the growth of population. However, self-centered consciousness has become the difficulty of compulsory education. In their daily life, they have nothing to worry about, which leads to the fear to stress and lack of curiosity for learning. As a result, they learn according to their own wills. For example, they will learn more on the subject if they are more interested in it. A survey says that 60% focus on their interested lessons and ignore other lessons, while about half of them are not target-oriented in their study. What's more, 20% loss heart in their study.

Requirements on the Teachers according to the New Curriculum. The new curriculum emphasizes the process objective from the perspective of teaching objective. According to the structure and the content of the textbook, it focuses more on the mathematics activity. Meanwhile, the ways of learning are no longer simple imitation and memory. Instead, they should be self-practice and scrupulous research and cooperation.

4.2 Measures for the Change of Teaching Methods

The change of teaching methods help the students to master the ways of learning during the process of self learning. By creating the live atmosphere,the students can experience the formation and application of mathematics knowledge. By focusing on research and discussion, the desire for knowledge will be stimulated. Meanwhile, the teachers should maintain unity and respect diversity.

4.3 Issue That the Teachers Are Confronted

Massive Class. In July, 2007, the Handan Municipal Government has promised that they will make the compulsory education balanced and no optional school across the city in the press. The Mayor, Guo Dajian says that the government should put all the efforts in education and suggests the governments of all levels take it as priority in their work, which has accelerated the development of compulsory education.

In Handan, the development of compulsory has been balanced. However, the volume of a class in some high schools is still beyond the requirement of new curriculum. In this way, it is difficult for the teachers to arrange the students for spontaneous research and discussion in order to finish the teaching objectives.

Entrance Examination-Oriented. It is the most important issue leading to the difficulty. It is hard for some teachers to change their mind because of the pressure brought by the exam. If the appraisal system of entrance examination is result-oriented, the change will still remain difficult.

In one word, the objectives for the change of teaching methods in the perspective of new curriculum are the psychological experience and new ideas gained by the students with the intention of self-improvement and self-development. Therefore, the main role should be the student. New way of class teaching is the dynamics between learning and teaching. During the process, the teachers and students share their views, experiences and knowledge and exchange their feelings and values, which enriches the teaching content. In this case, they can achieve the goal of co-development.

References

1. Wang, B.: Curriculum and Teaching. Higher Education Press, Beijing (2004)
2. Xu, J.: Analysis of the Changing of the Mathematics Teaching Methods of the New Curriculum in Junior High School. Consumer Guide (2) (2009)
3. Ministry of Education: Full-time compulsory education mathematics curriculum standard (experimental manuscript). Beijing Normal University Press, Beijing (2007)
4. Cui, Y.: Effective teaching. East China Normal University Press, Shanghai (2009)
5. Kong, F.: Innovative Instructional Designs for Senior High School Mathematics According to the New Curriculum. Northeast Normal University Press, Changchun (2005)
6. Wang, T., et al.: Teacher Action Handbook on Problem-oriented Learning. East China Normal University Press, Shanghai (2010)
7. Sun, H.: New High School Mathematics Teaching Methods. Central China Normal University Press, Wuhan (2007)
8. Ministry of Education: Into the New Curriculum - the Dialogue and Curriculum Implementers. Beijing Normal University Press, Beijing (2002)
9. Zhang, D., Song, N.: Introduction to Mathematics Education. Higher Education Press, Beijing (2004)
10. Ma, L.: Mastery and Teaching of Primary Mathematics. East China Normal University Press, Shanghai (2011)
11. Zhang, D.: The Mathematics Education I Witnessed. Jiangsu Education Press, Changshu (2009)
12. Zhang, J.: High School Students Self-monitoring Capability on Mathematics. East China Normal University Press, Shanghai (2003)

The Design of Aerobics Course Theory Examination Question Database Management System

Xiuling Ou[1], Baoming Yu[2], and Yukuo Wang[3]

[1] Department of Sports, Tianjin Agricultural University, Tianjin, 300384, China
xiulingou@126.com
[2] Department of Materials, Tianjin University of Sport, Tianjin 300381, China
baoming@163.com
[3] Department of Physical Education, Hebei Normal University of Science & Technology, Qinhuangdao 066004, China
wyk3003@126.com

Abstract. In order to solve the problems of the different scoring standards and low paper validity in the evaluation of aerobics course theoretical knowledge, this paper, combined with the specialty characteristics of aerobics course, proposes the construction of aerobics course theory examination question database management system by adopting SQL Server2000 and Visual Basic 6.0. This system includes five function modules: examination paper generation, examination paper output, examination question database editing, examination question database output and system maintenance, and it realizes the functions such as the batch input of examination questions, the random selection of examination questions and the automatic examination paper generation. Meanwhile, the paper also makes an analysis of the design basis and the treatment of key technical problems of the examination question database management system. This system is simple and practical, with strong expandability, and it improves teachers' working efficiency, improves the quality of teaching evaluation, has important application significance in reducing education investment cost and reusing test question resources, etc.

Keywords: examination question database management system, SQL Server2000, Visual Basic 6.0, aerobics course.

1 Introduction

Examination is an important link in teaching process of aerobic course, which is an important part of college physical education curriculum. In order to make the course evaluation more reasonable, technology practice evaluation and theoretical knowledge evaluation should be carried out according to the course characteristics, but the current questions choosing method of theoretical knowledge evaluation has the problems such as different paper level, different evaluation standard and low stable validity, etc., and this traditional questions choosing method is mainly based on the examiners' experience or subjective judgment, which can not reflect the requirements of course

C. Liu, J. Chang, and A. Yang (Eds.): ICICA 2011, Part I, CCIS 243, pp. 387–393, 2011.

and the examinees' level correctly. In order to improve the examination level and make the reliability, validity, degree of difficulty, differentiation, question type, question amount and coverage of the theory paper reach the requirements of teaching plan and examination syllabus, aerobics theory examination question database must be set up to carry out standardized examination. For this aim, this study tries to design and develop aerobics theory examination question database by adopting SQL Server2000 and Visual Basic 6.0 to improve the quality of aerobics theoretical knowledge examination.

2 The Construction Basis of Examination Question Database

2.1 Decomposing Teaching Goal

The syllabus stipulates the education goal and teaching contents, so constructing examination question database must base on aerobics course syllabus. First, distinguish grade of contents, that is, find out which contents are for general understanding, which contents are for comprehension, which contents are for mastering and application; which should be analyzed, integrated and the knowledge system should be restructured; which could help form the ability of solving practical problems by exercises and practice. Second, make clear connotation grade of the teaching contents, that is, which are basic knowledge, which are important contents, which are for general understanding or for research and discussion, etc.. Decomposing course teaching contents and teaching goal to layers and listing the knowledge units and competence units for mastering are very important. [1]

2.2 Screening Questions and Standardizing Question Types

The examination type is only a form, and the question type is related to the characteristics of the course contents, therefore, the questions should cover all contents and emphasize the key contents to test whether students have complete basic knowledge or have the ability of solving practical problems. Meanwhile, to standardize the paper, the questions should be classified into five types including blank filling, true or false statements, multiple choices, questions with simple answers and questions for argumentation. [2]

2.3 Determining the Weights of Knowledge Units and Competence Units

Determine the percentage of different knowledge units and competence units in the examination questions and the weights of their scoring according to their different position and role in the overall teaching goal, then build up quantity concept of examination keys and make the keys and their distribution not or less influenced by human factors.

2.4 Determining the Degree of Difficulty of Questions and Classifying the Questions According to their Difficulty Grade

Determine the degree of difficulty of each question according to the accumulated examination paper database and the analysis result of score distribution situation of real examination and classify the questions according to their difficulty degree, [3] and this classification is beneficial to the objective and fair evaluation of students' learning situation and makes their examination scores have a normal distribution. (Table 1)

Table 1. Evaluation Weight of Aerobics Course

Classification	Degree of difficulty	General elective course		Specialism course	
		Undergraduate	Junior college education	Undergraduate	Junior college education
Knowledge	Easiest	15	20	10	10
Comprehension	Easy	15	20	15	20
Application	Moderate	40	40	30	35
Analysis	Difficult	20	15	25	20
Integration	Most difficult	10	5	20	15

3 The Design of Examination Question Database Management System Structure

3.1 The Design of Examination Question Database Structure

In the designing of examination question database structure, the examination question database, according to the question type, are classified into five examination question databases: 1) blank filling examination question database;2) true or false statements examination question database;3) multiple choices examination question database;4) questions with simple answers examination question database; 5) questions for argumentation examination question database. Each examination question database has the same database structure consisting of five fields: code (C type, length is 2), contents of question (C type, length is 200), answers of question (C type, length is 200), difficulty of question (N type, length is 1), using marker (C type, length is 1). [4]

The designing aim of code is to give a range to each question and the difficulty of question shows its depth to adapt to the examination requirements to examinees of different levels. [5]It is controlled by a difficulty coefficient (values are 1, 2, 3), which is the important parameter to control the degree of difficulty of questions in selection process; the aim of using marker is to mark the selection times of the question and is designed for the examination questions selection module with the value range between 1 to 9 (among which, 1 represents the examination questions could be selected in the operation of system this time, 2 represents the examination questions selected last time, 3 represents the questions selected and used last time, 4 represents the questions selected the time before last time, and the like).

3.2 Functions Designing

The system is designed by adopting SQL Server2000 and Visual Basic 6.0, and operated by using pull-down menu. It consists of five modules including examination paper generation, examination paper output, examination question database editing, examination question database output and system maintenance, and each module also consists of several sub-modules. [6] (Figure 1)

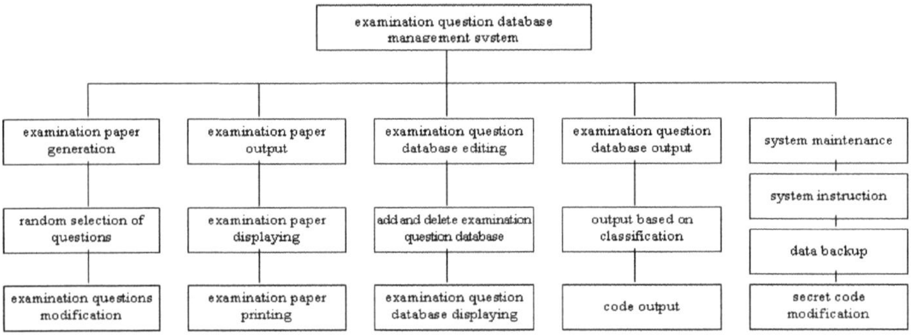

Fig. 1. Basic structure of aerobic theory examination question database

3.2.1 Examination Paper Generation Module

Examination paper generation module is an important function module in examination question database system, which is divided into two sub-modules: random examination questions selection module and examination questions modification module.

Random examination questions selection module. The function of this module is the computer automatically generates papers, that is, it automatically selects relevant examination questions from various examination question database. Every time when this system is started, it can generate several papers, and no repeated questions will appear in these papers. In order to achieve the aim of correct and reasonable selection of examination questions, the examination question database system adopts random question selection method combined with smallest coverage method.[7][8] The designing idea of random question selection method is to construct an algorithm which can generate random number and make it have a normal distribution in the range of examination question database and which can make sure that the repetition rate of questions is very small in the papers generated by using this system twice. The designing idea of the smallest coverage method is that when there are enough questions in the examination question database, the questions selected in the two adjacent (or more) generated papers have as low as possible repetition rate. The method to realize this algorithm is using the function of setting the field of using marker in the database structure of examination question database, in the operation of system it only selects the questions with marker “1”. Next time the system is started, it can reset the marker of the earliest used question as “1” to reset this question to the initial states which means it can be used again. By doing this it achieves the aim of smallest repetition rate.

Modification module. This module mainly makes analysis of the degree of difficulty of paper and deletes unsuitable questions to satisfy the different requirements of different specialty; it can add questions of the same type with the deleted questions to the paper.

3.2.2 Examination Paper Output Module

Examination paper output module can view various kinds of questions automatically generated by computer and view the standard answers. [9] This system can output the generated qualified papers in three ways, that is, the output of screen display, standard paper and file format for easy archiving; in the paper output printing it can realize examination paper arrangement, editing and printing, and the output format includes two kinds: compact format (leaving no blanks for answers in the paper) and non-compact format (leaving blanks for answers in the paper).

3.2.3 Examination Question Database Editing Module

Examination question database editing module is designed to make the examination question database accord with the requirements of education development and have expansibility and reality. Its main function is to realize the functions such as adding, modifying, deleting and consulting the examination question database according to the classification.[10]

3.2.4 Examination Question Database Output Module

This module has the functions of printing examination questions in the examination question database according to the classification or chapters and also has the functions of outputting examination questions by file format for archiving.

3.2.5 System Maintenance Module

The main functions of this module is to provide instructions for users unfamiliar with this system, backup the edited examination question database to soft disk for users, modify secret code, and provide other such special functions.

4 The Treatment of Key Technical Problems in Programming

4.1 System Help Information

A lot of help information is provided in the system, by entering online help system one can get to know the detailed instructions of various operations. Furthermore, there are various simple operation suggestions in every operating window, which can help even the unfamiliar users of this system complete the examination question selection smoothly and get a satisfactory paper. [11]

4.2 Error Processing

Error-processing program is set in the system, and when the user makes improper operation, the system will automatically execute the error-processing program and advise the user to make correct operation.

4.3 System Security

In the designing of this system, according to the high security characteristic of examination paper, the system is set double security function, which means when entering the use of the software and editing the examination question database, the operator must input secret code, and the operator who inputs wrong secret codes can not use this software, which can play the role of securing the examination paper.

5 Conclusions

Aerobics course theory examination question database management system can randomly generate various different aerobic theory examination papers according to different syllabus, different aim and requirements of examination, different educational system and teaching stages. This system can test and give feedback of students' learning effects in site, which expands the functions of examination question database system and achieves the aim of aiding teaching. This system can make quantitative analysis of various quality information indexes of examination questions to complete the selection of good questions and elimination of bad questions and perfect the quality of examination question database continuously. This system successfully uses various functions of SQL Server2000 and makes the users who don't know much about computer can operate and use computer well according to the menu suggestions and reduces teachers' labor intensity and improves working efficiency and improves the quality of examination paper. The development of aerobics course theory examination question database management system provides good conditions for gradually realizing standardized examination, improving examination quality and correctly evaluating teaching quality.

References

1. Wu, C.Q.: Development and Study of Examination question database Computer Management System. Sports Science 1, 57–61 (1998)
2. Ming, H., Sun, B.: The Design and Implementation of General Examination Question Database Management System. Computer Engineering and Design 9, 2185–2188 (2007)
3. Huang, W., Wang, Z.H.: Design of Examination paper generation System of Computer Application Basis Examination question database. Computer Era 4, 52–54 (2008)

4. Yang, Y., Liang, J.Q.: Design and Implementation of a General Examination Question Database System Based on the B/S Scheme. Computer Engineering and Science 4, 143–145, 148 (2009)
5. Zheng, K.D.: Design of a Examination question database and Examination paper Generation System for Foundation Courses of the Computer Science. Electronic Science and Technology 5, 113–114, 121 (2010)
6. Zhang, G.J.: Design and Implementation of Non-paper Test System Based on VB Language. Fujian Computer 11, 147–148 (2010)
7. Weng, Y.L.: Development and Implementation of Test Question Database System Based on Adaptive Technology. Computer Knowledge and Technology 36, 10201–10203 (2010)
8. Wang, H., Chen, Y.: The Development and Study of College Exam Question Bank Management System. Value Engineering 36, 225 (2010)
9. Zeng, X.Y., Li, T.: Development for the General-purpose Test Item Bank Management System. Journal of Changzhou Institute of Technology 6, 46–50 (2009)
10. Wang, W.: Design and Realization of General-purpose Test Question Database System Based on Net Technology. China Computer & Communication 4, 61–63 (2010)
11. Wei, D.: Realized a Simple Test Base by Authorware. Computer Knowledge and Technology 30, 8648–8649, 8663 (2010)

Exploration on Assessing-Method Reform of Engineering Management Major

Jiefang Tian, Xingguo Wang, and Wei Ming

College of Civil Engineering And Architecture, Hebei United University, 063009 Tangshan, China

Abstract. Course assessment is an important process of teaching. Traditionally the principal mode of assessment is through examinations, in which memory of facts is emphasized. Such a method does not encourage the development of practical capability of the students, or of their originality. A study of assessment reform is therefore significant. This thesis presents drawbacks of the traditional evaluation methods, particularly those still applied in high educational institutions. The study made in this thesis is based on the curriculum of the Management of Construction Projects, explores the approaches to course assessment. It also evaluates the validity of the assessing methods, and offers suggestions and improvements accordingly.

Keywords: exam reform, plans of implementation, effect assessment.

1 Introduction

Examination on courses is an essential assessing method to check knowledge acquisition and application on the part of the students, is also a gauge to judge the result and effect of teaching during the term. Examinations of various sorts are never missed or ignored in schools and universities. There is a need to study examinations on theoretical and practical levels. Project management is a relatively new discipline in China. The effective ways for training and educating personnel in this area are being explored and tried. This thesis has made efforts in looking at the course assessment on this new discipline, which is an important process in the education of project management.

2 Purpose of Assessing-Method Reform Conducted

2.1 Disadvantages of the Traditional Assessing Approach

At present, the assessing approaches adopted by most of the universities are mainly through examinations and tests, with the former being the commonest. The patterns of the examination are usually term explanation, gap filling, choice, judgment questions, answering questions, brief account, calculation, mapping, etc. with an aim of the

C. Liu, J. Chang, and A. Yang (Eds.): ICICA 2011, Part I, CCIS 243, pp. 394–399, 2011.

knowledge resurgence. This kind of examination is easy to be checked with a standard set for scores since there are books to be consulted and questions to be chosen. Moreover, this kind of examination is easy to be handled and can comparatively guarantee justice with a standard scoring system. The students can pass the examinations as long as they work hard. Evidently, this kind of assessing approach has restricted the thought of the students and does no good to the cultivation of creativity and employment adaptability because it doesn't permit varied opinions and different solutions to one single issue.

2.2 Research on Curriculum Assessing Approach Reform in Home Universities and Its Practice

Many educators have made explorations on curriculum assessing-approach reform. Citation [1] analyzes the disadvantages of the current assessing approach (examination and test), and puts forward specific suggestions on assessing approach covering the purely theoretical courses, courses integrating theory into practice and applied courses. Citation [2] proposes curriculum assessing reform for the public relations, including basic knowledge assessment, operation assessment and scoring, in the meanwhile, it puts forward the corresponding measures with the assessing approach reform. Citation [3] analyzes the problems in the curriculum assessing approach of Groundsill Management and puts forward the assessing approach of the curriculum teaching and design as well as the evaluation of the assessment effect. Citation [4] explores the improved measures of the internship assessing approach for Civil Engineering and Mapping. Citation [5] introduces the internship assessing ways and evaluates their effect. Citation [6] introduces the assessing ways of graduation design and makes a summary of its reform effect. Citation [7] to [12] puts forward suggestions on varied curriculum assessing approach respectively. Other similar research has been conducted which is not to be mentioned one by one.

From the domestic research results mentioned above, it is obvious that educators have all realized that the current curriculum assessing approach won't do any good to the training of applied talents since it attaches much importance to the knowledge resurgence and gravely confines the cultivation and training of the students' creativity. The citations mentioned above have mostly explored reform approach from the view point of a certain course while very few have done a systematic research on a major or conducted reforms really, therefore, the reform effect is to be tested yet. It is of great pragmatic value to research on assessing approach.

2.3 Suitable For Management of Construction Project Course to Reform Its Curriculum Assessing Approach

Management of Construction Project as a specialized and compulsory course in Management of Civil Engineering major, is about the overall management of construction project from the perspective of proprietor. Through the study, the students will become familiar with the whole process of management of the Civil Engineering, be cultivated on their research ability with an emphasis on practicability. The content of curriculum consists of an overview of the management of construction project, project planning and decision, project management organization, bidding, civil engineering project goal (quality, schedule, investment) control, contract management and information management.

This curriculum in question belongs to the management category, while management lies in practice. The traditional assessing approach can not achieve the practical and applied purpose which requires the recitation of textbook knowledge. Moreover, the training aim of the undergraduates requires the students' elementary research ability, which can be better facilitated by means of thesis writing and oral defense for the thesis. The students will be competent enough to write the graduation thesis through this training.

The teaching faculty of this major in question has practiced the approach for seminars on this issue and consulted the students for their opinions. As a result, they reached a unanimous agreement on it. Six courses of the management of Civil Engineering major of grade 2004 have conducted examination reform this term, the rest of the five are Management of Construction Enterprises, Project Financing, Marketing, Market Promotion for Real Estate, Professional Foreign Language Reading.

3 Implementation of the Program of Curriculum-Assessing Reform

3.1 Reform Goal

The reform means to integrate theory into practice, to enable the students to master the theory and approach of management in civil engineering and do a research on one aspect which interests themselves so as to cultivate their capability to analyze and solve problems, improve research ability as well as promote their confidence.

3.2 Grading

(1) The curriculum assessment consists of two parts: the daily assessment and curriculum thesis assessment.

(2) The daily assessment consists of class attendance, assignment, answering questions, and class discussion.

(3) The curriculum thesis consists of the thesis quality and oral defense. It also aims to set down the evaluation approach for thesis and that for the oral defense, which will be part of the thesis.

3.3 Grading Criterion

(1) Daily score (100 points in total, accounting for 20% of the total score)

1) Class attendance (40 points)
2) Assignment (40 points)
3) Answering to questions and class discussion (20 points)

(2) Curriculum thesis (100 points in total, accounting for 80% of the total score)

1) Thesis quality (70 points)
2) Score of oral defense (30 points)

3.4 Program Implementation

Principally the program means to full the following goals.

(1) To inform the students of the assessing approach in the first class, ask them to collect materials after each class and instruct them on the methods of consulting materials.

(2) To check a few students on their prepared material as well as their mastery of the relevant knowledge in the course of the class. To instruct at any time the thesis writing method and the format.

(3) To ask the students to submit the thesis titles to the teachers for their opinions and suggestions immediately before the end of the course.

(4) To have students submit the first draft of their theses within one week after the end of the course. The teachers give opinions on its revision according to the first draft of each student.

(5) To have students submit the final draft within three days after the check of the first draft.

(6) To have teachers check the theses and grade them within three days after submission of the final drafts.

A three-member oral defense committee is to be organized, which is to hold the oral defense within two days and grade each student.

4 Effect Evaluation of Curriculum-Assessing Reform

4.1 Advantages

(1) The students will be able to have gained a deeper understanding of the knowledge, widened to widen their horizon, and to improve their capability to analyze and solve problems.

(2) The students' research ability has been will be upgraded greatly after they have acquired a lot of knowledge beyond the textbooks by conducting pragmatic research and literature consultation over a long time. The students become familiar with the thesis writing method and are capable of writing it with standard format. Some of the theses are to be published on the journal of our university and other journals.

(3) The curriculum assessing reform has gained a compliment from the experienced teachers in our university. The examination paper of Management of Construction Enterprises made by Mr. Liu Yanfeng was checked in the mid-term supervision and received very well with "excellence" as a result.

(4) The course reform has been submitted to and approved by the authority as a research project, and a reformed examination assessment is being promoted throughout the school.

4.2 Shortcomings

(1) A few students are lowly motivated because there is no pressure from examination.
(2) There may be thesis plagiarism.

5 The Corresponding Countermeasures

The teaching faculty of this major in question have estimated the coming problems in the seminars held before and made the corresponding countermeasures below.

(1) Efforts are to be made to the improvement of the teaching effect in the class. To adopt the teaching method of case study, raise more questions, supplement more discussion classes, and organize more visits to projects, hence integrate theory into practice. Most of the students have an a good impression for this kind of teaching method and it has produced a better effect.
(2) Honesty is seen as a priority for education before the thesis composition. Once a plagiarism is discovered at the first draft stage, the thesis will be demanded to be revised, meanwhile, more questions will be popped up to it at the oral defense stage.
(3) Defense veto is to be adopted.
(4) Researches are to be conducted on the examination method and the corresponding teaching method, which has been permitted as a teaching reform project.
(5) Efforts are to be made on the teaching method reform with a correspondence with examination method reform.

References

1. Li, S.: An Analysis of the Assessing Approach Reform for the Higher Vocational Schools. Research on Vocational Education 1(2), 30–32 (2003)
2. Meng, H.: Integrating Teaching into Examination, Mutually Improving Teaching and Learning. Corps Educational College Journal 11(4), 42–44 (2005)
3. Pei, X.: An Exploration on the Curriculum Assessing Approach Reform for Groundsill Management. Changchun Engineering College Journal 2(3), 49–51 (2004)
4. Wang, Q.: An Analysis of Engineering Survey Internship Assessing Approach Reform. Sanming Vocational University Journal (3), 127–128 (2002)
5. Zhou, D.: An Elementary Exploration on Chemical Engineering Internship Assessing Approach Reform. Zhongshan University Journal 21(1), 201–202 (2001)
6. Wei, Q.: The Packing Major Graduation Assessing Approach Reform and Practice. Packing Engineering 23(4), 190–194 (2002)
7. He, J.: A New Mode of Curriculum Reform for Mathematics of Higher Vocational Electricity Major. Beijing Electronics Science & Technology Institute Journal 14(3), 75–77 (2006)

8. Qi, C.: Electronics Technology Curriculum Assessing Approach Reform and Practice. Journal of Technology College Education 22(6), 113–114 (2003)
9. Dan, Z.: Teaching Reform and Research in Electronic Accounting. Management and Technology of Small and Medium-sized Enterprises 9(4), 198–199 (2010)
10. Wang, J.: The Reform, Research and Practice of the Course of Project Charts and Graphs. Technological Information 33(2), 193 (2010)
11. Cheng, D.: A Study of Three-dimensional Approach for University Computer Basics Series. China Technological Information 22(5), 218–219 (2010)
12. Rong, X.: On Courses Teaching and Reform for Experiments in Junior Colleges. Journal of the Vocational School of Railway. Shi Jia Zhuang 3(4), 108–111 (2010)
13. Wang, N.: Course Research and Reform on Project Engineering Major Based on Field Work and Classroom Study. A Study on New Courses for Vocational Education 11(6), 23–24 (2010)

College Students' Mathematical Contest and the Training of Mathematics Quality

Cuilan Mi and Baoxiang Liu

College of Science, Hebei United University, Tangshan, Hebei, China
micuilan@163.com, liubx5888@126.com

Abstract. Mathematics quality is an important part of science and technology talents' scientific quality. To improve math quality is a crucial task of university mathematics education. With the help of college mathematical contests, the training method and approach of engineering students' mathematical quality is explored deeply. The paper puts forward with the cultivation of students' math quality in pre-competition exercises through ramming elementary knowledge, mathematical thinking ability, mathematics thoughtway and will character.

Keywords: College Mathematics Competition, mathematics quality, Mathematical Thought, mathematical way of thinking.

1 Introduction

With the rapid development of science and technology, the idea and method provided by mathematics have penetrated into various fields including natural science and humanities. Mathematics is playing an increasingly important role in all respects. More and more people realize that high technology is an essential mathematical technique. Mathematics quality is the most important part of modern talent quality as well as the key ring of talent training. Mathematics quality is an important part of scientific and technological personnel scientific quality and it is impossible to innovate science and technology without good mathematics quality.

Engineering college is a cradle of training high technical talents. Their mathematics quality will directly affect how they research and innovate science and technology. How to cultivate students' innovation ability and improve student's mathematics quality has become one of the important task of engineering mathematics teaching reform. At present, various levels of college mathematical competitions have become one of the most important parts of current university mathematics education and attract many college students. The student mathematics competition is the important ways to test students' mathematical knowledge, accomplishment and ability. It has been proved that the previous training and competition of college mathematical contests is playing an important role in the college students' mathematical quality education. Therefore, how to develop students' mathematical quality through college mathematical contest is worthy of discussion.

C. Liu, J. Chang, and A. Yang (Eds.): ICICA 2011, Part I, CCIS 243, pp. 400–405, 2011.

2 The Necessity of College Students' Mathematical Contest

Mathematics is the tools of training thought: Mathematics as the highest results of human rational thinking, Is the method and tools digestion and absorption of engineering principle, concept. Mathematics as a number of science form, Is the test data of processing tools. Mathematics quality education should include: combination "the number" and "form" with the objective to things, Develop the practical problem into mathematical language way of thinking, Have the basic ability of computing mathematics and mathematical software application, Get the habit of using mathematical thinking and the solution to the problem. So, we must strengthen a mathematics quality education in order to cultivate adapt to the development of the knowledge age applied talents.

Mathematics course not only teach the necessary mathematics knowledge, And the more important to cultivate the thinking ability of students' mathematical, Improve the students' mathematical literacy and cultural quality. in this aspect, College students' mathematical contest should play a role in promoting. For to cultivate engineering and technical personnel and management talent persons of engineering schools, is very necessary attend College students' mathematical contest. Mathematics competition is the platform of cultivate students' ability and quality. Mathematics competition not only can exercise the students' thinking ability, Expand thinking space, but also can measure a ability of flexible use of students knowledge and methods. training of the students' mathematics quality, more can train the student to analyze the question and solve the question ability, strengthen the enthusiasm of study mathematics and applied mathematics.

3 Mathematics Competition Coupled with Its Training Has Promoted Classroom Teaching

The earliest college students of Mathematics competition was held in the United States and the former Soviet union. From the 1980s, different provincial and domestic colleges and universities begin to hold their college students' mathematical contest in succession. The National Student Mathematics Competitions have been held since 2009 which are sponsored by China Mathematical Society with the test paper composed by unified experts from National Student Mathematics committee. various universities are eligible to take part in the contests. The national student mathematics competition received the welcome of teachers and students at the same time of becoming the largest extracurricular technological and cultural activities of all domestic universities. The engineering student mathematics competitions in our university have been held for years. We also joined the national college students mathematics competition twice with satisfactory results. We organized intensive training before the competition which is divided into three segments: The first section is basic training, during which experienced teachers are invited to carry on the elementary knowledge lecture in order to consolidate the higher mathematics knowledge system and guide the students to practice foundation knowledge related questions; The second section is comprehensive training which will focus on the contest syllabus in order to train students' comprehensive ability to solve problems with the help of some comprehensive exercises; The third section is improvement training of some typical examples appeared in the process of training. Experienced teachers will be invited to give instructions in order to check short of a leak and widen their thoughts.

It is proved by Liweip's practice that mathematics competition and its training have greatly enhanced classroom teaching and reform. For teachers, because mathematics competitions content request both to the teaching material, and to deepen and synchronous expansion textbooks, mathematical contest results can feedback some problems in teaching thus urging teachers' teaching research and reform. In order to help students attend the competition, teachers must have good mathematics attainment, teaching method, the satisfactory capability of solving problems and expressing themselves, which will in return promote teachers' awareness to conduct further research, to update their knowledge constantly, to improve the teaching level and to promote classroom teaching. It can be said that at the same time of cultivating a large number of outstanding students, mathematics competitions have also cultivated a group of excellent math teachers.

For students, the series of lectures before competitions play a crucial role in extending teaching flexibility hours, strengthening students' mathematical foundation and broadening their vision which enables the students to overlook classroom learning from a higher point, and to have a deeper understanding of mathematics knowledge structure. All o the above lay a olid foundation for students' follow-up study. Many students who have attended the contests got good insight and creativity through the pre-contest training. At the same time, these students were trained and exercised through the contests resulting in the improvement of their learning capabilities. In return, the enhancement of these abilities provides favorable conditions for their classroom learning. The mathematics competitions also helped in the discovery, training and selecting outstanding students to attend the national college students' mathematical modeling contest. Their significance has far exceeded the competition and winning the competition itself.

4 Mathematics Competition Coupled with Its Training Is an Effective Way of Training Mathematics Quality

Mathematics quality generally refers to people's savvy and potential in understanding and dealing with the law of count and shape, logic relation and abstract things, which is achieved through mathematical education. The insight, understanding, judgment and creative ability of some who is lack of mathematics quality will be greatly restricted. While the math competition activities provides effective way to improve the mathematics quality and ability of engineering students. The mathematics quality of engineering students should be integrated embodiment of mathematics knowledge and mathematical ability. We believe that the cultivation and improvement of college students' mathematical quality can be embodied in the following respects: Ramming mathematics elementary knowledge, improving mathematical thinking ability, focusing on mathematical thinking method in cultivating mathematics application ability and forming good will character.

4.1 Ram Mathematics Elementary Knowledge

Mathematics education is quality education in nature. As a matter of fact, through rigorous mathematical training, students can be endowed with some peculiar qualities which can not be replaced and achieve easily by other course study and practice. As engineering students, it is fundamental to have higher mathematical quality and solid basic mathematics knowledge. The most familiar content for mathematics teachers is to teach students to master the necessary basic knowledge of mathematics. But now all teachers are facing the problem of short teaching hours. For the Mathematics Olympiad, teachers use holidays to train students intensively, just to make up for the lack of hours.

In class, teachers often do not systematically summarize the knowledge acquired. In our basic training before the game, we invite experienced teachers to conduct basic lectures on solid basic knowledge of mathematics. Through tutoring before the game, students can coherent mathematics knowledge they learned systematically, understand the role of mathematics further and improve the logical reasoning ability with the help of the systematical knowledge summary, the training of certain skills and logical reason. Having laid a basis for the follow-up mathematical studying, many students benefit from it. In recent years, competition exams and the graduate student exams are closer and closer in content and form. Students who want to take part in the entrance exams for postgraduate schools benefit from the competition, Many students passed math competition training, PubMed substantial increase in math scores. In recent years, results from the study section to see. Therefore, Mathematical Competition is useful supplement to mathematics teaching in class.

4.2 Cultivate Mathematical Thinking Ability

Mathematics is not only a tool or a method, but also a kind of thinking mode, namely "mathematical thinking". Thinking ability is the highest level of human ability. While the cultivation of thinking ability is the most important of quality training. Besides ramming mathematics elementary knowledge, engineering students still should gradually improve mathematical thinking ability. Mathematical thinking is the one which takes mathematics for the object, mathematics activities as the carrier, including logical thinking, divergent thinking, analogy thinking, visual thinking and innovative thinking, etc. Mathematical contest questions are flexible, and can be used to effectively exercise students' mathematical thinking ability. Through the speculation, analysis and summing rules, it can effectively improve students' innovation consciousness and cultivate students' rational thinking ability, and it has improved the ability to analyze and solve problems thus fostering students' mathematical quality. So in competition training, we mainly cultivate students' mathematical thinking from mathematical contest questions:

(1) In the process of problem solving, we often need "guess" to induce innovation inspiration, which is necessary in the invention. It is in favor of cultivating innovation consciousness and creative ability. In addition, in teaching process, using a topic multi-solution and one problem changeful method can gradually active the students' thoughts, enable them to be think big, explore boldly and inspire their enthusiasm of study. Through the training of mathematical contest questions, students can not only learn to guess, conclude and summarize, but also learn to seek novelty. By this method, we can cultivate students' innovative thinking and develop students' creativity.

(2) There are a large number of open questions which are elaborate and carefully designed in mathematics contest questions. Training of open questions can help students get more interested in math. It will also cultivate the students' spirit of pursuing excellence and exploring boldly at the same time of cultivating students' applied mathematics ability., Effective training innovation ability of students. Because only in the strong sense of innovation under the guidance of the students was, May have a strong motivation for innovation, foster innovation goals, full innovation potential and talent, passion for the liberation of learning and innovation.

(3) The proof questions in math contest can help to develop students' abstract thinking ability. The argumentation of complex proof question always requires kinds of reasoning and thinking ways, so doing more proof questions is actually a good general training which can improve students' abstract thinking ability.

4.3 Focus on Ability of Mathematical Thinking and Develop the Ability of Mathematical Application

Mathematical thinking is the distillation and summary of the basic mathematics knowledge and methods. It is a bridge of knowledge into ability. After acquiring the mathematical way of thinking, students will be able to reveal the internal relations of the knowledge points, and make it possible to solve practical problems. Math contests contain a wealth of mathematical thinking. In the training of contests, students will encounter some important mathematical ideas, methods and examples. Focusing on solving practical problems, the applied problems require the ability to change abstract practical problems into mathematical problems and to establish mathematical models using mathematical principles and methods in order to train the students' ability to apply mathematical knowledge to problems solutions and enhance the initial capacity of numerical treatment and the numerical calculation.

4.4 Develop Good Will Character

In the modern era, the basis of business success is competitive awareness and strong perseverance. Mathematics competitions offer a platform for training students' sense of competition and perseverance. Character is a important constituent of mathematics quality for students. Through the training of the contest questions, we can cultivate indomitable perseverance and exploring spirit in students. Many universities attend the college students mathematics competition yearly. The match itself existed competition. As the apotheosis of the proposition, the contest questions is highly abstract and rigorous logic and exploratory. Solving mathematical contest questions needs continuous attempt and exploration which can promote the full development of self wisdom and willpower potential. Through the contest questions training, students can learn how to overcome difficulties, work with perseverance, dare to face difficulties, and dare to meet the challenges of the indomitable volition quality.

Above all, as a supplement of classroom exercise, college mathematical contest plays a promoting positive role in knowledge expansion, intelligence development, mathematics quality cultivation and teaching quality improvement.

References

1. Wang, X.: Quality education on Mathematical Reflections. Jouranl of Changsha University (4), 76–78 (2001)
2. Mi, C., Wang, X.: Research and Practice on Mathematics Competition Training Model for Students in Engineering. Education Technology and Training, 322–323 (2010)
3. Yuan, M., Zou, J., et al.: Analysis of Advanced Engineering Mathematics Competition counseling Corps College of Education, vol. (1), pp. 98–100 (2000)
4. Chen, H.-X., Guo, Y.-P., et al.: My Humble Opinion about Culture Mathematical Quality. Jouranl of Yanbei Normal University (6), 102–104 (2002)
5. Huang, Q., Zhu, L.: Higher non-science majors on the higher mathematics contest practice and understanding. Nantong Vocational University (3), 426–429 (2008)
6. Jin, J.-H.: Improving Teaching and Learning through Mathematics Competitions. Joumal of Research on Education for Ethnic Minorities (5), 53–55 (2005)
7. Huang, X.-M.: Discussion on Raising Students Mathematics Quality. Higher Education Forum (2), 76–78 (2007)
8. Joanne, L., David, C., Amy, B.E.: Initiating and Eliciting in Teaching: A Reformulation of Telling. Journal for Research in Mathematics Education (36), 101–136 (2005)
9. Li, M.: Cultivation of Mathematics Quality and Innovation of Mathematics Teaching. Jouranal of Wuhan Metallurgical Manager Institute (2), 52–54 (2006)
10. Ma, J., Wang, X.: Mathematical thinking in the 21st century with the mathematical quality of the training establishment. Higher Education of Sciences (1), 35–37 (2001)
11. Guo, S., Yu, W.: Mathematical Thinking on Education. Shanghai Education Publishing House (2000)
12. Zeng, J., Zang, Y.: Mathematical learning theory. Guangxi Education Publishing (2000)
13. Zang, T., Chen, C.: Mathematical problem-solving research competition. Higher Education Press (2000)
14. Shan, Z.: Mathematics is the science of thinking. Math Bulletin (6), 34–36 (2001)
15. David Jr., E.E.: Notics of American Mathematical Society 31(2), 142 (1984)
16. Liu, F.-C., Zhang, S.-Q.: On Reform in Teaching Technological Mathematics to Improve Mathematical Quality of Students. Journal of Guangdong University of Technology (3), 52–54 (2002)

Application of Digital Storytelling in Comprehensive Practice Activity Curriculums

Jiangyan Zheng, Jiongzhao Yang, Hao Zhang, Lili Wang, Zhongkui Sun, and Huan Xue

Qinggong College, Hebei United University
zjymm2005@126.com

Abstract. The increasing development of computer and information technology has brought new challenges as well as opportunities to education. As a way of personal multimedia storytelling, digital storytelling is very popular in foreign countries and begins to be widely used in the field of education, and have achieved some results. Firstly, digital storytelling is given detailed explanation. Then functions and advantages in applying digital storytelling in Comprehensive Practice Activity Curriculums are put forward. Finally, the feasibility of applying digital storytelling in Comprehensive Practice Activity Curriculums is confirmed by a teaching case.

Keywords: Digital storytelling Comprehensive Practice Activity Curriculums Teaching cases.

1 Introduction

1.1 Past and Present

Story is the most common way of transmitting knowledge and experience to people. Ages ago humans began to tell and record stories in many ways. Until recently, with the emergence of computers and the increasing development of multimedia technology, the general public has the opportunity to create their own digital storytelling. Digital stories produced in the early 1920s. As the starting figure of storytelling, Dana Winslow Atchley made a short autobiographical film by combining old photos and the statement of his past, which received all the praise. Then, Atchely together with his friends Lambert began to help other people describe their own personal digital storytelling, and more and more people began to this new form of creation. The first Digital Media Center was set up in San Francisco, which is now the digital storytelling center. (CDS).

According to statistics, there were more than 800 search results page about the digital storytelling and education related information in 1999, which meant that many people had been using the network digital media to tell their own stories, but at that time the stories were mostly demonstrated by text, photos and pictures. The writer inserted the key words "digital storytelling in education" with the search engine AltaVista in May 20, 2010, and found 2,630,000 related records; with the search

C. Liu, J. Chang, and A. Yang (Eds.): ICICA 2011, Part I, CCIS 243, pp. 406–414, 2011.

engine Google 4,020,000 related records were found; with yahoo 2,630,000 records were found accordingly. It is found that digital storytelling has changed a lot with the support of network technology and information technology. Compared with previous digital storytelling, the present stories add new transition effects, the narrator's voice, corresponding pictures, videos, background music etc, which make these stories more appealing, intuitive, attractive to the audience's attention, and increase the amount of information.

Digital storytelling integrates the old art of story telling and existing multimedia tools (including graphics, sound, vivid video and network publishing.) Specifically, the story is a brief description, with appropriate sound and various forms of visual media (such as pictures, videos, artwork, titles, and digital video, etc.). Personal digital storytelling are generally 2-5 minute video clips about the content related to life, art, history, education, character, and fairy tales, combining video, sound, animation and other forms of media, and production is transmitted on the network form of streaming media.

The reason why digital storytelling are popular in foreign countries is that its production is simple, as long as there is no less than WONDOWS2000 version of the computer and the corresponding simple-to-use editing software (such as Window XP comes with Movie Maker, iMovie, vivid, The most common PowerPoint, etc.), and no other expensive equipments are needed. You can create a wonderful multimedia video, making the non-professionals in the artist's camp.

In the view of people interested in movies, digital storytelling telling is more exciting than that of the story statement - achieving from the text description of video and audio recording life to the historic leap, liberated only by reading the computer screen, print media and the eyes, making the sound and video done. Being different from films, the digital storytelling is more interactive than the film; its audience is not passive recipients but active digital video creator according to their own life experience.

As a new way of teaching, digital storytelling is put into practice in primary and secondary schools in foreign countries. After investigating and interviewing the domestic primary and secondary students, it is known that students in the third and above grade have the ability to use PowerPoint.

Therefore, the research-oriented study combining digital storytelling and subjects has the development conditions.

1.2 The Characteristics and Production Process of Digital Storytelling

Upon completion of the task of digital storytelling, students under the guidance of teachers, search for relevant information about the subject through interviews, surveys, collect information from life or online stories, write the script, and tell the story with the help of multimedia. We can see that the production of digital storytelling does not only focus on the production of student work, and more emphasis is on cognitive, emotional and improvement of information literacy. Students can master the textbook knowledge, but more importantly let students be able to process through the acquisition of knowledge, handle the process of social relationships, and guide students to calmly face the complex relationship between the living worlds. In addition, promote student visual, musical, aesthetic and other abilities. In the course, practice is an essential part. In this process, teachers guide students to use various means and methods, from different angles to carry out inquiry learning, through a series of events, students acquire a certain amount of learning materials, the accumulation of certain knowledge can write a story after the script, through the forms of multimedia can make their knowledge visualized.

Digital storytelling as a teaching method are applied and developed continuously in the classroom teaching, but in the process two major restricted factors appear: the first one is the limited class time, and the second one is the hardware resources. As for these two issues, foreign experts made the following six steps in the production of digital storytelling:

(1) Write a script draft.
(2) Design a story and script series corresponding storyboard.

Storyboard shown in Figure:

Screen number	Diagrams or pictures	Narrative / sound track
1		
2		
…		

(3) Discussion, modify the script.
(4) Layout photos in the video time line of video editing software.
(5) Add narrative content to audio track.
(6) Add photo effects and transition effects.

When teachers design for students to create digital storytelling of these six steps, there are two very important benefits: first, to specify tasks, the extension of the student extra-curricular time to learn and experiment, while in video editing software, students can more clearly see senses of participation. Followed by the production of teachers into the blackboard or whiteboard on the steps, teachers can understand the progress of students easily and provide timely study guide.

2 The Role and Advantages of Stories in the Comprehensive Practice Course

Digital storytelling as a novel application of the comprehensive practical learning activities, have had a great impact on multiple intelligences of students, as well as cognitive, emotional and behavioral inputs, but also provide a form for curriculum integration of information technology.

2.1 To Make Up for Students in the Course of Comprehensive Practical Activities of Uneven Development of Multiple Intelligences

Comprehensive Practice Course is the existing knowledge and experience of students and based on real life. The curriculum design reflects the comprehensive application of knowledge, emphasizes the practice, students focus on analysis of issues and problem-solving skills development. In this process, teachers train students to develop multiple intelligences, but due to students' intellectual development vary, each other's strengths and weaknesses are different. So in the event there will be some students who are often actively involved in the activities while some students have cynicism problems. The digital storytelling is to let students use digital technology and multimedia tools learn. Digital storytelling consists of video, audio and other digital resources. These visual and auditory sensory involvement, provide a broad space for students' balance development of multiple intelligences, especially for introverted students to provide the advantages of intelligent stage show, enhancing their confidence and participation initiatives.

2.2 A Form of Information Technology and Curriculum Integration

In digital storytelling comprehensive practical activities, students can not only collect text, pictures, video and other data, but also find useful information from the network. Then these information and information technology serve as a platform to create creative and unique works. In the process, digital storytelling provides information processing support for the Comprehensive Practice Course, as well as support for the exchange of students' collaboration. In addition, digital storytelling provide students with creative thinking space, and realize the function of information technology in the curriculum resources collection, information processing, collaboration, communication and research, which truly reflect the organic information technology and curriculum integration.

2.3 Promote Students' Behavior Investment, Emotional and Cognitive Inputs. These Are Mainly Demonstrated in the Following Three Aspects

(1) Involvement of digital technology and media to promote the development of deep-level cognitive engagement.

Digital storytelling in the comprehensive practice activities requires students to undertake activities centered around one topic in the form of one group under the guidance of teachers. In this process, students can independently arrange group activities, such as the division of labor, taking initiatives to analyze the problems, taking timely solution to the problem, and reflecting on the problems. Digital storytelling can be seen in the integrated curriculum of practical activities to promote the investment of "live" component in learning theory, cultivate a student's cognitive strategies and metacognitive skills.

(2) Encourage students' emotional investment by storytelling.

The story can enhance communication and emotion among students, between students and teachers. Psychological research has demonstrated the learning process is closely related to emotion and emotional experience of penetration in all schools and students; creative thinking skills and emotional investment are directly related to students. When students are learning, once the emotional motivation works, the students' contact and cooperation will be easier and more effective, and inspiration will burst their peers and teachers' motivation.

(3) Digital storytelling centered around comprehensive practice activities promote the investment behavior.
When digital storytelling are used in the Comprehensive Practice Course, students are motivated to be more conscious to review the learnt knowledge and put what their have learned into practice, as well as take the initiative to apply the knowledge to solve practical problems. These are the performance of behavior investment, thereby promoting a better investment in the students learning to cultivate the students "live" capability, "innovation" ability and "contribution" capability.

3 "Causes and Prevention of Myopia," Teaching Case and Teaching Summary

Course Objectives:

(1) Cognitive goal: to understand the formation of internal and external causes of myopia.
(2) Emotional goals: to recognize the confusion caused by myopia, to make students aware of protecting their eyes.
(3) Motor skills objectives: the ability to collect information, make cooperation and exchange, and use multimedia software to display their achievements.

Contents:
Analysis phase:

(1) Divide students into different groups to investigate the number of students suffering from myopia and understand the troubles myopia brought them.
(2) To collect information and pictures on the causes of myopia through the network or the library.

Digital storytelling production phase:

(1) Complete program of activities
In order to facilitate activities, students from different groups, and name their own team. Each member is responsible for specific tasks. Then team members discuss the plan activities and arrangements. Here is the plan of a group's activities:

Group Name: Peas Team
General director: Liu Yang
Dubbing: Zheng Jiangwei
Script writers: Liu Xin
Information workers: Zheng Tong, Zheng Jiangwei
Computer Operator: Wang Shuo
Specific Arrangements of Activities
First step is that members of the group discuss the story theme

The second step is that script writers write the story and computer operator prints it and save it in the computer

The third step is that information workers collect and collate information

The fourth step is that the director guides the production of digital works and dubbing it.

The fifth step is to playback digital storytelling, and then proposes amendments suggestions.

The sixth step is to upload the digital storytelling to the internet.

(2) Manuscript writing.
Script was written after the students internalize the knowledge output of the process. Comprehensive Practice Activity Curriculums focus on the various curriculums integration, and pay attention to students' practice, so the Comprehensive Practice Course is more creative than other subjects.

Manuscript Content:
Myopia has become a prominent issue in my school. According to our survey, an average of 4-5 people per class is myopia. What causes myopia? One reason is that the genetic parents, especially the most vulnerable to high myopia genetic parents of the child. We can not control this factor. But the day after tomorrow development of our vision is also important, the expert survey, a large children's myopia is due to lack of physical exercise, eating, picky eaters, nutritional insufficiency, coupled with the lack of scientific knowledge with the eyes, and no eye protection, long-term adverse eye habits. It is more dangerous to spend much time watching TV and playing video games. In addition, the computer is one of the most important reasons causing myopia. Students' myopia is closely related to environmental conditions. In terms of students, poor lighting during homework, together with lack of reading and writing habits, forces the students to get close to the book, causing a series of near reflex. Near reflecting lets the biochemistry structural change in the eye wall and increases intraocular pressure to form a longer axial length that is true axial myopia. Therefore, we should seriously do eye exercises every day, for an instant 20 times, making the eyes flexible, comfortable and bright.

(3) Data collection
After the students write a good script, they will collect information and music in comprehensive practical activities. In this process, as primary students have relatively poor ability to identify information, teachers should provide timely help to guide them to collect online information and save them to different folders according to different types.

(4) Storyboard series
To alleviate the workload of students, teachers assist students to design a good storyboard series, students according to this template, fill in your own story board with pictures and sound blend together properly.

(5) Edit digital storytelling
Students input pictures and sounds collected into the computer, and adjust the picture based on the story boards and the location of the sound, making sound and picture harmonious, in line with the requirements of the theme. After adding some of these

images transition effects, as well as rendering the atmosphere add background music to the story, the final output of the story comes out. In the process, it is found that students are more focused on the transition effects and add special effects to avoid distracting the teacher works with the transition effects limit up to a maximum of 3.

(6) Show the work
Participate in activities with students from fourth and fifth grades, grouping mixed group, stage show in the works, let each group make the work of students participating in activities to demonstrate to the standard evaluation form for group peer review, suggest modifications, and then the revised works were located in their respective class player, form a learning community, promoting the development of students.

After the event, in order to understand the learning activities, teachers and students were interviewed:

After interviewing the lecturer Liu Haitao, it is known that the comprehensive practical activity plays a significant role in students' development, which is summarized as follows:

(1) Digital storytelling provides students with a platform to show themselves.
Since primary school pupils have poor self-control, and weak self-learning capability, especially for students with poor academic performance. They are prone to lose participation enthusiasm in the process of activities implementation and behave lazily. Digital storytelling for students, is a relatively new concept, they like to try and experience. Especially in the completion of the process of digital storytelling, it is to be fully mobilized that language expression, photography skills, aesthetics, music appreciation and computer operations and other areas. So students can easily find their strengths and weaknesses and develop a self-display space.

(2) Improve students' comprehensive knowledge, performing ability and social practice ability.
In digital storytelling-based activities, students use Powerpoint to create digital storytelling about myopia as their own learning goals, to promote comprehensive application of knowledge learnt in and out of school, explore the theme-related content and activities to complete the activity tasks. Thus the students' hands-on and practical ability are enhanced.

(3) To ensure the smooth implementation of activities, teachers should provide necessary support services.
In the activities, teachers' support services include emotional support and technical support. Emotional support is that in the activity implementation course, the group members may generate intense controversy for a certain issue. When the internal conflict is difficult to resolve, the teacher need to properly analyze problems, make reference, guide students to successfully carry out activities, and encourage students to persevere. Technical support refers to the fact that teachers need to give students the necessary support and assistance in the choice of theme, the flow of digital storytelling, and the application of video software and so on.

After the event, under the help of Liu Haitao, students are required to answer the following questions:

(1) Have you encountered difficulties in the comprehensive practice of digital activities? So what are the difficulties?
(2) Do you like digital storytelling of the Integrated Curriculum? Talk about your feelings on the event

I read students' response and find that some students write down the following sentences.

Class Two, Grade Four LiuYing

Since I do not like sharing with the students, so in the previous activities, I always try to hide myself in the group, do not participate in group discussions, and it seems that the activities have nothing to do with me. Of course, the students do not know my advantages. In this activity, our team leader gives me specific task, letting me write the script, which really makes me feel happy because making up stories is my hobby and I finally have a chance to show it! I like this event, and hope to engage in more activities like this.

(Second class in fifth grade Wang Shuo)

I have encountered difficulties. Our group made an appointment on Sunday to edit the information in the school, I feel like I have been very proficient in the use of the software Powerpoint and offered to be responsible for computer operation. I started very smoothly in inserting the picture into Powerpoint, and added the transitional effect. Our team leader Liu Yang praised me, followed by the sound input. When Zheng Jiangwei is ready and it becomes quiet all around, one problem appears. I cannot insert the sound and feel there is no problem in my operation. Then under the inspection of all my group members, I operated it again and suddenly realized that I ignored a tiny aspect the teachers emphasized. In this activity, I found myself too proud, dazzled by the joy, and I still feel the power of teamwork is very big!

I reap the benefits from the activity. I like digital storytelling, particularly like to produce their own digital storytelling, especially after finishing it I have a sense of accomplishment and build up my confidence.

Based on observation of students' performance and analysis of the survey results, through this event, most students recognize the influence myopia has on us and the importance of eye protection. Meanwhile, the activities promote students' ability to promote cooperation and exchange of information, help the students understand and memorize knowledge, as well as provide students with a stage to demonstrate their advantage. Generally speaking, the teaching objective is achieved. Some students say, they do not like the clear division of labor in groups. Another student says that his team members are inactive in carrying out the activity and have difficulty in cooperating with each other. It can be seen that students' division, together with group cooperation of digital storytelling in practical activities still need further exploration.

References

1. Jeo, L.: Digital Storytelling Cookbook, pp. 9–20 (February 2007)
2. The Educational Uses of Digital Storytelling, http://www.coe.uh.edu/digital-storytelling/examples.htm
3. Chen, J.: Application of Digital storytelling in Education, pp. 8–11 (2006)
4. Luo, Y.: Research and Practice of Comprehensive Practice Activity Curriculums, p. 4. Central China Normal University (2004)
5. Peng, X.: Social Science Front. On the basic characteristics of "Comprehensive Practice Activity Curriculums", 292–294 (2007)
6. Ping, J.: The overall course of comprehensive practical activities to promote and implement school-based, p. 4. Capital Normal University Press (2006)
7. Jason, O., Foreword by David T.: Digital storytelling in the classroom: new media pathways to literacy, learning, and creativity. Corwin Press (2008)
8. Aline, G.: Digital Storytelling: An Emergent Method for Health Promotion Research and Practice. Health Promotion Practice, 186–191 (2009)
9. Welch, T.: Digital Storytelling in the Classroom. Catechist Magazine, 21–24 (2009)
10. Xia, H.: The application of Digital Storytelling in education. Communications and Computer, 2 (2008)

Practice of "Design of Integrated Circuit Layout" Course Construction

Jian Wang and Liping Fan

College of Information Engineering, Shenyang University of Chemical Technology, Shenyang 110142, China
wj100_108@126.com, flpsd@163.com

Abstract. Design of Integrated Circuit Layout is an important course in the electric science technology Specialty. In this paper, using modern teaching philosophy, the practice of course construction in the course is introduced, and also the methods are put forward. Especially, the experiment teaching content and teaching methods are discussed in detail. Practice has proved that students master the practice ability of integrated circuits layout and raise the ability of autonomic learning.

Keywords: design of integrated circuits layout, course construction, modern teaching philosophy.

1 Introduction

In recent years, with the vigorous development of Integrated Circuit (IC) industry, the demands for IC design talent are increasing rapidly. Layout is the bridge from IC design to manufacturing; the IC layout technology is an important skill for design talent [1]. "Design of Integrated Circuit Layout" is the important Course of Electronic Science and Technology Professional, whose main task is to teach the structure and principle of integrated circuit layout, use of IC design software and design methods. Initially, traditional teaching ideological had been adopted, but it was found that stimulating enthusiasm and initiative of students is more difficult, teaching effect is not ideal. In order to improve the quality of teaching, for several years, the modern educational philosophy has been applied to teaching practice. As a result, student's learning autonomy is significantly enhanced and better master the skills of IC layout design.

2 Overview of Modern Teaching Philosophy

Teaching philosophy is the teaching ideals and concepts, which exists in teaching process and has a profound impact on teaching behavior. Modern teaching philosophy is Complexes of various beliefs and theories of teachers in the teaching process, which is related to teachers, students, knowledge, ability and quality [2].

C. Liu, J. Chang, and A. Yang (Eds.): ICICA 2011, Part I, CCIS 243, pp. 415–420, 2011.

Modern teaching should be established the following three concepts: (1) Teaching interaction. Teaching is a special interactive activity between teachers and students, which is a purposeful, organized and planned activity of teacher-student interaction. (2) Subject of student. Main body of students is specifically expressed in autonomy, initiative and creativity during teaching process. (3) The construction of knowledge. This concept requires teachers to focus on the exploration of knowledge structure, guide students to explore the inherent of knowledge, direct students in learning strategies, which allow students to explore a particular learning process, and then form their own unique learning style [2].

In recent years, the basic direction of college is to develop the ability of students with attention during imparting knowledge, strengthen the guidance of learning and research methods for improving students' independent ability to acquire knowledge, focus on practical ability and innovative ability for the development of student resilience, and enhance student adaptability and innovation.

3 The Practice of Modern Teaching Philosophy in Theory Teaching

For theory teaching, in order to implement the three concepts of modern teaching, curricula and teaching modes and methods are reformed.

3.1 Curriculum Reform

For undergraduate teaching, the practice not only is focused on, but also the theory; [3] Students should master not only the layout and software, but also the principles of layout architecture. Therefore, the basic objectives of the course are: (1) the ability to read and analysis circuit schematics accurately; (2) learning by heart basic common cells layout; (3) modifying and verifying the layout [4]; (4) mastering the IC failure mechanisms and the design approach of special device layout.

Standard bipolar is the oldest of the many available bipolar processes, most of which offer much faster switching speeds. The newer processes often replace junction isolation with partial or complete dielectric isolation to simultaneously reduce component area and minimize parasitic capacitance. Diffusions consist of much thinner layers, often created through innovative use of polysilicon as a doping source. Self alignment and improved dimensional control allow the construction of far smaller geometries. These improvements have increased switching speeds by two orders of magnitude, allowing modern bipolar transistors to operate at speeds approaching fifty gigahertz. The highly specialized processes used to obtain such performance are fully as complex and costly as the most sophisticated of CMOS processes.

The bipolar junction transistor (BJT) is among the most versatile of all semiconductor devices. In addition to its obvious applications as a voltage or current amplifier, it can also serve as the basis of voltage and current references, oscillators, timers, pulse shapers, amplitude limiters, nonlinear signal processors, power switches, transient protectors, and many other types of circuits. There are also certain applications for which bipolar transistors are ill-suited, the most important of these being low-power digital logic. Most logic is now constructed using CMOS circuitry. Bipolar transistors remain important for constructing most analog circuits, although many of these circuits now contain CMOS elements as well.

CMOS processes have undergone their share of evolutionary advances. Gate lengths have shrunk relentlessly as digital designers have sought to pack ever larger numbers of transistors onto limited amounts of silicon real estate. Once gate lengths fall below 1um, a variety of short-channel effects dictate the use of much more elaborate structures. The back gate doping levels must increase to combat premature punch through and elaborate implantation strategies become necessary to confine the channel to the desired region immediately beneath the gate oxide. Cost and complexity have soared as processes push steadily deeper into the submicron regime seeking the elusive ultimate limits of device performance [5].

The earliest MOS processes only offered PMOS transistors. These were soon superseded by processes that could produce both enhancement and depletion NMOS transistors. Demands for lower current consumption and greater design flexibility led to the introduction of processes that could simultaneously fabricate both NMOS and PMOS transistors. Although originally intended for digital applications, these CMOS processes could also be used to design a variety of analog integrated circuits. These soon began to replace bipolar integrated circuits in selected applications, but CMOS transistors were not able to duplicate all of the capabilities of bipolar. Many newer processes now merge both bipolar and CMOS transistors onto a common substrate.

BiCMOS technologies seek to merge the best of both worlds. They are therefore heir to both the complexities of submicron CMOS and the elaborate bipolar structures required to obtain high switching speeds. Almost any bipolar or CMOS innovation can be merged into a BiCMOS process, and most have been [5].

According to the teaching plan, referring to several textbooks, the syllabus has been worked out with unique feature. The main contents include: analog and digital IC basic circuit and principle; process technology of bipolar, CMOS and BICMOS; [6] IC failure mechanisms and protective measures; the layout of NPN and PNP transistors, NMOS and PMOS transistors, resistors, capacitors, inductors and other components; special device layout and working principle [5]; distribution, wiring and basic methods of standard cell design; reverse layout identification methods [6]; integrated circuit design software [7].

3.2 The Reform in Classroom Teaching

In teaching, the way that is from the emotional to the rational and then to practice is adopted, use the blackboard, multimedia and wall charts, [8] consequently, the interest of students is mobilized, students' initiative, participation and creativity is enhanced. [9]

In teaching consequence, first, the reverse layouts of bipolar and CMOS IC are demonstrated, which enable students to have an intuitive understanding of the layout and stimulate their desire. Second, with teaching bipolar, CMOS process, the basic components and working principle of layout, asking students to draw on the blackboard, and then identify the reverse layout, which reinforce the student's subjectivity. Third, students learn basic analog, digital integrated circuits and principle of the basic cells, distribution and wiring methods, which understand the actual layout route through the reverse analysis. Fourth, the principle of special device and IC layout development profile was taught. Finally, IC design software and workflow are taught. As a result, the students can master the basic design steps.

In summary, by the way, the students learning process conform to the human cognitive process; students master the basic skills of layout design.

4 Practical Application of Modern Teaching Philosophy

The purpose of learning is that students apply knowledge to practice, design products for the community and realize their own value, [10] therefore, the practice session is arranged reasonably, which combines the practice and teaching closely achieving the learning objectives.

4.1 Course Experiment

In the course experiments, two kinds of IC software are adopted, which are tools of most of IC companies. Experimental instructions in English are used to improve the students' professional foreign language level and self-learning ability. Course experiment includes: inverter design and verification, multi-selector design and verification, the amplifier circuit design and verification, the accumulator circuit design and verification. Through the design of experiment process, students grasp the basic concepts of IC and software operating methods.

4.2 Curriculum Design

In terms of curriculum design, students are required to design a complex trigger by using 0.6 micron N-well process. Design includes: standard cell schematics, symbols and layout of the inverter, NAND and NOR gates are designed and verified; the trigger circuit, symbols and layout are designed and verified. All circuit functional simulation, pad and ESD protection circuits are designed and tested.

In short, with the practices, students grasp integrated circuit design ideas and design processes.

5 The Reform in Assessment Methods

In order to objectively evaluate teaching effectiveness and teaching quality, it is necessary to improve and reform assessment methods [1]. Course score consist of the usual results (20%) and final examination (80%).Usual results include the theory Homework, class discussion, computer operation and discipline. In terms of curriculum design, score depends on the time of the experiment completion. The shorter time is, the higher score is. Reasonable, effective, fair and impartial assessment methods also help stimulate students to learn actively and on their own initiative.

6 Conclusions

In this paper, it is discussed that "design of integrated circuit layout" courses has been construction using modern teaching philosophy. Years of teaching practice has shown that the application of modern teaching philosophy achieve interactive teaching, student body and the construction of knowledge. Students master skills of IC layout design and integrated circuits layout structure methods, which raise ability to innovate from passive learning to active knowledge. Over the past five, many graduates are employed by the domestic IC companies; their professional ability has been well received.

Acknowledgments. This work was supported by the Project of Teaching Reform in Higher Education of Liao Ning Province, China (No.2010-2-3-53), and the Project of Teaching Reform in Education of Shenyang University of Chemical Technology (2009A006).

References

1. Shi, M., Sun, L., Xu, C.: Research on Construction of "Computer Aided Design of IC Layout" Course. China Integrated Circuit 12, 59–62 (2007)
2. Liu, S.: Reform of Teaching Methods of Modern Teaching Philosophy. China Higher Education 6, 11–13 (2009)
3. Li, B.: Teaching Reform of Two Integrated Circuits Course. Journal of EEE 31, 6–8 (2009)
4. Zhang, Z.: "Design of Integrated Circuit Layout" Instructional Practice Design. The Science Education Article Collects 10, 43 (2010)
5. Alan, H.: The Art of Analog Layout. Publishing House of Electronics Industry, Beijing (2008)
6. Zhu, Z., Zhang, H., Zhu, Y.: Semiconductor integrated circuit. Tsing Hua University Press, Beijing (2009)
7. Zheng, Q.: Design of Integrated Circuit Layout. China Machine Press, Beijing (2008)
8. Gu, S.: Grasp of Teaching Promote the Reform of Teaching Methods. China Higher Education 7, 31–33 (2009)
9. Yao, L.: Break the Ice of Education Reform Innovative Methods of College Teaching. China Higher Education 8, 40–42 (2010)
10. Chen, Y.: Strengthen Curriculum Development and the Foundation Works to Improve the Quality of Teaching. China Higher Education 24, 27–28 (2007)
11. Feng, X., Xu, J.: Evaluation of industrialization prospect of integrated circuits layout design based on neural network. Systems Engineering and Electronics 28(7), 1020–1023 (2006) (language: Chinese)

12. Sheng, P.S.: Integration of environmental factors in pre-layout design optimization for printed circuit boards. Siddhaye, Journal of Electronics Manufacturing 8(1), 1–14 (1998)
13. Rangel-Ortiz, H.: New Mexican Legislation on the Legal Protection of Integrated Circuit Layout-Designs. Patent World 102, 35 (1998)
14. Mehlhorn, K.: Hill System: A Design Environment For The Hierarchical Specification, Compaction, and Simulation of Integrated Circuit Layouts, pp. 139–149. MIT, Lengauer, Thomas (1984)
15. Wilmore, J.A.: Use of Bit Maps In Designing Efficient Data Bases For Integrated Circuit Layout Systems. Journal of Digital Systems 4(1), 71–95 (1980)

Mathematical Formula Design Based on Mobile Learning Environment

Yanan Li, Hao Zhang, Yanling Meng, and Honghui Wang

Qinggong College, Hebei United University, Tangshan 063009, China
liyanan312@163.com

Abstract. As the development of mobile communication technology and increasingly demand for education, mobile learning will make a huge improvement for education information, for all, and for lifelong around China. Given the structural features being studied, a mathematical formula structural model is proposed, based on which, a universal mathematical formula markup language is designed, to be as the transportation and expression of mathematical formulas in the mobile learning environment. This makeup language is easy to use and browse.

Keywords: mathematical formulas, markup language, mobile learning.

1 Introduction

In recent years, with mobile computing (Mobile Computing) technology, the rapid development of the intelligence level of the mobile terminal continues to improve, a new way of learning - mobile learning (M-learning) is generated, and it is considered a future of learning. Dr. Keegan predicted: "from the E-Learning and mobile phone technology where the combination of M-Learning study will show us the future." While the rapid development of mobile learning, mobile learning resource development has also attracted the attention of many researchers.

2 The Mathematical Formula Model

Mathematical formula is a recursive natural language, in a two dimensional structure to express its significance, after analysis, we put the mathematical formula involved in the structure is divided into three kinds of structure, based on this; establish a general mathematics formula of the model.

2.1 Fractal Mathematical Formula

(1) Basic type
The basic shape of the structure shown in Figure 1, consists of 11 forms, their names are shown in Figure 1-1 to 1-5, where A is defined as the subject.

C. Liu, J. Chang, and A. Yang (Eds.): ICICA 2011, Part I, CCIS 243, pp. 421–426, 2011.

(2) Composite form

In the mathematical formula, binomial, matrix, the determinant and formula is a special type of overall; this paper put this type structure called compound shape. Compound shape constitutes this special formula structure by the braces, brackets, the brackets and determinant symbols as the main body. Compound shape elements into three categories:

Formula elements, as a component of the compound shape only occupy a position in and are available in eight direction and other parts connected.

Block symbols occupy the ranks of complex shape in a few locations, and only one character, while its boundary is free. Block symbol character is generally "O", "o", "0", "1" and "*" a few, the shape of triangles and rectangles two, shown in Figure 2.

Repeated symbols, repeated symbols occupy the ranks of one or several locations, is to specify the formula elements → ↓ ↘ ↙ symbols arranged in a row direction. Repeat the same symbol at least three points of a straight line, shown in Figure 2. There are three types of repeated symbolic links first is to connect both ends of the formula elements. Connect one end of the second is a formula element, one end point to the beginning of the row or column or terminal part, as shown in Figure 2 (c) repeated symbols. Is not connected at both ends of the third element of any formula, take it directly to a row or column to indicate the repeated rows or columns, as shown in Figure 2 (d) the third line.

The first category is rule-complex-shaped, non-repeating symbols and symbols of the block-shaped complex called the rules of complex shape. For geometry of Figure 3. The second type is irregular-shaped complex, with block symbols and composite symbols repeated as irregular-shaped complex shape. This form is often seen in conditions of complex equations, determinants and matrices.

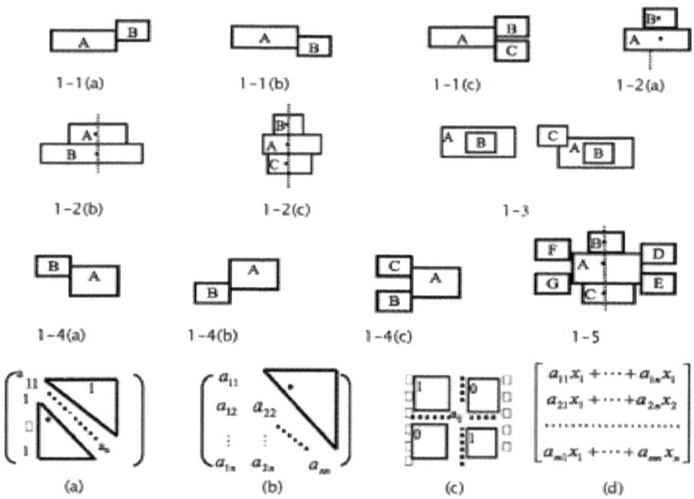

Figure 2

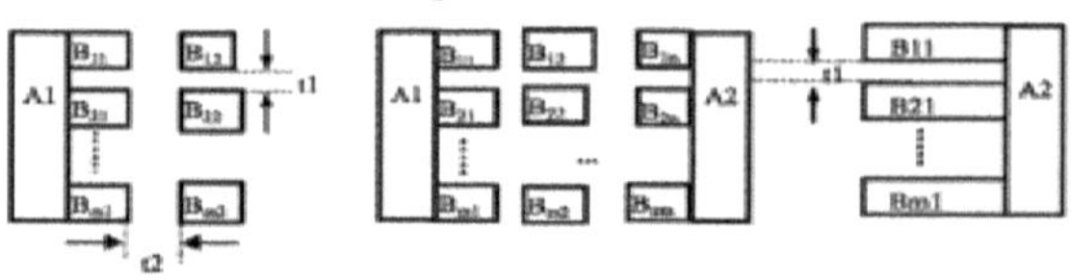

Complex-shaped structure is complex, given its characteristics according to the following representation:

(1) Rules in complex-shaped elements in the formula directly that the row and column labels.

(2) irregular-shaped compound is more complicated, the formula elements that are still using its row and column numbers, and define three functions, respectively, block symbols and repeated symbols.

• Use the function (,,,,,,) 1 1 2 2 3 3 Tri xyxyxyp said triangular block symbols, of which the first block of six parameters of the triangle symbols represent the three vertices occupied by the row and column numbers, the last parameter represents the block of symbols character type. To make that a consistent, low number of specified parameters ranks first, high in the post, and then down.

• With Re (,,,,) 1 1 2 2 cxyxyp said rectangular blocks of symbols, of which the first four parameters that left point and lower right point of the rectangle occupied by the ranks of the number, the last parameter indicates the type of block symbol character.

• With Re (,,,) 1 1 2 2 pxyxy that repeated symbols, repeat symbol indicates that the four parameters two vertices occupied by row and column numbers, a repeat sign may occupy more than one row and column numbers, just know that its two end points of the occupied ranks number can easily deduce that it occupies the ranks of the number. This provides: 1 2 1 2 X ≤ X, Y ≤ Y.

2.2 Mixed Connections

In some fractal, such as fractions $\frac{x^2+1}{x+y}$, using the above fractal can not express very well what is the molecular shape of the upper part, to solve this problem introduced the concept of mixed connections. Around the Internet from the above two forms, the most right side of the left-shaped form of the left and right side in the same vertical line, the shape of the main center is located in the same horizontal line, such as a whole constitutes a mixed connection. For example, the above formula is a mixture of molecular connections.

3 The Contents of Mobile Learning Resource for Interaction Design Strategy

In order to enable learners to actively and positively to the mobile learning, to improve the quality of learning, mobile learning content resources, interaction design should strive to be innovative in form, content, informative, lively, with leading, motivating, inspiring. Specifically, efforts should be done several ways:

3.1 Reasonable Content and Forms of Organization

Learners in the construction of meaning in mobile learning and learning content is mainly between the learning content of the trade-offs, forms and methods of direct interaction determines the degree of self-learners. First, the designer of the learning content to a reasonable choice, the choice of content to facilitate mobile learning; Secondly, a good choice of learning content but also the rational organization, but also think about what forms of learning content used for learning who learn best. In order to facilitate mobile learning, learning content can be used to render the card type, and some complex learning content, you can use the visual image such as graphics, images, video, animation and other exhibits, if necessary, can be explained by adding the appropriate sound. Of course, in the use of a variety of media to express the same content, we must take full account of the space occupied by the media and network transmission speed, not abuse. Otherwise, the media feedback delay would seriously dampen the enthusiasm of the learner's learning.

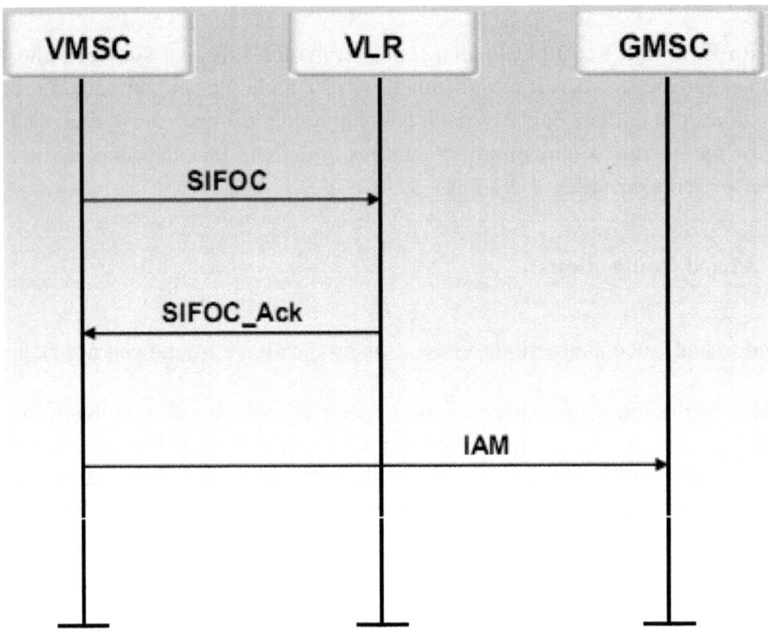

3.2 Mobile Network Under the Multi-perspective

First, the mobile network environment should take full advantage of information superiority, provide a lot of relevant information resources, making learning informative and detailed, so that students can learn the complex and uncertain resources, through various means to identify and select useful information; Second, students should use a variety of media resources, the same thing from different levels to grasp the essential characteristics or process. Finally, learners can use interactive tools and timely access to other people's decision-making information, different perspectives and feedback, so that they can on the knowledge or skills to repeat the study, and ultimately be able to learn course content with the representation of different perspectives access to knowledge of the depth.

4 Interpersonal Interaction for Mobile Learning Resources, Interactive Design Strategy

Communication session is the most basic form of interpersonal interaction. In mobile learning, mobile devices and networks can be achieved: the use of electronic bulletin board system at any time (BBS) or online chat (Chat) to guide learners to discuss issues; more easily through e-mail system (E-mail) or mobile phone short Information for interactive Q & A and so on. The tab as bellow:

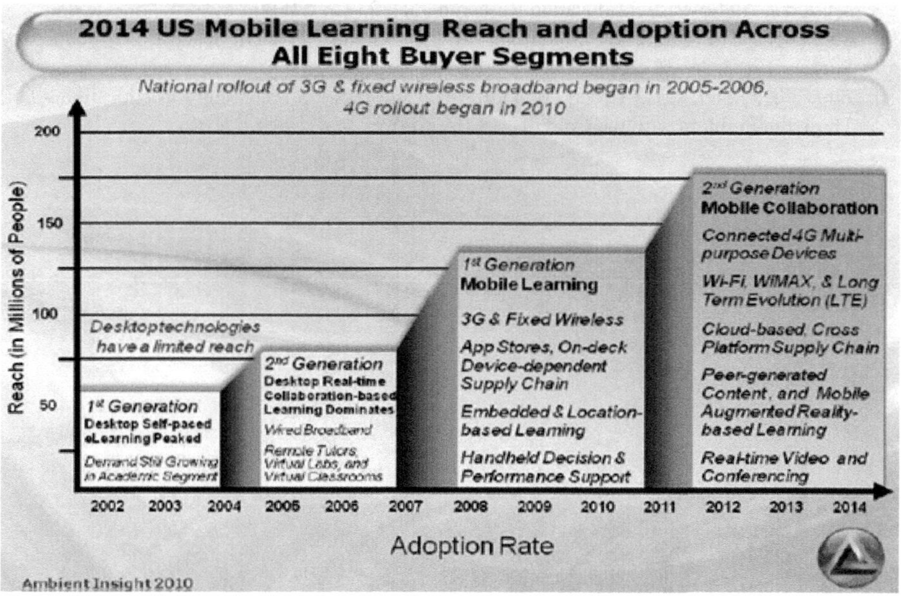

Achieve learners and learners, between learners and teachers of communication and more timely and efficient. You can also learn in the introduction of competition in training, is the competition-style interaction. It is divided into "single mode" and "double mode" two. The "double mode" is between two learners time by doing the exercises or other learning project approach, based on competitive results obtained corresponding points. In this way the interaction of interest to both strengthen the learner, but also effective in promoting active participation of learners, which is conducive to learning activities.

References

1. Yee, L.: Mobile and Interactive Learning Research. Software Navigation (4), 26 (2007)
2. Rosman, P.: M-learning – A paradigm of new forms in education. E & M Ekonomie a Management 11(1), 119–125 (2008)
3. Keegan, D.: Mobile Learning: The next generation of learning. Open Education (6), 40 (2004)
4. Gu, X.Y.: Based on situated cognition theory of interaction design of multimedia courseware. Nanjing Normal University Master thesis (2008)
5. Chan, K.F., Yeung, D.Y.: Recognizing online handwritten alphanumeric characters through flexible structural matching. Pattern Recognition 32(7), 1099–1114 (1999)
6. Jiang, L.B.: In Ling yun to based on 3G technology, mobile learning in adult education in the application. Modern Distance Education (3), 67–68 (2007)
7. Li, S.Q., Wu, X.: Based on WAP technology, mobile learning in high school English learning in the application of China. Education Information (14), 52–54 (2009)
8. Wang, L., Ma, X.: Opinion leaders in the Virtual Learning Community The role of social networks. Audio-Visual Education Research (11), 23–25 (2009)
9. Sun, J.H.: The future of computing in the "cloud". Modern Education Technology Surgery 19(8), 34–36 (2009)
10. Zhu, Z.T., Jiang, C.H.: Cloud computing and information technology in education - hot. Think the Problem with the Cold (4), 13–15 (2009)

Network-Based Construction of Open Virtual Laboratory Teaching Platform

Dong Lu, Chen Lian Qing, Xian Yu Dan Qian, Cui Ying Shan, Kan Lian He, and Song Li Chuan

Hebei Union University Modern technology education center Tang Shan 063000, China
{dl_ncmc,clq.555}@163.com, fsh484@sina.com,
{tsmycys,xinxislc}@126.com, kanlianhe@heuu.edu.cn

Abstract. Through expounding the importance of building up a network virtual laboratory, this paper introduces the key technology to construct the virtual laboratory, and the construction of the network virtual laboratory teaching platform, and the process of management background, and eventually set up a virtual experimental teaching platform, set the experiment management, experiment and test report and experimental evaluation at an organic whole, realized from the auxiliary teaching, independent experiment to the experiment report submitted online and reviews in the whole process of the operation and management, and meet the needs of the online experiment teaching. To strengthen the quality of the students in our school education and practice ability and to improve our education of information technology application level.

Keywords: virtual reality technology, virtual laboratory, virtual experiment teaching.

1 Introduction

According to China's national education development present situation and future development needs, fifteen years in education informationization to promote education modernization has become the important content of education reform. We to enhance the cultivation of students' innovation ability, the virtual experiment for the purpose of traditional experimental teaching as a supplement and evelopment, but also by experiment contents and experimental mode reform and innovation. Virtual laboratory can say is the application of information technology education field, by studying a kind of innovation to construct the virtual laboratory its key technologies, with virtual reality technology, network technology and database etc for support, modern information technology, To form a virtual laboratory[1], given the school campus and built to access the Internet circumstance, and combines practical situation, develop an open virtual experimental teaching system, reforming experiment teaching and cultivate creative talents.

C. Liu, J. Chang, and A. Yang (Eds.): ICICA 2011, Part I, CCIS 243, pp. 427–433, 2011.

2 The Establishment of Network Virtual Laboratory

2.1 The Establishment of the Virtual Laboratory Based on WEB

(1) Virtual reality technology Virtual Reality (is) in recent years and Reality of the rapid development of the information technology product, is a door in computer graphics, computer simulation technology, man-machine interface technology, multimedia technology and sensing technology developed on the basis of interdisciplinary. Computer generated by high technology simulation system, make the computer to produce a human virtual environment, make people in sight, hearing, touch on produce a immersed in the feeling of the environment, and realize the "experience" feeling. At present, in a foreign country, the virtual reality technology has already large used in classroom teaching. In China, the virtual reality technology in film and television, and cultural entertainment has wide application. In the higher education field, the virtual reality technology has been used in the virtual simulation campus, virtual teaching, virtual experiment, etc, such as China university of science and technology development of the geometry of the optical design experimental platform, radio university physical distance teaching system of virtual experiment. Our research on in higher education institutions and a small amount of research institutes.

Virtual reality has three basic characteristics. ①Immersion: Refers to the emotion of the virtual world observer reflects, and this feeling that the user can put into this virtual world in all, this is the first feature of virtual reality[2]. ②interactive: Refers to virtual reality is an open environment, can respond to user input by monitoring device, and can affect users and user influence. ③imaginary: Refers to virtual reality is not only a media, an advanced user interface, or an application system, it with vivid form reflect the mind of the designer. Virtual reality is stressing the three basic features in the system in the leading role. Virtual reality system according to the function is different, can be divided into three types: Tele-immersive virtual reality system, desktop type virtual reality system and distributed virtual reality system. Among them, the desktop type virtual reality system is using the software programming methods in monitors displayed 3d scene, users through the keyboard, mouse equipment and the virtual scene interaction, its characteristic is simple structure, low cost, easy to generalize.

(2) Network virtual laboratory The so-called virtual laboratory, is refers to the use of regional network or the Internet, from the virtual reality technology generated on a virtual experiment for the experimental system, including the corresponding lab environment, relevant experimental instrumentation equipment, the subjects and experimental information resources, etc[3]. Virtual laboratory can be a real laboratory real realization, also can be virtual idea laboratory, virtual experiment through the virtual laboratory. In virtual experiment, the volunteers have distinct feeling, were feeling, like is the real close in reality lab make site operation. In virtual experiments, not a tangible laboratory, nor take physical form exists with the experimental object, experimental tools for virtual experimental process is basically thing operation. Based on network platform of virtual laboratory has many advantages:

(1) Open platform In the traditional experimental mode, students must be the need for dedicated experiment field experiment. But limited experimental site is often

difficult to satisfy the infinite desire for knowledge, students. In order to solve this problem, this virtual experimental platform make full use of the Internet technology and server technology creating an open experimental platform, make teachers and students can at any time, through the classrooms and laboratories, dormitory or other local Internet access can the experiment.

(2) Innovation platform The traditional laboratory is commonly according to teaching syllabus and setting experiment item, students often only stipulated according to experimental instruction procedures to be conducted experiments, and in programming courses, students tend to be designed for the algorithm for verification. In order to solve this problem, this virtual experimental platform will be able to use the latest component and Web services technology, the students will according to their own ideas and not get bogged down in the textbook knowledge to experiment, expand its thinking[4].

(3) Extendable platform Information technology is developing rapidly, the content of courses, and constantly update to update the traditional laboratory experiment equipment is if requires completely changing equipment to meet the requirements, such costs are relatively large. In order to solve this problem, this virtual experimental platform has good scalability, make full use of component and Web service technical superiority, made in use process can quickly add new virtual set just keep modify platform code, and users can also according to their own needs to add corresponding in platform a virtual instrument.

(4) But online guide platform Experiment is exploration and practice knowledge learnt process, In this virtual experimental platform, students can at any time and any place, so when the experiment problem might often there is no guide teacher. In order to solve this problem, this virtual experimental platform provides online guidance function, students in the problem to the teacher or other students can request instruction, the teacher can also through the platform to all online his students experimental process.

(5) Low-cost platform Experimental construction is often the key school teaching investment, with the experimental course content renewal and the increase in student.

Numbers, laboratory investment also increasing. And some experiments is deteriorating experiments, In order to reduce operating costs, make students laboratory dare to try, this virtual experiment platform of experimental equipment can be reality is virtual, achieve the experimental effect of real equipment, but in the wrong operation will only give corresponding tip, and won't lead to improve the cost[5].

2.2 Based on the WEB Virtual Laboratory Building Key Techniques

(1) Java Technology. Java is a page from static into dynamic software programming language, Java is simple, object-oriented, interpreted, robust, and security and portable features[6], the more important is it cross-platform properties meet the network computer thoughts, Java or a dynamic code system, Java program downloaded to perform client port browsing, greatly enriched the customer forms, improve the ability to interact, realize visualization, auralization, can operationalization interactive

animation, Java these characteristics of the construction of virtual laboratory based on WEB useful.

(2) ActiveX technology. As for Internet application development technology, ActiveX is widely used in WEB server and client's each aspect, meanwhile ActiveX technology allows for the software development kit with each other in the network operation, it can be the code reusability also is in a virtual experiment in the development process, an experiment instrument in several experimental environment ActiveX components, including the environment of high efficiency and development is used the most accessible Visual Basic.

(3) VRML technology. VRML is a kind of three-dimensional scene descriptive language, it for users in the Internet, provided a new virtual world space. Will VEML based WEB virtual laboratory for the development process, can increase capacity, expressive and users can achieve good collaborative work virtualization environment[7].

(4) QTVR technology. QTVR is based on static image processing imaging modeling virtual reality technology can be applied to photos[8], video, QTVR or digital images to create virtual environment, make it more traditional multimedia technology, traditional virtual reality technology has higher realism, the more abundant images and details of more distinct characteristics.

(5) Safety and reliability System operation must be safe and reliable, request all-weather work, students at any time may log on the Internet, the network administrator of network maintenance regularly, the main data for backup.

3 How to Set Up Virtual Laboratory System

To build a network platform system, including hardware, software and management three aspects[9]. At present the schools have established the campus network and access to the Internet, these infrastructure can satisfy the demand, basic do not need much input. In software, a laboratory platform development of software system, its associated with website construction; Another is the web site's content (experiment content) construction, this is the key of laboratory construction. Virtual laboratory shall have can do experiments to support, or software platform is a mere skeleton, non-existing. Meanwhile, this platform also should have the support of the experiment management of experimental apparatus, test report, experiment guidance, experimental results and on-line question-answering etc, and the effective management of the virtual laboratory monitor. The computer network virtual laboratory the main function of each module in the system are as follows.

(1) The experiment management module By student management, teacher management, equipment management and student performance management etc. In the student management, students through the browser to register after landing successful login, you can visit experiment item, check the detailed material, booking experiment experimental projects and doing the experiment of time, online sending and receiving messages, carries on the discussion, to carry out experiments after completing the registration, the experiment by network lab report and submit the written report.

Teacher management of experimental contents, add, modify, sorting, delete, referred to the student experiment report lists, correcting the experiment report, fill in comments and achievements, submit result, and corrects students are discussed[10]. Instrument management, the development of new design for uploading and virtual instrument, so experiment classifies and use. Performance management aspects of students' experiment (test times, test report and complete the situation) gave the result, and statistical analysis and provide inquiry, etc.

(2) Instrument display module Available for virtual laboratory virtual components, virtual instrument equipment classify ground for the management, and to the graph way, for students presented intuitive choice in the experiment.

(3) Instrument display module Includes laboratory introduction, experiment method, experimental project emphasis and difficulty, experiment purposes, experimental principle, experiment preparation, experiment task, experimental process, test report requirements and experimental should note.

(4) Experiment report module Mainly to the students in the completion of experiments, provide related experimental report templates, for students to download by student fill in related content, the results of the experiment, and after completion, the experiment report upload softcopies reviews, and teachers accounts.

(5) Experimental question-answering module Experimental question-answering module of student experiment by professional teachers in the knotty problem appears to answer, helps the student to smoothly through the experiment. And understand students master degree of the of the experiment, and the timely feedback, adjusting teaching.

(6) BBS communication module Teachers and students can communicate via BBS sufficiently, students can will experiments of harvest, experience and experience and problems, and teachers to release it to the BBS of some typical problems can be brought out, for everybody discussion. Students in such relaxed environment their own opinions, teachers from which we can receive timely experiment teaching feedback information, so that the improvement.

(7) Virtual experiment modules Is an important part of the virtual laboratory construction. Students through the virtual experimental modules to strengthen the goal of knowledge. This module content according to the specific circumstances of professional study and experiment construction condition, can continue to increase. The computer professional network virtual laboratory system construction, may introduce other schools in the virtual laboratory. This method is simple and easy to implement, the effect quickly. But need to put more software purchase expenses, but also to the combination of the real situation some adjustment, have a period. Another kind is to adjust measures to local conditions, independent development. According to our practical teaching and experiment, and in combination with the student's actual level, teachers or hiring by the development team, composed some experts to conduct a series of virtual experiment project development research, and will be connected to the research achievement of virtual laboratory, expands gradually until perfect. This way is more agile, and less funding.

4 Network Virtual Laboratory Management

1. Strengthen the user management For every student distribution account. Virtual laboratory to students enter, use laboratory as virtual experiment register preservation. Background management mode is mainly to avoid administrator and user mix in a interface, and considering the security of the management system.
2. Round-the-clock open virtual laboratory. Students can always into virtual experiment real do-it-yourself organization experiment, to design the plan, begins to finish the experiment, sorting and summarized the experimental data and submit test report, cultivate the students' ability and the innovation ability, and analyzed by "gradually to the students as the center" the independent personality development model transformation.
3. Organize professional teachers online Guide to answer, Participate in BBS discussion, correcting the experiment report in time, For students finish the experiment provides services. Smooth. In virtual laboratory, the teachers should raise the question are students as soon as possible to help and solutions, and make the necessary guidance. Published in laboratory BBS view, questions let students thinking, make teachers and students in virtual laboratory, has the strong interactivity, teachers should act as a good student experiment collaborators and the construction of the knowledge of the role.
4. In virtual laboratory to students' performance and evaluation results. Each course for students of virtual experiment completion status, test report, online questions, BBS post, give students a grades and evaluation and feedback to students, and with the course of normal physical experiment with total credited experiment. The teacher also should on the student evaluation at the same time, asked the students for virtual laboratory's opinion, the information feedback to students rectification.

5 Conclusion

Teaching means, technology of digital and network, virtualization push education technology diversity, flexibility, intelligent, is the development trend of current higher education. Using the network virtual reality technology constructing virtual laboratory teaching platform solutions experimental operation under the network environment, can make up to mention interactive teaching especially remote network today to experiment teaching of the cognitive and practical problems. Can well solve the current hardware equipment can't keep up with the requirements, experiment with students' experiment time enough for such problems, improve students' practical ability and problem analysis and solution actual problem ability has the extremely vital significance. Believe based on network virtual reality technology in teaching field of teaching platform will play more and more important role.

References

1. Qu, Y.: Based on the campus network virtual laboratory of the design and research. Modern Education Technology 20(5), 133–134 (2010)
2. Wang, S.Y.: Virtual laboratory construction of the initial study. The Journal of Post and Telecommunications 10(2), 141–143 (2005)
3. Xu, H., et al.: Network virtual laboratory construction. Experimental Science and Technology Research 5(4), 132–134 (2007)
4. Zhang, H.S.: Based on the distance virtual laboratory. Modern Distance Education Research (2), 56–58 (2005)
5. Yang, J.: Based on campus network studios to construct the virtual laboratory. Sichuan University of Journal 21(10), 49–52 (2008)
6. Qiu, W.T.: Based on the virtual laboratory building WEB. Journal of Remote Education (6), 39–42 (2002)
7. Shen, J.H.: Vrml-based vr virtual laboratory development. Laboratory Research and Exploration 30(3), 342–346 (2011)
8. Zhou, M.Q.: Remote network virtual laboratory support technical analysis and comparison on computer age (8), 65–68 (2004)
9. Hu, C.W., et al.: Based on the network platform virtual laboratory technology research and implementation. Computer Applications 25(12), 319–321 (2005)
10. Xie, W.C., et al.: The virtual laboratory platform based on WEB design and software realization. Xihua University Journal 27(1), 69–72 (2008)

An Adaptive Routing Algorithm for Ad Hoc Network

Sihai Zheng, Layuan Li, and Yong Li

College of Computer Science and Technology,
Wuhan University of Technology, Wuhan, China, 430063
sihaizheng@sina.com

Abstract. In Ad Hoc network, the bandwidth is limited. If each node moves rapidly, it can easily lead to network congestion. Most of existing routing protocols can only provide single path, which will undoubtedly increase the network congestion. This paper proposes a new multipath routing protocol (i.e. MPDSR). The reliability of MPDSR is better than that of single path; it is adaptive to provide single path or multipath. The results of simulation show MPDSR can significantly increase the packet delivery ratio and decrease the average delay, the performance is better than DSR protocol.

Keywords: Ad Hoc, Multipath, Routing protocol, MPDSR.

1 Introduction

Ad Hoc networks are envisioned to have dynamic, sometimes rapidly changing, random, multihop topologies which are likely composed of relatively bandwidth constrained wireless links. Since every node in Ad Hoc network acts as both a host and a router, routing algorithm is a main research issue.

Some studies on multipath routing have carried out in Ad Hoc networks. MSR [1] is an extended multipath source routing algorithm based on DSR. It uses the path detection to reduce network congestion and network delay. But it assumes that the multipath is completely independent when the load is assigned, it does not achieve the complete independence among the paths to find a routing. Ref. [2] proposes a routing protocol called PARAODV, it only consider the nodes to participate path from the point of energy, which may lead to a path with excessive hops. Ref. [3] proposes a routing protocol called PTRSR, which considers the energy conservation and the traffic balance. However, the bottleneck node with the minimum residual energy in a path has not been considered, which may lead the network to split earlier.

The main contributes of this paper are as follow. We propose a adaptive multipath source routing protocol (i.e. MPDSR). In order to reduce the interference and make load balance between the multipaths, this paper focuses on the node disjoint path algorithm. Finally, the simulation analysis is completed. The results of simulation show MPDSR can significantly increase the packet delivery ratio, and greatly decrease the average delay, the performance of MPDSR is much better than that of DSR.

In the rest of this paper, we first discuss how to determine the number of multipath in section 2. MPDSR routing algorithm is analyzed in section 3. The results of simulation are shown in section 4. Finally, we offer the conclusion in section 5.

C. Liu, J. Chang, and A. Yang (Eds.): ICICA 2011, Part I, CCIS 243, pp. 434–441, 2011.

2 Number of Multipath

In the literature about multipath routing, generally only describes how to find the multipath routing, but the number of multipath is not clear illustrated and analyzed. In fact, the number of multipath is not the more the better. With the number of path increases, the routing overhead will be a corresponding increase too; protocol's performance not only has not been improved, but also has been decreased.

2.1 Mathematical Analysis

This paper uses a random variable to represent the life of a link between a pair of communication nodes. Assuming there is a routing from the source node S to the destination node D, it is composed the k links which step over k-1 intermediate nodes. Let L_i is the first i links in a routing (i=1,2, …,k-1); Its value of life is X_L. It is assumed that X_L is an independent and identically distributed variables, the average of each variable is l.

In the path P, it will interrupt as long as any link break. Therefore, the X_p, which is the life of the routing P, is a random variable; it can be express as follow:

$$X_P = \min(X_{L_1} X_{L_2} \ldots X_{L_k}) \tag{1}$$

According to the Ref. [4-5], we know that X_p is an exponentially distributed random variable; its average value is l/k. Now we derive the statistical properties of the T which is the interval between two consecutive routing searches in multipath routing.

Suppose there are N routings between the source node S and destination node D. P_1 is the first one, $P_2,P_3,\ldots,P_N$ are the others, the length of P_i is recorded as k_i. When the source node finds all routings are not available it will launch a process to search new routing. Then, the T can be expressed as follow:

$$T = \max\{X_{P_1} X_{P_2} \ldots X_{P_N}\} \tag{2}$$

Since X_{P_1}, X_{P_2}, …, X_{P_N} are exponentially distributed random variable, their probability density function is [6]:

$$f_{X_{P_i}}(t) = \lambda_i e^{-\lambda_i t} \,(\, \lambda_i = k_i / l \quad i = 1, 2, \cdots, N\,) \tag{3}$$

Because X_{P_i} is independent of each other, the cumulative distribution function $F_T(t)$ is:

$$\begin{aligned} F_T(t) &= P[T \le t] = P[\max\{X_{P_1}, X_{P_2}, \cdots, X_{P_N}\} \le t] \\ &= P[(X_{P_1} \le t) \cap (X_{P_2} \le t) \cap \cdots \cap (X_{P_N} \le t)] = \prod_{i=1}^{N} F_{X_{P_i}}(t) \end{aligned} \tag{4}$$

Since $f_{X_{P_i}}(t) = \lambda_i e^{-\lambda_i t}$, $F_{X_{P_i}}(t) = 1 - e^{-\lambda_{ii} t}$ are derived. Thus we get the probability density distribution function of T:

$$\begin{aligned} f_T(t) &= \lambda_1 e^{-\lambda_1 t}(1 - e^{-\lambda_2 t})(1 - e^{-\lambda_3 t}) \cdots (1 - e^{-\lambda_N t}) \\ &\quad + \cdots + \lambda_N e^{-\lambda_N t}(1 - e^{-\lambda_1 t})(1 - e^{-\lambda_2 t}) \cdots (1 - e^{-\lambda_{N-1} t}) \end{aligned} \tag{5}$$

According to (5), the mathematical expectation of T can be expressed as follow:

$$E(T) = \int_0^{+\infty} t f_T(t) dt \tag{6}$$

Here we give an example to illustrate the relationship between $E(T)$ and the number of multipath. If $N=2$, then:

$$E(T) = \int_0^{+\infty} t[\lambda_1 e^{-\lambda_1 t}(1-e^{-\lambda_2 t}) + \lambda_2 e^{-\lambda_2 t}(1-e^{-\lambda_1 t})]dt = \frac{\lambda_1^2 + \lambda_2^2 + \lambda_1\lambda_2}{\lambda_1\lambda_2(\lambda_1+\lambda_2)} \tag{7}$$

2.2 Data Analysis

For simplicity, we use two special cases of data for the statistics.

Case A: Suppose there are N routings between the source node S and destination node D. The original path is the shortest one, the length of other path is increased, and one unit increase in each path. That is:

$$k_1=k,\ k_2=k+1,\ \ldots,\ k_N=k+N\text{-}1;$$

Case B: Suppose there are N routings between the source node S and destination node D. The original path is the shortest one, the length of other path is increased, and two units increase in each path. That is:

$$k_1=k,\ k_2=k+2,\ \ldots,\ k_N=k+2(N\text{-}1);$$

In the calculation, $l=1$ and $k=3$, $N=1, 2, \ldots, 7$. The results are shown in Fig. 1.

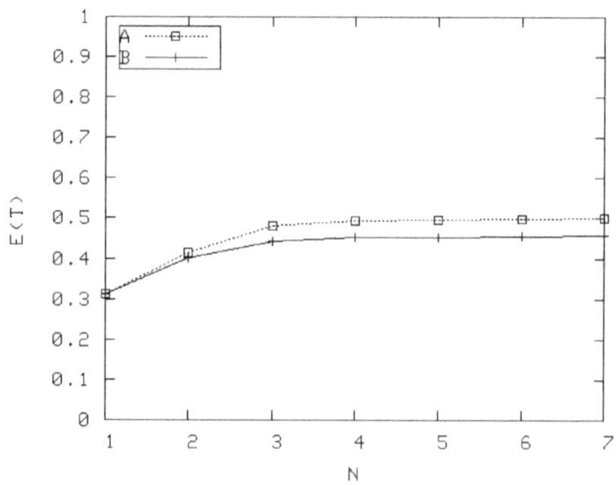

Fig. 1. The Relation Between E(T) and N

From Fig. 1, we find when N increases, E(T) also increases. When N>3, this trend is not obvious. Therefore, N=3 is enough in multipath routing, if N is more than 3, the performance is not improved obviously, and it will increase overhead of routing protocol.

3 Routing Algorithm

MPDSR protocol improves the RREQ packet of DSR; it increases several fields in the packet, which are convenient for recording multipath. The routing process is different from DSR, it consists of three parts. The first is routing request; the second is how to choose the node disjoint paths, and the third is routing maintenance.

3.1 Routing Request

In the process of the routing discovery, source node broadcasts RREQ packet to its neighbor nodes firstly. The format of RREQ is as follow:

Source_Addr	*Destination_Addr*	*Request_ID*	*Route_Record*	*Hops*

Source_Addr is the address of source node; Destination_Addr is the address of destination nodes; Request_ID is the serial number of routing request packet. Route_Record is the routing record. When routing request packet arrives at the destination node, the address of all nodes in this field is a available routing. Hops is the amount of the hops from source node to current node, which is used to prevent the excessive paths. <Source_Addr, Request_Addr > is used to uniquely identify a routing request packet.

3.2 Node Disjoint Path

When the destination node has collected several paths, MPDSR protocol begins to choose the node disjoint path in the cache. It will choose no more than three paths. At last, the destination node sends the information to source node using the least hops.

We define $G=<V,E>$ as a set of multipaths, which is directed acyclic graph. $V=\{ v_1,v_2,\ldots,v_n \}$ is the set of nodes in Ad Hoc networks, $E=\{e_1,e_2,\ldots,e_m \}$ is the set of links in V. If node n_i and n_j are neighbor nodes in one path, there is a directed link e_{ij} between n_i and n_j.

3.3 Correctness Verification and Complexity Analysis

Theorem 1. The routing selected by MPDSR is no loop.

Proof. Suppose p is a probe frame whose destination is node D, and $S(P, D)$ is the routing selected by MPDSR. If there is a loop in $S(P, D)$, then it show that there is a node i which have received p twice and forwarded it. It is conflict with DSR, which provides a node can only forward a probe frame. As MPDSR follows the mechanisms, $S(P, D)$ certainly has no loop.

Theorem 2. The time complexity of the routing algorithm in MPDSR is $O(6n)$.

Proof. MPDSR need to send a probe frame to find a routing, the time cost to successfully establish a path is s round trip. Assuming the cost each message pass a link is a unit, n is the maximum number of hops chosen multipath, in addition, MPDSR choose up to three paths. Therefore, the time complexity of the routing algorithm in MPDSR is $O(6n)$.

Theorem 3. The complexity of the message in MPDSR is $O(9n)$.

Proof. MPDSR mainly uses two messages, Route Request and Route Reply, to find routing. As the number of multipaths is 3, there will be 9 packets in each process of routing discovery. n is the maximum number of hops chosen multipath, then each message must be forwarded up to $9n$ times.

4 Experiment Analysis

To evaluate the new algorithm and compare it to existing algorithms, simulations are performed. A Mobility Framework for NS2 [7], a discrete event simulator written in C++, is used as a tool. Two sets of experiment were carried out. The scene is 800m × 800m, there are 50 nodes in the scene, and they are randomly distributed;

In the first set, Mobile nodes have the same maximum speed and different connections. The maximum moving speed is 10m/s. The connections are 5, 10, 15, 20, 25 and 30. Fig. 2, 3 and 4 show the results of the first set.

In the second set, Mobile nodes have the same connections and different maximum speed. The connections are 15. The maximum moving speed is 0, 5, 10, 15, 20 and 25. Fig. 5, 6 and 7 show the results of the second set.

Fig. 2 shows the packet delivery ratio when the connections are changed. When the connections are 5, their packet delivery ratio is about 95%, but when the connections increase to 30, the difference is obvious. The packet delivery ratio of MPDSR is always more than that of DSR. Especially, if there are more connections, and more network loads, the advantage of MPDSR is more obvious.

Fig. 3 shows the average delay when the connections are changed. With the connections increasing, it also increases. This is due to multipath transmission, which can reduce waiting time of the data in the queue, thus significantly reduce the delay.

Fig. 4 shows the routing overhead when the connections are changed. We find the routing overhead of MPDSR is more. That because it needs to search several paths simultaneously, more RREQ packets must be forwarded, that correspondingly increases the routing overhead. But the increasing overhead is in the acceptable range.

Fig. 5 shows the packet delivery ratio when the maximum node speed is changed as well as 50 nodes and 15 connections. Although when the connections increase, the packet delivery ratio both decrease much, MPDSR is better than DSR. MPDSR adopts several routings to work; only if all routing is not available it stops transmitting packet. Therefore, the routing of MPDSR can work longer hours.

Fig. 6 shows when nodes move rapidly, the end to end delay respectively increase, which increase the probability of re-routing. Because MPDSR makes use of multipath to transmit packet simultaneously, the end to end delay is less.

Fig. 7 shows routing overhead of MPDSR is more than that of DSR, but the difference is not obvious.

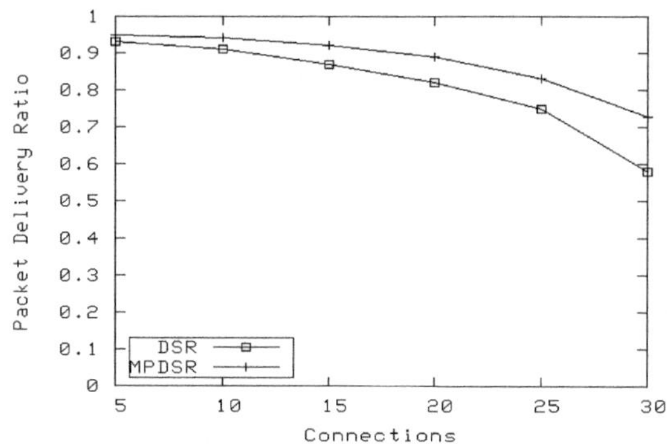

Fig. 2. Packet delivery ratio of different connections

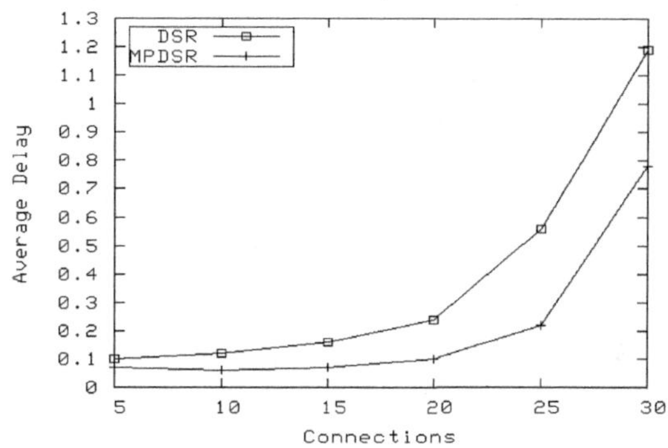

Fig. 3. Average delay of different connections

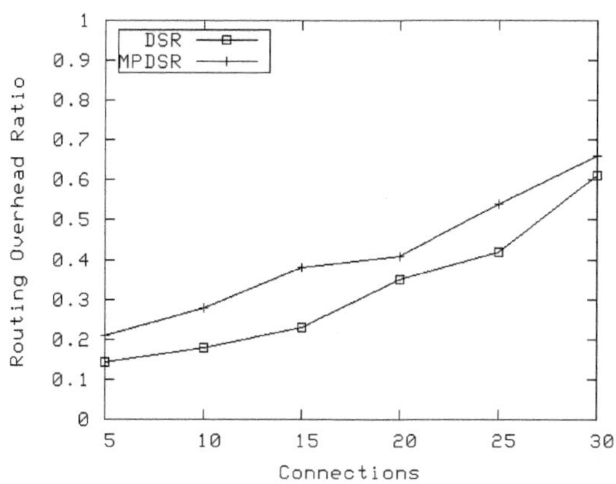

Fig. 4. Routing overhead of different connections

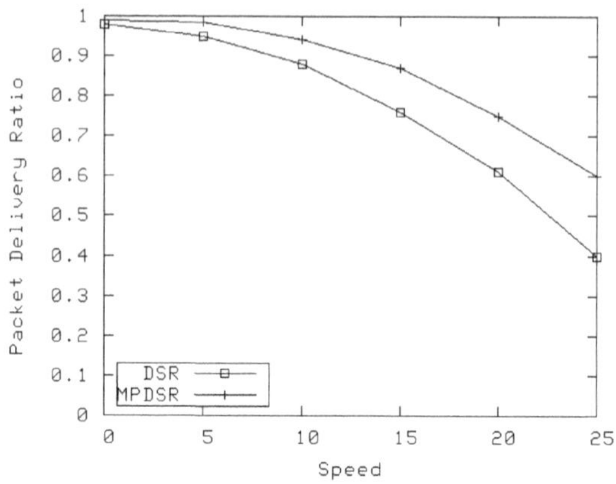

Fig. 5. Packet delivery ratio of different speed

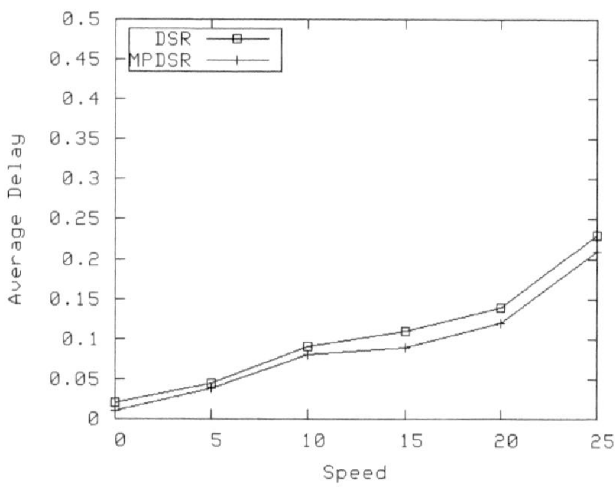

Fig. 6. Average delay of different speed

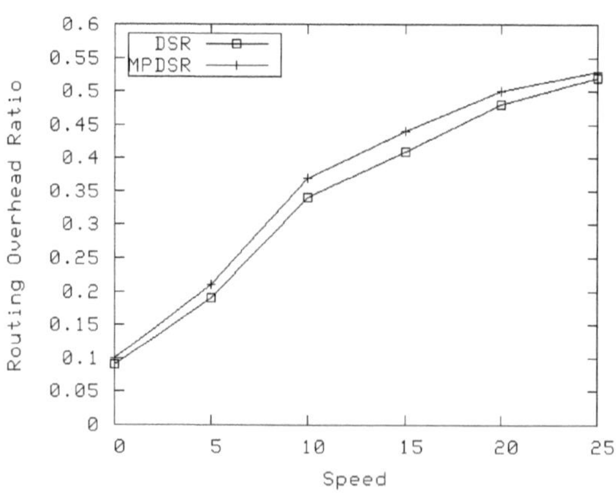

Fig. 7. Routing overhead of different speed

5 Conclusion

This paper proposes MPDSR routing protocol. By incorporating the multipath mechanism into DSR and employing a probing based on load balancing mechanism. We analyze its stability and how to determine the number of multipaths. Routing mechanism and routing maintenance are described in detail. Finally, simulation is completed. The results show its performance is better than DSR. In the future work, we might focus on how to include QoS support into MPDSR, so that it can provide a certain quality of service.

Acknowledgments. This paper is supported by National Natural Science Foundation of China(No: 60672137, 60773211, 60970064), Open Fund of the State Key Laboratory of Software Development Environment(No: SKLSDE-2009KF-2-02), New Century Excellent Talents in university(No: NCET-08-0806), Specialized Research Fund for the Doctoral Program of Higher Education of China(No:20060497105).

References

1. Wang, L., Zhang, L.F., Shu, Y.T.: Multipath source routing in wireless ad hoc networks. In: Proc. of Canadian Conference on Electrical and Computer Engineering, pp. 497–483. Institute of Electrical and Electronics Engineers Inc. (2000)
2. Lee, S.J., Gerla, M.: Split multipath routing with maximally disjoint paths in Ad Hoc networks. In: Proc. of IEEE International Conference on Communications, Helsinki, pp. 3201–3205 (2001)
3. Mateen, W., Raza, S., Uzmi, Z.A.: Adaptive multi-path on-demand routing in mobile ad hoc networks. In: Proceedings-Eighth IEEE International Symposium on Object Oriented Real-Time Distributed Computing, ISORC 2005, pp. 237–244. Institute of Electrical and Electronics Engineers Computer Society (2005)
4. Senouci, S.M., Pujolle, G.: Energy efficient routing in wireless Ad Hoc networks. In: IEEE International Conference of Communication, ICC (2004)
5. Xia, L., Song, Z., Su, X.: Ad-hoc multipath routing protocol based on load balance and location information. In: 2009 International Conference on Wireless Communications and Signal Processing, WCSP (2009)
6. Robert, A., Hunjet, E.: Power and Placement: Increasing Mobile Ad hoc Network Capacity and Power Efficiency. 978-1-4244-2322- 4/08/ Commonwealth of Australia (2008)
7. Chen, L.X.: NS2 based performance measurement of mobile ad hoc networks routing protocols. Journal of Computational Information Systems 3(1), 109–115 (2007)

An Efficient Clustering Algorithm for Mobile Ad Hoc Networks

Sihai Zheng, Layuan Li, Yong Li, and Junchun Yuan

College of Computer Science and Technology,
Wuhan University of Technology, Wuhan, China, 430063
sihaizheng@sina.com

Abstract. Most of clustering algorithms are too complicated and some computations about several factors are not reasonable. To effectively solve those problems, this paper proposes a new efficient clustering algorithm based on AOW, named EAOW. Then we use it to replace the minimum node ID clustering algorithm in CBRP routing protocol, i.e. EARP. New protocol takes into account the mobility and residual energy; it significantly improves network performance, enhance the overall network load balancing. Simulation experiments in NS2 validate its feasibility and correctness. The performance of EARP is much better than CBRP routing protocol.

Keywords: Ad Hoc, clustering algorithm, EAOW, routing protocol, EARP.

1 Introduction

For clustering algorithm in Ad Hoc network, nodes should been divided into several clusters. There are cluster head nodes, gateway nodes and member nodes in each cluster [1]. The routing protocol based on cluster algorithm can reduce the effect caused by the mobility of nodes and the flooding overhead in the process of routing discovery, and it can accelerate the process of routing seeking. In order to avoid the algorithm is frequently triggered, node usually maintains complete routing information only inside cluster. The routing between clusters shields the topology changes inside the cluster by means of virtual backbone.

Here are two well-known routing protocols based on clustering algorithm.

CBRP [2] (Cluster Based Routing Protocol) is a distributed, scalable and efficient routing protocol. It uses hierarchical mechanism to reduce flooding packets in the process of on-demand routing discovery. Also, local repair mechanism is used to increase the packet delivery rate, reduce delay and routing overhead. Each routing is optimized by shortening mechanism.

CEDAR [3] (Core Extraction Distributed Ad Hoc Routing Algorithm) is a clustering algorithm based on QoS; its goal is to build a stable virtual core structure which can spread routing information reliably. The core area of CEDAR consists of core nodes. Ordinary nodes select a core node as its ruler. The advantage of CEDAR is that the routing discovery and maintenance is carried out between the core nodes. When the network size is larger, the control overhead is less, which can better support the real time application based on QoS.

C. Liu, J. Chang, and A. Yang (Eds.): ICICA 2011, Part I, CCIS 243, pp. 442–449, 2011.

The main contributes of this paper are as follow. We have in-depth researched on the typical clustering algorithm, and propose a new efficient clustering algorithm (EAOW). Then we use EAOW algorithm to replace the minimum node ID clustering algorithm in CBRP routing protocol, named EARP. New protocol significantly improves network performance; enhance the overall network load balancing. Experiments validate its feasibility and correctness. The performance of EARP is much better than CBRP routing protocol.

In the rest of this paper, we first propose the related definitions in section 2. Then, EAOW algorithm is analyzed in section 3. The experiments and analysis are shown in Section 4. At last, we offer conclusions in Section 5.

2 Related Definition

Definition 1. Ad Hoc network topology is actually a graph which consists of nodes and links, denoted by $G=(V, E)$. Where V is the set of nodes, E is the set of edges. If there exists one edge denoted by (i, j) between node n_i and node n_j, then n_i and n_j are neighbors with one hop and they can communicate each other.

Definition 2. $d(x, y)$ is defined as the minimum *hops* between node n_i and node n_j. If n_i and n_j can directly communicate each other, then $d(x, y)=1$; Else $d(x, y)>1$. If n_i and n_j can not communicate at all, then $d(x, y)=\infty$.

Definition 3. A cluster $C_i \subset V$ is a set of such nodes, in which if $x, y \in C_i$ then $d(x, y) \leq h$, where h is a system parameter and $V=\cup C_i$. If $C_i \cap C_j=\varphi$, $i \neq j$, then C_i and C_j are called non-overlapping clusters; Else they are overlapping clusters.

Definition 4. In cluster C_i with cluster head h, if $\max\{d(x, h), x\in C_i\} \leq k$, then C_i is called the k-hops cluster with cluster head. In cluster C_j without cluster h, if $\max\{d(x, h), x, y\in C_j\} \leq k$, then C_j is called the k-hops cluster without cluster head.

Definition 5. If $N[k]=\cup_j \in_V\{j \mid d(k, j) \leq 1\}$, then the ruling set S consists of all nodes k. Each node in the network belongs to either S or the neighbors in S.

Definition 6. Node degree is the number of its neighbors with one hop. It is denoted by $ND(k)=|N[k]|-1$.

3 EAOW Algorithm

EAOW (Efficient Adaptive On-demand Weighting) algorithm is based on the following assumption:

1) When network is initialized, each node can obtain the ID of its neighbors in the process of exchanging control message.
2) A message sent by a node should be received correctly by all neighbors in a corresponding period.

3.1 Mobile Constrained Eigenvalue

Suppose $K=(k_1, k_2, \ldots, k_n)^T$ is constraint space, where k_i respectively denote the computing power of node n_i, physical link state, available bandwidth, residual energy, stability of cluster, etc.

Definition 7. Function $f_1(x), f_2(x), \ldots, f_n(x)$ are respectively the different constraints. If $n_i \in G$, then its function with constraints is denoted by *Deg*(*i*):

$$\mathrm{Deg(i)} = \lambda_1 \mathrm{f_1(x)} + \lambda_2 \mathrm{f_2(x)} + \ldots + \lambda_n \mathrm{f_n(x)} = \sum \lambda_i \mathrm{f_i(x)} \quad (1)$$

Where λ_i is the weight factor of constraint function, if R_i is the constraint degree of n_i, then $R_i = |Deg(i)|$.

R_i denotes the communication state and communication ability of node n_i. To simplify EAOW algorithm, the value space of R_i is divided into four intervals, which respectively represent four communication states.

$$s_i = \begin{cases} 0, 0 \le R_i < X_1 \\ 1, X_1 \le R_i < X_2 \\ 2, X_2 \le R_i < X_3 \\ 3, X_3 \le R_i < X_4 \end{cases} \quad (2)$$

Where $0<X_1<X_2<X_3<X_4<1$, n_i ($n_i \in G$) is in any above state (i.e. S_i). $S_i=0$ shows n_i has poor ability to communicate, that is n_i can not communicate with others; $S_i=1$ shows n_i has general ability to communicate with others, it can be act as a ordinary communication node; $S_i=2$ shows n_i has strong ability to communicate with others, it can be act as a cluster head candidate; $S_i=3$ shows n_i has stronger ability to communicate with others, it can be act as a cluster head.

3.2 EAOW Weight

When EAOW algorithm selects cluster head, it mainly takes into account the following four factors: node degree, transmission power, node mobility and residual energy. EAOW algorithm already treat the transmission power of node and residual energy as part of constraints, so in fact, there are only three factors need be considered: node degree, distance between nodes and its neighbors, node relative mobility. EAOW will assign each node involving in election a weight, nodes with minimum weight will be elected as cluster head. We can use equation (3) to calculate the weight of node [4].

$$\mathrm{W_i = w_1 M_i + w_2 D_i + w_3 \Delta_i} \quad (3)$$

Where W_i is the weight of node n_i, w_j (j=1, 2, 3) is respectively the coefficient of weight, which is different in different application. M_i is the relative mobility of node n_i. $\triangle_i$ is the deviation of node degree between the degree of n_i and the optimal node degree. D_i is the sum of distance between and its all neighbors.

In Ad Hoc network, we should consider the relative mobility instead of the speed of movement because most of nodes may randomly move. Comparing the signal strength received from its neighbors with the old value in cache, we can estimate the relative mobility. Suppose $M_y(x)$ is the relative mobility between n_y and n_x, then,

$$\mathrm{M_y(x) = 10lg(R_xP_{newr}x \rightarrow y / R_xP_{oldr}x \rightarrow y)} \quad (4)$$

Where $R_xP_r^{new}\, x \rightarrow y$ is the power current node n_y has received from n_x. $R_xP_r^{old}\, x \rightarrow y$ is the power node n_y has previously received from n_x. If $M_y(x)<0$, it shows two nodes is gradually moving away, else the two nodes is moving close to each other. The local relative mobility is expressed as follow:

$$M_y=\sum^{m}_{j=1}|M_y(x_j)|/m \tag{5}$$

If M_y is less, the relative mobility of node is also less, else it is stronger.

3.3 Optimal Size of Cluster

If there are too much member nodes in a cluster, the cluster head must manage a great number of packets simultaneously, which may cause congestion. On the contrary, if there are too few members in a cluster, the bandwidth of cluster head can not be fully utilized [5]. In order to get best throughput, we can derive the optimal size of cluster using equation (6).

$$R=\theta(W/\sqrt{n}) \tag{6}$$

Where W is the channel bandwidth. In EAOW algorithm, the cluster head will construct a high-level backbone network, in which the traffic of a cluster is the sum of all traffics. If N is the total number of all nodes, m is the number of cluster, and then the number of nodes in each cluster is N/m. The bandwidth within cluster is denoted by w_1, the bandwidth between clusters is denoted by w_2, the traffic of each member in cluster is expressed as equation (7).

$$R_{local}=\theta(w_1/\sqrt{N/m}) \tag{7}$$

The traffic of each backbone member node is expressed as equation (8).

$$R_{backbone}=\theta(w_2/\sqrt{m}) \tag{8}$$

The cluster head is in charge of the communication between inside and outside cluster, which has two interfaces. That is, it is not only a member of cluster, but also a node work in backbone network. Assuming network traffic is evenly distributed, the traffic which cluster head had exchanged to outside cluster is $(m\text{-}1)/m$ of total traffic of cluster head. To avoid congesting, we can derive the following inequality from equation (7) and (8).

$$((m-1)/m)R_{local}<R_{backbone} \tag{9}$$

Now, our goal is to derive the optimal size of cluster. If $m=M$, where M is the optimal size, then $((m\text{-}1)/m)R_{local}$ will be the maximum, which is in line with equation (10). If $m<M$, some bandwidth will be wasted. On the contrary, the backbone can not cover all business, which may cause seriously congestion [6].

According to equation (7) and (8), the ceiling of $((m\text{-}1)/m)R_{local}$ and $R_{backbone}$ is respectively expressed as following:

$$(M\text{-}1)/M\sqrt{8/\pi}\,(w_1/\Delta)\sqrt{N/M}\ ,\ \sqrt{8/\pi}\,(w_2/\Delta)\sqrt{M}$$

If $m=M$, then we can derive equation (11) from above analysis,

$$(M\text{-}1)/M\sqrt{8/\pi}\,(w_1/\Delta)\sqrt{N/M} = \sqrt{8/\pi}\,(w_2/\Delta)\sqrt{M} \tag{10}$$

The solution of equation is expressed as equation (11).

$$M=(w_1/w_2)\sqrt{N}+1 \tag{11}$$

If there are large number of N in network, equation (11) is simplified as (12).

$$M=(w_1/w_2)\sqrt{N} \tag{12}$$

Therefore, if the optimal size of cluster is denoted by δ, then,

$$\delta = N/M = (w_2/w_1)\sqrt{N} \tag{13}$$

3.4 Theorem and Proof

Theorem 1. In EAOW algorithm, if *ch* and *ch'* are respectively two different cluster head in $G=(V, E)$, then *ch* will find an available routing to *ch'*.

Proof. There are two cases should be proofed in this theorem.

Case 1. If *ch* and *ch'* are neighbors each other, suppose gw_1 and gw_2 are gateway between them, where gw_1 is in cluster *ch* and gw_2 is in cluster *ch'*. As *ch* and *ch'* are neighbors, then $(gw_1, gw_2) \in E$. gw_1 and gw_2 can receive HELLO message from each other. In addition *ch* can receive message from gw_1, so *ch* and *ch'* can receive message from each other. Therefore, *ch* can find an available routing to *ch'*.

Case 2. If *ch* and *ch'* are not neighbors. Suppose there are other clusters between *ch* and *ch'*, such as ch_1, ch_2, …, ch_i. According to case 1 the whole network is connected. *ch* and ch_1 communicate with each other through gateway *gw*, and ch_1 and ch_2 communicate with each other through gw_1, …, ch_i and *ch'* communicate with each other through gw_i. Therefore, there is at least one available routing between *ch* and *ch'*, such as $P=\{ch, gw, ch_1, gw_1, ch_2, gw_2, ch_3, gw_3, \ldots, ch_i, gw_i, ch'\}$.

Theorem 2. In EAOW algorithm, if n_1 and n_2 are any two nodes in $G=(V, E)$, then n_1 will find an available routing to n_2.

Proof. There are four cases should be proofed in this theorem.

Case 1. If n_1 and n_2 are both cluster head, then n_1 can find an available routing to n_2 according to theorem 1.

Case 2. If n_1 is not a cluster head and n_2 is a cluster, suppose n_1 belongs to a cluster *ch*. According to theorem 1, *ch* will find an available routing to n_2. As n_1 is the member node of *ch*, n_1 will find a routing to n_2.

Case 3. If n_1 is a cluster head and n_2 is not a cluster, suppose n_2 belongs to a cluster *ch'*. n_1 can communicate with *ch'*, and n_2 is the member node of *ch'*, then n_1 will find an available routing to n_2.

Case 4. If neither of n_1 and n_2 are cluster head, suppose n_1 belongs to *ch* and n_2 belongs to *ch'*. *ch* can communicate with *ch'*, n_1 can communicate with *ch* and n_2 communicate with *ch'* directly. Therefore, n_1 will find an available routing to n_2 through *ch* and *ch'*.

4 Experiment and Analysis

To evaluate the new algorithm and compare it to existing algorithms, simulations are performed. A Mobility Framework for NS 2 [7], a discrete event simulator written in C++, is used as a tool. Two sets of experiment were carried out. In the first set, the scene is 1000m × 1500m, there are 50 nodes in the scene, and they are randomly distributed; Data source is CBR, packet size is 512 bytes, it sends a packet in each second. Each experiment spent 600s; the maximum moving speed is 20m/s, the initial energy each node has is 400J. The pause time of nodes are respectively 0s, 50s, 100s, 150s, 200s and 250s. Network topologies are constructed by *setdest* [8]. The best size of cluster is 6 in EARP protocol, and w_1=0.4, w_2=0.2 and w_3=0.25. The results are shown in fig. 1. In the second set, the numbers of nodes are respectively 10, 60, 110, 160, 210, 26, 310 and 360 in scene; the pause time is 0s. The best size of cluster is approximately $\sqrt{N}$ in EARP protocol. The results are shown in Fig. 2, 3, 4.

From Fig. 1 we find their packet delivery rates are both continually increased when nodes pause longer. That is because the network topology is changed only a little when nodes pause longer, which make network is relatively stable and less packets are dropped. EAOW algorithm takes into account relative mobility of nodes, if nodes move frequently, its cluster is more stable than the minimum ID algorithm. If nodes pause longer, the clusters of CBRP protocol are also stable more and more, but the complexity of EARP protocol is higher. Therefore, its data delivery rate is less than CBRP.

Fig. 2 shows data delivery rate is rapidly increased while the number of nodes is less than 160, but it is slowly decreased while the number of nodes is more than 160. That is because some paths will become longer if there are more nodes in network, more and more packets are dropped in process of transmission, then the two data delivery rates are decreased.

Fig. 3 shows the relationship between network lifetime and the number of nodes. The network lifetime of EARP is apparently longer than that of CBRP. In CBRP routing protocol, a cluster head, the node with the minimum ID, will consume much more energy than member nodes. In general, the cluster head will soon run out of its energy. Whereas the cluster head will become a member node when its energy is less than the specific threshold in EARP, and a new cluster must be elected. This kind of mechanism can effectively prolong network lifetime.

Fig. 4 shows the relationship between routing overhead and the number of nodes. From fig. 4 we find more nodes, more routing overhead. As there are more nodes, both protocols must maintain more routing information in cache and great amount of control message should be forwarded. But the two lines are very close, showing EARP only increases a little routing overhead.

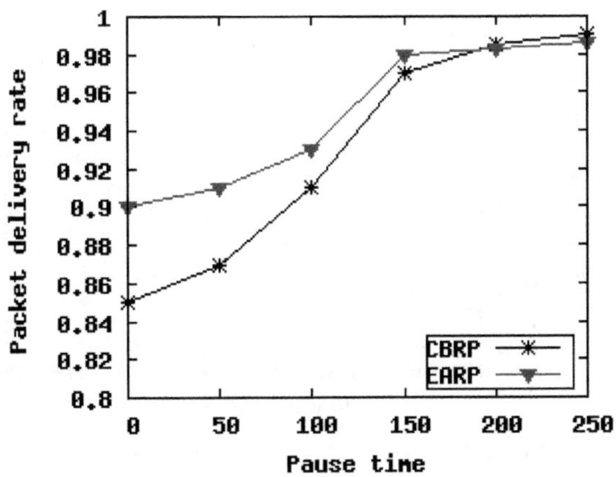

Fig. 1. Packet delivery rate of 50 nodes

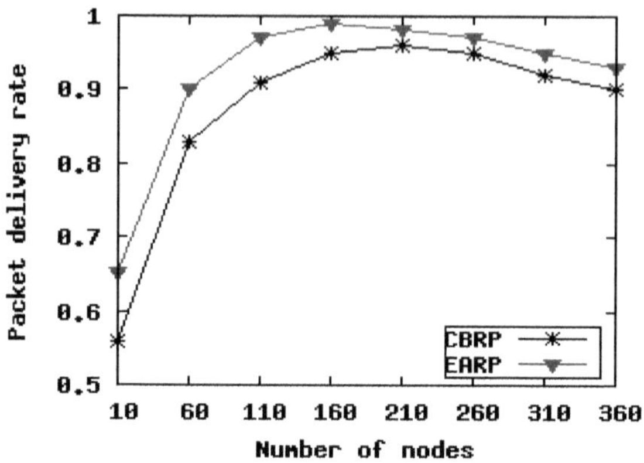

Fig. 2. Packet delivery rate and number of nodes

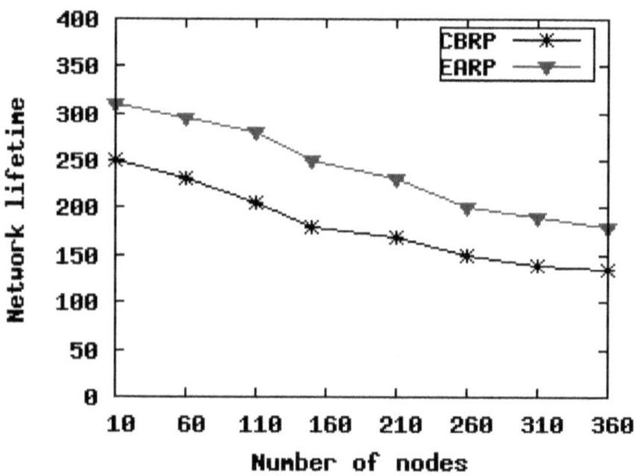

Fig. 3. Network lifetime and number of nodes

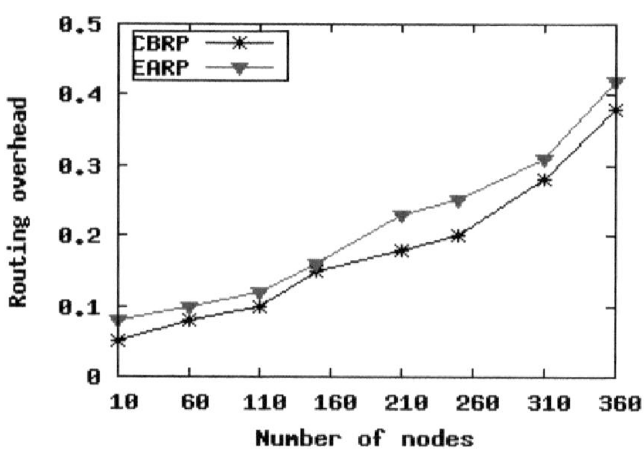

Fig. 4. Routing overhead and number of nodes

5 Conclusion

This paper proposes a new clustering algorithm (i.e. EAOW), then EAOW algorithm takes place the minimum ID algorithm in CBRP routing protocol, i.e. EARP routing protocol. New protocol can improve the performance of network and enhance the ability of load balancing. The results of simulation shows EARP can optimize clustering algorithm and prolong network lifetime, it also enhances the robustness of network. The drawback of EAOW is the routing overhead is more than AOW. Fortunately, the computer is becoming more powerful, so it may not be the obstacle to the deployment of EAOW algorithm. In the future work, we might focus on how to include QoS support into EAOW, so that it can provide a certain quality of service.

Acknowledgments. This paper is supported by National Natural Science Foundation of China (No: 60672137, 60773211, 60970064), Open Fund of the State Key Laboratory of Software Development Environment (No: SKLSDE-2009KF-2-02), New Century Excellent Talents in university(No: NCET-08-0806), Specialized Research Fund for the Doctoral Program of Higher Education of China(No:20060497105).

References

1. Jeng, J.T., Chuang, C.C.: Robust interval competitive agglomeration clustering algorithm with outliers. International Journal of Fuzzy Systems 12(3), 227–236 (2010)
2. Lee, K.H., Suh, H.S., Han, S.B.: An authentication protocol based on CBRP in ad hoc network. In: 6th International Conference on Advanced Communication Technology: Broadband Convergence Network Infrastructure, vol. 1, pp. 407–412 (2004)
3. Qi, W., Zhang, X., Yu, H.: An improved CEDAR routing protocol. In: The Fourth International Conference on Computer and Information Technology, CIT 2004, pp. 621–626 (2004)
4. Karunakaran, S., Thangaraj, P.: An adaptive weighted cluster based routing (AWCBRP) protocol for mobile Ad-hoc networks. WSEAS Transactions on Communications 7(4), 248–257 (2008)
5. Sheikh, Z., Moham, M., Fanian, A.: A cluster-based key establishment protocol for wireless mobile ad hoc networks. CCIS, vol. 6, pp. 585–592 (2008)
6. Wang, Y., Dong, L., Liang, T.: Cluster Based Location-Aided Routing Protocol for large scale mobile ad hoc networks. IEICE Transactions on Information and Systems E92-D(5), 1103–1124 (2009)
7. Chen, L.X.: NS2 based performance measurement of mobile ad hoc networks routing protocols. Journal of Computational Information Systems 3(1), 109–115 (2007)
8. Ruoshan, K.: The simulation for network mobility based on NS2. In: Proceedings - International Conference on Computer Science and Software Engineering, CSSE 2008, vol. 4, pp. 1070–1074 (2008)

Research on Semantic Web Service Composition Based on Ontology Reasoning and Matching

Jianfeng Zhang, Piyuan Lin*, Peijie Huang, and Guangfa Wu

College of Informatics, South China Agricultural University,
Guangzhou 510642, Guangdong, China
pyuanlin@163.com

Abstract. Semantic Web Service enables Web Service to become an entity which computer can understand, supporting automatic discovery, execution and composition of services. Thus it has gradually become a focus of service-oriented computing research. OWL-S,which is a W3C recommendation, lacks clear description of non-functional properties, effective service matching algorithms and dynamic adjustment of service, and it is executed just in one way strictly without much flexibility in the practical application, resulting in the limitation of its widespread adoption. In this paper, OWL-S is effectively extended by a proposed method based on ontology semantics reasoning and matching which is to support the automated discovery, matching and composition of Web Service, implemented by adding essential ontology information to expand Web Service ontology. Moreover, its effectiveness has been verified by a case study of veterinarian reservation service.

Keywords: Semantic Web Service, OWL-S, Ontology Reasoning, Ontology Matching.

1 Introduction

Internet environment's dynamic, heterogeneity and other features require that Web-based services provided should be of flexibly and reliably to meet customer needs, implement the target of "on-demand service" [1]. Web Services is a dynamic combination of automatic selection of program or agency, assembling the appropriate Web Service to complete the task with user a high-level format on a formal task description [2]. The expansion based on semantic description of Web Services will enable computers to better understand Web Services, achieving the automatic discovery automatic matching, automatic combination of Web Services in order to complete the user-specific needs [3]. Therefore, dynamic Web Services composition implemented by the extension based on semantic description of Web Services is a recognized method. Since the W3C OWL-S(Ontology Web Language for Services) has been accepted as a standard Web Service description, many combinations based on the semantics are OWL-S. Domestic researches are still relatively less, which

* Corresponding author.

C. Liu, J. Chang, and A. Yang (Eds.): ICICA 2011, Part I, CCIS 243, pp. 450–457, 2011.

mainly integrate semantic information to the WSDL language in OWL-S ontology to add geographic information [4], while foreign portfolio of Dynamic Service Composition researches focus on matching discovery algorithm [5], and integrate the semantic information into a traditional Web Service discovery mechanisms (e.g. UDDI).

2 Model of Dynamic Service Composition Based on OWL-S

2.1 Overview of Model

Overview of Ontology. The ontology concept is originated in the field of philosophy [6] and the first definition in the computer field of artificial intelligence disciplines is given by Neches's team, who defined ontology as "the field is given constitutes a basic vocabulary terms and relationships, and the use of these terms and relations constitute the provisions of these terms extension of the definition of the rules [7] ".

Experimental Model Based on OWL-S. OWL-S [8] is based on the OWL ontology language for Web Services. OWL-S has defined a set of core language components, which are used to make a logic description of Web Service whose generated description file supports semantic Web Services in order to achieve the automatic discovery [9], invocation, composition and monitoring.

As a body of knowledge describing Web Services, OWL-S aims to be the logic of a Web Service description [10]. However, OWL-S becomes inflexible and lack scalabilities if it is used only in this way, the next section of this paper is to show a experimental model to fine-tune and improve, directly adding a subclass on the "thing" Class of owl's as non-functional properties to support the corresponding reasoning and matching work.

The problem that lack of non-functional semantic description is partly solved by OWL-S ontology extension. Thus, a dynamic service composition model is designed by using the OWL-S framework. In this model, with the help of OWL-S Editor in WSDL2OWL-S Converter achieving the convert from a WSDL file to an OWL-S file [11], and then the necessary semantics are added into service ontology which can be used for matching afterwards. It will match the corresponding Web Service according to user requests and preferences and generate a combination sequence and then call the Web Service accordingly. The next section includes the design and implementation of Web Service ontology, the reasoning and matching of Web Service ontology and composition of Web Service.

2.2 Design and Implement of Web Service Ontology

This instance only uses a Web Service description WSDL in order to make this example become Web Services based on OWL-S. Because as long as the business logic is exposed as Web Services form, and Web Services are published in the UDDI registry, any user can via WSDL2OWL-S & QoS agent to dynamically discover and invoke these services, no matter what platforms their system bases on and what development of language they use [12].

This step makes a preparation for reasoning and matching services, which needs to abstract information of ontology required by service matching and saves it into the ontology library in order to ensure that it can be used in the course of reasoning and matching afterwards. In reality, the ontology library should be an ontology standard formed by experts in all walks [13], but a simply ontology (just an experimental one) is used for illustrating this instance.

2.3 Reasoning and Matching of Web Service Ontology

Jena 2 Ontology API, a Java framework hosted by HP, is universally used to implement the ontology reasoning and matching aiming to establish Semantic Web. It provides the programmable environment to manipulate objects like RDF and OWL. Meanwhile Jena is also a popular open-source project which the project Protégé is based upon and we can distinguish the relation of two given parameters using the Jena 2 Ontology API [14]. During the process of reasoning, exposed non-functional attributes added by the local entity can be first served and then the non-functional attributes can be reasoned out, namely the reasoning from parent node to child node or from child node to parent node. In the hierarchy chart composed by the ontology, the following operation can be done via the reasoning machine:

childNode --> fatherNode

During the process of matching, we can match the Web Service entities in the consideration of knowledge and users' references derived from the reasoning process.

2.4 Composition of Web Service

The composition of Web Service is implemented based on the requirement of different autonomous Web Services via the integration of service searching and interfaces between service, aiming to provide newer and more powerful Web Service or valuable Web Service [15]. Semantic Web Service Composition can dynamically figure out the best service to meet users' references [16] and generate a Web Service composition sequence, and then call relative Web Services depending on it.

3 Design and Implement of an Instance

The example is an information service system on veterinarian reservation. As long as users input the name of pet, the disease name and the required service references, the system will return relative veterinarian information, bringing convenience to various operations for users. Used ontologies in the experiment are as follows:

Disease ontology is presented in Fig.1. Animal ontology and Service ontology with semantic information are presented in Fig.2.

Fig. 1. Disease ontology

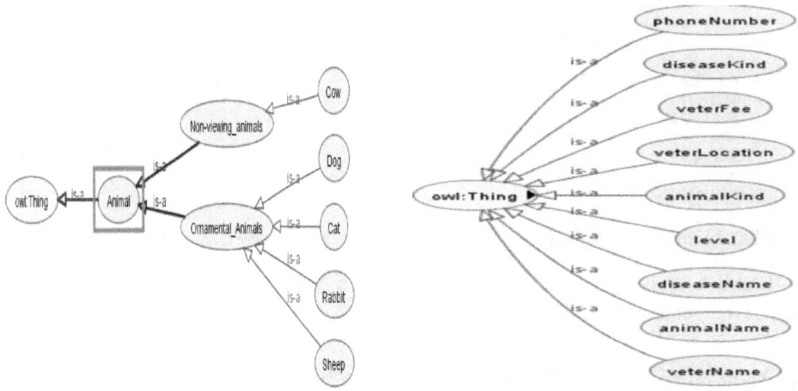

(a) Animal ontology (b) Service ontology with semantic information

Fig. 2. Animal ontology and Service ontology with semantic information

There are two service ontologies in the example: the first one is a service to determine the subordinate disease and the Class of the non-functional attributes added by the service are diseaseName and diseaseKind.

The other is a service to return the information of veterinarian to the users and the Classes of the non-functional attributes added to the service are animalKind, animalName, diseaseKind, diseaseName, veterName, veterLocation, veterFee, level and phoneNumber. And the added Property are level_value, phoneNumber and value. Besides, animalKind, animalName, diseaseKind and diseaseName are used for the reasoning and matching of the service ontology, and level and veterFee are used as the selection of service.

The processes to establish and store the service ontology are listed below:

(1) Configure Web Service in the IDE like Netbeans and generate the WSDL documents.
(2) Implement the convert from the WSDL document to OWL-S and generate the .owl files using the WSDL2OWL-S converter in the OWL-S Editor.
(3) Add operations like Class, Property and Individual to the generated .owl files applying the used semantic information to the service ontology.
(4) Store the content of processed .owl files in the database via Java technology and Jena 2 API.

Take veter1 for example to manifest the procedure discussed above:

Establish Web Service 'chooseVeterService' in Netbeans and generate the WSDL files and convert the generated .wsdl documents into .owl files, shown in Fig.3.

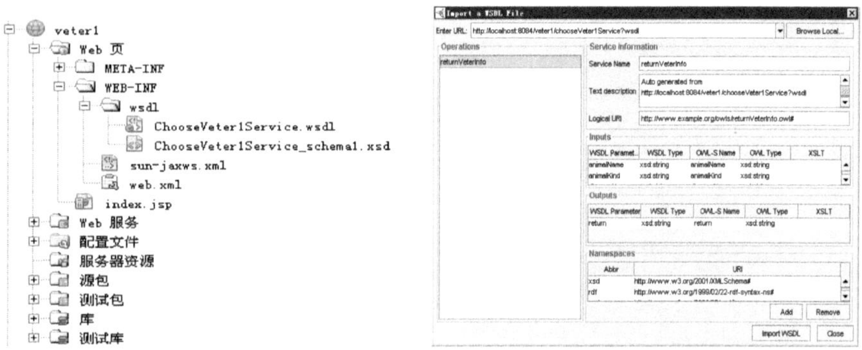

(a) Establish a Web Service (b) Convert .wsdl into .owl files

Fig. 3. Establish Web Service 'chooseVeterService' in Netbeans and generate the WSDL files and convert the generated .wsdl documents into .owl files

Add necessary Class and Property for the converted owl files, shown in Fig.4.

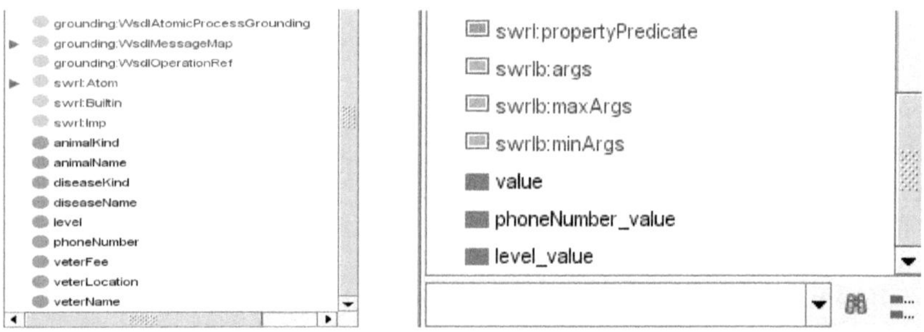

(a) Add Class (b) Add Property

Fig. 4. Add necessary Class and Property for the converted owl files

Build up relative individual examples in every Class and instantiate the information of a certain individual, shown in Fig.5.

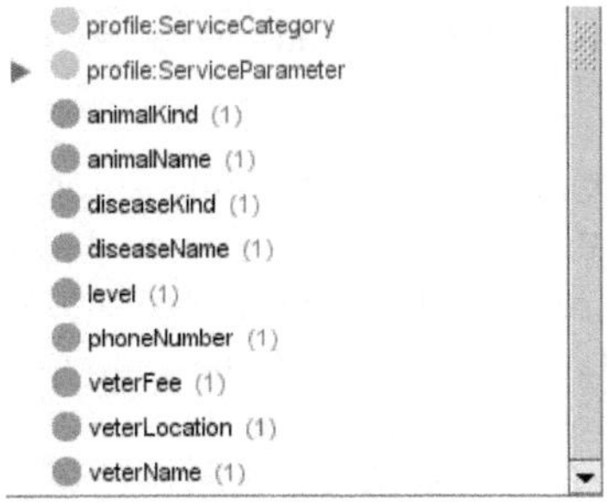

(a) Build up an individual instance

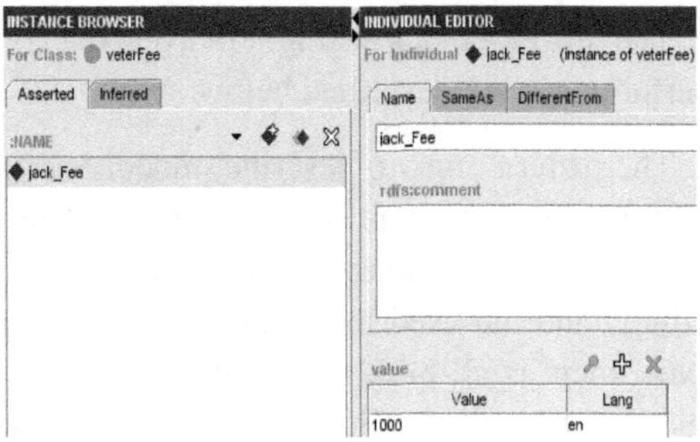

(b) Instantiate the information

Fig. 5. Build up relative individual examples and instantiate certain individual's information

The Java codes aiming to abstract the local ontology and store it into the database are listed below:

```
public static OntModel
createDBModelFromFile(IDBConnection
con,String name,String filePath) {
ModelMaker maker= ModelFactory.createModelRDBMaker(con);
Model base = maker.createModel(name);
```

The specific implementation of Web Service ontology reasoning and matching is as follows:

Firstly, operate the reasoning and matching process via the semantic diseaseName and diseaseKind added upon the optional judgment of disease sorting, which is derived from the users' input and thus gains the exact disease determination in this way. After gaining the disease sorting of the animal, the system can search in optional and multiple entities veter(i) on the veterinarian information and operate the reasoning and matching process based upon the users' references and semantic information added by the service ontology.

There are three kinds of references on veter service in the example, presented like below:

(1) Quality optimization: Substitute users to make a selection based upon the non-functional semantic attribute level added by the veter service, and select the veter service with the highest value of level.
(2) Cost optimization: Substitute users to make a selection based upon the non-functional semantic attribute veterFee added by the veter service, and select the veter service with the least value of veterFee.
(3) Cost-quality optimization: First define a ratio called rate as the cost of veterFee of the added non-functional attribute of veter against the grade of level of veter. Then make a selection based on the value of the variable rate and adopt the veter service with the highest value rate.

The development/testing environment in this experiment and relative running performance are described below:

The pattern aims to describe, model and implement the service composition based on OWL-S, and operates an extension. Due to the consideration of multi-pattern of distributed programming, this example adopts certain model tool (Protégé3.1,OWL-S Editor) and the used third-party API is all for Java programming, the pattern of the experiment is all built up based on JDK1.5, adopts MYSQL as the storing database, and operates all development and testing work in the NetBeans IDE 6.1, with the Tomcat 6.0.16 as the application server.

First configure OWL-S and Jena 2 Ontology API in the project, and use Protégé3.1 as ontology modeling tool. This system implements convert from original WSDL documents to the Web Service description of OWL-S files, the modeling of Web Service via the Ontology Modeling Tool and achieves the reasoning and matching operations with programming. After running this program, select three parameters of the animal name, the disease name of the animal, the service aim, and then commits the request, it will finally present the derived information in the scanner from the server which is based upon the requirements and references of users.

The service requirements and outcomes of quality optimization, cost optimization and cost-quality optimization are presented in Fig.6.

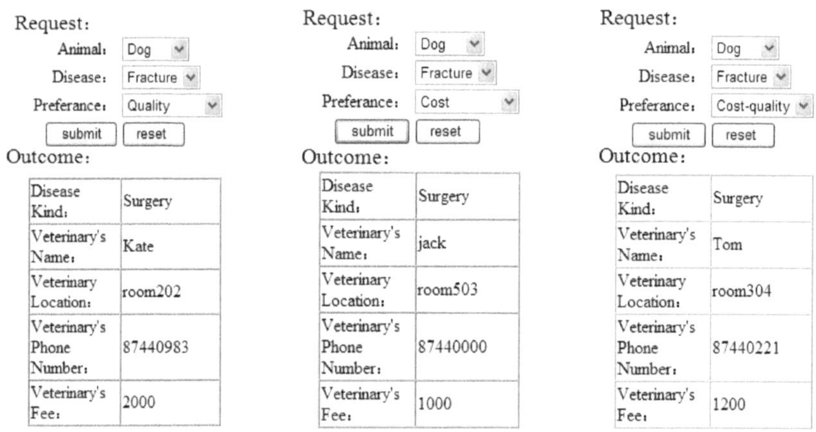

(a) Quality optimization (b) Cost optimization (c) Cost-quality optimization

Fig. 6. The service requirements and outcomes of quality optimization, cost optimization, and cost-quality optimization

4 Conclusion

This paper makes a research on the application of Web Service ontology reasoning based upon OWL-S, and attempts to add necessary semantic information into the Web

Service ontology to implement the description extension of non-functional attributes of OWL-S, which can operate the reasoning and matching process based on the Web Service ontology using an example for validation. The work of this paper acts as the technological preparation of the future work of automated Web Service Composition.

Acknowledgments. This work is supported by Science and Technology Research Planning Project of Guangdong Province under Grant No. 2010B020315024, the College Students' Innovation Experiment Project of Guangdong Province under Grant No. 1056410038, the Foundation for Distinguished Young Talents in Higher Education of Guangdong, China under Grant No. LYM09034.

References

1. Dustdar, S., Schreiner, W.: A Survey on Web Services Composition. Web and Grid Services 1, 1–30 (2005)
2. Rao, J., Su, X.: A Survey of Automated Web Service Composition Methods. In: Cardoso, J., Sheth, A.P. (eds.) SWSWPC 2004. LNCS, vol. 3387, pp. 43–54. Springer, Heidelberg (2005)
3. Cui, H., Ying, S., Yuan, W.J.: Review of Semantic Web Service Composition. Computer Science, 21–25 (2010)
4. Zhang, Z., Zuo, C., Wang, Y.: Web Service Discovery Method Based on Semantic Expansion. Journal on Communications 28, 57–63 (2007)
5. Michael, M., Singh, M.: A Framework and Ontology for Dynamic Web Services Selection. IEEE Internet Computing 8, 84–93 (2004)
6. Deng, Z.H., Tang, S.W., Zhang, M., Yang, D.Q., Chen, J.: Overview of Ontology. Acta Scicentiarum Naturalum Universitis Pekinesis 38, 730–738 (2002)
7. Neches, R., Fikes, R.E., Gruber, T.R.: Enabling Technology for Knowledge Sharing. AI Magazine 12, 36–56 (1991)
8. OWL-S Semantic Markup for Web Services, `http://www.w3.org/Submission/OWL-S/`
9. Feng, Z.W., He, K.Q., Li, B., Gong, P., He, Y.F., Liu, W.: A Method for Semantic Web Service Discovery Based on Context Inference. Chinese Journal of Computers 31, 1354–1363 (2008)
10. Wu, S.M., Shen, J.J., Han, Q.: Web Service Composition Method Based on Domain Ontology and OWL-S. Computer Engineering 35, 256–258 (2009)
11. Xu, D.Z., Tang, Y.H.: Automatic Semantic Web Service Composition Based on OWL-S. Application Research of Computers 27, 3767–3770 (2010)
12. Li, M., Wang, D.Z., Du, X.Y.: Dynamic Composition of Web Services Based on Domain Ontology. Chinese Journal of Computers 28, 644–650 (2005)
13. Li, S.P., Yin, Q.W., Hu, Y.J., Guo, M., Fu, X.J.: Overview of Researches on Ontology. Journal of Computer Research and Development 41, 1041–1052 (2004)
14. Zhou, Z.C., Sun, R.S.: Platform of Automatic Discovery, Match and Execution of Web Services Based on Semantics. Journal of Computer Applications 25, 233–235 (2005)
15. Xiong, W.: Summary of Composite Web Services. Informationization, 1-4 (2009)
16. Li, M., Li, J.H.: Study on Semantic Web Services Discovery Based on Filtrating and Selecting. Computer Engineering and Design 30, 3649–3652 (2009)

A Study of Indoor Distributed Calculation Model of Mobile Communication

Yinpu Zhang[1], Fang Wang[2], Yanchun Shen[1], and Wenfeng Huo[3]

[1] College of Tangshan,Tangshan, Heibei, China
[2] College of Electronic and Information Engineering, Heibei University, Baoding, Heibei, China
[3] Tangshan Kaiyuan Autowelding System Co., Ltd, Tangshan, Heibei, China
cnsyc@126.com

Abstract. As there are many high-rise buildings in the city, indoor coverage provided by outdoor station boasts great limitations. For the guarantee of the quality of indoor coverage, it will become hard to control the outdoor interference, influencing the overall planning and capacity of the network. Through the analysis of six common indoor distributed calculation models, this thesis studies the different coverage methods in different application environments, contributing to the improvement of the capacity of cellular network system. As the extension of the current cellular network, the flexible application of microcellular technology and relay station to build a microcellular network of high quality could obtain good effects both to improve the system utilization rate and deepness coverage of the network.

Keywords: Mobile Communication, Indoor Distribution, Calculation Model, Coverage.

The indoor environment is a closed and half-closed transmission environment. Because of the existence of walls, doors and windows, furniture and other objects, the electric wave from the sending antenna to receiving antenna not only includes indirect wave, reflection wave and transmission wave, but also diffracted wave generated from the diffraction of edges and corners of the object. The transmission of indoor radio signal is mainly affected by the following factors:

1. Reflection and diffraction from objects like indoor walls and floors, etc.
2. Transmission from walls, floors and other obstructions.
3. The tunneling effect of energy, especially for high frequency and passage.
4. The movement of persons or objects on one side or both sides of the radio link.

1 Keenan-Motley Model

In the indoor distributed system, Keenan-Motley model has already become semi-empirical model predicting the indoor electric wave transmission. A complete Keenan-Motley model is a formula that could predict the transmission properties of

C. Liu, J. Chang, and A. Yang (Eds.): ICICA 2011, Part I, CCIS 243, pp. 458–465, 2011.

three-dimensional indoor electric wave. It could concurrently predict the path loss of horizontal direction (of the same floor) and hierarchical direction (between different floors), but it only takes the path between antenna point and receiving point into consideration. In a simple indoor environment, however, it is already enough for this model to guarantee enough prediction precision [1].

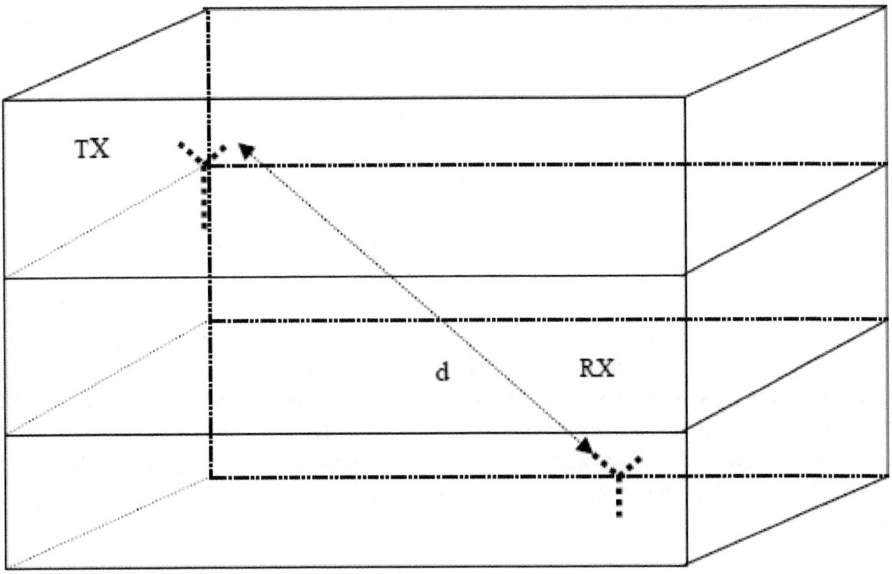

Fig. 1. Keenan-Motley model

$$Lp = 20\lg(\frac{4\pi d}{\gamma}) + kK - \omega W \tag{1}$$

d is the distance between the transmitter and receiver; k is the number of floors; K is the floor attenuation coefficient; ω is the number of walls; K is the attenuation coefficient of walls. The new Keenan-Motley model is a further improved and developed formula by adopting Matlab tool. The modified Keenan-Motley model formula is as below:

$$L = 20\lg(\frac{4\pi d}{\gamma}) + \frac{kK}{k^{b-1/(1+k)}} + (p_1W_1 + p_2W_2)10^{\frac{k^2}{5}} + p_3W_3 + p_4W_4 + \Gamma.\max(0, d - d_1) + C \tag{2}$$

d is the distance between the transmitter and receiver, λ is the wavelength, k is the building floors,K is the floor attenuation coefficient,b is the floor attenuation coefficient being 0.78 generally,P_i is the number of walls and W_i is the attenuation coefficient of walls.

Table 1. Default value of all the parameters

Parameters	Default value
K	12-30[dB]
W_i	2-7[dB]
Γ	0.2[dB/m]
d_1	65[m]

The first item in the formula is free space loss. If it is used to predict the same floor only, a further simplified Keenan-Motley model could be adopted. The specific formula is as follows:

$$L_p = 20\lg f + N\lg d - 28 \tag{3}$$

f is the frequency, N is the distance loss coefficient (being 30 generally) and d is the distance between sending antenna and the observation point.

The actual measurement finds that the signals measured might be higher than the predicted value, which is attributed to the influence of the electric wave phenomenon of passage effect. Passage effect is a kind of systematic error, and Keenan-Motley model thus boasts a lower predicted signal intensity value in some places, such as the passage end that is far from the antenna. The reason why signal intensity is underestimated is because that the model assumption signal goes through several walls, but actually, the signal has several times of refraction and reflection along the passage.

2 Log-Distance Path Loss Model

As the log-distance path loss model is rather simple, it is widely applied to the prediction of indoor path loss. In this model, the average path loss is n-degree power function of distance, represented as

$$L_{50}(d) = L(d_0) + 10n\lg\left(\frac{d}{d_0}\right) \tag{4}$$

In this formula, $L_{50}(d)$ is the average path loss (dB), d is the receiving-sending distance (m), $L(d_0)$ is the path loss of the transmitter to the reference distance d_0, d_0 is the reference distance (m) and n rests with the average path loss index.

Reference path loss could be obtained through the calculating expression testing or applying free space path loss. When d_0 of 1m is chosen to be the free space loss from the free space of 1m from the transmitter to the reference distance, then the free space loss $L(d_0)$ at 1m of 2150MHz is 39dB.

Path loss obeys lognormal distribution. Average path loss index n and standard deviation σ depends on the architectural type and the number of floors between the transmitter and the receiver. The path loss at a distance of d from the transmitting and receiving distance of L(d) is

$$L(d) = L_{50}(d) + X\sigma \tag{5}$$

In this formula, X is the random variable of lognormal distribution with a standard deviation of dB and an average value of 0, representing the influence of environment on the objects.

3 Common Site Model

As there is no or only a small amount of site information needed, this model is called a common site model. In this model, indoor radio path loss is described by the average path loss and its relevant shadow attenuation statistics. This model takes into consideration the loss resulting from going through various floors. Path loss index includes the influence from going through walls and other obstacles, as well as the loss from factors that others may experience on the same floor of the architecture [2].

$$L = 20\lg(f) + N\lg(d) + L_f(n) - 28 \tag{6}$$

In this formula, N is the path loss index, f is frequency (MHz), d is the distance between the base station and the mobile station (m) in which d >1m. L_f is the floor penetration loss factor (dB) and n is the number of floors between the base station and the mobile station (n≥1).

For the residential buildings of which the path loss index is not given, the corresponding value of office buildings could be adopted. It asks for attention that the isolation of various floors should have a certain upper limit. It is quite possible for the signal to achieve the receiver by going through other external paths with a smaller loss than going through various floors. If external path is excluded, the test result of 5.2GHz indicates that the average loss value of the concrete floor of a normal incidence of suspended ceiling is 20dB, and the standard deviation is 1.5dB. The lighting equipment adds a loss of 30dB and a standard deviation of 3dB, while the air-conditioning tubes under the floor makes the average loss value increase to 36dB and the standard deviation to 5dB. In specified point models like ray tracing, these data should be applied to replace L_f [3,4].

Indoor shadow attenuation relevant to this model obeys zero-mean lognormal distribution, of which the standard deviation is demonstrated in Table 2.

Table 2. Shadow attenuation standard deviation of indoor path loss

Frequency/GHz	residential buildings	office buildings	Commercial buildings
1.8~2	8	10	10
5.2	—	12	—

4 Attenuation Factor Model

Attenuation factor model is the experience model used to predict the path loss of the same floor or different floors. Its calculating formula is:

$$L = L(d_0) + 10n_1 \lg\left(\frac{d}{d_0}\right) + FAF \tag{7}$$

In this formula, n_l is the path loss index of the same floor and it depends on the architectural type. Its typical value is 2. 8[5, 6].

The typical value of $L(d_0)$ is 30dB for a frequency of 900MHz. FAF is floor attenuation factor, which is relevant to the number of floors and architectural type. Table 3 gives FAF (floor attenuation factor) and the standard deviation of the measured value and the difference of measured value.

Later, this model is modified, and the path loss after modification is

$$L = L(d_0) + 10n_1 \lg\left(\frac{d}{d_0}\right) + \alpha d + FAF \tag{8}$$

α is the attenuation factor of different indoor environment in this formula.

As the log path loss linearity depends on the distance between the transmitter and the receiver, this model is also called linear slope model. The tests of 850MHz, 1700MHz and 4000MHz indicate that for buildings of four floors, the attenuation factor changes between 0.62-0.47dB/m and for buildings of two floors, the attenuation factor changes between 0.48-0.23dB/m. [7].

Table 3. FAF (floor attenuation factor) and standard deviation

Test scenario		FAF/dB	α/dB
Office building 1	A penetration of one floor	12.9	7
	A penetration of two floors	18.7	2.8
	A penetration of three floors	24.4	1.7
	A penetration of four floors	27	1.5
Office building 2	A penetration of one floor	16.2	2.9
	A penetration of two floors	27.5	5.4
	A penetration of three floors	31.6	7.2

5 IMT-2000 Model

Since IMT-2000 becomes the standard of the third generation mobile communication system (3G), in order to evaluate the radio transmission techniques of IMT-2000, the characteristics of environmental transmission is widely studied and considered, including big cities, small cities, suburbs, villages and desert areas. Indoor office environment, indoor and outdoor pedestrian environment and vehicle environment constitute the working environment of IMT-2000 together. The key parameters of every transmission model include delay spread, multi-diameter attenuation features of signal envelop and radio working frequency band [8,9].

5.1 Indoor Office Environment Model

The transmission feature of this kind of transmission environment is small with a low reflection power. The various separations of walls and floors, the resistance of various obstacles and the scattering of the electric wave bring changes to path attenuation laws. These objects could also generate shadow effect and this shadow effect corresponds to the lognormal distribution of a standard deviation of 12dB. The movement of pedestrian users also produces the corresponding Doppler frequency migration. When the base station and the pedestrian users are in the city, the delay spread is between 35~460ns. The average path loss could be calculated according to the formula below:

$$L(d) = 37 + 30\lg d + 18.3^{[(F+2)/(F+1)-0.64]} \tag{9}$$

Among it, d is the distance (m) and F is the number of floors of the path.

5.2 Pedestrian Environment from Indoors to Outdoors

This kind of environment is characterized by a small district and low reflection power. The base station is outdoors with a low height of antenna. When the pedestrian users are on the street or in the building, the delay expands to a change of 100~1800ns. If the path is the visual distance on streets like valleys, the path loss follows the law of d^{-2} when there is Fresnel regional time slot. When there is a longer Fresnel regional time slot, the path loss law of d^{-4} is appropriate. Influenced by trees and other obstacles on the path, the loss range could achieve d^{-6}. The standard deviation of outdoor lognormal shadow attenuation is 10dB and the indoor lognormal shadow attenuation is 12dB. Under the circumstance of non-visual distance, the average path loss is

$$L(d) = 40\lg d + 30\lg f_c + 49(dB) \tag{10}$$

Among it, f_c is carrier frequency (MHz). The above describes the poorest transmission environment and the standard deviation of lognormal shadow attenuation is 10dB. [10].

5.3 Vehicle Environment

This kind of environment is characterized by a large district and high reflection power. In the environment of uplands and mountainous areas, the delay spread on the bump road might change between 0.4~12ms. In cities and suburbs, the lognormal shadow attenuation of a 10dB of path loss rule and standard deviation of d^{-4} is appropriate. The average architectural penetration loss is 18dB and the standard deviation is 10dB. In villages with a flat landform, the path loss is lower than that of cities and suburbs. In mountainous areas, if the base station is selected to avoid path obstacles, the path loss is close to d^{-2} rules. The average path loss in this kind of environment is

$$L(d) = 40(1 - 4\times10^{-2}\Delta h_b)\lg d - (18\lg\Delta h_b) + 21\lg f_c + 80(dB) \quad (11)$$

Among it, d is the distance between the base station and the mobile station (km), f_c is the carrier frequency (MHz), Δh_b is the antenna height (m) of the base station measured according to the average ridge level [11].

6 Free Space Transmission Model

While studying the transmission of electromagnetic wave, the transmission loss is a major property. The study of transmission loss asks for the study of the properties of two antennas in the uniform medium of the free space (isotropy, non-absorption, a zero electrical conductivity). Take the ideal Omni-directional antenna for example, when the transmission distance is much greater than the wavelength of the electromagnetic wave, the transmission loss of the free space is:

$$L_{BS} = 20\log f + 20\log d - 28 \quad (dB) \quad (12)$$

Among it, f is frequency (MHz) and d is distance (m).

The transmission loss of the free space is directly proportional to the square of distance d. When d doubles, the path loss in the free space increases by 6dB. Meanwhile, when frequency is improved, the path loss will increase. We could compensate these losses by increasing transmitting power and receiving antenna gains.

7 Conclusion

This thesis discusses the major methods to realize indoor coverage in the mobile transmission system of GSM. It gives a detailed analysis and introduction of six common calculation models of indoor distribution and the environments for the application of every kind of model. It is impossible to realize coverage by depending on outdoor station in the malls and recreation centers with a comparatively great depth. Therefore, the major method to solve indoor coverage is to set microcellular and to establish relay station. The above research provides a good reference for the selection of indoor distributed technique of different environments.

References

1. Wu, B.: Design of WCDMA Digital Fiber Repeater Monitor Terminal based on ARM. Modern Science & Technology of Telecommunications (5), 57–61 (2011)
2. Wang, X., Sujie.: Mobile indoor distribution system acceptance. Telecommunications Technology (3), 46–47 (2010)

3. Xia, J., Gu, N., Zhang, J.: Transceiver-based mobile communications technology, combined cable distribution system intensive indoor. Telecommunications Information (6), 35–38 (2010)
4. Zhao, L., Yu, Z., He, Z., Lin, K.: A Traffic Information Simulation System Based on Mobile Communications Dat. Acta Scientiarum Naturalium Universitatis Sunyatseni 48(4), 24–30 (2011)
5. Zhou, W.: Discussion of Technologies about the Mobile Communications Base Station Lightning Protection. Guangxi Communication Technology (3), 27–30 (2009)
6. Battelle Memorial Institute. Assessmentofautomated datacollection technologies for calculation of commercialmotorvehicle border crossing travel time delay. Battelle Memorial Institute, Columbus (2002)
7. Yim, Y.B., Cayford, R.: Investigation of vehicles asprobes using global positioning system and cellular phonetracking: field operational test. University of Califonia, Berkeley (2001)
8. Ygnace, J.L., Drance, C., Yim, Y.B., et al.: Travel time estimation on the San Francisco Bay area network using cellular phones as probes. University of Califonia, Berkeley (2003)
9. Yim, Y.B.: The State of Cellular Probes. University of Califonia, Berkeley (2003)
10. Yganace, J.L., Drance, C.: Cellular telecommunication and transportation convergence: a case study of aresearch conducted in California and in France on cellular position techniques and transportation issues. In: 2001 IEEE Intelligent Transportation Systems Conference Proceedings, Oakland, pp. 16–22 (2001)
11. Smith, B.L., Zhang, H., Fontaine, M.D., et al.: Wireless location technology-based traffic monitoring critical assessment and evaluation of an early-generation system. Journal of Transportation Engineering 130, 576–584 (2004)

Research of Semantic Web Model and Reasoning Based on F-Logic

Guorong Qin[1], Tao He[1], and Liping Li[2]

[1] Software Engineering Department,Shenzhen Institute of Information Technology, Shenzhen, China
[2] Computer and Information Institute, Shanghai Second Polytechnic University, Shanghai, China
{qingr,het}@sziit.com.cn, llping2000@yahoo.com.cn

Abstract. A formal modeling method of Semantic Web language OWL-S is proposed in this paper, to provide a core ontology modeling framework, and to map its global attributes into F-logic classes and formulas. At the same time it analyzes the construction of OWL-S model type, gives F-logic axioms, derivation rules and methods of its consistency and satisfiability etc. to reason the tasks and attributes of the system. The model and method can verify some global attributes of Semantic Web system by model checking based on first-order logic.

Keywords: Web Service, F-logic, Software Requirement, Model checking, Verification.

1 Introduction

Model theoretic semantics of Semantic Web description language OWL-S provides a formal method for the OWL-S ontology, and is used to represent the instance data. An OWL - S ontology usually consists of some classes, properties, and examples and justice component. These elements are represented by logic language. Moreover, the frame logic (F-logic[1]) allows the use of the same identifier as a class, instance or property identifier, while still had based on the first-order logical standard semantics. Antonio Brogi[2] presents a description from OWL-S to Petri net and designs a translation machines, so that many Petri net tools can also be used to verify the analysis. S. Narayanan and SA Mcllraith [3] proposed a model based on Petri nets to describe the Web services of OWL-S. They assume that services are composed of a number of atomic services, but this assumption is not entirely suitable combination of services in an open environment, and their method does not involve the static semantics of OWL-S. Jiang Yun-Chen [4] analyzes the semantic Web Services Description Ontology Language OWL-S formal semantics, and provides a reasoning theoretical basis for semantic Web services, but he did not develop effective reasoning engine to support the transaction and inference.

In this paper, F-logic specification language [5] gives a formal model for the Semantic Web language OWL-S, to provide a core ontology framework for Web

C. Liu, J. Chang, and A. Yang (Eds.): ICICA 2011, Part I, CCIS 243, pp. 466–472, 2011.

services-based software requirements model, and unambiguous, machine-explain capabilities to descript the nature of the Web service, at the same time, improve the reasoning mechanism and methods of verification under the Semantic Web. The advantage is to combine the concepts described, reasoning, logic programming and object-oriented description language as a unified form of the current methods; and to expand their skills in this regard. The model is not only an unambiguous formal model can be used for development and other related development tools, and can be used to identify and eliminate errors in the current document. This model and the method can use model checking method based on the first-order logical to verify some global property of OWL-S service system.

2 F-Logic Inference of Meta-model

In order to verify the OWL-S ontology, the consistency, satisfiability, implication, equivalence and examples of the F-logic models must be verified. When it comes to consistency of the model, check whether knowledge is meaningful, whether there are some model explanation I to O, whether there are some the possible explanations I to C, whether problems can be reduced to the consistency and so on. Regardless of whether the two classes are represented by the same instance set, we must check the equivalence of model with reasoning. For verifying the model, we must inspect whether the individual i is an example of class C, and retrieval the individual set of illustration C.

The F-logic reasoning logical task we consider is a standard reasoning task, usually being considered in the text:

Satisfiability Checking: The duty is to inspect whether the knowledge foundation of a F-logic is consistent (to have a model);

Class Satisfiability Checking: The expansion of class A is non-empty, for example, A may have at least one instance.

Classification Inspection of Class: The duty is to check whether a given class C is expansion subset of another class D, for example, C is subclass of D;

Example Inspection: The duty is to check whether to follow a specific description logic knowledge foundation. In this foundation a given individual is a member of a specified class;

Connection's Inquiry answer: The duty is when assigning a given variable, to check whether a connection inquiry is logical deduction of a description logic knowledge foundation.

2.1 F-Logic Rule

Regular F-logic procedure P is composed of the form of rules such as the following:

$$h \leftarrow b_1,\ldots,b_m,\text{not } c_1,\ldots,\text{not } c_n,$$

Where $h,b_1,\ldots,b_m,c_1,\ldots,c_n$ are the free equivalent atoms or molecules. h is the head atom of r, $B^+(r)=\{ b_1,\ldots,b_m \}$ is the positive body atom set of r, and $B-(r)=\{c_1,\ldots,c_n\}$ is the negative body atom set of r. If $B-(r)=\varnothing$, then r is positive. If each variable in r appears in B, r is safe. If each rule $r\in P$ is positive (is correspondingly safe), then P is positive (is correspondingly safe). Moreover, each F-logic program contains the following rules. These rules make semantic of molecular axiomatizable:

x::z ← x::y,y::z
x: z ← x:y,y:z
x::x

The first article rule axiomatizes the transmission of subclass relations; the second article rule axiomatizes the inheritance of class member; the third rule axiomatizes the fact that each class is a subclass of its own.

F-logic symbol A is a superset of function and predicate symbols appearing in P. Supposes L_P^F express F-logic language based on Σ_P. Suppose Σ_P contains at least a 0-ary function symbols or unique 0-ary predicate symbol.

B_H, Herbrand foundation of L_P^F, is basic set of atomic formula and molecular of L_P^F. The subset of B_H is called the Herbrand explanation. A basic logic program P expressed as gr(P), is union set of all possible basic instances of P. Each rule $r\in P$ is obtained in Σ_P with through substitution of an elemental term by rule r.

Supposes P is a procedure. M, a Herbrand interpretation of P, is a model of P. If for each rule, $r\in \mathrm{gr}(P)$, $B^{+}(r)\subseteq M$ means $H(r)\cap M\neq\varnothing$. A Herbrand model M is minimal if and only if for every model has $M'\subseteq M, M'=M$.

According to [10], a the simple logic program P of a Herbrand interpretation M, is expressed as P^M. It is obtained from the gr (P) by removing the following:

each rule r with B;

delete the non-c (not c) from each body of the remaining rules r with $c\in B-(r)$. If M is a minimal Herbrand model of P^M, then M is a stable model of P.

If P is a positive logic program, then for each rule, the corresponding Horn F-logic theory Φ replace arrow ← with ⊃, and replace each "," with ∧ in the rule body. [10]

2.2 F-Logic Inference of Metamodel

Theorem 1. Let P be a positive logic program and Φ is a corresponding Horn F-logic theory, then P has a corresponding model M, and for each basic atom or molecule a, $a\in$ M if and only if $\Phi\models a$.

Definition 2 (flat item) a basic flat item is a constant or a variable. An item is flat if and only if it is a basic flat item or a function item $f@(t_1,...,t_n)$, where f is a n-function symbol and $t_1,...,t_n$ is basic flat item. An atom $P@(t_1,...,t_n)$ is flat if and only if all $t_1,...,t_n$ items are flat. A text is flat if and only if its atoms are flat; a clause is flat if and only if it is all the text is flat.

For example, if c is a constant and a is a 0-ary function symbol, then P@(x,c,a),P(f@x;f@c) and $f@x \doteq g@c$ is flat, but P@(f@a,f@c) and $f@a \doteq g@c$ is not flat.

Random clause set may be transformed into flat clause set by "extracting" the clauses unneeded. It requires applying the following conversion rules to a given set of clauses to achieve as much as possible.

(1) If s_i is not a basic flat item, where x is a new variable, then use

$P@[t_1,\ldots,f@(s_1,\ldots,x,\ldots,s_m),\ldots,t_n]\rightarrow(\,)$ OR $H\leftarrow B, x \doteq s_i$.

to replace a clause like below.

$P@[t_1,\ldots,f@(s_1,\ldots,s_i,\ldots,s_m),\ldots,t_n]\rightarrow(\,)$ OR $H\leftarrow B$.

(2)If s_i is not a basic flat item, where x is a new variable, then use

$H\leftarrow B, P@(t_1,\ldots,f@(s_1,\ldots,x,\ldots,s_m),\ldots,t_n)\rightarrow(\,), x \doteq s_i$.

to replace a clause like below.

$H\leftarrow B, P@(t_1,\ldots,f@(s_1,\ldots,x,\ldots,s_m),\ldots,t_n)\rightarrow(\,)$.

Obviously, for any set of clauses, use a uniquely determined set of a flat clause (equivalent to renaming of variables and the sort of body atoms) to terminate its flattening.

Definition 3. (Equivalence transformation) Let P be a Σ-clause set. The P equal transformation expression is P^{eq}. It is a clause set obtained by flattening P and by adding the following clause:

$\leftarrow c \doteq d$ For any two different Σ-constants c and d

$x \doteq x\leftarrow$

$x \doteq y \leftarrow y \doteq x$

$x \doteq z \leftarrow x \doteq y, y \doteq z$

$P@(x_1,\ldots,y,\ldots,x_n)\rightarrow(\,) \leftarrow P@(x_1,\ldots,x_i,\ldots,x_n)\rightarrow(\,), y \doteq x_i$. Each n–predicate symbol P in Σ is different from $\doteq$, and all i are $1\leq i\leq n$

When axiom $\leftarrow c \doteq d$ is neglected, the only difference between equal transformation and the axiom equal processing lies in using function substitute the axiom. For example, axioms such as A, for each n-ary Σ-function symbols and all $i = 1,\ldots,n$, these axioms can be omitted or abandoned because of being flatten.

Theorem 2. (correctness and completeness of equivalent transformation) Let P be a set of clauses, then P is UNA-E-satisfied if and only if P^{eq} is satisfiable.

Proof: the proof of necessary conditions is not difficult. for the limited space this omitted its proof. Note that "extract" sub-item to keep E- satisfied.

Regarding sufficient condition's proof (completeness), suppose I is a Herbrand model of P^{eq}. some subset $R_I \subseteq I$ to demonstrate is a UNA-E- model of P (to make $R_I \subseteq I$ meaningful, and take every procedure $s \doteq t$ in I as two rules $s\rightarrow t$ and $t\rightarrow s$). More specifically, R_I will be a termination rewrite system without overlapping.

To Prove R_I is a P UNA-E-model needs three steps: First defines R_I and proves $R_I \models_E P^{eq}$, next infers $R_I \models_E P$, finally we prove R satisfies unique name supposition (UNA). Detailed proof is omitted here for limited space.

Therefore, any correctness and completeness theory prove provide a method to check UNA-E- satisfied. The essential condition (accuracy) is easy to prove. There are the similar explanation in [11,12], and it is easy to infer.

Definition 4. (Block transformation) Let P be a flat Σ-clause. Block transformation is expressed as P^{bl}. It can be obtained by application of the following four steps:

Domain restraint: Replace each rule H←B of P with rule H←B,dom@x_1,...,dom@x_k, where {x_1,…,x_k} is variable set occurs in H←B. There is k≥0.
(2) Extracts the function item: replaces each clause like

$$H \leftarrow B, P@(t_1,\ldots,f@(s_1,\ldots,s_n),\ldots,t_m) \rightarrow () \tag{1}$$

as far as possible in the result sub-clause, where f is a non-0 Σ-function symbol and has

$$H \leftarrow B, P@(t_1,\ldots,x,\ldots,t_m) \rightarrow (), f@(s_1,\ldots,s_n) \rightarrow_{ref} x \tag{2}$$

And finally to this step with clause:

$$x \rightarrow_{ref} x \leftarrow \tag{3}$$

$$x \rightarrow_{ref} y \leftarrow x \rightarrow y \tag{4}$$

(3) limited domain search: add the following clause to the result clause set, for each variable c, each n-ary function symbol f and all i=1,…,n, and for each m-ary Σ-predicate symbols P and all j=1,…,m,

$$dom@c \leftarrow \tag{5}$$

$$dom@x_i \leftarrow dom@(f@(x_1,\ldots,x_n)) \tag{6}$$

$$dom@x_i \leftarrow dom\_candidate@(f@(x_1,\ldots,x_n)) \tag{7}$$

$$dom\_candidate@(f@(x_1,\ldots,x_n)) \leftarrow dom@x_1,\ldots,dom@x_n \tag{8}$$

$$f@(x_1,\ldots,x_n) \rightarrow_{sub} x_1 \vee \ldots \vee f@(x_1,\ldots,x_n) \rightarrow_{sub} x_n \vee dom@(f@(x_1,\ldots,x_n)) \leftarrow dom\_candidate@(f@(x_1,\ldots,x_n)) \tag{9}$$

$$x \rightarrow c \leftarrow x \rightarrow_{sub} c \tag{10}$$

$$x \rightarrow (f@(x_1,\ldots,x_n) \vee x \rightarrow_{sub} x_1 \vee \ldots \vee x \rightarrow_{sub} x_n \leftarrow x \rightarrow_{sub} f@(x_1,\ldots,x_n) \tag{11}$$

$$P@(x_1,\ldots,x_{j-1},y,x_{j+1},\ldots,x_m) \leftarrow x_j \rightarrow y, P@(x_1,\ldots,x_m) \tag{12}$$

$$\leftarrow x \rightarrow y, dom@x \tag{13}$$

(4) uniqueness of →: add the following clause to the result clause set, for each n-ary Σ-function symbol f and all i = 1, ..., n:

$$\leftarrow x \rightarrow y, x \rightarrow z, y \neq z \tag{14}$$

$$x \neq y \leftarrow y \neq x \tag{15}$$

$$c \neq d \leftarrow \tag{16}$$

To random two different Σ-constant c and d

$$c \neq f@(x_1,\ldots,x_n) \leftarrow \tag{17}$$

$$g@(y_1,\ldots,y_k) \neq f@(x_1,\ldots,x_n) \leftarrow \quad \text{For each k-ary function symbol g different from f} \tag{18}$$

$$f@(x_1,\ldots,x_{i-1},y,x_{i+1},\ldots,x_n) \neq f@(x_1,\ldots,x_n) \leftarrow y \neq x_i, dom@(f@(x_1,\ldots,x_{i-1},y,x_{i+1},\ldots,x_n)), dom@(f@(x_1,\ldots,x_n)) \tag{19}$$

The f@(t_1,...,t_n) is mapped to a its child item to make f@(t_1,...,t_n) to be a new domain element. It is better termination behavior. After being tested, it is proved to be reliable. It set the model generation process to achieve this goal.

Lemma 1. Let T be a set of flattened clauses. If P^{bl} is not satisfiable, then P is not satisfiable.

Theorem 2. (correctness and completeness of block transformation) Let P be a set of flat clauses, then P is satisfiable if and only if P^{bl} is satisfiable.

Proof: the proof of necessity can be deduced from Lemma 1.

Proof of sufficiency: Let Ibl is a Herbrand Σ-model of Pbl. We proved that Ibl determines a Σ-model I (may be non-Herbrand) of P. The proof has two steps: First step we construct domain, constant, function symbol and predicate symbol explanation of I. Second step we proved that I is a model of P. For limited space, concrete proof is omitted in this process.

theorem "if S |- C then S|=C" of this paper can be used to verify the accuracy of F-logic deduction, with the theorem "If a basic set of clauses S is not met, then there exists contrary evidence to S" [6] to verify the completeness of the basic reasoning. The following theorem of this paper is given to improve model check and verify the properties of the system.

Let L be a symbol Σ=<F,P>, with its F-logic ontology language based on predicate expression, the corresponding classification of F-logic language LF signed Σ', so that the result transfer function express as δ.

Theorem 3. Let P be a positive logic program, KP be the corresponding Horn F-logic theory, and then P has a stable model M. For each basic atom or molecule α, it has $\alpha \in M$ if and only if $K_P \models \alpha$.

Theorem 4. Let $K \subseteq L$ be a F-logic theorem, and let $\kappa \in L$ be a formula, then $K \models \kappa$ if and only if $\delta(K) \models_f \delta(\kappa$.

Proof: it can be immediately driven from Theorem 3, and from the fact checking features $K \models \kappa$ can deduce the satisfiability by formula $(\wedge K) \wedge \neg \kappa$ (with similar characteristics in the F-logic).

Theorem. mapping:

Γ: {F-formula}→ {well-formed formula of predicate computation},

Φ: {F-structure}→ { semantic structure of predicate computation },

For any structure M and any F-formula ψ, $M \models_F \psi$ if and only if $\varphi(M) \models_{PC} \Gamma(\psi)$. Here "$\models_F$" and "$\models_{PC}$" express computing features of predicate logic in F-logic.

F-OWL and Flora-2 is OWL inference engines based on F-logic, which use the above theorem to complete reasoning tasks of the model. Its inference will observe information formal semantic during the coding process in OWL, thus discovers the inconsistency in the OWL-S data, simultaneously reasoning new information from known information.

3 Conclusion

This paper describes the conversion from the ontology of semantic Web services language OWL-S to ontology expressed by F-logic. To ontology language based on predicate, this conversion keeps the properties. This paper not only studies formalization of the dynamic evolved requirement of OWL-S process model, but also studies formalized concept, axiom, restraint and uniform frame semantics of the

OWL-S static model. This paper portrays the OWL-S static model with the F-logic formalization method, designs an F-logic model to confirm the OWL-S ontology, and express its global property and frame as F-logic class and formula. It also gives the validation of axioms, inference rules, and theorems to verify the consistency, satisfiability etc of model, to analyze the construction of OWL-S model type, and reasoning the tasks supported by OWL-S. This model and the method can use based on the first-order logical simulate to confirm the OWL-S service system's some global property. This model and method can use model checking based on first-order logical to verify some global property of OWL-S service system.

Acknowledgment. This work was supported in part by a grant from Basic Research Program of Shenzhen Science and Technology Research and Development under grants JC201006020791A and JC201006020820A, Natural Science Foundation of Guangdong Province, China, under grant S2011040000672, Guangdong Provincial Education and science project of the 11th "five-year plan", Research Fund of Shenzhen Institute of Information Technology.

References

1. Angele, J., Kifer, M., Lausen, G., Angele, J., Kifer, M., Lausen, G.: Ontologies in F-logic. In: Handbook on Ontologies. Springer, Heidelberg (2009)
2. Moldt, D., Ortmann, J.: DaGen: A Tool for Automatic Translation from DAML-S to High-Level Petri Nets. In: Wermelinger, M., Margaria-Steffen, T. (eds.) FASE 2004. LNCS, vol. 2984, pp. 209–213. Springer, Heidelberg (2004)
3. Coppola, B., Gangemi, A., Gliozzo, A., Picca, D., Presutti, V.: Frame Detection Over the Semantic Web. In: Aroyo, L., Traverso, P., Ciravegna, F., Cimiano, P., Heath, T., Hyvönen, E., Mizoguchi, R., Oren, E., Sabou, M., Simperl, E. (eds.) ESWC 2009. LNCS, vol. 5554, pp. 126–142. Springer, Heidelberg (2009)
4. Golbeck, J., Parsia, B., Hendler, J.: Linking Social Networks on the Web with FOAF: A Semantic Web Case Study. In: Proceedings of the Twenty-Third AAAI Conference on Artificial Intelligence, 2008, pp. 1138–1143 (2008)
5. Calì, A., Gottlob, G., Kifer, M., Lukasiewicz, T., Pieris, A.: Ontological Reasoning with F-Logic Lite and Its Extensions, Complexity. In: Proceedings of the Twenty-Fourth AAAI Conference on Artificial Intelligence (AAAI 2010), pp. 1660–1665 (2010)
6. Klyne, G.: Framework for Security and Trust Standards. SWAD-Europe, (December 2002)
7. Golbeck, J.: Trust and nuanced profile similarity in online social network. ACM Transactions on the Web (TWEB) 3(4) (September 2009)
8. Zou, Y., Finin, T., Chen, H.: F-OWL: An Inference Engine for Semantic Web. In: Hinchey, M.G., Rash, J.L., Truszkowski, W.F., Rouff, C.A. (eds.) FAABS 2004. LNCS (LNAI), vol. 3228, pp. 238–248. Springer, Heidelberg (2004)
9. Kattenstroth, H., May, W., Schenk, F.: Combining OWL with F-logic Rules and Defaults. In: International Workshop on Applications of Logic Programming to the Web,Semantic Web and Semantic Web Services (ALPSWS 2007), September 13, vol. 287, pp. 60–75 (2007)
10. Korovin, K.: iProver – An Instantiation-Based Theorem Prover for First-Order Logic (System Description). In: Armando, A., Baumgartner, P., Dowek, G. (eds.) IJCAR 2008. LNCS (LNAI), vol. 5195, pp. 292–298. Springer, Heidelberg (2008)
11. Robinson, J.A., Voronkov, A.: Handbook of automated reasoning, vol. 1, 2122 pages. Gulf Professional Publishing (2001)
12. Bachmair, L., Ganzinger, H., Voronkov, A.: Elimination of Equality Via Transformation with Ordering Constraints. In: Kirchner, C., Kirchner, H. (eds.) CADE 1998. LNCS (LNAI), vol. 1421, pp. 175–190. Springer, Heidelberg (1998)

Design and Implementation of Educational Administration System on the Basis of C/S and B/S Heterogeneous Architecture

Jiang Yan

Hebei United University, Tangshan 063000, China
Anthea488@hotmail.com

Abstract. This paper introdues an university educational administration system in "Independent College". From the user characteristics and main function of the system, combined with practical application,the core part of the educational administration system structure characteristics were analysed. Taking Jitang College,Hebei United University as an example,the college now uses URP of University Educational Administration System (referred to as UEAS), which is a large integrated teaching management information system combining Client/Server and Browser/Server technology, involving various aspects of teaching management and facing all levels and departments of colleges and users. The system achieves various functions in teaching management and provides a reference for the innovation of teaching management information in independent college.

Keywords: independent college, educational administration, UEAS, network.

1 Introduction

"Independent College" is a newborn subject appearing in the process of the extensional expansion of high-quality education resources in Chinese public universities and colleges. Its unique operation mode in the teaching management leads to its particularity in most process of its teaching management in contrary to that of the public universities. Therefore, Hebei United University Jitang College (referred to as Jitang College) requires a set of teaching management platform that is in line with their teaching rule and situation. In view of the particularity of Jitang College, based on the concept of system engineering and software engineering, this article adopts the combinative way of B/S and C/S to meet the requirements of management and information services. For the different types of users such as the school leadership, educational administrators, teachers, students and so on, all of whom have different requirements for system data processing and deployment, UEAS uses C/S technology to realize the management function with respect to fixed applying places, a large quantity of data, complex data processing, data processing time. B/S technology is used for realizing those functions about large operation and frequent visit by distributed concurrent users. Since its introduction from Tsinghua University,

C. Liu, J. Chang, and A. Yang (Eds.): ICICA 2011, Part I, CCIS 243, pp. 473–481, 2011.

the system has played an important role in all of Jitang College's teaching aspects and has been the core platform on the college teaching operation management. As it strengthens the unified planning concept of the education resources and intensifies the support for such modes as the complete credit system, many campuses, many terms and new students enrollment according to majors, it can greatly improve the application functions of the web interface inquiry for teachers, students and other users. I believe under the joint efforts of all the teachers and students, the system will be better adapted to my school education and teaching reform and development, promote the management modernization of independent colleges, improve teaching quality and provide better service for the whole school.

2 The Main Administration Problems in Jitang College[1]

2.1 Application of Information Network Management Means Is Insufficient

The basic Characteristics of university information network, from a technical perspective, are digital, networked, intelligent, multimedia and systematic. Networked feature makes information resources be shared online and activities have less time and space restraint and interpersonal collaboration easy to implement, which increases the flow and feedback of information so that the teaching management department will be able to use the Internet to release information to teachers and students. Network and Information Center in " Jitang College "begins to take shape but still needs to vigorously carry out the construction of the campus network. It should be considered that the educational administration is in public online, making full use of IT technology to improve the efficiency of educational administration.

2.2 Quality of Educational Administration Needs to Be Improved

Teaching administrative staffs are directly teaching organizers and managers whose work directly affects the overall level and quality of teaching management. "Jitang College" educational administration personnel independent from the parent schools needs a lot of time to learn, improve professional ability and level so as to handle the complex and various problems. Therefore, it is a long-term task to improve the overall quality and professional levels of teaching management, to change their work style, to enhance service awareness, to improve efficiency and to carry out all work creatively around "teaching center".

2.3 Educational Administration Mode Is Not Reasonable

With the constant introduction of credit system, new problems concerning educational administration appear continuously, the root cause of which is that it is still deeply influenced by traditional teaching management model and daily work of the current college teaching management department is complicated. Especially for "Jitang College", education management jobs may face more problems. How to make the teaching management more scientific, standardized while cultivating creative ability of students is the key to measure the level of teaching management. Unclear education management responsibilities, insufficient communication with teaching units and lack of comprehension about the daily work of the teaching affairs office, all of those result in lax teaching management and the reduction of teaching quality. But if engineering college teaching management model is simply transplanted, it may bound the creative ability of teachers and students in "Jitang College", and at the same time it is not conducive to the college development. How to adjust the status of the teaching management department without affecting its unique teaching mode is the common problem faced by teachers and students in Jitang College.

2.4 The Efficiency of Educational Administration Is Low

As the work of educational administration in "Jitang College" is complex and multifarious, low efficiency of educational administration is a common phenomenon. In order to improving efficiency, it is necessary to make full use of all resources. Now through UEAS, the educational management tends to be informationized, scientific and standardized. Standardized management of each teacher's curriculum, each student's credits, as well as the progress of each course, makes the whole educational management more systematic and more complete.

2.5 Existing Departmental Task Is Not Clear

As the divisions of the educational administration department are more refined, departmental tasks become more and more intersectional, leading to the unclearness of each departmental task, which may cause some work done by a lot of departments, and even cause dissension. Meanwhile, there is still some work no department is responsible for, just set aside. Those situations may cause discontent of teachers and students and the poor functioning of the school administration work, which also affects the competitiveness of the school. To solve this problem restructuring of existing institutions is necessary, making the division of labor more clear and accurate.Division of labor is divided according to the post function instead of department, which can increase the coordination between departments and make the task clearer. Through the establishment of a sound system of the educational administration post responsibility and rigorous posts and allocation, the responsibilities can be carried out to each academic worker. The quality of education management is ensured by the responsible educational workers. This can make various Academic departments in "Jitang College" more united and more cooperating so as to increase the capacity of the overall school's academic work.

2.6 Academic Information is Not Being Fully Utilized

In a point of view of management means, some parts of “Jitang College” educational administration work are still in the stage of the manual management or computer-aided management. In the stage of the manual management, management tasks mainly rely on manual way, the teaching information feedback in the teaching process lagging behind the other teaching activities, information exchange and preservation still using paper medium as the carrier, the scope of information collection limited by time and space. The way of information transmission is obsolete, speed low, lag phenomenon obvious, statistics means of information backward, data information not being fully utilized.

3 The Construction of UEAS

3.1 The Background of Educational Administration

With the gradual independent operation of teaching and reform implementation of credit program, school scale unceasingly expands from originally a campus to two campuses and the number of students continually increases from original more than 3,000 people to more than 5,000 people. At the same time learning branches and professions are continuously enriched. With the original methods of teaching management, information sharing can not be achieved and a lot of basic data need to be operated manually and repeatedly, which are the major amount of manpower consumption and high probability of error. In order to make full use of campus network, improve efficiency and make the academic management modernization, it is necessary to establish UEAS based on campus network, that is, the comprehensive educational administration system of multi- level, modularization, distribution and the unified identity authentication based on the campus network[2].

3.2 The Overview of the Overall System Design

UEAS condenses a wealth of teaching experience, abundant research and development, advanced management ideas; the colleges and universities user-oriented UEAS expands the service coverage area and achieves information interaction between the main academic business and other auxiliary functions; it improves software integration, enhances the software usability and improves and innovates human-machine interface by a wide margin, software architecture and software aspects; Meanwhile, a good interface with other systems seamlessly integrates overall framework of digital campus URP. UEAS can fully satisfy the needs of the teaching management mode of credit system, fully support the study period elasticity under the credit system, cover all aspects of the academic and teaching process;it achieves powerful functions on a structured training program system, the controlled curriculum arrangement mode that is chosen first and then arranged, minor mode that is taken course first and then registered; it reflects the features concerning the flexible management mechanism, teaching target management as the foundation, supervision control in the management process; it provides a powerful guarantee for implementation for the school teaching management model under the credit system.

3.3 Technical Framework of UEAS[3-5]

As just using C / S or B / S architecture can not meet the needs according to system requirements and goals, the system uses the popular combined system of C / S and B / S, the former mode used in educational administration business, the latter adopted in course selection subsystems and the related information inquiry and release. The system uses the Office of Academic Affairs and office management mode of department level 2 to provide a unified interface, achieving different operational control through rights management. From software architecture point of view, the system should be a typical 3-layer architecture of Browser-DB Server-Client (that is, multi-layer composite structure), which is a combination of C / S (Client / Server) and B / S, as shown in Figure 1.

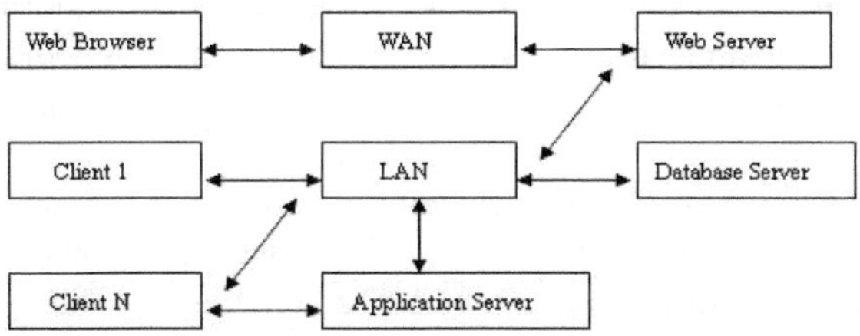

Fig. 1. Client/Server and Browser/Serverr mixed mode map

3.4 The Functions of UEAS[6,7]

1) Enrollment management.Teaching management department in Jitang College arranges all of student numbers as their unique identification throughout the student's registration, course selection, performance, evaluation of teaching and all the other academic management processes, which achieves various kinds of information management, including student enrollment information, personal information, rewards and punishments information, etc. It provides complete data exchange solutions so that relevant business systems (such as the card system) can obtain the accurate information related to the students in real time.

2) Registration management.In the beginning of each semester, each student should be registered through the registration system. With the powerful sub-registration management functions, it can be registered easily in sub-departments, sub-campuses and even allopatry; at the same time it can provide real-time centralized management and statistical analysis toward registration data.

3) Training program management.Training program management system makes training program for students in different grades mainly to maintain each professional curriculum, course plan as the standard of course selection and graduation audit. UEAS plays a key role in the training program as a programmatic document in teaching and learning activities, which standardizes it on the data structure so that it can correctly implement the teaching outline, standardize course arrangement, guide

course selection, and provide the operating basis as the standards of semester examination, graduation audits, degree grant and the implementation of teaching assessment, teaching workload statistics.

4) Teaching material management.Teachers and students can fill in and search teaching materials online and then the system automatically calculates the number and amount of teaching materials. It realizes the overall management for the teaching materials purchase, sale and storage.

5) Courses arranging management.Courses arranging management system arranges courses based on course plan and school teachers resources and sends the results to the elective course system. The whole college centralizes course arrangement, centralizes arrangement of time and place for courses, and makes overall arrangement about all kinds of laboratories and classrooms, greatly solving the problems of insufficient teaching resources and increasing the utilization rate of classrooms and laboratories, which provides constructive suggestions for school development scale and the campus planning. It achieves the management of school course system and the comprehensive support for the construction of school course system and the course content.

6) The management of Course Selection. Course selection sub-system adopts the B/S structure that students within the specified time can register their classes on any computer online. It realizes free customization about course stage, breaking the fixed course selection mode in course stage, enabling users to set up more than one elective period on their own. In the course of giving the students the full autonomy, it also meets the school requirements to strengthen the selection control.

7) Examination management. Examination management module makes unified management of various types of school examinations come true. It realizes the unified management of a variety of tests; it supports examination management in the normal teaching process and also supports the unified management of examination scheme unplanned like grade examinations; through the online exam registration functions, it realizes free registration concerning all kinds of tests. It supports multiple testing arrangement modes. It improves efficiency of overall exam schedule and assures the consistency and security of the business data.

8) Performance management. Teachers accomplish the entry to student achievement through the teaching management system and print report card for examination paper analysis.Incorporating advanced reporting tools can adjust the report flexibly based on the school's needs and adapt to the present situation of the management diversity according to different schools.

9) Graduation audit. The system reviews if the student has graduate qualifications according to the student's professional training program, achievements and his enrollment when he is about to graduate. Graduation examination system can not only do final graduation examination but also carry out the flexible review for a semester.

10) Teaching Evaluation management. Along with the establishment of various aspects of teaching quality standards in "Jitang College", UEAS module of the teaching evaluation is also being perfected, from the previous single teaching evaluation to the present students evaluating teachers, teachers' evaluating students, peer-peer assessment and teachers' self-evaluation, which enormously enriches data

sources on the teaching quality evaluation. The advanced teaching evaluation algorithm is introduced to ensure the scientific, fair and reasonable evaluation results. Teaching evaluation management model achieves a centralized management of the school teaching assessment.

4 UEAS Applications in Jitang College Educational Management

The teaching management department in Jitang College is equivalent to a functional department, using data source provided by each unit to aggregate, process and transmit the academic information data to shared data platform for each unit and individual to call and inquire. Every unit and individual can write and read in a central database through their access. Different interfaces of center database are opened with different access as shown in Table 1.

Table 1. Various departments of the academic use of the UEAS

Application department	The data disposed by the teaching management department for each unit's inquiry		
The students' affairs division	Inquiry of students' enrollment	Performance inquiry	Test information inquiry
The Personnel Department	Teaching status andyear-end performance	Job promotion	Learning and training qualifications
All the teaching units	Teaching plan inquiry	Course inquiry	Teachers' work task inquiry

4.1 The Effects on the Restructuring the Educational Administration

In the analysis of UEAS functional modules, we will find the current educational institutions establishment has some shortcomings, which requires restructuring of existing institutions and the more clear and accurate division of labor, thus we recommend that the Department of Teaching Management should set up teaching project management post, school management posts, performance management post, course arrangement and transfer post, the class election management post, test administration post, teaching materials management post and so on according to each function module of UEAS.

4.2 Effects on the Means of Teaching Information Process

At present, the scale of higher schools is generally larger with the large number of faculty and students, leading to the great amount of data.The traditional management mode causes easily to the delay of the educational information transfer and affect the accuracy of the data. With database and network technology collection range of expanding information, UEAS sets up verification mechanisms on information integrity and accuracy so as to transmit information rapidly and timely and share the teaching management information to the greatest degree.

4.3 The Impact of the Credit System Reform

The educational administration under the credit system mainly includes teaching plan management, the students' enrollment management, student performance management, the test information management, integrated information management, etc. Each part has both some independence and indivisible interdependent relationship with each other. Comprehensive educational administration system sets up subsystems for each part of the management and unifies system resources code in the entire system so that all resources can be shared between subsystems, which completely solves complex problems arisen during the transition from school year system to the credit system and makes management standardized and unified.

4.4 The Effect on Improving the Quality of Teaching Management Team

As the powerful function and advanced technology of UEAS can only be reflected through the use of operators, the level of the staff's quality is the key element whether comprehensive educational administration system is operated successfully and gives play to the greatest efficiency. Therefore, operators need a clear position and clear division of labor, unity of thinking and understanding, and actively technical training and business learning to enhance the level of using UEAS. A clear division of labor and close collaboration are needed to make the maximum of the strong function of UEAS.

4.5 Impact on the Efficiency of Educational Administration

As UEAS is put into operation, duplication and errors are greatly reduced in business management such as course arrangement, course selection, performance management, enrollment management. The entire school's teaching resources such as teachers, classrooms, laboratories, curriculum, teaching programs are shared for different identities of users.Resource sharing under the background of network improves overall working efficiency and quality of service for the teachers and students.

4.6 The Impact on Teaching Quality Monitoring[8]

In order to meet the practical needs of the current rapid development, the school enhances the informationization of teaching management and establishes a powerful teaching management information system. At the same time the school inspection and supervision work is summarized and analyzed by UEAS and the inspection feedback is sent to the relevant units to get suggestions of rectification. A sound monitoring system is established in Jitang College that can give full play to the function of the teaching supervision department in each institute, each department and each teaching and research section. As soon as the problems appear, the system can feed back timely and correct timely. Teaching quality assessment and inspection are carried out designedly to improve the quality of teaching.

5 Conclusion

To speed up the process of the educational administration of colleges and universities, the inform system of synthetically educational administration management is developed by advanced information technology. Based on all aspects and factors in the process of educational administration, UEAS design uses computer technology, network technology, database technology and modular technology to integrate and optimize educational administration data. It obtains the data sharing in campus to the greatest degree and meets requirements concerning collection, storage, manipulation, organization, management and utilization of information resources under the multi-campus centralized management model, thus it can centralize, share and unify information resources[9,10]. Based on the teaching goal management, it strengthens the monitoring of teaching management process, reflecting the people-oriented ideology and highlighting the business data management so as to provide mature management idea, strong management function, and convenient operation mode for the reform in Jitang College. It can help Jitang College solve all kinds of problems that may be encountered in the way to reform and ultimately hope to provide accurate and effective decision analysis, thus promoting the educational reform process in Jitang College and promoting scientific, networking and informationized construction in the independent college academic affairs management.

References

1. Han, J.: Research and practice on university information administration system. Journal of ChangChun University 20(10), 122–124 (2010)
2. Shen, P., Wang, Y., Wu, H., Bai, Y.: Modernization of education management and information system. Qing Hua University Education Research 01, 138–142 (2000)
3. Li, H.: Research on the implementation of educational administration system on the basis of C/S and B/S heterogeneous architature. Modern Computer 321, 195–197 (2009)
4. Zhang, H.: Educational administration information system research and implementation. China Education Information 23, 43–44 (2008)
5. Yang, H., Wang, J.: The design and realization of teaching affairs management system for universities and colleges based on C/S & B/S architecture. Journal of Hunan University of Technology 23(6), 69–72 (2009)
6. Jiang, H., Shi, J.: The design of electronic digital campus academic system. Education Information 12, 39–40 (2006)
7. Yang, Z., Zhang, Z.: Design of web-based campus network teaching system. Journal of Guangdong Technical College of WaterResources and Electric Engineering 2(3), 36–38 (2004)
8. Wan, Z.: The optimization of education system to improve teaching strategies. Jiangxi Educational Research 5, 57–60 (1997)
9. Wu, Q., Qiu, X.: The study and realization of educational affairs management system in independent college. Journal of Jilin Province Economic Management Cadre College 24(1), 98–100 (2010)
10. He, Y.: On the information technology educational administration. China Education Innovation Herald 16, 219 (2008)

Strategic Measures of Network Marketing of SME Brand

Zhou Zhigang

Hebei United University Tangshan, 063009, China
Amonzhou@163.com

Abstract. This paper analyzes main problems existed in the current network promotion of small medium enterprise (SME) brand in our country and puts forward solutions and strategic measures of SME brand network communication. Although Strategic Measures enterprise application network of sales increased, but in the sense of the use of network there exist in a number of disadvantages and the erroneous zone.

Keywords: SME, brand, sales network.

1 Introduction

Creating the largest market with less capital investment, is the problem that every business venture faces with when starting a business or promoting it and also the thing that enterprises expect to resolve. Through the Internet, corporate brand, which is sold in a geometrical way, has become a cost-effective marketing method, because this method can make the selling cost lower compared with the traditional selling method. Its powerful effect is incomparable for traditional media sales. Networks have become an important means of corporate brand marketing. Applying Internet marketing to increase core competitiveness of enterprises has become the only way for enterprises, in particular, many SMEs. Although Strategic Measures enterprise application network of sales increased, but in the sense of the use of network there exist in a number of disadvantages and the erroneous zone.

Strategic Measures brand sales network problems.

Strategic measures:

The construction of the website of Strategic Measuress

Due to the low cost, quick effect, short cycle, set up enterprise's websites have been influenced by many Strategic Measures of favor, a lot of medium and small enterprises and have done related aspects of the demonstration and analysis, also did not stand in network marketing strategy to consider the height of the construction of the website, the more did not have to website after website built by how to promote its own brand. Website construction is the enterprise network marketing plan condition, but most Strategic Measures in the website construction process has many problems:

The contents of the website.

In many Internet enterprises in the backdrop, a lot of medium and small enterprise is just a follow suit construction behavior. In its content, the enterprise is just a brief

C. Liu, J. Chang, and A. Yang (Eds.): ICICA 2011, Part I, CCIS 243, pp. 482–488, 2011.

introduction, product information to release it to the web site content such as. Many Web sites are only a few simple Web pages, the website information, whether in small function, or in the information is unable to achieve the purpose of brand sales.

The website localization is not clear.

Many Strategic Measures web site set up, and there is no rush to target customers and market analysis of the specific situation, are not considered website market position, the colour collocation of the website, main structure is not accorded with enterprise localization of target. The enterprise did not through the web site to its brand theme display to potential customers, it is difficult to keep visitors leave deep impression.

Update website information slowly.

Strategic Measures built after the web site, long time don't update web page content, so not only won't improve enterprise image, it will give the negative effects of enterprise image.2.

2 Strategic Measures Web Search Engine Promotion Erroneous Zone

2.1 Get Rich Quick, Lack of Patience

Search engine promotion has become a lot of medium and small enterprise promoting their own brand of important means, the enterprise is in first contact search bidding, to search for higher expectations, hope in the choice of the keywords begins to put right after received effect. Many enterprise to search for disappointment is from the within a period of time and didn't see significant effect and reduce or even cancel the search for service investment. In fact, for the first time to search for the Strategic Measures investment, it up the first key words is not completely suitable for enterprise's own scheme situation and characteristics, to find a more ideal on the scheme will have to put in a period of time after the continuously to modify and improve. Therefore, maintain a certain amount of patience is the enterprise the time in one key, not be eager to hope for success.

2.2 Select Key Words Much Too Conservative

Some enterprise worry about high cost, selected only limited key words, and it makes on the effect to sell at a discount greatly. Search for more, not keywords choice depends on the more the greater investment. Therefore, in the choice of keywords, enterprise should according to their own characteristics, combined with news events, in the full understanding of target customers based on the characteristics of the search, the authors choose more effective keywords, through the continuous optimization, and realize the cost of the investment promotion effect and the best balance.

2.3 Select Search Service Provider is Relatively Single

At present domestic search service has three big providers, respectively is Google, baidu, Yahoo. Three great services occupied the whole search sales service of the 80%, also is enterprise customers preferred search for service providers. Although three search engines provide nearly identical search service, and technology level, but is facing each target user groups have certain differences. Such as: yahoo's use objects to 35 years of age as business flow, users in the first; Baidu the target group, most of the older, small for students at school and a younger generation to search the majority of rendering entertainment; Young white-collar workers, scholars and technical personnel more accustomed to using Google search. From that, the enterprise in on the key words, should according to different target user group selection of different search engines are combined on the which keeps more target users can access the enterprise group website, to the ideal promotion effect.

	Search number	growth rate	Market share
otal	9,461,583	27.5%	100%
Google	5,945,064	40.8%	62.8%
Yahoo	1,528,779	8.7%	16.2
Microsoft	1,057,677	18.3%	11.2%
AOL	381,769	8.9%	4.0%
Ask.com	181,205	1.0%	1.9%
My Web	66,649	-6.9%	0.7%
Comcast	50,311	25.8%	0.5%
Yellow Pages	25,392	--	0.3%
AT&T	24,061	-2.0%	0.3%
NexTag	23,145	0.3%	0.2%

Data source: Nielsen Oline, MegaView Search

Fig. 1. Internet search provider rankings

2.4 Not in Time on the Plan. Maintenance

Lock core target users is the search for the main characteristics of the key words, the enterprise on the scheme are directly related to the release of an effect. Effective keywords can attract more users click on, they are all enterprise potential user groups. Along with the social hot, Internet users search habits and the changing market environment, first on the solution may be not suitable for the development of The Times, the needs of the enterprises, this needs the enterprise according to the circumstance of oneself make timely adjustments, the website information has good timeliness.

3 To Strengthen the Construction and Maintenance of Corporate Website

In order to fully make the website display products and instructions to consumers in the way of flexible and vivid information material, picture information and so on, enterprises should rich Website content timely and thus enhance consumers' understanding and trust to branded products.

Corporate brand image should be effectively promoted through the website. Consumer's understanding to corporate brand is inseparable from the information about the corporate brand he or she received. The Internet is the ligament that enterprises convey a variety of brand information to consumers on the initiative through the website. Enterprises can take advantage of website, the platform, to establish a brand image.

Corporate website is the publishing platform of enterprise information. Maintaining the timeliness of website information is the important work for enterprises in network marketing process. Enterprises should release the latest information of products on the website timely, in order to make users to understand more information about enterprises and relative products, thereby enhancing attraction of website to users. Website should have good online service function. Good online services can improve enterprises' efficiency to serve for consumers, and quickly solve customers' problems and provide the best solutions to enhance their creditworthiness.

4 Search Engine Optimization is Commonly Used Effective Method of Network Brand Promotion at Present

In order to win the market preferable and market its own brand, enterprises need to create website, enrich and improve the website function, content and services. What's more, they need to rely on search engine, the third party tool, to allow

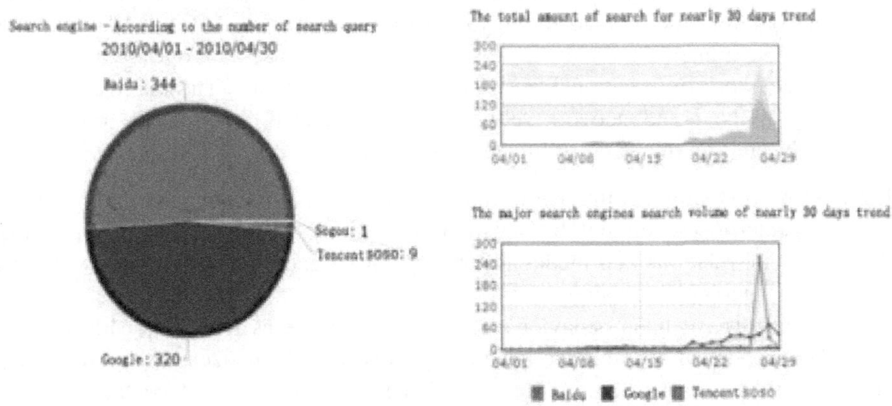

Fig. 2. A search engine rankings

consumers to quickly check the company website and click to access. This requires enterprises to use tools or purchase services to optimize search engine. Enterprises should make your website meet search rules of search engine as much as possible and let your website information and links appear in the front position of the search results to obtain better Website ranking. There are three main aspects of search engine optimization: web content optimization, key word optimization, and website external links optimization.

Optimization of Site Content. ① Enterprises must set up suitable website column structure and striking and clear navigation, in order that users can easily obtain corporate information when going to the website. ② The domain name of enterprises should be normative, and as simple as possible. The domain name can not include special characters such as symbols "*, #" and so on, which will not be detected by search engines. ③ On the webpage there should be content like text description and personalized page titles which are visible to search engines. Try not to use a large number of FLASH and pictures. ④ Frequently update website content and maintain the timeliness of the content.

Keyword Optimization. Keyword optimization is very important for website search. Choosing the right keywords has a direct impact on the results of visitors' searching for websites. When choosing keywords the following points need be paid attention to : ① Select product name, product type, enterprise name, brand name, industry name and so on. ② To improve the access rate, multiple similar main keywords should be used. ③ In view of the pressure of competition among enterprises, the ranking is more competitive as enterprises are more and more, so try not to use too popular words. ④ Taking regional feature of keywords into consideration, certain region keywords should be set.

External Links of Website Optimization. In order to improve the ranking of enterprises, enterprises need to do as much external links as possible. For example, they can set their own links in some websites with good quality, higher click rate in search engine, and relevance to the enterprises; or obtain the links permit by some industrial organizations; or go to the forum to comment and add corporate website link with the comment.

Select Network Information Transfer to sell corporate brand. Through the practice, the value of the brand network selling will be reflected, whereas the process of practice depends on the ways of information transfer.

Internet Advertising. As Internet technology continues to develop and Internet users increase, enterprises can not be satisfied with brand performance and marketing through social relations and media advertising. More and more enterprises will shift its target to Internet advertising.

In the 6th Ireli netizen behavior research report, netizens who frequently contact with the proportion of Internet advertising was 75.3%, netizens who frequently contact with the proportion of TV advertising was 71.59%, and contact rates of newspaper ads, magazine ads and outdoor advertising were 52.5% , 59.1% and 48.9%.

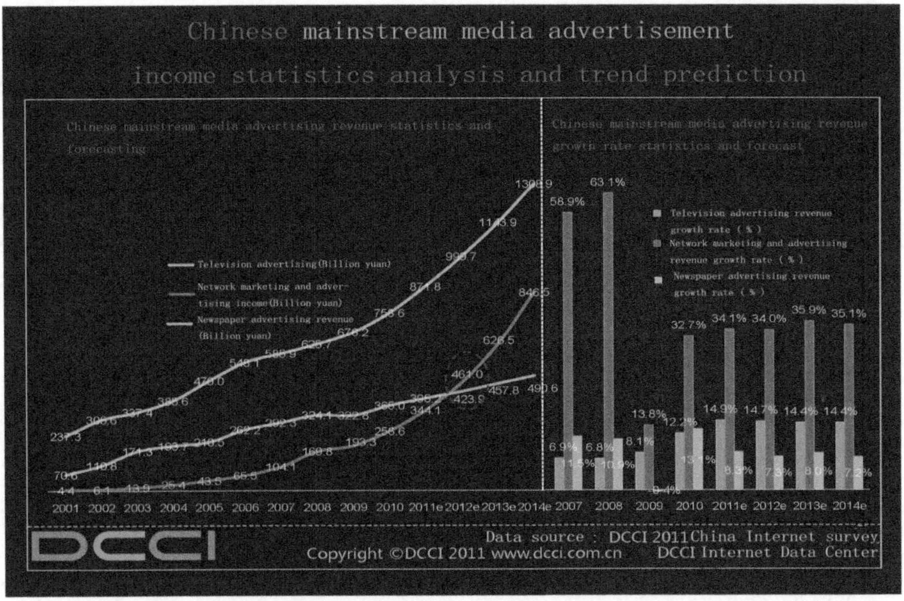

Fig. 3. China's mainstream media income statistics

Link Exchange. Link exchange is also called reciprocal link, which is the simple form of cooperation between websites with complementary strengths. That means placing website LOGO or website name of the other enterprise on their corporate website respectively and adding the corresponding hyperlinks, in order to allow users to find directly and click on their own enterprise's website from their cooperative partner's website. Link exchange is a common approach of brand promotion. As it was linked by other websites more and more, the effect will be more obvious. This is a commonly-used and free means of promotion, which has become a method which was adopted by a large number of SMEs.

E-mail. From the day that the first email came into being to today, e-mail not only simply means messages sending and receiving or is used as mutual communication tool; it has become a part of business operating activities gradually. With targeted, easy to handle, low cost, and efficient to communicate features, e-mail has become an important and universal means of information communication. It is also an important tool of brand network marketing.

Interactive Network Virtual Community. Network virtual community contains discussion groups, forums, chat rooms, paste bars, blogs and other forms of online communication platform. Each plate of network community is concentrated with visitors with common interest and common needs. In fact, due to large number of users' participation, virtual community has become a special marketing place.

Network Video. Network video is a common Internet marketing way. Enterprises can upload their own propaganda or product description to the Internet in the format of video. Through the WEB video player, consumers can watch the display of the products online. The real image enables consumers more intuitive and emotional to understand enterprise products, thus deepening consumers' understanding and trust to enterprise products.

Summary

SMEs should fully understand the impact of network on corporate brand, make the network become a powerful medium of brand marketing, put traditional brand marketing and network brand marketing together, establish and improve corporate website, select a variety of network information delivery methods to market corporate brand, to better enhance their visibility and establish corporate brand image.

References

1. Aake, D.A., Joachimsthaler, E.: Brand Leadership, pp. 273–299. The Free Press, New York (2000)
2. Deirdr: Cyberbranding:Brand Building in the Digital Economy, pp. 15–24. Prentice Hall P1.R, Indiana (2000)
3. Chen, S.: Assessing the Impact of the Internet on Brands. Brand Management 8(5), 288–302 (2001)
4. de Leslie: Succeeding with Brands on the lmemct. Brand Management 8(3), 186–196 (2001)
5. Braunatein, M., Levine, E.H.: Deep Branding Oll the Internat, p. 10. Prima Publishing, Roseville (2000)
6. Loosley, R.: The Effect on Brand management when a Business Migrates onto the Intemet. Brand Management I(4), 267–279 (2004)
7. Shi, D.: Customer relationship marketing, customer value and virtual community. Jiangsu Business Research (6) (2004)
8. Wang, C.: The enterprise brand network operation and management. Productivity Research (3), 36–39 (2000)
9. Philip, K.: Marketing management (Asian Edition). In: Hong, R., et al. (eds.), pp. 10126–10486. Renmin University of China press, Beijing (1997)
10. Fang, W.: Research on customer service based on Internet tools. Hohai Human Studies, Nanjing (2004)
11. Been: Network brand marketing strategy. Enterprise Management 4, 18–19 (2000)
12. Rong, L., Song, T.: Enterprise network management, p. 1. China Radio and Television Publishing House, Beijing (2002)
13. Wang, J.: The network brand characteristics. Technical Economy (10), 59–61 (2001)
14. Wang, X.: China: facing the Internet era of "new economy", p. 2. Sanlian Bookstore, Beijing (2003)
15. Yang, Z.: The network brand construction. The Journal of Jiangxi Administration Institute (2), 25–27 (2003)
16. Yu, M.: Brand. Anhui people's Publishing House, Hefei (2002)

Design and Accomplishment of Campus WebGIS Based on B/S Model—A Case-Study of Hebei Polytechnic University

Xiaoguang Li*, Fenghua Wu, and Shunxi Yan

College of Mining Engineering, Hebei United University, Tangshan Hebei 063009, China
Lxg96122@126.com

Abstract. In view of the present development situation and the significance of digital campus, an overall design and a detailed design for digital campus system are worked out based on Hebei Polytechnic University by using C#, .NET, SQL Server 2000, XML language, SuperMap IS.NET 5 and SQL Server 2000 database. What I did was the design and implementation of the ten modules including introducing the general situation, house property and the mien of the campus as well as the view of topic chart. These modules implement functions including issuance of map, view of information, information query, printout of map and tropic chart, etc.. And then spatial data sharing is implemented.

Keywords: SuperMap IS, WebGIS, digital campus, C#.

1 Introduction

Traditional university informatization is mainly MIS system based on Web, which attach importance to information management. The information shown by MIS is short of stereoscopic sensation and spatial data.

This article takes Hebei Polytecnic University for example. A digital campus system based on B/S is developed with the support of WebGIS. Users can acquire spatial information of campus through IE Browser. Hebei Polytecnic University is on the way of developing and extending. The construction of digital campus based on WebGIS improves the capacity of teaching resources and teaching efficiency.

2 Selection of Developing Platform

It is important to select the right software environment when designing the WebGIS system. The suitable operating system, database management system, front end development tool and WebGIS developing platform is important. There are tens of

* Please note that the LNCS Editorial assumes that all authors have used the westernnaming convention, with given names preceding surnames. This determines the structure of the names in the running heads and the author index.

C. Liu, J. Chang, and A. Yang (Eds.): ICICA 2011, Part I, CCIS 243, pp. 489–495, 2011.

WebGIS products in the markets based on Internet/Intranet so far. Comparing the advantages and disadvantages of these products, we chose SuperMap IS.NET at last. SuperMap IS.NET is a new generation developing platform of WebGIS. And it is based on Microsoft .NET techniques and SuperMap Objects component techniques. Its integration adopts the distributed computing technique which is Internet-oriented and complex and large-scale network apply system which supports cross-regional and cross-network. SuperMap IS.NET is composed of these components such as client-side user interface manifestation components, Web server extension, GIS sever, data sever, remote manager and so on.

The operation system is Windows XP(SP2 or advanced)or Windows Server 2003(SP2 or advanced)or Windows Server 2008. In addition, sever needs to install Microsoft Internet information sever(IIS), SuperMap Objects(DataViews or Developer Edition), .NET Framework 3.5 SP1, SuperMap IS.net hardware dog. Client-side should install operation system and IE Internet browser.

The Web GIS websites development based on SuperMap IS.net is conducted in the environment of Visual Studio.NET 2003. Therefore, the following is needed:

(1) Server Operating System: Windows 2000, Windows XP, Windows Server 2003 or advanced; install IIS, SuperMap IS.NET as well as software dog
(2) Client-side: Windows 95/ 98/ NT/ 2000/XP/ 2003(including IE Internet browser)
(3) Development environment: Microsoft Visual Studio.NET 2003

3 The Design of the System Function Module

Ensuring how to realize the Digital Campus based on WebGIS concretely lays an excellent foundation for the embodiment of the system and the embodiment of the module design which is on the stage of black box in the overall stage .According to the consequence of the overall stage, the Digital Campus based on SuperMap IS.NET has ten function modules, they respectively are the general situation of the science and engineering, campus map, house estates , browse of special subject, space analysis, information of teachers, information of students, elegant demeanor, online forum, Website management. The mission and the target of the detailed design are the concrete procedure and implementation algorithm of these modules, also including the establishment of the concrete module embodiment and the limiting surface of the module. Just doing so can have something in store for use and widen the speed in the coding stage.

Digital Campus is a digital space related to the show of the campus, it shows the stretch and the spread of the campus space. The system adopts C# , coupled with

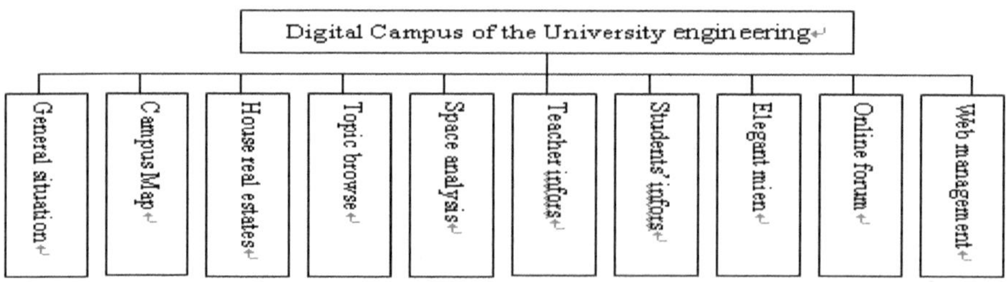

Fig. 1. Component of the module system

SuperMap IS.NET Website platform and Microsoft SQL 2000 database to develop and use the more mature Browse/Server structure. All servers are placed in the Website center, and the subscriber's access the servers through browsers, inquiring the information needed.

4 The System Achievement

4.1 The Allocation of the System Software

This system is used in the environment of Visual Studio.Net 2003, based on WebGIS contained in SuperMap IS.NET. So its operation needs the following situation:

(1) The Server operation system: Windows 2000, Windows XP, Windows Server 2003 or higher version; Installing IIS, SuperMap IS.NET, the software of sogo included.
(2) The Clients Side: Windows 95/98/NT/2000/XP/2003(including IE browser).
(3) The developed environment: Microsoft Visual Studio.NET 2003.

4.2 The Establishment of Database

This text use SuperMap Desktop to vectorize the relief map of Hebei Polytechnic University which scale is 1:10000, and to modify the transformations of features by the means of land survey. After successfully entering space information, collect and edit the corresponding attribute information. According to objects, system data can be classified as the following aspects: teaching buildings, sports sites, dormitory buildings, office building, library, canteen, earthquake remain, and so on. The type of data source adopts SQL data source.

4.3 The Realization of System Function

The following will take distance measurement and how to query attributes from map for examples to introduce the implementation process:
Distance measurement

The following flow chart is about the specific flow-sheet of distance measurement:

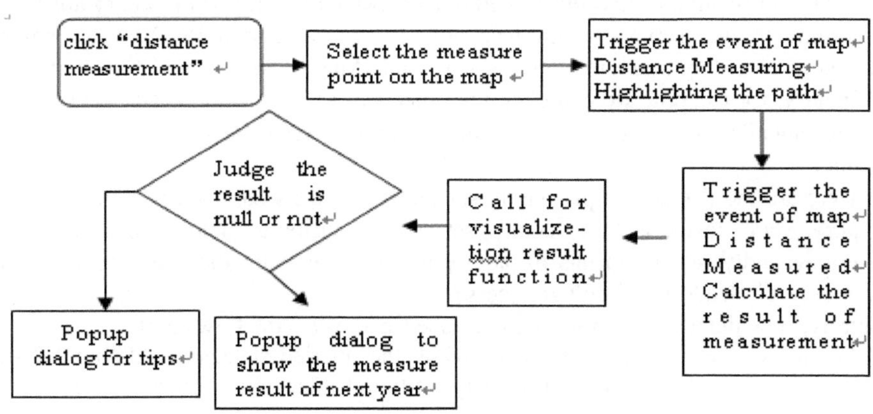

Fig. 2. Distance measuring follow chart

The specific implementation process of distance measuring:

Load the control component for area measurement to Web form.

Program function DisplayResult() which is the same as distance measurement's.

Add the following code to the event AreaMeasuring() of the map control component:

e.IsHighLight=true: //highlight the area, in which e is argument of function.

4) Add the following code to the event AreaMeasured() of the map control component:

String result = e.Area + "square meter"; //calculate the result of area measurement

This.DisplayResult(result); //display result

5) The operation result is the same as shown.:

(2)Inquiry attributes according to the map

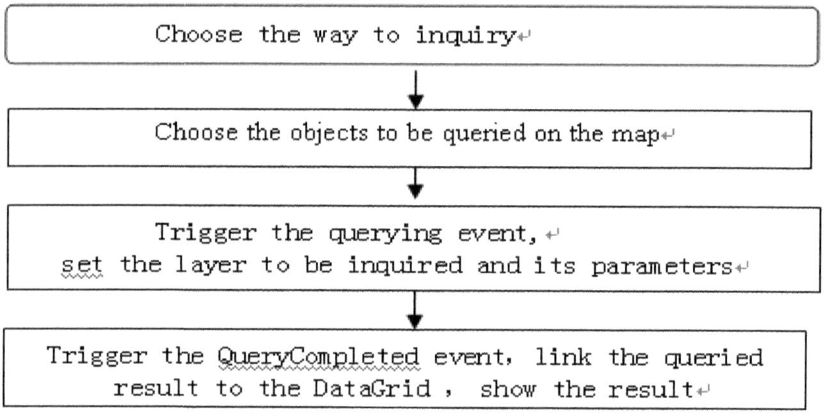

Fig. 3. The flow chart of querying attributes according to the map

There is another way of space information inquiry. We can inquiry corresponding attribute information to find the related objects ,which is referred to inquiry attributes according to the map.Now introduce how to use SuperMap IS .NET to inquiry attributes according to the map in this step. SuperMap IS.NET provides several ways to inquiry, for example we can click the objects directly to inquiry, and we can also set rectangular box range、circle range、polygon range and buffering range to inquiry.

Here are the detailed steps. Firstly set the lays and its parameters before that we inquiry. For instance, we could set some attribute fields information to return.Secondly, set the means to inquiry that is what states the map is(pointquery, rectquery, circlequery and polygonquery).

Thirdly,show the results on the user interface.Chart 5-9 is the flow chart.

We need a set of tool buttons to switch the queried state,and add four HTML elements images to present it. The images title attributes are pointquery , ectquery, irclequery and polygonquery separately, and the pictures are  ,click the HTML selections ,and switch the editing state to HTML mode,and try to find the HTML codes of the four images which is done on the former step,and add corresponding CLICK events and codes to corresponding buttons :

Pick out a picture by points:

```
onclick=" SMISActionStart ('MapControl1','Point QUERY');"
```

Pick out a picture by rectangles:

```
onclick=" SMISActionStart ('MapControl1','RECTQUERY');"
```

Pick out a picture by circles:

```
onclick=" SMISActionStart ('MapControl1','CIRCLEQUERY');"
```

Pick out a picture by polygons:

```
onclick=" SMISActionStart
('MapControl1','POLYGONQUERY');"
```

Then write the check code. Install the rogatory parameters, then return numeric field and so on in the code. Finally, bind the rogatory Spatial Database to DataGrid Database and display.

```
Private void MapControl1_Querying (object sender,
SuperMap.IS.WebControls.EventArguments.QueryingEventArgs e)
{
e.Params. Highlight.HighlightResult = true; // Install whether to return a highlighting map
e.Params.Layers = new QueryLayer [1]; // Install the rogatory objects of the layer
e.Params.Layers [0] = new QueryLayer ();
e.Params.Layers [0].Name = "World@World";// Install the rogatory layer
e.Params.Layers [0].ReturnFields = new string [2];
e.Params.Layers [0].ReturnFields [0] = "SMID"; // Set the attribute information which back to the layer
e.Params.Layers [0].ReturnFields [1] = "Country"; // Set the attribute information which back to the layer
// Bind the rogatory results to the DataGrid
Private void MapControl1_QueryCompleted (object sender,
SuperMap.IS.WebControls.EventArguments.QueryCompletedEventArgs e)
{
    ResultSet rs = new ResultSet ();
    rs.Recordsets = e.Recordsets;
    rs.TotalCount = e.TotalCount;
    DataSet ds = rs.ToDataSet ();
    dgResult.DataSource = ds;
    dgResult.DataBind ();
}
```

5 Discussion in the Key Technique

Web Service is a service based on XML and HTTPS. It's communication protocols are mainly based on SOAP,With the description of the services through WSDL and the discovery and acquirement of the metadata through UDDL.

Web Service is a new and important application program. Web Service is a length of code that can be discovered described and visited with XML. There are many activities in this field; however there are three XML standards that are mainly used in Web Service.

OAP: Originally it's Simple Object Access Protocol. SOAP defines a documental format which describes the approach to call for a length of remote code. My application program creates a XML document which describes the approach I wish to call for, and also pass down the essential parameter to it, then the application program transmit the XML document to that code via the Internet. The code receives the XML document, explain it, call for the approach that I requested, and then return a XML document that describes the result. SOAP standard edition 1.1 is located in w3.org/TR/SOAP/. Please visit w3.org/TR/ to understand all the activities that are related to SOAP.

WSDL: Web Services Description Language is a XML vocabulary chart used to describe the Web Service. It's possible to write a length of code which receive WSDL document and then call for the Web Service it never used before. The information of WSDL files defines the name of service, the name of its approach, the parameters of these approaches, and other detailed information. You can find the recent WSDL standards in w3.org/TR/WSDL (no symbol in the end).

UDDI:Universal Description, Discovery, and integration protocol defines SOAP interface for Web Service register center. If you have a length of code which is hoped to be regarded as Web Service to arrange, UDDI standard defines how to add your service description to register center. If you are looking for a length of code which provides some function, UDDI standard defines how to find out register center so that you can find the information you want. All the data sources that are related to UDDI can be found in uddi.org.

According to the traditional Internet map service software has many problems for instance complex-using, difficult-developing, difficult yin meeting big load operation and so on. SuperMap is used on opening architecture and it has many advantages such as easy and convenient, easy to expand, give full play to the function of map engine consequently.

Through this architecture, SuperMap can be achieve much server cluster, dynamic load balancing, compile and execution, directly response for HTTP, multistage cache, many maps engines to support, centralize management and so on. Consequently make it possible for users to release large quantities of data quickly as well as the map data from different sources.

SuperMap is using XML technology, it's characteristics for instance powerful map performance ability, easy to develop, easy to use, convenient operation. SuperMap IS not only can built Internet GIS website quickly, but also can be used to establish feature-rich Intranet-based and enterprise-class network based GIS application.

SuperMap Editor supports the large space database technology SDX and SDX+.

6 Conclusion

Digital campus is the embodiment of WebGIS application, it can provide students and social public teaching resources geographical spatial location information query and other related information service. This article mainly discusses the design and implementation of the function of network map which developed based on SuperMapIS.NET. Along with the development of a more profound "3S" technologies and faces the society and integrated application, school web will no longer be a single WebGIS application, but will be shirt-sleeve 3S integration. On this basis, the function design and forms of network map will be much more diverse and more practically, maps website will also give our survival and live earth home bring deeper interpretation.

Acknowledgments. The authors acknowledge the support by the Natural Science Foundation of Hebei United University (No. z200715).

References

1. Shuliang, Z., Guonian, L.: The network geographic information system. Science Press, Beijing (2005)
2. Yingxue, X., Jingshan, W.: The Design and Implementation of Digital Campus System Based on WebGIS. Journal of BeiJing Institute of Education (Natural Science) 5, 14–17 (2006)
3. Xiao-Ai, D., Ji-Yang, Y., Jian, J.: Design and Accomplishment of Campus WebGIS Based on B/S Model-A Case-study of Chengdu University of Technology. Surveying and Mapping 33, 13–17 (2010)
4. Chunrong, Z., Pinghui, L.: Design and Research of Campus Geographic Information System based on Supemap IS.NET-A Case Study of Fast China Institute of Technology. J. Technology Square 8, 49–52 (2008)
5. WuNian, Y., Guoliang, P., Yujun, D., et al.: Digitalizing campus: digital Chengdu University of Technology. Journal of Chengdu University of Technology (Science & Technology Edition) 32, 101–106 (2005)
6. Hong, X.: Implementation of Campus WebGIS System Based on. J. Microcomputer Applications 26, 21–23 (2010)
7. Xiaogang, F., Xiang Dong, W.: Research on the System of Digital Campus—A Case Study of the Xi'an University of Arch and Tech. J. Geomatics & Spatial Information Technology 33(6), 9–12 (2010)
8. Wei, Y., Weining, Y.: Design and Research of Campus Geographic Information System based on Supemap IS.NET-A Case Study of Ningxia University. J. Science & Technology Information 21, 21–22 (2010)
9. Wei, W., Xi, Y., Nan, L.: Application of WebGIS in Campus Spatial Information Visible Management. Journal of Xian University of Arts & Science (Nat. Sci. Ed.) 2, 11–14 (2009)
10. Xiaohong, X.: Design of Digital Campus System Based on GIS. J. Geospatial Information 1, 62–64 (2008)

Design and Implementation of WLAN Monitoring and Management System

Jiantao Gu[1,*], Qun Wei[1], and Wei Li[2]

[1] College of Sciences, Hebei United University, 063009 Tangshan, China
[2] College of Information Engineering, Hebei United University, 063009 Tangshan, China

Abstract. This paper aims at constructing a new wireless remote monitoring and management systems "WLAN Inspector". The system is designed to achieve a real-time monitoring (7 x 24 hours) and intelligent management systems. It has multiple functions: real-time network monitoring, real-time protocol analysis, information, statistics, safety testing and network performance monitoring, etc. This system can give Video Frame Capture for Mac, analyze the WLAN traffic characteristics, detect possible security vulnerabilities, and give the appropriate solution. The system deployment, interactive architecture, and graphical interface system structure are discussed with Graphics in this paper.

Keywords: Wireless LAN, WLAN Inspector, System deployment, Interactive architecture.

1 Introduction

As IEEE 802.11 Wireless LAN (WLAN) technology matures, the huge decline in the cost of WLAN devices, coupled with its mobility, flexibility, scalability, etc., wireless local area network (Wireless LAN) have been more widely used as an extension , supplement or replace of traditional wired networks in the enterprise, campus, and many other places. However, due to open space of radio waves, design flaws of IEEE 802.11 protocol, low prices of equipment, as well as easy installment, there are so many security problems of wireless LAN. The increasing popularity of wireless LANs brings a range of issues and challenges to network and information management. From the industry to the research community, it is widely recognized difficulties of wireless LAN monitoring and management, and a lot of research has begun.

This paper aims at constructing a new wireless remote monitoring and control systems "WLAN Inspector". The system is designed to achieve a real-time monitoring (7 x 24 hours) and intelligent management systems. It has multiple functions: real-time network monitoring, real-time protocol analysis, information,

* The research supported by Projects of Hebei Province Education Department (Z2010261) and Research Project of Hebei United University (z200716).

C. Liu, J. Chang, and A. Yang (Eds.): ICICA 2011, Part I, CCIS 243, pp. 496–502, 2011.

statistics, safety testing and network performance monitoring, etc. This system can give Video Frame Capture for Mac, analyze the WLAN traffic characteristics, detect possible security vulnerabilities, and give the appropriate solution.

2 System Deployment

As shown in Figure 1, it uses passive monitoring deployment mode. Monitoring laptop is a notebook computer equipped with wireless laptop card. Monitoring laptop supports many types of wireless local area network such as 802.11a, 802.11b, 802.11. It can be fixed in a physical location to do the monitoring and analysis works, it also supports the move monitoring. Monitoring results displayed through graphical user interface directly, critical information such as alarm will be recorded to do further analysis.

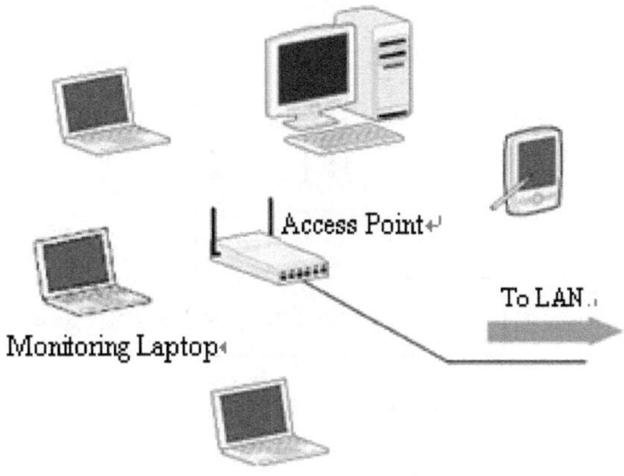

Fig. 1. System Deployment

At the same time in a simple graphical interface, the user can correspondingly get analysis reports which support a variety of formats.

3 Interactive Architecture

As shown in Figure 2, the entire system is divided into two parts, the graphical interface and the underlying modules. The graphical interface is responsible for completing system configuration, achieving display and query functions of results and alarm information. The underlying module is responsible for receiving the configuration commands, achieving generate and output functions of monitoring results and alarm information.

To maintain two connections in the graphical interface and the underlying modules, one is used for the extraction of monitoring and alarm information (defined as the first connection), the next one for graphical interface ordering configuration information, start and stop commands to underlying module (defined as the second connection).

Using TCP approach, the graphical interface and the underlying modules are maintained by two connections. The underlying module is in SERVER mode, the graphical interface is in CLIENT mode. The first connection is a long connection, that is, during system operation, this connection has been maintained always, and the underlying module will take the initiative to push the monitoring results to graphical interface; The second connection is a short connection that requires the graphical interface to establish a new connection with the SERVER of underlying module, and the connection will cut off after using.

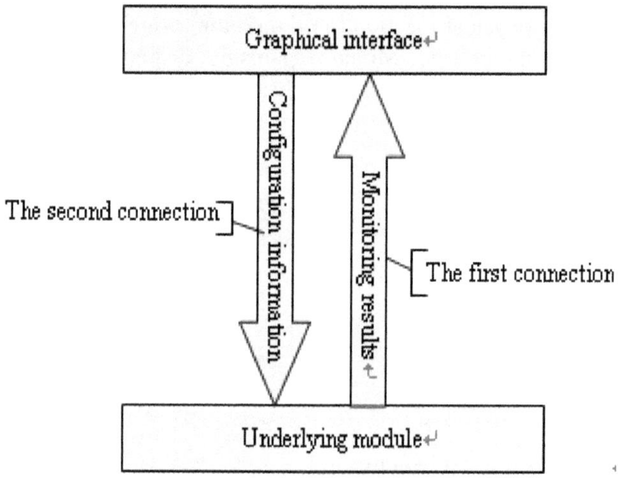

Fig. 2. Interactive Architecture

4 Graphical Interface System Structure

4.1 Overall Framework Design of Graphical Interface

As shown in Figure 3, the graphical interface mainly consists of five major component, they are basic information modules, channel information, modules, equipment information modules, alarm information modules and report modules. The five major parts use common data to complete the corresponding interface for data display functions.

The five major parts link through the main interface with the system configuration, interface and underlying database. It is an organic whole which is supported by data sources and underlying interface, and used interface dynamically displays as the theme with configuration management for the assistance.

4.2 Brief Description of Each Module

(1) Interface module:
It is used to maintain two connections in the graphical interface and the underlying modules. Using TCP approach, the graphical interface and the underlying modules are

maintained by two connections. The underlying module is in SERVER mode, the graphical interface is in CLIENT mode. The first connection is a long connection, that is, during system operation, this connection has been maintained always, and the underlying module will take the initiative to push the monitoring results to graphical interface; The second connection is a short connection that requires the graphical interface to establish a new connection with the SERVER of underlying module, and the connection will cut off after using.

(2) System configuration module:
It is used to complete system operation before and during the operation of the basic configuration, which Includes device block configuration, legal device configuration, monitoring parameters configuration, communication interface configuration, alarm configuration and channel configuration.

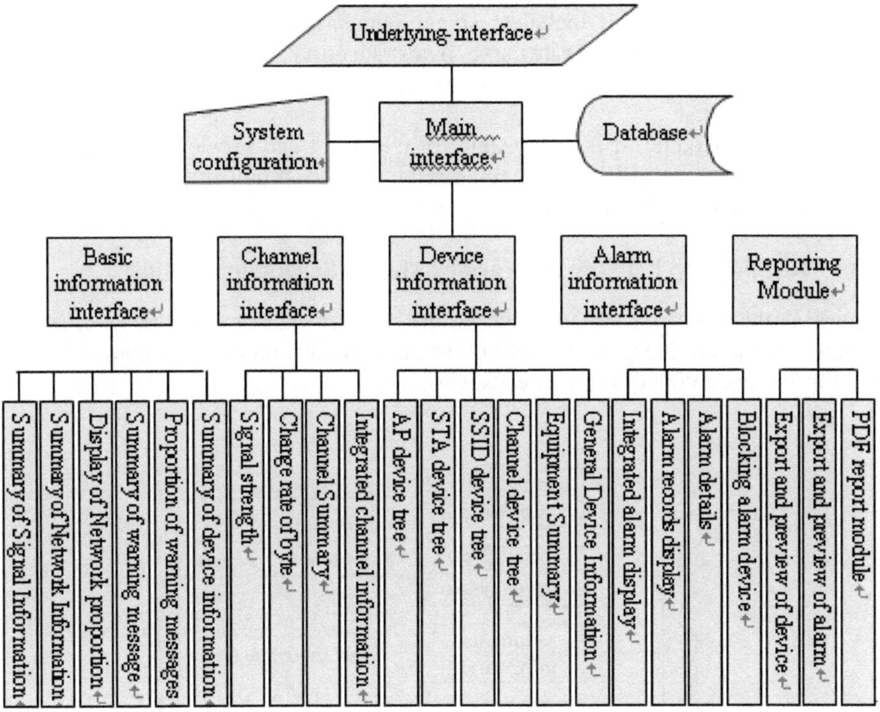

Fig. 3. Overall framework design of graphical interface

(3) Database module:
It is data-switching center of saving and reading of configuration data. It responsible for storing the data flow from the interface into the database, and data flow of system configuration, basic information, channel information, equipment information and alarm information.

(4) Main interface:
As a container, it unifies together with basic information, channel information, equipment information and alarm information, and is responsible for messaging in

each module, data transmission and related configuration information processing. At the same time, it is responsible for controlling and monitoring the underlying WLAN interface control.

- Basic information interface: Basic information is responsible for presenting a summary of information which is monitored in 802.11 networks. As shown in Figure 3, the displayed information includes: signaling information, network information, network proportion information, warning message, and device information.
- Channel information interface: It is responsible for displaying the channel details in a particular type of network (802.11a, 802.11b or 802.11g). This part mainly shows the following content: signal strength, change rate of byte, channel summary and integrated channel information.
- Device information interface: It is responsible for displaying the details change information on different devices, including by AP, SSID, STA and channel. The displayed information includes: signal intensity curve, noise intensity curve, signal noise curve, frame rate curve, bytes rate curve, etc.
- Alarm information interface: It is responsible for displaying the alarm information list.
- Reporting Module: It is responsible for exporting and previewing of device and alarm, storing as a PDF document to reference for administrators, and to analysis network status and fault location.

4.3 Relationship Between the Various Thread Scheduling Module

Figure 4 illustrates the system relationship between the various thread scheduling module. The main thread is responsible for the initialization of the graphical interface and for the scheduling of other threads work.

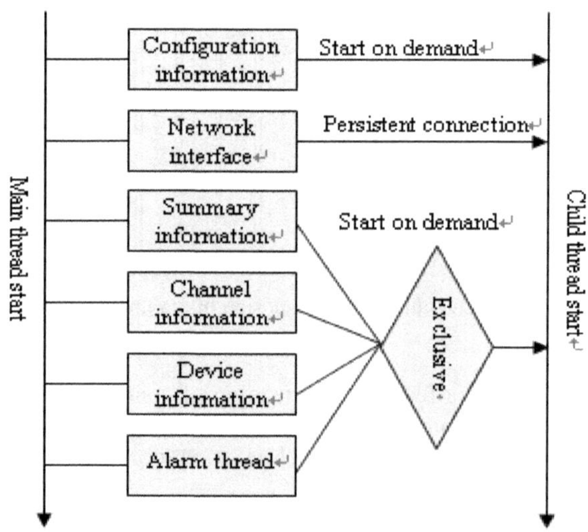

Fig. 4. Relationship between the various thread scheduling module

When you need to configure the system parameters, configuration information thread will start, and independent with other threads.

When the monitoring program starts, network interface thread will start, and independent with other threads.

If and only if the monitoring program is in start state, there only one thread is active in summary information thread, channel information thread, equipment information thread, and alarm thread, to ensure efficient use of system resources.

5 Technical Features

According to the 802.11 frame format, parse all types of data frames captured in the WLAN, extract the network ID and network traffic information, provide friendly and simple graphical interface.

Making use of specific characteristics and identity of Security vulnerabilities and specific traffic model, detect the Possible WLAN security threats and hacking, give warning message.

Based on 802.11 Protocol, construct special management frames, block the illegal equipment so as to disconnect to original AP.

References

1. Bhaiji, Y.: Network security technologies and solutions, 1st edn., March 30. Cisco Press (2008)
2. Garcia, Luis F., Eng, M.: Preventing layer-3 wormhole attacks in ad hoc networks with multipath Dsr. Ecole De Technologie Superieure, 94 pages (2009)
3. Issa, K., Saurabh, B., Ness, B.S.: LiteWorp: Detection and Isolation of the Wormhole Attack in Static Multihop Wireless Networks. The International Journal of Computer and Telecommunications Networking 51, 3750–3772 (2007)
4. Azer, M., El-Kassas, S., El-Soudani, M.: A Full Image of the Wormhole Attacks Towards Introducing Complex Wormholes Attacks in Wireless Ad Hoc Networks. IJCSIS of Computer Science and Information Security 1(1), 41–51 (2009)
5. Chiu, H.S., Lui, K.S.: Delphi: wormhole detection mechanism for ad hoc wireless networks. In: 1st International Symposium on Wireless Pervasive Computing, pp. 6–11 (January 2006)
6. Khalil, I., Bagchi, S., Shroff, N.B.: Liteworp: Detection and isolation of the wormhole attack in static multihop wireless networks. Computer Networks 51(13), 3750–3772 (2007)
7. Khalil, I., Bagchi, S., Shroff, N.B.: Mobiworp: Mitigation of the wormhole attack in mobile multihop wireless networks. Securecomm and Workshops 2006, 1–12 (August 2006)
8. Hu, L., Evans, D.: Using directional antennas to prevent worm hole attacks. In: Proceedings of Network and Distributed System Security Symposium (2004)
9. Sun, C., Doo-yong, Do-hyeon, Jae-il: WAP: Wormhole Attack Prevention Algorithm in Mobile Ad Hoc Networks. In: IEEE International Conference on Sensor Networks, Ubiquitous, and Trustworthy Computing, pp. 343–348 (2008)

10. Garcia, L.F., Robert, J.-M.: Preventing Layer-3 Wormhole Attacks in Ad-hoc Networks with Multipath DSR. In: 8th IFIP Annual Mediterranean Ad hoc Networking Workshop (2009)
11. Perkins, C.E., Belding-Royer, E.M., Das, S.R.: Ad hoc on-demand distance vector (AODV) routing. RFC 3561, The Internet Engineering Task Force, Network Working Group (July 2003), http://www.ietf.org/rfc/rfc3561.txt
12. Johnson, D.B., Maltz, D.A.: Dynamic source routing in ad hoc wireless networks. In: Imielinski, Korth (eds.) Mobile Computing, vol. 353, pp. 153–181. Kluwer Academic Publishers (1996)
13. Song, N., Qian, L., Li, X.: Wormhole attacks detection in wireless ad hoc networks: A statistical analysis approach. In: Proc. of 19th IEEE International Parallel and Distributed Processing Symposium, pp. 8–15 (April 2005)

Research on Layer 2 Attacks of 802.11-Based WLAN

Ji Zhao[1,*], Jiantao Gu[2], and Jingang Liu[1]

[1] Modern Technology and Education Center, Hebei United University, 063009 Tangshan, China
[2] College of Sciences, Hebei United University, 063009 Tangshan, China

Abstract. The layer 2 attack is the most easy to implement, and also the least likely to be found in the security threat. It can paralyze the network, or through illegal access to sensitive information to endanger the security of internet users. Layer 2 Attack methods can be divided into four categories: MAC layer attacks, VLAN attacks, spoof attacks, and attacks on switch devices. This paper aims at research on layer 2 attacks of 802.11-based Wireless LAN. It has been in this paper that the overall frame of layer 2 attacks based on 802.11 wireless LAN, description of process and module, and the preparatory work which has been completed. Its aim is to achieve an intelligent WLAN security monitoring and management system by studying the layer 2 attack.

Keywords: Wireless LAN, layer 2 attack, overall frame. Attack tactics.

1 Introduction

No matter how secure you make the TCP/IP fortress, if a hacker can get into any of the layers, he can rule the system. If the attacker can puncture the stack at layer 2, he can control all the above traffic. The layer 2 attack is the most easy to implement, and also the least likely to be found in the security threat. It can paralyze the network, or through illegal access to sensitive information to endanger the security of internet users. Layer 2 Attack methods can be divided into four categories: MAC layer attacks, VLAN attacks, spoof attacks, and attacks on switch devices.

Some of the common layer 2 attacks are listed below.

(1) ARP-based attacks;
(2) MAC Duplicating;
(3) DHCP Starvation attack;
(4) DHCP Rogue attack;
(5) CAM Overflow/ MAC flooding;
(6) VLAN Hopping attack;
(7) Spanning Tree attack;
(8) Virtual Trunk Protocol attack;
(9) VMPS attack (VLAN Management Policy Server);
(10) 802.1Q and ISL Tagging attack;

[*] The research supported by Projects of Hebei Province Education Department (Z2010261).

C. Liu, J. Chang, and A. Yang (Eds.): ICICA 2011, Part I, CCIS 243, pp. 503–509, 2011.

(11) Double-Encapsulated 802.1Q/ Nested VLAN attack;
(12) Private VLAN attack;
(13) Multicast Brute Force attack;
(14) Random Frame Stress attack.

2 Overall Frame of Layer 2 Attacks Based on 802.11 Wireless LAN

2.1 Technical Problems to be Solved

The following is some technical problems to be solved.

(1)For a wireless network card works on the half-duplex principle, use two network cards as monitors and bidding device. How to coordinate the two network cards working in parallel efficiently is one of technical difficulties to be solved.

(2) Monitoring strategy:

To quickly detect illegal AP and STA;
Make different criteria for illegal AP according to actual application requirements;
Make appropriate feedback for AP and STA which has been attacked, so as to notify bidding device to stop the block attack, and then minimize resource costs to achieve maximum blocking effect.

(3) Attack tactics:

When will it start?
To construct what kind of wireless network packets (data frame format)?
How to send it (only send to the STA, or transmission between STA and AP)?
Sending rate?
Sending time?
When to stop (to stop receiving feedback, or stop the time-out timer)?

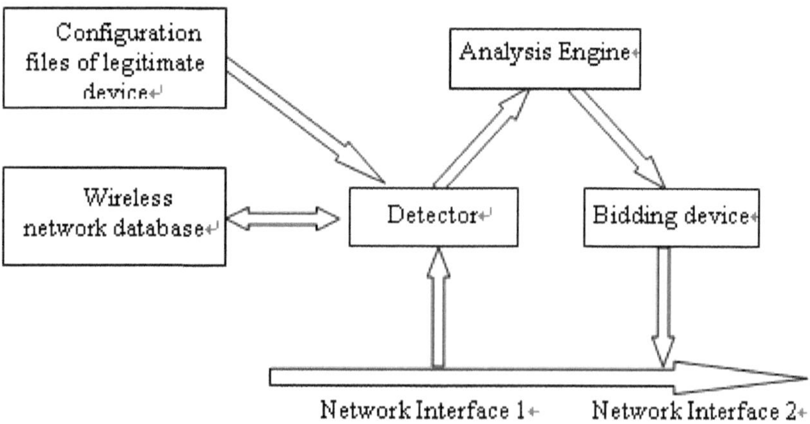

Fig. 1. Overall frame of layer 2 attacks based on 802.11 wireless LAN

2.2 Description of Process and Module

(1) In bypass listening mode, the monitor capture a variety of data packets on the coverage of the wireless network and audit, while the information about illegal websites are uploaded to analysis engine.
(2) According to website information uploaded by monitor, analysis engine assigns specific action command to bidding device through policy choices, to forcing illegal sites offline.
(3) The construction and sending action about special data packet are completed by bidding device.

2.3 Proposed Technology Solutions

(1) Strategic choice: Static security policy.

Illegal AP is defined as AP outside the network configuration file list. When the monitor captures a management frame, it quickly matches AP with a list of legitimate AP.

If match fails, then it is an illegal AP, its AP MAC address, SSID, MAC address of AP currently associated, and other information will be imported into the analysis engine, and then an order blocking the STA will be issued.

In scheduled time, if a packet containing the AP is not found, the STA will be thought to have been offline. You can cancel the attack thread.

(2)Synchronous model

Taking advantage of low resource consumption of multithread and fast switching between threads, we plan to use a multi-threaded Producer-Consumer model to coordinate and synchronize work of detector device and bidding device, act as producers monitor the role of contracting device to act as consumers.

The Monitor plays the role of producer, bidding device to act as consumers. Considering there may have more than one STA needed to block, we need a consumer management thread (analysis engine) to unify bidding device.

(3) Start or stop of bidding device

Monitor maintains a state list of all AP. Once the monitor finds an illegal AP, it judges its status information by looking for the list.

If it is judged need to be attacked, it will be sent to a public buffer. Analysis engine (consumer management thread) used to maintain a list of MAC addresses and a handle mapping table of bidding device, which each complete one selection for information from the public buffer.

If the type of information is judged to attack necessary, then a bidding device (the consumer) will start to attack with assigned type. If you need to stop the attack, then the current thread attack on the AP will be canceled. Making a timer in the attack, it will automatically end the thread if time approaches.

3 The Preparatory Work Which Has Been Completed

(1) 802.11 wireless network packet capture device has been fully realized, it's the base of detector.

(2) The test program of underlying bid has already passed. Packet injection has been realized.
(3) The producer-consumer model has been built.
(4) The experimental platform has been set up, which uses Cisco USB wireless card to achieve bidding and attack wireless card of desktop.
(5) STA block has been achieved by sending deauthentication data packets. Screenshot of effect function achieved are as follows:

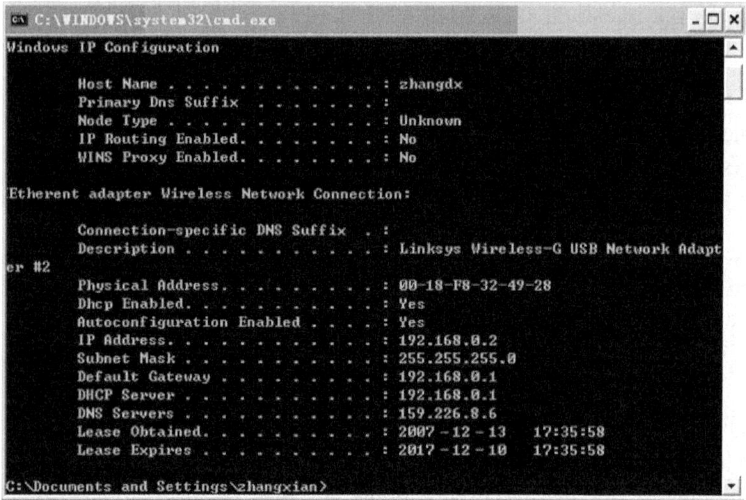

Fig. 2. The MAC information of attacked machine

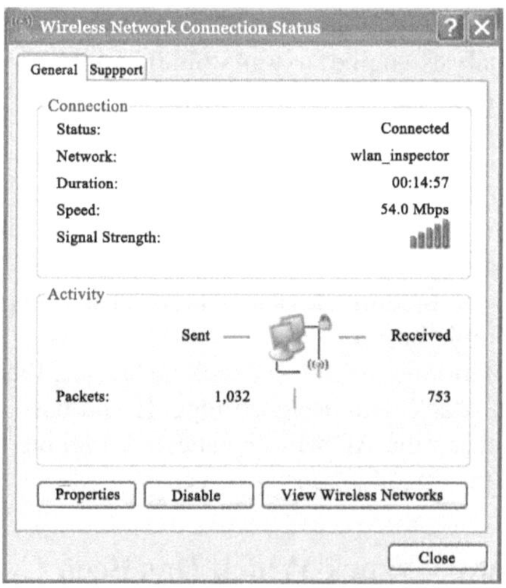

Fig. 3. The connection status of attacked machine

MAC address of wireless network card of the machine being attacked: 00:18:F8:32:49:28

Illegal MAC address of AP: 20:03:7f:e0:0d:09

Blocking mode: sent Deauthenticaion management frames.

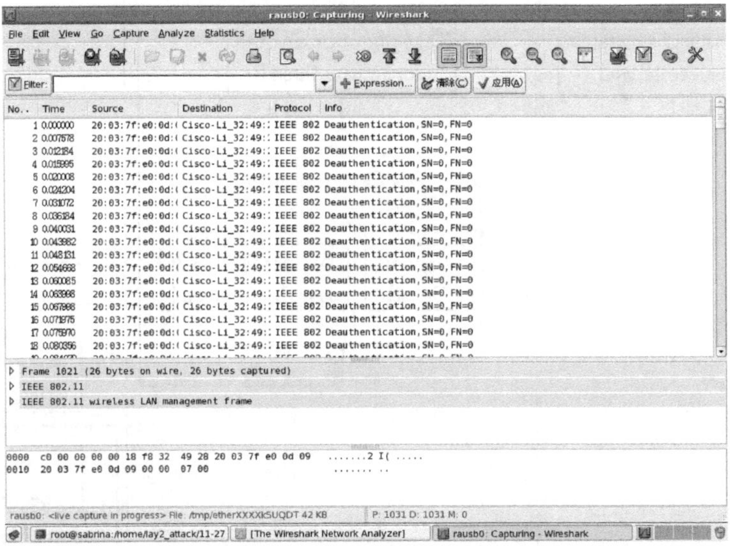

Fig. 4. Runs layer 2 block program in the client and capture packets using wireshark

After 5-10s the attacked machine is forced to disconnect the wireless connection. The figure 5 shows the flow chart of layer 2 attacked program.

4 The Next Step in the Work

During the experiment, it is found that to simply send a large number of Authentication management frames of fake AP can not achieve the effect of Dos attacks. Therefore we should consult related documents to understand the AP implementation mechanism and to designed block algorithms.

Weather or not the moment of forced offline for attack STA has law? Weather or not it has contact with the rate of sending Deauthentication packets? If you can find out these details, you can optimize the bidding device, to achieve blocking effect with a minimum cost of resources.

Therefore, you can design a test procedure to get the data we need. This test procedure continuously sends the ping command to test whether STA offline, and record the time interval.

Then further analysis on the basis of these data to identify which is the law.

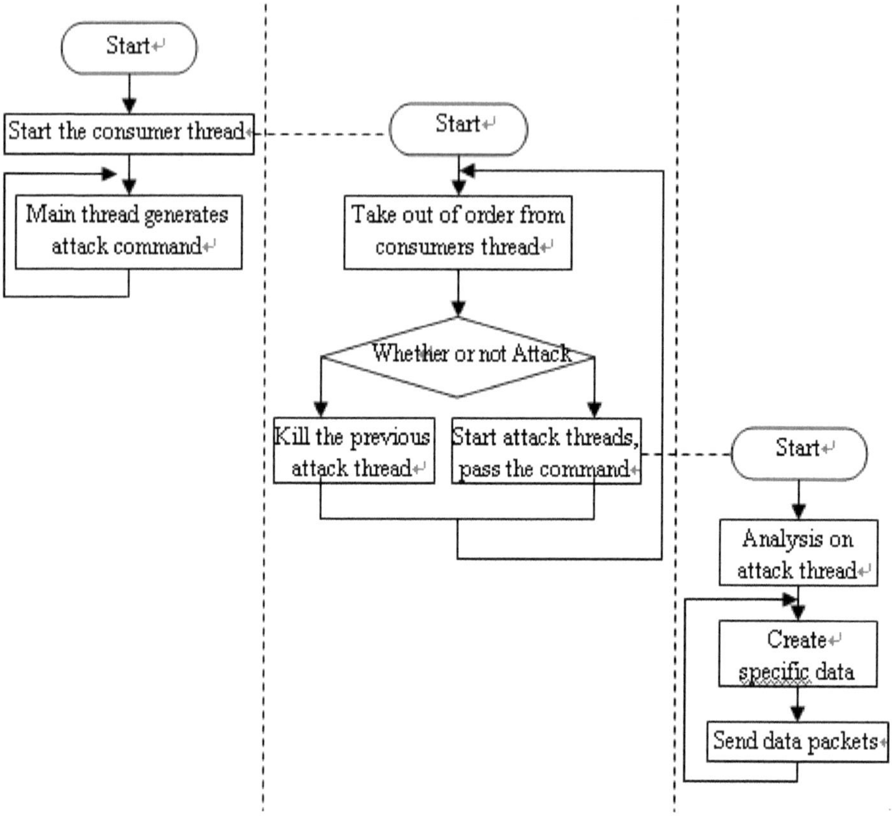

Fig. 5. The flow chart of layer 2 attacked program

References

1. Bhaiji, Y.: Network security technologies and solutions, 1st edn., March 30. Cisco Press (2008)
2. Garcia, L.F., Eng, M.: Preventing layer-3 wormhole attacks in ad hoc networks with multipath Dsr. Ecole De Technologie Superieure, 94 pages (2009)
3. Issa, K., Saurabh, B., Ness, B.S.: LiteWorp: Detection and Isolation of the Wormhole Attack in Static Multihop Wireless Networks. The International Journal of Computer and Telecommunications Networking 51, 3750–3772 (2007)
4. Azer, M., El-Kassas, S., El-Soudani, M.: A Full Image of the Wormhole Attacks Towards Introducing Complex Wormholes Attacks in Wireless Ad Hoc Networks. IJCSIS of Computer Science and Information Security 1(1), 41–51 (2009)
5. Chiu, H.S., Lui, K.S.: Delphi: wormhole detection mechanism for ad hoc wireless networks. In: 1st International Symposium on Wireless Pervasive Computing, pp. 6–11 (January 2006)
6. Khalil, I., Bagchi, S., Shroff, N.B.: Liteworp: Detection and isolation of the wormhole attack in static multihop wireless networks. Computer Networks 51(13), 3750–3772 (2007)

7. Khalil, I., Bagchi, S., Shroff, N.B.: Mobiworp: Mitigation of the wormhole attack in mobile multihop wireless networks. In: Securecomm. and Workshops 2006, pp. 1–12 (August 2006)
8. Hu, L., Evans, D.: Using directional antennas to prevent worm hole attacks. In: Proceedings of Network and Distributed System Security Symposium (2004)
9. Sun, C., Doo-yong, Do-hyeon, Jae-il: WAP: Wormhole Attack Prevention Algorithm in Mobile Ad Hoc Networks. In: IEEE International Conference on Sensor Networks, Ubiquitous, and Trustworthy Computing, pp. 343–348 (2008)
10. Garcia, L.F., Robert, J.-M.: Preventing Layer-3 Wormhole Attacks in Ad-hoc Networks with Multipath DSR. In:8th IFIP Annual Mediterranean Ad hoc Networking Workshop (2009)
11. Perkins, C.E., Belding-Royer, E.M., Das, S.R.: Ad hoc on-demand distance vector (AODV) routing. RFC 3561. The Internet Engineering Task Force, Network Working Group (July 2003), http://www.ietf.org/rfc/rfc3561.txt
12. Johnson, D.B., Maltz, D.A.: Dynamic source routing in ad hoc wireless networks. In: Imielinski, Korth (eds.) Mobile Computing, vol. 353, pp. 153–181. Kluwer Academic Publishers (1996)
13. Song, N., Qian, L., Li, X.: Wormhole attacks detection in wireless ad hoc networks: A statistical analysis approach. Proc. of 19th IEEE International Parallel and Distributed Processing Symposium, 8–15 (April 2005)

Stability Model on Website Competition and Cooperation of Establish and Analysis Evidence

Xu Huianxin[1], Jiang Wenchao[2], and Zhao Guoqi[1]

[1] Hebei Software Institute, Baoding, Hebei, China
[2] Yanshan University, Qinhuangdao, Hebei, China
superxhx@163.com

Abstract. In this paper, through the establishment of the stability model to discuss the competition and cooperation of portal and search engine. For cooperation model of portals and search engines, By using Lotka-Volterra Mutualism model to describe and establish; for competition model of portals and search engines, then it is established using a prey item - Predator model with Lotka-Volterra of Logistic. As the paper designed to competition model of portals and search engines, from the mathematical analysis the stability of the model, and prove the global stability of the model, then given a series of competitive strategy for portals and search engines.

Keywords: Search engine, portal website, Cooperation model, Competitive model.

1 Introduction

The dawning of the information age has been the rapid development of Internet, now already exists on a large number of Internet sites, no matter what type of site,it can be divided into two categories:portals and search engines, therefore, this paper is to discuss the portal and search engine of competition and cooperation.

Search engine is based on a certain strategy, the use of specific computer programs to gather information on the Internet, and after the organization of information processing, and processing the information is displayed to the user and is providing search services for users. In this article, search engine is a specialized site of providing search services[2].

Portal is a major producer and provider of Information on the Internet, its importance is beyond doubt, however, there is massive information on the Internet, search engines have become the tools of users search for information, is an indispensable tool on the Internet. "25th China Internet Development Survey Report" show, using search engines has reached 73.3%[3] for Internet users in 2009.So, it has important implications further understanding of the Internet,which is establishing the dynamic model of portals and search engines,qualitative and quantitative research between their cooperation and competition.

According to the literature [4] and [5] in the relevant statistical information, very few sites share with most users click-through ratea in the market,(web site users click-through rate is per unit time the number of users accessing the site),and most of

C. Liu, J. Chang, and A. Yang (Eds.): ICICA 2011, Part I, CCIS 243, pp. 510–517, 2011.

the site's click rate close to zero, the Internet exist winner-take-all phenomenon. As the click rate and advertising revenue of the site is closely related, web site click-through rate is too low which is difficult to survive in the Internet market. Therefore, for most sites, it is very important that how to survive in the highly competitive market, how to ensure your click rate is not to zero.

Contention system by the introduction of Maurerand Huberman [6]is describe to the n-dimensional Lotka-Volterra competitive model, the numerical calculations show that, when the fierce competition between sites, Internet will be "winner takes all" phenomenon. Lopezand Sanjuan[7]had used the same model with [6], research competing systems by composed of three sites, numerical calculations show that, two smaller sites of initial click rate overcome the higher site of initial click rate through mutual cooperation.So, [7] gives a series of strategies for small Web site against big Web site.

Wu Hong and Wang Yuanshi[8] had qualitative analysis for the model of the literature [7], theoretically proved the strategy of correctness and feasibility.

Above literature,they discussed model of competition and cooperation or discussed cooperation model of the portal and search engine,for competition model of the portal and search engine, there is little relevant research literature.

Here we will build portals and search engines cooperation and competition model, through theoretical analysis ,then discuss the global stability of the system.

As the mass number of sites on the Internet, in order to facilitate the processing, Only set upa competition and cooperation model of portal and search engine, This model is easily extended to multi-dimensional case. Goal is to create a model of stability, Used to describe competition and cooperation of the portal and search engine.

2 Cooperation Model of Portal and Search Engine

Lopez and Sanjuan established a competitive system of three sites to use Lotka-Volterra, the model as follows:

$$\begin{cases} x_1^{'} = x_1(b - bx_1 - a_{12}x_2 - a_{13}x_3) \\ x_2^{'} = x_2(b - bx_2 - a_{21}x_1 - a_{23}x_3) \\ x_3^{'} = x_3(b - bx_3 - a_{31}x_1 - a_{32}x_2) \end{cases} \tag{3.1}$$

The model's advantage is when each axis of equilibrium point are asymptotically stable, system (3.1) almost all solutions tend to the set of points by formed balance the axis. very few sites share with most users click-through ratea in the market, and most of the site's click rate close to zero.

However, there are shortcomings in the model: consider all aspects of the site is essentially equal, suitable for describing different types of competition between sites is questionable; in practice, cooperation may exist between the various sites, the model is not well reflect the partnership website.

So, we use Lotka-Volterra model of mutualism to establish the cooperation model of portals and search engines:

$$\begin{cases} x_1^{'} = x_1(b_1 - a_{11}x_1 + a_{12}x_2) \\ x_2^{'} = x_2(-b_2 + a_{21}x_1 - a_{22}x_2) \end{cases} \quad (3.2)$$

Where: $b_i, a_{ij} > 0, (i, j = 1,2)$; x_1 and x_2 indicates users click-through rate of the portal and search engine, $x_i^{'} = \dfrac{dx_i}{dt}$ indicates rate of change for x_i $(i = 1,2)$; b_1 and $-b_2$ indicates intrinsic growth rate of the portal and search engine; a_{11} and a_{22} indicates blocking effect coefficient of the portal and search engine; $a_{ij}(i, j = 1,2, i \neq j)$ indicates support site with j to i, reflect the number of hits where the site j brought for the site i.

The model show different points of the portals and search engines, that search engines can not exist independently, but the portal can, and portals and search engines that can achieve a win-win. However, the two sites may not be cooperation in practical, they exists the fierce competition in many cases.

3 Competition Model of Portal and Search Enginen

Fig. 1 shows changes of the two hits the site.Notes: site i to site i arrows indicate the density constraints $(i = 1,2)$, we can see from the assumption 3 that $M < N$.

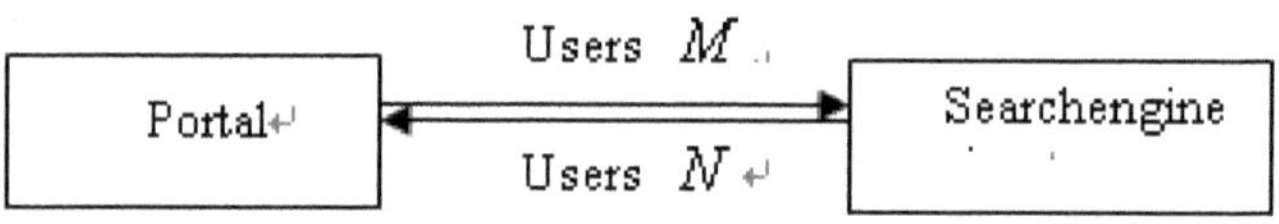

Fig. 1.

According to background analysis Fig. 1, we created the following model:

$$\begin{cases} x_1^{'}(t) = x_1(t)(b_1 - a_{11}x_1(t) - a_{12}x_2(t)) \\ x_2^{'}(t) = x_2(t)(-b_2 + a_{21}x_1(t) - a_{22}x_2(t)) \end{cases} \quad (3.3)$$

Where: $x_i(t)$ indicates the user hits of site i at time t, $x_i^{'}(t) = dx_i(t)/dt$ indicates rate of change of $x_i(t)$ $(i = 1,2)$. In order to facilitate, let $x_i = x_i(t)$, $i = 1,2$. Since x_1 and x_2 are positive, we discuss the range

$$\{(x_1, x_2) : x_1 > 0, x_2 > 0\}.$$

Parameter $b_1 (b_1 > 0)$ indicates the intrinsic growth rate when no other website impact, is its own content, update rate and other aspects of comprehensive measures, reflects the attractiveness of the site to users. If the portal provides a lot of interesting contents and can adapt to the needs of users, and update speed, then the site will have a relatively high intrinsic growth rate b_1 , $b_1 > 0$ because there is no other site, the portal can be viable.

Parameter $a_{11}(a_{11} > 0)$ indicates portal hits the blocking effect of their own growth factor. As the portal may click-through rate is limited, therefore, the higher the click rate of website, click on the lower rate of growth. In fact, b_1/a_{11} is a maximum rate of user clicks for the portal. In other words, if there is no impact on search engine, portal will increase in accordance with $\log istic$, portal will increase in accordance with $x_1^{'} = x_1(b_1 - a_{11}x_1)$.

Parameter $a_{12}(a_{12} > 0)$ indicates the competition rate of search engine on portal, is used to measure portals lost hits to the emergence of search engine. $a_{12}x_1x_2$ indicates that because of the emergence of search engines, the percentage of users in the unit of time to access the search engine instead of access the portal. The competition rate and search engine technology, internal algorithms have a great relationship, for example, in the search results display, search engine allows the content of the portal very front row, you can also row after, These two cases which search engine bring the portal hits is different. If the search engine portal site has a high rate of competition, that portal unfriendly, more users away from the portal. the higher the competition rate, the more users will become the portal search engine users. For parameter $a_{12} > 0$,we assume that $M < N$.

Parameter $-b_2(b_2 > 0)$ indicates the intrinsic growth rate when portal search engine hasn't. As the main and most search engine users from the portal, if the portals, search engines will not searchable content, or the contents of the user's requirements is not found in line , the user clicks will be negative growth rate.

Parameter $a_{21}(a_{21} > 0)$ indicates the ratings of portal for search engine, Used to measure the number of users of the search engine from the portal, the support rat indicates the associate degree for portals and search engines. If the portal search engine has a high support rate,it is said that portal users prefer to use search engines to search relevant information. In addition, a_{21} have a great relationship with the quality of search engine, if users find the search engine's speed is quickly , then the user will be more willing to use it. In short, the more the support rate, more users become the portal search engine users.

Parameter $a_{22}(a_{22} > 0)$ indicates search engine hits the blocking effect of their own growth factor. As the search engine may click-through rate is limited, therefore, the higher the click rate of website, click on the lower rate of growth.

We have established a competition model of portal and search engine , the following qualitative analysis the the model.

4 The Model of Stability Analysis

We will analyze the singularity toof of the global stability by a global phase diagram of the system.

Let isocline: $l_1 : b_1 - a_{11}x_1 - a_{12}x_2 = 0 \quad l_2 : -b_2 + a_{21}x_1 - a_{22}x_2 = 0$

the slope of l_1, l_2 respectively: $k_1 = -a_{11}/a_{12}$, $k_2 = a_{21}/a_{22}$ .Intersection of l_1, l_2 and x_1 - axis are: $(b_1/a_{11}, 0)$ and $(b_2/a_{21}, 0)$. Intersection of l_1, l_2 and x_2 -axis are: $(0, b_1/a_{12})$ and $(0, -b_2/a_{22})$,as Fig. 2.

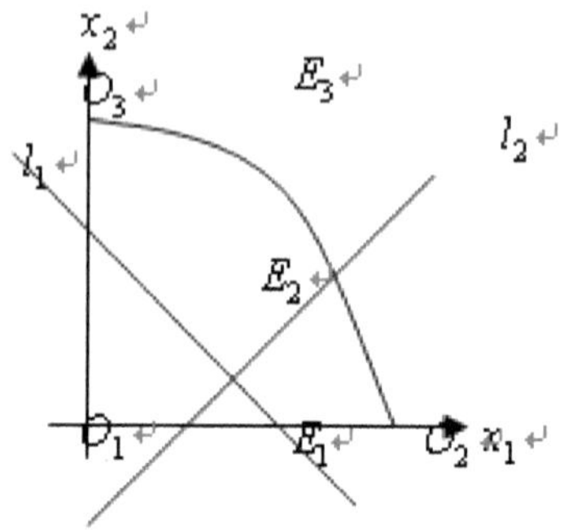

Fig. 2.

We are based on the relative position of a and b, we discuss the six cases,

①$b_2a_{11} > b_1a_{21}, a_{22} > a_{12}$ ②$b_2a_{11} > b_1a_{21}, a_{22} \le a_{12}$
③$b_2a_{11} = b_1a_{21}, a_{22} > a_{12}$ ④$b_2a_{11} = b_1a_{21}, a_{22} \le a_{12}$
⑤$b_2a_{11} < b_1a_{21}, a_{22} > a_{12}$ ⑥$b_2a_{11} < b_1a_{21}, a_{22} \le a_{12}$

Here we discuss the six cases in detail:

Case ① : when $b_2a_{11} > b_1a_{21}, a_{22} > a_{12}$, l_1 and l_2 do not intersect in $\operatorname{int} R_+^2$, $\operatorname{int} R_+^2$ is divided into three regions with l_1 and l_2 ,that is I , II and III .In I , $x_1' < 0$, $x_2' > 0$;in II , $x_1' < 0$, $x_2' < 0$;in III , $x_1' > 0$, $x_2' < 0$. These directions are given relative to rail line. $a_{22} > a_{12}$, then $(a_{11} + a_{21})/(a_{22} - a_{12})$ $> a_{21}/a_{22}$,that is E_3 top of the l_2 .In addition, we know from Theorem 3.2 and 3.3, at this point O_1 and E_3 is a saddle point, O_2 and O_3 is the unstable node, E_1 is asymptotically stable node. Here we show that E_1 is a globally stable on the $\operatorname{int} R_+^2$.

According to the trend of rail line, the trajectory left movement as t increases from the region I , must enter the area II . The rail line departure from the regional II , movement to the lower left, or tend to E_1, or enter the area III . However, it is impossible to enter the area I , If a rail line enter into I the at a time t_1 by a straight line l_2 , then $x_2'(t_1) = 0$,and $x_1'(t_1) < 0$. From the equation (3.1) can be calculated $x_2''(t_1) = a_{21}x_1'(t_1)x_2(t_1) < 0$, indicates $x_2(t)$ achieve maximum, This is impossible, because the value of $x_2(t)$ has been decrease in II . The rail line departure from the regional III , movement to the lower right, but it can not enter the area II .

This is because if the rail line enter into II at some point by line l_1 ,then $x_1^{'}(t_2)=0$,and $x_2^{'}(t_2)<0$,but $x_1^{''}(t_2)=-a_{12}x_1(t_2)x_2^{'}(t_2)>0$, $x_1(t)$ obtain minimum in t_2 .But in III , $x_1(t)$ must be increase, this is a contradiction. Therefore, rail line will eventually tend to E_1 from the region III .

Case ② :when $b_2a_{11}>b_1a_{21}, a_{22}\le a_{12}$, l_1 and l_2 do not intersect in $\text{int}\,R_+^2$, $\text{int}\,R_+^2$ is divided into three regions with l_1 and l_2 ,that is I , II and III .In $\text{int}\,R_+^2$, $x_1^{'}<0$, $x_2^{'}>0$;in II , $x_1^{'}<0$, $x_2^{'}<0$;in III , $x_1^{'}>0, x_2^{'}<0$. These directions are given relative to rail line. In addition, we know from Theorem 3.2 and 3.3, E_3 is not in $\text{int}\,R_+^2$ or does not exist O_1 is a saddle point, O_2 is the unstable node, O_3 is a saddle point , E_1 is asymptotically stable node. And analysis of the situation is same as case 1 ,here we show that E_1 is a globally stable on the $\text{int}\,R_+^2$, global phase diagram shown in Fig. 4.

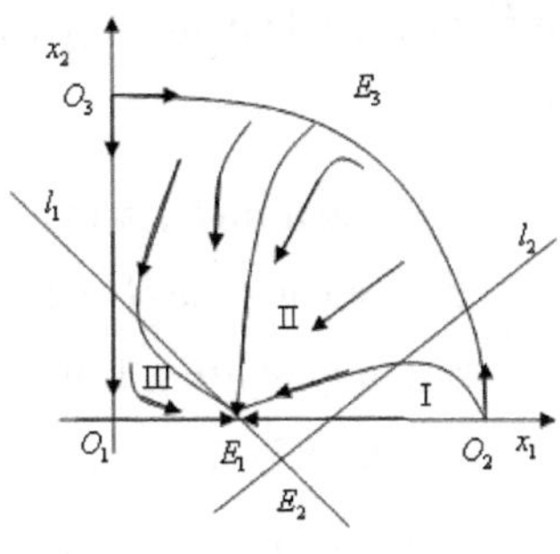

Fig. 3.

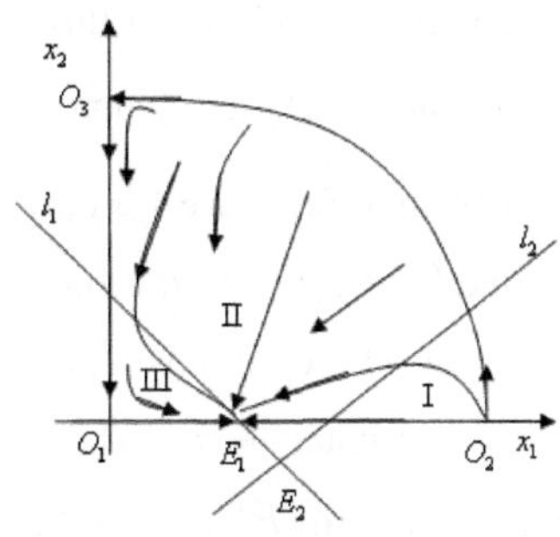

Fig. 4.

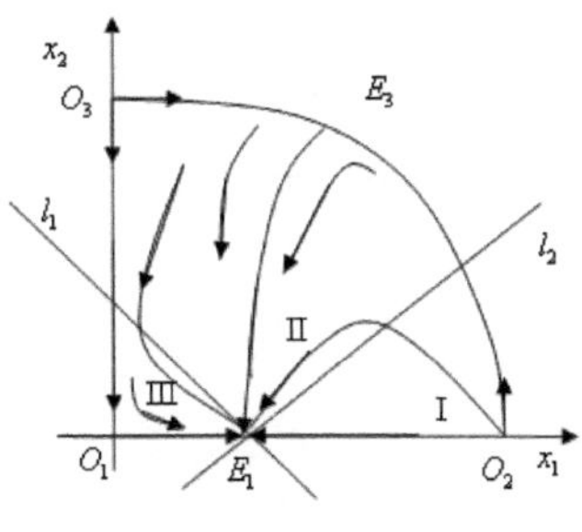

Fig. 5.

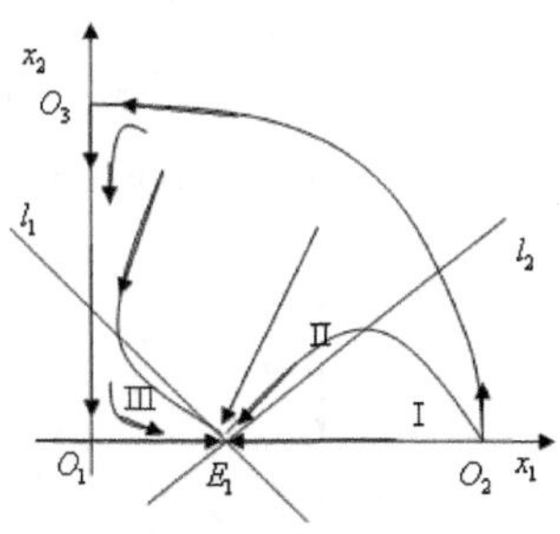

Fig. 6.

Case ③ : when $b_2a_{11}=b_1a_{21}$, $a_{22}>a_{12}$, l_1 and l_2 intersect in E_1 , E_1 and E_2 coincide. Theorem 3.2, E_1 is a saddle point,they are locally asymptotically stable node in $\text{int}\,R_+^2$, other singular point is consistent with case 1, trajectory's trendence is also consistent with case 1, E_1 is a globally stable on the $\operatorname{int} R_+^2$, global phase diagram shown in Fig. 5.

Case ④ : when $b_2 a_{11} = b_1 a_{21}$, $a_{22} \le a_{12}$, l_1 and l_2 intersect in E_1 , E_1 and E_2 coincide. Theorem 3.2, E_1 is a saddle point,they are locally asymptotically stable node in $\operatorname{int} R_+^2$, other singular point is consistent with case 2, trajectory's trendence is also consistent with case 2, E_1 is a globally stable on the $\operatorname{int} R_+^2$, global phase diagram shown in Fig. 6.

Case ⑤ : when $b_2 a_{11} < b_1 a_{21}$, $a_{22} > a_{12}$, l_1 and l_2 intersect in E_2 on $\operatorname{int} R_+^2$, $\operatorname{int} R_+^2$ is divided into four regions with l_1 and l_2 ,that is , II , III and IV .In I , $x_1' > 0$, $x_2' > 0$;in II , $x_1' < 0$, $x_2' > 0$;in III , $x_1' < 0$, $x_2' < 0$,in IV , $x_1' > 0, x_2' < 0$. These directions are given relative to rail line. $a_{22} > a_{12}$,then $(a_{11} + a_{21})/(a_{22} - a_{12}) > a_{21}/a_{22}$,that is E_3 top of the l_2 .In addition, we know from Theorem 3.2 and 3.3, at this point O_1 , E_1 and E_3 is a saddle point, O_2 and O_3 is the unstable node, E_2 is asymptotically stable node.

The analysis similarcase 1 is easy to show, trajectory starting from I , or trends E_2 , or enter the II ; trajectory starting from II , or trends E_2 , or enter the III ; trajectory starting from III , or trends E_2 , or enter the IV ; trajectory starting from IV , or trends E_2 , or enter the I . Then by Theorem 3.1, system (3.3) there is no closed trajectory in the $\operatorname{int} R_+^2$,all rail line will tend to E_2 from the region $\operatorname{int} R_+^2$, E_2 is globally stable in $\operatorname{int} R_+^2$, global phase diagram shown in Fig. 7.

Case ⑥ : $b_2 a_{11} < b_1 a_{21}$, $a_{22} \le a_{12}$,And the analysis is same as case 5 ,then E_3 not in $\operatorname{int} R_+^2$, O_3 is a saddle point. Global phase diagram shown in Fig. 8.

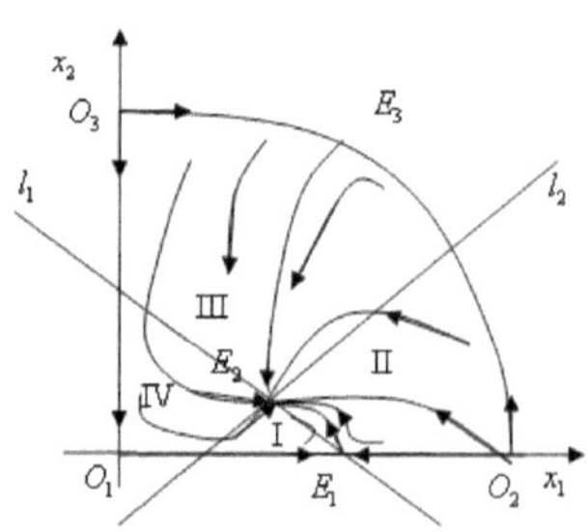

Fig. 7.

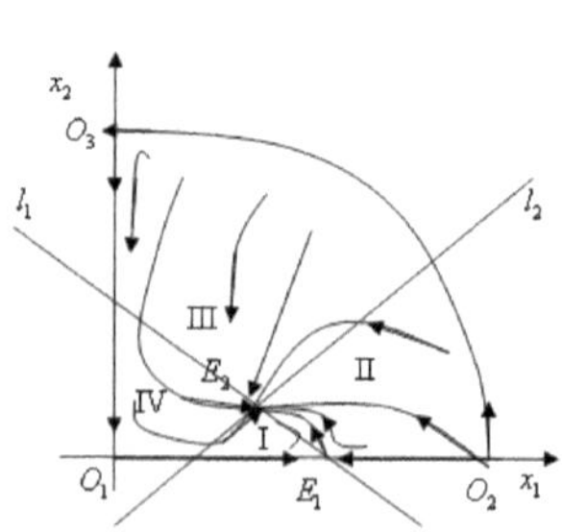

Fig. 8.

In summary, we have the following important conclusions:

when $b_2 a_{11} \geq b_1 a_{21}$, E_1 is globally stable in $\operatorname{int} R_+^2$, the search engine will die;

when $b_2 a_{11} < b_1 a_{21}$, E_2 is globally stable in $\operatorname{int} R_+^2$, that portals and search engines will coexist, the ratio of their market share are determined by the parameters of system (3.3).

5 Conclusion

Through the above analysis can be obtained:

Prey - predator model can describe competition of the portal and search engine, In this type of competitive systems, search engines rely on the portal, more like a predator; portal is the main provider, like a predator.

In a variety of parameters, the system always has a globally stable equilibrium point, the initial click-through rate is not important in this type of system. We believe that a strong web site should be the site of strong environmental adaptability, not just those sites with high click-through rate. Of course, with a high click-through rate ,it may be greater benefits in return, so that better fit their strong competitive environment.

References

1 http://baike.baidu.com/view/9803.htm
2 http://baike.baidu.com/view/1154.htm
3 http://research.cnnic.cn/html/1263531336d1752.html
4 Adamic, L.A., Huberman, B.A.: Power-law distribution of the world wide web. Science 287(8), 2115 (2000)
5 Adamic, L.A., Huberman, B.A.: The nature of markets on the world wide web. Q.J.Electron.Commerce 34(1), 5–12 (2000)
6 Maurer, S.M., Huberman, B.A.: Competitive dynamics of web sites. Journal of Economic Dynamics & Control 27, 2195–2206 (2003)
7 Lopez, L., Sanjuan, M.A.F.: Defining strategies to win in the Internet market. Physica A 301, 512–534 (2001)
8 Wu, H., Wang, S.: Site competition model of qualitative analysis. Control Theory and Applications 22(2), 218–228 (2005)
9 Zhang, Z.: Qualitative theory of differential equations. Science Press (1985)
10 Wang, G.: Ordinary Differential Equations, 2nd edn. Higher Education Press (1983)
11 Jiang, Q.: Mathematical model, 2nd edn. Higher Education Press (1992)
12 Ma, Z., Zhou, Y.: Qualitative and stability methods of ordinary differential equations. Science Press (2001)
13 Li, X.: Gray estimation method of research for Logistic and Lotka-Volterra model parameter. College Mathematics 20(6), 82–87 (2004)

On the Improvement of Motive Mechanism to Enhance the College-Enterprise Corporation on Vocational Education

Guoqing Huang, Tonghua Yang, and Sheng Xu

Jiangxi Agricultural University, Occupation technical College, Nanchang, China
Hgq99@126.com

Abstract. Aim at currently an our country occupation education college and enterprise cooperation to be placed in the realistic problem that the shallow layer cooperate, this paper begins with a profound analysis upon the factors that motivate vocational and professional institutions to cooperate with enterprises, while followed with a conclusion that this cooperation is not adequately motivated. Accordingly, the writers suggest a government ensuring mechanism, a win-win cooperation mechanism, a mutual engagement mechanism, an evaluation and incentive mechanism and a cultural penetration mechanism. Those are argued to be valid motive mechanisms to push forward the college-enterprise cooperation on vocational education.

Keywords: vocational education, college-enterprise cooperation, motive mechanism.

Motive mechanisms are believed to be the valid forces to drive the cooperation between the enterprises and vocational and professional institutions. Therefore a successful cooperation can only be made when enterprises and institutions are both fully motivated, and they are both rewarded. That is, they are mutually benefited. This is a key that pushes their cooperation to go further and deeper.

1 A Profound Analysis Upon the Factors that Motivate Vocational and Professional Institutions to Cooperate with Enterprises

1.1 The Driving Forces Behind the Institutional Participation into the College-Enterprise Cooperation

1.1.1 To Improve Graduates' Employment Rate and Quality

Recently, with the expanded population of college students and the transformation of social values and beliefs, graduates' employment rate has been publically viewed as an

C. Liu, J. Chang, and A. Yang (Eds.): ICICA 2011, Part I, CCIS 243, pp. 518–523, 2011.

important criterion to evaluate the schooling quality of a college or university. Under this growing pressure of employment, a higher employment rate and quality has become the first driving force behind the institutional participation into the college-enterprise cooperation.

1.1.2 To Optimize Talents Training Model and Improve Education Quality

Under the background of college-enterprise cooperation, an advisory committee of professionals and scholars can be set up, and enterprises should be allowed access to academic development and to talents training objectives, regulations and approaches. In that case, enterprises and institutions join hands to train talents and improve training quality.

1.1.3 To Solve the Problem of Capital Inadequacy in School Running and Schooling Conditions

Because of capital shortage, lack of school buildings, limitations of campus and inadequacy of training equipments are severe. Those problems can never be solved by institutions alone or government alone. Thus, training and practice are suggested to be set up in enterprises, professionals from enterprises can help lessen the severe lack of teachers. After then, students' hand-on proficiency can be improved, graduates' employment can be enhanced. Hence, a stronger institutional force to cooperate with enterprises.

1.2 The Motives Behind Corporation Participation into the College-Enterprise Cooperation

1.2.1 To Meet Requirements of Market Competition and Corporation Development

In the market economy, corporation survival and development depends on its own key competitive strength, which then depends on the initiation and creation of talent. Enterprises then look to institutions for new talent in order to improve their own personnel.

1.2.2 To Improve Its Research Capacity and Provide Enterprises with Advanced Technologies

Vocational and professional institutions are better equipped with research capacity. Some of its teachers can be professional experts. They are able to apply governmental research project and study some problems with corporation production and management and to make technical and managerial breakthroughs. Thus, enterprises can take advantage of those advanced technologies and be more competitive in the market.

1.2.3 To Create a Better Social Image

Corporation cooperation with institutions — participation of academic development, curriculum development, training management and professional practice — is a public activity. Meanwhile, the setup of scholarships, bursaries and assistance-ships, all named after the relative enterprise, is an effective advertisement in the society. It can improve the corporation image in the public.

2 Analysis Upon Inadequate Motivation for the College-Enterprise Cooperation

2.1 Inadequate Governmental Investment and Lack of Effective Operational Regulations

In recent years, though the government has been attached great importance to vocational and professional education and invested more to it, the educational investment is still far from enough. Even when the government place great value on the college-enterprise cooperation, the related effective operational regulations are still in lack. Besides, the incentive mechanism to further this cooperation has not been installed, which fails to motivate either institutions or enterprises.

2.2 Flawed Realization of a Win-Win Principle for this Cooperation

Mutual benefit, realization's totally winning is the inside core motive that the college cooperates with business enterprise.Because of the flawed principles that regulate the assignment of profits between the enterprises and institutions, profits can be improperly or controversially assigned. That, obviously, can impede corporation or institutional participation.

2.3 Inadequate School Running Capacity with the Institutions

In most institutions, the teaching personnel can be not qualified enough, not creative enough and in lack of research capacity. The institutions can also be lack of school running capital or competent management conditions. Those make it hard to compensate enterprises. The institutions, therefore, fail to help enterprises to settle their problems, and then fail to motivate the corporation cooperation.

2.4 Corporation Short Effect

At present, institutions and enterprises are not fully aware of the cooperation. The enterprise has not fully realized that the institutions can help them solve their key problems. The present performance standards also hinder the cooperation between these two parties. The enterprise still shoulders great risks in technology development.

Because the student of occupation college is just some talented persons of apprentice types, most occupations abilities which practice a student also can't create more benefitses for business enterprise and the business enterprise doesn't have the actual benefitses which get to immediately show sex and also obstructed a business enterprise to participate the motive that the college cooperates with business enterprise to some extent.

3 Effective College-Enterprise Cooperation Mechanism

3.1 A Government Ensuring Mechanism

As the leading role, government is supposed to maximize the efficiency of cooperation through regulating policy and economic lever. First of all, government should bring its macroeconomic regulating function into full play, coordinating with college and enterprise, improvement relevant laws so as to restrict the behaviors of both sides, and encouraging enterprises engaged in vocational education. Educate supervisor's section wants the result which cooperates with business enterprise college as to investigate college to do index sign of learn level or valuation education special features, actively promote national certificate system of the occupation qualifications, strongly open an exhibition to train before the Gang, aggressive implement the labor force be quasi- into the system.Secondly, taking funds as the lever, government could make favorable policies to college-enterprise cooperation, such as subsidies, tax remission and easy access to loans.

3.2 A Win-Win Cooperation Mechanism

The institutions need to improve their own teaching quality and research capacity to emphasize their advantages. They also need to help solve corporation problems like technical problems and management problems, help them to develop new products and advance new technologies and equipments. During this cooperation, an effective cooperation mechanism needs to be set up in order to joins hand to study problems and to develop projects. On the other hand, the enterprise can help the institution to improve their faculty quality.

3.3 A Mutual Engagement Mechanism

The devotion that college and business enterprise cooperate includes a government, business enterprise, college three squares' common devotions.The government needs to invest more to enhance the college-enterprise cooperation. The government must be the driver of it, and the mediator in it as well as the bridge between these two. The most important problem in this cooperation is capital. A greater investment can lessen pressure on these two parties. Thus, this cooperation can be enhanced through (1) set-up of joint enterprises, (2) corporation investment into education, (3) corporation investment into campus building, (4) opening institutional practice garden to the enterprises, and (5) building out-of-campus training gardens.

3.4 An Evaluation and Incentive Mechanism

Nation and profession supervisor section in response to enlargement evaluation the reform of mechanism, go deep into thin chemistry hospital and business enterprise to cooperate the procedure, evaluation of the evaluation implement standard, raise college and business enterprise to cooperate science and operability of evaluate the mechanism, encourage business enterprise and occupation college to cooperate.

Some contracts can be singed to ensure the effective cooperation between these two parties. And then the relative responsibilities and rights can be clear. The college-enterprise cooperation thus can be enhanced.

3.5 A Cultural Penetration Mechanism

Enterprises are the best places to practice students' knowledge and technologies. With learning new knowledge, students can go to hand-on practice, and get access to management and services. Their humanity, teamwork, quality awareness and service attitude can thus be improved. On the other hand, students, as would-be workers or even professionals, are energetic and ambitious. Their entrance into enterprises can be a flow of new impetus, and then enhance the college-enterprise cooperation.

4 Conclusion

Aim at currently an our country occupation education college and enterprise cooperation to be placed in the realistic problem that the shallow layer cooperate, this paper begins with a profound analysis upon the factors that motivate vocational and professional institutions to cooperate with enterprises, while followed with a conclusion that this cooperation is not adequately motivated. Accordingly, the writers suggest a government ensuring mechanism, a win-win cooperation mechanism, a mutual engagement mechanism, an evaluation and incentive mechanism and a cultural penetration mechanism. Those are argued to be valid motive mechanisms to push forward the college-enterprise cooperation on vocational education.

References

1. Wei, W.: Create an orientation business enterprise a demand of occupation education mode. Occupation Technique Education (18), 43 (2002)
2. Huang, G.: The qality and quality guarantee of higher vocational education under popularization background. Journal Of Hebei Energy Institute Vocation and Technology (6), 24 (2009)

3. Kuang, P.: Occupation education produce, study, science research cooperation long the study of effect mechanism. Occupation Technique Education 17 (2006)
4. Huang, G.: Inquiry Into of Higher Vocational Education College and Enterprise Motive Mechanism of Diversified Cooperation. Education Research Monthly (10), 97 (2010)
5. Wu, W.: Benefits and obstacle that college and business enterprise cooperate are analytical. The College Journal of the University of Hunan 5 (2004)
6. Dixon, G., Westbrook, J.: Followers revealed. Engineering Management Journal 15, 19–25 (2003)
7. Collinson, D.: Rethinking followership: A post-structuralist analysis of follower identities. Leadership Quarterly 17(2), 179–189 (2006)
8. Kellerman, B.: Followership: How Followers are Creating Change and Changing Leaders. Harvard Business Press, Boston (2008)
9. Ehrhart, M.G., Klein, K.J.: Predicting followers preferences for charismatic leadership: The influence of follower values and personality. The Leadership Quarterly 12, 153–179 (2001)
10. Padilla, A., Hogan, R., Kaiser, R.B.: The toxic triangle: Destructive leaders, susceptible followers, and conducive environment. The Leadership Quarterly 18, 176–194 (2007)
11. Useem, M.: Leading Up: How to Lead Your Boss So You Both Win. Georgia, Crown Business (2001)
12. Huang, X., Wu, J., Zhang, S.: Architecture of Distance Learning Management System. Computer Engineering and Applications. J. Mol. Med. (12) (2003)
13. Gu, J.: Efficient Local Search for Very Large-scale Satisfiability Problems. Sigart Bulletin 3(1), 8–12 (1992)
14. Li, Y.-J., Lu, C.-W.: The Use of Ant Colony Genetic Algorithm in Intelligent scheduling course of Colleges and Universities. Modern Electronic Technology. J. Mol. Med. (14) (2010)
15. Sun, X.-B., Xu, T.-Z., Li, W.: Study on Scheduling Course System Based on GIS on Campus. Computer and Digital Engineering. J. Mol. Med. (3) (2009)
16. Chen, X.-F.: Class Arrangement Algorithm Constraint Conditions and their Realization in Teaching Management System. Journal of Dongguan University of Technolegy. J. Mol. Med. 16(1) (2009)
17. Li, F.-L.: Design and Realization of Intelligent Scheduling Course System for Middle Vocation Schools. Beijing University of Technology. J. Mol. Med. (3) (2009)
18. Wang, L., Wen, W.-S.: Study and Realization of Scheduling Course System Based on Aglet platform. Computer Engineering and Science. J. Mol. Med. (9) (2009)
19. Xie, J.J., Liu, C.P.: Fuzzy mathematics methods and its application. Mol. Huazhong University of Science and Technology (2000)

Reform of Biochemistry Teaching for Municipal Engineering Graduate Based on the Theory of Brain Science

Changhong Jia[1], Lixin Chang[1], Weijie Wang[1], Yuxin Pan[1], and Liyan Feng[2,*]

[1] College of Life Science, Hebei United University, Tangshan, Hebei, China 063009
[2] College of Foreign Languages, Hebei Union University, Tangshan, Hebei, China 063009
jiachanghong66@163.com, fengliyan2002@yahoo.com.cn

Abstract. Based on the theories of brain science, the teaching methods of municipal engineering graduate biochemistry were reformed. The main methods were as follows: the teaching material was reconstructed, three-dimensional objective and implementation plan were established, and these teaching methods were researched: fantasy association method;teaching method of combining infiltration with steps; study case teaching method; combining "miniature practice" with classroom teaching.

Keywords: brain science, municipal engineering graduate, biochemistry.

1 Introduction

Nowadays, based on the development of scientific research and education, China's postgraduate education succeeded in improving students' comprehensive ability through teaching, researching, practicing and thesis writing. Students develop a scientific way of thinking and make a solid foundation of professional knowledge as well.

Municipal engineering takes water supply and drainage works as the research object, developing the study around the projects and systems of the water collection, treatment, transportation. Biochemistry, as the professional degree courses, not only lays the foundation for the principle of biological treatment of water, microbiology and other courses, but also provides new ideas and methods for the professional scientific research, such as wastewater treatment theory and technology.

However, the biochemistry teaching for municipal engineering is facing specific difficulties. First, the teaching content is miscellaneous. There is a large number of biochemical knowledge to remember. Second, the suitable teaching materials are rare. With the bio-technology engineering's booming, a number of suitable materials for different biochemical engineering profession also appeared, but no biochemical materials for graduate students of municipal engineering is found. Third, the teaching

* Corresponding author. Teaching reform project of Hebei Union University: (K0902,Y0915-04).

C. Liu, J. Chang, and A. Yang (Eds.): ICICA 2011, Part I, CCIS 243, pp. 524–531, 2011.

hours for biochemistry are limited. There are only 40 hours for municipal engineering graduate students' biochemistry, the students are lack of specific knowledge and experimenting opportunities.

For these problems, we made some attempt to impart the boring, tedious biochemical knowledge to students in a vivid way based on brain science theory, developing students' ability to analyze and solve problems, helping them forming an active and critical thinking.

2 A Theory Based on Brain Science [1,2,3]

In recent years, brain research has developed quickly, many innovations appear, such as X-ray photography based on the calculation level, computer axial tomography (CAT) brain imaging technologies, positron emission tomography (PET), and the capture of the rapidly changing neurons of EEG (EEG), etc. All these contribute to the rapid development of brain research, and make it the forefront of scientific research, one of the most active subjects. Many countries have involved brain research in national key research programs, such as the "brain decade" program in America", the European Community's "EC brain decade in Europe", Japan's "Brain Science Times", etc. Gratifying achievements have also been made in the field of brain science in China. Professor Shu Siyun in the First Military Medical University found a new area deep in the brain, closely related to learning and memory. This new "Marginal zone" is referred to as "Shu's area" by the international authority.

The results of brain research reveal the basic understanding of some difficult diseases and the treatment basis; on the other hand the results provide a guideline for the reform of teaching methods. The following will analyze briefly the content of brain science that relates closely to teaching and learning.

2.1 The Two Hemispheres of the Brain

The human's brain is divided into two "functional asymmetry": the left and right hemispheres connected by the corpus. Left hemisphere, regarded as the "academic hemisphere", is mainly responsible for language, logic, mathematics, and order functions; right hemisphere, regarded as "creative hemisphere", deals with rhythm, music, images and fantasies, intuitive and divergent thinking. Function of the left hemisphere is mainly used in traditional teaching, but insufficient attention is paid to right brain function.

2.2 Trinity

From another perspective, the brain can also be divided into: brain stem; cerebellum; the limbic system and cerebral cortex. The new research results show that the cerebellum plays an important role in the cognitive domain (such as planning and imagination activities). Above the brain stem is the limbic system, at the bottom of the limbic system, there are two groups of neuronal cells shaped like almond, named the amygdala, it is solely on the emotional affairs, if the brain is an early warning system, then the amygdala is the brain's mental guard. Owing to the amygdala, you can make "rational memory and reaction", that is to say, the process of "information → thalamus →new cortex → reaction" is formed. "Short circuit" is: the information → thalamus → direct response to the amygdale, thus form the "emotional memory and reaction". Things with the emotional significance most likely cause this kind of reaction, and resulting in a strong memory.

There are seven different intelligence in the cortex, that is ① language intelligence; ② logical-mathematical intelligence; ③ visual spatial intelligence; ④ bodily kinesthetic Intelligence; ⑤ Music Intelligence; ⑥ interpersonal intelligence; ⑦ penetrating into other people's inner intelligence. How to develop these seven intelligence should be our main issues to consider in teaching.

Based on the theory of brain science, we strive to fully inspire the function of right brain and limbic system in teaching and pay more attention to cooperation of the seven intelligence centers.

3 The Ideas and Methods of the Teaching Reform

3.1 The Construction of Teaching Materials[4,5,6]

The construction of teaching materials is the basic work of graduate education and the basic guarantee for achieving teaching aims. While, because graduate teaching materials are profound, lack of reader and not profitable, it is difficult to see "Biochemistry" text book for municipal engineering graduate on the market today, let alone the suitable one. In our teaching reform, modeling on Biochemistry (the national textbook for The Eleventh Five -Year Plan), we prepared and built materials in the attitude of innovative thinking, and strived to enhance the effectiveness of teaching.

3.1.1 Adding Basic Knowledge of Biology to Help Students' Understanding

Based on municipal engineering graduate students' lack of general biological knowledge, our teaching materials enrich the basic biological knowledge. For example, we involved the basic content of cytology in the first chapter in order to make students understand the relationship between biochemistry and organisms; involved the concept, types and characteristics of the metabolism in Chapter VIII, to develop the complex dynamic biochemical metabolic pathways understand. In this way, learning content can be arranged progressively, the transfer of knowledge is more easy to be achieved , thus students can enter the learning process with pleasure

3.1.2 Constructing a Flexible Form of Knowledge

According to the cognitive laws provided by brain research, we pay attention to modulating the structure of teaching materials and the teaching method. We try to develop a complete thought, organize a large number of cumbersome into a complete knowledge system. The main approach is: In the introduction to each chapter a question is brought up, pointing to the main content of this chapter; in front of each chapter and each section, through the Knowledge Network form the main link between the knowledge points; after each chapter there are some questions to help students sum up the main issues in this chapter. In addition, some biological phenomena, examples have been inserted to explain the relevant knowledge.

3.1.3 Focusing on the Combination with Practice, Improving Learning Motivation

In the textbook, we focus on basic knowledge and at the same time integrate traditional experimental methods and new experimental methods, to form the basis for scientific research; we also focus on the combination with other municipal engineering graduate courses. In addition, the emphasis is laid on basic knowledge and practical application. For instance, more specialized applications for the microbial and biochemical characteristics of static and dynamic have been highlighted and some of the problems associated with research have been involved into teaching materials, for example, the biological treatment of wastewater is written in the dynamic biochemical part.

3.1.4 Understanding the Frontier Research Through Internet

The life science is developing rapidly and the knowledge of biochemistry updates day after day. In order to enable students' access to the frontier of knowledge as soon as possible, we provide some relevant professional website at the back of each chapter for students to find the latest information.

3.2 Setting Up the Three-dimensional Teaching Objectives and Implementation Plan

The results of brain science research show that clear learning aim will stimulate students' interest in learning and desire, and making the various parts of the brain take part in the learning process rapidly. However, in traditional teaching, although teachers are well aware of teaching aims and the implementation programs, most of them didn't stress enough to students.

In the teaching reform, the three-dimensional teaching objectives are given before the class which includes three aspects: (1) knowledge points; (2) knowledge objectives; (3) ability and emotional goals. Knowledge objectives include three levels: knowing, understanding and mastering. The increasing requirements can be seen clearly and difficult points are marked. Ability target includes memory, creativity, divergent, observation, imagination, analysis, logical reasoning, deductive reasoning, etc.; the emotional goal is to focus on improving students' learning interest, and the infiltration in students' world view and values, etc.

For example, in learning the first chapter about "enzyme chemistry", Table 1 is given which clearly shows the contents of this section for students to achieve. In the lecture process, methods of achieving the specific objectives of each part are set out (referring to Table 2), thus students can preview, learn in class and review with a clear idea.

Table 1. The Three-dimensional Teaching Objectives

Emotion/ability / Knowledge	Analysis ability Divergent Thinking	Analysis ability Divergent Thinking	Analysis ability
Knowing	1. the comparison between enzyme and general catalyst (common and specificity)		
Understanding		2. characteristics of the enzyme: 2) efficiency 3) mild effect	3. the chemical nature of enzymes
Mastering		2. characteristics of the enzyme 1) specificity	

Table 2 takes "enzymes as biological catalysts" as an example to show the implementation program.

Table 2. Implementation Program

Content		Implementation Program	Target
II. The Characteristics of Enzymes as Biological Catalysts	the concept of specificity	chart and pictures	remember the knowledge
	four pairs of the concept of enzymes specificity (1)show some terms from all aspects (2)examples on different kind of specificity (3)explain through the examples in the textbook (4)let students think about the reason for different "specificity" and its advantage.	intuitive understanding focus on an example typical example students to answer	remembering firmly by focusing on thinking, deeper understanding through divergent thinking, deepen the knowledge, and make a summary
	knowing the efficiency and mild effect	teacher's brief explanation	remember the knowledge

3.3 Reforms in the Teaching Methods of Municipal Engineering Graduate Biochemistry[7-11]

3.3.1 Fantasy Association Method

Fantasy association method is to visualize memorizing material, making it as vivid and intuitive as possible, or even we can exaggerate the material with imagination to make it absurd. In this way the material will form a singular image in the brain and leave deep impression.

For example: in order to remember the source of the atoms on the pyrimidine ring, we can make up a story of a farmer and his son.

3.3.2 Teaching Methods of Combining Infiltration with Steps

The "infiltration" is to help students understand roughly the whole system of knowledge as soon as possible through some teaching methods. "Infiltration" can not be exhaustive, but it can focus on the important points, establish the framework for students rapidly. The whole process is just like we first look at a panorama map, which is conducive to the overall understanding of the whole problem. While the "Step Mode" focuses on learning step by step. From the aspect of knowledge, the knowledge will be shown from simple to complex, which will help students' understanding, and avoid their fear of hardship; From the aspect of means, the Learning → Research → exploration process is followed, this will be conducive in helping students grasp the learning method. Infiltration combined with the step-mode will help student learning the details of knowledge step by step while keeping the final goal in sight.

For example, when explaining 4 pairs of concept of Specific enzymes, (see Table 2), we first show a few "comprehensive terms" (infiltrating forms the basic framework); then we "focus on one specific example to explain various types of contact" (vivid, and easy to understand); Next "explain concepts, and examples in the textbook" (leading to the extensive and in-depth understanding of knowledge); Finally, let students consider the reason for different "specificity" (deepen the knowledge, and make a summary).

3.3.3 Study Case Teaching Method

"Study case" is an "outline" to guide students to learn, it includes teacher's teaching ideas, the main framework of knowledge, the supplementary to other versions of teaching materials, student learning experience and so on. Specific use of "study case": before class let students, guided by the case, finish the task of considering and consulting, and come to the class with their own problems and what they have learned; after-school organize their notes according to the case. Let students check whether their self-study objectives are achieved, and communicate with the teacher frequently.

For example, the "study case" for the first chapter of enzyme chemistry includes: Table 1, Table 2, and the following questions. Some of the issues are conducive to both learning and teaching. a. Is knowledge framework established? Show it in the form of tables and diagrams. b. Which part of knowledge is grasped and which part is not? c. Some suggestions for teachers. d. Consulting reference of this part such as scientific knowledge, history of the progress of modern biotechnology, and knowledge that are closely related with water.

3.3.4 Combining "Miniature Practice" with Classroom Teaching

Biochemical verification experiment, production practice and dissertation research experiment all play an important role in training students' competitive ability, such as: practical ability, innovation capacity, the ability of connecting theory with practice. The classroom teaching of biochemistry for Municipal Engineering graduate is not equipped with validation experiments and production practice, and the thesis research experiment would be done later, so we try to "shrink" these links in the classroom teaching. For example, by watching "polyphenol oxidase preparation, chemical properties and influencing factors on the role of enzyme" in the video, students can understand in-depth the enzyme extraction, separation, purification as well as its applications. At the same time some questions are given in the "study case", guiding students to integrate knowledge in textbook and the application of the knowledge. Again, by showing students the video of "how the sewage treatment plant deals with domestic wastewater treatment", we can analyze the biochemical principles that involve biological treatment method. What's more, the research subject "A Study on Wastewater Treatment in Coking Plant" is given to students, since they may be involved in the project. Let students access to information in a method which is in accordance with the basic ideas of graduate thesis research. Let them summarize research significance, list the required equipments and drugs, decide the basic approach, get the expected results in theory, analyze the results, and draw a conclusion. In this process, a clear purpose and science requirements are given in the "study case".

4 The Effect of the Teaching Reform

The practice shows that the implementation of these new teaching methods, achieves positive effect. Fantasy association method generates vivid visual image, makes the boring contents of Biochemistry colorful and learning an exciting experience, thus the knowledge system can be quickly set up between the brain networks, it is conducive to students' rapid devotion in the initial phase of learning, and guide the learning process to a deep and broad development. The combination of theory and practice is conducive to the formation of solid neural network, and it shows important significance in stimulating students' motivation for study and the integration of knowledge.

In short, it is proved that the above reformed teaching methods take full advantage of the right brain hemisphere and "limbic system", and effectively develop the intellectual center of the brain. All the methods keep students in high spirits and motivated in the whole learning process. A Survey showed that the rate of students who consider the course more difficult declines, while 100% of the students believe that these methods can achieve greater efficiency. The students also find these methods can be applied to other curricula. All these show that these reforms not only achieve the efficiency and effectiveness in classroom teaching, but also have a wide effect in further study.

References

1. Vos, J., Dryden, G.: The Learning Revolution. Sanlian Bookshop, Shanghai (1998)
2. Sprenger, M.: Learning & Memory/The Brain in action. Light Industry Press of Chain, Beijing (2005)
3. Wolfe, P.: Brain Matters. Light Industry Press of Chain, Beijing (2005)
4. Dong, X., Jia, C.: Biochemistry. Higher Education Press, Beijing (2010)
5. Ji, Z., Chen, J.: Biochemistry. Higher Education Press, Beijing (2007)
6. Zhang, X.: A Three-tiered Model for Developing Textbooks for Graduate. Higher Education of Sciences 5, 66–69 (2009)
7. Zheng, W., Zhang, J.: Correlation Between Construction of R & D Infrastructure and Improvement of Post-graduate R & D Capability. Tropical Agricultural Engineering 8, 63–65 (2009)
8. Chen, Y., Yang, L.: Teaching Reforms in Advanced Biochemistry for Post-graduates. Journal of Shanxi Medical University(Preclinical Medical Education Edition) 8, 422–424 (2008)
9. Chen, H., Qiu, G.: Reforming Curriculum System and Cultivating Graduates' Creative Ability. Academic Degrees & Graduate Education 6, 27–29 (2005)
10. Hou, J., Li, G.: Reform Postgraduate Courses System Cultivate Creative Talents. Higher education Forum (6), 56–58 (2008)
11. Ye, L.: Consideration on Practising Learning Project Instruction Method in the Teaching of Electron Technology Foundation. Vocational and Technical Education 27(14), 58–60 (2006)

Numerical Analysis of Wu-Yang Highway Tunnel Excavation and Support

Lu Hong-Jian, Gan De-Qing, Yang Zhong-Jian, and Lu Xiao-Na

Hebei United University ,Tangshan 063009, China
luhongj2006@sina.com

Abstract. This paper applied the finite element analysis software MIDAS/GTS, taking use of ground structure method analysis stability in the process of tunnel excavation and support the of Wu-Yang. The results showed that the different sections during the excavation the maximum principal stress within the rock focused on steel feet, it is timely lock pin bolt when steel erection, taking use of small catheters grouting and other methods reinforcement of the rock arch foot when necessary. From the perspective of lining deformation, the maximum deformation at the end of the foot and the location of the vault subsidence, Thus, we should pay attention to the monitoring of settlement of vault, the gradual excavation of core soil, Ensure the construction and structural safety, and should be based on engineering facilities in time to control the chamber deformation.

Keywords: highway tunnel, excavation, supporting, numerical analysis.

1 Project Overview

Wu-Yang highway tunnel is located in foothills of Yan Shan, The type of landscape is structure of ablation hilly area, the more complex topography, hilly gully development. Tunnel surrounding rock is mainly to Sandy mudstone interceded conglomerate, Jurassic conglomerates in the system after the city group, Jurassic sandstone system after the city group. The tunnel was designed by the standard of two-way six-lane highway, the length of left line was 385m, the right one was 428m, net width of the main tunnel for the tunnel construction clearance was 14.50m, and net height is 5.0m. The surrounding rock of tunnel entrance with low quality and there is bias, the stability of the excavation and support has relatively strong effect. This paper applied finite element analysis software MIDAS / GTS made in-depth analysis to the stability during the process of construction.

2 Establish of Tunnel Excavation Numerical Simulation Model

2.1 Calculation Methods and Underlying Assumptions

The calculation method selected stratigraphic structure method. It was analyzed by two-dimensional plane strain, the rock material is assumed to be isotropic material in finite element analysis. Rock material criterion used.

C. Liu, J. Chang, and A. Yang (Eds.): ICICA 2011, Part I, CCIS 243, pp. 532–538, 2011.

Druker-Prager yield criterion, and selected the associated flow rule to calculate, assuming that material more than tensile stress, which cannot withstand tensile stress. In addition, the concrete lining and concrete support, structural materials are assumed to be elastic.

2.2 Finite Element Model and Material Parameters

Select the left line IV rock typical cross section ZK34+160 to simulate.

Calculation of material parameters was shown as table 1-2.

Table 1. Solid element calculation parameter table

Material name	Modulus/MPa	Poisson's ratio	Bulk density/KN/m³	Cohesion/KPa	Friction angle/°
Strong weathering	1200	0.40	19	80	22
Medium Weathering	1500	0.38	20	120	24

Table 2. Beam, bar unit calculates parameter table

Material name	Modulus/ MPa	Bulk density /KN/m³	Cross-sectional area /m²	Moment of inertia I/ m^4
Anchor	210000	78.5	0.000380	50
Initial lining	23000	25	0.26	80
Second lining	29500	25	0.45	400

3 Numerical Simulation Results and Analysis

In this paper applied structural design finite element analysis software---MIDAS / GTS, numerical simulation according to the construction steps, the simulation results shown in Figure 1 ~ 8.

3.1 The First Step Results and Analysis

The section after excavation, the maximum horizontal displacement occurs in the cutting face, arch around the waist position was maximum 1.16mm, vertical displacement occurred in the vault, the top was sinking 7.0mm, bottom uplift 6.2mm; Displacement there is a greater value, and the corresponding place with large compressive stress, shear stress is large.

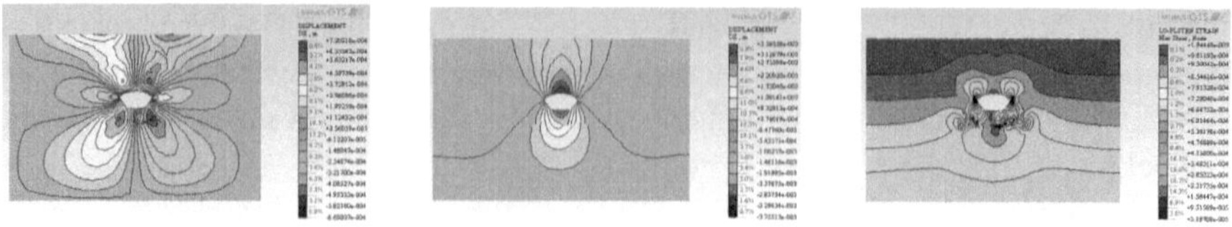

Horizontal displacement contour　　Vertical displacement contour　　Maximum shear strain contour

Fig. 1. The first step the simulation results

3.2 The Second Step Results and Analysis

The displacement and stress have been effectively controlled after support, Maximum bolt axial force was took place in the vault and the arch lumbar, the maximum was 0.56KN ; Axial force, shear force, bending moment which lining bolt in the lock at the foot was greater, respectively, 16.9KN、5.1KN、1.12KN/M.

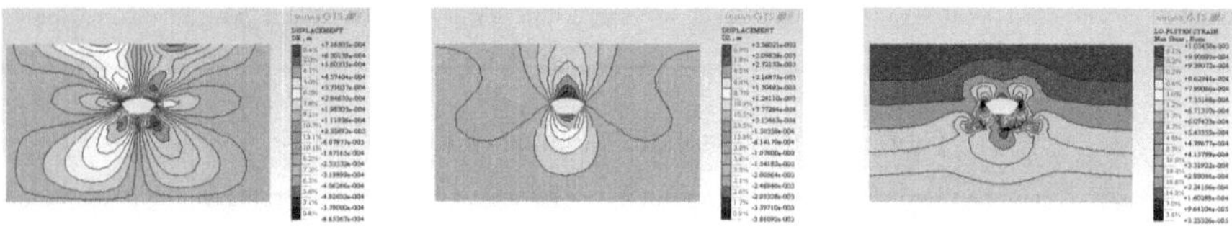

Horizontal displacement contour　　Vertical displacement contour　　Maximum shear strain contour

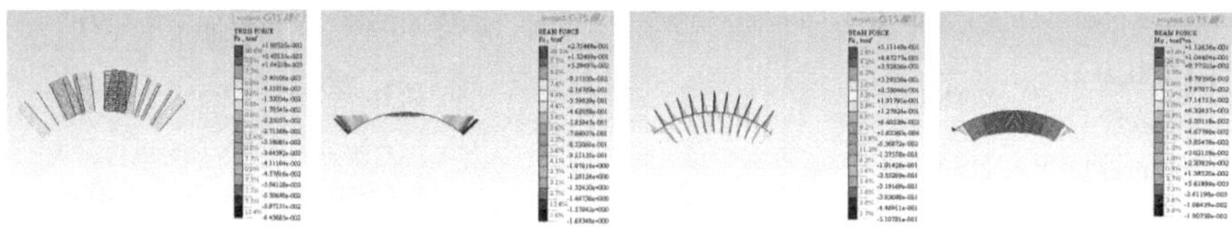

Bolt axial force figure　　Lining axial force figure　　Lining shear diagram　　Lining moment diagram

Fig. 2. The second step the simulation results

3.3 The Third Step Results and Analysis

Section on the left after excavation, initial support in the end is controlled under the displacement of small change; horizontal displacement occurred hence excavation face is 1.75mm,because volley surface increases after the left section excavation is completed, vertical displacement of 5.31mm in position at the tunnel crown.The lining on the face and the bolt support force are all into growth trends, the maximum bolt axial force occurred in the position of vault and the arch lumber, the maximum is 11.5KN ; lining locks the foot in the axial force of bolt, shear, bending moment greater, respectively, 608KN、217KN、55.7KN/M.

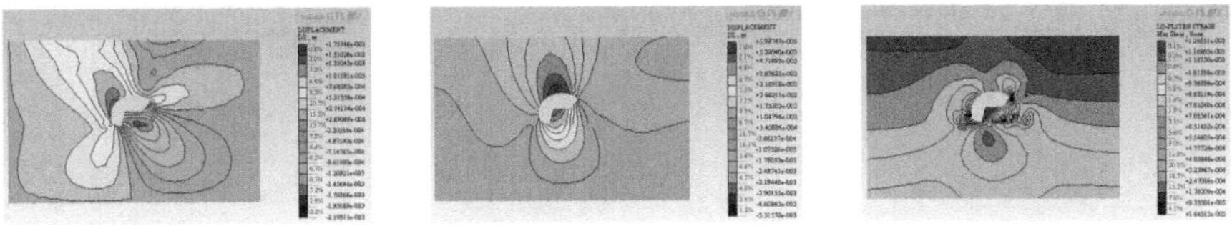

Horizontal displacement contour | Vertical displacement contour | Maximum shear strain contour

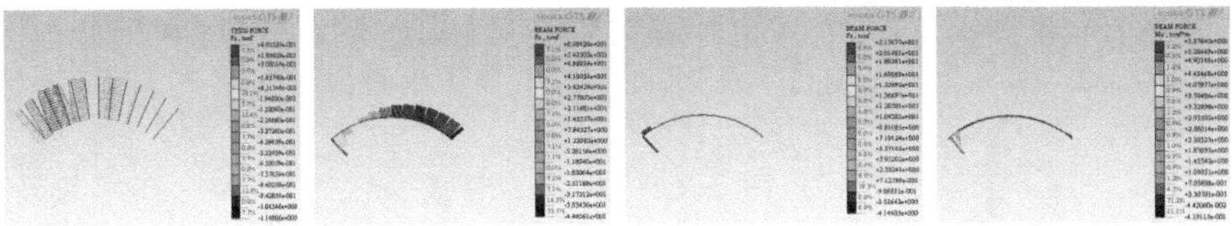

Bolt axial force figure | Lining axial force figure | Lining shear diagram | Lining moment diagram

Fig. 3. The third step the simulation results

3.4 The Fourth Step Results and Analysis

Support section on the left, the displacement and the support structure, the resulting change of control value was smaller.

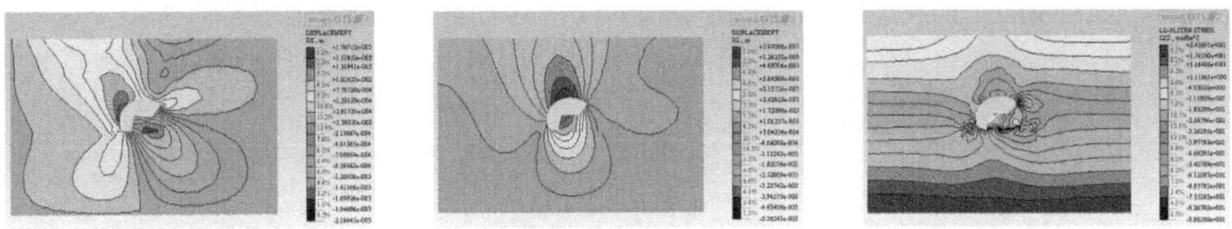

Horizontal displacement contour | Vertical displacement contour | Maximum shear strain contour

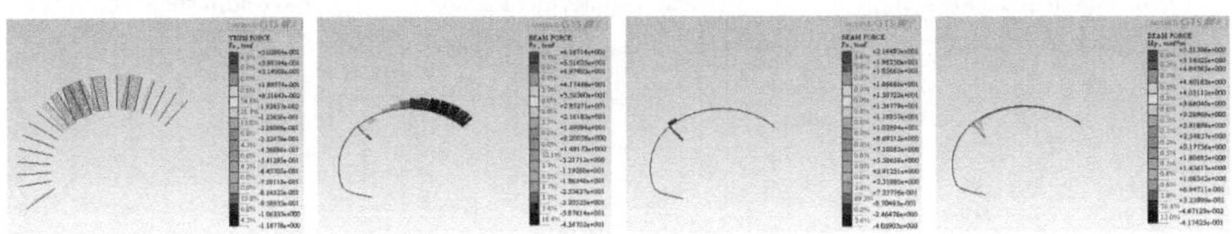

Bolt axial force figure | Lining axial force figure | Lining shear diagram | Lining moment diagram

Fig. 4. The fourth step simulation results

3.5 The Results and Analysis of the Fifth Step

Right section after excavation, as volley surface after section excavation was increased, the increase in displacement. The force on the left section support structure was increased, Vertical displacement occurred on the position of tunnel crown 6.61mm, the maximum bolt axial force occurred in the position of vault and the arch lumber, the maximum is39.6KN; lining locks the foot in the axial force of bolt, shear, bending moment greater, respectively, 511KN、214KN、56.4KN/M.

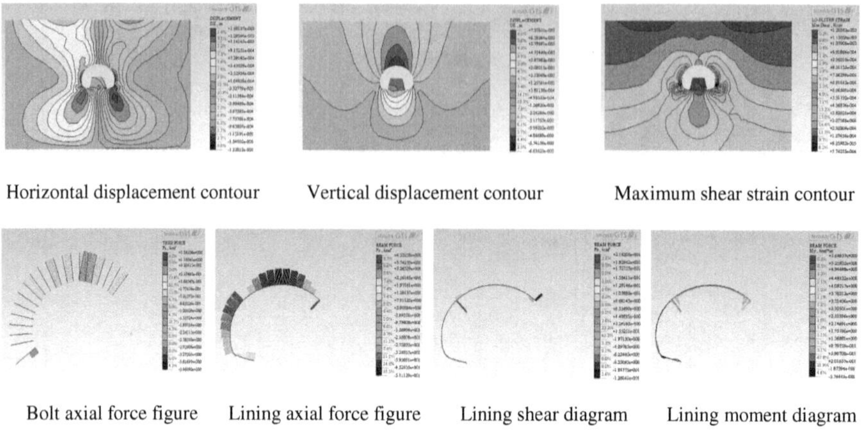

Fig. 5. The fifth step simulation results

3.6 The Results and Analysis of the Sixth Step

Supporting the right cross section, the displacement and force support structure have been effectively controlled, the change is smaller.

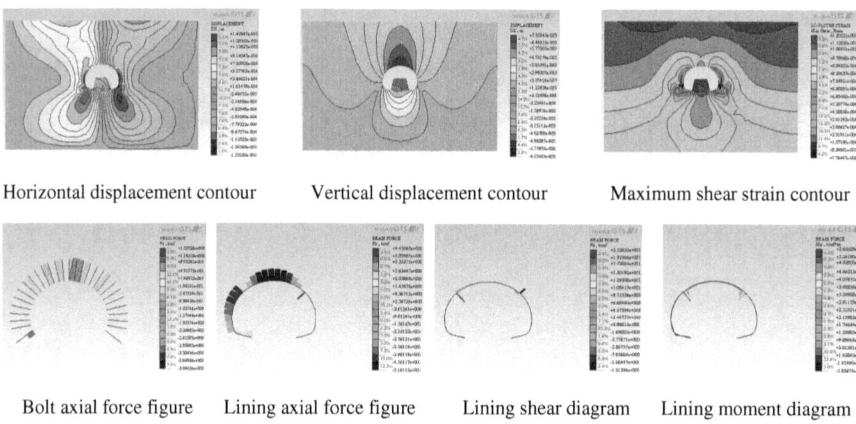

Fig. 6. The sixth step simulation results

3.7 The Results and Analysis of the Seventh Step

Core soil under the section after excavation and support, the force on the displacement and support structure are small changes because of no change in free surface.

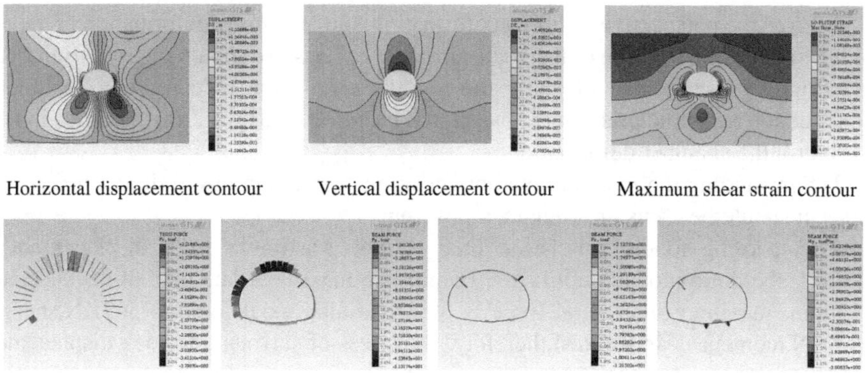

Horizontal displacement contour Vertical displacement contour Maximum shear strain contour

Bolt axial force figure Lining axial force figure Lining shear diagram Lining moment diagram

Fig. 7. The seventh step simulation results

3.8 The Results and Analysis of the Eighth Step

After pouring the second lining, two lining displacement and stress values is small, tunnel surrounding rock displacement and structural changes in the value of supporting small, which play a primary support better control effect.

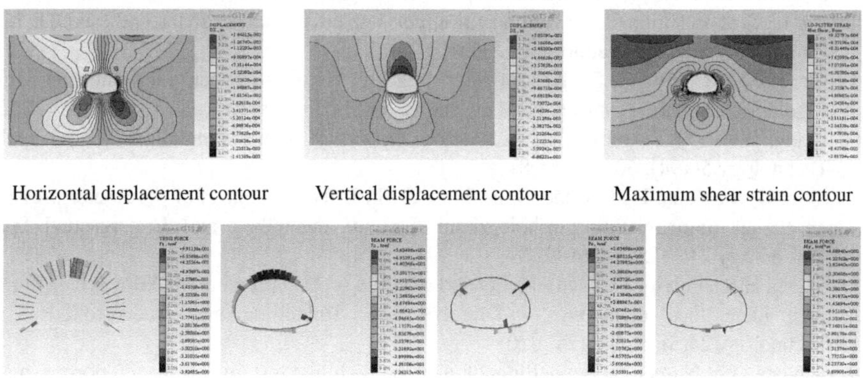

Horizontal displacement contour Vertical displacement contour Maximum shear strain contour

Bolt axial force figure Lining axial force figure Lining shear diagram Lining moment diagram

Fig. 8. The eighth step simulation results

4 Conclusions

1) Different sections during the excavation, the maximum principal stress within the surrounding rock concentrated on the steel foot, when steel erection you should lock the foot bolt and construction on time, taking use of small catheters grouting and other methods reinforcement of the rock arch foot when necessary.

2) From the perspective of lining deformation, the maximum deformation at the end of the foot and the location of the vault subsidence, Thus, we should pay attention to the monitoring of settlement of vault, the gradual excavation of core soil, Ensure the construction and structural safety, and should be based on engineering facilities in time to control the chamber deformation.

3) Surrounding the most unfavorable position, appears in the vault and invert both sides, it should be focus on strengthen position.

4) According to the simulation final results: Maximum vault displacement of 6.86mm,the bottom of the uplift of 7.05mm, the maximum lateral wall displacement 1.44mm; maximum bolt axial force is 39.2KN,lining axial force is 563KN,shear is 63.5KN,moment is 46.8KN/M,therefore, the stress of surrounding rock displacement and institutions are in a safe range, indicating a reasonable tunnel construction, structural design to meet the strength requirements.

References

1. Tan, R., Wang, C., Yang, Q.: Tunnel engineering. Chongqing University Press, Chong Qing (2001)
2. Liu, T., Lin, T.: Soft rock engineering design theory and construction practice. China Building Industry Press, Beijing (2001)
3. Weng, Q., Yuan, Y., Du, G., et al.: Three-dimensional numerical analysis of integrity state of double-arch tunnel. Underground Space and Engineering 2(1), 96–100 (2006)
4. Yu, L.: Soft rock tunnel excavation and support numerical analysis [Master thesis]. Da Lian: Dalian University of Technology (2003)
5. He, M., Li, C., Wang, S.: Kenton room large section of soft rock excavation numerical simulation of nonlinear mechanical properties. Public Process of Rock 4, 483–485 (2002)
6. Wang, Z., Li, L.: Analysis of excavation support of tunnel simulation. Shanxi Traffic Technology 5(194), 60–63 (2008)
7. Shin, H.-S., Youn, D.-J., Chae, S.-E., Shin, J.-H.: Effective control of pore water pressures on tunnel linings using pin-hole drain method. Tunnelling and Underground Space Technology 24(5), 555–561 (2009)
8. Seung, H.K., Fulvio, T.: Face stability and required support pressure for TBM driven tunnels with ideal face membrane – Drained case. Tunnelling and Underground Space Technology 25(5), 526–542 (2010)
9. Sanavia, L.: Numerical modelling of a slope stability test by means of porous media mechanics. Engineering Computations 26(3), 245–266 (2009)
10. Park, K.H., Tontavanich, B., Lee, J.G.: A simple procedure for ground response curve of circular tunnel in elastic-strain softening rock masses. Tunneling and Underground Space Technology 23(2), 151–159 (2008)

Minimal Surface Form-Finding Analysis of the Membrane Structure

Nan Ji[1] and Yuanyuan Luo[2]

[1] College of Science, Hebei United University, Tangshan, Hebei Province, 063009, China
[2] Tangshan Radio and TV University, 063000
pumpkinji@163.com

Abstract. With the rapid development of science engineering calculation and the membrane building structure system, membrane structure has been widely used in many kinds of architectural style. This paper focuses on the minimal surface form-finding analysis of membrane structure, which is mainly solved through the nonlinear iteration. Through analyzing the surface iterative solution of the initial solution, a higher degree approximation of the initial solution surface can be found, which also can be used for an approximate form of the membrane surface in the structure design.

Keywords: minimal surface, membrane structure, form-finding analysis.

1 Introduction

Membrane structure is the structure with a thin, flexible surface (membrane) that carries loads primarily through tensile stresses. There are two main types: tent structures and pneumatic structures. The membrane structure is originated in ancient times structure system of human living in tent rope and animal skins, because of the properties of high strength, waterproof, pervious to light and the surface is bright and clean, easy to clean, the membrane material has been a kind of new developed form of building structure in nearest 20-30 years, which is adored by most of the people in the word for its special, elegant sculpt and the power of tensile force.[1] With the rapid development of science engineering calculation and the membrane building structure system, Membrane structure has been widely used for the coastal tourism, fair, art, sports and other large space of the public buildings, such as the world exposition Fuji museum in Osaka (see figure 1) and Water Cube in Beijing (see figure 2)

Fig. 1. The world exposition Fuji museum. Osaka

C. Liu, J. Chang, and A. Yang (Eds.): ICICA 2011, Part I, CCIS 243, pp. 539–545, 2011.

Fig. 2. Water Cube Beijing

Membrane structures refer to those structures of which the main structural components are thin sheets of membrane made of resin coated fabrics. Design of membrane structures typically involves three stages i.e. form finding, cutting pattern determination and structural analysis.

2 Overview of the Minimal Surface Form-Finding

Stiffness of the membrane structure is provided by surface curve and pre-stresses, therefore, form — finding is the first and foremost step in design of membrane structure. Form-finding is a process to predict the membrane shape or the behavior of the membrane shape when subjected to a given boundary or loading condition. As the specificity of membrane materials and membrane structural design requirements, pre-distribution of minimal surface tension is commonly used to membrane structure for the form-finding objectives. The minimal surface form-finding analysis of membrane structure is a nonlinear problem. Its strong nonlinearity makes its computation to be a great challenge which usually needs a lot of iterations. Then it is necessary to find a rational initial solution to guarantee the convergence of the solution process. As we all know, the initial solution is the minimal surface that we seek.

3 Preliminaries for Minimal Surface

From the mathematical point of view, the process of finding a minimal surface within a boundary with specific constraints is determined by the calculus of variations. [3] The mathematical model of minimal surfaces is based on differential geometries and is strictly related to the standard computational method of visualization used in most of the cases. Minimal surfaces may be also characterized as surfaces of minimal surface area for given boundary conditions. When a closed wire is dipped into a soap solution and afterward raised up from the solution, the surface spanning the wire is a soap film. The soap film is in a state of equilibrium. Soap films are classical examples of minimal surfaces. A minimal surface is a geometry concept which refers to a surface with zero mean curvature that has the property of being locally area-minimizing, in a sense of having the smallest area within a given boundary.

Given the parameters of the surface in 3- dimensional space R^3, (see figure3)

$$\vec{r}(u,v)=\{x(u,v), y(u,v), z(u,v)\}\ ,\ u\in(-\infty,+\infty)\ ,\ v\in(-\infty,+\infty) \tag{1}$$

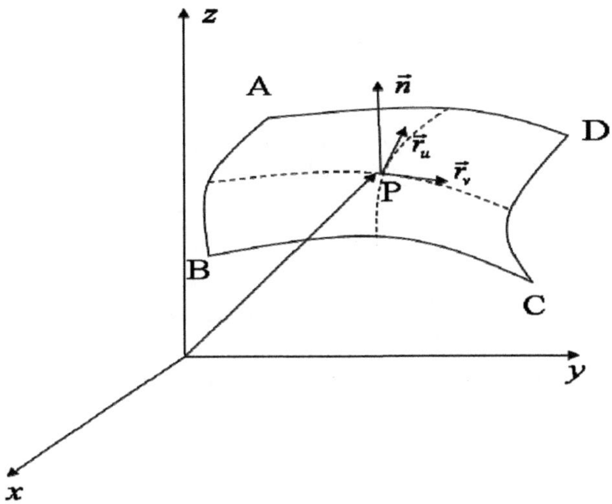

Fig. 3. Surface

The first fundamental form is

$$I = Edu^2 + 2Fdudv + Gdv^2 \tag{2}$$

In which, $E=\vec{r}_u\cdot\vec{r}_u = x_u^2+y_u^2+z_u^2$, $F=\vec{r}_u\cdot\vec{r}_v = x_u x_v + y_u y_v + z_u z_v$, $G=\vec{r}_v\cdot\vec{r}_v = x_v^2+y_v^2+z_v^2$.

The second fundamental form is

$$II = Ldu^2 + 2Mdudv + Ndv^2 \tag{3}$$

In which, $E=\vec{r}_{uu}\cdot\vec{n}=(\vec{r}_u,\vec{r}_v,\vec{r}_{uu})$, $M=\vec{r}_{uv}\cdot\vec{n}=(\vec{r}_u,\vec{r}_v,\vec{r}_{uv})$, $N=\vec{r}_{vv}\cdot\vec{n}$ $=(\vec{r}_u,\vec{r}_v,\vec{r}_{vv})$, $\vec{n}$ is the normal vector at point $P(x,y,z)$, $(\ ,\ ,\ )$ is mixed product.

The mean curvature H and Gauss curvature K is defined as follow:

$$H = \frac{EN - 2FM + LG}{\sqrt{EG - F^2}}, K = \frac{LN - M^2}{EG - F^2} \tag{4}$$

Definition 1. If the mean H of a parameter surface M: $\bar{r} = \vec{r}(u,v)$ satisfies H=0, then the surface is minimal.[2]

As we all know, the surface M is minimal if the variation of the area of M is zero.[4]

4 Approximate Solution of the Minimal Surface

Firstly, the membrane surface is subdivided into Quadrilateral surface element, now the area of the surface element (M_0) is as follows:[5,6]

$$\text{Area}(M_0) = \iint_{M_0} |\vec{r}_u \times \vec{r}_v| \, dudv \tag{5}$$

Because

$$\left|\vec{r}_u \times \vec{r}_v\right|^2 = (\vec{r}_u \cdot \vec{r}_u)(\vec{r}_v \cdot \vec{r}_v) - (\vec{r}_u \cdot \vec{r}_v)(\vec{r}_v \cdot \vec{r}_u) = EG - F^2 \tag{6}$$

According to the geometric meaning of the cross product

$$\left|\vec{r}_u \times \vec{r}_v\right| = |\vec{r}_u| \cdot |\vec{r}_v| \cdot \sin\theta = \sqrt{E}\sqrt{G}\sin\theta \tag{7}$$

In which, θ is the angle of $\vec{r}_u$ and $\vec{r}_v$.

From (5), (7) and integral mean value theorem, we get

$$\text{Area}(M_0) = \xi \iint_{M_0} \sqrt{EG} \, dudv \tag{8}$$

In which, ξ is the mean value and we don't know the value of it.

When the unit division is reasonable, and the shape of unit is closed to parallelogram, ξ is approximated by the mean value of sine value of the unit four angles. If the side length of the unit is not known, the length of the straight line which connects two endpoints of this side is used to calculate the approximation of the angles. Then, we denote the mean value of $\sqrt{E}$ and $\sqrt{G}$ in the unit is $\overline{\sqrt{E}}$ and $\overline{\sqrt{G}}$ respectively. When the surface unit is parallelogram, we can get $\overline{\sqrt{E}}$ and $\overline{\sqrt{G}}$ as following:

$$\overline{\sqrt{E}} = \frac{1}{2}(\overset{\frown}{AB} + \overset{\frown}{CD}), \ \overline{\sqrt{G}} = \frac{1}{2}(\overset{\frown}{BC} + \overset{\frown}{AD}) \tag{9}$$

In which, $\frac{1}{2}(\overset{\frown}{AB} + \overset{\frown}{CD})$ is the mean value of the arc lengths of $\overset{\frown}{AB}$ and $\overset{\frown}{CD}$.

If $\overline{\sqrt{E}} \approx \sqrt{E}$, $\overline{\sqrt{G}} \approx \sqrt{G}$, we can get the following conclusion,

$$\begin{aligned} \text{Area}(M_0) &= \xi \iint_{M_0} \sqrt{E}\sqrt{G}\, dudv \approx \xi \iint_{M_0} \sqrt{E}\overline{\sqrt{G}}\, dudv \\ &= \xi \iint_{M_0} \sqrt{E}\lambda \overline{\sqrt{E}} dudv \approx \lambda\xi \iint_{M_0} E\, dudv \end{aligned} \tag{10}$$

In which, we denote $\overline{\sqrt{G}} \big/ \overline{\sqrt{E}} = \lambda$. When surface unit is closer to parallelogram, the error caused by is smaller. the area of the surface M is

$$\text{Area}(M) = \sum \text{Area}(\text{M}_0) \approx \sum \lambda\xi \iint_{M_0} E\, dudv \tag{11}$$

Then we seek the minimal surface which satisfies the boundary condition to cause the surface area smallest, i.e. the variation of the area function is 0.

$$\delta[Area(M)] = \delta\sum \text{Area}(\text{M}_0) \approx \sum \lambda\xi \iint_{M_0} \delta E\, dudv = 0 \tag{12}$$

Since $Area(M)$ is positive definite quadratic function, with the use of conventional discrete methods, derived equations are a set of linear equations, easily solved and no iteration,

The variation of the area of surface unit M_0 is as follows,

$$\begin{aligned} \delta[Area(M_0)] &= \lambda\xi \iint_{M_0} \delta E\, dudv = \lambda\xi \int_{-1}^{1}\int_{-1}^{1} \delta E\, dudv \\ &= 2\lambda\xi \int_{-1}^{1}\int_{-1}^{1} (x_u \delta x_u + y_u \delta y_u + z_u \delta z_u)\, dudv = 0 \end{aligned} \tag{13}$$

Then we can get a set of linear ordinary differential equations, and the solution is an approximate solution of minimal surfaces.

Taking (6) into (5), we get

$$\text{Area}(M_0)=\iint_{M_0}\sqrt{EG-F^2}\,dudv \tag{14}$$

Then variation of the area of surface M is as follows

$$\delta[Area(M)]=\delta\sum\text{Area}(\text{M}_0)=\sum\iint_{M_0}\frac{E\delta G+G\delta E-2F\delta F}{2\sqrt{EG-F^2}}dudv \tag{15}$$
$$=0$$

The above equation is the variation equation of the form-finding analysis for the minimal surface. From this we may derive the corresponding nonlinear differential equation. We use the initial solution surface in the area element to replace the correspond minimal surface quantity in the formula (12), then we obtains the equation of variation after Revised, which is variation equation of minimal surface iterative solution.[8,9,10,11] From this derives governing equation is still nonlinear differential equation, but the nonlinearity is weak, and it is more easily solved.

5 Process of Form-Finding of Minimal Surface

By using the initial solution of minimal surface to iterate, we may obtain a higher accuracy solution. If the solving surface satisfies the error limit, it is the minimal surface which we seek. But if it doesn't satisfy the error limit, we will seek the initial solution again. the process of the form-finding iteration algorithm is as follows:

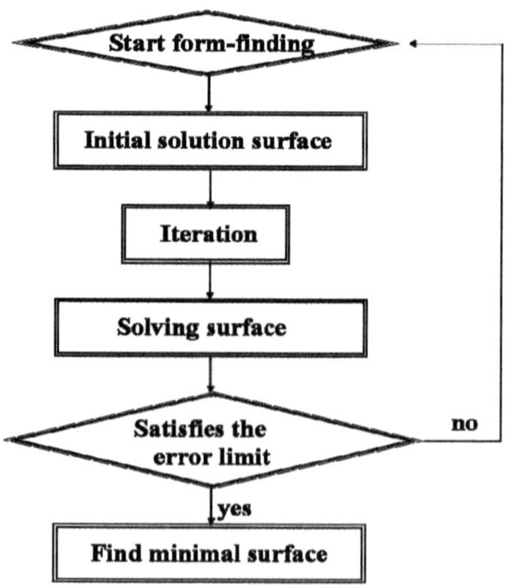

Fig. 4. Process of Form-finding of minimal surface

6 Conclusion

Through analyzing the surface iterative solution of the initial solution, a higher degree approximation of the initial solution surface can be found, which also can be used for an approximate form of the membrane surface.

Acknowledgment. This work is supported by the Scientific Technology Research and Development Plan Project of Tang Shan City (No.10110214C)

References

1. Loong, T.S., Abdul Razak, H., Ismail, Z., Keong, C.K.: Experimental and Numerical Form-finding of Membrane Structures. Asian Journal of Civil Engineering 8(1), 1–12 (2007)
2. Grabe, M., Neu, J., Oster, G., Nollert, P.: Protein Interactions and Membrane Geometry. Biophysical Journal 84, 854–868 (2003)
3. Yi, F.-A., Hu, J.-Z., Yue, Y.-F.: The Minimal Surface Analysis of Cable-Nets and Fabric Structures. Engineering Mechanics (2004)
4. Osserman, R.: A Survey of Minimal Surface. Dover Publications Inc., New York (2002)
5. Su, B.: Differential Geometry. People's Education Press (1980)
6. Mei, X., Huang, J.: Differential Geometry. Higher Education Press (2008)
7. Zhang, H., Shan, J.: Dynamic Relaxation Method Study of Membrane Structures. Chinese Journal of Applied Mechanics 19, 84–86 (2002)
8. Gao, B.: A Study of Form–Finding Methods for Membrane Structure by Nonlinear Finite Element. Journal of Yan shan University, 331–334 (2002)
9. Yuan, S., Liu, X., Ye, K.: FEMOL solution for minimal surface form finding of tensile membrane structures. China Civil Engineering Journal, 1–7 (2010)
10. Li, Z., Niu, D., Fan, Y.: Form-Finding of Prestressed Membrane Structure. Journal of ShiJiaZhuang Railway Institute 13(2), 39–43 (2002)
11. Deng, X.-Y.: Form-finding analysis of tensile membrane structures using nonlinear finite element. ShanXi Architecture 33(18), 71–72 (2007)

Influence of Coal Price to Exploitation Mode in China

Chen Shuzhao[1,2], Wang Haijun[1,2], Li Kemin[1,2],
and Xiao Cangyan[3]

[1] State Key Laboratory of Coal Resources and Mine Safety,
China University of Mining and Technology, Xuzhou,
Jiangsu 221008 China
[2] School of Mining Engineering, China University of Mining and Technology,
Xuzhou, Jiangsu 221008, China
[3] College of Light Industry, Hebei Polytechnic University,
Tangshan, hebei 063020, China

Abstract. Based on the continuously improve of coal market and rise of coal price in recent years, we analyze the development of open pit coal mine in China, put forward the standards of transformation from underground into open pit mining, and take Yuanbaowan Coal Mine of China National Coal Group Corp. for case study in this paper. The paper consider that the higher growth speed of open pit mine production in recent years prove that the rising of coal price beneficial to the development of open pit mine. With the total benefit, annual benefit, and net present value of open pit mining are bigger than underground mining, we should actively consider the transformation from underground into open pit mining. The Case studies shown that when the coal price is greater than 241 yuan/t, the Yuanbaowan Coal Mine should exploit by open pit mining, and the terminal condition of transformation from underground into open pit mining will rise with the rising of underground mining rate and open pit mining cost.

Keywords: coal price, open pit mining, underground mining, transformation from underground into open pit mining.

1 Introduction

Compared with underground mining, open pit mining of coal resource have advantages such as: higher mining rate, higher safety level, larger production, higher mechanization, higher production efficiency[1~3]. While the other major coal producing countries in the world, such as Germany, Australia, India, United States, Russia and South Africa and so on take open pit mining as the priority exploitation method[4~7], the main coal resource exploitation method of China in a long time is underground mining, and more than 90% of the total coal output come from underground mining. The coal output of China since 2003 shown in Table 1.

C. Liu, J. Chang, and A. Yang (Eds.): ICICA 2011, Part I, CCIS 243, pp. 546–553, 2011.

Table 1. Coal production of China

Year	Total production (Mt)	Open pit mine production (Mt)	Open pit mining ratio (%)	Remarks
2003	1668	80	4.80	
2004	1956	131	6.70	
2005	2190	132	6.03	
2006	2381	139	5.84	
2007	2524	170	6.74	
2008	2716	210	7.73	
2009	2850	295	10.35	
2010	3250	350	10.77	

2 Relationship Between Coal Price and Open Pit Mine Production

Because the coal resources exploited by open pit mining in China are lignite and low metamorphic grade bituminous coal, the coal price is generally lower. While coal market downturn, the open pit mine production are more susceptible. As coal price index is not uniform in China, we determine the relationship between coal price and calorific value shownn in Figure 1 based on coal price of Qinhuangdao Port and other ports at the end of 2010. The coal production growth rate of open pit mine in recent years shownn in Figure 2.

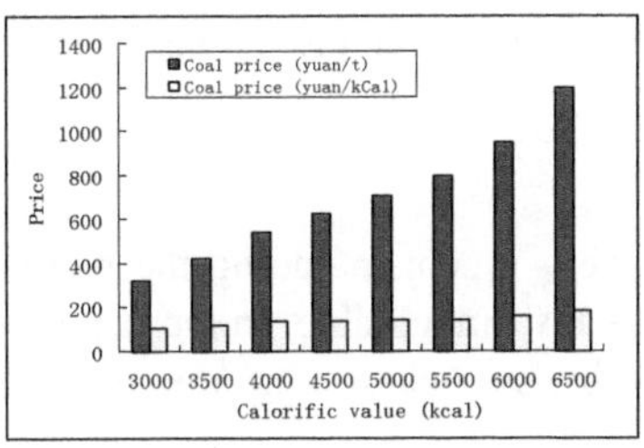

Fig. 1. Relationship between calorific value and coal price

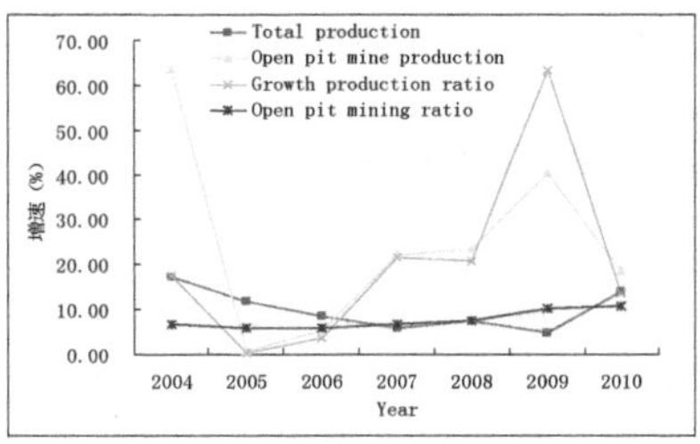

Fig. 2. Comparison of growth rate

Table 1 and Figure 2 showns that, in nearly seven years, with the development of national economy and the expansion of energy demand, coal production and open-pit mining open the proportion of rapid growth, and open pit coal production has grown faster than total output growth speed, the new production in the open-air production is higher than the proportion of total production in the open air. The analysis of reasons for this are as follows.

(1) Because of the lower coal prices, the economic transport distance of low metamorphic grade coal is shorter, so the relevance degree between open pit production and regional economic development is higher.

(2) The benefits of open pit mine decline with coal prices, or even loss, so they tend to reduce production.

(3) While coal price increases, downstream firms tend to use low metamorphic grade coal which relatively low price and high cost-effective.

Thus, the coal prices rising is conducive to the open pit mining development.

3 Efficiency Comparison

The benefits of transformation from underground into open pit mining are mainly from resource mining rate improve and production capacity expansion [8].

3.1 Total Benefit

Resources under certain conditions, the total benefits of open-pit mining and underground mining are:

$$\text{Underground: } S_{jz} = 100 \times Q_0 \times \eta_j \times (A - C_j) \times (1 - 25\%) \quad (1)$$

$$\text{Open pit: } S_{lz} = 100 \times Q_0 \times \eta_l \times (A - C_l) \times (1 - 25\%) \quad (2)$$

Where: S_{jz} - Total benefits of coal resources underground mining, 104yuan. Q_0 - Coal reserves, Mt. η_j - Underground mining rate, %. A - Coal prices, yuan/t. C_j - The full costs of underground mining (including production costs, taxes, washing costs etc.), Yuan/t. 25% - Income tax rate. S_{lz} - Total benefits of coal resources open pit mining, 104yuan. η_l - open pit mining rate, %. C_l - The full cost of open pit mining, Yuan/t.

3.2 Annual Benefit

Factors affect the production capacity of mine is very much, including the national standard requirements for mine service life which is insurmountable. In the paper, we take the maximum production capacity allowed by service life as the basis for comparison annual benefits:

$$\text{Underground: } \begin{aligned} S_j &= 100 \times q_j \times (A - C_j) \times (1 - 25\%) \\ &= 100 \times \frac{Q_0 \times \eta_j}{n_j \times k_j} \times (A - C_j) \times (1 - 25\%) \end{aligned} \quad (3)$$

$$\text{Open pit: } \begin{aligned} S_l &= 100 \times q_l \times (A - C_l) \times (1 - 25\%) \\ &= 100 \times \frac{Q_0 \times \eta_l}{n_l \times k_l} \times (A - C_l) \times (1 - 25\%) \end{aligned} \quad (4)$$

Where: S_j - Annual benefit of coal resources underground mining, 104yuan/a. q_j - The largest underground mining production capacity, Mt/a. n_j - The legal service life of underground mining (the Standard shown in Table 2), a. k_j - The reserves standby coefficient of underground mining. S_l - The annual benefit of coal resources open pit mining, 104yuan/a. q_l - The largest open pit mining production capacity, Mt/a. n_l - The legal service life of open pit mining (the Standard shown in Table 3), a. k_l - The reserves standby coefficient of open pit mining.

Table 2. Service life in old and new mine standards

Old mine standards		New mine standards	
Mine production capacity (Mt/a)	Service life(a)	Mine production capacity (Mt/a)	Service life(a)
>15	90	>30	90
>10~15	80	>10~30	80
>8~10	70	>5~10	70
>5~8	70		
>3~5	60	>2~5	60
1~3	50	<2	30~50

Table 3. Service life of open pit mine

Mine type	Production capacity (Mt/a)	Service life(a), more than	
		New open pit coal mien	Extension open pit coal mien
Large	≥10	35	30
	≥4~<10	30	20
Medium	≥1~<4	20	15
Small	<1	10	10

3.3 Net Present Value

Consider the timeliness, the net present value of open pit mining and underground mining are.

Underground: $$S_{jx} = \sum_{i=0}^{n_j-1} (1-e)^i \times S_j \quad (5)$$

Open pit: $$S_{lx} = \sum_{i=0}^{n_l-1} (1-e)^i \times S_l \quad (6)$$

Where: S_{jx} - the net present value of coal resources underground mining, 10^4yuan. e - discount rate, %. S_{lx} - the net present value of coal resources open pit mining, 10^4yuan.

We consider that, if the total benefits, annual benefit and net present value of open pit mining are greater than underground mining, should priority consider open pit mining. If one or two indicators index is larger, should be carefully considered, and if necessary should pause the exploitation.

4 Case Study

4.1 Mine Profile

The Yuanbaowan Coal Mine of China National Coal Group Corp. Shanxi Jinhaiyang Co., Ltd. is restructured by the Shanyin Yuanbaowan Coal Co., Ltd. and the Shanyin Shangmanwan Coal Mine. The geological reserves of Yuanbaowan Coal Mine is 136.31Mt, and the designed production capacity is 900kt/a. The main coal seams of Yuanbaowan Coal Mine shown in Table 4.

Table 4. Coal seam

No.	Coal seam thickness (m) Min—Max / Average	Coal seam texture (Parting layer)	Coal seam interval (m) Min—Max / Average	Admissibility
3^{-1}	0.96-4.36 / 2.71	Simple (0—2)	13.20-20.50 / 16.64	Whole can mining
4	2.37-12.94 / 7.26	Relative complex (1—3)	16.02-31.83 / 24.39	Whole can mining
6	1.04-9.14 / 3.47	Simple (0—2)	6.35-12.63 / 9.29	Whole can mining
9	4.25-12.77 / 6.60	Simple—Complex (0—4)	4.08-7.65 / 5.81	Whole can mining
10	0-3.27 / 1.08	Simple (0)	11.20-14.92 / 12.63	Local can mining
11	0-6.42 / 2.03	Relative simple (0—3)		Local can mining

4.2 Comparison of Exploitation Methods

Based on the production data of Yuanbaowan Coal Mine, and reference to the experience of some surrounding mines, we determine the economic indicators in Table 5.

Table 5 shows that, with the existing market conditions, the total benefits, annual benefit and net present value of open pit mining are larger than underground mining, so the Yuanbaowan Coal Mine transfer from underground into open pit mining is suitable.

Table 5. Economic indicators of Yuanbaowan Coal Mine

Project	Unit	Original design	Underground extension	Open pit
Production capacity	Mt/a	0.9	1.5	400
mining rate	%	50	50	95
Reserves coefficient		1.3	1.3	1.05
Service life	a	58	35	30
Coal price	yuan/t	500	500	500
Total cost	yuan/t	198.5	198.5	249.5
Profit	yuan/t	226.125	226.125	187.875
Annual benefit	10^4yuan/a	20351.25	33918.75	75150.00
Total benefit	10^4yuan	1185503.80	1185503.80	2243857.33
Discount rate	%	5	5	5
Net present value	10^4yuan	386247.65	565708.18	1180397.94

Note: Sales tax and additional were considered in the all costs, which accounting for 18.7% of the price.

4.3 Influence of Coal Price

With other factors remain unchanged, consider the fluctuations of market coal price (based on historical experience determine the fluctuations range is 200 to 600 yuan/t). The relationship between coal resource development benefits and coal price shown in Figure 3.

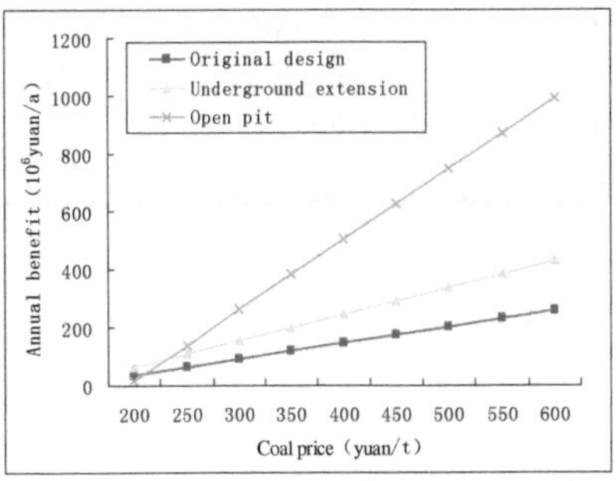

(a) Annual benefit and coal price

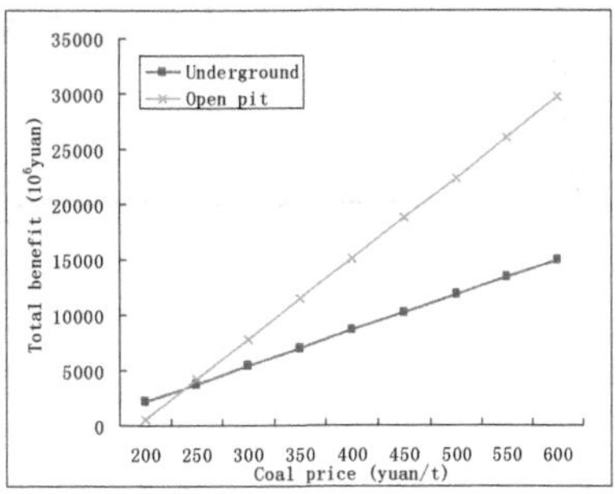

(b) Total benefit and coal price

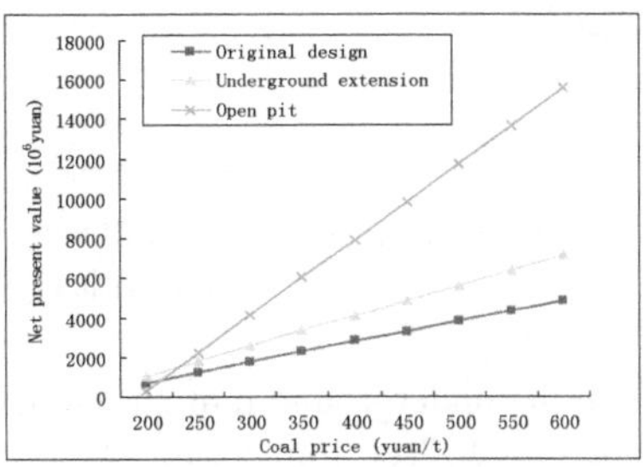

(c) Net present value and coal price

Fig. 3. Benefit and coal price

We can see from the figure, when coal price is higher than 241 yuan/t, the three indicators of open pit mining were higher than underground mining, so open pit mining should be given priority. when coal price less than 230 yuan/t, open pit mining can not get enough benefit to make up for the drawbacks bring by higher production costs, so open pit mining should be carefully considered. when coal price less than 129 yuan/t, should maintain the origin capacity or stop production.

4.4 Other Factors

Other factors which influence the economic effect of open pit mining, mainly including the underground mining rate and open pit mining costs. Reference to the mining rate of large state-owned underground mines, and consider technical progress. The influence of underground mining rate to development benefits shown in Table 6, and the influence of open pit mining costs to development benefits shown in Figure 4.

Table 6. Influence of mining rate to benefit

mining rate (%)	Production capacity (Mt/a)	Service life (a)	Annual benefit 10^4yuan/a	Total benefit (10^4yuan)	Net present value (10^4yuan)
30	0.9	35	20351.25	711302.3	339424.9
40	1.2	35	27135	948403	452566.5
50	1.5	35	33918.75	1185504	565708.2
60	1.8	35	40702.50	1422605	678849.8
70	1.8	41	40702.50	1659705	714665.4
80	1.8	47	40702.50	1896806	740993.2
90	1.8	52	40702.50	2133907	757520.1

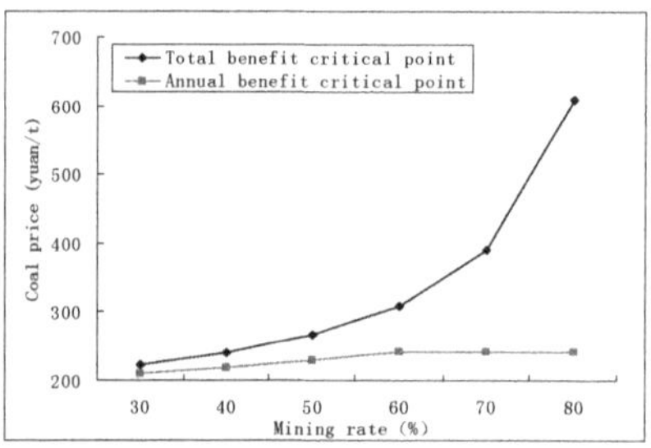

Fig. 4. Influence of mining rate to open pit mining critical point

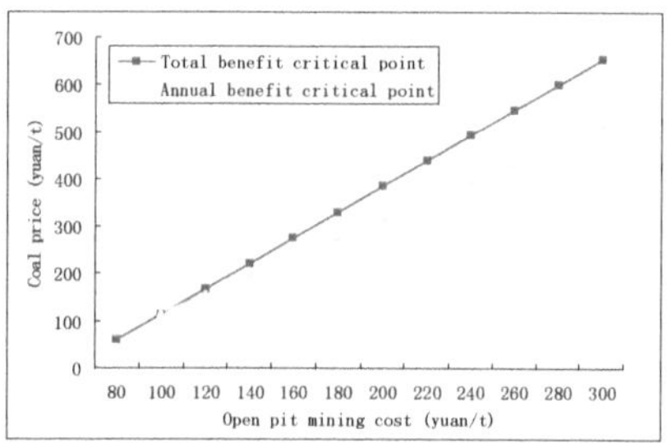

Fig. 5. Influence of mining cost to open pit mining critical point

Table 6 shows that, with the underground mining rate increase, the benefits of coal resources exploitation increased. But limited to the service life requirements of underground mine, the growth rate of annual benefit and net present value is less than the total benefits. Comparing Table 5 and Table 6 we can know that, restricting by the production capacity, the annual benefit and net present value of underground mining always less than open pit mining.

The main influence factors of open pit mining costs are resources occurrence conditions and mining technology. With the open pit mining technology development, the unit cost of open pit mine is gradually decreased. The influence of open pit mining cost to Yuanbaowan Coal Mine shown in Figure 5.

5 Conclusions

Conclusions of this paper as following:

(1) With the coal market improved, the coal amount of open pit mining accelerating growth, and the growth rate higher than the national total coal production growth rate.
(2) We established the evaluation criteria of transformation from underground into open pit mining from the total benefits, annual benefit, and net present value in this paper.
(3) with the existing market conditions, the total benefits, annual benefit and net present value of open pit mining are larger than underground mining, so the Yuanbaowan Coal Mine transfer from underground into open pit mining is suitable.
(4) When the coal price is greater than 241 yuan/t, the Yuanbaowan Coal Mine should exploit by open pit. The critical point of transformation from underground into open pit mining will rise with the rising of underground mining rate and open pit mining cost.

References

1. Luo, Z.: Surface Mining (Mining Technology). China University of Mining and Technology Press, Xuzhou (1996) (in Chinese)
2. Yu, R., Zhang, R., Wang, B., Liu, G.: Optimization Theory and Practice of Open Pit Mining. China Coal Industry Publishing House, Beijing (2005) (in Chinese)
3. Zhang, Y., Zhang, D.: The Strategic Development of Surface Coal Mining in China. China Mining Magazine 2(1), 17–21 (1993) (in Chinese)
4. Zhang, D., Zhang, Y.: New Technology of Open pit Mining. China University of Mining and Technology Press, Xuzhou (1992) (in Chinese)
5. Yan, T., Zhang, S., Li, D.: Status – Quo of Coal Industrial Structure of China and Its Differences from Major Coal Producing Countries. China Coal 26(4), 28–33 (2000) (in Chinese)
6. Zhang, Y., Cai, Q., Li, K., Zhou, C.: Technology Development Characteristics of the World Open Pit Mining and Planning Proposals of Open Pit Coal Mining Research in China. China Coal 10, 10–14 (1996) (in Chinese)
7. Zhang, H., Jin, X., Li, G., Yang, Z., Jia, J., Jiang, Z., Han, B.: Comparison of Coalfields and Coal-mining Geological Conditions of the Main Coal-producing Countries in the World. Coal Geology & Exploration 35(6), 1–9 (2007) (in Chinese)
8. Wang, H., Li, K., Chen, S., Wang, B.: Analysis of the Conditions of Resource Adapt to Transferring From Underground into Open Pit Mining. Metal Mine 6, 54–56 (2010) (in Chinese)

Finite Element Analysis on the Drum of Concrete Mixing Truck

Li Dong-mei[1] and Ma Xing-hua[2]

[1] Tangshan Industrial Vocational Technical College, Tangshan, Hebei , 063000, China
[2] College of Science, Hebei United University, Tangshan, Hebei , 063009, China
{nhnhldm,mxh332}@163.com

Abstract. Applied the finite element method and finite element analysis software ANSYS, the static analysis of the drum and blade is carried out, and which provides an important basis for further analysis and optimized design.

Keywords: Concrete mixing truck, Spiral blade, Finite element analysis.

With the popularity of computers, computer and application technology with its powerful calculation and simulation capabilities, product design analysis of all walks of life, is playing an increasingly important role. CAD , CAE and CAM are the most common computer application technology in designing and manufacturing field. CAE (Computer Aided Engineering) or Computer Aided Engineering, is the use of computer systems supporting people to carry out engineering analysis and simulation technology. Compared with traditional design and analysis tools, CAE design and analysis technology is revolutionary, it is for the majority of engineering design provides a good calculation, design, analysis platform, the use of CAE technology to the successful completion of product design and simulation work.

1 Finite Element Method

Finite element method (or the finite element method) is a computer-aided engineering (CAE) of the most important and most widely used numerical methods. Because of its versatility and effectiveness, computer-aided engineering is based on the formation of an independent discipline by the engineering community attaches great importance to the finite element.

Finite element method to deal with complex engineering problems of a numerical calculation method, a complex shape that it will break down into a finite number of continuum shape of a simple unit, through the discretization, to solve the continuum of stress, strain, temperature, converted to solving problems finite element problem.

2 Introduction of ANSYS Software

ANSYS is a multi-purpose finite element analysis software, which can be used for structural analysis and thermal analysis of linear, and the fluid, electricity,

C. Liu, J. Chang, and A. Yang (Eds.): ICICA 2011, Part I, CCIS 243, pp. 554–559, 2011.

electromagnetic fields and collision analysis. ANSYS has been widely used in mechanical, electrical, civil, electronics and aerospace industries. ANSYS contains the finite element analysis, computer graphics and optimization technology together, which has become a problem to solve a powerful tool of modern engineering. This article only research for static analysis of the tank truck.

ANSYS analysis software typically consists of three main steps:

(1) General Preprocessor
A. The geometry model (or finite element model)
B. Set the unit type
C. Set the material properties and cell constants
D. Divide geometry model into units
(2) Solution Processor
A. Set boundary conditions and applied load
B. Set solving options and solve
(3) General Postprocessor POST1 or Time-History Postprocessor POST26
A. POST1 is used for static structural analysis, buckling analysis and mode analysis, and the results of the variable are listed or graphical displayed.
B. POST26 is used for dynamic structural analysis, listing or displaying the results of time-domain variables change over time.

3 Finite Element Analysis of Concrete Mixer Truck Tank

3.1 Finite Element Model of the Concrete Mixing Truck Tank

Concrete mixer truck tank is the main bearing component, in particular, the shape of spiral blade mixing performance of concrete has a direct impact. This article mainly concrete mixer truck tank and spiral blades of the finite element method.

Analysis of the object to 9m^3 concrete mixer truck, dimensions shown in Figure 1. Tank material 16Mn, elastic modulus Pa; tank shell thickness: 4.0mm; front and

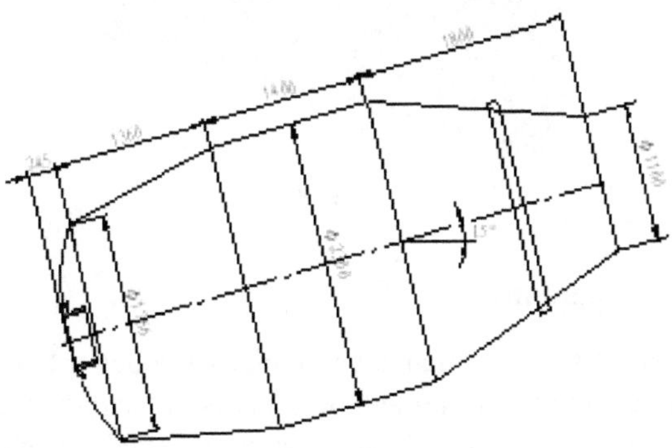

Fig. 1.

middle sections of the spiral bevel blade oblique angle: $11.1°$; after the oblique cone angle of the helical blade: $0°$; concrete density : 2.352 N/m^3.

The figure researches for the analysis of the post ring cone support rail, the use of solid elements and the tank using shell element.

3.2 Meshing

Blades the tank and the spiral shape is complex, so we use free mesh, element edge length of about 30.0mm, quadrilateral grid. Among them, the tank and the helical blade used by shell element Shell63 unit, supporting unit Solid185 rail unit with body. The overall finite element model and mesh the results shown in Figure 2.

model within the finite element mesh can be seem from Figure 3 by opening the tank , while the local helical blade finite element mesh is shown in Figure 4.

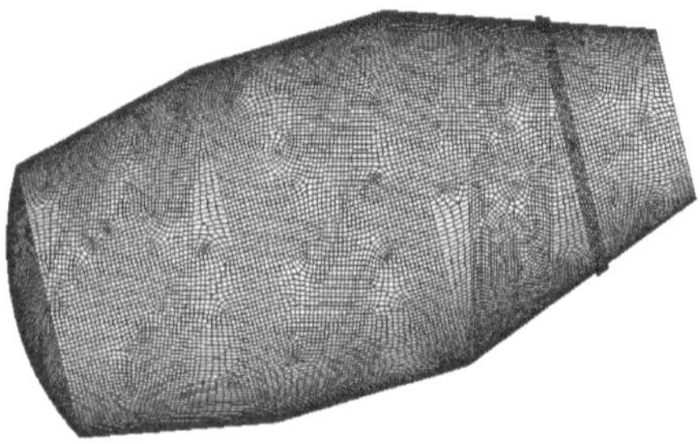

Fig. 2.

Fig. 3.

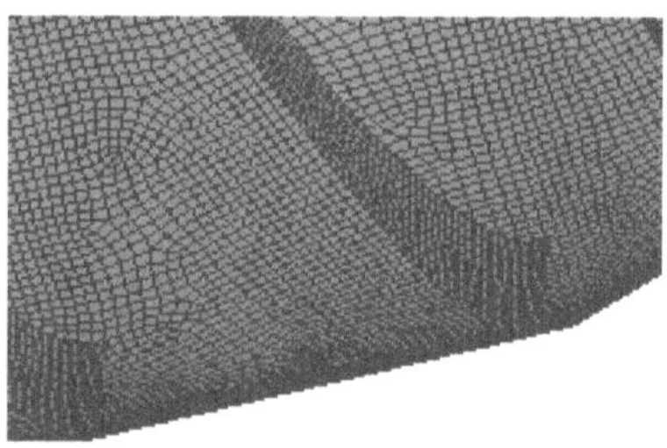

Fig. 4.

3.3 Constraint Conditions

Tank before the end of the cone flange and reducer through a fixed connection, after the cone tank installed in the car through the chassis rail and the bracket on the wheel connection, according to the actual situation of the tank support, the constraints imposed is shown in Figure 5 and Figure 6.

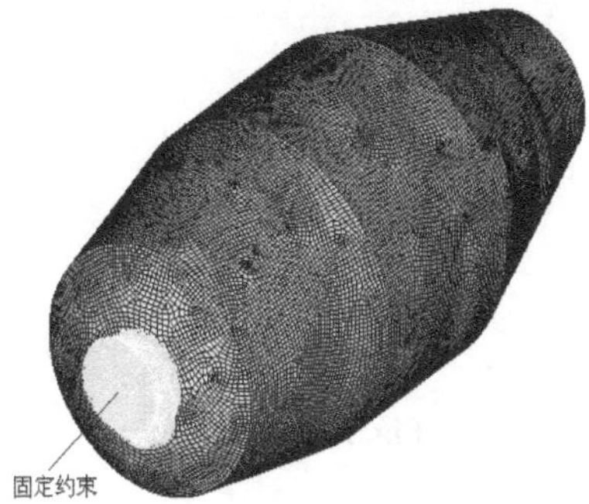

Fig. 5.

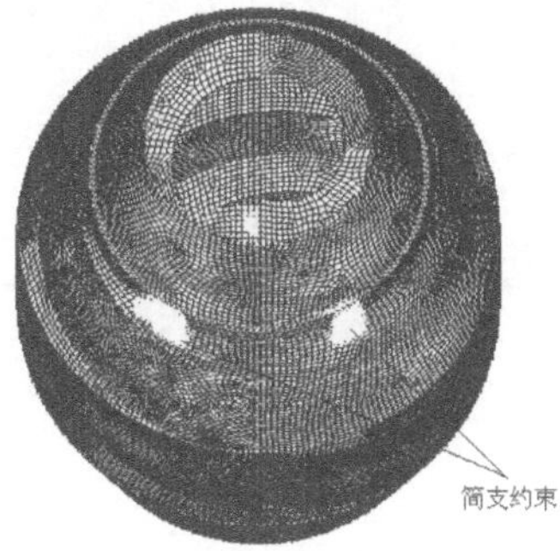

Fig. 6.

3.4 Load

Tanks are under load have two kinds: one is that tank of material of costumed inside tank, 2 it is the weight the weight itself. Applied load, the tank inside the dresses weight of the material changes with height in the form of the pressure exerted on the inner surface of the tank (Figure 7). Weight of the tank itself in the form of gravity applies to the tank.

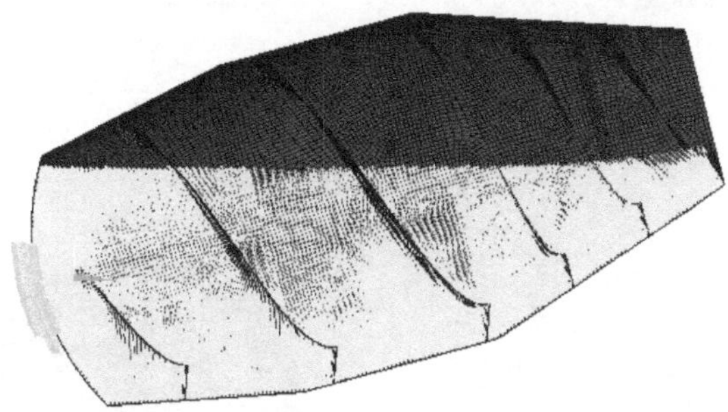

Fig. 7.

3.5 Finite Element Analysis Results of Concrete Mixing Truck Tank

This paper researches on static analysis of tank body and spiral blades. Model for sealing heads the constraint conditions in for all constraints set the flange connection with roller, the guides below the contact point for the rigid constraints set. Considering concrete liquid property, we applies load with function loading method, so tanks with the liquid surface force decreases. Solving the deformation after loading the tank is shown in figure 8 and figure 9.

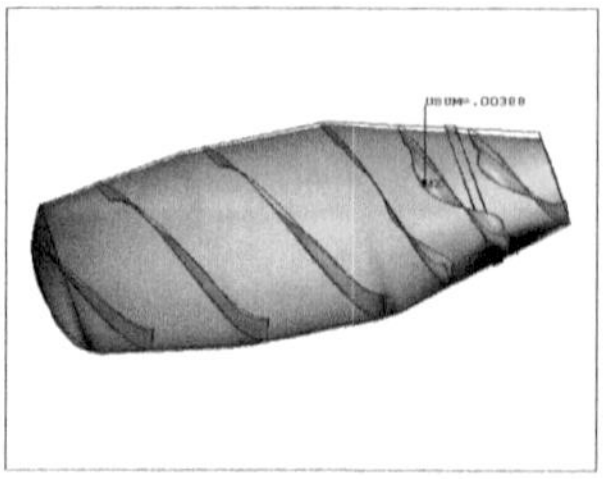

Fig. 8. Left view

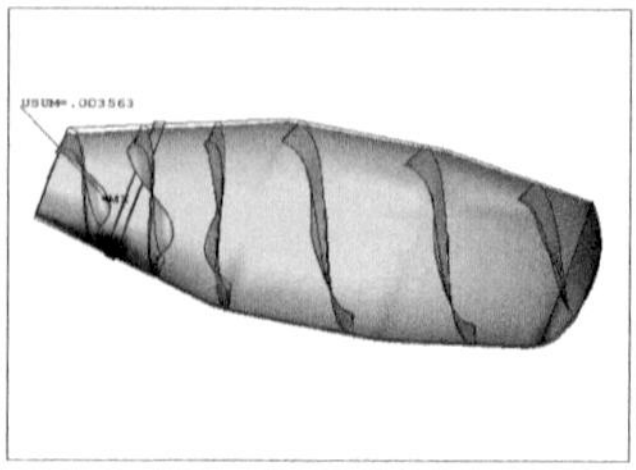

Fig. 9. Right view

Figure 8 and Figure 9 show that the spiral blade at the back has a great cone deformation and the left view and right view respectively, while the maximum deformation of 3.5 mm and 3.88mm. ANSYS software in the post-processor, you can query the deformation at any point.

Blades the tank and spiral cloud Von mises stress and the stress data are shown in Figure 10 to Figure 14.

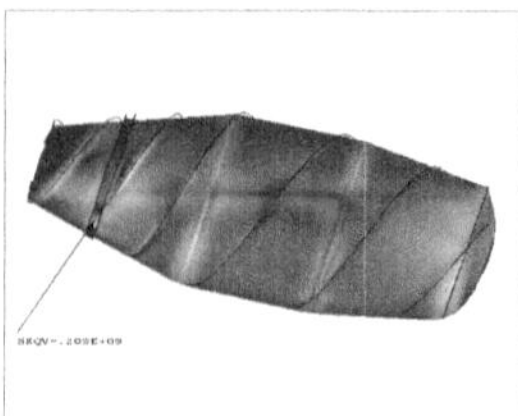

Fig. 10. Left lateral view of von Mises stress of the tank

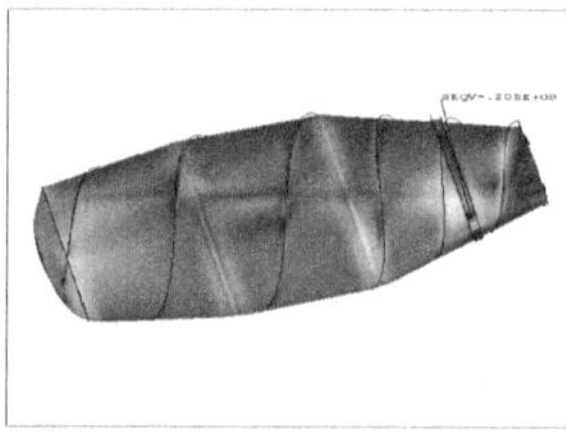

Fig. 11. Right lateral view of von Mises stress of the tank

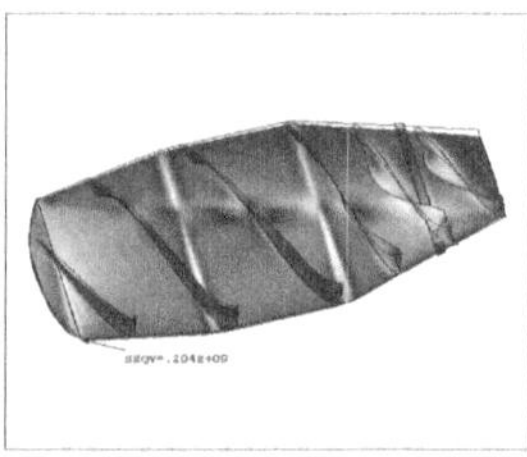

Fig. 12. Front lateral view of von Mises stress of the tank

Fig. 13. Right view of Von Mises stress inside the tank

ANSYS software in the post-processor, you can check at any point the stress and strain. If all the graphics in this chapter is set to color, according to the diagram shown in different colors can also be intuitively understand the parts of the corresponding stress value. The maximum stress value is given in a group of view above. Various views show that cylinder and blade have occurred a significant elastic

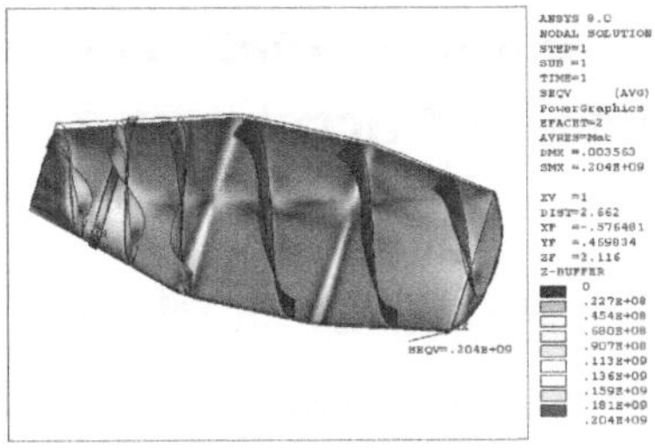

Fig. 14. Left view of Von Mises stress inside the tank

deformation. The maximum stress which occurs in the tank outside the tank with the wheel touching the rails at a maximum stress value of 209.0MPa . Von Mises stress within the tank maximum stress cone in the bottom of the tank before the intersection with the head office, the maximum stress value of 204.0MPa . Maximum stress on the spiral blade is lower than the maximum stress tanks.

The above analysis shows that the tank did not produce plastic deformation, although the large elastic deformation of the helical blade, but the stress away from the plastic deformation stress. The overall design of the tank and blade to meet the requirements, and there is room for improvement.

References

1. Jianguo, T.: Finite Element Analysis Using ANSYS 6.0. Beijing University Press (2002)
2. Game Creation Studio. Analysis and Application of APDL Parametric Finite Element Techniques. China Water Power Press (2004)
3. Moabeni, S.: Finite Element Analysis - ANSYS Theory and Applications. Electronic Industry Press (2003)
4. Xingpu, Yi, C., Guo, J.: Simulating design and model analysis of the concrete mixer-blade. Machinery Design & Manufacture (August 2007)
5. Zhai, X., Ge, J.: Optimum Design of Mixing Blade of the Concrete Truck. Mechanical Engineering & Automation (October 2007)
6. Huang, G.: Application of Finite Element-based and AYSYS. Machinery Industry Press, Beijing
7. Feng, Z.: Concrete Mixing Theory and Equipment. People's Communications Press, Beijing (2001)
8. Wei, J., Hao, M., Zhu, J.: CAD System for the Mixing Drum of Concrete Transit Vehicle. Construction Machinery and Equipment (1) (2000)
9. Du, J.: Determine the Mixer Drum Screw-Angl of Truck Mixer. Journal of Xi'an Highway University
10. Cheng, S.: Design of Concrete Mixer Truck Mixing Blade. Construction Mechanization (4) (2006)

Lateral Escape Capability Analysis with Probabilistic Pilot Model for Microburst Avoidance

Gao Zhenxing, Gu Hongbin, and Gao Zheng

Research Center of Flight Simulation and Advanced Training,
Nanjing University of Aeronautics and Astronautics, P.R. China
{Gao Zhenxing,Gu Hongbin,Gao Zheng LNCS}@Springer.com

Abstract. Low altitude wind shear presents a significant hazard to aircraft during takeoff and landing operations. Much of the prior research on aircraft escape procedures during microburst encounters has assumed that the aircraft penetrates the center of the microburst in straight flight. Based on a parameterized three-dimensional microburst model and flight dynamics model with wind effects, the lateral escape was studied. The escape strategy and occasion was studied by changing the parameters. Since single pilot's control behavior cannot stand for a group of pilots, a parameterized human pilot model was developed to simulate pilots' characters. A pilot-aircraft-microburst environment model was constructed for further study. To study the safety of lateral escape, the Monte Carlo Simulation was adopted to obtain a numerical approximation of the probability density function of the minimum altitude and F-factor. The results show that although lateral escape capability is affected by pilots' characters and microburst parameters, escape from the weaker side of the wind field is favorable than longitudinal escape.

Keywords: microburst, lateral escape, wind shear, pilot model, Monte Carlo.

1 Introduction

Low altitude wind shear, in particular the microburst, presents a significant hazard to aircraft during takeoff and landing. As far as landing is concerned, an aircraft which penetrates the centre of a microburst will initially experience an increasing headwind and consequent upward force. As the aircraft proceeds along the glide slope, the downdraft increases while the headwind shifts into a tailwind causing the aircraft to loose speed and altitude.

Most of the prior research on microburst escape strategies has focused on longitudinal escape. The FAA wind shear training aid recommended three kinds of longitudinal escape procedures which are pitch guidance, altitude guidance, and dive guidance[1]. Longitudinal escape is equivalent to the aircraft penetrating the center of the microburst. In this way, only the effect of the horizontal wind components and the vertical downburst are considered. However, with the advent of warning systems that can remotely detect microburst, the possibility of lateral maneuvering for escape should be considered [2][3].

This paper will study the escape capability of lateral maneuver. Firstly, a parameterized three-dimensional (3D) microburst model and a flight dynamics model

C. Liu, J. Chang, and A. Yang (Eds.): ICICA 2011, Part I, CCIS 243, pp. 560–567, 2011.

(FDM) with wind shear effects are built. Then a probabilistic pilot model is designed whose parameters can subject to specific probabilistic distribution. The lateral escape strategy was realized in the compensatory system of the pilot model. With the frame of "pilot-aircraft-microburst environment", the lateral escape capability was deeply studied by selecting different flight condition, microburst and pilot parameters. Furthermore, the Monte Carlo method is used to judge the robustness and adaptability of lateral guidance strategy. Based on the simulation, some results and discussion are explained in the last part of this paper.

2 Microburst Wind Shear and Flight Dynamics Modeling

The microburst model used for this study is a parameterized 3-D wind field model quoted from [4]. It is built by vortex ring and Rankine vortex principle. Given its flexibility and re-configurability, the model can be used in real time simulation. The model parameters can be described as follows:

$$\vec{\vartheta} = [x_P, y_P, z_P, \Gamma, R, r]$$

(x_p, y_p, z_p) stands for the spatial position of the model. Γ represents the strength of the microburst. R and r stand for the radius of the vortex ring and the radius of the vortex core respectively. The above parameters can define a concrete microburst wind field. The 3D characters can support lateral escape research.

A group of nonlinear equation of motion describing the aircraft dynamics in the 3D space is derived from [5]. It is a general dynamics model with wind effects. Besides, the simulation used a nonlinear aerodynamic model of the Boeing747. The thrust performance of JT-9D engine can also be simulated by data interpolation. Given that the fuselage and wingspan are comparable with the microburst wind field, the wind gradient effects should be taken into consideration on FDM [6].

The whole model can be described by the following figure:

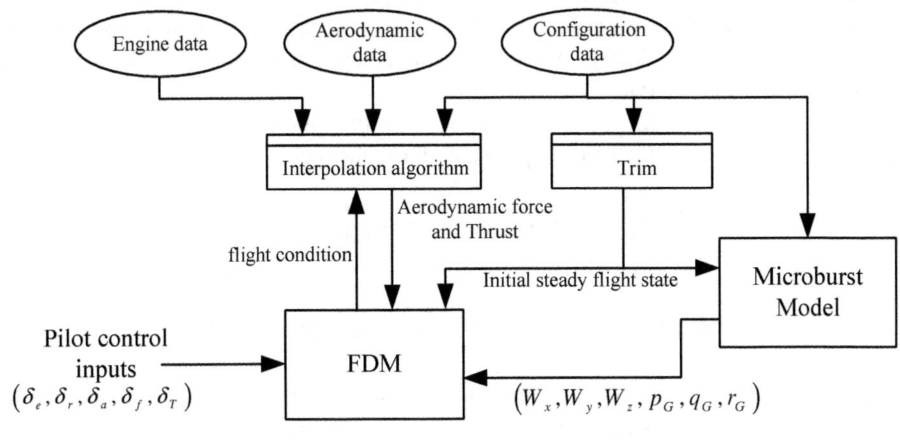

Fig. 1. Microburst and Flight Dynamics Model

3 Probabilistic Pilot Modeling

A time domain pilot model was used in this paper for it considers the actual human processing characteristics [7]. The effect of pilot model is applied to the aileron and rudder deflection. As far as lateral escape is concerned, the pilot needs to do nothing on elevator deflections. Furthermore, maximum throttle settings are also prerequisite for any escape strategies.

3.1 Single Pilot Modeling

A single pilot model was constructed as shown in Fig. 2. Several simulation blocks were adopted to describe the pilots' characteristics:

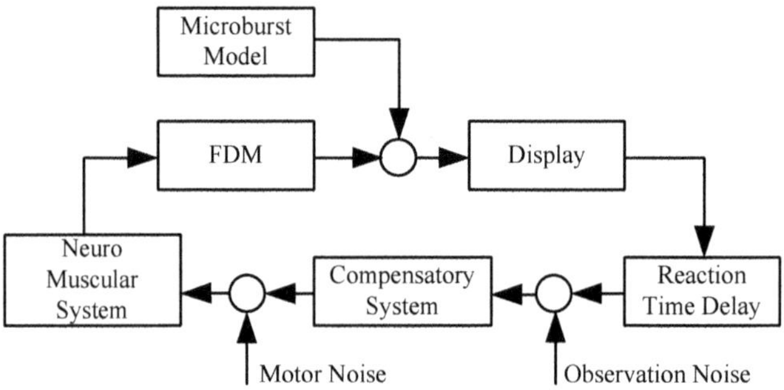

Fig. 2. Structure of Pilot Model

The Display block forms the medium by which the pilot observes the instantaneous state of the aircraft. Pilot's decision is based on his experience and the readings of all kinds of flight instruments. Various sources of error such as observation and instruction error will be included in this procedure.

Reaction time delay describes pilot's observation delay, processing and decision making delay, etc. Evidently, the overall time delay depends on the pilot's training, experience and knowledge.

Compensatory system, which forms the core of pilot model, is analogous to an automatic controller. For lateral escape, a coordinate turn controller is designed as follows:

$$\delta_a = K_{P\phi}(\phi-\phi_c)+K_{D\phi}(\dot{\phi}-\dot{\phi}_c)+K_{I\phi}\int_0^t(\phi-\phi_c)d\tau \tag{1}$$

$$\delta_r = K_{P\psi}(\psi-\psi_c)+K_{D\psi}(\dot{\psi}-\dot{\psi}_c)+K_{I\psi}\int_0^t(\psi-\psi_c)d\tau \tag{2}$$

Neuromuscular dynamics system characterizes the personality, skill and experience of each pilot. Besides, a kind of motor noise is caused due to natural factors such as physical stability, mental stress and intensity of concentration.

3.2 Probabilistic Pilot Modeling

As stated earlier, single pilot may not be sufficient to make decisions in case of research study that might involve pilots with a wide variation in characters. In such cases, there is a need incorporate a model for not a single pilot, but a group of pilots. To model a group of pilots, the variations can be expressed as random variables with suitable probability density functions.

According to single pilot model, the parameters that will vary depending on the level of pilot's training, experience, mental state, are as follows:

(1) The time constant τ , in the reaction time delay.

(2) The time constant τ_N , in the neuromuscular dynamics system.

(3) The noise power n_o in the observation noise.

(4) The noise power n_m in the motor noise.

Even in case of a pilot with the best performance, the parameters listed above will not be zero. These parameters in a group of pilots are modeled by Rayleigh distribution. Rayleigh random variable is a good model for measurement error in a number of different physical situations generally [8].

With regard to τ , based on the prior experience with the behavior of most pilots, it is known that varying the parameter τ from 0.15s to 0.3s models the entire range of pilots encountered in practice [9]. Similarly, the range of values for τ_N can be selected as 0.1s to 0.2s.

It is assumed that the maximum observation error does not exceed 5% of the corresponding command values. When it comes to lateral escape strategy, the noise power for the roll angle and pitch angle measurements are 0.0017 rad^2 .

The limits of the motor noise depend on the training, experience, and the emotional stability. In our study, the value of noise power for rudder and aileron deflections, is assumed to be equal to that of corresponding observation noise.

4 Monte Carlo Simulation of Microburst Escape

Based on microburst model and FDM of Boeing747, together with the probabilistic pilot model, the lateral escape strategy is examined in this paper. In Fig. 3, the real lines show the trimmed approaching flight state. The microburst was set to locate near the runway with the parameters [7000, 2000, 2000, 10, 2000, 500]. Assuming that the aircraft probes the microburst at 30s, the pilot would control the aircraft to change its azimuth with a roll angle of 13.5deg. From Fig. 3 we can see the flight states change acutely when encountering the wind field including crosswind, downburst, tailwind or headwind. During the escape procedure, the wind vectors the aircraft encountered are shown in Fig. 4.

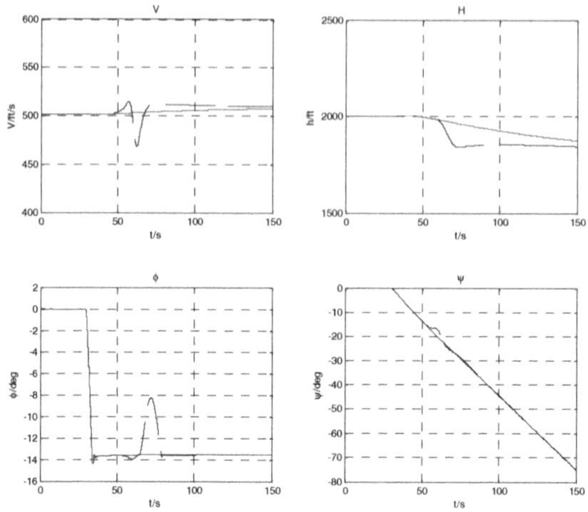

Fig. 3. Flight through Microburst with fixed Control

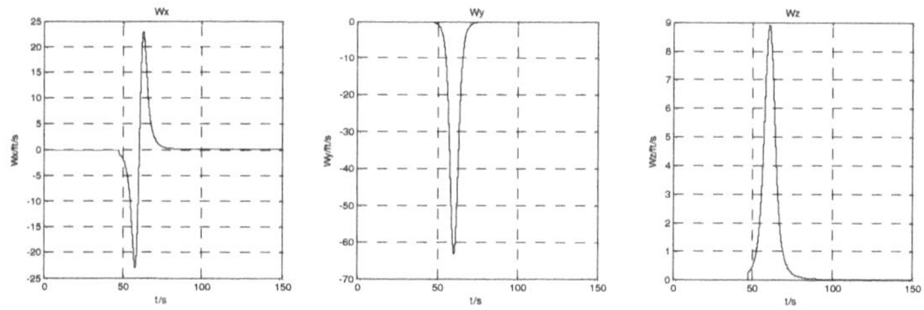

Fig. 4. Wind Vector during lateral Escape

4.1 Microburst Escape Simulation

Effects of lateral escape occasions were simulated in Fig.5.

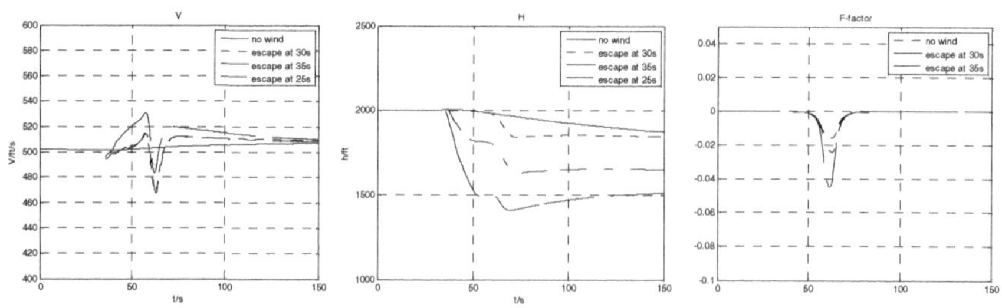

Fig. 5. Lateral Escape with Different Occasion

The first picture shows the airspeed, the middle one shows the altitude while the latter shows the F-factor variation during escape. Evidently, when detecting the wind shear, both lateral and longitudinal escape should be adopted as soon as possible. Earlier escape is advantaged to flight safety.

Fig. 6 shows the effects of lateral offset on lateral escape. According to radar detection, pilot could make the aircraft escape from the weak side of the microburst. Under this circumstance, the aircraft would be much safer by escaping from the weaker side than penetrating directly from the center field. Once the wind field is detected clearly, lateral escape is a better choice than longitudinal maneuver.

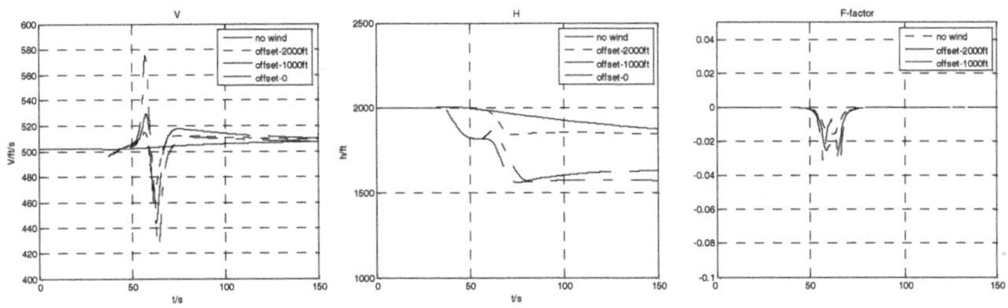

Fig. 6. Lateral Escape with Different Lateral Offset

4.2 Monte Carlo Simulation

Section 4.1 only shows a single simulation with specifically microburst, flight and pilot parameters. Single simulation cannot be proved that the aircraft will or will not escape the wind field affirmatively. So a Monte Carlo method was used to get some statistical laws for the escape capability of lateral escape.

The safety of escape strategies can be qualified by the minimum altitude the aircraft flies during escape maneuver and the F-factor [10]. Both $h_{\min}$ and F-factor would become random variables since both the microburst and pilot parameters are random variables. Obviously, it is difficult to formulate $h_{\min}$ and F-factor to be an algebraic function of the microburst and pilot parameters. Therefore, the Monte Carlo simulation is adopted to obtain a numerical approximation of the probability density function of the two safety index.

Both $h_{\min}$ and F-factor depend on the initial condition at which the aircraft enters the microburst, the parameters of the microburst, and the guidance strategies. Hence,

$$h_{\min} = h_{\min}(\vec{h}_0, \vec{\vartheta}, \vec{K}) \tag{3}$$

$$F = F(\vec{h}_0, \vec{\vartheta}, \vec{K}) \tag{4}$$

In this paper, $\vec{h}_0$ stands for the flight states as follows:

$$\vec{h}_0 = \left[V_x, V_y, V_z, p, q, r, \phi, \theta, \psi, x_E, y_E, z_E\right]^T$$

The microburst parameters including:

$$\vec{\vartheta} = [x_P, y_P, z_P, \Gamma, R, r]$$

And the pilot parameters are:

$$\vec{K} = [\tau, \tau_N, n_o, n_m]^T$$

The probability distribution function of $h_{\min}$ can be defined as:

$$F_{h_{\min}} = Probability(h_{\min} \le h) \tag{5}$$

Note that $F_{h_{\min}}(0) = \Pr(h_{\min} \le 0)$ is the probability of crash. In this study, the microburst strength, Γ is assumed to be Rayleigh distributed because it is utilized to fit the statistical data from JAWS [6]. Other parameters subject to uniform probability density functions. By practice, the pilot parameters used in this paper are [9]:

$$[\tau, \tau_N, n_o, n_m]^T = [0.225, 0.15, 0.007, 3]^T$$

The probabilistic density functions of $h_{\min}$ and F-factor can be acquired based on thousands of experiments, as shown in Fig. 7:

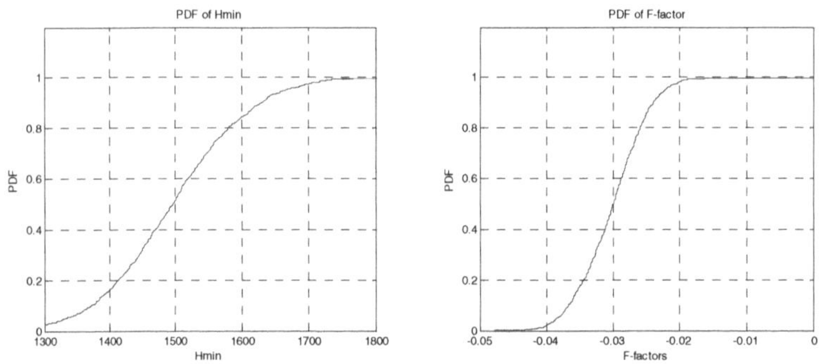

Fig. 7. Probability Density Function of $h_{\min}$ and F-factor

5 Conclusions

In this paper, the escape capability and safety of lateral escape was studied. With the development of wind shear detection technology, lateral escape may be much safer than longitudinal escape by escaping from the weaker side of the wind field. As far as any escape strategies are concerned, make escape maneuvering as soon as possible is much more advantaged.

According to the research by Monte Carlo simulation, lateral escape is affected by the following factors:

(1) Pilot characters, including their skills, experiences, knowledge, emotion, etc;
(2) Microburst conditions, including its outburst dimensions, the strength, etc;

Besides, there are many kinds of unknown factors affecting the escape performance. By Monte Carlo Simulation, the numerical approximation of some key factors could be acquired instead of complicated reasoning or flight tests.

Acknowledgments. This work was supported by postdoctoral foundation (1001013C) and National Natural Science foundation (61039002).

References

1. Dogan, A.: Guidance Strategies for Microburst Escape. ProQuest Dissertations and Theses, AAI9977147 (2000)
2. Visser, H.G.: Lateral Escape Guidance Strategies for Microburst Windshear Encounters. Journal of Aircraft 34(4), 515–521 (1997)
3. Visser, H.G.: Minimax Optimal Control Analysis of Lateral Escape Maneuvers for Microburst Encounters. Journal of Guidance, Control, and Dynamics 20(2), 370–376 (1997)
4. Gao, Z., Gu, H.: Research on Modeling of Microburst for Real Time Flight Simulation. Journal of System Simulation 20(23), 6524–6528 (2008) (in Chinese)
5. Brian, L.S., Frank, L.L.: Aircraft Control and Simulation. John Wiley and Sons, Canada (2003)
6. Gao, Z., Gu, H., Hui, L.: Real-Time Simulation of Large Aircraft Flight through Microburst Wind Field. Chinese Journal of Aeronautics 22(5), 459–466 (2009)
7. Schroeder, J.A., Grant, P.R.: Pilot Behavioral Observations in Motion Flight Simulation. In: AIAA Modeling and Simulation Conference and Exhibit (2010)
8. Dogan, A., Kaewchay, K.: Probabilistic Human Pilot Approach: Application to Microburst Escape Maneuver. Journal of Guidance, Control, and Dynamics 30(2), 357–369 (2007)
9. Gestwa, M., Michael Bauschat, J.: Development of a Fuzzy-Controller with a State Machine as a Cognitive Pilot Model for an ILS Approach. In: AIAA Modeling and Simulation Conference and Exhibit (2007)
10. Beukers, J.T., Stroosma, O., Pool, D.M.: Investigation into Pilot Perception and Control During Decrab Maneuvers in Simulated Flight. Journal of Guidance, Control, and Dynamics 33(4), 1048–1063 (2010)

On the Development of Engineering Management and the Education of Such Personnel in This Area

Jiefang Tian, Xingguo Wang, and Wei Ming

College of Civil Engineering And Architecture, Hebei United University.
063009 Tangshan, China

Abstract. Engineering management is a new discipline with a lot of development potential. This major is aimed at producing advanced management personnel of versatility. Our country's membership of WTO has set a higher demand for such personnel. This paper discusses the characteristics of Engineering management, the current situation facing this discipline, and the problems unsolved so far, and on such basis, the solution and strategies in coping with the problems.

Keywords: engineering management, discipline development, education of personnel.

1 Introduction

Although Engineering Management is closely connected with Engineering Technology, Engineering Management is more of an independent discipline, and is not a subordinate to Engineering Technologies. Both are important and have equal status. For Engineering Management to be classified into Management Science and Engineering is out of the consideration convenience of management of research and study for such majors, because of the identical theoretical basis of management science. The parallel approach to the two-division of management and engineering management shows the recognition of the importance of management on the part of the state.

2 Implication and Characteristics of Engineering Management

Engineering management is a cross-disciplinary and complex major, uniting both "hard" and "soft" aspects of engineering mechanism. Compared with general management disciplines, engineering management has the following characteristics [1]:

(1) There is an emphasis on the acquisition from courses of engineering technologies. This is so because of the special characters existing building engineering areas and the related products. To be specific, these characters relate to engineering charting, home building engineering, building construction techniques, project pricing, materials, equipments, mechanics, as well as project measurement and management software courses. A good command of this approach requires an involvement a series of practices, such as project measurement practice, the design and home engineering,

C. Liu, J. Chang, and A. Yang (Eds.): ICICA 2011, Part I, CCIS 243, pp. 568–573, 2011.

project pricing. In this way what is learned in classrooms can find the right subjects in reality.

(2) Another aspect of these characters is professional trait bordering on economics, management and law. There are only a few courses, such as management science, marketing, strategies, which are similar to general course of economics, management and law. A great many of courses have to do with project management and cross-disciplinary capacity, such as engineering economics, building construction accounting, engineering price estimation, estate accounting, management of construction enterprises, claim on international engineering and the dealing with FIDIC contracts

(3) A third character is the cultivation of ability to work on self. The filed-practice level of teaching for this course is decided on requirements and aims, thus the education plan comprising observation practice, production practice, course design, application of computer technology, final-term practice, semi-operation of project, final-term design and thesis writing. There can be 40 weeks of requirement for the completion of the course, amounting to one fourths of the whole campus study time. This is not only necessary but also a guarantee of the practical capability.

3 Current Situations Facing the Major of Engineering Management at Home and Abroad

3.1 Oversea Situations

In the developed countries and regions engineering management of high education has undergone a half-century of building and development, and has become a relatively independent, stable and mature course. The Florida University of USA has had this course set since the 30s of the last century. By 1994, more than 80 universities and departments have included engineering management, though they are not industry and commerce oriented. CIOB is a special association related to construction management in Britain, and so far more than 50 schools have been assessed by this institution. All the schools mentioned above have provided construction management major, independent of Industry and Commerce Management School. In Reading University, Britain, for example, has set up urban development college, under which there are department of Construction Engineering Management, Estate Study, Geography. The University of Hong Kong has established Building Construction and Estate Studies, while the Singapore National University Construction Management and Estate Studies.

In these countries and regions there is a focus on the training and evaluation of construction management personnel. In each country and region there is a professional association to judge and qualify the professionals. These professional associations, including the British CIOB, RICS, FIDIC, ICE, guarantee the quality of the professionals.

3.2 The Current Situations of EM at Home

In China about 200 higher education institutions have had EM set as an undergraduate pursuit. There are pioneers, such as Tongji University, Tianjin University, the Southeast University and Harbin Industries University. Most other university which have done so started the plan after 1999. In this sense, EM is a new specialty. Among those which have done so, there are both complex-discipline universities and single-oriented colleges. On the basis of EM undergraduate pursuit, there are cases in close connection with Economics Management School, such as the practice of Tongji University; there are also those which collaborate with Civil Engineering School, which is the practice of Southeast University. Still others have established their own Economics Management School or set aside such a major, which is the case of Chongqing University. Also on the EM basis, some universities have specified their specialties, and have formed their own prominent ways, such is the case with the International EM orientation, Tianjin University. There are also universities who have found it unnecessary to specify those majors. [3]

4 Issues Related to Personnel Training and Education

4.1 Shortage of Highly Qualified Personnel

For a long time it is wrongly believed that building construction industries are labor intensive, and that highly technical personnel are only necessary in conducting large-scale and very complicated projects, and that since most people work on site, doing labor work, they do not need much education. Such belief leads to a negligence of EM personnel training. Such being the case, it is not surprised that low quality projects, construction time delay, investment out of control, the failure of the developers' intentions, the chaotic and disorderly competitions are prevalent in building construction markets. Developed countries have done a lot to ensure that the involved personnel have the necessary training in consultation and contract. They have already established an advantage for themselves for being very competitive. They pay particular attention to the education and assessment of such professionals. Various associations and boards have been established to qualify these people and their quality.

4.2 Problems Facing the Training of EM Personnel in Higher Institutions

(1) Vague orientation for the majors

Viewing the origin and growth of this major in universities around China; such a major is generally placed in schools of management or civil engineering. Some universities have an independent EM. Related information gathered from Australia, GB, Singapore and Hong Kong indicates a tendency of independent discipline, in a management department, or construction environment department, or simply a branch of architecture or civil engineering. Without any exception there are major of management in these universities. Information gather from questionnaires shows that most experts in this filed are in favor of an independent management major or part of a civil engineering arrangement.

(2) Low quality of a EM teaching team

As a new academic major, most of the higher institutions are fully ready with qualified teaching staff. Excellent academic leaders are even greater a problem. Besides, the structure of age, specialties, learning resources are either insufficient or unreasonably allocated.

(3) Backward and inadequate experiment conditions for EM teaching

The idea of EM education is immature and still on experiment stage, with poor and inadequate teaching facilities. To a large extent, the lab construction meant for EM teaching is still a bottle neck and the people for this end are perplexed as to where to go. Such indecision and confusion will surely lead to a stagnant situation for EM lab development and construction, and ultimately affects the undergraduate education of EM students.

(4) The practice stage of EM teaching being loose and inefficient

According to a survey made on the universities which have provided EM courses, most universities have done more about theoretical teaching and learning than practical teaching. So practical training remains a gap in most places.

5 Strategies for Consolidating and Managing EM Personnel

5.1 Being Aware of the Characteristic of the Discipline as the First Step to Specialty Profession Development

EM is cross-over discipline bordering on civil engineering, management and economics. The discipline of EM should be advanced in the direction of management science and construction science. It also overlaps with the science of economics and that of management. It is necessary to balance the relationship of the three disciplines in order to develop in depth and breath. It is also necessary to upgrade the structure of knowledge system, so that the special ways of EM can be formed, to facilitate discipline construction.

5.2 Formulating Featured Education Plan for the Undergraduate Syllabus

The formulation of the syllabus should be made in accordance to the practical requirements of the markets, an emphasis on students' operational and practicing capability. Furthermore the long-term learning on the part of students is to be another priority. There is a focus on the education of certification of the construction field, namely certified consultants, certified pricing engineers, certified supervising engineers, certified builders, and certified estate estimation specialists.

5.3 Upgrading the Teachers' Structure of EM Major

(1) It is necessary to establish a high-quality, competent EM staff. For this purpose the selection of academic elites, one or two persons, and a competent team.

(2) Attention should be paid to ladder development of teaching staff, made up the old, the young and the middle age teachers.

(3) For individual teacher development, he or she will have to be equipped with specialized theories and knowledge, and rich practical experience. Such a person should be able to combine classroom teaching with research, and raise the level of teaching through research.

5.4 Improvement of the Lab Facilities to Enhance Teaching

(1) Toward the new major there should be a right attitude, that EM major is not a pure classroom activity, therefore experiment means should be established for personnel training.

(2) The investment on EM majors should be long-term and constant, for the purpose of the staff construction. The labs are not there to meet the routine assessment from state or higher academic levels. Rather it should serve the right purpose for teaching and personnel development. There should be preparation of long time development, patience, and resource accumulation.

(3) The specific ways and features are to be formed in developing lab facilities and resources. The aims and purposes are to be withheld so a practicable curriculum is formed to ensure classroom learning and filed practice. Plans are to be made concerning lab teaching and conditions.

5.5 The Improvement of EM Practice and on-Site Teaching

(1) The process of EM majors includes practice, design, and project operation observation. The process should be integrated and treated as a whole.

(2) The guidance of practical teaching can be tailored with the guidance from students' own tutors and also from tutor of other schools. In this way social resources can be made full use of. At the same time, classroom teaching and practical filed learning are brought together, so that the quality of teaching for EM is improved.

(3) The focus on outside school filed learning is also needed.

References

1. Jin, C.: On the Development Engineering Management for Undergraduate Students in China. For Construction Enterprises' Improvement 26(4), 79–81 (2005)
2. Ren, H., et al.: Future and Prospect for Engineering Management, vol. (6), pp. 33–35. Higher Education Press (2001)
3. Dai, Z., Yang, P.: On Training and Education of Engineering Management Personnel at Undergraduate Level, vol. 15(3), pp. 38–42. Higher Education Press (2006)

4. Li, S., Liu, M.: Where Engineering Management Goes in Face of Merging Situations for Higher Education Institutions. Construction Structure (10), 10–13 (2000)
5. Jiang, H.: On the Training Mechanism for Applied Engineering Management Personnel. Xu Zhou Engineering Journal 21(2), 76–79 (2006)
6. Xiao, Y.: Practitioner Certification System and the Training of Engineering Management Personnel, vol. 15(1), pp. 32–35. Higher Education Press (2006)
7. Zhang, X.: A Discussion of the Curriculum Design for Project Management. China Construction Education 1(4), 35–37 (2010)
8. Zhang, L., Li, H., Liu, Y.: An Analysis and Survey on the Current Situation and prospect of Project Management Personnel. Science and Technology Information 23(7), 56–59 (2009)
9. Wu, Y.: A Study of Practice Teaching Reform for Project Management Major. The Journal of Science and Technology Institute of Hunan 8(5), 40–41 (2010)
10. Guo, S.: On Situation and Strategy for the Education of Project Management Personnel, vol. 5(3), pp. 43–46. Higher Education Press (2009)

Research on the Urban Ecological Bearing Capacity of Resource-Based Cities----Tangshan as an Example

Ma Jingzhong

Department of Scientific Research and Production, Tangshan College,
Tangshan, Hebei 063000, China
mjz04013@sina.com

Abstract. Ecological bearing capacity is one of the research methods which can be used to study the sustainability of a city's economy and society. Bearing exponents, as a research method on ecological bearing capacity, have the advantage of conciseness and comparability. The bearing exponents of Tangshan between 2006 and 2010 are calculated based on Tangshan's resource and environment data. The results indicate that Tangshan's overall bearing capacity has been improved in recent years with abundant water and land resources. Still, transportation and environment call for greater improvement.

Keywords: Eecological Bearing Capacity, Sustainable Development.

1 Introduction

As the over-exploitation of natural resources and the damage to the environment intensifies, it is recognized that resources are limited, environmental capacity is limited, and human activity and urban development will be subjected to the constraints of the resources and the environment. The concept of bearing capacity, which is originally a mechanical concept, has been gradually introduced into the study of urban development [1]. Bearing capacity can be better quantified. Therefore, it's been widely studied and used. Resource bearing capacity, environmental bearing capacity, population bearing capacity and other ecological bearing capacities become research hotspots. Tangshan, as a resource-based city, has been developing rapidly in recent years. However, the heavy-industry-based industrial structure exerts enormous pressure on the sustainable development of Tangshan's economy. A scientific evaluation of its ecological bearing capacity is of great practical significance for Tangshan, and also has important reference value for other similar cities in China. In this paper, bearing exponents, which are easily comparable, are used to study the basic condition of Tangshan's ecological bearing capacity. Hopefully, it can provide a scientific reference for the urban development of Tangshan.

2 City Bearing Capacity Evaluation Method

The research methods of ecological carrying capacity mainly includes support, supply and demand analysis, concept model method, ecological footprint method and index

C. Liu, J. Chang, and A. Yang (Eds.): ICICA 2011, Part I, CCIS 243, pp. 574–579, 2011.

system method etc., but there is no unified research method currently. There are also other studies employing methods such as value analysis method, system dynamics model and multi-objective decision analysis method [2-6]. There is not much research about the ecological bearing capacity of Tangshan; LuYugong, ShiBaojuan [7] constructed the Tangshan city ecosystem evaluation model based on the method of evaluation index model, and WuQinglin, GaoRuihua, LiuGuifang [8]carried out related researches about water resources carrying capacity in Tangshan. This paper adopts the simple bearing capacity measurement method based on the evaluation model comparable principle. The measurement methods are as follows:[9]

(1) single factor evaluation
Bearing index equals to the ratio between the capacity of the existing elements and precaution level, say, the comparison between the bearing capacity of the existing elements and the precaution index, and then judge the level of the bearing capacity.

Bearing index calculation formula is as follows:

Bearing index = existing element numerical/elements precaution value bearing capacity (elements) (type 1 standard bearing capacity)

Among them, precaution index refers to precaution condition of the elements of the bearing capacity. precaution index values' change has a direct impact on the bearing capacity index. Concrete meanings of the elements of the bearing index are shown in table 1.

System /load index

The water resources bearing capacity/

water resources bearing index = per capita useable water resources/average water consumption per person

The bearing capacity of land

Land bearing index = per capita construction land use/health per capita construction land level

Traffic bearing capacity

traffic load bearing capacity index = city traffic flow situation/theory of saturated

Environmental bearing capacity

environment bearing capacity index (state) = / present situation emissions (pressure)

(2) Comprehensive evaluation
Comprehensive index is one of the basic form of total index, it is a method of comprehensive evaluation which calculates the comprehensive value of the index system on the basis of individual indexes and the various index weighted average,. Because of the differences in the values and units of each index numerical calculation, this research should use statistical methods to standardize the index statistics to make statistics comparable. The index values after standardization should be weighted by analytical hierarchy process together with summation of comprehensive carrying capacity.

Comprehensive index method evaluation model of computation formula is as follows:

$$F = \sum_{i=1}^{n} w_i f_i$$

Type: F score for comprehensive carrying capacity, wi for the weights of the I indicators, fi standardization value. The greater the index weight, the larger the influence is on the factors. the greater the F (comprehensive score) is, the greater the bearing capacity is, namely city population, social economy bearing capacity .

3 Weight Index Evaluation

There are many methods to determine the weight index, such as Delphi method, the AHP method, the comparative method, A.J.K lee, least-square method, entropy weight coefficient method and so on. This study adopts the AHP method which can better reflect the principle of the combination of the quality and the quantity to determine the index weight. The basic procedure is as follows:

a. Tectonic judgment matrix

The questionnaire is used to investigate the index, factors ad points on the investigation, the importance of factors to the same level of evaluation, and comparative judgment matrix A={aij}.

Table 1. Connotation of each element bearing index

	A1	A2	A3	·······	An
A1	a11	a12	a13	·······	a1n
A2	a21	a22	a23	·······	a2n
⋮	⋮	⋮	⋮	·······	⋮
An	an1	an2	an3	·······	ann

The evaluation rule of aij is magnitude scale method by A.L.Saaty. The importance of each factor is rated into 9 levels, and it is shown below.

Table 2. Saaty's 9 scale method and meaning

Scale	Meaning
1	Factor i is as important as j
3	Factor i is slightly more important than j
5	Factor i is slightly much more important than j
7	Factor i is slightly far more important than j
9	Factor i is absolutely much more important than j
2,4,6,8	The median value between two adjacent judgments
Reciprocal	indicates the ratio between i and j is equal to the reciprocal of the ration of j and i

b. calculate $W_i = \frac{\left(\prod_{j=1}^{n} a_{ij}\right)^{\frac{1}{n}}}{\sum_{i=1}^{n}\left(\prod_{j=1}^{n} a_{ij}\right)^{\frac{1}{n}}}$; Wi0 can be got through the normalization of Wi.

(Formula 3)

c. consistency index calculation C.I.:

$$C.I. = \frac{\lambda_{\max} - n}{n-1}, 其中 \lambda_{\max} \approx \frac{1}{n}\sum_{i=1}^{n}\frac{\sum_{j=1}^{n} a_{ij}W_j}{W_i}. \quad \text{(Formula 4)}$$

d. calculation consistency proportion C.R.

$$\text{C.R.} = \frac{\text{C.I.}}{\text{R.I.}} \text{(C.R.<0.1 namely to meet consistency requirements)} \quad \text{(Formula 5)}$$

The average consistency index can be got from the table.

The judgment matrix of the index system and the weight calculation results are shown in table 3.

Table 3. Evaluation index weights

Urban comprehensive bearing capacity	Water resource bearing capacity	Land resource bearing resource	Transportation bearing capacity	Environment bearing capacity
Water resource bearing capacity	1	1/2	2	3
Land resource bearing resource	2	1	3	5
Transportation bearing capacity	1/2	1/3	1	2
Environment bearing capacity	1/3	1/5	1/2	1
Single weight	0.2717	0.4832	0.1569	0.0882

λmax=4.0145; CI=0.0048; RI=0.9; CR=0.0054<0.1 namely to meet consistency requirements.

4 Bearing Capacity Evaluation of Tangshan City

Based on the statistical yearbook of Tangshan city as well as the investigation data from the Bureau of Land and Resources, the Weather Bureau, Water Authority, and other units, this article selects the relevant data from 2006 to 2010 and makes calculation accordingly, thus gaining the result of the bearing capacity evaluation of Tangshan city, which is shown in the following table 4.

Table 4. Bearing Capacity Evaluation of Tangshan Resources (2006-2010)

year	comprehensive bearing capacity	bearing capacity of water resources	bearing capacity of land	bearing capacity of traffic	bearing capacity of environment
2006	1.38	2.61	1.12	0.62	0.36
2007	1.43	2.85	1.13	0.52	0.40
2008	1.73	3.90	1.17	0.47	0.41
2009	1.77	3.90	1.22	0.39	0.70
2010	1.67	3.46	1.28	0.31	0.76

Following is the direct statistical description which is made respectively from the single factor score and the comprehensive score of the bearing capacity. According to the score of the four essential elements of the bearing capacity of Tangshan city in table 4, the bar graph of the single factor score is made as shown in figure 1 below.

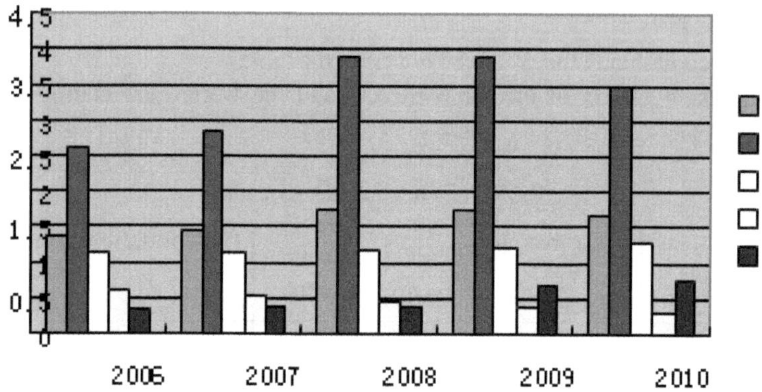

Fig. 1. Bearing Capacity Level of Tangshan City (2006-2010)

As can be seen from the graph, the bearing capacity of transportation and environment are the main factors to restrain the development of Tangshan city. The bearing capacity of land has been relatively stable, and it is basically able to meet the development needs of the city. In addition, the bearing capacity of water resources is higher, which indicates that the amount of water can better support the development of Tangshan. While, known from the research, the water structure that lays too much emphasis on the groundwater has also brought great pressure upon the urban development. This, on the other hand, reflects the water-use features of such a city with abundant water and land resources.

This shows the evaluation results of the bearing capacity of Tangshan in recent years, and the overall situation is relatively optimistic. Especially since 2008, the comprehensive bearing capacity of Tangshan has been greatly improved. And it is closely related to the change of economic development mode influenced by the financial crisis.

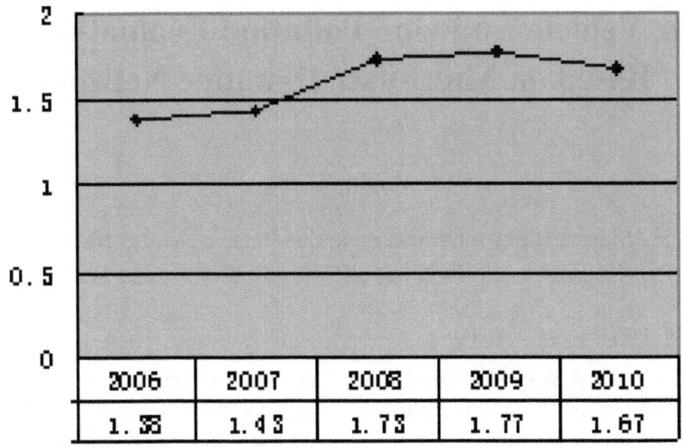

Fig. 2. Comprehensive Bearing Capacity of Tangshan City (2006-2010)

5 Conclusion

This paper measures the bearing capacity of Tangshan city (2006 - 2010) with the exponents. The research shows that: the comprehensive bearing capacity of Tangshan has elevated somewhat recent years; the bearing capacity of water resources is comparatively good, which proves that Tangshan is a city with abundant water and land resources; the bearing capacity of land resources is more steady, which can satisfy the needs for the urban development, while the bearing capacity of traffic is hard to meet the demand and needs to be improved; the bearing capacity of environment is elevated on a larger scale, but it still faces huge pressure.

References

1. Xu, L., Yang, Z.: Urban ecosystem carrying capacity, vol. (1), pp. 1–2. Normal University Press, Beijing (2011)
2. Hoekstra, A.Y., Chapagain, A.K.: The water foot-prints of Morocco and the Netherlands: Global water use as a result of domestic consumption of agricultural commodities. Ecological Economics 64(1), 143–151 (2007)
3. Gerbens-Leenes, P.W., Hoekstra, A.Y., Van Der Meer, T.: The water footprint of energy from biomass: Aquantitative assessment and consequences of an increasing share of bio - energy in energy supply. Ecological Economics 68(4), 1052–1060 (2009)
4. Hubacek, K., Guan, D., Barrett, J., et al.: Environmental implications of urbanization and lifestyle change in China: Ecological and water footprints. Journal of Cleaner Production 17, 1241–1248 (2009)
5. Wang, Y.: Beijing ecological carrying capacity and sustainable development research. Beijing University of Mining PhD thesis (6), 1-16 (2010)
6. Xie, G., Cao, S., Lu, C.: Chinese ecological carrying capacity research, vol. (10), pp. 272–298. Science Press (2010)
7. Lu, Y., Shi, B.: Tangshan city ecosystem carrying capacity asssessment. Hebei Polytechnic University Journal (2), 102–105 (2009)
8. Wu, Q., Gao, R., Liu, G.: Analysis of ecological carrying capacity of Tangshan water resources. Hebei Water Conservation (1), 80–81 (2008)

Motor Vehicle Emission Pollution Evaluation Model Based on Multi-user Dynamic Network

Aiping Lian

Beijing Municipal Environmental Protection Bureau, Beijing, 100048, China
aiplian@sohu.com

Abstract. This paper established the urban road vehicle emission pollution evaluation model based on multi-user dynamic network traffic flow distribution, this model used the method of unit cell transfer, simulated mixed models of microcosmic running characteristics on the urban traffic network, and at the same time, it realized the dynamic network traffic flow of the users optimal distribution, it also can output the network traffic flow when reached to the users optimal operation state, each section and all kinds of models in every time, every area of the speed and flow, by combining exhaust emission model to analyze on network the motor vehicle exhaust emission pollution condition.

Keywords: multi-user, dynamic network traffic flow distribution, urban road, vehicle emission pollution evaluation.

1 Introduction

With the acceleration of urbanization process and the development of the car industry, motor vehicle quantities rapid growth, the road exhaust pollution are intensifying, road traffic environment problem are increasingly, now to control vehicle emissions pollution has become a focus of the social concern. There are three major types in all kinds of vehicle emission pollution control method at present. First, through the motor vehicle design and manufacture technology, and improve pavement characteristics to reduce pollution discharge; Second, through each level road layout, and the building setting reach to reduce in specified area of vehicle emission pollution degree goals; Three, through the traffic control and management measures to realize the control of vehicle emission pollution. Among them, the first and second class measures have been as main ways and research is more, but by the experiences of developed countries, its existing technology has reached or come close to the limit, emission reduction potential is extremely limited; While the third kind of measure at the present research is less, using the modern intelligent transportation improvement ease and improve the traffic environment pollution methods are beginning to be taken seriously, thus it become a key-point research of control vehicle emission pollution.

Therefore, in view of the current urban road transportation exhaust pollution problems, this paper using intelligent transportation system (ITS) improve traffic management and control to improve the efficiency of traffic and the alleviation and

C. Liu, J. Chang, and A. Yang (Eds.): ICICA 2011, Part I, CCIS 243, pp. 580–587, 2011.

improve the traffic environment pollution theory and method, by combining the road traffic flow model with the motor vehicle exhaust emissions model, it established city road motor vehicle emission pollution evaluation model based on multi-user dynamic network traffic flow distribution, this model used the method of unit cell transfer, simulated mixed models of microcosmic running characteristics on the urban traffic network, and at the same time, it realized the dynamic network traffic flow of the users optimal distribution, it also can output the network traffic flow when reached to the users optimal operation state, each section and all kinds of models in every time, every area of the speed and flow, by combining exhaust emission model to analyze on network the motor vehicle exhaust emission pollution condition. The model can not only provide real-time network at each section and each local points of the traffic emissions pollution condition, also provided the theory and the method for the user optimal control policy caused environmental effect, in order to realize the goal that using ITS to users provided the most optimal route guidance thereby control and reduce the goal of vehicle exhaust pollution.

2 Based on Multi-user Dynamic Network Traffic Flow Distribution Model

First established based on micro road traffic flow of multi-user dynamic network traffic distribution model, using CTM model unit cell transmission method, depicting multi-user of mixed traffic flow micro operating characteristics, and carrying the network multi-user traffic flow through dynamical optimum allocation, enabling the network traffic flow in time and space to realize the optimal distribution, all kinds of users the best travel impedance, thus reducing network congestion, and controlling motor vehicle exhaust emission pollution.

2.1 Symbol Definition

In order to describe the multi-user dynamic network traffic flow model, at first introduces the following variables.

$u_a^m(t)$ is the inflow of the type m users entering into road section a at the time of t ,

$u_a^{sm}(t)$ is the inflow of the type m users entering into road section a at the time of t and reach to the point s .

$U_a^m(t)$ is the accumulated inflow of the type m users entering into road section a at the time of t .

$O_a^m(t)$ is the accumulated outflow of the type m users entering into road section a at the time of t .

$o_a^m(t)$ is the outflow of the type m users leaving off road section a at the time of t .

$X_a^m(t)$ is the vehicle number on the road section a at the time of t

$X_a^{sm}(t)$ is the vehicle number of the type m users leaving off road section a at the time of t and reach to the point s.

$g_l^{sm}(t)$ is the quantity demanded of the type m users setting out from nodal points l and reach to the point s.

$\tau_a^m(t)$ is the vehicle actual travel impedance of the type m users entering into road section a at the time of t.

$\pi_l^{sm}(t)$ is the least actual travel impedance of the type m users setting out from nodal points l and reach to the point s.

2.2 Multi-user of the Traffic Flow Evolution

In order to accurately simulated road various driving characteristics of mixed traffic flow state, Wong and Wong expanded the traditional traffic flow LWR model, using car driving speed to distinguish between various driving characteristics, and structured of the multi-user traffic flow model—MCLWR.

In a section, it distributes m different speed types of user, ordering $q^m(x,t)$, $\rho^m(x,t)$, $\vartheta^m(x,t)$ respectively represent the flow, density and speed of user at the time t at x.

The LWR formula of multi-user expanded continuous conservation equation:

$$\frac{\partial \rho^m(x,t)}{\partial t} + \frac{\partial q^m(x,t)}{\partial x} = 0 \ \forall m = 1,2,\ldots,M \tag{1}$$

All kinds of user's speed and secret relations:

$$\vartheta^m(x,t) = \Upsilon^m(\rho^1, \rho^2, \ldots, \rho^M) \ \forall m = 1,2,\ldots,M \tag{2}$$

2.3 Actual Road Section Impedance Calculation

In the network condition, the calculation methods of the actual road impedance are as follows: due to road section inlet and outlet capacity constraints, congestion gateway road line and signal control factors, type m of users in the moment k set out of the section of inflow $u_a^m(k)$ will be divided into number N flows respectively outflow this section at the time interval of $k+1, k+2, \ldots, k+N$,assuming time interval $k+n$ corresponding son flow is a_n^m ,$1 \le n \le N$, $a_n^m \ge 0$ and $\sum_{n=1}^{N} a_n^m = u_a^m(k)$. The following are the calculation method of the son flow to be satisfied with the type users conditions of FIFO.

For a certain time interval n greater than k :

$$a_n^m=\begin{cases}0 & if \quad O_a^m(k+n)<U_a^m(k-1)\\ O_a^m(k+n)-U_a^m(k-1) & if \quad O_a^m(k+n-1)<U_a^m(k-1)\le O_a^m(k+n)\le U_a^m(k)\\ y_{d+1,a}^m(k+n)\cdot 1 & if \quad U_a^m(k-1)\le O_a^m(k+n-1)\le O_a^m(k+n)\le U_a^m(k)\\ U_a^m(k)-O_a^m(k+n-1) & if \quad U_a^m(k-1)\le O_a^m(k+n-1)\le U_a^m(k)<O_a^m(k+n)\\ 0 & if \quad U_a^m(k)<O_a^m(k+n-1)\end{cases} \tag{3}$$

So, there are given in the following calculation methods of user m sections practical average trip the impedance:

$$\tau_a^m(k)=\frac{a_1^m\cdot(k+1-k)+a_2^m\cdot(k+2-k)+\cdots+a_N^m\cdot(k+N-k)}{a_1^m+a_2^m+\cdots+a_N^m}=\frac{a_1^m+2a_2^m+\cdots+Na_N^m}{u_a^m(k)} \tag{4}$$

2.4 Multi-users Dynamic Network Traffic Flow Distribution Problems

First of all, give in the multi-user dynamical user optimum allocation the need to meet the constraints, such as the defined constraints:

$$u_a^m(t)=\sum_s u_a^{sm}(t)\ \forall a, \forall t, \forall m \tag{5}$$

$$o_a^m(t)=\sum_s o_a^{sm}(t)\ \forall a, \forall t, \forall m \tag{6}$$

The road section $a=(l,m)$ related constraints:

$$\sum_{a\in A_l} o_a^{sm}(t)+g_l^{sm}(t)=\sum_{a\in B_l} u_a^{sm}(t)\ \forall l\neq s\ \forall s, \forall t, \forall m \tag{7}$$

Annotation: If the node l is a network node, $\sum_{a\in A} o_a^{sm}(t)$, $\forall s$ can be regarded as zero.

$$\int_0 u_a^m(t)dt=\int_0^{t+\tau_a^m(t)} o_a^m(t)dt\ \forall a, \forall t, \forall m \tag{8}$$

$$\frac{dX_a^{sm}(t)}{dt}=u_a^{sm}(t)-o_a^{sm}(t)\ \forall a, \forall t, \forall s, \forall m \tag{9}$$

$$X_a^{sm}(t) \geq 0,\ u_a^{sm}(t) \geq 0,\ o_a^{sm}(t) \geq 0\ \forall a, \forall t, \forall s, \forall m \tag{10}$$

$$X_a^{sm}(0) = 0,\ o_a^{sm}(0) = 0\ \forall a, \forall s, \forall m \tag{11}$$

If $u_a^{sm}(t) > 0$, the road section a at the time of t was used by the m type user make s as the destination node. Order that feasible flow set was satisfied with these constraints (5) ~ (11) as $\widetilde{\Omega}$.

The multi-class dynamical user optimum conditions can be described used to the complementary problem:

$$[\tau_a^m(t) + \pi_{l_2}^{sm}(t + \tau_a^m(t)) - \pi_{l_1}^{sm}(t)]u_a^{sm}(t) = 0\ \forall a, \forall s, \forall t, \forall m \tag{12}$$

$$\tau_a^m(t) + \pi_{l_2}^{sm}(t + \tau_a^m(t)) \geq \pi_{l_1}^{sm}(t)\ \forall a, \forall s, \forall t, \forall m \tag{13}$$

$$u_a^{sm}(t) \geq 0\ \forall a, \forall s, \forall t, \forall m \tag{14}$$

Therein: $a = (l_1, l_2)$, $\pi_{l_1}^{sm}(t) = \min_a\{\tau_a^m(t) + \pi_{l_2}^s(t + \tau_a^m(t))\}$.

If record $\Omega_a^{sm}(t) = \tau_a^m(t) + \pi_{l_2}^{s\,m}(t + \tau_a^m(t))$, and the last formula to write for:

$$[\Omega_a^{sm}(t) - \pi_{l_1}^{sm}(t)]u_a^{sm}(t) = 0\ \forall a, \forall s, \forall t, \forall m \tag{15}$$

$$\Omega_a^{sm}(t) - \pi_{l_1}^{sm}(t) \geq 0\ \forall a, \forall s, \forall t, \forall m \tag{16}$$

$$u_a^{sm}(t) \geq 0\ \forall a, \forall s, \forall t, \forall m \tag{17}$$

Based on the above multi-class network flow evolution model, here adopt MSA algorithm to solving content multi-class dynamical user optimum conditions (12) ~ (17) dynamic network traffic flow distribution problems.

Algorithm specific steps are as follows:

Step 0: Given the initial inflow sections $\{u_a^{sm(0)}(k)\}$ ($\forall m$, $\forall a$, $\forall s$),and order $n = 0$ .Use the user network flow evolution model implementation of network traffic flow of many users loading.

Step 1: Order $k = 0$.

Step 2:Calculate all kinds of user minimum path impedance, Use "all or none" method calculate $\{\bar{u}_a^{s\,m(n)}(k)\}$ and $\{\bar{u}_a^{\,m(n)}(k)\}$ ($\forall m, \forall a, \forall s$).

Step 3: Updated inflow:

$$u_a^{s\,m(n+1)}(k) = u_a^{s\,m(n)}(k) + \frac{1}{n}[\bar{u}_a^{s\,m(n)}(k) - u_a^{s\,m(n)}(k)]\ \forall a, \forall s, \forall m$$

Step 4:If $k = K$, turn to the step 5; otherwise order $k = k+1$, turn to the step 2.

Step 5: Convergence test:

$$RGap(k)^{m(n)} = \frac{\sum_a\sum_s u_a^{sm(n)}(k)\cdot\Omega_a^{sm(n)}(k) - \sum_l\sum_s(\sum_{a\in A_l} o_a^{sm(n)}(k) + g_l^{sm}(k))\cdot\pi_l^{sm(n)}(k)}{\sum_l\sum_s(\sum_{a\in A_l} o_a^{sm(n)}(k) + g_l^{sm}(k))\cdot\pi_l^{sm(n)}(k)}$$

If to all type m users, it contented with $RGap(k)^{(n)} < \varepsilon$, get sections inflow $\{u_a^m(k)\}$ ($\forall m, \forall a$),stop iteration; Otherwise order $n = n+1$, turn to the step 1.

3 Checking Model Validation

3.1 Parameters Input

As shown in graph 1 the below shows the one-way traffic network to check that multi-user traffic flow characteristics and network flow distribution results. The main parameters are taken from Bliemer, Bovy (2003) and Boel, Mihaylova (2006), and slightly increased.

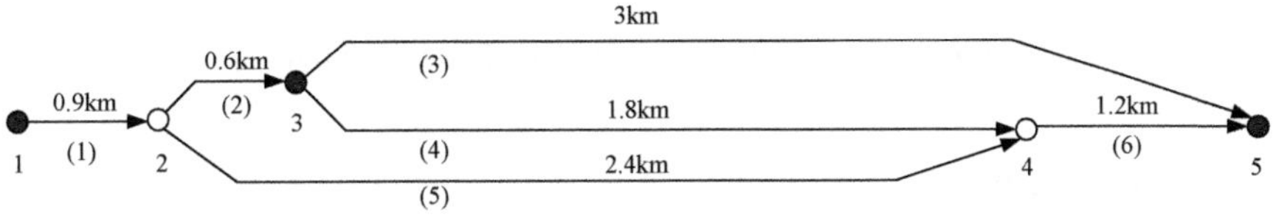

Fig. 1. Example network

Network for section 4 is dedicated truck trickle outside, the rest are various vehicles mixed running lanes, including sections (1), (2), (3) and (5) all are 2 lanes, (6) is the 4 lane; the length of the various sections as shown in Fig 1.

There are two types of vehicle cars and trucks in road net, the vehicle length respectively is 4 meters or 8 meters, and with their own freedom velocity to distinguish between types of vehicle, the car: ϑ_f^{car} =108km/hour, the truck: ϑ_f^{Truck} =72 km/hour.

Simulation time is 1800 seconds, length of time is Δt =10seconds, and the unit cell partition is Δt =500meters, ρ_{critic} =50cars/km. And the minimum safety interval is t_d =2seconds, $\vartheta^{m}_{j,\min}$ =7.4km/hour, density weight is α_j =0.15, speed weight is

$$\beta_j(k+1)=\begin{cases}0.3 & if \quad \left|\rho^{antic}_{j+1}(k+1)-\rho^{antic}_{j}(k+1)\right|\geq 1\\ 0.7 & otherwise\end{cases}$$

3.2 Analysis of Results

Fig. 2 described the various types of vehicle position of the space-time evolution. As you can see, the same type of vehicles running meet first in first out rules, and different types of vehicle can exist overtaking. In addition, in the case of the multi-users meet dynamical user optimum conditions of the assignment result, such as the following form shows, cars running in section 1 and 2 as an example. The results show that Vehicles according to dynamical user optimum conditions make path selection, but also for the guidance system provides comprehensive sections misleading information.

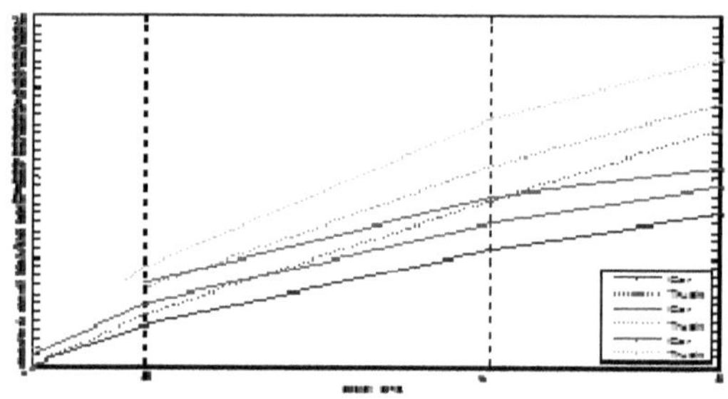

Fig. 2. Vehicles position variation of space and time

4 Conclusion

Compared with the previous research, this paper established model has the following characteristics: First, described the micro a single road traffic flow characteristics of the multi-user model expands to network layer, maintain the original model characteristics, and can also to simulate multi-user traffic flow evolution in the network. Second, it can reflect the saturated crowded under the condition of line network flow operation and many users of mixed traffic flow various influence each other. Third, it based on the evolution model structure of the impedance function calculation method, can reflect the microscopic traffic flow characteristics, describe the physical line up and extended, overcome traditional analytical function qualitative attunements of the defects. Fourth, it established multi-user mixed running dynamic network user optimum distribution model, can make user optimum allocation to network traffic flow, make different type vehicles overtake at the same time, the same type vehicle running according to FIFO rules , thus reasonable solute the mixed traffic flow does not meet the FIFO phenomenon. Fifth, in network traffic flow when achieve the optimal allocation of users, output the motor vehicle exhaust emissions calculation model need of the car model, time, speed, position etc. vehicle parameters, it can real-time calculate analysis of various sections vehicle exhaust emissions and the spread of pollution, from the view of the medium and the microscopic realized the urban road network emission pollution condition assessment.

References

1. Wong, G.C.K., Wong, S.C.: A multi-class traffic flow model-an extension of LWR model with heterogeneous drivers. Transportation Research A 36, 827–841 (2002)
2. Daganzo, C.F.: The cell transmission model part II: network traffic. Transportation Research B 29, 79–93 (1995)
3. Boel, R., Mihaylova, L.: A compositional stochastic model for real time freeway traffic simulation. Transportation Research B 40, 319–334 (2006)
4. Ran, B., Boyce, D.E.: Modeling dynamic transportation network: an intelligent transportation system oriented approach. Springer, Heidelberg (1996)
5. Feng, X., Chen, S.: Improve the city road vehicle emission pollution intelligent transportation means. Journal of Traffic and Transportation Engineering 2, 73–77 (2002)
6. Bliemer, M.C.J., Bovy, P.H.L.: Quasi-variational inequality formulation of the multiclass dynamic traffic assignment problem. Transportation Research B. 37, 501–519 (2003)
7. Boel, R., Mihaylova, L.: A compositional stochastic model for real time freeway traffic simulation. Transportation Research B. 40, 319–334 (2006)
8. Kadalbajoo, M.K., Arorar, P., Gupta, V.: Collocation method using artificial viscosity for solving stiff singularly perturbed turning point problem having twin boundary layers. Computers and Mathematics with Applications 61, 1595–1607 (2011)
9. Wang, R.-H., Li, C.-J., Zhu, C.-G.: Computational Geometry. Science Press, BeiJing (2008)
10. Ren, Y.-J.: Numerical Analysis and MATLAB Implementation. Higher Education Press (2008)

Application of Fuzzy Mathematics in Real Estate Valuation

Yanwei Zhu[1], Yongli Zhang[2], Shufei Lin[3], and Xiaohong Liu[2]

[1] Department of Mathematics and Information science,Tangshan Normal University, Tangshan, China
[2] College of Light Industry, Hebei United UniversityTangshan, China
[3] Department of Computer, the North University for Ethnics, Yinchuan, China
{zhyw79,zhyl01,linshufei197937}@163.com

Abstract. Similarity degree and the principle of selection are analyzed in this paper. Fuzzy mathematics is used to Market comparison approach. By applying fuzzy theory into real estate valuation, calculation example shows that the application of the method of real estate assessment can overcome the shortcomings of traditional methods, the valuation results are more scientific and rational and fair.

Keywords: Market Comparison Approach, Fuzzy Mathematics, Fuzzy Similarity Degree, Membership Functions, Real Estate Valuation.

1 Introduction

Real estate is a special commodity. In order to really grasp the formation of its price, it is necessary fully to understand the theory of price formation, and for specific analysis. Real estate prices are the core of the real estate market [1][2][3][4]. It reflects the needs of the relationship between the real estate investors and consumers. So assessment includes speculation and judgments of between people and real estate on real estate prices. The process of estimating the valuation, real estate appraisers is essentially the process of economic studies. Since the actual situation in each country or region different, real estate development and application of valuation methods are also different. At present, the property valuation used in the more popular methods are: cost approach, income approach, market comparison approach [5][6]. In order to achieve a better valuation effect, the fuzzy thinking will be applied to the market comparison approach. Using fuzzy similarity degree in mathematics, the examples are analyzed [7][8][9]. Choose to be estimated with the most similar to the real estate transaction as a comparable instance. Calculate the price of real estate to be estimated.

2 Fuzzy Mathematics Theories

Fuzzy Mathematics are founded by L. A. Zadeh Professor in 1965.It is an approximation of accuracy and fuzzy. It set up a bridge between mathematics and the real world.[10]

C. Liu, J. Chang, and A. Yang (Eds.): ICICA 2011, Part I, CCIS 243, pp. 588–595, 2011.

2.1 Fuzzy Similarity Degree

Similarity degree is a measure of fuzzy sets and fuzzy sets near the level. Its values is $[0\ 1]$.When the similarity degree is equal to 1,the two fuzzy sets are completely close. When the similarity degree is equal to 0, the two fuzzy sets are not completely close.

Definition: let $\tilde{A}$, $\tilde{B}$ are two fuzzy sets in number field U, then

$$\tilde{A}\cdot\tilde{B}=\vee_{i=1}^{n}\left(A(x_i)\wedge B(x_i)\right)=\vee_{x=U}\left(A(x)\wedge B(x)\right) \tag{1}$$

$\tilde{A}\cdot\tilde{B}$ is called with the inner product $\tilde{A}$ and $\tilde{B}$.

$$\tilde{A}\otimes\tilde{B}=\wedge_{i=1}^{n}\left(A(x_i)\vee B(x_i)\right)=\wedge_{x=U}\left(A(x)\vee B(x)\right) \tag{2}$$

$\tilde{A}\otimes\tilde{B}$ is called with the outer product $\tilde{A}$ and $\tilde{B}$.

$$\sigma\left(\tilde{A},\tilde{B}\right)=\frac{1}{2}\left[\tilde{A}\cdot\tilde{B}+\left(1-\tilde{A}\otimes\tilde{B}\right)\right] \tag{3}$$

$\sigma\left(\tilde{A},\tilde{B}\right)$ is called with the similarity degree $\tilde{A}$ and $\tilde{B}$.

2.2 Near the Principle of Selection

Sets of known model $A^{(1)},A^{(2)},\cdots A^{(n)}\in F(X),A\in F(X)$ will be recognized. If $N(A^{(i)},A)=\vee_{k=1}^{n}(A^{(k)},A)$, then A and $A^{(i)}$ are the most closely. Because similarity degree of A and $A^{(i)}$ is Maximum, A and $A^{(i)}$ are the most closely, A is belong to $A^{(i)}$,It is near the principle of selection.

Set There are 6 elements in the U. The standard model library is consisted by the following fuzzy vectors:

$$a_1=\left(1,0.8,0.5,0.4,0,0.1\right) \tag{4}$$

$$a_2=\left(0.5,0.1,0.8,1,0.6,0\right) \tag{5}$$

$$a_3=(0,1,0.2,0.7,0.5,0.8) \tag{6}$$

$$a_4=\left(0.4,0,1,0.9,0.6,0.5\right) \tag{7}$$

$$a_5=\left(0.8,0.2,0,0.5,1,0.7\right) \tag{8}$$

$$a_6=\left(0.5,0.7,0.8,0,0.5,1\right) \tag{9}$$

Fuzzy vector b will be identified

$$b=(0.7,0.2,0.1,0.4,1,0.8) \tag{10}$$

σ_1 as the standard by proximity, and seek

$$\sigma_1(b,a_1)=0.3333 \tag{11}$$

$$\sigma_1(b,a_2)=0.3778 \tag{12}$$

$$\sigma_1(b,a_3)=0.4545 \tag{13}$$

$$\sigma_1(b, a_4) = 0.4348 \tag{14}$$
$$\sigma_1(b, a_5) = 0.8824 \tag{15}$$
$$\sigma_1(b, a_6) = 0.4565 \tag{16}$$

$\sigma_1(b, a_5)$ is the maximum, according to near the principle of selection, b is classified a_5.

2.3 Fuzzy Evaluation Model

Steps:

(a) Data collection and building a database;
(b) Building Property Database;
(c) Fuzzy similarity degree calculation;
(d) Real estate prices calculation;

Let: There are n trading instances of real estate transactions $A_1, A_2, \cdots A_n$. T_i is i instance of a feature vector of real estate transactions. $T_i = (t_{i1}, t_{i2}, \cdots t_{in})$, t_{ij} is i th feature vector of real estate transactions j,Characteristic matrix T and price matrix E :

$$T = \begin{bmatrix} t_{11} & t_{12} & \cdots & t_{1n} \\ t_{21} & t_{22} & \cdots & t_{2n} \\ \\ t_{n1} & t_{n2} & \cdots & t_{nn} \end{bmatrix} \tag{17}$$

$$E = \begin{bmatrix} e_1 \\ e_2 \\ e_{n-1} \\ e_n \end{bmatrix} \tag{18}$$

$t = (t_1, t_2, \cdots, t_n)$ is feature vector of estimated based real estate. Using formula (3) to calculate real estate t and similarity degree σ_i of examples of real estate transactions T_i. $\sigma_1 \rangle \sigma_2 \rangle \cdots \rangle \sigma_n$, transaction price are $E_1, E_2, \cdots E_n, (E_i \neq e_i)$, similarity degree E_1 is the maximum. E_2 is the second and so on. If similarity degree is same size, need to use the fuzzy correlation coefficient in order of:

$$T = \sum_{j-1}^{m} t_{ij} / \left[\max_{i-1}^{n} \sum_{j=1}^{m} t_{ij} \right] \tag{19}$$

Let E_i^* is i th the assessed value of transaction price. $E_i - E_i^*$ is valuation error. $i-1$ th the assessed value of transaction price is

$$E_{i-1}^* = E_i^* + \sigma_i \left(E_i - E_i^* \right) = \sigma_i E_i + (1 - \sigma_i) E_i^* \tag{20}$$

Using formula (20) expand, calculate the assessed value of real estate:

$$\begin{aligned} E_0^* &= \sigma_1 E_1 + \sigma_2(1-\sigma_1)E_2 + \sigma_3(1-\sigma_1)(1-\sigma_2)E_3 + \cdots \\ &+ \sigma_n(1-\sigma_1)(1-\sigma_2)\cdots(1-\sigma_{n-1})E_n + (1-\sigma_1)(1-\sigma_2)\cdots(1-\sigma_n)E_n^* \end{aligned} \tag{21}$$

E_n^* is assessment initial. From (21), Real estate price is mean of the weighted average of each transaction instanced the instance of the arithmetic. Weight change gradually descending to zero. Ownership value is equal to 1.

$$\begin{aligned} &\sigma_1 + \sigma_2(1-\sigma_1) + \sigma_3(1-\sigma_1)(1-\sigma_2) + \cdots + \\ &\sigma_n(1-\sigma_1)(1-\sigma_2)\cdots(1-\sigma_{n-1}) + (1-\sigma_1)(1-\sigma_2)\cdots(1-\sigma_n) = 1 \end{aligned} \tag{22}$$

Integrated (21), (22), To be estimated with a real estate transaction instance and the right approach degree value of the composition to be estimated real estate prices. In practical work, because the weights are exponentially decreasing. Weight is very small of Example 4. As long as transactions take previous 3 examples to fully meet the accuracy requirements. Evaluation model can be simplified as

$$\begin{aligned} E_0^* = \lambda[&\sigma_1 E_1 + \sigma_2(1-\sigma_1)E_2 + \sigma_3(1-\sigma_1)(1-\sigma_2)E_3 \\ &+ (1-\sigma_1)(1-\sigma_2)(1-\sigma_3)(E_1 + E_2 + E_3)/3] \end{aligned} \tag{23}$$

λ is correction factor. $\lambda \in [\ 0.95 \sim 1.07\ ]$.

3 Application Examples

Area of a building A is $124.3m^2$. It needs to be valued. According to market research, B, C, D, E are comparable examples. Feature elements are Location, traffic, environment, structure, into a new, renovated. They are criteria to judge .As the field U . Try to assess the real estate market prices in July 2011.

Table 1. Membership function value

Feature Elements	A	B	C	D	E
Location conditions	0.95	0.90	0.85	0.75	0.80
Traffic	0.95	0.95	0.85	0.75	0.80
Environmental Quality	0.80	0.80	0.80	0.85	0.85
Building structure	0.80	0.85	0.80	0.80	0.80
Condition	0.85	0.85	0.85	0.80	0.85
Renovation case	0.85	0.85	0.90	0.80	0.85
Unit price /(Yuan/m^2)		6720.0	6521.0	7244.0	6723.0

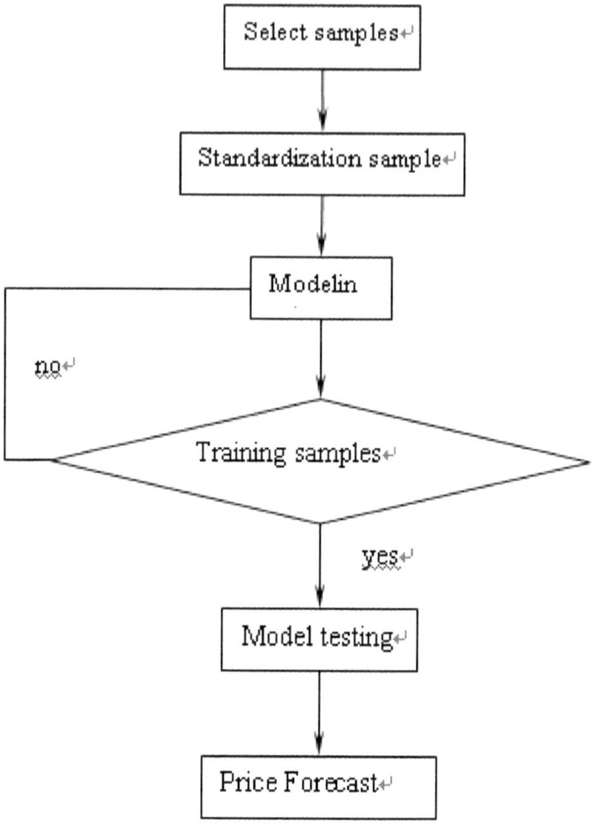

Fig. 1. Fuzzy price forecasting algorithm flow chart

Characteristic matrix:

$$T = \begin{bmatrix} T_1 \\ T_2 \\ T_3 \\ T_4 \end{bmatrix} = \begin{bmatrix} 0.90 & 0.95 & 0.80 & 0.85 & 0.85 & 0.85 \\ 0.85 & 0.85 & 0.80 & 0.80 & 0.85 & 0.90 \\ 0.75 & 0.75 & 0.85 & 0.80 & 0.80 & 0.80 \\ 0.80 & 0.80 & 0.85 & 0.80 & 0.85 & 0.85 \end{bmatrix} \tag{24}$$

Fuzzy set of real estate to be estimated $t = (0.95, 0.95, 0.80, 0.80, 0.85, 0.85)$.

3.1 Closeness Degree Calculation

t and T_1 closeness degree:

$$\begin{aligned} t \cdot T_1 = & (0.95 \wedge 0.85) \vee (0.95 \wedge 0.95) \vee (0.80 \wedge 0.80) \\ & \vee (0.80 \wedge 0.85) \vee (0.85 \wedge 0.85) \vee (0.85 \wedge 0.85) \end{aligned} \tag{25}$$

$$= 0.90 \vee 0.95 \vee 0.80 \vee 0.80 \vee 0.85 \vee 0.85 = 0.95 \tag{26}$$

$$\begin{aligned} t \otimes T_1 &= (0.95 \vee 0.90) \wedge (0.95 \vee 0.95) \wedge (0.80 \vee 0.80) \\ &\quad \wedge (0.80 \vee 0.85) \wedge (0.85 \vee 0.85) \wedge (0.85 \wedge 0.85) \\ &= 0.95 \wedge 0.95 \wedge 0.80 \wedge 0.85 \wedge 0.85 \wedge 0.85 = 0.80 \end{aligned}$$

$$\sigma(t,T_1) = \frac{1}{2}\left[t \cdot T_1 + \left(1 - t \otimes T_1\right)\right] = \frac{1}{2}\left[0.95 + \left(1 - 0.80\right)\right] = 0.575 \tag{27}$$

t and T_2 closeness degree:

$$\begin{aligned} t \cdot T_2 &= (0.95 \wedge 0.85) \vee (0.95 \wedge 0.85) \vee (0.80 \wedge 0.80) \\ &\quad \vee (0.80 \wedge 0.80) \vee (0.85 \wedge 0.85) \vee (0.85 \wedge 0.90) \\ &= 0.85 \vee 0.85 \vee 0.80 \vee 0.80 \vee 0.85 \vee 0.85 = 0.85 \end{aligned} \tag{28}$$

$$\begin{aligned} t \otimes T_2 &= (0.95 \vee 0.85) \wedge (0.95 \vee 0.85) \wedge (0.80 \vee 0.80) \\ &\quad \wedge (0.80 \vee 0.80) \wedge (0.85 \vee 0.85) \wedge (0.85 \wedge 0.90) \\ &= 0.95 \wedge 0.95 \wedge 0.80 \wedge 0.80 \wedge 0.85 \wedge 0.90 = 0.80 \end{aligned} \tag{29}$$

$$\sigma(t,T_2) = \frac{1}{2}\left[t \cdot T_2 + \left(1 - t \otimes T_2\right)\right] = \frac{1}{2}\left[0.85 + \left(1 - 0.80\right)\right] = 0.52 \tag{30}$$

t and T_3 Closeness degree:

$$\begin{aligned} t \cdot T_3 &= (0.95 \wedge 0.75) \vee (0.95 \wedge 0.75) \vee (0.80 \wedge 0.85) \\ &\quad \vee (0.80 \wedge 0.80) \vee (0.85 \wedge 0.80) \vee (0.85 \wedge 0.80) \\ &= 0.75 \vee 0.75 \vee 0.80 \vee 0.80 \vee 0.80 \vee 0.80 = 0.80 \end{aligned} \tag{31}$$

$$\begin{aligned} t \otimes T_3 &= (0.95 \vee 0.75) \wedge (0.95 \vee 0.75) \wedge (0.80 \vee 0.85) \\ &\quad \wedge (0.80 \vee 0.80) \wedge (0.85 \vee 0.80) \wedge (0.85 \wedge 0.80) \\ &= 0.95 \wedge 0.95 \wedge 0.85 \wedge 0.80 \wedge 0.85 \wedge 0.85 = 0.80 \end{aligned} \tag{32}$$

$$\sigma(t,T_3) = \frac{1}{2}\left[t \cdot T_3 + \left(1 - t \otimes T_3\right)\right] = \frac{1}{2}\left[0.80 + \left(1 - 0.80\right)\right] = 0.500 \tag{33}$$

t and T_4 Closeness degree:

$$\begin{aligned} t \cdot T_4 &= (0.95 \wedge 0.80) \vee (0.95 \wedge 0.80) \vee (0.80 \wedge 0.85) \\ &\quad \vee (0.80 \wedge 0.80) \vee (0.85 \wedge 0.85) \vee (0.85 \wedge 0.85) \\ &= 0.80 \vee 0.80 \vee 0.80 \vee 0.80 \vee 0.85 \vee 0.85 = 0.85 \end{aligned} \tag{34}$$

$$\begin{aligned} t \otimes T_4 &= (0.95 \vee 0.80) \wedge (0.95 \vee 0.80) \wedge (0.80 \vee 0.85) \\ &\quad \wedge (0.80 \vee 0.80) \wedge (0.85 \vee 0.85) \wedge (0.85 \wedge 0.85) \\ &= 0.95 \wedge 0.95 \wedge 0.85 \wedge 0.80 \wedge 0.85 \wedge 0.85 = 0.80 \end{aligned} \tag{35}$$

$$\sigma(t,T_4) = \frac{1}{2}\left[t \cdot T_4 + \left(1 - t \otimes T_4\right)\right] = \frac{1}{2}\left[0.85 + \left(1 - 0.80\right)\right] = 0.525 \tag{36}$$

Closeness degree of T_2 and T_4 is same.

$$T_2 = \sum_{j=1}^{6} t_{2j} \Big/ \left[\max_{i-1}^{2} \sum_{j=1}^{6} t_{ij} \right] = 5.02/5.20 = 0.971 \tag{37}$$

$$T_4 = \sum_{j=1}^{6} t_{4j} / \left[\max_{i-1}^{4} \sum_{j=1}^{6} t_{ij} \right] = 4.95/5.20 = 0.952 \tag{38}$$

$$\sigma_1 = \sigma(t, T_1) = 0.575 \tag{39}$$

$$\sigma_2 = \sigma(t, T_2) = 0.525 \tag{40}$$

$$\sigma_3 = \sigma(t, T_3) = 0.500 \tag{41}$$

$$\sigma_4 = \sigma(t, T_4) = 0.500 \tag{42}$$

3.2 Calculate Real Estate Prices to be Estimated(let $\lambda = 1.07$)

$$\begin{aligned} E_0^* &= \lambda[\sigma_1 E_1 + \sigma_2 (1-\sigma_1) E_2 + \sigma_3 (1-\sigma_1)(1-\sigma_2) E_3 \\ &\quad + (1-\sigma_1)(1-\sigma_2)(1-\sigma_3)(E_1 + E_2 + E_3)/3] \\ &= 1.07 \times [0.575 \times 6720 + 0.525 \times (1-0.575) \times 6521 \\ &\quad + 0.525 \times (1-0.575)(1-0.525) \times 6423 + (1-0.575) \\ &\quad (1-0.525)(1-0.525)(6720 + 6521 + 6423) \div 3] \\ &= 1.07 \times (3864 + 1454.998 + 680.7376 + 628.531) \\ &= 7092.25(yuan/\, m^2) \end{aligned} \tag{43}$$

The total price of real estate: $7092.25 \times 124.3 = 88.15$(Million yuan)

4 Conclusions

There are many advantages of fuzzy mathematics. By applying fuzzy theory into real estate valuation, calculation example shows that the application of the method of real estate assessment can overcome the shortcomings of traditional methods, the valuation results are more scientific and rational and fair. But this method will be further improved in the future.

Acknowledgments. This project was supported by the Science Foundation of Hebei United University (qd201007) and teaching and research to guide the project(qgjg201019).

References

1. Liu, Q., Ren, R.: Study on Model of Chinese Real Estate Appraisal. Journal of Anhui Agri.Sci. 35(16), 5013–5017 (2007) (in Chinese)
2. Huang, H., Li, S., Yang, Q.: Comparison Method of Real Estate Appraisal Based on GIS and Fuzzy Theory. Chongqing Jiaotong University (Natural Science) 28(5) (2009) (in Chinese)
3. Qilin, Z.: On the improvement of real estate valuation methods. China Construction (08) (2009) (in Chinese)
4. Kuang, D., Yang, L.: Application of BP Neural Network in Real Estate Valuatio. Quanzhou Normal University (Natural Science) (11) (2006) (in Chinese)

5. Tang, H.: The Models of Quantitative Analysis in Real Estate Appraisal. Dalian Maritime University 10 (2005) (in Chinese)
6. Lu, H.: Use of Artificial Neural Network in Market Comparison Approach. Journal of Lianyungang College of Chemical Technology (4) (1999) (in Chinese)
7. Wei, L.: Research basis on fuzzy mathematics's real estate appraisal method. Shanxi Architecture (02) (2010) (in Chinese)
8. Fen, H.: Fuzzy application in the real estate valuation. Chongqing Institute of Technology (Natural Science) (3) (2009) (in Chinese)
9. Lele, C.L.: Fuzzy math project cost estimate of the real estate. Modern-Commerce Industry (03) (2010) (in Chinese)
10. Peng, Z., Sun, Y.: Fuzzy Mathematics and its Applications, 3rd edn. Wuhan University Press, Wuhan (2002) (in Chinese)

On the Compound Poisson Risk Model with Debit Interest and a Threshold Dividend Strategy

Chunwei Wang*, Xigang Du, and Qiaoyu Chen

School of Mathematics and Statistics, Henan University of Science & Technology
471003, Luoyang, China
wangchunwei@yeah.net

Abstract. In this paper, a compound Poisson risk model with debit interest and a constant dividend barrier is considered under absolute ruin. When the surplus is below a fixed positive level, the surplus is kept as liquid reserves, which do not earn interest. When the surplus attains the level, the excess of the surplus over the level will receive interest at a constant rate. On the contrary, when the surplus is negative but not too far to zero, the insurer would loan some money from the bank. Integro-differential equations satisfied by the expectation of discounted aggregate dividend payments with certain boundary conditions are obtained. When the claim sizes obey the exponential distribution, explicit solutions are obtained.

Keywords: Absolute ruin, Dividend payments, Debit interest, Integro-differential equation, Liquid reserves.

1 Introduction

Consider the classical risk model

$$U(t) = u + ct - S(t), \qquad t \geq 0, \tag{1}$$

where u is the initial surplus, $c > 0$ is the premium rate, $S(t) = \sum_{n=1}^{N(t)} X_n$ is the aggregate claim process, $\{N(t),\ t \geq 0\}$ is a Poisson process with intensity $\lambda > 0$, which counts the claim times in the interval $(0, t]$, and $\{X_n,\ n \geq 1\}$ (representing the sizes of claims) is a sequence of independent and identically distributed nonnegative variables with a common distribution function $F(x)$ that satisfies $F(0) = 0$ and has a positive mean μ. In addition, $\theta = \frac{c}{\lambda\mu} - 1 > 0$ is the security loading factor, $\{X_n,\ n \geq 1\}$ is independent of $\{N(t),\ t \geq 0\}$.

* Thanks to the Research Fund for the doctoral program of higher education of China (No. 20093705110002), the basic research and cutting-edge technology of Henan Province(No. 092300410178) and the doctoral research fund of Henan University of Science & Technology(No. 09001443).

C. Liu, J. Chang, and A. Yang (Eds.): ICICA 2011, Part I, CCIS 243, pp. 596–603, 2011.

To adapt a surplus model closer to reality, we employ the idea from Embrechts and Schmidli [1]. We assume that the insurer could borrow an amount of money equal to the deficit at a debit interest force $\delta > 0$ when the surplus is negative. Meanwhile, the insurer will repay the debts continuously from his premium income. When the negative surplus attains the level $-c/\delta$ or is below $-c/\delta$, absolute ruin occurs at this moment. Papers of the risk model with debit interest can be seen in [2-8]etc. We also assume that the insurer is allowed to make investment only if the insurers surplus attains a level of $\Delta \geq 0$ and only the excess of the surplus over the level will receive interest at the interest force $\tau > 0$. The surplus below the level is kept as liquid reservoir(here means Δ), which do not earn interest. The research of risk model with liquid reservoir could be seen in [9,10]etc. When the surplus attains another level $b \leq \Delta$, we assume the insurer would pay part of his premium $\rho \in (0, c]$ to the shareholders as dividends. Thus the modified surplus $\overline{U}(t)$ can be seen as the solution to

$$d\overline{U}(t) = \begin{cases} (c - \rho + \tau(U_b(t) - \Delta))dt - dS(t) & u \geq b, \\ (c + \tau(U_b(t) - \Delta))dt - dS(t) & \Delta \leq u < b, \\ cdt - dS(t) & 0 \leq u < \Delta, \\ (c + \delta U_b(t))dt - dS(t) & -c/\delta < u < 0, \end{cases} \quad \overline{U}(0) = u, \; t \geq 0.$$

Since the barrier strategy was initially proposed by De Finetti [11] for a Bernoulli model, research on dividend strategies has been carried out extensively. For example, see [12-17]. Among of them, [16,17] considered the risk model (1) with a constant threshold dividend strategy. In this paper, we assume the insurance company will pay dividends to its shareholders. Let $D(t)$ denote the aggregate dividends paid by time t.

For the modified surplus process $U_b(t)$, we define the time of absolute ruin by $T_b = \inf\{t \geq 0 : U_b(t) \leq -c/\delta\}$ and $T_b = \infty$ if $U_b(t) >\leq -c/\delta$ for all $t \geq 0$. We denote the force of interest for discounting the dividends by $\alpha \geq 0$ and the present value of all dividends until time of absolute ruin T_b by

$$D_{u,b} = \rho \int_0^{T_b} e^{-\alpha t} dD(t) = \rho \int_0^{T} e^{-\alpha t} \mathbf{I}(U_b(t) > b)dt, \qquad 0 \leq u \leq b.$$

where $\mathbf{I}(C)$ is the dictator function of event C. For $-c/\delta \leq u \leq b$, we denote the expectation of $D_{u,b}$ by $V(u, b) = E[D_{u,b}]$.

Since $V(u, b)$ behaves differently when u is in differen interval, we define

$$V(u, b) = \begin{cases} V_1(u, b) & u \geq b, \\ V_2(u, b) & \Delta \leq u < b, \\ V_3(u, b) & 0 \leq u < \Delta, \\ V_4(u, b) & -c/\delta < u < 0, \end{cases}$$

The structure of the paper is as follows: In Section 2, we obtain the integro-differential equations satisfied by the expected discounted dividend payments with certain boundary conditions. In Section 3, we give the integro-differential equations satisfied by the moment generating function and higher moments of the dividend payments with certain boundary conditions, and obtain the explicit expressions of them for a special case. In Section 4, we present the integro-differential equations satisfied by the expected discounted penalty function and give its explicit expressions for some special cases.

2 Integro-Differential Equations for $V(u,b)$

At first, we derive the integro-differential equations satisfied by $V_i(u,b)$ $(i = 1,2,3,4)$ in their respective domains in the following theorem.

Theorem 1. For different value of u, $V_i(u,b)$ satisfies the following integro-differential equations in their respective domains

$$((u-\Delta)\tau + c - \rho)V_1'(u,b) - (\lambda+\alpha)V_1(u,b) + \lambda\left(\int_0^{u-b} V_1(u-x,b)f(x)dx\right.$$
$$+ \int_{u-b}^{u-\Delta} V_2(u-x,b)f(x)dx \int_{u-\Delta}^{u} V_3(u-x,b)f(x)dx$$
$$\left.+ \int_u^{u+c/\delta} V_4(u-x,b)f(x)dx\right) = -\rho, \tag{2}$$

$$((u-\Delta)\tau + c)V_2'(u,b) - (\lambda+\alpha)V_2(u,b) + \lambda\left(\int_0^{u-\Delta} V_2(u-x,b)f(x)dx\right.$$
$$\left.+ \int_{u-\Delta}^{u} V_3(u-x,b)f(x)dx + \int_u^{u+c/\delta} V_4(u-x,b)f(x)dx\right) = 0, \tag{3}$$

$$cV_3'(u,b) - (\lambda+\alpha)V_3(u,b) + \lambda\left(\int_0^{u} V_3(u-x,b)f(x)dx\right.$$
$$\left.+ \int_u^{u+c/\delta} V_4(u-x,b)f(x)dx\right) = 0, \tag{4}$$

$$(\delta u + c)V_4'(u,b) - (\lambda+\alpha)V_4(u,b) + \lambda\int_0^{u+c/\delta} V_4(u-x,b)f(x)dx = 0. \tag{5}$$

Proof. When $u \geq b$, consider a small interval $(0,t]$ and assume that the surplus at time t without claims is denoted by $h_b(t) = (u-\Delta)e^{\tau t} + (c-\rho)\frac{e^{\tau t}-1}{\tau} + \Delta$. By conditioning on whether there is a claim in the time interval $(0,t]$ and on the amount of the claim if it occurs, we obtain

$$V_1(u,b) - e^{-(\lambda+\alpha)t}(\rho t + V_1(h_b(t),b)) - \lambda\int_0^t e^{-(\lambda+\alpha)s}ds$$
$$\times\left(\int_0^{h_b(s)-b} V_1(h_b(s)-x,b)f(x)dx + \int_{h_b(s)-b}^{h_b(s)-\Delta} V_2(h_b(s)-x,b)f(x)dx\right.$$
$$\left.+ \int_{h_b(s)-\Delta}^{h_b(s)} V_3(h_b(s)-x,b)f(x)dx + \int_{h_b(s)}^{h_b(s)+c/\delta_2} V_4(h_b(s)-x,b)f(x)dx\right)$$
$$= 0. \tag{6}$$

Taylor's expansion gives

$$V_1(h_b(t),b) = V_1(u,b) + ((u-\Delta)\tau + c - \rho)V_1^{'}(u,b)t + o(t). \quad (7)$$

Substituting (7) into (6), dividing t on both sides of (6) and rearranging it, we obtain (2). Similar arguments as that of obtaining (2), we can obtain (3)-(5). □

In the following theorem, we will prove the continuity of $V(u,b)$ at 0, Δ, b.

Theorem 2. $V_i(u,b)$ and $V_i^{'}(u,b)$ $(i=1,\cdots,4)$ satisfy

$$V_1(b+,b) = V_2(b-,b), \quad V_2(\Delta+,b) = V_3(\Delta-,b), \quad V_3(0+,b) = V_4(0-,b), \quad (8)$$

$$((b-\Delta)\tau + c - \rho)V_1^{'}(b+,b) = ((b-\Delta)\tau + c)V_2^{'}(b-,b) - \rho, \quad (9)$$

$$V_2^{'}(\Delta+,b) = V_3^{'}(\Delta-,b), \quad V_3^{'}(0+,b) = V_4^{'}(0-,b), \quad (10)$$

$$\lim_{u\to+\infty} V_1(u,b) = \frac{\rho}{\alpha}, \quad V_4(-c/\delta,b) = 0 \quad (11)$$

Proof. Using similar method of the proof (4.4) in Fang and Wu [12], we obtain the three equation of (8). Letting $u \downarrow b$ in (2) and $u \uparrow b$ in (3) and in view of the first equation of (8), we obtain (9). Similar arguments of obtaining (9), we obtain the two equations of (10).

When $u \to +\infty$, absolute ruin will not occur and dividend are paid at constant premium rate ρ. Thus, we obtain the first equation of (11). Letting $u \downarrow -c/\delta$ in (5), we obtain the second equation of (11).

3 Exponential Claims

In this section, we assume the claim sizes are exponentially distributed with parameter β. Substituting $f(x) = \beta e^{-\beta x}$ into (2) and rearranging it, we obtain

$$((u-\Delta)\tau + c - \rho)V_1^{'}(u,b) - (\lambda+\alpha)V_1(u,b) + \lambda\beta e^{-\beta u}\left(\int_b^u V_1(x,b)e^{\beta x}dx \right.$$
$$\left. + \int_\Delta^b V_2(x,b)e^{\beta x}dx + \int_0^\Delta V_3(x,b)e^{\beta x}dx + \int_{-c/\delta}^0 V_4(x,b)e^{\beta x}dx\right) = -\rho. \quad (12)$$

By applying the operator $\frac{d}{du} + \beta$ to (12), we obtain the following differential equation

$$((u-\Delta)\tau + c - \rho)V_1^{''}(u,b) + ((u-\Delta)\tau\beta + (c-\rho)\beta + \tau - (\lambda+\alpha))V_1^{'}(u,b)$$
$$- \alpha\beta V_1(u,b) + \rho\beta = 0. \quad (13)$$

Using similar method to obtaining (13) from (2), from (3)-(5) we can obtain the following differential equations satisfied by $V_i(u,b)$ $(i=2,3,4)$ in their respective domains

$$((u-\Delta)\tau+c)V_2''(u,b)+((u-\Delta)\tau\beta+c\beta+\tau-(\lambda+\alpha))V_2'(u,b)$$
$$-\alpha\beta V_2(u,b)=0, \quad (14)$$
$$cV_3'(u,b)+(c\beta-(\lambda+\alpha))V_3'(u,b)-\alpha\beta V_3(u,b)=0, \quad (15)$$
$$(\delta u+c)V_4''(u,b)+((\delta u+c)\beta+\delta-(\lambda+\alpha))V_4'(u,b)-\alpha\beta V_4(u,b)=0. \quad (16)$$

By transforms $V_1(u,b)=g_1(y)+\frac{\rho}{\alpha}$, $y=-\frac{\beta}{\tau}(\tau(u-\Delta)+c-\rho)$, (13) is changed to

$$yg_1''(y)+\left(1-\frac{\lambda+\alpha}{\tau}-y\right)g_1'(y)+\frac{\alpha}{\tau}g_1(y)=0, \quad (17)$$

where $y<-\frac{\tau(b-\Delta)+c-\rho}{\tau}<0$. By (13.1.15) and (13.1.18) of Abramowitz and Stegun [18], the general solution to the above equation is a linear combination of two independent solutions in the following

$$g_1(y)=a_{b1}e^yU\left(1-\frac{\lambda}{\delta},1-\frac{\lambda+\alpha}{\delta};-y\right)$$
$$+a_{b2}(-y)^{\frac{\lambda+\alpha}{\delta}}e^yM\left(1+\frac{\alpha}{\delta},1+\frac{\lambda+\alpha}{\delta};-y\right),$$

for $y<-\frac{\kappa(b)}{\tau}<0$, where $M(l_1,l_2;y)$ and $U(l_1,l_2;y)$ are the confluent hypergeometric function of the first and second kinds respectively, and a_{b1} and a_{b2} are arbitrary constants, $\kappa(b)$ is the value of $\kappa(u)=\tau(u-\Delta)+c-\rho$ at $u=b$. Thus, for $y<-\frac{\kappa(b)}{\tau}<0$,

$$V_1(u,b)=g_1\left(-\frac{\beta}{\tau}\kappa(u)\right)+\frac{\rho}{\alpha}=a_{b1}h_{b1}(u)+a_{b2}h_{b2}(u)+\frac{\rho}{\alpha}, \quad (18)$$

with

$$h_{b1}(u)=e^{-\frac{\beta}{\tau}\kappa(u)}U\left(1-\frac{\lambda}{\delta},1-\frac{\lambda+n\alpha}{\delta};\frac{\beta}{\tau}\kappa(u)\right), \quad (19)$$

$$h_{b2}(u)=\left(\frac{\beta}{\tau}\kappa(u)\right)^{\frac{\lambda+\alpha}{\delta}}e^{-\frac{\beta}{\tau}\kappa(u)}M\left(1+\frac{\alpha}{\delta},1+\frac{\lambda+\alpha}{\delta};\frac{\beta}{\tau}\kappa(u)\right). \quad (20)$$

Obviously, we know that

$$\lim_{u\to+\infty}h_{b1}(u)=0, \qquad \lim_{u\to+\infty}h_{b2}(u)=+\infty. \quad (21)$$

Letting $u\to+\infty$ in (18) and with the help of Theorem 2.2 and (21), we obtain $a_{b2}=0$. Thus, (18) reduce to

$$V_1(u,b)=a_{b1}h_{b1}(u)+\rho/\alpha, \quad (22)$$

Let $\nu_1(u) = \frac{\beta(\tau(u-\Delta)+c)}{\tau}, \nu_2(u) = \frac{\beta(\delta u+c)}{\delta}$. Using similar method to obtaining (18), we obtain the solutions of (14) and (16) respectively as the following

$$V_2(u,b) = a_{\tau 1}h_{\tau 1}(u) + a_{\tau 2}h_{\tau 2}(u), \quad \Delta \le u < b, \tag{23}$$
$$V_4(u,b) = a_{\delta 1}h_{\delta 1}(u) + a_{\delta 2}h_{\delta 2}(u), \quad -c/\delta < u < 0, \tag{24}$$

with

$$h_{\tau 1}(u) = e^{-\nu_1(u)}U\left(1-\frac{\lambda}{\delta}, 1-\frac{\lambda+n\alpha}{\delta}; \nu_1(u)\right), \tag{25}$$

$$h_{\tau 2}(u) = (\nu_1(u))^{\frac{\lambda+\alpha}{\delta}} e^{-\nu_1(u)}M\left(1+\frac{\alpha}{\delta}, 1+\frac{\lambda+\alpha}{\delta}; \nu_1(u)\right), \tag{26}$$

$$h_{\delta 1}(u) = e^{-\nu_2(u)}U\left(1-\frac{\lambda}{\delta}, 1-\frac{\lambda+\alpha}{\delta}; \nu_2(u)\right), \tag{27}$$

$$h_{\delta 2}(u) = (\nu_2(u))^{\frac{\lambda+\alpha}{\delta}} e^{-\nu_2(u)}M\left(1+\frac{\alpha}{\delta}, 1+\frac{\lambda+\alpha}{\delta}; \nu_2(u)\right). \tag{28}$$

Obviously, the general solution of (15) is the following

$$V_3(u,b) = a_{01}e^{\theta_1 u} + a_{02}e^{\theta_2 u}, \quad 0 \le u < b, \tag{29}$$

where a_{01} and a_{02} are arbitrary constants, θ_1 and θ_2 are the two roots of

$$c\theta^2 + (c\beta - (\lambda+\alpha))\theta - \alpha\beta = 0, \tag{30}$$

that is to say

$$\theta_1 = \frac{\lambda+\alpha-c\beta+\sqrt{c^2+4c\alpha\beta}}{2c}, \quad \theta_2 = \frac{\lambda+\alpha-c\beta-\sqrt{c^2+4c\alpha\beta}}{2c}. \tag{31}$$

By the property of the confluent hypergeometric function of the first and second kinds, if $\delta \ne \lambda + n\alpha$, we obtain

$$\lim_{u\downarrow -c/\delta} h_{\delta 1}(u) = \frac{\Gamma(\frac{\lambda+\alpha}{\delta})}{\Gamma(\frac{\delta+\alpha}{\delta})}, \quad \lim_{u\downarrow -c/\delta} h_{\delta 2}(u) = 0. \tag{32}$$

Letting $u \downarrow -c/\delta$ in (18) on both sides, substituting the second equation of (11) and (32) into it, we obtain $a_{\delta 1} = 0$. Thus

$$V_4(u,b) = a_{\delta 2}h_{\delta 2}(u), \quad -c/\delta < u < 0. \tag{33}$$

From Theorem 2.2, (18) and (27)-(29), we obtain

$$a_{b1}h_{b1}(b) = a_{\tau 1}h_{\tau 1}(b) + a_{\tau 2}h_{\tau 2}(b), \tag{34}$$
$$a_{\tau 1}h_{\tau 1}(\Delta) + a_{\tau 2}h_{\tau 2}(\Delta) = a_{01}e^{\theta_1\Delta} + a_{02}e^{\theta_2\Delta}, \tag{35}$$
$$a_{01} + a_{02} = a_{\delta 2}h_{\delta 2}(0), \tag{36}$$
$$a_{\delta 2}h'_{\delta 2}(0) = a_{01}\theta_1 + a_{02}\theta_2, \tag{37}$$
$$a_{01}\theta_1 e^{\theta_1\Delta} + a_{02}\theta_2 e^{\theta_2\Delta} = a_{\tau 1}h'_{\tau 1}(\Delta) + a_{\tau 2}h'_{\tau 2}(\Delta), \tag{38}$$
$$(c-\rho)a_{b1}h'_{b1}(b) + \rho = c(a_{\tau 1}h'_{\tau 1}(b) + a'_{\tau 2}(b)), \tag{39}$$

Solving the above equations, we obtain

$$a_{b1} = \frac{\rho(h_{\tau 2}(b)(h_{\tau 1}(\Delta) - Mh'_{\tau 1}(\Delta)) - h_{\tau 1}(b)(h_{\tau 2}(\Delta) - Mh'_{\tau 2}(\Delta))}{N(b)},$$

$$a_{\tau 1} = \frac{-\rho h_{b1}(b)(h_{\tau 2}(\Delta) - Mh'_{\tau 2}(\Delta))}{N(b)},$$

$$a_{\tau 2} = \frac{\rho h_{b1}(b)(h_{\tau 1}(\Delta) - Mh'_{\tau 1}(\Delta))}{N(b)},$$

$$a_{01} = \frac{\rho M_1 h_{b1}(b)(h_{\tau 1}(\Delta)h'_{\tau 2}(\Delta) - h_{\tau 2}(\Delta)h'_{\tau 1}(\Delta))}{N(b)},$$

$$a_{02} = \frac{-\rho M_2 h_{b1}(b)(h_{\tau 1}(\Delta)h'_{\tau 2}(\Delta) - h_{\tau 2}(\Delta)h'_{\tau 1}(\Delta))}{N(b)},$$

$$a_{\delta 2} = \frac{\rho(\theta_1 - \theta_2)h_{b1}(b)(h_{\tau 1}(\Delta)h'_{\tau 2}(\Delta) - h_{\tau 2}(\Delta)h'_{\tau 1}(\Delta))}{N(b)},$$

with

$$\begin{aligned} N(b) &= (h_{\tau 2}(\Delta) - Mh'_{\tau 2}(\Delta)[(c-\rho)h_{\tau 1}(b)h'_{b1}(b) - ch'_{\tau 1}(b)h_{b1}(b)] \\ &\quad -(h_{\tau 1}(\Delta) - Mh'_{\tau 1}(\Delta))[(c-\rho)h_{\tau 2}(b)h'_{b1}(b) - ch'_{\tau 2}(b)h_{b1}(b)] \\ M &= \frac{(h'_{\delta 2}(0) - \theta_2 h_\delta(0))e^{\theta_1 \Delta} - (h'_{\delta 2}(0) - \theta_1 h_{\delta 2}(0))e^{\theta_2 \Delta}}{(h'_{\delta 2}(0) - \theta_2 h_{\delta 2}(0))\theta_1 e^{\theta_1 \Delta} - (h'_{\delta 2}(0) - \theta_1 h_{\delta 2}(0))\theta_2 e^{\theta_2 \Delta}}, \\ M_1 &= \frac{h'_{\delta 2}(0) - \theta_2 h_{\delta 2}(0)}{(h'_{\delta 2}(0) - \theta_2 h_{\delta 2}(0))\theta_1 e^{\theta_1 \Delta} - (h'_{\delta 2}(0) - \theta_1 h_{\delta 2}(0))\theta_2 e^{\theta_2 \Delta}}, \\ M_2 &= \frac{h'_{\delta 2}(0) - \theta_1 h_{\delta 2}(0)}{(h'_{\delta 2}(0) - \theta_2 h_{\delta 2}(0))\theta_1 e^{\theta_1 \Delta} - (h'_{\delta 2}(0) - \theta_1 h_{\delta 2}(0))\theta_2 e^{\theta_2 \Delta}}. \end{aligned}$$

When $\rho = c$, we assume that the barrier is constant and consider the problem of finding the optimal level for the barrier. To do so, we need to find $b^* \geq 0$ which maximize $V(u,b)$. By (22) and (28), we find that the numerators of them do not depend on b and the denominators of them are all $N'(b)$. Hence, an optimal dividend barrier b^* is found by maximizing $V(u,b)$ i.e. minimizing $N'(b)$. Thus b^* is a solution to $N''(b) = 0$.

Table 1. Influence of τ and δ on b^* with $c = 2,\ \lambda = 1,\ \beta = 1,\ \alpha = 0.04,\ \Delta = 0$

Optimal barrier b^* $(V_2(1,b^*))$					
	$\delta = 0.06$	$\delta = 0.07$	$\delta = 0.08$	$\delta = 0.09$	$\delta = 0.10$
$\tau = 0.020$	0.221	0.798	1.299 (24.85)	1.745 (24.63)	2.145 (24.43)
$\tau = 0.025$	0.560	1.201 (25.18)	1.744 (24.97)	2.218 (24.79)	2.639 (24.63)
$\tau = 0.030$	1.103 (25.47)	1.822 (25.29)	2.413 (25.14)	2.918 (25.01)	3.360 (24.90)
$\tau = 0.035$	2.176 (25.60)	2.989 (25.50)	3.631 (25.41)	4.166 (25.33)	4.627 (25.26)

Table 1 provides numerical results for the optimal dividend barrier b^* for various τ and δ. We find that the optimal dividend barrier increases as the credit interest or debit interest increases.

References

1. Embrechts, P., Schmidli, H.: Ruin estimates for a general insurance risk model. Adv. Appl. Prob. 26, 404–422 (1994)
2. Dickson, D.C.M., Egídio dos Reis, A.D.: The effect of interest on negative surplus. Insurance Math. Econom. 21, 1–16 (1997)
3. Gerber, H.U., Yang, H.: Absolute ruin probabilities in a jump diffusion risk model with investment. N. Amer. Actuar. J. 11(3), 159–169 (2007)
4. Cai, J.: On the time value of absolute ruin with debit interest. Adv. Appl. Prob. 39(2), 343–359 (2007)
5. Cai, J., Gerber, H.U., Yang, H.: Optimal dividends in an Ornstein-Uhlenbeck type model with credit and debit interest. N. Amer. Actuar. J. 10(2), 94–108 (2006)
6. Wang, C., Yin, C., Li, E.: On the classical risk model with credit and debit interests under absolute ruin. Statist. Probab. Lett. 80(5-6), 427–436 (2010)
7. Wang, C., Yin, C.: Dividend payments in the classical risk model under absolute ruin with debit interest. Appl. Stoch. Models Bus. Ind. 25, 247–262 (2009)
8. Yin, C., Wang, C.: The perturbed compound Poisson risk process with investment and debit interest. Methodol. Comput. Appl. Probab. 12(3), 391–413 (2010)
9. Cai, J., Feng, R.H., Willmot, G.E.: The compound Poisson surplus model with interest and liquid reserves analysis of the Gerber-Shiu discounted penalty function. Methodol. Comput. Appl. Probab. 11(3), 401–423 (2009)
10. Cai, J., Feng, R.H., Willmot, G.E.: Analysis of the compound Poisson surplus model with liquid reserves interest and dividends. Astin. Bull. 39(1), 225–247 (2009)
11. Dickson, D.C.M., Waters, H.R.: Some optimal dividends problems. Astin. Bull. 34, 49–74 (2004)
12. Fang, Y., Wu, R.: Optimal dividend strategy in the compound Poisson model with the constant interest. Stoch. Models 23, 149–166 (2007)
13. Yuen, K.C., Wang, G., Li, W.K.: The Gerber-Shiu expected discounted penalty function for risk processes with interest and a constant dividend barrier. Insurance Math. Econom. 40(1), 104–112 (2007)
14. Li, S.: The distribution of the dividend payments in the compound Poisson risk model perturbed by diffusion. Scand. Actuar. J. 2, 73–85 (2006)
15. Wan, N.: Dividend payments with a threshold strategy in the compound Poisson risk model perturbed by diffusion. Insurance Math. Econom. 40(3), 509–523 (2007)
16. Lin, X.S., Kristina, P.P.: The compound Poisson risk model with a threshold dividend strategy. Insurance Math. Econom. 38(1), 57–80 (2006)
17. Lin, S.X., Willmot, G.E., Drekic, S.: The classical risk model with a constant dividend barrier: analysis of the Gerber-Shiu discounted penalty function. Insurance Math. Econom. 33, 551–566 (2003)
18. Abramowitz, M., Stegun, I.A.: Handbook of Mathematical Function: with Formulas, Graphs, and Mathematical Tables. U.S. Government Printing Office, Washington, D.C (1972)

Research of Distributed Heterogeneous Database Query Technology Based on XML

Honghui Wang,Zhihui Chen, Hao Zhang, and Yanan Li

Qinggong College, Hebei United University, Tangshan 063009, China
wanghui6819526@126.com

Abstract. This study uses XML as a middleware transparent access to heterogeneous databases, and uses the standard database language based on SQL-99 to implement the operation of global data and global query, enabling users to make global data in the system tables are created, deleted, the global data insert, update, delete, and global query and other database operations.

Keywords: heterogeneous databases, XML, global table, global query.

1 Introduction

Heterogeneous database research is mainly used for multiple geographically distributed heterogeneous databases, to realize transparent access to heterogeneous databases without affecting its local autonomy, to support the global application of the database and the flexibility of information exchange and sharing of database .The key point is to based on the local database model, to realize the establishment of global data model or global external view. Meanwhile the collected data also supports the historical data access, then data warehouse users can use the provided unified data interface for decision support queries.

2 Implementations of the Global Query

Heterogeneous database access is needed for inquires transparent information service, and the global inquires is the important segment of the whole design system. When users submit queries,the system will extract the content with form and do the input string processing to get the query information, then traverse the related data dictionary to take data. The users' inquires are mainly proposed for the global view, and these inquires are must taken breaks down into inquires for the partial view in order to get the data the users want, thus realize the data transparent access.

Global query Can be divided into four steps:

To transform the query of users into to visit sequence to the local database.

To visit heterogeneous database, it is necessary to transform the inquire conditions, namely visit parameters.

C. Liu, J. Chang, and A. Yang (Eds.): ICICA 2011, Part I, CCIS 243, pp. 604–610, 2011.

Traverse the data dictionary to get search results, and translate them into an XML document.

Filtering repetitive data and combining the incomplete data of the XML document.

3 The Design of Global Query

Query processing module is center execution transparent parts of the heterogeneous database access to system. Query is the global mode based on XML. Global users are different from local users , local users control a local node, while the global users only have operating permissions of the sharing part that included in the joint use, and different global users also should have the difference between operating permissions. When the users inquire, the first step is the operation of XML query. When inquire each local database, the query should be decomposed into local mode, that is the subquery of various heterogeneous database. In this process ,XML queries should be transformed into database queries.

3.1 The Global Query

The global query is the core technology of this system which involves the compiler processing ,decomposition translation ,query optimization, execution of local database, results summary and so on . The realization process is as shown in figure 1 below:

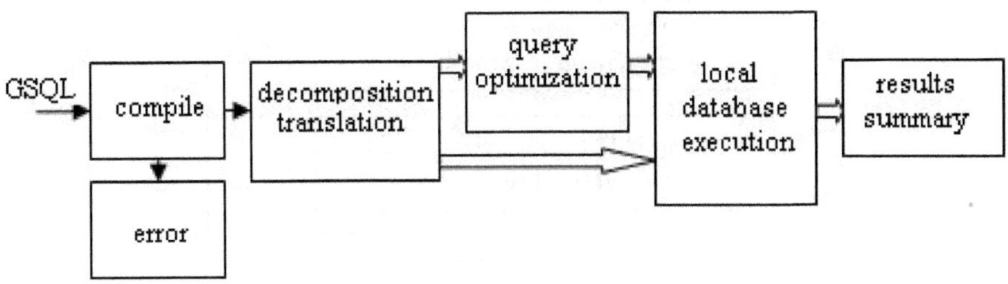

Fig. 1. The implementation of GSQL

To inquire a record, firstly analyze the SQL language is whether the SQL statement or not. If it is the SQL statement, then get the table name and the query conditions, and judge that if the table name is in global data dictionary, if in, then judge the table is whether in the global table, then obtain the name of node database which the table storages, and generate the query statement of every node, do the query operation for the node database, incorporate the query data. The query operation is shown as figure2:

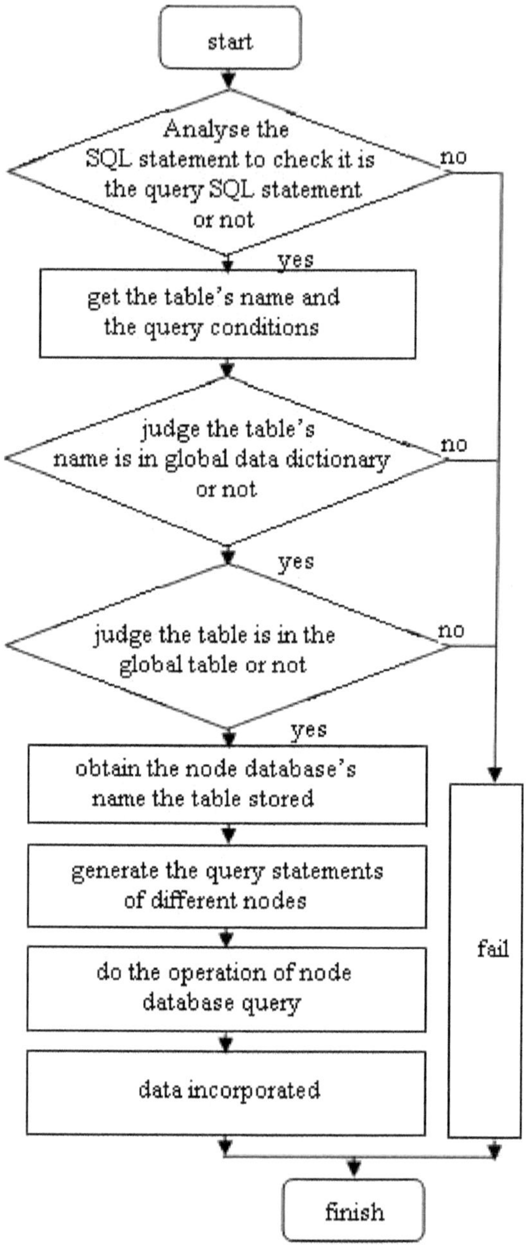

Fig. 2. Flow chart of global query

3.2 The Decomposition of Query

During the process of global query, the query is often translated for many times. When the query system through the different level, it will be converted into the language and data representation in the corresponding level, and solve the problem of difference between different levels. The data dictionary realized the system overall concept layer and local concept layer, so the query decomposition and translation are based on the data dictionary , the translation runs through in the process of decomposition, so here the query decomposition and translation process are combined into a component to be realized.

The process of query decomposition is shown as follows:

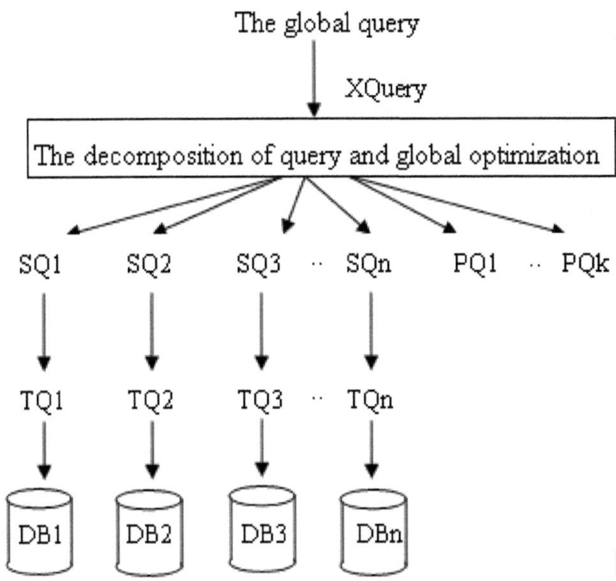

Fig. 3. The query decomposition

The steps of query decomposition are shown as follows:

1) the replacement of the key words. Replace the key words of SQL and functions with the corresponding key word in the data dictionary.
2) the replacement of constants. Replace the special express of some data type constants in the local database system with the corresponding forms.
3) the replacement of the identifier. The identifier includes names of the field and the global table. According to the data dictionary, replace the global table name and field name with the local database table name and the local column name which constituted the local database of the global table.

3.3 Transform of XML Documents

Display the XML document With XSL technology. XML documents will be tested to decide that the XSLT transformation is necessary or not by the data validity. If the data validation fails, then error page tips. If the data is effective, transform the XML into HTML by the XSLT transformation.

Display the XML document With XSL technology. XSLT is an important part of the XSL, which is used to transform XML documents into XML and HTML documents or pure text documents. By XSLT, the input file can be added/removed elements and attributes, some elements also can be hidden. XSLT document has a root element used for the definition of the version information"stylesheet". XSL: out elements are used to specify the need of pure text output rather than HTML or XML output. Use the browser open XML files, then create an XSL style sheet with a conversion template. And connected the XSL style sheets to XML documents, then the XML document can be transformed into HTML successfully. Of course, the browser should be compatible with XSLT. If there is XSLT namespace declaration on the top of document, it will be allowed to visit the XSLT elements, attributes and characteristics. The content of the<xsl: template> elements define the HTML code. The process of transformation is shown as follows:

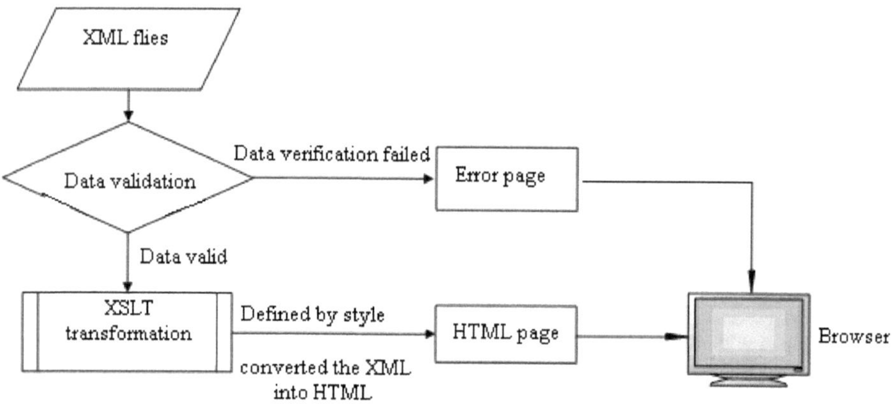

Fig. 4. Flow chart of XML document conversion

3.4 Using JDOM Technology to Analyze XML Documents

JDOM is a Java tool package using XML, JDOM based on tree structure, using Java technology for parsing XML documents and other operations, it also uses the standard Java coding mode. it aims to simplify the interaction with XML, it faster than using DOM, it will be Java-specific document model.

XML file will be analyzed into Document object if operate as the following three steps:

Create a DocumentBuilderFactory. The object will be created DocumentBuilder.

Create a DocumentBuilder. Document DocumentBuilder to analyze the actual object.

Analysis of the file to create a Document object. For example, to achieve test results table generated MY_SCORETABLE_CJB.

The core code translated into Document object code is as follows:

```
this.xmlFile="MY_SCORETABLE_CJB.xml";// The XML file which need to be converted
// Create DocumentBuilderFactory
DocumentBuilderFactory docBuilderFactory=
DocumentBuilderFactory.newInstance( );
// Create DocumentBuilder
DocumentBuilder docBuilder=docBuilderFactory.newDocumentBuilder( )
//Analyse XML file
document=docBuilder.parse(xmlFile);
```

The flow chart of processing XML files used JDOM, modifying and adding node is as follows:

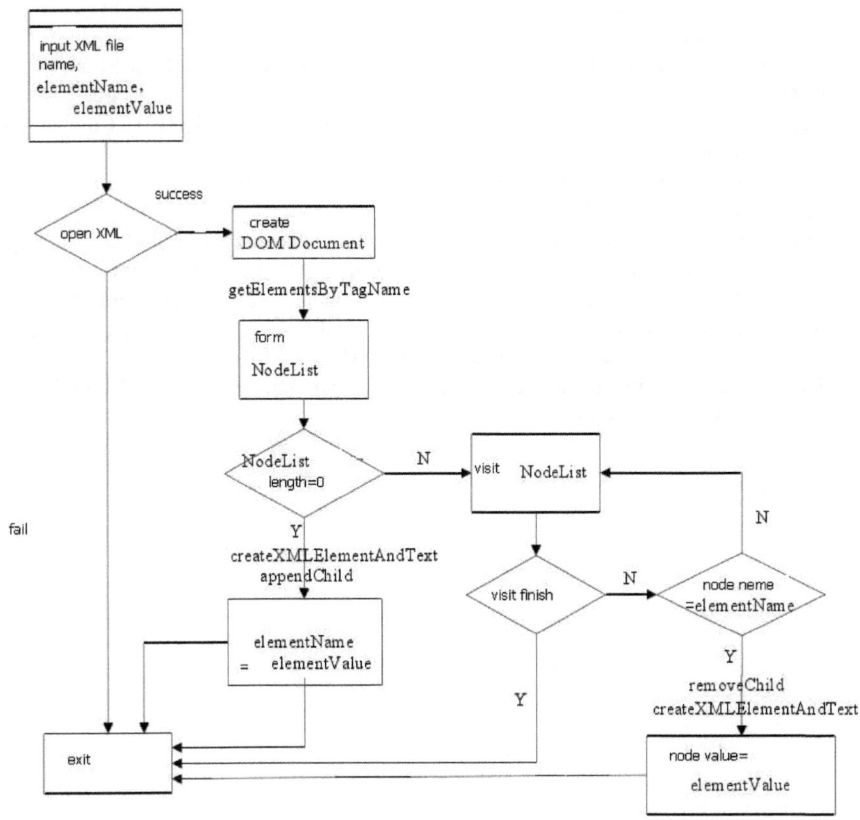

Fig. 5. Flow chart of JDOM handle XML documents

4 Conclusion

This paper puts forward the scheme of the global inquires, does the related study about integration technology problems of heterogeneous database integration. And according to the correlation analysis, makes the theory research about the query decomposition, gives a specific decomposition method.

References

1. Chen, M., Yu, P.: Interleaving a join sequence with semijoins in distributed query processing. IEEE Trans. on Parallel and Distr. System 3, 611–621 (2008)
2. Mullin, J.: Optimal semijoins for distributed database systems. IEEE Trans. Software Eng. 16, 558–560 (2007)
3. Dede, C.: The Evolution of Constructivist Learning Environments: Immersion in Distributed Virtual Worlds. Educational Technology, 352–361 (2005)
4. Bright, M.W.: A Taxonomy and Current Issues in Multidatabases Systems. IEEE Computer 25(3), 50–59 (2008)
5. Bernstein, P., Chiu, D.: Using semi-joins to solve relational queries. J. ACM 28(1), 25–40 (2008)
6. Berstein, P.A., Goodman, N.: Power of NationalSemioins. SIAM J. Comput. 10(4), 602–625 (2008)
7. Mullin, J.: Optimal semijoins for distributed database systems. IEEE Trans. Software Eng. 16(5), 558–560 (2007)
8. Chen, M., Yu, P.: Interleaving a join sequence with semijoins in distributed query processing. IEEE Trans. on Parallel and Distr. System 3(5), 611–621 (2008)
9. Lee, W.F., Olson, P.L., Thomas, G.F.: A remote user interface for the ADDS multidatabase system. In: Proceeding of the 2nd Oklahoma workshop on Applied Computing, The Univ. of Tulsa, pp. 194–204 (2008)
10. Shipman, D.: The functional data model and the data language DAPLEX. ACM Trans. Database Syst. 6(1), 140–173 (2007)

Risk Quantitative Analysis of Project Bidding Quotation Based on Improved AHP Method

Hong Wang, Wei Liu, and XiaoLi Cai

Jiangxi University of Sciece and Technology, Nanchang, Jiangxi, 330013, China

Abstract. Project bidding quotation is a process of uncertainty; bidders always face some risks in bidding. This paper tries to find out the risky factors which affect the bidding, and then put forward a kind of quantitative quotation methods by Blurry Mathematics and Weighing Determination ---which is called Improved AHP method. By this new method, it is favorite to provide the bidding quotation of the new projects. And last the paper will use an example to explain how the method will be employed in project bidding quotation.

Keywords: AHP, bidding quotation, risk, quantitative analysis.

1 Preface

Project bidding quotation is a process of uncertainty, which is affected by some factors, such as the location prices, the complex competitive situation and the needed technical skills of the bidding. This process also requires some factors such as technical content. Besides, the time, resources and environment are also the factors affected the bidding quotation. Project bidding is a kind of risky job, which has three functions, there are washing out people who don't have ability to get the project, inspiring the one who want to get the project and adjusting the resources[1]. Bidders who face enormous risks during the process, because after winning bidding, they will carried out the long duration contract, and also will couple with the complex economical and regional environment. The most risky situation they will face is the uncertainty of the project itself may cause higher cost than the bidding quotation which is led to a great loss. Therefore, before going to have project bidding, bidders must have a risk analysis about the price quotation[2].Besides, they should build a control system, cooperating well with sales department, investing department, project managing and financial, supervising departments. All of these departments should take their responsibilities and try to decrease the bidding risks[3].

At present, the domestic and foreign project bidding quotation risk analyses are mostly the qualitative analysis. In the current flourishing construction market, the competition is more serious than before; bidders in order to win in the competition must give a quantitative risk analysis to the bidding quotation. This paper proposes a kind of quantitative risk analysis of bidding quotation that is improved AHP method; which can assist the bidders to decrease or avoid risks.

C. Liu, J. Chang, and A. Yang (Eds.): ICICA 2011, Part I, CCIS 243, pp. 611–617, 2011.

2 The Factors Affect the Bidding Quotations

With the reforms of economical system and enterprise managing mechanism, the construction market is becoming more and more prosperous. If the bidders want to win from the serious competitions, they should analyze the factors affected bidding quotation and then carry out some proper strategies to deal with the risks[4].

The affected factors of the bidding prices are the followings: estimates the profitability of the bidding project; bidding competition; bottom or control price; the facts of owner funds; contract conditions; management fee; workers' wages; material price; mechanical equipment rental price; the level of bidding units and their experience; the conditions of the projects and their future opportunities[5,6].

3 The Quantitative Analytical Method of Bidding Quotation Risks

The article uses the expert evaluation method[7] to do the quantitative analysis. This method is used in this way, first ,for a new bidding project, we should make the weight W to the above 12 factors, then measure the bidding by using these 12 factors, and next marking off each factor into five ranks according to bidding blurry mathematic[8] method and give each rank score C(1.0,0.8,0.6,0.4,0.2), last, calculate each factor score of C which is given by experts, multiply W and C, and accumulate summation Σ WC, compared with the results of similar projects haven before, and try to decide whether bid or not. if did ,then try to handle the risks according with the knowledge which have done before to the previous situations.

By the improved analytic hierarchy processes (AHP) [9] determine the risk factors weights are as follows:

3.1 Analytic Hierarchy Processes (AHP)

AHP method tries to get the persuasive result through building matrix, sorting calculation and check consistency. This method has obvious superiority, and it is suitable for employing in project to measure the risky weight of the bidding quotation; At the same time, this method use quantity form to reflect the subjective basis, it is scientific and well-organized, and it is better to avoid contradictions caused by people's subjectivity and overcome the difficulties made between policy makers and policy analyzer. This method also overcome the personal preference of policy maker, it helps to improve the efficiency of the policy.

3.2 The Shortage and Improvement of Analytic Hierarchy Process (AHP)

The experts and policy makers are hard to get the standard of the bidding, so the judgments are difficult to keep the consistency. Therefore, the method is needed to revise. When use power iterative eigenvalue method to solve the weight vectors, because of the different judgment matrixes, convergence slower, the iteration calculation is also very big. For this is disadvantage, this paper proposes the way to improve AHP method, and the way is to formatting the two-phase judgment matrix. The first stage adopts people's familiar three scale method (0,1,2) to compare with the factors .After comparing between each two, establish a comparison matrix and compute of the element's sort index, and then the second stage is to change the comparative matrix into the judgment matrix, and prove it can completely keep the consistency. So it can avoid the inconsistency of judgment matrix made by analytic hierarchy process, and in the consultation process just the three scale method can be adopted, as to the expert is easy to make the right judgment, and the calculation is greatly reduced.

3. 3 The Steps to Determine the Weighing of Risk Factors

(1) For the situation which it can construct a fully judgment matrix [5]

①decomposing and combining the problems, establishing hierarchical structure, showing the relationships between those levels clearly;

②Using three scales method to establish a comparative judgment matrix after compare the elements in the same level, and then calculate the sort index of the element. And last change the comparative matrix into judgment matrix.(the judgment matrix can be constructed by using range method.)

(a) using range method to construct the judgment matrix, because $f(r_i, r_j) = c_{ij} = c_b^{(ri - rj)/R}$, and the matrix $C = (c_{ij})_{n\times n}$ is the consistence judgment matrix, c_b is a constant, is a certain standards of poor elements of a given the relative important degree (usually in a practical application often take $c_b = 9$); $R = r_{max} - r_{min}$, called range, $r_{max} = \max\{ r_1, r_2, \ldots, r_n \}$,$r_{min} = \min\{ r_1, r_2, \ldots, r_n \}$.

(b) use extremely analogy method to construct the judgment matrix, by transform the $f(r_i, r_j) = c_{ij} = \left(\frac{r_i}{r_j}\right)^{\log_{r} c_b}$ to get $C = (c_{ij})_{n\times n}$,it is a consistency judgment matrix, and the $r = \frac{r_{max}}{r_{min}}$ called extremely ratio.

③ to exam the consistency (after check ,using the method mentioned above can reduce the iteration numbers).

(2) For the situation which can not construct for the fully judgment matrix [6]

①the effective incomplete judgment matrix $A = (a_{ij})n\times n$, and to calculate the equivalent matrix $\overline{A}$, to design the calculate steps is L, when L = 1;

② using AHP method to calculate the W (k) of $\overline{A}$ matrix;

③ according to the consistency principle, to test the index $P_{C.I} = (\lambda_{max} - n)/(n-1)$, and to check the consistency (λ_{max} is the maximum eigenvalue, n is evaluation index number), when L = 1.3, it can use the $\delta(k) = \max\{|w_i^{(k)} - w_i^{(k+1)}|/|w_i^{(k-1)}|\} \le \varepsilon$ to validate the consistency (Among them ,ε is the maximum number to satisfy the consistency , general according to the specific circumstances to determine), if meet the requirements of the check, the calculation should be stop, W (k) is the weight should be calculated. Otherwise, when L = 1.3, then turn to ④, when L = 2, then turn to ⑤, k is the iteration number;

④ According to the revise, it can get the judgment coefficient

$r_{ij} = \frac{\partial p_{C.I}}{\partial a_{ij}} = \frac{1}{n-1} \left| v_i w_j - w_i v_i / a^2_{ij} \right|$ (Where the vi, wi its largest eigenvalue matrix is equivalent to the corresponding eigenvectors V and weight W of the i-th component).Aij to rij, the greater the effect of that of consistency, the greater the correction aij, make corresponding L = 2 turn ②.

⑤ by $\frac{\partial P_{C.I}}{\partial_{a_{ij}}} = (| A - \lambda_{max} I|)^{-1} [(v_i w_j - v_j w_i / a^2_{ij})[W]_0 - [X]_0]$ type of weight sensitivity; $[W]_0$ refers to the n a component is 0 W vector, $W = (w_1, w_2, \ldots, w_n)$; $[X]_0$ refers to the n a component is 0 X vector, including $X = (0, \ldots, 0, wj, 0, \ldots, 0, -w_j / a_{2ij}, 0, \ldots, 0)$, $- w_j / a2_{ij}$ for the i term; i as the unit matrix for the unknown Yuan attributes the sensitivity of information value, and additional into A, making L = 3, computational W (k + 1), turn ②.

In short, each method has its advantages and disadvantages, to comprehensive speaking, the project bidding quoted price risk factors to determine the weighing of the AHP method, and improvement is relatively advisable.

4 The Case --- Quantitative Risk Analysis of the Project Bidding Quotation

Before project bidding on its bidding quotation, it needs to have quantitative risk analysis as to decide whether to participate in the project bidding. Hypothesis to consider the bidding project profitability estimated size (c_1), bidding competition (c_2), mark-bottom or control price (c_3), truth owners funds conditions (c_4), contract conditions (c_5), management rate fare size (c_6), the project is artificially wages (the c_7), the project material price (c_8), the project machinery equipment rental price (c_9), bidding unit their own level and similar engineering experience (c_{10}), project conditions (c_{11}) and future opportunities (c_{12}) etc 12 risk factors; Concrete analysis process is as follows:

(1) Establish comparative matrix

$A = (a_{ij}) =$

A	c1	c2	c3	c4	c5	c6	c7	c8	c9	c10	c11	c12	ri
c1	1	2	2	2	2	2	2	2	2	2	2	2	23
c2	0	1	1	1	1	2	2	2	2	2	2	2	18
c3	0	1	1	1	1	2	2	2	2	2	2	2	18
c4	0	1	1	1	1	2	2	2	2	2	2	2	18
c5	0	1	1	1	1	2	1	2	2	2	2	2	17
c6	0	0	0	0	0	1	2	2	2	1	2	2	12
c7	0	0	0	0	0	0	1	2	2	0	2	2	9
c8	0	0	0	0	0	0	0	1	1	0	2	2	6
c9	0	0	0	0	0	0	0	1	1	0	2	2	6
c10	0	0	0	0	0	1	2	2	2	1	2	2	12
c11	0	0	0	0	0	0	0	0	0	0	1	1	2
c12	0	0	0	0	0	0	0	0	0	0	1	1	2
rj	1	6	6	6	6	12	14	18	18	12	22	22	

$$a_{ij} = \begin{cases} 2 & c_i \text{ is important than } c_j \\ 1 & c_i \text{ and } c_j \text{ are equally important} \\ 0 & c_i \text{ is important than } c_j \end{cases} \quad (i,j=1,2,\ldots,12), r_i=\sum_{j=1}^{12} a_{ij}, \; r_j=\sum_{i=1}^{12} a_{ij}$$

(2) establish the judgment matrix

$C = (c_{ij}) =$

c	c_1	c_2	c_3	c_4	c_5	c_6	c_7	c_8	c_9	c_{10}	c_{11}	c_{12}	M_i	W_i	
c_1	1	2	2	2	2	3	4	6	6	3	9	9	1105441.83	3.19	0.21
c_2	1	1	1	1	1	2	3	4	4	2	5	5	2075.53	1.89	0.12
c_3	1	1	1	1	1	2	3	4	4	2	5	5	2075.53	1.89	0.12
c_4	1	1	1	1	1	2	3	4	4	2	5	5	2075.53	1.89	0.12
c_5	1	1	1	1	1	2	2	3	3	2	5	5	898.69	1.76	0.12
c_6	0	1	1	1	1	1	1	2	2	1	3	3	1	1	0.07
c_7	0	0	0	0	0	1	1	1	1	1	2	2	0	0.77	0.05
c_8	0	0	0	0	0	1	1	1	1	1	2	2	0	0.53	0.03
c_9	0	0	0	0	0	1	1	1	1	1	2	2	0	0.53	0.03
c_{10}	0	1	1	1	1	1	1	2	2	1	3	3	1	0.99	0.07
c_{11}	0	0	0	0	0	0	0	1	1	0	1	1	0	0.35	0.02
c_{12}	0	0	0	0	0	0	0	1	1	0	1	1	0	0.35	0.02

Type of $M_i=\prod_{j=1}^{12} c_{ij}$, $W_i=\sqrt[12]{M_i}$, $\overline{W_i}=\dfrac{W_i}{\sum_{i=1}^{12} W_i}$, $\sum_{i=1}^{12} W_i=15.14$, $\sum_{i=1}^{12}\overline{W_i}=1$

(3) Validate the consistency

Suppose: $C=(c_{ij}), D=(d_i)_{n\times i}=C\cdot \overline{W_i}^{T}=(2.52,1.50,1.50,1.50,1.40,0.79,0.61,0.42,0.42,0.78,0.28,0.28)^T$,

Then maximum eigenvalue $\lambda_{\max}=\sum_{i=1}^{12}\dfrac{d_i}{nw_i}=\dfrac{1}{12}\left(\dfrac{2.52}{0.21}+\dfrac{1.50}{0.12}+\dfrac{1.50}{0.12}+\dfrac{1.50}{0.12}+\right.$

$\left.\dfrac{1.40}{0.12}+\dfrac{0.79}{0.07}+\dfrac{0.61}{0.05}+\dfrac{0.42}{0.03}+\dfrac{0.42}{0.03}+\dfrac{0.78}{0.07}+\dfrac{0.28}{0.02}+\dfrac{0.28}{0.02}\right)=12.0067$

$P_{C.I}=\dfrac{\lambda_{\max}-n}{n-1}=\dfrac{12.0067-12}{11}=0.0006 < \varepsilon$ (because $\varepsilon=0.001$, meet the consistency test)

(4) According to the determined weight of risk factors, determine the WC as follows:

tender considerations	Weight(W)	expert scoring (C)	WC
Estimates of the bidding project profitability size	0.21	1	0.211
Bid competition situation	0.12	0.9	0.112
Mark-bottom or control price actual situation	0.12	0.9	0.112
Owner funds conditions	0.12	0.9	0.112
Contract conditions	0.12	0.8	0.093
The size of the structure of management fee rate fare	0.07	0.7	0.046
The project location's artificially wage standard	0.05	0.5	0.025
The project location's material price	0.03	0.3	0.01
The project location's mechanicale equipment retal prices	0.03	0.3	0.01
The tenderers' own level and similar project experience	0.07	0.7	0.046
Engineering project conditions	0.02	0.2	0.005
Future opportunities	0.02	0.2	0.005
ΣWC = 0. 778			

According to the bidders' experience, the ΣWC above 0. 6 can be bided. This example Σ WC = 0. 778, therefore bidders decide to bid, and according to Σ WC, the bidders should make the risky strategies from previous similar project .therefore, bidders can determine the final bidding quotation.

5 Conclusion

The proposed quantitative risk analysis can assist the bidders to analyze the risk of bid price quotation, and according to previous bid price quotation, we can set new method to make the bidding quotations.

References

1. Long, A.: Project bidding strategies of bid. Journal of Systems Engineering 11, 39–41 (1994)
2. Wang, P., et al.: Judgement matrix in AHP method to construct. Journal of System Engineering Theory and Practice, 134–138 (August 1998)
3. Xiao, W.: Fundamentals and applications of fuzzy mathematic. Beijing aviation industry press (1992)
4. Deng, T.: Project risk management. People's traffic press, Beijing (2004)
5. Sun, J., Jiang, D.: Analytic hierarchy process (AHP) method to construct judgment matrix. Journal of Southeast University 21(3), 69–75 (1991)
6. Hu, P.: Not completely judgment matrix decision-making method. Journal of Southwest Jiaotong University 30(5), 573–578 (1995)
7. Li, G., Liao, O.: Based on BP neural network engineering project bidding price risk premium prediction research. The Chinese Market, China Market in the editorial mailbox, 45 (2010)
8. Chen, W.: Engineering project risk management. People's traffic press, Beijing (2008)
9. Yang, L., Xu, Z., Zhang, J.: The Method of The order for Bidding associated stream. Scientific Research Management, Management of young, The editorial E-mail (2000) (period)
10. Niu, Q.: Decision-making order associated-of the bidding. Railway Engineering Cost Management, Railway Engineering Management ranks, The editorial department (2009)
11. Li, Y.: Construction on The show: Study of Bidding Assessment. Bought associated north China electric power university (HeBei), master's thesis (2009)

Prediction Based on Wavelet Transform and Support Vector Machine

Xiaohong Liu[1], Yanwei Zhu[2], Yongli Zhang[1], and Xinchun Wang[3]

[1] Qinggong College, Hebei United University, TangShan, China
[2] Department of Mathematics and Information science,Tang Shan normal university, Tang Shan,China
[3] Hebei United University, China
lily130203@yahoo.cn

Abstract. In this paper, a model combining the wavelet transform and support vector machine to predict the time series is set up. First, wavelet transform is applied to decompose the series into sub series with different time scales. Then, the SVM is applied to the sub series to simulate and predict future behavior. And then by the inverse wavelet transform, the series are reconstructed, which is the prediction for the time series. The prediction precision of the new model is higher than that of the SVM model and the artificial neural network model for many processes, such as runoff, precipitation, temperature. The universal applicability of the new Wavelet-SVM model and the improvement direction are discussed in this paper.

Keywords: Support vector machine, Wavelet Transformation, Regression.

1 Presentation of the Questions

In the time-domain statistical analysis, researchers have paid much attention to empirical risk minimization (ERM) for the past many years. ERM is rational as the empirical risk is approaching the expected risk when nember samples are large. However, results based on ERM cannot reduce the real risk in the state of finite samples; that is to say, small training error doesn't always lead to sound outcome of forecast and simulation. People often refer to the ability of correct prediction using learning machine with the output as generalization ability. In certain cases, the ability to generalize will decline when the training error is too small and the real risk is raised, which is called overfitting[1].That's because samples are inadequate and the design of learning machine is unreasonable. The two reasons are interrelated. In the neural network, when samples are limited, the learning ability of network is overfit to remember each sample and the empirical risk will quickly converge to a small value or even zero, which cannot guarantee reasonable forecast of future samples. The theory of effective learning and generalizing method needs to be built up under the condition of small samples based on minimizing both empirical risk and fiducial range (VC dimension (VaPnik-Chervonenkis Dimension) of learning machines capacity) because of the contradiction between complexity and generalization of

C. Liu, J. Chang, and A. Yang (Eds.): ICICA 2011, Part I, CCIS 243, pp. 618–625, 2011.

learning machine, which leads to the production of structure risk minimization (SRM). Actually, support vector machine [2-4] (SVM) is the realization of this theory aimed to pattern recognition.

Compared to traditional neural network [5, 6], SVM method replaces traditional empirical risk with structure risk minimization and solves a quadratic optimization problem which can get the global optimal solution in theory. The method has avoided local extreme value problem in neural network. The theory of support vector machine has become popular since 1990s. The algorithm of SVM is applied to pattern recognition, regression estimate and probability-density function estimate. It is considered as an alternative method of artificial neural network in the classifications of text and recognitions of hand-written character, speech and face because of its excellent performance of study [7, 8].

In recent years, SVM method has been applied to time-series analysis [9~11]. Time-series is usually regressed by SVM and then its trend will be predicted in the time-series prediction, which cannot reflect the impact of the blend. However, a lot of time-series are always the superposition of periodic terms and trend terms with the changes of both short-term and long-term characteristics. If the method is used, the impact of short-term will be weakened or even disappears. Wavelet analysis with good time-frequency property just covers the shortage.

Time series are decomposed into different time and scale by wavelet transformation, and thus we can get the property of time series in different frequency bands as time goes by[12]. The method has been widely used in multi-scale analysis of time-series. Regularities of short-term (high frequency) and long-term (low frequency) are reflected in different frequency bands after wavelet decomposition of time-series including many process changes by various time scales. If wavelet coefficients in different frequency bands are regressed by SVM, the tendencies of development and the regularities for change of time-series by different time scales will be obtained, which can reflect its natural information better.

In the paper, Firstly, wavelet coefficient on different time scales of time-series is regressed by support vector machine. Secondly, the mathematical model of time-series will be reconstructed by inverse wavelet transformation. Finally, the changes of time-series in the future will be analyzed and forecast taking the process of runoff for instance.

2 Design of the Trend Analysis Model for the Time Series Based on Wavelet and SVM

2.1 Pretreatment of Hydrological Time Series

At present, wavelet multi-resolution analysis in hydrological process always decomposes original sample data, and then extracts wavelet scale information. This method can reduce time for calculation and simplify calculation process. But there is a problem ignored. In wavelet multi-resolution analysis, what should be decomposed is wavelet coefficient instead of original sample data. Generally, some new information could be obtained by decomposing the original sample directly. However, there is no theoretical support [13].

$x(n)$ is the direct input to the filter banks, and let $x_s(t)$ is a continuous time function. $x_s(t)=\sum_n x(n)\psi(t-n)$, where $x(n)$ is the coefficient. Only when $\psi(k)=\delta(k)$ (where $\delta(k)$ is a sign function), $x_s(t)$ has correct coefficient $x(n)$. Commonly, hydrological time series $\psi(t)$ dissatisfy this condition, which is often ignored in wavelet scale analysis for hydrological process. Hence we could construct the known sample $x(n)$ by adjusting the coefficient $a(n)$, and then we could get $a(k)$ by $x(t)=\sum_n a(n)\psi(t-n)$. In fact, time series $x(n)$ is often replaced by

$$a(n)=\sum_t x(t)\tilde{\psi}(t-n) \tag{1}$$

Where $\tilde{\psi}(t-n)$ is the conjugate function of $\psi(t-n)$. Then the continuous time function is expressed as followed:

$$x_s(t)=\sum_n a(n)\psi(t-n)$$

2.2 Wavelet Transformation and Multi-scale Decomposition

Suppose that $\psi(t)$ is a basic wavelet or mother wavelet. After translation and dilation for it, the following expression is obtained:

$$\psi_{a,\tau}(t)=\frac{1}{\sqrt{a}}\psi\left(\frac{t-\tau}{a}\right) \qquad (a,\tau\in R, a>0)\cdot$$

Where, a is the dilation factor and τ is the translation factor. $\psi_{a,\tau}(t)$ is the mother wavelet depending on parameters a and τ .

For any signal $f(t)$ with finite energy, we construct a continuous wavelet transform (CWT) as follows.

$$WT_f(a,\tau)=\left[f(t),\psi_{a,\tau}(t)\right]=\frac{1}{\sqrt{a}}\int_R f(t)\psi\left(\frac{t-\tau}{a}\right)dt$$

If C_ψ satisfies admissible condition [13] and the signal $f(t)$ satisfies the condition

$$\int_{-\infty}^{+\infty} f(t)dt<\infty$$

Then we can reconstruct $f(t)$ without loss of information as followed.

$$f(t)=\frac{1}{C_\psi}\int_0^{+\infty}\left[\int_{-\infty}^{+\infty}WT_f(a,\tau)\frac{1}{\sqrt{a}}\psi\left(\frac{t-\tau}{a}\right)dt\right]\frac{da}{a^2}$$

The DWT can be thought as a judicious sub sampling of $WT_f(a,\tau)$ in which we just deal with 'dyadic' scales (i.e., we pick a to be the form $2^{j-1}, j=1,2,3,\cdots$) and then, within a given dyadic scale 2^{j-1}, we pick times that are separated by multiples of 2^j, namely $\tau = 2^j k$;then the wavelet and scaling coefficient of level j is defined as followed,

$$W_{j,t} = \sum_{l=0}^{L-1} h_l V_{j-1,(2t+1-l \bmod N_{j-1})} = \sum_{l=0}^{L_j-1} h_{j,l} X_{2^j(t+1)-1-l \bmod N}$$

$$V_{j,t} = \sum_{l=0}^{L-1} g_l V_{j-1,(2t+1-l \bmod N_{j-1})} = \sum_{l=0}^{L_j-1} g_{j,l} X_{2^j(t+1)-1-l \bmod N}$$

Where $V_0 = X$ and it represents the initial hydrological time series. t is time, $W_{j,t}$ is wavelet coefficient of level j of time t , $V_{j,t}$ is scaling coefficient of level j of time t, h_l, g_l is equivalent wavelet and scaling filters of level j, and 'umodN' stand for 'u modulo N'.

If W, V represents the DWT wavelet and scaling coefficients respectively, then the following functions can be derived.

$$W = PX \ , V = QX$$

Where P is a $N \times N$ real matrix and satisfies $P^T P = I_N$, so we could reconstruct the expression of X.

$$X = \sum_{j=1}^{J} P_j^T W_j + Q_J^T V_J = \sum_{j=1}^{J} D_j + S_J$$

Each D_j is a time series related to variations in X at the scale of 2^j. In a multi resolution analysis, D_j is called the wavelet detail of level j, and $S_j = \sum_{k=j+1}^{J} D_k + S_J$ is called the wavelet smooth of level j for X. The wavelet detail reflects the detail variations on different time scales, and the wavelet smooth reflects the general trend on different time scales.

From the decomposition process above, original time series are decomposed to different scales. On one hand, long-term change process of series can be observed and analyzed; on the other hand, information about short-term series change and the singularity of the time series can be obtained.

2.3 Support Vector Machine Regression and Predication

Calculate the regression function through the support vectors using the obtained coefficient, and then forecast the trend change of the future. The basic idea of support vector machine regression is nonlinear mapping the original data x into its high dimensional feature space.

Make $G = \{(x_i, a_i)\}_{i=1}^{n}$ a given training data set (x_i is the input vector, a_i is the observed value and n is the total number of data). The form of SVM decision function is as following.

$$f = \omega\psi(x_i) + b \tag{2}$$

Where, $\psi(x_i)$ is the non-linear mapping turning input vectors into high dimensional feature space. The coefficients ω and b are estimated by minimizing the regularized risk function

$$r(f) = C\sum_{i=1}^{N}\Gamma_\varepsilon(a_i, f_i) + \frac{1}{2}\|\omega\|^2 \tag{3}$$

The first term is the empirical error (risk); the second term $\frac{1}{2}\|\omega\|^2$ is a measure of the flatness of the function. C is the regularized constant determining the tradeoff between the empirical risk and the flatness of the model. $\Gamma_\varepsilon(a_i, f_i)$ is called loss function. Among loss functions ε-insensitive function [27] is most widely used, and it takes the following form.

$$\sum_{i=1}^{N}\Gamma_\varepsilon(a_i, f_i) = \begin{cases} 0 & |a_i - f_i| < \varepsilon \\ |a_i - f_i| - \varepsilon & otherwise \end{cases} \tag{4}$$

ε is called tube size and the ε-insensitive function doesn't penalize the error below ε. The smaller is ε and the higher is the approximation accuracy placed on the training data. C and ε are both user-defined parameters.

By introducing positive slack variables ξ and ξ^*, Eq. (3) is transformed to the following primal problem.

Min

$$r(\omega, \xi, \xi^*) = \frac{1}{2}\|\omega\|^2 + C\sum_{i=1}^{N}(\xi_i, \xi_i^*) \tag{5}$$

s.t. :

$$\omega\psi(x_i) + b - a_i \le \varepsilon + \xi^*, i = 1,2,\cdots,N$$
$$a_i - \omega\psi(x_i) - b \le \varepsilon + \xi_i, i = 1,2,\cdots,N$$
$$\xi_i, \xi_i^* \ge 0, i = 1,2,\cdots,N$$

The optimization of the above constraints can be solved by the form of Lagranian [14].

$$\begin{aligned} & L(\omega, b, \xi, \xi^*, \alpha, \alpha^*, \beta, \beta^*) \\ & = \frac{1}{2}\|\omega\|^2 + C\sum_{i=1}^{N}(\xi_i + \xi_i^*) - \sum_{i=1}^{N}\beta_i(\omega\psi(x_i) + b - a_i + \varepsilon + \xi_i) \\ & - \sum_{i=1}^{N}\beta_i(a_i - \omega\psi(x_i) - b + \varepsilon + \xi_i^*) - \sum_{i=1}^{N}(\alpha_i\beta_i + \alpha_i^*\beta_i^*) \end{aligned} \tag{6}$$

And the following functions can be deduced according to extremum conditions.

$$\frac{\partial L}{\partial \omega} = \omega - \sum_{i=1}^{n} (\beta_i - \beta_i^*)\psi(x_i) = 0 \tag{7}$$

$$\frac{\partial L}{\partial b} = \sum_{i=1}^{n} (\beta_i^* - \beta_i) = 0 \tag{8}$$

$$\frac{\partial L}{\partial \xi_i} = C - \beta_i - \alpha_i = 0 \tag{9}$$

$$\frac{\partial L}{\partial \xi_i^*} = C - \beta_i^* - \alpha_i^* = 0 \tag{10}$$

Next, Karush-Kuhn-Tucker condition is applied to regression, and the conjugate Lagrangian function (11) is deduced when the expressions of (7) and (10) are applied in function (5).

$$L = \frac{1}{2}\sum_{i=1}^{n}\sum_{j=1}^{n}(\beta_i - \beta_i^*)(\beta_j - \beta_j^*)\psi(x_i)\psi(x_j) - \varepsilon\sum_{i=1}^{N}(\beta_i - \beta_i^*) + \sum_{i=1}^{N}\alpha_i(\beta_i - \beta_i^*) \tag{11}$$

So, when $K(x_i, x_j)$ equals to $\psi(x_i)\psi(x_j)$, the conjugate Lagrangian function (11) can be obtained.

$$\text{Min}\ \vartheta(\beta_i, \beta_i^*) = \sum_{i=1}^{n}\alpha_i(\beta_i - \beta_i^*) - \varepsilon\sum_{i=1}^{n}(\beta_i + \beta_i^*) - \frac{1}{2}\sum_{i=1}^{N}\sum_{j=1}^{N}(\beta_i - \beta_i^*)(\beta_j - \beta_j^*)K(x_i, x_j) \tag{12}$$

s.t. :

$$\sum_{i=1}^{n}(\beta_i - \beta_i^*) = 0$$
$$0 \le \beta_i \le C, i = 1,2,\cdots,N$$
$$0 \le \beta_i^* \le C, i = 1,2,\cdots,N$$
$$\beta_i * \beta_i^* = 0$$

Calculate value of β_i and β_i^*, the optimal weight of vector of regression hyperplane is as following.

$$\omega^* = \sum_{i=1}^{n}(\beta_i - \beta_i^*)\psi(x_i) \tag{13}$$

Finally, when the above expressions are applied to the function (2), the regression function can be obtained and it is as follows.

$$g(x,\beta,\beta^*)=\sum_{i=1}^{n}(\beta_i-\beta_i^*)K(x_i,x_i)+b \tag{14}$$

$K(x_i,x_i)$ is called kernel function. The value of the kernel equals to the inner product of two vectors of $\psi(x_i)$ and $\tilde{\psi}(x_i)$ in the feature space. Namely, $K(x_i,x_i)=\psi(x_i)\tilde{\psi}(x_i)$. Any function satisfying Mercer condition can be named kernel function [15].

After the regression function is derived, the scale of runoff prediction time is inputted, the prediction is obtained corresponding to the wavelet coefficient.

2.4 Wavelet Reconstruction

By using support vector regression, the prediction data is obtained corresponding to the wavelet coefficient, and then a_n is reconstructed.

2.5 The Calculation Steps of the Wavelet-SVM Model Based on MEXHAT Wavelet

According to the result of analysis, a model can be set up to predict the time series by combining the wavelet transform and support vector machine. Based on literature [13], the Mexican hat wavelet is selected.

3 Conclusion and Discussion

Different scales of some time series are reflected on different frequency bands. Therefore it is not rigorous to predict the trend in the future using SVM regression this processes. The regression on Wavelet coefficients based on SVM on different scales on time series is presented, which gives full consideration of the impact of regularity for series on various scales and frequencies. The shortcoming of high frequency part (short period) weakened by SVM has been overcome. The result indicates that the accuracy obtained from SVM method based on wavelet transform is significantly higher than that based on SVM and BP models.

The method based on wavelet-SVM can dig up deeper information contained in the process of time-series and produce better results of prediction. The method could be applied to many processes, such as runoff, precipitation, temperature and so on.

Trial is used for the selection of the SVM parameters and the number of input parameters for SVM training and predicting. Selection of parameters is an important part of the model building. How to choose suitable parameters need further study. Besides, the paper only takes the radial basis function as kernel function for study. Different kernel function has direct impacts on the establishment of SVM model. For this reason, choosing other types of kernel function for comparative research is worth discussing deeply.

References

1. Bian, Z., Zhang, X.: Pattern recognition. Tsinghua university press, Beijing (1999)
2. Vapinik, V.N.: Statistical learning theory. Wiley Interscience (1998)
3. Cristianini, N., Shawe-Taylor, J.: An introduction to support vector machines and other kernel-based learning methods. Cambridge University Press (2000)
4. Xu, J., Zhang, X., Li, Y.: Advances in support vector machines. Control and Decision 19(5), 481–484 (2004)
5. Jin, L., Qing, W.: A Multi-Step Prediction Model of Wavelet Neural Network. Scientia Atmospherica Sinica 24(1), 79–86 (2000)
6. Chen, R., Liu, J.: The Area Rainfall Prediction of Up-river Valleys in Yangtze River Basin on Artificial Neural Network Modes. Scientia Meteorologica Sinica 24(4), 483–486 (2009)
7. Jonsson, K., Matas, J., Kittler, J., Li, Y.P.: Learning support vector machines for face verification and recognition. In: Proc. IEEE Intl. Conf. Automatic Face and Gesture Recognition, pp. 208–213 (2000)
8. Byun, H.-R., Lee, S.-W.: Applications of Support Vector Machines for Pattern Recognition: a Survey. In: Lee, S.-W., Verri, A. (eds.) SVM 2002. LNCS, vol. 2388, pp. 213–236. Springer, Heidelberg (2002)
9. Tripathi, S., Srinivas, V.V., Nanjundiah, R.S.: Downscaling of precipitation for climate change scenarios: A support vector machine approach. Journal of Hydrology (April 2009)
10. Wei-Chiang, H., Ping-Feng, P.: Potential assessment of the support vector regression technique in rainfall forecasting. Water Resour. Manage. (2006), doi:10.1007/s11269-006-9026-2
11. Lin, J., Cheng, C.: Application of support vector machine method to long-term runoff forecast. Journal of Hydraulic Engineering 37(6), 681–686 (2010)
12. Strang, G., Nguyen, T.: Wavelets and filter banks, Wellesley College (1996)
13. Wang, H.R., Ye, L.T., Liu, C.M., et al.: Problems existing in wavelet analysis of hydrologic series and some improvement suggestions. Progress in Natural Science 17(1), 80–86 (2007)
14. Schölkopfy, B., Simard, P., Smola, A.J.: Prior Knowledge in SuPPort Vector Kernels. In: Advanced in Neural Inofrmation Processings Systems, pp. 640–646. MIT Press, MA (1998)
15. Smits, G.F., Jordnaa, E.M.: Improved SVM regression using mixtures of kemels. In: Proceedings of the 2002 International Joint Conference on Neural Networks, pp. 2785–2790. IEEE, Hawaii (2008)

Schur Convexity for a Class of Symmetric Functions

Shu-hong Wang, Tian-yu Zhang, and Bo-yan Xi

College of Mathematics, Inner Mongolia University for Nationalities,
Tongliao City, Inner Mongolia Autonomous Region, 028043, China
{shu-hongwang,shuhong7682}@163.com

Abstract. The Schur-convex function was introduced by I. Schur in 1923, and it has many important applications in analytic inequalities, generalized means, statistics experiment, chart and matrix, combinatorial optimization, reliability, information security, random sorting, etc. So it is important that Schur-convexity for symmetric functions of several variables is researched. In this paper, Guan's symmetric function was improved, and a class of symmetric functions were derived. By so-called Schur's condition, Schur-convexity and Schur-geometric convexity and Schur-harmonic convexity are studied for a class of symmetric functions.

Keywords: symmetric function, schur-convex, schur-geometric convex, schur-harmonic convex.

1 Introduction

Suppose

$$R = (-\infty, +\infty), R_+ = \{x | x \in R^n, x_i > 0, i = 1, 2, \cdots, n\}.$$

The Schur-convex function was introduced by I. Schur in 1923 [1], and it has many important applications in analytic inequalities[1,13], generalized means[1], statistics experiment[2], chart and matrix[3], combinatorial optimization[4], reliability[5], information security[6], random sorting[7], etc. Now, we introduce the definition of Schur-convex function as follow:

Definition 1.1[1]. Let$x = (x_1, x_2, \cdots, x_n), y = (y_1, y_2, \cdots, y_n) \in R^n$. x is said to be majorized by y(in symbols $x \prec y$) if

$$\sum_{i=1}^{k} x_{[i]} \le \sum_{i=1}^{k} y_{[i]} k = 1, 2, \cdots, n-1 \quad , \quad \sum_{i=1}^{n} x_{[i]} = \sum_{i=1}^{n} y_{[i]},$$

where $x_{[1]} \ge x_{[2]} \ge \cdots \ge x_{[n]}$ and $y_{[1]} \ge y_{[2]} \ge \cdots \ge y_{[n]}$ are rearrangements of x and y in a descending order.

Definition 1.2[1]. Let $\Omega \subset R^n$ be a symmetric convex set. A real-valued function f:$\Omega \to R$ is said to be Schur-convex(Schur-concave) on Ω if $f(x) \le (\ge) f(y)$ for all $x, y \in \Omega$ and $x \prec y$.

C. Liu, J. Chang, and A. Yang (Eds.): ICICA 2011, Part I, CCIS 243, pp. 626–634, 2011.

For $n \geq 2$, $r \in \{1, 2, \cdots, n\}$ and $x = (x_1, x_2, \cdots, x_n) \in [0, 1)^n$, the symmetric function was defined by Guan [8] in 2007 as follows:

$$G_n(x;r) = G_n(x_1, x_2, \cdots, x_n; r) = \sum_{1 \leq i_1 < i_2 < \cdots < i_r \leq n} \prod_{j=1}^{r} \frac{x_{i_j}}{1 - x_{i_j}}, \tag{1}$$

and some results on the Schur-convexity of $G_n(x;r)$ was derived by Guan [8]. Unfortunately, in [8] Guan did not discuss the Schur-convexity or concavity of $G_n(x;r)$ for $n \geq 5$ and $3 \leq r \leq n-2$. Chu, et al.[9] gave the answer of this open problem in 2009:

Theorem 1.1[9]. If $n \geq 2$, and $2 \leq r \leq n$, then

(1) $G_n(x;r)$ is the Schur-convex on $\left[\frac{r-1}{2(n-1)}, 1\right)^n$;

(2) $G_n(x;r)$ is the Schur-concave on $\left[0, \frac{r-1}{2(n-1)}\right]^n$.

Now, a class of symmetric function is defined as follows:

$$G_n(x, r, m) = E_n(x^m, r) = \sum_{1 \leq i_1 < \cdots < i_r \leq n} \prod_{j=1}^{r} \frac{x_{i_j}^m}{1 - x_{i_j}^m}, \tag{2}$$

where $x = (x_1, x_2, \cdots, x_n) \in (0, 1)^n, n \geq 2, r \in \{1, 2, \cdots, n\}, m > 0$ and $i_1, i_2, \cdots, i_n$ are positive integers. The purpose of this paper is discussing Schur-convexity [8,9] and Schur-geometric convexity [11] and Schur-harmonic convexity [12] of $G_n(x, r, m)$.

2 Lemmas

In order to prove our main results, we establish and introduce several lemmas, which we present in this section.

Lemma 2.1(Schur-Ostrowski Theorem)[8,9,12]. Let $\Omega \subset R^n$ be a symmetric convex set with nonempty interior, and $f : \Omega \to R$ be a continuous symmetric function on Ω. If f is differentiable in Ω°, then f is Schur-convex(Schur-concave) onΩif and only if

$$(x_1 - x_2)\left(\frac{\partial F}{\partial x_1} - \frac{\partial F}{\partial x_2}\right) \geq 0 (\leq 0), x \in \Omega^\circ.$$

Lemma 2.2[11]. Let $\Omega \subset R_+^n$ be a symmetric geometric convex set with nonempty interior, and $f : \Omega \to R_+$ be a continuous symmetric function onΩ. If f is differentiable in Ω°, then f is Schur-geometric convex(Schur-geometric concave) on Ω if and only if

$$(\ln x_1 - \ln x_2)\left(x_1 \frac{\partial f(x)}{\partial x_1} - x_2 \frac{\partial f(x)}{\partial x_2}\right) \geq 0 (\leq 0), x \in \Omega^\circ.$$

Lemma 2.3[10]. Let $\Omega \subset R^n$ be a symmetric harmonic convex set with nonempty interior, and $f : \Omega \to R$ be a continuous symmetric function on Ω. If f is differentiable in Ω°, then f is Schur-harmonic convex (Schur-harmonic concave) on Ω if and only if

$$(x_1 - x_2)\left(x_1^2 \frac{\partial f(x)}{\partial x_1} - x_2^2 \frac{\partial f(x)}{\partial x_2}\right) \geq 0 (\leq 0), x \in \Omega^\circ.$$

Lemma 2.4[9]. If $1 \leq r \leq n-1$, then

$$E_n^2(t,r) \geq E_n(t,r-1)E_n(t,r+1)t = (t_1,t_2,\cdots,t_n) \in (0,\infty)^n, (n \geq 2).$$

Lemma 2.5. If $n \geq 2, 1 \leq r \leq n-1$, and $m > 0$, then the function

$$\varphi_n(x,r,m) = \varphi_n(x_1,x_2,\cdots,x_n;r,m) = \frac{G_n(x_1,x_2,\cdots,x_n;r+1,m)}{G_n(x_1,x_2,\cdots,x_n;r,m)}$$

is increasing with respect to each $x_i \in (0,1), i = 1,2,\cdots,n$.

Proof. By the symmetry of $\varphi_n(x_1,x_2,\cdots,x_n;r,m)$ with respect to $(0,1)^n$, we only need to prove that $\varphi_n(x_1,x_2,\cdots,x_n;r,m)$ is increasing with respect to $x_i \in (0,1)$.

The proof is divided into three cases.

Case 1. If $r = 1$, then

$$\frac{\partial \varphi_n(x_1,\cdots,x_n;1,m)}{\partial x_1} = m x_1^{m-1}\left((1-x_1^m)\sum_{i=1}^{n}\frac{x_i^m}{1-x_i^m}\right)^{-2}\left[\left(\sum_{i=2}^{n}\frac{x_i^m}{1-x_i^m}\right)^2 - \sum_{2\leq i<j\leq n}\frac{x_i^m x_j^m}{(1-x_i^m)(1-x_j^m)}\right] \geq 0.$$

Case 2. If $r = n-1$, then

$$\frac{\partial \varphi_n(x,n-1,m)}{\partial x_1} = m x_1^{m-1}\left(\sum_{i=1}^{n}\frac{1-x_i^m}{x_i^m}\right)^{-2} \geq 0.$$

Case 3. If $n \geq 4$, and $2 \leq r \leq n-2$, then

$$\begin{aligned}\frac{\partial \varphi_n(x,r,m)}{\partial x_1} &= \frac{m x_1^{m-1}}{\Delta^2}[G_{n-1}^2(x_2,\cdots,x_n;r;m)\\ &\quad -G_{n-1}(x_2,\cdots,x_n;r-1;m)G_{n-1}(x_2,\cdots,x_n;r+1;m)]\\ &= \frac{m x_1^{m-1}}{\Delta^2}[E_{n-1}^2(t_1,\cdots,t_{n-1};r;m)\\ &\quad +E_{n-1}(t_1,\cdots,t_{n-1};r-1;m)E_{n-1}(t_1,\cdots,t_{n-1};r+1;m)].\end{aligned}$$

where

$$\Delta = x_1^m G_{n-1}(x_2, \cdots, x_n; r-1; m) + (1 - x_1^m) G_{n-1}(x_2, \cdots, x_n; r; m),$$

$$t_i = \frac{x_{i+1}^m}{1 - x_{i+1}^m}, i = 1, \cdots, n-1.$$

By Lemma 2.4, we get

$$\frac{\partial \varphi_n(x_1, x_2, \cdots, x_n; r, m)}{\partial x_1} \geq 0.$$

Thus the proof of Lemma 2.5 is complete.

Lemma 2.6. Let $n \in N_+, n \geq 2, 2 \leq r \leq n$, and $m \geq 1$, then the function

$$f(u) = (n-r)\frac{1}{u^{m-1}} + [(n-1)m - (n-r)]u - (n-1)mu^{m+1}$$

is decreasing on $\left[\sqrt[m]{\frac{r-1}{(m+1)(n-1)}}, 1\right)$.

Proof. Since

$$f'(u) = (n-1)m - (n-r) - (n-r)(m-1)\frac{1}{u^m} - (n-1)m(m+1)u^m \leq 0,$$

we have $f(u)$ is decreasing on $\left[\sqrt[m]{\frac{r-1}{(m+1)(n-1)}}, 1\right)$.

Thus the proof of Lemma 2.6 is complete.

Lemma 2.7. Let $m > 0$, then the functions

$$g(u) = \frac{u}{1 - u^m}, h(x) = \frac{u^{m+1}}{(1 - u^m)^2}$$

is increasing on$(0, 1)$.

Proof. Since

$$g'(u) = \frac{1 + (m-1)u^m}{(1 - u^m)^2} \geq 0, h'(u) = \frac{u^m[(m+1) + (m-1)u^m]}{(1 - u^m)^3} \geq 0,$$

we have $g(u)$ and $h(u)$ is increasing on $(0, 1)$.

Thus the proof of Lemma 2.7 is complete.

3 Main Results

In this section, we discuss the Schur-convexity and the Schur-geometric convexity and the Schur-harmonic convexity of $G_n(x, r, m)$, our main results are the following.

Theorem 3.1. Let $n \in N_+, n \geq 2, 2 \leq r \leq n$, and $m \geq 1$, then $G_n(x,r,m)$ is Schur-convex on $\left[\sqrt[m]{\frac{r-1}{(m+1)(n-1)}}, 1\right)^n$.

Proof. According to Lemma2.1 and Lemma2.6, we only need to prove that

$$\nabla_S(x,r,m) := (x_1 - x_2)\left(\frac{\partial G_n(x,r,m)}{\partial x_1} - \frac{\partial G_n(x,r,m)}{\partial x_2}\right) \geq 0$$

for $x = (x_1, x_2, \cdots, x_n) \in \left[\sqrt[m]{\frac{r-1}{(m+1)(n-1)}}, 1\right)^n$.

The proof is divided into four cases.

Case 1. If $n \geq 2, r = n$, and $x \in \left[\frac{1}{\sqrt[m]{m+1}}, 1\right)^n$, then

$$\frac{\partial G_n(x,n,m)}{\partial x_1} = \frac{mG_n(x,n,m)}{x_1(1-x_1^m)}, \quad \frac{\partial G_n(x,n,m)}{\partial x_2} = \frac{mG_n(x,n,m)}{x_2(1-x_2^m)},$$

therefore

$$\nabla_S(x,n,m) = \frac{(x_1-x_2)mG_n(x,n,m)}{x_1x_2(1-x_1^m)(1-x_2^m)}[x_2(1-x_2^m) - x_1(1-x_1^m)] \geq 0.$$

Case 2. If $n \geq 3, r = 2$, and $x \in \left[\frac{1}{\sqrt[m]{(m+1)(n-1)}}, 1\right)^n$, then

$$G_n(x,2,m) = \frac{x_1^m x_2^m}{(1-x_1^m)(1-x_2^m)} + \left(\frac{x_1^m}{1-x_1^m} + \frac{x_2^m}{1-x_2^m}\right)\sum_{i=3}^{n}\frac{x_i^m}{1-x_i^m} + \sum_{3\leq i<j\leq n}\frac{x_i^m x_j^m}{(1-x_i^m)(1-x_j^m)},$$

and

$$\frac{\partial G_n(x,2,m)}{\partial x_1} = \frac{mx_1^{m-1}x_2^m}{(1-x_1^m)^2(1-x_2^m)} + \frac{mx_1^{m-1}}{(1-x_1^m)^2}\sum_{i=3}^{n}\frac{x_i^m}{1-x_i^m},$$

$$\frac{\partial G_n(x,2,m)}{\partial x_2} = \frac{mx_2^{m-1}x_1^m}{(1-x_2^m)^2(1-x_1^m)} + \frac{mx_2^{m-1}}{(1-x_2^m)^2}\sum_{i=3}^{n}\frac{x_i^m}{1-x_i^m},$$

therefore

$$\begin{aligned}\nabla_S(x,2,m) &= \frac{(x_1-x_2)mx_1^{m-1}x_2^{m-1}}{(1-x_1^m)^2(1-x_2^m)^2}\Bigg[x_2(1-x_2^m) - x_1(1-x_1^m) \\ &\qquad + \left(\frac{(1-x_2^m)^2}{x_2^{m-1}} - \frac{(1-x_1^m)^2}{x_1^{m-1}}\right)\sum_{i=3}^{n}\frac{x_i^m}{1-x_i^m}\Bigg] \\ &\geq \frac{(x_1-x_2)mx_1^{m-1}x_2^{m-1}}{(1x_1^m)^2(1-x_2^m)^2[(n-1)m+(n-2)]}\Bigg\{(n-2)\frac{1}{x_2^{m-1}} \\ &\qquad + [(n-1)m-(n-2)]x_2 - (n-1)mx_2^{m+1} \\ &\quad -(n-2)\frac{1}{x_1^{m-1}} - [(n-1)m-(n-2)]x_1 + (n-1)mx_1^{m+1}\Bigg\} \geq 0.\end{aligned}$$

Case 3. If $n \geq 4, r = n-1$, and $x \in \left[\sqrt[m]{\frac{n-2}{(m+1)(n-1)}}, 1\right)^n$, then

$$\begin{aligned}
&G_n(x, n-1, m) \\
&= \left[\frac{x_1^m x_2^m}{(1-x_1^m)(1-x_2^m)} \sum_{i=3}^{n} \frac{1-x_i^m}{x_i^m} + \frac{x_1^m}{1-x_1^m} + \frac{x_2^m}{1-x_2^m}\right] \prod_{i=3}^{n} \frac{x_i^m}{1-x_i^m},
\end{aligned}$$

and

$$\frac{\partial G_n(x, n-1, m)}{\partial x_1} = \left[\frac{m x_1^{m-1} x_2^m}{(1-x_1^m)^2(1-x_2^m)} \sum_{i=3}^{n} \frac{1-x_i^m}{x_i^m} + \frac{m x_1^{m-1}}{(1-x_1^m)^2}\right] \prod_{i=3}^{n} \frac{x_i^m}{1-x_i^m},$$

$$\frac{\partial G_n(x, n-1, m)}{\partial x_2} = \left[\frac{m x_2^{m-1} x_1^m}{(1-x_2^m)^2(1-x_1^m)} \sum_{i=3}^{n} \frac{1-x_i^m}{x_i^m} + \frac{m x_2^{m-1}}{(1-x_2^m)^2}\right] \prod_{i=3}^{n} \frac{x_i^m}{1-x_i^m},$$

therefore

$$\begin{aligned}
&\nabla_S(x, n-1, m) \\
&= \frac{(x_1-x_2) m x_1^{m-1} x_2^{m-1}}{(1-x_1^m)^2(1-x_2^m)^2} \prod_{i=3}^{n} \frac{x_i^m}{1-x_i^m} \left(\sum_{i=3}^{n} \frac{1-x_i^m}{x_i^s}\right) \Bigg\{ [x_2(1-x_2^m) - x_1(1-x_1^m)] \\
&\qquad + \left[\frac{(1-x_2^m)^2}{x_2^{m-1}} - \frac{(1-x_1^m)^2}{x_1^{m-1}}\right] \left[\sum_{i=3}^{n} \left(1 - \frac{x_i^m}{x_i^s}\right)\right]^{-1} \Bigg\} \\
&\geq \frac{(x_1-x_2) m x_1^{m-1} x_2^{m-1}}{(1-x_1^m)^2(1-x_2^m)^2[(n-1)m+1]} \left(\prod_{i=3}^{n} \frac{x_i^m}{1-x_i^m}\right) \left(\sum_{i=3}^{n} \frac{1-x_i^m}{x_i^s}\right) \Big\{ 1/x_2^{m-1} \\
&\qquad + [(n-1)m-1] x_2 - (n-1) m x_2^{m+1} - x_1^{1-m} \\
&\qquad - [(n-1)m-1] x_1 + (n-1) m x_1^{m+1} \Big\} \geq 0.
\end{aligned}$$

Case 4. If $n \geq 5, 3 \leq r \leq n-2$, and $x \in \left[\sqrt[m]{\frac{r-1}{(m+1)(n-1)}}, 1\right)^n$, then

$$\begin{aligned}
G_n(x, r, m) &= \frac{x_1^m x_2^m}{(1-x_1^m)(1-x_2^m)} G_{n-2}(x_3, \cdots, x_n; r-2; m) \\
&\quad + \left(\frac{x_1^m}{1-x_1^m} + \frac{x_2^m}{1-x_2^m}\right) G_{n-2}(x_3, \cdots, x_n; r-1; m) + G_{n-2}(x_3, \cdots, x_n; r; m),
\end{aligned}$$

and

$$\begin{aligned}
\frac{\partial G_n(x, r, m)}{\partial x_1} &= \frac{m x_1^{m-1} x_2^m}{(1-x_1^m)^2(1-x_2^m)} G_{n-2}(x_3, \cdots, x_n; r-2; m) \\
&\quad + \frac{m x_1^{m-1}}{(1-x_1^m)^2} G_{n-2}(x_3, \cdots, x_n; r-1; m),
\end{aligned}$$

$$\begin{aligned}
\frac{\partial G_n(x, r, m)}{\partial x_2} &= \frac{m x_2^{m-1} x_1^m}{(1-x_2^m)^2(1-x_1^m)} G_{n-2}(x_3, \cdots, x_n, r-2; m) \\
&\quad + \frac{m x_2^{m-1}}{(1-x_2^m)^2} G_{n-2}(x_3, \cdots, x_n, r-1; m),
\end{aligned}$$

therefore

$$\nabla_S(x,r,m) \geq \frac{(x_1-x_2)mx_1^{m-1}x_2^{m-1}G_{n-2}(x_3,\cdots,x_n;r-2;m)}{(1-x_1^m)^2(1-x_2^m)^2[(n-1)m+(n-r)]}$$
$$\cdot\Big\{(n-r)x_2^{1-m}+[(n-1)m-(n-r)]x_2-(n-1)mx_2^{m+1}$$
$$-(n-r)x_1^{1-m}-[(n-1)m-(n-r)]x_1+(n-1)mx_1^{m+1}\Big\}\geq 0.$$

Thus the proof of Theorem 3.1 is complete.

Theorem 3.2. Let $n\in N_+, n\geq 2, 2\leq r\leq n$, and $m>0$, then $G_n(x,r,m)$ is Schur-geometric convex on $(0,1)^n$

Proof. According to Lemma2.2, we only need to prove that

$$\nabla_G(x,r,m) := (\ln x_1-\ln x_2)\left(x_1\frac{\partial f(x)}{\partial x_1}-x_2\frac{\partial f(x)}{\partial x_2}\right)\geq 0$$

for$x=(x_1,x_2,\cdots,x_n)\in(0,1)^n$.

The proof is divided into four cases.

Case 1. If $n\geq 2$, and $r=n$, then

$$\nabla_G(x,n,m)=\frac{(\ln x_1-\ln x_2)(x_1^m-x_2^m)mG_n(x,n,m)}{(1-x_1^m)(1-x_2^m)}\geq 0,$$

Case 2. If $n\geq 3$, and $r=2$, then

$$\nabla_G(x,2,m)$$
$$=\frac{(\ln x_1-\ln x_2)(x_1^m-x_2^m)m}{(1-x_1^m)^2(1-x_2^m)^2}\left[x_1^m x_2^m+(1-x_1^m x_2^m)\sum_{i=3}^{n}\frac{x_i^m}{1-x_i^m}\right]\geq 0.$$

Case 3. If $n\geq 4$, and $r=n-1$, then

$$\nabla_G(x,n-1,m)=\frac{(\ln x_1-\ln x_2)(x_1^m-x_2^m)m}{(1-x_1^m)^2(1-x_2^m)^2}$$
$$\cdot\left[x_1^m x_2^m\sum_{i=3}^{n}\frac{1-x_i^m}{x_i^m}+(1-x_1^m x_2^m)\prod_{i=3}^{n}\frac{x_i^m}{1-x_i^m}\right]\geq 0.$$

Case 4. If $n\geq 5$, and $3\leq r\leq n-2$, then

$$\nabla_G(x,r,m)=\frac{(\ln x_1-\ln x_2)(x_1^m-x_2^m)m}{(1-x_1^m)^2(1-x_2^m)^2}[x_1^m x_2^m G_{n-2}(x_3,\cdots,x_n;r-2;m)$$
$$+(1-x_1^m x_2^m)G_{n-2}(x_3,\cdots,x_n;r-1;m)]\geq 0.$$

Thus the proof of Theorem 3.2 is complete.

Theorem 3.3. Let $n \in N_+,\ n \geq 2, 2 \leq r \leq n$, and $m > 0$, then $G_n(x, r, m)$ is Schur-harmonic convex on $(0, 1)^n$

Proof. According to Lemma2.3 and Lemma 2.7, we only need to prove that

$$\nabla_H(x, r, m) := (x_1 - x_2)\left(x_1^2\frac{\partial f(x)}{\partial x_1} - x_2^2\frac{\partial f(x)}{\partial x_2}\right) \geq 0$$

for$x = (x_1, x_2, \cdots, x_n) \in (0, 1)^n$.

The proof is divided into four cases.

Case 1. If $n \geq 2$, and $r = n$, then

$$\nabla_H(x, n, m) = mG_n(x, n, m)(x_1 - x_2)\left(\frac{x_1}{1 - x_1^m} - \frac{x_2}{1 - x_2^m}\right) \geq 0.$$

Case 2. If $n \geq 3$, and $r = 2$, then

$$\begin{aligned}\nabla_H(x, 2, m) = {} & \frac{m x_1^m x_2^m (x_1 - x_2)}{(1 - x_1^m)(1 - x_2^m)}\left(\frac{x_1}{1 - x_1^m} - \frac{x_2}{1 - x_2^m}\right) \\ & + m(x_1 - x_2)\left[\frac{x_1^{m+1}}{(1 - x_1^m)^2} - \frac{x_2^{m+1}}{(1 - x_2^m)^2}\right]\sum_{i=3}^{n}\frac{x_i^m}{1 - x_i^m} \geq 0.\end{aligned}$$

Case 3. If $n \geq 4$, and $r = n - 1$, then

$$\begin{aligned}& \nabla_H(x, n-1, m) \\ & = \frac{m x_1^m x_2^m}{(1 - x_1^m)(1 - x_2^m)}(x_1 - x_2)\left(\frac{x_1}{1 - x_1^m} - \frac{x_2}{1 - x_2^m}\right)\sum_{i=3}^{n}\frac{1 - x_i^m}{x_i^m} \\ & \quad + m(x_1 - x_2)\left[\frac{x_1^{m+1}}{(1 - x_1^m)^2} - \frac{x_2^{m+1}}{(1 - x_2^m)^2}\right]\prod_{i=3}^{n}\frac{x_i^m}{1 - x_i^m} \geq 0.\end{aligned}$$

Case 4. If$n \geq 5$,and$3 \leq r \leq n - 2$,then

$$\begin{aligned}& \nabla_H(x, r, m) \\ & = \frac{m x_1^m x_2^m}{(1 - x_1^m)(1 - x_2^m)}(x_1 - x_2)\left(\frac{x_1}{1 - x_1^m} - \frac{x_2}{1 - x_2^m}\right)G_{n-2}(x_3, \cdots, x_n; r-2; m) \\ & \quad + m(x_1 - x_2)\left(\frac{x_1^{m+1}}{(1 - x_1^m)^2} - \frac{x_2^{m+1}}{(1 - x_2^m)^2}\right)G_{n-2}(x_3, \cdots, x_n; r-1; m) \geq 0.\end{aligned}$$

Thus the proof of Theorem 3.3 is complete.

References

1. Marshall, A.W., Olkin, I.: Inequalities: Theory of Majorization and Its Applications. Academic Press, New York (1979)
2. Stepniak, C.: Stochastic Ordering and Schur-Convex Functions in Comparison of Linear Experiments. Metrika 36, 291–298 (1989)

3. Constantine, G.M.: Schur-Convex Functions on the Spectra of Graphs. Discrete Math. 45, 181–188 (1983)
4. Hwang, F.K., Rothblum, U.G.: Partition-optimization with Schur Convex Sum Objective Functions. SIAM J. Discrete Math. 18, 512–524 (2004/2005)
5. Hwang, F.K., Rothblum, U.G., Shepp, L.: Monotone Optimal Multipartitions using Schur Convexity with Respect to Partial Orders. SIAM J. Discrete Math. 6, 537–547 (1993)
6. Forcina, A., Giovagnoli, A.: Homogeneity Indices and Schur-Convex Functions. Statistica (Bologna) 42, 529–542 (1982)
7. Shaked, M., Shanthikumar, J.G., Tong, Y.L.: Parametric Schur Convexity and Arrangement Monotonicity Properties of Partial Sums. J. Multivariate Anal. 53, 293–310 (1995)
8. Guan, K.-Z.: Some Properties of a Class of Symmetric Functions. Journal of Mathematical Analysis and Applications 336, 70–80 (2007)
9. Chu, Y.M., Xia, W.F., Zhao, T.H.: Schur Convexity for a Class of Symmetric Functions. Sci. China Math. 53, 465–474 (2010)
10. Xia, W.-F., Chu, Y.-M.: Schur-Convexity for a Class of Symmetric Functions and Its Applications. Journal of Inequalities and Applications, Article ID 493759, 15 pages (2009)
11. Shi, H.-N.: Schur-Geometric Convexity for Differences of Means. Applied Mathematics E-Notes 10, 275–284 (2010)
12. Shi, H.-N., Jiang, Y.-M., Jiang, W.-D.: Schur-Convexity and Schur-Geometrically Concavity of Gini Mean. Comp. Math. Appl. 57, 266–274 (2009)
13. Xia, W.-F., Chu, Y.-M.: Schur-Convexity for a Class of Symmetric Functions and Its Applications. Journal of Inequalities and Applications, Article ID 493759, 15 pages (2009)

The Study on Clutch Shift Control Based on Sliding-Mode

Zhang Guang Hui

Shandong Transport Vocational College,Weifang, Shandong 261206, China
jyjcbwg@163.com

Abstract. This paper has presented a systematic approach for the pressure-based clutch fill and engagement control of wet clutches in automatic, dual clutch, or hybrid transmissions. The clutch fill and engagement controls have been critical for the clutch-to-clutch shift technology, which is the key enabler for fuel-efficient, compact, and low-cost transmission designs. The main challenges of the pressure-based clutch control design lie in the complex dynamics, the ON/OFF behavior during the clutch fill phase, the pressure chattering effect induced by inappropriate control gain design, and the precise pressure –tracking requirement during the dynamic loading condition transient. To address these challenges, first, a dynamic model capturing the bulk modulus variation and the piston motion wiggling effect has been constructed based on extensive experimental results.

Keywords: clutch shift control, pressure-based control, sliding-mode.

1 Introduction

With the increasing demand for fuel efficiency and reduced emissions, new technologies have emerged in the automotive transmission systems [1]–[3]. Clutch to clutch shift control [3]–[7] is a key enabler for fuel-efficient, compact, and low-cost transmission designs, including automatic transmissions [3], dual clutch transmissions [8], and hybrid transmissions [9]–[11]. For a smooth clutch-to-clutch shift, proper control of two consecutive processes is necessary. First, precise coordination of the on-coming clutch and off-going clutch is critical, which otherwise will cause undesirable torque interruption and oscillations [3]. To ensure precise synchronization, before clutch engagement, it is necessary to fill the on-coming clutch to a position where the clutch packs are just in contact. This process is called clutch fill. Second, during the clutch engagement process, which typically occurs right after the clutch fill, smooth and precise torque control is crucial.

2 System Dynamics Modeling

The proportional pressure-reducing valve controls the flow in and out of the clutch chamber. When the clutch fill begins, the valve will connect the clutch chamber to the

C. Liu, J. Chang, and A. Yang (Eds.): ICICA 2011, Part I, CCIS 243, pp. 635–642, 2011.

high-pressure source, which is regulated by a relief valve, and the high-pressure fluid flows into the chamber and pushes the piston toward the clutch pack. Once the clutch fill ends, the valve will control the chamber pressure to further increase until the clutch packs are fully engaged. When the clutch is disengaged, the proportional pressure-reducing valve connects the clutch chamber to the tank, and the clutch return spring pushes the clutch piston back to the disengaged position. The clutch dynamic model consists of the valve dynamics, the clutch mechanical actuator dynamics, and the clutch chamber pressure dynamics, which will be presented in the following sessions.

2.1 Modeling of the Proportional Pressure-Reducing Valve

When there is no control voltage, the spool is kept at the top position by the return spring. At this position, port 3 is connected to port 1. Therefore, the fluid inside the clutch chamber will flow to the tank. When a positive voltage is exerted on the magnetic coil, the induced magnetic force will push the spool toward port 1. As the spool connects port 1 to port 2, the high-pressure fluid will flow into the clutch chamber. The increased pressure in port 1 will push the spool upward and eventually close the orifice between port 1 and port 2. Clearly, the spool position is determined by the magnetic force Fmag , the returning spring force Fspring , and the chamber pressure Pr .

The spool dynamics can be described as follows:

$$\dot{L}_{spool} = v_{spool}, \quad \dot{v}_{spool} = \frac{1}{M_{spool}}[F_{mag}(Vol) - K_{spring}(L_{spool} + L_{preload}) - D_{spool}v_{spool} - A_{spool}P_r] \tag{1}$$

$$F_{mag}(Vol) = K_f \times i = K_f \times (\frac{i_{\max} - i_{\min}}{Vol_{\max}} Vol + i_{\min}) \tag{2}$$

Where

L_{spool} is the spool position, v_{spool} is the spool velocity, M_{spool} is the spool mass, K_{spring} is the spool spring constant, A_{spool} is the cross-sectional area of the spool, and D_{spool} is the damping coefficient. $L_{preload}$ is the spool position, where the orifice between port 1 and port 2 is just closed. F_{mag} is the magnetic force, which is determined by the coil magnetic constant K_f and the current i. The current i is generated by the power amplifier and can be calculated using the input voltage Vo 1 . i_{max} and i_{min} are the maximum and minimum current that can be generated from the power amplifier, and Vol_{max} is the maximum control voltage corresponding to i_{max} .

Given the spool position L_{spool} , the orifice area Aorifice between the high-pressure port 2 and chamber pressure port 1 is

$$A_{orifice}(L_{spool}) = \pi L_{spool}\sin(\theta) \times (d_{spool} - L_{spool}\sin\theta\cos\theta) \tag{3}$$

where dspool is the diameter of the spool, and θ is the spool surface slant angle.

Similarly, the orifice area Adump between the tank port 3 and the pressure port 1 is

$$A_{orifice}(L_{spool}) = -\pi L_{spool}\sin(\theta) \times (d_{spool} + L_{spool}\sin\theta\cos\theta) \tag{4}$$

Then, the flow dynamics across the valve orifice is

$$Q(L_{spool}, P_r) = \begin{cases} \mathrm{sign}(P_h - P_r) C_d \sqrt{\dfrac{2|P_h - P_r|}{\rho}} A_{orifice}(L_{spool}), L_{spool} > 0 \\ 0, L_{spool} = 0 \\ -C_d \sqrt{\dfrac{2|P_r|}{\rho}} A_{orifice}(L_{spool}), C_d \sqrt{\dfrac{2|P_h - P_r|}{\rho}}, L_{spool} < 0 \end{cases} \tag{5}$$

where ρ is the fluid density, Cd is the discharge coefficient, Aorifice is the orifice area connecting the clutch chamber (port 1) and the supply pressure (port 2), and Adump is the orifice area connecting the clutch chamber (port 1) and the tank (port 3). When the spool position Lspool > 0, the clutch chamber is connected to the high pressure. When the spool position Lspool < 0, the clutch chamber is connected to the tank.

2.2 Mechanical System Modeling

The dynamics of clutch motion can be modeled as [20]

$$\dot{x}_1 = x_2 \tag{6}$$

$$\dot{x}_2 = \frac{1}{M_p} \times [A_p \times P_r + P_c - P_{atm}] - D_p x_2 - F_{drag}(P_r + P_c, x_2) - F_{res}(x_1 + x_{p0})] \tag{7}$$

where x_1 is the clutch piston displacement, x_2 is the clutch piston velocity, M_p is the effective mass of the piston, A_p is the piston surface area, D_p is the clutch damping coefficient, P_{atm} is the atmospheric pressure, xp 0 is the return spring preload. P_c is the centrifugal force [21] induced pressure generated from the rotation of the clutch assembly.

F_{res} is the displacement-dependent resistance force. During the clutch fill, the resistance force comes from the return spring; thus, the force F_{res} depends on the spring stiffness constant K_{cs} . During the clutch engagement, the resistance force is due to the squeezing of the clutch pack, and therefore, the resistance force F_{res} can be modeled as

$$F_{res} = \begin{cases} K_{cs} \times (x_1 + x_{p0}), (x_1 \le x_{fill}) \\ F_{en}(x_1 + x_{p0}), (x_1 > x_{fill}) \end{cases} \tag{8}$$

where the function Fen (x1 + xp0) includes both spring force and the nonlinear clutch pack reaction force, xfill is the clutch piston position at the end of the clutch fill. Fdrag is the piston seal drag force, which is dependent on the piston motion. It is modeled as

$$F_{drag} = \begin{cases} [k_m(P_r + P_c) + c_m] \times sign(x_2), (x_2 \ne 0) \\ F_{stick}, (x_2 = 0) \end{cases} \tag{9}$$

where km and cm are constants, and F_{stick} is the static stick friction force from the Kanopp's stick-slip model. Further detail of the mechanical dynamic model can be found in our recent paper [20].

2.3 Modeling of the Clutch Chamber Pressure Dynamics

When the orifice between the high-pressure port and the clutch chamber is open, the fluid will flow into the clutch chamber, which results in the pressure rise in the chamber. The pressure dynamics is modeled as

$$\dot{P}_r = \frac{\beta(P_r)}{V}[Q(L_{spool}, P_r) - A_p x_2]$$

where V is the chamber volume, which is assumed constant due to small clutch piston displacement, and β is the effective bulk modulus.

As the clutch fill typically occurs in a low pressure range (1.68–1.97 bar) while the clutch engagement occurs in a much higher range, the air entrained in the oil could cause the bulk modulus variation. The variation is modeled with respect the pressure as [19]

$$\beta(P_r) = \frac{\beta_e(1+10^{-5}P_r)^{1+1/\gamma_b}}{(1+10^{-5}P_r)^{1+1/\gamma_b} + 10^{-5}R(1-c_1P_r)(\beta_e/\gamma_b - 10^5 - P_r)} \tag{10}$$

where β_e is the bulkmodulus in ideal fluid with no air entrained, γ_b is the ratio of specific heats for air, c1 is the coefficient of air bubble volume variation due to the variation of the ratio of the entrained air and dissolved air content in oil, R is the entrained air content by volume in oil at atmospheric pressure. β_e , R, γ_b, and c1 are fixed when the oil temperature and pumping conditions are constant.

2.4 Overall System Dynamics Model

The overall clutch system dynamics model including the valve dynamics, the mechanical actuator dynamics, and the chamber pressure dynamics can be summarized as follows:

$$\dot{L}_{spool} = v_{spool},\ \dot{v}_{spool} = \frac{1}{M_{spool}}[F_{mag}(Vol) - K_{spring}(L_{spool} + L_{preload}) - D_{spool}v_{spool} - A_{spool}P_r] \tag{11}$$

$$\dot{P}_r = \frac{\beta(P_r)}{V}[Q(L_{spool}, P_r) - A_p x_2] \tag{12}$$

$$\dot{x}_1 = x_2 \tag{13}$$

$$\dot{x}_2 = \frac{1}{M_p} \times [A_p \times P_r + P_c - P_{atm}] - D_p x_2 - F_{drag}(P_r + P_c, x_2) - F_{res}(x_1 + x_{p0})] \tag{14}$$

Further investigation reveals that the time constant of the pressure-reducing valve is far less than the time constant of the clutch-actuation system pressure dynamics, which means that the dynamic behavior of the reducing valve can be neglected. A step voltage is applied to the valve at 0.07 s. Once the step signal is ON, the valve quickly opens to its full orifice, which is reflected from the near step jump of the flow rate measurement close to 0.08 s and indicate that the valve time constant is around 10 ms. this slow response is partially due to a low bulk modulus value at the low pressure.

Therefore, to simplify the control design, the proportional valve spool dynamics is converted into a static mapping

$$L_{spool} = \frac{1}{K_{spool}}[F_{mag}(u) - K_{spring} \times L_{spool} - A_{spool}P_r] \tag{15}$$

Here, we denote u = Vol as the control input to the proportional valve.

Therefore, the system dynamics [see (11) and (12)] becomes

$$\dot{P}_r = \frac{\beta(P_r)}{V}[Q(u,P_r) - A_p x_2] \tag{16}$$

Where

$$Q(u,P_r) = \begin{cases} \mathrm{si}\,gn(P_h - P_r)C_d\sqrt{\frac{2|P_h - P_r|}{\rho}}A_{orifice}(L_{spool}), L_{spool}(u,P_r) > 0 \\ 0, L_{spool}(u,P_r) = 0 \\ -C_d\sqrt{\frac{2|P_r|}{\rho}}A_{orifice}(L_{spool}), C_d\sqrt{\frac{2|P_h - P_r|}{\rho}}, L_{spool}(u,P_r) < 0 \end{cases} \tag{17}$$

Finally, the reduced-order system dynamics includes (13)–(17).

In addition, for a given flow rate q, the required control input u can also be determined based on (3), (4), (15), and (17). This relationship will be used in the following section, and the mapping from q to u can be written as

$$U(q,P_r) = \frac{Vol_{\max}}{i_{\max} - i_{\min}} \times \left[\frac{(L_{spool}K_{spring} + K_{spring}L_{preload} + A_{spool}P_r)}{K_f} - i_{\min}\right] \tag{18}$$

where Lspool is defined by (19), shown at the bottom of this page.

Equation (19) is used to calculate the spool position Lspool corresponding to a specific valve opening orifice based on (3) and (4). The relationship between (17) and (18) can be written as Q{U (q, Pr), Pr } = q.

$$L_{spool} = \begin{cases} \frac{d_{spool} - \sqrt{d_{spool}^2 - (4q\cos(\theta)/(\pi sign(P_h - P_r)C_d(\sqrt{2|P_h - P_r|})/\rho)))}}{\sin(2\theta)}, q > 0 \\ 0, q = 0 \\ \frac{-d_{spool} + \sqrt{d_{spool}^2 + (4q\cos(\theta)/(\pi C_d(\sqrt{2|P_h - P_r|})/\rho)))}}{\sin(2\theta)}, q < 0 \end{cases} \tag{19}$$

3 Robust Nonlinear Controller and Nonlinear Observer Design

The clutch system [see (13)–(17)] is a third-order nonlinear system. As both the control input u (the valve voltage) and the control output Pr (the chamber pressure) appear in the dynamic equation (16), the system has a nonlinear dynamics with relative degree 1. Equations (13) and (14) are the system internal dynamics, the equilibrium point of which is asymptotically stable (the proof is straightforward, thus is omitted here). Therefore, the nonlinear system is minimum phase. Note that the internal dynamics in this application is a spring mass damper system; therefore, the minimum phase feature also suggests that the whole system will be stabilized as long as the states other than the internal dynamics states could be stabilized. This unique feature suggests applying the sliding-mode controller, which can ensure system robustness with a relatively low order controller design.

Define the tracking error e2 as the difference between the desired pressure trajectory r and the actual measurement P_r

$$e_2 = P_r - r \tag{20}$$

and define another error terme1 , the derivative of which is equal to e2

$$\dot{e}_1 = e_2 \tag{21}$$

With the pressure dynamics in (16), we have

$$\dot{e}_2 = \dot{P}_r - \dot{r} = \frac{\beta(P_r)}{V} Q(u, P_r) - \frac{\beta(P_r)}{V} A_p x_2 - \dot{r} + \Delta_1(P_r) + \frac{\beta(P_r)}{V} \Delta_2(u, P_r) \tag{22}$$

where Δ1 (Pr) represents the model uncertainty of the pressure dynamics (16), and Δ2 (u, Pr) represents the model uncertainty of the pressure-reducing-valve flow dynamics (17). Bounds of the uncertainty term swill are obtained experimentally in the later session.

Define the sliding surface S as

$$S = k_1 e_1 + e_2 \tag{23}$$

where k1 is a weighting parameter. Then, the controller can be designed as

$$u = -U\left\{\frac{V}{\beta(P_r)} \times [k_1 e_2 - \frac{\beta(P_r)}{V} x_2 - \dot{r}] - v_u, P_r\right\} \tag{24}$$

Where U is defined in (18) and vu is a controller term to be designed later. As the piston velocity x2 cannot be measured directly due to the lack of a displacement and velocity sensor, an observer is needed to estimate x1 and x2 . The estimated states can not only be fed back to the controller (24), but also used to evaluate the piston displacement and, therefore, the clutch fill status. The observer design for piston motion will be presented in the next session. With the observed x2 , the control input becomes

$$u = -U\left\{\frac{V}{\beta(P_r)} \times [k_1 e_2 - \frac{\beta(P_r)}{V} (x_2 + \Delta_3(\hat{x}_2) - \dot{r}] - v_u, P_r\right\} \tag{25}$$

where $\hat{x}_2$ is the estimate of x2 and Δ3 ($\hat{x}_2$) is the estimation error.

4 Conclusion

A precise estimation of the bounds for unmodeled dynamics is also obtained. Then, a sliding-mode-based robust controller has been designed to track the desired pressure. To avoid chattering, the controller gain has been designed based on the nonconservative uncertainty bound. To ensure precise tracking, a nonlinear observer has been designed to estimate the clutch piston motion, which is a necessary term in the controller structure to further alleviate the high-gain demand. In addition, the observer estimation can also be used to diagnose the clutch fill status. Finally, experimental results show the effectiveness of the proposed control methods. Future works include the investigation with a miniature pressure sensor, the model uncertainty calibration in various environments, and the vehicle test of the proposed control algorithm.

References

1. Wagner, G.: Application of transmission systems for different driveline configurations in passenger cars. SAE Technical Paper 2001-01-0882 (2001)
2. Lee, C.J., Hebbale, K.V., Bai, S.: Control of a friction launch automatic transmission using a range clutch. Presented at the 2006 ASME Int. Mech. Eng. Congr. Expo., Chicago, IL (2006)
3. Sun, Z., Hebbale, K.V.: Challenges and opportunities in automotive transmission control. In: Proc. 2005 Amer. Control Conf., Portland, OR, June 8-10, pp. 3284–3289 (2005)
4. Hebbale, K.V., Kao, C.-K.: Adaptive control of shifts in automatic transmissions. Presented at the 1995 ASME Int. Mech. Eng. Congr. Expo., San Francisco, CA (1995)
5. Bai, S., Moses, R.L., Schanz, T., Gorman, M.J.: Development of a new clutch-to-clutch shift control technology. SAE Technical Paper 2002-01-1252 (2002)
6. Marano, J.E., Moorman, S.P., Whitton, M.D., Williams, R.L.: Clutch to Clutch transmission control strategy. SAE Technical Paper 2007-01- 1313 (2007)
7. Han, W., Yi, S.J.: A study of shift control using the clutch pressure pattern in automatic transmission. Proc. Inst. Mech. Eng. D, J. Automobile Eng. 217(4), 289–298 (2003)
8. Zhang, Y., Chen, X., Zhang, X., Jiang, H., Tobler, W.: Dynamic modeling and simulation of a dual-clutch automated lay-shaft transmission. ASME J. Mech. Des. 127(2), 302–307 (2005)
9. Grewe, T., Conlon, B., Holmes, A.: Defining the general Motors 2- Mode hybrid transmission. SAE technical paper 2007-01-0273 (2007)
10. Kim, S., Park, J., Hong, J., Lee, M., Sim, H.: Transient control strategy of hybrid electric vehicle during mode change. SAE Technical Paper Series 2009-01-0228 (2009)
11. Levin, M., Kozarekar, S., Chottiner, J., Maucher, E., Karamavruc, A., Shankland, R.: Hybrid powertrain with an engine-disconnecting clutch. SAE Technical Paper Series 2002-01-0930 (2002)
12. Glielmo, L., Iannelli, L., Vacca, V.: Gearshift control for automated manual transmissions. IEEE/ASME Trans. Mechatronics 11(1), 17–26 (2006)
13. Langjord, H., Johansen, T.: Dual-mode switched control of an elec- tropneumatic clutch actuator. IEEE/ASME Trans.Mechatronics 15(6), 969–981 (2010)
14. Montanari, M., Ronchi, F., Rossi, C., Tilli, A., Tonielli, A.: Control and performance evaluation of a clutch servo system with hydraulic actuation. J. Control Eng. Practice 12(11), 1369–1379 (2004)

15. Horn, J., Bamberger, J., Michau, P., Pindl, S.: Flatness-based clutch control for automated manual transmissions. J. Control Eng. Practice 11(12), 1353–1359 (2003)
16. Sanada, K., Kitagawa, A.: A study of two-degree-of-freedomcontrol of rotating speed in an automatic transmission, considering modeling errors of a hydraulic system. J. Control Eng. Practice 6(9), 1125–1132 (1998)
17. Gao, B., Chen, H., Sanada, K., Hu, Y.: Design of clutch-slip controller for automatic transmission using backstepping. IEEE/ASME Trans. Mechatronics, doi:10.1109/TMECH.2010.2045391
18. Gao, B., Chen, H., Zhao, H., Sanada, K.: A reduced order nonlinear clutch pressure observer for automatic transmission. IEEE Trans.Control Syst. Technol. 18(2), 446–453 (2010)
19. Yu, J., Chen, Z., Lu, Y.: The variation of oil effective bulkmoduluswith pressure in hydraulic systems. J. Dyn. Syst., Meas., Control 116(1), 146–150 (1994)
20. Song, X., Mohd Zulkefli, A., Sun, Z.: Automotive transmission clutch fill optimal control: An experimental investigation. In: Proc. 2010 Amer. Control Conf., Baltimore, MD, pp. 2478–2753 (June/July 2010)
21. Song, X., Sun, Z., Yang, X., Zhu, G.: Modeling, control and hardware- in-the-loop simulation of an automated manual transmission. Proc. Inst. Mech. Eng. D, J. Automobile Eng. 224, 143–159 (2010)

Numerical Simulation Program of an Elastic Membrane Considering the Fluid-Structure Interaction*

Liu Jian-Min and Cai Zhen-Xiong

Marine Engineering Institute, Jimei University, Xiamen 361021, China
liujm501@gmail.com

Abstract. The airship placed in the stratosphere flow field is a flexible body with low rigidity and therefore can be taken as an elastic membrane structure. The distribution of the peripheral flow field around the membrane structure is closely related to its shape, which is essentially a fluid-structure interaction problem. Accordingly, to investigate the coupling of the peripheral flow field of the membrane structure and its deformation in the stratosphere, the numerical simulation program to this problem was developed. The iteration method was introduced, and the three-dimensional flow around the airship was studied numerically by means of SIMPLE method based on the Finite Volume Method. The nonlinear finite element method was employed to investigate the large deflection of the elastic membrane structure. Afterwards, the validation of the computation was shown. And then, a comparison of the pressure distribution and the changes of flow parameters between the rigid model and the aeroelastic model of the large airship was provided.

Keywords: Membrane, Fluid-Structure Interaction, Numerical Simulation.

1 Introduction

With its membrane structure and large volume—the overall dimension can reach 220 meters--the stratosphere airship shows low rigidity[1]. Therefore it is considered a flexible envelop. As a result, the areoelasticity of the fluid flow around the airship should be closely connected with the configuration. On one hand, the structure of the airship is affected by the surrounding fluid flow. On the other hand, the shape of the airship determines the distribution of the flow. Because there is still not a similarity law to meet aerodynamic model test for flexible body, numerical computation is an effective measure to investigate the aeroelasticity of the airship. With the numerical simulation of the coupling of the flexible aeration configuration and the three-dimension flow, it is definite to understand the respective aerodynamic influences of the rigid and flexible models on the flexible airship. All the results can be valuable references to the structure design, control and shape optimization of flexible aircrafts. According to the current study at home and abroad, the numerical simulation of the

* Project supported by the Natural Science Foundation of Fujian Province (Grant No. 2009J01010).

C. Liu, J. Chang, and A. Yang (Eds.): ICICA 2011, Part I, CCIS 243, pp. 643–650, 2011.

aeroelasticity of flexible membrane structures has just gotten off the mark. Based on the previous work, the fluid-structure coupling computation is introduced in this paper to investigate the aerodynamic force of flexible airship and its aeroelasticity. Meanwhile, a corresponding computing software is developed.

2 Physical Model of Fluid Flow and Its Solver

In this section, the physical model of fluid flow around the airship and the fluid flow solver are presented. The governing equations for fluid flow are mass conservation equation and Reynolds-Averaged Navier-Stock (RANS) equations. In a more explicit manner for these equations with Cartesian coordinate in a three-dimension framework, they can be commonly expressed as:

$$\frac{\partial(\rho\phi)}{\partial t} + \mathrm{div}(\rho\vec{u}\phi) = \mathrm{div}(\Gamma\,\mathrm{grad}\,\phi) + S_\phi \tag{1}$$

By setting general variable   equal to 1, u, v, w, and selecting appropriate values for the diffusion coefficient and source term , we can obtain the special form of the partial differential equations of mass conservation and RANS equations.

For simulating the turbulent, the standard two model (Jones and Launder) [2] turbulence closure model has been proposed. The success of such model largely depends on the treatment of the solid wall boundary conditions which are fairly complicated in the turbulent flow. Near the wall boundary, the local Reynolds number is low and the viscous effects are important. However, the two model is based on the high Reynolds number assumption in which the turbulent stress forces are dominated. In order to solve these difficulties, two approaches are commonly employed: one is the wall function treatment, and the other is the low Reynolds number version of the turbulent model. In our program, LL-Low Reynolds modified model (Lien and Leschziner)[3] is employed. The kinetic energy k equation is expressed as follows:

$$\frac{\partial(\rho k)}{\partial t} + \mathrm{div}(\rho\vec{u}k) = \mathrm{div}((\mu + \mu_T)\,\mathrm{grad}\,k) + P - \rho\varepsilon \tag{2}$$

The dissipation equation for ε is:

$$\frac{\partial(\rho\varepsilon)}{\partial t} + \mathrm{div}(\rho\vec{u}\varepsilon) = \mathrm{div}((\mu + \mu_T\frac{\mu_T}{\mathrm{Pr}_Z})\,\mathrm{grad}\,\varepsilon) + f_1 C_{\varepsilon 1}\frac{\varepsilon}{k}P - f_2 C_{\varepsilon 2}P\frac{\varepsilon^2}{k} \tag{3}$$

where μT is the coefficient of eddy viscosity, defined by:

$$\mu_T = \rho f_\mu c_\mu \frac{k^2}{\varepsilon} \tag{4}$$

More details about these terms and parameters can be found in Ref. 3. Since Eqs. (2) and (3) have their similar forms of Eq. (1) with the exception of the diffusion coefficient and the source term, they can be discretized accordingly.

The finite volume method is employed for numerical discrete in our work. After integrating Eq. (1) over a three-dimensional control volume CV and applying Gauss' divergence theorem, the equation can be written as follows:

$$\frac{\partial}{\partial t}\left(\int_{CV}\rho\phi dV\right)+\int_{A}n\cdot(\rho\phi\vec{u})dA=\int_{A}n\cdot(\Gamma\,\mathrm{grad}\,\phi)dA+\int_{CV}S_{\phi}dV \qquad (5)$$

where A is the boundary surface of CV. In our program, the diffusion scheme is approximate to central differences. To achieve accurate results of these problems, a high-order resolution TVD (Total Variation Diminishing) [4] scheme is adopted in convection schemes. All the unknowns are stored at the center of CV.

SIMPLE method, which is an iterative procedure for the calculation of pressure and velocity fields, is used for calculating the solution algorithms of pressure and velocity. The principal steps in our program for the fluid flow solver are:

1) Start the flow with an initial pressure field p*;
2) Solve the discrete momentum equation to yield the intermediate velocity fields (u, v, w, p);
3) Solve the continuity equation in the form of an equation pressure correction;
4) Correct pressure and velocity;
5) Solve the k and ε transporting equation;
6) Repeat the above steps until the fields p, u, w, v, and others all converge.

The algebraic equations are solved by the strongly implicit procedure (SIP) proposed by Stone[5].

3 Fluid-Structure Coupling

In this coupling of fluid and structure interaction, to predict the aeroelasticity of the membrane structure, the fluid flow equation and the structure equation need to be solved together. The three-dimensional flow solver has been mentioned above. The influence of inherent nonlinear structure has to be taken into consideration for the deformation of the airship membrane structure is comparatively large. To account for the deformation of the membrane structure a three-dimensional membrane model is proposed. The deflection of the airship membrane is considered as large displacement but small strain condition. For the description of large deformation we introduce the Green-Lagrange strain tensor [6]. The strain-displacement relation with nonlinear terms reflecting large deformation is given by:

$$\begin{aligned}
\varepsilon_X &= \frac{\partial u}{\partial X} + \frac{1}{2}\left(\left(\frac{\partial u}{\partial X}\right)^2 + \left(\frac{\partial v}{\partial X}\right)^2 + \left(\frac{\partial w}{\partial X}\right)^2\right) \\
\varepsilon_Y &= \frac{\partial v}{\partial Y} + \frac{1}{2}\left(\left(\frac{\partial u}{\partial Y}\right)^2 + \left(\frac{\partial v}{\partial Y}\right)^2 + \left(\frac{\partial w}{\partial Y}\right)^2\right) \\
\varepsilon_{XY} &= \frac{1}{2}\left(\frac{\partial v}{\partial X} + \frac{\partial u}{\partial Y}\right) + \frac{1}{2}\left(\left(\frac{\partial u}{\partial X}\frac{\partial u}{\partial Y}\right) + \left(\frac{\partial v}{\partial X}\frac{\partial v}{\partial Y}\right) + \left(\frac{\partial w}{\partial X}\frac{\partial w}{\partial Y}\right)\right)
\end{aligned} \tag{6}$$

where u, v, and w are displacements in X, Y, and Z directions respectively, from the unstrained position in the initial coordination system. A general form of the principle of virtual work in Lagrangian description is given for equilibrium equations of membrane as follows:

$$\int_v \delta\mathbf{E}^T \sigma dv = \int_v \delta\mathbf{u}^T q dv + \int_A \delta\mathbf{u}^T p dA \tag{7}$$

where δuT are the virtual displacements, δET represent the corresponding virtual strains, p is the external surface force, and q is the body force.

The close coupling iterative method is employed to solve the problem. Fig. 1 illustrates the computation method. In the course of iteration, after the deformation computation is completed, the facial boundaries of the flow around the airship undergo changes. This requires that the computational grid of the flow should be re-developed. In the exchange, the geometry and external load values of the two grids are obtained with the Thin Plate Spline [7].

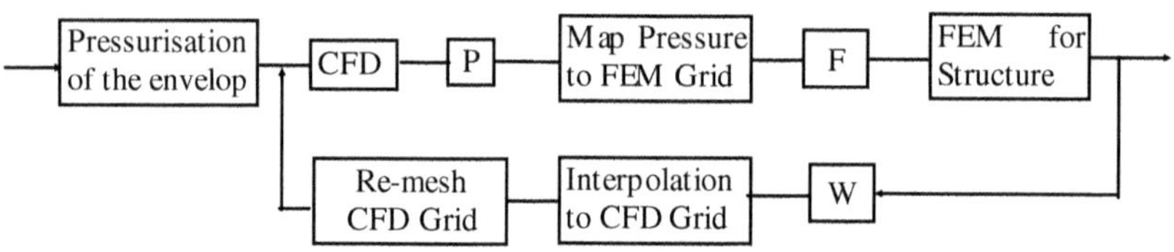

Fig. 1. Coupled Fluid-Structure Flow Diagram

4 Numerical Results and Discussion

In order to ensure the reliability and accuracy of the computation program developed in this paper, we compare our results with the experimental results by LOTTE in Lit. 8. In Fig. 2 the computation and experimental values of drag coefficient of LOTTE airship are compared. And in Fig. 3 the comparison of lift coefficient is presented. In these two figures, the abscissa is the attack angle of the inflow. The figures shows the computation results are well in accordance to the experimental ones in both bare hull and full-hull. The drag coefficient is fairly sensitive in the aerodynamic computation.

The consistency of the computation and experimental results fully proves the reliability and accuracy of the computation method developed in this paper. The contours of pressure of LOTTE airship at the attack angle of 20 when Re=3.9×106 are plotted in Fig. 4. The left picture gives the experimental results, and the right, the numerical ones. These pictures show that the pressure distribution of the numerical computation and the experiment is well corresponding. It is obvious that the computation program we develop is fairly reliable to realize the visualization of the fluid flow.

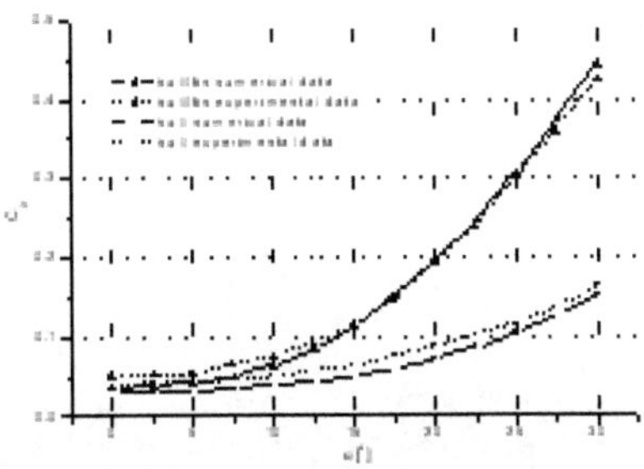

Fig. 2. The volumetric drag coefficient vs. angle of attack

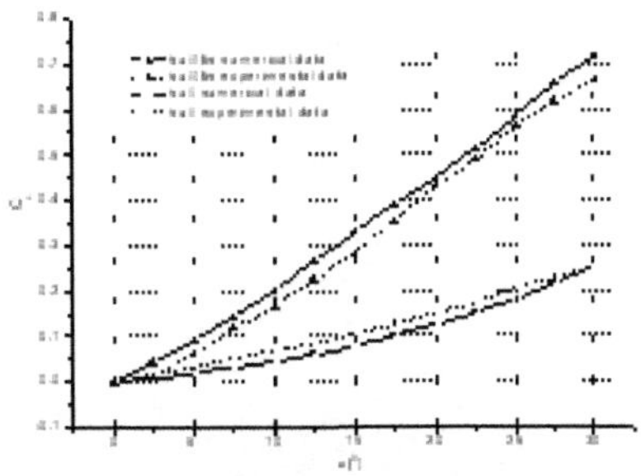

Fig. 3. The volumetric lift coefficient vs. angle of attack

Based on Lits. 9 and 10, the structural deformation is calculated in the program. Fig. 5 presents the deformation of a quadrangular membrane under pressure in the experiment and numerical computation respectively. The detailed computation parameters please refer to Lit. 9. In Fig. 5, six different points on the membrane and the grid we adopted are displayed. The computation values at the six different points are compared in Table 1. It is clear that the program we exploited is able to calculate accurately the nonlinear deformation of the membrane structure. The configuration of the membrane face when deformed under pressure is presented in Fig. 6.

Table 1. Displacement of different points on membrane surface

Displacement (mm)	Points on membrane surface					
	1	2	3	4	5	6
Exp.(Shore *et al.*) [10]	3.76	7.25	8.19	14.81	16.94	19.48
Irvine[10]	3.41	6.69	7.57	14.31	16.08	19.22
Han and Olson[9]	3.59	6.79	7.50	14.49	16.62	19.32
Results from our Program	3.34	6.55	7.21	14.02	16.29	19.01

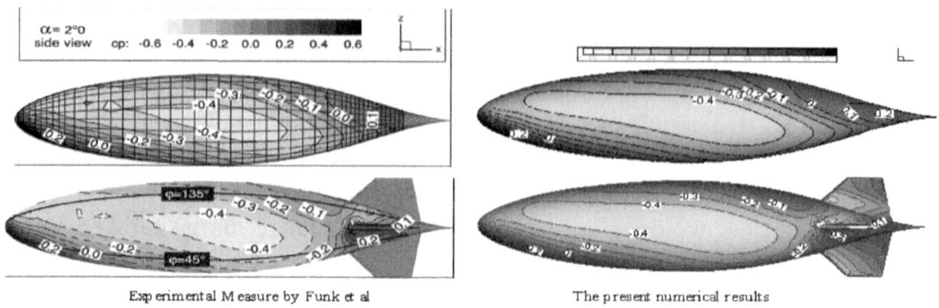

Fig. 4. Surface pressure distribution of bare hull and hull-fin configuration, side view $\alpha=20^0$, $Re_v=3.9\times10^5$

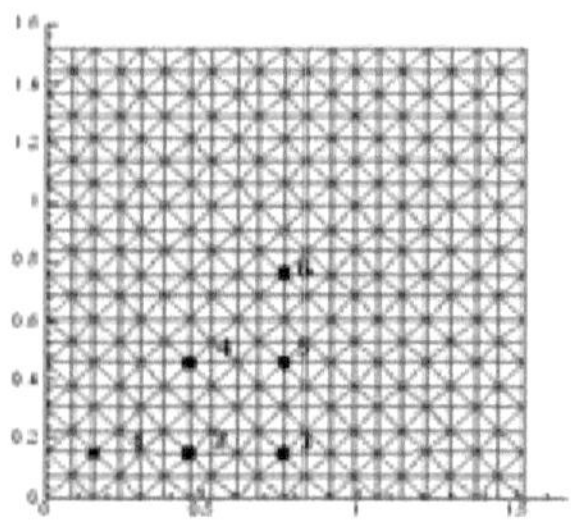

Fig. 5. Quadrangular membrane under surface pressure

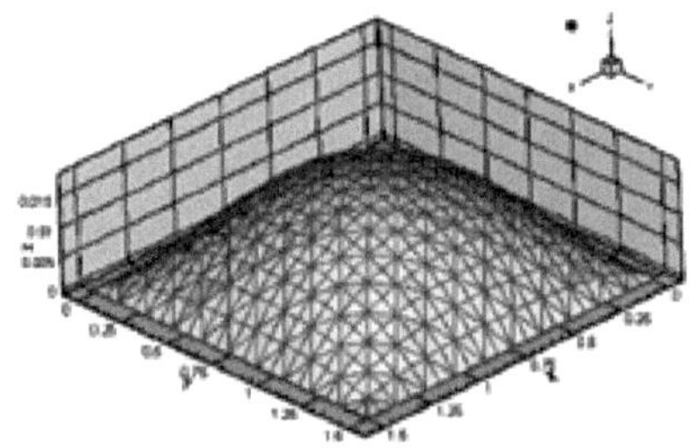

Fig. 6. Deformation when the membrane is under pressure

Based on the computation method mentioned above, the aeroelastic characteristics of 220-meter airship is investigated. The relation curves of drag coefficient against attack angle in the rigid and areoelastic models are given in Fig. 7, and, the curves of lift coefficient against attack angle are in Fig. 8. Accordingly, the contours of surface pressure coefficients of the hull at the attack angle of 20 are plotted in Fig. 9 and Fig, 10 respectively.

From the above curves, we can see: the aeroelastic model exhibits higher values than the rigid one in both drag and lift coefficients; both of the coefficients appear the same rising trend with the increase of the attack angle, within which the drag coefficient goes up about 9 percent, while the lift coefficient about 3 percent; the areoelasticity seemingly produces more effect on the drag coefficient than on the lift coefficient. Now let's compare the contours of pressure coefficient. It can be observed that there exists greater negative pressure zone on the lee face of the aeroelastic hull than on that of the rigid model. Fairly big difference is present at the pressure distribution near the tail vane. All these changes are valuable for the overall design, control, and optimization of the airship.[11]

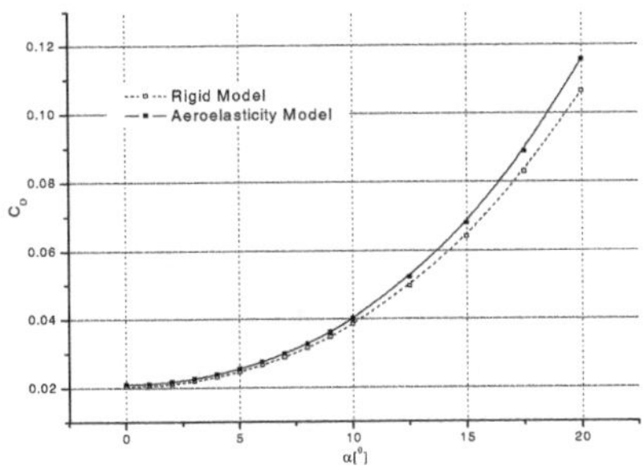

Fig. 7. The volumetric drag coefficient vs. angle of attack (220 meters)

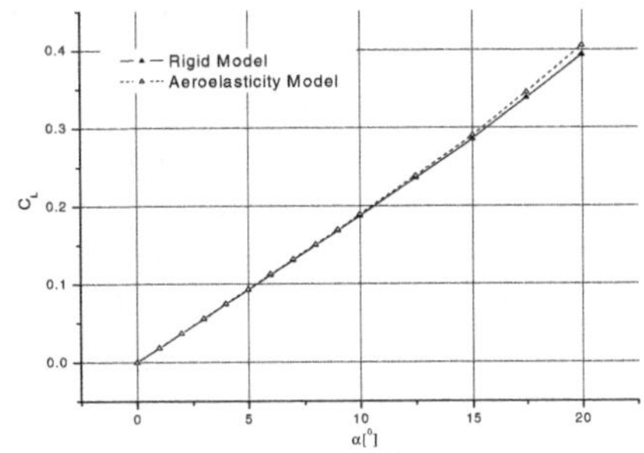

Fig. 8. The volumetric lift coefficient vs. angle of attack (220 meters)

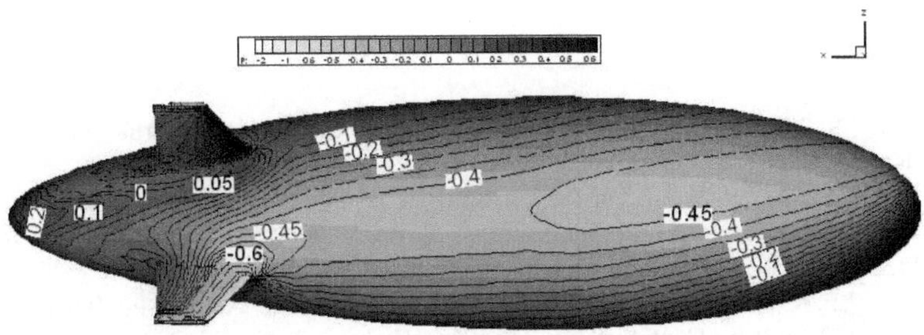

Fig. 9. The contour of pressure coefficient C_P of the rigid model ($\alpha=20^0$)

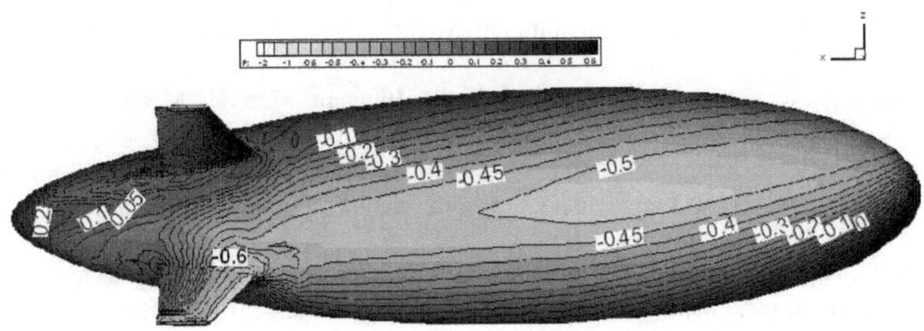

Fig. 10. The contour of pressure coefficient C_P of the aeroelastic model ($\alpha=20^0$)

5 Conclusion

The coupled fluid-structure alternative manner adopted in this paper is a three-dimensional turbulence numerical model, which is based on the finite volume method and SIMPLE algorithm, and the membrane structure nonlinear finite element method. This method can preferably solve the complicated problem of fluid-structure coupling of the ambient flow around the large gas-filled airship on the stratosphere and the flexible deformation.

Verified with examples, the numerical computation program of coupled fluid-structure of the flexible membrane structure developed in this paper is valid and accurate. With this program, we analyzed the aeroelastic characteristics of the large airship. It can be concluded that the flexibility of the airship places a pretty great effect on the aerodynamic parameters. With the increase of the attack angle, both the drag and lift coefficients shows the rising trend, and the pressure distribution on the surface of the airship undergoes changes, too. All these achievements are worthwhile to the further study of the aeroelasticity of the airship.

Acknowledgments. This work was supported by the Science Foundation of Jimei University, China (Grant No. ZQ2009009).

References

1. Bessert, N., Frederich, O.: Nonlinear Airship Aeroelasticity. Journal of Fluids and Structures 21, 731–742 (2005)
2. Balabel, A., Askary, W.A.: On the Performance of Linear and Nonlinear k-ε Turbulence Models in Various Jet Flow Applications. European Journal of Mechanics-B/Fluids 30, 325–340 (2011)
3. Liu, J., Lu, C., Xue, L.: Numerical Inverstigation on the Aeroelastic Behavior of an Airship with Hull-fin Configuration. Journal of Hydrodynamics 22, 207–213 (2010)
4. Anguelov, R., Lubuma, J., Minani, F.: Total Variation Diminishing Nonstandard Finite Difference Schemes for Conservation Laws. Mathematical and Computer Modelling 51, 160–166 (2010)
5. Ferziger, J.H., Peric, M.: Computational Methods for Fluid Dynamic. Springer, Berlin (2002)
6. Zienkiewicz, O.C., Taylor, R.L.: The Finite Element Method. McGraw-Hill, London (2005)
7. Xiang, S., Bi, Z., Jiang, S., Jin, Y.: Thin Plate Spline Radial Basis Function for the Free Vibration Analysis of Laminated Composite Shells. Composite Structure 93, 611–615 (2011)
8. Funk, P., Lutz, T., Wagner, S.: Experimental Investigations on Hull-fin Interferences of the LOTTE Airship. Aerospace Science and Technology 7, 605–610 (2003)
9. Han, P.S., Olson, M.D.: Interactive Analysis of Wind-loaded Pneumatic Membrane Structures. Computers & Structures 25, 699–712 (1987)
10. Irvine, H.M.: Analytical Solution for Pretensioned Cable Nets. The Engineering Mechanics Division, ASCE 102, 43–57 (1976)
11. Li, Y., Nahon, M., Shart, I.: Airship Dynamics Modeling: A Literature Review. Progress in Aerospace Sciences 47, 217–239 (2011)

Green Theory Research and Practice on Indoor Air Pollution by Overall Process Controlling

Liu Jun and Zhuo Yuguo

Environmental Management College of China, Qinhuangdao, 066004, P.R. China

Abstract. On the base of the residential interior decoration and the air pollution status in China, as the requirements of indoor air quality at present are increasing, from the concept of healthy house, new idea is proposed that indoor air pollution is controlled by overall process through green interior design, selecting environmentally friendly materials and green decoration for safety, healthy and environmental green home so that indoor air quality could be further improved.

Keywords: Indoor air pollution, overall process controlling, green interior design, green decoration, green ornament.

1 Introduction

While more than 80% life time is spent in indoor, indoor air quality directly affects human health. With the improvement of people's living standard and housing conditions there is serious indoor air pollution caused by residence decorating in all over China such as Beijing [1], Lanzhou [2], Changsha [3], Hangzhou [4-5], 13 municipalities [6] in Jiangsu and so on [7-12], at the same time, along with the unceasing enhancement in environmental consciousness, more and more people require that indoor air quality is further improved based on the indoor air quality assurance.

The world health organization puts forward the concept of healthy residence that refers to kilter residence in that people feel completely comfortable from physical, mental to social and its aim is to make the people who live in the residence achieve happiness and well-being.

From the concept of healthy residence the paper points out new idea – overall process controlling indoor air pollution, so the passive state is get rid that after the interior decoration causes severe pollution and hazards indoor air pollution control is go on. From design, decoration to living, possible pollutants in every link are targeted controlled and safe, healthy, environmental green household environment is created.

2 Green Interior Design

Green interior design is as far as possible to use natural elements and natural material in space organization, decorate adornment respect and indoor display art, to create natural and plain living and working environment and to pay attention to rational utilization of

C. Liu, J. Chang, and A. Yang (Eds.): ICICA 2011, Part I, CCIS 243, pp. 651–656, 2011.

natural energy and materials.

Green interior design is the inevitable requirement of developing low carbon economy, which should be evaluated in many-sides from material selection, transportation, product resources life, to recycling. Briefly materials used in a green interior design should be plain for example it can be obtained materials from local sources or recycling materials.Then natural lighting and ventilation should be mostly utilized so that not only energy is saved but also environment suitable for living could be created. The green design thoughts melt into the interior design to build the green indoor space.

Fresh air requirement is $30m^3$/ (person·h) in GB18883-2002 indoor air quality standard. Therefore using design technique for example opening window in the architectural design or modification of architectural design can make indoor and outdoor keep fully so that habitants have more fresh air and indoor pollutants are discharged easily. More natural model arts such as pot plant, potted landscape, waterscape, flower arrangement and so on are introduced, the application of natural color and natural materials is be emphasized and to imitate natural sound and smell effect is used in interior design. In the original design step at greatest degree new air volume is enough kept and wood-based panels quantity is reduced considering interior space load capacity.

Reasonable space organization arrangement is an important part in green interior design. In addition to satisfying human body engineering and improving space function, the designer should futher analyse the client requirements in order to avoid all kinds of waste from reconstruction. For example the space design for couple's should be a forcasting design that as far as possible considering the future baby's appearance. Thus when the couple has a baby the space inconvenience will not occur.

The application of new materials and natural material must be emphasiazed in green interior design. To the greatest extent avoid making use of large areas of wooden panels and select some environmental wallpaper and natural wallcoverings that use cotton, hemp, cane products, etc.as base material. Such green materials as microlite, plastic floor, composite floor, bamboo floor and so on which save energy are used in the floor.

3 Green Environmental Material Selection

It is the most important to make use of interior decoration and ornament materials which meet the national standards. Regular decoration companies should be chosen and key materials that will be used in the indoor decoration had better buy brand products. When buy finishing materials not only quality of products but also energy conservation should be payed attention to. To select decoration materials renewable, recycle and reuse principle should be more considered.Three mainly used materials that are wood-based panels, floorings and coatings are introduced in the interior decoration.

3.1 Wood-Based Panels

Because natural timbers in the growth process inevitably have some defects and lots of waste are produced in wood processing for improving timber availability and the quality of products wood-based panels have been widely put into use which is made of crushed aggregates that come from timber or other fibers. The main pollutant in wood-based panels is formaldehyde and according to the limit of formaldehyde there are E1 and E2 classes in current national standard. E1 class can be applied to indoors directly, while E2 class can used indoors after decorative surface processing. E1 wood-based panels should be chosen in the interior decoration.

3.2 Coatings

According to the diluent type, coatings are divided into solvent-thinned coatings and water based coatings. Water based coatings which is low toxicity should be chosen. Water-based coatings that use water as diluent and do not contain organic solvents, benzene, toluene, xylene, formaldehyde, free TDI and toxic heavy metals are harmless to human body and do not pollute environment.

In addition to considering the coating effect, the first choice is anion functional coating and natural plant coating of all the developing products on the market at present. When coatings which are added into anion additives are painted on metope, it can release negative ions for a long time and make air fresh.

3.3 Floorings

At present there are five categories that are solid wood flooring, engineered wood flooring, bamboo flooring and cork flooring. The price of engineered wood flooring is moderate, so the market share is higher. Formaldehyde is the main pollutant in the floor but formaldehyde removal agent is difficult to penetrate because engineered wood flooring has a hard surface. So high-quality composite floor should be selected and don't buy inferior floor.

4 Green Decoration

Green decoration is a decoration that environment materials are used and after decoration indoor environment meets national standards. For example wood that comes from renewable forests is used. In decoration construction people are first, do not endanger building structure and disturb neighbour. Green decoration contains two respect contents that are green decoration and environmental construction.

4.1 Green Decoration

Because many pollutants have additive effect, although formaldehyde releasing quantity of sola wood based panel meet the standard, if in a certain space many wood based panels are used, serious pollution will be caused. To uttermost reduce formaldehyde releasing quantity one is to control the use of total wood based panels, the other is when decorating to use formaldehyde scavenging agents spraying panels.

In green decoration avoid unnecessary lighting facilities and make use of water-saving sanitary fittings. If saving idea is put into design and energy conservation products at least 20% fitment cost can be saved.

4.2 Environmental Construction

Professionalization construction troops are prioritized in decorative finishing which can use materials to the greatest extent and control attrition rate within 3%. In specific work progress for top house thermal insulation material is filled between hang ceiling and roof and in the floor fishing thermal insulation fillers are lain down the floor. Light thermal insulation walling can be used as indoor partition.

During construction save electricity and water, at the same time do not work in spare time in order to reduce the noise influence on residents. The waste from construction should be properly handled and cannot be optional dumped.

5 Green Ornament

There are two aspects that are added environmental furniture and indoor air purification in green ornament and there are three ways to achieve indoor air purification which are indoor air cleaner, purification materials and plant purification.

5.1 Environmental Furniture

When buying furniture the priority choose is the furniture that has get environmental certification. In a certain space don't place too much furniture. Otherwise although sola furniture is met the standards, pollution is still serious. Meanwhile before furniture is assembled, bio-enzyme, photocatalyst [13] and so on is used to effectively remove formaldehyde, benzene content, TVOC pollutants in the furniture.

5.2 Indoor Air Cleaner

It is an effective way to make use of air cleaner for improving indoor air quality and creating comfortable office and house environment. Air cleaner in home should be often started and kept clean. At present indoor air purifier can effectively remove formaldehyde, benzene content, TVOC, particles [14], germs and so on and can also release negative ion so it is an effective way to improve the indoor air quality.

5.3 Indoor Purification Materials

Recently indoor air purification materials that meet the demand of indoor air pollution market have developed. In a few short years many new products such as formaldehyde capture agent, benzene scavenger, photocatalyst and so on are put on the market.

Activated carbon and carbon carving products belong to indoor purification materials which have certain purification effect and improve the indoor air quality when it are placed indoors.

5.4 Plant Purification

As is well-known that bracketplant, aloe and so on can absorb much formaldehyde. Gerbera, lily and sago cycas can eliminate benzene in the air while cactus can take up electromagnetic radiation. So it is good chioce to purify indoor air by plants.

Such ornamental plants as bracketplant, aloes, bunting, ivy that are placed indoors can purify air make environment beautiful but just when the pollution is within 1 times national standard requirement certain effect could get, so only as auxiliary means [15].

6 Summary

With the enhancement of environment consciousness more and more people require high air quality. Control pollution sources, select green material, adopt high-efficiency purification technics and ventilation and put green plants in the room. From design, selecting material, decoration and ornament, linked together, reducing pollution and controlling pollution by overall process healthy houses will be build.

References

1. Jiang, C., Li, S., Zhang, P., Wang, J.: Level and Characteristics of Indoor Air Pollutants in a Furniture Mall in Beijing. Environ. Science. 31, 2860–2865 (2010)
2. Huang, W., Lu, Y., Chang, Q., et al.: Indoor Air Pollution in Newly Redecorated Rooms. J. Environ. Health 24, 101–103 (2007)
3. Fang, D., Jing, H., Weihong: Investigation of Indoor Air Pollution in Docorative Bedrooms in Changsha. J. Environ. Health 25, 732–733 (2008)
4. Zhang, X., Zhou, Z., Xu, L., et al.: Investigation on airborne pollution caused by room decoration. Chinese Journal of Health Laboratory Technology 19, 669–671 (2009)
5. Li, F., Zheng, S., Xiang, J., et al.: Survey on indoor air pollution in decorative rooms in Yuhang district in Hangzhou. Chi. Prev. Med. 11, 952–953 (2010)
6. Wang, Y., Zhang, Q.: Monitoring Appraisal of the Environment Pollutants of Civil Construction Engineering of the 13 Cities in Jiangsu Province in Winter and its Counterplans. Jiangsu Construction 123, 85–88 (2008)
7. He, A., Yang, S., Li, C., et al.: Investigation on Formaldehyde Pollution of Indoor Air and its Control Measures in Zhuzhou City. Practical Preventive Medicine 16, 140–141 (2009)
8. Huang, H.: Current situation analysis of indoor air polltion and its countermeasures in Zhongshan. Guangdong Building Materials 6, 71–73 (2006)
9. Zhao, W., Bai, Z., Ma, L.: Concentration of Formaldehyde, Benzene Homologues and TVOC in Indoor Air in Shijiazhuang. Urban Environment & Urban Ecology 21, 9–11 (2008)
10. Liu, S., Liu, Y., Li, L., et al.: Investigation on indoor air pollution to health in decorated houses. Chin. J. Public Health 23, 400–401 (2007)

11. Liu, F., Sun, Z., Wang, C.: Investigationon People Cognition of Indoor Air Pollution and Human Health. J. Environ. Health 26, 242–243 (2010)
12. Franklin, P.J.: Indoor air quality and respiratory health of children. Paediatric Respiratory Reviews 27, 281–286 (2007)
13. Qi, F., Li, F.: Experiment research on curbing indoor pollution by photocatalyst. Chemical Engineer. 179, 44–46 (2010)
14. Xu, Y., Zhao, J., Chen, J., et al.: Study on pollution characteristics of particulate matter in indoor air. Environmental Pollution & Control 33, 52–56 (2011)
15. Zhang, C., Huangyanning, D.X.: Improving Indoor Environment of Ornamental Plant. Chinese Agricultural Science Bulletin 24, 301–305 (2008)

Regularization Method Combined with Parameter Competitive Criterion for Model-Plant Performance Matching of Aircraft Engine

Lifeng Wang[1] and Datian Zhong[2]

[1] North China University of Technology, Field Bus Technology & Automation Lab, 100041
[2] Beijing Aerospace Propulsion Institute, Beijing, 100070
Lf_wang@ncut.edu.cn

Abstract. The model-plant performance matching of aircraft engine can be used to solve several problems, such as fault diagnosis, model calibration and deterioration estimation etc. A partially mixed high bypass ration turbofan in civil aviation is modeling in simulating environments to constitute a model-plant performance matching benchmark. Depending on the nonlinear thermodynamic model between measured residuals and health factors, the regularization method with parameter competitive criterion is used to optimize the object value of components health factors. Several sets of simulated deterioration and fault data are naturalized as the invaliding cases, the better matching of model-plant is obtained from the simulating results.

Keywords: Engine model-plant matching, fault diagnosis, regularization, deterioration estimation.

1 Introduction

Performance simulation model of aircraft engine is playing an important role in design, development and availability. The complex performance simulation models of aircraft engine are developed by manufacturer, which is based on design information and the many measurements taken during product development. But the much complaint from the customers happens when it is put into use in the application because of the mismatching of model-plant testing data.

It may be caused by three situation, as follows:a) The problem of healthy plant, such as the individual product quality, changes over time of the plant design and manufacturing process, performance differences between part vendors, deterioration of engine during testing and service. b) The problem of modeling, the analysis assumptions of model, un-modeled, imperfectly modeled or incorrectly modeled physical phenomena in engine, c) The faulty plant, the faults of one or more plant components occur during service.

The deviation between model and plant is observed from residuals of the measured quantities and model predicting output. The matching problem is to seek a solution to determine the values of the tuning health factors from a given series of measured residuals.

C. Liu, J. Chang, and A. Yang (Eds.): ICICA 2011, Part I, CCIS 243, pp. 657–664, 2011.

Not only can it be used in model-plant matching, but also be applied to fault detecting and diagnosis. So the algorithm techniques of tuning the model parameter factors to achieve the model-plant matching have been developed in many published paper. Gas Path Analysis(GPA) are introduced in fault detecting and diagnosis by Doe[1,2], Mathiodakis[3]. It include the linear, nonlinear adaptive modeling techniques [4], multiple discrete points optimization approach [5]. The adaptive GPA and genetic algorithm is also proposed into matching of model and testing data by Li[6,7,8]. As well as the probabilistic fusion wit GPA derived from diagnosis methods is applied to the model and testing data matching[9]. While matching is treated as inverse problem is brought forwards[10,11], so many choice can be adopted to solve the inverse problem[12,13]. The most difficulties faced on model-plant matching are the limited number of measured quantities and data noise. So model-plant matching can be treated as the ill-posed problem.

In present paper, a partially mixed high bypass ration turbofan in civil aviation is modeling in simulating environments to constitute a model-plant performance matching benchmark. Depending on the nonlinear thermodynamic model between measured residuals and health factors, the regularization method combined with parameter competitive criterion is used to optimize the object value of components health factors. Several sets of simulated deterioration and fault data are naturalized as the invaliding cases, the better matching of model-plant is obtained from the simulating results.

2 Inverse Problem and Regularization Method

The inverse problem typically involves the estimation of certain quantities based on indirect measurements of these quantities. For aircraft engine, the component characteristic is stand for the engine health status, which cannot be directly measured but severely influence the engine performance. The performances include the aerodynamic parameter through the gas path, rotor speed, force and specific fuel consume etc. If the residuals of model–plant testing data exists, the task of inverse problem is calculating the health parameter.

According to the detailed components level thermodynamic model of engine, at engine steady state, the formula of interrelation between the scaled residuals and health factors can be described as follows:

$$\begin{aligned} d_1 &= g_1(f_1, f_2, \ldots, f_n) \\ d_2 &= g_2(f_1, f_2, \ldots, f_n) \\ &\;.. \\ d_m &= g_m(f_1, f_2, \ldots, f_n) \end{aligned} \tag{1}$$

where the n health factors and m residuals factors, where m<n. Vector formula of equation (1) can be represented for

$$\mathbf{d} = \mathbf{g}(\mathbf{f}) \tag{2}$$

The residual is deviation of measured y_{mi} relative to model refer y_{ri}. The scaled residuals defined as:

$$d_i = (y_{mi} - y_{ri}) / y_{ri} \quad \text{i=01...m} \tag{3}$$

The health parameter employed to characterize the fault of rotating components are an efficiency η and flow capability ω. The health factor is deviation of estimated h_{mi} relative to the model refer health parameter h_{ri}. The scale factor is defined as follows:

$$f_i = (h_{mi} - h_{ri}) / h_{ri} \quad \text{i=01...m} \tag{4}$$

In equation (2), there are n fault factors but only m equations are available, where m<n . If the scaled residuals are knows, there are infinite number of sets of health parameter values satisfying the equations. It belongs to ill-posed problem.

The health factors are more than the number of equations, so the regularization method is used to optimize the object value on the health factors of engine components. The optimizing target function is defined as follows:

$$\min \phi(\mathbf{f}) = \left\|\mathbf{g}(\mathbf{f}) - \mathbf{d}_m\right\|^2 + \alpha\left\|\mathbf{f} - \mathbf{f}^*\right\|^2 \tag{5}$$

Where $\mathbf{d}_m$ is measurement residuals vector, α is Tikhonov regularization coefficients, it representing the accuracy related with data noise, its range 0.001~0.1 in paper. $\left\|\mathbf{f} - \mathbf{f}^*\right\|$ is norm, representing for regularization items of health factor. $\mathbf{f}^*$ is initial guess value of health factors, means that the seeking health factors is not far to its initial values. In order to gain the $\min \phi(\mathbf{f})$, it is satisfied as follows:

$$\frac{\partial \phi(\mathbf{f})}{\partial \mathbf{f}} = \mathbf{J}(\mathbf{f})^T (\mathbf{g}(\mathbf{f}) - \mathbf{d}_m) + \alpha \mathbf{I}(\mathbf{f} - \mathbf{f}^*) = 0 \tag{6}$$

I is unit matrix. The iteration equation steps of solving equations (6) are as follows:

$$\begin{aligned} &(\mathbf{J}(\mathbf{f}^k)^T \mathbf{J}(\mathbf{f}^k) + \alpha \mathbf{I})\delta\mathbf{f} = \mathbf{J}(\mathbf{f}^k)^T (\mathbf{d}_m - \mathbf{g}(\mathbf{f}^k)) - \alpha \mathbf{I}(\mathbf{f}^k - \mathbf{f}^*) \\ &\mathbf{f}^{k+1} = \mathbf{f}^k + \delta\mathbf{f} \end{aligned} \tag{7}$$

Where $\mathbf{J}(\mathbf{f}^k) = \dfrac{\partial \mathbf{g}(\mathbf{f})}{\partial \mathbf{f}}$ is the Jacobian matrix of function $\mathbf{g}(\mathbf{f})$ at $\mathbf{f}^k$, $\mathbf{J}(\mathbf{f}^k)^T$ is the transfer matrix of $\mathbf{J}(\mathbf{f}^k)$, superscript *k* is iteration step.

3 Parameter Competitive Criterion

The calculating results of health factors using regularization method is usually not satisfied, because its values beyond the reasonable scope referring to engineering experience. So parameter competitive criterion is selected to improve the method.

The first parameter competitive criterion is trend of health factors. The effect of engine degradation due to aging or fault is modeled in the nonlinear simulation by modifying the efficiencies and flow capacities of key engine components, such as: fan, booster, compressor, main burner, high pressure turbine, low pressure turbine and nozzle etc. From the reference [14,15], the degradation or fault level has its regular pattern. For example, the efficiency and flow capability of fan, booster and compressor decrease, the efficiency of burner decrease, but flow capability of turbine increase but efficiency decrease, nozzle flow capability increase. The trend of regular pattern is summarized as Table 1.

Table 1. Trend of engine health parameter,(-):decrease (+):increase

Health factor **f**	Fan	Booster	Compressor	Main burner	High turbine	Low Turbine	Nozzle
Efficiency $\boldsymbol{\eta}$	-	-	-	-	-	-	
Corrected Flow **w**	-	-	-		+	+	+

The second parameter competitive criterion is quantitative of health factors. Because of data noise and measurement accuracy, the health factors accuracy is limited in scope. If the magnitudes of health factors too small, it is no meaning to engineering. So threshold is selected for health factors:

$$|\mathbf{f}| \le \delta_c, \quad or \qquad |\mathbf{f}| \ge \delta_c, \qquad \delta_c > 0 \tag{8}$$

Now the regularization method combined with parameter competitive criterion diagram refer figure 1. In criterion judgment steps, the variables which not meet the criterion will be eliminated.

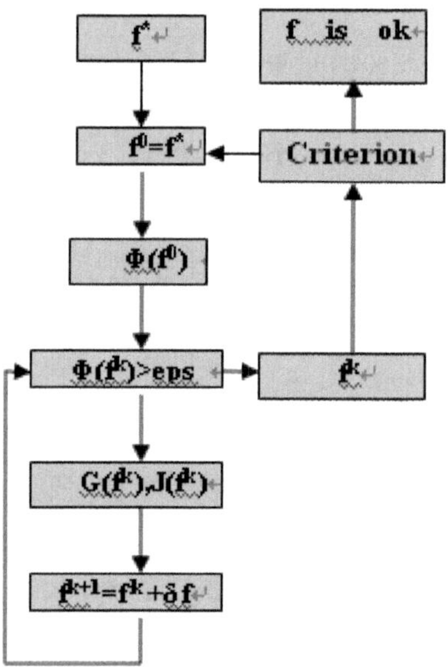

Fig. 1. Regularization with criterion

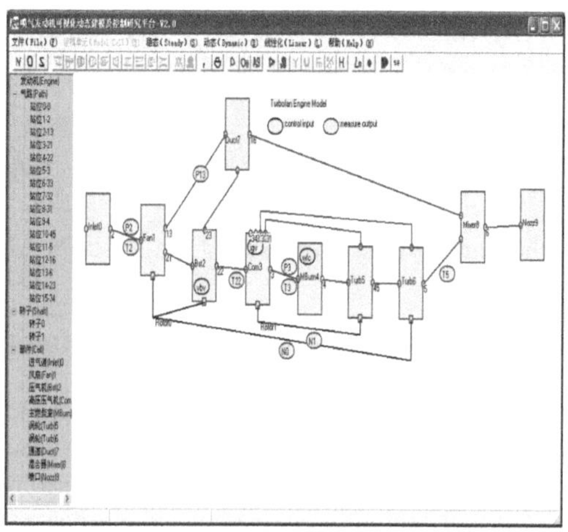

Fig. 2. Turbofan engine model skeleton

4 Commercial Turbofan Engine Layout

A partially mixed high bypass ratio turbofan engine which is representative of the type used in civil aviation today is selected as a demonstrating object. Refer figure 2, the turbofan engine have been modeling in simulation environment[16]. It is high bypass ratio and a two-spool configuration. The five rotating components consist of the fan(Fan), Booster (Bst), and low pressure turbine (Lturb) on the fan shaft, and the high pressure compressor (Com) and high pressure turbine (Hturb) on the core shaft. The hot gas is generated by burning in main burner(Mburn), which drive the turbine shaft to rotate. The gas is exhausted through the Nozzle(Nozz).

Some perspective of the engine is modeling to operate with a bypass ratio of 5.2 and an overall pressure ratio of 29. The design speeds for the fan and core shafts are 2450 and 9300 rpm respectively, refer to ref[17]. The control inputs to this engine are fuel flow (*wf*), inlet guide vane (igv) angle, and variable bleed valve (vbv) position. Two spool rotation and seven gas path sensors are considered as measured quantities for control: *N*0, *N*1, *P*2, *T*2, *P*13, *T*22, *P*3, *T*3, *T*5. This is representative of the sensors used in most commercial turbofan engines.

The steady state operating point of engine is defined by the control inputs, ambient temperature (*T*2) and pressure (*P*2), which is referring operating point. The set of measurements used for monitoring is follows: *N*0, *N*1, *P*13, *T*22, *P*3, *T*3, *T*5. The listing of measured quantities is referred to Table 2:

Table 2. Listing of measured quantities

Measured quantity	Fan shaft	Core shaft	Fan Outer Pressure	Bst Outlet Temp	Com Outlet Pressure	Com Outlet Temp	LPT Outlet Temp
y_{mi}	*N*0	*N*1	*P*13	*T*22	*P*3	*T*3	*T*5
d_i	d_1	d_2	d_3	d_4	d_5	d_6	d_7

The health parameter include Fan, Bst, Com, Hturb, LTurb. But the health parameter of Mburn is burner efficiency η, and the health parameter of Nozz is flow capability ω. So Listing of health parameter is refer the table 3.

Table 3. Listing of health parameter for engine component

Components	**Fan**		**Bst**		**Com**		**Mburn**	**Hturb**		**Lturb**		**Nozz**
Health h_{mi}	η	ω	η	ω	η	ω	η	η	ω	η	ω	ω
Fault f_i	f_1	f_2	f_3	f_4	f_5	f_6	f_7	f_8	f_9	f_{10}	f_{11}	f_{12}

5 Case Evaluate and Validation

In order to evaluate the effectiveness of proposed approach applying to model-plant match of aircraft engine, the cases, which cover the fault, calibration and deterioration, are performed compared with regularization approach. All measured quantities is simulated on simulation environment and testing data is average using 10 points with sample time. Where α=0.03,and with noise data

Case A: component fault
Component fault is consequently occurring when engine working, but we may not know the location of fault in prior. Now assumed that the Bst and Com have faults, which the efficiency of Bst reduced by 1%, flow capability reduced by 0.8%, and Com reduced by 1.8%, flow capability reduced by 0.2%. The health factors of components distribute refer the figure 3, the scaled residuals distribute refer 4.

The best results is gained through regularization with parameter competitive criterion, but the results through regularization method, some health parameter does not meet the criterion, so it is eliminated when second optimization.

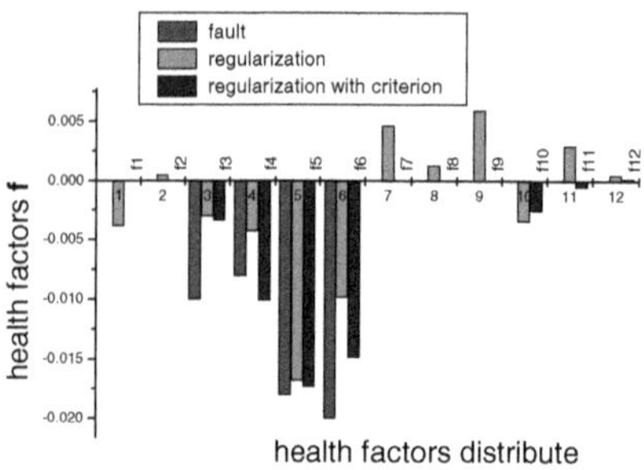

Fig. 3. Health factors distribute of case C

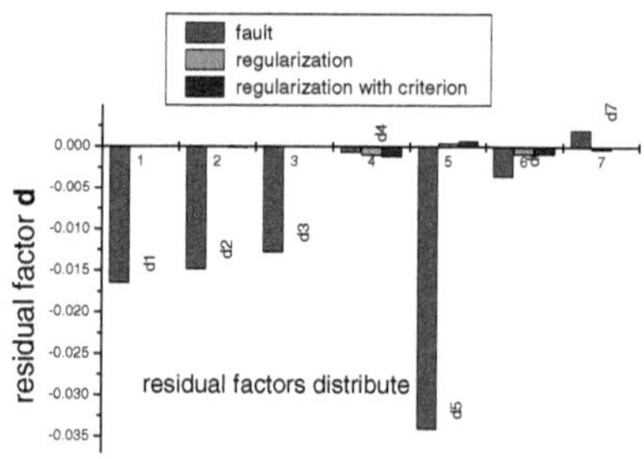

Fig. 4. Measured residuals distribute of case C

Case B: calibration
The normal performance model stands for the average of all product line, so the deviation between individual plant and the normal model exist because of product quality. For example, at standard atmosphere in ground, the health factors of components distribute refer the figure 5, the scaled residuals distribute refer 6.

The criterion of calibration is different from the fault. The criterion is health factors less than the limit. The same results is gained for regularization with criterion and regularization.

Although the same fine tuning measured residuals of 1% and 3% disturbance inputs around refer adjacent points, the better health factor distribute have been gained from the 3% disturbance inputs. This may be caused by the extent of nonlinear equations at 3% disturbance inputs.

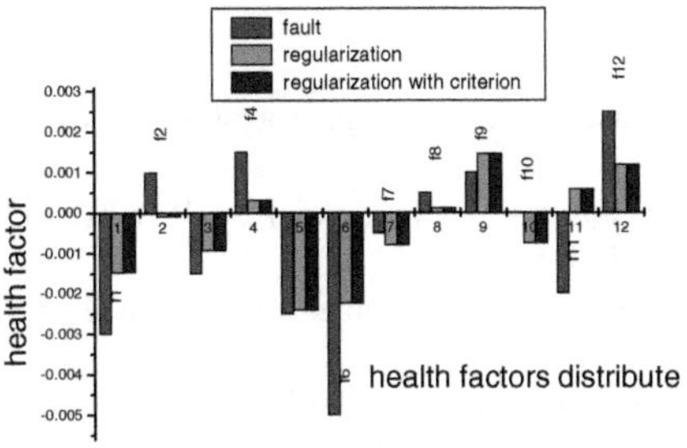

Fig. 5. Health factors distribute of case A

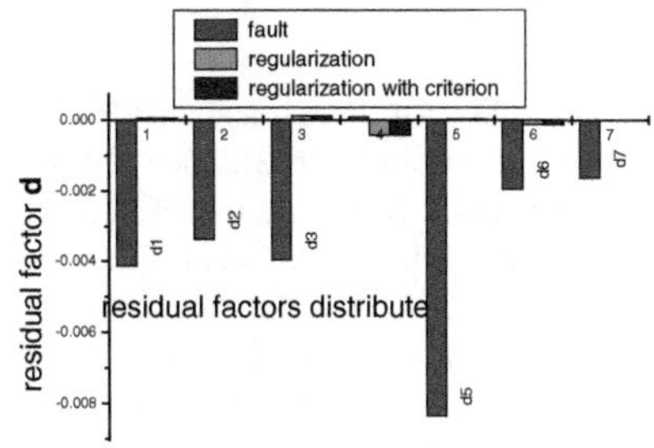

Fig. 6. Measured residuals distribute

Case C: deterioration

The deterioration of engine happens with service cycles. The deterioration level may be higher than effects of loads and rub. In ground, the health factors of components deterioration distribute refer the figure 7, the scaled residuals distribute refer figure 8.The margin of health factor is larger than calibration. The effects of regularization with criterion is better than pure regularization.

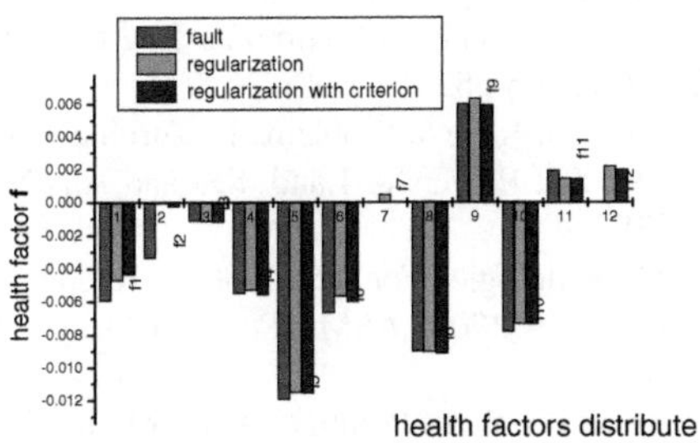

Fig. 7. Health factors distribute of case B

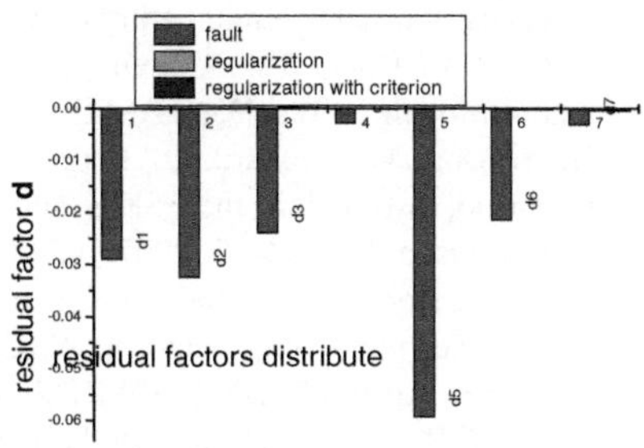

Fig. 8. Measured residuals distribute of case B

6 Conclusions

Regularization combined with parameter competitive criterion for model-plant performance matching is invalidated through calibration, deterioration and fault case. The better matching effect is obtained from the simulating results. The method is more stable for next step study.

Acknowledgement. The work for this paper is sponsored by Beijing Municipal Education Commission funds (KM200410009006, KM200610009001) & PHR(IHLB). Many thanks for supporting my works from my friends.

References

1. Doel, D.: An assessment of weighted-least-squares based gas path analysis. J. Eng. Gas Turbines Power 116(2), 366 (1994)
2. Doel, D.L.: Interpretation of Weighted-Least-Squares Gas Path Analysis Results. Journal of Engineering for Gas Turbines and Power 125, 625 (2003)
3. Mathioudakis, K., Kamboukos, P.: Assessment of Gas Path Diagnostic Schemes. ASME Turbo Expo paper GT2003-53862 (2003)
4. Aretakis, N., Mathioudakis, K.: Non-linear engine component fault diagnosis from a limited number of measurements using a combinatorial approach. In: Proceedings of ASME Turbo Expo 2002 ASME-GT-2002-30031 (2002)
5. Gulati, A., Taylor, D., Sign, R.: Multiple operating point analysis using genetic algorithm optimization for gas turbine diagnostic. In: XV ISABE, Bangalore, India, September 3-7 (2001), paper ISABE-2001-1139
6. Li, Y.G., Abdul Ghafir, M.F., Wang, L., et al.: Nonlinear Multiple Points Gas Turbine Off-Design Performance Adaptation Using a Genetic Algorithm. J. Eng. Gas Turbines Power 133(7), 071701(9 pages) (2011)
7. Li, Y.G., Marinai, L., Lo Gatto, E., Pachidis, V., Pilidis, P.: Multiple Point Adaptive Performance Simulation Tuned to Aerospace Test-Bed Data. J. Propul. Power 25(3), 635–641 (2009)
8. Li, Y.G.: Gas Turbine Performance and Health Status Estimation Using Adaptive Gas Path Analysis. Journal of Engineering for Gas Turbines and Power 132 (April 2010)
9. Roth, B.A., Doel, D.L., Cissell, J.J.: Probabilistic Matching of Turbofan Engine Performance Models to Test Data. ASME Paper No. GT2005-68201 (2005)
10. Henriksson, M., Léonard, O., Borguet, S., et al.: On Inverse Problems In Turbine Engine Parameter Estimation. In: ASME Turbo Expo 2007: Power for Land, Sea and Air, Montreal, Canada, May 14-17 (2007), GT2007-27756
11. Cerri, G., Borghetti, S., Salvini, C.: Inverse Methodologies For Actual Status Recognition Of Gas Turbine Components. In: Proceedings of PWR2005,ASME Power, Chicago, Illinois USA, April 5-7 (2005), PWR2005-50033
12. Vogel, C.R.: Computational Methods for Inverse Problem. Frontiers Appl. Math. (2002) ISBN: 0-898715-50-7
13. Krisch, A.: An Introduction to the Mathematical Theory of Inverse Problems. Applied Mathematical Sciences. Springer, New York (1996)
14. Chatterjee, S., Litt, J.S.: Online Model Parameter Estimation of Jet Engine Degradation for Autonomous Propulsion Control, NASA/TM—2003-212608,vol. 8 (2003)
15. lee, G.P.: Performance Deterioration Based on Existing (Historical) Data – JT9D Jet Engine Diagnostics Program, NASA-CR-135448. Pratt and Whitney Aircraft Group
16. lifeng, W.: Study on Visual Dynamic Modeling Environment of Turbojet Engine. In: 12th Conference on Aerodynamic & Thermodynamic of Propulsion System of China, Sichuan, vol. 9 (2009)
17. DeCastro, J.A., Litt, J.S., Frederick, D.K.: A Modular Aero-Propulsion System Simulation of a Large Commercial Aircraft Engine", NASA/TM—2008-215303 (September 2008)

Study of Flow Control System Model Based on Bypass Protocol Analysis

Sujuan Zhang[1], Yanli Zhang[2], and Zhijie Fan[3]

[1] Nerwork Centre, Hebei United University, Tangshan,China
[2] Tangshan Jidong Petroleum Mechanical CO., LTD, Tangshan, China
[3] Library, Hebei United University, Tangshan,China

Abstract. The paper has proposed a bypass protocol analysis method in the design of flow control system to change the traditional working style. In this new method, the network packets can be controlled after its protocol is identified. To improve the performance of the system, a zero-copy implementation, based on flow control system, is designed to realize the memory sharing between kernel space and user space. The applications enable the direct access to the kernel data through memory sharing. Thus, the time spent on data copying and context switching is greatly reduced.

Keywords: bypass analysis, zero-copy, regular expression.

1 Introduction

Ideally, the network should be able to carry any unexpected traffic, until the maximum throughput over the network. However, if the network overload, network performance will plummet [1]. The traffic schedule will also directly affect network performance, so burst traffic belongs to one area or one business will seriously affect the utilization of network resources [2].

To maximize use of resources, a set of reasonable control strategy is formulated. Traffic control based on business characteristics can increase the bandwidth unit yield [3]. In addition, the large number of region's non-adapted data stream can lead to network performance reduction, even lead to some network services paralysis, such as the worm that seriously affected network security and performance in recent years, therefore [4], that the non-adapted data steam is effective distinguished is an important task in flow control system.

2 Traditional Flow Control System

The traditional workflow of flow control system is shown as follow: firstly analysis of captured data packets, secondly identifying the appropriate protocols, and then processing the data packets according to the corresponding strategies. Flow control system that work in traditional style must process each data packet [5], and then to control network traffic, so it is difficult to improve the efficiency of the system.

C. Liu, J. Chang, and A. Yang (Eds.): ICICA 2011, Part I, CCIS 243, pp. 665–672, 2011.

LIBPCAP is usually used to capture network data packet, there are much data copy in the transmission process of data packets from network card to applications, and there are a large amounts of in the backbone. The data copy will occupy a lot of CPU resources, which will reduce the system performance.

3 Overall Design Model

Protocol identification is more resource-intensive part of the flow control system. To avoid that protocol identification affects the system performance, the bypass protocol identification is used in the system. The entire platform is divided into two parts: straight control and bypass analysis. The system entirety structure is shown in figure 1.

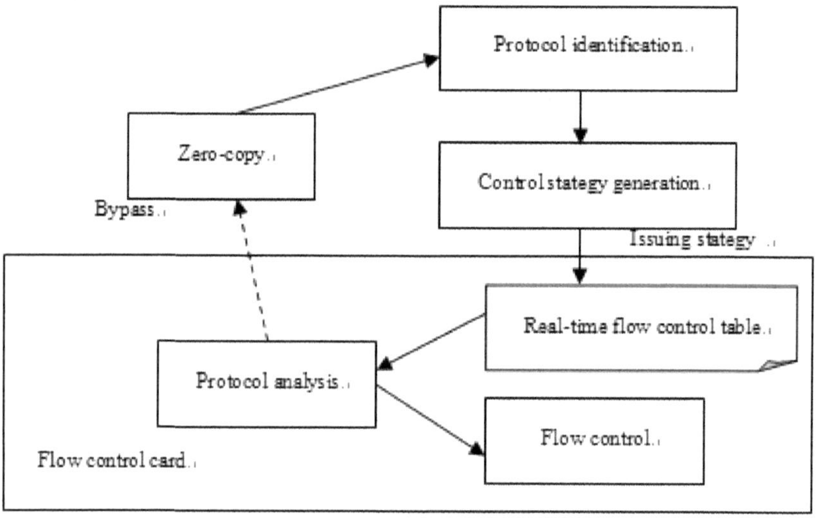

Fig. 1. The system entirety structure

In the straight, protocol analysis module first analyzes the network packet captured and extracts four-tuple [6], then find corresponding control strategy in the real-time flow control table. The next action is executed if the strategy match successfully, otherwise the packet is sent to bypass analysis, and the packet is transmitted at the same time. In the bypass analysis, the packet to be analyzed is obtained in zero-copy, and then protocol identification module detects and identifies the content of the packet, finally, the result is output to control strategy generation module.

3.1 The Straight Control

In the protocol analysis module, packets are simple analyzed by TCP/IP stack that is offloaded to flow control card, packet is split up to transport layer, the four-tuple that can uniquely represent a connection is extracted, the four-tuple includes source IP, destination IP, source port and destination port. The module calls real-time flow control table for match strategy, the corresponding control strategy is executed if the connection can successfully match, otherwise two actions are executed: (1) copying the total data packet to bypass analysis by zero-copy module; (2) releasing the packet.

Real-time flow control table is actually a hash table that stores all of the current network connections. Each line represents a current connection, and each connection is processed by the protocol identification module and consists of five basic information, they are: source IP, destination IP, source port, destination port and control strategy. The table is updated by control strategy generation module and provided to the protocol analysis module for inquiry

Flow control module takes appropriate control action using the existing flow control techniques according to output result of protocol analysis module.

3.2 The Bypass Analysis

The bypass analysis must achieve two goals that is less time-consuming and high accuracy. Zero-copy technology can decrease memory copy in the process of transmitting data packets [7], in other words the flow control card directly sends network packets to user space when packets need to be identified. User layer direct exchange data with network interface layer, which can shorten walk path of the data packet and save CPU overhead and improve network and system processing performance.

DPI (Deep Packet Inspection) technology is used to improve the accuracy of protocol identification. This method is suitable for real-time environment, and it is high accuracy.

The bypass analysis is the key part of the system, and the detailed design is as follows.

4 Zero-Copy Module

4.1 Theoretical Analysis

PF_RING is a closest implementation of zero-copy. It maintains a circular buffer in kernel, and the ring buffer has two interfaces, one for the card to write data packets, one for the application to read data. When the external data packet arrives, the NIC receive data and copy it into the ring, and then the data packet itself is discarded, no into kernel protocol stack of Linux. Application gets read pointer of the ring buffer by opening the socket descriptor of PF_RING types [8], and then access the ring buffer by mmap.

PF_RING is a relatively mature zero-copy program, but it still includes a copy [9]. By analyzing the PF_RING source, we know that data needs be copy in the process of transmission from kernel space to user space. PF_RING allows memory map between kernel space and user space, thus the user can directly access data in kernel space as in their own space, but PF_RING ring buffer size is fixed---- 1024 slot. The processes that card receive packets and put it into the ring is a hardware deal, very fast.

Application must remove the packets as soon as possible, and empty the memory; otherwise there is no space to receive data in NIC, so it has to copy the packets to its own space. That is so-called the producer and consumer issues. Of course, if the user program processes data fast enough (for example, just do a statistics), it need not do so, you can use the pointer, not copy, then it is zero-copy. However, in the flow control system, the flow analysis module must systematic analyze the packet, its processing speed can not meet the requirement, so data must be copied to user space before being processed.

To solve this problem, a data area managed (zc_buf) is built in kernel in my design. It that records all the information of the packets is actually a control structure. The kernel distributes not only the storage space but also control structure zc_buf to network packets. User program and the NIC apply for available memory from the management area when data needs be processed and free it when data has been processed. The way of continuous application and free of memory ensure that there is enough available space for the NIC to write.

4.2 Zero-Copy Program Design Flow

A ring buffer is built in kernel as PF_RING, however, it storages in the ring is not the packet but the packet descriptor which includes the packet start position and offset in memory. Figure2 shows the system structure of zero-copy:

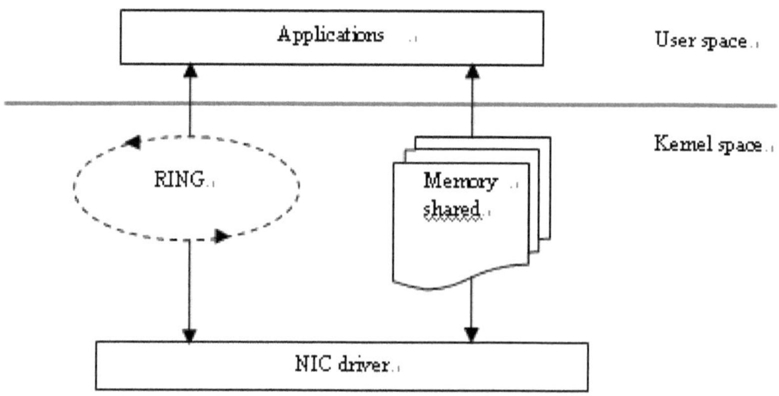

Fig. 2. System structure of zero-copy in flow control system

The work process of zero-copy is as follows:

Number of consecutive pages in kernel mapped to user space;

These pages are managed kernel module, and as the DMA address of NIC drive to receive and send packets;

If the packets which are received the NIC drive need to be sent to user space, their descriptor is wrote the kernel module into the specific buffer for the user space to read, corresponding the memory used counter plus 1;

The application reads the packets descriptor and calculates the corresponding address, that is, the address of packets which need to be processed; after the end of the life cycle of the packets, the application informs the kernel space to reduce memory count by COW, if the memory count is 1, the memory is freed;

It that the application sends packets takes a similar approach, the difference is that the packet memory is applied the user space, allocated the kernel module and then handed to the user space.

4.3 Synchronization

Synchronization is a key problem in zero-copy technology. On the one hand the NIC drive of the kernel space write data packets in the memory, on the other hand the user process directly analyses data packets [10]. They work in different space, which makes the synchronization very complex.

There are many ways to solve the synchronization, in this program we use the ring (ring buffer mentioned above), as follow:

A ring buffer which storages the packet descriptor is built in kernel;

The ring buffer is divided into four types. 1 free buffer waiting the NIC to write, 2 data buffer and the data is waiting to be processed, 3 data buffer and the data is being processed, 4 data buffer and the data has been processed and the memory can be freed;

After the NIC receive data packets, the NIC drive puts the packets descriptor into the buffer marked 1, if there is no, into the buffer marked 2;

The same time, the user space reads this ring, if founds any buffer marked 2, the first marks to 3, then processes data in it;

When the user space processed data, the corresponding buffer is marked to 4;

At the same time, a timer thread in kernel scans this ring buffer, if founds any buffer marked 4, the corresponding memory is freed and the buffer is marks to 1.

5 Protocol Identification Module

Each new connection request is analyzed by protocol identification module, and most are the application layer protocol. The module flow chart is shown in figure15. Non-application layer protocol is identified by reading the protocol header information, which is the corresponding layer information in zc_buf. The protocol analysis of application layer is the most important and most complicated in this module, and pattern-matching technology based DPI is used to filter the contents of the packet.

Pattern-matching algorithm compares contents of packet and protocol features that have been identified, and the packet is considered to be some kind of protocol if matching successful. All data of a connection belong to the same application, so system only needs to match the first few packets, and the number of packets is defined as 10 in this system. We think that the data stream can be identified if a few packets in front of the stream contain some protocol features. The other packets will be given up to match and if the first few packets fail to match, and the steam can be identified.

The modular approach is adopted to implement the protocol identification module, the big module includes rules management module, connection management module and rule matching module according to different functions, and their relationship is shown in figure 3.

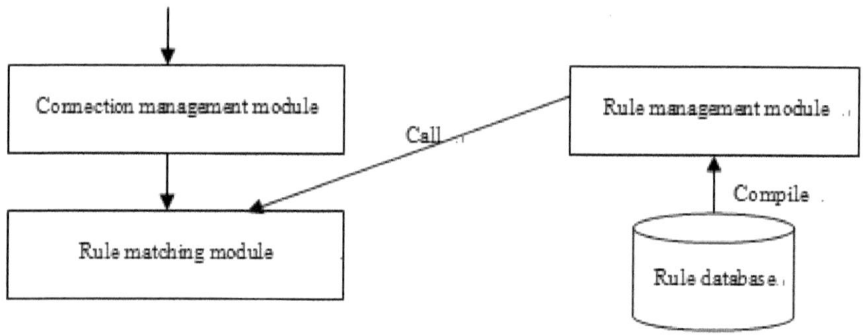

Fig. 3. Module structure of protocol identification

5.1 Rule Management Module

There are two ways in rule management of protocol: one is to compile the protocol features into the main program, and it needs to be timely updated according to internet changes; another is to compile the protocol features into some plus-ins that include dynamic link library and shared library, and the plus-ins are responsible for registering new features into main program. The first way involves changing the main program when protocol features are updated, so the first way is poor operability and the second way is used.

There is rule configuration file protocol.config in system directory /etc/. A packet only matches a rule when identifying protocol, the file lists the matching order of rules. The contents of protocol.config are shown as follows:

Segment checked in the first line (such as 10.16.1.0);
Network mask in the second line (such as 255.255.255.0);

Protocol names in the third line and the follow lines (each line corresponds to a file of pat).

Pat files are placed in system directory /etc/regexps/. The directory contains all the rules available, and the files are named with the corresponding protocol names. Pat file format is as follows:

#comment line;
Protocol name;

Matching rule, that is regular expression of protocol feature.

Rule management module is loaded in the following order: firstly, rule configuration file is read; secondly, rule files are loaded according to the rule order of rule configuration file; lastly, the regular expressions of rule files are compiled and loaded into memory.

5.2 Connection Management Module

Connection management module is designed to improve matching speed and efficiency of regular expression. The module is responsible for managing the connections of packets to identify. The four-tuple is still used to represent a connection in this module, when a connection matches more than 10 times, system thinks the connection failed to match and the protocol could not be identified.
The module works as follows:

Extracting the four-tuple when a packet arrives;
Searching the current connection database, and reading the old connection if the four-tuple is a old connection, otherwise, creating a new connection;
Return if the connection has matched successfully, otherwise, calling rule matching module;
If matching successful, go 6), otherwise, matching times add 1;
Protocol can not identified and go 6) if times more than 10, else return;

Output result and return.
A data structure connection is defined to represent a connection representation and storage:

```
struct connection
      {
       unsigned int   packetsnumber;/*matching times*/
        char          protocol;      /*protocol name*/
       unsigned int    key;          /*index*/
       unsigned short  scrsport; /*source port*/
       unsigned int    scrip;    /*source IP*/
       unsigned int    dstip;    /*destination IP*/
       unsigned short  dstsport;   /*destination port*/
      }
```

5.3 Rule Matching Module

Rule matching module reads data from connection management module, and then compares the data with the regular expression link compiled. The module works as follows:

Removing 0x00 from the application layer data to avoid matching incomplete;
Traverse the regular expression link to match one by one;
Return protocol name if matching successful, otherwise return null.
The input data of rule matching module is the contents and length of application layer data, and the output data is the protocol name or null.

6 Conclusion

In this paper, the work style traditional flow control system is changed, and a new bypass analysis architecture is designed to improve system efficiency and performance.

In the part of data transmission, system is improved in the application and distribution of PF-RING, and the RING function is changed, so that a true zero-copy is achieved, and the change can save CPU overhead and increase network throughput.

Acknowledgments. This paper is supported by the Natural Science Foundation of Hebei Province of China (Grant No.E2010000932) and by the Key Scientific and Technological Project of Tangshan City of China (Grant No.10150201A-4).

References

1. Keny, F.P., Maulloo, A.K., Tan, D.K.H.: Rate control for communication networks: shadow prices, proportional faimess and stability. Joumal of the 0perational Research Society, 237–252 (1998)
2. Bansal, D., Ward, P.: Third-Party Flow Control. In: Proc of the 3rd Annual Communication Networks and Services Research Conference, New York, pp. 118–124 (2005)
3. Huan, Y.W., Ying, D.L.: A Survey and Measurement Based Comparison of Bandwidth management Techniques. IEEE Communications Surveys and Tutorials, 10–21 (2003)
4. Thiran, P., Le Boudec, J.-Y.: Network Calculus: A Theory of Deterministic Queuing Systems for the Internet. LNCS, vol. 2050, pp. 3–81. Springer, Heidelberg (2001)
5. Chen, Y., Jiao, Z., Xie, J.: Design and Implementation of a High Performance VIA Based on Myrinet. Journal of Software, 285–292 (2006)
6. Han, D., Nassn.: A NAS-based storage network. Journal of harbin Institute of Technology, 95-99 (2007)
7. Li, Y.C.: LyraNET: A zero-copy TCP/IP protocol stack for embedded systems. Real-Time Systems, 76–81 (2006)
8. Yousif, M.F: On generalizations of PF-rings. Communications in Algebra, 65–69 (2004)
9. Xia, H., Chen, K.: Research and Performance and Optimization of Gigabit network based on Zero-Copy technology. Micro-Computer Information, 155–157 (2008)
10. Jerry, H.K., Chu, L.: Zero-Copy TCP in Solaris. In: Proceedings of the USENIX 2005 Annual Technical Conference, pp. 21–22 (2005)

Research on the Application of Improved K-Means in Intrusion Detection

Mingjun Wei[1], Lichun Xia[2], and Jingjing Su[2]

[1] College of Sciences, Hebei United University, 46 West Xinhua Road, 063009 Tangshan, China
[2] College of Information Engineering, Hebei United University, 46 West Xinhua Road, 063009 Tangshan, China
weimj@heut.edu.cn, xialichun77@126.com

Abstract. To solve the shortages of traditional k-means algorithm that it needs to input the clustering number and it is sensitive to initial clustering center, the improved k-means algorithm is put forward. In the improved algorithm, each data object will be represented by the number of points around it in a certain region. Data objects will be clustered on the basis of that the distances between data objects belonging to different kinds are farther than the ones between the same. Both k-means and improved k-means are used in intrusion detection, which shows that the improved can overcome inherent disadvantages of k-means and has good clustering results.

Keywords: k-means, cluster, anomaly, intrusion detection.

1 Introduction

Intrusion detection is one of the main research directions of network security technology [1]. Its method [2] mainly includes two kinds: misuse detection and anomaly detection. Misuse detection, which is the detecting behavior based on the matching of attack characteristic pattern, will compare the collected network data with characteristics of intrusion behavior existing in attack characteristics database. This method can detect known attacks perfectly, but for some unknown ones or variations of known ones it can not detect accurately. Anomaly detection is the detecting behavior based on the analysis of behavior statistic. It utilizes users' normal behavior data to construct normal behavior models and determines whether the data is judged as an attack by comparing data to be detected with normal behavior models. Therefore, one of the advantages of the anomaly detection is that it can detect unknown intrusions. By applying k-means and approved k-means to anomaly detection in intrusion detection, the paper aims to summarize some normal models to enhance the intrusion detection accuracy and reduce the rate of false negative rate and false positive rate [3].

C. Liu, J. Chang, and A. Yang (Eds.): ICICA 2011, Part I, CCIS 243, pp. 673–678, 2011.

2 K-Means Algorithm

K-means algorithm [4-6] is a classic clustering method based on division. It, which treats the number of the clusters to be generated as input parameters, will divide n objects into k groups (k < = n), in which each group stands for a cluster. First of all, it will choose k objects randomly and each object represents the initial average of a cluster. For each remaining object, it will be assigned to the nearest cluster according to the distance between it and center of each cluster. Then, the average of each cluster will be recounted, which will repeat until criterion function converges. Usually the distance is Euclidean distance and the square error rule function is adopted as criterion function [7].

Define 1 Euclidean distance

$$d(x_i, y_j) = \sqrt{(x_{i1} - y_{j1})^2 + (x_{i2} - y_{j2})^2 + \cdots + (x_{is} - y_{js})^2} \tag{1}$$

During this formula, $x_i = (x_{i1}, x_{i2}, \cdots, x_{is})$ and $y_i = (y_{i1}, y_{i2}, \cdots, y_{is})$ are two s d data objects.

Define 2 Square error rule function

$$J_e = \sum_{i=1}^{k} \sum_{X \in C_i} | X - m_i |^2 \tag{2}$$

During this formula, J_e is the sum total of the square error of all the data objects; X is the data object belonging to cluster C_i; m_i is the average of cluster C_i.

K-means algorithm is described as follows:

Input: $X = \{x_1, x_2, \cdots, x_n\}$ is a data collection which contains n objects.

K, the number of clusters to be clustered

Output: k clusters

Process:

Choose k objects randomly, initialize $m_1, m_2, \cdots, m_k$ respectively

Do

Calculate the distances between x_i and m_i from different clusters, and then distribute x_i to the closest cluster

Recount the average of each cluster as the new cluster center

Until the center of each cluster doesn't change

The time complexity of k-means algorithm is O (tkn), t standing for iteration times, k for the cluster number. Its space complexity is O (k+ n). K-means algorithm has inherent weakness [8-9]:

(1) Before clustering, k-means requires the defined k and k objects to be selected randomly as the initial clustering centers. K-means can not define the clustering

number according to the characteristics of the data, so it is difficult to achieve best clustering.

In the addition, because of defining the clustering number randomly, different initial centers can result in different results or even no results. That is to say the results of k-means are not stable. In different situation the results may be different distinctly.

(2) It's easy for k-means to fall into the local optimal solution. This algorithm is based on the objective function, usually using gradient method to solve the extremum. But because search direction of the gradient method is in direction of energy reducing, this makes the algorithm easy to fall into the local extremum. Therefore, the results k-means finds is local optimal solution not the global optimal solution. These defects largely limit the scope of its application.

3 Improved K-Means Algorithm

In order to improve the disadvantages of k-means, the new algorithm makes some improvement. In the improved k-means algorithm clustering guiding function is introduced. It can help the algorithm determine clustering in direction of the high point density.

Define 3 Clustering guiding function

$$f(x_i) = \{p \mid Dist(p, x_i) \prec r, p \in X, x_i \in X\} \tag{3}$$

During the function, X is the data object collection, r is distance radius and is used to be Manhattan distance, p and x_i are data objects.

Define 4 Manhattan distance

$$d(x_i, y_j) = |x_{i1} - y_{j1}| + |x_{i2} - y_{j2}| + \cdots |x_{is} - y_{js}| \tag{4}$$

During the function, $x_i = x_{i1}, x_{i2}, \cdots, x_{is}$ and $y_j = (y_{j1}, y_{j2}, \cdots, y_{js})$ are s d data object.

Define 5 R in the clustering guiding function

$$r = \frac{1}{2n(n-1)} \sum_{i=1}^{n} \sum_{j=1}^{n} d(x_i, y_j) \tag{5}$$

During the function, x_i and y_j are data objects.

According to the three functions referred above, each object can obtain a value of clustering guiding function, which will be used as the basis of clustering. Improved k-means algorithm aims to find object with the maximum of clustering guide function in a small range, which will be treated as the representative of the cluster it belong to. Each cluster will be made of representative of the cluster and the object belonging to the representative.

Improved k-means algorithm is described as follows:

Input: $x = \{x_1, x_2, \cdots, x_n\}$ is the data collection of n objects

Output: k clusters

Process:

Do

For representative of each cluster, find x_j, $i \neq j$, distance between x_j and x_i is less than r, and $f(x_j)$ is the least among all the $f(x_j)$;

Compare $f(x_i)$ with $f(x_j)$, if $f(x_i) \prec f(x_j)$ cluster x_j distributed to cluster x_i, else cluster x_i doesn't change

Until for each $i = 1, 2, \cdots, n$, cluster x_i doesn't change any more

4 Experiment and Analysis

4.1 Description of Experimental Data Set

Whether clustering algorithm can be used in intrusion detection is based on the following basic assumption:

(1) The amount of normal data is much more than that of attacking data;
(2) The value of some properties of attacking data has a marked departure from the normal.

The selected data "kddcup.Data_10 percent" is from authoritative test data set KDD cup99 [10] in intrusion detection field. There are 494021 records in the data set, among which 97278 are normal and the other abnormal. The abnormal data contains four categories: DoS (Denial of Service), U2R (Root) to the User, R2L (Remote User) and Probe.2000 records are chosen from the test data set as experimental data, among which the number of normal data is 1966. The percentage of normal data is 98.3%, which satisfies the assumption that the number of normal data is much more than that of abnormal. For every TCP/IP connection, except for some basic properties, some properties are expanded by using domain knowledge. Each connection has 41 kinds of symbolic and numeric attributes, but symbol characteristic attributes is difficult to be changed into numerical model. Therefore, 15 properties are chosen from all the 38 ones. From results of clustering which is normal (less than a predetermined threshold [11]) or abnormal can be directly defined. In order to evaluate the analysis results, false positive rate and detection rate are used to measure the performance of the algorithm.

False positive rate=the number of normal records which are treated as abnormal/the number of all the normal records in the data set chosen

Detection rate=the number of attacks detected/the number of all the attacks in the data set chosen

4.2 Data Preprocessing

Before the experiment the data should be standardized. That is to say that processing data will be translated from original place into a standardized space. The method of standardization is as follows:

Define 7 Average

$$m_f = \frac{1}{n}(x_{1f} + x_{2f} + \cdots + x_{nf}) \tag{6}$$

$x_{1f}, x_{2f}, \cdots, x_{nf}$ are data objects.

Define 8 Mean absolute error

$$s_f = \frac{1}{n}(|x_{i1} - m_f| + |x_{i2} - m_f| + \cdots |x_{mf} - m_f|) \tag{7}$$

Define 9 Standardization formula

$$z_f = \frac{x_{if} - m_f}{s_f} \tag{8}$$

4.3 Experimental Results and Analysis

The test data is experimented both in k-means and approved k-means to compare the performance of the two algorithms. Because k-means needs initial k and different k may result in different clustering results, the experiment will be repeated by using different k. The performance of k-means algorithm is described as table 1.

Improved k-means algorithm does not need the specified cluster number. It can decide cluster number independently according to data features. Performance of improved k-means algorithm is as table 2.

From table 1 and table 2 it can be seen that, compared with k-means algorithm, improved k-means algorithm can find out the appropriate cluster quantity according to data without initial cluster number k and have a good false positive rate and detection rate. Therefore, improved k-means algorithm is feasible.

Table 1. Performance of k-means algorithm

No.	Clustering number	False positive rate	Detection rate
1	36	1.424%	20.588%
2	40	0.102%	67.647%
3	44	2.747%	88.235%
4	50	5.239%	91.177%
5	55	6.205%	91.177%

Table 2. Performance of improved k-means algorithm

No.	Clustering number	False positive rate	Detection rate
1	44	1.984%	91.177%

5 Conclusion

For perfecting k-means algorithm, this paper puts forward improved k-means algorithm based on k-means. It can overcome the disadvantages of k-means. By performing experiment on KDD cup99, it shows that the improved k-means has higher detection performance and is feasible.

Acknowledgments. Our thanks go to Hebei Province Department of Education (grant number: 2008457), which grant us enough fund to support our research. Also, we extend our sincere gratitude to editors, the anonymous reviewers and the sponsor. Last but not least, without the help of our colleagues, our paper will not be completed in the form.

Reference

1. Gao, L., Zhang, Y., Liu, H.: Research on development status and application of network intrusion detection. J. Science&Technology Information 92 (2011)
2. Yang, Z., Tian, D., Xiao, J.: Survey of intrusion detection technology. J. Computer Engineering and Design 27, 2119–2123 (2006)
3. Zhang, D., Zhang, X., Chou, J.: Application of improved k-means Algorithm in Intrusion Detection. J. Microcomputer Information 26, 11–13 (2010)
4. Jain, A.K., Dubes, R.C.: Algorithms for clustering data. Prentice-Hall, New Jersey (1988)
5. Zhang, Y.: An Improved K-means Algorithm. J. Computer Applications, 31–33 (2003)
6. Han, L., Wang, Q., Jiang, Z., Hao, Z.: Selection method of initial clustering center of an improved k-means. J. Computer Engineering and Applications 46, 150–152 (2010)
7. Guo, H., Li, T.: Research on the application of K^+ mean in network intrusion detection. J. Software Guide 8, 152–154 (2009)
8. Chinrungrueng, C., Sequin, C.H.: Optimal adaptive k-means algorithm with dynamic adjustment of learning rate. Columbia University (2002)
9. Yan, X., Chu, X.: Application to Cluster Algorithm in Anomaly Detection of Network Intrusion. J. Applications of the Computer Systems 10, 34–37 (2005)
10. Zhang, X., Zeng, H., Jia, L.: Research of intrusion detection system dataset-KDD CUP99. J. Computer Engineering and Design, 4809–4816 (2010)
11. Portnoy, L., Eskin, E., Stolfo, S.J.: Intrusion Detection with Unlabeled Data Using Clustering. In: ACM CSS Workshop on Data Mining Applied to Security, Philadelphia, pp. 5–8 (2001)

Application Research of Analytic Hierarchy Process in the Evaluation of College Cadres

Xuejun Wang, Haijing Bai, and Yujing Shi

Information Science Technology College of Shijiazhuang Tiedao University,
050043, Shijiazhuang, Hebei, China
wangxj_sjzri@tom.com, baihaijing@126.com, shiyujing@stdu.edu.cn

Abstract. Analytic Hierarchy Process(AHP), using the combination of qualitative and quantitative analysis methods, can achieve the multi-objective decision-making effectively. In this paper, the AHP method is applied in the evaluation of College Cadres so as to establish a performance evaluation system which aims at determining the weights of each subsystem and index and at working out the composite score of the Cadres by correlation algorithms, hence, determining the evaluation ranks of them. Experiments show that the method is scientific, effective, and can play a positive role in the evaluation of College Cadres .

Keywords: AHP, Cadre Evaluation, Hierarchical Structure.

1 Introduction

The management of the people is the first part of the management work. How can we evaluate one person's ability by the scientific method is the key to achieve optimal use of talents. In the past, the main way of Personnel assessment is voting or scoring. For the vote, the entire enterprise or department employees are the voting body, regardless of the length of working hours, whether voting bodies are in correct attitude to vote, their voting weights are the same; In addition to the above question, there is a reasonable fraction of the settings, this simple method will result in the voting results can't accurately reflect a person's overall abilities. Analytic Hierarchy Process(AHP), the combination of qualitative and quantitative point of view, to explore new ways of talent evaluation [1].

2 Analytic Hierarchy Process(AHP)

AHP[2] is a decision analysis method which combined the methods of qualitative and quantitative. Decision makers can make their thinking process modeling and quantitative by this method when they make decisions on complex system. By using this approach, decision-makers divide the complex problem into several levels and several factors, compare and calculate between the various factors, and they can get the different weights to provide the basis for selection of the best programs.

C. Liu, J. Chang, and A. Yang (Eds.): ICICA 2011, Part I, CCIS 243, pp. 679–685, 2011.

2.1 The Principle of AHP

The first question of AHP is to make the problem hierarchical, dividing the problem into different layers according to the character and the overall goal of the program, forming a multi-level structural model of analysis, it includes the lowest level (for decision-making programs, measures, etc.), and the scheduling problem of the highest level (The overall goal) about the determination of relative importance weight and the order of the relative merits.

2.2 The Steps of AHP

Explicit Problems. We must first have a clear understanding of the problem, understand the scope of the problem, have a good knowledge of the factors about the issues contained, and then determine the relationship and affiliation between the factors.

The Establishment of Hierarchical Structure. Based on the analysis and understanding of problem, sectionalize factors included in the problem, according to whether there are certain characteristics, and make the factors of same features as a new level of the system, and these factors themselves also in accordance with other features combine together, forming the factors of higher level, until finally the highest level of the formation of a single feature. The top is the target layer. The middle layer is the rule layer. The lowest layer is the program layer or measures layer.

Established Matrix of Pair-Wise Comparison Judgments. Judgment matrix represents a unit for the previous level (element); the level is related to the importance of correlation between the units[3,4,5]. General forms are as shown in Table1.

Table 1. Judgment matrix of compared with each other

C_S	P_1	P_2	…	P_n
P_1	b_{11}	b_{12}	…	b_{1n}
P_2	b_{21}	b_{22}	…	b_{2n}
…	…	…	…	…
P_n	b_{n1}	b_{n2}	…	b_{nn}

Judgment matrix has features as follows: $b_{ii}=1$, $b_{ji}=1/b_{ij}$, $b_{ij}=b_{ik}/b_{jk}$ (In which i, j, k=1, 2…n).

Single Ordering. Single ordering is to list evaluating sorting on all the elements of the layer based on the further layer, it is to calculate the maximum eigenvector of judgment matrix; the most common method is to accumulate the law and the square root law.

Composite Ordering. According to the result of single ordering ,Further get the more comprehensive merits of the order of the previous level, that is the task of composite sorting of the layer.

3 Evaluation Model of College Cadres

Use AHP to evaluate cadres, first make these facets about the cadre's evaluation element, according to the nature concerned and the requirements in actual work, dividing these facets into different components, and then to form a multi-level model based on the inter-relationship, influence, and affiliations between components. Through mathematical calculations and testing, obtained the weights of each evaluation index, that may let us make a comprehensive evaluation, to achieve the effect of cadre's evaluation. Take the following examples to represent the concrete application of AHP method. A university evaluates three cadres, and measured by six attributes: health, business level, writing skills, eloquence, policies, and work styles, represent respectively by P_1, P_2, P_3, P_4, P_5, and P_6.

3.1 The Establishment of Hierarchical Structure

In order to ensure the scientific evaluation, we must establish the structural levels of cadre's evaluation [6,7] . In this problem, we select the results of Evaluation as the target layer; consider the state of health, business level, writing ability, eloquence, policies, style of work six factors. Hierarchical structure is shown in Fig. 1.

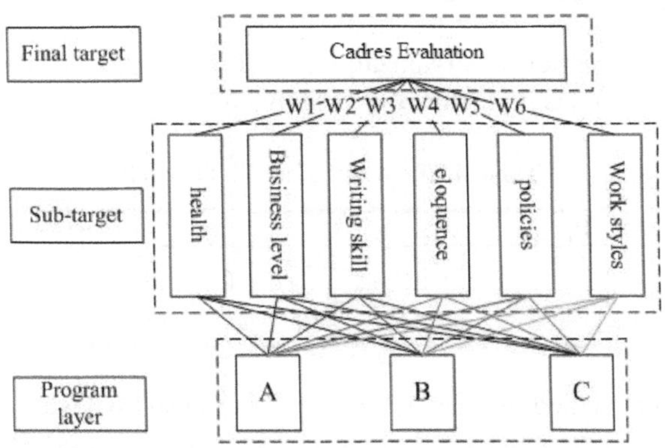

Fig. 1. Hierarchical structure graph of cadre's evaluation

Judgment matrix B is given in Table 2.

Table 2. Judgment Matrix B

B	P_1	P_2	P_3	P_4	P_5	P_6
P_1	1	1	1	4	1	1/2
P_2	1	1	2	4	1	1/2
P_3	1	1/2	1	5	3	1/2
P_4	1	1	1/5	1	1/3	1
P_5	1	1	1/3	3	1	1
P_6	2	2	2	3	1	1

3.2 The Establishment of Pair-Wise Comparison Matrix

After the establishment of hierarchical structure, the subordinate relationship between upper levels is identified. Assume above a layer of element C as the rule, the elements of the next layer which be dominated by element C is u_1, u_2, $u_3 \ldots u_n$. Our purpose is to give the element corresponding weights, according to the elements to the relative importance of rule C .which AHP had used is Weight Export Method, and it is so called Pair-wise comparison method [8,9]. In this step, decision makers answer the questions repeat, to rule C, elements to elements, which is more important, how important it is .Give a value to the degree of importance, according to the proportion scale of 1~9. The definition of 1~9 are as shown in Table 3.

Table 3. The number of rating scales is in different situations

Scale	Definition and description
1	These two factors are equally important
3	One element is slightly more important than the other one
5	One element is obviously more important than the other one
7	One element is more important than the other one
9	One element is most important than the other one
2,4,6,8	It need to choose between the above two scale
$1/b_{ij}$	The inverse comparison of two elements

Through the discussion of organization, score to the target layer (A, B, C). For example, the result of health factor (P_1) as shown in Table 4.

Table 4. The result of health factor (P_1)

P_1	A	B	C
A	1	1/4	1/2
B	4	1	3
C	2	1/3	1

Using the same method, we can get the results of business level factor (P_2), writing skills factor (P_3), eloquence factor P_4, policies factor (P_5) and work styles factor (P_6).

3.3 Weight Calculation

There are many ways for weight calculation[9,10], in this paper; we used Asymptotic Normalization Coefficient (ANC) method to calculate the maximum eigenvector of the judgment matrix B (Table 2).

Normalize the elements in each column of the judgment matrix, the general term for the elements is:

$$b_{ij} = \frac{b_{ij}}{\sum_{1}^{n} b_{ij}} (i, j = 1,2,\ldots,n) \tag{1}$$

The results after normalizing are as shown in Table 5.

Table 5. The results after normalizing

B	P_1	P_2	P_3	P_4	P_5	P_6
P_1	0.16	0.17	0.15	0.20	0.14	0.13
P_2	0.16	0.17	0.30	0.20	0.14	0.13
P_3	0.16	0.09	0.15	0.25	0.42	0.13
P_4	0.04	0.04	0.03	0.05	0.05	0.09
P_5	0.16	0.17	0.05	0.15	0.14	0.26
P_6	0.32	0.34	0.30	0.15	0.14	0.26

According to the formula 2, Add the line of the normalized judgment matrix.

$$W_i = \sum_{1}^{n} b_{ij} (i = 1,2,...,n) \tag{2}$$

Normalize the vector $W = (W_1, W_2,...W_n)^t$ and the result is:

$$W_i = \frac{W_i}{\sum_{1}^{n} W_j} (i = 1,2,...,n) \tag{3}$$

Calculate the maximum eigenvector:

$W = (W_1, W_2,...W_n)^t = (0.16, 0.18, 0.20, 0.05, 0.16, 0.25)$ is the approximate solution of the eigenvector which we need.

Calculate the maximum eigenvalue of the judgment matrix by formula 4:

$$\lambda_{Max} = \sum_{1}^{n} \frac{(BW)_i}{nW_i} \tag{4}$$

$$\lambda_{Max} = \frac{1.025}{6*0.16} + \frac{1.225}{6*0.18} + \frac{1.305}{6*0.20} + \frac{0.309}{6*0.05} + \frac{1.066}{6*0.16} + \frac{1.640}{6*0.25} = 6.35.$$

The consistency index of judgment matrix is:

$$C.I. = \frac{\lambda_{Max} - n}{n - 1} = 0.07 \tag{5}$$

Random consistency ratio is:

$$C.R. = \frac{C.I.}{R.I.} = 0.056 < 0.10 \tag{6}$$

In which n=6. R.I=1.24.

3.4 Find Out the Maximum Eigenvector of Project Layer on Target Layer

Using the same method, the maximum eigenvectors of all indicators on project layer are calculated and results are as follows:

P_1: $(W_1^1\ W_2^1\ W_3^1) = (0.14, 0.62, 0.24)^t$

P_2: $(W_1^2\ W_2^2\ W_3^2) = (0.10, 0.32, 0.58)^t$

P_3 :($W_1^3\ W_2^3\ W_3^3) = (0.14, 0.62, 0.24)^t$

P_4: $(W_1^4\ W_2^4\ W_3^4) = (0.28,0.65,0.07)^t$

P_5: $(W_1^5\ W_2^5\ W_3^5) = (0.47, 0.47, 0.06)^t$

P_6: $(W_1^6\ W_2^6\ W_3^6) = (0.80, 0.15, 0.05)^t$

Calculate the total score of each: A's total score is $\sum W_i * W_i^1 = 0.3576$.B's total score is $\sum W_i * W_i^2 = 0.4372$ .C's total score is $\sum W_i * W_i^3 = 0.2182$. According to the scores we get the results of cadres evaluation.

4 Conclusions

In this paper, the evaluation method of AHP is proposed for the evaluation of college cadres .Experiments show that the method is scientific, effective, and can play a positive role in the evaluation of college cadres.We hope this method be useful in solving other unstructured management.

Reference

1. Tang, M., Hu, J.: A Research of Fuzzy Comprehensive Evaluation on Network Class Based on AHP. J. Research on Higher Education 3, 77–81 (2008)
2. Qiao, P., Yao, L.: The Research on the training model combining Engineering Evaluation System of vocational. J. China Higher Education Evaluation 4, 69–72 (2009)
3. Ling, D., Li, N.: Application of AHP in cadre selection and evaluation system of university students. J. Data of Culture and Education 1, 217–219 (2009)
4. Jin, M., Tian, J.: Application of AHP in the evaluation of university teachers. J. Research on Chinese University Teaches 5, 17–23 (2008)
5. Li, S.: Engineering Fuzzy Mathematics and Application. Harbin Institute of Technology Press, Harbin (2004)
6. He, A.H.: Study on the decision-making of coal industry technology development based on AHP. J. Advanced Materials Research 204-210, 911–914 (2011)
7. Gu, W.: Analysis on the human factors to the air pollution in large supermarket based on analytic hierarchy process (AHP). J. Advanced Materials Research 255-260, 2658–2662 (2011)

8. Perez-Vega, S.: Analytical hierarchy processes (AHP) for the selection of solvents in early stages of pharmaceutical process development. J.Process Safety and Environmental Protection 89, 261–267 (2011)
9. Lee, S.-H.: Using fuzzy AHP to develop intellectual capital evaluation model for assessing their performance contribution in a university. J. Expert Systems with Applications 37, 4941–4947 (2010)
10. Lin, H.-F.: An application of fuzzy AHP for evaluating course website quality. J. Computers and Education 54, 877–888 (2010)

The Research of Finacing Higher Education in the Context of Financial Crisis

Yuxin Liang, Zhenhai Lei, and Yu Zhang

Qinggong College, Hebei Polytechnic University, Tangshan Hebei 063000, China
18931539199@189.com

Abstract. Financing higher education is the economic behavior to finance the higher education by using fiscal measures, market mechanisms and financial innovations in the market economy. In the 1990s Asian financial crisis, to stimulate consumption, Chinese universities began to enlarge the enrollment, and higher education assumed the task of stimulating the domestic demand. Now the financial crisis took place again, of course, we can not take enrollment approach any more. At the national launch of 4,000 billion yuan economic stimulus plan, education and health together only occupy 40 billion, representing only one percent, and the funds related to education is only 4.4 billion which is to be invested in basic education in the Midwest. With no hope in the increase of the government funding and tuition fees, colleges and universities should expand the financing channels and financial capacity to meet the demand for funds of their own development. In this paper, the financing of higher education and the status are analyzed; the main problems and reasons of the financing of higher education has been identified, and therefore the strategy has been made to improve the financing of higher education.

Keywords: Financial crisis, higer education, finacing strategy.

1 Introduction

Higher education is a costly undertaking, if there is no certain amount of capital investment, the university can hardly be properly developed. Although the amount of money is not the sole determinant of the development of universities, but to a large extent it determines the college's development. China's higher education system has its own peculiarities. The financial crisis on the direct impact of higher education is not obvious, but the potential crisis can not be ignored. Especially the financing of higher education will have a direct impact, weakening the government's direct investment, school-enterprise cooperation in business investment will reduce the ability of the community fund-raising will be more difficult, personal income would impact on tuition to pay, especially is relatively weak strength of the impact of colleges and universities would be more apparent. This is the reality facing China's higher education financing difficulties and challenges. The purpose of this paper is to learn from foreign universities in financing the accumulation of useful theory and

C. Liu, J. Chang, and A. Yang (Eds.): ICICA 2011, Part I, CCIS 243, pp. 686–694, 2011.

practical experience. Through the financing of higher education at home and abroad, analyze the status compared with the actual development of higher education, and propose in the context of the financial crisis to further expand the financing channels and ways to prevent and defuse financial risks and realize the sustainable development of higher education.

2 Higher Eudcation Financing Status and Main Problems

2.1 Government Funding Is Still Insufficient

Over the years, the absolute number of financial provision of higher education is growing, but its growth rate continued to decline, and compared with the United States, Japan and other developed countries, China's ratio of investment in higher education is significantly lower. In recent years, China's expenditure on education by the rapid rise between 1996 and 2004, budget expenditure on education, an increase from the 121.19 billion yuan to 402.78 billion yuan, an average annual increase of 16.2%; education budget from the 165.42 billion yuan to 446.59 billion average annual increase of 13.2%, exceeding the average annual GDP growth of 9.1% over the same period the level. However, relative to the enrollment enlargement rate, the increase in financial allocation is still lagging behind, so most colleges and universities will depend on the banks financing channels, which in today's college history, is still "Chinese characterized development path of universities."

2.2 The Space of Increasing the Tuition Fee Is Limited

Compared with developed countries, although China's university tuition fee of the total revenue is on the rise, construction and development of universities increasingly depend on the tuition, but because of many social and economic reasons, the cost of higher education sharing mechanism is still in the early stages of development, which leads to limiting tuition increases, and the charges have not yet adjusted since 2001. In most developed countries, tuition is an important source of funding for universities, especially for private colleges and universities. In 1991-1995, tuition increased by 41%, 39%, 39% and 25% respectively in U.S. universities, state universities, community colleges and four-year private universities. In Japan's public universities, approximately 10% of the budget comes from tuition fees, while private universities rely on tuition income for about half. Canadian college tuition has doubled the past 10 years, and has continued to raise, the general running costs of school fees account for about 21%. Australia's "Higher Education Contribution Scheme" is essentially a collection of tuition fees system. Our colleges and universities to increase government input in the same time, colleges and universities should increase tuition fees in the share of funding and improve higher education cost-sharing mechanisms, to establish differential tuition policy or pattern. Government policies and regulations can be introduced, according to different levels of colleges and universities, the cost of education required for different disciplines and their possible future rate of return and social rate of return individuals to develop a more rational differential tuition policy or pattern. In India, scholars Wajis proposed a tuition payment plan which required people with different abilities to pay different fees, that is, the people with highest income pay 75% of total cost of education; people with higher incomes pay 50%; people with general income pay 25% and the lowest income people exempt from tuition fees.

2.3 Scientific Research and Technological Development Show Slow Income Growth

In the field of capital, innovation, science and technology system, China's low level of higher education research activities could be improved. Colleges and universities should use its technological strength to carry out research projects. They should to obtain research funding from social enterprises (institutions) organizations and government. On our funding and government funding of science and technology education in terms of relative importance between 1996 and 1999, the Government allocated funding for university research funding was only occupying 11.71% of government funding for education, while the ratio of U.S. government at all levels in 1992-1993 school year was equivalent to 31.48%, which shows that government funding for tertiary education in China focusing on education and teaching activities. In developed countries, universities and colleges are the second largest research departments second only to corporates, and our colleges and universities are ranking third, listing behind R & D institutions and corporates. From 1997 to 1999, the proportion of our national research expenditure in universities and colleges decreased from 12.1% to 6.6%.

2.4 The Funds and Donations from the Alumini Associations and Foundations Are Limited

The channel is one important source in the colleges and universities of the developed countries. In 1994 the top of U.S. top five universities which accepted highest amount donation is Harvard University and the amount is $ 6.201 billion; the lowest is Stanford University which reached $ 2.751 billion. From the history development of higher education, the school funding initially mainly came from the personal property in the universities named after the creators. The presidents of universities of developed countries use about 2 / 3 of the time to publicize the school policy, academic achievement to the community, in order to obtain the support of the whole society, and raise more funds for running schools. And our domestic colleges and universities get comparatively less from all these sources of funding. The main reason is the state's tax system and non-scale private donations.

2.5 The Revenue from Non-teaching Service Is Significantly Low

China's current higher education funding sources are not effective, and social investment in higher education is insufficient. Fundings among the universities are increasingly competitive, and obtaining funds from the non-teaching services has become an important way. With the international source of funding for colleges and universities becoming more competitive, the funding of colleges and universities are also more innovative. China's higher education funding in tuition, personal community school funding, donations and other sources of funding is significantly occupying lower proportion, in particular, the proportion of tuition and other sources are lower than the United States similar proportion by 10 percentage points or more.

2.6 The Main One among Various Financing Models Is Using Bank Loans

Potential financial risk diversification of university financing model is based on the premise of relying on tuition income diversification, other sources of financing for community, and some just started, and some development is still not sufficient, some better financing only a partial, typical, not universal, or in a wide range of uses, especially through capital market financing little start. China's college funding sources are mainly concentrated in bank loans. With the deepening of reform of higher education, our colleges and universities by the "elite education mode" to "public education model" into 2005, the national college entrance 504 million, 4.7 times in 1998, enrollment in colleges and universities up to 23 million people; 639 million college and university admissions in 2009, the number of university students in 29 million, the scale has been ranked first in the world. And with the peak of enrollment, it is a large-scale expansion of the university wind. In order to attract and accommodate more students, many universities have planned to construct enclosure made floor, and even to competing, "forward to the world-class university," a variety of high-rise buildings, etc., comparisons of colleges and universities have become a bargaining chip. Expansion of the natural need of funds, the main source of funding for our colleges and universities with financial grants and tuition fees, because these two are relatively limited income, so the bank credit has become a major source of university funds for construction. According to the Academy of Social Sciences published "2006: China Social Situation Analysis and Prediction," Social Blue Book shows that in 2005 the total bank loans in our colleges and universities around between 150 to 200 billion yuan, including engineering building contractors, if Loaning (debt delay), the introduction of direct investment in social capital and through the Trust's internal financing and other hidden liabilities, estimated liabilities to reach 4,000 billion yuan. Almost all colleges and universities have a loan, some institutions of the debt has more than twice the annual budget revenues, and investment planning and actual demand is far from over, resulting in high interest payments is difficult to balance the budget, capital chain is very fragile. In recent years, Hebei Province, only 26 universities in the provincial bank loans of up to 50 billion, of which 10 key universities on loans of more than 40 billion yuan, accounting for 80.2% of total loans. Not only in financial dilemma of local colleges and universities, is some of the central government also “elite” in debt. March 29, 2007, the Audit Commission announced the 18 colleges and universities directly under the Ministry of Education, the 2003 financial accounts of the results of the audit, 18 colleges and universities in total debt 7.275 billion yuan, up 45 percent over the end of 2002, including capital formation accounted for 82% of debt. The huge expansion of credit has become troubled by the university's development of a severe test. Bank is optimistic that "public universities would not go bankrupt", and enrollment fees, "making money" and therefore fails in the loan approval process conditions for critical review of commercial loans, mortgages do not create security or property, but by virtue of the basic school the credibility of the implementation of credit loans, loans for the final randomness caused, contributed to this university's financial crisis. In the March 23, 2007, Jilin University, the school issued notice said: "Since 2005, Jilin University each year to pay interest on loans up to 150 million to 170 million yuan, and the expenditure exceeds the income of the school is becoming more serious." "A ripple", college loan has caused widespread concern and discussion, and the financial crisis rapidly emerges.

3 The Basic Features of Raising Funds for US Higher Education

The basic features of raising funds for US higher education summed up from analyzing funds sources of U.S. institutions of higher education are as below:

(1) U.S. funding of institutions of higher education is diversified. Government, students, persons, colleges and uiversities are providers of higher education funding, and investment from all levels of government ranks the first on both the amount and ratio.
(2) The second highest proportion is tuition fees, which are rising; sales and service revenue in list third place, and the proportion is slowly rising, while the proportion of pure donation revenue remaines stable.
(3) American universities attach great importance to raise funds. Raising funds can not only make up an inadequate investment in education, but also set the school's image and position in the industry, enhancing the school's brand, which is a reflection of the university's comprehensive ability and overall image. Fund-raising is "number one project". University Presidents and Deans will regard raising funds as the first major work to manage the school. University set up a special fund-raising department, individual responsibility and allocated special funding for the work. The universities establish fund-raising department and the responsible person provide the funds. They also have many fund-raising channels and set the foundation, and get the donation information through the Alumni Association.

4 Diversified Financing Strategy of Higher Education

Mr. Li Yining, who wrote: "The important way to further develop the education is to use the capital market, and the most common methods are as follows: first, issue education bonds; second, appear school-run enterprise on the market; third, establish the education industry funds; fourth, develop education development companies; the fifth, the listed companies establish the training center by using its raised funds. The five channels can help education industry to develop. By make full use of capital market, the development of education can be accelerated". This is the earlier proposed point of view which is education should develop by financing through market.

The adapted ways of national captial into higher education

(1) Through the commercial banks and other financial institutions, make full use of financial means or the introduction of social capital financing fund raising, student housing construction and logistics to speed up the process of socialization speed. Banks involved in supporting institutions of higher learning, is conducive to the development of institutions of higher learning, in terms of the bank itself is a low-risk high-return investments. Development needs of commercial banks, universities, banks to participate in institutions of higher learning can play the following functions: One is to play in investment banking, financing, financial planning advisory role. As the bank has close ties with all sectors of national economy, he understood the financial operations, investment finance to understand the various techniques, and institutions of higher learning in the future development of investment and financing needs more, hoping banks play a consultant role. The second is to promote, assist and even participate in various colleges and universities to support the development of the Fund. With the further development of market economy, all economic entities in the growing economic strength, social groups and individuals to invest in education and attitudes are formed, will have more invested enterprises and individuals willing to support education industry. Foundation funding is in the form of an effective choice. And fund formation, management and operation, requires a certain expertise, the bank's participation can make it run more smoothly. Third, it could provide long-term loans directly to institutions of higher learning and short-term loans. Especially the new campus construction loans for school development with direct help. Fourth, the payment of student loans for students to help students complete their studies with a role in promoting the employment of these students will become the bank after the potential of high-quality customers. For commercial banks, institutions of higher learning is the quality customers, can bring stability to the commercial bank deposit sources. Birth of the scientific and technological achievements of the institutions of higher learning market is the banks are looking for new business growth. Institutions of higher learning in the middle of a rich business, consumer credit business is banks are looking for low-risk, high return business sources. "Silver school co-operation" mode can produce a "win-win" result. However, the Government shall have the required conditions to encourage the participation of banks limited the development of supporting institutions of higher learning, to guard against financial risk schools.

(2) Improve the current government investment mode in infrastructure to the universities, using "a combination of grants and loans," or using the discount method allows the government to attract bank capital to accelerate the pace of infrastructure construction in colleges and universities, so to encourage institutions with more potential students and working chances to reform or expand the education infrastructure.

(3) Stock market is one way to absorb the social direct investment. We can combine the industrial capital with it to realize the diversity of the educational capital the forms of education, just like Tsinghua Tongfang, Peking University Founder,

Shanghaicaida of Technology Development Co. They are all successful examples. Some of the colleges and universities holding or shareholding companies have listed, and developed rapidly. The listed companies have become very active investment area. Data shows that, with further improvement of the stock market, university-run industry will further expand the market space, which will undoubtedly open up new ways to finance the higer education by using capital market.

(4) Issue higher education bond. Through the central government and local government bonds issued by special education, or increase the allocation of university bonds, etc. to raise the proportion of idle funds, and increase government investment in higher education. Prestigious universities in the process of marketization of higher education resources available is a university's reputation, with the reputation of the University, the University in accordance with business practice, to issue a certain number of bonds to relieve the school of sustainable development in the "urgent needs." Only the United States, for example for a description and analysis. In the United States, institutions of higher education bond issue in 1995 has reached 160, totaling $ 2.67 billion bond. In 1996, the school bond issue has increased to 189, total debt to 4.14 billion U.S. dollars. The form of bonds can be common bonds and tax-free bonds. The bonds can be sub-and long-term bonds. Long-term bond repayment period is of 25-30 years, and interest is the 5-6 per cent. Long-term bond has much longer repayment period, and interest rates should be slightly higher. For example, Yale University in 1996 issued a "century bonds", 100-year maturity. What are the uses of bonds? In a nutshell: First, for working capital; second, the current in order to repay other debts; third is to build large-scale projects for schools. Harvard College verde was issued in 1996 totaling $ 24 million bond for the renovation project the college buildings. Through the issuance of bonds, money soon in place, construction will soon be completed, the effect is immediate. In the U.S., a variety of bonds too numerous to cite, but the University still has a certain bond market. For universities, especially elite universities have a certain reputation, it is not only emotional sense of identity, but also clearly knows the money's use. Thus, people not only feel safe, beneficial, and that contribute to the development of society.

But for the university to issue bonds there are differing views. Supporters argue that "from the federal government to every family, every part of society has a debt of the university is no exception." Dean of Harvard Verde C Wind thinks that "The payment was balanced but school buildings are poor, which is not always a good thing." Therefore, it is unimpeachable to issue the bonds.

(5) The fixed assets required, like school teaching and research space and equipments, can be solved by the way of finance and lease.

(6) Encourage and support a variety of forms, a variety of property rights to establish stock hold higher education institutions; introduce private capital investment in higher education, to develop tax incentives to mobilize the enthusiasm of the majority of those shares, to achieve social provision of education, we Office of Education, and jointly promote the education industry. Held by an independent public university colleges, or colleges and universities, created a number of "state-run" of the two colleges, the government bank loans to private colleges and universities to raise

capital to provide security and give education discount, set up a "private higher education development fund", etc.

(7) Issuing lotteries can bring together social idle capital to make up for the lack of state financial resources. China has issued a large number of sports lotteries, the welfare lottery, gathering a huge amount of money for a particular purpose. It is based on the public welfare lottery, monopoly, voluntary on the basis of the game, which has the accumulation effect. So this might seem a quick way to raise education funds. From the welfare lottery and sports lottery issuance of view, from 1987 to now, China's estimated 90 million people bought lottery tickets, this is the issue size is strictly limited under the conditions of the number of participants. Reference lottery market in developed countries 60% to 80% participation rate, China's lottery market participation rates, there should be much room for growth. According to the Shanghai Welfare Lottery Issuing experience, after deducting the required return, we can raise about 40% to 50% useful funds.

(8) Government support and regulatory institutions of higher learning based on knowledge production and technological innovation, entrepreneurial behavior; University is the place where the invention is an important center of knowledge creation. With patents, creating new knowledge, it is necessary to promote scientific research into productivity quickly. How quickly the advantages of technological innovation into the benefits and economic advantages, it is currently exploring the direction of the university. In this regard, is divided into several levels. First, the implementation of technology transfer, that is to take knowledge directly in exchange for return; the second is the implementation of scientific and technological development, with their own inventions, develop their own products; third is to buy someone else's technology to develop their own products. The first approach is technology development increases the transfer of technology; the latter two is to combine technology and development. Here is a brief on the transfer of the patent. In 1995, U.S. colleges and universities rely on patents to obtain the transfer of funds of 3.18 billion U.S. dollars. Harvard University in 1980, the patent transfer fee is only $ 24,000, and by 1994, rising to $ 5.4 million, an increase of 200 times. Patent transfer varies with the different schools.

Patents and technology transfer is a form to obtain economic return. Although the patent is not very substantial transfer fee, the funds in the universities the proportion of revenue is still negligible. But taking into account its rapid development, patent transfer may not only become an important form of cooperation between business and university, but also the highlight of university income.

References

1. Hu, J.: Hold high the great banner of sociallism with Chinese characteristics and fight for winning new victories in building a moderately prosperous society. People's Publishing House, Beijing (2009)
2. Wang, Y.: The theory and practice of Education Industrialization. China Economic Publishing House, Beijing (2007)

3. Chen, L., Lu, G., Zhang, X.: Characteristics and revelation of social donation in American colleges and universities. Modern Educational Science (Higher Education Research) (1) (2010)
4. Yang, Z., Shi, J.: Research of comprehensive evaluation on the university finance. China Renmin University Press, Beijing (2002)
5. Liu, R.: The basic form of market-oriented higher education raising funds. Educational Science (1) (2004)

Study on the Theorem Proving of Plance Pencil Equation

GuoKun Xia[1], LinTao Kong[1], YinLi Liu[1], Jia Liao[1], RuiHai Zhang[1], and YingJie Zhu[2]

[1] College of Science, Tianjin University of Science & Technology, Tianjin 300457,China
{xiagk,klt8341,liuyinli,ridge78}@tust.edu.cn,
zhangruihai@126.com
[2] College of Science, Changchun University, Changchun 130022, China
zhuyingjie2004@sina.com

Abstract. In the higher mathematics and space analytic geometry materials, the plane pencil equation has important application value, but some of the materials did not give a strict proof about the definition of the plane pencil equation, even no proof. It caused great confusion and perplexity to the readers and teachers with using the materials. The paper mainly focus on the study of the definition of plane pencil equation. For the need of theorem proving, we first give a lemma, and give the detailed proof of plane pencil equation on the basis of the lemma. The purpose of the article is to make the reader can get clear understanding to this problem.

Keywords: plane pencil, plane pencil equation, space point, straight line, distance between point and plane.

1 Introduction

In the higher mathematics teaching, we find that the contents about straight line and plane are very important chapter. The set of all plane through the same line is called the plane pencil with axis, referred to as the plane pencil. Plane pencil equation for solving a plane Equation meet certain conditions is an effective method, Such as, Finding a straight line projection in the plane; Finding plane equation through point and line; Finding plane equation perpendicular to the known plane through two points; Finding plane equation paralleling to the both known planes and having Equal distance with them. Because of the importance of this part, the section can be introduced in the general space analytic geometry materials (including the section of space analytic geometry in higher mathematics teaching materials).

2 Problem Description

Set a straight line L by the equation

$$\begin{cases} \pi_1 : A_1x + B_1y + C_1z + D_1 = 0, & (1) \\ \pi_2 : A_2x + B_2y + C_2z + D_2 = 0, & (2) \end{cases}$$

C. Liu, J. Chang, and A. Yang (Eds.): ICICA 2011, Part I, CCIS 243, pp. 695–702, 2011.

Where the coefficient A_1, B_1, C_1 and A, B_2, C_2 is not proportional.

The plane pencil Equation is

$$A_1x + B_1y + C_1z + D_1 + \lambda(A_2x + B_2y + C_2z + D_2) = 0 \tag{2}$$

Where λ is an arbitrary constant.

To prove this conclusion, based on relationship of the graphics and equation, we need to prove two aspects:

① The equation of form (3) are all though the straight line L;

② Arbitrary Plane $Ax + By + Cz + D = 0$

(except the plane $\pi_2 : A_2x + B_2y + C_2z + D_2 = 0$) through straight line L can be written the form (3).

References 1 explaines one aspect of the problem: the equations of form (3) are all though the straight line L, which is the pure character of the equation (3). But, equation (3) is an arbitrary plane through the line L (except $\pi_2 : A_2x + B_2y + C_2z + D_2 = 0$)? It needs to be proved. In other words, we still need to prove the completeness of the equation (3). However, references 1 explain only through the following a word.

"Conversely, any plane through the straight line L (except plane (2)) is included in the equation (3)."

Why? Suppose a plane $Ax + By + Cz + D = 0$ is any a plane through the straight line L (except the plane (2)), Why it is included in the gens plane of the equation (3)? Is this not the need to prove?

In summary, we think in fact the references 1 did not prove the second aspect, the proof was fallacious. Below we will give strict proof of the theorem.

3 Lemma

In order to prove the theorem, we first look at a lemma.

Lemma. Space (except itself) will be divided into two parts U_1 and U_2 by the plane $\pi : Ax + By + Cz + D = 0$. On part U_1, the symbol of $Ax + By + Cz + D$ is not change; On part U_2, the symbol of $Ax + By + Cz + D$ is also not change. And on parts U_1 and U_2, on the one side $Ax + By + Cz + D > 0$, on the other side $Ax + By + Cz + D < 0$.

Proof

Any point $P(x, y, z)$ in the plane satisfy $Ax+By+Cz=-D$,

Take a number D_1, and $-D_1<-D$, then

$$Ax+By+Cz+D_1<Ax+By+Cz+D=0,$$

Take another number D_2, and $-D_2>-D$, then

$$Ax+By+Cz+D_2>Ax+By+Cz+D=0.$$

Thus, the point out of the plane π satisfy $Ax+By+Cz+D>0$ or $Ax+By+Cz+D<0.$

But, Points with different symbols of $Ax+By+Cz+D$ can not be the same side of the plane. Because, if Continuous function $Ax+By+Cz+D$ have Different symbols on U_1 or U_2, according to the intermediate value theorem of continuous functions, the point of $Ax+By+Cz+D=0$ is exist on the line connecting these two points. While, the point must be on the plane π. So, on the two parts U_1 or U_2, one side $Ax+By+Cz+D>0$, the other side $Ax+By+Cz+D<0.$

Now, We Give Two Instructions:

(1) For the general plane, the positive and negative symbols of $Ax+By+Cz+D$ can be determined by the location of Coordinates origin and the value D. When $D>0$, $Ax+By+Cz+D>0$; when $D<0$, $Ax+By+Cz+D<0$. when $D=0$, Plane $Ax+By+Cz$ through the Coordinate origin, the symbols of $Ax+By+Cz$ can be Independently determined by the value A,B,C. When $A>0$, the symbol of the space of positive *x*-axis is positive, when $A<0$, the symbol of the space of the negative *x*-axis is positive, similarly, the positive and negative symbol of the space can also be determined by the value B,C (see Fig. 1, Fig. 2 and Fig. 3).

(2) For the gens of the parallel plane, the symbol of the one side of the planes is determined.(see Fig. 4)

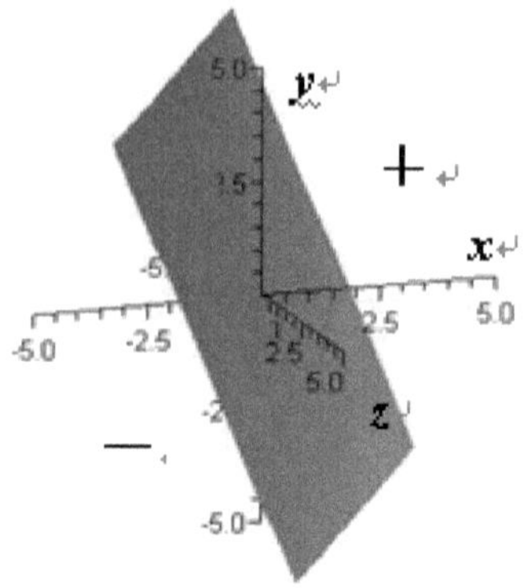

Fig. 1. D=0

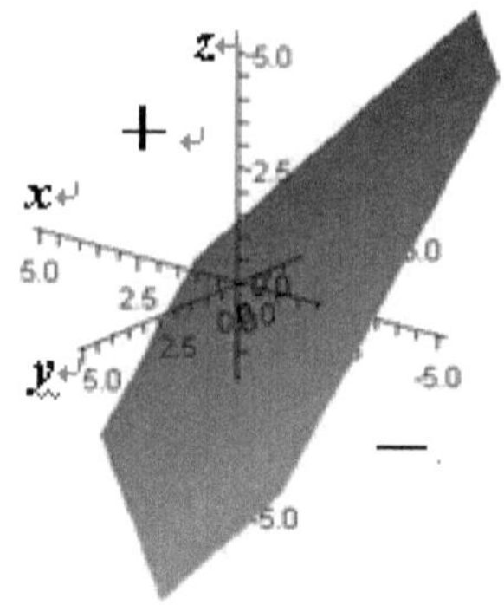

Fig. 2. D$\neq$0

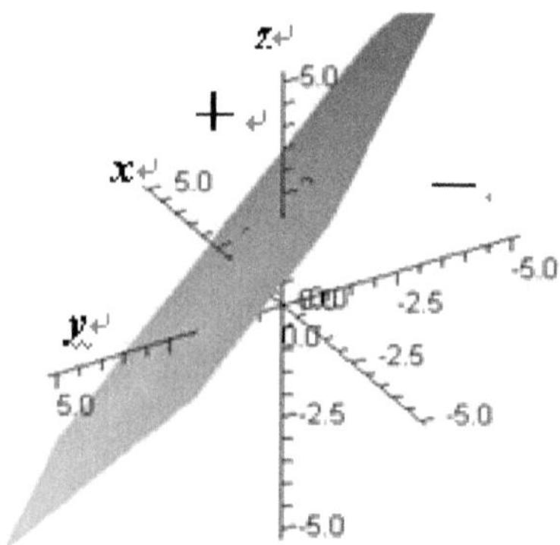

Fig. 3. D<0

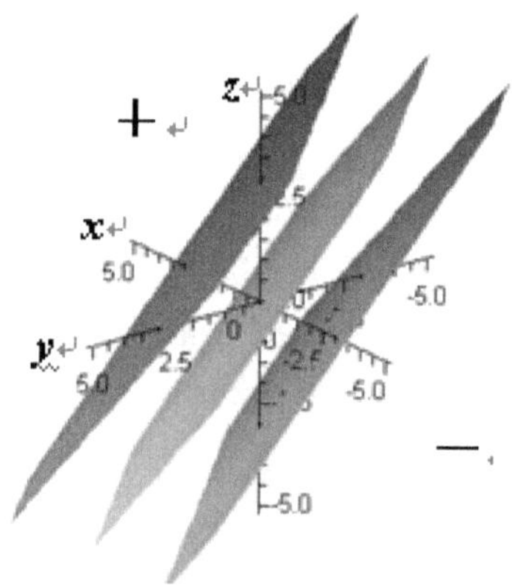

Fig. 4.

4 Proof of Theorem

Theorem the plane $Ax + By + Cz + D = 0$ through the straight line

$$L:\begin{cases}\pi_1 : A_1x + B_1y + C_1z + D_1 = 0, & (4)\\ \pi_2 : A_2x + B_2y + C_2z + D_2 = 0, & (5)\end{cases}$$

Can be written as the form

$$A_1x + B_1y + C_1z + D_1 + \lambda(A_2x + B_2y + C_2z + D_2) = 0 \tag{6}$$

Where λ is an arbitrary constant.

Proof

The plane $\pi_1 : A_1x + B_1y + C_1z + D_1 = 0$ can write form (3), when we let $\lambda = 0$.

Suppose that the plane $\pi: Ax+By+Cz+D=0$ is an arbitrary plane through staight line L except plane π_1 and π_2, the angle between plane π two place π_1 and π_2 are separately α, β $(0<\alpha<\beta<\frac{\pi}{2})$. Let point $P(x,y,z)$ is any point on the plane π (Fig. 5).

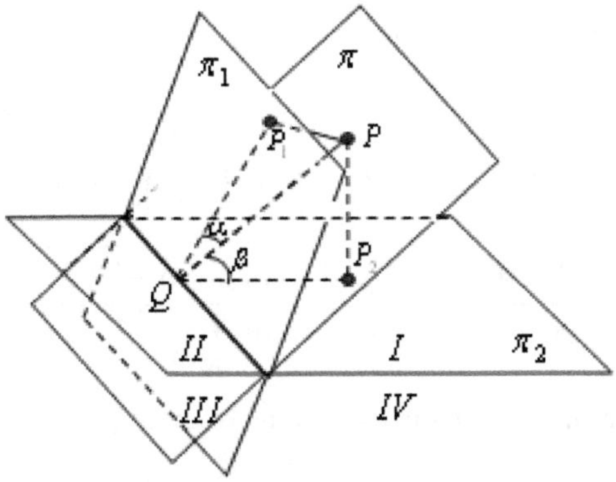

Fig. 5.

The distances between point and two planes are

$$|PP_1| = \frac{|A_1x+B_1y+C_1z+D_1|}{\sqrt{A_1^2+B_1^2+C_1^2}} = |QP|\sin\alpha$$

and

$$|PP_2| = \frac{|A_2x+B_2y+C_2z+D_2|}{\sqrt{A_2^2+B_2^2+C_2^2}} = |QP|\sin\beta.$$

hence

$$\frac{|PP_1|}{|PP_2|} = \left[\frac{|A_1x+B_1y+C_1z+D_1|}{\sqrt{A_1^2+B_1^2+C_1^2}}\right] \Bigg/ \left[\frac{|A_2x+B_2y+C_2z+D_2|}{\sqrt{A_2^2+B_2^2+C_2^2}}\right]$$

$$= \frac{|A_1x+B_1y+C_1z+D_1|}{|A_2x+B_2y+C_2z+D_2|} \cdot \frac{\sqrt{A_2^2+B_2^2+C_2^2}}{\sqrt{A_1^2+B_1^2+C_1^2}}$$

$$= \frac{\sin\alpha}{\sin\beta}$$

We can obtain

$$\frac{|A_1x+B_1y+C_1z+D_1|}{|A_2x+B_2y+C_2z+D_2|}=\frac{\sin\alpha}{\sin\beta}\cdot\frac{\sqrt{A_1^{\,2}+B_1^{\,2}+C_1^{\,2}}}{\sqrt{A_2^{\,2}+B_2^{\,2}+C_2^{\,2}}} \tag{4}$$

Now we have to prove that removing the absolute symbol of the left, the following two equations have one and only one.

$$\frac{A_1x+B_1y+C_1z+D_1}{A_2x+B_2y+C_2z+D_2}=\frac{\sin\alpha}{\sin\beta}\cdot\frac{\sqrt{A_1^{\,2}+B_1^{\,2}+C_1^{\,2}}}{\sqrt{A_2^{\,2}+B_2^{\,2}+C_2^{\,2}}},$$

$$\frac{A_1x+B_1y+C_1z+D_1}{A_2x+B_2y+C_2z+D_2}=-\frac{\sin\alpha}{\sin\beta}\cdot\frac{\sqrt{A_1^{\,2}+B_1^{\,2}+C_1^{\,2}}}{\sqrt{A_2^{\,2}+B_2^{\,2}+C_2^{\,2}}}.$$

The space is divided into four parts by two intersecting planes, we recorded as Ⅰ, Ⅱ, Ⅲ, Ⅳ.

(1) Firstly, we discuss the condition of P in part Ⅰ.

①If the two inequalities have the opposite sign on point P, let's assume that

$$A_1x+B_1y+C_1z+D_1>0,\quad A_2x+B_2y+C_2z+D_2<0,$$

Where $\dfrac{A_1x+B_1y+C_1z+D_1}{A_2x+B_2y+C_2z+D_2}$ is Negative, the formula (4) change into

$$\frac{A_1x+B_1y+C_1z+D_1}{A_2x+B_2y+C_2z+D_2}=-\frac{\sin\alpha}{\sin\beta}\cdot\frac{\sqrt{A_1^{\,2}+B_1^{\,2}+C_1^{\,2}}}{\sqrt{A_2^{\,2}+B_2^{\,2}+C_2^{\,2}}},$$

Let $\dfrac{\sin\alpha}{\sin\beta}\cdot\dfrac{\sqrt{A_1^{\,2}+B_1^{\,2}+C_1^{\,2}}}{\sqrt{A_2^{\,2}+B_2^{\,2}+C_2^{\,2}}}=\lambda,$ then

$$\frac{A_1x+B_1y+C_1z+D_1}{A_2x+B_2y+C_2z+D_2}=-\lambda,$$

And we have

$$A_1x+B_1y+C_1z+D_1+\lambda(A_2x+B_2y+C_2z+D_2)=0.$$

②If two inequalities have the same sign on poite P, let's assume that

$$A_1x+B_1y+C_1z+D_1>0,\quad A_2x+B_2y+C_2z+D_2>0,$$

Where $\dfrac{A_1x+B_1y+C_1z+D_1}{A_2x+B_2y+C_2z+D_2}$ is Positive, formula (4) change into

$$\frac{A_1x+B_1y+C_1z+D_1}{A_2x+B_2y+C_2z+D_2}=\frac{\sin\alpha}{\sin\beta}\cdot\frac{\sqrt{A_1^2+B_1^2+C_1^2}}{\sqrt{A_2^2+B_2^2+C_2^2}},$$

Let $\dfrac{\sin\alpha}{\sin\beta}\cdot\dfrac{\sqrt{A_1^2+B_1^2+C_1^2}}{\sqrt{A_2^2+B_2^2+C_2^2}}=-\lambda,$ then

$$\frac{A_1x+B_1y+C_1z+D_1}{A_2x+B_2y+C_2z+D_2}=-\lambda,$$

And we have

$$A_1x+B_1y+C_1z+D_1+\lambda(A_2x+B_2y+C_2z+D_2)=0.$$

(2) Secondly, we discuss the condition of point P in part Ⅲ.

We Noted that the point P' in the plane π and the point P of (1) are on both sides, So, at this time, on the point P, the symbol of $A_1x+B_1y+C_1z+D_1$ and the the situation of the problem (1) have just the opposite of the symbol. Similarly, the symbol of $A_2x+B_2y+C_2z+D_2$ and the the situation of the problem (1) have just the opposite of the symbol, So the symbol of $\dfrac{A_1x+B_1y+C_1z+D_1}{A_2x+B_2y+C_2z+D_2}$ is also determined, which is Positive or negative. Therefore, adopting the same mathod of (1), we also have

$$A_1x+B_1y+C_1z+D_1+\lambda(A_2x+B_2y+C_2z+D_2)=0$$

Thus, to any point on the plane, we can get the equation of plane π has form (3).

end

Here we give a little description, for general two intersecting planes, the symbol of the area of the two intersecting planes can not be determined, we need discusse and analyze the different situation, but if the angle of them is the acute angle, we can draw the conclusion that the symbol of them is different, leaving the reader to think.

5 Conclusion

Plane pencil equation is a very available tool insettfing problems of an alytic geometry .This paper first gives definition and application of the equation of plane pencil. Then , we give the complete proof of theorem using Point to plane distance formula on the basis of the given lemma. In summary, in the teaching of line and plane, we should be good to explain the definition of the plane pencil equation, and pay attention to students with a plane pemcil equation to deal with some exercises.

References

1. Department of Mathematics, Tongji University. Higher Mathematics, 6th edn., vol. 2, pp. 47–49. Higher Education Press, Beijing (2008)
2. Lv, L.: Analytic Geometry, pp. 137–138. Higher Education Press, Beijing (1992)
3. Department of Mathematics, Nankai University. Analytic Geometry of Space Introduction. People's Education Press, Beijing (1978)
4. Shi, J.: Higher Mathematics Examples and Problem Sets, pp. 56–58. Xi'an Jiaotong University Press, Xi'an (2002)
5. Jiao, S.: Point to the straight line distance. Studies in College Mathematics 6(1), 8–10 (2003)
6. Yan, G.: Teaching and learning of mathematics refer to (First Volume), pp. 105–107. Northwest Industry University Press, Xi'an (2002)
7. Shen, Y., Gao, Z.: Multi-function differential calculus of several basic relationship between the concepts. Studies in College Mathematics 2(12), 33–36 (2009)
8. Wu, Z.: Mathematical analysis of engineering-based counseling to the book, vol. 2, p. 223. Higher Education Press, Beijing (2007)
9. Liu, D.: Straight-line distance between two different surfaces of a variety of formulas derived. Studies in College Mathematics 12(2), 21–23 (2009)
10. Wang, J., Fu, R.: Analytic geometry of space, pp. 81–84. Beijing Normal University Press, Beijing (2003)
11. Peng, F., He, S.: Space linear beam and equation. Journal of Mathematics for Technology (1), 110–112 (2000)
12. Chen, Z.: Advanced Algebra and Analytic Geometry, pp. 45–47. Higher Education Press, Springer (2002)
13. Hui, M.: Study on the Definition of Planes Equation. Journal of Tianjin Normal University (Natural Science Edition) 22(3), 38–39
14. You, H., Wu, B., Dong, Z.: Linear algebra and analytic geometry, pp. 38–40. Beijing Science Press (2001)
15. Xu, X., Yin, T.: A method for spatial point to straight distance-the application of beam plane. Studies in College Mathematics 7(2), 25–26 (2004)

The Reserching of the Second-Order Matrix Eigenvalue Problem

Shujuan Yuan* and Yafeng Yang

Qinggong College, Hebei United University, Tangshan 063000, China
yuanshujuan1980@163.com

Abstract. This paper discusses the second-order matrix eigenvalue problem $\varphi_x = M\varphi$, the Bargmann constraint of this problem is given.by the relation between the potential (q,r) and the eigenfunctor φ is set up, by means of the nonlinearization of the Lax pairs,we found the Bargmann system of the eigenvalue problem.It can be equal to the Hamilton canonical systems in real symplectic space.By the end,the infinite-dimensions Dynamical systems can be transformed into the finite-dimensions Hamilton canonical systems in the symplectic space.Moreover,the representations of the solutions forthe evolution equations are generated.

Keywords: eigenvalue problem,integrable system, evolution equation, lax representation.

1 Introduction

To seek a new completely integrable system which is associated with the development of non-linear equations is an interesting issue in the international mathematical physics Union. In this paper, we obtain a new finite-dimensional completely integrable system by using the nonlinear eigenvalue problem.

2 Lax Representation and the Evolution Equation Hierarchy Related to Eigenvalue Problem

We consider the second order matrix eigenvalue problem:

$$\begin{pmatrix}\varphi_1\\ \varphi_2\end{pmatrix}_x = \begin{pmatrix}\lambda-q & \lambda\\ \lambda+r & q-\lambda\end{pmatrix}\begin{pmatrix}\varphi_1\\ \varphi_2\end{pmatrix} = M\varphi, \tag{1}$$

$$u = \begin{pmatrix}r\\ q\end{pmatrix},$$

* Corresponding author.

C. Liu, J. Chang, and A. Yang (Eds.): ICICA 2011, Part I, CCIS 243, pp. 703–709, 2011.

Let $W = \sum_{j=0}^{\infty} \begin{pmatrix} W_{11} & W_{12} \\ W_{21} & W_{22} \end{pmatrix} \lambda^{-j}$,

from $W_x = [M, W]$,

we can get the following result:

$$w_{11} = -qa_{j-1} - \frac{1}{2} a_{j-1x} + \lambda a_{j-1},$$

$$w_{12} = \lambda a_{j-1},$$

$$w_{21} = -qa_{j-1} - \frac{1}{2} b_{j-1x} + \lambda a_{j-1},$$

$$w_{22} = qa_{j-1} + \frac{1}{2} a_{j-1x} - \lambda a_{j-1}$$

Definition:

$$\boldsymbol{K} = \begin{pmatrix} \partial \boldsymbol{r} + \boldsymbol{r} \partial & \boldsymbol{q}\partial - \frac{1}{2}\partial^2 \\ \partial \boldsymbol{q} + \frac{1}{2}\partial^2 & 0 \end{pmatrix},$$

$$J = \begin{pmatrix} -2\partial & \partial \\ \partial & \frac{1}{2}\partial \end{pmatrix} \tag{2}$$

$KG_{j-1} = JG_j$, $j = 0, 1, 2, 3, \ldots,$

$$G_j = \begin{pmatrix} a_j \\ b_j \end{pmatrix} \tag{3}$$

Note: Operators K, J are double *Hamilton* operator [1], it is that K, J have the Properties of antisymmetry, bilinear, non-degeneracy, and satisfy the *Jacobi* equation.

The definition of second-order matrix as follows:

$$W_m = \sum_{j=0}^{m} \begin{pmatrix} -qa_{j-1} - \frac{1}{2} a_{j-1x} + \lambda a_{j-1} & \lambda a_{j-1} \\ -qa_{j-1} - \frac{1}{2} b_{j-1x} + \lambda a_{j-1} & qa_{j-1} + \frac{1}{2} a_{j-1x} - \lambda a_{j-1} \end{pmatrix} \lambda^{m-j}$$

We have the following proposition:

Proposition 2.1: The Evolution Equation Hierarchy related to eigenvalue problem is ($u=(r,q)^T$):

$$u_{tm}=\begin{pmatrix} r_{tm} \\ q_{tm} \end{pmatrix}=JG_m,\ m=0,1,2,\dots \tag{4}$$

It is equivalent to Lax Equation[2]:

$$M_{tm}=(w_m)_x+w_m M-Mw_m \tag{5}$$

In other words, Equation (4) is consistency condition of spectrum-preserving for the following two linear equations:

$$(\varphi_{xt_m}=\varphi_{t_m x},\lambda_{t_m}=0)$$

$$\begin{cases} \varphi_x=M\varphi \\ \varphi_{tm}=w_m\varphi \end{cases} \tag{6}$$

Let

$$JG_{-1}=0,$$

so $G_{-1}=\begin{pmatrix} 4 \\ 0 \end{pmatrix}$,

from

$$KG_{m-1}=JG_m,$$

$$G_0=\begin{pmatrix} 2q-r \\ 4q+2r \end{pmatrix} \tag{7}$$

$$G_1=\begin{pmatrix} \frac{1}{2}q^2-\frac{3}{2}rq+q_x+\frac{3}{8}r^2 \\ 3q^2+rq-r_x-\frac{3}{4}r^2 \end{pmatrix}$$

Then we have the evolution equation:

$$u_{t0}=\begin{pmatrix} r_{t0} \\ q_{t0} \end{pmatrix}=\begin{pmatrix} 4r_x \\ 4q_x \end{pmatrix} \tag{8}$$

$$u_{t1}=\begin{pmatrix} r_{t1} \\ q_{t1} \end{pmatrix}=\begin{pmatrix} 4qr_x+4rq_x-3rr_x-r_{xx}-2q_{xx} \\ 4qq_x+(qr)_x+q_{xx}-\frac{1}{2}r_{xx} \end{pmatrix} \tag{9}$$

Proposition 2.2: Let $\varphi=(\varphi_1,\varphi_2)^T$, If the trace of the second- order matrices M over the reals is 0, so

$\int_\Omega (\varphi_1,\varphi_2)\begin{pmatrix}0 & -1\\ 1 & 0\end{pmatrix}\dot{M}\begin{pmatrix}\varphi_1\\ \varphi_2\end{pmatrix}dx=0$, the Functional derivation is denoted by Symbol[3] .

Proposition 2.3: If φ_1,φ_2 is the characteristic function that the eigenvalue problem (1) relates to λ, so the functional gradient[4] as follows:

$$grad\lambda=\begin{pmatrix}\dfrac{\delta\lambda}{\delta v}\\ \dfrac{\delta\lambda}{\delta u}\end{pmatrix}=\begin{pmatrix}\lambda\varphi_1^2\\ -2\lambda\varphi_1\varphi_2\end{pmatrix},$$

and $Kgrad\lambda=\lambda Jgrad\lambda$.

3 The Hamilton Equation and Its Complete Integrability under the Bargmann Constraint

We suppose that $\lambda_1<\lambda_2<\ldots<\lambda_N$ is N different eigenvalues of Equation (5). $\varphi_{1j},\varphi_{2j}$ are characteristic function of λ_j ($j=1,2,\cdots,N$), so

$$\begin{pmatrix}\varphi_{1j}\\ \varphi_{2j}\end{pmatrix}_x=M\left(u,\lambda_j\right)\begin{pmatrix}\varphi_{1j}\\ \varphi_{2j}\end{pmatrix}, \tag{10}$$

$$\begin{pmatrix}\varphi_{1j}\\ \varphi_{2j}\end{pmatrix}_{t_m}=w_m\left(u,\lambda_j\right)\begin{pmatrix}\varphi_{1j}\\ \varphi_{2j}\end{pmatrix}, \tag{11}$$

Let $\Lambda=diag(\lambda_1,\lambda_2,\cdots,\lambda_N)$,

$$\varphi_{1j}=(\varphi_{11},\ldots,\varphi_{1N})^T,\varphi_{2j}=(\varphi_{21},\ldots,\varphi_{2N})^T,$$

from $Kgrad\lambda=\lambda Jgrad\lambda$ [5], we can get the result:

$$K\begin{pmatrix}\langle\Lambda^k\varphi_1,\varphi_1\rangle\\ \langle\Lambda^k\varphi_1,\varphi_2\rangle\end{pmatrix}=J\begin{pmatrix}\langle\Lambda^{k+1}\varphi_1,\varphi_1\rangle\\ \langle\Lambda^{k+1}\varphi_1,\varphi_2\rangle\end{pmatrix} \tag{12}$$

From (7) and (11), we have

$$G_j = \begin{pmatrix} \langle \Lambda^j \varphi_1, \varphi_1 \rangle \\ \langle \Lambda^j \varphi_1, \varphi_2 \rangle \end{pmatrix}, \; j = 0,1,2, \ldots,$$

$$\Lambda = diag(\lambda_1, \cdots, \lambda_N);$$

At the same time, we have

$$\begin{cases} a_{j-1} \\ b_{j-1} \end{cases} = \begin{pmatrix} \langle \Lambda^j \varphi_1, \varphi_1 \rangle \\ \langle \Lambda^j \varphi_1, \varphi_2 \rangle \end{pmatrix}, \; j = 1, 2, \cdots \tag{13}$$

The constraint condition is Bargmann constraint condition:

$$G_0 = \begin{pmatrix} 2q - r \\ 4q + 2r \end{pmatrix} = \begin{pmatrix} \langle \varphi_1, \varphi_1 \rangle \\ \langle \varphi_1, \varphi_2 \rangle \end{pmatrix},$$

$$\begin{pmatrix} q \\ r \end{pmatrix} = \begin{pmatrix} \frac{1}{4}\langle \varphi_1, \varphi_2 \rangle + \frac{1}{4}\langle \varphi_1, \varphi_1 \rangle \\ \frac{1}{2}\langle \varphi_1, \varphi_2 \rangle - \frac{1}{2}\langle \varphi_1, \varphi_1 \rangle \end{pmatrix} \tag{14}$$

The Poisson bracket [6]of Smooth Function H and F in symplectic space $(R^{2N}, \sum_{k=1}^{N} d\varphi_{2k} \Lambda d\varphi_{1k})$ is defined as followed:

$$\{H, F\} = \sum_{k=1}^{N} \left(\frac{\partial H}{\partial \varphi_{2k}} \frac{\partial F}{\partial \varphi_{1k}} - \frac{\partial H}{\partial \varphi_{1k}} \frac{\partial F}{\partial \varphi_{2k}} \right)$$

Proposition 3.1: (10) and (11) can be written as a finite-dimensional system:

$$\begin{cases} \varphi_{1x} = \dfrac{\partial H}{\partial \varphi_2} \quad \varphi_{2x} = -\dfrac{\partial H}{\partial \varphi_1} \\ \varphi_{1t_m} = \dfrac{\partial H_m}{\partial \varphi_2} \; \varphi_{2t_m} = -\dfrac{\partial H_m}{\partial \varphi_1} \end{cases} \quad m = 1, 2, \ldots \tag{15}$$

H and H_m are *Hamilton* function here.

$$H = -\frac{1}{4}\langle \Lambda\varphi_1, \varphi_1 \rangle \langle \varphi_1, \varphi_2 \rangle - \frac{1}{8}\langle \Lambda\varphi_1, \varphi_2 \rangle \langle \varphi_1, \varphi_2 \rangle + \langle \Lambda\varphi_1, \varphi_2 \rangle$$
$$+ \frac{1}{8}\langle \Lambda\varphi_1, \varphi_1 \rangle \langle \varphi_1, \varphi_1 \rangle + \frac{1}{2}\langle \Lambda\varphi_2, \varphi_2 \rangle - \frac{1}{2}\langle \Lambda\varphi_1, \varphi_1 \rangle \tag{16}$$

$$\begin{aligned}H_m &= -\frac{1}{2}\langle\Lambda^m\varphi_1,\varphi_1\rangle\langle\varphi_2,\varphi_2\rangle - 2\langle\Lambda^{m+1}\varphi_1,\varphi_1\rangle \\ &+\frac{1}{2}\langle\Lambda^m\varphi_1,\varphi_1\rangle\langle\varphi_1,\varphi_1\rangle + 4\langle\Lambda^{m+1}\varphi_1,\varphi_2\rangle + 2\langle\Lambda^{m+1}\varphi_2,\varphi_2\rangle \\ &-\langle\Lambda^m\varphi_1,\varphi_1\rangle\langle\varphi_1,\varphi_2\rangle + \frac{1}{2}\sum_{j=0}^{m}\begin{vmatrix}\langle\Lambda^j\varphi_2,\varphi_2\rangle & \langle\Lambda^j\varphi_2,\varphi_1\rangle \\ \langle\Lambda^{m-j}\varphi_2,\varphi_1\rangle & \langle\Lambda^{m-j}\varphi_1,\varphi_1\rangle\end{vmatrix}\end{aligned} \tag{17}$$

The generator E_k is as followed:

$$E_k = \frac{1}{2}\lambda_\kappa\Gamma_k - \varphi_{1k}^2\langle\varphi_1,\varphi_2\rangle + 4\lambda_\kappa\varphi_{1k}\varphi_{2k} + \frac{1}{2}\varphi_{1k}^2\langle\varphi_1,\varphi_1\rangle + 2\lambda_\kappa\varphi_{2k}^2 - \frac{1}{2}\varphi_{1k}^2\langle\varphi_2,\varphi_2\rangle$$

among them, $\Gamma_k = \sum_{\substack{j=1 \\ j\neq k}}^{N}\frac{(\varphi_{1k}\varphi_{2j}-\varphi_{2k}\varphi_{1j})^2}{\lambda_k-\lambda_j}$.

Proposition 3.2: (1) $\{E_k, k=1,2,...N\}$ is involutive system[7]: so that $\{E_k,E_j\}=0,\forall k, j=1,2,...N$, and $\{dE_k\}$ has nothing to do with the gradient;

(2) $H_\lambda = \sum_{k=1}^{N}\frac{1}{\lambda-\lambda_k}E_k = \sum_{m=0}^{\infty}\lambda^{-m-1}H_m$ [2]

Among them, $H_m = \sum_{k=1}^{N}\lambda_\kappa{}^m E_k, m=1,2,\cdots$ [3]

Proposition 3.3: (1) $\{H,E_k\}=0, k=1,2,...N.$

(2) $\{H,H_m\}=0, m=0,1,2,...$

(3) $\{H_n,H_m\}=0, m,n=0,1,2,...$

(4) $(R^{2N},\sum_{k=1}^{N}d\varphi_{1k}\Lambda d\varphi_{2k},H),(R^{2N},\sum_{k=1}^{N}d\varphi_{1k}\Lambda d\varphi_{2k},H_m)$ is the completely integrable system in the Liouville sense[8].

Proposition 3.4: if φ_1, φ_2 are involutive solution of the Hamilton regular system[9],so

$$\begin{pmatrix} r \\ q \end{pmatrix} = \begin{pmatrix} \frac{1}{2}\langle\varphi_1,\varphi_2\rangle - \frac{1}{2}\langle\varphi_1,\varphi_1\rangle \\ \frac{1}{4}\langle\varphi_1,\varphi_2\rangle + \frac{1}{4}\langle\varphi_1,\varphi_1\rangle \end{pmatrix}$$

is the solution of evolution equation hierarchy (4)[10].

References

1. Olver, P.J.: Applications of Lie Groups to Differential Equations, 2nd edn., pp. 13–53, 452–462. Springer, Heidelberg (1999)
2. Cao, C.: Confocal involutive system and a class of AKNS eigenvalue problem. Henan Science 5(1), 1–10 (1987)
3. Gu, Z.: Two finite-dimensional completely integrable Hamiltonian systems associated with the solutions of the MKDV hierarchy. Math.Phys. 32(6)
4. Arnold, V.I.: Mathematical Methods of Classical Mechanics. Springer, Heidelberg (1978)
5. Cao, C.W.: A classical integrable system and involutive representation of solutions of the KDV equation. Acta. Math. Sinia, New Series 7(3), 436–440 (1991)
6. Chen, D.: Soliton Theory, 1st edn., pp. 194–199. Science Press (April 2006)
7. Gu, Z.: The Neumann system for 3rd-order eigenvalue problems related to the Boussinesq equation II. Nuovc Cimento 117B(6), 615–632 (2002)
8. You, F., Xia, T.: Integrable Couplings of the Generalized AKNS Hierarchy with an Arbitrary Function and Its Bi-Hamiltonian Structure. International Journal of Theoretical Physics (12), 46 (2007)
9. Chen, D., Zhang, D., Bi, J.: New double Wronskian solutions of the AKNS equation. Science in China Series A: Mathematics (1), 51 (2008)
10. Long, F.: Nonlinear Integrable Systems and Related Topics. In: CNKI:CDMD 1, 25 (2009)

Author Index

GPSR Compliance

The European Union's (EU) General Product Safety Regulation (GPSR) is a set of rules that requires consumer products to be safe and our obligations to ensure this.

If you have any concerns about our products, you can contact us on ProductSafety@springernature.com

In case Publisher is established outside the EU, the EU authorized representative is:

Springer Nature Customer Service Center GmbH
Europaplatz 3
69115 Heidelberg, Germany

Batch number: 10682580

Printed by Printforce, the Netherlands